INTERNATIONAL HANDBOOK OF EDUCATIONAL
RESEARCH IN THE ASIA-PACIFIC REGION

A publication of the Asia-Pacific Educational Research Association

Kluwer International Handbooks of Education

VOLUME 11

A list of titles in this series can be found at the end of this volume.

International Handbook of Educational Research in the Asia-Pacific Region

Part One

Editors:

John P. Keeves
Flinders University Institute of International Education, Australia
and
Ryo Watanabe
National Institute for Educational Policy Research of Japan, Tokyo, Japan

Section Editors:
John P. Keeves, *Flinders University Institute of International Education, Australia*
Rupert Maclean, *UNESCO-UNEVOC International Centre for Education, Bonn, Germany*
Peter D. Renshaw, *Griffith University, Southport, Australia*
Colin N. Power, *University of Queensland, St Lucia, Queensland, Australia*
Robyn Baker, *New Zealand Council for Educational Research, Wellington, New Zealand*
S. Gopinathan, *National Institute of Education, Nanyang Technological University, Singapore*
Ho Wah Kam, *National Institute of Education, Nanyang Technological University, Singapore*
Yin Cheong Cheng, *Hong Kong Institute of Education, Hong Kong*
Albert C. Tuijnman, *Institute of International Education, Stockholm University, Sweden*
Ryo Watanabe, *National Institute for Educational Policy Research of Japan, Japan*

APERA

KLUWER ACADEMIC PUBLISHERS
DORDRECHT / BOSTON / LONDON

Library of Congress Cataloging-in-Publication Data is available.

ISBN 1-4020-1007-9

Published by Kluwer Academic Publishers
PO Box 17, 3300 AA Dordrecht, The Netherlands

Sold and distributed in North, Central and South America
by Kluwer Academic Publishers,
101 Philip Drive, Norwell, MA 02061, U.S.A.

In all other countries, sold and distributed
by Kluwer Academic Publishers, Distribution Centre,
PO Box 322, 3300 AH Dordrecht, The Netherlands

A publication of the Asia-Pacific Educational Research Association

Printed on acid-free paper

All Rights Reserved
© 2003 Kluwer Academic Publishers
No part of this publication may be reproduced or utilized in any form or by any means, electronic, mechanical, including photocopying, recording or by any informations storage and retrieval system, without written permission from the copyright owner.

Table of Contents

Overview and Introduction
John P. Keeves and Ryo Watanabe   xiii

PART ONE

SECTION 1: TRENDS AND ISSUES
Section Editor – John P. Keeves

1. Trends in Educational Reform in the Asia-Pacific Region
   Yin Cheong Cheng   3

2. Achieving Education for All in the Asia-Pacific Region
   Rupert Maclean and Ken Vine   17

3. Educational Expenditure and Participation in East Asia and Australia
   Gerald Burke, Robert Lenehan, and Hing Tong Ma   29

4. The Family and Schooling in Asian and Pacific Countries
   Kevin Marjoribanks   43

5. Cultural and Social Capital in Asian and Pacific Countries
   Lawrence J. Saha   59

6. Secondary Education Reform in the Asia-Pacific Region
   Rupert Maclean   73

7. Educational Research and Educational Policy-Making in Asian and Pacific Countries
   T. Neville Postlethwaite   93

8. Evaluation and Accountability in Asian and Pacific Countries
   Ramon Mohandas, Meng Hong Wei, and John P. Keeves   107

9. Educational Research in the Asia-Pacific Region
   John P. Keeves, Ryo Watanabe, and Peter McGuckian   123

SECTION 2: ACCESS AND EQUITY

Section Editor – Rupert Maclean

Education of Special Groups

10	Equality of Opportunity in Education *Rupert Maclean*	143
11	A Case Study of Learning Achievement in South Asia *Rupert Maclean and Ken Vine*	155
12	Education of Children in Remote Areas *Tiedao Zhang*	171
13	Education of Gifted and Talented Learners *Kenneth Kuen Fung Sin*	189
14	Inclusive Education for Students with Special Needs *David Mitchell and Ishwar Desai*	203
15	Issues for Urban Youth in Asia and the Pacific *Kerry J. Kennedy*	217
16	Drop-outs from School and How to Cope with this Problem *S. Srinivasan and S. Anandalakshmy*	231
17	Ethnicities, Minorities and Indigenous Groups in Central Asia *Joseph and Rea Zajda*	241
18	Sex and Gender Differences in Educational Outcomes *John P. Keeves and Malcolm Slade*	257
19	Gender-Sensitive Education for Bridging the Gender Gap *Namtip Aksornkool*	269
20	Gender Differences in Access to Education and Employment *Sharada Jain*	279

Lifelong Learning

21	Adult Literacy in the Asia-Pacific Region *Inayatullah*	293
22	Learning Across the Adult Lifespan *Erlinda C. Pefianco, David Curtis, and John P. Keeves*	305
23	Workforce Education *David N. Wilson*	321
24	Nonformal Education *Steve Wilson and Mona Shrestha*	335

SECTION 3: LEARNING AND HUMAN DEVELOPMENT

Section Editors – Peter Renshaw and Colin Power

25	The Process of Learning *Peter Renshaw and Colin Power*	351
26	Cognitive Development *Alison F. Garton*	365
27	Lifespan Human Development *Candida C. Peterson*	379
28	Values Education in a Changing World *Lourdes R. Quisumbing and Joy de Leo*	395
29	Measuring Attitudes by Unfolding a Likert-Style Questionnaire *David Andrich and Guanzhon Luo*	409
30	Bullying in Schools *Phillip T. Slee, Lang Ma, Hee-Og Sim, Keith Sullivan, and Mitsura Taki*	425
31	Student Learning: A Cross-Cultural Perspective *David N. Watkins*	441
32	Classroom Learning Environments *Barry J. Fraser and Swee Chiew Goh*	463
33	Metacognition *Christina E. van Kraayenoord and Merrilyn Goos*	477
34	Motivation and School Learning *Chi-Hung Ng and Peter Renshaw*	495
35	Problem Solving *Michael J. Lawson*	511
36	Technology and Learning *Kwok-Cheung Cheung*	525

SECTION 4: CURRICULUM AND TECHNICAL EDUCATION

Section Editor – Robyn Baker

Curricula of the Schools

37	Change in the School Curriculum: Looking to the Future *Robyn Baker and Andy Begg*	541
38	Civics and Citizenship *Thomas Kwan-Choi Tse*	555

39	Environmental Education and Education for Sustainable Development *John Fien and Debbie Heck*	569
40	Literacy and Reading *Warwick B. Elley and Ho Wah Kam*	585
41	Mathematics Curricula *Andy Begg*	599
42	Science Curricula *Robyn Baker and Rosemary Hipkins*	615
43	Assessment Research in Second Language Curriculum Initiatives *Kathryn Hill and Tim McNamara*	629
44	Education for Peace and International Understanding *Yoshiyuki Nagata and G.R. (Bob) Teasdale*	641

Education and the World of Work

45	Planning Technical and Vocational Education and Training in Asia *David N. Wilson*	657
46	Vocational Education and Training in Asia *Jandhyala B.G. Tilak*	673
47	Pacific Island Issues in Vocational Education and Training *Perive Tanuvasa Lene*	687
48	Transition from School to Work in East Asia *David Atchoarena and Efison Mujanganja*	701
49	Enterprise Education in Australia and New Zealand *Michael Long and Chris Selby Smith*	715

PART TWO

SECTION 5: TEACHING, TEACHERS AND TEACHER EDUCATION

Section Editors – S. Gopianathan and Ho Wah Kam

Teaching

50	Issues and Concerns Regarding Teaching, Teachers and Higher Education *S. Gopinathan and Ho Wah Kam*	733

51	Class Size and Classroom Processes *Peter Blatchford and Gemma Catchpole*	741
52	Homework and Coaching *Ian David Smith*	755
53	Teacher Self-Evaluation *John MacBeath*	767
54	Time: Allocated, Institutional and Task Oriented *Maurice Galton*	781
55	Monitoring of Student Learning *Geoff N. Masters*	793

Higher Education and Teacher Education

56	Higher Education and Development *Jandhyala B.G. Tilak*	809
57	Financing Higher Education in the Asia-Pacific Region *N.V. Varghese*	827
58	Selection for Higher Education in the Asia-Pacific Region *V. Lynn Meek*	839
59	Adult Education in Universities in the Asia-Pacific Region *Darryl Dymock and Barrie Brennan*	853
60	Teaching as an Occupation and Learning Profession *Kerry J. Kennedy*	867
61	Research into Teacher Education *Sim Wong-Kooi*	883
62	The Recruitment and Reparation of Teachers *Chen Ai Yen, Lim Cher Ping, and S. Gopinathan*	899

SECTION 6: ORGANISATION AND MANAGEMENT OF EDUCATION

Section Editor – Yin Cheong Cheng

63	Organisation and the Management of Education: Development, and Growth *Yin Cheong Cheng, Magdalena Mo Ching Mok, and King W. Chow*	915

64	Decentralization and the Self-Managing School *Brian J. Caldwell*	931
65	Quality Assurance and School Monitoring *Magdalena Mo Ching Mok, David Gurr, Eiko Izawa, Heidi Knipprath, Lee In-Hyo, Michael A. Mel, Terry Palmer, Wen-Jing Shan, and Zhang Yenming*	945
66	Staffing in School Education *Young-Hwa Kim*	959
67	School Leadership and Management *Allan Walker*	973
68	Effective Schooling in the Asia-Pacific Region *Clive Dimmock*	987
69	School Leadership Development *Philip Hallinger*	1001
70	Public and Private Education *Ramsey Ding-Yee Koo, Andy Man-Sing Yung, Kip Yuen Ip, and Wei-Chen Chuang*	1015
71	Policy-Making, Planning and Change in Tertiary Education *Alan Wagner and Philip Kwok-Fai Hui*	1031
72	Financing Education in Asian and Pacific Countries *Mark Bray*	1047
73	Family and Community Participation in Education *I-Wah Pang, Eiko Isawa, Anna Kim, Heidi Knipprath, Michael A. Mel, and Terry Palmer*	1063

SECTION 7: EDUCATIONAL RESEARCH AND NATIONAL DEVELOPMENT

Section Editor – Albert C. Tuijnman

74	Educational Research for National and Regional Development *Albert Tuijnman*	1081
75	Globalisation and Education in Asia *Francis O. Ramirez and J. Chan-Tiberghein*	1095
76	Comparative Educational Achievement Studies *Don Spearritt*	1107
77	Comparative Indicators in Education *Lawrence J. Saha and Albert Tuijnman*	1123

78	Dissemination of the Findings of Educational Research *Grant J. Harman and Kay Harman*	1137
79	Donor Support for Educational Research *William A. Loxley*	1151

SECTION 8: TOWARDS THE FUTURE

Section Editor – John P. Keeves

80	Educational Research for Educational Reform *John. P. Keeves and Rung Kaew Dang*	1167
81	The Impact of Educational Research on Decision Making and Practice *Victor Ordonez and Rupert Maclean*	1181
82	Research in Education: Nature, Impact, Needs and Priorities *Zhou Mansheng and John P. Keeves*	1193
83	University Education for National Development *Molly N.N. Lee and Suk Ying Wong*	1207
84	Culturally Inclusive Teacher Education in Oceania *Konai Helu Thaman*	1221
85	Reforming Secondary Education and the Education of Adolescents *Phillip W. Hughes*	1231
86	Reform in Science and Technology Curricula *Kok-Aun Toh and Ngoh-Khang Goh*	1243
87	Emerging Information and Communications Technology in Education *Sivakumar Alagumalai*	1257
88	Education Reform and the Labour Market in Pacific Island Countries *Gerald Burke*	1271
89	Training of Educational Research Workers *Barry J. Fraser and Angela F.L. Wong*	1285
90	Regional Cooperation in Educational Research *M.S. Kharparde and Ashok K. Srivastava*	1301
91	Challenges for Research into Educational Reform in the Asia-Pacific Region *Yin Cheong Cheng*	1315

92　Monitoring the Impact of Gobalisation on Education and Human Development
　　John P. Keeves, Hungi Njora, and I. Gusti Ngurah Darmawan　　1331

Index of Names　　1347

Index of Subjects　　1365

Overview and Introduction

JOHN P. KEEVES
Flinders University Institute of International Education, Australia

RYO WATANABE
National Institute for Educational Policy Research of Japan, Japan

1. FURTHERING COOPERATION AMONG EDUCATIONAL RESEARCH WORKERS

In early October, 2000 representatives of educational research organisations in the Asia-Pacific region met at the offices of the National Institute for Educational Policy Research of Japan in Tokyo to attend a regional seminar titled 'Educational Research for Policy and Practice'. This meeting was sponsored by the UNESCO Asia-Pacific Centre of Educational Innovation and Development and followed similar meetings that had been held in Melbourne in 1995, in Bangkok in 1996, and in Tokyo in 1998. It was recognised at this time that there were several very active national educational research associations in the region including the All India Association for Educational Research, the Educational Research Association of Singapore, the Hong Kong Educational Research Association, the Australian Association for Research in Education and the New Zealand Association for Research in Education. The last four associations listed above had held a joint conference in Singapore in 1997. However, the discussions that had taken place over the past five years had indicated the need to establish an Asia-Pacific Educational Research Association.

From this regional seminar, the Tokyo Declaration on joint action to advance educational research for improved policy and practice in education in the Asia-Pacific region was issued.

Recognising the rich and unique traditions, cultural diversity and common challenges – including obstacles of language and geographical separation – we, the assembled educational research leaders meeting in Tokyo in October 2000 under the auspices of the Japanese National Institute for Educational

Research and UNESCO, hereby commit ourselves to joint action to support and advance the conduct and use of educational research to improve policy and practice in the Asia-Pacific region.

To this end, we agree to establish an Asia-Pacific Educational Research Association, the objectives of which will be to:

- promote collaboration of researchers in the region;
- facilitate the publication of Asia-Pacific research for improved educational policy and practice;
- organise professional meetings; and
- support the training and professional development of educational researchers in the region.

There are several reasons why improved collaboration among educational researchers in the Asia-Pacific region is desirable. First, researchers frequently work alone or in small research teams, sometimes unaware of similar research being carried out elsewhere. Often, when research workers do look beyond their own national borders, it is to Europe or to the United States, rather than to research being carried out within the region. Language barriers and infrequent opportunities to meet and consider research issues and findings have worked against the development of a substantial and systematic Asia-Pacific body of knowledge in education.

Second, educational change is occurring very rapidly in many Asia-Pacific countries. However, these changes are often made on the basis of fashion or on ideological grounds rather than on dependable research-based evidence. In addition, there is often little systematic evaluation of new initiatives. Since education is a major area of public expenditure in all systems in the region, it seems reasonable to expect that the allocation of resources and the introduction of new educational processes and structures would be based on reliable research evidence and subjected to systematic study and evaluation.

Third, there is recognition worldwide, that educational research could be better directed towards pressing issues of policy and practice. Some educational research is conducted with limited consideration for its practical implications or subsequent implementation. Results often are communicated primarily within the research community rather than to policy makers and practitioners. Regional collaboration could be effective in identifying ways of enhancing the impact and adoption of the findings of research in countries within the region. Greater coordination and collaboration might also be effective in supporting the national implementation of research findings and in enhancing the ways in which educational research is perceived, supported and used within the Asia-Pacific region. Finally, greater cooperation among research workers in the Asia-Pacific region is likely to be effective in enhancing levels of research expertise within the region. Training workshops to introduce researchers to new research methods, if conducted under the auspices of a regional association, are likely to be a very effective way of raising the quality of research within the region (see *Training of Educational Research Workers*).

2. NEW DIRECTIONS FOR RESEARCH IN THE ASIA-PACIFIC REGION

The Asia-Pacific region contains countries and school systems at very different stages of development. Consequently, it is perhaps not surprising that each school system has its own unique set of problems that require research in order to facilitate the resolution of these problems. Thus it is difficult to summarise the new directions for research within the region. Nevertheless, among the 14 education systems that sent representatives to the Regional Seminar in Tokyo in October 2000, there were few issues or problem areas that were cited by a particular system that were not referred to by another system within the region. It is clear that the education systems of these countries are not so disparate that they do not have something to discuss and learn from the research being carried out in a neighbouring system within the region.

Perhaps the issue that was most common across systems involved the nature of the curriculum, which was already seen to be overburdened, and yet needed reform with new curriculum areas included, or existing curriculum areas extended in order to meet the changes that were occurring rapidly within society. Many systems were concerned with the inculcation of moral values among their youth, and this area relates to concern for adolescent behaviour, life skills and the structure of schools in the future, as well as preparation for adult life, that involves lifelong learning and development. Several systems were concerned with issues and problems relating to information technology and the individualisation of education. Furthermore, many systems were interested in the policy making process and the implementation of change since there was recognition that the simplistic view of direct implementation was no longer adequate at a time of rapid change.

The problems encountered in the region not only differ among the countries within the region, but also differ from those that are present in the other major zones of the educational world, North America, Latin America, Europe and Africa. Consequently, the turning to Europe and North America for guidance by the countries within the region would no longer seem appropriate. Only countries on the fringe of the Asia-Pacific region like Australia and New Zealand, because of both their location and their traditions are likely to make gains from occasionally turning to Europe and North America. The time has come for by far the great majority of education systems within the Asia-Pacific region to see that they are part of a dynamic and vibrant zone of a world in which changes are occurring at an increasing rate.

It was within this context that a decision was made to review the field of educational research in the Asia-Pacific region and to publish on behalf of the Asia-Pacific Educational Research Association a *Handbook of Educational Research in the Asia-Pacific Region*. This *Handbook* would focus on the problems and issues facing education at all levels in the region. It would also review the findings of the research that has been conducted within the region, and would provide new directions for research in the decades ahead that would be directed towards the problems confronting education in the region. The pages that follow in this *Overview and Introduction* contain the views and writings of scholars who are concerned with the problems of educational policy and practice in the Asia-Pacific region. Most, but not all authors, live or work in the region. Their writings reveal the strength and extent of research that has been conducted or is currently being undertaken in the region, but has remained hidden because of the dominance of the journals and books that are issued in Britain and the United States and that are published in the English language. In countries like China, India, Japan and Korea in particular, there is a wealth of findings of research studies in the field of education that are reported in the national language of the country and that are not seen outside their country of origin. Unfortunately, this *Handbook* does not achieve full access to this large body of research findings. Nevertheless, it does represent an initial attempt to present information on the research being carried out in the Asia-Pacific region. Furthermore, the authors contributing to the *Handbook* argue strongly for greater collaboration between educational research workers in the Asia-Pacific region. They seek to foster the sharing of the findings of research across the countries of the region that have common problems, which differ from those of the more highly developed countries that currently dominate the field of educational research.

This *Handbook* is prepared as a source book of ideas for those who advise policy makers and practitioners in education. It is too large to have a strong appeal to politicians and policy makers who must draw on the counsel and advice of policy analysts. Moreover, it is too large to appeal to many teachers in schools who must obtain guidance from teacher educators as well as superintendents and administrators of school systems. The *Handbook* is written for these people who need to keep abreast of the latest findings from educational research studies in order to foster change and development in both policy and practice in schools and education systems. The *Handbook* should also prove to be very useful for graduate students, who are planning research studies, as well as research workers in education who seek support in their work from replication through similar studies conducted in different settings, or who seek ideas for future investigation. Likewise, curriculum developers and teachers at university and college levels need to be well-informed about the changes that are occurring in the field of education in the region and the relevance of the findings of research for curriculum development and teacher education programs. With these many different users of this *Handbook* in mind, the editors argue very strongly for the development of a sense of unity in the field of educational research. There is increasing variety in the strategies and tactics that are employed in research into educational problems, as well as in the methods of inquiry, theoretical perspectives and procedures of analysis that are used to investigate the practices and processes of education, the contexts and conditions under which educational services are provided, and the policies and products that influence change and development. Nevertheless, there is a unity of purpose that cuts across the different disciplinary perspectives and approaches to inquiry that are employed.

The purpose of scholarly inquiry and research in education is the building of a coherent body of knowledge that has been examined against evidence from the real world and that is available for transforming the real world through human agency and social action. This *Handbook* presents the coherent body of knowledge that is currently available and is related to educational policy and practice in the Asia-Pacific region (see *Research in Education: Nature, Impact, Needs and Priorities*).

3. THE STRUCTURE OF THIS HANDBOOK

The articles in this *Handbook of Educational Research in the Asia-Pacific Region* are assembled in eight major sections:

(a) Trends and Issues,
(b) Access and Equity,
(c) Learning and Human Development,
(d) Curriculum and Technical Education,
(e) Teaching, Teachers, and Teacher Education,
(f) Organisation and Management of Education,
(g) Educational Research and National Development,
(h) Towards the Future.

The structure of the *Handbook* is in many ways greatly influenced by a decision that the *Handbook* should be contained in two volumes, each of approximately 700 pages for the purposes of printing and production. This demands that the length of articles must necessarily be limited, which has required that the initial drafts of some articles unfortunately needed substantial pruning, so that the articles did not exceed the specified word limit. In total, 90 articles were sought with each article not exceeding a word limit of 6000 words. The use of sections served primarily the purposes of sub-dividing the workload of inviting contributing authors and the supervision and editing of contributed articles. The use of section editors and the general editors also ensured that each article was systematically reviewed by two reviewers who examined the material presented in each article for content, style and appropriateness for inclusion in the *Handbook*.

At the beginning of each of the six middle sections there is an introductory article, written by the section editor that not only reviews developments in the area and discusses issues, but also comments on how the entries in the section are clustered together and organised for reference purposes. Thus, within each section, and where sub-sections also exist, the articles are grouped in such a way as to provide a coherent perspective across the topics considered in the articles that contribute to the particular section or sub-section. The sections that comprise the complete volume seek to focus on the major issues that are seen to confront educational research in the region. In a similar way the topics that are addressed in each of the articles seek to direct attention to particular problems that are seen to exist within the region. These problems frequently do not exist in other parts of the world and, in particular, the highly developed countries of Europe and North America, or the less developed countries of sub-Saharan Africa. Nevertheless, there are likely to be major issues that exist in the Asia-Pacific region, that have not been considered in this *Handbook*, as well as issues that are discussed in this *Handbook* that reflect a European or North American bias, and that might well have been treated in a different way.

While such possible shortcomings are to be regretted, it is the view of the editors that this *Handbook* serves well its intended purpose to draw attention to problems and issues as well as research findings and perspectives that are of critical importance in the Asia-Pacific region and are not addressed in the widely distributed publications that arise from Europe and North America.

3.1. *Trends and Issues*

In the opening section of the *Handbook* there are nine articles that address issues that help to set the scene for the reading of the articles that follow on subsequent pages of the *Handbook*. The leading article arises directly from recent discussions in the Asia-Pacific region that seek to identify the trends in educational reform within the countries of the region (see *Trends in Educational Reform in the Asia-Pacific Region*). The second article considers the major issue facing education not only in the Asia-Pacific region, but also in many countries of the world, but excluding perhaps the more highly developed ones, namely the achievement of the goal of 'Education for All' (see *Achieving Education for All in the Asia-Pacific Region*). The social and economic problems of the region and the larger world would appear to be solvable only by raising the standards of education through increased levels of participation. The next article in the introductory section examines the important issues that relate the expenditure on education within a country to the level of participation achieved within the schools and universities of the country (see *Educational Expenditure and Participation in East Asia and Australia*). This article addresses the major issue that faces decision makers in education in many countries of the region, namely, the obtaining of the financial resources necessary for running the schools and tertiary institutions. These education systems are commonly expanding both because of growth in the sizes of the age cohorts as well as the trend to stay longer in education to lift the standards of learning. The fourth article in the section extends the discussion of issues beyond the schools to consider the relationships between the home and the school in the provision and conduct of education in the Asia-Pacific region (see *The Family and Schooling in Asian and Pacific Countries*). The article that follows extends this perspective further to consider the effects of the society and the cultural setting on education within the region (see *Cultural and Social Capital in Asian and Pacific Countries*). Both of these articles provide theoretical perspectives and information on the application of these ideas to future research studies as well as the making of policy for schools in the region. The sixth article is concerned with a major problem, particularly in the least developed and developing countries in the region, on the reform, strengthening and upgrading of secondary education (see *Secondary Education Reform in the Asia-Pacific Region*). Since the 1950s there has been marked expansion in the region in the provision of secondary education, but the overall quality has often declined, because resources have been limited and systems have become less efficient. While much has been accomplished in recent decades, a great deal remains to be done to meet the level of high quality and innovative secondary education that is desired by the countries of the region. The next article in the first section presents an approach to the design and conduct of research studies in order to meet the specific needs of those who make educational policies within a country. This approach is being employed in one country in the region, namely Vietnam, in a trial way (see *Educational Research and Educational Policy-Making in Asian and Pacific Countries*). The following article in the introductory section addresses the issues of evaluation and accountability and provides a theoretical framework for the undertaking of evaluation research studies of schools, curricula and programs. Such studies also serve the purposes of accountability. The article argues for a prospective view rather than a retrospective view in evaluation, and gives examples of how this approach has been and is being applied within the Asia-Pacific region. The examples given relate to the conduct of national examinations, the evaluation of a major program to improve learning within schools, and the collection of data for indicators on the effectiveness of schools within the region (see *Evaluation and Accountability in Asian and Pacific Countries*). The concluding article in the introductory section provides a brief account of the historical development of educational research activity within the region, and identifies those countries that are contributing to the worldwide body of knowledge about education through their research efforts. The article considers briefly the way in which educational research has grown in these leading countries of the region. Furthermore, it argues strongly for greater collaboration between the countries of the region in order to strengthen the educational research efforts within each country as well as to improve educational policy making and practice within the region (see *Educational Research in the Asia-Pacific Region*).

3.2. *Access and Equity*

This section takes up the issues involved in the provision of education for all in the Asia-Pacific region. It addresses the particular problems of providing access for all children to primary and secondary education, in ways that are fair and just, and in ways that are free from race, religion, sex, and social class bias. The section is divided into two sub-sections that focus on particular problem areas, namely *Education of Special Groups*, and *Lifelong Learning*, while the issues being addressed in specific articles are considered in the introductory article to the section that is titled '*Equality of Opportunity in Education*'.

3.3. *Learning and Human Development*

This section, titled '*Learning and Human Development*' examines the problems facing education in the Asia-Pacific region from a largely psychological perspective. The introductory article (see *The Process of Learning*) considers the links between the different articles in the section. The important conclusion drawn from these articles is that learning and human development should be viewed as processes that are set within social, cultural and institutional systems that interact with each other and the individuals within them.

3.4. Curriculum and Technical Education

Perhaps the most challenging problems facing educators in the Asia-Pacific region are associated with the design and development of curricula for the schools of the region and the issues that exist between the provision of general education and the provision of a technical and technologically based education. As a consequence this section is sub-divided into two parts: *Curricula of the Schools* and *Education and the World of Work*. The introductory article to the section *Change in the School Curriculum: Looking to the Future*, considers the laying of sound foundations for later stages of education and throughout a lifetime. The issues addressed in this section are being made very complex by the rapid growth of knowledge and the marked changes needed in some countries to respond to the changing nature of work as a consequence of globalisation and the advances of technology.

3.5. Teaching, Teachers and Teacher Education

The introductory article to this section, as its title implies, addresses the *Issues, and Prospects Regarding Teaching, Teachers and Teacher Education*. The section is sub-divided into two sub-sections; the first sub-section is primarily concerned with *Teaching*, while the second sub-section considers *Higher Education and Teacher Education*. The issues addressed in this section extend beyond education in schools at the primary and secondary levels to include the tertiary phase of education and further into adult education.

3.6. Organisation and Management of Education

This section considers education not only in schools, but also at the levels of tertiary and higher education, as well as through the family and through community participation in education. The introductory article to the section (see *Organisation and Management of Education: Development and Growth*) reviews the articles included in the section and discusses the changes that are occurring in the provision of educational services within the region. There are, however, great disparities between the countries of the region, with some children, who live in countries with large populations, never having the opportunity to attend school or learning to read and write. It is evident that the costs of educational provision are in all countries of the region an important issue, with the private sector being increasingly involved in providing educational services.

3.7. Educational Research and National Development

The penultimate section is concerned with the relationships between educational research and economic and human development. The introductory article addresses these issues and briefly reviews the articles in the section, extending the scope of development to include regional as well as national development (see *Educational Research for National and Regional Development*). The role of donor agencies in supporting and promoting national development through programs that provide and assist with the supply of educational services is also discussed in an article on *Donor Support for Educational Research*.

3.8. Towards the Future

The concluding section of the *Handbook* is concerned with the future development of education in the Asia-Pacific region. The opening article is concerned with the relationships between educational research and reform in education. Following an introductory statement on the theory of the processes of change, examples are provided to illustrate the nature of the processes of reform from five countries in the region that used in different ways the findings of educational research. However, it is argued that the nature of the processes of reform and change in education remains a fruitful area for research, since relatively little is known about the reform process itself (see *Educational Research for Educational Reform*). The second article arises from discussions at seminars within the region on two occasions, and draws together the views of decision-makers on what they expect from educational research studies that would assist them in the making of policy-related decisions (see *The Impact of Educational Research on Decision Making and Practice*). This article challenges educational research workers in the region to design and conduct their investigations in such a way that their findings meet directly the needs of the decision-makers. It is also necessary to ensure that the findings of their research studies are presented in ways that can be readily comprehended by those who are involved in the making of decisions. The following article examines the nature, needs and impact of educational research in the region, with consideration given to the identification and the setting of priorities for research into educational problems in several countries of the region (see *Research in Education: Nature, Impact, Needs and Priorities*). The next issue addressed in this section is concerned with the contribution of university education to national development, particularly in East and South-East Asia (see *University Education for National Development*). Among the issues that must be addressed is the question of whether or not, with limited resources, the money available should be directed to raising both participation and standards at the primary, the secondary or the tertiary levels, in order to meet the needs of a particular country at a particular stage of development. The article that follows considers the issues of educational reform in the Pacific Island countries (see *Culturally Inclusive Teacher Education in Oceania*). It is clear that very different strategies are required for the smaller Pacific Island countries than for the larger Asian countries in undertaking change and planning programs for educational reform.

The next article in the section considers an important issue relating to the education of adolescents and the need for reform in the second phase of education (see *Reforming Secondary Education and the Education of Adolescents*). This article is followed by a provocative article on the need for and the nature of reform in the curricula of science and technology at the secondary school stage (see *Reform in Science and Technology Curricula*). The subsequent article in this section follows on from the previous one and addresses the controversial issue of the role of new technology, particularly information and communications technology (ICT), in education (see *Emerging Information and Communications Technology in Education*). The use of ICT and other technology in the provision of education in order to enhance learning is gradually emerging, but there is little doubt that the use of ICT is occurring before the questions of how education should relate to ICT have been clearly answered.

In some countries of the region, particularly in Oceania, advances in the standards of living of the people in these countries are dependent on developments in the labour market, which in turn are dependent on educational reform. The article that follows addresses these issues with respect to the many small island countries that are spread across the Pacific Ocean (see *Educational Reform and the Labour Market in Pacific Island Countries*).

The major problem in expanding educational research activity in the region involves the training of educational research workers. In the past, many research workers have been trained in institutions outside the Asia-Pacific region, in ways that do not necessarily address the problems of the region. It is clear that the time has come for training programs to be regionally based with a focus on the problems of education within the Asia-Pacific region (see *Training of Educational Research Workers*). This article is followed by an article arguing very strongly for regional cooperation and collaboration in educational research between countries and groups within the Asia-Pacific region because of the common problems of so many countries and the urgent need for sound solutions to these problems (see *Regional Cooperation in Educational Research*). Cooperation and collaboration in the future can build on what has been achieved in the past, particularly through the programs introduced by the National Institute for Educational Policy Research of Japan (NIER) and the UNESCO Centre in Bangkok.

The two concluding articles in the *Handbook* seek to draw together the issues addressed by the articles presented in the earlier sections. The article on *Challenges for Research into Educational Reform in the Asia-Pacific Region* redirects attention to the opening article in the *Handbook* (see *Trends in Educational Reform in the Asia-Pacific Region*) and examines both the challenges that confront education in the region, as well as the research needed in order to respond in appropriate ways to these challenges. The final article considers an issue that is raised repeatedly in earlier articles, namely the impact of globalisation on the countries and peoples of the Asia-Pacific region. This article argues that while the problems raised by globalisation are regarded in the main to be economic, political, scientific and technological, environmental, or societal issues, the primary concern in examining the effects of globalisation is for issues involving human development. There would appear to be no simple way in which the effects of globalisation can be advanced or retarded by educational policy decisions that apply across countries. Giddens (1999) has described the existing situation in terms of the *Runaway World*. However, within each country educational policy decisions might be made to accelerate or decelerate change. What is required is the systematic monitoring of the effects of change not only in terms of indicators that assess the economic, political, scientific and technological, environmental and societal effects of global change, but also the impact of change on human development within each country and across the countries of this region. In the light of evidence collected through systematic monitoring it might be possible for countries within the Asia-Pacific region to cooperate in the finding of common solutions to specific problems that emerge and that are shown to have reached a critical stage. The challenge for educational research workers and other research workers in the social and human sciences is to assemble evidence on human development that has been carefully collected, and through the use of indicators to monitor systematically the changes that are taking place. Only if the evidence provided by the indicators is sound can plans be made and policies developed to tackle major problems as they arise (see *Monitoring the Impact of Globalisation on Education and Human Development*).

4. HOW TO USE THIS HANDBOOK

Educational research in the Asia-Pacific region is a highly diverse enterprise, drawing on many disciplinary areas, many different cultural traditions, and using many different approaches to inquiry. Over recent decades a substantial body of theoretical knowledge concerned with the processes of education has been built up that relates to the particular problems facing education in the region. While these problems and the body of knowledge that has been assembled are likely to have much in common with the corpus of knowledge derived from educational research studies in other parts of the world, there is clearly sufficient that is unique to the Asia-Pacific region to warrant the preparation of a separate *Handbook* that focuses on educational research in the region. Thus, it is the editors' contention that there is a unity and coherence running through this volume that is provided by the common problems of the region. This warrants the *Handbook* being seen as more than a compendium of articles, written by different scholars drawn from different disciplines and different countries and with different approaches to inquiry. It is thus the focus on the educational problems of the region that provides this *Handbook* with its purpose and design and makes it a source book for those who are engaged in the many different aspects of educational activity in the region.

Thus, the *Handbook* is intended as a reference work or a source book: (a) for administrators and policy makers and policy analysts who seek to grapple with the educational and societal problems of particular countries and education systems within the region; (b) for graduate students to use as a first introduction to particular issues within the region that they are planning to investigate, review or debate; (c) for university and college teachers to read in their preparation of lectures and discussions with their students; and (d) for practising research workers who seek to obtain information and knowledge about specific problems in the region that they plan to examine in greater depth and to research in their scholarly inquiries. As a consequence of the inclusion of articles on so many topics in two volumes, it is evident that no individual entry can be complete in itself. Thus, every article seeks not only to be relevant and up to date, but also to provide guidance, through a concise set of references to key articles or publications that are likely to be readily available, from which the administrators, policy makers, policy analysts, students, teachers, research workers and scholars might obtain further information. Furthermore, in order to facilitate the search for information, references are provided within each article to other articles in the volume where related information has been presented.

In addition, both a detailed *Index of Names* and an *Index of Subjects* based on key words or phrases have been compiled to assist the reader in the search for information. Consequently, the reader of this *Handbook* who is searching for information on a particular problem or topic could commence by looking up appropriate words in the *Index of Subjects* in order to locate an article related to the problem or topic and to identify articles that are referenced by key words where the topic is considered. In a similar way, the *Index of Names* can be used to locate references to the work of a particular author or scholar who is known to have made a substantial contribution to a sphere of research related to the topic on which information is sought. In order to assist in this task, page numbers are given both for the bibliographic reference and for the point at which the reference is cited in the text. Furthermore, as well as the specified authors of particular articles, there are many other scholars who have contributed directly or indirectly to the preparation of particular articles. As far as is possible, every effort has been made to list the names of all who have contributed to the preparation of articles for this *Handbook*, together with their institutional affiliations.

ACKNOWLEDGEMENTS

No work of the size of this *Handbook* could be published without considerable efforts being made by many people. To several people a special debt of gratitude is due. First, we are grateful to Rupert Maclean, Yin Cheong Cheng and Geoff Masters who conceived the idea of a *Handbook* and persuaded Kluwer Academic Publishers to undertake the publication of the two volumes that have been prepared. They have also assisted in very tangible ways with the editing of a section of the *Handbook* and the preparation of articles for publication and in providing advice and guidance on the development and editing of the *Handbook*. In addition, we are grateful to Neville Postlethwaite and Albert Tuijnman who from their extensive experience with the preparation of similar works, not only contributed through a particular article, but also gave very helpful advice and assistance with the preparation of other articles for inclusion in this *Handbook*. Second, we are grateful to the many authors who prepared articles, carefully checked galley proofs, revised their articles and in many cases acted as consultants for other articles in the *Handbook*. Third, a very great debt is due to the section editors, who willingly undertook the work required of them, by selecting authors for the section for which they were responsible, revising the list of articles for their section, reviewing and editing the articles that they received and preparing the articles in their section for publication. Fourth, we are very grateful to Michel Lokhorst, who took responsibility for the carrying of the manuscript through the process of publication and to Irene van den Reydt who undertook the detailed work required for the successful publication of the *Handbook*. Finally, we are very grateful to Dianne and John Harris who helped maintain contact with authors around the world, and typed and retyped articles to prepare them for publication. To them all, our very sincere thanks are offered.

REFERENCE

Giddens, A. (1999). *Runaway World: How Globalization is Reshaping our Lives.* London: Profile Books.

SECTION 1:

TRENDS AND ISSUES

Section Editor – John P. Keeves

1

Trends in Educational Reform in the Asia-Pacific Region*

YIN CHEONG CHENG
Hong Kong Institute of Education, Hong Kong

1. INTRODUCTION

Educational reform in the Asia-Pacific region, which is one of the fastest developing areas in the world, is receiving strong and intensive local and global attention. Since the 1990s, huge national resources have been invested in education and related initiatives in nearly every country in the region for bringing about substantial improvement and development in many different aspects of society (Cheng & Townsend, 2000). Unfortunately, many countries are still very disappointed with their education systems in view of the challenges of the new century. In order to redress the problems in their education systems, more and more reforms are now proposed to improve the practice and effectiveness of education at different levels. The major question to be asked is: what lessons can be learnt and shared from these ongoing educational reforms in the region such that we can avoid repeating failure, thus, preparing for policy formulation and implementation of educational changes in each of our own countries?

Particularly for policy makers, educators and researchers, the following questions should receive due attention in considering educational reform.

- What are the major trends and characteristics of the ongoing educational reforms in this region? The answer to this question will furnish a basis for delineating an overall profile for understanding the direction, nature and progress of the national initiatives and efforts in the region.
- What are the major challenges that the policy makers and educators are facing in the current educational reforms particularly in such a new era of globalisation, information technology, competition and the knowledge-driven

---

* Parts of the material in this article were adapted from Cheng (2001d), Cheng (1999b) and Cheng and Townsend (2000). (See also *Challenges for Research into Educational Reform in the Asia-Pacific Region*).

economy? The answers will provide a common ground for sharing the concerns, discussing issues, exchanging ideas and even developing related strategies to cope with the challenges.
- What implications can be drawn from these trends and challenges for research? The answers may bridge the gaps between research and policy-making, for a knowledge base can then be built by research to inform policy-making and practice.

In response to the concerns with educational reforms in the region, a group of scholars in the region had already begun in 1997 to organise a symposium of country reports to describe and analyse the educational changes and developments that had occurred in mainland China, Hong Kong, Korea, Malaysia, Singapore, Taiwan and Thailand. These reports were then edited and published as a special issue in *School Effectiveness and School Improvement: An International Journal of Research, Policy and Practice* (Cheng, 1999a).

Following this issue, a broader and larger regional effort was organised in 1999 to continue the discussion on educational change and development. In addition to the country reports from Hong Kong, Japan, Korea, Malaysia, P.R. China, Singapore, Taiwan, and Thailand for sharing among a wide readership are country reports from Australia, New Zealand and the Islands in the South Western Pacific. These reports were then edited and published in the form of a book chapter in *Educational Change and Development in the Asia-Pacific Region: Challenges for the Future* (Townsend & Cheng, 2000).

These scholarly efforts are not undertaken in a vacuum, as the educational reforms in the region have received increasing attention from both national and international organisations. In October 2000, the National Institute for Educational Policy Research of Japan and United Nations Educational, Scientific and Cultural Organisation (UNESCO) organised an international seminar on educational research for improved policy and practice in the Asia-Pacific region. At the conference, participants from different countries and organisations in the region presented their country reports on educational reform and discussed the current issues regarding the relationship between educational research and policy making. The reports were from a wide range of countries and areas in the region, including Australia, China, Hong Kong, India, Indonesia, Japan, Lao P.D.R., Malaysia, New Zealand, Philippines, Korea, Sri Lanka, Thailand and Vietnam.

With the support of delegations from more than 16 countries, the Hong Kong Institute of Education also organised in February 2001 an international forum on educational reform in the region. The plenary country reports revealed a wide range of experiences and progress of educational reforms in different countries and areas in the region. At the forum, educators, policy makers, researchers and practitioners had intensive and stimulating discussion on the trends and directions of educational reforms in individual countries and the whole region, in response to the impact of globalisation and technology, the demand for localisation and the expectations of individualisation in education in the new century.

In July 2001, the Office of the National Education Commission in Thailand organised another international forum on educational reform, with the support of a number of national and international organisations. Again, this international forum represented the continuing national and regional effort and commitment to educational development and change with a hope of meeting the challenges of the new millennium. The representatives of selected countries, in the region with some from the United Kingdom and the United States, reported their country experiences in formulating and implementing educational reforms and related strategies.

Since 1998, the *Asia-Pacific Journal of Teacher Education and Development* (*APJTED*) has published numerous articles and country reports on the change and development in teacher education in the region. The articles, particularly country reports at the symposium of Korea (2000, Vol. 3, No. 1), of Singapore (1999, Vol. 2, No. 1), of Malaysia (2000, Vol. 3, No. 2), of Australia (Vol. 1, No. 2) and of China (Vol. 4, No. 2), as well as those from Taiwan, Thailand and India, are being released in *APJTED*, and are an important source of information for understanding the context and issues of educational reform in these countries.

2. MAJOR TRENDS IN ONGOING EDUCATIONAL REFORM

The above country reports and documents become the updated, comprehensive and relevant sources of information for understanding the trends and issues of educational reform in the region. Based on these reports and documents, this article aims to provide an overview of the trends in educational reform in the Asia-Pacific region in recent years. It addresses the first of the three questions posed in the preceding section, with the other two questions (regarding challenges and implications from these trends for research) to be addressed in a later chapter in the closing section of this Handbook (see *Challenges for Research into Educational Reform in the Asia-Pacific Region*).

After reviewing the above reports with reference to Cheng (1999a) and Cheng and Townsend (2000), some major trends of ongoing educational reforms in the region can be observed and are discussed in the following paragraphs. The discussion that follows is guided by a conceptual framework for a four-level analysis which reflects the scope, focus and general nature of the trends, as shown in Figure 1. In brief, at the macro-level, the main trends include: (a) towards re-establishing new national visions and educational aims; (b) towards restructuring the education system at different levels; and (c) towards market-driving, privatising and diversifying education. At the meso-level, (d) towards parental and community involvement in education and management is a salient trend. At the site-level, the major trends are: (e) towards ensuring education quality, standards and accountability; (f) towards decentralisation and school-based management; and (g) towards enhancement of teacher quality and continuous lifelong professional development of teachers and principals. At the

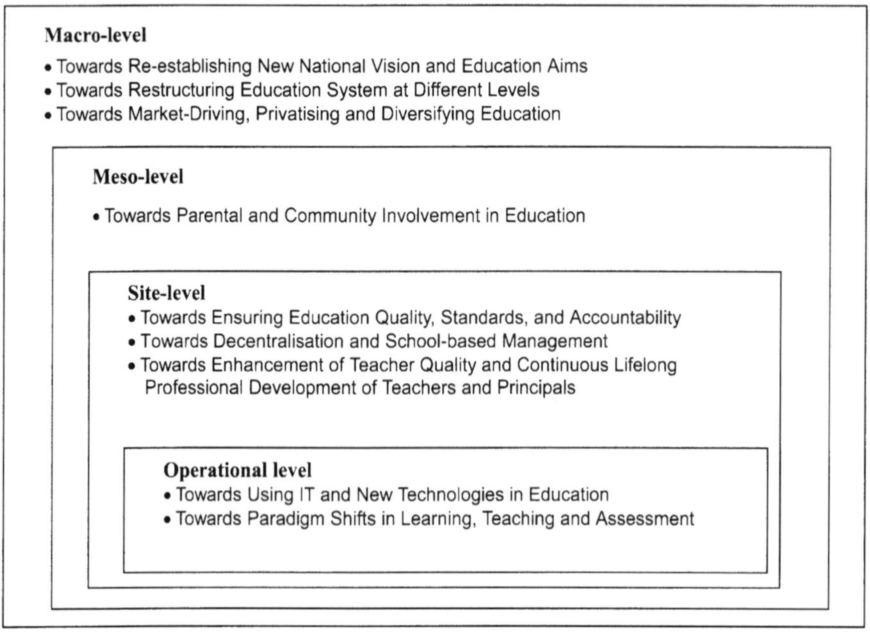

Macro-level
- Towards Re-establishing New National Vision and Education Aims
- Towards Restructuring Education System at Different Levels
- Towards Market-Driving, Privatising and Diversifying Education

Meso-level
- Towards Parental and Community Involvement in Education

Site-level
- Towards Ensuring Education Quality, Standards, and Accountability
- Towards Decentralisation and School-based Management
- Towards Enhancement of Teacher Quality and Continuous Lifelong Professional Development of Teachers and Principals

Operational level
- Towards Using IT and New Technologies in Education
- Towards Paradigm Shifts in Learning, Teaching and Assessment

Figure 1. Trends of educational reforms at different levels

operational level, the main trends include: (h) towards using information technology in learning and teaching and applying new technologies in management; and (i) towards paradigm shifts in learning, teaching and assessment.

2.1. *Towards Re-establishing New National Visions and Educational Aims*

Many national leaders in the region take a functionalist perspective of educational reform as a means of supporting the economic, political and cultural development of society (Blackledge & Hunt, 1985). In facing the rapid changes and global challenges from economic, cultural and political transformations, national leaders have become dissatisfied with the short-term achievements of their education systems. Political leaders increasingly draw connections between the role of education and the achievement of their national visions for growth and prosperity in the new era (Brown, 1999). They propose new educational visions and long-term aims to prepare their new generations for the future in a globally competitive environment.

Malaysia provides a typical example of this connection between national visions and educational goals. Under Dr. Mahathir Mohammed's leadership, the Malaysian government put forward its *Vision 2020*. This plan developed during the 1980s proposed that Malaysia would transform itself from a commodity-export country to an industrialised and developed country by the year 2020. Education played a central role in *Vision 2020* as an instrument for promoting national unity, social equality and economic development (Lee, 2000).

By way of further example, Singapore's national leaders took a similarly strategic view of education in their plans for nation-building. Indeed, they accepted the challenge of making learning part of the national culture. Accordingly, they proposed the slogan 'Thinking schools, a learning nation' as a vision for directing national educational changes. This is illustrated in Gopinathan and Ho (2000, p. 161):

> ... While the national economy (Singaporean) is adjusting through structural shifts, such as liberalisation, deregulation, and privatisation, which help integrate a national economy with the larger world economy ... the education system must also adjust structurally to a changing national economy.

Many similar examples can be found in Australia, Cambodia, P.R. China, Hong Kong, India, Japan, Korea, New Zealand, the Philippines, Taiwan, Thailand and Singapore. Leaders in these countries and areas have reviewed their educational aims and established new goals that reflect new national and global visions (see, e.g., Baker, 2001; Caldwell, 2001; Castillo, 2001; Cheng, 2001a, 2001b; Rajput, 2001; Rung, 2001; Sereyrath, 2001; Shan & Chang, 2000; Sharpe & Gopinathan, 2001; Suzuki, 2000; Tang, 2001; Townsend, 2000; Yu, 2001).

2.2. *Towards Restructuring the Education System at Different Levels*

The development of the education system often has to meet the needs of the development of the economy in the country (Chabbott & Ramirez, 2000). In the past two and three decades, most developing countries or areas in the Asia-Pacific region made great efforts to expand their compulsory education to nine years when they were establishing their industries. Now, some of them are making efforts to expand their senior secondary school sectors and improve enrolment to higher education. Hong Kong, Korea, Malaysia and Taiwan are representative cases (Cheng, 2001a, 2001b; Kim, 2000; Lee, 2000; Shan & Chang, 2000). Comparatively, some countries like Cambodia, Vietnam and Laos put more effort into further expanding their compulsory education (Pok, 2001; Sereyrath, 2001; Sisavanh, 2001). Singapore and Taiwan provide more vocational and technical training opportunities at the secondary and post-secondary levels (Gopinathan & Ho, 2000; Shan & Chang, 2000).

Many countries in the region have invested more and more resources in educational development in the past decade. Some developed countries, such as Australia, Japan and New Zealand, after expansion of their education systems a few decades ago, are no longer concerned with their compulsory or universal education (Baker, 2001; Suzuki, 2000; Townsend, 2000). They are more concerned with the accountability and quality of their education systems than with quantity.

In facing the challenges of globalisation, the knowledge-based economy and international competition, such countries and areas as Korea, P.R. China, Hong Kong, Malaysia, Taiwan and Singapore are very concerned with the effectiveness and relevance of their education system to their national development in a highly competitive global context. They have started to review and change their education systems from early childhood education to citizenship and lifelong education. For example, they put more emphasis on early childhood education, enhancing the provision of vocational education in terms of quantity, quality, variety and relevance and to reviewing the interface between levels of school education. The reform of the examination system is also an important area of review in education systems. For example, in P.R. China, Japan, Korea, Singapore, and Malaysia, there are many different types of policy efforts being made to review and change their examination systems. The purposes of these changes are to reflect the changes towards new educational aims, to improve the process of selection and allocation of students, to promote multiple intelligences of students, to enhance educational equality, to re-direct educational practice and to redress serious drawbacks in the examination-oriented culture particularly in some Asian countries.

2.3. *Towards Market-Driving, Privatising and Diversifying Education*

There are tight financial constraints on meeting the rapidly increasing needs of diverse developments in nearly all countries in the region. Policy makers in some countries are trying to shift the exclusive public funding model to privatisation as one approach to expanding, diversifying and improving education. For example, P.R. China, being caught in the stream of development with its market economy playing an increasingly important role, is confronting more complicated and tighter financial constraints in developing its education system to satisfy the huge and diverse needs for education (Tang & Wu, 2000).

Particularly when more and more people want to pursue higher education in order to survive in a very competitive job market, privatisation of tertiary education will inevitably become more common in, for example, Korea, Taiwan, Japan, P.R. China and the Philippines. It is generally believed that privatisation will allow educational institutions to increase their flexibility of use of physical and human resources. How to create a market or semi-market environment for promoting competition between educational institutions has become a salient issue in reform at the turn of the century. Some countries (e.g., Australia) are experimenting with funding methods designed to encourage self-improvement as well as competition among schools. Other areas (e.g., Hong Kong and Singapore) are trying out different types of parental choice schemes.

2.4. *Towards Parental and Community Involvement in Education*

During the past several decades, parents and the community have increased expectations of education and are becoming more demanding of better school performance for their children. Also, there is an increasing demand for educational accountability to the public and to demonstrate value for money because education is mainly financed with public funds (Adams & Kirst, 1999). Inevitably, educational leaders at the school, district and national levels have to provide more direct avenues for parents and the community to participate in developing the schools.

In some developed countries, such as Canada and the United States, there is a long tradition of parental involvement in their schools. In many Asian areas like Hong Kong, Japan, Korea, Malaysia, Taiwan and Thailand such a tradition has been largely absent. Recently, people in these countries have become more aware of the importance of involving parents and local communities in school education (Wang, 2000). Although there is seldom legislation in some areas to guarantee parents' involvement in school education, sentiment is growing that parents should be given this right (Tik, 1996).

In addition to parents, the local community and the business sector are also direct stakeholders in education. Their experiences, resources, social networks and knowledge are often very useful to the development and delivery of education. From a positive perspective, community involvement in education can benefit the educational institutions by providing more local resources, support and intellectual input, particularly when facing the increasing but diverse demands for quality education, the community resources and support become extremely important and necessary. Also, parents and community leaders can share the management responsibility; strengthen communication between families, the community and the school; motivate teachers; monitor school operations; and even assist the school in combating negative influences inherent in the local community (Goldring & Sullivan, 1996).

2.5. *Towards Ensuring Education Quality, Standards and Accountability*

As reported by Cheng (2001c), there have been three waves of educational reform in different parts of the world during the past three decades that pursue internal quality, interface quality and future quality in education. The first wave focuses on the pursuit of internal quality and effectiveness through improvement of internal processes particularly teaching and learning. The second wave emphasises achievement of interface quality through ensuring educational accountability to the public and meeting stakeholders' concerns. The third wave aims at assurance of the future quality of education with a strong emphasis on enhancement of educational relevance for the future needs of the new millennium.

From the country reports, it was seen that many countries in the region were mainly in the second wave of educational reforms with some starting on the third wave. Since the beginning of the 1990s, there have been a lot of initiatives with a strong emphasis on educational quality assurance and accountability due to the growing demands from stakeholders. Particularly following quality movements in the business and industry sectors over the last two decades, such concepts as quality control, quality assurance, total quality management and benchmarking have been brought into the educational sector (Mukhopadhyay, 2001). In practice, the definition of educational quality is often associated with fitness for use, the satisfaction of strategic constituencies and conformity to strategic requirements and expectations. Different indicators are being developed and used to assess educational quality and to set educational standards or benchmarks for school performance and accountability (Fitz-Gibbon, 1996).

In the region, such countries and areas as Australia, P.R. China, Hong Kong, India, Singapore and Thailand, have introduced different types of quality assurance initiatives to monitor and promote educational quality and accountability (Abdullah, 2001; Cheng, 1997; Lloyd, 2001; Mukhopadhyay, 2001; Townsend, 2000).

2.6. *Towards Decentralisation and School-Based Management*

The emerging international trend in educational administration from external control to school-based management for effective use of resources and promoting human initiatives in education was evident in the 1990s and is continuing today. Centralised management often ignores school-based needs and human initiatives and it is often too rigid to meet changing school needs (Cheng, 1996). Current reforms in many parts of the world are seeking to facilitate school-based initiatives for development and effectiveness in education.

This is the case, for example, in such developed nations as Australia and New Zealand. In New Zealand, public schools were changed into self-managing schools in 1998. In the state of Victoria, Australia, schools were turned into self-managing schools in 1993. More recently, they have started the process of further decentralising authority to promote self-governing schools (Townsend, 2000).

Similar trends are now also apparent in some developing areas of the region. In Hong Kong, the School Management Initiative was implemented in 1991 with the goal of enhancing educational quality through school-based management. Hong Kong's Education Commission further reinforced school-based management as one facet of its quality assurance process for all schools in 1997. In Korea, hundreds of public primary and secondary schools experimentally organised a School Governing Board involving teachers, parents, principals, alumni and community leaders to promote school self-management and to enable schools to provide diverse educational services to meet the needs of their local communities (Kim, 2000). In Malaysia, the administrative system is being decentralised to encourage school-based management and teacher empowerment (Lee, 2000). In Singapore, the government set up autonomous schools as early as 1991, as a mechanism for improving quality in education (Gopinathan & Ho, 2000). In P.R. China, decentralisation of power from the central government to local communities and to the school level is becoming evident. School autonomy and the participation of local communities are now being encouraged to facilitate school development and effectiveness (Tang & Wu, 2000).

2.7. *Towards Enhancement of Teacher Quality*

In response to the fast changing educational environment and the increasing and demanding challenges from the local and global communities, there is a trend for educational reforms in many countries of the region with an emphasis on teacher quality and continuous lifelong professional development of both teachers and principals. Many policy makers understand that teacher quality is the key to success in educational reform and development. For example, Australia, China, Korea, Hong Kong, Malaysia, Taiwan, Thailand, Singapore and Vietnam have made major policy efforts in recent years to enhance the quality of teachers and principals. More and more professional training is provided to teachers through in-service education programs. The required professional qualifications for entering the teaching profession also tend to be gradually enhanced even though the extent of progress may be different in different countries.

Traditionally, it is often assumed that educational goals are clear and static, and educational practices should be improved if these goals cannot be successfully achieved. Nowadays, educational environments in the region are changing very quickly, and goals are not so clear and unchanging anymore. In the past decade, numerous changes have been imposed on schools and teachers in different parts of the region, and this trend seems to be further accelerated in the new century. If teachers, principals and their schools are not enabled and prepared to deal with these changes, all the efforts for enhancing educational quality and effectiveness will result in failure. Since educational change and development are ongoing in such a changing environment, there is inevitably a strong need for continuous lifelong professional development of school practitioners. Most areas in the region like China, Hong Kong and Korea have already reviewed their teacher education programs and put lifelong professional development of teachers and principals onto their agenda for educational reform.

2.8. *Towards Using Information Technology and New Technologies in Education*

The increasing and tremendous impact of information technology (IT) on every aspect of society are evident to most national leaders and educational leaders. Many policy makers take IT in education as one of the most strategic initiatives in ongoing educational reforms (Birch & Maclean, 2001). Countries like Australia, Japan and Singapore implemented their strategies to promote IT in education a few years earlier while other countries have developed their IT plans during the last three years (Gopinathan & Ho, 2000; Suzuki, 2000; Townsend, 2000). In Hong Kong, schools are getting more and more computers and other IT facilities, and they are also being helped to network both locally and internationally through the intranet and internet. More and more training is provided for teachers in the use of IT in teaching. Teachers and students are often expected to become IT competent in a very short time (Education and Manpower Bureau, 1998).

In addition to IT in education, there has been a clear shift of emphasis from using simplistic techniques towards applying sophisticated technology in educational management in the past decade. Traditionally, schools or educational institutions were all under external control and dependent on management by central authorities. Educational leaders or managers did not see a need to use sophisticated management technologies. Today, however, the environment is changing much more rapidly. Consequently, such management technologies as strategic management, development planning, participative management and quality assurance are increasingly emphasised. Policy makers in the region and other parts of the world are promoting the use of these methods (see, e.g., Bush & Coleman, 2000).

2.9. *Towards Paradigm Shifts in Learning, Teaching and Assessment*

In response to the challenges of globalisation, IT and a knowledge-based economy in the new millennium, there is a growing trend for educational reforms to emphasise paradigm shifts in learning, teaching and assessment in many areas of the region. For example, Australia, Hong Kong, Korea, Singapore and Taiwan have started new initiatives with the support of IT and networking to promote major changes in curriculum, pedagogy and assessment with a hope of bringing about a paradigm shift in learning and teaching in the classroom.

As pointed out in Cheng (2000b), the whole world is moving towards multiple globalisations and becoming a global village with boundless interactions among countries and areas in the new century. Many societies in the region are now more diverse and are moving towards becoming learning societies. In such a fast changing environment, the aim of educational reform tends to develop students as lifelong learning citizens who will contribute creatively to the formation of a learning society and a learning global village with multiple developments in technological, economic, social, political, cultural and learning aspects. Cheng (2000b) has further urged that there should be a paradigm shift in education from the traditional site-bounded paradigm to a new paradigm with an emphasis on the development of contextualised multiple intelligence (CMI) for the new generations through the processes of globalisation, localisation, and individualisation in education.

In fact, the ongoing educational reforms in some parts of the region like Australia, Hong Kong, Singapore and Japan have already provided evidence of moving in the direction of a new organisation with various types of initiatives in globalisation, localisation and individualisation for education. The learning and teaching will tend to be globalised, localised, and individualised in the coming years with the help of IT and boundless multiple networking. Unlimited opportunities and multiple global and local sources will be created for lifelong learning and development by both students and teachers.

3. CONCLUSION

In response to the challenges of globalisation, IT, international competition, the knowledge-based economy, and rapid societal developments in the new millennium, there are numerous educational reforms launched in nearly all countries and areas in the Asia-Pacific region. To optimize the reforms, policy makers, educators and researchers must pay due attention to three important questions in considering educational reforms. The first question – 'What are the major trends and characteristics of the ongoing educational reforms in this region?' – is addressed here, with the answer furnishing a basis to delineate an overall profile for understanding the direction, nature and progress of the national initiatives and efforts in the region. In sum, based on the observations from the country reports, nine major trends of educational reform in the Asia-Pacific region are identified and discussed in this article, with the discussion guided by a conceptual framework that reflects the scope, focus and general nature of the trends.

From the country reports and documents, some key concerns and issues arising from each trend in educational reform can be observed. In addition, we may understand that the trends of educational reform at these four levels may mutually influence the development of education. It is hardly a surprise that the educational environment shaped by the educational reforms at the macro- and meso-level will often influence the management, functioning, process and output of education at the site and operational levels. Clearly, the effectiveness and quality of educational outputs from the more micro-levels may also produce impacts on the development of policies and initiatives at the macro- and meso-levels. Even though the congruence or mutual support between educational reforms of different trends and of different levels is strongly expected in policy making and implementation, unfortunately it is often not the case in the reality of educational reforms. In the past decade, policy gaps between initiatives inevitably became one of the major problems and challenges accounting for reform failure in education (Cheng & Cheung, 1995).

'What are the major challenges the policy makers and educators are facing in the current educational reforms?' and 'what implications can be drawn from the above trends and challenges of education reforms for research?' are also important questions in the ongoing discussion of educational reform in the Asia-Pacific region. The answers to these questions would provide a common ground for understanding the concerns and challenges of the educational reforms and bridging the gaps between research and policy making, with a hope of building up a knowledge base by research to inform policy making and practice of educational reform in the region and in other parts of the world.

REFERENCES

Abdullah, H. M. (2001). *Policy Dialogue on Quality Improvement in Education: A Malaysian Experience*. Paper presented at the Second International Forum on Quality Education: Policy, Research and Innovative Practices in Improving Quality of Education, Beijing, China, 12–15 June 2001.

Adams, J. E., & Kirst, M. W. (1999). New demands and concepts for educational accountability: Striving for results in an era of excellence. In J. Murphy & K. S. Louis (Eds.), *Handbook of Research on Educational Administration* (pp. 463–490) (2nd ed.). San Francisco: Jossey-Bass.

Baker, R. (2001, February 14–16). *A Challenge for Educational Transformation: Achieving the aim of 'Thinking and acting locally, nationally and globally' in a devolved education system*. Plenary speech presented at the International Forum on Education Reforms in the Asia-Pacific Region 'Globalization, Localization, and Individualization for the Future', HKSAR, China.

Birch, I., & Maclean, R. (2001). Information and communication technologies for education and teacher development in the Asia-Pacific region: Issues and challenges. In Y. C. Cheng,, M. M. C. Mok & K. T. Tsui (Eds.), *Teaching Effectiveness and Teacher Development: Towards a New Knowledge Base* (pp. 347–370). Dordrecht, The Netherlands: Kluwer Academic Publishers.

Blackledge, D., & Hunt, B. (1985). *Sociological Interpretations of Education*. Sydney: Croom Helm.

Brown, T. (1999). Challenging globalization as discourse and phenomenon. *International Journal of Lifelong Education, 18*(1), 3–17.

Bush, T., & Coleman, M. (2000). *Leadership and Strategic Management in Education*. London: Paul Chapman.

Caldwell, B. (2001). *Setting the Stage for Real Reform in Education*. Plenary speech presented at the International Forum on Education Reforms in the Asia-Pacific Region 'Globalization, Localization, and Individualization for the Future', HKSAR, China.

Castillo, E. S. (2001). *Educational Reform: The PCER strategy and findings/recommendations*. Plenary speech presented at the International Forum on Education Reforms in the Asia-Pacific Region 'Globalization, Localization, and Individualization for the Future', HKSAR, China.

Chabbott, C., & Ramirez, F. O. (2000). Development and education. In M. T. Hallinam (Ed.), *Handbook of the Sociology of Education* (pp. 163–188). New York: Kluwer/Plenum.

Cheng, Y. C. (1996). *School Effectiveness and School-based Management: A Mechanism for development*. London: Falmer Press.

Cheng, Y. C. (1997). A framework of indicators of education quality in Hong Kong primary schools: Development and application. In H. Meng, Y. Zhou & Y. Fang (Eds.), *School Based Indicators of Effectiveness: Experiences and Practices in APEC Members* (pp. 207–250). China: Guangxi Normal University Press.

Cheng, Y. C. (1999a) (Ed.). Recent education developments in South East Asia. Special Issue of *School Effectiveness and School Improvement, 10*(1), 3–124.

Cheng, Y. C. (1999b). Recent education developments in South East Asia: An introduction. *School Effectiveness and School Improvement, 10*(1), 3–9.

Cheng, Y. C. (2000a). Educational change and development in Hong Kong: Effectiveness, quality and relevance. In T. Townsend & Y. C. Cheng (Eds.), *Educational Change and Development in the Asia-Pacific Region: Challenges for the Future* (pp. 17–56). Lisse, The Netherlands: Swets & Zeitlinger.

Cheng, Y. C. (2000b). A CMI-triplization paradigm for reforming education in the new millennium. *International Journal of Educational Management, 14*(4), 156–174.

Cheng, Y. C. (2001a). *Towards the Third Wave of Education Reforms in Hong Kong: Triplization in the New Millennium*. Plenary speech presented at the International Forum on Education Reforms in the Asia-Pacific Region 'Globalization, Localization, and Individualization for the Future', HKSAR, China.

Cheng, Y. C. (2001b). *Education Reforms in Hong Kong: Challenges Strategies, and International Implications*. Country report at the First International Forum on Education Reform: Experiences of Selected Countries, Bangkok, Thailand, 30 July – 2 August 2001.

Cheng, Y. C. (2001c). *Paradigm Shifts in Quality Improvement in Education: Three Waves for the Future*. Plenary speech presented at the Second International Forum on Quality Education: Policy, Research and Innovative Practices in Improving Quality of Education, Beijing, China, 12–15 June 2001.

Cheng, Y. C. (2001d, October). *Educational Reforms in the Asia-Pacific Region: Trends, challenges and research*. Paper presented at the Second APIED International Conference on Education Research, Seoul National University, Seoul, Korea.

Cheng, Y. C., & Cheung, W. M. (1995). A framework for the analysis of educational policies. *International Journal of Educational Management, 9*(6), 10–21.

Cheng, Y. C., & Townsend, T. (2000). Educational change and development in the Asia-Pacific region: Trends and issues. In T. Townsend & Y. C. Cheng (eds), *Educational Change and Development in the Asia-Pacific Region: Challenges for the Future* (pp. 317–344). Lisse, The Netherlands: Swets & Zeitlinger.

Education and Manpower Bureau (1998). *Information Technology for Learning in a New Era*. Hong Kong: Government Printer.

Fitz-Gibbon, C. T. (1996). *Monitoring Education: Indicators, quality, and effectiveness.* London: Cassell.

Goldring, E. B., & Sullivan, A. V. (1996). Beyond the boundries: Principals, parents, and communities shaping the school environment. In K. Leithwood, J. Chapman, D. Corson, P. Hallinger & A. Hart (Eds.), *International Handbook of Educational Leadership and Administration* (pp. 195–222). Dordrecht, The Netherlands: Kluwer Academic Publishers.

Gopinathan, S., & Ho, W. K. (2000). Educational change and development in Singapore. In T. Townsend & Y. C. Cheng (Eds.), *Educational Change and Development in the Asia-Pacific Region: Challenges for the Future* (pp. 163–184). Lisse, The Netherlands: Swets & Zeitlinger.

Kim, Y. H. (2000). Recent changes and developments in Korean school education. In T. Townsend & Y. C. Cheng (Eds.), *Educational Change and Development in the Asia-Pacific Region: Challenges for the Future* (pp. 83–106). Lisse, The Netherlands: Swets & Zeitlinger.

Lee, M. N. N. (2000). The politics of educational change in Malaysia: National context and global influences. In T. Townsend & Y. C. Cheng (Eds.), *Educational Change and Development in the Asia-Pacific Region: Challenges for the Future* (pp. 107–132). Lisse, The Netherlands: Swets and Zeilinger Publishers.

Lloyd, S. (2001). *The Impact of National Goals and Policies on Educational Quality at Local and National Levels.* Paper presented at the Second International Forum on Quality Education: Policy, Research and Innovative Practices in Improving Quality of Education, Beijing, China, 12–15 June 2001.

Mukhopadhyay, M. (2001). *Total Quality Management in Education.* New Delhi: National Institute of Educational Planning and Administration.

Pok, T. (2001, February 14–16). *Educational Reforms in Cambodia.* Plenary speech presented at the International Forum on Education Reforms in the Asia-Pacific Region 'Globalization, Localization, and Individualization for the Future', HKSAR, China.

Rajput, J. S. (2001, February 14–16). *Reforms in School Education in India.* Plenary speech presented at the International Forum on Education Reforms in the Asia-Pacific Region 'Globalization, Localization, and Individualization for the Future', HKSAR, China.

Rung, K. (2001, February 14–16). *Educational Reform in Thailand: Implementation and strategy.* Plenary speech presented at the International Forum on Education Reforms in the Asia-Pacific Region 'Globalization, Localization, and Individualization for the Future', HKSAR, China.

Sereyrath, S. (2001). *Major Movements of Education Reform in Cambodia.* Country report at the First International Forum on Education Reform: Experiences of Selected Countries, Bangkok, Thailand, 30 July – 2 August 2001.

Shan, W. J., & Chang, C. C. (2000). *Social Change and Educational Development in Taiwan, 1945–1999.* In T. Townsend & Y. C. Cheng (Eds.), *Educational Change and Development in the Asia-Pacific Region: Challenges for the Future* (pp. 185–206). Lisse, The Netherlands: Swets & Zeitlinger.

Sharpe, L., & Gopinathan, S. (2001, February 14–16). *After Effectiveness: New directions in the Singapore school system?* Plenary speech presented at the International Forum on Education Reforms in the Asia-Pacific Region 'Globalization, Localization, and Individualization for the Future', HKSAR, China.

Sisavanh, K. (2001). *Curricular Reform in Lao PDR Today and Tomorrow.* Paper presented at the Second International Forum on Quality Education: Policy, Research and Innovative Practices in Improving Quality of Education, Beijing, China, 12–15 June 2001.

Suzuki, S. (2000). *Japanese education for the 21st century: Educational issues, policy choice, and perspectives.* In T. Townsend & Y. C. Cheng (Eds.), *Educational Change and Development in the Asia-Pacific Region: Challenges for the Future* (pp. 57–82). Lisse, The Netherlands: Swets & Zeitlinger.

Tang, X. (2001, February 14–16). *Educational Reform and Development in the People's Republic of China: Issues and trends.* Plenary speech presented at the International Forum on Education Reforms in the Asia-Pacific Region 'Globalization, Localization, and Individualization for the Future', HKSAR, China.

Tang, X., & Wu, X. (2000). *Educational Change and Development in the People's Republic of China:*

Challenges for the Future. In T. Townsend & Y. C. Cheng (Eds.), *Educational Change and Development in the Asia-Pacific Region: Challenges for the Future* (pp. 133–162). Lisse, The Netherlands: Swets & Zeitlinger.

Tik, C. Y. (Ed.) (1996). *New Trends in Home-School Cooperation.* Hong Kong: Breakthrough.

Townsend, T. (2000). The Challenge to Change: Opportunities and dangers for education reform in Australia. In T. Townsend & Y. C. Cheng (Eds.), *Educational Change and Development in the Asia-Pacific Region: Challenges for the Future* (pp. 229–266). Lisse, The Netherlands: Swets & Zeitlinger.

Townsend, T., & Cheng, Y. C. (Eds.) (2000). *Educational Change and Development in the Asia-Pacific Region: Challenges for the Future.* Lisse, The Netherlands: Swets & Zeitlinger.

Wang, Y. (Ed.) (2000). *Public-Private Partnership in the Social Sector.* Tokyo, Japan: Asian Development Bank Institute.

Yu, F. Z. (2001). *Education Development and Reform in China.* Country report at the First International Forum on Education Reform: Experiences of Selected Countries, Bangkok, Thailand, 30 July – 2 August 2001.

2

Achieving Education for All in the Asia-Pacific Region

RUPERT MACLEAN
UNESCO-UNEVOC International Centre for Education, Bonn, Germany

KEN VINE
University of New England, Armidale, Australia

1. INTRODUCTION: THE QUEST TO ACHIEVE EDUCATION FOR ALL

The Education for All movement has gained considerable momentum throughout the world over the past ten years, as countries work increasingly closely together to stamp out illiteracy and so empower individuals and their communities and help create a better quality of life for their citizens. This is to be expected, for as the Organisation for Economic Cooperation and Development (OECD) has noted the attainment of basic literacy and numeracy skills has been identified repeatedly as the most significant factor in reducing poverty and increasing participation by individuals in the economic, political and cultural life of their societies (OECD/DAC, 1996). This realization is not new, and is not limited to organisations like the OECD. Many development agencies such as the Swedish International Development Co-operative Agency (SIDA, 2001), the World Bank (1997, 2000), the Department for International Development in the United Kingdom (DFID, 2000), and non-government organizations such as Oxfam (Watkins, 2000) strongly share this same view.

More than 50 years ago, the nations of the world, speaking through the *Universal Declaration of Human Rights*, asserted that "everyone has a right to education". Yet world-wide, and particularly in the Asia-Pacific region, the current provision of education remains seriously deficient. The situation is so serious that many governments and members of the international aid community believe that more decisive and better coordinated action must be taken if education and schooling are to be made relevant, to improve qualitatively, and to be universally available to all. Education as a fundamental right for all people, women and men, of all ages, world-wide is regarded as crucially important to the welfare of humankind. The reason is that effective education can help ensure a safer, healthier, more prosperous and environmentally sound world, while simultaneously contributing to social, economic, and cultural progress, tolerance, and international cooperation. It contributes to economic, social and political development, to rising income levels and to improved standards of living. Sound basic education is also fundamental to the strengthening of higher levels of education and of scientific and technological literacy and capacity and thus to self-reliant, sustainable development. In addition, as the *Report to UNESCO of the International Commission on Education for the Twenty-first Century* (Delors Report, 1996) has so persuasively argued, education is not just a human right but is also fundamental to the survival of our human societies.

The term 'education for all' does not just concern itself with primary education for all, but is concerned with six key target dimensions, these being:

- expansion of early childhood care and development;
- universal access to completion of primary education;
- improvement in learning achievement;
- increase in adult literacy rates;
- expansion of provision of basic education and training in essential skills required by youth and adults; and
- increased acquisition by individuals and families of the knowledge, skills and values necessary for better living and an improved quality of life.

Despite notable efforts by countries around the globe to ensure the right to education for all, the current reality is that, worldwide: (a) more than 100 million children, including at least 60 million girls, have no access to primary schooling, while millions more attend school but do not acquire essential knowledge and skills; (b) more than 960 million adults, two-thirds of whom are women, are illiterate, while functional illiteracy is a significant problem in all countries, industrialized and developing; and, (c) more than one-third of the world's adults have no access to the printed knowledge, new skills and technologies that could improve the quality of their lives and help them shape, and adapt to, social and cultural change.

At the same time the world faces a wide range of other daunting problems which adversely impact on the ability of countries to strengthen and upgrade education and schooling, most notably: (a) mounting debt burdens, (b) the threat of economic stagnation and decline, (c) rapid population growth, (d) widening economic disparities among and within nations, (e) war, (f) occupation, (g) civil strife, (h) violent crime, (i) the preventable deaths of millions of children, and (j) widespread environmental degradation. Some argue that these problems constrain efforts to meet basic learning needs, while the lack of basic education among a significant proportion of the population prevents societies from addressing such problems with strength and purpose (*World Declaration on Education for All*, 1990a). However, it may also be argued that for many developing countries it is not only a lack of resources, but also a matter of government priorities, where a greater proportion of GNP is spent on so-called 'weapons of war' (such as armies, tanks and armaments) than on 'weapons for peace' (schools, health care and clean water).

Whatever the root causes of these problems, over the last decade they have led to major setbacks in improving basic education in many of the least developed countries. In some other countries, economic growth has been available to finance educational expansion but, even so, many millions remain in poverty and are unschooled or illiterate. In certain industrialized countries, too, cutbacks in government expenditure have led to the deterioration of education in terms of access, equity and quality assurance.

As a result of such problems, in order to ensure everyone has a better opportunity to exercise their right to education, governments, along with international aid organizations and members of civil society, decided in 1990 to band together at the World Conference on Education for All (EFA), in Jomtien, Thailand, to make a concerted effort to achieve education for all (EFA) by the end of the year 2000. At this international conference on EFA, some 1,500 participants comprising delegates from 155 governments, policy makers and specialists in education and health, social and economic development from around the world, met to discuss major aspects of education for all. Representatives were ambitious in their goals, in that they agreed to take combined action to universalize primary education, massively reduce illiteracy, and to work together towards making basic education available to everyone, by the end of the twentieth century.

The *World Declaration on Education for All* (1990a) and the *Framework for Action to Meet Basic Learning Needs* (1990b), adopted at Jomtien, foresaw the need for an end-of-decade (2000) assessment of progress as a basis for a comprehensive review of policies concerning basic education. The World Education Forum (Dakar, Senegal, April 2000) was the first and most important event in education at the dawn of the new century. Unfortunately no region of the world was successful in achieving the goal set at the Jomtien conference of achieving EFA by 2000 and so, by adopting the *Dakar Framework for Action*, the 1,100 participants of the Forum reaffirmed their commitment to achieving Education for All, this time by the year 2015.*

2. CONTEXTUAL FACTORS: DEVELOPMENT AND EDUCATION

The region of Asia-Pacific, which is home to almost 60 per cent of the world's population, is outstanding for the vast range of diversities that encompass almost all aspects of life, whether geographical, socio-economic, cultural, political or developmental. In this region there are countries of vast landmasses (China,

---

* In addition, six years after the Jomtien Conference, the Mid-Decade Meeting of the International Consultative Forum on Education for All, in Amman, Jordan (June 1996) brought together some 250 decision-makers from 73 countries, including ministers of education, and multilateral and bilateral agencies and non-governmental organizations. Their aim was to assess the advances made since the Jomtien Conference, and to take stock of progress and shortcomings to enable adjustments to be made prior to and as a run up to the end of decade EFA evaluation.

India and Australia) and also island countries lying in expansive ocean areas (the Maldives, and Pacific Island countries). Countries with the largest populations (China – 1.3 billion; India – 1 billion) and the most rapidly growing megacities are to be found in the region, as are countries with relatively small populations (Bhutan, 600,000; Niue in the Pacific, with just 2,300 inhabitants). The levels of economic development also vary widely, with some of the richest countries (such as Japan and Australia) and some of the poorest countries on earth (such as Bangladesh and Burma) (UNESCO, 2001b).

The enormous disparities between rich and poor are brought home graphically if one considers that it is estimated that 60 per cent of those living in the region have never used a telephone, while at the same time millions of others can afford access to the latest computers and communications technologies in their own homes, and use these facilities routinely in either their workplace or in their schools and colleges (UNESCO, 1998, 2000c).

Asia contains the largest number of poor of any region in the world and in overall terms the number is increasing. The incidence of those living below the poverty line remains as high as 45 per cent in some developing economies in the Asia-Pacific region. Such widespread poverty is a destabilizing factor affecting adversely health, social and educational services, and levels of educational attainment. It also intensifies gender disparities (UNESCO, 2000b). Some of the major educational problems currently facing humankind are evident in the Asia-Pacific region. Despite a commitment in 1990 by international aid organizations and the donor community to achieving Education for All by the year 2000, the Asia-Pacific region contains the largest proportion of the world's illiterates. At present there are estimated to be 625 million illiterates in the Asia-Pacific region: 71 per cent of the world's total, of whom 64 per cent are women and girls (UNESCO, 2000a). Moreover, some of the disparities that exist between sub-regions in the Asia-Pacific region are particularly disturbing, for example, in South Asia the literacy rate is 42 per cent compared with 72 per cent in East and South-East Asia; in South Asia, life expectancy is ten years lower than for those living in East and South-East Asia (UNESCO, 2000a).

In the Asia-Pacific region, 56 per cent of the school-age population (6 to 11 year olds) is not enrolled in primary education. Of those who do enrol, at least one-third abandon, or drop-out, of school before completing the primary cycle. The reasons are compelling and well known: poverty, social exclusion, socio-economic gaps, urban-rural disparities, rampant mismanagement, and lack of adequate and relevant educational programs. Moreover, gender disparities make the picture bleaker: of the out-of-school children in the region, 62 per cent are girls, concentrated especially in South Asia.

In spite of such challenges and diversity there is a common, positive thread in that all countries in Asia and the Pacific believe that in order to achieve poverty eradication, sustainable human development, justice and equity in all respects, there is a need to make greater efforts to improve the quality, effectiveness and relevance of education and schooling. The reform and re-engineering of education and schooling is receiving increasing attention from governments in the region, especially in the less developed countries, with particular reference to achieving universal literacy and education for all.

3. END-OF-DECADE EFA 2000 ASSESSMENT: THE PROCESS

The International Consultative Forum on Education for All, the EFA Forum, was established by the principal sponsors of Jomtien (1990). Its purpose was to guide the follow-up, plan the assessment process and determine the General and Technical Guidelines for preparing Country Assessment Reports. As the basis for the end-of-decade (2000) assessment of progress towards EFA, the EFA Forum established an inter-agency Global Technical Advisory Group (GTAG) in early 1998 consisting of technical representatives from each of the five Jomtien partner agencies: UNDP, UNESCO, UNFPA and the World Bank. The GTAG was assisted by 11 Regional Technical Advisory Groups (RTAG). The RTAG in Asia and the Pacific was created in November 1998 and included representatives from the five Jomtien partner agencies, the regional agencies, such as ESCAP and the Asian Development Bank (ADB), and the donors. The RTAG for the Asia-Pacific region was coordinated by UNESCO, Bangkok.

In May 1998, the GTAG team first met at UNESCO, Bangkok, and by June 1998 a set of *EFA 2000 Assessment: General Guidelines* and *EFA 2000 Assessment: Technical Guidelines* had been prepared. The *Technical Guidelines* proposed a number of characteristics and phenomena, as well as a set of 18 core EFA indicators that describe or measure the main components of basic education, that were grouped according to the six target dimensions of EFA, referred to earlier in this article. These core indicators were decided upon by UNESCO and UNICEF after discussions with countries taking part in the EFA 2000 Evaluation. Each country EFA Assessment Report referred directly to these 18 core EFA indicators.

From October 1998, EFA 2000 Assessment activities in the Asia-Pacific region commenced in collaboration with regional and field offices from EFA Forum Partners throughout the region. Member States designated EFA coordinators, EFA Assessment teams and technical sub-groups to implement this major endeavour. Between October 1998 and April 1999, technical teams from UNESCO and UNICEF conducted a series of workshops in a number of Member States in order to launch the EFA Assessment activity and to provide technical assistance to enable countries to prepare their EFA Status Country Reports. Countries were encouraged to assess critically their achievements in education and identify more effective and appropriate strategies for laying down the foundations of lifelong learning for all. The assessment sought to identify progress and shortcomings in basic education. This assessment was seen as vital for planning effective and achievable solutions and policies for the twenty-first century to achieve education for all. Areas examined included: (a) life skills for youth for the new millennium; (b) adolescent reproduction and sexual health education; (c) distance learning by satellite; (d) inclusive education; and

(e) scientific, technological and environmental literacy for all. The Asia-Pacific Conference adopted a regional action plan for education that eventually fed into the Global Plan for Education in the Twenty-first Century.

The culmination of the whole world-wide Education for All 2000 Assessment exercise was the World Education Forum in Dakar, Senegal, in April 2000, at which the results from the six regional conferences were presented and debated. The outcomes of the Dakar Conference have helped to motivate and re-energize decision makers and policy makers towards achieving EFA, this time by 2015, with new commitments and ideas to accelerate the EFA process.

4. EFA 2000 ASSESSMENT IN THE ASIA-PACIFIC REGION: OVERVIEW OF RESULTS

No region of the world, including the Asia-Pacific region, was successful in achieving the goal set at the Jomtien Conference (1990) of achieving EFA by the year 2000. However, over the decade 1990 to 2000 the Asia-Pacific region made some progress towards achieving the EFA objectives set at Jomtien, and the rate of growth of enrolment of primary school children outpaced that of other regions of the world. The Asia-Pacific region, however, is still far from achieving the various EFA goals set at the Jomtien Conference and the challenge remains of expanding access to quality basic education for all to include marginalized groups such as the poor, women and girls, ethnic minorities and those living in remote areas.

What follows is a brief overview and synthesis of the 42 country EFA 2000 Assessment Reports prepared for the Bangkok conference (January 2000) to discuss EFA 2000 Assessment in the Asia-Pacific region in March 2000. The aim here is to convey the essential flavour of these country reports, by identifying the main quantitative trends emerging and the principal qualitative factors that warrant consideration in designing future policy and practice to achieve EFA. In addition to examining what happened in the past decade the aim is also to identify what trends and points of emphasis are likely to occur in the future.

This overview stresses the overall situation in the region and does not detail the often considerable disparities that exist between and within regions. Readers who need to examine such details are directed to the country reports and, in particular, the sub-regional synthesis reports. The main results of the EFA 2000 Assessment exercise in the Asia-Pacific region, regarding the key target dimensions, are given in the sections that follow (UNESCO, 2000d, 2000e, 2000f, 2000g, 2001a).

4.1. *Early Childhood Education*

Although the sub-sector of early childhood education (ECE) in many countries is smaller, and at an earlier stage of development than is the case with primary education, this sub-sector has achieved an impressive growth rate over the past decade, in all-sub regions in Asia-Pacific except for the Central Asian States, where central financing for early childhood programs was one of the victims of the process of transformation for a market driven economy. Enrolment in early childhood programs was 30 million in 1990, and it reached an estimated 48 million in 2000, an average increase of almost 50 per cent. This expansion has mainly been achieved through an increasing community support for ECE. However, early childhood education is largely urban based, teachers are generally poorly trained, and programs are difficult to sustain due to their heavy reliance on local community resources.

It must also be noted that data on ECE are usually of low quality because in most countries in the Asia-Pacific region the sub-sector is loosely regulated by government, and responsibility for ECE policy and planning is spread over a number of Ministries. Typically, in these circumstances, no one Ministry assumes responsibility for monitoring ECE development and, hence, the data collected by each Ministry are incompatible with that collected by the other Ministries. Moreover, ECE programs are characterized by a wide diversity of providers both public and private, ranging from institutions that provide occasional day care facilities that are little more than child minding operations, to pre-schools that implement educational curricula designed to stimulate intellectual development. Consequently, it is difficult to interpret figures that give the same status to part- and full-time enrolments, irrespective of the type of institution. Most worrying, though, is the frequent absence of a regulatory framework. This circumstance can permit the operation of child care centres and pre-schools within which children may be abused. Enactment and enforcement of appropriate legislation is probably the most pressing need in the ECE sub-sector in the Asia-Pacific region.

4.2. *Primary Education*

The good news regarding primary education is that participation in primary schooling has grown considerably over the past decade, outpacing the population growth of the school-age cohort. Total primary school enrolments in 2000 approached 400 million for the region as a whole, compared to 331 million enrolled in 1990. This represents an average annual growth rate much higher than the 1.4 per cent population growth rate. However, despite the appreciable growth in primary enrolments there is an increasing disparity of access within many countries. In many of the larger countries, internal disparities are alarming in that rural areas, geographically remote communities, ethnic and racial minorities, and the less disadvantaged in general, demonstrate slower or no progress when compared to the more accessible target populations. In addition, the gender gap has not appreciably narrowed, in spite of major efforts that have been made to improve this situation.

In many countries the stress has been on the expansion of systems of primary education to improve access to this level of education. But this focus may have distorted resource allocations away from support for quality and retention measures. Many countries now realize that resources may have been better spent on improving the holding power of schools, and on reducing repetition and drop-out rates, rather than merely adding to the infrastructure of education systems whose internal efficiency allows massive wastage in terms of too many children dropping out after a few years. Empirical data support this view in that several countries in South Asia, for example, have registered credible progress in expanded enrolments without registering appreciable reductions in what are currently high drop out, repetition and survival rates. For example, in some South Asian States by the end of the decade it was still the case that only 50 per cent of the primary cohort completed five years of schooling.

4.3. Learning Achievement

The dimension of learning achievement and assessment has become a renewed priority in many countries of the region. The reason is that there is an increasing concern about quality assurance, which has driven policy reform and project activities in the areas of curriculum reform, teacher training, textbook revisions, and the reorientation of testing procedures. The matter of quality of learning is important, but difficulties arise when it comes to matters such as how universal standards and learning needs are balanced with local and community needs, how to allocate resources to the various quality inputs such as textbooks and teacher training, and these need to be carefully scrutinized and balanced. One of the problems with the greater stress on evaluation and assessment in countries is that in many cases this is used as a tool to evaluate the individual student, rather than as a diagnostic tool to help improve the learning achievements of students. In addition, a greater emphasis needs to be given to assessment as a diagnostic tool to evaluate education systems and, in the light of such evaluation, to make improvements. In a few countries there is unfortunately a move to use tests to exclude learners from the next stage of education and schooling.

The dominant impression gained from many Asia-Pacific countries' sub-regional and regional EFA 2000 Assessment reports, is that in nearly all countries substantial progress was made over the last decade in improving access to, and participation in, primary education. Unfortunately, however, the dominant impression is also that this quantitative expansion of the provision of educational opportunities has been accompanied by diminution of learning quality, and this is particularly the case in South Asia. This matter is examined in a later article, where a case study is provided regarding learning achievement in the countries of South Asia (see *A Case Study of Learning Achievement in South Asia*).

4.4. Adult Literacy

Over the past decade, adult literacy has increased in almost all countries, although, given the fact that there are different ways of measuring this success, and there are different rates of success between countries, it is difficult to generalize about a consistent pattern of improvement in this area. One trend has been the increasing stress on functional literacy for the world of work and for citizenship, and an increasing number of Community Learning Centres. For

Asia as a whole, the adult literacy rate is currently about 73 per cent with the lowest rate being just above 50 per cent in South Asia. One of the concerns is the uneven growth, and the insufficient resources devoted to, and low status of, adult literacy. One trend in countries where a greater emphasis is being given to adult literacy is an increasing emphasis on adult literacy as a vehicle for empowerment, not as an end in itself, but for skills development for increasing agricultural productivity, better employment, more effective citizenship, or entrepreneurship, or as a vehicle for nutrition, sanitation and other health messages. One important matter which many countries are addressing is that of sustainability regarding literacy programs, to avoid relapse into illiteracy, which is all too common in some countries, and particularly for communities in rural areas.

The development of adult literacy programs in the region is uneven, and much remains to be done to expand access and improve quality. One reason is that many countries do not recognize adult education and literacy as being a key aspect of education for all, and part of the notion of lifelong learning. Instead, some focus almost exclusively on the education of the young and youth, which, although important, are only some of the dimensions of EFA. A key recommendation of the Dakar Forum is that governments should allocate a greater percentage of their basic education budgets to adult learning programs rather than mainly relying on NGOs and local communities to carry the main cost of financing this sub-sector.

4.5. Skills Training and Education for Quality of Life

Countries in the Asia-Pacific region tended to interpret the fifth and sixth dimensions of EFA 2000 Assessment differently. This is probably due to a lack of conceptual clarity in their definition by the EFA Forum, and because many different providers deliver life skills and vocational training for youth, only some of which are government funded and operated. Consequently, life skills and vocational training for youth and adults is an area that attracted relatively little attention in the various country reports.

This is unfortunate because there is a global trend to conceptualise vocational and skills training for youth differently from how it has been seen in the recent past. Specifically, there is a growing recognition of the need for flexible vocational training systems that represent partnerships between industry, business and government, and which balance acquisition of tightly specified job skills with broader, more generic knowledge that will facilitate life-long learning. The need for such an approach to vocational training of youth is no doubt as pressing in the Asia-Pacific region as in the most developed of the Western economies, and will assume growing importance with increasing trade liberalization and consequent increased emphasis on economic competitiveness, which, in turn, requires a highly skilled workforce.

In many countries in the Asia-Pacific region life skills training is provided through nonformal education (NFE) channels. This is especially the case with programs designed to assist marginalised groups such as homeless youth, migrant workers and those living in severely impoverished circumstances. The programs are intended to develop a range of life skills that will prepare individuals and groups to take advantage of opportunities as they arise in their communities, or to create such opportunities.

It is impossible to provide a comprehensive account of the scale of NFE in the Asia-Pacific region because it is often implemented by community organisations with limited, if any, funding from local, provincial or central governments. Also, most NFE training programs are of short duration and offered in different modes: for example, full time for two weeks; part time for three months; two evenings a week for six months. In these circumstances, simple head counts of the number of participants each year are misleading. Additionally, many of the smaller providers lack the administrative capacity to design and maintain information systems of the complexity needed to monitor closely and to evaluate their operations. Similarly, NFE providers vary enormously in scale of operation and breadth of program offerings. Consequently, statistics such as the number of NFE providers are not particularly useful.

Notwithstanding these difficulties of assessment, it is apparent from their reports that many countries in the Asia-Pacific region have experienced a growth in demand for NFE programs in a wide variety of areas and for diverse client groups. However, this component of the education sector is possibly the least well understood by policy analysts and planners, and has received the least attention from governments in the context of EFA.

5. CONCLUSION: THE WAY AHEAD

The EFA 2000 Assessment exercise revealed many successes and uncovered many issues that need urgent attention. As previously remarked, the gains made in access and participation rest on insecure foundations, not least because there is compelling evidence that over the last decade there has been a trade-off between quantitative expansion of national systems and reduction in quality of education.

This must change, and change rapidly, because education is both a cultural imperative and an economic necessity. In respect of the latter, the increasing rate of globalisation leaves many traditional industries in developing countries exposed to market forces that are insensitive to local circumstance, and which spur the migration of labour intensive manufactures to low wage economies. The only effective, longer-term protection that developing countries can have to the liberalization of world trade is rapidly to skill their workforce so that they can make the necessary adjustments to their economies. However, the origins of a skilled and flexible workforce lie in high quality education at all levels of schooling.

Moreover, global economic development will not await upon changes in education systems in developing countries, and this implies that the rate of change in education systems will have to outpace that of economic development.

This poses an enormous challenge to all countries but especially to those in the developing world where, in terms of quality of education, there is a need both to catch up quickly and then to maintain best education practice. It is clear from the EFA 2000 Assessment exercise that, with few exceptions, developing countries lack the resources needed for such an undertaking. In these circumstances, the most developed nations must find the means to provide such resources, not because of altruism, though that would be laudable, but because education, health and dignified employment are basic human rights, and to the extent that they are denied to anyone we are all diminished.

REFERENCES

Delors Report (1996). *Learning: The Treasure Within*, Report of the International Commission on Education for the Twenty First Century. Paris: UNESCO.

DFID (2000). *Education for All: The Challenge of Universal Primary Education*. London: Department of International Development.

OECD/DAC (1996). *Shaping the 21st Century: The Contribution of Development Cooperation*. Paris: Organization for Economic Cooperation and Development.

SIDA (2001). *Education for All: A Human Right and a Basic Need*. Stockholm: Swedish International Development Agency.

UNESCO (1990a). *World Declaration on Education for All*. Paris: UNESCO.

UNESCO (1990b). *Framework for Action to Meet Basic Learning Needs*. Paris: UNESCO.

UNESCO (1996). *Education for All: Achieving the Goal. Meeting of the International Consultative Forum on Education for All*, Amman, Jordan, 16 to 19 June. Paris: UNESCO.

UNESCO (1998). *Development of Education in Asia and the Pacific: Issues and Prospects*. Bangkok: UNESCO Principal Regional Office for Asia and the Pacific.

UNESCO (2000a). *Conference Report: Asia-Pacific Conference on Education for All 2000 Assessment*. Bangkok: UNESCO Principal Regional Office for Asia and the Pacific.

UNESCO (2000b). *Asia-Pacific Conference on Education for All 2000 Assessment: Background Information*. Bangkok: UNESCO Principal Regional Office for Asia and the Pacific.

UNESCO (2000c). *World Education Report 2000: The Right to Education*. Paris: UNESCO.

UNESCO (2000d). *A Synthesis Report of Education for All 2000 Assessment in the South and West Asia Sub-Region*. Bangkok: UNESCO Principal Regional Office for Asia and the Pacific.

UNESCO (2000e). *A Synthesis Report of Education for All 2000 Assessment in the Pacific Sub-Region*. Bangkok: UNESCO Principal Regional Office for Asia and the Pacific.

UNESCO (2000f). *A Synthesis Report of Education for All 2000 Assessment in the Trans-Caucasus and Central Asia*. Bangkok: UNESCO Principal Regional Office for Asia and the Pacific.

UNESCO (2000g). *A Synthesis Report of Education for All 2000 Assessment in the East and South East Asia Sub-Region*. Bangkok: UNESCO Principal Regional Office for Asia and the Pacific.

UNESCO (2001a). *Regional Action Plan: Follow-Up to the World Forum on Education for All (2001–2006)*. Paris: UNESCO.

UNESCO (2001b). *Statistical Reports and Studies*. Paris: UNESCO.

World Bank (1997). *Development in Practice*. Washington: The World Bank.

World Bank (2000a). *Education for All: From Jomtien to Dakar and Beyond*. Paper prepared by the World Bank for the World Education Forum in Dakar, Senegal, April 26 to 28, 2000. Washington: The World Bank.

World Education Forum (2000b). *Global Synthesis: Education for All 2000 Assessment*. Paris: UNESCO.

Watkins, K. (2000). *The Oxfam Education Report*. Oxford: Oxfam.

3

Educational Expenditure and Participation in East Asia and Australia

GERALD BURKE, ROBERT LENAHAN and HING TONG MA
Monash University – ACER Centre for the Economics of Education and Training, Melbourne, Australia

1. INTRODUCTION

This article reviews (a) the population and income levels of some selected economies to provide a broad indication of their educational need and of the capacity to finance them; (b) the main features of the level of participation in education, the resources provided, and the degree of public and private provision and finance; and (c) education strategies pursued in the selected economies. The article draws on an earlier study by Lenahan, Burke and Ma (1998) of educational expenditure and participation in selected economies in the Asia-Pacific region. The economies considered here in order of their income per head in 2000 are Japan, Hong Kong, Australia, Singapore, Republic of Korea, Malaysia, Thailand, Philippines, China, Indonesia and Vietnam.

There are considerable deficiencies in the data available, which means that the information presented and the findings of the article must be considered as tentative. The data limitations include the time lags involved in collecting and presenting data by the international agencies, inconsistencies in the nature of data presented in the various international publications and absence of any data at all for certain time periods and certain economies. The article relies mainly on data from UNESCO, *Education at a Glance, OECD Indicators* reported by the OECD (2001) and *World Development Indicators* reported by The World Bank (2001).

2. POPULATION AND POPULATION CHANGE

The populations of the selected economies vary enormously. Population data for all of the selected economies for the year 2000 are given in Table 1. The huge range of population sizes is illustrated by these data. China has a population

Table 1. Indicators of population and national product

Economy	Population (millions) 2000	Population average (annual growth rate %) 1980–2000	Population average (annual growth rate %) 2000–15	Population (% aged 0–14) 2000	GNI per capita (US$) 2000	GNI per capita ($PPP) 2000	GDP per capita (% average growth per annum) 1990–00
Japan	127	0.4	−0.1	15	35,620	27,080	1
Hong Kong	7	1.5	0.6	16	25,920	25,590	2
Australia	19	1.3	0.8	21	20,240	24,970	3
Singapore	4	2.5	1.3	22	24,740	24,910	5
Korea, Repub	47	1.1	0.4	21	8,910	17,300	5
Malaysia	23	2.6	1.5	34	3,380	8,330	4
Thailand	58	1.3	0.8	27	2,000	6,320	3
Philippines	76	2.5	1.7	38	1,040	4,220	1
China	1,263	1.3	0.7	25	840	3,920	9
Indonesia	210	1.7	1.2	31	570	2,830	3
Vietnam	74	1.9	1.2	33	390	2,000	6

Source: World Development Indicators (World Bank, 2001) and *Education at a Glance* (OECD, 2001).
Gross National Income in US$ estimated by World Bank Atlas method, mainly using exchange rates.
PPP – Purchasing power parity dollars, i.e. converted at the rate that would equalise the cost of a similar basket of goods and services across countries.

nearly 70 times as large as Australia. The smallest ones are Hong Kong and Singapore. The rate of growth of population in the selected economies is slowing. The simple average population growth rate from 1980 to 2000 was 1.6 per cent per annum but is projected to fall to 0.9 per cent. The projected rate is highest for the Philippines at 1.7. The population is falling in Japan.

3. STUDENT-AGE POPULATION

The growth in population, and whether it is by natural increase or migration, affects the age distribution of the population. The relative size of the young population provides some insights into the demand for education. Column 4 in Table 1 presents the percentage of the population aged 0 to 14 years. This gives an indication of likely enrolment in the compulsory years of education in the coming year. Consistent with the data for population growth, the richer countries tend to have low proportions of their population in this age group. Only 15 per cent of Japan's population is in this category whereas Vietnam and the Philippines have a third of their total population in this group. The additional burden of educational provision for these countries is clear.

4. FINANCIAL CAPACITY

Measures of national income or national product can be used to provide an indication of the standard of living in a country and also of the capacity to provide for social services including education. The data in Columns 5 and 6 in Table 1 show the gross national income per capita of the selected economies estimated at current exchange rates and by the purchasing power-parity method (PPP), which is based on a conversion factor representing the cost of an equivalent basket of goods and services for all countries. Column 7 gives the average annual rate of growth of the period in per capita GDP for the period 1990 to 2000.

There are four high-income economies, Japan, Hong Kong, Australia and Singapore. They have a Gross National Income (GNI) per capita of $25,000 to $27,000 on the PPP measures. Korea is not far out of the high-income group. Malaysia is in an upper middle group. Thailand, the Philippines and now China, with its very rapid rate of economic growth, are classified as lower middle-income economies. Indonesia with particular economic problems in the period since 1997 has fallen to the low-income list. It joins Vietnam which is growing rapidly from a very low base. The average rate of growth of the lower or low income economies is higher than for the rich countries, but their income is relatively very low and the demands of their population structure is high.

5. EDUCATION SYSTEMS AND THEIR FINANCING

This section provides a broad overview of the extent of participation, the structures of the education systems of the selected economies, the main forms of financing and the broad levels of expenditure. Detailed diagrams and descriptions of the education systems are included in Postlethwaite (1995).

5.1. Structure and Participation

The selected economies vary substantially in the levels of educational provision. Table 2 presents the estimated gross and net enrolment in the main sectors of education. Table 3 provides a very broad and tentative indication of the recent attributes of the economies, which are listed in order of their per capita incomes as shown in Table 1.

UNESCO provides estimates of gross enrolment ratios, which are total enrolments in a sector regardless of the age of students, divided by the population of the official age group for that sector. Net enrolment ratios are the enrolments of the official age group divided by the population of that age. Both gross and net enrolment ratios are shown for primary and secondary education in Table 2 but only gross for pre-primary and for tertiary. Table 2 also shows data on enrolment rates by age from the World Education Indicators reported for some of the selected countries by the OECD (2001).

The UNESCO data for pre-primary are highly variable and show that Hong Kong and Korea have high proportions of young children in educational programs. It should be noted that the Korean rates are for five-year-olds and that the World Education Indicators show Korea with a low rate of enrolment of persons aged 4 years and under. The data are for full- and part-time enrolment, not full-time equivalent data.

The information in the table for primary education is reasonably consistent. All of the economies appear to be implementing policies of universal primary education. The gross ratios vary within a narrow range from 87 in Thailand to 123 in China, and indicate that, in the main, the vast majority of students of primary school age in the selected economies are enrolled at schools. In Indonesia and Vietnam only half of the students of secondary age are enrolled, but virtually all students at this level in Japan and Korea are enrolled. The gross rate for Australia has been affected by the way that adult enrolments in technical and further education are distributed in these statistics across both secondary and tertiary education.

Japan, Australia and Korea have gross rates of 40 per cent or more in tertiary education. The very high rate for Australia, of over 70 per cent, reflects the high rates of participation of older adults. Of lower-middle income economies, the Philippines has a high rate of secondary enrolment and a quite high rate of tertiary enrolment. As will be considered, this is achieved through fairly low unit expenditures and by considerable private finance. For Malaysia and Hong Kong there are a very large number of tertiary students who study in other economies. On the other hand, overseas students make up about ten per cent of university students in Australia.

In summary, the high- and middle-income economies appear to have achieved universal primary education. The low-income economies are close to achieving

Table 2. Estimated enrolment ratios

| | Pre-Primary | | UNESCO 1996* | | | | | World Education Indicators about 1999** | | | |
	Age group	Gross	Primary	Primary gross	Secondary net	Secondary gross	Tertiary gross	4 and under as % population aged 3 to 4	5 to 14	15 to 19	20 to 29
								Net enrolment rates by age group of full- and part-time students in public and private institutions			
Japan	3–5	50	100	101	na	103	41	76	101	na	na
Hong Kong	3–5	83	90	94	69	73	na	na	na	na	na
Australia	4	78	95	101	89	148	72	34	98	80	27
Singapore	3–6	na	92	94	na	74	39	na	na	na	na
Korea, Rep	5	88	92	94	97	102	52	16	92	81	22
Malaysia	4–5	42	100	101	na	64	12	3	97	44	6
Thailand	3–5	62	na	87	na	56	22	49	99	58	3
Philippines	5–6	11	100	114	59	77	29	na	85	62	4
China	3–6	29	100	123	na	70	6	na	na	na	na
Indonesia	5–6	19	95	113	42	51	11	na	76	37	2.6
Vietnam	3–5	38	na	113	na	47	7	na	na	na	na

Source: UNESCO (www)and OECD (2001).
Net enrolment ratios are the enrolments of the official age group divided by the population of that official age.
Gross enrolment ratios are the enrolments of any age in the sector of any age as a percentage of the population of the official age.

Table 3. Participation, finance and structure of education: a tentative classification, mid-1990s

	Japan	Hong Kong	Australia	Singapore	Korea	Malaysia	Thailand	Philippines	China	Indonesia	Vietnam
Participation											
Universal primary	Yes	Yes	Yes	Yes	Yes	Yes	Yes?	Yes?	Yes?	Yes?	No
Universal junior secondary	Yes	Yes	Yes	Yes	Yes	Yes	No	No	No	No	No
Senior secondary – greater than 50% completion	Yes	Yes	Yes	Yes	Yes	Yes	No	Yes	No	No	No
Post secondary -greater than 40% participation	Yes	No	Yes	No	Yes	No	No	Yes?	No	No	No
Vocational											
Specialist vocational senior secondary – 20% or more of total	Yes	Yes*	No	Yes	Yes	No	Yes	Yes	Yes	Yes	Yes
Non-university tertiary – share of total greater than 30%	?	Yes?	Yes	Yes	Yes	Yes?	Yes	Yes	Yes	Yes	Yes
Private funds greater than 20% in public education											
Primary	No	No	No	No	No	No	No	–	No	No	No
Junior secondary	Yes**	No^	No	No	No	No	?	–	No	Yes	Yes
Senior secondary	Yes	No^	No	No	Yes?	No	?	–	No	Yes	Yes
University	Yes?	No	Yes	No	Yes	No?	?	No	No	Yes	Yes
Non-university tertiary	Yes?	No?	No	–	Yes	–	?	–	No	Yes	Yes
Private provision greater than 20% of total enrolments											
Primary	No	No	No	No	No	No	No	No	No	No	No
Junior secondary	No	Yes	Yes	No	Yes	Yes	No	Yes	No	Yes	No
Senior secondary	Yes	Yes	Yes	Yes*	Yes	Yes	No	Yes	No	Yes	No
Secondary vocational	Yes	?	No	Yes?	Yes	Yes	Yes	Yes	No	Yes	Yes?
University	Yes	No	No	No	Yes	No	Yes	Yes	No	Yes	Yes?
Non-university tertiary	Yes?	–	No	No	Yes	Yes	Yes	Yes	No	Yes	Yes

Source: ** Postlethwaite (1995); * Mingat (1995); ^ Cheng (1992); ? further data required to confirm; – data not found.

it. Universal junior secondary schooling has been accomplished in the high-income economies and the wealthier of the middle-income economies but has not yet been reached in the low-income economies. Table 3 summarises this and related information about the system and its financing.

The high- and middle-income economies have achieved 50 per cent completion of senior secondary education and participation of 40 per cent in some form of post-secondary education. Among the lower income countries the Philippines has secondary and tertiary participation rates above what might be expected from its level of income.

A part of secondary schooling is devoted to vocational education in nearly all the economies. In all but Australia this tends to take the form of specialist technical or vocational schools, usually at senior secondary level. In the formal secondary system in Australia, there are scarcely any schools that can be classified as vocational though there has been a rapid growth in the last five years in vocational programs in senior secondary schooling, many of which yield a vocational certificate and many involving industry experience. Around 34 per cent of all senior secondary students in Australia were engaged in at least one subject in such programs in 1999 (McIntyre & Pithers, 2001).

5.2. Public and Private Provision of Education

Quite rapid change is occurring in a number of economies in the patterns of finance so the snapshot of recent provision may provide only a rough indication of either past or future arrangements. There is considerable variation across the economies in the extent of: (a) fees charged for publicly provided education, (b) the size of the private sector, (c) public subsidy to the private sector, and (d) student assistance. Indeed the extent of public subsidy to private institutions and the charging of fees in public ones make the division of institutions into public and private a somewhat unclear one. Table 3 includes a classification on the first two factors.

The classification for fees in public education is set at fees greater than 20 per cent of costs – an arbitrary dividing line. Public primary education is provided without significant tuition fees. Fees are more likely to be charged the higher the level of education. There is not a simple relationship with level of income as there was for participation. Some low-income economies, such as the Socialist Republic of Vietnam, have introduced fees for all but primary education. China has not officially introduced fees but they exist in practice (Bray, 1996a). Fees appear to be charged in most economies for public post-secondary education but only in a few of them do they exceed 20 per cent of costs, the indicator chosen here.

There is again substantial variation in the proportion of formal education that is privately provided (often with government subsidy) and in the level of education at which private provision is common. Australia is unusual in having substantial private provision at the primary level. A large part of costs of Australian private schools is covered by government grants. This means that the distinction of public from private is not the same across economies or even across levels within economies.

Nearly all Australia's and Singapore's university enrolments are in public institutions whereas in Japan and Korea most university students are in private institutions in which fees cover more than half the costs (Mingat, 1995). Private provision at the university level is also common in Thailand, Indonesia, the Philippines and Vietnam. Malaysia from 1996 has permitted the establishment of private universities including foreign owned universities but as yet they account for only small enrolments. Malaysia has large numbers of students in private colleges taking degrees at foreign universities.

5.3. Expenditure on Education

As income per head rises in a country so too will average wages and salaries in the community. This will affect the major cost of education, staff salaries, though not necessarily evenly across all sectors of education. Because of this, the variation in expenditure per student across economies expressed in say, US dollars, may very much overstate the variation in teacher resources per student. Expenditures expressed as a percentage of GDP do not have this problem, though they tend to understate the purchasing power of non-staff expenditures in the richer economies.

Public expenditure data derived mainly from UNESCO and OECD data are given in Table 4. The public expenditure on education in low-income economies is usually a small proportion of GDP. Most middle- and high-income economies tend to show a higher proportion of GDP given to public expenditure on education but Hong Kong has a surprisingly low proportion. Australia, Malaysia and Thailand have the highest percentage of public expenditure. Table 4 also shows public expenditure on education as a percentage of all government expenditure. Singapore also appears to devote a large part of a relatively small public outlay to education. In general, the Asian economies do not have large public sectors. In passing, it can be noted that most European economies have larger public sectors and larger proportions of expenditure devoted to education (OECD, 2001).

5.4. Staffing Ratios

The major element of expenditure is for teachers. The intensity of staffing and the salaries of staff are the major component of education expenditures. Table 5 provides information on the ratio of students to teachers, which offers some insights into the expenditure data just considered.

Table 5 gives student-teacher ratios for primary and secondary schools. Tertiary ratios are not presented as the ratios are affected by the large numbers of part-time students and teachers in some economies. Pre-primary enrolments are affected by part-time attendance and are also not presented here. In the selected economies only Australia and Japan have low ratios of primary students to staff. Thailand and Malaysia have ratios not much higher, in line with their

Table 4. Expenditure on education

	UNESCO 1996*		World Education Indicators 1998**		
	Public expenditure % GNP	As % of all public outlays	Public expenditure on educational institutions as % of GDP	Private expenditure on institutions as % of GDP	Public expenditure on education including subsidies to households as % of GDP	Public expenditure on education including subsidies to households as % of total public expenditure
Japan	3.6	10	3.6	1.2	na	na
Hong Kong	2.9	na	na	na	na	na
Singapore	3.0	23	na	na	na	na
Australia	5.5	14	4.3	1.1	5.0	14
Korea, Rep	3.7	18	4.1	3.0	4.1	17
Malaysia	5.2	15	4.5	na	4.8	14
Thailand	4.8	na	4.3	3.4	4.7	27
Philippines	3.2	18	3.5	2.7	3.5	20
China	2.3	na	na	na	na	na
Indonesia	na	na	1.4	0.6	1.5	7
Vietnam	2.9	na	na	na	na	na

* *World Education Report 2000*, UNESCO (2002).
** OECD (2001).

Table 5. Staffing levels

	UNESCO 1996* Ratio of students to teaching staff		World Education Indicators 1999** Ratio of students to teaching staff (public and private institutions based on full-time equivalents)	
	Primary	Secondary general	Primary	Secondary
Japan	19	14	21	15
Hong Kong	24	20	na	na
Australia	17	12	17	13
Singapore	25	20	na	na
Korea, Rep	31	25	32	22
Malaysia	19	19	22	19
Thailand	na	na	21	23
Philippines	35	32	34	33
China	24	17	na	na
Indonesia	22	14	23	19
Vietnam	32	29	na	na

* *World Education Report 2000*, UNESCO (2002).
** OECD (2001).

high levels of public expenditure as a percentage of GDP. The student to staff ratios are relatively high in Hong Kong, Singapore and in Korea in particular among the wealthier economies, again in line with their relatively small public expenditures. Australia has the lowest ratio at secondary level. Indonesia, Japan and China have relatively low ratios. The Philippines has the highest ratios at both primary and secondary levels, explicable by its low income, relatively high participation rates.

6. STRATEGIES FOR PLANNING AND POLICY MAKING

The education and training strategies of the Asian economies are not obvious from the basic statistical data reported here. The considerable deficiencies in data contribute to the difficulty in drawing out what the strategies have been and whether they have been effective. A further issue is that the data show variability in participation and expenditure even among economies with fairly similar income levels or growth rates. Hence, very close analysis is needed of the relationships among the variables and the economic and social development of the economies to tease out what the strategies have been and the apparent consequences of them.

To offer a commentary on the strategies of these economies it is necessary to draw on the research literature and in particular such overviews as are provided by Bray (1998), Mingat (1995), Middleton, Ziderman and Van Adams (1993) and Ziderman and Albrecht (1995). These studies draw on the international data sets, and also on a range of other data and research analyses. After considering this literature in conjunction with the data presented in this report, several issues that are important in the educational strategies of the economies considered have been identified. They are:

- the emphasis the economies place on particular levels of education;
- the emphasis on vocational education at secondary level;
- the emphasis on particular fields of study at tertiary level;
- the extent of public and private financing and provision of education;
- the unit costs of education at various levels and especially the salaries of teachers; and
- mechanisms to ensure efficiency, quality and equity.

Given the limitations of space only three brief comments are offered here in relation these matters.

- Given the variations noted in the participation and expenditures it appears that many different forms of education and training systems may be compatible with economic development.
- There is usually a lower unit cost in private institutions. But this is not necessarily an indicator of efficiency. It could reflect lower quality, in the absence of effective monitoring. On the other hand, studies of pupil performance tend to suggest higher achievement in private secondary schools even after controlling for socio-economic background (e.g., Jimenez & Lockheed, 1995). The problem is that such controls can never fully compensate for the motivation of persons of similar social background who choose, or do not choose, private education. Nor does it account for the widespread use of private tutoring which is not accounted for in the private school costs. Bray (1996b) warns against generalisations about private schools which range from high quality elite academic schools to low resourced, low quality, second-chance schools for students not catered for in the public system.
- Advocates of competition argue that privatisation is the primary way to ensure efficiency in all areas, including education. However, externalities and equity justify some government finance even in post-secondary education and training. Lack of knowledge and natural monopoly, provide a case for government regulation and possibly provision.

7. CONCLUSION

This article has reviewed a wide range of data on the educational participation and educational finance of the selected economies. Educational participation and, to some extent, expenditure as a percentage of GDP, are related to the level of income per head. Malaysia, Australia and Thailand appear to make the largest commitment of public expenditure. Australia has high rates of educational participation and low ratios of students to staff in its schools. Hong Kong and Singapore have lower public expenditures than other high-income economies, which may be accounted for by the relatively high ratios of students to staff for their primary and secondary schools and only middling levels of tertiary participation.

Data on private outlays are sparse but Korea and Japan have much of their higher education in the private sector and have relatively large private expenditures. Korea has high ratios of students to staff ratios in primary schools which is a means of containing its public outlays. The economies also vary in the degree of government subsidy of private education and the charging of fees in public education. Somewhat surprising is socialist Vietnam which has fairly recently embraced fees as a means of expanding its educational participation. More data are needed on all of these factors if precise comparisons are to be undertaken.

Educational participation tends to be lower in upper secondary education and tertiary education the lower a country's income per head, though there are anomalies. The Philippines has higher levels of participation than might be expected from its income levels and educational expenditures, achieved by very high ratios of students to staff and by a large private sector. Most of its public outlays are directed at primary education.

There are a number of areas in which specific research on particular economies could lead to a better understanding of the variations across economies. Such areas are:

- the extent to which education in public institutions is supported by fees;
- the extent of student assistance for living costs or support for fees;
- the extent to which the private sector is subsidised by the government;
- the level of teachers' salaries relative to income per head in each country;
- the nature of vocational education in upper secondary education;
- more precise documentation of recent policy changes in educational finance; and
- measures of educational performance and of outcomes in relation to social and economic needs.

The identification of effective strategies requires a detailed study of a wider range of data than available for this article and an analysis of each economy's particular experience and needs. In order to offer commentary on the strategies of the Asian economies, the data in the article have been supplemented with the findings of a range of reviews of education and development. The main issues identified for educational strategies include the:

- emphasis the economies place on particular levels of education;

- emphasis on vocational education at secondary school levels and on fields of study at tertiary levels;
- extent of public and private financing of education and public and private provision of education;
- unit costs of education at various levels and the salaries of teachers; and
- mechanisms to ensure efficiency, quality and equity.

Some, but not all, of the high-income Asian economies rely on private finance for a substantial part of their upper secondary and tertiary education. The ability to increase levels of funding for education may be related increasing the extent of private finance of various forms. Mechanisms to ensure quality and efficiency may involve increased private provision and market forces but the evidence reviewed is not conclusive. Governments in all economies remain the major source of educational funds and improved government administration is an important part of educational strategies.

The data compiled for this article provide only a partial view of the nature of education and training in the economies under consideration. Comparative studies need to be based on more detailed and wide-ranging data than are likely to be provided by international agencies. More detailed studies, which focus on a small number of economies and consider a particular aspect of education and training, may yield greater insight into their strategies. The great variation in participation and expenditures reported in the article imply that more than one strategy may be compatible with successful economic development. Strategies have to be developed appropriate to the particular economic and social needs of each economy.

REFERENCES

Bray, M. (1996a). *Counting the Full Cost, Parental and Community Financing of Education in East Asia.* Washington: World Bank.

Bray, M. (1996b). *Privatisation of Secondary Education: Issues and Policy Implications,* International Commission on Education of the Twenty-first Century. Paris: UNESCO.

Bray, M. (1998). *Financing Education in Developing Asia: Patterns, trends and policy implications, Asian Development Bank, Working paper for the Study of Trends, Issues and Policies in Education.* Hong Kong: University of Hong Kong.

Jimenez, E., & Lockheed, M. E. (1995). *Public and Private Secondary Education in Developing Countries,* World Bank Discussion Papers 309. Washington, DC: World Bank.

Middleton, J., Ziderman, A., & Van Adams, A. (1993). *Skills for Productivity, Vocational Education and Training for Developing Countries.* New York: Oxford University Press.

McIntyre, J., & Pithers, B. (2001). *Structured Workplace Learning 2000: ECEF numbers compared to all senior students.* Sydney: Enterprise and Career Education Foundation.

Mingat, A. (1995). *Towards improving our understanding of the strategy of high performing Asian economies in the education sector,* IREDU CNRS. France: University of Dijon.

OECD (2001). *Education at a Glance, OECD Indicators.* Paris: OECD.

Postlethwaite, T. N. (Ed.) (1995). *International Encyclopedia of Comparative Education and National Systems of Education.* Oxford: Pergamon.

UNESCO Institute for Statistics [www.uis.unesco.org/en/stats/stats0.htm]

UNESCO (2002). *World Education Report.* Paris: UNESCO.
World Bank (2001). *World Development Indicators.* Washington, DC: World Bank.
Ziderman, A., & Albrecht, D. (1995). *Financing Universities in Developing Countries.* Washington, DC: Falmer Press.

4

The Family and Schooling in Asian and Pacific Countries

KEVIN MARJORIBANKS
University of Adelaide, Australia

1. INTRODUCTION

One of the persistent challenges confronting societies is how to reduce inequalities in the educational attainment of students from different socioeconomic, ethnic and race group backgrounds. Such inequalities are typically intensified between females and males, and for students from different residential and geographic locations. It is generally agreed that if parents are involved positively in activities associated with children's learning, then the school outcomes of those children are likely to be enhanced.

As families and households increasingly experience disruptive and often dramatic upheavals it is not always obvious, however, how teachers should respond to optimise their relationships with parents. Coleman (1993) observed that with the changing nature of societies, schools now interact more than ever, with particularly varied groups of families. He suggested that some parents:

> are deeply involved and have the skills to be effective. Others are involved, but in ways that are ineffective or harmful. And still others take little time to inculcate in their children those personal traits that facilitate the school's goals. (Coleman, 1993, p. 6)

If educational policies and practices that attempt to reduce inequalities in students' school attainment are to be more cogent, then we need to increase our understanding of the complexity of relationships among family background, family and school learning environments, students' individual characteristics, and school outcomes. It is the purpose of this article to examine research that has investigated the intricate nature of these relationships. In the following section a number of theoretical orientations are presented that might be combined to form a framework to examine family-school relationships in Asian and Pacific countries.

2. THEORETICAL ORIENTATIONS

In the construction of a bioecological model of human development, Bronfenbrenner and Ceci (1994) proposed that students' outcomes are related to proximal processes, which are enduring forms of interaction that occur in immediate settings such as families and classrooms, and to more remote contexts in which the immediate settings are embedded. They indicated:

> The form, power, content and direction of the proximal processes affecting development vary systematically as a joint function of the characteristics of the developing person, of the environment – both immediate and more remote – in which the processes are taking place, and the nature of the developmental outcome under consideration. (Bronfenbrenner & Ceci, 1994, p. 572)

In addition, the model suggests that the relationships between individual characteristics, immediate settings and school outcomes are likely to be moderated by distal family contexts, while the intervening measures mediate the effect of family background on outcomes. The nature of the relations between family background and school outcomes was emphasized by Ceci, Rosenblum, de Bruyn and Lee (1997) who stated:

> The efficacy of a proximal process is determined to a large degree by the distal environmental resources. Proximal processes are the engines that actually drive the outcome but only if the distal resources can be imported into the process to make it effective. (Ceci et al., 1997, p. 311)

If the bioecological model is to be adopted as part of a framework to examine family-school relationships, then there is a need to determine the nature of the proximal processes operating in families and schools. In the development of a theory of the social trajectory of individuals, Bourdieu (1998) presents a two-dimensional model of social space. The overall volume of economic and cultural capital possessed by individuals or available to them defines the vertical dimension. In contrast, the horizontal dimension indicates the structure of individuals' capital and it is assessed by the relative amounts of economic and cultural capital within the total volume of their capital. While economic capital refers to financial resources and assets, cultural capital includes: (a) those tastes and habits acquired by individuals as they grow up in family and school settings; (b) cultural objects such as paintings, antiques and books accumulated by individuals or families; and (c) formal educational qualifications attained by individuals. Bourdieu (1998) claimed:

> The school, once thought of introducing a form of meritocracy by privileging individual aptitudes over hereditary privileges, actually tends to establish,

through the hidden linkage between scholastic aptitude and cultural heritage, a veritable social nobility. (Bourdieu, 1998, p. 22)

Similarly, in the construction of a general social theory, Coleman (1990, 1997) proposed that family and school influences are analytically separable into components such as economic, human and social capital. Human capital provides parents and teachers with resources to create proximal learning settings and it can be measured by indicators such as parents' and teachers' educational attainment. In contrast, social capital is defined by the resources children may access through social ties. It is the amount and quality of academically oriented interaction between children and their parents and teachers that provide them with access to adults' human capital. (see *Cultural and Social Capital in Asian and Pacific Countries*)

In families, the potentially valuable social capital related to a child's successful schooling includes: (a) the amount and quality of interest, support, encouragement, and knowledge that other family members have about education; and (b) the extent that such resources are transmitted to the child in interactions with family members. Favourable social capital in schools involves the networks students establish with academically oriented peers, and it is associated with the success students have in developing strong and positive relationships with teachers and other educators. Such theoretical orientations suggest that investigations of family and schooling need to examine relationships among distal family contexts, the cultural and social capital of families and schools, individual characteristics, and students' school outcomes. In the following sections of this article, research is examined that has explored such relationships.

3. FAMILY BACKGROUND AND STUDENTS' OUTCOMES

Rumberger (1995) observed that:

> Family background is widely recognized as the most significant contributor of success in schools. Research has consistently found that socioeconomic status, most commonly measured by parental education and income, is a powerful predictor of school achievement and dropout behavior. (Rumberger, 1995, p. 587)

Even in societies that have adopted policies to eliminate class-based inequalities in educational opportunities, there continue to be significant family background differences in individuals' life chances. In an examination, for example, of the so-called 'send-down' policy that operated in China during the Cultural Revolution, Zhou and Hou (1999) investigated the impact of family background on the life course of students who were sent from cities to live and work in rural communities. Although the average time students stayed in rural regions was six years, the probability of students returning early to cities was related significantly to their family background. The study indicated:

> As the political tides subsided, high-rank cadres did have advantages in reducing the adverse impact of state policies by bringing their children back earlier to the cities, compared with children of other occupational groups. An early return was extremely valuable ... children of cadres and professionals were especially advantaged in attending college. (Zhou & Hou, 1999, p. 32)

Zhou and Hou (1999) concluded that the process of social class reproduction was only temporarily interrupted by the events of the Cultural Revolution. They suggested that their findings were a further indication of the enduring significance of social stratification structures in mediating associations between state policies and students' life opportunities, even in dramatic political situations.

In a further analysis of relationships between distal influences and career mobility in China, Walder, Li and Treiman (2000) examined the importance of education and party membership for elite occupational status. They indicated that party membership was the most important single credential for an elite cadre position, with a college education not conferring any advantage over a high school education. In contrast, educational qualifications were related strongly to positions in the elite professions, with party membership mattering very little. Walder et al. (2000) concluded:

> In China the enforcement of meritocratic principles has not been permitted to interfere with principles of party loyalty – and vice versa. The regime has created two segmented 'markets' for elites in which educational credentials are paramount for the attainment of elite professionals while political credentials are paramount for the attainment of elite administrative positions. (Walder et al., 2000, p. 206)

Similarly, in an analysis of relationships between family background and job placement in South Korea, Lee and Brinton (1996) examined whether graduation from an elite university generated advantages for men in the labour market. They found that men who had fathers with a university education were more likely to attend the most prestigious universities. Further, attendance at such elite universities had an important effect on the early labour market destination of South Korean men. Lee and Brinton proposed that "The close relationships among family background, human capital, and university prestige mean that a highly select group of South Korean men acquire the best jobs" (Lee & Brinton, 1996, p. 177). Such a conclusion supports Ishida's (1993) finding in Japan of very strong relationships among family social status, entrance to prestigious universities, and students' eventual educational attainment.

These investigations provide support for the general proposition that differences in family background have strong associations with inequalities in students' school success and in young adults' eventual educational and occupational attainment. The proposition raises the question, how do families from certain distal family contexts optimize their children's schooling opportunities?

4. FAMILY CAPITAL AND A SCHOOL'S INSTRUCTIONAL ORGANISATION

There is a body of research, often controversial, which suggests that a school's instructional organisation has a substantial impact on differences in students' progress. Investigations have shown, for example, that ability grouping in schools is likely to favour students in high-ability groups in relation to course taking, academic performance and school engagement, at the expense of students in lower-ability groups. Hallinan (1992) suggested, however, that "Surprisingly little empirical research has examined how ability groups are formed and how students are assigned to them. The paucity of research on the assignment process is particularly curious, given the potential consequences of placement" (Hallinan, 1992, p. 115).

In an analysis of the relationship between school practices and group placement, Le Tendre (1996) examined the process of placement counselling in Japanese middle schools. Le Tendre observed that competition for entry to selective secondary schools was fierce and that being a graduate of an elite university was vital for privileged job opportunities. Using survey and ethnographic research orientations, Le Tendre investigated how students in middle schools made decisions about choosing to attend high schools that ranged from technical to academic. He described the role that teachers had as placement counsellors. While they used grades and test scores as their primary indicators for advice, they also considered family background and gender as important components of their recommendations. Le Tendre indicated that for teachers it was important that placement was related to an appropriate balance of students' effort and motivation, family circumstances, ability, and aspirations. The study concluded:

> Students whose fathers had higher levels of education tended to have higher grades, to enter high-ranked high schools, and to change their plans less – which supports the theory that social background affects how students fare in the competition for high school entrance. (Le Tendre, 1996, p. 207)

In addition, the analysis suggested that as a result of placement counselling, parents could expect their children to be placed in appropriate high schools that prepared them for social positions not too dissimilar to those of the parents.

In a further analysis of the relationships between family background and group placement, Broaded (1997) examined whether ability group placement in Taiwan reinforced educational inequalities associated with family background, or whether it enhanced the educational opportunities of high-ability students from economically disadvantaged families. Broaded indicated that junior high schools were ranked in communities according to the number of their students who graduated to prestigious academic high schools. As a result, "some parents seek to enroll their children in schools outside their own neighborhoods, in the hope that attending a better school will enhance their chances on the high school entrance examinations" (Broaded, 1997, p. 28).

Broaded observed that ability grouping in junior high schools created a context in which classroom instruction was related to the entrance examinations for different types of high schools. Parents and teachers expected students in high-ability groups to do well, and to be placed in academic high schools. In contrast, students in low-ability classes were expected to perform poorly on entrance examinations and to gain admission to the lowest-prestige vocational schools, or to dropout from school. The study concluded that the educational attainment process in urban Taiwan appeared to be guided by meritocratic principles. It was suggested that:

> Students from advantaged households cannot automatically reproduce their parents' status, but must compete successfully on the high school entrance examinations. Conversely, talented students from disadvantaged households face fewer barriers to educational achievement and advancement than do children from similar backgrounds in the United States. (Broaded, 1996, p. 48)

The analysis indicated, however, that the findings did not erase the advantages and disadvantages of family background on academic outcomes and high school placement. Higher-income families, for example, were able to afford more intensive and higher quality supplementary schooling, such as home tutoring or cram schooling, and they could choose to enrol their children in private high schools.

These investigations begin to indicate the intricate nature of relationships among family background, a school's instructional organisation, and students' eventual educational attainment. If the meritocratic nature of Asian school systems is to be examined, for example, then research is required that explores with greater sensitivity relationships among family background, proximal family social and cultural capital, the instructional organisation of schools, and students' outcomes.

5. PROXIMAL FAMILY CAPITAL

The potential impact that supportive proximal family capital may have on students' success is suggested in the following claims by Coleman (1991) and Wang, Haertel and Walberg (1993). Coleman stated:

> Research shows conclusively that parents' involvement in their children's education confers great benefits both intellectual and emotional on their children. Thus, a major issue facing education today is this: How to improve educational outcomes for children in the face of contradictions in family functioning, when strong families are so important for children's learning? (Coleman, 1991, p. 1)

Similarly, Wang, Haertel and Walberg (1993) observed:

> In contrast with distal variables, which are more removed from students' day-to-day lives, the home is central to students' daily experience. Consequently, the home functions as the most salient out-of-school context for student learning, amplifying or diminishing the school's effect on school learning. (Wang et al., 1993, p. 278)

Using New Zealand longitudinal data, Caspi, Entner Wright, Moffitt and Silva (1998) attempted to identify individual and family predictors of youth unemployment. They classified their predictors into three types of capital: human, social and personal, and these were assessed at ages ranging from 3 to 15 years old. Human capital included measures of parents' occupational status and educational attainment. Social capital was defined by family structure (single-parent families), family conflict that gauged the degree to which families were characterised by conflictual relations, the adolescents' attachment to their parents, and the school involvement of adolescents. Personal capital included measures of students' delinquency and behaviour problems, mental illness and overall physical health.

Caspi et al. observed that "adolescents who lacked high school qualifications, had poor reading skills, who were uninvolved in school, who grew up in single-parent households, and who were involved in antisocial behavior were at risk for unemployment regardless of when they exited educational settings" (Caspi et al., 1998, p. 443). They indicated, however, the need to interpret their findings with caution as it was not possible to determine whether relationships between unemployment and measures of family structure, family conflict, and parental attachment reflected limited access to monetary resources or perhaps the failure of family and non-family members to provide supportive proximal learning contexts. In general, the study demonstrated that labour-market outcomes were shaped by family and personal characteristics that began to emerge years before young people entered the labour force.

In an investigation that did measure proximal family capital with greater sensitivity, Marjoribanks (1998a) examined relationships among family background, social and academic capital, and the aspirations of a sample of Australian students. When the children in the study were 11-year-olds, parents were interviewed to measure their aspirations for their children, their individualistic-collectivistic orientations, and parents' involvement in children's schooling. The academic capital of the children was assessed using a combination of ability, reading and mathematics scores. When the students were 16-year-olds, family social capital was measured by the adolescents' perceptions of their interactions with fathers and mothers. Distal family background was defined by ethnicity and social status.

The findings revealed that the family and academic capital predictors combined to have medium to large associations with adolescents' aspirations, and that the associations were larger for educational aspirations than for occupational aspirations, and stronger for males than for females. In addition, after taking into account family social and childhood academic capital, there were ethnic group differences in adolescents' occupational aspirations and sons of fathers with high social status continued to have higher occupational aspirations than did other male adolescents.

The persistence of significant residual effects of ethnicity and fathers' social status on males' occupational aspirations may reflect differences in the cultural value placed on education by parents from different distal family backgrounds. Bourdieu (1984) argued, for example, that families from certain social backgrounds have cultural capital that is elaborated in a taste for education and reflected in an emphasis on the intrinsic value of scholastic success. It is likely, however, that the transmission of family cultural capital was not captured by the proximal measures used in the Marjoribanks (1998a) study. In more detailed analyses of relationships among distal capital, proximal family capital and students' outcomes, measures should be included that assess both social and cultural capital.

In an investigation involving 14-year-old Hong Kong students, Marjoribanks and Kwok (1998) adopted the Bourdieu and Coleman theoretical orientations to examine relationships between family capital and academic achievement. Students completed schedules that provided information about the economic, human, social, and cultural capital of their families. Social capital, for example, was measured by two 20-item scales that included items such as 'My father/mother tells me that it is important for me to do well at school,' 'My father/mother supports me by attending activities at school.' In contrast, a 15-item scale assessed the frequency that parents and children joined in cultural activities over the preceding two years. Academic achievement was measured by performance in Chinese language, English language, and mathematics.

The findings revealed gender differences in the nature of the relationships. In regression models, economic and cultural capital continued to have significant associations with girls' English and mathematics achievement, while economic, human and social capital were related to the girls' Chinese language scores. In contrast, family social capital was the only significant predictor of boys' academic performance.

Such differences reflect the possible complexity of relationships between family capital and school outcomes. As Sternberg and Grigorenko (2001) proposed, there is a need to examine the extent that students' school outcomes are related to the possible incongruity between their proximal learning settings and the expectations of mainstream society. Similarly, Stanton-Salazar (1997) argued that family capital should be considered in relation to the wider social networks available to children. He proposed that children from different distal family backgrounds have networks of relationships that are differentially "converted into socially valued resources and opportunities" (Stanton-Salazar, 1997, p. 8). That is, in an elaborated theoretical model, social capital might be expanded to include children's interactions with a network of institutional agents such as community leaders, counsellors, social workers, and teachers as well as family members.

6. SCHOOL CAPITAL AND STUDENTS' OUTCOMES

Although there may be significant and even dramatic school events that influence students' life chances, it is a proposition of this article that relationships between family background and school outcomes are mediated, in part, by students' perceptions of their classroom and school experiences. There is now a growing body of research that has defined classroom and school learning environments by the shared perceptions of students and sometimes of teachers (see *Classroom Learning Environments*) The schedules that have been constructed to assess these perceptions are often referred to as high-inference measures. In contrast, low-inference techniques measure specific explicit phenomenon such as the number of questions asked by students in a certain section of a lesson.

Typically, perceptual measures are related to modest or moderate amounts of variance in learning outcomes, often beyond the variance that can be attributed to student characteristics such as pretest performance or general ability. In Singapore, for example, Teh and Fraser (1995) found significant associations between a perceptual scale designed for computer-assisted instruction classroom environments and measures of geography students' achievement and attitudes. Using multilevel statistical techniques, Goh, Young and Fraser (1995) demonstrated that scores on a modified version of the *My Class Inventory* were related substantially to the mathematics achievement of Grade 5 students in Singapore. Fraser (1998) reported on the development of the *What Is Happening In This Class Questionnaire*, which combines scales from a wide range of existing questionnaires and adds new items to assess issues such as equity and constructivism in classrooms. When the Questionnaire was used in a large comparative study of Australian and Taiwanese junior high school science students the results indicated, for example, that "the scales of Involvement and Equity had the largest differences in means between the two countries, with Australian students perceiving each scale more positively than students from Taiwan" (Fraser, 1998, p. 26).

In a national longitudinal study of Australian students, Marks (1998) examined Grade 9 students' perceptions of the quality of school life. The perceptions were assessed using a scale consisting of 30 items, that measures four dimensions of schooling: (a) General satisfaction with school (e.g., 'I get excited about the work we do,' 'I really like to go to school each day'); (b) Relationship with teachers (e.g., 'My teachers take a personal interest in helping me with my school work,' 'My teachers help me to do my best'); (c) Relevance of school (e.g., The things I learn will help me with my adult life,' 'The work I do is good preparation for my future'); and (d) Success in school (e.g., 'I always achieve a satisfactory standard in my work,' 'I am a success as a student'). The findings indicated that: (a) students with more highly educated parents were happier at school; (b) female students expressed higher general satisfaction, were more positive about their teachers, and were more satisfied about their perceived success at school; and (c) perceptions of general satisfaction and success in school, had significant associations with Grade 10 students' self-perceived achievement.

Such studies of students' perceptions have the implication that school outcomes might be improved by establishing classrooms that match those perceived learning environments that have been shown to be associated with improvements in students' learning. A limitation of many classroom learning environment schedules, however, is that they measure an individual student's perceptions of a whole class, as distinct from students' perceptions of their own roles in classrooms. There is a distinction between the private or idiosyncratic perception that each person has of a learning environment and the consensual perceptions that the members of a group share about that environment (see Fraser, 1998). It is likely that future classroom and school capital research will be enhanced if personal as well as group perception schedules are adopted.

Many educators argue that school learning environments need to be examined with greater sensitivity than can be generated from perceptual measures. Researchers using these scales generally acknowledge that the measures provide only one portrayal of school capital that would be enriched by adopting more interpretive analyses of classroom settings. In such an interpretive investigation, Okano (1995) examined the job-referral system that operated in two Japanese vocational high schools. Data were collected from a yearlong participant observation of students' decision making about job opportunities. Okano observed that students in Japanese vocational high schools had limited opportunities to enter higher education and a restricted range of potential jobs. From observations, interviews, documents, questionnaires and photographs, the study indicated that the job-referral system restricted some students' choices but promoted a rational decision-making process. Okano concluded that for "students who can rely on a family network for employment openings and related advice and information, the referral system may seem like a restrictive and unnecessarily bureaucratic institution that limits freedom of choice, whereas for those with fewer resources, the system offers a wider range of opportunities" (Okano, 1995, p. 46).

In a further intensive study of Japanese high schools, Yoneyama (1999) examined relationships among teacher-student interaction, school organisation, bullying, and school refusal by students. Yoneyama observed:

> Attending school is still a taken-for-granted norm for the majority of students who live in a 'super-meritocratic' society. The most distinct characteristic of this 'mass-education society' is that students feel more or less the same degree of academic pressure, regardless of their future educational prospects. (Yoneyama, 1999, p. 244)

From her analysis, however, Yoneyama concluded that many Japanese high schools were stifling places with formal, rigid and autocratic organisational structures. In particular, it was proposed that in such a meritocratic society, "teachers' power to convert students' behaviour into academic opportunity is considerable, especially in junior high schools, where the [teacher's] report is subsequently used as part of the selection criteria for admission to senior high school" (Yoneyama, 1999, p. 245). As a result, Yoneyama claimed that peer relationships in schools tended to be characterised by competition, surveillance and threat, rather than by friendship and solidarity. Further, she examined the phenomenon of school refusal that refers to the large group of students who withdraw from school. As one mother recalled:

> I thought that if my son stopped going to school his whole world would be destroyed. I could not think of his future outside the framework of schools. One day, however, he looked so distressed that I said to him "You can do anything. I will never get angry." He then started violently to throw away everything related to school. When I saw this I thought what a stupid parent I had been, forcing him to go to school while he was suffering so much. I cried with him. (Yoneyama, 1999, p. 206)

Similarly, in a study of Australian aboriginal students, Groome and Hamilton (1995) used interviews with students, parents and teachers to address the questions: "What are the blockages to Aboriginal students succeeding? And, How can these be overcome?" (Groome & Hamilton, 1995, p. xviii). The investigation concluded that "The majority of the students who were achieving well believed that much of the credit for their success needed to go to one or other of their parents. Their support and encouragement had given them the courage and determination to persevere through the difficult periods of racism and depression" (Groome & Hamilton, 1995, p. 30). In addition, many Aboriginal students indicated that while they had high aspirations and wanted to be academically successful, they found it difficult to deal with the confrontational and alienating contexts of many schools.

These studies of school capital suggest that our understanding of the relationships between proximal school settings and students' outcomes might be enriched if investigations integrated perceptual and interpretive analyses of student-teacher interactions. In addition, the analysis of relationships between school capital and outcomes is likely to become more meaningful if investigations include students from diverse social and cultural distal contexts (see Tobin, 2000).

7. DISTAL FAMILY BACKGROUND, PROXIMAL SETTINGS AND STUDENTS' OUTCOMES

In an analysis of the Bronfenbrenner and Ceci framework, that adopted the orientations of Bourdieu and Coleman, Marjoribanks (1998b) examined the environmental and individual influences on Australian students' likelihood of attending university. Data were collected when students were 11-, 16-, and

21-years-old. In the initial survey, parents were interviewed to provide information about their involvement in their children's learning. In addition, the children's ability, attitudes to school and academic achievement were assessed. During the second survey, the adolescents' perceptions of mothers', fathers' and teachers' support for schooling were measured, as well as the students' aspirations.

The initial results indicated that distal family background, early family learning environments, and individual attributes all contributed to students' eventual academic success. Adolescents' perceptions of their family and school influences mediated many of the earlier relationships, while the students' educational aspirations mediated the associations between their perceptions of proximal learning settings and academic success. Such a longitudinal study begins to investigate Bourdieu's primary concern of the extent that families and schools operate to convert social hierarchies into academic hierarchies.

An interesting set of studies is emerging that examine the school outcomes of students from immigrant Asian families. In an analysis of American Grade 10 students, Goyette and Xie (1999) concluded, for example, that students from seven Asian groups had higher educational aspirations than did Anglo Americans. They suggested that it was remarkable that so many Asian American adolescents from diverse cultural backgrounds and with different immigration experiences, expected to attain higher educational levels than did other Grade 10 American students. Similarly, in a large scale Australian study, Marjoribanks (2002) found that adolescents from Asian families expressed the highest aspirations, even after taking into account proximal family and school environments and measures of individual characteristics (also see Marks, Fleming, Long & McMillan, 2000). Such studies of immigrant families could provide insights into those factors that are related to students' school outcomes in the immigrants' home countries. They suggest, for example, that distal family background differences in academic success may be related to between-family as well as within-family influences. For immigrant groups, Hao and Bonstead-Bruns (1998) proposed that between-family influences are reflected in the premium that some groups place on education, ambition and persistence. Another form of between-family capital is trustworthiness and solidarity that allows families in certain immigrant groups to distribute economic and educational resources in order to support children's education. Zhou (1997) suggested that children of immigrant groups react to schools with varying strategies that may also be applicable in their home countries. These strategies include using the social capital of extended families and communities to assist them in being successful at school; rejecting the norms of the larger society and resisting the culture of schooling; and giving up the struggle at school and dropping out.

8. CONCLUSION

The studies that have been presented in this article indicate that students' school outcomes are influenced by distal family background, proximal learning settings and individual characteristics. They suggest that when students perceive their parents and teachers to be supportive of their learning, they are more likely to have positive attitudes to schooling, express stronger aspirations, and be more academically successful. It is important, therefore, that when educational innovations are introduced to improve learning outcomes, that they involve participation of parents and other family members. A number of literacy projects have been implemented in Asian and Pacific countries, for example, that provided children with access to high-interest illustrated storybooks. The results in Niue (De'Ath, 2001), Fiji (Mangubhai, 2001), the Solomon Islands and Vanuatu (Singh, 2001), Brunei (Ng, 2001), Sri Lanka (Kuruppu, 2001), and The Philippines (Lituanas, Jacobs & Renandya, 2001) are particularly encouraging. If such projects could be related to programs that involved parents in truly meaningful partnerships with teachers, then it is likely that children's school outcomes would be even more richly enhanced.

This article suggests that investigations of individual characteristics and proximal learning settings have provided an initial, but incomplete, understanding of family-school differences in students' educational outcomes. For a more complete understanding of those differences, there is a need to extend such investigations and identify those between-family and between-school factors that may be related to the school outcomes of students from Asian and Pacific countries. As Keeves suggested "the problems investigated [in education] should be those that contribute most, both to change in the real world, as well as to the building of a coherent body of knowledge about education and educational processes" (Keeves, 1999, p. 14).

REFERENCES

Bourdieu, P. (1984). *Distinction: A social critique of the judgement of taste*. London: Routledge & Kegan Paul.

Bourdieu, P. (1998). *Practical Reason: On the theory of action*. Cambridge, UK: Polity Press.

Broaded, C. M. (1997). The limits and possibility of tracking: Some evidence from Taiwan. *Sociology of Education, 70*, 36–53.

Bronfenbrenner, U., & Ceci, S. J. (1994). Nature-nurture reconceptualization in development perspective: A bioecological model. *Psychological Review, 101*, 568–586.

Caspi, S. J., Entner Wright, B. R., Moffitt, J. E., & Silva, P. A. (1998). Childhood predictors of unemployment in early adulthood. *American Sociological Review, 63*, 424–451.

Ceci, S. J., Rosenblum, T., de Bruyn, E., & Lee, D. Y. (1997). A bio-ecological model of human development. In R. J. Sternberg & E. L. Grigorenko (Eds.), *Intelligence, Heredity, and Environment* (pp. 303–322). Cambridge, UK: Cambridge University Press.

Coleman, J. S. (1990). *Foundations of Social Theory*. Cambridge, MA: Harvard University Press.

Coleman, J. S. (1991). *Parental Involvement in Education*. Washington, DC: U.S. Department of Education.

Coleman, J. S. (1993). The rational reconstruction of society. *American Sociological Review, 58*, 1–15.

Coleman, J. S. (1997). Family, school, and social capital. In L. J. Saha (Ed.), *International Encyclopedia of the Sociology of Education* (pp. 623–625). Oxford: Pergamon.

De'Ath, P. (2001). The Niue literacy experiment. *International Journal of Educational Research, 35*, 137–146.

Fraser, B. J. (1998). Classroom environment instruments: Development, validity and applications. *Learning Environments Research, 1,* 7–33.

Goh, S. C., Young, D. J., & Fraser, B. J. (1995). Psychosocial climate and student outcomes in elementary mathematics classrooms: A multilevel analysis. *Journal of Experimental Education, 64,* 29–40.

Goyette, K., & Xie, Y. (1999). Educational expectations of Asian American youths: Determinants and ethnic differences. *Sociology of Education, 72,* 22–36.

Groome, H., & Hamilton, A. (1995). *Meeting the Educational Needs of Aboriginal Adolescents.* Canberra: Australian Government Publishing Service.

Hallinan, M. T. (1992). The organization of students for instruction in the middle school. *Sociology of Education, 65,* 114–127.

Hao, L., & Bonstead-Bruns, M. (1998). Parent-child differences in educational expectations and the academic achievement of immigrant and native students. *Sociology of Education, 71,* 175–198.

Ishida, H. (1993). *Social Mobility in Contemporary Japan.* Stanford, CA: Stanford University Press.

Keeves, J. P. (1999). Overview of issues in educational research. In J. P. Keeves & G. Lakomski (Eds.), *Issues in Educational Research* (pp. 3–14). Oxford: Pergamon.

Kuruppu, L. (2001). The 'books in schools' project in Sri Lanka. *International Journal of Educational Research, 35,* 181–191.

Lee, S., & Brinton, M. C. (1996). Elite education and social capital: The case of South Korea. *Sociology of Education, 69,* 177–192.

Le Tendre, G. K. (1996). Constructed aspirations: Decision-making processes in Japanese educational selection. *Sociology of Education, 69,* 193–216.

Lituanas, P., Jacobs, G. M., & Renandya, W. A. (2001). An investigation of extensive reading with remedial students in a Philippines secondary school. *International Journal of Educational Research, 35,* 217–225.

Mangubhai, F. (2001). Book floods and comprehensible input floods: Providing ideal conditions for second language acquisition. *International Journal of Educational Research, 35,* 147–156.

Marjoribanks, K. (1998a). Family background, social and academic capital, and adolescents' aspirations: A mediational analysis. *Social Psychology of Education, 2,* 177–197.

Marjoribanks, K. (1998b). Environmental and individual influences on Australian students' likelihood of attending university. *The Journal of Genetic Psychology, 159,* 261–272.

Marjoribanks, K. (2002). Family background, environmental and individual influences on adolescents' aspirations. *Educational Studies, 28,* 33–46.

Marjoribanks, K., & Kwok, Y. (1998). Family capital and Hong Kong adolescents' academic achievement. *Psychological Reports, 83,* 99–105.

Marks, G. N. (1998). Attitudes to school life: Their influences and their effects on achievement and leaving school. *Longitudinal Surveys of Australian Youth* (Research Report Number 5). Melbourne: Australian Council for Educational Research.

Marks, G. N., Fleming, N., Long, M., & McMillan, J. (2000). Patterns of participation in Year 12 and higher education in Australia: Trends and issues. *Longitudinal surveys of Australian youth* (Research Report Number 17). Melbourne: Australian Council for Educational Research.

Okano, K. (1995). Rational decision making and school-based job referrals for high school students in Japan. *Sociology of Education, 68,* 31–47.

Ng, S. M. (2001). The Brunei reading and language acquisition project. *International Journal of Educational Research, 35,* 169–179.

Rumberger R. W. (1995). Dropping out of middle school: A multilevel analysis of students and schools. *American Educational Research Journal, 32,* 583–625.

Singh, G. (2001). Literacy impact studies in Solomon Islands and Vanuatu. *International Journal of Educational Research, 35,* 227–236.

Stanton-Salazar, R. D. (1997). A social capital framework for understanding the socialization of racial minority children and youths. *Harvard Educational Review, 67,* 1–40.

Sternberg, R. J., & Grigorenko, E. L. (2001). Degree of embeddedness of ecological systems as a measure of ease of adaptation to the environment. In E. L. Grigorenko & R. J. Sternberg (Eds.), *Family Environment and Intellectual Functioning* (pp. 243–262). Mahwah, NJ: Lawrence Erlbaum.

Teh, G., & Fraser, B. J. (1995). Associations between student outcomes and geography classroom environment. *International Research in Geographical and Environmental Education, 4*, 3–18.

Tobin, K. (2000). Catalyzing changes in research on learning environments. *Learning Environments Research, 2*, 223–224.

Walder, A. G., Li, B., & Treiman, D. J. (2000). Politics and life chances in a state socialist regime: Dual career paths into the urban Chinese elite, 1949 to 1996. *American Sociological Review, 65*, 191–209.

Wang, M. C., Haertel, G. D., & Walberg, H. J. (1993). Toward a knowledge base for school learning. *Review of Educational Research, 63*, 249–294.

Yoneyama. S. (1999). *The Japanese High School*. London: Routledge.

Zhou, M. (1997). Growing up American: The challenge confronting immigrant children and children of immigrants. In J. Hagan & K. S. Cook (Eds.), *Annual Review of Sociology, 23*, 63–95. Palo Alto, CA: Annual Reviews.

Zhou, X., & Hou, L. (1999). Children of the cultural revolution: The state and the life course in the People's Republic of China. *American Sociological Review, 64*, 12–36.

5

Cultural and Social Capital in Asian and Pacific Countries

LAWRENCE J. SAHA
Australian National University, Canberra, Australia

1. INTRODUCTION

This article investigates the relevance of cultural and social capital in school achievement and attainment in the Asian and Pacific countries. The Western concepts of 'cultural and social capital' are first defined in the Asian and Pacific context, and their relevance for understanding educational processes is developed in this article, together with a selection of the research that documents the extent to which cultural and social capital play a role in this region of the world. Where possible, comparisons are made with research evidence from Western societies. The article concludes with an evaluation of the importance of cultural and social capital in Asian and Pacific schooling.

2. DEFINITIONS OF CULTURAL AND SOCIAL CAPITAL

The concepts of 'cultural and social capital' have their origin in Western sociological research and are related to the notions of 'economic and human capital'. The four concepts focus on resources that are distributed in society by means of social practices and social institutions. It is the unequal distribution of these resources that has attracted the interest of social scientists. While the concepts of 'economic and human capital' are the older of the four, they are also more easily defined as the total expendable economic resources, including income and inheritance, and human resources, including health and education, belonging to individuals or groups. The concepts of 'cultural and social capital', however, are more recent and more sociological in their focus.

The first use of the concept of 'cultural capital' occurred in the research of Bourdieu and Passeron (Bourdieu & Passerson, 1977, 1979) in which the main focal point was the way in which social relations and social institutions are reproduced through specific agents. The content of cultural capital includes knowledge and possessions that are reflected in books, art, and other cultural artifacts. The possession of cultural capital facilitates the participation or movement of the possessor in society, thereby bringing advantage in lifestyle or access to the valued institutions of society. In an early writing, Bourdieu also recognized the existence of social capital which he described as the total amount of a "network of relationships" which can be mobilized to support both cultural and economic capital (Bourdieu, 1986). Bourdieu regarded both cultural and social capital as forms of investment, which required time and energy to acquire and maintain.

Coleman (1988) applied and popularized the concept of social capital in his research on government and private schools. However he argued that the concept was first used by Loury in 1977, although Schneider (2000) argues that the concept can be traced to the earlier sociological work of Park, Burgess and Mead in the 1920s and 1930s.

In contrast to cultural capital, social capital, according to Coleman, can be defined as "... social resources that children and youth have available to them outside schools in their family or community" (Coleman, 1997, p. 623). As Coleman explains, social capital consists primarily of the social relationships with adults, which the young person possesses, and which provides advantages in a range of activities, including those related to school. Social capital includes the interests of parents, the patterns of norms in the family that relate to schooling, and similar relationships outside the family in the wider community (see *The Family and Schooling in Asian and Pacific Countries*).

This wider application of the concept of 'social capital' is found in Putnam's analysis of the decline in community involvement in the United States (Putnam, 2000). Putnam has argued that a major characteristic of modern American life is the withdrawal in participation in a wide range of civic institutions, including politics and religion. A consequence of this decline, according to Putnam, is the loss of social capital and its replacement by formal arrangements whereby the same needs are met.

Narayan and Cassidy (2001) approach their review of the concept of 'social capital' by first demonstrating the difficulty in its measurement. Therefore it is not always easy to plot its presence or absence. However, they agree with Putnam and argue that the influence of social capital is particularly important when the relationships cut across social boundaries, such as social class or ethnicity. In this way, social capital becomes a means of attaining social mobility, social and political mobilisation, and social and economic development.

In his overview, Portes (1998, p. 9) identifies three uses of social capital that are found in the sociological literature: (a) as a mechanism for social control, (b) as a source of support from family, and (c) as a source of support from members of the community. Social capital as a source of social control focuses on the use of tight-knit communities to maintain discipline and compliance among their members. The notion of social capital as a form of support is consistent with its use by Coleman and Putnam.

In summary, 'cultural capital' is a concept that refers to the knowledge-related resources of a society, while 'social capital' refers to social resources based on relationships with family, other adults and the community. In the educational context, both concepts are seen as providing possible advantages to young people as they progress through schooling and later into their occupational careers. Both concepts can function as independent and dependent variables, and both have received considerable attention in educational research.

3. CULTURAL AND SOCIAL CAPITAL AND SCHOOLING

In what ways do cultural and social capital affect educational performance and educational attainments? In order to provide an adequate answer to this question it is important to take each concept in turn, for each relates to schooling in a different manner.

3.1. *Cultural Capital and Schooling*

Cultural capital is related to knowledge and culture, and in particular the knowledge and culture that is valued in a society and is transmitted in many ways, including schooling. It becomes relevant in understanding how some social groups are advantaged in plural or complex societies where there are social divisions with competing cultural capital. Thus the important question is "Whose culture has more capital?" (Collins & Thompson, 1997). Because the notion of 'culture capital' is embodied in symbolic resources reflected in the curriculum, testing standards, classroom practices, and similar school activities and structures, the answer to the question depends on who makes the decisions regarding these aspects of schooling, namely the social group with power, or the dominant group.

In its original application, Bourdieu and Passeron (Bourdieu & Passerson, 1970, 1977) operationalised cultural capital as high culture and studied the differential uses of art museums, music concerts and similar activities. They argued that participation in these activities contributed to the knowledge necessary to negotiate the adult world. However, the concept is much broader and includes language (accent), certain kinds of travel, and a range of family practices. Thus the notion of 'cultural capital' is class-based and also applies to the relationships between the family and the school. These forms of cultural capital are acquired through the family and the school and remain a positive resource throughout educational and occupational careers. An early study that applied the concept of culture capital in the Asian-Pacific region is one by Lamb (1990) in Australia. In this study the concept was found to be a useful tool for the examination of how cultural knowledge and educational attainment are related.

3.2. *Social Capital and Schooling*

In contrast to culture capital, social capital is concerned with relationships. This form of capital is found in family interaction patterns, in schools, and in communities. It constitutes an advantage for educational performance and attainment because it consists of patterns of behaviour that support and reinforce the goals of education. Thus parents who help their children with homework, or are even sufficiently interested in the schooling of their children to talk and ask questions about it, represent an important social capital resource.

However, the concept has even more widespread application. Social capital is available to students in schools not only in the opportunities it provides for schooling, and the quality of interactions with teachers, but also in the networks of friendships and other contacts made with other students and their parents. In this respect, the type of school and the selectivity and composition of the other students represent potential differences in the amount of social capital available to students. Coleman (1987) has argued that this difference in social capital is one of the benefits that private schools provide for their students. Private schools, because parents deliberately choose them, and because they are selective according to a number of criteria, represent educational communities which are beneficial not only while the students attend them, but also afterwards in the job market. The notion of the 'old school tie', and the potential advantages it brings later in life, is an example of social capital as an outcome of schooling.

3.3. *The Conflicting Effects of Cultural and Social Capital*

The original development of the concepts of 'cultural and social capital' was deterministic in that they were assumed either to exist or not exist in a community, family or an individual. These concepts of capital were seen to operate from the perspective of the dominant values of society. Thus the possession of cultural and social capital, so defined, was seen as beneficial for the educational performance and attainment of students. However, as Demerath (2000) has pointed out, students can be subjected to two forms of cultural and social capital, particularly in those environments where there is a clash of value systems between the home and the school. Thus the possession of one form of capital may be detrimental to the possession of another. A student in a developing country, for example, who acquires the cultural and social capital of the school, may lose it with respect to his or her integration in their traditional community.

In this context, the analysis of cultural and social capital with respect to education becomes more complex. In many Western and non-Western countries, both developed and less developed, there are traditional subcultures that conflict with the culture of the school. Both cultures possess forms of cultural and social capital that in one way or another can serve as an advantage to the student. This is particularly true where the culture of the home is collectivist whereas the culture of the school is individualist.

4. COLLECTIVISM, INDIVIDUALISM AND SCHOOLING

A collectivist or communitarian culture is one in which the social self is embodied in a network of social relationships such that the boundaries of the self and those of the community are not clearly defined. In contrast, an individualist culture is one in which the social self is more autonomous, competitive, and clearly delineated from the community. Social psychologists often use the terms the 'independent self' and the 'interdependent self' (Moghaddam, 1998). However the boundaries between these two notions of the self are not necessarily fixed, so that it is likely that some variation in the social self occurs as individuals find themselves in different social contexts. In other words, persons from a collectivist culture may find themselves in an environment that assumes a more individualist orientation in behaviour.

This distinction in orientation is important because both individualist and collectivist cultures possess culture and social capital, and the acquisition and importance of these forms of capital and the school become more problematic. This interplay between the two has often been described as a conflict or struggle whereby a collectivist traditional culture attempts to resist or hold together when confronted with the culture of the school that attempts to dismember it.

The understanding of cultural and social capital, and their relationship to schooling, in the Asia-Pacific region needs to use this extended view of the two concepts. Many cultures from this region, both in developed and developing countries, are characterised by a collectivist rather than an individualist orientation. However, the structures of the educational systems are uniformly Western, and therefore assume, at least in part, an individualist orientation. Furthermore, because there are different types of schools in these countries, it is highly likely that the relationship between schooling and the acquisition of cultural and social capital will vary considerably.

In the following section a selective review of educational research on the role of cultural and social capital in schooling in the Asia-Pacific region of the world is summarized. The interpretations of the concepts here are broad, as many studies on the effects of home background, and on the effects of schooling, do not specifically mention cultural and social capital. However, implicitly these concepts are represented in much of the research.

5. EMPIRICAL STUDIES OF CULTURAL AND SOCIAL CAPITAL

Some school systems in the Asian region have attracted worldwide attention because of the comparatively high educational performance of their students on standardized academic tests. For example Japan, Republic of Korea, Singapore, and to a lesser extent Taiwan and Hong Kong, are examples of systems which have attracted research in order to explain why their children seem to perform better in schools than comparable children in Western schools. Some of this research attention is motivated by the implementation of policies to improve the school performance of Western children. This was the underlying motivation for the study of Stevenson and Stigler (1992) who compared elementary school children in three cities: Sendai (Japan), Taipei (Taiwan), and Minneapolis (USA).

Other studies, however, have focused on non-Western cultural and traditional educational behaviours and outcomes simply to understand better their importance. In this context some religious or interpersonal practices that are directly related to schooling can be interpreted as non-Western forms of cultural and social capital.

In the following section, an analysis of selected studies is used to illustrate the ways in which cultural and social capital operate in Asian and Pacific countries. In some cases, cultural and social capital function in much the same ways as in Western cultures. However, it is apparent that the manifestations of these forms of capital are culture-specific, so that some unique features of some Asian and Pacific countries can produce forms of culture and social capital not found in the West.

5.1. *The Family Environment*

There are forms of cultural and social capital in Asian and Pacific countries which are similar to that found in Western societies, but which are practised to a different degree. Thus the structure and processes of the family in some Asian societies contain a richness of cultural and social capital which are important determinants in academic performance.

Stevenson and Stigler never mention cultural or social capital in their comparative study of Asian and American education. However, in their findings they point to aspects of the Japanese and Chinese educational outcomes which reflect high levels of cultural capital. Primary students in the Asian schools they studied are embedded in home and family environments that not only are supportive, but also participative in the work of the school. There is continuity between the home and school that they did not find in their study of American schools. Furthermore, there is complementarity between Asian home and school environments rather than duplication: "Parents and teachers work together, but do not duplicate one another's roles …. Americans, by contrast, seem to expect that schools will take on responsibility for many more aspects of the child's life" (Stevenson & Stigler, 1992, p. 83).

The differences in culture capital between the Asian and American education environments do not end with the nature of home and school relationships. Stevenson and Stigler found that Asian schools stressed more cooperative and group learning activities than did American schools, and that differences in academic performance were less likely to be attributed to differences in ability, but rather to differences in effort. The latter, they argue, is significant in explaining their finding that Asian children were more persistent in trying to succeed academically: "In sum, the relative importance people assign to factors beyond their control, like ability, compared to factors that they can control, like effort, can strongly influence the way they approach learning" (Stevenson & Stigler, 1992, p. 106).

Clearly in the study by Stevenson and Stigler, culture capital and social capital are highly interrelated. It is the cultural capital of the Japanese family which provides support for educational attainment, while it is the social capital of the cooperative and group learning of the school environment which increases the social resources for the learning process. The difference between the Japanese and American views regarding educational performance lies in the greater recognition, and dependence upon, the amount of cultural and social capital the Japanese parents and students can mobilize in expending educational effort. (See *The Family and Schooling in Asian and Pacific Countries*)

5.2. Single-Mother Families

An indication of the unusual ways that culture and social capital manifest themselves in Asian educational settings is found in the study by Pong (1996) of the school participation of children in single-mother families. The findings from studies in most Western societies, in particular the United States, Great Britain and Australia, are consistent in showing a negative relationship between single-parent families and educational attainments. Pong found that in Malaysia much depends on the cultural status of a single-parent family, and that children from some single-parent environments do not show this negative relationship. She distinguished between the reason for single-family status (divorce/separation or widowhood), and the ethnic background of the single-families (Malay, Indian, and Chinese). She then controlled for other family characteristics (mother education, income, and sibship size) and found that widowhood among Malay mothers does not necessarily result in lower school participation among children.

In her discussion, Pong observed that divorced or separated mothers generally cut their ties with their collectivist extended families. Widowed mothers do not. Hence they continue to receive intangible social help, and financial help, from their extended families. In effect, collectivist ties provide the social capital necessary for the education of children. Pong concluded: "This differs sharply with the U.S. situation, where economic deprivation plays an important role in mediating the detriment of family disruption" (Pong, 1996, p. 249).

5.3. Teacher Expectations

In some Asian contexts cultural capital and social capital are highly interrelated. Robinson (1994) found that Korean schoolteachers hold strong beliefs about the relationship between the social status background of students and their academic ability. This belief is grounded in traditional Confucian cultural practices in the home, which are regarded as indicators of social status. In addition to the normal sources of information which teachers have about the social status of students, the extent to which parents make contact with the teacher about their child is also interpreted as a sign of concern, and therefore of status.

Parents also participate in the custom of *ch'onji*, or the practice of giving "tokens of appreciation" to the teacher. Although the teachers deny that these gifts influence their treatment of students, nonetheless they are seen as a "reflection of the parents' concern" for children (Robinson, 1994, p. 516). As a result Robinson found that teachers tended to call on students in class more often, a practice generally seen as contributing to *palp'yo*, or the acquisition of classroom speaking skills which consist of honorific language forms that are important in later public life. Thus from the parents' point of view, the practice of *ch'onji* helps acquire the social capital necessary to ensure the child's academic success, and ultimately the social success of their children. This complex process that Robinson documents "is an example of how economic capital can be converted to social capital" (Robinson, 1994, p. 528).

This example illustrates how cultural capital and social capital are interrelated. It is the possession of cultural capital, that is, a knowledge of how the social system functions, which enables the acquisition of social capital. Parents who know about *ch'onji*, most of whom would be of upper status background, possess the cultural capital which helps build social capital, namely the perception of teachers that they care about their children's academic performance. The teachers in turn interact with the relevant students in such a way that contributes to higher academic performance.

5.4. *Sons and Daughters*

Families play an important role in the distribution of cultural and social capital among its members. This is particularly true in patriarchal families regarding the differential treatment of older and younger children, as well as between sons and daughters. This pattern of differential treatment has been widely studied in Western and non-Western societies, and has been found to be changing somewhat as societies become more wealthy, and family sizes become smaller (Parish & Willis, 1993). In many Asian cultures sons traditionally are favoured over daughters in the use of family economic capital for educational attainment. However, as elsewhere, this practice is not normally interpreted in terms of the distribution of cultural and social capital, but rather as a rational response to economic constraints. Yet many studies have documented the manner in which there is differential treatment of sons and daughters in Asian families with respect to education, and in which it is possible to identify the role of cultural and social capital as well.

A good example that illustrates how family dynamics provide the arena for the interaction between economic, cultural and social capital is that by Post and Pong (1998), on Hong Kong families. Using census data from 1981 and 1991, they found that the effects of family composition on the unequal educational attainments of boys and girls declined during this period. More importantly, however, they were able to identify the factors that contributed to this process.

A decision by the Hong Kong Government in 1978 to make secondary education free for all Hong Kong students might have been expected to reduce sex differences in educational attainment. However, Post and Pong explored the changing effects of household behaviour on these differences in attainment as well. They found that even though fathers' income and mothers' education increased during this period, it was the latter that independently brought about the greatest reduction in the negative effect of sibling size and birth order (male or female, older or younger), on the increasing educational attainment of Hong Kong girls.

Post and Pong argued that mothers' educational attainment represents "an omnibus measure of culture capital" (p. 108). Furthermore, they contended that this variable reflects the increased status and power of the mother, as well as the mother's values regarding the education of children. In this respect mother's education can also represent a form of social capital, since increased status and power are relational phenomena, and they imply that the mother's ability to influence decisions regarding the education for her children also increased. These forms of cultural and social capital operated independently of the economic capital provided by the increase in fathers' income, and independently of the increased provision of education for all Hong Kong children.

These findings are significant for other Asian cultures where sons and daughters are differentially valued with respect to educational attainment. Some studies, such as that reported by Parish and Willis (1993) in Taiwan, suggest that concern over resource dilution, or restraints in economic capital, is the primary explanatory variable in the differential treatment of sons and daughters in Taiwan. On the other hand, Pong's (1993) analysis of ethnic, gender and socioeconomic status differences in educational attainment in Malaysia demonstrates that both structural (economic) factors, and cultural factors operate in educational differentiation. In the case of Malaysia, the government's preferential educational and economic policies of 1961 and 1971 respectively did increase the educational attainment of the Malay population. However, the propensity for males to receive more education than females diminished considerably during this period. Furthermore, Pong found that, as in Hong Kong, mother's education (a form of cultural capital) was an important family variable in influencing the educational attainment of children.

From these studies of Hong Kong and Malaysia it is clear that government policies can influence the effects of cultural and social capital in educational processes and outcomes. In the case of Hong Kong, the provision of free schooling by the government did, indirectly and in the long-term, affect the amount of cultural and social capital in the home by raising the educational attainment of mothers. Similarly the preferential educational policies did increase the educational attainments of the Malay population, but also reduced the preferences of sons and daughters in schooling. In both of these examples, the effects of cultural and social capital continued to operate. In this manner, and independently of the economic capital available, the cultural and social capital of the household served further to reduce sex inequalities in educational attainment.

5.5. *Examination Practices*

As with many Asian societies, Japan, Taiwan and China have rich traditional cultures that guide the daily lives of people. The knowledge of these cultures, and the practices which flow from them, constitute a form of cultural capital that can be directly related to education. One area not often explored in this context is practices that are available to students to assist in academic performance, especially examinations. Although Asian families are rich in cultural and social capital that assist in improving student achievement, there are also other practices outside the family that are available to bring about higher academic performance.

The various religious-cultural practices of school students in Japan and Taiwan to assist in passing examinations are mechanisms that give personal confidence and solace to those students who practise them. In this context, Zeng (1996) describes the use of the *ema* ("painted horse" or prayer tablet) in Shinto shrines and the *hachimaki* (headband) by Japanese students, or the use of *guangming deng* (brilliance lamp) or *omamori* (charms) by Taiwanese students. Access to these practices by many students differentiate them from others who choose not to, or for one reason or another cannot resort to them, in terms of cultural capital. Unfortunately little attention has been given to these unique practices in Asian and Pacific societies.

5.6. *The Culture of Authority and Education*

There are examples of Asian countries where the form of culture capital acts as an obstruction to educational processes, and in addition, an obstruction to the formation of educationally relevant social capital. In a macro-level study of the relationship between socio-economic development and educational expansion in Cambodia, Ayres (2000) focussed attention on the historical and political circumstances that impeded both development and education. However, even when concerned with macro-level processes, Ayres noted that culturally imbedded traditions in interpersonal relationships impeded attempts to modernize Cambodian society. What Ayres and others have called the "distinct Khmer way" (p. 455) consists of the traditional patron-client relationships that date before the Angkor period of Cambodian history. This tradition of patron-client relationships, even in the most supportive environment for the promotion of educational expansion, hindered the kind of political and social negotiation and cooperation necessary for the introduction of modern institutions necessary for educational expansion to occur. Even in Western democratic societies, the existence of so-called 'patronage politics' tends to mitigate against effective and innovative government. (Putnam, 2000, p. 347) In the Cambodian patronage context Ayres notes that "... the notion of mutual obligation did not exist" (Ayres, 2000, p. 456).

Given this cultural context, Cambodian society has consisted of the powerful and the governed. Without any mutual obligation, power relations flowed only in one direction, the result being that power became an end in itself. The traditional culture that defined power relations was also the obstacle to the establishment of new modern institutions, including successful education.

> Put simply, the provision of formal education in Cambodia has been embraced to build a nation-state that looks modern, yet is concerned almost exclusively with sustaining the key tenets of the traditional polity, where leadership is associated with power and where the nature of the state is perceived to be a function of that power. (Ayres, 2000, p. 459)

The type of conflict between the traditional and the modern, as found in Cambodia, represents a form of culture capital which can be an obstacle to the functioning of a modern education system. It also prevents the formation of culture capital that supports the individual values and ambitions that make education a desirable goal. Finally it ultimately deprives individuals of the social capital which makes access to education possible.

Many societies in the Asia-Pacific region are in stages of social and economic development where traditional cultural institutions coexist with modern institutions. In these contexts, it is likely that forms of cultural and social capital may be unavailable or inappropriate to support modern institutions. Education as a modern institution, both in terms of its expansion, as well as in the attainment of students, is hindered in this context.

5.7. *Literacy and Women*

The relationship between cultural and social capital, and education, can be found in other non-school contexts where learning takes place. The participation in literacy classes for women in Arutar, a remote village in Western Nepal, provides an example of the importance of these forms of capital. Robinson-Pant (2000) approached the study of literacy programs from the ideological perspective whereby meanings of literacy are seen as imbedded in a cultural context. Thus for Robinson-Pant there are several literacies in a community, the literacy of adult men and women, of young people, and whether literacy learning is "imposed" or "self-generated". Although she did not use the concepts of 'cultural and social capital', Robinson-Pant's findings concerning the way literacy was regarded and acquired by men and women, and for the different types of literacies, namely 'everyday literacy' and the 'class literacy' taught through a development agency.

Using an ethnographic approach, Robinson-Pant (2000) found that both cultural capital and social capital were involved in the way literacy was valued and practised. 'Cultural capital', as a concept, underpinned the differences between the men and women in the acquisition of literacy. For the women, literacy was seen as a form of empowerment and autonomy, while for the men, their authority was preserved even if they were illiterate. Social capital, in turn, was clearly important in the consequences of class literacy. The objective of the literacy program sponsored by the development agency was to provide the women of the village with the opportunity to improve numerical skills, to keep accounts, and to improve the family income. Ironically these skills were not necessary because of the numerical skills in a culture that relied on "oral calculations and memory" (p. 358). However, the women did acquire social capital as a result of the formal literacy classes. They became empowered as a result of coming together for classes and acquiring the skills which enabled them to record and communicate their own thoughts and feelings in writing, and the attainment of a new social identity (that is, as a 'literate' person), and the social space this gave them. As Robinson-Pant commented: "... literacy for many of the women was viewed as an empowering process, in contrast to the aid agency's 'efficiency' objective" (Robinson-Pant, 2000, p. 361).

5.8. *Overseas Study as Cultural Capital*

Overseas university study, either government or privately funded, has been an increasing phenomenon for many Asian and Pacific countries during the past decade, although the practice can be traced to the late nineteenth century. Over 425,000 international students were enrolled at American universities for bachelor studies in 2001, and over 220,000 in Britain. In Australia, between 1994 and 2001, the number of international students grew 73 per cent. The largest numbers came from Asian countries, with China, Japan, Korea, India and Taiwan being the main source for study in the United States. The students from the Asia-Pacific region have tended to travel to Western countries such as Australia, Canada, the United Kingdom, the United States, and recently to Japan from China and Korea (McMurtrie, 2001).

The reasons for this phenomenon have been the limited access to tertiary education places in the home country, the desire to acquire unique educational credentials, or the marketing success of outside universities. Studies of the effects of the overseas study experience have typically focused on culture conflict, brain drain, or prospects for social mobility in the home country. However, another sociological aspect of this important phenomenon is the acquisition of overseas education as a form of cultural capital for the home country.

In order to demonstrate the formation of cultural capital from overseas education, Huang (Huang, 2002) investigated the careers of 120 young peasant students, aged between 10 and 16 years, who were sent by the Chinese government to study in the United States between 1872 and 1875. They were recalled to China in 1881 for fear that they might become too 'Americanised'. In his analysis, Huang showed how these students later became personally successful and also how they contributed significantly to the early social transformation of modern China. Huang showed how these early students through their achievements gradually acquired a positive social identity as returned students (*liuxuesheng*), and that they brought with them knowledge and skills, that is, foreign cultural capital, which became positively valued in their home country. Furthermore, their success contributed to the rise of a Western-style education in China in recent years.

It could be argued that the generations of students who have subsequently followed these early Chinese students in study abroad, not only from China but also from other Asia-Pacific countries, have acquired a form of cultural capital which accrues to them personally, and also contributes to changes in their home countries. This is a perspective which has been largely neglected in the study of overseas education in the Asia-Pacific region.

6. CONCLUSION

The illustrations of cultural and social capital found in these studies suggest that these phenomena are present and operate in Asian and Pacific societies in much the same way as they do in Western societies. However, the analysis of how these forms of capital are manifested suggests that the uniqueness of some Asian and Pacific cultural patterns provide unusual and unexpected examples. Clearly cultural and social capital are useful concepts for the analysis of social processes across cultures. Furthermore they provide ways of understanding how cultural practices and social connectedness can have both positive and negative effects on education processes and outcomes.

Very few studies of education in Asian and Pacific countries have explicitly used these concepts in the analysis of education. Yet the studies analysed here provide sufficient evidence that these concepts would be useful in future studies of education in non-Western societies (see also *The Family and Schooling in Asian and Pacific Countries*).

REFERENCES

Ayres, D. M. (2000). Tradition, modernity, and the development of education in Cambodia. *Comparative Education Review, 44*(4), 440–463.

Bourdieu, P. (1986). The forms of capital. In J. G. Richardson (Ed.), *Handbook of Theory and Research for the Sociology of Education* (pp. 241–258). New York: Greenwood Press.

Bourdieu, P., & Passeron, J.-C. (1977). *Reproduction in Education, Society and Culture*. London: Sage. (French original published in 1970).

Bourdieu, P., & Passeron, J.-C. (1979). *The Inheritors: French Students and Their Relation to Culture*. Chicago: University of Chicago Press. (French original published in 1965).

Coleman, J. S. (1987). Social capital and the development of youth. *Momentum, 18*(4), 6–8.

Coleman, J. S. (1988). Social capital in the creation of human capital. *American Journal of Sociology, 94*(Supplement), 95–121.

Coleman, J. S. (1997). Family, school and social capital. In L. J. Saha (Ed.), *International Encyclopedia of the Sociology of Education* (pp. 623–625). Oxford: Pergamon Press.

Collins, J., & Thompson, F. (1997). Family, school and cultural capital. In L. J. Saha (Ed.), *International Encyclopedia of the Sociology of Education* (pp. 618–623). Oxford: Pergamon Press.

Demerath, P. (2000). The social cost of acting 'extra': Students' moral judgements of self, social relations, and the academic success in Papua New Guinea. *American Journal of Education, 108*(3), 196–235.

Huang, H. (2002). Overseas studies and the rise of foreign cultural capital in modern China. *International Sociology, 17*(1), March, 35–55.

Lamb, S. (1990). Cultural selection in Australian secondary schools. *Research in Education, 43*, 1–14.

McMurtrie, B. (2001). Foreign enrollments grow in the U.S., but so does competition from other nations. *The Chronicle of Higher Education*, November 16, 2001.

Moghaddam, F. M. (1998). *Social Psychology: Exploring Universals Across Cultures*. New York: Freeman and Company.

Narayan, D., & Cassidy, M. F. (2001). A dimensional approach to measuring social capital: Development and validation of a social capital inventory. *Current Sociology, 49*(2), 59–102.

Parish, W. L., & Willis, R. J. (1993). Daughters, education and family budgets: Taiwan experiences. *Journal of Human Resources, 28*, 863–898.

Pong, S.-L. (1993). Preferential policies and secondary school attainment in peninsular Malaysia. *Sociology of Education, 66*(3), 245–261.

Pong, S.-L. (1996). School participation of children from single-mother families in Malaysia. *Comparative Education Review, 40*(3), 231–249.

Portes, A. (1998). Social capital: Its origins and applications to modern sociology. *Annual Review of Sociology, 24*, 1–24.

Post, D., & Pong, S.-L. (1998). The waning effect of sibship composition on school attainment in Hong Kong. *Comparative Education Review, 42*(2), 99–117.

Putnam, R. D. (2000). *Bowling Alone: The Collapse and Revival of American Community*. New York: Simon and Shuster.

Robinson, J. (1994). Social status and academic success in South Korea. *Comparative Education Review, 38*(4), 506–530.

Robinson-Pant, A. (2000). Women and literacy: A Nepal perspective. *International Journal of Educational Development, 20*(4), 349–364.

Schneider, B. (2000). Social systems and norms: A Coleman approach. In M. T. Hallinan (Ed.), *Handbook of the Sociology of Education* (pp. 365–385). M. T. Hallinan, New York: Kluwer. Academic/Plenum Publishers.

Stevenson, H. W., & Stigler, J. W. (1992). *The Learning Gap: Why Our Schools Are Failing and What We Can Learn from Japanese and Chinese Education*. New York: Summit Books.

Zeng, K. (1996). Prayer, luck and spiritual strength: The desecularization of entrance examination systems in East Asia. *Comparative Education Review, 40*(3), 264–279.

6

Secondary Education Reform in the Asia-Pacific Region

RUPERT MACLEAN
UNESCO-UNEVOC International Centre for Education, Bonn, Germany

1. INTRODUCTION: THE IMPORTANCE OF SECONDARY EDUCATION

The reform, strengthening and upgrading of secondary education is one of increasing world-wide concern. This is particularly the case for least developed and developing countries, those going through a period of rapid transition and countries in a post-conflict situation. Nowhere is this concern greater than in the vast and diverse Asia-Pacific region which is home to approximately 60 per cent of the world's population of six billion people, and 71 per cent of the world's total number of illiterates.

Since the 1950s an increasing number of countries have been successful in expanding their education systems, as they are successful in moving towards achieving education for all and the universalisation of primary education. However, this has at the same time resulted in a significant increase in upwards pressure on expanding gross enrolments in secondary education. Figure 1 shows the growth of secondary education in the Asian region compared to the world as a whole. As access to secondary education has expanded its overall quality has often been in decline, since resources have been stretched thin and systems have become more inefficient. In many countries secondary education has become the weakest link in the education chain.

There is widespread agreement as to the need for a fundamental re-thinking of the role and place of secondary education as part of the re-engineering of education systems. Most countries recognise the priority of secondary education, as an indispensable link in the whole education system. It is also an area of particular importance for youth in preparing them for the world of work and to become fully functioning and effective citizens. At the World Education Forum in Dakar (2000) the matter of what happens after primary education was raised as being an important issue in a number of regions where secondary education is now regarded as being part of basic education. At the Dakar Forum, a Roundtable on "After Primary Education: What?" discussed the reform of the secondary education curriculum.

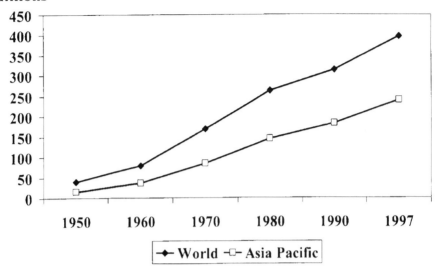

Figure 1. Expansion of secondary education enrolments (Asia compared to the world). [Source: based on figures in UNESCO *World Education Report*, 2000a]

Important problems are emerging which require the strengthening and upgrading of secondary education. For instance, there is an urgent need to address the problem of the sudden, overwhelming increase in the number of qualified applicants for secondary education. Providing access to secondary education is a more difficult and complex process than is the case for primary schooling since it is in secondary schools that subject-specialization begins. There is also an even larger number of stakeholders for this level of education, whose views need to be accommodated, than is the case for primary education. Secondary education is also generally more expensive than is primary schooling.

Figure 2 presents the gross enrolment rates for a selection of countries in the Asian region. Gross enrolment rates in secondary education vary enormously between countries: from 23 per cent in Cambodia to 100 per cent in the Republic of Korea and Japan. There are clearly millions of out-of-school secondary school aged youth in many countries, and these young people cannot be accommodated by existing facilities. In other cases they have no access to, or interest in undertaking, secondary education, for a variety of reasons such as economic poverty, living in an isolated location, or feelings of alienation. This problem is commonly greater for girls than for boys, and for those living in South Asia compared to those in Eastern Asia and Oceania, as can be seen from Figure 3 that presents the gender breakdown of out-of-school secondary school aged youth in these two sub-regions.

In order to help address these types of difficulties, increasing attention is being given to inter-related matters, such as: (a) ways of cost effectively expanding access to secondary education without sacrificing equity considerations, so that

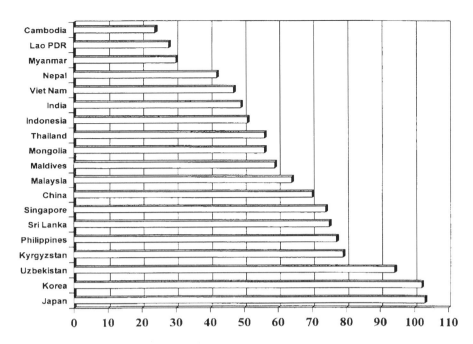

Figure 2. Secondary education in Asia (gross enrolment ratios by %). [Source: based on UNESCO *World Education Report*, 2000]

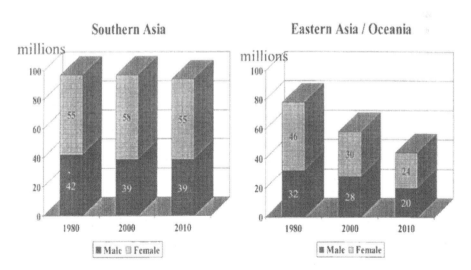

Figure 3. Gender breakdown of out-of-school secondary-school age youth (Asia and the Pacific). [Source: UNESCO *World Education Report*, 2000]

all sections of society regardless of gender, socio-economic background, ethnicity or geographical location have access to a high-quality, relevant secondary education; (b) identifying ways of reducing drop-out and repeater rates; (c) achieving quality assurance so that expanding access is not at the expense of the quality of programs; (d) improving the relevance and effectiveness of the content of the secondary education curriculum as one way of reducing high drop-out and repeater rates; (e) the importance of recruiting, adequately training and then keeping good and effective teachers in the teaching force; (f) utilizing the most effective modalities for delivering secondary education programs, including reinforcing mainstream formal education systems while at the same time also utilizing nonformal practices and innovative modes of delivery such as distance education and harnessing existing and new information and communication technologies; and, (g) coping with financial pressures on the funding of secondary education through such means as encouraging the private funding of secondary education, financial partnerships with employers including cost-sharing considerations, and through improving the internal efficiency of secondary education.

Major regional and international conferences have been held, such as the 1998 International Conference on Education organised by UNESCO's Asia-Pacific Centre for Educational Innovation for Development on 'Secondary Education and Youth at the Crossroads', and the 'International Expert Meeting on General Secondary Education in the Twenty-first Century: Trends, Challenges and Priorities' (UNESCO, 2001b). These conferences have repeatedly stressed the urgent need to upgrade, diversify and expand education at the secondary level. This is essential in order to respond adequately to the types of concerns referred to above and challenges emerging due to rapid changes in societies, globalisation and the changing nature of work.

A major difficulty facing governments, educational policy makers and practitioners, is the general paucity of good quality, comprehensive and relevant research data to provide concrete guidance on best practices to adapt for secondary education reform. There is also a lack of comparative research data which maps developments in secondary education reform in the Asia-Pacific region, compared to other parts of the world, and between countries in the region, and so provides useful benchmarks for comparative purposes.

In this article a brief overview is provided of the main areas of interest to aid agencies and the donor community concerning the reform and development of secondary education in various parts of the world. After sketching out the international context regarding such reforms, a more detailed analysis is then provided of what is known about strategic issues and policy analysis of secondary education in the Asia-Pacific region.

2. SPECIAL IMPORTANCE OF THE DELORS REPORT

Youth who are living in what for many is a turbulent, rapidly changing world need values-orientated anchors, and the knowledge, skills and understandings, to enable them to find effective ways of coping with the tensions, pressures and contradictions that are apparent in their societies, and in their daily lives. When it comes to examining the renovation, renewal and diversification of secondary education, with particular reference to meeting the educational needs of youth, the Report to UNESCO of the International Commission on Education for the Twenty-first Century, *Learning: the Treasure Within*, (Delors Report 1996) raises some important matters and provides a helpful conceptual framework for analysing and guiding the content, organisation and management of secondary education reform and the education of youth.

In Chapter 6 of the Delors Report, in a Section called 'Secondary education: the crossroads of life', the authors of the Report note:

> Many of the hopes and criticisms aroused by formal systems seem to focus on secondary education. On the one hand, it is often regarded as the gateway to social and economic advancement. It is accused, on the other hand, of being inegalitarian and not sufficiently open to the outside world and, generally, failing to prepare adolescents not only for higher education but also for the world of work. In addition, it is also argued that the subjects taught are irrelevant and that not enough attention is paid to the acquisition of attitudes and values. It is now generally recognized that, for economic growth to take place, a high proportion of the population has to have received secondary education. It would thus be useful to clarify what secondary education needs to do to prepare young people for adulthood.
>
> The view of learning as a process that continues throughout life leads us to reconsider both the content and globalisation of secondary education. The requirements of the labour market create a pressure owing to which the number of years of schooling tends to increase. (Delors, 1996)

Secondary education must be linked in the context of lifelong education to three major principles: diversity of courses, increased emphasis on the alternating of study and professional or social work, and attempts to improve quality.

3. SECONDARY EDUCATION PROGRAM ACTIVITIES WORLD-WIDE

The purpose of this section of this article is to survey main areas of emphasis concerning the policy and practice of countries throughout the world regarding the reform of secondary education. This has been achieved by examining the current range of activities, and priority areas, in secondary education being implemented by the United Nations Educational, Scientific and Cultural Organisation (UNESCO) and by other international agencies active in this area, such as UNICEF, OECD, UNDP, the ILO, the British Council, Education International, USAid, the World Bank, the Commonwealth of Learning, DFID, and the International Baccalaureate Organisation. This provides a measure of the priorities of countries concerning secondary education reform, since each of these organisations frame their program activities in the light of the wishes and priorities of their member states, as expressed through their various Governing Boards or Councils. In other words, the priorities and activities undertaken in these organisations reflect the expectations and wishes of the constituents of each of these organisations concerning secondary education reform. Two different surveys are reported upon here (Maclean & Caillods, 2002).

The first survey sought to ascertain the essential flavour of what is currently being undertaken by UNESCO with regard to secondary education reform. This helps identify the priority areas (and gaps) of program areas requested by member states. Information for this survey comes from professional staff working in UNESCO Headquarters, Paris, UNESCO Field Offices and UNESCO Institutes and Centres, worldwide. They were approached in August 2000 to provide details on current and planned program activities concerning secondary education reform and the education of youth. The information gathered through the survey has been augmented with details from UNESCO files and publications.

Table 1 provides a summary overview of what UNESCO is currently doing to assist member states strengthen and upgrade their systems of secondary education, and indicates the means by which these activities are being undertaken. As the details show, a wide range of activities are being undertaken concerned with the renovation and expansion of secondary education, worldwide. Priority program areas attracting the greatest attention are concerned with:

- expanding access to secondary education;
- quality assurance;
- curriculum reform (with particular reference to values education, science and technology education and preventative education for HIV/AIDS, and education for the world of work); and
- alternative delivery systems.

Other major program activities concern:

- equity considerations, with particular reference to the education of girls;
- improving teaching methods;
- reducing school drop-out;
- the development of teaching and learning materials;
- teacher recruitment; and
- strengthening the professional development of teachers.

Overall, less attention is being given to the management of education (with particular reference to the decentralisation of decision making), the financing of education, and monitoring and evaluation at both the systems and classroom levels.

With regard to the areas of coverage in various regions of the world, those in the Arab States are less involved with program areas relating to matters of equity, girls education, reducing drop-out, HIV/AIDS and alternative delivery

Secondary Education Reform in the Asia-Pacific Region 79

Table 1. UNESCO activities world-wide in secondary education reform and the education of youth

Program Areas	UNESCO HQ	UNESCO field offices					UNESCO Institute		
		Africa	Arab States	Asia-Pacific	LAC	IIEP	IBE	IITE	UIE
Expanding Access	*	*	*	*	*	*			*
Equity/Girls education		*		*	*				
Reducing drop out		*		*	*				*
Quality Assurance	*	*	*	*	*	*	*		
Curriculum reform	*	*	*	*	*		*		
* HIV/AIDS	*	*	*	*	*	*			
* STE	*	*	*		*		*		
* Values Education	*	*	*	*	*			*	*
* TVET	*	*	*	*				*	
* Other									
Teaching Methods	*	*					*	*	
Teaching Learning Methods			*	*	*		*	*	
Monitoring/Evaluation		*				*			
Alternative Delivery Systems	*			*		*			*
Teacher recruitment/ Professional development	*	*	*	*					
Management						*			
Financing						*			

Modalities

Project Formulation	*					*			*
Project Implementation	*			*					*
Project Evaluation	*	*	*	*	*	*	*		*
Conferences	*	*	*	*	*	*	*		*
Workshops/Seminars					*	*	*		
Research Studies				*	*	*	*		
Publications	*		*	*	*	*	*	*	
Utilisation of New ICT								*	

systems than are those in other regions of the world. Countries in the Asia-Pacific region are involved with a greater range of program areas and modalities of operation relating to secondary education reform than are those in other regions of the world, and are particularly concerned with listening to the 'voice of youth' when devising, implementing and evaluating programs. Concerning the range of modalities being used to undertake these activities there is widespread use of conferences, workshops and seminars. Publications, the undertaking of research studies and, to a lesser extent, project evaluation are also popular. Relatively little is currently occurring with regard to project formulation or implementation, and with utilizing the new information and communication technologies.

The second survey was conducted in February 2000. It sought to ascertain the views of partner agencies, who are members of the Inter-Agency Consultative Group on Secondary Education Reform and the Education of Youth, which was established by UNESCO in Paris in 1999, concerning future action to assist countries with secondary education reform. Since these organisations also respond to the wishes of their members states with regard to educational policy and practice, the findings provide a good overview of what countries want to achieve concerning secondary education reform. Table 2 shows the 'areas of emphasis', with regard to program activities concerning the reform of secondary education undertaken by the various agencies surveyed. It is not intended to show all the areas with which they are involved.

As Table 2 illustrates, program activities attracting most attention by the greatest number of these agencies concern the management of secondary education, financing considerations, quality assurance, curriculum reform with particular reference to health education, technical and vocational education and training for the world of work, teacher recruitment, career-long professional development, and the role of youth as the consumers of secondary education. Less explicit attention is given to program areas concerned with equity considerations including the education of girls, expanding access to secondary education, the development of teaching and learning materials, improved teaching methods, and to the monitoring and evaluation of secondary education. With regard to modalities, the emphasis is on research studies, publications, and the use of ICT and websites to publicise case studies of best practice and innovative approaches to the reform of secondary education.

4. SECONDARY EDUCATION IN THE ASIA-PACIFIC REGION

Attention is now directed in this article more specifically to an examination of the particular situation in countries in the Asia-Pacific region. Over the past four decades, large amounts of government and private finance have been injected into a variety of developments related to secondary education. The Asian Development Bank, as a significant financial contributor to such developments in the region over this period, commissioned in 1994 the Asia-Pacific Centre of

Secondary Education Reform in the Asia-Pacific Region 81

Table 2. Program activities undertaken by various agencies world-wide in secondary education reform

Program Areas	UNESCO	OECD	UNICEF	UNDP	ILO	Comm. of Lng	DFID	WB	USAID	Ed Int	Council of Europe	British Council	Comm Secr	IBO	AI France	GINIE
Expanding Access	*	*														
Equity/Girls Education	*	*														
Reducing Dropout	*															
Quality Assurance		*		*												
Curriculum Reform			*				*									
* HIV/AIDS	*															
* STE	*							*								
* Values Education			*	*										*		
* TVET	*	*			*			*					*			
* Other																
Teaching Methods											*					
Teaching Learning Materials		*														
Monitoring/Evaluation				*												
Alternative Delivery Systems						*										
Teacher recruitment/Teacher Education	*				*					*						
Role of Youth	*		*							*	*	*				
Management	*									*	*	*	*	*	*	
Financing	*	*					*	*			*					
Modalities																
Sector Case Studies	*							*								
Project Implementation	*							*	*							*
Project Evaluation	*								*							*
Conferences	*							*	*	*	*	*				*
Workshops/Seminars	*	*							*	*	*	*	*		*	
Research studies. Database	*								*		*	*	*	*	*	*
Publications	*						*		*		*	*				
ICT and Website	*	*	*				*				*					

Educational Innovation for Development (ACEID), UNESCO, Bangkok, and the Colombo Plan Staff College for Technician Education (CPSC), Manila, to undertake a comparative survey of developments in secondary education. This is a unique study, being the first Asia-Pacific regional inter-country comparative review of secondary education over the past 30 years.

This comprehensive, comparative survey of secondary education provided comparative information about alternate patterns of secondary education in the region and about implications for the future development of that education. The research was directed at educational planners, country level policy makers, politicians, members of non-government organisations interested in sponsoring quality secondary education, bilateral and international agencies, and major donor and lending agencies, including their technical staff and senior management. Data for the study were obtained through commissioned case studies in seven selected countries (Bangladesh, Indonesia, Republic of Korea, Pakistan, Philippines, Sri Lanka, and Thailand), from the review and analyses of secondary education in the Asia-Pacific region using international and national consultants, discussions with representatives from countries in the region and an examination of various publications on secondary education. These data provided the bases for a comparative analysis of the effects of alternative patterns and strategies for secondary education development in the region. The study was a large scale one, being conducted by two international consultants, 14 national consultants, and several UNESCO-ACEID consultants.

A total of 17 developing countries in the Asia-Pacific region were included in the overview analysis. In addition to countries used for the detailed case studies referred to above, other countries surveyed were Afghanistan, Bhutan, China, India, Lao PDR, Malaysia, Mongolia, Myanmar, Nepal, and Papua New Guinea. The 17 countries included in this overview were grouped according to the classification developed by the Asian Development Bank for its major review publications *Education and Development in Asia and the Pacific* (see Table 3).

The report of the Asian Development Bank study (ADB, 1995) was not published for wide circulation. Instead it was used as an internal discussion paper and strategy document for determining future Bank policy regarding secondary education reform, and in the Bank's dealings with countries in the Asia-Pacific region regarding loan applications for secondary education. The findings of the ADB study, which are published here in summary form for the first time, have been updated, drawing on recent sources such as paper presentations at the UNESCO-ACEID International Conference on Secondary Education and Youth at the Crossroads (UNESCO, 2000) and recent reviews of the latest developments in secondary education reform in the Asia-Pacific region (e.g., International Bureau of Education, 2000, 2001; *Journal of Educational Change*, 2000; Wilson, 2000). In essence, based on the ADB overview analysis and the case studies undertaken, the following may be said about key trends in secondary education in the Asia-Pacific region for the countries surveyed for the ADB study.

Table 3. Countries included in the overview analysis of secondary education in Asia

Large population, low income, high potential countries	
China	India

High technology exporting countries	
Malaysia	Republic of Korea

Middle income industrializing countries	
Indonesia	Pakistan
Philippines	Sri Lanka
Thailand	

Low income industrializing countries	
Bangladesh	Mongolia
Myanmar	

Subsistence agricultural countries	
Afghanistan	Bhutan
Lao PDR	Nepal
Papua New Guinea	

4.1. Structure and Participation

There is a great diversity across the Asia-Pacific region with respect to the structures of secondary education, enrolments, and retention rates in secondary education. While primary education may be offered for three or more, up to, eight years, secondary schooling may be offered from four or more, up to eight years in the various countries. Thus primary plus secondary education may occupy from 10 up to 13 years, depending on the country. In 11 countries surveyed secondary education is not compulsory but in another six it may be so for three, four or five years. Generally there is a lower and upper stage in secondary schooling, with a smaller proportion of students enrolled in the latter. However, there are also points in these structures where a higher proportion of males or females may discontinue.

The absolute magnitude and growth rates in gross enrolment ratios vary across countries. By and large subsistence agricultural countries (Afghanistan, Nepal, Papua New Guinea, Lao PDR and Bhutan) are low in both; for high technology exporting ones (Malaysia, Republic of Korea) the magnitude is between 57 and 87 per cent with an increase in growth since 1980; while for low income industrializing countries (Bangladesh, Myanmar, and Mongolia) the magnitude is between 17 and 24 per cent, with modest growth since 1980. Apparent retention rates have increased to 80 per cent in the high technology countries since 1980 and have been consistently low (12 to 15%) in the subsistence agricultural countries, with a decline since 1984.

Although there have been remarkable increases in the secondary education population in countries experiencing rapid expansion in population, many still have a long way to go to raise their gross enrolment ratios. Furthermore, there have been declines overall in vocational secondary education enrolments and great variations in the growth of primary schooling, with some countries experiencing an increase and others a decrease. There are variations in participation rates in the different educational structures which suggest interactions between the structure and the participation. But there are many subtleties which remain to be teased apart in order to understand the phenomenon (see *Educational Expenditure and Participation in East Asia and Australia*).

4.2. *Financing*

There has been a growing commitment across the region to secondary education over the past 40 years. Even so, the relative share of GDP which goes to education is low in the Asia-Pacific region compared to many other parts of the world. About 3.2 per cent goes to education currently, of which about a third is allocated to secondary education, and there appears to be scope to lift both these proportions.

While it is the case that the proportion of GDP allocated to education has risen (albeit unevenly) across the countries there is also great diversity regarding the means of financing education (for example, from tuition fees or from the private sector) and a great diversity regarding the capacity of countries to finance further expansion in secondary education. Tuition fees contribute about 18 per cent of unit costs to public sector secondary education, and private sources can also help, but the implications of the latter sector's involvement are not clear. The greater involvement of the private sector is a matter for further consideration and resolution. At present, due to a complex interplay of factors, there are great variations between countries as to the contributions the sector makes to secondary schooling.

Multilateral banks and funds are providing increasing support for education in the region and generally there has been a greater use of loans for educational purposes. In recent years the region has received about half of total lending for education from multilateral banks and funds. The Asian Development Bank has supplied about 26 per cent of this amount.

Some questions yet to be resolved are: (a) how to finance more effectively, expansions in secondary education, with particular reference to lower secondary; and (b) how to finance the greater participation of females. There is also the issue of the greater use of private sector funding for secondary schooling and the concomitant matter of the control and quality of that schooling.

4.3. *Access and Equity*

Although there has been a three-fold increase in secondary enrolments over the past 40 years (1960–2000) there is unequal access to this level of schooling for females, persons with disabilities, and members of various societal or racial subgroups. The proportion of females in secondary education has increased; although it is lower than that for primary education. It is highest in the high technology exporting countries such as Malaysia and Republic of Korea (where it is approaching 50%) and lowest in the low income industrializing ones such as Bangladesh, Myanmar and Mongolia (about 27%). In subsistence agricultural countries (Nepal, Papua New Guinea and Lao PDR) there have been significant gains since 1985 with the proportion now at about 37 per cent.

The female retention rates, though a fraction lower than for primary retention, vary from between 80 to 90 per cent for the high technology exporting countries (Malaysia, Republic of Korea) to about ten per cent for the low income industrializing ones (Bangladesh, Myanmar, Mongolia). A higher proportion of females than males participate in secondary education which contains teacher education. While there has been a decline in female drop-out rates throughout secondary education, there is a lower proportion of females in the final years of secondary. There can also be peaks in female drop-out after the first year, at about the transition point from lower to upper secondary or just prior to entry into the final secondary year. There are also inter-country variations. However, there is currently little statistical information to enable clear comparisons between rural and urban populations regarding access, although inequities appear to exist across countries. There is also very little data about the relative access for religious, racial and disabled sub-groups.

4.4. Internal Efficiency

A major policy question concerns the extent to which the additional resources allocated to secondary education have, or are, being efficiently used. Assessments about the internal efficiency of secondary education involve judgements about whether the desired educational output has been maximized given certain levels of resourcing. Some of the indicators include the cost of the education provided, expenditure per student, proportion of per capital GDP, student-teacher ratios and drop-out or wastage rates.

The expenditure on secondary education in the Asia-Pacific region is comparable to that of other developing countries in the world. Although there are some differences between countries, the costs of secondary education, however, are about twice that for primary education, but only 25 per cent that for tertiary education. There has been a substantial increase over the past 20 years in the level of public expenditure per student but at the same time administrative costs have increased proportionately from about 5 per cent to 18 per cent of recurrent costs. Of total expenditure the recurrent budget accounts for about 80 per cent and capital works, 20 per cent. Teachers' salaries take about two-thirds of the recurrent education budget.

Generally student teacher ratios have declined since 1980 to below 20:1 in the majority of countries. School sizes on the other hand can vary from about 300 to 1,100 which also affects student teacher ratios and the range of curriculum offerings for students. Although due caution must be exercised when comparing the costs of private and public schools, generally it is the case that expenditure in private schooling is less than that on public schooling. Furthermore, technical and vocational education costs are about five or six times more than those for secondary education.

Wastage or drop-out rates and repetition rates vary across the region from low and almost negligible to high. At certain points throughout secondary education peaks can occur in the drop-out rates. In some countries repetition rates reach 13 per cent of a grade enrolment. However, there has been a diminution in the wastage rates since the early 1980s. There is a greater likelihood than previously that a student will complete a secondary education. But with respect to output, it is not yet completely clear what it is that students have gained as a result of their attendance at secondary school.

4.5. *Quality Assurance*

This is difficult to measure but there are indicators related to curriculum, teaching and teacher education, educational assessment, globalisation and management, and education policies, that can be used. All countries accord a high priority to curriculum reform and believe curriculum should be responsive to emerging needs. Curriculum Development Centres have been established to help with this and the number of relevant school texts has increased. There are, however, still calls for more and better quality texts, additional curriculum courses to meet new emerging needs, research on curriculum, and for a constant, sustained review and modification of curricula. Flexibility of the curriculum is needed to suit a rapidly changing world, new teaching areas are also necessary. Curricula need relevance and balance. The teaching-learning process needs much improvement with more student participation, the use of teaching aids and better quality textbooks and teaching materials. Research in secondary education is insufficient and is a weak point in school systems. Definite steps have been taken to meet the great demand for teachers but more are still required. As teachers are the key to a high quality secondary education the quality of their training needs to be upgraded, revised and modernized. This must also occur with regard to their conditions of service, status and salary.

Countries have taken account of the universities' requirements for selection and so, as a consequence, there is a predominance of examinations in secondary education. Student assessments needs reform and the place for national examinations revised. Since there are fundamental questions about the reliability and validity of these, there are calls for a greater variety in the forms of student assessment including continuous assessments set by teachers and for standardised testing. Concomitant calls are for training programs to upgrade teachers (and others) competencies in test construction, administration, and interpretation.

The importance of educational policies, management and good globalisation have been acknowledged throughout the region and changes have occurred in all three areas. Most countries have overarching educational plans and national co-ordinating and advisory bodies, although some are not very active. Devolution of authority, decentralisation, and the privatisation of schooling are occurring with varying degrees of success. More attention must be directed to rationalising decentralized structures, and to monitoring, evaluating and fine tuning what is occurring with respect to privatisation, decentralisation and the devolution of authority. Management training programs are required as is the installation and greater use, than at present, of computer systems to assist with management. There is a trend for increased decentralisation but communications within such systems is weak especially training for administrators and managers of the system. Countries need to pay special attention to management at the classroom level.

4.6. *External Efficiency*

Continuing efforts are needed by countries to ensure that students are provided with curricula and learning experiences that are relevant to the economic and social environments they are about to enter.

The countries lack systems for providing advice and counselling for students about their educational and employment expectations. In the East Asian region there is strong evidence that rising levels of educational attainment have had a positive impact on economic growth (see *Educational Research for National and Regional Development*). Most countries experience the phenomenon of educated unemployment. Much can be done to reorient curricula and student advisory services to reflect more the realities of the labour market. It is also observed that the per student costs of vocational programs are higher than for general secondary education in countries with diversified curricula.

4.7. *Regional Views on Issues and Policy Options*

There was a high degree of common concern on the themes identified by the ADB study, speakers at the ACEID conference (UNESCO, 1999), and in recent publications about secondary education reform in the region (IBE, 2000, 2001; *Journal of Educational Change*, 2001), on, for example, curriculum deficiencies including deficient links to the world of work, on equity of access, teacher shortages and teacher quality, private sector involvement in secondary education, decentralisation and management, nonformal secondary education, assessment and examinations. To be more detailed, the broad areas for further attention, even though advances have occurred in each, may be summarized as follows:

- further improvement in access to education and in gender equity, but with due care to ensure that there will not be a decline in the excellence of secondary education as a consequence;
- decentralisation of decision making about the curriculum, improvement of curriculum and associated textbooks, strengthening of the links between curriculum and industry and the world of work, and greater use of English for instruction while retaining the national language;

- reviews of the structure of secondary education;
- reviews of the systems of examinations and assessment;
- greater decentralisaton, devolution of authority, and privatisation of schooling;
- greater, and more frequent, monitoring and evaluations of changes in schooling and to its administration;
- clarification of the roles of administrative and policy-making bodies;
- quality training programs for educational administrators and supervisors;
- revisions of policies and practices with respect to financing education; and
- revision, upgrading and improvement in the quality of teacher education and training.

4.8. *Technical and Vocational Education at the Secondary Level*

There have been some impressive developments in Technical and Vocational Education and Training (TVET) in the region, but many of these developments have also been uneven. TVET, which consists of a diverse range of courses, including the trades, is usually offered at upper secondary levels and beyond, lower secondary being only for general vocational skills and for providing an awareness and appreciation of the world of work to all students. There is a general desire within the region: (a) for the further development of TVET (but not in ways where there would be a demise of agricultural education); (b) for the better integration of TVET into lower and upper secondary; (c) for better partnerships to be developed between the public and private sector with respect to TVET; (d) for a review of TVET financing; for more formal and nonformal TVET courses; and, (e) for there to be a greater number of revised, upgraded and modernized training programs for TVET teachers.

With the restructuring of industry, secondary education TVET needs reorienting, curriculum revision, new technology-oriented courses, removal of obsolete curriculum materials and the modernization of equipment and teaching-learning materials. Strong school-industry links need to be established.

Donor agencies, in view of their significant contributions in the past, need to assist countries in the regular updating of existing facilities to enable them to serve continually the requirements of industry and also be in a position to spearhead industrial structuring. The restructuring of TVET should take into account curricula, resources, teachers, assessment and examinations, and certification, school-industry links, nonformal TVET options and the involvement of the private sector.

4.9. *Future Considerations in the Asia-Pacific Region*

Although the foundations of secondary education in the region are firm there is still much to be done to achieve the vibrant, rich, high quality education desired by the countries. There are a number of matters, not mutually exclusive, to be considered, accorded a priority, and resolved, as deemed appropriate by planners, policy makers and donors. They include the ones listed below. Most have been named explicitly by the countries. Three, 'educational indicators', 'benefit monitoring' and 'research' were not, although they are implied. These matters may be clustered into broad groups: (a) those dealing with education personnel, (b) with teaching, learning and curriculum, (c) with assessment, (d) with research and innovation, (e) with women and girls, and (f) with the inter-relationship of finance and policy.

Briefly, the matters for consideration are listed below.

- Effective ways are needed of developing the potential and expertise of the human resources involved in secondary education (for example, teachers, principals, administrators, managers and supervisors) through training and other programs. This human resource development also involves considerations about recruitment and conditions of service.
- The devolution and decentralisation of authority in secondary education and various associated matters such as the degree of school autonomy, communication within the system, monitoring management and leadership, and leadership and management training are needed.
- The specification and greater use of educational indicators are needed at the institutional, system and regional levels to provide reference points for management (including management to the school and classroom), planning, policy and financing. Countries will require assistance in specifying and defining their relevant indicators, in establishing data banks, and in determining ways of disseminating and sharing information throughout their systems and between countries.
- Benefit monitoring will help to ascertain whether persons or groups actually benefit from particular educational policies and can also involve determination of the most cost-effective ways to ensure anticipated benefits.
- Alternative modes are needed for delivering secondary education, including nonformal means, the use of modern communications technologies and the vernacular as well as English as the medium of instruction.
- Innovations are needed in curriculum with particular attention to: (a) basic education to cater for the majority, (b) environmental and preventative education programs, (c) values and ethics, (d) linkages between school-industry-world of work, and (e) technical and vocational education.
- Relevant curriculum resources are needed such as national textbooks, and other learning materials (including low cost and no cost teaching and learning materials) in the vernacular.
- Alternative models are needed of assessment including internal assessment procedures by teachers, modifications of present practices, assessment training programs, and the role of item banks and standardized testing.
- Research is needed to provide: (a) reliable information to inform innovation, management and policy; (b) extended projects yielding evidence for decision making on the effects of socio-cultural factors on schooling, the impact of school and class size, and factors affecting school drop-out and repetition rates; and (c) monitoring of the extent to which individuals or members of

sub-groups are actually benefiting from secondary education. The adoption of innovation methods is also very limited.
- Ways are needed of increasing the access of women and girls, and members of other societal, generally minority sub-groups (disabled, rural, ethnic, racial and religious) to secondary education. Matters to be considered include revision of curricula, provision of learning centres, teacher development, and financial support. While increasing attention has recently been given to the participation of females, similar levels of interest and support are required for improving the education of such groups as minorities, the disabled and those living in remote areas.
- Major considerations are: (a) the levels of financing to sustain quality education which is maintainable over the long term; (b) the monitoring of the trends in education costs; and (c) the interactive effects of policies with respect to drop-out or wastage rates, student-teacher ratios (class sizes) and private financing of education on government budget allocations for a quality secondary education.

5. CONCLUSION

The matters examined in this article are ones which governments, educational planners and policy makers, in particular, must assign priority. However, setting priorities is a complex process and the resultant orderings will vary from country to country depending upon the intricate interaction between societal, cultural, economic, educational and political forces. Nevertheless, the priorities are important as they determine educational policies and the allocation of material, human and monetary resources.

With respect to several of the matters, for example, educational indicators, item banks, data bases and standardized testing of competencies, a number of the countries in the region would benefit from further technical assistance, through grants, to help them establish a base on which they could subsequently build and support from their own budgets. A matter to be considered by donor agencies is the provision of seeding grants for technical support for particular purposes. This may imply that the agencies will expand their role in providing technical assistance with corresponding changes in their budgets for this purpose.

Agencies could help countries to establish databases regarding the competencies of students at different levels of schooling; and, strengthen the countries' research capabilities in secondary education. It is also essential that personnel should be trained in order to sustain competency testing and to ensure that indicators are used effectively. Assistance could also be provided through cultural exchanges or inter-country visits whereby delegates become acquainted first hand with each others' educational achievements, educational centres of excellence and exemplary practices.

There are firm foundations to secondary education in the Asia-Pacific region. Much has been accomplished in the last few decades. But, as this article has shown, there is still a great deal to be done to put into place the vibrant, rich, diverse, relevant, high quality and innovative secondary education desired by countries in the region. Resolutions, and especially actions, on the issues mentioned above, by members of the audience to whom his article is directed, will contribute to the realization of that desire. The challenges are great, and numerous, but the future for secondary education in the Asia-Pacific region appears bright and full of promise.

REFERENCES

Asian Development Bank (1988 and later versions). *Education and Development in Asia and the Pacific.* Manila: Asian Development Bank.
Asian Development Bank (1995). *Secondary Education in the Asia-Pacific Region: Strategic Issues and Policy Analysis.* Unpublished report prepared by the UNESCO Asia-Pacific Centre of Educational innovation for Development (ACEID), Bangkok and the Colombo Plan Staff College for Technician Education (CPSC), Manila: ADB.
Journal of Educational Change (2001). Special Issue on 'Educational Change in Asia'. Guest Editor Rupert Maclean. 2(3). Dordrecht: Kluwer Academic Publishers.
National Institute for Educational Research (1995). *Reorienting Secondary Education in Asia and the Pacific.* Tokyo: National Institute for Educational Research.
Maclean, R., & Caillods, F. (2002). *Overview of UNESCO Activities Regarding the Renewal and Diversification of Secondary Education.* Unpublished, internal discussion paper. Paris: UNESCO.
UNESCO (1996). *Learning: The Treasure Within.* Report to UNESCO of the International Commission on Education for the Twenty-first Century. Chair, Jacques Delors. Paris: UNESCO.
UNESCO (1999). *Secondary Education and Youth at the Crossroads.* Bangkok: UNESCO, ACEID.
UNESCO (2000a). *World Education Report: The Right to Education.* Paris: UNESCO.
UNESCO International Bureau of Education (2000b). *Prospects: Quarterly Review of Comparative Education* (Special Issue on 'Education in Asia'. Guest Editors Victor Ordonez and Rupert Maclean), No. 115. Geneva: IBE.
UNESCO International Bureau of Education (2001a). *Prospects: Quarterly Review of Comparative Education* (Special Issue on 'Secondary Education Reform'. Guest Editors Rupert Maclean and Cecilia Braslavsky). No. 117. Geneva: IBE.
UNESCO (2001b). *International Experts meeting on General Secondary Education in the Twenty-first Century: Trends, Challenges and Priorities.* Final Report. Paris: UNESCO.
Wilson, J. D. (Ed.) (2000). *Snapshots of Primary and Secondary Education in Asia-Pacific.* Bangkok: UNESCO.

7

Educational Research and Policy-Making in Asian and Pacific Countries

T. NEVILLE POSTLETHWAITE*
University of Hamburg, Germany

1. INTRODUCTION

If educational research is to play a role in educational reform then it is imperative that there is a cadre of good educational researchers in the country concerned and that there is a healthy relationship between those in a position to ensure change in an education system and the researchers. Education is not a discipline in itself but rather an amalgam of various other disciplines in the social sciences: psychology, sociology, economics and so on. The organisation of education is concerned with the learning and socialisation of children and adults living within the boundaries of the country.

2. CENTRALISED AND DECENTRALISED SYSTEMS

In some cases, the national Parliament is content to leave the matter of education to the regional, state, or district levels of authority in the country as in Australia and Japan. Even where there has been a national authority for education there was, at the end of the 1900s, a decentralisation movement to hand over more authority to the regions and districts. In Indonesia, there is a central Ministry but several decisions are left to the provincial level. In Vietnam there is the national government and 61 provinces and all decisions concerning education are made at one of these two levels. In some of the emerging ex-communist regimes in Eastern Europe, there was demand from the public that more power be given to the local regions and the national authorities concurred. Nevertheless, in some countries, particularly small ones, the national authorities are responsible

---

* The author is grateful to the following persons for the information that they supplied to him for this article: Yeoh Oon Chye (Singapore), Molly Lee (Malaysia), Sukhum Moonmuang (Thailand), K.C. Cheung (Macao), Mark Bray (Hong Kong), Yong Fang (China), Ryo Watanabe (Japan) and Moegiadi (UNESCO, New Delhi) for information on India and Indonesia.

and run education nationally. However, even in small countries there is some decentralisation in so far as the nationally defined, intended, and desired pupil outcomes are translated by school boards, principals, and teachers for each school. Schools have a good deal of autonomy in this translation process including how to deploy their annual school budgets.

Stated briefly, a system of education provides learning places for people to learn, namely, schools. These schools are then equipped with certain basic materials. The children from the community are placed into the schools at a particular age for a period of time. A curriculum is developed, teachers trained and placed in the schools, and then learning and socialisation is meant to ensue. Of course, learning and socialisation also take place in the home and when planning education it must be recognised that some homes develop their children more than others.

3. QUESTIONS ABOUT A SYSTEM OF EDUCATION

There are several clusters of issues that are typically asked in research about systems of education. These include the following questions.

- *School Buildings.* What is the most effective least cost architecture, optimal total enrolment, best type of laboratory, useful kinds of sports facilities, efficient provision of maintenance and appropriate classroom size and who pays?
- *Basic Equipment for Schools and Classrooms.* Which equipment is required for effective learning?
- *Structure of the System.* What is the best structure for the system in terms of the number of years of primary and secondary education, selective or comprehensive schools, heterogeneous or homogeneous grouping of pupils, length of school year, number of terms per year, number of hours of instruction per day and year, curricula and syllabi and cross-curricular activities?
- *Teacher Training and Allocation of Teachers to Schools.* Which forms of training are most effective for different kinds of outcomes? How are rural and isolated areas best assured of good teachers?
- *Homework.* How much and how often should homework be given at different grade levels and how often corrected and worked through with pupils?
- *Feedback and Corrections.* Which forms of feedback to teachers and correctives by teachers are most effective to improve pupil learning?
- *Grade Repetition.* How much grade repetition should occur and how is it determined, or should there be none?
- *Decentralisation and Cost.* How much decentralisation in education should there be and how should education be financed?
- *Educational Outcomes.* Is the variance among regions, among schools and among pupils for various forms of outcomes reasonable? How is it checked and how frequently?

This is but a short list of the many areas in education where questions are asked.

The questions will differ somewhat for the different school types: primary, secondary, or vocational schools. No educational system exists in a vacuum. There is a societal and political context as well as a tradition of education. Planners of systems must and do take these factors into account. Furthermore, there is the question of funds available for an education system. If the money is not available, then however desirable a particular course of action might be, there is little use in suggesting it, if there is not hope of the money being made available. Or even though there is no hope for the money now, it might be worth suggesting it now in order to plant the idea in the heads of those in charge of the source of funding. Despite these constraints, it can be argued that the planners need to know the answers to most of the questions if they are able to take a stance on a particular issue. What, then, is the evidence that educational planners and administrators can use in order to answer the above questions?

4. EVIDENCE FOR PLANNING

There is systematic and non-systematic evidence. Systematic evidence is that which refers to all schools of interest to the planner (the target population) and also across time (i.e. on several occasions). Non-systematic evidence is that which reports an example of a phenomenon in a particular school or pupil but with only one observation, often a casual one. The sources of such evidence are historical (through documentary analysis), from current observation (typically from the inspectorate in a country), and from empirical research conducted by educational researchers. However, there are some questions that cannot be answered from historical research. Take, for example, the issue of computers in schools. The advent of computers in schools began only in the late 1980s. The field is still developing rapidly and it is unlikely that the analysis of historical documents would be likely to have much to say on this issue. Each source of evidence is important and not to be discarded lightly. In the best of worlds, all three sources should yield the same results. It is with the last source of evidence that this article is concerned, namely the evidence supplied by empirical educational researchers.

5. THE RELATIONSHIP BETWEEN RESEARCH AND REFORM

Educational research is a growing industry. Its major aim is to make a contribution to knowledge by supplying the kind of information needed to answer the question posed at the beginning of this article. How this knowledge can be used, and in some cases if it can by used, to reform education forms the focus of this article.

In 1899, William James in his *Talks to Teachers on Psychology* emphasised that education was an art and not a science and could therefore not deduce schemes and methods of teaching for direct application from psychology: "An intermediary inventive mind must make the application by using its originality"

(James, 1899, p. 8). Nearly 100 years later De Landsheere (1994, p. 1871) stated "Like medicine, education is an art. That is why advances in research do not directly produce a science of education, in the positivistic meaning of the term, but yield increasingly powerful foundations for practice and decision-making". Masters, on the other hand, while making comparisons with medical research, has suggested that in education research syntheses, sharper-focussed research questions, and better communications between researchers and research utilisers, would do much to improve the link between research and school reform (Masters, 1999).

In 1960, there seemed to be general agreement in the institution where this author worked that it would take at least one generation, about 15 years, between the results being produced by any of the then current research projects and their implementation at the school or classroom level. As empirical educational research has become a larger enterprise, sponsors have increasingly hoped that research would provide pointers to the elements of reform that could either help to raise cognitive achievement, affective development and skills or cut the costs of education without damage to the desired outcomes.

6. RESEARCH AND POLICY-MAKING

The following sections of this article deal with some of the different aspects of educational research, the contexts in which policy-making and research take place, models of research utilisation, and also, with some examples of the establishment of links between research results and action or reform.

6.1. *Different Aspects of Educational Research*

Before proceeding with the link between research and reform, it would be desirable to deal with the various aspects of research. Most policy-makers want, as mentioned above, clear results from research for the problems they have. These results should preferably be accompanied by a set of suggestions for reform or action. The research from which the results emanate should be sound.

Given that it is often extremely difficult if not impossible to conduct good experiments in education from which cause and effect can be safely identified, researchers often have to depend on natural variation using survey samples. But, this depends on natural variation being there for the phenomenon under investigation. Class size is an example of where there is some variation in school systems but it is often within fairly narrow limits. Within a country, the average class size may be 25 children per class at a certain grade level. But the range is only 20 to 30. Yet, in other countries, the average class size may well be over 40 or even over 60. And in these other countries the range will be small. As another example, a country may wish to examine the differences between private and public schools but if there are few private schools, then there is little natural variation. Furthermore, there is always the criticism that cross-sectional and longitudinal studies are correlational and assumptions must be made about cause and effect.

The research must be found to be 'sound'. Yet it can be argued that there are many studies that have technical deficiencies such that the results cannot be trusted. These deficiencies can include poor conceptualisation, poor measurement, poor sampling and incorrect estimates of sampling error, inappropriate analyses, and false interpretations and conclusions. Some could argue that more unsound than sound research is produced in the field of education. The International Academy of Education produced a summary of 'The requirements of a good study' for sample surveys in international educational achievement studies (IAE, Appendix 2, 1999). This described in lay terms the kinds of points in research publications that policy-makers should look for when trying to decide whether or not the research was well conducted and trustworthy. It would be useful if summaries such as this one were to be produced for different types of research. It is important that readers of research reports can identify if the research conducted was unsound and could not be trusted. Many senior policy-makers do not have this ability and must rely on those skilled in these matters in their own ministries of education. Unfortunately, not all ministries have such people. The dangers of implementing policy based on poor research are obvious.

It is also the case that policy-makers need results that have, if possible, been replicated and that are generalisable to a grade level or general level (e.g., junior high school or elementary levels of education) in an education system, and where the effects are large. Research that is only applicable to a few specific schools (case-study approach) is not of interest to them. Furthermore, the research should ideally be applicable to several key subjects in school and not just to one subject. Ministries allocate resources to schools and they want the resources to have a wide application in each school and not just to one subject. Unfortunately, having results on the effect of variables on several subjects at the same time is costly and time consuming.

Keeves (1994) has distinguished between research studies associated with the generation of change and those that serve to maintain and consolidate existing conditions. It is the second type of research that he calls 'legitimatory research'. Thus, the motivation for commissioning research must also be taken into account when viewing the links between research and change.

6.2. *Contexts for Policy-Making and Research*

As already stated, policy-makers are interested in their problems within their current frame of reference and understanding of education. They perceive of what researchers know as 'fundamental' research to be of no, or only peripheral, interest to them. What the policy-makers perceive to be of interest can change with a change of government. For example, the matter of bussing, educational vouchers, and private schools had quite different priorities under the Carter and Reagan administrations in the United States. Equality of educational opportunity, on the other hand, has had a high priority under various administrations in various countries. In the second project of the Southern Africa Consortium for Monitoring Educational Quality (SACMEQ), chief policy-makers in 15 southern African countries were asked to rate issues that were of interest to them in primary schooling. One of the issues was that of private tuition outside of school. This was given very low priority despite the fact that the first study of SACMEQ had shown the practice to be very widespread, and for the most part to affect achievement even after home background had been accounted for. It was later given a higher priority after the researchers had interacted more with the policy-makers.

Policy-makers have allegiances that influence both what they regard as relevant, innocuous or even dangerous research and also their willingness to take account of research findings. Stories abound of ministries or government departments either ignoring research results or delaying the publication of government sponsored research because the results did not accord with the current political interests. Ways of delaying the publication of research results that governments do not like have been hilariously resumed in *Yes Minister* (Lynn & Jay, 1982). Not only can research be delayed or ignored but only partial results can also be selected to help argue a case. Keeves (1994), has dealt with many of the problems that arise with those in authority when conducting legitimatory research.

Governments, as a rule, last only a few years. The research they sponsor should be completed within that time period and preferably in less than two years. There are few research projects that can be completed in this time period when it is considered that the instruments have to be developed and tried out before the major data collection can begin. The findings should be made available in time for the decisions that have to be taken and which will go ahead with or without the necessary knowledge base. Operational decision-making cannot wait for the results of specifically sponsored research results.

6.3. Contexts for Researchers to Conduct Research

The researchers often tend to have different backgrounds and value systems from those of the policy-makers. Researchers have usually undertaken their work in research institutes or university settings. Researchers have been trained to think widely and to question all things. Their allegiance tends to be more to fundamental or conclusion-oriented research. They pay much more attention to how the quality of their research is received by their research peers than by government agencies.

In most cases, researchers are not involved in the planning and implementation of reform. They rarely have any interest in how to plan the costs involved in any reform. They can rarely phrase their results in the language of planning and implementing reform. Indeed, once they have published their research report they tend to lose interest in what happens after that.

Status in the research system depends on the reputation the individual researcher gains from his or her research work. Status in the administrative world tends to be based on seniority and length of service and not on the quality of the research work undertaken.

6.4. *Models of Research Utilisation*

Weiss (1979) distinguished between seven different models of research utilisation in the social sciences.

(1) *The R and D model.* This is a linear process from basic research to applied research and development to application. Weiss pointed out that the applicability of this model was limited in the social sciences because knowledge in the field does not lend itself easily to "conversion into replicable technologies, either material or social" (Weiss, 1979, p. 427).

(2) *The Problem-Solving Model.* Here the results from a specific project are expected to be used directly in a decision-making situation. The process consists of the identification of missing knowledge, leading to the acquisition of research information either by: (a) conducting a new study; or (b) reviewing the existing body of knowledge leading to an interpretation of the results given the policy options available. These steps lead to a decision about which policy to pursue. This model has sometimes been known as the 'philosopher-king' approach where researchers are supposed to provide the information from which policy-makers derive guidelines for action. The problem-solving model often tacitly assumes agreement about goals, but social scientists do not agree among themselves about the goals of certain actions. Nor is there necessarily agreement among all policy-makers about goals.

(3) *The Interactive Model.* This model assumes an ongoing dialogue between researchers and policy-makers. This is often a disorderly set of interconnections and back-and-forthness.

(4) *The Political Model.* Research findings are used as ammunition to defend a particular point of view. It is often the case that policy-makers have already made up their minds about taking a particular course of action and should there be research results that legitimise this, then they will use that research.

(5) *The Tactical Model.* This is a negative approach in that it is a way of deferring any decision. Thus, a controversial issue can be buried or postponed by policy-makers calling for more research or further analyses.

(6) *The Enlightenment Model.* According to Weiss (1979, p. 428) this is the model where social science research most frequently enters the policy arena. Research can enlighten policy-makers because as research results become available they sensitise informed public opinion about ways of thinking of educational problems and come to shape the way in which people think about social issues. This is sometimes known as the percolation effect. People are helped to redefine problems through research so that they begin to think of the problems in a different way.

(7) *Research-oriented model.* Weiss refers to this as the "research-as-part-of-the-intellectual-enterprise-of society" model. Social science research together

with other intellectual inputs, such as philosophy, history, journalism and so on, contribute to widening the horizon for the debate on certain issues and to reformulating the problems. This is somewhat akin to the enlightenment model outlined above.

It can be seen that these models do not exist in isolation but that quite often two or three of them co-exist in countries at the same time.

Shavelson (1988, pp. 4–5), when dealing with the utility of social science research, sought to reframe the issue of "utility" by suggesting "that the contributions lie not so much in immediate and specific applications but rather in constructing, challenging, or changing the way policy-makers and practitioners think about problems". He suggested that it cannot be expected that educational research would lead to practices that made society happy, wise and well educated in the same way that the natural sciences lead to a technology that makes society wealthy. The assumption that "educational research should have direct and immediate application to policy or practice rests on many unrealistic assumptions" (pp. 4–5). Among these are relevance to a particular issue, provision of clear and unambiguous results, research being known and understood by policy-makers, and findings implying other choices than those contemplated by policy-makers. It is thus, called the 'enlightenment model' that has been the major way in which research has had an effect.

6.5. Some Examples

It is relatively easy to identify some research that has had an enlightenment effect. The work of Piaget in identifying stages of development began to have an effect on work in curriculum development by the end of the 1950s. Bloom's *Taxonomy of Educational Objectives* and Biggs and Collis' Solo Taxonomy had a marked effect on many later research projects the results of which entered the market place and influenced educational thinking. Coleman's *Equality of Educational Opportunity* study produced the concepts of 'school climate' and later 'social capital', both of which entered educational thinking. The *Plowden Report* in England produced the concepts of 'parental attitudes' and 'educational priority areas', both of which entered general educational thinking. Carroll's *Model of School Learning* and later his *Human Cognitive Abilities* research both influenced how educators thought about school learning. But, in all of these cases, the process took a long time. In some special cases, for example in Sweden in the late 1950s and early 1960s, research studies led directly to some action especially in the revision of the curriculum. However, the direct effects examples are rare.

In the first two decades (1960–1979) of the work of the International Association for the Evaluation of Educational Achievement (IEA) (Postlethwaite, 1994), a massive amount of effort went into attempting to identify the major determinants of educational achievement in each of the participating countries. It was to the chagrin of the research workers that very little attention was given to the results. It was rather the so-called 'horse race' national mean achievement levels that gained the attention of the Press and the policy-makers. In the 1970s, one Minister of Education talked of the results being like an electric shock because they showed that the gap between north and south Italy was much larger than had been expected. The Third International Mathematics and Science Study (TIMSS) of IEA in the 1990s presented only aggregate estimates for the test scores and selected questionnaire variables in their first set of publications. They did not present analyses identifying the major determinants of either between-country differences, or between-school or between-student differences within countries. Nevertheless, it was these aggregated estimates that attracted enormous media publicity and comment. In some cases the comment was appropriate, such as, about the high achievement scores, but the low attitudinal scores towards the learning of the subject in Japan. In other cases, several of the journalists' comments and even those of some ministry officials proffering policy suggestions assumed wrongly that the relationships between certain variables between countries would be the same as those within countries (Ross, 1997). The question must be asked as to why the Press and the Ministries seem to be more interested in the mean score differences rather than in the determinants of such differences. Is it possible that an interface of persons skilled in translating research findings into policy suggestions is needed?

7. THE IMPACT OF RESEARCH

At the outset, it should be mentioned that in many research institutions or units, especially those within ministries of education, many of the research papers produced are for internal use and are not published as academic research papers in academic journals. It is often difficult to obtain these kinds of research papers and hence the research productivity of some institutions can be dangerously underestimated. However, the work conducted in Asia has covered nearly all aspects of education. Beeby (1979) in his book on educational planning used the example of Indonesia but was so wide that it covered planning in education in any Ministry of Education anywhere in the world. He wrote of research that was either being conducted or should be conducted in the areas of drop-out, literacy levels, the financing of education, the teacher training college inefficiencies, the length of the school day, the problem of language, manpower demands, grade repeating rates, the implementation of reforms (formative evaluation) and the impact of reforms (summative evaluation). Many of the countries have entered the field of assessment of the achievement levels in their countries at the end of primary and at the end of lower secondary schooling. Such studies have been often conducted as part of the IEA endeavour and the assessment has been in various subject areas. There were many other investigations, such as the assessment studies carried out at the end of the 1970s in Indonesia (see Moegiadi, Magindaan & Elley, 1979; Jiyono & Ace Suryadi, 1982) and both Indonesia and Thailand showed great initiative in conducting studies (Mappa, 1982, Viboonlak, Nonglak & Kanjani, 1982) in nonformal education.

Suggestions in terms of educational policy directions are made to ministries either from within the ministry or from outside the ministry. Some of these have been based on research findings but not exclusively so. For example, in Japan such agencies as the Central Council for Education, the Curriculum Council, the Science Education and Vocational Education Council, the Educational Personnel Training Council, the Textbook Authorisation Council, the Life-long Learning Council all make recommendations about policy directions to the Ministry of Education. Based on these policy directions the Ministry develops specific measures and implements them. In this sense, educational research percolates through to the formulation of new policies and practices in schools.

In general in Malaysia, educational research has had relatively little direct impact on practice. Two studies are worthy of note: the study on pre-school intervention on Primary 1–3 pupils (EPRD, 1996a) and a study to review the per capita grant rates for the teaching and learning of Secondary School Science and Language subjects (EPRD, 1996b). More typical was, however, the inclusion or research findings in national policy reports. Examples were the Murad Report on Drop-outs (1973), the Cabinet Report on Educational Policies (1980), and the Rahman Arshad Report on Teachers (1996).

While it cannot be claimed that educational research has had much direct impact on school and classroom practice or in policy formulation in Singapore, few would dispute that research in education has always responded to the social and political needs, through developing closer articulation between theory and practice, and research and training (Deng & Gopinathan, 2000) especially pre-service and in-service education. Other institutions such as ISEAS (Institute of South East Asian Studies), EAI (East Asian Institute) and RELC (the SEAMEO-Regional Language Centre) and RIHED (Regional Institute of Higher Education) in the region also engage in studies that relate to different aspects of social and educational policies.

In China, two examples of educational research studies can be cited as having had an impact on practice. One was predominantly theoretical in the area of educational economics (Li Yining, 1984) and one was on the scale and benefit of higher educational institutions (Ming Weifang, 1986). The first study resulted in four per cent of GNP being set aside for educational expenditure.

In India, the National Council of Educational Research and Training (NCERT) has had success in its work especially in curriculum development. For example, the PECR (Primary Education Curriculum Renewal) project undertaken in the late 1970s formed the basis of the curriculum in all primary schools at the beginning of the third millennium. The same is true of the minimum levels of learning (MLL) that were developed by the NCERT in the mid-1980s.

In the United States, the United States Department of Education published a booklet in 1986 under the title *What Works: Research about Teaching and Learning*. This booklet reported the results of research syntheses. It was aimed at all involved in education and presented in one or two pages the results of research and the practical implications of those results. This was followed by a series of similar booklets on different aspects of education. These booklets were made available to all schools in the United States. The International Academy of Education (IAE) in conjunction with the International Bureau of Education (IBE) in Geneva has begun a series of similar publications (see the web site: www.ibe.unesco.org).

Nearly all of the examples given above have indicated that it is major policy reports that have had an impact and that research, to the extent that it feeds into these kinds of reports, has an indirect impact.

8. THE PLANNING OF RESEARCH FOR POLICY-MAKING

By the beginning of the 1990s, some progress was being made in the attempt to have educational planners and administrators work more closely with educational researchers in order to have more direct links between research and policy-making. One international study in the 1990s had the strategy of identifying the research questions, in conjunction with ministries of education and then working out the actions to be taken. This latter step was undertaken *before* the research reports were finalised for publication. This study was that of the Southern Africa Consortium for Monitoring Educational Quality (SACMEQ). The last chapter of each national publication listed the suggested policy actions categorised by cost and time needed for implementation.

The Ministry of Education in Vietnam undertook a similar approach in its 2001 Grade 5 study of Reading and Mathematics and before the study began over 100 policy research questions had been advanced. A selection of one small sub-set of policy questions has been presented below in Table 1. It will be noted that at the side of each question some cross-references have been made. These indicate the table in each chapter of the final report where the answer to the question is to be found and also to the number of the question in the questionnaires where the data came from.

9. CONCLUSIONS

A great deal of money goes into educational research and yet the results are rarely used directly. Indirectly and over time research results percolate down, referred to as the 'enlightenment model', to the district and school levels and then demands are made on the policy-makers to do something. If research is, in some cases, to have a more direct link to school reform it would seem as though several steps should be taken.

- Researchers should talk to the policy-makers before the research begins and ensure that the design and proposed analyses will answer the policy-makers' concerns.
- Projects should be conducted in a sound technical way. This requires that the funders have a cadre of persons who can advise them about the technical

Table 1. Policy questions, tables and questionnaires for Vietnam Grade 5 study

Group	Question number	Policy question	Table reference	Questionnaire reference
01		Pupils		
	1.01	What are the characteristics, including home background, of the Grade 5 pupils? What actions do these characteristics require the Ministry to take? Do these characteristics and the home background have an influence on achievement?	3.1	P02 D
	1.02	What is the age distribution of Grade 5 pupils? Are there distribution patterns requiring corrective action and/or having an influence on teaching methods and/or the curriculum?	3.1	P03 D
	1.03	What is the sex distribution of Grade 5 pupils? Are there imbalances in the enrolment of male and female pupils requiring corrective action?	3.1	P05 D
	1.04	What is the ethnic group of the children?	3.1	P10
	1.05	How regularly do Grade 5 pupils eat meals?	3.1	P04 D
	1.06	What percentage of Grade 5 pupils speaks the language of the test at home?	3.2	P11 D
		What is the level of the parents' education of Grade 5 pupils?	3.1	PD12 D
	1.07	How many books are there in pupils' homes?	3.1	P06 D
	1.08	What is the socio-economic status of the pupils and their parents? (measured in terms of possessions, parental education, and books at home)	3.1	PD07 D and R, P06 P11 + P12 R for SE5
	1.09	Do the pupils have a quiet corner at home in which to work?	3.2	P08
	1.10	How many hours per day did the pupils have to work to help their families?	3.2	P09 D
	1.11	How many minutes do pupils take to travel to school?	3.2	P13
	1.12	On how many days were the pupils absent from school in the previous month?	3.2	P14 & 15

[a] Tabulation of policy questions, tables in chapters addressing them, and references to questions in the questionnaires.
P = Pupil questionnaire   D = Derived variable to be computed
R = Rasch score to be computed

soundness of the proposed research. This is a big step because there are not many ministries even in highly developed countries that possess such persons.
- Projects should, wherever possible, be replicated.
- Researchers should, after consultation with the policy-makers, make a list of suggested actions for reform.
- Ministries of education should train and employ a cadre of policy-researchers who are able to translate the research results into suggested actions that constitute the crucial actions and not only those easy to conduct. These persons may not necessarily be within the ministry but could be in university departments.
- Policy suggestions should be acted upon and well implemented.
- Studies should be conducted to assess the effect of the implementations.

Until these kinds of steps are taken, research will continue to have its indirect enlightenment effect.

Finally, it should be remembered that there are certain reforms that do not depend on research. When the great debate raged in the 1960s in Europe about comprehensive schooling versus selective schooling it was the then Minister of Education in England and Wales who wrote, when asked why England had not preceded 'going comprehensive' with research such as that conducted in Sweden,

> It implied that research can tell you what your objectives should be. But it can't. Our belief in comprehensive reorganisation was a product of fundamental value judgements about equity and equal opportunity and social division as well as about education. Research can help you to achieve your objectives, and I did in fact set going a large research project, against strong opposition from all kinds of people, to assess and monitor the process of going comprehensive. But research cannot tell you whether you should go comprehensive or not – that's a basic value judgement. (Husén & Kogan, 1984, p. 202)

REFERENCES

Beeby, C. E. (1979). *Assessment of Indonesian Education: A Guide to Planning.* Wellington: New Zealand Council for Educational Research, and Oxford: Oxford University Press.

De Landsheere, G. (1994). Educational research, history of. In T. Husén & T. N. Postlethwaite (Eds.), *International Encyclopedia of Education* (pp. 1864–1873). Oxford: Pergamon Press.

Deng Zongyi & S. Gopinathan (2000). *An Analysis of Research on Teacher and Teacher Education in Singapore (1989–1999): Preliminary Findings.* Paper presented at the Annual Conference of the Education Research Association. Singapore (mimeo), 10 pp.

EPRD (Educational Planning and Research Division) and UNICEF (1996a). *The Impact of Preschool Intervention on Primary 1–3 Pupils in Malaysia.* Kuala Lumpur: EPRD.

EPRD (Educational Planning and Research Division) (1996b). *A Study to Review the Per Capita Grant Rates for the Teaching and Learning of Secondary School Science and Language Subjects.* Kuala Lumpur: EPRD.

Husén, T., & Kogan, M. (Eds.) (1984). *Educational Research and Policy: How Do They Relate?* Oxford: Pergamon Press.

International Academy of Education (IAE) (1999). *The Benefits and Limitation of International Studies of Educational Achievement*. Paris: IIEP.

James, W. (1899). *Talks to Teachers on Psychology: And to Students on Some of the Life's Ideals*. London: Longmans Green.

Jiyono & Ace Suryadi (1982). The planning, sampling, and some preliminary results of the Indonesian repeat 9th grade survey. *Evaluation in Education*, 6(1), 5–30.

Keeves, J. P. (1994). Legitimatory research. In T. Husén & T. N. Postlethwaite (Eds.), *International Encyclopedia of Education* (pp. 3368–3373). Oxford: Pergamon Press.

Li, Yining (1984). *Educational Economics*. Beijing: Beijing Press.

Lynn, J., & Jay, A. (1982). *Yes Minister: The Diaries of a Cabinet Minister by the Rt Hon., James Hacker MP*. London: British Broadcasting Corporation.

Mappa, S. (1982). Radio broadcasting program for out of school education in South Sulawesi (Indonesia). *Evaluation in Education*, 2(1), 31–51.

Masters, G. N. (1999). Valuing educational research. *ACER Newsletter Supplement* (The Australian Council for Educational Research), 94. Autumn.

Ming, Weifang (1986). *Research on the Scale and Benefits of Higher Education Institutions*. Beijing: Peoples' Education Press.

Moegiadi, Mangindaan C., & Elley, W. B. (1979). Evaluation of achievement in the Indonesian education system. *Evaluation in Education*, 2, 281–351.

Postlethwaite, T. N. (1994). Educational achievement: Comparative studies. In: T. Husén & T. N. Postlethwaite (Eds.), *International Encyclopedia of Education*, 3 (pp. 1762–1769). Oxford: Pergamon Press.

Ross, K. N. (1997). Research and policy: A complex mix. *IIEP Newsletter*, XV(1).

Shavelson, R. (1988). Contributions of educational research to policy and practice: Constructing, challenging, changing cognition. *Educational Researcher*, 17(7), 4–11, 22.

United States Department of Education (1986). *What Works: Research about Teaching and Learning*. Washington, DC: US Department of Education.

Viboonlak, T., Nonglak, P., & Kanjani, J. (1982). *Evaluation in Education*, 6, 53–81.

Weiss, C. (1979). The many meanings of research utilisation. *Public Admin. Rev.*, 39, 426–431.

8

Evaluation and Accountability in Asian and Pacific Countries

RAMON MOHANDAS
National Institute for Research and Development, Jakarta, Indonesia

MENG HONG WEI
China National Institute for Educational Research, Beijing, The People's Republic of China

JOHN P. KEEVES
Flinders University Institute of International Education, Australia

1. INTRODUCTION

The use of both evaluation and accountability in education systems has been of long standing, although the ways in which they are used have changed markedly over the past century. Where schools and universities are run as private, fee paying organisations, the clients, who are the students and their parents, must make their own judgments of the effectiveness and value of the education provided. However, where schools and universities are paid for out of public funds the need arises to evaluate and account for the spending of public monies. With the expansion across the world of the education systems in each country, province and municipality, the call for evaluation and accountability of those systems has increased, because of the substantial and rising expenditures involved. Over the past 100 years, not only has the size of the school-aged population grown markedly, but the demand has also grown, initially for universal primary education, subsequently for widespread secondary and technical education, and more recently for greatly increased provision of higher education and training in technology and commerce. The costs of providing these services are substantial and often relatively larger in those countries that can least afford to provide such services, but have the greatest need. This article considers the nature of both evaluation and accountability and examines how they are practised and developed in the region.

2. DEVELOPMENT OF EDUCATION SERVICES IN THE REGION

The expansion of education in the countries of the Asia-Pacific region was initially undertaken by the colonial powers that ruled those countries, namely, Great Britain (in the Indian subcontinent, Australasia, many of the Pacific Islands, Hong Kong, and Singapore, as well as countries like Malaysia where the British influence was strong), France (in the Indo-China, New Caledonia and Tahiti regions), the Netherlands and Portugal (in the Indonesian archipelago), and the United States (in the Philippines, the Hawaiian islands, and American Samoa). In addition some influence of Russian education is to be found in China, and such countries as Vietnam, North Korea and the Central Asian republics. Consequently, it is not surprising to find that the curricula and instructional practices employed in the countries of the Asia-Pacific region should reflect the traditions of Western Europe, and in particular, Great Britain, the Netherlands, Russia and France, as well as the United States. Nevertheless, it must be acknowledged that in many countries of the Asia-Pacific region there was a well-established education system, largely of a private nature, in operation in the eighteenth and nineteenth centuries prior to the introduction of influences from Western Europe. Today these education systems maintain longstanding traditions, even though Western influences have introduced many changes and produced a global uniformity of educational provision.

The explanation of the development of a largely common curriculum across not only the countries of the Asia-Pacific region, but also across the whole educational world is rather more complex than the simple process portrayed here in terms of the influence of dominant countries in Western Europe and the United States. Meyer, Kamens and Benavot (with help from Asian colleagues Yun-Kyung Cha and Suk-Ying Wong) (1992, p. 172) have examined the world-wide institutionalisation of primary school curricula and have considered the possibility of world-wide influences from: (a) evolving educational knowledge and theory, (b) general changes in world society, and (c) the interests and qualities of the world powers that have been politically and educationally dominant. In addition, there has been the influence of certain key individuals whose ideas, as is shown in this article, have been accepted across the world in many different and modified forms.

In Western Europe evaluation and accountability of the school systems were initially achieved by such policies as 'payment by results' to school principals. These policies were transferred to systems in the region (for example, see Hearn, 1872). Moreover, the examination system that the Jesuit Order introduced into their schools and colleges across Europe in the sixteenth century in order to lift the standards of education provided in European universities (Madaus & Kellaghan, 1992, p. 121) was carried by them to other parts of the world including Asia and Australasia, where schools of a largely academic nature were set up. The examination programs of these schools grew into national examination systems primarily for the purposes of selection into universities, but these examinations also served a function of certification as the school systems expanded.

Furthermore, the public examination systems in each country also provided a basis for evaluation and accountability, in so far as schools could be and were judged by their successes in the examinations that were conducted at the different levels of schooling.

With the expansion of education that took place in different countries at different times during the twentieth century, the examination systems in some countries collapsed under their own weight, since with rapidly growing numbers of candidates it became increasingly difficult to operate a system of public examinations. It was in the affluent United States during the early decades of the twentieth century where alternatives first emerged. This article is primarily concerned with the procedures that have been set up and are being introduced in the Asia-Pacific region to provide for the evaluation of the schools and school systems in the countries of this region.

3. EVALUATION, ACCOUNTABILITY, AND ASSESSMENT

It is necessary to distinguish between the meanings of three terms that are often used in ambiguous ways, namely 'evaluation', 'accountability', and 'assessment' before discussing in this article the procedures for evaluation and accountability that are employed.

3.1. *Evaluation*

In general, the use of the term 'evaluation' is reserved for application to entities, such as programs, curricula and organisations. The word 'evaluation' implies a general weighing of value or worth. Moreover, evaluation commonly involves the making of comparisons with a standard, or against criteria derived from stated objectives, or with other programs, curricula or organisations. Evaluation is primarily an activity that is associated with research and development. It generally involves consideration of the attainment of identifiable outcomes by both individuals and groups. Consequently, its potential importance for the improvement of educational practice is widely recognized, but fierce controversy sometimes surrounds the methods that should be employed in the conduct of an evaluation.

3.2. *Accountability*

Accountability is a process that involves the responsibility of systems and organisations to submit at regular intervals an account of the tasks they have performed to the body or bodies that have authorized or delegated to the system, or organisation the duty to perform those tasks. All educational organisations and systems have some form of accountability to a body or bodies that may sanction or reward the organisation or system (Neave, 1988, p. 19). In the field of education, schools, colleges, organisations and systems are accountable to a wide range of stakeholders. These include: (a) students, (b) teachers, (c) parents,

(d) school principals, (e) school councils, (f) school district personnel, (g) other educational organisations, (h) state, regional, and national educational agencies, (i) the national or regional parliament, and (j) the public at large. In so far as provision for education is made by many agencies with considerable expenditure involved, these agencies may require that an evaluation study should be conducted as part of the accountability process or may simply require that the organisations to which responsibility is delegated should report periodically. Alternatively, these agencies may require that an assessment study should be carried out to provide information on the performance of those individuals who benefit from the provision of educational services. However, the process of accountability generally involves much more than the supplying of information obtained through student assessment, since the use made of the inputs provided, must be considered as well as the outputs obtained.

3.3. Assessment

In general, the employment of the term 'assessment' in the field of education is reserved for use with reference to people, since it involves estimating the amount of learning or development that has occurred, or the level of performance attained. It may involve the administration of tests that relate to specific outcomes. Alternatively, it may simply involve the activity of grading or classifying student performance with respect to specified criteria. The evaluation of a curriculum or program may require the collection of information through the assessment of student performance with regard to the objectives of the curriculum or program, but it is the value of the curriculum or program that is being considered in an evaluation study, and not the value or worth of those students whose performance is assessed. It is, nevertheless, unfortunate that the term 'student evaluation' is now being widely used as a consequence of the growing emphasis on the evaluation of educational programs.

Education is primarily concerned with the learning and development achieved by individuals in organisations and systems. At the core of the educational process is the curriculum provided by these organisations and systems for individuals. Consequently, any consideration of evaluation and accountability in education must focus on the curricula of educational organisations and systems and on the instruction provided by those organisations.

4. CURRICULUM, INSTRUCTION AND ASSESSMENT IN SCHOOLS

In the early decades of the twentieth century the industrialized countries faced the tasks of (a) expanding secondary education, (b) meeting the vocational needs of a technical revolution, and (c) reforming education to make it more efficient, as was required of industry and commerce. Cubberley (1917) in the United States argued that no longer could the efficiency of the school system be solely determined by personal opinion and inspection. A better method for the evaluation of the work of schools and their teachers had been developed that involved the use of standardized tests. The outcomes of education could be measured by such tests, and school superintendents could use the results of testing to evaluate the instructional program of a school (Munroe, 1917). Moreover, these tests would provide teachers with a standard by which they might judge the performance of their students in comparison with the performance of other students in the same school or the same school district. The idea of measuring the outcomes of education using the assessment of student performance was further developed during the first four decades of the twentieth century to meet the changing nature of the schools that were influenced by the Progressive Education Movement.

In 1933, a major study was set up to examine the effects of this reform movement in secondary education in the United States with R.W. Tyler as Research Director of the Evaluation Staff. From the work of this study, the Eight Year Study, a new approach to the evaluation of the work of schools emerged, that was formulated in *The Basic Principles of Curriculum and Instruction* (Tyler, 1949). These ideas were further developed by Bloom and his colleagues in the *Taxonomy of Educational Objectives Handbook 1, Cognitive Domain* (Bloom, 1956) and *Handbook 2, Affective Domain* (Krathwohl, Bloom and Masia, 1964). In 1971, these ideas were disseminated widely through a workshop in Sweden conducted under the auspices of the International Association for the Evaluation of Educational Achievement (IEA) at which teams of six people from selected countries involved in curriculum development and evaluation studied together for a period of six weeks. Asian teams came from Thailand and Malaysia.

Thus, this new approach to curriculum development and evaluation spread throughout both the developed and developing countries of the world. Bloom directed this workshop and the *Handbook of Formative and Summative Evaluation of Student Learning* (Bloom, Hastings & Madaus, 1971) was the set text for the workshop. Tyler attended for all six weeks as a key speaker and resource person with his monograph on the basic principles of curriculum and instruction being reprinted for the occasion. The Tyler model of evaluation has gradually became a guiding model for developments in evaluation and accountability in many countries of the world, although the model has undergone many changes over time (see Tyler, 1986).

4.1. *The Tyler Model*

The Tyler Model for evaluation in education may be shown as a triangle, with curriculum objectives at the apex of the triangle, that lead to instruction and the provision of learning experiences, which in turn lead to an evaluation of the extent to which the objectives are realized. The relationships in this triangle are reciprocal in nature, in so far as evaluation feeds back to instruction and to the curriculum objectives. The curriculum triangle is shown in Figure 1 (Tyler, 1949).

While evaluation refers to both the curriculum objectives and to the learning experiences provided, at the student level the process involves the assessment of

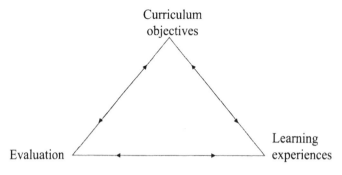

Figure 1. The curriculum triangle

student performance. Although the approach that Tyler proposed was a model for developing curricula, it has tended to become a framework for test development, with the provision of learning experiences frequently overlooked. Tyler's approach was reduced to seven steps: (a) formulating objectives, (b) classifying the objectives, (c) refining and defining the objectives, (d) identifying ways of assessing student performance with respect to the objectives, (e) trying out appropriate ways of assessing student performance, (f) improving methods of assessment, and (g) interpreting the results with a reexamination of the objectives. Tyler (1986) subsequently questioned the over-emphasis on testing and assessment by psychologists and psychometricians at the expense of examining the curriculum objectives and the learning experiences employed in schools.

A further widespread shortcoming in the use of this approach has been a reliance on assessment using relative performance with respect to other students in a specified reference group, rather than the employment of standards of performance to be attained. Thorndike (1918) recognized the need to specify degrees of proficiency in the assessment of student performance. However, several decades passed before Mager (1962) emphasized the setting of standards as a step associated with the specification of curriculum objectives. Bloom (1968) in the consideration of learning for mastery, and Tyler (1973) in detailing the place of testing in programs of student assessment have both subsequently acknowledged the importance of identifying standards of performance.

The curriculum triangle in Figure 1 requires modification and extension in order to (a) introduce the standards of performance; (b) indicate that assessment takes place with students; and (c) that evaluation and accountability apply to all four other vertices of the curriculum-evaluation diamond as presented in Figure 2. The idea that evaluation only relates to the learning outcomes and to student assessment introduces a fallacy, which is unfortunately all too common, and is detrimental to the best interests of educational policy and practice. Research workers in Australia (Keeves, 1999, pp. 128–130) have argued for the recognition of underlying scales associated with the curriculum objectives, the standards of performance, and the assessment of student outcomes and have shown how measurements can be made to test the measured structures of the

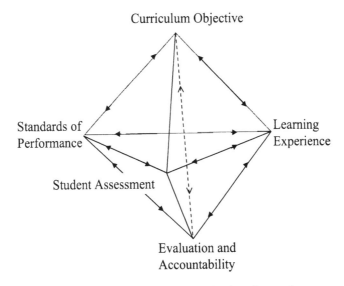

Figure 2. The curriculum-evaluation diamond

curriculum objectives, the performance standards, and the outcomes achieved by students. Teachers in planning instruction for classroom groups of students should examine the structures that are measured, and proceed with the provision of appropriately sequenced learning experiences.

4.2. *The Evaluation of the Mastery Learning Project in Korea*

The Mastery Learning Project that directly involved standards of performance was conducted in Korea and was evaluated within the Tylerian framework and Bloom's notions of a model of school learning to examine the effectiveness of strategies of mastery learning. This large-scale evaluation study was associated with one of the most systematic and most successful innovations in Korean education during the second half of the twentieth century. The introduction of mastery learning strategies that has had a marked impact on learning in Korean schools (Kim, 1975, pp. 13–22) was built upon a soundly conducted evaluation study.

5. PUBLIC EXAMINATIONS AND ACCOUNTABILITY

Public examinations, whether conducted at the national, systemic, or regional levels provide an important form of accountability and direct evidence of the effectiveness of a school or organisation in terms of the number and level of preparation of students, who are successful in the examinations. In general, the success rate of a school becomes public knowledge, and judgments can be made about the effectiveness of the school and the organisation's contribution to student success. However, the use of examination results in this way suffers from two major shortcomings. First, schools differ in the quality of the intake that they receive, either because they use selection procedures in recruiting students or they have catchment areas in which students of higher quality live. Second, schools differ in their retention rates, and even if schools had intakes of students of similar quality, their graduating classes would differ in quality because of differing retention rates. Consequently, it would seem appropriate for a school to be judged by what it achieves with the students it recruits. Nevertheless, these shortcomings are largely ignored in the comparisons that are made about a school's performance from a consideration of the successes of its students in public examinations. There is no doubt that public examinations provide evidence, which is widely used in the evaluation of schools and organisations (Keeves, 1994).

5.1. *The Certification of Graduating Students*

Public examinations provide for the certification of students at the terminal stages of schooling as well as selection for further education. Consequently, public examinations at the middle and upper secondary school levels are sometimes maintained in order to award successful students with a graduation certificate. However, the functions of selection and certification that are associated with the provision of public education are to some extent incompatible. This sometimes leads to the conduct of examinations at the terminal stage of schooling in two forms, namely a certification examination that is held at a regional level and a selection examination that is conducted by or on behalf of the institutions of higher education. China, India, Indonesia, Japan, and the Republic of Korea maintain different examinations to serve these two purposes of selection and certification. Nevertheless, where such public examinations are conducted there is a clearly identified form of accountability that publicly provides evidence for the evaluation of both schools and their teaching methods, as well as the curriculum that is laid down for the schools by the examination system.

5.2. *Large-Scale Testing Programs*

Australia, New Zealand and American Samoa, are countries where public examinations are, in general, not held in any form during the years leading up to the terminal secondary school stage. Moreover, at the terminal stage, teachers through their assessment of students' work during the final year of schooling contribute to the gradings assigned for the purposes of selection and certification, sometimes in conjunction with, or moderated by public examination scores. Consequently, in these countries there is seen to be a serious lack of evidence for accountability purposes that was formerly provided by a system of public examinations at levels below the terminal stage of schooling. This has led to the widespread use of standardized tests for the purposes of accountability that are prepared in New Zealand by the national Department of Education, and in the territories of the United States largely by commercial publishing houses. In Australia, each of the States and Territories of the Commonwealth of Australia conducts its own state-wide testing programs for all students at Grades 3 and 5 and increasingly at Grade 7 in order to provide evidence for accountability purposes to the different stakeholders in the Australian school systems. While the tests conducted in the different States are not strictly comparable, work is in progress to provide comparable results as part of an accountability program that compares the performance of students in different regions of Australia.

6. NATIONAL APPROACHES TO PUBLIC EXAMINING – AN EXAMPLE

In 1973, the Indonesian Government through the *President's Instruction Number 10, 1973* started an educational program to provide better opportunities for learning by school-aged children in elementary schools. The success of this six-year program of compulsory education inevitably led to the next educational program, namely the commencement of the nine-year compulsory basic education program. This program was officially declared by the President of the Republic of Indonesia on 2 May 1994. However, this rapid expansion of education has been accompanied by a demand to ensure that standards were being maintained, which has led to the development of an extensive examination system.

The structure of the school system in Indonesia consists of the Elementary School (6 years), the Junior Secondary School (3 years), the Senior Secondary School (3 years), and the University. At the end of each cycle of schooling in Primary and Secondary Education (Grade 6 of the Elementary Schools, Grade 9 of the Junior Secondary Schools, and Grade 12 of the Senior Secondary Schools), a final examination is administered. For Elementary and Junior Secondary Schools, the final examination serves two purposes, namely for certification and selection to a higher level of education. However, for Senior Secondary Schools, the final examination only serves as certification, because universities, both state and private, do not use the final examination results for selection into the universities, they administer their own entrance examinations.

The final examinations in Indonesia have experienced several major changes in recent decades. Until the early 1970s, the final examination for the Primary and Junior Secondary Schools in Indonesia was administered using a system referred to as 'State Examination.' In this system, a national committee at the central level prepared examination papers for all subject-matter areas tested throughout Indonesia. Students from all over Indonesia at the same level of schooling, taking the same school subjects, would take the same set of items for the final examination.

From the early 1970s to the early 1980s, there was a major change in the system. The State Examination was changed into the Schools Examination. In this new system, every school was given the authority to construct its own tests, to score them, and to decide the passing grade for the students taking the tests. This system was referred to as the 'Schools Examination'. This change gave greater freedom to the schools across the country at a time of marked expansion.

From the 1980s up to the present, there was a further change in the system, referred to as *EBTANAS* (this is an acronym in Indonesian language which means 'National Final Examination of Students' Achievement'). These changes were introduced in an effort to raise the standards of education across the country during the period of continued expansion of the school system. In this new examination system, the test specifications for the subject matter to be tested at the end of each stage of schooling in both Primary to Junior Secondary Education were prepared by a national team in Jakarta.

Thus for both primary and secondary schools, the administration of the teaching-learning process and the conduct of the examinations have been the responsibility of the Directorate General of Primary and Secondary Education. However, the Examination Development Centre, as a research and development institution within the Office of Educational and Cultural Research and Development, has been responsible for the design and development of the examination papers. Among its specific tasks in the development of the examination system have been the construction of a national item bank, as well as the provision of technical guidance to teachers in item writing, both tasks serving the purpose of raising the quality of the examination papers employed across the country.

Formerly for the Primary and Junior Secondary Schools, the provincial committees developed three to seven test forms for each subject-matter area. The Provincial Offices were given the authority to review, finalise, and administer these tests in their respective provinces and to undertake the scoring of students' test papers. The passing score for the test, however, was determined by the Directorate General of Primary and Secondary Education in Jakarta. For the Senior Secondary Schools, the provincial committees developed one set of items for each subject-matter area. These test items were then sent to Jakarta for further review by the national team, which developed the test specifications. The national team was responsible for the preparation of seven sets of items out of the 26 sets received from the 26 provinces. The final versions of the sets were then sent back to each province for duplication and for administration in the final examination. Each province was given the authority to make decisions on the results of this examination.

Beginning in the 2000/2001 school year, there was a slight change in these arrangements. By the decree of the Minister of National Education issued in February 2001, the Examination Development Centre is now given full authority to administer the examinations. However, the examination at the end of Primary Schooling was subsequently abandoned. This Centre is now responsible for the construction and administration of the test items for all subject matter areas in Junior Secondary, and Senior Secondary Schools. The construction of the test items at both levels of schooling are carried out primarily by choosing for each subject matter area at each level appropriate items that are available in an Item Bank which is managed by the Examination Development Centre.

For entry to a higher level of schooling (from Junior Secondary Schools to Senior Secondary Schools), the scores of *EBTANAS* are used as criteria for selection. These scores, referred to as *NEM (Nilai EBTANAS Murni*, meaning Purely *EBTANAS* Scores), are recorded on separate sheets as a supplement to the certificates. As the name suggests, the scores obtained by the students in *EBTANAS* are recorded without change on the separate sheets.

In this system, comparability of test scores becomes a very important issue in order to make fair decisions in selection. If the different test forms were not comparable, the students who happened to take a more difficult test form would be disadvantaged compared to those who might take an easier test form. From the way the different test forms were constructed without pretesting, it would be methodologically wrong to assume that the different test forms would automatically provide comparable results.

In the 1994 administration of the *EBTANAS*, the Examination Development Centre introduced the use of common items in the five different test forms for six subject matter areas in the Junior Secondary Schools. The six subject matter areas are: (a) Pancasila Moral Education; (b) Indonesian Language; (c) Social Science; (d) Science; (e) Mathematics; and (f) English. The purpose of using these common items is to make the equating of the different test forms in each subject possible. By using these common items for linking the different forms, Rasch equating can be employed to obtain comparable scores across the different test forms.

In the current selection system, the scores of the students in the *EBTANAS*, regardless of which forms they are taking, play a major role in the decision to admit or to reject students into the schools they have chosen to attend. In most cases, the favourite schools, which are naturally the better schools, set their criteria of selection in such a way that only those students with high scores are admitted to the schools. Since there are different forms of tests used in the *EBTANAS* for security reason, the comparability of test scores is essential in order to make fair decisions about which students to admit and which students to reject. This comparability must be maintained even though the students take different test forms in the *EBTANAS*.

In an effort to raise the standards of education across the country, there should also be reliable information about the achievement of the students in different places and at different times. The information about the increase or the decrease of the students' achievement over the years in different parts of the country can only be obtained when the measures of their achievement are also comparable over time and place. Comparability of students' scores in *EBTANAS*, to a certain extent, also serves the purpose of monitoring the achievement levels of students over the years and the different locations, so that this information can also be used in an effort to improve the quality of education provided by the schools.

7. SURVEY STUDIES OF EDUCATIONAL ACHIEVEMENT

The introduction of survey studies involving testing programs at the primary and lower secondary school levels in order to assist with the advancement of education at those stages of schooling has become recognized as a way in which the work of the schools can be evaluated at less expense than is involved in conducting nationwide testing programs (see *Case Study of Learning Achievement in South Asia*). These survey types of testing programs have been developed over the past 20 years.

In 1980, the International Association for the Evaluation of Educational Achievement (IEA) and the National Institute for Educational Research (NIER) in Japan organised training seminars for teams of evaluators drawn from the Office of Educational and Cultural Research and Development in Indonesia, the National Education Commission in Thailand, and the Ministry of Education in Malaysia. The seminars were held in two stages. At the first seminar, general instruction was provided in evaluation techniques, and detailed plans of evaluation were developed by the six team members from each country. At the second seminar held 18 months later in 1982, data analyses were undertaken and national reports prepared. While full national reports were written on each of the two survey studies conducted by each team in the national languages, short reports were also prepared for journal publication (Amara, Abu & Jiyono, 1982). This program provided highly effective training for research workers to carry out evaluation studies, using survey research procedures and the monograph prepared on this program indicated the type and quality of work in educational evaluation in countries in the Asia-Pacific region. Such training programs have been replicated from time to time in the different countries in the Asia-Pacific region.

8. SCHOOL-BASED INDICATORS OF EFFECTIVENESS

In 1995, the Human Resources Development Working Group of the Asia-Pacific Economic Cooperation (APEC) organisation initiated a study of school-based indicators of effectiveness. Nine countries participated in the study, namely Brunei Darussalam, People's Republic of China, Chinese Taipei (Taiwan), Hong Kong, New Zealand, Singapore and Thailand from the Asia-Pacific region and Canada and the United States who were from outside the region, although they were APEC members. The economic growth and social development of the APEC member states had created an increased interest in monitoring and improving the quality of education provided. In order to improve the educational system of each country, it was considered necessary to improve the performance of individual schools and to strengthen the effectiveness of each school. The aim of the study was to provide an overview of existing indicators of school effectiveness in the Asia-Pacific region through a survey and through a series of case studies. More specifically the study looked at:

(a) policy issues in the evaluation of school effectiveness,
(b) a historical description of the study of school effectiveness,
(c) existing indicators and programs of school effectiveness, and

(d) how these indicators and programs catered for needs at the school level.

The project sought to prepare through a cooperative study, a guidebook that described the methods, programs of supervision of school effectiveness, and use of school-based indicators that were valid and reliable, and that identified common approaches and strategies to answer several questions.

1. Whether the resources devoted to education were achieving the desired effects?
2. What standards of achievement should be expected of schools?
3. How could it be shown that standards had improved over time?

The orientation of the study was for schools to be responsible for evaluating their own effectiveness and reporting to their stakeholders including their teachers, students and parents on how each school performed.

Each country participating in the project undertook a case study of practices within the country and submitted a report for publication. In addition, consultants presented invited papers on:

(a) monitoring school effectiveness: conceptual and practical possibilities and dilemmas in developing a framework (Cheng, 1997a);
(b) framework of indicators of education quality in Hong Kong primary schools: development and application (Cheng, 1997b); and
(c) developing indicators on the performance of education systems in an international context: The OECD Education Indicators (Schleicher, 1997).

The report of the study (Meng Hong Wei, Zhou Yigun & Fang Yihua, 1997), found that member states saw educational outcomes as an important indicator of school effectiveness, with growing concern for the physical and emotional development of students. A critical issue was the need to maintain a balance between the school's internal development and accountability to the public through the monitoring of school effectiveness. Consequently, there was a need to manage the balance in both evaluation and accountability between the school level and the system level. The information collected through this project also showed that most schools had little systematic knowledge of the nature and extent of their effectiveness and used few indicators of institutional performance.

9. CONCLUSION

In most of the countries of the Asia-Pacific region educational evaluation studies have had only a short life of no more than 30 years. During that time the conduct of educational evaluation studies has changed markedly throughout the world. The advance of the electronic computer has for many investigators changed the way in which evaluation studies could be carried out because large bodies of data could now be conveniently stored and readily processed. Under these circumstances the vision is not merely the conduct of on-off studies of evaluation and accountability, but the undertaking of a planned sequence of related investigations that monitor the changes that are occurring. Consequently it should be possible over the coming decades to provide advice for policy and practice, from an ongoing series of studies involving both evaluation and accountability, that examine national systems of education and monitor the changes that are occurring. Questions must be asked not only about the direction of change, but also the rate of change and the factors that influence both direction and rate. Unfortunately governmental policies vary markedly from occasion to occasion, in a reaction to perceived changes that have occurred and new situations that have arisen. What is needed is a longer term vision of the development of an education system with perceptive monitoring of the changes taking place.

REFERENCES

Aikin, W. M. (1942). *Adventure in American Education, Volume 1, The Story of the Eight-Year Study.* New York: Harper.

Amara Sawadisevee, Abu Bakar Nordin & Jiyono (1982). Six educational evaluation projects in South East Asia. *Evaluation in Education,* 6(1), 1–158.

Bloom, B. S. (Ed.) (1956). *Taxonomy of Educational Objectives: The Classification of Educational Goals. Handbook 1, Cognitive Domain.* New York: McKay.

Bloom, B. S. (1968). Learning for mastery. *University of California Comment,* 1(2), 1–12.

Bloom, B. S., Hastings, T. J., & Madaus, G. F. (1971). *Handbook of Formative and Summative Evaluation of Student Learning.* New York: McGraw-Hill.

Cheng, Y. C. (1997a). Monitoring effectiveness: Conceptual and practical possibilities and dilemmas in developing a framework. In Meng Hong Wei et al. (1997), *School Based Indicators of Effectiveness: Experiences and Practice* (pp. 179–206). Guilin, China: Guangxi Normal University Press.

Cheng Y. C. (1997b). A framework of indicators of education quality in Hong Kong primary schools: Development and application. In Meng Hong Wei et al. (1997), *School Based Indicators of Effectiveness: Experiences and Practices* (pp. 207–249). Guilin, China: Guangxi Normal University Press.

Cubberley, E. P. (1917). Editor's introduction. In W. S. Munroe (1924), *Educational Tests and Measurements* (pp. xi–xv). Boston: Houghton Mifflin.

Hearn, W. E. (1872). *Payment by Results in Primary Education.* Melbourne: Stellwell and Knight.

Keeves, J. P. (1994). *National Examinations: Design, Procedures and Reporting.* Paris: UNESCO, IIEP.

Keeves, J. P. (1999). Research into curriculum change. In J. P. Keeves & K. Marjoribanks (Eds.), *Australian Education: Review of Research* (pp. 113–144). Melbourne: ACER.

Kim, H. (1975). Evaluation of the mastery learning project in Korea. *Studies in Educational Evaluation,* 1(1), 13–22.

Krathwohl, D. R., Bloom, B. S., & Masia, B. B. (1964). *Taxonomy of Educational Objectives. The Classification of Educational Goals, Handbook 2, Affective Domain.* New York: McKay.

Madaus, G. F., & Kallaghan, T. (1992). Curriculum evaluation and assessment. In P. W. Jackson (Ed.) (1992), *Handbook of Research in Curriculum* (pp. 119–154). New York: Macmillan.

Mager, R. F. (1962). *Preparing Objectives for Programmed Instruction.* San Francisco: Fearon Publishers.

Meng Hong Wei, Zhou Yigun & Fang Yihua (1997). *School Based Indicators of Effectiveness: Experiences and Practices.* Guilin, China: Guangxi Normal University Press.

Meyer, J. W., Kamens, D. H., & Benavot, A. with Yun-Kyung Cha and Suk-Ying Wong (1992). *School Knowledge for the Masses.* London: Falmer Press.

Munroe, W. S. (1917). *Educational Tests and Measurements.* Boston: Houghton Mifflin.

Neave, G. (1985). Accountability in education. In T. Husén & T. N. Postlethwaite (Eds.), *The International Encyclopedia of Education* (pp. 19–29). Oxford: Pergamon.

Schleicher, A. (1997). Developing indicators on the performance of education systems in an international context: The OECD education indicators. In Meng Hong Wei et al. (1997), *School Based Indicators of Effectiveness: Experiences and Practices* (pp. 251–264). Guilin, China: Guangxi Normal University Press.

Thorndike, E. L. (1918). The nature, purposes and general methods of measurements of educational products. In G. M. Whipple (Ed.), *The Measurement of Educational Products* (17th NSSE Yearbook) IL (pp. 16–24). Bloomington: Public School Co.

Tyler, R. W. (1949). *Basic Principles of Curriculum and Instruction*. Chicago: University of Chicago Press.

Tyler, R. W. (1973). Testing for accountability. In A. C. Ornstein (Ed.), *Accountability for Teachers and School Administrators*. Belmont, CA: Fearon Publishers.

Tyler, R. W. (1986). Changing concepts of educational evaluation. *International Journal of Educational Research, 10*(1), 1–113.

9

Educational Research in the Asia-Pacific Region*

JOHN P. KEEVES
Flinders University Institute of International Education, Australia

RYO WATANABE
National Institute for Educational Policy Research of Japan, Tokyo, Japan

PETER McGUCKIAN
The Australian Council for Educational Research, Melbourne, Australia

1. INTRODUCTION

Perhaps the most impressive achievement of the twentieth century in the Asia-Pacific region is the creation within each country in the region of an organised system of education that aims to provide schooling for all. The rate and extent of development of the system in each country have differed, depending on existing traditions, the financial resources available and the size and structure of the population (see *Educational Expenditure and Participation in East Asia and Australia*). Nevertheless, the educational services that are being provided extend from early childhood education, through primary and secondary schooling, workforce and technological training to higher education in universities and adult recurrent education. This explosion in the provision of education has been costly and not without controversy within each country and between countries. In spite of the complexity of the issues involved and the wide range of problems that have been seen to exist, the countries in the region were initially slow to see the potential importance of research into educational problems. Education was seen to be an art, rather than a wide field with many problems that were amenable to investigation and research from a range of different perspectives with many different approaches to inquiry (see *Educational Research and Educational Policy-Making in Asian and Pacific Countries*).

These formerly held views have changed, and educational research is now a vigorous field of social inquiry. This article in the *Handbook* seeks to trace the

---

* The assistance of T.N. Postlethwaite in the preparation of this article is gratefully acknowledged.

development of research into educational problems in the Asia-Pacific region, to identify key organisations and associations within the region which lead the research endeavours in their respective countries, and to set the educational research conducted within the region into a world-wide context. However, this context is still strongly oriented towards the Western world and is dominated by the United States and the United Kingdom. Yet, approximately 60 per cent of the world's people live in the Asia-Pacific region, where a rapidly growing proportion of the educational research being conducted world-wide is now being carried out. The time has come for the educational problems of the Asia-Pacific region to be seen more clearly, and for the growing body of research being conducted within the region not only to become more visible but also to have greater impact on both the policy and practice of education worldwide.

2. DEVELOPMENTS IN EDUCATIONAL RESEARCH: WORLD PERSPECTIVES

Educational research as disciplined inquiry into educational problems with an empirical basis had its origins in Europe and North America in the latter decades of the nineteenth century in (a) the child study movement, (b) the work by Wundt in Germany in experimental psychology, and (c) the development of mental tests by Binet and Simon in France (De Landsheere, 1982). In the early decades of the twentieth century, educational research expanded in the United States, with the establishment of the National Society for the Scientific Study of Education (NSSE), a movement towards educational change led by Dewey, initially at the Department of Education, University of Chicago and later alongside E.L. Thorndike at Teachers College, Columbia University in New York. The progressive education movement prospered in the 1930s in both the United States and Europe. However, it was only in the late 1950s and early 1960s, when the educational world sought to reform the provision of education, in order to cater for the remarkable growth of knowledge which had occurred during the first half of the twentieth century that educational research started to flourish. This was the period when the need for widespread research into educational problems was first seen to be essential. Moreover, this advancement coincided with the advent of the electronic computer that greatly facilitated the storage of information and the processing of data.

In the late 1960s and 1970s educational research thrived, in spite of the cultural crisis in many of the more highly industrialized countries that had an important impact on scientific epistemology. Initially, there was a strong belief that social and educational research would provide a scientific basis for the solving of societal problems through the provision of evidence and the advancement of knowledge that could be directly used to guide the making of policy and the improvement of practice. However, in the latter decades of the twentieth century there was a so-called 'crisis of confidence' in educational research in many countries (Kogan & Tuijnman, 1995). This crisis would appear to have been based on criticisms involving the fragmentation of research effort, the apparent irrelevance of some of the research, as well as the perceived low quality, usefulness and effectiveness of some of the research undertaken. Some of these criticisms would seem to have been founded on a lack of understanding on how research in the social and behavioural sciences, as contrasted with the natural sciences, operated. In addition there was a failure to recognize the complexity of the problems and of the factors influencing educational change. Educational research, particularly in the Asia-Pacific region is today gaining in strength as it emerges from this 'crisis of confidence' (see *Research in Education: Nature, Impact, Needs and Priorities*).

3. DEVELOPMENTS IN THE ASIA-PACIFIC REGION

Initial developments in the field of educational research would seem to have occurred in the Asia-Pacific region during the early decades of the twentieth century through scholars from universities and teachers colleges, travelling to Germany, the United Kingdom and to the United States to study. These scholars returned to their home countries and set up small psychological laboratories, that gave rise to an interest in experimental education. Very little original research was carried out in the Asia-Pacific region during this period. However, the number of people interested in and involved in educational research in Australia was sufficient for the Carnegie Corporation of New York to found and support financially the Australian Council for Educational Research in 1930, and shortly after to establish a similar organisation in New Zealand in order to foster the advancement of educational research in these countries. Little happened in the region to advance the undertaking of educational research until the influence of developments in the United States and the United Kingdom was felt in the mid-1960s, partly as a result of greatly increased opportunities for travel by air from the Asia-Pacific region to Europe and North America and greatly improved telecommunication services.

In 1967, Dr Mansumori Hiratsuka, the Director General of the National Institute for Educational Research in Japan, working in collaboration with Dr Raja Roy-Singh who was Director of the Unesco Bangkok Office, initiated a regional Cooperation Programme for Educational Research in Asia. This program implemented a comparative study of curriculum and educational content in the schools of Asian countries. Subsequently in 1974, the Asia and Pacific Programme of Educational Innovation and Development (APEID) was established on the recommendation of the Third Regional Conference of Ministers of Education in Asia held in Singapore in 1971. A centre devoted to this work has been maintained in Thailand for nearly 30 years.

From these beginnings the Asia-Pacific region has been seen as a zone of the world where educational research could guide the making of policy and influence the advancement of practice in schools during the marked expansion of education that has occurred and is continuing to occur at all levels and in most countries of the region. In 1971, Cronbach from Stanford University in the United States ran a training course in Thailand known as the Seminar on Learning and the Educational Process (SOLEP) that was similar to seminars held at Stanford, California in 1965 and in subsequent years in Sweden, France and Germany. At the seminar in Thailand there were mainly participants from Asia. The participants had to have a PhD degree and two years of post-doctoral experience. There was an international faculty and the standard was high. Those who attended this seminar have never forgotten the experience, and universities in some countries in the Asia-Pacific region subsequently introduced courses geared specifically to providing training for educational research workers. This seminar was followed for a decade or more by the activities of the South East Asia Research in Education Group (SEAREG) that established and maintained collaborative links between educational research workers in this region.

In 1979, Dr Hiroshi Kida of the National Institute for Educational Research in Japan, again at the request of the Unesco Regional Office for Education in Asia and the Pacific in Bangkok, organised a Regional Seminar on Educational Research in Relation to Educational Reform in Asia and Oceania (Kida, 1979), that paid special attention to the training of educational research workers. Since that time, and largely as a consequence of this initiative and the seminars subsequently held at the National Institute for Educational Research in Tokyo on an annual basis, and in some years more frequently, there has been a marked expansion of educational research activity in the Asia-Pacific region.

During the intervening years in some of the countries of the region, educational research associations were set up: (a) to provide opportunities for debate, discussion and training among research workers; (b) to hold annual conferences, sometimes jointly between two or more countries; (c) to publish on a regular basis a journal reporting research; and (d) to prepare and publish monographs presenting the findings of educational research studies. Some of these associations are considered in a later section of this article (see Section 5 of this article).

Furthermore, since 1964 the International Association for the Evaluation of Educational Achievement (IEA) has maintained a program of cross-national research studies that has involved many of the countries in the region, with 13 education systems within the Asia-Pacific region at present being members of IEA (see *Comparative Educational Achievement Studies*). The systems involved in IEA at the beginning of the twenty-first century were Australia, People's Republic of China, Taiwan (Chinese Taipei), Hong Kong (SAR), Indonesia, Japan, Republic of Korea, Malaysia, New Zealand, Philippines, Russian Federation, Singapore and Thailand. Other countries that have been involved in IEA studies in the past include India, Iran, and Papua New Guinea. In addition, the OECD Programme for International Student Achievement (PISA), had over 40 member countries world-wide at the beginning of the twenty-first century, with Australia, People's Republic of China, Indonesia, Japan, Korea, New Zealand, Philippines, and Thailand being members from the Asia-Pacific region. In both the IEA and the OECD studies, the national research workers have been able to learn a great deal from each other through their participation.

Moreover, these international studies also have set a standard for quality in the conduct and execution of research studies.

4. MAJOR RESEARCH INSTITUTIONS IN THE ASIA-PACIFIC REGION

In many of the countries within the Asia-Pacific region there are major research institutions that have led and supported the development of educational research within those countries. Some of these institutions are described briefly in the pages that follow, where it is known that the institution has made an important contribution not only to educational research within the country but also to educational research within the region. This discussion of major research institutions is limited to 12 countries where productivity, as assessed by international publications is known to be greatest in the Asia-Pacific region (see Section 4 of this article).

4.1. *Australia*

In 1930, The Australian Council for Educational Research (ACER) was established with a central office in Melbourne and with affiliated Institutes in each of the Australian States. In the early years, the State Institutes participated in the research program and activities of the Council in a way that helped build expertise in educational research in the States. In the mid-1940s the State and Commonwealth Governments agreed to assist with the funding of the ACER's program of research thus enabling the Council to undertake an innovative and leadership role in the field of educational research and to maintain an active program of publication and dissemination of the findings of research. This support has also enabled the ACER to build a strong reputation as an international research organisation that has taken a major role in both the IEA and PISA research studies. In 1967, a conference was convened by the ACER that had a marked impact on the amount of educational research conducted in Australia, mainly in universities and government agencies, and on improving the value of research to policy and practice in education (Radford, 1967). Many of the universities have since carried out vigorous educational research programs, but research activity within governmental agencies has largely died out, although in some Australian States it has some times been strong and well supported.

4.2. *New Zealand*

The New Zealand Council for Educational Research (NZCER) was founded in 1933 and was subsequently constituted as a statutory, largely government funded, but autonomous body that has had an important influence on the development of educational research in the country. The Council's research priorities have been directed towards national concerns, and have included studies of educational achievement, policy issues and studies of the Maori language and the education of Maori students. The commitment of university teachers to research has been maintained over the years and has strengthened, particularly since the mid-1960s, often working in collaboration with the NZCER.

4.3. Thailand

In Thailand, the first educational research unit was founded in 1943. Its name was the International Institute for Child Study. It formed part of the Education College that was under the Ministry of Education. In time, the Education College became part of Srinakarinwirot University and was no longer under the Ministry of Education. The Office of the National Education Commission (ONEC) in Thailand was established in 1959 and directly served as an advisory body to the Prime Minister and Cabinet on all matters concerning education. In 1978, ONEC was designated to function as a national educational policy and planning agency and also to engage in research and evaluation in relation to planning and policy formulation. It conducted a great deal of educational research especially in the period from the 1960s to 1980s. Another well-known institution conducting educational research at the national level has been the Institute for the Promotion of Science and Technology (IPST).

4.4. Japan

The National Institute for Educational Research of Japan (NIER) was founded in 1949. In 2001, the name of the Institute was changed to the National Institute for Educational Policy Research of Japan although the acronym of NIER remained. This change occurred at the same time as other changes in government organisations when the Ministry of Education was merged with the Agency for Science and Technology and the new ministry was called the Ministry of Education, Culture, Sports, Science and Technology. At the beginning of the twenty-first century, the NIER was the only educational research institution to remain within the governmental structure. Other institutions, such as the National Institute of Special Education, became independent and autonomous agencies. In addition, many educational research centres at the prefectural level, many private educational research institutes and many educational research institutes or centres attached to national universities have been established. In all some 400 small educational research centres have been formed, including two centres for educational research in developing countries at the universities of Tokyo and Hiroshima.

4.5. China, People's Republic of

In China, the Central Institute of Educational Research (CIER) was founded in 1957 and the Central Institute has not only undertaken commissioned research but has also participated in international studies. Two Special Administrative Regions (SARs) of the republic are Hong Kong and Macao. In Hong Kong, educational research is well established (see Section 4.11 of this article). Macao on the other hand has carried out very little educational research and it is likely that mostly outsiders have conducted the research that has been undertaken. Systematic educational research in the sense of scholarly publications by insiders is a recent development that is mainly undertaken by students at the University of Macao and the Universities of China.

4.6. Malaysia

Educational research in Malaysia started in 1959 soon after independence in the form of bibliographic documentation. At the beginning of the twenty-first century most of the research was undertaken by the universities, the Ministry of Education, the Ministry of Science, Technology and Environment as well as in regional centres such as RECSAM (Regional Education Centre for Science and Mathematics). The research has been conducted by university lecturers, ministry officials, lecturers at teachers training colleges, teachers and others. The main foci of this research have been on curriculum, language education, teacher education and on the educational development of the system. The Educational Planning and Research Division (EPRD) was instituted in 1963 within the Ministry of Education. In addition, within the Malaysian Ministry educational research has been undertaken in the Curriculum Development Centre, the Teacher Training Division, the Schools Division, the Technical and Vocational Education Division, and the Department of Moral and Islamic Education Division.

4.7. India

In India, the National Council of Educational Research and Training (NCERT) was established in 1961. Its mandate has been to advise and assist the Ministry of Human Resource Development, the Government of India and the Departments of Education in each of the States. It has established a large decentralized network of constituent units that have included the National Institute of Education in New Delhi, the Regional Institutes of Education at Ajmer, Bhopal, Bhubaneswar, Mysore and Shillong, the Central Institute of Educational Technology at New Delhi, the Pandit Sunderlai Sharma Central Institute of Vocational Education at Bhophal, and the Offices of the Field Advisers in each of the States. The NCERT has provided leadership and has built up research capacity through activities such as the formulation and revision of frameworks for national curricula. It should not be forgotten that there have been other institutions such as universities and private research institutes that have also undertaken educational research, but the NCERT is the best known both within and outside India.

4.8. Russia

From 1967 to 1991, the USSR Academy of Pedagogical Sciences was the most important body supporting and undertaking educational research in Russia. In the early 1990s, this institution was renamed the Russian Academy of Education and since then there has been a tendency towards decentralization of its activities. Over 20 research institutes have been set up within the Academy and approximately 2000 researchers have been employed, some of whom have undertaken theoretical research, while others have prepared curricula, syllabuses and educational materials. Moreover, since the early 1990s, the Academy has been interested in research at all levels of education and not only in the schools. In addition, educational research has been conducted in all universities and in all teacher-training institutions.

4.9. Indonesia

Educational research in Indonesia was introduced after the Second World War in universities. It was only in the 1960s that the government became interested in research as an integral part of an education system. In 1969–70, an office was created within the Ministry to conduct a national assessment of education so that planners might have sound data on which to build programs under the successive five-year development plans (Beeby, 1979). By 1980, the originally small office had evolved into a fully-fledged Research and Development Unit (*Balitbang Depdiknas*) within the Ministry of Education. This organisation has several centres within it: a secretariat, a policy research centre, a curriculum centre, an assessment centre, an educational statistics' centre, and an educational innovation centre. Each of these centres conducts its own research and development program.

4.10. Singapore

In Singapore, educational research grew incrementally to keep pace with the socio-economic and political developments in the country. A number of policy-directed reports formed the backdrop for the creation of the National System of Education after independence in 1965. These reports have set the agenda for education to upgrade and to sustain the standards of education in schools, polytechnics and universities. From the mid-1980s, the research effort has been aided significantly by access to the comprehensive computer-based School, Teacher and Student Data Banks, in the Research and Testing (R and T) Division of the Ministry. Since 1991, the National Institute of Education (NIE), at Nanyang Technological University (NTU) has been responsible for accelerating teacher training at all levels, including the leadership programs for school principals and the heads of departments. Concurrently, the training of educators in research content and methods has been undertaken through postgraduate masters and doctoral degree programs in education, by coursework and with thesis. Participation in the IEA studies in 1980s and 1990s has helped Singapore to compare its achievement levels in science and mathematics with the levels in other countries.

4.11. Hong Kong, SAR

The University of Hong Kong was established in 1911 and the Chinese University of Hong Kong was founded in 1964. These two universities together with the Hong Kong Institute of Education (founded in 1994) have made major contributions to educational research. The Comparative Education Research Centre (founded 1994) at the University of Hong Kong has begun to play a major role in educational research. The Baptist University, the Open University of Hong Kong, and the City University of Hong Kong have played more modest roles in the field. Output of research by universities has been encouraged and supported by the University Grants Committee's Research Assessment Exercises (RAEs). Nevertheless, educational research has had a very chequered history in Hong Kong. There was considerable activity in the late 1960s and the 1970s in the universities, but this was reduced in the mid-1980s because of lack of suitably qualified personnel. However, it was revived again in the mid-1990s as a result of the introduction of post-graduate courses at the University of Hong Kong, the Chinese University of Hong Kong and the Hong Kong Institute of Education. The Educational Research Establishment within the Hong Kong Educational Department has, in the past, undertaken many evaluation and research studies that have focused on the government's policies and programs. Financial support for research in the institutions of higher education has been largely funded by the government through a research council.

4.12. Republic of Korea

The major educational research institute in Korea has been the Korean Educational Development Institute, (KEDI) that was founded in 1972. In 1998, KEDI split into two additional research institutes, the Korean Institute of Curriculum and Evaluation (KICE) and the Korean Research Institute for Vocational Education and Training (KRIVET). KEDI has had a staff of over 350 specialist research workers and has undertaken studies of educational objectives and curriculum content, as well as instructional methods for improving the quality of learning. Especially in curriculum development and mastery learning, the Institute has achieved a very high reputation. It has also been very active in the development of instructional radio and television as well as curriculum materials and textbooks. KICE has conducted research for educational testing programs and has developed a wide variety of testing instruments. KRIVET has aimed to support vocational education and training in Korea through research into vocational skills, industrial labour policy and the qualifications system. In addition, city and provincial research institutes conduct research related to the improvement of teaching methods and counselling, and the development of instructional materials together with the operation of pilot programs and the in-service training of teachers. In 1999, the Korean Education Research and Information Service (KERIS) was set up to establish a comprehensive educational and research information network.

4.13. Overview

Initially, all of these research institutes originally had relatively small staffs. The people who worked there were mostly from the discipline of psychology and, in particular, educational psychology. They were people who had undertaken self-training after having completed their first or second degrees at universities. In the late 1960s, the institutes increased the number of members of staff who were recruited from the universities and from disciplines other than psychology, such as sociology, social psychology, anthropology, and economics. These developments in the Asia-Pacific region have reflected developments that had taken place a little earlier in Europe and the United States. By the end of the 1990s, nearly every country in the region had a national research institute or a research unit (often a Planning Unit) that conducted research for the Ministry of Education.

5. PERFORMANCE IN RESEARCH, AN INTERNATIONAL PERSPECTIVE

In this section the performance of countries in educational research is viewed from an international perspective. Performance is assessed in terms of articles appearing in educational journals that have been indexed by the Institute for Scientific Information (ISI). It should be noted that much of the research findings that are reported in the Asia-Pacific region are not published in journals which are indexed by ISI, but are published in books, monographs and journals that have only a national circulation in the national language and in newsletters that are distributed directly to teachers or as reports that go directly to policy making bodies. Nevertheless, the ISI indexing system does provide a basis for comparisons not only in the Asia-Pacific region but across the world of educational research, and does give some indication of the productivity of the educational researchers within a particular country, when viewed in a world or perhaps North American context.

The work on the bibliometric analysis that has been summarized in this section was carried out by Phelan et al. (2000) in the Research School of Social Sciences at the Australian National University. Table 1 records a ranking of systems in the Asia-Pacific region with respect to a composite index of productivity in educational research. The period reviewed was from July 1987 to June 1998, and the index was formed from seven specific measures: international share of citations, international share of publications, citations per publication, publications per capita, citations per capita, publications relative to GNP, and citations relative to GNP. The summary index reported in Table 1 was created by combining the seven measures, after normalizing each measure with the highest score set at 100, and the other scores calculated as a proportion of the highest score. The seven measures were combined with equal weights and an average calculated. The cross-national rankings both for systems in the Asia-Pacific region and across the world are given in Table 1 together with the value of the combined

Table 1. Productivity of leading systems in educational research

System	Composite index	A-P ranking	World ranking	Trends over time periods (%)[a] 1987–91	1993–97
New Zealand	53.3	1	3	0.80	0.81
Australia	44.8	2	5	3.33	3.80
Hong Kong	18.1	3	9	0.35	0.60
Singapore	9.5	4	17	0.14	0.23
Malaysia	5.7	5	26	0.12	0.11
Japan	5.2	6	27	0.43	0.50
India	4.3	7	29	0.50	0.40
Taiwan (Chinese Taipei)	4.1	8	31	0.07	0.18
China	2.2	9	34	0.28	0.36
Russian Federation	0.8	10	35	0.40	0.64

Source: Phelan et al. (2000, p. 594 and p. 596).
[a] A proportion of total international publications on educational research is recorded.

index. Table 1 also shows the trend in the proportion of international publications in educational research produced by each education system, over two time periods, but only data for the top ten systems in the Asia-Pacific region are presented.

New Zealand and Australia hold first and second rankings in research productivity in the Asia-Pacific region and high rankings of third and fifth in a world setting. While New Zealand remained at a steady level of productivity in the period under review, Australia moved upwards in educational research productivity.

Moreover, of the ten systems under consideration seven had increased their proportion of the world publications in the period 1987 to 1998, two systems had remained at a steady level and one system had declined. While the United States dominates the world production in educational research with 67 per cent of total productivity and the United Kingdom is second with 10 per cent, the contributions of Hong Kong and Singapore that hold third and fourth rankings in the Asia-Pacific region, as relatively small systems, are clearly gaining rapidly in productivity. However, it should be noted that the systems in the Asia-Pacific region as assessed by these data are only producing approximately seven per cent of the measured output of educational research in the world, with Australia producing approximately half of this regional output. This method of assessing productivity of educational research clearly favours the two education systems that control journal publication, namely the United States and the United Kingdom, implying that only publication in English is of value, and that only publication in a select set of refereed journals is worthwhile. It would seem that serious consideration must be given in the coming decades to the wider dissemination of the findings of educational research that has been conducted within the Asia-Pacific region as well as the training of research workers and the setting of priorities for research within the region.

6. DEVELOPMENT OF EDUCATIONAL RESEARCH ASSOCIATIONS

Some years after the expansion of activity in the field of educational research that started in the mid-1960s, several countries in the region, as the need arose, formed educational research associations. These associations have served to support and promote the conduct of educational research through (a) increasing collaboration in research within each country, (b) holding regular conferences, (c) publishing journals and reports of research, (d) training research workers, and (e) arguing the case for greater funding for educational research. Information on several of these national educational research associations is provided in the following section.

6.1. *Australia*

An outline of the events leading to the founding of the Australian Association for Research in Education (AARE) can be found in the history of the Association (Bessant & Holbrook, 1995). The first national meeting of educational researchers in Australia was convened by the Australian Council for Educational Research in May 1967. The theme was 'Research into Education: Improving its Value to the Practice of Education' (Radford, 1967). The possibility of forming a national organisation was canvassed during the conference. Planning was undertaken during the following two years and a meeting of educational researchers held in Melbourne on 13–14 March 1970 resolved to form the AARE. The highly significant contribution of Dr W.C. Radford, then Director of the ACER towards the formation of the AARE is recognised in the official history.

The purpose of the new organisation was "to encourage and improve research in education and the application of its results in education". The first interim committee was based at Macquarie University and the foundation conference was held in November 1970. Approximately 100 researchers attended the first conference. While the initial membership criteria restricted membership to researchers with postgraduate qualifications in a relevant area of educational research, in the early years of AARE major revisions were made to open up membership criteria to all those involved in educational research. The *Australian Educational Researcher (AER)* and the *AARE News* are distributed to members and sold to others. Members are entitled to AARE annual conference abstracts and papers, which are distributed by the internet and on disk. An important area of activity for AARE is the Special Interest Groups (SIGS). AARE encourages members to form SIGS for those with specialist research interests (for instance, Teachers' Work and Lives SIG). Each SIG requires a minimum of 10 members and a convener. Each SIG is also given the opportunity at each AARE Annual Conference to hold meetings, symposia and paper presentations.

The AARE annual conference has grown to become a major event. Participants are attracted from many countries, particularly from the Asia-Pacific region. Collaboration with the Singapore Educational Research Association in recent years has seen a strong participation by researchers from Singapore. The place of the annual conference in the life of AARE was described by W.F. Connell to members in 1974, as 'the principal event' and:

> ... a valuable means of keeping up-to-date on research and gossip, of renewing old associations, and forming new and congenial friendships. It is an opportunity to hear about one's colleagues' recent work and to explain to them the errors they are committing; it is also a chance to find out quite a range of unknown developments in other fields and in other States. The association by its conference should be a forum for uninhibited and exacting criticism, for a broadening of research horizons, for inspiration to new lines of research, for the planning of cooperative ventures, and for mutual respect and good fellowship among the community of educational research workers in Australia. (Bessant & Holbrook, 1995, p. 160)

6.2. *People's Republic of China*

The Chinese Society of Education (CSE) was established in 1979. It is a national mass education academic organisation operated under the professional guidance and supervision of both the Ministry of Education and the Ministry of Civil Affairs. The CSE holds its general assembly every five years and its fifth general assembly was held in year 2000 with nearly 200 representatives from the branches of education associations at the provincial level, teacher universities and educational research institutes.

Membership. The CSE has a membership of 30 education associations at the provincial level, 45 branches and professional committees throughout the country and 850,000 individual members. There are 33 elected managing directors and 165 board directors.

Activities. The Constitution of the Chinese society of Education was substantially revised at the fifth general assembly to:

- carry out mass activities in educational research, pilot programs on pedagogical and teaching reform, and academic exchange;
- disseminate knowledge of educational science and introduce the latest information on educational research, important research findings, and experiences with educational reform at home and abroad;
- provide educational policy makers with scientific analysis, information feedback and consultancy;
- organise the accreditation and dissemination of educational research findings as well as the results of pedagogical and teaching reform pilot programs;
- carry out research, write teaching materials, publish academic journals, run

experimental schools at the basic education stage, and engage in training activity;
- offer professional, policy and legal consultancy;
- organise educational assessment activities;
- promote educational academic exchange and cooperation with the Hong Kong, Macao and Taiwan regions, as well as foreign countries;
- carry out other related activities.

6.3. *New Zealand*

The New Zealand Association for Research in Education was established in December 1979. It consists of individuals and organisations with an interest in educational research. The aims of the Association are to foster a high standard in the practice of educational research in New Zealand by organising conferences and special interest seminars, publishing a newsletter, commissioning publications, promoting discussion about research and development, disseminating the results of research and advising and making representations on matters relevant to the use of research in education.

Individual membership of the Association is open to any person who has been or is actively involved in the conduct, promotion or application of research in education. There are three categories of individual members: (a) regular members, (b) student members, who are enrolled as students in tertiary education at least half-time and employed less than half-time, and (c) retired members. The prime benefit for personal members is the opportunity to meet and interact with others with similar interests at the NZARE Annual Conference. Members also receive (a) three issues a year of the Association's newsletter *Input*, (b) two issues a year of the *New Zealand Journal of Educational Studies*, (c) a copy of each monograph in the Association's *State of the Art Monograph Series*, and (d) a discount on personal subscriptions to the NZCER's research information series *Set*. NZARE conducts special interest seminars on specific topics of interest to members. The Early Childhood Special Interest Group is particularly active, running an annual conference in conjunction with the NZARE annual conference. The NZARE annual conference is combined with the annual conference of the AARE, the Australian Association for Research in Education, where a regular session is held in which New Zealand research teams present a symposium.

6.4. *Singapore*

The first annual general meeting of the Singapore Educational Research Association (SERA) was convened by Dr Sim Wong Kooi in August 1986. Professor William Taylor, Chairman of the National Foundation for Educational Research for England and Wales at the time spoke at the meeting. The first executive committee was elected to serve for two years with Dr Sim as the inaugural President. The main objective of the association as outlined by Dr Sim was "to promote the practice and utilization of educational research, particularly in the schools with the view to enhancing the quality of education in Singapore". The aims of SERA are to:

- promote the practice and utilisation of educational research with the view to enhancing the quality of education;
- encourage schools to carry out action research;
- stimulate and facilitate collaborative research efforts;
- promote critical discussion into problems, methods, presentation and use of educational research;
- disseminate the findings of educational research; and
- facilitate closer ties with the international research community.

Membership of the Association is open to any qualified person or institution that supports its objects. There are five categories of members: (a) ordinary, (b) associate, (c) corporate, (d) life, and (e) honorary.

The SERA annual conference is the major annual activity. There has been a conference each year since 1987, providing a forum for Singaporean and international researchers to gather and report on their work. The conference has been particularly important in bringing researchers from across the East-Asian region together. Collaborative conferences with Australian and Malaysian educational research associations have been an important feature in recent years.

The various activities undertaken by SERA include:

- organising workshops and seminars to deal with educational problems and issues, and to improve research skills;
- working on collaborative projects with schools to assist in the solution of educational problems;
- conducting an annual conference to encourage dissemination of research findings and encourage collaboration in research;
- enabling local and international experts to share findings and experiences;
- disseminating information through newsletters and other publications about the latest developments in educational research; and
- holding social functions to enable educationists and researchers to interact informally.

6.5. *Hong Kong, SAR*

The Hong Kong Educational Research Association was established in 1984 and currently has a membership of over 400. Membership comprises teachers, principals, administrators, counsellors, social workers, graduate students, researchers and publishers. There are two basic types of membership, professional and associate. Professional membership is open to educators with at least a first degree or equivalent qualification who are actively engaged in educational research. Educators who are interested in educational research but do not meet these requirements may apply to be associate members. Both categories are entitled to participate in the Association's forums and annual conference and receive free issues of the newsletter and journal. The Association aims to improve the educational process by promoting a scholarly approach to the study and practice of education. It encourages discussion and collaboration among its members, and supports the dissemination and application of research results. Each year the Association runs a major conference and a number of forums. The Association also publishes a newsletter and an internationally refereed journal.

6.6. *India*

The All India Association for Educational Research was founded in 1987. The major activities of the Association in recent years have been the conducting of annual conferences of national and state levels, the publication of a journal and the conducting of seminars in the different States. The objectives of the Association are to:

- develop and promote educational research;
- provide a forum for discussion of problems related to educational research;
- conduct workshops, seminars and conferences on educational research;
- publish journals, monographs and other types of literature on educational research;
- cooperate with organisations engaged in educational research; and
- carry out all such other activities as may be conducive to the attainment of the above objectives.

There are several categories of membership: individual members, individual life members, institutional members, institutional life members, and donor members.

The Malaysian Educational Research Association (MERA) was formed by Professor Zainal, who died shortly before the inaugural conference in 1998. However, no further information about this Association is known to the authors of this article.

7. FORMATION OF APERA

The Asia-Pacific region has rich and unique traditions, cultural diversity and common challenges, including obstacles of language and geographical separation. It is home to approximately 60 per cent of the world's population and it faces major educational challenges in an environment of ongoing social and economic change. The idea of increased collaboration in educational research among the nations of the Asia-Pacific region was discussed during a meeting in 1995, which was co-sponsored by the UNESCO Asia-Pacific Centre of Educational Innovation for Development (ACEID) and the Australian Council for Educational Research (ACER). Fourteen countries were represented at that meeting. Discussions centred on the identification or research priorities in the region and on ways of collaborating to address them. Several follow-up meetings were held over the next few years involving research and development institutes in the region. These meetings included discussion of the formation of a regional educational research association. It was in Tokyo in October 2000 that participants in a UNESCO regional meeting, hosted by NIER, Japan, and attended by organisations from across the region, agreed to the establishment of the Asia-Pacific Educational Research Association (APERA). It was also decided at this meeting that the Australian Council for Educational Research (ACER) would provide secretarial services for the first few years, and that the APERA office would initially be located at the ACER offices in Melbourne, Australia. The launch of APERA took place at the 2001 UNESCO-ACEID conference in Bangkok in December 2001.

APERA is a not-for-profit organisation. The founding Board of Directors comprises eight members drawn from the initial APERA founding membership of 22 organisations from 14 countries in the region. Membership is open to institutions, individuals and students. There are four membership categories.

Institutional Membership: for institutions that implement research activities or train educational professionals; associations of professionals that coordinate activities for educational researchers at the national level; universities and colleges of advanced learning; organisations having an interest in educational research and having a presence in the Asia-Pacific region; government departments, entities, agencies or semi-governmental entities having an interest in educational research.

Fellowship Membership: for those recognised by their colleagues as deserving recognition for meritorious service to educational research.

Individual Membership: for individual educational research professionals.

Students Membership: for those in the process of undertaking or completing a university (or other tertiary level) qualification in education.

APERA's mission is:

- to support and encourage educational research in the Asia-Pacific region, and;
- to build stronger links between research, policy and practice in education.

APERA's objectives are:

- to support educational research and researchers in the Asia-Pacific region;
- promote greater communication between researchers and policy makers, administrators and educational practitioners;
- disseminate educational research findings; and
- support the development of educational research skills in the Asia-Pacific region.

8. COLLABORATION AND COOPERATION IN RESEARCH

The major purpose of the Asia-Pacific Educational Research Association (APERA) is to foster greater collaboration and cooperation between individuals and institutions in the conduct of educational research within the region in order to support both policy-making and practice in education in the region. It is in the fulfilment of this major purpose that this *Handbook* has been produced.

REFERENCES

Beeby, C. E. (1979). *Assessment of Indonesian Education: A Guide in Planning.* Wellington: NZCER.
Bessant, B., & Holbrook, A. (1995). *Reflections on Educational Research in Australia: A History of the Australian Association for Research in Education.* Coldstream, Victoria: AARE.
De Landsheere, G. (1982). *Empirical Research in Education.* Paris: Unesco.
Kida, H. (1979). *Educational Research in Relation to Educational Reform in Asia and Oceania. UNESCO/APEID-NIER Seminar Report.* Tokyo: NIER.
Kogan, M., & Tuijnman, A. (Eds.) (1995). *Educational Research and Development Trends, Issues and Challenges.* Paris: OECD.
Phelan, T. J. Anderson, D. S., & Bourke, P. (2000). Educational research in Australia: A bibliographic analysis. In Australia, Department of Education, Training and Youth Affairs. *The Impact of Educational Research* (pp. 573–671). Canberra: The Department (DETYA).
Radford, W. C. (1967). *Research and Education: Improving Its Value to the Practice of Education.* Melbourne: ACER.

SECTION 2:

ACCESS AND EQUITY
Section Editor – Rupert Maclean

Education of Special Groups

10

Equality of Opportunity in Education

RUPERT MACLEAN
UNESCO-UNEVOC International Centre for Education, Bonn, Germany

1. DIMENSIONS OF EDUCATIONAL DISADVANTAGE

The notion that there should be equality of opportunity in education, where everyone has fair and equal access to a good quality education regardless of social background, race, gender or religion, and where people achieve success in education according to their efforts and ability, free of any form of discrimination, is enshrined in several International Conventions. Article 26 of the *Universal Declaration of Human Rights* (United Nations, 1948) proclaims that "everyone has the right to education", that "education shall be free, at least in the elementary or fundamental stages" and that "education shall be directed to the full development of the human personality ...".

With regard to promoting equality of opportunity in education, Article 1 in the *Convention against Discrimination in Education* (UNESCO, 1960) notes that the term discrimination includes any distinction, exclusion, limitation or preference which, being based on race, colour, sex, language, religion, political or other opinion, national or social origin, economic condition or birth, has the purpose or effect of nullifying or impairing equality of treatment in education and in particular: (a) of depriving any person or group of persons of access to education of any type or at any level; (b) of limiting any person or group of persons to education of an inferior standard; and (c) of inflicting on any person or group or persons conditions which are incompatible with the dignity of man. For the purposes of the Convention, the term 'education' refers to all types and levels of education, and includes access to education, the standard and quality of education, and the conditions under which it is given. In these Declarations and Conventions, equal opportunity in education is generally taken to mean that individuals have equality of opportunity "on the basis of individual capacity" (Article 28 of the *Convention on the Rights of the Child*, United Nations, 1989; Article 26 of the *Universal Declaration of Human Rights*; *World Education Report*, UNESCO, 2000.)

Despite such International Conventions, which seek to promote equal access and equity in education, in reality we live in a world where equality of opportunity in education does not currently exist on most occasions. Instead, many individuals throughout the world receive a second class education, or no education at all, not because they lack ability, are lazy or do not value education, but due to circumstances beyond their immediate control. In those developing countries where access is available, the education programs offered are often basic and of low quality, so that learners relapse back into illiteracy just a few years after completing their schooling. Nowhere is this more apparent than in the Asia-Pacific region, when it comes to the matter of access and equity, and equality of opportunity, in education and schooling. Despite efforts that have been made, particularly over the past 50 years, to promote and achieve equality of opportunity in education, there are still populations that are totally excluded from good quality and effective education and schooling.

The figures on education in the Asia-Pacific region speak for themselves. In 2000, there were 875 million illiterate adults (aged 15 years and over) in the world, and 649 million of these lived in the Asia-Pacific region. Of these, 62 per cent were women and girls. Currently there are 74 million out-of-school children in the school age population (6 to 11 year-olds) in Asia's developing countries. As a general rule, those living in cities have a better chance of receiving a good education than do those in remote rural or isolated parts of a country. Moreover, boys have a better chance of achieving an effective education than do girls; the rich have greater opportunities for a good education than do those living under conditions of poverty; and those who belong to the mainstream of a society have access to better educational opportunities than do ethnic, racial and religious minorities.

There are great variations between and within the different sub-regions in Asia. For example, the combined illiteracy rate for males and females in Southern Asia in 2000 was 44 per cent while for Eastern Asia and Oceania it was 14 per cent. Likewise, there are differences between illiteracy rates in Southern Asia for males (33%) compared to females (56%). However, there have been some substantial improvements over time: for instance, the estimated adult illiteracy rate in Asia in 2000 was 25 per cent, while 50 years earlier (1950) the rate was a massive 63 per cent.

The most comprehensive recent study of access and equity in education in the Asia-Pacific region is that by Lee (2002). In his excellent analysis of access and equity in education in developing countries in Asia, Lee (2002) identifies four main factors as being related to equity, these being: (a) gender-related equity; (b) income-related equity; (c) region-related equity; and (d) sociocultural-related equity. Lee demonstrates that those who receive the poorest education (or no education at all) are girls and women, those who live in poverty, those in slum areas in large cities or in remote or isolated parts of a country and ethnic or racial or religious minority groups.

The statistics referred to above about access and equity in education in the Asia-Pacific region do not tell the full story, for, as the UNESCO *World Education Report* (2000) graphically illustrates, the right to education has a qualitative as well as a quantitative aspect to it. As Article 26 of the *Universal Declaration of Human Rights* puts it, when referring to the qualitative aspects of education, "education shall be directed to the full development of the human personality and to add to the strengthening of respect for human rights and fundamental freedoms", and "it shall promote understanding, tolerance and friendship among the nations, racial or religious groups and shall further the activities of the United Nations for the maintenance of peace." In the Asia-Pacific region there is an increasing emphasis on the qualitative aspects of education: on education for peace, international understanding, human rights and democracy, and on values in education (UNESCO International Conference on Education, 1995), rather than just on the promotion of the skills of literacy and numeracy, that are, however, the prerequisite for all further learning.

There has also been an expanding vision over time of what educational opportunity actually means (World Education Report, 2000). As a result, the stress is no longer just on basic education, but on a larger vision that extends beyond that of meeting basic learning needs. Elementary education is no longer seen as complete in itself, and for the masses, while only a minority go onto higher levels of education such as secondary education and studies at the tertiary level. Instead the emphasis is on 'lifelong learning', 'lifelong education' and on 'career long occupational development', for all.

Most recent statistics (1997) show that of the 1,155 million people enrolled in formal education, 58 per cent were studying at the primary level, 34 per cent at the secondary level, and eight per cent at the tertiary level. This compares to the situation in 1950, when of the 252 million students, 82 per cent were studying at the primary level, 16 per cent at secondary, and three per cent at the tertiary level. Thus there has been a substantial expansion of learning opportunities beyond primary education, although the distribution of these opportunities varies considerably between developed and developing countries, and between different population groups, such as the poor compared to higher income groups, girls and women compared to boys and men, and between population groups in different geographical areas.

2. EXPLANATIONS OF EDUCATIONAL SUCCESS AND FAILURE

Worldwide, it has been widely accepted for several decades that, for example, individuals from different socio-economic backgrounds vary in their level of academic achievement at school; but the reasons advanced to explain this difference, and the ideological views about what should be done to rectify this situation, have varied over time. A debate continues to this day in countries in the Asia-Pacific region as to 'why do individuals and groups perform differently in education and schooling?' The answer to this question has far-reaching implications for educational policy and practice.

The prevailing view in many countries in the Asia-Pacific region appears to be that tenable arguments can be advanced to support the view that environmental factors are vitally important in affecting a child's educational achievement, although at the same time it is recognized that innate ability may be the most powerful single influence. Reasons can be advanced in support of this stance. Although there is no conclusive evidence to prove either point of view, few would deny that environment has some affect on educational performance, the disagreement being over how much. Even if it is accepted that environment only accounts for 20 per cent of educational performance and intellectual ability, it is not justified to presume that this is not a significant amount and large enough to affect considerably a person's educational performance. In addition, even if some psychological traits are inherited, this does not mean that they cannot be environmentally modified. Finally, if countries deny the importance of environmental factors the issue of equality of educational opportunity becomes virtually meaningless, a stance which is unacceptable in most democratic societies.

The Asia-Pacific region is one of enormous diversity, with countries at very different stages of economic, social and political development: for instance, the region contains some of the poorest countries (such as Bangladesh and Pakistan) and richest countries (such as Japan and Australia) on earth. The education systems of countries in the region are also at very different stages of development, with some nations struggling to achieve universal literacy and primary education for all, while in others most learners complete secondary education and even go onto tertiary studies. Perhaps as a result of this diversity, each of the views on reasons for differences in the educational careers of individuals and groups are reflected to differing degrees in the various countries in the region. In addition, it can be argued that countries that are struggling to achieve the universalisation of primary education simply do not have the funds to mount programs aimed at achieving positive discrimination in favour of disadvantaged population groups. This they regard as being a luxury they simply cannot afford.

3. RESEARCH ACCESS, EQUITY AND EQUALITY OF OPPORTUNITY

One of the problems faced by developing countries in the Asia-Pacific region is that there is currently insufficient educational research specifically generated within the developing countries in Asia, on a whole range of education-related topics. This is due to a range of factors such as funding constraints and resources available for research activities. Moreover, there is an insufficient number of researchers with the necessary skills and experience to conduct high quality and rigorous research studies. Also, in many of these countries, when research is conducted it is undertaken by government departments, which are likely to have a biased interest in the research outcomes, rather than by independent bodies such as universities. In some countries the stress is almost exclusively on quantitative research studies, which may be helpful in identifying cause and effect relationships, but more qualitative research may still be necessary to get behind the numbers in order to generate explanations for the existence of such correlations. Often there is also not a well developed educational research culture in many developing countries in the region.

As a result of these problems there remains an over reliance on educational research generated in developed countries, particularly in the United States and the United Kingdom, but also increasingly from Australia and New Zealand. An important limitation of this reliance on overseas research is that the findings from such research often do not travel well when interpreting the situation in developing countries in the Asia-Pacific region, or when framing effective educational policies and practices in these countries.

Worldwide, there is a vast research literature which examines similarities and differences in the educational careers of learners. Much of this research is within educational psychology, and as such is often concerned with identifying and explaining reasons for similarities and differences in the personal and psychological characteristics of learners, in an attempt to explain why some learners are more successful in education than are others. Other influential research studies, mainly within the sociology of education, tend to examine the socio-economic and background characteristics of learners to help explain differences in their level of educational performance and educational careers, according to social, cultural and economic factors.

4. FACTORS THAT INFLUENCE THE EDUCATIONAL CAREERS OF LEARNERS

There is an abundance of research conducted over the last 40 years which seeks to explain why there are differences in the educational careers of children and youth. The purpose here is to sketch out briefly, in broad brush strokes, the main research findings on factors that explain differences and similarities in the educational careers of learners. The aim is not to provide a formal literature review as such, since much of what is examined here is taken up in detail in the various articles, which follow in this *Handbook* in the section on Access and Equity, and in other articles in the *Handbook*.

4.1. Family and Community Environment

There is a great deal of research evidence from all regions of the world indicating the considerable importance of family and community environment on the educational careers of children, youth and adults; and much is also known about the ways in which these variables affect the learner's educational performance. In fact, in referring specifically to young learners, environmental factors within the child's family and neighbourhood are the most important influences on future academic success at school. It is also known that the effects of these early learning factors on educational success tend to increase as the child rises in the school, so the chances of the disadvantaged child failing or deciding to dropout of the system progressively increases with age. This is an important reason why the pre-school level, and the early years of schooling, have been focused upon by those concerned with implementing compensatory education policies.

The family, as the primary unit of society, is particularly important because it is the child's immediate environment for the first several years of life, when he or she is most impressionable and models much of his or her behaviour on that of parents and siblings. The attitudes of parents to the education of their children and to learning are particularly important. Neighbourhood and community environment have implications for the child's educational career, because they act to reinforce many home influences and values, as well as creating some of their own.

4.2. Economic Poverty

Those children who come from economically impoverished backgrounds, characterized by sub-standard housing, inadequate food and clothing, and where they have often to undertake paid employment outside school hours, do not generally perform as well at their studies as do those who come from environments where these features do not exist. Apart from the effects of such conditions on a child's health, overall development and rate of absenteeism from school, the home also tends to lack some important pro-educational facilities (such as books) known to be conducive to achieving success at school in developing countries. A significant number of children in the Asia-Pacific region probably underachieve at school because of the economic poverty of their parents. In addition to affecting school performance, poverty often means that the child is expected to leave school at the earliest possible time in order to contribute to the income and maintenance of the family.

4.3. Family Size and Structure: Parental Interaction

Children from small families tend, on average, to perform better on intelligence tests and at school than do those from larger families. One reason given by educational researchers is that the child in a larger family, where overcrowded conditions often prevail, tends to suffer from a poverty of experience. Because parents have less time to devote to each child in the family, the visual, mental and audio stimulation each is subjected to is said to be less than it normally would be in a small family, so development is frequently inhibited. This is said to occur particularly in the parent-child verbal interchange which in the large family tends to be more limited in quality and content. This often means that the child goes to school more poorly equipped to take part in its activities than does the child from a smaller family. Large families, overcrowded conditions and low economic status tend to go together.

4.4. Parental Attitudes to and Interest in Education

Parental attitudes toward education are extremely important in affecting the school success of children. Parents are important in conveying to the child a set of expectations and attitudes regarding the value of educational success, and so affect motivation to perform well at school and the desire not to leave school at the earliest possible opportunity. The available research evidence indicates that disadvantaged children tend to come from homes where parental attitudes to and interest in a child's education is low, and where they do not see education as important and so neglect to motivate their children to be successful at school. A child's scores on intelligence, arithmetic and reading are positively related to parental interest in their child's education. The degree of involvement of parents in the school their child attends also has an impact on the child's school performance. The view that the child has of the school and education affects his or her educational success. If the child has a positive view of the school rather than an antagonistic one, he or she is more likely to do well. The image of the school is acquired in the first instance from parents, from siblings, and from neighbourhood community peers. Child rearing methods adopted by different groups in the community can be important in affecting the attitudes of children to education, and their response to it when they attend school. It has been shown, for example, that the child rearing practices of some disadvantaged groups do not inculcate the idea of deferred gratification, as others do, so that the child lacks values which are conducive to success in the education system. Some parents tend to encourage passiveness on the part of the child in their response to school, encouraging their children to have a passive role at school by saying "when you go to school be quiet and do what the teacher says."

4.5. *Cultural and Value Orientations*

Some of these have already been dealt with earlier. When children attend school they take with them a set of attitudes and beliefs which have been internalized during the period of socialisation within the family and neighbourhood. For some children, these tend to correspond to those of the school, but for the disadvantaged child this generally is not the case. The values of the school tend to be different to those of the disadvantaged child. So some degree of culture shock and clash can occur when the child attends school. In some disadvantaged areas the residents may considerably undervalue education and may in fact be actively hostile to it, the child often developing a self-imposed barrier to educational achievement and social and economic mobility. This can result in pupils switching off school from an early age, and seeing it as alien.

4.6. *Language Patterns*

Some researchers argue that for learners from disadvantaged backgrounds there may be a clash in the language patterns used and valued by the school, and the language used in the home. This language clash does not occur for those from more privileged background. Of special importance is the disadvantage suffered by children for whom the language of instruction in the school is not the language of the home. This has an impact on educational careers and learning outcomes.

4.7. *Regional Differences*

There are often substantial regional differences in the age of school, the availability and quality of teachers, and the amount of money spent on learning materials such as library books and textbooks, and teaching and learning materials available to students. There are marked differences between urban and rural areas in many countries in the Asia-Pacific region.

5. STRATEGIES OF COMPENSATION

Various programs have been adopted in various countries in the Asia-Pacific region, to promote equality of opportunity and to discriminate positively in favour of the educationally disadvantaged through compensatory education programs. The main areas of policy and practice with regard to promoting equality of opportunity in education have been in the following areas.

5.1. *Pre-school Education*

Evidence indicates that this is the best time to change the pattern of a child's life. The aim is to reach children before they enter school and to bring about changes which would improve their educational performance and ability to take advantage of the educational opportunities available. The preschool teacher can be seen as having the job of compensating for the varying family and neighbourhood backgrounds of children which could adversely affect their educational careers.

5.2. *Home Visit Programs*

In view of persuasive evidence which indicates the importance of parental attitudes to education in affecting the educational careers of children, many researchers and policy makers believe that contact with the family on a regular basis should be established as early as possible in a child's life, and attempts made to increase its positive educative influences on factors such as the development of the child's language abilities and his or her image of the school. There is also a belief, with regard to home visit programs, that there is a need to move outside the traditional school setting if significant changes are to be achieved. In many projects parents have been found to be receptive to the home visiting contact, and success has been achieved in improving the educative attitudes of parents and the language skills of children.

5.3. *Improving Links Between Schools and their Social Setting*

Attempts have been made to break down the barriers existing between schools and the local community, for it is felt that a lack of adequate communication exists between parents and the school, and that this is one of the main reasons for parents' lack of support of educational programs within the home. The main outcome of communal commitment to the school is in the field of improving parental and public knowledge of its activities, in order that parents and others might be better placed to support the children's education. It is believed that for some, one of the main reasons for the lack of communication between school and home is that the norms and values of each may differ enormously, so attempts have been made to reduce these differences. In many places, it is felt that the school should become a Community School that is more open to the influences and values of the local community, and that the curriculum should meet the interests and needs of the local community more than has been the case in the past. As a theoretical goal the Community School is one which ventures out into and welcomes in the community until a visionary time arrives when it is difficult to distinguish school from community. The school should take account of the particular needs and interests of its local area, and not attempt to be uniform throughout the whole country. For example, in some places local community control of the school has been introduced with a joint Board being formed which is made up of professional educators and local parents, with power to select staff, determine curriculum, and allocate resources. The curriculum is framed to meet the needs of the local community and to handle community issues. In other places school buildings are used out-of-school hours, for local community activities such as adult education classes, local meetings and for entertainment related activities.

5.4. Improving the Quality of Teaching

As the Delors Report (1996) puts it, "good schools require good teachers." The stereotyped image of a middle class teacher working in a poor area is frequently one of someone who is either hostile and unsympathetic to the children being taught, but who, despite good intentions, is poorly equipped to handle problems arising in such schools. Partly as a result of such views, in many countries it is felt that something must be done specifically to train people to work in schools in disadvantaged areas. Attempts have been made to achieve greater staff stability by, for example, giving material incentives such as 'hardship allowances' or 'post adjustments' to help reduce the turnover of staff, improve morale and attract suitable people to work in these schools. In some countries a special effort is made to recruit teachers from disadvantaged areas, such as rural slums, and remote areas or communities where ethnic racial minority groups reside. These recruits are then encouraged to return to teach in these communities on completion of their teacher training.

6. CONCLUSION: THE WAY AHEAD

This article has argued that many of the causes of inequality of educational opportunity in countries in the Asia-Pacific region are directly traceable to the family and community environment of the disadvantaged learner, particularly to the parent and child relationship. It is only by enriching the relationship between the young child and his or her family and neighbourhood community that real success can be achieved. This raises the question of whether the state should have the right to try to alter this relationship, which for some people would be a more important issue than that of equality of opportunity itself.

Evidence from the various compensatory education programs that have been conducted demonstrates that the ability of an education system to compensate for disadvantaged environments, and to bring about changes that are not widely supported by other agencies in society, needs to be reexamined. Instead a holistic approach needs to be adopted which involves better education, health care, clean water, access to decent work, empowerment in the political sense, better housing and the like. In other words, it is clear from the available evidence that education on its own cannot compensate for deficiencies in the society in which the school is located.

It may be argued that so-called 'educational priority areas (EPAs)' should be seriously considered by educational policy makers, and that many communities would benefit if traditional schools were dispensed with and replaced by the concept of the 'community school'. It can be demonstrated that such schools can be more relevant to meeting the needs of the communities involved. The important question that has to be asked is 'knowledge and education for what?', which leads to the conclusion that children are often being taught knowledge which is not relevant to their particular values and needs, and which does not motivate them to remain in school. Although this is true, it is possible that the main problem with the community school is that it is not really preparing the child to compete in the wider society in which the child will live. It is not helping achieve the goal of equality of opportunity. Whether or not we wish it to be the case, the reality is that certain kinds of knowledge are currently the prerequisite for economic success in many industrializing and globalising countries in Asia-Pacific region, and unless an individual possesses this knowledge he or she is at a distinct disadvantage, and is likely to be marginalised.

There is a growing realization that educational reforms must be co-ordinated with social and economic reforms, and this needs to be considered in any moves to achieve equality of opportunity in education, and to provide effective compensatory education programs. If compensatory education programs are to be undertaken in a serious way, large allocations of funds are necessary. If this is looked at in terms of a purely economic cost-benefit approach, it is necessary to ask, "what financial return is society going to get for these resources?" This is the type of question which countries will want to answer before mounting expensive educational programs. It is hard to avoid the conclusion that those parts of the education service which impact most directly on increasing productivity will take priority over any proposals, however desirable, in the field of social welfare, which do not impact on the solving of existing economic problems.

The problem of compensating for the disadvantaged child seems to be an enormous one, and a problem which cannot be forcably tackled unless action is taken on a society-wide basis to achieve the aims envisaged. Compensatory education which is limited to that which occurs within the school system does not work. There must be a systems approach to the problem with action also being taken in areas other than education, and by trying to overcome some of the other problems which are part of the disadvantaged child's environment.

Education cannot achieve the reform of society on its own, since as has been said before, "education cannot compensate for society".

7. ARTICLES IN THIS SECTION

The articles in this section of the *Handbook* all examine key aspects of access and equity to education and schooling, with particular reference to the matter of equality of educational opportunity and action being taken by countries throughout the region to promote justice and equity in education. As the articles commissioned here graphically demonstrate, more needs to be done to address various aspects of the learning needs and the education of special groups. It is clear from the evidence presented (see *Case Study of Learning Achievement in South Asia*) that for many countries in South Asia, increasing access to education has not been accompanied by an improvement in the level of learning achievement, but, instead, as access has been improved, there has also been a drop in the quality of education provided and in learning outcomes. Particularly disadvantaged groups in the East and South Asia sub-regions are those children living in remote and rural areas, and special programs are needed to provide effectively for the education of these children (see *Education of Children in Remote Areas*). In addition, school drop-out rates continue to be high and so innovative ways need to be found to attract and keep learners engaged in the educational process (see *Drop-outs from School and How to Cope with this Problem*). Youth in urban areas face special problems due to increasing feelings of alienation in their lives, and difficulties regarding what they perceive to be the lack of relevance of much of what is taught in schools (see *Issues for Urban Youth in Asia and the Pacific.*)

Special challenges exist concerning how to provide an education which is relevant for those living in a particular society who have different ethnic, racial and cultural backgrounds to those who form the mainstream of the society concerned, and who may be from minority population groups. And how at the same time to strike a balance between providing an education which respects and celebrates such cultural diversity, while at the same time achieving important areas of agreement to promote social cohesion and harmony in the country concerned (see *Ethnicities, Minorities and Indigenous Groups in Central Asia*). There are also some interesting approaches being adopted to provide a relevant education for students with various forms of disability (see *Inclusive Education for Students with Special Needs*) but also for those with special talents (see *Education of Gifted and Talented Learners*).

A key set of issues which affect access and equity in education concerns gender issues in education since there are considerable differences between the educational careers of males and females in terms of the process of education and the outcomes achieved (see *Sex and Gender Differences in Educational Outcomes*). There is also often a lack of fairness, justice, equity and consistency in the ways in which boys and girls are treated in schools and classrooms (see *Gender-Sensitive Education for Bridging the Gender Gap*) and in their access to education and well paid, suitable employment, particularly in South Asian countries (see *Gender Differences in Access to Education and Employment*.)

An important trend throughout the Asia-Pacific region is that of lifelong learning. For those who have missed out on educational opportunities early in life, there is also a second or third chance to receive an education, as part of the increasingly widespread policy of universal literacy (see *Adult Literacy in the Asia-Pacific Region*). Learners also have the opportunity to return to and continue their studies at various stages in their lives (see *Learning Across the Adult Lifespan*). The move for lifelong learning includes the notion of career long development in the workplace (see *Workforce Education*) and that of utilizing informal and nonformal, as well as the more traditional formal education modalities (see *Nonformal Education*).

REFERENCES

Delors Report (1996). *Learning: The Treasure Within*. Report of the International Commission on Education for the Twenty-first Century. Paris: UNESCO.

Lee, W. O. (2002). *Equity and Access in Education: Themes, Tensions and Policies*. Education in Developing Asia, Volume 4. Manila: Asian Development Bank, and Comparative Education Research Centre, The University of Hong Kong.

UNESCO (1960). *Convention against Discrimination in Education*. Adopted by the General Conference at its Eleventh Session, 14 December, Paris: UNESCO.

UNESCO (1995). Final Report. *Declaration on Education for Peace, Human Rights and Democracy*. International Conference on Education, Final Report, Geneva: UNESCO/IBE.

UNESCO (2000). *The Right to Education: Towards Education for All Throughout Life*. World Education Report. Paris: UNESCO.

United Nations (1948). *Universal Declaration of Human Rights*. Adopted and Proclaimed by the General Assembly of the United Nations on the Tenth Day of December 1948. Final Authorized Text. New York: United Nations.

United Nations (1989). *Convention on the Rights of the Child* New York: United Nations (A/RES/44/25).

11

A Case Study of Learning Achievement in South Asia

RUPERT MACLEAN
UNESCO – UNEVOC International Centre for Education, Bonn, Germany

KEN VINE
University of New England, Armidale, Australia

1. INTRODUCTION

In this article the area of learning achievement in the primary cycle is examined, where the discussion is expansive and research findings are presented in greater detail than was the case in an earlier article in this *Handbook* (see *Achieving Education for All in the Asia-Pacific Region*). This emphasis upon learning achievement is presented on the grounds that by far the most concerning outcome of education for all and EFA 2000 Assessment in the Asia-Pacific region was the emerging evidence that in South Asia (UNESCO, 2000), with the exception of The Maldives, the often impressive gains in primary access and participation rates were accompanied by alarmingly low levels of learning achievement.

2. THE SOUTH ASIAN SITUATION

It is not clear that national governments in South Asia fully appreciate that their gains over the last decade in access and participation rest on insecure foundations, and that unless evident and rapid improvements are made in the quality and relevance of primary education, enrolment levels will drop as families become increasingly less willing to shoulder the opportunity costs of having their children attend school. For this reason, some of the evidence concerning learning achievement in a few selected South Asia states is presented in this article. It should here be noted that a comprehensive survey of the evidence concerning learning achievement in the Asia-Pacific region is well beyond the scope of this article. The intention is only to present some of the more important issues, and a sample of the related evidence.

Primary school examination processes in all South Asian countries produce results expressed in terms of pass percentages. As a consequence, educators cannot easily translate examination results into statements about what children can be said to know and what they can and cannot do in relation to curriculum objectives. Moreover, they cannot make accurate assessments concerning maintenance of standards from year to year, and when the examinations are set by provincial or district examination boards, they cannot make accurate comparisons within a particular year from province to province or between years.

Moreover, there are examination paper construction problems that limit the usefulness of the process from an educator's, as compared with an administrator's, perspective. Consequently, scrutiny of past papers usually reveals a predictability of questions and an emphasis on the reproduction of facts and algorithmic knowledge. In the mathematics papers, for instance, there is often a more thorough testing of a students' skill in doing long multiplication than probing their understanding of the concept of multiplication and the applicability of the concept in problem solving. It may be argued that these limitations of the examination process should not be seen as important as is using the results as a gate-keeping mechanism for the selection of who is promoted to lower secondary schooling. Undoubtedly, that administrative perspective is important but so, too, is the educator's need to assess the quality of learning achievement in the nation's schools.

Another common problem with the end of primary cycle examinations in nearly all countries in the Asia-Pacific region is that the weighting, implicit in the question scoring procedures, yields essentially ordinal scores that are treated as though they were interval scores for purposes of computing total marks for each candidate. For example, a particular mathematics question might be said to be worth six marks if answered correctly, while the correct answer for another question might yield only three marks. These judgments of relative question difficulty are not derived from empirical testing; usually they represent the views of expert panels of teachers and curriculum developers. Consequently, there is no way of knowing whether the difference in achievement between a child who scores 45 per cent on a test and one who achieves 50 per cent on the same test is the same as the difference between the latter child and another who scores 55 per cent. All that can be done with confidence is to place these three children in a rank order of achievement. When the pass mark is determined by the number of places available in the following school year in the first grade of lower secondary schooling, this method of scoring lacks the level of accuracy and precision that is necessary for making such decisions.

For these, and other reasons, there is a tendency in South Asia for the end of cycle primary examination to become the *de facto* curriculum, and for the standard textbook to become the focus of all instruction, thus shaping teaching and learning practices in the classroom. Educators require examinations and national testing programs that allow for cross-sectional and longitudinal analyses of examination data, both of which are needed to make developmental assessments of student progression through the curriculum, and to assess movement in standards from year to year. They also need data that will allow them to make so-called 'value added judgements' concerning the effects of schooling within and between school districts that are meaningful and consistent. Perhaps most importantly, they need examination and national testing systems that link classroom practice, curriculum development, teacher training and retraining, and assessment in an evolutionary dynamic that will ultimately benefit children (Irvine, 2000).

3. EVIDENCE FROM COUNTRIES IN SOUTH ASIA

These deficiencies have been known and discussed for some time, particularly in academic journals and at international conferences, and, in some measure, motivated the sample based studies that UNESCO and UNICEF carried out in many developing countries during the 1990s. Evidence from these and other studies assumed prominence in the context of EFA 2000 Assessment as, almost without exception, they produced results that indicated low levels of attainment of national curriculum objectives. A brief summary of the findings of a few of these and other similar studies follows.

3.1. *India*

Yadav, Bhardwaj, Sedwal and Gaur (2000) carried out an extensive review of learning achievement studies conducted over the period 1989 to 1999, which were directed at measuring performance on a range of subjects by Grade 4 and Grade 5 students. The studies reviewed included the following investigations.

- A baseline achievement study of Grade 4 students by the National Council for Education Research and Training (NCERT) in 1989 in 22 states and the union territory of Delhi.
- A learning achievement study of 5381 Grade 4 and Grade 5 students in eight districts in four states in 1997 under the auspices of Action Aid.
- A baseline assessment study of Grades 1 and 2 and Grades 4 and 5 students in 42 districts and seven states in Mathematics and Language carried out by NCERT in 1994.
- A baseline assessment study of Grades 1 and 2 and Grades 4 and 5 students in 60 districts and 11 states in Mathematics and Language carried out by NCERT in 1997.
- A baseline assessment study of Grade 4 and 5 students in ten districts of Rajasthan in Mathematics and Language carried out by the Rajasthan State Institute of Education Research and Training in 1997.

The 1989, NCERT baseline study tested 65,842 children and covered basic language skills and arithmetic. The national mean score on the combined test was 45.2 per cent, with a range extending from 32 per cent in Karnataka to 69 per cent in Bihar. The 1997 Action Aid study tested 3719 Grade 4 and 1662 Grade 5 children and covered Language, Mathematics and Environmental Science. The mean scores ranged from 47 per cent (Grade 4 Mathematics) to 63 per cent (Grade 5 Language). The 1994 NCERT baseline study also produced similar findings for Grades 4 and 5 children. The mean scores for Language ranged from 24 per cent in Karnataka to 47 per cent in Tamil Nadu, while those for Mathematics extended from 28 per cent in Assam to 49 per cent in Karnataka. The larger scale 1997 NCERT baseline study yielded findings with an even wider range of achievement levels for Grades 4 and 5 children. The mean scores for Language ranged from 16 per cent in Madhya Pradesh to 74 per cent in Kerala, and those for Mathematics from 28 per cent in Andhra Pradesh to 60 per cent in Kerala. The 1997 Rajasthan study reported a mean score for Grade 5 children on Hindi of 42 per cent (standard deviation = 20), and on Mathematics of 19 per cent (standard deviation = 17).

Because these studies used different instruments, analytical processes and administrative procedures it is difficult to make direct comparisons between them. Moreover, it has not been possible to acquire the raw data to re-analyse students' responses using a common metric. However, they were all designed for the same purpose of assessing student performance in terms of movement through a set of specified curriculum objectives and, hence, they offer informed guidance on the quality of learning in the nation's primary schools. In that regard, it is noteworthy that, in general, the findings across these studies are similar in that they sometimes portray, on average, disturbingly low levels of learning. This is especially the case in Mathematics. The findings also show wide variation across states and the union territory of Delhi. It is understood that there are equally wide variations in mean levels of performance between districts within states, and there is wide gulf in learning achievement between urban and rural areas.

There are other studies summarized in a World Bank (1997) *Development in Practice* publication that show a similar pattern of low levels of achievement and wide inter- and intra- state variation. The World Bank summarized the situation as follows:

> Children who reach the final year of lower primary school (Grade 4 in some states and Grade 5 in others) often have mastered less than half the curriculum taught the year before. (World Bank, 1997, p. 84)

Perhaps the most disturbing finding was that reported by Govinda and Varghese (1993). They found that in a rural zone of Madhya Pradesh no Grade 4 or Grade 5 students had mastered the Grade 2 competencies.

In considering the significance of these findings it should be remembered that the Net Enrolment Ratio for India is about 75 per cent and that fewer than 50 per cent of the children who start primary school in India complete Grade 5. Even if it is assumed that 50 per cent, a most optimistic assumption, of the children who do complete primary school in India have attained only 50 per cent of the competencies expected of them in Language and Mathematics, it follows that most children will have achieved a barely sustainable level of literacy and numeracy. Having regard for the demonstrated links between education and economic development, and especially between levels of adult female literacy and fertility rates, this situation has grave consequences for India.

3.2. Nepal

Nepal recognized many of the difficulties inherent in using end-of-primary-cycle examinations for making a summative assessment of learning achievement, and as part of the Basic Primary Education Project (BPEP) instituted two large scale surveys of learning achievement in primary schools (Khaniya, 1999). The first was conducted in 1997 and tested Grade 3 children in Nepali, Mathematics and Social Science. The second was carried out in 1999 and tested Grade 5 students on the same three subjects. Stratified, proportional, random sampling procedures were used in both surveys in an attempt to derive a representative sample that would allow for the comparison of results on regional and zonal bases. Additionally, the questions used in the surveys were developed by expert teachers and curriculum developers and were directly related to curriculum learning objectives. They were pilot tested and were found to have good psychometric properties, such as high reliability and discrimination indices.

The results of the surveys are given in Table 1.

The results of both surveys caused considerable concern as not only were the mean scores in all three subjects lower than would reasonably have been expected, but the large standard deviations also indicated a wide spread of scores. Of particular concern were the very low scores for Mathematics, especially those achieved by Grade 5 students in 1999; a mean of 27.3 and SD of 17.1 suggests a heavily skewed distribution. Both surveys also compiled distributions of mean scores by administrative region and ecological zone. Although there were regional and zonal differences they were of lesser concern than the low levels of national performance.

The test instruments used in 1997 and 1999 employed a weighting system for scoring students' responses that reflected expert judgment of relative test difficulty. In order to test the effect of the weightings used in the 1999 Mathematics paper, student responses were re-analysed to derive weightings of question difficulty on an empirical basis. For this purpose, the partial credit form of the Rasch model (Masters, 1982), as implemented in the QUEST software package (Australian Council for Educational Research, 1996), was employed. The Rasch

Table 1. Nepal 1997 and 1999 Learning Achievement Studies Findings (per cent scores recorded)

Year	Grade	Sample Size	Mathematics Mean	Mathematics Standard Deviation	Nepali Mean	Nepali Standard Deviation	Social Sciences Mean	Social Sciences Standard Deviation
1997	3	3472	43.8	21.6	45.7	15.9	50.4	16.1
1999	5	3510	27.3	17.1	51.5	15.9	41.8	15.2

model estimates question difficulty and student ability on the same underlying interval scale using a metric expressed in logits.

The Rasch analysis confirmed the psychometric properties of the 1999 Mathematics test. The values of the parameters that measured the construct validity, reliability, consistency, and discrimination characteristics of the test far exceeded the threshold levels considered necessary for a well-constructed test. However, the estimates of student ability and question difficulty produced by the Rasch analysis suggested that overall student performance was even more worrying than that reported in the 1999 survey report. Figure 1 illustrates the distribution of question difficulty, with question numbers plotted on the x-axis and question difficulty on the y-axis.

It is noted that the scale of measurement is calibrated so that all but six of the questions have difficulty levels greater than 0.0 logits and that the gradient of question difficulty is steady for all except the six most difficult questions. Remembering that question difficulty and student ability are estimated on the same logit scale, these characteristics of the calibrated scale and the question difficulty gradient should be borne in mind when considering the frequency distribution of the estimates of student performance given in Figure 2.

It is noted from considering Figures 1 and 2 together that the majority of students have performance estimates that are less than 0.0 logits; that is they have performance levels such that they can be expected to succeed on only six of the 32 questions on the test. This implies that nearly all students found most of the questions far too difficult, and that the mean Mathematics scores reported in the survey findings over-estimate the performance of Grade 5 students.

It must be remembered that the Grade 5 test was soundly based on curriculum

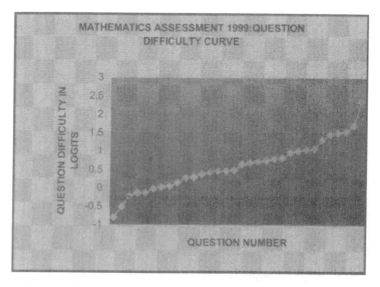

Figure 1. Question Difficulty Gradient for 1999 Mathematics Test.

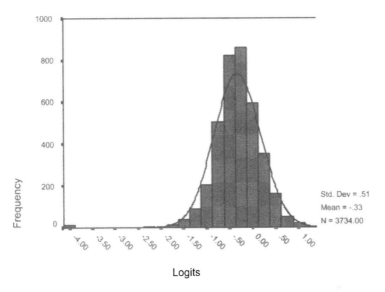

Figure 2. Frequency Distribution of Estimates of Student Performance Derived from 1999 Mathematics Test.

objectives and that it had excellent psychometric properties. Consequently, it must be concluded that very few Grade 5 children, on this analysis fewer than 10 per cent, achieved the competencies expected of them in Mathematics. Given that more than 75 per cent of primary school graduates go on to lower secondary schooling in Nepal this implies that the very large majority of those children are ill prepared by their primary school experience to cope with lower secondary school mathematics. The further implication is that lower secondary teachers are faced with a need to redress rapidly those shortcomings, or decide to teach to a lower curriculum standard. Given the onerous demands placed on lower secondary school teachers in Nepal the more likely response is the latter, and the effects of that decision may be propagated throughout the whole of secondary schooling thereby reducing the academic quality of secondary school graduates.

3.3. Pakistan

The Pakistan education authorities also recognized the limitations of end-of-primary-cycle examinations from the standpoint of gaining an understanding of national levels of performance. Consequently, in the context of EFA 2000 Assessment UNESCO-Islamabad and UNICEF-Islamabad, in collaboration with the Pakistan Academy of Education Planning and Management (AEPM), carried out in 1999 a nation-wide sample study of learning achievement in primary school mathematics. The sample was drawn to be representative of government primary schools. In all, 2783 children were tested, 1406 boys and 1377 girls.

The test items were constructed by specialists in the primary mathematics curriculum in Pakistan and were closely related to curriculum objectives. A total of 35 items was used, including problem solving exercises. Standard procedures for assessing construct validity and test-retest reliability were employed and pupils' responses were analysed using two methods. The first was to mark responses as being correct or incorrect without taking explicit account of the difficulty of each question. The second method used the Rasch model to estimate question difficulty and student performance. On the basis of the first method the mean scores and standard deviations were found and are presented in Table 2. The maximum score was 35.

On this basis, it may be said that the students displayed a reasonable level of performance and that there was no difference between boys and girls. However, the Rasch analysis, which took account of empirically derived weights of question difficulty, yielded a different set of findings. Figure 3 illustrates the question difficulty gradient.

The question difficulty gradient shown in Figure 3 reflects a generally even gradient except at either end of the range. Importantly, there are an approximately equal number of questions on both sides of 0.0 logits since the calibration procedure in this case sets the average difficulty level of the items to be zero. This should be compared with the student ability gradient shown in Figure 4.

A comparison of the question difficulty and student performance gradients reveals that although approximately 50 per cent (54%) of the questions had difficulty levels greater than 0.0, only 29 per cent of students had performance

Table 2. Mean Scores on Pakistan Primary Mathematics Test

Group	Number	Mean	Standard Deviation
Boys	1406	20.62	8.04
Girls	1377	20.04	8.53

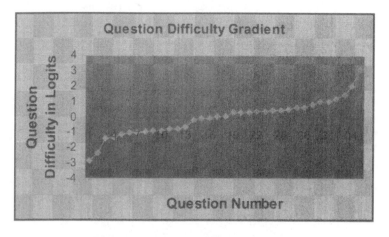

Figure 3. Question Difficulty Gradient.

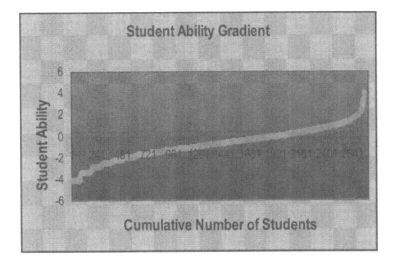

Figure 4. Student Ability Gradient.

levels exceeding 0.0. In other words, the test was far too difficult for the majority of students. An indication of the level of achievement of the lower half, in terms of estimated performance of the students can be gauged from the information recorded in Table 3.

The questions listed in Table 3 are all drawn from the curriculum and it is reasonable to expect that they would be within the capacity of Grade 5 children. It is noteworthy that the questions that were most difficult were word problems that required the children to understand first the problem before applying the

Table 3. Response Frequencies for Selected Questions

	Question Type	Correct	Incorrect	No Attempt
9	Write odd numbers between 2 and 9	1431	964	387
31	Fraction diagram	1203	726	853
16	Write seven thousand two hundred and forty in figures	1414	1047	321
33	Read numbers off a graph	1175	741	866
29	Division by powers of ten	1303	1009	470
27	Subtraction word problem	1308	1071	403
18	How many metres in a kilometre	1236	1181	365
26	Adding fractions with the same denominator	1182	1304	296
25	Multiplication of fractions	1172	1333	277
32	Which shape is a square	939	1015	828
35	Transitivity of addition of fractions	908	1284	590
23	Multiplication (4*3) word problem	754	1797	231
10	Place value – multiplication	397	2018	367

correct arithmetical procedure. A close study of the response patterns indicates that many of the children who were unable to handle such questions could cope with other questions that tested directly their capacity to carry out correctly the arithmetical procedure. It is not clear from the data, however, whether the children's difficulty was more one of decoding the language or being able to select the appropriate arithmetical procedure.

It should also be mentioned that there were substantial differences between provinces in mean levels of performance. The best performing provinces were the Punjab and Sindh, the two most populous provinces. Interestingly, in these two provinces the girls' mean level of performance was significantly higher than the boys', though the reverse was the case in the other provinces.

As is the case with India, when considering these findings it should be borne in mind that the national net enrolment rate for primary school in Pakistan is only about 70 per cent, and that fewer than 50 per cent of the children who commence primary school complete the five year cycle. Consequently, these findings, which relate to children enrolled in Grade 5, are of grave concern as they indicate that the current low levels of adult literacy and numeracy in Pakistan will persist for another generation of citizens, unless massive programs to redress the situation are introduced in the very near future.

3.4. *Summary*

The burden of the evidence from the learning achievement studies that have been conducted over recent years is that in sub-continental South Asia it is most probable that fewer than 50 per cent of the children who complete the last grade in the primary cycle have acquired 50 per cent or more of the competencies expected of them in Language and Mathematics. The magnitude of this problem is further compounded by the fact that in some South Asian primary school systems fewer than 50 per cent of the children who start Grade 1 complete all years of the primary cycle.

There are many factors that contribute to this outcome. The factors explored in the publication *Development in Practice* (World Bank, 1997) certainly apply to other countries in the sub-continent, though the relative contribution of each factor may change. The factors include level of national investment in primary education, household spending on schooling, physical school quality, instructional materials, teacher quality, teaching practices, school policy and management, school and class context, and levels of attendance. The World Bank has argued that, even if approached only from the standpoint of economic efficiency, the need to improve the primary education system in India is a national imperative. Its modelling indicates that the cost of the following list of improvements would be 10,300 million rupees in 2000; rehabilitation of classrooms, provision of water and toilets, classroom instructional materials, school instructional materials, and in-service teacher training. This is the set of quality improvements specified under the Indian Government's District Primary Education Programme (DPEP), which is the main means by which the government proposes to universalize primary education and improve the quality of learning.

The level of investment advocated by the World Bank is substantial but it should be viewed in the context of the magnitude of the educational wastage of the present system in which fewer than 50 per cent of the children who enrol in Grade 1 actually complete Grade 5. Based on the estimates of grade-wise survival given in the Government of India's Ministry of Human Resource Development's *EFA 2000 Assessment* report, the number of students in the 1990–91 cohort who dropped out at Grades 2 to 4 during 1992, 1993 and 1994 total 39.2 million. Using the National Institute of Educational Planning and Administration's 1991 expenditure estimate of approximately 400 rupees per year per primary enrollee, this amounts to 15,700 million rupees, annually, in 1991 prices. In other words, if it is assumed that investment in primary education is not fully realised unless the child completes the primary cycle and that investment in each non-completer constitutes so-called 'wastage', then the magnitude of that educational wastage in India is approximately 15,700 million rupees annually. This estimate does not include investments and opportunity costs of primary schooling borne by families and households. It should be emphasized that the cost of the improvements advocated by the World Bank approximates only 65 per cent of the annual wastage inherent in a system that fails to retain at least 50 per cent of the Grade 1 cohort for five years.

Although this kind of investment would exert a positive influence on student demand and retention, with the exception of teacher training, the proposed improvements would affect only indirectly the quality of pedagogy, the efficacy of classroom practice, and ultimately the quality of learning. Strategies are needed which directly address the quality of learning problem and which build upon investments made in other areas so as to increase demand for schooling and retain those who enter at Grade 1 until completion of the primary cycle.

The above comments concerning wastage in the primary system in India and the costs of various improvements apply with equal force to all South Asian systems. The policy tension may be seen as either expanding an inefficient system, thus increasing aggregate levels of wastage, or investing in measures designed to increase quality and, hence, improve student demand and retention. Of course, this is a false dichotomy because quality of education and aggregate demand are, in a Hegelian sense, linked dialectically. Indeed, it may well be the case that unless the quality of primary education is improved families will question the value of sending their children to school and this will reduce enrolment and retention levels.

4. SOME ISSUES REGARDING EFA EVALUATION AND ASSESSMENT

When it comes to governments devising and implementing policies and strategies to achieve EFA, countries vary considerably with regard to the extent to which they are guided by the best research findings available to them. The bridge between educational research, policy and practice is often weak, for reasons that have been examined in detail elsewhere in this *Handbook* (see *The Impact of Educational Research on Decision Making and Practice*). In essence, it appears that policy makers often have difficulty in digesting much of the educational research available, and in framing policies that take account of such research. In addition, educational decision making is often driven by a political agenda that ignores empirical evidence drawn from high quality, policy relevant research.

In the developing countries, there is often a paucity of educational research and researchers examining local issues, within the local context. The bulk of educational research is conducted in Western countries and reflects concerns that may have little relevance to the circumstances in which educational services are provided in the developing world. Moreover, acute financial pressures on national education budgets often result in monitoring and evaluation and applied research being considered as luxuries, which few can afford, rather than as being essential for informing policy and guiding educational planning.

In the case of EFA, the research findings that are available in many of the developing countries are almost always quantitative in nature. They are necessary and useful to answer so-called 'what type' questions, such as "what percentage of the primary cohort is enrolled in school?" However, such data rarely provide answers to so-called 'why type' questions, such as "why do so many students have difficulty applying their arithmetical knowledge in novel problem solving situations?" Answers to questions of this kind tend to require qualitative research methodologies, which are rarely employed in most countries in the Asia-Pacific region. Indeed, educational phenomena tend to be conceptually complex and usually require the application of both quantitative and qualitative methods if a comprehensive understanding is sought.

There is, therefore, a pressing need for more qualitative research involving techniques such as participant and non-participant observation of classroom processes, individual and group interviews, and dynamic assessment of cognitive development. Moreover, researchers interested in developing even proximate models of causality must be encouraged to look outside the school to the family and local community, especially if an objective of the research is to offer strategies for intervention.

The characteristics of qualitative research also mitigate against its adoption by researchers in developing countries in Asia-Pacific where resources are scarce and the range of potential research questions is enormous. Qualitative research is nearly always labour intensive, usually employs small sample sizes, and frequently collects large amounts of textual or observational data which are not susceptible to quick analysis using computer-based techniques. In addition, and in contrast to quantitative research studies, qualitative research studies can regarded as being 'data heavy but sample light', and consequently do not provide findings that can be generalized to large populations. In such studies generalization depends upon many replication studies and the gradual accretion of evidence. These are not characteristics that are appealing to politicians or policy makers seeking quick answers to complex problems.

A further difficulty that emerged during EFA 2000 Assessment is that there are insufficient, highly trained, educational researchers, whether of a quantitative or qualitative persuasion, in developing countries in the Asia-Pacific region to carry out the research that is clearly needed to inform decision making at the national level. Indeed, it was also evident that there were insufficient qualified education planners and statisticians to undertake these national assessments. This deficiency was most clearly demonstrated in the absence in country reports of any systematic attempt to simulate, or model, the growth of national education systems over the next decade so as to assess the resource implications of achieving their new EFA goals.

In order to improve teacher effectiveness, there is also a need to promote the notion of 'teacher as reflexive practitioner and researcher' to help improve the performance levels of pupils. National policies may change, new curricula may be developed and innovative forms of assessment may be promulgated, but unless teaching and learning practices in the classroom change there will be little effect on learning outcomes. For this to happen, it is not sufficient simply to expose teachers to new forms of classroom practice through in-service training schemes. It is necessary to encourage teachers to see themselves and their role differently, and persuade them to adopt the kind of perspective that underpins action research.

Because of the sheer size of the task, the gathering of educational statistics on EFA requires the efforts of national governments. In countries that are very poor, the gathering of such statistics is regarded as being a luxury, which they feel they can ill afford. Even national censuses in those countries are conducted infrequently and are notoriously unreliable. Furthermore, sometimes governments may not want to publicize or reveal the true situation regarding their education systems, particularly, for example, when they have not made as much progress in achieving EFA as they had publicly committed to at the Jomtien Conference in 1990. It, therefore, can become a matter of national pride not to reveal the true situation.

Once the statistics are collected for a particular country, if they are unfavourable it is often difficult to get a high ranking government official to sign them as correct, since the person involved does not want to take this responsibility and perhaps be held accountable for the adverse publicity that the interpretation of such statistics brings to the country in question. Thus, unfavourable statistics may remain indefinitely in the in-tray of the official who has the authority to sign, but who is unwilling to do so. Moreover, in some countries all educational researchers are in the employ, directly or indirectly, of the government. It is therefore difficult to obtain an independent viewpoint when it comes to the collection and interpretation of research findings, since the researchers in question may be concerned not to present statistics or research findings which may displease their political masters and which, therefore, may have an adverse impact on their careers.

The figures collected for a whole country are often processed in a manner that enables statements to be made about the national situation, but not about regional differences (Irvine, 2000). This is partly for convenience, because it requires less time and may reduce the complexity of analysis; but it is often also done for political reasons since politicians may not want to reveal regional differences, especially if these are likely to show that the situation is better in urban areas than in remote rural areas, and for the mainstream population rather than for ethnic, racial or religious minorities.

Some key dimensions for analysis are often not included in government statistics. For example, the analysis of data according to socio-economic status, gender, geographical location, ethnic and racial background or religion could draw unwelcome attention to such differences. For example, when during the EFA 2000 Assessment countries were asked to present information on education performance according to gender differences, at least one country declined to do so this because they said that gender was not a problem in their country. However, as the international researchers pointed out at the time, how does a country know that this is not a problem unless there are statistics to demonstrate it?

Countries may also be concerned that their progress in achieving EFA is going to be measured against their promises and prior commitments, and that they will be found to be wanting in certain areas. They may be reluctant to reveal the true situation if progress has been slow, and if they feel that they are going to be compared unfavourably with other countries. Because of these problems, one of the outcomes of the EFA 2000 Assessment was a recommendation to help countries improve their systems of monitoring and evaluation, so that future assessment exercises can cope with the types of problems identified earlier. This is being achieved in the following ways.

- Financial assistance is being obtained with regard to the gathering of research findings.
- Training of researchers is being carried out in both quantitative and qualitative methods.
- Technical assistance is being provided with regard to research design, analysis, interpretation and report writing.
- Assurance is being given to government officials that the research on EFA monitoring is intended to assist countries in monitoring progress, and to devise future strategies, and not to make comparisons between counties. As was the case with the End of Decade 2000 Assessment EFA Monitoring and Evaluation meetings the point is stressed that the emphasis is not on comparing countries, and no so-called 'league table of EFA results' is constructed.

5. CONCLUSION

This article examines in some detail one aspect of the Education for All 2000 Assessment, with a considerable amount of material on learning achievement being presented, including empirical data drawn from various studies. The vexed issue of learning achievement has been given special attention here because in the Asia-Pacific region this is the most pressing matter confronting educational policy makers. The gains made in access and participation are quickly lost unless the current situation is redressed. Moreover, not fixing this problem will have dire economic consequences for the countries, communities and individuals concerned.

REFERENCES

Australian Council for Educational Research (1996). *QUEST – The Interactive Test Analysis System*. Melbourne: ACER.

Govinda, R., & Varghese N. V. (1993). *Quality of Primary Schooling in India – A Case Study in Madhya Pradesh*. Paris: International Institute for Educational Planning, and New Delhi: National Institute of Educational Planning and Administration.

Irvine, J. (2000). South Asia and basic education: Changing UNICEF's strategic perspectives on educational development and partnerships. *Prospects, 30*(3), 297–311.

Khaniya, T. (1999). *National Assessment of Grade 5 Students*. Kathmandu: Academy for Educational Development.

Masters, G. N. (1982). A Rasch model for partial credit scoring. *Psychometrika, 47*, 149–74.

UNESCO (2000). *A Synthesis Report of Education for All 2000 Assessment in the South and West Asia Sub-Region*. Bangkok: UNESCO Principal Regional Office for Asia and the Pacific.

UNESCO (2001). *Statistical Reports and Studies*. Paris: UNESCO

World Bank (1997), *Development in Practice*. Washington: The World Bank.

Yadav, M. S., Bhardwaj, M., Sedwal, M., & Gaur, G. (2000). *Learner Achievement in Primary Schools*. New Delhi: National Institute of Educational Planning and Administration.

12

Education of Children in Remote Areas*

TIEDAO ZHANG

Beijing Academy of Educational Sciences, P.R. China

1. INTRODUCTION

It is an internationally observed phenomenon in education provision that rapid quantitative expansion is often out of step with quality. How to maintain a balance between more opportunities and better quality has been a critical dilemma for educational policy-makers. Almost 50 years ago the General Assembly of the United Nations adopted the Universal Declaration of Human Rights proclaiming that: "Everyone has the right to education. Education should be free, at least in the elementary and fundamental stages. Elementary education shall be compulsory" (United Nations, 1956). In spite of the most praiseworthy efforts, for many children in today's world, especially those in developing countries, this minimum right still remains a distant dream. According to UNESCO's *World Education Report* (1995b), there are 75 million school-aged children in Asia and Oceania who have no access to education. Over half of the total of 884.7 million adult illiterates in the world live in China and India, namely, 166.2 and 290.7 million respectively. As the most populous continent, Asia has been and will remain the major battlefield for the international campaign toward a more literate World.

International experience also informs us that maintaining an effective education system, both quantitatively and qualitatively, depends very much upon the extent to which curricula are responsive to actual development needs of the targeted population. This article is therefore focused on how the learning programs at the primary level could be more effectively oriented to meet the basic learning needs of rural children in Asian developing countries. For this purpose,

---

* This study was made possible with the sponsorship of the Graduate School for International Development and Co-operation (IDEC), Hiroshima University. The author wishes to acknowledge his personal gratitude to Gansu Institute for Educational Research (GIER) for their institutional support. This study also benefited from the stimulating insights and devoted personal help from many scholars, in particular, Shuichi Nakayama, Shigekazu Takemura, Raja Roy Singh, Li Binde, Ma Peifang, Rupert Maclean, Penkae Matrakul, and John Fox.

it deals first with the progress of universal primary education (UPE) between 1960 and 1990. After briefly mentioning the World Conference on Education for All, poverty is analyzed in relation to the basic needs issue. A tentative framework for a needs-based empowerment curriculum is proposed with a view to meeting the basic learning needs of rural children in Asia.

2. UNIVERSALIZATION OF BASIC EDUCATION: AN UNFINISHED TASK

Most developing nations obtained their political independence after the Second World War. They adopted the European pattern of formal schooling to train a young generation desperately needed to achieve an efficient economy and to launch national development. In response to these educational aspirations, UNESCO convened a series of regional meetings of Ministers of Education in the late 1950s and early 1960s with the aim of facilitating national planning to achieve universal primary education (UPE). In Asia this move was accepted by the education ministers during their meeting in Karachi, Pakistan, in 1959: "every country of this region should provide a system of universal, compulsory and free primary education of seven years or more within a period of not more than twenty years (1960-1980)" (UNESCO, PROAP, 1985). This goal, later known as the Karachi Plan, gave rise to the Asian Model, the first quantified plan for educational development at primary, secondary and tertiary levels.

In order to achieve this target, the governments of the developing countries in the region adopted legislation for compulsory UPE, thus making the provision of education a governmental responsibility. Since 1961, UNESCO's Regional Office held regular Conferences of Ministers of Education and Those Responsible for Economic Planning in Asia and the Pacific (MINEDAP). It was also responsible for two programs, namely, the Asia and the Pacific Program of Educational Innovation for Development (APEID) since 1972, and the Asia-Pacific Program of Education for All (APPEAL) since 1987 (Singh, 1996).

Alongside the spread of democracy, global enrolments in primary to tertiary levels expanded rapidly from 250 million in 1960 to 906 million in 1985. The number of adult literates in the world doubled from 1,134 million to 2,314 million during the same period. In developing countries, the primary enrolment ratio increased by 25 per cent and adult literacy ratio by 21 per cent respectively. A World Bank specialist commented: "During the last three to four decades, the world has experienced an educational explosion" (Tilak. 1989). Asian countries, with their sustained investment in education, also achieved remarkable progress towards UPE, as illustrated in Tables 1 and 2.

However, such progress resulted in higher costs and lower quality. Unpredicted population growth outnumbered the enrolment increase, leaving an ever greater number of children without access to school. The number of out-of-school children in Asia, particularly in South Asia, was noteworthy. The World Bank statistics give more specified data on the five most populous countries in Asia, as illustrated in Table 3.

Education of Children in Remote Areas   173

Table 1. Estimated Public expenditure on education (US$, billions at current prices) and as a percentage of GNP

	Africa US$	Africa per cent GNP	Asia US$	Asia per cent GNP	Latin America US$	Latin America per cent GNP	Arab States US$	Arab States per cent GNP
1960	0.4	2.6	3.9	2.2	1.5	2.1	0.8	4.6
1970	1.4	3.9	13.5	3.0	5.3	3.3	1.9	4.9
1980	10.7	5.2	92.5	4.6	31.4	3.9	18.1	4.5
1990	7.7	4.8	104.9	4.3	25.4	3.8	25.6	6.6

Source: UNESCO statistics presented in Husén and Postlethwaite (1994, p. 466)

Table 2. Estimated public expenditure at primary level in developing countries, by world regions (in millions)

Year	Africa	Asia	Latin America Caribbean	Arab States	Total
1960	14.1	85.0	26.0	7.1	133.0[a]
1970	20.3	239.5 (105.8)[b]	46.6	12.6	319.0
1980	45.7	323.7 (146.3)[b]	64.8	20.6	454.8
1985	51.5	336.6 (133.7)[b]	69.6	24.8	482.5
1990	80.8	361.9	22.1	30.4	495.2

[a] Not including China. [b] Figure for China only.
Source: Based on Husén and Postlethwaite (1994) and the UNESCO (1995c) Statistical Yearbook.

Table 3. 6–11 year olds enrolled in primary schools and proportion of 6–11 year old population in most populous Asian countries

Country	Total (000) 1965	Total (000) 1975	Total (000) 1985	6–11 year olds enrolled as per cent of population 6–11 year-olds 1965	1975	1985
Bangladesh	3,576	6,955	8,353	38.2	53.9	48.6
China	81,958	100,562	100,813	90.5[a]	81.4[a]	93.1[a]
India	41,828	55,811	73,495	63.8	68.7	80.8
Indonesia	8,859	13,773	23,591	64.1[a]	78.7[a]	111.1[a]
Pakistan	2,823	4,668	6,613	28.7	35.7	42.5

[a] Primary school starts at age 7, figure adjusted accordingly.
Source: Based on Lockheed and Verspoor (1991).

It was revealed in UNESCO's (1991) *World Education Report* that over two-thirds of the world's illiterate population lived in the nine most populous developing countries, five of which were in Asia. In addition to the population factor, there has been a high cost in meeting the UPE target as measured by repetition, drop-out and cohort completion rates during primary schooling. According to the regional investigations organized by ACEID during the 1980s, the cost-effectiveness of education in almost all developing countries was mediocre. Table 4 records the repetition rate by grade for seven Asian countries and shows the marked differences between countries in grade repetition, with, in general, little change over time for the periods recorded.

These studies concluded that the poor performance of the education systems had resulted in a huge wastage of limited resources and would, in the long run, prolong the process of universalisation of primary education. Several in-depth studies (Hallak, 1990; Lockheed & Verspoor, 1991; Singh, 1991, 1996) have identified that the failure to achieve UPE by 1980 or even by 1990 is primarily due to the population boom, economic stagnation and unpredictable policy changes in the Asian states. Consequently, there was a consensus that emphasis should be maintained not only on access but also on retention and achievement. Beeby (1966) was among the first advocates on quality issues in developing countries, referring to it as the essence of all educational problems. He was apparently warning the Third World policy-makers when he suggested:

> Quantity in education is inseparably linked with quality, and nowhere more so than emergent countries where money and manpower are wasted in the schools because many of the pupils fail to achieve a level of education that is of even minimal use. (Beeby, 1996, p. 49)

Table 4. Repetition rate by grade in primary education

Country	Year	Average	Grade 1	Grade 2	Grade 3	Grade 4	Grade 5	Grade 6
Bangladesh	1988	6.9	6.5	6.2	7.2	7.5	7.2	
China	1987	7.4	15.2	7.6	6.4	5.7	2.4	0.7
	1989	6.4	13.1	7.0	5.9	5.2	2.3	0.5
India	1984	4.5	4.9	4.0	4.4	5.1		
	1986	4.5	4.6	4.2	4.3	4.8	4.4	
Indonesia	1979	8.8	15.2	9.8	7.8	5.7	4.0	1.4
	1989	9.6	16.1	11.7	10.3	8.4	6.4	1.4
Lao PDR	1978	23.1	39.8	28.1	19.8	15.9	13.6	
	1986	21.2	27.3	22.9	20.7	19.8	15.5	
Sri Lanka	1981	10.9	7.7	11.1	12.3	13.0	18.3	
	1988	8.6	5.7	9.9	10.0	9.8	8.3	
Thailand	1986	3.7	8.8	3.9	2.3	2.5	3.1	
	1987	3.4	7.4	3.6	2.2	2.3	2.9	

Source: UNESCO (1990–91) *PROAP Bulletin, No. 31.*

Unfortunately his voice was not heard in the developing world in their rush for UPE. In summary, looking back at UPE in the developing countries of Asia, the Karachi Plan, though paralyzed with so many unpredicted constraints, stood out as the most significant regional landmark, not only for the joint national pursuit of primary education as a minimal precondition for economic development, but also as regionalised co-operation in education. Two lessons can be drawn from this brief review: (a) educational development planning, as an integral component of national development, should be tuned to the actual national contexts in which the education system operates, especially the demographic and socio-economic contexts; and (b) effective progress is sustained with properly balanced policy decisions paying due emphasis to quantitative expansion and qualitative improvement.

3. FOCUS ON QUALITY EDUCATION: A GROWING DEMAND

In March 1990, the World Conference on Education for All (WCEFA) was held at Jomtien, Thailand. The conference was a response to the widespread concern over inadequacies in education systems around the world and the growing recognition of the key role of basic education for human development. The conference proved most significant in establishing a general consensus on an expanded vision of 'education for all' (EFA), confirmed in the World Declaration on Education for All (UNESCO, 1990). WCEFA pronounced a continued international commitment to provision of basic learning for all children, youths and adults particularly in disadvantaged contexts.

It was proposed in the Framework of Action that to meet the basic learning needs of children, youths and adults would require the contribution of all pertinent strategies, including pre-school interventions, enhancing the relevance and quality of educational programs for children both by formal and nonformal means, functional training of youths and adults, employing mass media and modern information technologies for EFA purposes, involving families and communities for a more conducive learning environment, and strengthening the link between educational programs and the socio-economic contexts. Apparently, the WCEFA succeeded in bringing about renewed commitment and consequently increasing investments, particularly for universal primary education. The major funding agencies indicated their commitment to boost their support for EFA initiatives.

The developing nations in Asia, especially those with large populations, have also made great commitments since 1990. It was revealed in a UNESCO (1995a) report that Bangladesh initiated a food supply program as an incentive for poor families to send their children to school. It succeeded in increasing the primary enrolment from 76 per cent in 1991 up to 87 per cent in 1994. India decided to argue for government spending on education from the current 3.7 per cent of GNP to 6.3 per cent by the year 2000. In Indonesia, the government expanded its mass literacy campaign by 5.8 million and had consequently reduced the national illiteracy rate from 15 to 13 per cent by 1994. China publicized its decision to allocate to this sector an additional total amount of approximately US$470 million during 1995–2000, together with a doubling of input from local governments. This forms part of a special project to reduce the widening gap between the developed regions and poverty-stricken areas. Late in 1993, the national leaders of the nine most populous countries (Bangladesh, Brazil, China, Egypt, India, Indonesia, Mexico, Nigeria and Pakistan) gathered in New Delhi to review progress and to reconfirm their commitment to EFA goals. WCEFA was a historic landmark in the global education development in that it redirected investment in human development. However, the conference also stimulated a higher public demand for quality education conducive to development, both in urban and rural contexts.

4. POVERTY: REALITY IN RURAL CONTEXTS

In order to achieve the grand goal of 'education for all' (EFA) the developing countries of Asia are confronted with at least two major obstacles: 'financial inadequacy' and 'curriculum irrelevance'. The former is concerned with the question of to what extent we can afford the intensive and long-term investment in the development of human resources. The latter is more directly related to what type of curriculum, both in terms of contents and delivery modes, could adequately accommodate the basic learning needs of children, particularly in disadvantaged rural areas, where the majority of the EFA target population lives.

Any attempts to examine these issues will inevitably be confronted with the notion of 'poverty' that particularly affects Asian and African rural areas. According to United Nations (1993) Statistics, there were 1,100 million people in developing countries suffering from poverty in 1985, the majority of whom live in Asia. More recent statistics show that, of the 5.7 billion people in the world, 1.5 billion are desperately poor with one billion of the world's poor living in rural areas; and the number of poor is increasing by approximately 25 million a year. Asia is severely affected.

Currently, the largest concentration of severely impoverished people, about half of the world's total, lives in South Asia (i.e. Bangladesh, Bhutan, India, Maldives, Nepal, Pakistan and Sri Lanka) (United Nations, 1996). Nevertheless, China still numbers 65 million poor people, according to the latest official report (Chen, 1996). Moreover, the income distribution disparity between different regions and between urban and rural areas has been increasing at an alarming rate. This message is clearly stated in the *Report on the World Social Situation* (United Nations, 1993).

The phenomenon of poverty is more than mere economic deprivation. Robinson (1976) concluded that, once a person was caught up in poverty, it meant in most cases a loss of power and could result in apathy, despair and detachment. Recent studies on rural poverty in China (Mu, 1994; Ye, 1995) have further identified that three other outcomes are frequently associated with rural populations living in economic poverty, namely, illiteracy, lack of productive skills and mis-oriented perceptions. The notion of 'mis-oriented perceptions' is used to refer to a passive dependence on material aid, with no desire to change their own situation. This aspect is also known as 'spiritual poverty'.

From this perspective, poverty seems not only imposed upon the poor by external factors, such as a disastrous natural environment, the population explosion, economic stagnation, and political instability or military conflicts, but is also a psychological condition of the prescribed population themselves. Therefore, the poverty phenomenon could be understood as, first of all, a state of scarcity of the minimum resources for survival such as food, water, shelter, clothing and land. However, poverty is also a state of condition where human beings are unable to take actions to maintain their own survival and development. Such inability is separate from intellectual factors, such as illiteracy, productive skills and problem-solving techniques. Furthermore, poverty is, in a more concealed manner, a spiritual anguish leading to lack of self-respect and confidence, thus a readiness to accept poverty as a preordained fate and, therefore, apathy.

These factors work together to reinforce and reproduce poverty. In this case, any effective efforts to eradicate poverty should therefore start with the empowerment of the poor and to promote their readiness with literacy, productive skills and, most critically, confidence to change their life. For such an empowerment process education could make the most significant contribution. Contrary to this assumption, however, the current schooling system in the developing countries has been observed to prepare children to flee from the hardships of rural poverty through the so-called 'academic ladder', rather than to empower them with abilities necessary for self-reliance. In his examination of the relationship between educational provision and poverty in rural areas in Asian and African developing countries, Harrison (1993) made the most striking criticism about the irrelevance of schooling:

> Political independence in Africa did not bring with it cultural independence. The style and contents of education continued along largely European lines. Education was oriented to theory and distant facts, not to the practical life of the village. (Harrison, 1993, p. 324)

During his field trips to the rural villages, Harrison (1993, p. 318) was shocked by the academic dominance of the school system: "None of the earlier stages are self-sufficient, each is a preparation for the next, more academic phase, not a preparation for real life and work". Doubting the purpose of schooling, he wrote in a cynical tone:

> Today a school certificate is seen as a one-way ticket out of the poverty and depression of rural life and the curse of manual labour it has turned into yet another device for ensuring high rewards for the few and continued poverty for the many. It is an alienation machine, distancing young people

from their families, and from manual work, making them turn their backs on the villages that so desperately need their promise, vigour and adaptability. It does not even turn out enough people with the skills that the modern sector needs. But produces a large class of disoriented drones and impractical mandarins. (Harrison, 1993, p. 306)

Certainly, one of the fundamental functions of the schooling system is to enable young people, particularly those in disadvantaged contexts, to find employment in urban enterprises or, better still, in government offices. However, wants are too many while chances are very few, especially with population pressure and economic stagnation. The majority of the survivors from the schooling system in rural areas cannot find jobs in the cities and have to remain in villages, for which they have been inadequately prepared. They are then likely to become alienated from the rural community life in which they were brought up.

Although urbanization could continue to absorb migrants, there is certainly a limit of the urban cities to accommodate the population rush due to economic conditions and social infrastructure. In spite of the speed-up of urbanization in the developing world, rural production will remain a primary way of life in the coming century. In 1985, rural inhabitants made up 72 per cent of the total Asian population (Ogawa et al., 1993). According to the estimation of the United Nations (1994b), the rural population still amounted to 66 per cent in 1994 and will probably decline to 45 per cent by 2025. Rapid urbanization and growing income discrepancy in developing countries have also contributed to increasing mass poverty (United Nations, 1993). Consequently, the problem, from a developmental perspective, has become: 'what type of education should we provide in order to cater to the basic needs of the rural population so that they can effectively pursue a gradual improvement in their living standards?' There is no doubt that the curriculum, as an integral component of the infrastructure, should be reoriented so as to empower rural populations for more development options.

In this perspective, it is assumed that the rural education curriculum should be no longer confined merely to employment in industry or so-called 'white-collar' occupations, but rather be further expanded to cater to both community and household development needs as well. In other words, the future education curriculum should not only be oriented solely to the needs of continuing urbanization but, more necessarily, to the urgent needs for improvement in the quality of rural life. In addition to such critical reassessment of the problems, it is also necessary to review the alternative approaches.

5. INNOVATION: CASE STUDIES IN CURRICULUM DEVELOPMENT

Along with the evolution of universalisation and literacy in Asia, there has been a growing intention to reorient the existing educational programs, particularly the curriculum, thus to suit the actual needs of rural population groups. For instance, India formulated a Minimum Learning Levels Program (MLLP) in the 1990s for a functional core curriculum framework covering the most essential level of acquisition of literacy, numeracy and life skills in rural daily life (NCERT, 1995). In Pakistan, Alma Ikbal Open University started to introduce nonformal literacy and productivity training programs for rural populations a few decades ago. In China, fundamental reform initiatives have been introduced in the last few years. The curriculum framework for the nine-year compulsory program has been modified to allow variation, though still rather limited, including local contents and school-based extra-curricular learning activities. Furthermore, the previously unified textbook that provided one set of books for all children throughout the country has been replaced with eight sets of textbooks, newly developed to cater for the needs of children in different regions. The on-going rural education reform is now geared to serving farmers' aspirations for higher productivity, more income and a better quality of life (Zhang, 1995). Most recently a brand new National Guideline for Basic Education Reform was released officially by the Ministry of Education in 2001, calling to regulate and change the curriculum goals, structure, contents and delivery systems thus to ensure the desired quality education (MOE, 2001). For a specific discussion of this point, three cases are presented below.

5.1. *Nonformal Primary Education Program in Bangladesh*

The Nonformal Primary Education Program (NFPE), a non-governmental project, was introduced from 1979 in Bangladesh. First of all, it was on an experimental basis in special response to the educational needs of rural girls from poor families by the Bangladesh Rural Advancement Committee (BRAC), the largest non-governmental organization in the country. NFPE consisted of a three-year program for 8–10 year-olds and a two-year program for the 11–16 year age group. By the end of 1992, BRAC had established 11,108 single-class schools with a total enrolment of 333,240 children (over 70% were girls) and 10,093 female teachers recruited from local communities. BRAC planned to increase the number of NFPE schools to 100,000 by 1997.

During the field investigation on the project, BRAC-NFPE schools were found effective with the following features. Basic facilities were most functional. The classrooms, normally 30 square meters in area rented from a local landlord, were equipped with a blackboard, a school calendar, a stool and a teaching-kit box for the teacher. Children, generally 30 in number, sat on the floor in a semicircle, each on a mat, with a few textbooks and exercise books, and a small wooden chalkboard and a bunch of chalks, their learning tools, in front of them. The curriculum was composed of Bangladesh language, mathematics, social studies and English. BRAC staff and university scholars, taking into consideration both local needs and the official curriculum prepared the learning materials. After completing NFPE, the children were expected to continue their learning from Grade 4 in the government schools, where English was compulsory. The learning process was highly intensive with two-and-a half hours a day, six days a week and 270 days in total for one year. Children had 40 minutes every day for after-class activities such as physical exercise, singing and dancing, drawing, playing games and storytelling. No long vacations were assigned since it was feared that the children might forget what they had learned. The instruction time arrangement was decided by the teacher and the parents.

BRAC developed a unique teacher selection and training system. All teachers were selected from the local villages. They were usually housewives with no less than nine years of education, aged between 20–35 years, responsible and willing to teach for NFPE. The procedure included individual interviews by BRAC staff. Those selected candidates were given two weeks of intensive training at the regional training centres. Here, the trainees studied the textbooks, learned some basic teaching methods and, in the end, were assessed by both paper test and demonstration teaching. Recruitment of the successful candidates then took place. The training needs of the teachers were also served through short-term refresher programs, varying from two to four days, prior to every semester and a one-day training session in each month. The regular operation of NFPE was coordinated by field supervisors, who were usually college graduates, with special training for instructional work. The field supervisors worked in teams, each in charge of a school district, 50 to 70 in size. Each supervisor was responsible for 15 schools. They travelled to each school once a week or fortnight, by motorbikes or bicycles. For each school, a committee was set up with parent representatives (normally one mother and one father), a village leader and the teacher. The committee was expected to assist the teacher in ensuring children attended and in solving day-to-day problems. In terms of the financial supply, BRAC was successful in acquiring funding from many international donor agencies, thus making the program almost free to the beneficiary communities, while parents bore only one per cent of the total cost. The per capita annual expenditure was US$18, which appeared minimal compared to the government schools.

The study team was informed that 90 per cent of BRAC school students continued at the government schools, compared to 53 per cent retention rate from Grade 3 to Grade 4 in these schools. With the information provided by BRAC and the above-mentioned field observation, the study team had the impression that NFPE proved to be an effective alternative primary education system for disadvantaged rural girls in remote areas. The team was also deeply impressed with the praiseworthy commitment and skills of the BRAC staff throughout the system. Their ability to make the impossible possible was highly commended. However, the retention rate was unstable as about 50 per cent of BRAC students were reported to drop out in the later grades of government schools. Probably, this was due to the different curriculum arrangement, economic constraints and other factors.

The team was told that the NFPE funding was primarily dependent upon foreign donations. As BRAC decided to expand the programs to cater to a rapidly growing population, it became a question of whether overseas donor agencies could increase or sustain the necessary financial support for the future NFPE in the coming years.

5.2. Asian-Pacific Joint Production Program of Materials for Neo-literates in Rural Areas

The Asia-Pacific Cultural Centre for UNESCO (ACCU) is a national non-profit-making organization established in 1971 by the private sector on the initiative of the Japanese National Commission for UNESCO and with the full support of the Japanese Government. ACCU has three major on-going programs: culture through the co-production of musical materials, book development with the co-production of children's books, and literacy through the joint production of materials for neo-literates in rural areas and basic literacy materials. The Asian-Pacific Joint Production Program has been one of the most popular projects that ACCU has, in collaboration with UNESCO, organised to address, in particular, the learning needs of the remote rural population for combating poverty. Over the last 20 years, the accumulated experience of ACCU has formulated a needs-based curriculum development model which, so as to link training programs to the promotion of the quality of life in rural households and communities.

The preparation of ACCU learning materials abides by the following six criteria.

Awareness. The learners, either individually or as a group, should be first of all made aware of the conditions under which they live and work. They should be motivated to undertake an analysis of the factors contributing to their existing problems and be encouraged to think of possible ways in which they could help themselves change their situations for the better, namely, need for learning to make a difference.

Functionality. The literacy training programs should be related in a practical manner to the environment, work and family situation of the learner.

Flexibility. The literacy curriculum should allow for modifications, alternatives and additions so as to respond to the learner's needs and environmental requirements.

Diversity. The curriculum should be sufficiently varied to cater to the interests and needs of particular groups, such as peasants, women, urban dwellers and cultural communities.

Appropriateness of the learning relationship. The experience and potential abilities of the adult learners and their needs should influence the instructor-learner relationship, so as to build on what the learners already know and can do.

Action-oriented. The curriculum should aim at mobilizing the learners to take action to improve their own lives (ACCU, 1992, p. 6).

In order to carry through this philosophy, ACCU/AJP learning materials follow an interrelated sequence. By the end of 1994, ACCU produced in this manner 49 kinds of AJP materials as listed in Table 5.

The most useful contribution that ACCU has made is an alternative approach to reach the remote rural poor with training materials developed in response to their concrete daily problems. ACCU has made this possible by applying a bottom-up needs-assessment procedure to address the actual problems for effective preparation of training materials. This practice, as suggested by numerous program documents, is then strengthened with assimilation training workshops at national level by ACCU mobile training teams. While the available training contents are quite practical, as shown in Table 5, the participating countries need to develop valid mechanisms to carry through the curriculum in order to achieve the desired changes in eliminating poverty among the target population. Therefore, the commitment of the respective countries is required to complete the curriculum development cycle down to the grass roots level.

5.3. *Appeal Training Materials for Literacy Personnel*

The UNESCO Asia-Pacific Program of Education for All (APPEAL), soon after its establishment in 1987, introduced a curriculum initiative named 'APPEAL Training Materials for Literacy Personnel' (ATLP). ATLP was geared to revitalize national efforts in the eradication of illiteracy by jointly developing a literacy curriculum acceptable to all countries. In order to upgrade literacy program managers, trainers and instructors or teachers, and to cater to the diversified learning needs at the grassroots level, a 12-volume set of materials was produced during 1987–1988. The contents cover the following major aspects.

- Principles of curriculum design for literacy training,
- Principles of resource design for literacy training,
- Manual for senior administrators of literacy training programs,
- Manual for supervision resource development and training programs,
- Exemplar training manual – Extra money for the family,
- Exemplar training manual – Our forests,
- Exemplar training manual – Village co-operatives,
- Exemplar training manual – Health services,
- Specifications for additional exemplar training manuals,
- Post-literacy activities and continuing education,
- Evaluating a literacy training program, and
- Implementing a literacy training program.

The underlying rationale of ATLP was that the literacy curriculum must, first of all, be agreeable to all the people concerned. The most important areas of social concern, particularly in rural contexts, were defined as: family life, income, health and civic consciousness. Twenty-four other subjects were also identified and their scope outlined. In consideration of the different needs of the rural learners, three entry levels were set with varying degrees of progress. It was also

Table 5. List of ACCU/AJP materials (prototypes)

Content Areas	Level 1 (Beginning level)	Level 2 (Middle level)	Level 3 (Self-learning level)
A. Family life	▲ Let's make the home clean (poster)	▲ Home gardening ◆ Women's literacy for happier and healthier life (box puzzle) ■ Why literacy for women (booklet) ▲ Let's think about our population (poster)	■ Useful and simple knowledge for everyday living (booklet)
B. Economics, income and production	◆ Let's plant trees (step by step game)	■ Bamboo handicrafts (booklet) ▲ Tree planting (poster) ● Poultry for additional income (slide kit, video)	■ Grow mushrooms (booklet) ■ More income by tree planting (booklet) ■ Raising chickens (booklet) ■ Use of gas from daily wastes (booklet) ■ Fish need a lot of oxygen (booklet)
C. Health, sanitation and nutrition	● Water in everyday life (slide kit, video) ▲ Let's wipe out worms (poster) ▲ Sanitation (poster) ▲ Everyone's water (poster)	◆ Nutrition (card game) ◆ A balanced diet (rotating pie-graph) ● Pit latrine for a clean village (kamishibai) ▲ Charcoal water filter (poster)	■ Mari and the festival – let's eat more vegetables (booklet)
D. Civic consciousness	◆ Save the village (puppet play) ● Let's repair the road (endless cartoon strip) ▲ Public pollution inside the bus (poster) ▲ Let's read (poster)	◆ Building up a happy community (sugoroku game) ▲ Good use of water	● Let's form a farmers' cooperative (cassette drama/radio program) ■ Cooperatives for better life (booklet) ▲ We can take action! (poster)
E. Culture, science and others	▲ Let's safely use electricity (poster) ▲ Do you know numbers? (poster) ◆ Animal sugoroku (game) ▲ The river and us (poster)	▲ How to improve the well system (poster) ◆ Proverb card game (card game) ◆ Around Asia and the Pacific (sugoroku)	■ The life of water (booklet)

▲ = poster. ■ = booklet. ● = audio-visual material. ◆ = game.
Source: ACCU (1992).

stated that the actual contents would correspond closely to both national goals as well as the local problems and needs of the targeted clientele. The time allocations at the three levels were scaled in a ratio of 3:2:1 and about 200 contact hours were considered as a minimum to achieve a level of literacy competency that would allow the learner to continue on to further leaning. Table 6 illustrates the curriculum framework.

It was reported in 1994 that the ATLP series had already been translated into the languages of 12 countries and were being used extensively for literacy personnel training programs (Sakya, 1994). UNESCO has been trying to develop a functional curriculum package for literacy personnel at different levels. The ATLP series appear to convey the general curriculum development principles of literacy training in rural areas, a domain where most academics or professionals in the developing countries rarely trespass. It is, nevertheless, an area where the education authorities badly need such expertise. However, there is currently little feedback on what kind of impact this package has actually had. The time is now right to evaluate it from the forefront of the program, among the targeted rural household communities.

5.4. *Overview*

These three programs share at least two matters in common. The learning was specifically oriented as a special aid to the rural poor to enhance their capability to cope more effectively with their daily problems; and their actual needs were addressed as the foundation for relevant curriculum development.

6. EMPOWERMENT FOR DEVELOPMENT: CURRICULUM REORIENTATION

It has become apparent from the previous sections that the UPE efforts in remote rural areas of Asian developing nations are now more challenged than ever in terms of relevance and quality of learning in meeting the actual needs for survival and for promotion of quality of life. The poverty phenomenon, no matter whether perceived economically, intellectually and spiritually, is identified as the ultimate obstacle holding back any attempt for sustainable development. Consequently, education, as the most empowering process for personal and national capacity, should therefore be reoriented to equip the disadvantaged with basic qualities, such as literacy skills, entrepreneurial competencies, and positive values and affective traits, so that they are enabled to tackle a wider range of development options.

Education for All, as first advocated by the World Conference on Education for All in 1990 and reclaimed at the 2000 EFA Forum in Dakar, is, by contrast, so different from the formal schooling currently provided in many ways that we are led to believe that an alternative, more contextualized curriculum framework is necessary. As a tentative effort, the following proposal is suggested.

Education of Children in Remote Areas   185

Table 6. APPEAL-ATLP curriculum grid, the scope of the training manuals

Content areas	Level I (Basic level)			Level II (Middle level)		Level III (Self-learning level)
	I.1	I.2	I.3	II.1.	II.2	III
A. Family life	IA.1 Family members, their roles and their responsibilities 1	IA.2 Supplementing family income 5	IA.3 Extra money for the family 9	IIA.1 Family needs and budgeting 13	IIA.2 Family customs and traditions 17	IIIA Responsible parenthood 21
B. Economics and income	IB.1 Work & income 2	IB.2 Daily savings 6	IB.3 Improved agriculture 10	IIB.1 Home gardening 14	IIB.2 Village cooperatives 18	IIIB Entrepreneurship 22
C. Health	IC.1 Food, nutrition and water 3	IC.2 Family health 7	IC.3 Common diseases 11	IIC.1 Health problems 15	IIC.2 Community health 19	IIIC Health services 23
D. Civic consciousness	ID.1 Rights & duties 4	ID.2 People's participation in development and cleanliness 8	ID.3 Our forests 12	IID.1 Our culture 16	IID.2 all people are equal 20	IIID. My country 24

Source: UNESCO (1988).

6.1. *A Tentative EFA Curriculum to Empower the Rural Population*

Objectives. EFA is, by its very nature, geared to foster the basic empowerment of every individual, thus to enable them to continue learning and to deal effectively with their life and work. Such individual empowerment will, in return, lay the foundations for the community and national development.

Target group. EFA is committed to meeting the basic learning needs of all learners specially the disadvantaged population groups, regardless of age, gender, ethnicity, and social and economic status.

Curriculum contents. A needs-based curriculum framework is perceived applicable so as to integrate the basic learning skills (e.g., literacy and numeracy), basic knowledge and skills for life and work, and the acquisition of positive values and attitudes. Curriculum development should not only relate to the structure and organization of learning contents in a pedagogical perspective, but also address the actual conditions of the local community in a constructive manner. The term 'constructive' is used to indicate that poverty can also be employed didactically as a resource for the empowerment process, thus preparing learners to combat poverty effectively and to implement self-reliant development. Therefore, the curriculum may cover such areas as the understanding of causes for poverty, and the human potential to combat poverty in terms of personal capacity building, skills and attitudes required to face poverty, initial experience in making a positive change in one's daily life, All of these will prepare future adults with capability and confidence in overcoming poverty for a better quality of life.

Delivery modes. EFA should provide learners with more alternative learning programs in terms of objectives, contents, learning patterns in response to the particular conditions of the target group. To this end, a facilitative system should be made available to enable the learners with different needs in various contexts too benefit from such learning experience; for example, literacy for an effective citizenship, technical or entrepreneurial skills for employment either by themselves or by local economic institutions, and readiness to pursue further learning.

Teachers. EFA places new demands on teachers, or rather facilitators, who are expected not only to be academically qualified but also with the ability to apply their learning as a resource for constant promotion of quality of life, both of themselves and the community, thus to motivate the community involvement in learning. Local teachers, technicians, community elders, parents and even the learners themselves can fulfil such roles.

Evaluation. Evaluation of such learning is, in a similar vein, to be expanded from simply measuring scholastic performance to enlisting the learners' participation and ability obtained to contribute to community development. These features, incomplete as they are, present a different perspective from the existing formal system and may perhaps place new demands on curriculum reorientation. Generally speaking, the current curriculum in Asian developing countries has been dominated by governmental requirements for a better-trained labour force and, to some extent, for desired citizenship. However, the system is still operated within traditional scholastic domains, namely reading, writing, arithmetic and other cognitive skills, principally geared to prepare learners for further schooling. While this model appears self-justifying in theory, for social mobility in favour of the individualistic success of an elite group, it is contradictory to the very nature of meeting the basic learning needs of all community members who are entitled to such social service. As a result, only a few find their way out of the disadvantaged context through the academic ladder, while the majority oftentimes find themselves ill-prepared for the betterment of their rural life.

Therefore, the EFA curriculum in the Asian developing countries should be redefined to address the basic learning needs of the target population, taking such factors not only as the national employment needs, but also those of rural communities and households. EFA, means to enable every learner with beneficial learning experience which could empower every person with basic cognitive, enterprise or productivity and affective faculties necessary for their constructive participation in development at individual or household, community and national levels, so as to prepare all the learners for rural transformation.

The proposed curriculum shift from a nation-dominance model towards an EFA model requires fundamental changes to the very basic assumptions on why we learn, what we learn, how we learn. Education will no longer be the privilege of the minority as the result from the so-called 'social selection' by academic standards, but rather a basic instrument for the empowerment of the whole populace. To this end, it is inevitable for us to undertake the redefinition of educational goals and corresponding curriculum reorientation in the light of the capacity building at the national, community as well as individual or household levels.

Sustainable national development relies on the human resource empowerment of the total populace. Past experiences have demonstrated that the universalisation goals of primary education in developing countries could neither be fulfilled by the national governments alone nor be justified simply by the benefit of the national work force. It is therefore simply impractical for the government to finance fully a huge uniform education system and to provide adequate employment opportunities for school-leavers. Unconventional approaches must be sought if we are determined to carry out such EFA goals. It is proposed therefore that the policy-makers and curriculum developers should undertake a systematic critical reassessment, in the light of EFA visions, the relevance and quality of learning programs, so as to reorient our education system for the benefits of all.

REFERENCES

Asian Cultural Centre for UNESCO (1992). *New guide book for development and production of literacy materials.* Tokyo: ACCU.

Beeby, C. E. (1966). *The quality of education in developing countries*. Cambridge, MA: Harvard University Press.

Chen, J. H. (1996). On eradication of poverty by 2000. In *Guangmin Daily*. 9 March [Text in Chinese].

Hallak, J. (1990). *Investing in the future: Setting educational priorities in the developing world*. Paris: UNESCO: International Institute for Educational Planning. Oxford: Pergamon Press.

Harrison, P. (1993). *Inside the Third World*. Harmondsworth, U.K: Penguin Books.

Husen. T., & Postlethwaite T. N. (Eds.) (1994). *International Encyclopaedia of Education* (2nd ed.) Oxford: Elsevier Science Ltd.

Lockheed, M., & Verspoor, A. (1991). *Improving primary education in developing countries*. Oxford: Oxford University Press.

Ministry of Education (MOE) (2001). National guidelines for the curriculum reform of basic education. In the *Proceedings of the National Working Meeting on Basic Education*. Beijing: Tuanjie Publishing House [Chinese ed.].

Mu, G. Z. (1994). Population quality and eradication of poverty. *Journal of Social Science Front (TOWN)*, September, 44–53 [Chinese ed.].

NCERT (1995). National minimum learning levels for primary schools in India, In *Learning Quality and Basic Standards* (pp. 417–85). New Delhi: National Center for Educational Development and Research, Guangxi Educational Press [text in Chinese].

Ogawa, N. et al. (1993). *Human Resources in Development Along the Asia-Pacific Rim*. Oxford: Oxford University Press.

Robinson, P. (1976). *Education and Poverty*. London: Methuen.

Sakya, T. M. (1994). PROAP's Report on APPEAL and ACCU's Contribution to EFA. In *ACCU 1994 Planning Meeting for Neo-Literates in Rural Areas (AJP)*. Tokyo: ACC.

Singh, R. R. (1996). *Education in Asia and the Pacific: Retrospect and Prospect*. Bangkok: UNESCO.

Singh, R. R. (1991). *Education for the Twenty-first Century: Asia-Pacific Perspectives*. Bangkok: UNESCO.

Tilak, J. B. G. (1989). *Education and its relation to economic growth, poverty and income distribution: Oast evidence and further analysis*. Washington, DC: World Bank. (A World Band discussion paper.)

UNESCO (1990). *World declaration on education for all and framework for action to meet basic learning needs, adopted by the World Conference on Education for All: Meeting basic learning needs*. Jomtien: Thailand.

UNESCO (1991). *World Education Report*. Paris: UNESCO.

UNESCO (1995a). *Bulletin of EFA 2000 (Paris)*. No. 19, April-July.

UNESCO (1995b). *World Education Report*. Paris: UNESCO.

UNESCO PROAP (1988). *APPEAL training materials for literacy personnel*. Bangkok: UNESCO.

UNESCO PROAP/APEID (1985). *Towards universalisation of primary education in asia and Pacific: Regional Overview*. Bangkok: UNESCO.

UNESCO (1990–91). *PROAP Bulletin, No. 31*. Bangkok: UNESCO.

UNESCO (1995c). *Statistical Yearbook*. Paris: UNESCO.

United Nations (1956). Final authorized text of universal Declaration of Human Rights, adopted and proclaimed by the United Nations on the tenth day of December 1948. New York: UN.

United Nations (1993). *Report on the world social situation*. New York: UN.

United Nations (1994). *Summary of the Program of Action of the International Conference on Population and Development*. Cairo: UN.

United Nations (1996). *International Year for the Eradication of Poverty, an advocacy pamphlet*. New York: UN.

Ye, C. H. (1995). Reflections on education for socially disadvantaged population groups. *Jiangxi Education Research Journal*, 2(1–4) [Chinese ed.].

Zhang, T. D. et al. (1995). Study report on BRAC NFPE. In W. Zhou (Ed.), *Action Research on Girls' Education in West-China*. Ningxia: Ningxia People's Education Press [Chinese ed.].

13

Practices and Development of Gifted and Talented Education

SIN KUEN-FUNG
Hong Kong Institute of Education, Hong Kong SAR, China

1. INTRODUCTION

The challenges of meeting the needs of gifted and talented children attract growing attention in the fields of educational psychology, curriculum instruction and special education. Focusing on the various research and policy issues, this article highlights the complexity of gifted and talented education by illustrating the multidimensional development and changing notions of giftedness in selected education systems in the Asia-Pacific region. Some practices and research work on gifted and talented education in the sub-regions and countries of China, including mainland China and the Hong Kong Special Administrative Region (hereafter Hong Kong), Republic of Korea, Singapore, Taiwan and Thailand are discussed for global sharing generally and for sharing within the Asia-Pacific region in particular.

2. CATERING FOR INDIVIDUAL DIFFERENCES

In 1994, The Salamanca Statement asserts the importance of 'education for all' by urging policy makers to address the special needs of children with all ranges of abilities (UNESCO, 1994). Catering for individual differences of children with or without disabilities becomes a major concern in the processes of pedagogical practice, curriculum reform, teacher training and school development. With the provision of additional resources and collaborative effort, schools are expected to achieve success in creating culture, producing policies and evolving good practices for including students with all ranges of abilities (Booth & Ainscow, 2000).

However, there are identified difficulties in the processes of optimising the different potentials of gifted and talented children (Sin, Lyon, & Chan, 1998). Owing to limited resources and the immediate care of the needy group, 'egalitarianism and elitism' and 'equality and equity' are always the controversial issues in resource allocation and priority of work. Some object to the rationale of extra resource allocation to gifted and talented children, who to many people are always the advantaged group with privileges in the community. Others insist that the 'education for all' objective also implies 'quality education for all', with the goal of optimising the potentials of all children with all ranges of abilities.

Despite the ongoing debates and hesitation in resource allocation, gifted and talented education is widely and strongly accepted in many education systems. For example, in a survey conducted in mainland China, a country with a legacy of proletariat equalitarianism, students, teachers and administrators were invited to express their concerns for gifted and talented education (He, 1999). The findings reveal that many supported gifted and talented education and argued for a national policy and further development.

Currently, the aims of gifted education in Taiwan are clearly stated in the public ordinance for feasible implementation and resource allocation (Wang, 1999). The foci of work include the following: (a) to offer regular education and prepare for further education; (b) to promote critical and logical thinking; (c) to develop creativity; (d) to enhance social development; (e) to promote self-understanding and mental health; (f) to develop moral and spiritual values; and (g) to explore career opportunities. All these objectives become the practical guidelines of work in gifted education.

In comparison, the curriculum needs and educational opportunities of gifted children in Hong Kong were highlighted in educational reports (Education Commission, 1990, 2000; Board of Education, 1996). From the official policy perspective, the aim of education is that every school should help all its students, whatever their ability and including those with special educational needs, to develop their potential as fully as possible in both academic and non-academic directions. More importantly, the current Hong Kong education policy considers that giftedness in children may be manifested in academic and non-academic areas. This conception brings about a diversity of practice in school programs.

Review of pertinent educational literature in the Asia-Pacific region indicates that it is generally agreed that, in quality education for all, the aims of gifted and talented education are to develop the potentials of gifted students and to meet their educational needs (Cho, 1999; Lim, 1999; Phothisuk, 1999a; Wu, 1999). In view of the support and opportunities, it seems that the public has achieved consensus in elaborating the issues of 'egalitarianism and elitism' and 'equality and equity'. Schools in different regions take every possible measure to realise the objectives of gifted and talented education and to cater for individual differences. However, due to differences in the availability of only limited resources, the priority of work in gifted and talented education is different in different regions. Also, the complexity of intelligence theories may lead to a wide range of understanding and a diversity of classroom practices and policy plans.

3. CURRENT TRENDS IN DEFINING THE GIFTEDNESS AND TALENTS

The way to define 'giftedness and talents' is always a difficulty in gifted education. Generally speaking, 'giftedness' refers to acquired and inborn ability while talents are exceptional performance or high potential in particular areas. However, the two terms are generally used together to describe those school children with high ability, good achievement and excellent performance. In line with the examination of human intelligence, many scholars and psychologists have advocated the significance of giftedness and developed theories on gifted and talented education (see, Guilford, 1967; Renzulli, 1986; Gardner, 1993; Sternberg, 1996).

In short, there are many conceptions of giftedness and talents. It appears that the theories of intelligence encompass multiple dimensions and that giftedness extends from academic foci to non-academic areas. Reflecting the view that educational reform is research-based, in the evaluation report on the pilot school-based program for academically gifted children in Hong Kong, it was concluded that there were a series of changes and interpretations in the development of the definition on giftedness.

> From the historical point of view, the concept of 'giftedness' has been evolving from unidimensional to multidimensional; from convergence to divergence; and the focus of attention has shifted from cognitive to affective aspects, and from latent potentials to the development of performance.
>
> (Education Department, 1999, p. 4)

Facing reality, however, teachers may feel frustrated or incompetent in comprehending the theories and conceptions, particularly in linking them with classroom practices. This is a major practical implication that must be underscored in both the research and reformulation of education policy impacting on gifted and talented children.

The fourth report of the Education Commission (1990) provides a definition of gifted students in Hong Kong. The description of gifted and talented children has become more explicit and operational, in terms of intelligence, aptitude, creative thinking, superior talent, leadership and psychomotor performance. The research-based notion is helpful for the identification of children with high ability, good achievement and excellent performance, while the nurture of multiple intelligences has great implications for recent curriculum reform (Education Commission, 2000).

In Taiwan, the changing conceptions of giftedness and talents from the heredity, intelligence performance, creativity and thinking model; to multiple intelligences are well noted in the literature (Chien, 1999). Indeed, the all-round development of the individual child, particularly the holistic development of the cognition, motor skill and affection, is the final consensus in gifted education (Wang, 1999). Wu and Chien (1999) further summarise the multiple intelligences of Gardner (1983) and the successful intelligence of Sternberg (1996) for application in Taiwan's educational context. Sternberg focuses on the successful life with a balanced development of four intelligences. These are academic (analysis) intelligence, personal intelligence, management (practical) intelligence and creative intelligence. Some of his propositions have been verified by developing scales and curricula for personal intelligence. Positive personal intelligence and coping behaviors have also been reported in an elementary school program (Wu & Chien, 1999).

In short, notwithstanding the definitional issues of giftedness and talent, efforts and attempts define 'giftedness' is in the various education systems in the Asia-Pacific region. The changes in the concept of giftedness have brought about changes in the emphasis of identification, placement and nurturing of multiple intelligences as well as in the foci of research. The conceptions of giftedness and talent are still controversial in the Asia-Pacific region. The changing conceptions of giftedness and talent in different education systems also reflect the changes in the trends of education for the gifted and talented in the respective systems.

4. THE REVIEW OF THE GIFTED AND TALENTED EDUCATION IN DIFFERENT REGIONS

In view of the multifaceted nature of giftedness, the ways and strategies of development are the concerns to many scholars, policy makers and educators in the region. There are criticisms that many studies and research investigations were individual-based, incidental and short-term-oriented (Wu, 1999). In the Symposium of Research on Gifted and Talented Education (1999) held in Taipei, the participants from mainland China, Taiwan, Hong Kong, Korea, Singapore and Thailand jointly affirmed the theme "Global development of gifted and talented education". All the presentations revealed the efforts expended in various education systems in offering learning opportunities as well as undertaking research work into gifted and talented education (Chinese Association of Gifted Education, 1999). The critical review of the current and future development in different sub-regions and countries illustrated the success, difficulties and strategic work involved.

In Korea, since 1980, many research projects on gifted and talented education have been carried out by the National Research Institute and the Research Center for the Gifted and Talented at Korean Educational Development Institute (Cho, 1991, 1999a and b). These research studies involved efforts to address the needs for a multidimensional examination at different levels, particularly in educational policy, assessment and identification, psychological characteristics and teacher training. Also, studies for optimising the potential of gifted and talented children, the success of learning programs, web-based instructional service systems and program evaluation have been undertaken. The longitudinal studies of giftedness, involving the effects of social and cultural variables, are required in the future.

In Thailand, there has also been a growing concern about these issues during the past 20 years. Research into gifted and talented education has been carried out in the areas of teaching strategies, modelling, attitudes and program efficiency (Phothisuk, 1999a). The implementation of many programs for gifted and talented children has been reported at the secondary school level and subject areas, such as mathematics, science, art, or music. Efforts have also been made to start programs at the elementary school level, by developing the assessment tools and materials, sharing experiences and disseminating information (Phothisuk, 1999b). Schools have attempted to develop a school management system with gifted and talented programs in mathematics, Thai language, English, arts and music. The modes of delivery include enrichment, extension and acceleration programs. In view of a need for future development, the National Center for the Gifted and Talented was set up, so as to formulate policy and a national plan on gifted and talented children. It is also expected that the establishment of the National Research and Development Institute would facilitate the coordinating of future plans, follow-ups, resource support and research work.

In Singapore, gifted and talented education started in 1984, with the identification of gifted pupils in some primary and secondary schools (Lim, 1999). Since then, there have been research studies conducted on curriculum, learning characteristics, socio-emotional development, independent research program and teacher training in gifted and talented education (Lim, 1997; Quah & Teo, 1998). The government's Gifted Education Program and the programs of the Chinese High School for gifted pupils are particularly noteworthy with respect to the effectiveness of the implementation of their programs. The former provides a curriculum with enrichment content and a stimulating environment, and it helps the gifted students to develop higher order thinking and reflection across the different subjects. The latter provides gifted pupils with a challenging, differentiated and enriched curriculum, particularly in the subjects of Mathematics, Science and Computer Science. In addition, some exceptionally talented children participate in an independent research program. The training, focuses on library research skills, inquiry skills, critical and creative thinking skills, learning-how-to-learn skills, and written and communication skills. With the help of mentors from the universities and research institutes, the children are provided with the necessary assistance they need through an independent research program (Lim, 1999).

In Hong Kong, it is the government's policy to have the gifted and talented students educated in mainstream schools. In 1990, the government was advised by the Education Commission to set up a professional team and a resource centre, launch pilot projects, devise identification programs, initiate school-based programs, develop resource materials; and provide training programs for teachers and parents (Education Commission, 1990). The recommendations were encouraging and promising, regarding the strong implications for educational policy and resource allocation. In 1992, the Education Department launched research studies, including designing tools to identify gifted children and examining the distribution of gifted children in primary schools as well as the identification of their educational needs (Ku et al., 1994a,b, 1995, 1998). After that, a three-year pilot school-based program for academically gifted children was launched in 19 primary schools in 1994. The Resource Centre of Gifted Education was set up in 1995 and a professional team was formed in 1996. They supported and delivered educational services for gifted and talented students, as well as developing school-based programs and teaching materials (Education Department, 1999).

The above examples from Korea, Thailand, Singapore, and Hong Kong show that different education systems in the Asia-Pacific region have strived to enhance the education of gifted and talented children and have made efforts to ensure that the respective programs are research-based. The above review of the contextual development and outcomes in these sub-regions also illustrates the strategies adopted in promoting the gifted and talented education.

5. THE MULTIDIMENSIONAL GROWTH OF GIFTED AND TALENTED EDUCATION

In light of the future development, the multidimensional development is always the hot issue for discussion (Chou, 1999; He, 1999; Liu, 1999; Wu & Cho, 1993; Zha, 1993). For example, in mainland China, it has been recognised that schools should formulate clear mission, vision and policy. The establishment of the innovative gifted educational research centre, for example, in Shanghai, will help conclude the successful experience and launch try-outs projects in all sorts of educational institutions. Parental involvement and community support, innovation in education reform and institution and school partnership are all considered to be the successful elements in the development.

Although the foci of the work carried out appear to be diversified across the region, the commonality of the approaches and areas for examination are very similar in the process of development of gifted and talented education programs. The evaluation study conducted in Hong Kong, referred to in the previous Section, summarised the issues of identification and assessment, characteristics and needs of gifted and talented students, resource development, program implementation, teacher training, community and policy support. These topics should be considered further through in-depth examination both locally and internationally.

This evaluation study draws implications of future development. At the policy level, this study also recommends formulating a comprehensive strategy, setting up a cross-sector advisory body learning from international experience and strengthening the functions of the Gifted Education Centre. At the implementation level, the strategies recommended include emphasising (a) multiple abilities, (b) devising assessment standards, procedures, and tools, (c) developing a flexible admission mechanism, (d) strengthening teachers' training, and (e) course development in teacher training institutions. At the community level, the approaches include wider participation and collaboration, avoiding a labeling effect and seeking parental support.

In short, an all-round development program is undoubtedly the current view for the process of development and research work in the area of gifted and talented education. However, the resource implications of the multidimensional work are always the difficulties in setting the priorities or reorganising the outcome from different areas. A unified effort in both plans and practices is expected.

6. INTEGRATED RESEARCH ON GIFTED AND TALENTED EDUCATION

The notion of frameworks at the policy level, implementation level and community level will help to increase the feasibility of the research. In Taiwan, a five-year integrated research project (1994 to 1999) with comprehensive strategies was systematically planned and launched. With the joint-effort of scholars and practitioners, the project not only reviewed the advantages, disadvantages and problems of gifted and talented education in Taiwan, but also strengthened theoretical foundations, integrated theories and practices and incorporated research professionals and resources in the area (Wu, 1999).

In the five-year plan, eight areas of research, including (a) policies and conceptions, (b) identification and placement, (c) ecological issues, (d) curriculum and instruction, (e) thinking skills and social-affective development, (f) counselling and following-up, (g) evaluation; and (h) gifted disadvantaged, were identified for examination. By examining the details of the action plans, the objectives were clear and explicit. They included (a) the review and formulation of the policy and provision of gifted education, (b) the strengthening of basic research of the psychosocial characteristics of gifted children, (c) the conducting of longitudinal study and evaluation of program effectiveness, (d) the evaluation of teacher training program, and (e) the dissemination of outcome in a unified effort. Also, a different number of sub-studies was implemented in each year of the five-year plan. The remarkable outcomes of all the sub-studies have been presented in the 1999 Symposium of Research on Gifted and Talented Education (CAGE, 1999).

The second five-year joint research project (1999–2004) was launched, focusing on "Development of multiple talents (DMT): program design and empirical studies". The construction of a framework of multiple talents with three dimensions is the basic idea of the second joint research project. The research model is constructed with three dimensions (a) form of talent (10 forms, mainly based on Gardner's multiple intelligences), (b) function of talents (three functions, basing on Sternberg's view of successful intelligence) and (c) developmental stages (four levels, from pre-school to senior high school) (Wu, 1999). Further examination or try-outs will be undertaken into the five identified sub-themes, including: (a) DMT program research, (b) identification of multiple talents, (c) DMT program design, (d) DMT program effectiveness, and (e) establishment of DMT systems. The clear structural framework and the wide coverage of investigation have attracted the attention and interest of scholars and practitioners in the field.

In short, under the systematic and integrated approach of the five-year project, the joint effort surely links effectively the individual studies and induces a substantial and fruitful outcome. The result is not only to promote the understanding of the intelligence theories, but also to put theory into practice. It is expected that the framework of the development of DMT can remedy the gap between theory and practice and set a good example of reference or practice with respect to other sub-regions. Furthermore, the notion of collaboration between universities and schools is also taken into consideration in the integrated project. For example, with respect to program evaluation, Chang and Chieh (1999) have claimed that the current practice of external evaluation would be unable to provide timely feedback for school improvements. School-based internal evaluation should be advanced through school-university collaboration in the development of models for evaluating gifted programs in the schools. The principles of parity, reciprocity, common language, mutual inquiry, participatory nature and being equitable and consensual were argued to be the essential elements of success.

7. PLACEMENT OF IDENTIFIED GIFTED AND TALENTED CHILDREN

The placement of identified gifted and talented children is another major concern in the Asia-Pacific region. The identification of gifted and talented children follows the service arrangement or placement (Chan, 1996, 1997). Considering the small sample size, the psychological needs, limited resources available and the diversified curricular needs, the mode of delivery is one of the important considerations. While the usual forms of placement are acceleration, enrichment or segregation, the issue of 'the most appropriate placement' for the identified children is always the problem to be solved.

Some examples of the modes of delivery in supporting the exceptionally talented children in mainland China have been advanced (Chou, 1999). The arrangements and practices have signified a unified effort of identification and placement. For example, in 1978, the China Technology University of Anhui Province organised the first class for talented children. Currently, many universities run classes for talented youth in China. This practice was considered highly satisfactory as a great number of the graduates have undertaken further studies in local or overseas universities.

Further, the first try-out class for primary gifted children was set up in Tianjin in 1984. Up to 1999, over 70 primary and secondary schools had launched try-outs and research into gifted and talented education. The modes of organisation included 'within-class teaching', 'individual teaching' and 'schools within schools'. In within-class teaching, many innovative practices were identified for meeting the needs of gifted children. These included small group teaching with a class size of 24 to 30, split group teaching with self-learning and tutor assistance for gifted children, individual subject teaching, advancement or exemption in some subjects, enrichment electives or project learning in the extra-curricular activities. For individual teaching, some schools provided gifted children with individual educational plans. The enrichment and extension activities were helpful towards class skipping and early entry. The talented classes for language, art, music, dance and physical education were also set up in many schools of the country. Activities, competitions, awards for talent adolescents and Olympiads in different subjects from the levels of school, county, province and nation were arranged from time to time. These practices all become channels to identify the talents or opportunities for optimising potential.

In Taiwan, the current support system includes enrichment, acceleration and ability grouping after the identification. Through extra-curricular activities, self-learning, and independent research, the enrichment programs are in form of in-depth programs with logical thinking and problem solving elements and widening programs with horizontal thinking and creativity components. For acceleration, early entry, early graduation, advancement, curriculum compacting and exemption are the practices while for ability grouping, the provision of special class, resource class, withdraw class, and honour class are arranged (Wu, 1999). Diversity in the support system is well noted. However, among enrichment, acceleration and ability grouping, the enrichment program has the first priority for being taken into consideration.

In Hong Kong, a special school for gifted and talented children was not supported (Education Commission, 1990; Education Department, 1999). Instead, schools are encouraged to take the initiative to start school-based programs. The policy assumption is that through grouping, acceleration, extended curriculum or extra-curriculum programs, gifted children would receive appropriate education in the school as well as supplementary educational experiences from the Gifted Education Center.

The levels of support are further divided into three: (a) whole class, (b) pullout, and (c) individual. Enrichment is in the forms of generic or specialised modes. First, for all students, the teachers integrate in all subject curricula the three core elements of creativity, problem-solving and social development. Second, for the top 10 per cent of students in the school, the teachers arrange extension and enrichment activities in various Key Learning Areas. Third, for the top two to four per cent, the teachers gain curriculum support from different channels. These include support from (a) the guideline and framework for systematic enrichment work within the Key Learning Areas, (b) curriculum samplers from previous school-based and centre-based programs, (c) vetting of proposals for school-based curriculum development projects for program funds, as well as (d) school consultation on planning of school-based gifted programs. Finally, for the top 0.1 per cent, schools are advised to take some special measures. The support includes specially designed curricula; consideration for acceleration or class skipping; and centre-based programs. Whenever it is feasible, the support also includes the early entry, mentorship, scholarship, attachment to university or business corporations, individualised support, counselling and guidance, and individual educational programs. In short, the strategies in Hong Kong practice highlight the significance of community involvement and a whole school approach in the process of development.

The above contextual analysis not only illustrates the modes of delivery, but also brings out the issue of implications in the considerations. There are ongoing controversial debates about providing the most appropriate arrangements (Chan, 1997; Chou, 1999; He, 1999; Wu, 1999). Gifted children may start school early, skip grades, do combined grades or work through a non-graded system or curriculum acceleration. The practices are supported because of the provision of more challenging curricula and the shortening of school years. However, there are also some objections that the children may also have difficulties in some areas of learning. Alternative arrangements may create unnecessary emotional or social maladjustment among peers.

Some prefer enrichment to acceleration. Gifted children remain in the same grade but are provided with extra learning opportunities in the formal and informal curriculum. They may be in the form of horizontal enrichment, vertical enrichment or supplementary enrichment. The disadvantage may be the teacher inadequacy as regular class teachers may have difficulty in providing appropriate enrichment plan for the gifted children in the group.

Some insist that a separate school is also a placement option. In the segregated environment, the children are provided with a tailor-made curriculum, a creative learning environment and educational opportunities. The claims are likely to be justified if we consider that the facilities, environment, teaching staff, curriculum, resources and teaching methods will be more consistent in a special school. However, the arrangement is questioned because it creates a long-term intense learning atmosphere for gifted children. Also, it is difficult to avoid creating psychological superiority or inferiority among gifted children, as the psychological implications of the so-called 'small fish in a large pond' and 'large fish in a small pond' always exert effects on self-concept development.

In short, a diversity in providing services is the trend, but school-based development is the focus. Indeed, Chen (1999) has highlighted the feasibility of the integration of gifted and regular education, and an educational model with integrated enrichment and an acceleration program is suggested. With a multi-method approach, every student is encouraged to develop his or her unique giftedness and talents.

8. CONCLUSION

The review of the research and work on gifted and talented education in different education systems in the Asia-Pacific region demonstrates the consensus and goals as well as the different approaches in the processes of development. Although the discussion might not fully reflect the whole picture of each sub-region, the notions of achievement are all highlighted.

In China, the wide variety of practices in gifted and talented education indicates the advantages of a flexible policy in providing the support services. Although the resources for the gifted and talented children always appear to be limited, schools are encouraged to offer a wide range of programs to gifted and talented children at different levels. Provided with these opportunities, the children are able to maximise their potentials.

In Taiwan, the explicit effort of adopting an integrated approach in the research project for gifted and talented education has enhanced the growth of knowledge and experiences, particularly the linking of theories with practices. The outcomes of the two five-year integrated research projects are the most substantial, comprehensive and multidimensional in the region. The university and school partnership in research and practice helps the advancement of gifted and talented education.

In Hong Kong, the emphasis on the school-based support for the majority in all subject curricula and pull-out support for a minority provides a clear and explicit framework of implementation for teachers. Schools are alert to support their high potential students with the appropriate learning opportunities and challenges. It signifies a more systemic approach to nurture high potential students within the schools as well as to mobilise teachers to include the core elements of creativity, problem-solving and social development in the subject curricula. In other words, gifted and talented education may be seen as part of quality education since the needs of high ability students are met in their own school.

In countries like Korea, Singapore, and Thailand, there are ongoing efforts and attempts to provide opportunities for gifted and talented children. The issues of policy development, identification and assessment, characteristics and needs, resource development, program implementation and effectiveness, teacher training, setting up of centres, and community support are the foci of work and research. These attempts represent the similarity of holistic development in the field in all education systems in the region.

In conclusion, while there is a diversity of approaches in the process of development, the commonality in achieving a quality education for gifted and talented children appears to be the ultimate goal. As a mission of 'quality education for all', it is agreed that schools have the responsibilities to support their high ability students. This global view may minimise further segregation, which is not the most appropriate placement if the social and emotional development of the children is the concern. It is also clear that schools in the region are trying to make efforts to nurture students with multiple intelligences that have been immersed in the school curricula. Although the identification or placement of gifted and talented children is always considered as the professional work of educational psychologists, an increasing number of teachers are able to identify and select students for extension work and enrichment activities in schools. Their competency is strongly linked with the growing work of joint research and training in the form of the university and school partnership.

9. THE WAY FORWARD

The effective implementation of gifted and talented education should be on the basis of global development. Those issues at policy, implementation and community level support are expected for in-depth examination locally and internationally. Without validated data in these areas, it is difficult to link the theories of intelligence with practice or to meet the needs of gifted and talented children. In light of Taiwan's integrated research project, future work will include the systematic review of the problems of gifted education, the strengthening of the gifted theories and conceptions, the linking of the theories and practices, and the greater utilisation of research findings and community resources.

All in all, while the process of development may be different in each region, the approach of holistic development in gifted and talented education is generally accepted among scholars and practitioners. It is believed that only joint effort of work and systematic plans for research help the advancement of gifted and talented education in the region. Further research is awaiting; so is further sharing, both regional and global.

REFERENCES

Board of Education (1996). *Report of the sub-committee on special education.* Hong Kong: Hong Kong Government Printer.

Booth, T., Ainscow, M. et al. (2000). *Index for inclusion: Developing learning and participation in schools.* UK: Centre for Studies on Inclusive Education.

CAGE. (Chinese Association of Gifted Education) (Ed.) (1999). *Proceedings of the 1999 Symposium of Research on Gifted and Talented Education: Global development of gifted and talented education.* Taiwan: Chinese Association of Gifted Education.

Chan, D. W. (1996). Program evaluation: Evaluating gifted programs in Hong Kong. *Education Research Journal, 11,* 101–105.

Chan, D. W. (1997). Education for the gifted and talented: What programs are best suited for Hong Kong? *New Horizons in Education, 38,* 22–27.

Chang, H. G., & Chieh, J. J. (1999). An application of collaborative research to the development of models for evaluating gifted programs in elementary schools. In CAGE (Ed.), *Proceedings of the 1999 Symposium of Research on Gifted and Talented Education: Global development of gifted and talented education* (pp. 298–322). Taiwan: Chinese Association of Gifted Education.

Chen, M. F. (1999). *Integrated of gifted and regular education: A model construct.* Paper presented at the 1999 Symposium of Research on Gifted and Talented Education, Taiwan.

Chien, M. F. (1999). Gifted and talented concepts and education. In Chinese Association of Gifted Education (Ed.), *Global Development of Gifted and Talented Education* (pp. 25–40). Taiwan: Psychology Publishing Co., Ltd.

Chinese Association of Gifted Education & Department of Special Education of Taiwan Normal University (Eds.) (1999). *Proceedings of the 1999 Symposium of Research on Gifted and Talented Education: Global development of gifted and talented education.* Taiwan: Chinese Association of Gifted Education.

Cho, S. (1991). Gifted student in Korea. *International Journal of Special Education, 6,* 1–5.

Cho, S. (1999a). *Gifted educational research in Korea.* Paper presented at the 1999 Symposium of Research on Gifted and Talented Education, Taiwan.

Cho, S. (1999b). Nurturing creativity for the gifted in Confucian culture. In CAGE (Ed.), *Proceedings of the 1999 Symposium of Research on Gifted and Talented Education: Global development of gifted and talented education* (pp. 199–208). Taiwan: Chinese Association of Gifted Education.

Chou, W. (1999). Developing talent potentials and nurturing creative talents In CAGE (Ed.), *Proceedings of the 1999 Symposium of Research on Gifted and Talented Education: Global development of gifted and talented education* (pp. 3–17). Taiwan: Chinese Association of Gifted Education.

Education Commission, (1990). *Education Commission Report No. 4.* Hong Kong: Hong Kong Government Printer.

Education Commission (2000). *Learning for life, learning through life: Reform proposals for education system in Hong Kong.* Hong Kong: Hong Kong Government Printer.

Education Department (1999). *Evaluation report of the pilot school-based program for academically gifted children: Executive summary.* Hong Kong: Hong Kong Government Printer.

Gardner, H. (1983). *Frames of mind.* New York: Basic Books.

Gardner, H. (1993). *Multiple intelligences: The theory in practice.* New York: Basic Books.

Guilford, J. P. (1967). *The nature of human intelligence.* New York: McGraw-Hill.

He, S. M. (1999). Study on the results of 'questionnaire on talent education in Chinese. In CAGE (Ed.), *Proceedings of the 1999 Symposium of Research on Gifted and Talented Education: Global development of gifted and talented education* (pp. 19–20). Taiwan: Chinese Association of Gifted Education.

Ku-Yu, H. S. Y., Shek, D. T. L., & Yung, K. K. (1994a). *The Hong Kong Chinese Behavioural Checklist for Teachers (HKBC-T).* Hong Kong: Hong Kong Government.

Ku-Yu, H. S. Y., Shek, D. T. L., & Yung, K. K. (1994b). *The Hong Kong Chinese Behavioural Checklist for Parents (HKBC-P).* Hong Kong: Hong Kong Government.

Ku-Yu, H. S. Y., Shek, D. T. L., Spinks, J. A., & Bacon-Shone, J. (1995). *Norming of Hong Kong Torrance Tests of Creative Thinking (HK-TTCT): Executive summary report.* Hong Kong: Hong Kong Government.

Ku-Yu, H. S. Y., Shek, D. T. L., Yung, K. K., Spinks, J. A., & Bacon-Shone, J. (1998). *The identification and distribution of gifted children in Hong Kong.* Hong Kong: Hong Kong Government.

Lim, T. K. (Ed.) (1997). *Maximizing academic achievement. The Chinese high gifted education program in Singapore.* Singapore: Times Academic Press.

Lim, T. K. (1999). Gifted education research in Singapore. Paper presented at the 1999 Symposium of Research on Gifted and Talented Education: Global development of gifted and talented education. Taiwan: Chinese Association of Gifted Education.

Liu, Z. P. (1999). Gifted education: Supernormal enlightenment on Mathematics. In CAGE (Ed.), *Proceedings of the 1999 Symposium of Research on Gifted and Talented Education: Global development of gifted and talented education* (173–198). Taiwan: Chinese Association of Gifted Education.

Phothisuk, U. (1999a). *Gifted researches in Thailand.* Paper presented at the 1999 Symposium of Research on Gifted and Talented Education, Taiwan.

Phothisuk, U. (1999b). Gifted programming in elementary level in Thailand. In CAGE (Ed.), *Proceedings of the 1999 Symposium of Research on Gifted and Talented Education: Global development of gifted and talented education* (pp. 135–138). Taiwan: Chinese Association of Gifted Education.

Quah, M. L., & Teo, C. T. (1998). A study of the relationship between creative thinking and academic achievement of intellectually gifted adolescents in Singapore. In Quah, M. L., & Ho, W. K. *Thinking processes: Going beyond the surface curriculum.* Singapore: Prentice Hall.

Renzulli, J. S. (1986). The three-ring conception of giftedness: A developmental model for creative productivity. In R. J. Sternberg & J. E. Davidson (Eds.), *Conceptions of giftedness* (pp. 53–92). New York: Cambridge University Press

Sin, K. F., Lyon, P. E., & Chan, H. K. (1998). The education of gifted children in Hong Kong. In J. L. Fortson (Ed.), *Interdisciplinary Studies* (Vol. VI, pp. 153–168). USA: Society of Educators and Scholars.

Sternberg, R. J. (1996). *Successful intelligence: How practical and creative intelligence determine success in life.* New York: Simon & Schuster.

UNESCO. (1994). *The Salamanca statement and framework for action on special needs Education.* Salamanca: UNESCO.

Wang, J. D. (1999). Policy development of gifted and talent education. In CAGE (Ed.), *Proceedings of the 1999 Symposium of Research on Gifted and Talented Education: Global development of gifted and talented education* (pp. 109–110). Taiwan: Chinese Association of Gifted Education.

Wu, W. T., & Chien, M. F. (1999). Curriculum design and experimental study on personal intelligence in elementary school. In CAGE (Ed.), *Proceedings of the 1999 Symposium of Research on Gifted and Talented Education: Global development of gifted and talented education* (pp. 279–296). Taiwan: Chinese Association of Gifted Education.

Wu, W. T., & Cho, S. (1993). Programs and practices for identifying and nurturing giftedness and talent in Asia. In K. A. Heller, F. J. Monks & A. H. Passow (Eds.), *International Handbook of Research and Development of Giftedness and Talent*. Oxford: Pergamon.

Wu, W. T. (1999). *Integrated research project on gifted education in Taiwan*. In Chinese Association of Gifted Education (Eds.). *Global Development of Gifted and Talented Education* (pp. 1–24). Taiwan: Psychology Publishing Co., Ltd.

Zha, Z. (1993). Programs and practices for identifying and nurturing giftedness and talent in People's Republic of China. In K. A. Heller, F. J. Monks and A. H. Passow (Eds.), *International Handbook of Research and Development of Giftedness and Talent*. Oxford: Pergamon.

14

Inclusive Education for Students with Special Needs

DAVID MITCHELL
University of Waikato, New Zealand

ISHWAR DESAI
University of Melbourne, Australia

1. INTRODUCTION

At the most fundamental level, inclusive education starts with all students with special needs (SWSN) having access to the same educational opportunities as other children. According to Kholi (1993), however, in developing countries in Asia, only one per cent of such children actually have access to any education. However, inclusive education implies much more than SWSN having access to education. In particular, as emphasised in *The Salamanca Statement and Framework for Action on Special Needs Education* (UNESCO, 1994), it requires that they have access to regular schools, and preferably regular classrooms, which in turn means that all schools should make appropriate adaptations to the curriculum, and teaching and assessment methods.

Apart from in Australia and New Zealand, and a few developing countries, there has been little research into inclusive education in the Asia-Pacific region. Much of it has focused on (a) documenting policies (or the lack of them), (b) action research into implementing inclusive education projects, and (c) surveys of attitudes towards inclusion. There have been few studies of its impact or on comparing different approaches. This article summarises some of the studies that have been carried out in 12 selected countries in the region, with more detailed coverage of four of them: Australia, China, India and Japan. Space permits the selection of representative studies only in most of the countries.

2. RESEARCH

2.1. *Australia*

In Australia, education is a legislative responsibility of the states and territories, with the Federal Government providing financial assistance to State

Governments and to the non-government education sectors, and parent groups to develop, implement and evaluate appropriate programs for SWSN. Not surprisingly, therefore, there is considerable variation in the way inclusive practices for such students are implemented in the six Australian states and the two territories.

There is no legislation in Australia mandating inclusive education. In the absence of such legislation, both Federal and State anti-discrimination and equal opportunity laws are often the only avenues for redress for persons with disabilities. In regard to education, for example, the Federal Disability Discrimination Act 1992, prohibits school authorities from refusing to admit a child with a disability as a student. It also prohibits the denial of access to any benefit that may be provided by a school authority. This is sometimes interpreted as a mandate for inclusion should a parent or student request it. There is, however, a loophole that renders this legislation ineffective in some situations. If, for example, school authorities are able to prove that they would suffer what is referred to as 'unjustifiable hardship' in accepting a child to a particular school then they may refuse entry of that child at the school (Commonwealth of Australia, 1997). Unjustifiable hardship can include the expense of educating a child with a disability, teacher stress, or making modifications to buildings (Commonwealth of Australia, 1997). The lack of legislative frameworks for inclusion in Australian jurisdictions emphasises the need to develop suitable legal models (Forlin & Forlin, 1998).

Since the late 1980s and early 1990s, both the Federal and State Governments in Australia have developed explicit policy statements about the education of SWSN and about inclusion (Elkins, in press). Although there is some diversity in the policy statements of the various states and territories, they all recognise the ability of every student to learn, the need to focus on the students' strengths rather than weaknesses, and the importance of parent involvement in the planning and development of the child's educational program (Dempsey, 2001).

The number of SWSN receiving support in regular schools has been steadily increasing, most noticeably in the state of Victoria where there are currently more students with a disability enrolled in a regular school than in a special school. Thus, in 1984 there were 214 students with a disability enrolled in regular schools and 5,300 in specialist settings, whereas in 2001 the number of students with a disability in regular schools rose to 10,900 in contrast to 5,900 who attended specialist settings (Tar, 2001). In New South Wales (NSW), too, the number of SWSN receiving support in regular schools has increased from 1,135 in 1988 to over 12,000 in the year 2000 (Foreman, Bourke, Mishra, & Frost, 2001).

Australian academics and researchers would very likely divide sharply in their interpretation of such statistics as indicators of significant progress towards inclusive education. Wills and Jackson (2001) recently completed a Report Card on Inclusive Education in Australia with a team of researchers drawn from each of the states and the Australian Capital Territory (ACT). They reported the following findings.

(1) Most children with disabilities across the country are not physically included in their local schools although many more are integrated than a decade ago. In this regard Victoria was rated significantly higher than South Australia (SA), Western Australia(WA), New South Wales (NSW) and Queensland (QLD). Tasmania was rated significantly higher than WA, NSW and QLD.
(2) Of those children with a disability who attended regular schools, the raters judged their social inclusion to have been predominantly determined by their peers and not by the adults in their schools. Victoria was rated significantly higher than SA, WA, NSW and QLD. Tasmania was rated significantly higher than QLD.
(3) Of the three dimensions of inclusion studied, namely, curricular, physical and social, curricular inclusion was found to be the least developed and understood. Victoria was once again rated significantly higher than SA, NSW and QLD.

Difficulties in implementing an effective policy for the social and curriculum inclusion of students with disabilities have been highlighted in studies in a number of countries, including Australia (Elkins, in press). Loreman (2000), who recently completed a study on secondary school inclusion for students with moderate to severe disabilities in Victoria, found many teachers having difficulties in delivering a multi-level curriculum. He stated that an inappropriate curriculum seemed, in part, to be responsible for the poor academic performance of some students. He also found that most students had difficulties making and keeping friends, and were viewed as having poor social skills. Notwithstanding these and other barriers facing the implementation of inclusion in Australia, there are reasons to be optimistic. Several surveys of teachers and principals during the past two decades have shown educators to be generally positive in their attitudes to inclusion (Bailey & du Plessis, 1998; Centre, Ward, Parmenter, & Nash, 1985; Desai, 1995).

2.2. *China*

Historically, as Deng, Poon-McBrayer and Farnsworh (in press), point out, people with disabilities occupied the lowest social status under the hierarchic feudal pyramid of roles that dominated China for 2,000 years under the influence of Confucianism. Even though superstition and fatalism were common, and are probably still present among some sectors of the population, sympathetic attitudes were also present. In recent times, laws and policies reflect endeavours to bestow equal rights to persons with disabilities. For example, the Compulsory Education Law of the People's Republic of China (1986) mandated that schools should accept SWSN. Laws do not always lead to practice, however, as illustrated by Deng and Manset (2000) who cite 1991 figures showing that only ten per cent of SWSN attended school. A somewhat more positive picture was presented by Chen (1996) who cited 1987 statistics on the placements of children with disabilities that showed that 55 per cent of SWSN were enrolled in some form of education (1.0% in special schools and 54% in regular schools), while the remaining 45 per cent were either kept at home or were placed in welfare institutions.

In 1989, a classroom integration project was initiated in two-thirds of China's provinces (Chen, 1996). This was deemed to be a success and led to the formulation of National Guidelines of Classroom Integration for Disabled Children. Among the perceived benefits were the provision of education for SWSN living in remote rural areas, an increase in the enrolment rates of SWSN, improved adaptation of SWSN to school and society, and the cultivation of mutual understanding between SWSN and other students. More recently, the Learning in Regular Classrooms movement has further advanced inclusive education (Deng & Manset, 2000), although it provides no guarantee of an appropriate education, parent involvement, appropriate assessment or individual education programs. Furthermore, many SWSN have been observed to be 'drifting in the regular classroom', taking no part in activities and even remaining at home while nominally being on the roll.

As noted by Mitchell and Chen (1996), the growing emphasis on mainstreaming in China reflects three main factors. First, since it is not possible to fund special schools, special class or mainstream class placement is seen as being more cost effective. Second, 80 per cent of SWSN live in rural areas and it is impossible for their families to send them to residential schools far from their homes. Third, such an arrangement is seen as good for helping SWSN understand each other.

Mitchell and Chen (1996) and Chen (1996) identified several obstacles to the development of inclusive education in China. One obstacle is that Chinese parents have conservative ideas about disability, doubting the learning capacities of SWSN and frequently shielding them from public view. A second obstacle is that non-academic study is generally neglected in schools and scores on academic tests are regarded as the sole criteria for evaluation. An associated view is that priority must be given to the education of normal children and that that accepting SWSN would interfere with study habits and achievements of the other students. Finally, there are inadequacies in educational facilities, teachers' abilities, support services, equipment, class size, and early intervention.

2.3. Hong Kong

According to Crawford (2000), despite the fact that Hong Kong has had an integration policy for over 30 years, an increasing number of SWSN are segregated from regular classrooms, especially at the secondary level. Earlier, Crawford (1995) noted that "there is a difference ... between the rhetoric of integration and inclusive schools and what occurs in practice." For example, a recent Green Paper on Rehabilitation arguing that the process of integration must be expedited, while at the same time the Education Commission was proposing segregative policies, even for students with mild learning difficulties.

In a recent initiative, the Department of Education set up a two-year pilot project to support integration in nine schools. This project extended from 1997 to 1999 and was evaluated by a team of researchers from the Hong Kong Institute of Education. In one of the studies, King (2000) investigated the social interactions of the 48 SWSN involved in the project. While most of them said they enjoyed life in mainstream schools, they also experienced some difficulties in making friends outside their group and at times felt isolated. Other findings, reported by Yuen (2000), included changes in teachers' attitudes and beliefs in educating diverse learners in ordinary schools, despite the fact that the data showed that they lacked the expertise or the time to develop and implement curricular adaptations and they rarely used such strategies as peer tutoring, cooperative learning and co-teaching.

2.4. India

Recent estimates of the number of school-aged children with disabilities in India have ranged from 30 to 35 million (Singh, 2001). Since its independence, India has witnessed a phenomenal growth in the establishment of special schools (Pandey & Advani, 1997). While the majority of these schools are located in urban areas, approximately 70 per cent of children with disabilities live in rural areas. According to Rao (2000), special schools cater for only one per cent of students with disabilities. Therefore, integrated education (the term preferred in India) remains the only viable option (Chadha, 2000; Swaroop, 2001).

In order to promote integrated education, the Government of India has taken a number of initiatives, such as the Project Integrated Education of the Disabled (PIED) in1987 and, more recently, the passage of The Persons with Disabilities Act (Equal Opportunities, Protection of Rights and Full Participation). With its emphasis on educating students with disabilities in regular school settings wherever possible, this legislation has the potential to change the educational status of more than 30 million children with disabilities who currently do not have access to any form of education. However, researchers note that providing education to such a vast number of children with disabilities in regular school settings will require a number of challenges and issues to be addressed.

School personnel, parents, students and the community generally hold deeply rooted negative attitudes toward people with a disability. A belief in the doctrine of Karma has often militated against such persons because it is believed that since their disability represents retribution for sins committed in a previous incarnation, any efforts to improve their lot would interfere with the workings of divine justice (Baquer & Sharma, 1997).

The majority of school personnel in India are not trained to design and implement educational programs for students with disabilities in regular schools (Das, 2001; Dev & Belfiore, 1996; Jangira, Singh, & Yadav, 1995). In 1974, the Central Government of India initiated a scheme to promote the integration of students with mild to moderate disabilities into regular schools. However, the program met with little success. Mani (1988) reported that by 1979–80, only 1,881 children from 81 schools all over the country had benefited from it. Jangira

(1990) attributed the lack of progress in implementing this scheme largely to the shortage of teachers specifically trained to work with children with disabilities.

Alur (2000) points out that because of the lack of direction from the government and from non-government organisations (NGOs), services for persons with disabilities are extremely fragmented. Her research suggests that the government has tended to rely too heavily on NGOs to educate children with disabilities. The NGOs, on the other hand, have contributed to this fragmentation by setting up centres of excellence which have removed the education of children with disabilities out of the public domain. In so far as the education of children with disabilities is concerned, Alur states that there exists no cohesive policy.

The majority of schools in India are poorly designed and equipped to meet the unique needs of students with disabilities (Alur, 2000; Sharma, 2001). Studies have shown that the lack of adequate equipment and appropriate instructional materials are major impediments to the inclusion of children with disabilities in regular education classrooms (Dev & Belfiore, 1996; Sharma, 2001). Researchers have reported that over-crowded classrooms are a major challenge to the implementation of inclusive education (Sharma, 2001, Swaroop, 2001). They warn that it may not be possible for educators to accommodate students with disabilities in their classes unless this issue is given serious attention.

Much of the research into inclusive education during the past decade has been directed at exploring factors related to educators' attitudes and their training needs to implement effective inclusive practices. The following provides a brief synthesis of selected research on these aspects. In 1991, Jangira and Srinivasan (1991) surveyed a number of educators who were involved in the implementation of the 1974 Integrated Education of Disabled Children Scheme to determine their attitudes to the education of children with disabilities in regular schools. They found that the special education teachers expressed the most positive attitudes, followed by educational administrators and school principals. Regular classroom teachers exhibited the least positive attitudes. Sharma (2001) explored the attitudes and concerns of 310 primary school principals and 484 teachers in Delhi regarding the integration of students with disabilities into regular school programs. He found that the best predictors of teachers' attitudes toward integrated education were their length of teaching experience, their contact with students with disabilities and perceived parental support for integrated education; while for the principals, perceived parental support for integrated education was the only significant predictor of their attitudes. He also found that both principals and teachers were concerned about the lack of resources, such as special education teachers and para-professional staff, the non-availability of instructional materials, the lack of funding, and their lack of training to implement integrated education.

Jangira, Singh and Yadav (1995) conducted a large-scale investigation involving 1907 teachers to identify their training needs relative to integration. The teachers expressed high levels of needs in the following areas: content of school subjects, methods of teaching, multigrade teaching, play-way techniques for teaching and the preparation and use of improvised teaching aids. More recently,

Das (2001) surveyed teachers in Delhi. They indicated a need for training in such aspects as professional knowledge, classroom climate, collaboration, assessment, classroom management, goal-setting, resource management, instructional techniques, individualised instruction and evaluation. They particularly emphasised their need for intensive training in professional knowledge and assessment. They identified conferences and conventions related to special education and workshops conducted by experts from outside India as their preferred mode for in-service training.

2.5. Japan

As noted by LeTendre and Shimizu (1999), there is very little research into how SWSN are integrated into regular schools in Japan. Ministry of Education statistics for 1999 show that only 1.02 per cent of students are placed in special schools or special classes. However, according to three sets of figures presented by Takuma, Ochiai and Munekata (2000), the number of students needing extra support is considerably higher than this figure. First, a 1967 survey revealed a prevalence rate of 3.69 per cent of students with disabilities in Japanese schools. A second survey, reported in 1995, found that by Grades 5 and 6, nearly one in ten students were rated as being two or more years behind the expected level of achievement in Japanese language or mathematics. The third study, carried out in 1998, noted that by junior high school and high school more than one student in five could not understand most of the content of their lessons. As well, so-called 'school refusal' is a growing problem, the rate in elementary and junior high schools having climbed from 0.5 per cent in 1987, to 1.26 per cent in 1998 (Monbusho, 2000). The discrepancy between the proportion of SWSN and the actual number receiving special education might suggest that Japan has a policy of including such students in regular education. This is true up to a point as almost all of them are in regular classrooms. For the most part, however, they receive few or no adaptations to their educational programs and teachers receive little specialist support or training (Mitchell, in press).

In 1993, the Ministry of Education introduced a policy in which some SWSN would attend resource rooms for several hours each week, while maintaining their enrolments in regular classes. Approximately two-thirds of such students have to travel outside of their home schools to attend resource rooms. It is suggested that this policy be reviewed, particularly with regard to the continuity of the programs between resource rooms and regular classes, the support provided to regular class teachers, and the wisdom of having students travelling outside their home schools.

In his research, Mitchell (in press) found generally positive views towards including students with disabilities in regular classes. However, to achieve this goal, there would have to be adaptations to the curriculum, the development of appropriate teaching and assessment methods, the institution of individual education programs (IEPs), the employment of assistant teachers, and modifications to teacher education. In his review of special education in Japan, Abe (1998) pointed out that "many students with mild handicaps or learning difficulties are being placed in regular classes without adequate support" (p. 93).

As noted by Mitchell (in press), Japan's approach to inclusive education can best be understood with reference to its cultural values. Three are of particular relevance. First, as Shimizu (1998) observed, Japanese schools are concerned more with providing education according to collectively established frames of reference than with catering for individual differences. Second, Japanese believe that, with rare exceptions, people are born with equal capacities to achieve and that where individual differences exist, they are created through cumulative effort, not innate ability. Third, since all students are seen as being equal, any special attention is seen as discriminatory.

2.6. Malaysia

Although Malaysia has no specific legislation mandating the inclusion of students with disabilities in regular schools, the term 'inclusive education' was introduced for the first time in the Education Act, 1996 and in Selected Regulations, 1998, as part of the continuum of services to be made available for SWSN. Eligibility for placement in special education programs is based on a student's educability as determined by a team of professionals (Jelas, 2000). Such students are initially placed in special education classrooms and then transferred to inclusive classrooms if they are deemed able to cope with the academic and social demands of these settings (Haq, 2000). Special education teachers and general education teachers share responsibility for educating these students.

According to Haq (2000), an increasing number of children with disabilities are being educated in regular classrooms. Perceptions of inclusive practices in Malaysian schools have recently been examined by Jelas (2000). Using a case study approach, she interviewed and observed three special education teachers, three regular classroom teachers and three mothers whose SWSN were integrated into a local primary school. The special education teachers felt that placement of these students in mainstream classrooms enhanced their school experiences. The regular teachers, while initially apprehensive and feeling unqualified for their role, were positive in their attitudes. All three mothers preferred their children to be in the mainstream classroom.

2.7. Pakistan

Pakistan's national policy, initiated in 1985 and revised in 1988, has as its primary goal raising the percentage of disabled children in schools to ten per cent. More recently, the government has accepted the general philosophy of the Salamanca Framework (UNESCO, 1994). However, a major constraint to inclusion is the historical separation of special and regular education. Thus, responsibility for the education of SWSN rests with the Ministry of Health, Special Education and Social Welfare, not the Ministry of Education.

Over the past decade, a few pilot projects have been initiated, with mixed success. A recent example of a successful project was reported by Khatoon

(2000). In this study, students with mild to moderate mental retardation were integrated into a regular school and were taught their special syllabus by a regular and a special teacher. Compared with a special school control group, they made gains in reading and mathematics and their developmental quotient increased.

2.8. Philippines

In the Philippines, legislation and various policy documents provide a mandate for inclusive or integrated education. For example, the 1992 Magna Carta for Disabled Persons declared that "Disabled persons are part of Philippine society, thus the State shall give full support to the improvement of the total well-being of disabled persons and their integration into the mainstream of society ...". Despite this philosophy and the fact that the incidence of SWSN is estimated to be between 15 and 25 per cent, estimates in the late 1980s showed that fewer than 2 per cent of such students were being provided for. Recent figures show that even in the Metro Manila region, fewer than ten per cent of SWSN received special education services.

According to Adorio (2000), a number of children with special educational needs have been placed in regular education classrooms with conditions for mainstreaming jointly set by both special and regular teachers. In a comparative study of teacher attitudes towards mainstreaming, Leyser, Kapperman and Keller (1994) found that teachers in the Philippines had generally neutral attitudes. A 1997 country report noted that although the ultimate goal of special education in the Philippines is integration, the reality is that not all SWSN can be integrated in regular classes and thus various options and plans for educational placement have remained open. Moves to adopt a more inclusionary model are faced with such problems as an inherited exclusionary system, limited geographical coverage, shortage of qualified and well-skilled teachers for inclusive education, the slow pace of curricular change in regular teacher education and limited fiscal and human resources.

2.9. Singapore

In Singapore, approximately one per cent of students are placed in segregated special schools that are under the control of voluntary welfare organisations with substantial, but not full, government funding (Lim & Nam, 2000), As well, since 1992, learning support coordinators work in just under half the primary schools to assist them cater for students with learning difficulties (Quah & Jones, 1997). Other programs provided by voluntary welfare organisations support students with physical disabilities and autism in regular schools.

A recent study by Ee and Cheng (2000) reported on the views of 750 teachers and parents of intellectually disabled and non-intellectually disabled children with regard to inclusion. They found that while there was general agreement as to the mutual benefits to be derived by both groups of students, the respondents were concerned that intellectually disabled students might not obtain necessary services and it might not be possible to modify lessons. According to Lim and Nam (2000), the principles of marketisation that drive Singapore's education system, as reflected, for example, in the ranking of schools, deter schools from accepting students who might depress their scores.

2.10. Turkey

In Turkey, an Act relating to special education was put in place in 1997. Integration practices constituted the general approach throughout this legislation. Thus, it was considered "a priority, as far as possible, to educate children with special needs with their normal peers in their social and physical environment and to make the necessary adaptations at the educational setting in terms of purpose, content, and educational processes ..." However, according to Uzundemir (2000), fewer than ten per cent of SWSN have access to any form of education and only 0.59 per cent receive special education services, with another 0.25 per cent being provided for in private and governmental rehabilitation centres; those with profound and multiple disabilities are excluded altogether. Sari (2000) concludes that the struggle to develop compulsory education for the majority of children takes precedence over the needs of SWSN in Turkey.

Some 13 research studies on inclusion in Turkey have been identified by Eripek (2000). Most concern students with mental retardation and employ a descriptive methodology. Their subjects ranged from attitudes towards inclusion to the involvement of parents. An example of one such study is that reported by Diken and Sucuoglu (2001) who compared the attitudes towards inclusion held by two groups of teachers who had and did not have students with mental retardation in their classrooms. They found that of the former, 87 per cent received no training in teaching such students and 75 per cent received no support. Both groups had negative attitudes towards inclusion, those with mentally retarded children in their classrooms being the more negative.

2.11. Vietnam

As described in a recent paper by Le Van Tac (2000), inclusive education in Vietnam got under way in the mid 1990s as staff in the National Institute of Educational Science, in association with Rädda Barnen from Sweden, set up some pilot projects. Evaluations of these projects that were carried out in 1995 showed positive changes of attitudes and an awareness among the general public that children with disabilities could be educated in regular schools. As well, however, the evaluation indicated a lack of knowledge among teachers and educational leaders as to how children learn and a lack of cooperation among various ministries and agencies. The former problem led to the introduction of a one-year pre-service teacher education program on inclusive education in two colleges in 1999. The latter was addressed through changes to the education law and the transfer of responsibility for the education of students with disabilities from the Ministry of Labor, Invalids and Social Affairs to the Ministry of Education.

3. CONCLUSION

Inclusive education focusing on students with special needs that arise from disabilities is a relatively new concept for most countries in the Asia Pacific region. The philosophy of inclusion has been widely adopted in principle, although countries vary greatly in their interpretation of it and the extent to which they implement it in practice. For the most part, countries have adopted the philosophy more for reasons derived from ideology (e.g., equality of educational opportunity) or pragmatism (e.g, segregated special schools are too expensive) than from the results of systematic research. Although indigenous studies have generally played a negligible role in determining the introduction of inclusion, they are playing an increasing role in guiding its implementation.

Research has thrown light on three main issues. First, reports show that in many of the countries in the region, SWSN do not have access to any form of education or special education. In this sense, inclusive education has not been widely accepted. Second, the range of literature contains many descriptive studies of the extent to which countries have accepted the principles of inclusive education. These include historical analyses, some of which provide cultural explanations for the presence or absence of inclusive education policies. Several studies refer to the frequent occurrence of disparities between policies and practices, and between rhetoric and reality. Third, the bulk of studies focus on the barriers to inclusive education. These include negative attitudes, large class sizes, lack of support services, inadequate teacher education, the presence of dual systems of general and special education, lack of coordination among government bodies and NGOs, uniform curricula, the utilisation of assessment for ranking purposes, inappropriate school design, negative cultural values, and funding.

Future research on inclusive education, will of course depend on country-specific interests, but there are some general issues worthy of attention. Two areas warrant study: investigations into the nature of inclusive education which goes beyond mere placement and looks at the nature of pedagogical practices and curricular adaptations, and investigations of the outcomes of inclusive education in terms of how it can enhance student learning.

REFERENCES

Abe Y. (1998). Special education reform in Japan. *European Journal of Special Needs Education*, *13*(1), 86–97.

Adorio, P. (2000). Inclusive education in Philippine schools: Issues and challenges. Paper presented at the International Special Education Conference, Manchester, UK.

Alur (2000). Invisible children: A study of policy exclusion. Paper presented at the International Special Education Congress, Manchester, UK.

Bailey, J., & du Plessis, D. (1998). An investigation of school principals' attitudes toward inclusive education. *Australasian Journal of Special Education, 22*, 12–29.

Baquer, A., & Sharma, A. (1997). *Disability: Challenges vs Response*. New Delhi: Concerted Action Now.

Center, Y. Ward, J., Parmenter, T., & Nash, R. (1985). Principals' attitudes towards the integration of disabled children into regular schools. *The Exceptional Child, 32,* 149–161.

Chadha, A. (2000). Special education: Empowerment through education. *The Journal of the International Association of Special Education, 3*(1), 17–22.

Chen, Y. Y. (1996). Making special education compulsory and inclusive in China. *Cambridge Journal of Education, 26*(1), 47–58.

Commonwealth of Australia (1997). *Disability Discrimination Act, 1992.* Canberra: Commonwealth of Australia.

Crawford, N. (1995). Enabling or disabling policies for children and young people. In G. Postiglione and L. W. Oh (Eds.), *Schooling in Hong Kong.* Hong Kong: Hong Kong University Press.

Crawford, N. (2000). Integration in Hong Kong: A framework for reform. Paper presented at the International Special Education Conference, Manchester, UK.

Das, A. (2001). *Perceived training needs of regular primary and secondary school teachers to implement inclusive education programs in Delhi, India.* Unpublished doctoral dissertation, The University of Melbourne.

Dempsey, I. (2001). Principles and policies for integration and inclusion. In P. Foreman (Ed.), *Integration and inclusion in action* (pp. 35–58). Sydney: Harcourt.

Deng, M, Poon-McBrayer, K. F., & Farnsworth, E. B. (in press). The development of special education in China: A socio-cultural review. *Remedial and Special Education.*

Deng, M., & Manset, G. (2000). Analysis of the learning in regular Classrooms movement in China. *Mental Retardation, 38,* 124–130.

Desai, I. P. (1995). Primary school principals' attitudes toward mainstreaming in Victoria, Australia. *International Journal of Special Education, 10*(2), 22–36.

Dev, P. C., & Belfiore, P. J. (1996). Mainstreaming students with disabilities: Teacher perspectives in India. Paper presented at the Annual International Convention of the Council of Exceptional Children, Orlando, FL.

Diken, I. H., & Sucuoglu, B. (2001). Attitudes of Turkish teachers towards inclusion. Paper presented at CEC Convention, Kansas City, USA.

Ee, J., & Cheng, S. K. (2000), Perceptions of Singaporean teachers and parents about inclusive educational placements of students with intellectual disabilities. *Saudi Journal of Disability and Rehabilitation, 6*(4), 272–275.

Elkins, J. (in press). The school context. In A. Ashman & J. Elkins (Ed.), *Educating Children with Diverse Abilities.* NSW: Pearson Education Australia.

Eripek, S. (2000). An evaluation of the research base about inclusion of special needs students in Turkey. Paper presented at the International Special Education Conference, Manchester, UK.

Foreman, P., Bourke, S., Mishra, G., & Frost, R. (2001). Assessing the support needs of children with a disability in regular classes. *International Journal of Disability, Development and Education, 48*(3), 239–252.

Forlin, P., & Forlin, C. (1998). Constitutional and legal framework for inclusive education in Australia. *Australian Journal of Education, 42*(2), 204–217.

Haq, F. S. (2000). From divided responsibility to shared responsibility: Inclusion in Malaysia. Paper presented at the International Special Education Conference, Manchester, UK.

Jangira, N. K. (1990). Education for all: What about these forgotten children? *Education and Society, 1*(4), 2–4.

Jangira, N. K., & Srinivasan, A. (1991). Attitudes of educational administrators and teachers toward education of disabled children. *Indian Journal of Disability and Rehabilitation* (July-December), 25–35.

Jangira, N. K., Singh, A., & Yadav, S. K. (1995). Teacher policy, training needs and perceived status of teachers. *Indian Educational Review, 30*(1), 113–122.

Jelas, Z. M.(2000). Perceptions of inclusive practices: The Malaysian perspective. *Educational Review, 52*(1),187–196.

Kholi, T. (1993). Special education in Asia. In P. Mittler, R. Brouilette & D. Harris (Eds.), *Special Needs Education* (pp. 118–129). London: Kogan Page.

King, H. W. (2000). Social integration of students with disabilities integrated in ordinary schools in Hong Kong. Paper presented at the International Special Education Conference, Manchester, UK.

Le Van Tac (2000). Inclusive education – A new phase in Vietnam. Paper presented at the International Special Education Conference, Manchester, UK.

LeTendre, G. K., & Shimizu, H. (1999). Towards a healing society: Perspectives from Japanese special education. In H. Daniels & P. Garner (Eds.), *Inclusive Education* (pp. 115–129). London: Kogan Page.

Leyser, Y., Kapperman, G., & Keller, R. (1994). Teacher attitudes toward mainstreaming: A cross-cultural study in six nations. *European Journal of Special Needs Education*, 9(1), 1–12.

Lim, L., & Nam, S. S. (2000). Special Education in Singapore. *The Journal of Special Education*, 34(2), 104–109.

Loreman, T. J. (2000). Secondary school inclusion for students with moderate and severe disabilities in Victoria, Australia. Unpublished doctoral dissertation, Monash University.

Mani, R. (1988). *Physically Handicapped in India*. Delhi: Ashish Publishing House.

Mitchell, D. (in press). Japanese schools' accommodation to student diversity. *The Journal of School Education*.

Mitchell, D. R., & Chen, Y. (1996). Special Education in Asia. In R. Brown, A. Neufeld and D. Baine (Eds.), *Beyond Basic Care: Special Education and Community Rehabilitation in Low Income Countries* (pp. 8–42). North York, ONT: Captus Press.

Monbusho (2000). *Statistical Abstract of Education, Science, Sports and Culture: 2000 edition*. Tokyo: Monbusho.

Pandey, R. S., & Advani, L. (1997). *Perspectives in Disability and Rehabilitation*. New Delhi: Vikas Publishing House.

Quah, M. L., & Jones, K. (1997). Reshaping learning support in a rapidly developing society. *Support for Learning*, 12(1), 38–42.

Rao, I. (2000). A comparative study of UN rules and Indian Disability Act 1995. Email obtained from cbrnet@vsnl.com on 17th March 2000.

Sari, H. (2000). Development of special education provision in Turkey: From the inclusive perspective. Paper presented at the International Special Education Conference, Manchester, UK.

Sharma, U. (2001). The attitudes and concerns of school principals and teachers regarding the integration of students with disabilities into regular schools in Delhi, India. Unpublished doctoral dissertation, The University of Melbourne.

Shimizu, H. (1998). Individual Differences and the Japanese Education System. In R. W. Riley, T. Takai & J. C. Conaty (Eds.), *The Educational System in Japan: Case Study Findings* (pp. 79–134). Washington DC.: National Institute on Student Achievement, Curriculum, and Assessment, Office of Educational Research and Improvement, U.S. Department Of Education.

Singh, R. (2001). Needs of the hour – A Paradigm Shift in Education. Paper presented at the North South Dialogue on Inclusive Education, Mumbai, India.

Swaroop, S. (2001). Inclusion and beyond. Paper presented at the North South Dialogue on Inclusive Education, Mumbai, India.

Takuma, S., Ochiai, T., & Munekata, T. (2000). Contemporary issues and trends in special needs education in Japan. In C. Brock & R. Griffin (Eds.), *International Perspectives on Special Needs Education* (pp. 251–275). Great Glenham, Saxmundham, Suffolk: John Catt Educational.

Tar, P. (2001). Policies, program management and leadership in special education and integration in Victoria. Seminar presented to post-graduate students at the University of Melbourne, 4th July, 2001.

UNESCO (1994). *The Salamanca Statement and Framework for Action on Special Needs Education*. Paris: UNESCO.

Uzundemir, E. (2000). Situation analysis of the excluded in the Turkish education system. Paper presented at the International Special Education Conference, Manchester, UK.

Wills, D., & Jackson, R. (2001). Report card on inclusive education in Australia. *Interaction*, 14(2&3), 5–12.

Yuen, C. (2000). Re-engineering the Hong Kong school curriculum for functional inclusive practice: A joint effort between general and special schools. Paper presented at the International Special Education Conference, Manchester, UK.

15

Issues for Urban Youth in Asia and the Pacific

KERRY J. KENNEDY
Hong Kong Institute of Education, Hong Kong

1. INTRODUCTION

There are a number of converging trends in Asia and the Pacific that are of particular significance for the future of urban youth. These include:

- projections concerning increasing urbanization (Gizewski & Homer-Dixon, 1995);
- the reported growth in urban poverty (Chapman, Dutt, & Bradnock, 1999);
- the cyclical patterns of regional economic downturn (ESCAP, 1998).

This convergence provides the structural context in which issues relating to urban youth in Asia need to be considered. On the one hand, it might seem that there is little that young people themselves, or even their governments, can do about the macro-context that drives social and economic developments. Governments often seem to be in responsive mode to forces that lie outside national jurisdictions. This is particularly true in relation to the economy and the increasing strength of globalization. On the other hand, governments do have access to policy-making processes and to resources that can be targeted at national issues if there is a will to do so. In the same way, young people themselves have a resilience that can be utilized in pursuing policy solutions that materially affect their quality of life. Thus structural issues should not be seen as impervious to human agency although the difficulties of dealing with such issues should not be underestimated.

Yet, there needs to be a realization that urban environments are confronting societies with significant issues for the future. Traditionally, investment in urban poverty reduction has not always been high on the policy agenda (Lipton, 1996) while it is becoming clear that urban populations are becoming increasingly more vulnerable. Within those populations, youth are particularly susceptible when they are denied access to education, employment, health care, social stability and emotional security. Given the potential contribution that youth can make to the cultural, economic and social development of nations, solutions need to be found that will integrate young people more effectively into future scenarios for national growth and development. To exclude them will risk alienation and disenchantment on a very large scale to the extent that the very survival of some nation states might well be threatened.

The purposes of this article, therefore, are to:

- outline the broad structural contexts that currently influence urban youth in Asia;
- analyse the conditions that put urban youth in particular at risk; and
- propose policy and practical solutions that recognize the agency of young people themselves in confronting these but also require action, support and commitment on the part of governments.

2. STRUCTURAL CONTEXTS AND URBAN YOUTH IN ASIA

In 2000, 35.1 per cent of the population in East Asia and the Pacific was classified as urban having grown from 32.8 per cent in 1996 (World Bank, 2001). It has been estimated that by 2021 more than half of India's population will live in urban areas and half of its population of poor people will also live in urban areas (Chapman, Dutt, & Bradnock, 1999, p. 244). This trend is not confined to just one country in the region (UNICEF, 1996).

While part of this growth can be understood in traditional terms such as natural growth and net migration rates (Gizewski & Homer-Dixon 1995) there are also new processes at work. Webster (1999, p. 1), for example, has identified peri-urbanization as one such issue by which he means "urbanization occurring beyond contiguously built-up core and suburban areas, or outside established urban boundaries". He has estimated that by 2025 some 450 million people in East Asia will live in these peri-urban areas. He has identified significant growth forecasts in the peri-urban areas of Jakarta, Bangkok and different parts of China. The proliferation of these areas is directly relevant to young people and to the international community.

A second issue that also gives current processes of urbanization a different edge is the growth of mega cities. The definition of mega cities has changed over time so that at present a mega city is defined by a population of ten million or more, compared with eight million under an earlier definition (Brockeroff, 2000). In 1970, the ten largest cities in the world ranged in population from 8.1 million (Beijing) to 16.5 million (Tokyo). Of these ten, three were in Asia. By 2015 it is predicted that the ten largest cities will range from 17.3 million (Jakarta) to 28.2 million (Mumbai) and six of these ten cities will be in Asia (Brockeroff, 2000, p. 50). The provision of services and basic infrastructure in these cities, particularly in new growth areas like Dhaka, Karachi and Dehli, will provide policy makers with significant challenges in the early years of the new century.

The growth of these urban conglomerates, therefore, adds a new dimension to traditional ways of thinking about urbanization and its problems. It is important to take this perspective when dealing with the Asia-Pacific region because many of the problems that are being created and will be created require new ways of thinking by national jurisdictions. A significant issue in addressing these problems is the gap between the theory and practice of market based economies.

Developing countries need to cope with structural adjustment and immense social change all at the one time. The role and functions of governments in this context will be severely challenged as governments decide where strategic interventions on behalf of the market are necessary and where they should leave outcomes to be solely determined by market forces.

As populations become increasingly urbanized across the region and as decision-making by governments becomes more complex, it seems clear that youth population in urban and peri-urban centres will increase. Nevertheless it is difficult to provide an exact picture of urban demographics (Brockeroff, 2000; Jones, 1997; Skeldon, 1997). If migration rather than natural increase continues to be the driving force of urbanization then it can be expected that young male workers will continue to be a large component of new urban populations. Males will not necessarily dominate the sex composition of the youth population because much will depend on the nature of labour market demand. In South East Asia, for example, low skilled and low wage assembly workers in export oriented industries are usually female (Brockeroff, 2000, p. 2). As Skeldon (1998) has pointed out in commenting on the ESCAP region, homogeneity does not characterize the region's growing urbanization so that any generalization will always need to be modified based on local contexts and conditions. Skeldon recognizes this in his analysis of urbanization in the ESCAP region by dividing the region into four distinct sub-regions based on a number of well defined characteristics. This is a methodological issue that is well to remember in seeking to provide an overview of the Asia-Pacific region as a whole.

Jones (1997) is similarly cautious in making generalizations about youth demographics for the ESCAP region as a whole. He uses an age range from 10 to 24 years in making projections about the demographic composition of the region. This age range covers what is officially recognized by the United Nations as adolescents (10–19 years) and youth (15–24 years). Drawing on his data it is possible to develop a statistical picture of both the current and projected adolescent and youth population in Asia. This picture is outlined in Tables 1 and 2.

The trends evident in Table 1 of a general decline in the proportion of the adolescent and youth population over time, with that trend more pronounced in East Asia than South and South East Asia, can also be seen in the statistics for selected countries as shown in Table 2.

The variation within the region can be further appreciated when the projected growth rates for 1995–2020 are examined. These are shown in Table 3.

The reasons for such variation are not the focus of this paper. What is of interest, however, is that urbanization is proceeding apace in all of the above

Table 1. Percentage of adolescents and youth in Asia and its sub-regions

	1980	1995	2020
East Asia	31.6	25.9	19.8
South East Asia	32.9	31.2	25.7
South Central Asia	31.5	30.5	27.3
Asia – Average	31.7	28.6	24.2

Based on Jones (1997).
Data have been drawn from official United Nations data bases but the countries of Oceania have been excluded.

Table 2. Percentage of adolescents and youth in selected Asian countries

	1980	1995	2020
China	32.6	26.3	20.0
India	31.0	29.9	26.1
Pakistan	31.2	30.7	30.0
Indonesia	29.0	31.7	24.0

Based on Jones (1997).

Table 3. Projected growth rates (%) for adolescent and youth populations in selected Asian countries, 1995–2020

Country	Growth Rate (%)
Pakistan	85
India	24
Philippines	18
Thailand	10
Indonesia	1
China	−7
Asia-Average	20

Based on Jones (1997).

countries that have more than the world's share of mega cities and where peri-urbanization is growing. Currently, the majority of adolescents and youth are living in rural areas. Both Jones (1997) and Gubhaju, Seetharam and Huguet (2001) agree that adolescents and youth will make up a significant proportion of rural-urban migration flows over the coming decades and "an increasing proportion of adolescents will be living their lives in urban environments, increasingly in big city and metropolitan environments" (Jones, 1997). It is this phenomenon of growing urban youth populations that requires the urgent attention of policy-makers.

Just as caution is needed in making generalizations about urban demographics there is also conflicting evidence about links between urbanization and poverty. On the one hand, Webster (1999, p. 2), in relation to the growth of peri-urban areas, has noted the development of a "new geography of poverty" characterized by a lack of basic infrastructure, poor service delivery and inadequate technical resources. Gubhaju, Seetharam and Huguet (2001), on the other hand have identified positive outcomes that can result from rural-urban migration flows. These outcomes relate to the reduction of poverty in both rural and urban areas and the promotion of greater gender equity. Skeldon (1997) has also identified the possibility of positive outcomes resulting from rural-urban migration. The real issue appears to be the state of readiness of urban areas and their ability to provide basic services and access to employment. As Brockeroff (2000) has pointed out it is the newer urban areas such as Mumbai that may have more difficulty in achieving positive outcomes more so than well-established areas like Calcutta. It is, therefore, the capacity of urban areas to absorb migration flows that remains the fundamental issue for the future.

What can be concluded from this is that the urban future of the region is in the hands of policy makers and governments. They will make the difference in preparing the region for its urban future. This is as true for preparing urban centres for future influxes of population and seeking to eliminate urban poverty as it is for the third structural feature of urban environments that will influence young people in the future: cyclical patterns of economic downturn. Both Heller (1999) and Varma (nd) have pointed to the impact of the 1997 Asian financial crisis on the most vulnerable groups in society and in particular young people. It can be assumed that the impact of the current downturn, occasioned to some extent, although not entirely, by the events of September 11, is having a similar effect on the region: less money is available for services such as health and education and unemployment increases. These fluctuations in services and jobs can have potentially serious impacts on productivity, skill development, health levels and perhaps most importantly on social capital. Governments will need to find constructive ways to deal with these fluctuations in the future, if young people are to be an asset rather than a liability to nation building.

The issue of youth's role in nation building is an important one. Any of the three issues discussed above can all influence the nation building process: (a) the growing pace of urbanization, (b) the problems of urban poverty, and (c) cyclical economic downturns. Young people need to feel a commitment to the nation and a commitment to fellow citizens if nation states are to survive. Recent geopolitical events have demonstrated only too clearly just how susceptible young people can be to ideology and prejudice when their own conditions of well being compare unfavourably with others. It is essential, therefore, that governments and policymakers seek to build positive environments that will nurture youth and allow them to become constructive citizens in the new century. How this might be done will be addressed in the next two sections of this article.

3. ISSUES CONFRONTING URBAN YOUTH

The structural issues confronting youth in the future have already been discussed in the first section of this article. Assuming that these structural features continue to characterize the macro level of most societies in the region, issues to be confronted by youth at the micro level include lifelong education, adequate health services and counselling, employment opportunities, conducive physical and social environments and more general opportunities for youth to contribute to developing the social fabric of their societies. These are not mutually exclusive issues: they interact and relate to each other in important ways as is shown in this section. There are two ways of considering these issues: (a) from the perspective of the service providers, which for the most part are governments, and (b) from the perspective of youth themselves. These are important perspectives to consider since it will take action by both governments and youth themselves to secure positive outcomes.

4. EDUCATION AND HEALTH

Lifelong education is a key policy objective for most countries of the region. The single most important aspect of such an objective, as far as youth are concerned, has been highlighted by Jones (1997, p. 29): "many of these adolescents will still lack access to secondary schooling and in some cases, even to primary schooling". Access to education, therefore, will be a key issue for young people. Providing access will be a key issue for governments: valuing education will be a key issue for young people themselves. For young people, education will be the means by which they will be prepared for turbulence and uncertainties in a rapidly changing world. For governments, it will be a momentous undertaking since many governments in the region are still struggling with the achievement of universal primary education. As significant as access is, it is not the only educational issue to confront governments: it is a necessary but not sufficient condition for the future of young people.

A second issue has to do with the physical conditions that we have come to associate with the processes of schooling. For the most part, modern schooling has been a process associated with the development of industrial societies and schools themselves have been very much instruments, and some would say replicas, of industrial processes. Visiting schools in China, Japan, Malaysia, Korea or India attests to the uniformity of modern schooling processes. Yet can these be the schools of the future? As urbanization outstrips the capacity of governments to provide much needed services, ways need to be devised to locate educational services in central locations that will enhance access and participation for young people. The priority needs to be access to the ideas, information and skills that young people will need to become active and engaged citizens and productive members of society: this access maybe provided in a variety of ways but these may not necessarily include the traditional plant and equipment associated with industrial style schools.

It is tempting in this context to focus on the potential of information technology to provide access to educational services. This potential has been explored recently in a number of scenarios for future schools (OECD, 2001). Yet there needs to be some realistic assessment of IT's capacity to be utilized in locations such as the peri-urban areas of some of Asia's rapidly growing cities. There is little doubt that the potential exists, but it requires will and resources on the part of governments to realize this potential. IT is a solution with very high cost implications.

Acknowledging the potential of IT, it is perhaps more important to focus on nonformal education (NFE) in general as a means of delivering education for young people in these newly urbanized areas. In the *Education for All 2000 Assessment Regional Report for Asia and the Pacific*, nonformal education was identified as a common aspiration for the future. It was also seen as one of the most resource efficient ways to deliver education. Currently, it is not well resourced in the region, receiving a declining share of declining education budgets. Yet its importance is undoubted.

The advantages of NFE are that it has always recognized that formal structures are not needed for learning to take place. It has involved service providers other than governments, and often goes to where learners are rather than insist that learners must come to a particular physical location. It recognizes the importance of the way adults learn and that this is often different from the way children learn. Underlying all this is the inherent flexibility of NFE – a characteristic that will be essential in light of the rapidly changing economic and social contexts facing young people in the future.

A third major issue related to education has to do with the substance and nature of the school curriculum. Most advanced industrial societies have found that in the move to mass secondary education curriculum reform has to be high on the agenda. The traditional academic curriculum is not good enough for societies undergoing change and seeking new directions. The school curriculum has to be relevant, meaningful and engaging for young people. It has to have some degree of cultural orientation that will enable youth to situate themselves within the larger culture and it has to have some vocational application that will provide a pathway to the future. At the same time, it cannot be assumed that employment will always be available for young people. Any curriculum, therefore, has also to assist in the development of skills and values that will equip young people to deal with this uncertainty. Curriculum reform must be a central issue if access and participation are to be meaningful. Without fundamental curriculum change and reconfiguration, particularly in the context of NFE, increased access will mean very little to young people.

Against this background, it is also useful to consider the needs of youth for health education, in particular, education about reproduction and safe sex. The

World Bank has acknowledged the important role health education will play in the future for young people:

By 2020, 87 per cent of young people will be living in developing countries and a large percentage of these young people will live in developing countries and a large percentage of them will be confronted with a range of social health problems (World Bank, 1998).

There is little doubt that health education must be a core component of any curriculum designed for young people. They must have access to information and they must also have access to the means by which they can practise safe sex. As with school education in general, this cannot depend on the formal education system. The means of education must be more community based and it must be available in ways that will connect with young people where they are. It may well be that what are needed in the future are centres for community education that are neither schools in the traditional sense of that term nor community health centres. Rather, such centres will serve a broad range of community functions including both education and health promotion. Integrated service provision must be the way of the future.

A natural question that follows from the reconceptualisation of service provision is how might quality be provided? Part of the answer lies in the quality of the personnel employed to maintain these centres. They will need to be teachers, but of a different kind from the ones that are employed in today's schools. They will need to be health workers but not of the traditional kind. They will need to know how to reach out to young people, how to build relationships with them, how to encourage them to value education and good health practices. They will need to know how to design curricula that can be delivered in nonformal contexts and they will need to be able to teach and work in such contexts. They will need to be skilled at one-on-one interactions as well as working with small groups and larger groups. Without such education and health personnel, the kind of flexibility provided by NFE will be of no benefit.

5. EMPLOYMENT OPPORTUNITIES

The generation of employment opportunities has traditionally been seen as a function of macro economic conditions in any society. Youth have often been a so-called 'at risk' group when it comes to the distribution of these opportunities. Jones (1997) has pointed to two characteristics of youth unemployment that deserve to be noted here because they have implications for the future: (a) unemployment affects youth more seriously than other groups within the population; and (b) unemployment rates for the over 24 years age group seem to drop significantly across countries within the region suggesting that unemployment is a structural feature of young people's transition to adulthood even where there are higher levels of education within the population.

Given these trends, it seems that unemployment is likely to be an issue that will confront urban youth in the future. The point concerning structural unemployment even for individuals with high levels of education is consistent with OECD predictions for this age group (Kennedy, 2001). Education is essential for young people in the future but it will not guarantee employment – at least not in the short term.

Visaria (1998) has pointed to the limitations of macro-economic policy in solving the problems of youth unemployment in a country like India. O'Higgins (1997) has also pointed to the limited effectiveness of government subsidized youth training programs that themselves depend on the existence of good economic conditions. The same points could be made in relation to many countries in the region. Macro economic policy that creates economic growth and therefore jobs is a blunt policy instrument when it comes to the kind of structural unemployment confronted by youth. Untargeted training programs that assume the problems of youth are lack of skills rather than lack of employment opportunities are similarly limited. It is for these reasons that Visaria (1998) points to initiatives in India that have tried and are trying to tap the creativity and ingenuity of youth themselves to be involved in volunteer work or other kinds of community service. Such approaches shift the focus from governments to individuals and civil society. This refocusing maybe the way of the future.

The International Labor Organisation (2000), for example, has talked about the role of entrepreneurship skills in assisting young people to be self-reliant when it comes to the generation of employment opportunities. Curtain (2000) has indicated the benefits of focusing on developing entrepreneurship skills as part of an employment strategy and in particular the way in which entrepreneurship "builds on their (i.e. youth's) own preference for work such as self-employment where they have a high degree of autonomy."

The idea that youth contain within themselves the capacity and capability to generate employment opportunities is an important one although it needs to be stressed that this is neither a reason for governments to abrogate their responsibilities in relation to youth nor to blame youth for their unemployment. Yet it does highlight two important issues: (a) the need to develop resilience in youth so they can respond positively to adverse circumstances; and (b) the need to align education programs both in and out of school with the development of entrepreneurship skills.

As Curtain (2000) has pointed out, entrepreneurship development cannot be the only employment strategy to be used by governments. Yet in the context of rapid urbanization it seems that the more self-reliant young people can become, the better equipped they will be to handle uncertainty and insecurity. Such a strategy would need to be supported with a more vocationally oriented curriculum, greater access to work experience programs, the creation of targeted employment and volunteer opportunities alongside entrepreneurship and enterprise development programs. Governments may also need to consider micro credit programs to ensure that young people have access to the means that can help them get new ideas off the ground (Curtain, 2000). Developing self-reliant young people will not be resource neutral.

6. SOCIAL AND PHYSICAL CONDITIONS OF URBAN AREAS

Not a single one of the issues discussed so far will be resolved if the physical and social environment for youth in newly urbanized areas is not conducive, safe and supporting of young people's growth and development. The prognosis for achieving such conditions is not good. The literature is replete with exemplars of urban environments that do not support children and youth (Blanc, 1994; Nangia, 1994; Gizewski & Homer-Dixon, 1995; Chapman, Dutt, & Bradnock, 1999; Witoelar, 2000). Perhaps more significantly, it is not only that conditions are not conducive for youth, they can be positively harmful.

Young people in the future, like their counterparts today, may well face deterioration in the urban environment as cities expand and services decline, economic and sexual exploitation, homelessness, increasing pressures to drop out of education and training and an inability to see themselves as part of the social fabric of their societies. Specific examples of the current issues facing young people are the sexual abuse of young female street children in Indonesia (Asian Development Bank, 2000), high adolescent childbearing rates in countries like Bangladesh (Islam, 1999), the pressing need for contraceptive education in the growing mega-cities in the region(Guest, 1994) and the growing threat of HIV/AIDS in Asia (World Health Organisation, 2001). These are examples of real and growing issues that will continue to confront young people. Some of them may be able to be solved by education. The development of a more resilient youth population may help young people to resist the risks and abuse that has unfortunately come to characterize urban growth. Yet, for the most part, it is governments that must attend to the physical plant of cities, provide the much-needed services, support good governance and provide a generally conducive environment. The private sector and NGOs may well be called on to help with these processes but in the end it is in the public interest to ensure such an environment and this is a responsibility for governments.

7. YOUTH IN SOCIETY: THE NEED FOR ACTIVE CITIZENS

The conditions surrounding youth will not always be likely to foster within them commitment to and support for the institutions that underpin their societies. Yet if youth are to be a positive part of the future their commitment must be won and if it is to be won, they must be made to feel less marginalized and less excluded from their societies. This will be one of the most significant challenges facing youth and their governments in the future.

UNESCO has recognized the significance of this issue by establishing the Education to Fight Exclusion Project which "aims at the social reinsertion of youth in urban and rural communities on one hand, and their insertion in the local economy, through odd jobs of popular (or informal) economy" (UNESCO, 1999). To date, this project has been responsible for a distance education initiative for marginalized urban youth in Mongolia, a nonformal training program for unemployed youth in the Philippines, nonformal literacy training for women and young girls in Laos and a nonformal basic education program for out of work and out of school youth in Ho Chi Minh City. For the most part these are relatively small initiatives but they are a recognition that concerted efforts must be made to include young people in the mainstream of their societies if they are not to be alienated.

Youth themselves have recognized the need to be included in decision-making processes on issues that are of concern to them. They brought this issue to public attention by formulating the Dakar Youth Empowerment Strategy in which they requested, among other things, for governments to commit themselves to implementing participatory policies across a broad range of areas including health, education and the provision of equal opportunities for all citizens.

Governments would do well to take notice of this request by youth because contained within in it is an important principle: youth are not only aware of the issues that confront them, they are aware of the kind of processes that would allow them to contribute to the solutions. These processes importantly include youth as active participants. This will be important to recognise in the future. To ignore them will be to contribute to further exclusion and social isolation.

8. CONCLUSION

There are two basic concepts that policy makers will need to be aware of if they are to confront the curriculum issues facing urban youth in the future. These concepts are 'social exclusion' and 'social capital'. In different ways, these concepts are capable of framing a constructive policy agenda.

Sen (2000) has analysed the first of these concepts in an attempt to bring some conceptual clarity. If youth are excluded from education and training, adequate health care and counselling, employment opportunities and safe physical and social environments, they are excluded from important social relationships that are enjoyed by other community members. This is one aspect of the potential social exclusion that youth face if governments do not provide a minimal level of basic social relationships in these important areas. For Sen, however, these kinds of deprivations not only constitute social exclusion itself but they also lead to other kinds of more instrumental forms of exclusion: poverty, homelessness, hunger, chronic illness, alienation and other kinds of socially dysfunctional behaviour.

Thus when governments are pondering the advisability or not of investing in what might be called the 'basics for youth survival' much more is at stake than a mere resource assessment. The consequences of not providing education, employment, health care and a safe physical and social environment go beyond the financial investment involved. It is not too much to assert that social breakdown on a large scale can be anticipated if governments cannot respond to the issues that urban youth will confront. Preventing social exclusion, in both its constitutive and instrumental senses, will be a key issue for governments in relation to urban youth in the future. Recognising the interaction between the two forms of social exclusion needs to be a key understanding for policy makers. Investment in basic services in the future will be an investment in social stability.

From a different perspective, Habisch (1999) has argued the need for social capital investment at the local level as a key strategy in poverty reduction. His views, though ideologically worlds apart from those of Sen's, are also complementary. If social exclusion risks widespread social alienation, then ways need to be found to rebuild trust among youth and to make them feel part of the community. This has to be a policy priority for the future. From Habisch's perspective, this means providing incentives for youth to be involved in the community and finding ways in which they can contribute (see *Cultural and Social Capital in Asian and Pacific Countries*).

A key priority in the future, therefore, must be the development of policies that will involve youth in networks and in campaigns directed at solidarity. In this way the constructive energy of youth can be harnessed for the good of the community and at the same time youth can be shown that they have a relational role within their communities. The rebuilding of trust among youth must be a key policy priority for the future.

The 'avoidance of social exclusion' and the 'promotion of social capital' will be essential in the future. These concepts must become the cornerstones of youth policy and youth action. If they do, young people can be provided with a future that will enable them to make their own contributions to what must seem like an uncertain and at time unfair society. It is up to policymakers, and all citizens, to convince them that the opposite is the case and that their contributions are valued and worthwhile.

REFERENCES

Asian Development Bank (2000). *Report of the President to the Board of Directors on a Grant (Funded by the Japan Fund for Poverty Reduction) to the Republic of Indonesia for Assisting Girl Street Children at Risk of Sexual Abuse*. http://www.adb.org/Documents/RRPs/INO/jfpr_00002.pdf Accessed 26 February 2002.

Blanc, C. (Ed.) (1994). *Urban Children in Distress*. Florence: International Child Development Centre (UNICEF).

Brockeroff, M. (2000). An urbanizing world. *Population Bulletin, 55*(3), 1–57.

Chapman, G., Dutt, A., & Bradnock, R. (1999). *Urban Growth and Development in Asia. Vol 11: Living in the Cities*. Brookfield, USA: Ashgate.

Curtain, R. (2000). Concept Paper: Identifying the basis for a youth employment strategy aimed at transition and developing economies. A paper prepared for the Secretary-General's Youth Employment Network. http://www.un.org/esa/socdev/youthemployment/1-curtain.pdf Accessed 25 February 2002.

Dakar Youth Empowerment Strategy (2001). http://www.un.org/esa/socdev/unyin/forum/dakar.doc Accessed 25 February 2002.

ESCAP. (1998). *HRD Newsletter No 11* (December). http://www.escap-hrd.org/news/n11 aceid.htm.

Gubhaju, B., Seetharam, K., & Huguet, J (2001). Population dynamics in the ESCAP region: Implications for sustainable development and poverty. *Asia Pacific Population Journal, 16*(1), 45–66.

Guest, P. (1994). The impact of population change on Mega-cities. *Asia-Pacific Population Journal, 9*(1), 37–56.

Gizewski, P. and Homer-Dixon, T. (1995). *Urban Growth and Violence Will the Future Resemble the Past?* Occasional Paper, Project on Environment, Population and Security, Washington, D. C.: American Association for the Advancement of Science and the University of Toronto, June http://www.library.utoronto.ca/pcs/eps/urban/urban1.htm. Accessed 25 January 2002.

Habisch, A. (1999). Social Capital, Poverty Reduction and 'Gesellschaftsordnungspolitik'. A German contribution to the World Development Report 2000/1. Villa Borsig Workshop Series. http://www.dse.de/ef/poverty/habisch.htm. Accessed 26 February 2002.

Heller, P. (1999). Human Dimensions of the Asian Economic Crisis. Presentation to World Bank Regional Meeting on Social Issues Arising from the East Asia Crisis and Policy Implications for the Future. Bangkok: January 21. http://www.stern.nyu.edu/globalmacro/ Accessed 25 February 2002.

International Labor Organisation (2000). Decent work for young people: Key messages http://www.ilo.org/public/english/employment/skills/targets/youth/decent.htm. Accessed 12 February 2002.

Islam, M. (1999). Adolescent childbearing in Bangladesh. *Asia-Pacific Population Journal, 14*(3), 73–87.

Jones, G. (1997). Population dynamics and their impact on adolescents in the ESCAP region. *Asia-Pacific Population Journal, 12*(3), 3–30 http://www.unescap.org/pop/journal/1997/v12n3a1.htm. Accessed 2 February 2002.

Kennedy, K. (2001). A new century and the challenges it brings for young people: How might schools support youth of the future? In OECD. (2001). *What Schools for the Future?* (pp. 203–215) Paris: OECD.

Lipton (1996). *Successes in Anti-Poverty, Issues in Development.* Discussion Paper No. 8. International Labor Organisation.

Nangia, P. (1994). Children in the urban informal sector: A tragedy for developing countries in Asia. In A. Dutt, F. Costa, S. Aggarwal & A. Noble, (Eds.), *The Asian City: Processes of Development, Characteristics and Planning* (pp. 279–293). Dordrecht The Netherlands: Kluwer Publishers.

OECD. (2001). *What Schools for the Future?* Paris: OECD.

O'Higgins, N. (1997). The challenge of youth unemployment. *Employment and Training Papers, 7.* Paris: International Labor Organisation.

Sen, A. (2000).Social Exclusion: Concept, Application, and Scrutiny. Social Developments Paper No. 1. Office of Environment and Social Devleopment, Asian Development Bank. June. http://www.adb.org/Poverty/Forum/frame_social.htm. Accessed 25 February 2002.

Skeldon, R. (1997). Rural-to-urban migration and its implications for poverty alleviation. *Asia-Pacific Population Journal, 12*(1), 3–216.

Skeldon, R. (1998). Urbanization and migration in the ESCAP region. *Asia-Pacific Population Journal, 13*(1), 3–24.

UNESCO. (nd).*The Asia Pacific Draft Synthesis Report – Education for All Assessment 2000.* http://204.29.171.50/framer/1000/default.asp?realname=UNESCO&cc=US&lc=en%2DUS&frameid=1565&providerid=112&url=http%3A%2F%2Fwww%2Eunesco%2Eorg. Accessed 9 February 2002.

UNESCO. (1999). *Éducation Contre Exclusion – About the Project.* http://www2.unesco.org/ece/uk_f_projet.htm Accessed 9 February 2002.

UNICEF. (1996). *Towards Child-Friendly Cities,* http://www.design.ncsu.edu/research/publications/moore/cities.html Accessed 31 January 2002.

Varma, K. (nd). *The Social Impact of the Asian Economic Crisis On Cities.* http://www.worldbank.org/html/extdr/offrep/eap/urban/kvspeech.htm Accesed 25 February 2002.

Visaria, P. (1998). Unemployment among youth in India – Level, nature and policy implications *Employment and Training Papers, 36,* International Labor Organisation. http://www.ilo.org/public/english/employment/strat/publ/etp36.htm#4.a Accessed 12 February 2002.

Webster, D. (1999). *Peri-Urbanisation in East Asia: Issues and Research Priorities.* Asia Pacific Research Center, Stanford University. July http://www.worldbank.org/wbi/urbancitymgt/singapore/assets/s-webster-mod01.pdf Accessed 24 January 2002.

Witoelar, E. (2000). Urban Poverty in Indonesia: The Impact of Crisis and Government's Response. Key Note Address, World Bank Urban Forum: Urban Poverty Reduction in the 21st Century. Chantilly, Virginia 3-5 April. lhttp://www.worldbank.org/html/fpd/urban/forum2000/papers/indonesia.pdf Accessed 31 January 2002.

World Bank. (1998). Investing in Young Lives: The Role of Reproductive Health http://www.worldbank.org/html/extdr/hnp/population/ynglives/ynglives.htm Accessed 31 January 2002.

World Bank. (2001).*World Bank Development Indicators* http://devdata.worldbank.org/external/CPProfile.asp?SelectedCountry=EAP&CCODE=EAP&CNAME=07+East+Asia+%26+Pacific&PTYPE=CP Accessed 24 January 2002.

World Health Organisation. (2001). HIV/AIDS in the Asia Pacific Region. Document prepared for Sixth International Congress on AIDS in Asia and the Pacific, Melbourne, 5-10 October. http://w3.whosea.org/hivaids/hiv_aids.htm Accessed 7 February 2002.

Yusuf, S. (1999), *World Development Report 2000 – Development Policy: Entering the 21st Century –* An Outline. http://www.dse.de/ef/papers/yusuf.htm Accessed 23 January 2002.

16

Drop-outs from School and How to Cope with this Problem

S. SRINIVASAN and S. ANANDALAKSHMY
Barefoot College, Tilonia, Rajasthan, India

1. INTRODUCTION

The problem of school drop-out is a major one in Asia, which is home to two-thirds of the world's illiterates. It is a region which contains more than half of the world's population of six billion people, and where financial resources are spread very thinly when it comes to providing a good quality education for all regardless of the learner's socio-economic background, gender, ethnicity, race, religion or geographical location. There are currently 74 million out-of-school children in the school-age population in Asia's developing countries, mostly in South Asia. Of those who do enrol in school, at least one third abandon or drop out before completing the primary cycle. In the state of Rajasthan in India, which is referred to in detail in this article, the literacy rate is 55.1 per cent for males and 20.8 per cent for females. In terms of primary education, the overall drop-out rate among children in the 6 to 14-year-old age group is 64.7 per cent, while it rises to 72.5 per cent for girls.

The big challenge facing Asia is to encourage learners, both young and adults, to undertake an organized education program, whether it be through formal or nonformal means, in order to enable them to become literate and numerate, with a particular stress on functional literacy for decent work and good citizenship. To be literate is to become empowered in life, and so it is a matter of great importance, and a key dimension of humanity. The problem of access to education remains a major one throughout Asia's developing countries, since in many communities there is no school, and suitable teaching and learning facilities for conducting nonformal classes are lacking. Moreover, even in those communities where access to education is possible, the problem of school drop-out is a major one since many learners do not find that what is being taught is relevant to meeting the immediate needs of their daily lives. In essence the matter is a simple one: if the schooling and education being provided are largely irrelevant to life, why should a learner forego an income, no matter how modest, to attend school or nonformal learning centres?

The purpose of this article is to provide an analysis of an alternative school in a rural community in Rajasthan where, like thousands of other rural communities throughout Asia, it is very difficult to attract learners to attend school in the first place, and where the problem of drop-out is severe among those who do take part in the education programs offered. The purpose is not to provide a statistical analysis of the problem of drop out in many communities in the developing world in Asia, and so the approach adopted here is very different from the other articles, which appear in this *Handbook*. Rather, this is a qualitative rather than a quantitative analysis of the problem of school drop-out, in order to get behind the figures to understand better the core reasons for such high rates of drop-out and to see what can be done to reduce effectively this major problem, particularly in economically impoverished rural communities in Asia's developing countries. The authors do not apologize for the approach adopted in this article, since in so doing they seek to provide an insiders' view of what actually works in such communities to attract learners to undertake education programs and not to follow the pathway of the drop-outs.

2. A GRASS ROOTS PERSPECTIVE

The Social Work and Research Centre (SWRC) was established in 1972, in Rajasthan, in the small village of Tilonia, as a registered, non-profit, voluntary organization. Tilonia is one of 110 villages of Silora Block in Ajmer District. The terrain in and around Tilonia is arid and rocky: large expanses of dusty land, peppered with rounded rocks and thorny trees. Only camels could thrive here; the people merely survive. One realizes this when one overtakes camel-driven carts on the road or passes camels in the fields, reaching out for what edible greenery they can find on the lanky shrubs. There are no perennial rivers here and no abundant monsoon. Any rain is treated as manna from the heavens; water is a perpetual scarcity.

This was the spot chosen by a small group of young, idealistic university graduates fired by an inner call to work for the poor, to set up shop and work with the people. This group, which soon attracted other like-minded people to join them, began working without a set agenda, determined to understand the culture and identify gradually, the needs of the community. From its inception, therefore, there was a continuing dialogue with the rural communities. In the early years, the SWRC team also worked out the principles that would govern their approach and activities. These came to be called the non-negotiables, and they included a commitment to gender and caste equality, to honesty and integrity and to environmental protection.

The process was not one of social workers implementing a program for the poor, but one of young university graduates planning with the community and putting the plans into operation. The core team of the SWRC was constituted of people from different parts of the country, with varied educational qualifications and talents. For the group the process of developing coherence and a symbiotic functioning was time-intensive. But it did happen. As the scale of SWRC's initiatives grew, it moved in the direction of becoming what was called a 'barefoot college', a system that was open for the common man, woman and child. The organization was able to identify two major objectives and give them concrete shape.

(1) The first objective was to create a conducive environment for participatory decision making, involving both the community and the SWRC team of workers.
(2) The second objective was to decentralise the focus of SWRC's initiatives to Field Centres, situated away from Tilonia, in villages in different directions.

These two processes of participatory decision making and decentralisation resulted in the link between development and education becoming clearer. Education was recognised as the foundation for any development-related initiative. Thus the need to provide education, with a focus on issues related to development, was perceived as an imperative. The dialogue consisted of a review of the critical aspects of the education of children, as they relate to development. There were several issues that confronted them. In the main, they were the following questions.

- How can rural children be attracted to primary education?
- How can primary education be made more relevant to them?
- Will the education system prepare them to work in their villages?
- Can the education system be made accountable to the community it serves?
- What is the learning process that will prepare them for responsible citizenship?
- What will prepare the children to work for development in their own settings?
- How can children demand attention to their aspirations?
- Can their large numbers enable them to develop a collective voice?
- How can the community be involved in planning for itself?
- What are effective strategies for the sharing of knowledge between the educated and those who have not had the opportunities to get an education?

These were the questions asked. The story that follows contains some of the answers.

3. THE BAREFOOT COLLEGE APPROACH

The formal schools were found to run at timings convenient for the teachers. Most of the teachers were from nearby towns and cities; none lived in the villages where they worked. The timing of the daily schedule was fixed to enable them to catch the trains and buses, which would take them back to their urban homes.

The curriculum followed in the school was alien to the everyday reality of the children and this resulted in a mutual indifference between the community and the school system. The Barefoot College was planned as an alternative, that could fill the lacunae. Its major thrust was to value and reinforce the skills and abilities of the people in the village: the artisan, the craftsman, the story teller, the puppeteer, the manual worker, the herder of sheep and goats and the woman who could cook, sew and conserve resources. A secondary thrust was to demystify academic expertise and to translate the formal knowledge received in higher education into viable and feasible strategies for the rural communities.

The project was aimed at supporting the community in identifying its own needs and to make plans to address them. The children had to realise that the schooling they had missed could be recovered at their very doorsteps. Literacy and numeracy would help them to be active participants in the processes of development and to take control over their own lives. When all the alternatives to make schooling relevant to village life were discussed at length, the following aspects emerged:

- parents must be involved in planning;
- the school timings must be convenient for the children;
- teachers who live in the village must be selected; and
- curricula and methods of teaching must relate to their environment.

The children in the villages in and around Tilonia herded goats or helped their parents in the tasks of subsistence farming. Also, there were the never-ending household chores for the girls, which effectively kept them occupied for the whole day. The families lived on the fringes of sustenance and could be termed marginal, in both economic and social aspects. They were invariably on the lower rungs of the caste hierarchy. This profile would surely qualify them to be considered 'unteachable' in the regular formal schools!

The Tilonia Night School project began in a small way, with three schools in the year 1975. This number grew to nine in 1980 and to 29 in 1981. In the beginning, only boys attended these schools. Gradually, one or two girls joined in. Today, 20 years later, more than 60 per cent of the students in the Night Schools are girls.

According to the decisions taken by the communities and the Barefoot College, the teachers must be residents of the village. There are two teachers, on average, for every school. The enrolment size of the schools vary, but it can be as high as 50. The schools are located in far flung villages, but are easily identified if driving in at night, by the solar lamp that lights up the school. The school works for two to three hours every evening, not enough to cover the standard curriculum, but the motivation of the children is so high that they do cover a lot of ground. The curriculum is developed with the specific communities in mind and contains both what is familiar and what is relevant. The selection and the continuous training of the teachers are in-built for the system to work. Young men and women with at least two or three years of High School education and an aptitude for teaching are trained on the job. The monthly meetings constitute an important part of the training. The meetings are, at once, a forum for the sharing of ideas and experiences and an educational process. After attending these meetings, the teachers feel a renewed energy and enthusiasm for their jobs. They are also glad to have greater clarity on both teaching and learning objectives and methods. The monthly meetings have proved to be the crucible for new learning, through the discussion of classroom and administrative issues that concern the teachers. But if the methods had been established, what were the new thought processes? In what way can the Barefoot College claim to have broken new ground?

When development issues began to be discussed at the teachers' meetings, the importance of the Night School as a nucleus for awareness-building, began to emerge. In fact, it came to be seen as one of the primary functions of the Night Schools. In the process of examining the aim of education, its potential leverage in the development of the village got recognized. The teachers of the Night Schools were also the same people involved in planning and implementing development programs. They saw the link between what they taught the children and how it would serve the rural communities in the future. At the start the curriculum had been planned, drawing on the environment of the child. The focus was further broadened, to relate the curriculum to the concerns of development. After many hours of deliberation, the teachers of the Barefoot College came to a consensus on the guiding principles and the objectives of the Night School system. They were all agreed that the conventional school, which imparted literacy and numeracy, up to the level of Standard V, did not satisfy the requirements of the community. The rural people considered education as a vehicle of social mobility and as a method for increasing the market value of their employment related labour. Formal schooling, as they could observe, did not satisfy either of the objectives they had defined. Further it served only to alienate the children from their surroundings. Consequently, they rejected the system.

The Barefoot College, by its very definition, did not see education as an isolated input in the lives of children, but as a process that must be strongly founded in their own concerns. Ultimately, the best input for the children is that which enables them to break the stranglehold of poverty. Knowledge, which had come to be traditionally defined as that which is taught in school, had to be redefined in the local context. Literacy is definitely necessary and useful to deal with the matters of the world outside; and literacy and numeracy are generally recognized as tools that increase access to development. However literacy, it was found, was not sufficient in itself to help the children get employment and to deal with various aspects of the power structure. The realization of this fact caused a shift in thinking.

3.1. *The Children's Parliament*

It was decided that if the children were to understand the linkages between the education system, the schemes for development and the political process, they needed to begin with hands-on experience in self-government. Thus the concept of a Children's Parliament was born. To begin with, the constituencies were defined. Two or three adjoining Night Schools would be one constituency. The electorate was made up of all children attending the Night School for a period of two years or more. The criteria for eligibility were determined by the children themselves. The children wanted Bunker Roy, the Director of the Barefoot College, to act as the President and be in over-all charge of their elections.

They also decided that children in the age group 11 to 12 years would be eligible for filing nomination papers, as candidates. Polling, by secret ballot, and in the presence of impartial observers, would be held in each of the Night Schools, where polling booths would be set up. Polling would be held simultaneously in all the booths, and the ballot boxes sealed, and transferred overnight, to Tilonia or to one of the Field Centres. The counting of votes would take place the next day and the results announced to the children gathered there. The elected members would then select, from among themselves, the Prime Minister, the Cabinet and the Speaker of the House. The President (the Director of the Barefoot College) would administer the oath of office to all the members of the Parliament on the same day. When the term of two years comes to an end, the President would announce the holding of fresh elections. This process, of electing independent, non-party members, to the Children's Parliament, every two years, has provided the children with an opportunity for first hand experience with democracy.

The Children's Parliament takes seriously the role of monitoring the Night Schools. The elected members occasionally make comments about the administration of the village. They are known to have written to the Director of the Barefoot College protesting about the absenteeism of a teacher or the lack of slates and books, and requesting the provision of educational and play materials. The members of the Children's Parliament work in coordination with the Village Education Committees. The nucleus of the idea of self-government, through duly elected representatives, appears to have generated a veritable movement. The children are not playing with models of democratic functioning: they consider democracy to be real and viable for them.

The major shift in thinking referred to earlier, was the change of focus in the purpose of education. Normally, the school system has a curriculum, which is expected to prepare the children for the future. The fact that literacy is a means of making books, newspapers and magazines comprehensible to the children was obvious. Providing them with the tools of communication to deal with a literate officialdom was also incontrovertible. Self government was seen adding value to education. In the Night Schools, literacy shared the space, with practice in democratic functioning. This, in turn, made the children more effective in dealing with the present, as well as in being equipped for the future.

3.2. *The Key Role of the Teacher*

There were two criteria for the selection of the teacher.

- He (or she) had to be from the village community and be accepted and respected by the people.

- He (or she) had to have adequate literacy and numeracy skills, and be confident to impart them to children.

The exact level of education was not fixed, but the aptitude and motivation for teaching were considered important.

Once selected, the teachers would come to Tilonia for training, for a period of one month. The first half of the month is spent on informal, wide-ranging discussions ranging from methods of teaching to socio-political problems in the village. The time would also be utilised for workshops in which learning situations would be simulated. On the basis of the insights from such an experience, the teaching aids for future use would be identified and made. At the end of the fortnight, the teachers would return to their villages to conduct a survey of the children in the age group of 6 to 14 years. How many children are in school and how many are out of it? This would begin the collection of demographic information about all the families in the village community. With the information about the occupation and socio-economic status of the families, the teachers would return to Tilonia to synthesize the data and to make a tentative plan of action. At this time, they would also be oriented to methods of evaluation of academic progress and the maintenance of school records.

The teacher is constantly supported and reinforced in the attempt to involve the community in the Night School. In the regular school system, the public is not welcomed into the schools. The curriculum is treated as a matter for specialists, who have been trained in Colleges of Education. It is just the reverse in the Barefoot College. The local bard, the wandering story-teller, the midwife, the health worker – any one of them could be a resource person for the Night School. This brings the local community into the school; but what is more important, it enables the children to respect their own cultural traditions and to learn directly from practitioners.

3.3. *Enlivening the Methods*

Rajasthan is famed for its puppetry, as everyone knows. The Barefoot College, which already had the experience of using puppets for the communication of development messages, introduced puppetry as pedagogy in the Night Schools. Children and teachers together made the puppets, wrote the scripts and presented the programs. In the first instance, the community was not certain that a puppet show, normally connected with entertainment and frivolity, was appropriate for the education of their children. But soon, the scepticism dissolved.

The SWRC had a Media Centre, where film strips and slides were developed. These were used for campaigns and for educating the adults about developmental issues. Some of the materials were adapted to be used for the children in the Night School. The Night Schools had a flexible approach to the use of modern technology; where it was feasible, it was adopted; where an older method would suffice, it was used. The intention was to make the school a lively place for acquiring relevant information and a positive mind set. In this context, the Night

Schools were often labelled as 'nonformal' by funding agencies and others. While the Barefoot College was not under the control or regulation of the Government, and could be deemed to be nonformal, it was clear that the education that the children were receiving in the Night Schools shared many properties of the regular system. The debate between formal and nonformal schools was found to be unproductive and the decision at Tilonia was to use the term, alternative school.

The Night Schools have a wide spectrum of activities and inputs, which emerged as responses to the expressed needs of the children. For example, the children wanted an opportunity to meet the children from other villages and other parts of the district. So the idea of the Children's Fair arose, rather similar to the village fairs meant for adults in the area. This became the Night School children's very own fair, organized annually. The fairs are held in different villages each year, with the community taking up the responsibility, through voluntary labour, for logistics and arrangements. The Annual Fair could range from one day to three days. The children look forward, excitedly, to the Fair and participate in the activities with vigour and enthusiasm. Some of them arrange for their older siblings to herd the goats on those days. The Fair has a variety of activities which combine learning with a great deal of fun. These include games, puzzles, Origami, toy-making, use of waste material and so on. For instance, out of old newspapers the children would learn to make more than a hundred types of caps and hats. Making caps and wearing them were very popular with the children.

Educational excursions and exposure trips were organized for both teachers and children. Most of them had never had an opportunity to go beyond a neighbouring village. These visits opened the world out to them and to say that the children enjoyed them was to make an understatement. They would have loved to see a new place every week, but the Barefoot College had its constraints.

For the children, who wished to learn a skill thoroughly, a residential training period of one year was ear-marked. Sewing, fabricating at the mechanical workshop, candle-making, chalk-making and carpentry were some of the skills taught in the Night Schools and taken beyond, for advanced work.

A mobile library functioned for the school system. This enabled children to get acquainted with the vast world of books. Although, many of them had only moderate reading levels, they could take the occasional story book home, for a week or two. Once in a while, there would be a video screening arranged for the children on themes of legal literacy, health, women's rights or environmental regeneration.

3.4. *The Curriculum*

The curriculum is prepared by a team, which incorporates the suggestions of the teachers, adults in the community and even the children. It is presented below.

Language. Reading, writing and correct articulation of Hindi, ability to express thoughts in their own words, writing formal applications for bank loans and jobs. Ability to decipher the script of the money lender, understanding bills and receipts.

Mathematics. Numbers, addition, subtraction, multiplication and division, knowledge of Indian currency, measurements of length, area, weight, volume of liquids, time, knowledge of different shapes, like triangle and square; knowledge of measurement of farm land and building, quantity of soil dug in cubic feet; simple and compound interest, profit and loss, ratio and proportion, calculation of wages.

Animal Husbandry. Knowledge about animals, their diet, their internal organs, their diseases and simple cures, immunisation, use of lactometer, cross breeding, artificial insemination.

Agriculture. Different types of soil, functions of different parts of a plant, various crops, disease of plants and their treatment, cross breed seeds, grafting, types of fertilizers, water and soil testing, proper storage of food grains, awareness of harmful effects of chemical fertilisers and pesticides.

Geography. Knowledge of directions (East, West, North, South), maps of the village and the farms, boundaries of the village, origin and shape of the earth, earthquakes, volcanoes, climate, day and night, subsoil water and its properties, geographical setting of Ajmer, map of India, the names of the Indian States.

History. Tales of local heroes, knowledge of local festivals and melas and their origin, history of their village, national festivals and tales of brave men and women, tales of Ramayan and Mahabharat, history of social customs, origin of man, discovery of fire and the wheel.

Knowledge of Rural Institutions. Panchayat (local self-government), Development Officer, *Pradhan* (elected Head of Village Council), their work and inter-relationships; *Patwari* (Revenue official) roles of Agricultural Extension Officer, School, Hospital and Post Office, information about veterinary worker, Village Cooperative Society.

Health. Knowledge about the human body, health and hygiene, importance of clean drinking water, immunisation, nutrition, symptoms of common diseases and their prevention and treatment, nutritional content of local food products.

Science. Air and pressure; heat as a source of energy and light, expansion due to heat; water; knowledge about space satellites; gravitational force, phases of the moon, North star, Milky Way, solar system, planets and stars.

4. THE UNIQUE FEATURES OF THE CHILDREN'S PARLIAMENT

Of all the innovations and new thrusts of the Night Schools, the most dramatic one is the Children's Parliament. This program has been described at length in various publications about the Barefoot College. It is easily the most successful of the steps taken in the Night School system. What was initially started as an experiment to teach children about the electoral process, has become a situation where children exercise real power, political and social power. Some of the highlights follow.

- As a result of being members of the Children's Parliament, they are able to ensure student and teacher attendance in the schools. (This is clearly more than the members of the *Lok Sabha* are able to do.
- They also put pressure on the SWRC and their local government for solar power, water pumps and other improvements in the village.
- It has reversed the thrust of socialization: children teach the parents and older relatives about the functioning of democracy and demonstrate its effectiveness.
- Every year, about 10 per cent of the children join the regular formal schools.
- Children of the Night Schools are involved in almost all the developmental activities of the SWRC: hand pump/water management, solar energy, dairy, crafts, puppetry and theatre.
- Almost all the alumni are members of the Youth Forum in their own villages.

There are several anecdotes and success stories, but two of them stand out for their boldness and uniqueness. One was the case of Dev Karan, the Speaker of the Children's Parliament, who was able to bring two rival politicians together, a feat hailed by all in the village as a miracle. The second is the story of Kaushalya, who was the Prime Minister, until she left her village to get married. As a young daughter-in-law she was able, after months of persuasion, to get her village to agree to implement a piped water supply. Single-handed she persuaded 56 families to pay a monthly fee of Rs 20 for water connections. The result was the installation of the first solar-operated pump for filling water in a 100,000 litre tank, which supplied safe drinking water regularly, to the whole village. And this in a State where no village pays for water supplied by the Government. Both these examples speak for the creative energy of the children, when allowed to think and speak for themselves.

17

Ethnicities, Minorities and Indigenous Groups in Central Asia

JOSEPH ZAJDA
Australian Catholic University, Melbourne, Australia

REA ZAJDA
James Nicholas Publishers, Melbourne, Australia

1. INTRODUCTION

One of the emerging problems with representation and treatment of minorities and indigenous groups in education in the transitional economies of the Central Asian states is the dichotomy between the emancipatory logic of egalitarianism (the continuation of the Enlightenment) and the rhetoric of nation building through a process of ethno-nationalism. How does one build a democratic, empowering and culturally pluralistic post-Soviet society, which is already characterised by a dominance of one ethnicity and the resulting marginalisation of other ethnicities and minorities, a growing social differentiation, income inequality, and inequitable access to education, exploitation and poverty? This is the question that can be asked of any nation in Central Asia. This article explores the directions in educational research dealing with the political, cultural, and educational developments in Central Asia, new citizenship and language policies and inter-ethnic tensions and conflict.

2. DEVELOPMENTS IN EDUCATIONAL RESEARCH

A key shift in the organisation and focus of research into ethnicity and minorities in Central Asia took place after the fall of the Soviet Union (USSR) and the declaration of independence of the former Soviet republics in Central Asia. The ideological collapse of the communist model has become the pivotal issue for all subsequent research. Since that time the organisation of research, once substantially the dominion of Institutes within the Russian Academy of Sciences, has become largely dominated by researchers in the United States, and to a lesser extent those in universities and other organisations in Europe. In Russia, a nation which, despite the dissolution of the Union, retains close strategic and economic interests in Central Asia, research on ethnicity and minorities is still continued by Russian scholars. Only China, among those remaining nations immediately adjacent to the Central Asian republics (including, Iran, Afghanistan, and Pakistan), engages in a significant amount of research in this field, although only very few Chinese contributions on Central Asia have been published in English or European languages (Zhang & Azizian, 1998, p. 5). Meanwhile, a slowly increasing proportion of Russian academic research in the area reaches a wider audience through English and European-language journals and books. Another significant collection of the Western research literature also focuses on the relationship of the Central Asian republics with nations on the southern tier of the Central Asian states, as well as that of Turkey to the north, which have been active in providing aid and educational support in the republics. In this respect Western interest focuses on the possible rise of pan-Islamic and pan-Turkic communities and whether they pose a threat to the stability and security in the region (Gleason, 1997, p. 7).

2.1. Directions of Educational Research

The collapse of communism and the question mark it raised over the future direction of the successor states of the USSR has tended to dictate the direction of research in the first ten years after 1992. A significant objective of much of this initial research output on the region's ethnicities and minorities has been directed towards examining the extent to which their existence affects the development of nation-building, national and regional stability, and most importantly, national regional economic growth, within the newly-independent nations of Central Asia. To this end a large proportion of the early research on the region in the post-Soviet era has been weighted towards country profiles, reports, and regional profiles whose primary purpose has been to examine the potential of the republics for national stability and its relationship to economic development and international trade and cooperation for each new nation. With some exceptions, research on the education of ethnicities and minorities has only tended to be included where it impacts on these primary interests of the countries and organisations funding the research. Indeed, it could be argued that what some scholars have referred to as "the modern Great Game" (Gleason, 1997, pp. 136–137), or competition between powers with interest in the region has to some extent influenced the organisation and direction of recent research. Central Asia has become a region of contention involving both states with Central Asian borders, and also those world powers and nations whose interest, while less direct, is also significant. The imperatives of this post-colonial rivalry have become a significant dimension in the direction of the research and also accounts for the gaps within the literature which are only recently being addressed.

Inasmuch as research priorities were essentially dictated by political and economic imperatives such areas as equality and equity, inclusivity, education for citizenship, language policies, global versus local history and culture tend to be cursory, if addressed at all, while the body of literature dealing with these areas in more detail is sparse.

3. ETHNICITY AND MINORITIES IN CENTRAL ASIA

The Central Asian states of Kazakhstan, Kyrgyzstan, Tajikistan, Turkmenistan and Uzbekistan, formerly a sub-region of the USSR, have been described as "a maze of ethnic groups" (Liu, 1998, p. 73). All five states are multi-ethnic with the number of groups in a particular state ranging from 100 different ethnic groups in Kazakhstan and 80 in Kyrgyzstan, to at least two dozen groups in other states. In four out of five of the Central Asian Republics, Russians are the second largest ethnic group. In Kazakhstan, Kazakhs comprise 51 per cent of the population, while Russians make up 34 per cent. In Kyrgyzstan, the relative proportions are 52.4 per cent Kyrgyzs and Russians 21.5 per cent. In Tajikistan, Russians only account for 7.6 per cent of the population yet are the third largest ethnic group behind Tajiks and Uzbeks (Liu, 1998, p. 74).

3.1. *Ethnicity and Minority under the USSR: Soviet Nationalities Policy*

At the turn of the twentieth century Central Asia consisted of multi-ethnic Islamic states or khanates and territorial pastures of nomads (Glenn, 1999, p. 3). After the 1917 Revolution the Bolshevik objective of promoting the so-called 'flourishing' (*ratsvet*), 'coming together' (*sblizhenie*), and 'merging' (*sliyanie*) of nations, including the regions of Central Asia, into a new union of Soviet people (*Sovetskii narod*), was tempered by a pragmatic policy of divide and rule. In Central Asia the region was divided into five national republics, largely to break up the large linguistic and cultural blocs founded on language (Turkic) and religion (Islam) (Roy, p. viii; Glenn, 1999, p. 5; Nahaylo, 1998), thus meeting the Soviet leaders' principle of "national in form, socialist in content". Where they did not exist, nations were created, so that paradoxically, the Soviet nationalities policy, intended to bring about the demise of nationalism, actually created some modern national identities in Central Asia and the Caucasus (Bremmer, 1993, p. 10; Hobsbawm, 1990, p. 166). There, and in the Caucasus, "internal borders were frequently arbitrarily imposed" (Nahaylo, 1998).

By means of *korenizatsia* or nativization, certain dominant cultures or ethnicities were promoted as the titular nationality in each region, given administrative power within their own region and were to be given preference for state-controlled benefits like education, housing, and employment. The USSR's "federation of ethno-territorial units organised into an elaborate administrative hierarchy" (Zaslavsky, 1993, p. 31) of the 15 Union republics, ASSRs or autonomous regions and autonomous areas, all with dominant titular nationalities and subordinate non-titular nationalities, owes much to Stalin's 1913 definition of nationality (*natsionalnost*) with its linkage of ethnicity, territory and politics. In Central

Asia, as in other areas, each national political entity was linked to "a corresponding titular nationality, defined as an ethnic community which had preserved an identity founded on language throughout the whole process of history" (Roy, 2000, p. viii).

The federal structure therefore had the result of crystallizing and fostering ethnic nationalism rather than achieving its hoped for gradual withering away. Ethnic nationalism was also further institutionalised by the registering of each citizen's ethnic origin on 'line five' of the internal passports. Introduced by the Stalinist regime in 1932, one only recorded nationality had to be chosen on "more or less voluntary self-indication" (Zaslavsky, 1993, p. 34) from a list drawn up by the state. Justified as a means of preserving special rights of all ethnic minorities, such as access to higher education, the element of choice was later removed so that for the past 50 years a citizens' nationality was registered according to parental passport entry.

3.2. Ethnicities and Minorities in Soviet Research

The impact of research in the Soviet era was to define titular nationalities and legitimate them as officially recognised national identities, as well as to consolidate ethnic identity, and define minorities. Hobsbawm's argument that the creation of what he refers to as "ethno-linguistic territorial and national administrative units" like Kazakhstan, Kyrgyzstan, Uzbekistan, Tajikistan and Turkmenistan "was a theoretical construct of Soviet intellectuals rather than a primordial aspiration" of any of these peoples (Hobsbawm, 1990, p. 166) is echoed by Roy, who suggests that the status of objective reality given to the Central Asian "re-groupments of populations" were in fact "largely artificial" and piecemeal arrangements among the Muslim population of the former Russian empire' (Roy, 2000, p. viii). He goes on to demonstrate that in respect to the ethnic conception of a 'people' it was:

> ... left to the anthropologists, linguistics experts and historians to explain how this virtual people had been waiting for centuries for its political incarnation to be achieved. (Roy, 2000, p. ix)

Soviet ethnography, a "legitimation discourse produced in the Soviet era by official academics (linguists, ethnologists, and archaeologists as creation of national culture" (Roy, 200, p. xiv) constructed, according to Roy, out the combination of two very different traditions: the idea of 'the people' from German Romanticism and developed by German and Russian theoreticians in second half of nineteenth century, and a simplified Marxist reading of developmental stages of modes of production. The founding text was Stalin's *Marxism and the National Question* published in 1913. Marxist theory required that the people in question pass through stages of political organisation related to the development of the means of production: from the tribe (*plemya*), through to the stage of primitive community, to the capitalist stage, that of nation (*natsya*) which is defined by a market, and thus territory (Roy, 2000, p. 63). Stalin believed that the unvarying element that maintains itself through history was language.

4. SOVIET LANGUAGE POLICY

After the consolidation of Soviet power in Central Asia, language policy played a key role in Soviet policy in the region. What has been referred to as "Moscow's deliberate efforts at social engineering" (Gleason, 1997: 45) saw all five titular languages of Central Asia transliterated from Arabic script into the Roman alphabet between 1927 and 1930 in order to foster a move away from Islam. This had the effect of further isolating the Central Asian republics from their neighbours, and also alienating the inhabitants from their shared history, literature and culture (Glenn, 1999, p. 81). Between 1939 and 1941 the Roman alphabet was exchanged for Cyrillic script in all republics. Justified in terms of promoting the greater unification of the Soviet people by linguistically integrating Central Asia into the Union, its added objective was also to stem influence of pan-Turkic links between Central Asia and Turkey which during its modernisation adopted the Roman script in 1928 (Glenn, 1999, p. 82).

4.1. *Literacy During the Communist Period*

The first policy of the Bolshevik Party proclaimed the right of the population to receive education in their native language and guaranteed this program by the state provision of schools for this purpose. This measure had the effect of defining identity in not necessarily territorial terms but also explicitly in ethnic terms, endowing ethnic groups with extra-territorial language rights (Glenn, 1999, p. 82).

Soviet education produced a vast improvement in literacy in the region, which in 1926 ranged from two per cent to seven per cent: Tajiks having the lowest with two per cent, whilst Kazahks had 7.1 per cent. By 1970 all these groups had literacy rates of over 99 per cent.

4.2. *Ethnicities, Minorities and Soviet Language Policy*

Soviet language policy moved in stages towards the ultimate goal of unity and internalisation, based on the dominance of the Russian language. Until the 1930s nativization (*korenizatsia*) aimed at increasing the involvement of Central Asians in the state apparatuses by cultivating the use of the national language of each republic in an official capacity alongside Russian. The growing predominance of Russian in the 1930s coincided with the internationalising of the local languages by the introduction of Russian loan words, culminating in the 1938 decree making the teaching of the Russian language compulsory in non-Russian schools throughout Soviet Union. These integrative tendencies continued under Khruschev with the enhancement of the status of the Russian language through the 1958 reform laws which allowed parents to chose whether their children attended schools taught in their mother tongue or Russian, the latter option being taken up by national elites of republics to ensure better career opportunities. In the late 1970s the use of Russian was further promoted by a mandatory increase in the number of teaching hours of Russian as a second language. Roy notes that this preeminence of Russian had perverse effects in the long term: those who were excluded from Russian schools developed a reactive national identity. For them the imposing of the national language became a way, after 1991 independence, of taking the place of Russian-speaking elites (Roy, 2000, p. 120).

5. POST-COMMUNIST RESEARCH

5.1. *Russian Post-Soviet Research*

For Russians, Central Asia remains the so-called 'near abroad', "a natural sphere of influence in which Russia has strategic as well as economic interests" (Zhang & Azizian, 1998, p. 4). In post-communist Russia, one important area of research involves attempts at a re-assessment and re-conceptualization of the former Soviet discourse on ethnicity and minorities. Prazauskas acknowledges that the Soviet nationalities policy, "particularly its strategic aim of moulding diverse nationalities into a single 'Soviet people'", the propaganda of the multi-national Soviet state, and the 'flourishing of nations' masked a situation where the Russian language and major elements of Russian culture became normative all over the Union, while languages and cultures of non-Russian groups were relegated to the periphery of public life and survived mainly in rural areas (Prazauskas, 1998, p. 52).

In a critique of representation policies and projected images in the Russian ethnographic discourse on indigenous peoples, Sokolovski analysed the historical construction of the category 'indigenous peoples' noting that the concept of 'indigenous peoples' (*korennye narody*) as applied to non-Russian groups in Russia is a recent innovation introduced under the influence of international legislation, (mainly due to the ILO *Convention Concerning Indigenous and Tribal Peoples in Independent Countries #169*) since the 1980s. He also traces the roots of the distinctly Russian comprehension of the 'Other' or 'non-Russian', which was achieved by the latter's adoption of foreign (Russian) ways and the politics of *prirodnenie* (a concept which can be interpreted as making someone similar to its own peoples or relatives, or making 'akin' or creating 'kinship'). In these terms Russians never conquered lands, they only attached (*prisoedinial*) them to the motherland, and then developed(*osvaivali*) them. During the sixty-year taboo for using the term 'indigenous peoples', the latter were referred to in the 1920s by the term 'tribe' (*plemena*) which was replaced in the 1930s with nationalities (*narodnosti*) or *small numbered peoples*. In the late 1980s, the USSR representative to the UN Indigenous Population Working Group explained the official Soviet position: the term 'indigenous people' was only valid in a colonial context and since the USSR had no colonies it had no 'indigenous people'.

5.2. Ethnicity in the Central Asian Republics Since 1992

Since the Central Asian republics declared their independence at the end of 1991, "ethnic harmony has been seen as the most fundamental condition for political stability" (Liu, 1998, p. 73). Edgar reminds us that the Central Asian nations and the ethnic groups on which they are based is a post-colonial creation, explaining:

> They are creation of the twentieth century. One hundred years ago, there was no Kyrgyzstan or Turkmenistan ... Central Asia was long home to a rich and complex mix of peoples, languages and cultures ... Our notion that an ethnic group brings together language, territory, and descent in a single package did not apply in Central Asia. (Edgar, 2001, p. 1)

Both the linguistic and cultural boundaries applicable to traditional ethnic groups are difficult to apply to some nations in Central Asia. For instance, the linguistic boundary between Uzbeks and Tajiks, even though they do speak two different languages is not sufficient to define the two distinct ethnic groups. Edgar argues that some nations are more defined by their cultural heritage relating to "history, genealogy and way of life". Her example refers to some ex-Soviet citizens now in the new Central Asia sub-region:

> Sometimes siblings within a single family would claim different ethnic identities. To this day, there are people living in Uzbekistan who declare themselves to be Uzbeks, yet speak Tajik as their first language. (2001, p. 3)

Different forms of ethnic identities are a part of life in Central Asia. Koroteyeva and Makarova (2002) show that multi-ethnic social identities are sometimes defined and constructed by territorial (political) boundaries and argue that it demonstrates "the territorial notion of nationhood":

> Telling their life stories our respondents spontaneously referred to themselves sometimes as Uzbeks, sometimes as Tajiks, without seeing any contradiction in this. They would not deny that their native language was Tajik nor that they grew up in a Tajik environment. One of our respondents explained that if he lived in Tajikistan, he would be a Tajik, but here, in Uzbekistan, he is an Uzbek. (Koroteyeva & Makarova, 2002, p. 4)

Is it the case of blurring boundaries and multiple levels of identity within and between minorities and indigenous groups?

A pluralistic definition of 'collective identities' may well be the key to understanding the minorities in post-Soviet Central Asia. The newest approach in defining and regulating multi-ethnic and transnational identities in Central Asia for the third millennium is characterized by a genuine policy of multiculturalism, which addresses both local and national (including clanship identity, that transcends national and political boundaries and borders) and transnational (a policy of 'open regionalism', where all minorities are equal) paradigms. Some leaders, like Karimov, Akaev, and Nazarbaev prefer to use a multicultural metaphor in their policies. As Wagner shows, Akaev has coined a doctrine of the 'Region of the Road' (his metaphor for the Silk Road), reflecting "the Central Asian version of the politics of globalization" (Wagner, 2002, p. 8). Similar ideas on global multiculturalism are found in the work of Smolicz (1981) who was one of the pioneers of multicultural education and policy, and argued that in order to achieve multiculturalism in a multi-ethnic society, education must provide opportunities for all minorities "to learn the shared values of society, including the national language", and "to study their own mother tongue in its cultural context" (Smolicz, 1981, p. 33).

It can be argued also that the current transitional period in the ex-Soviet Central Asia republics is a Hegelian dialectic in reverse – the rejection of the multifaceted *sovietski narod* as an ideological synthesis and the re-claiming of the lost traditional heritage of the past. Niyozov (2001) calls it a "dialectical negation", where beneath the rhetoric of social transformation and modernisation is found the genealogy of feudalism and traditionalism:

... at the surface things appear to have progressively changed, but in essence these countries have reverted to where they were before Russia's annexation of Central Asia at the end of the 19th century. (Niyozov, 2001, p. 2)

Since the collapse of the Soviet Union, political, cultural and economic transformations in Central Asia, which created new geo-political identities and nation building, have been accompanied also by negative manifestations: increased inter-ethnic hostility and conflict, civil wars, economic instability, and massive migration of the non-indigenous population, notably the ethnic Russians from the region. Ethnic conflicts resulted in numerous clashes and bloodshed in various parts of Central Asia. The re-invention process, involving indigenous groups, resulted in a new wave of fundamentalism and nationalism, which was threatening to turn back the clock, and abandon the hard won Soviet education legacy of scientific progress and development.

5.3. *Minorities, Indigenous Groups and Inequality*

The new economic transformation from the state to private enterprise has produced a new inequality, unemployment, and violence. The transformation also witnessed dramatic changes to education in Central Asia, where enrolment rates fell between 14 and 19 percentage points over 1989–96 in "Kazakhstan and the Kyrgyz Republic respectively" (Vandycke, 2001, p. 1). This is confirmed by Niyozov (2001) who believes that the new socio-economic transition has "provided access to unimaginable wealth for the few" and poverty for the majority, resulting in a serious "inequitable access to schooling" (Niyozov, 2001, p. 3). The dominant approaches to educational reform "remained mainly top-down, bureaucratic and largely rhetorical" and lacked in research and empirical data (Niyozov, 2001, pp. 3–4).

Extreme poverty is one of the key factors in the rising educational inequality in Central Asia. As Eshanova (2002) observes, education has become the privilege of the rich:

> Parents and children in Uzbekistan used to look forward to the start of the school year ... Today ... the start of the new year is bringing little joy to parents and children in Uzbekistan, or elsewhere in Central Asia. Although primary and secondary education remains free, preparing children for the start of school places a heavy burden on the majority of families. (Eshanov, 2002, p. 1)

Today, elite schools with modern computer facilities exist in the capitals of Central Asia. However, these schools are only for the children of government officials and wealthy businessman (Eshanova, 2002, p. 1). Similar signs of educational inequality can be seen in Tajikistan, where 80 per cent of the population lives in rural areas. In addition to urban and rural inequality, there is the divided schools syndrome, one school for the rich and another school for the poor. Parents are forced to open fee-paying schools and classes (Niyozov, 2001, p. 4). There are serious equity and equality problems in Tajikistan, that are relevant to the Central Asia region as a whole. The economic collapse in Central Asia, partly triggered of by the collapse of the USSR and its trading partners within the Soviet block, resulted in unforseen social, political and economic problems – poverty for the majority of ethnic groups in the Central Asia region, interethnic conflict, civil wars, unemployment, and isolation. For many ethnic and indigenous groups in the region the unfavourable economic and political climate brought for them extreme poverty and degradation. Confronted with these monumental economic and social problems how is a democratic and post-Soviet multi-ethnic Tajik society built? Tajikistan, like other nations in the Central Asia, has inherited a socio-political and economic infrastructure that is "unsustainable, ineffective and riddled with continuing tensions" (Niyozov, 2001, p. 3).

5.4. *Gender and Education in Central Asia*

Gender inequality in access to education is increasing in the Cental Asian region. Within the Central Asia the availability of educational opportunities for women is "exceedingly limited" (Ismagilova, 2002, p. 1). In a recent survey dealing with the violation of women's rights, the majority of the respondents indicated that they could not study as they were not "allowed to leave home", they "had no money for education" or and they "had no time". The least educated females had also the highest rates of physical abuse:

> ... the least educated women have the highest percentage of the various forms of violence in their community: 96% of women with no high or primary education experienced physical violence. (Ismagilova, 2002, p. 2)

6. ETHNICITY, EDUCATION AND POLICY SINCE 1992

One of the key problems for the multi-ethnic State engaged in promoting and practising pluralist democracy is reconciling the notion of genuine cultural diversity (and linguistic diversity) and political unity. Consequently, one of the central policy issues in some multi-ethnic nations in Central Asia is the status and position of the official state language(s) in relation to the languages of the minorities in the school curriculum and society.

6.1. *Language as the Medium of Instruction: The Constitutional and Legal Position*

There is no greater problem about the legal and political status of minorities than the medium of instruction in the school. It is at the school level that the genuine linguistic diversity is put to test. In Central Asia, particularly in Kazakhstan, Kyrgyzstan, Uzbekistan, Tajikistan, and Turkmenistan (former Soviet republics) the language of choice is the mother tongue for the dominant groups. However, of the small groups in Central Asia, some use Tajik, some use Turkmen, and others use Kazakh as their regional *lingua franca*.

After the 1991 break up of the Soviet Union, the ethnic Russians in Central Asia numbered 9.5 million, or 19.5 per cent of the total population. By 1994, the Russian population of Kyrgyzstan dropped to 18 percent (from 21.5 in 1989). In 1996 alone, some one million immigrants arrived in Russia, the majority of them were refugees from the Central Asia (Partridge, 2002, p. 2).

The Central Asian languages have another aetiological problem. Some groups had no written language prior to the 1917 Revolution. They had to adopt the Roman or the Cyrillic alphabet as a basis for mass literacy. During the 1970s in Kazakhstan, the preference for Russian was growing, even among the Kazakhs, who used it as a vehicle for upward social mobility. Educated Kazakhs became bilinguals, and Kazakhs, after the Tatars, had the highest proportion of fluent Russian speakers (59.5 per cent in urban areas) of the entire Turkic people (Grant, 1981, pp. 76–80).

When comparing ethnicity, indigenous culture and academic achievement among the major Central Asian nationalities in 1980, it became evident that Bashkirs, Chuvash, Tajiks, Kazakhs and Kirgiz had more individuals completing higher education. All had ratios of above 120 as a percentage of increase over a five-year period than the Russians, with their figure of 107.

In contrast, some 20 years later, modern Kazakh society is characterised by an inter-ethnic conflict, and by 'deep ethnic contradictions', arising from an increased competition between the Kazakhs and the ethnic Russians for power, privilege, high status and well-paid jobs, as well as the language problem (Kurganskaia, 2000, p. 3). Increasingly, the non-indigenous groups, especially the Russians, now feel like the 'second-class citizens' in the land where they were born, and grew up. In Kazakhstan, for instance, where there is a large Russian minority group and where Russian was the *lingua franca* of the region, there are moves to down-grade the strategic and political importance of Russian, much to the annoyance of the Russians residing in Kazakhstan (who had enjoyed the dominant status for decades) and enforce universal and compulsory literacy for all Kazakh citizens.

As part of the Russian exodus from Central Asia, some 250,000 Russian left Kazakhstan in 1994 (Partridge, 2002, p. 1). The exodus was prompted by the following three reasons: (a) the economic downturn in Central Asia, due to the collapse of the USSR, (b) the loss of privileged status enjoyed by the Russians, and (c) the initiation of cultural nationalisation by the indigenous elite.

The Language Law now defines and reaffirms the political and cultural significance of the state language. Article 4 of the Law states: "It is the duty of every citizen of the Republic of Kazakhstan to master the state language". The dominance of the state language was reinforced by the 1998 government decree *On the Use of the State Language in State Institutions*. The problem is that some Kazakhs themselves prefer to communicate in Russian and 14 per cent of them have a "problem performing their official duties" due to a poor command of the state language. Recently, a republic-wide opinion poll showed that 71.1 per cent of the respondents, including 54.1 per cent of Kazakhs, supported the idea of introducing the second state language (Kurganskaia, 2000, p. 7).

In Uzbekistan, where Russians, as a minority, comprise eight per cent of the population, language policy, first passed as the *Language Law* in the Uzbek Supreme Soviet in 1989, declaring Uzbek as the state language (but accepting Russian as the 'language of inter-ethnic communication'), and mandating that Uzbek be "the sole method of official communication", has contributed to a growing ethnocentrism against minorities, resulting in the massive exodus of the Russians during the 1990s. By 1992, some 800,000 individuals, mostly Russians, had left Uzbekistan (Soros, 2002, p. 1). The Russians, as a minority, when forced to learn the state language, as a condition for employment, and future career prospects, felt being discriminated against, and nick-named the language law 'a language of emigration'. The new citizenship law of 1992 also required all minorities to become Uzbek citizens by 1993 or be denied access to health and education, and other privileges accorded to citizens. Grass-roots nationalism, and the officially sanctioned discriminatory policies legitimated by the language law and the new citizenship law have certainly contributed to an inter-ethnic tension and conflict. Uzbek President Islam Karimov denies the existence of discrimination or the inter-ethnic tensions. It is difficult to reconcile his claim with the annual migration figures to Russia, where the number of emigrants to Russia had increased from 27,400 in 1996 to 33,000 in 1997 (Soros, 2002, pp. 1–3). Even if the rhetoric of the new laws on citizenship and language appear to be non-discriminatory, and offer the non-indigenous population an opportunity of becoming 'nationalized citizens', for those already residing in the country, the ethnic Russians feel marginalised and there were outbreaks of ethnic conflict and violence (Partridge, 2002, p. 1).

The closure of the Russian television channel, newspapers, and private publishing houses, meant total control of the media by the government. This could have serious implications for the education of the Russian-speaking minorities. Furthermore, to distance itself even more from the former Soviet or Russian dominance in education, Uzbekistan is planning to replace its Cyrillic alphabet with the Roman one in 2005. As many textbooks are published in the Cyrillic alphabet it would mean a complete transformation of the textbook industry.

6.2. The Re-Construction of National Identity

Koroteyeva and Makarova (2002), from the Institute of Ethnology and Anthropology in Moscow, are critical of the assertion of the Uzbek national identity, which, they argue, is divisive, as it excludes many non-indigenous people, particularly the Russians. The State, by using the concept of 'restoration of the national tradition' is legitimating ethnocentrism. The example of the *malhalla* (neighbourhood, and closely-knit Muslim community), where traditional Uzbek mores have been celebrated, which is an appeal to popular tradition and a crucial part of the nation building, stressing its separation from Russia. *Naruz*, a celebration of the New Year in the Iranian tradition, is an example of the large-scale invention of tradition that has become a national holiday. No attempt has been made to adopt multiculturalism, which would facilitate the formation of a multi-ethnic republic. Instead, the state's use of traditional institutions, and the process of indigenisation has created 'even more pronounced' divisions between the indigenous and the non-indigenous population (Koroteyeva and Makarova, 2002, 4).

What are the political, social and ethnic aspects of integration in Kyrgystan? Toktomyshev (2002), Vice-Chancellor of the Kyrgyz State National University, and Member of Parliament, believes that Kyrgystan inherited some of the ambivalent legacies from the Soviet past, when the Bolsheviks created separate ethnic republics, and artificial borders (especially across the multi-ethnic Fergana valley (the Osh and Jalal – Abad regions, with the three largest Kyrgyz, Uzbek, and Russian minorities, which was the local 'Babylon of Central Asia'). This was done in a completely arbitrary manner, displacing large minorities outside their own republic. Some parts of the Fergana valley have much in common with Uzbekistan and Tajikistan. President Askar Akaev claims that "Kyrgyzia inherited the burning fuse of the Osh (region) conflict and intra-republican confrontation between North and South" (Toktomyshev, 2002, p. 2).

The most obvious signs of education and policy change are the current moves to blend cultural and historical achievements of both the Fergana valley and the Kyrgyz North. The official policy is to ensure equality and access of educational opportunities for all minorities in the Fergana valley and throughout Kyrgystan. This has been achieved by the opening up of the National Academy of Sciences in the South, the establishment of research institutions, a number of new higher education institutions, and various other education centres, designed to promote the development of "the intellectual potential of all ethnic groups" (Toktomyshev, 2002, p. 4).

A very promising case study of nation building of multi-ethnic communities is in the Republic of Bashkortostan, near the Urals, which represents some 100 minorities, with the three major ethnic groups – the Bashkirs, Tatars and the Russians. As a result of the Soviet-inspired border policy, and demographic processes, Bashkirs are now in the minority. Here, the official policy of multicultural education affirms that all languages are equal and "deserve equal protection and development under the law" (Graney, 2002, p. 2). The Ministry of Education has been promoting the language policy, based on the concept of the "cult of the indigenous language" (Graney, 2002, p. 2).

6.3. Ethnicity and Values Education

Ambivalent legacies and new challenges. The Mountainous Badakhshan Autonomous Province (MBAP) of Tajikistan, which is located in the high Pamir Mountain Range, and culturally is a homeland of six small ethnic groups, represents a very useful case study of the influence of schooling and values education on such a culturally diverse region. Apart from the six ethnic groups, there are Turkic Kyrgyz and Iranian Tajiks, who had lived there for centuries. It is the only place in the world where Ismaili Shi'ite followers constitute a majority of the population and one of the few areas in central Asia where the Sunni Muslim tradition does not predominate.

The post-Soviet transitional period (1992–2002) has resulted in the revival of the Badakhshani multi-ethnic community – cultural and linguistic identities, nationalism, and globalism. The current situation of post-Soviet Badakhshan, Tajikistan, and Central Asia is one of ethnic transformation and dislocation. One way of preventing the process of ethnic fragmentation, which brings conflict, violence and ethnocentrism, is to teach the values of equality, tolerance and peace in the classroom.

Values education and the continuity of ethical authority of the teacher play a significant part in the teaching and learning process. The values of the good society are found in the writings of progressivist and humanistic thinkers. Equality, justice, peace, tolerance, cooperation, and friendship seem to provide a global bridge between modernity and tradition, where the values of Allah, prophet Mohammad, and the Imam intersect with the values and the promise of modernity. A history teacher in the region explains the similarity between the emancipatory spirit of Islam and the egalitarian logic of communism:

> I was a bit disturbed by the excess of talk about Islam, but then I realised that the major principles of the "code of the constructor of communism" are similar to those of *'javonmardi'* (chivalry) in Islam. The problem is how to apply them in practice. (Niyozov, 2001, p. 13)

Values education, particularly teaching peace and tolerance, is referred to by a school principal in the Kursk region, who believes, that the most crucial role of the school is to teach various ethnic groups to live in peace:

> The new reality and the new school's task is to teach tolerance to the

Russians, Armenians, Tajiks, Tatars, Moldavians and others. (*Uchitleskaia Gazeta*, 3 September 2002, p. 6)

Citizenship Education in Central Asia. Fagerlind and Kanaev (2000) argue for the importance of citizenship education in the Central Asian Countries undergoing a traumatic social and economic transformation. They explain that the process of building a new independent nation requires "new approaches to the study of national history, culture, and national identity, which form the core of civic education" (Fagerlind & Kanaev, 2000, p. 95).

The heritage that the Central Asian nations have received from the former USSR includes patterns of standard institutions, such as political and educational structures. Fagerlind and Kanaev argue that in the Central Asia nations the fostering of their national identities is "considered as a priority in the social sciences" (ibid., p. 108). This process should be assisted by the advantage of the common heritage legacy of the Central Asian countries which allows for the educational transformation "to be comparable across the region" (ibid., p. 105). All five countries have highly comparable education systems.

7. EVALUATION

Educational research on race and ethnicity in Central Asia deals with the constructivist nature of culture-making and nation-building. It focuses more on conceptual aspects of ethnicity and national identity, the borders issues, inter-ethnic conflict, cultural stereotypes, discrimination and inequality. In its attempts to solve the political and moral dilemmas of ethnic or national identity and citizenship it represents the ambivalence between the desire to re-discover and construct so-called 'authentic' nations, using, among other things, consensus-building cultural, political and religious slogans in Central Asia, that would satisfy both local and political agendas, and address the imperatives of modernity, particularly the continuation of the Enlightenment and the triumph of reason, science and progress, and the construction of a Western paradigm of the civil society.

In evaluating ethnicity and indigenous cultures the focus of educational research has been on language policies, citizenship, inter-ethnic inequality and discrimination. Problems in inter-ethnic conflict, and ethnic identity in Central Asia have been attributed to political (the contesting nature of the inter-state boundaries), economic (the problem of transitional economies), and social (temporary decline in welfare and other provisions) factors.

Very little educational research on race and ethnicity deals with the Western-driven models of globalisation, marketisation and information technology. The internet, which is "both global and local in its reach", can be a powerful tool of empowerment of marginalised and disadvantaged minorities (Ciolek, 2002, p. 1). In contrast, Mitter (1993) finds that in many countries the notion of 'democracy' has eroded, leading to "nationalism, ethnocentrism and racism" (pp. 464–465).

There is a need for a radical policy shift to address ethnic or racial conflict, which is a growing global problem.

One of the unresolved issues in educational research on race and ethnicity in Central Asia is a growing ethnic polarisation, differentiation, discrimination and inequality. The role of the State, in confronting and addressing social and psychological origins of prejudice and discrimination, has been one of adopting effective and multicultural in nature educational policies that focus on finding solutions to ethnic discrimination, and attempted regulation of transnational and multinational identities in Central Asia.

REFERENCES

Bremmer, I. (1993). Reassessing Soviet nationalities theory In I. Bremmer & R. Taras (Eds.), *Nation and Politics in the Soviet Successor States*. Cambridge: Cambridge University Press.

Ciolek, M. (2002). *Internet and Minorities*. http://www.ciole.com/PAPERS/minorities2001.html

Edgar, A. (2001). *Identities, Communities, and Nations in Central Asia: A Historical Pespective*. http://socrates.berkeley.edu/~iseees/

Eshanova, Z. (2002). *Central Asia: Class Struggles – Extreme Poverty Endangers Education*. www.rferl.org/nca/features/2002/08/300082002151006.asp

Fagerlind, I., & Kanaev, A. (2000). Redefining citizenship education in the central Asian countries. *Educational Practice and Theory*, 22(1), 95–113.

Graney, K. (2002). *Russia: Bashkortostan – A Case Study on Building a National Identity*. http://www.rferl.org/nca/features/1997/08/F.RU.97086152920html

Grant, N. (1981). The education of linguistic minorities in the USSR. In J. Megarry, S. Nisbet & E. Hoyle (Eds.), *World Yearbook of Education 1981: Education of Minorities*. London: Kogan Page.

Gleason, G. (1997). *The Central Asia States*, Boulder CO: Westview.

Glenn, J. (1999). *The Soviet Legacy in Central Asia*. Houndsmill: Macmillan.

Hobsbawm, E. J. (1990). *Nations and Nationalism since 1780*. Cambridge: Cambridge University Press.

Ismagilova, N. (2002). *Women in Mind: Educational Needs of Women in Central Asia – General Recommendations and Strategies for Development*. www.mtnforum.org/resources/library/isman02a.htm

Koroteyeva, V., & Makarova, E. (2002). *The Assertion of the Uzbek Natioanal Identity*. http://www.iias.nl/iiasn6/central/uzbek.html

Kurganskaia, V. (2000). *Kazakhstan: The Language Problem in the Context of Ethnic Relation*. www.ca-c.org/journal/eng01_2000/08.kurganskaia.shtml

Liu, G. (1998). Ethnic harmony and conflicts in Central Asia: Origins and policies. In Y. Zhang and R. Azizian (Eds.), *Ethnic Challenges Beyond Borders*. Houndmills: Macmillan.

Mitter, W. (1993). Education, democracy and development in a period of revolutionary change. *International Review of Education*, 39(6), 464–465.

Nahaylo, B. (1998). Population displacement in the former Soviet Union. *After the Soviet Union (Issue 98)* http://www/unhcr.ch/pubs/rmo98/rmo9801.htm

Niyozov, S. (2001). *Education in Tajikistan: A Window to Understanding Change through Continuity*. Paper presented at the ANZCIES, Curtin University of Technology, Perth, WA.

Partridge, B. (2002). *Central Asia: Ethnic Russian Population Decreases*. http://www.rferl.org/nca/features/1999/01/F.RU.990107130240.html

Prazauskas, A. (1998). Ethnopolitical issues and the emergence of nation-states in central Asia. In *Ethnic Challenges Beyond Borders. Chinese and Russian Perspectives of the Central Asian Conumdrum*. Houndmills: Macmillan.

Roy, O. (2000). *The New Central Asia. The Creation of Nations*. London: I. B. Tauris.

Smolicz, J. J. (1981). Culture, ethnicity and education: Multiculturalism in a plural society. In J. Megarry, S. Nisbet & E. Hoyle (Eds.), *World Yearbook of Education 1981: Education of Minorities*. London: Kogan Page.

Sokolovski, S. (2002). Classification as representations: The category of indigenous peoples in Russian Academy and Law. http://www.abdn.ac.uk/chags9/1sokolovski.htm

Soros Foundation (2002). *Relationship Between Language Policy: The Case of Uzbekistan*. http://www.soros.org/fmp2/html/laws/Zakons/Uzbekistan/UzbekIntoEngl.html

Toktomyshev, S. (2002). *The Political, Economic and Ethno-Social Aspects of Integration*. http://www.cpss.org/casianw/sovetbek.txt

Uchitleskaia Gazeta (Teachers' Newspaper), 3 September 2002, p. 6.

Vandycke, N. (2001). *Access to Education for the Poor in Europe and Central Asia*. Washington, DC: The World Bank.

Zaslavsky, V. (1993). Success and collapse: Traditional Soviet nationalities policy. In I. Bremmer & R. Taras (Eds.), *Nation and Politics in the Soviet Successor States*. Cambridge: Cambridge University Press.

Zhang, Y., & Azizian, R. (1998). Introduction. In Y. Zhang and R. Azizian, *Ethnic Challenges Beyond Borders*. Houndmills: Macmillan.

18

Sex and Gender Differences in Educational Outcomes

JOHN P. KEEVES
Flinders University Institute of International Education, Australia

MALCOLM SLADE
Flinders University Institute of International Education, Australia

1. INTRODUCTION

The Asia-Pacific region includes countries with a wide range of ethnic and racial groups and with a great variety of cultural traditions. Within these traditions, women and men may have very different roles in the societies in which they live, work and play. However, the expansion of educational services within the region during the twentieth century has raised the issues of whether there should be equality of educational opportunities for girls and boys and whether equality of educational outcomes should be expected between the sexes. The proper handling of the biological and psychological differences between boys and girls remains a challenging problem for education in all countries. Consequently, it is necessary to consider whether boys and girls have different innate abilities, have different capacities to read or to calculate, to memorize or to formulate and to express their ideas. Moreover, it is important to consider whether they have different emotional drives to participate or to succeed and need different types of preparation for the different tasks required of them in their adult lives. It is also inappropriate to assume that research conducted in North America, which often dominates the debate in educational settings, necessarily applies outside the particular culture in which that research was conducted. This article is primarily concerned with differences between the sexes in educational outcomes. Where possible it considers changes that have occurred in outcomes over time and whether there are differences in these outcomes between countries in the Asia-Pacific region. The existence of change or differences over time and between countries provides evidence that such differences as are observed are societally based. In addition, in situations where the societies are themselves changing, it must be asked whether further change in the differences between the sexes in educational outcomes might be expected.

2. SOCIETAL CHANGE AND THE ROLES OF WOMEN IN SOCIETY

From the Second IEA Science Study, Keeves (1992, pp. 28–29) reported that between the ten countries which tested in the first study in 1970 and again in the second study in 1984, with three countries being drawn from the Asia-Pacific region (Australia, Japan and Thailand), there was clear evidence of rapid social and economic change. Marked change had occurred in most countries in: (a) GNP per capita, indicating an increasing affluence within the society; (b) a reduction in the proportion of the labour force engaged in agriculture, indicating an increasing urbanization of the society; (c) a marked increase in the electrical energy consumed per person, indicating rapid technological development; and (d) a striking rise in living standards as assessed by drop in infant mortality per 1000 births. These changes were reflected in the changing roles of women in society (Keeves, 1992, p. 143) that involved: (a) an increase in the proportion of women in the labour force; (b) a marked decline in the total fertility rate; (c) a corresponding decline in family size and; (d) an increase in the age of women at first marriage. These changing societal circumstances were enabling women to continue for longer periods in employment and to return to work earlier after child bearing. Furthermore, Keeves (1992, p. 145) argued that increased participation in the labour force among females would appear to have led girls and women to: (a) stay longer at school; (b) increase their study in higher education and; (c) increase participation as secondary school teachers.

From a secondary analysis of IEA data from the First and Second IEA Mathematics Studies conducted in 1964 and 1982, Baker and Jones (1993) have shown a clear relationship between the increasing rate of participation of women in the labour force and the rate of reduction of differences between boys and girls in Mathematics achievement at the lower and middle secondary school levels. This study would seem to provide evidence for a relationship between societal forces that influence participation in the labour force and educational outcomes in so far as differences between the sexes are involved. Thus as a consequence of the changing roles of women in society, it might be expected that there would be changes in the sex differences in observed educational outcomes. Moreover, it is clear that the last three decades of the twentieth century have been highly significant ones for change in the roles of women in society, not only in many countries of the Asia-Pacific region, but also in many of the Western countries.

One change of interest that has taken place in this context during this period has been the preference of many scholars in education to refer to 'gender' rather than 'sex' differences. Megarry (1984) has argued for the use of 'gender' to refer to "the set of meanings, expectations and roles that a particular society ascribes to sex". Consequently, gender is considered to be a social construct, while sex refers to the biological category to which a person belongs and to genetically based influences. This article is concerned with differences in educational outcomes between males and females, both with respect to biological differences and those that are societally based. Nevertheless, it is acknowledged that there is an interaction between these biological differences and the effects of gender-related differences of an environmental, cultural, economic or social basis. As a consequence there remain sometimes very striking differences in the magnitudes of the educational outcomes achieved by males and females in the different school systems in the region, that would seem to be related to differences in the forces that are operating in the different countries of the region and that have largely societal origins.

3. DIFFERENCES IN PARTICIPATION

Among the areas where marked disparities between males and females occur in the region, are the opportunities provided and the expectations of the society for young people to take part in education at the successive levels of primary, secondary and tertiary stages of education. Since the age ranges for these three stages of education are specified differently in different countries, UNESCO reporting systems employ six year intervals: 5 to 11 years of age for the primary stage, 12 to 17 years of age for the secondary stage, and 18 to 23 years of age for the tertiary stage. Table 1 records the estimated participation rates or net enrolment rates for these three age groups in the two major zones of the Asia-Pacific region when compared with the developed countries of North America and Europe. These data are taken from the Delors Report (Delors, 1996, p. 76), which considers some of the consequences of such differences.

In East Asia and Oceania, as in the developed countries, the participation rates at the primary stage (5–11 years) are relatively high with approximately equal levels of participation between the sexes. However, although the participation rate in South Asia for boys is comparable with that in East Asia and Oceania, it is much lower for girls with only approximately two girls in three being enrolled in schooling in the South Asia region. At the secondary stage, significant drop-out occurs in East Asia and Oceania, falling to a level of a little over 50 per cent, but without a marked difference between the sexes. Nevertheless, in the South Asia region, while half the boys are in schooling at the secondary stage, less than one girl in three is enrolled at school. At the tertiary stage a similar pattern to that recorded at the secondary stage is shown, but with marked

Table 1. Estimated participation rate in education in the Asia-Pacific region, 1995

Net enrolment rates	Primary Ages 5–11 years		Secondary Ages 12–17 years		Tertiary Ages 18–23 years	
Participation rates %	Male	Female	Male	Female	Male	Female
East Asia and Oceania	88.6	85.5	54.7	51.4	19.5	13.6
South Asia	84.3	65.6	50.5	32.2	12.4	6.6
Developed countries	92.3	91.7	87.1	88.5	40.8	42.7

Source: Delors (1996, p. 76).

drops in the proportions recorded both for males and females and for the two regions under consideration.

Overall, it would appear that girls rather than boys are more likely to leave school prematurely and with lower levels of literacy. Moreover, these girls are more likely to marry at an early age, or to remain at home to help their mothers care for younger siblings, thus maintaining a high fertility rate that is associated with a low level of education, and thereby continuing a cycle of poverty, illiteracy and early mortality. Only through education and economic development can this cycle be broken. The girls play a major role in this cycle, but the boys also contribute, since it is the boys living in poverty who leave school earlier and fail to gain employment. Retention of students in education is a major challenge for education in the Asia-Pacific region, particularly in South Asia, and the problem is far greater for girls than for boys. Furthermore, this problem has very serious consequences for the failure to curtail population growth within the South Asia region.

4. DIFFERENCES IN LITERACY AND ILLITERACY

Adams and Chapman (1998) have examined data for the Asia-Pacific region on adult illiteracy rates with a marked difference between the East Asia region (6.2%) and the South Asian region (55.5%). There were also marked differences in the illiteracy rates between males and females for the countries in these two regions. Table 2 records the illiteracy rates presented by Lee (1998, p. 670) for males and females for countries within East Asia and South Asia.

In East Asia, it is only in Laos where the illiteracy rate for females exceeded 50 per cent. However, in South Asia, six of the countries listed: India, Afghanistan, Bhutan, Bangladesh, Nepal and Pakistan all had illiteracy rates for females of 50 per cent and above. Moreover, in all countries listed with the exceptions of Taiwan and Cambodia the illiteracy rate was greater for females than for males. The social, demographic and economic problems facing many of these countries arise at least in part from the very low levels of literacy among females. The six South-Asian countries listed above involve approximately two billion people, and more than a third of the world's population, and nearly half of these people are illiterate. The raising of the literacy rates, particularly among women represents one of the major educational problems in the Asia-Pacific region.

Lee (1998, p. 677) draws attention to the pressing need to develop policies in the South Asia region to achieve three important goals.

- *Increase educational opportunities for females.* The high levels of illiteracy in the South Asia region is largely attributable to females. Consequently, there is a need of the highest priority to increase the educational opportunities for females, with subsequent improvement in health, nutrition and reduced fertility rates of women and a resulting reduction in poverty in the country and region over time.

Table 2. Illiteracy rates between males and females for countries in East Asia and South Asia

	% Illiteracy East Asia				% illiteracy South Asia		
Country	Males	Females	F/M	Country	Males	Females	F/M
Singapore	4	14	3.5	Myanmar	11	22	2.0
Hong Kong, China	4	12	3.0	Papua New Guinea	19	37	1.9
Korea, Rep of	1	3	3.0	Sri Lanka	7	13	1.9
China, P.R.	10	27	2.7	Fiji	6	11	1.8
Vietnam	4	9	2.3	India	35	62	1.8
Indonesia	10	22	2.2	Afghanistan	53	85	1.6
Mongolia	11	23	2.1	Bhutan	44	72	1.6
Malaysia	11	22	2.0	Bangladesh	51	74	1.5
Thailand	4	8	2.0	Nepal	59	86	1..5
Laos PDR	31	56	1.8	Pakistan	50	76	1.5
Philippines	5	6	1.2	Maldives	7	7	1.0
Cambodia	9	9	1.0				
Taiwan	7	7	1.0				

F/M is the ratio of percentages for Females to Males.
Source: Lee (1998, p. 670).

- *Increase retention rates for females.* Not only is it essential to improve initial access to education for females, but it is also necessary to increase the retention rates for girls in countries in the South-Asia region, particularly at the secondary school level.
- *Develop specific educational programs for girls and boys.* Providing access to education and raising retention rates in schooling is not enough. There is also need to develop appropriate programs not only for the girls but also for the boys that will prepare them for suitable employment in their societies. Programs that do not differentiate between the needs of boys and girls are said to be merely passive measures (McDonald, 1995, p. 55). Only by more active measures would it be possible to achieve greater equality between women and men. Such measures must be directed towards the social and economic needs of each country in the region. Literacy and numeracy are necessary skills, but training for suitable employment is also essential, together with skills associated with health and home maintenance.

5. DIFFERENCES IN ACHIEVEMENT OUTCOMES

It is now widely accepted in more developed countries from studies of sex differences in achievement outcomes that girls consistently perform better than do boys when school grades are considered, are less frequently failed, and are more frequently accelerated through the years of schooling than are boys. However, when achievement outcomes are measured by standardized tests, the differences between the sexes are less consistent and frequently small. These comparisons of performance on achievement tests are commonly undertaken in testing programs of all sizes and at all levels of schooling, but, the results are generally confounded by: (a) self-selection effects at those levels of schooling where education ceases to be obligatory; (b) subject selection in those situations where the study of the subject ceases to be compulsory; (c) where schools or classes are the primary sampling unit and students are sampled or tested within groups, no allowance is made for the cluster sample design in testing for statistical significance; and (d) where schools differ in type, either single-sex or coeducational, no provision is made in the analysis of the data for the complex structure of the sample. As a consequence it is only with large, carefully designed samples with high response rates testing at levels where selection bias does not arise and with statistical analyses which allow for the complex structure of the sample in the testing of the observed differences for statistical significance and magnitude of effect, that meaningful results are obtained.

Over a long period of nearly 40 years, the International Association for the Evaluation of Educational Achievement (IEA) has maintained high standards of sample design, conduct of studies, with high response rates, and with appropriate methods of analysis. As a consequence the results reported from IEA studies are generally considered to be meaningful and strong.

Table 3 records information on the performance in Mathematics, Science and Reading of students at three stages of schooling, the middle primary school stage, the middle secondary school stage and the final year of secondary schooling for those countries in the Asia-Pacific region which participated in these IEA studies. In Mathematics at both the primary (Grade 4) and middle secondary school (Grade 8) levels was only in Korea where a significant difference between the sexes was recorded. Moreover, Korea recorded a significant difference only because it employed a well-designed sample with very small sampling errors and this led to the increased possibility of detection of a significant difference between the sexes. At the final year of schooling stage, the boys in all three countries involved, namely, Australia, New Zealand and the Russian Federation, performed significantly better than the girls. However, these differences were influenced by differences in retention rates and subject selection rates between the sexes in the different countries.

In Science, at both the primary and middle secondary school stages, three systems, namely Hong Kong, Japan and Korea recorded significant differences between the sexes with the boys doing significantly better than the girls at both levels. In Australia at the primary school stage in Science, a significant effect was recorded but not at the middle secondary school stage where the sample that was tested failed to satisfy the sampling requirements for strong comparisons to be made between the male and female groups of students. However, at the final year of secondary schooling in all three systems, namely, Australia, New Zealand and the Russian Federation, significant differences were recorded

Table 3. Sex differences in achievement in mathematics, science and reading from recent IEA studies

	Primary (Grade 4)		Lower Secondary (Grade 8)		Final Year Secondary	
	Male	Female	Male	Female	Male	Female
Mathematics (1995)						
Australia	63 (0.7)	63 (0.8)	†57 (1.2)	†59 (1.1)	†*540 (10.3)	†*570 (9.3)
Hong Kong	73 (1.1)	73 (0.8)	72 (1.7)	68 (1.7)		
Iran, Islamic Republic	39 (1.4)	37 (1.1)	39 (0.8)	36 (0.8)		
Japan	75 (0.5)	74 (0.5)	74 (0.5)	73 (0.4)		
Korea	*77 (0.4)	* 75 (0.5)	*73 (0.6)	*70 (0.7)		
New Zealand	52 (1.3)	54 (0.9)	55 (1.4)	53 (1.3)	*536 (4.9)	*507 (6.2)
Russian Federation	—	—	59 (1.4)	61 (1.3)	*488 (6.5)	*460 (6.6)
Singapore	75 (0.9)	76 (1.0)	79 (1.1)	79 (1.0)		
Thailand	49 (1.3)	52 (1.0)	56 (1.4)	58 (1.7)		
Science (1995)						
Australia	*67 (0.6)	*65 (0.6)	†61 (1.0)	†59 (0.8)	†*547 (11.5)	†*513 (9.4)
Hong Kong	*63 (10.8)	*61 (0.7)	*60 (1.1)	*55 (1.1)		
Iran, Islamic Republic	41 (1.0)	39 (0.9)	*49 (0.8)	*45 (0.8)		
Japan	*70 (0.4)	*69 (0.4)	*67 (0.5)	*64 (0.4)		
Korea	*75 (0.5)	*73 (0.5)	*67 (0.5)	*64 (0.5)		
New Zealand	59 (1.2)	61 (0.9)	60 (1.0)	56 (1.0)	*543 (7.1)	*515 (5.2)
Russian Federation	—	—	60 (0.9)	57 (0.7)	*510 (5.7)	*463 (6.7)
Singapore	65 (0.9)	64 (1.0)	71 (1.2)	69 (1.1)		
Thailand	49 (1.2)	49 (0.8)	57 (0.9)	58 (1.0)		
	Population A 9 year olds		Population B 14 year olds			
Reading (1990)						
Hong Kong	*512 (3.7)	*524 (3.6)	533 (4.0)	538 (3.8)		
Indonesia	394 (3.6)	397 (3.7)	—	—		
New Zealand	*519 (4.1)	*539 (4.0)	544 (5.9)	549 (5.5)		
Philippines	—	—	427 (3.4)	432 (2.6)		
Singapore	*510 (1.3)	*521 (1.3)	434 (1.6)	434 (1.6)		
Thailand	—	—	*464 (7.3)	*488 (5.5)		

Sources: Mathematics, IEA (1996, 1997, 1998); Science, IEA (1996, 1997, 1998); Reading, Elley (1994).
* Significant differences between males and females. Note: standard errors given in parentheses.
† System did not satisfy sampling guidelines.

between the male and female students in science achievement, with the boys clearly performing better than the girls. Again, at the upper secondary school level selection bias effects were in operation.

In Reading, at the nine-year-old (or Population A) stage in three of the four systems, namely, Hong Kong, New Zealand and Singapore, that participated in the study from the Asia-Pacific region, significant differences were recorded between the levels of achievement of boys and girls with the girls performing better than the boys in reading literacy. However, by the middle secondary school stage, while the girls sometimes do marginally better than the boys, it is only in Thailand where the difference recorded is found to be statistically significant.

The findings of these IEA studies show that where significant differences are recorded for large, well designed samples, the results are generally consistent with studies conducted in other parts of the world, with only small differences in mathematics achievement, some differences in science achievement that are significantly in favour of the boys, and likewise small differences in reading achievement, that favour the girls. Nevertheless, the differences between the sexes recorded in these studies are generally small, and would not contribute greatly to the differences between the sexes that are observed in work force participation in the different countries of the Asia-Pacific region.

6. SCHOOL ACHIEVEMENT AND COMPLETION RATES FOR BOYS

In discussing the problems of the declining rates of achievement and retention of boys, a focus is placed on the situation in Australia in the years 2000 and 2001. There is little doubt that a problem existed in Northern Europe, and in particular, in Hungary and Finland at least a decade earlier, but Australia seems to be the first country in the Asia-Pacific region to be confronted by a problem that is without doubt becoming world-wide in affluent countries (Keeves, 1992).

Less than a decade ago, challenges to education in Australia involved the education of girls (Yates, 1993), and social justice (Sturman, 1997); both issues referred to the education of boys as if there were few problems in the area. The release and analysis of information on changing patterns of retention rates in Australia (Lamb, 1998) showed that school completion rates had peaked in 1992 at approximately 77 per cent and by 1995 had fallen markedly to 72 per cent, with a far greater drop for boys than for girls from an already lower level of participation. In 1999, the retention rate for boys was 12 per cent lower than for girls (ABS 2000). These changes led to a study of early school leaving in South Australia (Smyth et al., 2000), and a national study of factors influencing the academic performance of boys and girls and their initial destinations after leaving school (Collins et al., 2000). These were followed by a study that focused particularly on the concerns of boys (Slade, 2002).

Although rates of achievement cannot easily be discussed in terms of the overall performance of boys compared with girls, the indicators suggest that the academic performance of boys is declining in real terms and that although high achieving girls and boys perform equally well in Year 12 examinations, the average girl continues to outperform the average boy. Furthermore, the academic performance of boys is more varied than that of girls, with larger numbers of boys performing at the lower end of the scale (Collins et al., 2000).

The possible reasons for the recent changes in academic performance and school completion rates found between boys and girls are manifold. Despite its prominence in the current debate, there appears to be little evidence to support the view that declining rates for boys are the outcome of either the over representation of women as secondary school teachers, or of girls at the upper secondary and tertiary levels. There is also little evidence to show that the apparent success of programs to improve the achievement and retention rates of girls at this level, particularly in the traditionally more male dominated subject areas, is any more than coincidental. Indeed, although there are gender issues remaining in education, it appears that recent trends in rates of achievement and retention are less to do with gender related programs and gender issues than is often thought, and that attempts to deal with these changes in terms of gender difference and gender equity, may be making matters worse.

Slade (2002), in an extensive study that involved interviewing groups of both boys and girls, found that both boys and girls are largely clear and uniform in their views about the nature and value of their educational offering. Based on their experiences of education, the issues and problems they identify and the reasoning they use to make sense of their views, there is a growing social, cultural and philosophical gap between the perceptions and expectations of young people and what the adult world is offering them in the form of learning environments and educational outcomes. The views expressed by students indicate that secondary schools in Australia have not managed to keep up with the technological, social and cultural changes and influences of recent decades. Most notably these involve the globalisation of the Australian economy, the growth of information and communication technology, the changing role of women, the quickening pace of liberalisation and democratisation, the impact of an aging population and the despairing realisation that we may be facing a global survival crisis. Together, these changes and influences are shaping and directing the lives and the future of young people in ways that are neither well understood nor suitably addressed in their educational programs. Furthermore, during the closing decade of the millennium, it became increasingly apparent that these changes were already having a more formative impact on the perceptions and expectations of young Australians than they were on many in the adult world around them.

Contemporary youth in highly developed countries, such as Australia, are far more aware of themselves and the complex and changing nature of the world than they have been in the past. At a much earlier age they find themselves needing to live more independent lives, to be more individually aspiring and self-motivating, prepared to make choices for themselves, and to work with others, but for reasons that they must clearly see as their own and not those of their world of adult mentors. They are more judgmental of others, particularly the adult world, and far more likely to act, or feel driven to act, on their own judgements, whether this amounts to a choice to comply and conform, or to a declaration of difference and, if necessary, defiance.

In light of these changes, students, particularly the boys, are decreasingly prepared to accept an educational offering that they believe to lack the appropriate content, rewards and relevance to the contemporary and rapidly changing world, in which they see themselves living and working. Furthermore, they are also less inclined to accept traditional pathways and practices in education, and to accede to the demands of structured authority. They show a distinct preference to act for reasons that are clear to them and to cooperate by choice, on the basis of trust and mutual respect. The sense in which this has changed the way young Australians seek to develop relationships with adults, particularly educative relationships with teachers, is of major significance in shaping the issues and problems that are currently producing indicators like the changing patterns of behaviour and performance in schools.

Slade (2002) found that, despite the diversity of their educational experiences and achievements, and of their lives in general, secondary school students, irrespective or whether they are girls or boys, are largely in agreement about the key issues and problems in education, and about the ways in which these are interconnected. Their central concern is that school presents too many contradictions and creates intensely paradoxical, cultural dilemmas. It is, however, more likely to be the boys who cease to work hard at their school studies and who decide to drop out from school.

There is also general agreement among secondary school students that although most girls choose to conform and comply, many boys, and some girls clearly do not. This is generally seen to be done for pragmatic reasons and are rarely discussed in terms of right or wrong. Conformity and compliance are seen strategically, as a means to an end, and that while some can maintain the strategy, others cannot. At present, it seems that many more boys than girls choose not to conform and comply and many more choose to resist without regard for the consequences, most of which inevitably lead to lower academic achievement and non-completion. Furthermore, there seems to be an increasing number, again mostly boys, who are losing interest in the notion that consequences, in general, are factors that might be considered when making behaviour choices.

7. CONCLUSION

The countries of the Asia-Pacific region are confronted with a very wide range of problems. The developed and the developing countries face very different problems as the different sections of this article have shown. Solutions would seem to lie in the many different situations that exist, through the provision of more flexible educational institutions that make use of information and communication technology to provide an appropriate range of educational services to meet the needs of individual countries and the different social groups within those countries. The focal groups for these services may be the girls and the women of the South Asia countries and the boys and young men of such countries as Australia, where new problems in the education of boys have recently emerged.

It seems likely that radical changes are required over the coming decades in the more highly developed countries to provide more flexible educational institutions at the upper secondary school level, in universities and institutes of technology and in centres for lifelong learning. This would seem to require the provision of an entitlement for specified periods to educational services, together with a sustentation entitlement that would provide support while studying full-time. Such programs become possible through the advances in information and communication technology. However, a clearly formulated youth policy would seem to be needed to ensure that all youth, whatever their sex, racial and ethnic background, and social status share equitably. One of the problems of social justice in Western societies is that youth of higher social status generally profit more from the higher educational opportunities provided than do youth of lower social status. Consequently, it is commonly the youth from lower social status homes who suffer. Nevertheless, the issues involved in the more developed countries are clearly greater than those of social and gender equity and a rethinking of the nature of all educational programs at all levels is required, before developing countries in the Asia-Pacific region copy Western models that are in need of change.

REFERENCES

Adams, D., & Chapman, D. W. (1998). Education and national development in Asia: Trends and issues. *International Journal of Educational Research, 29*, 583–602.

Baker, D. P., & Jones, D. P. (1993). Creating gender equality: Cross-national gender stratification and mathematical performance. *Sociology of Education, 66*, 91–103.

Delors, J. (Chairman) (1996). *Learning: The Treasure Within. Report to Unesco of the International Commission on Education for the Twenty-first Century.* Paris: UNESCO.

Elley, W. B. (Ed.) (1994). *The IEA Study of Reading Literacy: Achievement and Instruction in Thirty Two School Systems.* Oxford: Pergamon.

IEA Reports
  Martin, M. O. et al. (1997). *Science Achievement in the Primary School Years.*
  Mullis, I. V. S. et al. (1997). *Mathematics Achievement in the Primary School Years.*
  Mullis, I. V. S. et al. (1996). *Science Achievement in the Middle School Years.*
  Beaton, A. E. et al. (1996). *Mathematics Achievement in the Middle School Years.*
  Mullis, I. V. S. et al. (1998). *Mathematics and Science Achievement in the Final Year of Secondary School.* IEA: Boston, MA.: TIMSS.

Keeves, J. P. (Ed.) (1992). *The IEA Study of Science III: Changes in Science Education and Achievement: 1970–1984.* Oxford: Pergamon.

Lamb, S. (1998). Completing school in Australia: Trends in the 1990s. *Australian Journal Education, 42*(1), 5–31.

Lee, W. O. (1998). Equity and access to education in Asia: Levelling the playing field. *International Journal of Educational Research, 29*, 667–683.

Megarry, J. (1984). Sex, gender and education. In S. Acker (Ed.), *Women and Education, World Yearbook of Education, 1984*. London: Kogan Page.

McDonald, M. (1995). *Women in Development: Vietnam*. Manila: Asian Development Bank.

Slade, M. (2002). *Listening to the Boys*. Adelaide: Shannon Research Press.

Smyth, J. et al. (2000). *Listen to Me I'm Learning*. Adelaide: Flinders Institute for the Study of Teaching.

Sturman, A. (1997). *Social Justice in Education, Australian Education Review, No. 40*. Melbourne: ACER.

Yates, L. (1993). *The Education of Girls, Australian Education Review. No. 35*. Melbourne: ACER.

19

Gender-Sensitive Education for Bridging the Gender Gap

NAMTIP AKSORNKOOL
UNESCO, Paris, France

1. INTRODUCTION

Gender could be described as being the socially defined differences between the sexes as ascribed to men and women in their particular community or society. These man-made differences can change and vary from region to region, according to race, religion, class and social values. But they all have one thing in common – their enormous influence on the lives of girls and women and on society's attitude and behaviour to girls and boys, and women and men. They influence the relationships between the sexes: sex being the physical differences between women and men over which we have no control. The Dakar Framework of Action (UNESCO, 2000) pinpoints gender-based discrimination as

> ... one of the most intractable constraints to realizing the right to education. Without overcoming this obstacle, Education for All cannot be achieved.

Despite the World Bank's recent research findings that countries with a smaller gap between women and men in education, employment, and property rights have lower child malnutrition and mortality as well as better business, government and faster economic growth, countries are still not seriously addressing the issue of closing the gender gap (World Bank, 2000). Seven years on from the Beijing Conference information gleaned from the Asian region indicates that little has changed. There have been some initiatives and although promising they are scattered and bring little sustainable change on a large scale and therefore leave the global situation unchallenged.

This paper discusses the gender gap in both formal and nonformal education in Asia and the Pacific. It argues for the need for countries to look beyond access into quality of education if the gender gap is to be permanently eliminated. An overview of sexism in learning contents and materials is given. It ends by presenting a recent development of promoting gender-sensitisation as a prerequisite to successful reduction of the gender gap both quantitatively and qualitatively.

2. FIGURES SPEAK

Gender disparity in primary education is still prevalent in all regions. In 1990, 57 million out-of-school children were girls. Since 1990, there has been progress. Primary net enrolment rates have been increasing in all countries in Eastern Asia and Oceania although much variation exists in this broad region. In South Asia more than one-third of girls are unlikely ever to receive a formal education, and adult women have the lowest literacy rate in the world. There have been some signs of improvement, however, with girls' enrolment at the primary and secondary levels growing more rapidly than that of boys (Siniscalco, 2000).

Among the adult population, gender disparity is even greater. Unfortunately, illiteracy largely concerns women. Limited access to education affects girls and women disproportionately in most developing countries. The 1990 estimates indicate that there were 322 million illiterate men and 560 million illiterate women or over 30 per cent of the adult female population in the world (UNESCO *Statistical Yearbook* 1999). In 2000, the situation had not changed substantially with 563 million women (26.4 per cent), against 313 million illiterate men. The gender gap has decreased only marginally from 13.3 percentage points in 1990 to 11.7 in 2000. Of these, 865 million live in developing countries: 429 million are in South Asia ... 185 million in East Asia and Oceania (Siniscalco 2000). The number of illiterate adult women continues to grow, fuelled by high population growth and inadequate supply of educational services.

Measures, in both formal and nonformal education, to redress gender inequalities have been undertaken in many countries. Some initiatives which can be cited are: separate girls' schools, providing special scholarships to girls, free education for girls, including university, drives to recruit female teaches (e.g., India), special attention to villages where separate schools for girls do not exist, where primary school enrolment for girls is low or where women's illiteracy rates are particularly high (e.g., Pakistan) (UNESCO, 2000). However, it is clear from these examples that these measures are generally geared to improving girls' access only. While this is an important necessary step, it is, in itself, not enough.

3. SOCIAL, CULTURAL AND ECONOMIC REASONS

The world over, the female sex has traditionally been branded as inferior to men. New-born boys are a cause for celebration, but the birth of a girl spreads fear and foreboding and is seen as a financial burden. In certain parts of the Terai region of Nepal, the community weeps when a girl is born. Folk sayings degrading women abound in the region. Here are but some examples and their sources: women in the field damage the crops (Bangladesh); a woman has to live nine lives to become a man (Bhutan); respect men, degrade women (Japan and Vietnam); women, drums, illiterates and animals need beating (India).

Parents in traditional societies see girls as transient members of the family to be married off to another family, while boys are heirs to carry on the family name. This belief is universal, from Africa to Asia and from Oceania to Latin America. While men identify themselves in terms of what they do, women describe themselves in relation to others, especially men (Bisaria, 1985).

Economic restructuring has severely affected the education of girls, particularly in the poorest and least developed countries (LDCs) where poverty is the major obstacle to education (UNESCO, 1995). Faced with the cost of lunches, uniforms and learning materials, parents favour boys' schooling over that of girls. It is widely documented that when parents have to choose, they prefer to spend their money on boys. In rural Bangladesh, people of all classes spend up to 83 per cent of their educational budget on boys (Stromquist, 1994).

Practical issues also contribute to girls' absence from school or low achievement. A lack of toilets for girls in some schools forces them to stay at home when they are menstruating. Long distances in sparsely populated areas of countries like Bhutan raise concerns for children's security as they go to and from school. Harsh weather conditions can also add to the problem. In the cold season, when classrooms are not heated, Mongolian parents keep their children home (UNESCO, 1995).

There is no evidence that boys are inherently superior to girls. Indeed, no groups have superior cognitive capabilities to any others. Girls are on a par with boys in terms of learning achievement. Chinapah (1997) describes primary school test results in five countries where girls actually performed better than boys, but only in the earlier grades. In subsequent grades, girls, who were spending two or more hours per day on household chores, fared worse in literacy, numeracy and life skills tests than those who devoted one hour or less to housework.

Illiterate parents fear that educating daughters can be harmful. A genuine concern exists that educated girls will have more difficulty getting a husband. In the communities of Papua New Guinea and elsewhere where brides carry a price, any delay in the marrying of the daughter is seen as a risk. Many people are afraid that educated girls might pose a threat to their prospective mates, a challenge to their authority. Some societies do not welcome women rivalling their husbands in terms of their knowledge (UNESCO, 1995).

In some countries, parents fear that daughters who go to school may fall victim to sexual harassment by classmates, teachers and other men (UNESCO, 1995). In addition, exposure to life outside the home, according to parents, might lead to sexual promiscuity, early marriage and unwanted pregnancy. Baden and Green (1994) emphasize the enormous threat that potential sexual harassment poses to girls' and women's access to education. In some countries, girls are not permitted to attend school if their parents are not convinced that the environment is safe for girls. A safe environment has recently been taken up seriously as a category under the key five dimensions of quality education.

4. SEX STEREOTYPE: OBSTACLE TO QUALITY EDUCATION

In the post-Dakar era where countries are seen to be demonstrating political will to increase girls' access to education, it is important that the quality dimension be addressed alongside access in closing the gender gap. Quality, with its five dimensions: learners, content, process, environment and outcomes, is a prerequisite to sustaining the gains resulting from increased access to education. Stereotypes play a major role in this issue and are an obstacle to realizing content, materials and process.

It has now become clear that girls' access to schooling will not, in itself, guarantee a quality education and a better future. One of the most cited obstacles to that is that traditional learning contents, materials and methods are not designed to be girl-friendly. Often, these are downright hostile to girls and alienate them. They do little to reinforce girls' sense of self. Consequently, girls dropout before acquiring sufficient literacy and other basic skills.

In many cases, the underlying principle, deliberate or not, in curricula, materials and methods is to refer to men as the principal wage earners and family supporters and women as dependent housewives and domestics. The significant contribution that women make to the economy and to the well being of their families is all too often ignored. Moreover, the exclusion of this reality in learning contents and materials goes unnoticed or uncontested by the users as well as the public.

In textbooks and other educational resources, women and girls are mentioned less frequently than men and boys. The same goes for female activities, functions, concerns and aspirations. Invariably the female face appears in a man's world where girls and women are marginal and dispensable (UNESCO, 1995). A comparison of characteristics typically assigned to males and females according to their sex, derived from a review of primary school textbooks from around the world is revealing. In these books, girls and women are presented as passive, shy, weak, fearful, mild, awkward, sweet and nurturing. Boys and men, on the other hand, are projected as adventurous, intelligent, active, inquisitive, strong and heroic. While girls and women are shown as passive onlookers, listening to men, taking orders from others, boys and men are engaging in decision-making, order-giving, inventing, problem-solving and generally enjoying life.

Female preoccupations, often belonging to the world of mothers and wives, grow into low-paid jobs related to women's role as nurturers, such as kindergarten teachers, secretaries and nurses. UNESCO's analysis of post-literacy reading materials in 1990 found an overwhelming emphasis on women as mothers and nurturers. Women's potential for excelling in non-traditional endeavours receives scanty mention in educational materials. Materials rarely picture women in roles that have now become accessible to them in most countries of the region such as managers, politicians, leaders, pilots, doctors, armed and police forces, technicians, taxi, bus or train drivers, film producers, heads of state. The list expands day-by-day.

Based on the views of primary education experts, a UNESCO (1996) report entitled *The Education of Girls in Asia and the Pacific*, concluded that curricula and materials reinforced the stereotype of dependent and exclusively domestic roles for women. These limited views have been a guiding principle in the treatment of female pupils. As a result, at both the pre-school and primary school levels, girls lack opportunities to develop spatial skills and perform weakly in technical areas, mathematics and the sciences. Sex stereotypes also determine how girls and boys choose their subjects and ultimately their careers. Though women and girls account for more than half of technical and vocational enrolment, they keep choosing female fields such as health and home economics. Men, on the other hand, constitute three quarters of entrants to industry, engineering and agricultural courses (UNESCO, 1997). In Korea, for example, girls occupy 80 per cent of the places in business, but only 0.2 per cent are enrolled in fishery and marine sciences.

A paper presented at the UNESCO Workshop on Technical and Vocational Education for Girls in Seoul in 1995 indicates that stereotypes are often the guiding principle in the official policy:

> ... curriculum design of vocational education for women has become more rational with more courses adapted to social needs, the quick development of the third production and women's characteristics. There are courses in secretarial work, filing, accounting, fashion, nursing, childhood education, tourism, cosmetology, textile, hotel service and administration, and public relations. These are offered in girls' vocational schools and are chosen mostly by girls ... (Zu-Guang Yu, 1995: p. 4).

Slowly people are becoming aware of the danger of limiting the choice of subjects to those traditionally assigned to their sexes regardless of their aptitudes and talents. Mishra et al. (1995), for example, regretted the so-called 'home-science syndrome' in India where stereotyping practices prevent girls from being engaged in highly demanded jobs in the technology and science sectors.

5. GENDER SENSITISATION: A PROBLEM

The Dakar Framework for Action (UNESCO, 2000) condemned gender stereotyping in curricula and materials and advocated the elimination of stereotypes from formal and nonformal education programs. As early as 1994, in her studies of educational programs funded by development agencies around the world, Stromquist (1994) cautioned that funding agencies concentrated too much attention on access issues and not enough on issues related to program content, materials and methods. She examined a large number of programs and discovered that sexist materials featured predominantly in them and that little, if any, efforts were being made to render the material gender-sensitive. Efforts to sensitise relevant personnel in matters of gender have been timid. But program and material developers are increasingly realizing the importance of projecting the roles of the sexes in non-sexist ways. Stereotyped literacy programs and school curricula are being questioned with greater and greater insistence. Despite periodic attempts to adjust textbooks and other resources, most countries are reporting that gender sensitivity on a large scale has not been a guiding principle in curricular reforms.

Changes are slow because alterations in learning materials will only take place when the authors of such materials have become convinced of the need to change. Yet activities aimed at sensitising material developers, illustrators, publishers and others involved in the development of learning materials have been extremely rare. When such activities do occur they are centred on information-giving thus concentrating on the participants knowledge level. In the best case scenario, the trainees might be expected to talk or write about what gender means. It is not for enhancing people's attitudes towards the sexes, which comes, among other things, from putting people in conflict with their own long-held attitudes, values and beliefs.

Production of gender-sensitive materials is still rare and their impact weak. It is important to increase the awareness of the need for preparing materials free of sex stereotypes within government agencies and civil society organizations and to establish a monitoring mechanism to ensure that sensitivity continues as a guiding principle at the implementation level. However, examination of literacy readers across the region during the 1990s reveals that progress, although timid, has been made regarding portrayal of the sexes and their relationships. In the late 1980s women and girls did not appear or appeared very rarely in learning materials. Slowly, women began to appear. Yet they were still presented without regard to the specific and important contributions they make, such as sowing and weeding. Men working together, for example on their rice paddies, was the standard picture.

Later, women started to appear in their productive roles but still rather separate from men and far fewer in number, as compared to men. Their tasks were shown to be clearly 'lighter women's tasks'. This gradually changed when women and girls appear to be working alongside men and boys undertaking the same tasks requiring physical exertion such as on construction sites. In small vending and trading activities it is now possible to see women actively engaged in not only buying but also selling and handling money. Lessons on accounting and management occasionally show women as key characters. Even when there is no accompanying text, showing a picture of women in accountancy sends a strong subliminal message that it is a normal and acceptable state of affairs for women to be involved in such activities.

While illustrations of women and girls are appearing more in non-stereotype ways, the same cannot be said to be true of men and boys. It is extremely rare, for example, to see an illustration of men bathing or feeding babies, or cooking and washing-up. Exclusion of these contents illustrates that educational materials are not keeping up with the reality of the twenty-first century. On the contrary they represent the outdated and anachronistic view of people. They reinforce in readers' minds the reality of the past and not the dynamic and changing present.

Unless serious changes take place in the preparation and use of learning materials, quality can never be achieved. Yet, so little attention has been given to gender sensitisation as a means to raise the quality of content in real terms. It may be concluded then, that even when the Dakar Goal 4 is reached, people of both sexes will still lack access to equality of choices especially as it relates to girls and women.

Despite the repeated call for the elimination of gender stereotypes by the Beijing Conference on Women and the Dakar World Education Forum, it could be said that responses to these calls are still rather insignificant and scattered.

Though it is an abstract concept, gender-sensitisation is observable in people's behaviour, reflecting their attitudes, values and beliefs. If a gender sensitisation activity is successful, trainees will be able to treat people of both sexes in certain ways as a result of it. It will become clear, from the way they behave, speak and interact with others, that they have become more gender-sensitive than before. Very little attention has been given to gender sensitisation as a means to improve the quality of contents and materials both in formal school and nonformal education around the world. In Asia, there has been little or no systematic and deliberate effort at integrating gender sensitisation into either pre-service or in-service teacher training. What follows is an example of deliberate, albeit scattered, efforts in the Asia-Pacific region at rendering learning materials gender-sensitive in nonformal education settings.

6. GENDER SENSITISATION – A METHOD

Over the past 12 years, UNESCO has been building its experience in developing gender sensitisation with practical, easy to follow guidelines to help education practitioners, particularly those involved in materials development. Based on research indicating that information alone is insufficient to produce lasting change in people's perceptions and opinions about the roles of men and women, the manual relies heavily on activities that encourage participants' involvement and two-way communication. This approach has proved useful in helping people question traditional practices, their own and others' beliefs and attitudes regarding the sexes. It encourages participants to explore alternatives that are fair to people of both sexes. The activities include games, role-playing, analysis of case studies, newspaper clippings and textbooks and literacy readers. In the first part of the sensitisation, specific activities help people recognize the biases and prejudices that have become associated with gender. For example, when asked to draw a picture of a farmer, a majority of the participants, men and women alike, will usually draw men. This occurs at a time when an average of 50 per cent of food in the world is grown by women. The same kind of gender-biased assumptions are typically made when training participants are asked to describe a scene involving doctors, lawyers or politicians. This kind of exercise helps participants see for themselves the result of sexist socialization on their own psyches. Since no one can dictate to others how to feel, the sensitisation uses films and stories to make important points and evoke certain emotions. It draws, for example, on videos such as *The Impossible Dream*. The video shows the daily routines of different members of a family. It reminds viewers of their own lives, where in all too many cases, some members of the family are unfairly overworked. All this, without a word being said! Case studies, in which women and men appear in a broad range of roles and situations, are also used to stimulate reflection and discussion among the participants. One story describes the case of women scientists, successful and proud, but lonely at science conferences. Other topics treated through case studies include the sharing of housework and decision-making between husbands and wives, how a woman coped with her HIV infected husband, women in the sex trade, the biases reflected in the media's reporting of women and men holding high official posts, women's access to technology, legislation affecting women's employment opportunities and the transformation one woman experiences upon learning, as an adult, how to read and write. Another activity, a sort of time-use analysis, uses a series of drawings to describe and compare the daily routines of a typical village woman and man. The unavoidable conclusion of an unequal and unfair division of labour always generates a great deal of discussion.

The 12 years experience has been captured in a user-friendly manual, *Gender Sensitivity* (UNESCO, 2002). Its primary objective is to raise the sensitivity of educators to gender issues so they can incorporate a gender-sensitive perspective in their work. With respect to material development, it is encouraging to note that experience confirms that women and men can work together to develop sharper sensitivity to the specific needs and conditions of men and women. This is indicative in the learning materials they produced after the sensitisation.

7. CONCLUSION

Prejudices and stereotypes follow learners from home to the places they go to learn. Statistics paint a compelling picture of the nature and extent of inequality of opportunity for male and female learners. Simple enrolment or dropout rates, for example, tell their own story. While the total number of illiterate adult men has declined, the number of illiterate women has increased consistently. The ratio between men's and women's literacy rates has not substantially changed over the past 15 years and is a clear indication of warped development in education. Data describing the areas of education and career specialisation for women and men provide another clear indication that sex has played too great a role in determining which learner (i.e. which sex) was encouraged to enter the most well-compensated and prestigious fields.

Unfortunately gender biases are easily and unconsciously incorporated into learning materials. All too often, the men in these materials are shown strictly as the wage earner while women are portrayed as economically passive and dependent. At a time when women head one third of the world's households, this demonstrates how significantly educational materials may be at odds with reality. Curriculum and learning materials are only one aspect of education. Educators must be made aware that their attitudes, unconscious or not, affect people's aspirations and career choices. For administrators and planners of educational programs, awareness of gender issues is essential in priority setting, budget and task allocation, awarding of training and scholarship opportunities, monitoring of classroom activities and projections of role models.

Addressing the gender gap needs does not mean 'pitting women against men' and is a myth that has no *raison d'être*. For gender-sensitive materials and methods to be effective, their developers and users must be convinced that this approach to education offers benefits beyond the potential of education in the traditional sense of the word. Gender-sensitisation education must be recognized as a powerful tool; one that could lead to the creation of a more humane, more just world for all people of both sexes. Educational leaders need to broaden their vision and option to the possibility of seriously combining gender sensitisation with development of learning and training materials, content, environment and process. Doing so will greatly contribute to quality improvement. Certainly the focus on girls' education from a gender perspective has raised important issues about boys' education, and it is fully recognized that a gender-sensitive education will be more effective in addressing them.

What is now needed is a concerted, world-wide shift on the part of leaders in the Education For All (EFA) movement from the traditional view of access as the sole indication of bridging the gender gap to a holistic vision of considering access and quality as one necessary prerequisite to achieving EFA. Indeed the five dimensions of quality education are what determine whether, ultimately, members of both sexes are being fairly given equality of choices. One of the greatest challenges of the EFA movement of this century will therefore be to embrace gender sensitisation. Will nations have the courage and the resolve to rise to this challenge?

REFERENCES

Baden, S., & Green, C. (1994). *Gender and Education in Asia and the Pacific*. Institute of Development Studies, University of Sussex, Brighton, UK.: Report commissioned by the Australian International Development Assistance Bureau.

Bisaria, S. (1985). *Identification and Elimination of Sex Stereotypes in and from Education Programs and School Textbooks: Some suggestions for Action in Asia and the Pacific*. Paris: UNESCO.

Chinapah, M. (1997). *Handbook on Monitoring Learning Achievements: Towards Capacity Building*. Paris: UNESCO.

Chinapah, M. (2000). *Gender! A Partnership of Equals. Education and training*. Geneva, ILO, Bureau for Gender Equality.

Siniscalco, M. T. (2000). *Achieving Education for All: Demographic Challenges*. Thematic Study for the Education for All 2000 Assessment, World Education Forum, Dakar. Paris: UNESCO.

Stromquist, N. (1994). *Gender and Basic Education in International Development Co-operation*. Staff Working Paper No. 13. New York: UNICEF.

UNESCO (1995). *The Education of Girls and Women – Towards a Global Framework for Action*. Paris: UNESCO.

UNESCO (1996) *The Education of Girls in Asia and the Pacific*. Paris: UNESCO.

UNESCO (1997). *Adult Education in a Polarizing World, Education for All, Status and Trends*. Paris, UNESCO.
UNESCO (1999) *Statistical Year Book, 1999*. Paris: UNESCO.
UNESCO (2000). *World Education Forum – Framework for Action*. Paris: UNESCO.
UNESCO (2002). *Gender Sensitivity*. Paris: UNESCO.
World Bank. (2000). *Mainstreaming Gender*. Washington DC.: The World Bank
Zu-Guang Yu. (1995). *China Country Paper*. Presented at the International Expert Meeting on the Promotion of Equal Access of Girls and Women to Technical and Vocational Education, in Seoul, Republic of Korea.

20

Gender Differences in Access to Education and Employment

SHARADA JAIN*
SANDHAN, Jaipur, India

1. INTRODUCTION

This article looks at the broad pattern of disparities that exist between women and men (girls and boys) in their access to education and employment in South Asian countries. It focuses primarily on the situation in India, Pakistan, Bangladesh, Nepal and Bhutan. These countries constitute a major section of the total population of the Asia-Pacific region and present sharply discernible patterns with respect to gender, which need to be analysed in depth. These questions are addressed in this article.

- What is the difference in the situation with respect to the access of girls and boys to education? Has there been a shift in the pattern over the past decades?
- Is there a gender-based discriminatory pattern in employment in these countries? Is it linked to educational access?
- What are the underlying causes for continued disparity? Are there some possible ways of redressing these disparities?

The main claim of this article is that gender discrimination in South Asian countries is situated within the deeply ingrained systems of patriarchy, which limit and confine women to subordinate roles. Discrimination against South Asian women begins at or even before birth. This further manifests itself in discriminatory investments in nutrition, education and mobility, the three essential inputs in access to employment as an equal member of society. Consequently, the perceptible scenario is not just of inequality but systemic subordination.

---

* The author is grateful to the following individuals who have helped in the preparation of this article: Dr. Mridula Seth (Consultant, UNFPA, New Delhi), Dr. Usha Nayyar (Retd. Prof. & Head of Women's Studies, NCERT, New Delhi), Dr. Sanju Sharma (Project Coordinator, Doosra Dashak, Jaipur), Dr. Shobhita Rajgopal (Associate Fellow, IDS, Jaipur), Ms Shobha L. Kavoori (Sandhan, Jaipur).

Redressal of this situation demands shedding off the reluctance to go to the roots of the problem, analysing the social construction of femininity and masculinity and bringing these issues to centre stage in the debate on natural development and educational planning.

2. ACCESS: EDUCATION

Access to education is an issue, which clearly has two dimensions: quantitative and qualitative. At the quantitative level assessment of access to education is made by treating education as synonymous to schooling. It therefore takes note of literacy rates, enrolment data in schools and years of schooling with as much detailed information with regard to these issues as possible. This level of inquiry leaves out any consideration of the quality of education received by the participants. Quality is treated as a concern other than that of access. The issue of whether or not this schooling matches the educational expectations of the people is seldom addressed in any discourse on access.

The qualitative dimension, on the other hand, takes the second concern as central. The issue here refers to access to what can truly be called education, namely, genuine learning opportunities, which empower people to deal with life in an informed and confident manner. Development discourse across the countries has focused primarily on the quantitative aspect while it has notionally recognised the significance of the qualitative dimension of education. This choice possibly has its roots in the non-availability of hard data for making valid generalisations about qualitative concerns, which go much beyond graduation from school. It is clearly difficult to reduce and express these concerns, particularly relating to confidence, reflective skills and learning attitudes, in quantitative terms. This difficulty subsequently gets converted or relegated to become a secondary or later issue. These two dimensions, however, are equally significant in assessing discriminatory access to education in South Asia. While country based micro studies have emerged focussing on quality of education, they too do not see this as an essential dimension of access to education.

In order to get a broad picture of gender differences in access to education across countries, the following section restricts itself only to the quantitative interpretation or perspective of access. It attempts to look at three main issues in this regard:

(a) differences between South Asia and developed countries;
(b) disaggregated pattern in five countries of South Asia, in literacy and enrolment in primary school; and
(c) average years of schooling in the five countries of South Asia under consideration.

The overall pattern that emerges across these countries is that there is a glaring gender disparity in the literacy rates, enrolment ratios and average years of schooling. The issue of access to quality education has not surfaced as an integral issue in this discourse.

Gender gaps in education, namely the difference between the net enrolment ratio of boys and girls and the percentage of out of school children exist in all regions of the developing world. But in South Asia, these gaps are the widest. If the profile of the gender gap is examined the situation in South Asia is much worse than the aggregate of all developing countries. Table 1 presents the net enrolment ratio and percentage of out of school children for South Asia compared to other developing countries.

Most regions of the world have been trying to close the gender gaps by mainstreaming women's issues and by seeking to provide equality of opportunity by removing all gender-based discriminations. While South Asian countries are beginning to make similar efforts, gender gaps remain very large and they have a long way to go in closing them.

As a whole, educational status is low in all the five countries. However, the gender disparity in all the countries is what is really alarming. It raises a concern for the redressal measures in view of the unequal absorption capacity of investments made in education. Table 2 shows the gender differences in education in the five countries under consideration with respect to the primary enrolment ratios for girls and boys and the literacy rates for 1995.

Figure 1 shows the average number of years of schooling for male and female students in these five countries.

Table 1. Access to education in South Asia and developing countries

Access to education in South Asia compared to other developing countries: Gender gap		South Asia	*All developing countries*
Net enrolment ratio in primary school (%) (1995)	Girls	69	81
	Boys	88	86
Out-of-school children	Girls	40	19
	Boys	26	14

Source: Haq, M. and Haq, K., (1998, p. 86).

Table 2. Gender difference in education in five South Asian countries

Gender differences in education in South Asian Countries: Primary enrolment and literacy		India	Pakistan	Bangladesh	Nepal	Bhutan
Primary enrolment ratio (Net) 1995	Girls	76	25	78	46	47
	Boys	98	36	89	80	58
Literacy rate (%) 1995	Female	38	24	26	14	28
	Male	50	50	49	41	56

Source: Haq, M. and Haq, K. (1998, p. 87).

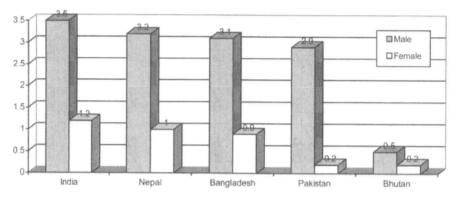

Figure 1. Average years of schooling for male and female students in five South Asian countries.

Source: Mahbub ul Haq Development Centre (2000, p. 105).

2.1. Why do Gender Gaps Persist in Education?

South Asia is one of the poorest regions in the world, with over 500 million people in absolute poverty, two-thirds of them women. Educating girls does not get the highest priority among family concerns for survival, in an all-pervading framework of patriarchy. It affects girls' chances of schooling in a striking manner. When household income is limited, boys tend to get preference over girls for schooling. The severe discrimination that women face in the labour market, including fewer chances for a job and less pay than men, reduces the incentive for their schooling. The family is also unable to bear the indirect costs of sending to school, girls who perform tasks that are essential to the household economy.

The distance of schools from the homes is another important deciding factor. A distant school places girls' safety at risk and it also keeps them away from domestic chores for longer periods of time. School-related factors play an important role in motivating girls to enrol and stay in schools. In certain cultures, a girl's chances of going to school may be directly dependent upon the availability of separate school facilities for girls and the presence of a female teacher. Numerous studies have shown that enrolment rates for girls have improved and dropout rates reduced significantly with female teachers in schools during recent decades. Other important factors are flexible school timings, which allow girls to perform household and agricultural chores, toilet facilities in schools, and relevant and gender-sensitive curricula.

Despite the persistence of gender gaps there have been some positive shifts in education patterns in the region during the past two decades. The enrolment percentages of girls and women at primary and secondary school levels have risen significantly during this period. Significant gains in higher education are also on record. The most outstanding achievement is in the area of literacy and closing of gender gaps in the literacy rates. Table 3 presents a balance sheet on the provision of education for girls and women over the past three decades.

3. ACCESS: EMPLOYMENT

There are differences in the economic scenario and women's participation in the economy within the different countries of South Asia. Yet, there are certain key issues that remain common to all of them.

Reliable, accurate and comprehensive information about women's activity and labour force participation is almost non-existent in all the countries. Gender roles have, over centuries, been determined on the basis of the reproductive roles of women and their contribution to activities related to this role, which includes household activities. Although women have always contributed to the economic well being of the family, this has been seen as an extension of their home-making role. Since this role is seen as a non-economic one, both men and women hold the view that it is the men alone who are workers. The issue of recognising women's labour and productive work as such, lies neglected. The dominance of women's reproductive roles and the lack of emphasis on their productive role has resulted in the widespread belief that when it comes to labour, men work more than women and must therefore be paid more, a misconception that is internalised by both men and women.

The glaring lack of gender-disaggregated statistics makes it impossible to obtain a true picture of women's contributions to the economy of each country within South Asia or to compare one country with another. Some degree of statistical invisibility of women in the economy is a worldwide phenomenon, but in South Asia it is particularly pervasive because of historical, traditional and cultural reasons. Statistics show that the majority of economically active women work in the informal sector for little or no wage and are restricted to activities that can fit with their role definition in society, namely, assisting in all economic activity of the family as well as care of children, old people and cattle. In effect, their contribution to the economy is much more than is widely recognised. Table 4 records the percentage of women in the labour force in the five countries under consideration in South Asia.

The invisibility of women's work in economic accounting systems is due to a flawed definition of economic activity. While dealing with women's invisibility in contributing to gross domestic product (GDP), two sets of issues arise. The first relates to the exclusion of household services from GDP, which is more or less a universal phenomenon. The second relates to the socio-cultural perception and reporting bias that women are engaged only in household maintenance activities and therefore ignores all market and non-market activities. Thus, the System of National Accounts (SNA) includes only products and services that are attributed to men. These two problems combine to ensure that much of women's work remains invisible as many of their activities and productions which are classified as services, such as cooking, care of the sick, the old and

Table 3. Balance sheet of education of girls and women over decades

SOUTH ASIA

Progress	Failures
Primary Education Gross primary enrolment of girls went up from 54% in 1970 to 87% in 1993.	More than 40% of girls drop out of primary school before reaching Grade 5. There were 28 million girls out of primary school in 1995.
Secondary Education Between 1980 and 1992 girls' secondary enrolments almost doubled. Over 9 million additional girls went to secondary school between 1985 and the early 1990s.	Only 33% of South Asian girls enrol in secondary school, compared to 52% of the boys. Secondary enrolment ratio for girls 20 percentage points lower than the average of 53% for East Asia.
Higher Education Girls' tertiary enrolment (per 100,000 people) increased from 241 in 1980 to 342 in 1992. Girls' enrolment at the tertiary level as a percentage of boys' enrolment went up from 28% in 1970 to 47% in 1990.	The enrolment ratio for girls at the tertiary level is only 3.6% in South Asia compared to 16.1% in Latin America and the Caribbean.
Literacy Profile Women's literacy has doubled from 17% in 1970 to 36% in 1995.	South Asia's female literacy rate of 35% is lower than any other region in the world. Of the total illiterate female population in the world, South Asia's share is 45%.
Gender Gaps Female literacy rate doubled between 1970 and 1995, while male literacy rate went up by less than one half, thus closing the gender gap.	Out of the total illiterate adult population of 400 million people in South Asia, nearly two-thirds are women. Mean years of schooling for girls are one third that for boys. The gender disparity in literacy was reduced by only 10% in South Asia in the last 15 years, this reduction being lower than most of the other regions of the world.

Source: Haq, M. and Haq, K. (1998, p. 91).

Table 4. Female percentage of labour force

Country	Percentage
India (1997)	32
Pakistan (1997)	27
Bangladesh (1997)	42
Nepal (1997)	40
Bhutan (1994)	32

Source: Mahbub ul Haq Development Centre (2000, p. 56).

the children, and household maintenance are still outside the SNA production boundary.

Micro-level studies specifically target the kinds of information that large surveys miss out. This is especially true for the agricultural sector where a majority of women workers are concentrated. A large part of the work that women do in rural areas is non-market work, including extremely time-intensive tasks such as cutting fodder, fetching wood and water. Some observers suggest that typically, South Asian women work between 10 and 12 hours a day, while men work 2 to 4 hours less. On the basis of studies in a number of countries, this seems to be a conservative estimate. In Pakistan, rural women are said to work between 12 and 16 hours in a day (Elson and Evers, 1996).

An analysis of women's labour force participation in South Asia yields the following findings.

(1) The majority of South Asian women work in the informal sector or as unpaid family helpers. In *India*, 96 per cent of economically active women work in the informal sector. In *Nepal*, 75 per cent are self-employed and 28 per cent are unpaid family workers. In *Pakistan*, 65 per cent of the female labour force is officially accounted for in the informal sector. In *Bangladesh*, 75 per cent of women earned a living in the informal sector in 1995–96.
(2) Work done by women accounts for the largest proportion of non-mechanised agricultural labour.
(3) Although more women are entering the paid labour force, many still face severe impediments in entering and participating in the work force.
(4) Gender-specific inequalities in pay and job security are widespread.
(5) Outside the agricultural sector, women are concentrated in a limited number of sectors, the majority in traditional or service-sector employment, others in poorly paid manufacturing work. More and more young women are entering the work force in these sectors (Human Development in South Asia, 2000).

Table 5 gives the percentage employment in the major industrial and service sectors for men and women in the mid-1990s in four countries. Women in formal

Table 5. Employment in South Asia by major sectors (%)

Country[a]	Gender	Agriculture	Industry	Service
Bangladesh	Male	53.9	19.2	26.8
(1996)	Female	41.7	27.8	30.5
India	Male	58.3	16.5	25.2
(1994)	Female	78.0	10.9	11.1
Nepal	Male	78.9	4.9	13.2
(1996)	Female	93.7	1.4	4.5
Pakistan	Male	40.7	20.2	39.0
(1997)	Female	66.4	10.6	23.2

[a] Data for Bhutan are not available.
Source: Mahbub ul Haq Development Centre (2000, p. 58).

sector employment are concentrated at lower levels in unskilled and low paid work in the industrial and services sectors, with little job security and few benefits.

Only 13.5 per cent of formal sector workers in Pakistan are women. They occupy less than a quarter of one per cent in the combined categories of legislator, senior official and manager; 0.83 per cent of professionals and one half of one per cent in the combined category of technicians and associate professionals. A miniscule percentage of women are clerks and plant and machine operators and assemblers. However, women's participation in the formal sector, especially the export sector, is rising. In Bangladesh's garment industry, 90 per cent of the workers are women and more urban women are now employed in the pharmaceutical, electronics and fish processing industries.

It is argued that many employers prefer to employ women because they tend not to unionise and can be paid less. Where cultural norms of women's seclusion exist they are minimised by employing an exclusively female workforce. However, the other costs of a female workforce, such as perceptions about greater absenteeism, the need for maternity and childcare benefits and high turnover, may play a role in depressing the demand for female labour in skilled activity relative to the demand for male labour. These factors are also likely to contribute to the vastly unequal pay scales for men and women.

The declining proportion of Nepalese women in the production and services sectors indicates a reduction in women's access to jobs created in the modern expanding sectors of the economy. In India, only 15.4 per cent of formal sector manufacturing employees are women. The actual number of women engaged in manufacturing, in India as elsewhere in South Asia, is much higher.

The service sector, across South Asia is also an insecure one because demand fluctuates, according to the state of the broader economy, both domestic and foreign. There are large wage differentials between men's and women's work. For the majority of women engaged in paid economic activity, the fact of being female means being paid less than men for their work. Overall in rural areas the differentials are much higher. Women in rural areas are paid about 60 per cent of what men are paid, compared to women in urban areas who make almost 80 per cent of what men make. In Nepal there is considerable fluctuation in the earnings profile of women across different sectors. However, the national statistics suggest that women get paid about 57 per cent of what men are paid.

To a large degree, South Asian women have borne the brunt of the negative effects of globalisation, adjustment policies in particular lead to an intensification of women's market work, interruption of girls' education and an increase in the amount of time women spend to obtain services or self-provide to them. It is clear that as yet there has not been a significant increase in the number of jobs available to South Asian women to take advantage of the globalisation process. Richer, educated women have gained from globalisation, at least in economic terms. But globalisation tends to increase income inequality between different sectors and groups, which, if not countered through redistributive fiscal and employment policies, will further marginalise vulnerable groups. Women form the vast majority of these in South Asia.

4. THE ROOTS OF DISCRIMINATION

Why are women so severely disadvantaged in their access to education? Moreover, if they work so hard for long hours, why do they remain in subordinated roles in employment, simply by virtue of being women? Why do women work for lower wages than men? Why are women mostly found employed in the informal sector?

Answers to such questions lie in the cultural ethos prevalent in the entire South Asian region. Gender bias here pervades all spheres of life and society and informs intra-familial attitudes and values, which in turn determine options available to men and women. The nature and intensity of this bias varies across economic systems and regions and over the life cycle of individuals. Thus the gender gap in education may be understood in the wider context of female disadvantage in South Asia. By virtue of being 'South Asian' and 'women' there are several factors cutting across class, culture and religion that affect the lives of women in these countries.

Patriarchal societies ensure that the levels of education of women remain lower than that of men. Women's mobility is highly restricted, which in turn hampers their access to education and employment opportunities. Linked to such factors is the stereotyping of women that confines them to subordinate roles. Sanctioned by religion, the primary and ultimate identity of a woman is that of a sister, daughter, wife and mother. Very little value is placed on her professional being. This is quite in contrast to the situation for men, where their professional roles are given priority. Much less emphasis is laid on a man's role as a brother, son, husband and father. Gender stereotypes have continued in social and institutional decision making, which has enforced and reinforced women's subordinated position in society. Equally, the stereotype of masculinity has also contributed to considerable stress in men, preventing them from playing a pro-active role in an adequate and effective manner for gender equality.

The problem is further exacerbated by the fact that women have internalised the ideology of subordination. Women themselves accept their condition and position in society with associated role expectations. They are equal partners in condemning any departure from the set patterns of expected behaviour. Such social conditioning of women begins early in life. This explains their self-image and low self-worth.

5. CONCLUSION

The question then is how is the cycle of disadvantage to be broken? There have been sporadic movements and policy efforts at addressing the problem particularly during the past two decades. The strategies adopted for this purpose have been varied. However, it is possible to discern two broad strands in these attempts. The first strategy provides an economic understanding of the social issue, whereby it is argued that the status of women would automatically improve with increasing participation in labour markets and development processes. The other strategy looks at women's empowerment as the key to addressing the issue of gender emancipation. It is believed that empowerment would increase visibility and give women more autonomy and bargaining power within the household and the society. While it is true that there is validity in both these perspectives, they are not mutually exclusive. The important point is that both perspectives accept that education has a central role to play in breaking the cycle of female disadvantage. Education must provide skills to enhance capabilities and education must also serve as a catalyst for emancipatory struggles.

The South Asian region as a whole fares very poorly in the education of women and children. There are various reasons that affect women's access to education. Cultural biases and social apathy may be singled out as being the most serious impediments. Cultural ethos affects both women and men by constructing basic stereotypes of femininity and masculinity. It is therefore clear that in order to achieve any significant change in the status of girls and women, serious recognition would also have to be given to issues involving boys and men. Up to the present time emphasis has been placed on working out the needs of girls and women. The needs of boys and men within the framework of women's rights is yet to become an accepted agenda in educational discourse.

It is only at a theoretical level that there is recognition of the fact that gender issues cannot be sufficiently addressed, through focusing on women alone. The transition from Women in Development (WID) to Gender and Development (GAD) has occurred with limited reference to men. There has been an overall lack of understanding of male issues at both the policy-making and grassroots levels, and few concrete interventions regarding male roles have been undertaken. Important exceptions include UNFPA's work on men's role in reproductive decision making, and UNICEF's research on fatherhood. Figure 2 presents a

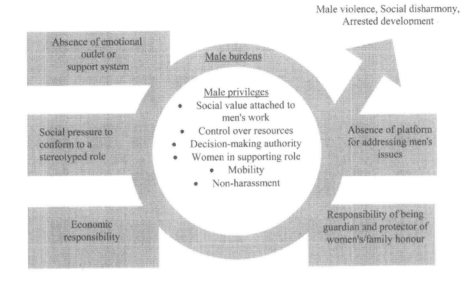

Figure 2. The other gender – men's issues in the development process.

Refer: Ahmad and Khan (1998); Levack and Rahim (1998–99).

model of men's issues in the development process that is accompanied by the statement given in Panel 1.

> *In 1998, in order to initiate discussions surrounding men's issues and development, the UNDP Gender Unit in Islamabad hosted a seminar on the other gender (see Figure 2). Seminar presentations touched upon the relationships between sons and mothers, and husbands and wives; the socialisation of boys into acceptable male roles; the sexual abuse of boys; and male violence. During discussions, participants identified several types of problems faced by males due to the gendered and patriarchal nature of society. The group also identified several privileges generally afforded men within the same patriarchal systems.*

Panel 1. The model of men's issues in the development process.

In order to understand the situation with all its complexities, it appears that redressal of the problem of gender bias demands multiple level interventions that include policy and implementation. First, there must be sufficient and intense policy pressure for treating girls and boys as equals. Second, women's empowerment for improved participation in all spheres must be emphasised. The ability to control their fertility and sexuality would serve as a landmark for any effort to reduce gender inequality. Third, there is need for social recognition that girls have as much competence as boys. Consequently, the candidature of girls for investment in education must be recognised. The initiatives would eventually change the overall scenario in employment opportunities.

The few policy pronouncements alone cannot help in a situation where female disadvantage is the result of social attitudes. Breaking the cycle of female disadvantage entails new forms of realisation and mobilisation of not merely resources but communities too. For this, there have to be major attitude shifts in society to break out of a culture of patriarchy. This entails renegotiations of roles in the family. It is essential to help women understand the importance of change and to break out of a mode of dependence and realise their worth. Also there is a growing realisation for the need to reinterpret roles and expectations of men. This would mean a departure from the prevailing stereotypical understanding of femininity and masculinity at societal level.

REFERENCES

Ahmad, K., & Khan, G. R. (Ed.) (March 1998). *The Other Gender: A Seminar on Men's Issues.* Islamabad: UNDP.

Elson, D., & Evers, B. (1996). *Gender Aware Country Economic Report: Pakistan.* Manchester: University of Manchester.

Haq, M., & Haq, K. (1998). *Human Development in South Asia.* Karachi and Oxford: Oxford University Press.

Levack. A., & Rahim, T. (1998–1999). The concept of men as partners in Pakistan. *Populi,* 25(4), 6–9.

Mahbub ul Haq Development Centre (2000). *Human Development In South Asia 2000, The Gender Question.* Oxford: Oxford University Press.

Lifelong Learning

21

Adult Literacy in the Asia-Pacific Region

INAYATULLAH
Pakistan Association for Continuing/Adult Education, Pakistan

1. A WORD ABOUT THE REGION

The Asia-Pacific region covers a vast area extending from Iran in the west to Japan and the two Koreas to the east and stretching from Kazakhstan in the north to New Zealand in the south. It has a number of sub-regions. (a) Trans Caucasus and Central Asia, (b) East and South East Asia, (c) Pacific, and (d) South and West Asia.

The region accounts for more than half of the world's population distributed very unevenly over large land masses and island states encompassing an extraordinary ethnic diversity. It is particularly noteworthy that five of the world's E 9 (largest population) states are in this region, namely, China, India, Indonesia, Pakistan and Bangladesh.

The region has been marked by social and economic upheavals of great magnitude, the effects of which will be evident for at least a further decade. They include: (a) the breakup of the former Soviet Union in 1991; (b) the extraordinary growth of the East Asian tiger economies in the early to middle years of the 1990s followed by the financial crisis that hit the sub-region in mid-1997; (c) the rapid growth of the economies of India and China; (d) the continuation of border and territorial conflict in parts of South Asia, (e) migration and settlement of economic and political refugees; and (f) the stagnation of the Pacific Island economies.

The diversity of the Asia-Pacific region makes it impossible to paint a generalized picture of its cultural backdrop. The ocean-based cultures of the Pacific have little in common with the traditions of the peoples of the steppes and mountain ranges of Central Asia. Although some traditions are less documented than others, most cultures in the Asia-Pacific region have been developing for centuries and even millennia. With different philosophies, religions, and cultures of Hindu, Buddhist, Confucian, Taoist, Islamic, and animist origins, it has correctly been said that Asia is a cradle of civilizations.

The history of countries of the region also varies dramatically, as centres of global power and geopolitical demarcations shift over time. Some countries have cherished histories of independence over centuries; others have emerged from their colonial roots at the turn of the century or after the Second World War. Still others have recently re-established their identities after breaking away from the Soviet Union. It may be said that, for different reasons, many are simultaneously old countries and new nation states. The historical-cultural context influences learning content in formal education, shapes education systems and structures, affects pedagogy, and informs the explicit and implicit values conveyed by the whole educational process.

2. VARYING CONCEPTS AND DEFINITIONS OF LITERACY

Over the years literacy has been interpreted as the capabilities which enable people to acquire the basic skills of reading and writing and the ability to make elementary arithmetical calculations. Increasingly, however, a broader concept has emerged which involves active participation in social, economic and political areas. As observed in the *Education For All 2000 Assessment Global Synthesis* (UNESCO, 2000b), literacy has come to be accepted as a product of a complex interplay of factors: cultural, socio-economic and educational and not a disorder or disease that can be swiftly eradicated. The older operational notions of literacy (grade-level, decoding or deciphering competence with written text) were complemented in the 1960s by the broader idea of functional competence in society. This refers to higher level abilities, those enabling people to function in the community and the workplace to achieve personal goals and develop knowledge and realize their potential. This broadening of the concept implies very close attention to contexts, uses, applications and changing relationships between the individual and society. A crucial example is the impact of technology and the consequent need for more people to become technologically literate and capable of making effective use of the instruments for communication and information processing that are becoming available.

An interesting instance of the definition of literacy as understood in the 1950s and early 1960s is contained in the *Chinese Regulations on Eradicating Literacy*:

> the recognition of 1,500 Chinese characters for peasants and 2,000 characters for staff and workers in business/enterprises and urban dwellers, the ability of reading simple and easy newspapers and articles, the ability of keeping simple accounts, and the ability of writing simple practical writings.

3. THE IMPERATIVE OF LITERACY

It is no exaggeration to say that the spread of literacy is a necessary step to remove impediments in the growth of the individual and the countries' socio-economic progress. It helps create responsible and productive citizens which in turn leads to the democratisation of the society and encourages popular participation in the decision making process by fostering a keen awareness of rights and responsibilities of the individuals and the community at large.

3.1. The Size of the Problem

According to UNESCO there were 875 million illiterates in the world in the Year 2000. Of these, East and South Asia had the highest number with an estimated 69 per cent of the total illiterates. In 1980 this percentage was 76.7 per cent. There is also a wide variation of the literacy rate in the region with three out of 31 member states having already achieved universal literacy more than two decades ago namely, Japan, Australia and New Zealand.

3.2. Adult Literacy Figures for the Region in 1983

It is instructive to look back at the figures relating to adult literacy as compiled in a UNESCO Report published in 1984 and recorded in Table 1. The data recorded in Table 1 show that over the ten-year period from 1970 to 1980 while the literacy rate greatly improved in all countries listed, only in about half of these countries did the number of illiterates decline.

Table 1. Literacy in Asia and the Pacific

Country	Number of illiterates (15+) 1970 (000)	1980 (000)	Variation (%)	Literacy rate 1970 (%)	1980 (%)
Afghanistan	6,388	7,391	+15.7	7.6	15.8
Bangladesh	27,694	32,606	+17.7	24.5	31.8
Bhutan	520	631	+21.1	14.0	16.4
Burma	4,901	5,003	+2.1	70.4	75.9
China	243,300	220,200	−9.5	52.8	66.7
Dem. Kampuchea	2,099	1,796	−14.4	46.7	58.1
Fiji	77	70	−9.1	73.8	82.4
India	209,350	235,937	+12.7	34.0	42.4
Indonesia	32,196	29,111	−9.6	54.0	67.7
Iran, Islamic Rep. of	11,023	11,906	+8.0	28.6	42.8
Korea, Rep. of	2,778	2,101	−24.4	85.0	91.7
Lao People's Dem. Rep.	1,167	1,209	+3.6	32.4	43.6
Malaysia	2,414	2,536	+5.1	59.5	69.8
Mongolia	137	100	−27.0	80.4	89.5
Nepal	5,785	6,558	+13.4	12.6	20.1
Pakistan	28,014	33,999	+21.4	20.6	28.9
Papua New Guinea	1,034	1,107	+7.1	26.1	39.1
Philippines	3,730	3,074	−17.6	81.8	89.2
Singapore	394	364	−7.6	68.9	79.1
Sri Lanka	1,675	1,722	+2.8	77.0	81.7
Thailand	4,246	3,409	−19.7	79.0	87.7
Turkey	9,868	9,749	−1.2	52.5	64.9
Vietnam	5,980	4,847	−18.9	76.5	84.5

Source: UNESCO (1984, pp. 7–11).

3.3. *Adult Literacy Data from 1990 to 1999*

The latest figures compiled in the *Synthesis Report of Education for All: Assessment Report for the Asia-Pacific Region* (UNESCO, 2000a) compiled the Year 2000 are given in Table 2.

4. SALIENT POINTS EMERING FROM LITERACY STATISTICS

4.1. *Dominant Themes*

The dominant themes for each of the four sub-regions may be stated.

- There is a persistent gender gap in the large countries of South Asia,
- Education management reforms are needed in the changing economies of the Trans Caucasian and Central Asian countries.
- The need to address the problems of youth in the particular circumstances of the Pacific Island states.
- A need for sustaining Education for All (EFA) gains in economic crisis situations in East and Southeast Asia.

In general, the data on Adult Literacy indicate that remarkable progress was achieved in a few countries and modest progress in others over the last decade. The most backward sub-region is South and West Asia. Here the crucial issues are the continuance of high levels of adult illiteracy and the persistence of significant sub-national, urban-rural and gender disparities in participation. A major factor is the unrelenting impact of rapid population growth (Pakistan rate is still 2.4%). If the number of school-age boys and girls grows in excess of the expansion of the primary sector and adequate funds for it are not forthcoming, the increase in the numbers of adolescents and adult illiterates is bound to go up. This phenomenon is well illustrated in the statement that in Pakistan the number of illiterates today exceeds that of the total population of the country in 1947, the year it came into existence. Consequently, the illiteracy rate in Pakistan and the sub-region as a whole has gone down in varying degrees, but there has been an actual increase in the number of illiterates. This is partly accounted for by lower participation of female and rural area populations. There is also the fact of a relapse for a lack of viable post-literacy programs. The high drop out rates in the primary school is yet another contributing factor. Thus there is a correlation between levels of adult female literacy and the rate of expansion of the school-age population which provides a structural barrier to an increase in participation rates and the reduction of disparities. A significant reason for laying greater emphasis on female literacy is the established relationship between it and fertility. Summers (1992) reported on a World Bank study linking female education and fertility wherein educating 1000 women would have averted 600 births saving $250,000 in sustenance costs. Thus there is a clear and strong relationship between literacy, population and participation in

Adult Literacy in the Asia-Pacific Region 297

Table 2. Adult literacy rate – of population aged 15 years old and over (Total)

Country/Region	1990–91	1991–92	1992–93	1993–94	1994–95	1995–96	1996–97	1997–98	1998–99
Central Asia									
Azerbaijan	97.3	97.3	97.3	97.3	97.3	97.3	97.3	97.3	97.3
Armenia	–	–	–	–	–	–	–	–	99.3
Georgia	–	–	99.3	99.4	–	–	99.5	99.6	–
Kazakhstan	99.5	99.6	99.6	99.6	99.7	99.7	99.8	99.8	99.9
Kyrgyzstan	–	–	–	–	–	97.0	–	–	–
Mongolia	–	–	–	–	–	–	97.2	–	–
Tajikistan	94.4	94.6	94.7	94.6	94.4	94.3	94.1	92.2	90.6
Turkmenistan	–	–	–	–	–	–	–	–	–
Uzbekistan	95.0	95.9	96.6	97.7	98.7	99.0	99.1	99.2	99.3
East/South-East Asia									
Cambodia	57.7	–	–	65.3	–	65.9	–	68.0	–
Indonesia	79.8	80.3	81.5	83.3	85.2	84.1	85.3	87.4	87.9
Lao PDR	–	–	–	–	–	60.2	–	–	–
Malaysia	–	–	–	–	–	91.0	93.0	93.3	93.7
Philippines	93.5	–	–	–	93.6	–	–	–	–
Republic of Korea	96.3	96.6	97.0	97.3	97.7	98.0	98.2	98.3	98.5
Thailand	–	–	–	–	96.4	96.6	94.3	96.0	97.7
Pacific									
Nauru	–	–	–	–	–	–	–	–	94.5
Samoa	–	97.9	–	–	–	–	–	–	–
Tonga	–	–	–	–	–	–	74.9	–	–
Tuvalu	–	–	–	–	98.0	–	–	–	–
South & West Asia									
Bangladesh	–	–	–	–	–	–	–	–	55.9
India	62.9	48.5	–	–	–	–	–	57.7	–
Iran	–	65.2	66.9	68.5	70.1	71.5	72.9	74.0	75.5
Maldives	–	–	–	–	–	–	–	98.6	–
Nepal	–	33.0	–	–	–	–	–	44.8	–
Pakistan	–	–	–	–	–	–	–	42.7	–

Source: UNESCO (2000a, pp. 69–72).

primary education. If adult female literacy rates move up, the rate of increase of the school population goes down.

4.2. Synthesis Report for EFA Assessment 2000

The *Synthesis Report for EFA Assessment 2000* (UNESCO, 2000a) has highlighted three powerful aspects that have influenced what has been achieved and will to a large extent determine what may be realized in the years to come:

- besides the increase in participation in primary education and enhancement of its quality there is the pressing need for reduction in gender and urban-rural disparities;
- there is an inadequacy of funding and a need for enhanced governmental support as well as the desirability of increased community involvement and contributions, and decentralized management with a special emphasis on information technology and a streamlined monitoring or evaluation;
- advocacy is required to secure larger contributions from international agencies.

A welcome move in this connection was the pledge at the World Education Forum in 2000 that no country seriously committed to EFA would be thwarted in the achievement of the Dakar goals by lack of resources. This resolve has been recently stressed by the Assistant Director General (Education) UNESCO at a meeting in Islamabad held in March 2002.

Some relevant factors identified by the authors of the *EFA 2000 Global Synthesis* may also be mentioned (UNESCO, 2000b).

- The data bases are so inadequate as to require a much greater effort at systematization if firm conclusions and reliable inferences are to be drawn and if coherent policies are to be developed and implemented. Audits are needed to ensure open and honest reporting.
- Long standing disparities and inequities remain within countries. There is need for better focused equity targets. The poorest countries, the poorest regions and the poorest groups are not receiving adequate support although they are targets of several donors and aid agencies; in the least developed countries one half of the adults are still illiterate.
- Adult literacy and nonformal education more generally are in many countries accorded insufficient priority and are at the margins of reform efforts.
- Successful programs depend upon a variety of conditions: (a) mobilizing many and varied resources, local, national and international; (b) sound organization and persistence of activity often over long periods; (c) community involvement and leadership; and (d) attention to the life conditions of illiterate people and to their motivation and incentives to become fully literate.
- Policies for adult literacy need to take account of problems being experienced by school-age children and the literacy standards they attain.
- Literacy of the most rudimentary kind is a useful intermediate target, as a step towards a broadly defined culture of literacy.

- Regular, reliable reporting of performance on agreed targets of basic literacy would enable concentration on the most difficult problems and areas of greatest need.

4.3. *EFA Assessment 2000 Thematic Studies*

The conclusions reached in *EFA Assessment 2000 Thematic Studies* (UNESCO, 2000c) published by the International Consultation Forum also must be stated. At the Jomtien conference, the literacy goal was to reduce the illiteracy rate in each country by 50 per cent in one decade. This has not happened in any country. And yet there is widening recognition that low literacy and poor basic learning competencies, by varying standards, are even more prevalent today than had been assumed a decade ago. Furthermore, with population growth the absolute number of illiterates has declined very little since Jomtien.

On the one hand, agencies which support or engage in literacy work need to be more realistic about what can be achieved within budget constraints. Such realism entails lowering expectations about major changes in individual, social and economic outcomes, while at the same time holding literacy-service providers to higher standards of accountability and professionalism. As in formal schooling, literacy and adult education do not provide a magic answer for any society, but they are part and parcel of all aspects of national development. On the other hand, agencies can enhance adult literacy programs by the following actions:

- building a more solid knowledge base for field based innovations;
- improving professional development and human resources capacity;
- providing better pathways from nonformal youth and adult literacy programs into the formal school system;
- combining nonformal programs for adults and early childhood programs;
- taking advantage of new technologies (especially for distance education in countries with remote areas lacking communication facilities and the ones consisting of large numbers of scattered small islands); and
- investing resources in assessment, evaluation and monitoring, surveys and applied research, and creating new synergies and collaborations between governmental and non-governmental agencies.

5. CASE STUDIES OF FIVE COUNTRIES IN THE REGION

5.1. *Literacy and Nonformal Education in China*

In response to the socio-economic and cultural needs of learners, the definition of literacy in China has come to encompass functional knowledge and vocationally oriented skills. With 90 per cent illiterates living in rural or remote, poverty stricken areas, nonformal education played a vital role in the provision of education to all citizens. Intending to help most young and middle-aged people throughout the country to join the ranks of literates, the Government legislated literacy education and put the system under a unified leadership. At the same time, the relevant government agencies mobilised human resources in all sectors of the society and optimised the co-operation among all concerned, right down to the grassroots level. This, together with post-literacy education and continuous efforts to improve the enrolment and retention rates of school-age children and popularising primary education in rural areas especially among girls, has helped in making about five million people literate each year. Due attention was given to ethnic minorities. Together with literacy, the people mastered the basic functional knowledge and vocational skills to improve their competence, quality of life and economic status.

The three main strategies to achieve universal literacy in China were blocking, elimination, and further improvement (UNESCO, 2000d).

- *Blocking*. This means reducing the number of new illiterates and popularising primary education while improving enrolment, retention, and graduation rates of school-age children.
- *Elimination*. This is the practice whereby literacy education is offered to the youth and middle-aged people who did not have an opportunity to receive education in school.
- *Further improvement*. This aims at consolidating the results of literacy education through continuing education programs for neo-literates.

The Government mobilised all sectors of society in order to make the integrated system of rural literacy and nonformal education workable. Grass-roots government agencies were entrusted with various responsibilities from planning to implementing, all in accordance with the national policy. In an agrarian society such as rural China, the farmers' needs were taken into consideration as they were prerequisites for the development of literacy and nonformal education in order to boost their own socio-economic progress. But farmers differed from one another in their learning needs and learning conditions, therefore teaching methods, hours and venues had to be flexible. Success of the program was also contingent upon sufficient numbers of competent teaching personnel. Universities and research institutes were encouraged to lend educational and technical support to promote modernisation of rural areas whereas NGOs maintained their active participation to the grass-roots government agencies.

A bottom-up approach of formulating future education policies by focusing on the practical needs for local, social and economic development were favoured. Greater commitment and fairer remuneration of rural education personnel, advocacy, revision and expansion of the content and modernisation of teaching methods were no less important.

5.2. *Nonformal Adult Education and Literacy for Sustainability: The Philippines Experience*

The Philippines is a country of contrasts in terms of literacy. While the country has one of the highest literacy rates in Asia, there are still 12 million people who are functionally illiterate. Since the beginning of the 1990s, the Government has intensified its efforts to eradicate illiteracy by implementing a number of programs in basic literacy and functional literacy in a more concerted manner. Worthy of note is the Functional Education and Literacy Programme (FELP), which caters for learners at basic literacy level, neo-literates, literate out-of-school youth and adults, and elementary and secondary school dropouts, using community-based materials that are mainly facilitator-aided instructions. FELP plans to expand its services and improve the quality and relevance of community-based adult literacy programs. The Continuing Education and Development Program (CED) helps adults and out-of-school youth to integrate into the learning system chiefly through the use of nonformal and informal education focussing on the minimum essential learning needs of adults in functional literacy and numeracy. The Female Functional Literacy Program (FEL) targets mothers and caregivers and aims to improve the health of women and children through provision of functional literacy skills. It also enables women to recognize their capabilities, strengths, and potential (UNESCO, 2000d).

For the millions of cultural minorities, an integrated community-based approach was used to develop Nonformal Education (NFE) programs. Committed prospective literacy facilitators were selected from the most remote villages of the indigenous groups and provided with intensive training for four months. By the end of the training period they were expected to be able to implement an NFE project, assess and determine learning needs of the target group, facilitate learning, develop and utilize materials for learning, monitor and evaluate learners' progress, and establish linkages and networks with other organizations in the community. The self-paced, Nonformal Education Accreditation and Equivalency (NFE A&E) System provides learning support for out-of-school youth and adults, functional illiterates, and school dropouts and industry-based workers who are 15 years or older. The system aims at improving learner's basic education skills and competencies using materials comparable to that of the formal school system, and at preparing the learners for certification of learning achievement equivalent to the formal elementary and secondary education system. To a certain extent the success of the program depends on the Instructional Managers' critical and essential skills such as in counselling, recruitment, placement, and managing the learning process. The Instructional Managers are required to attend the prescribed training programs, which are conducted in three phases: pre-service, in-service, and post-service.

In an attempt to remedy a weakness of the Government's education program, advocacy and social mobilization strategies in this program help to recruit new learners and bring together those who are affected by the problem and those who can contribute to its solution. The study notes that there have been 122 non-government organisations (NGOs) and community-based organizations active in the area of adult education since the late 1960s. Due to short-term foreign funding, NGOs sometimes had to accelerate their programs, which can be counter-productive to the learning process. NGOs also rely mainly on voluntary teachers who are not necessarily competent in capacity building and the development program they have to implement.

5.3. *The Indian Case*

Literacy rate in India, according to official figures, has reached 65 per cent, an impressive achievement considering that it was 24 per cent in 1961, 30 per cent in 1971 and 36 per cent in 1981 although the absolute number of illiterates also increased from 334 million in 1961 to 437 million in 1981. This sustained and substantial increase in the rate of literacy in India during the last two decades has primarily been due to the launching of the National Adult Education Programme started in 1978. It was a country wide effort in which all three tiers of the government (central, state and local) participated. Three marked features of it were: (a) the setting up of resource centers in each state, (b) a fairly well-designed monitoring system, and (c) the involvement of NGOs and universities. In 1998, it graduated into one of the five National Missions and is now known as the National Literacy Mission. Under this mission the Government and the voluntary agencies came up with a number of innovative approaches involving among others, district administration and diverse groups and organizations across the length and breadth of the country. Some of these programs and operations are listed below (India, 2002).

(1) *TLCS – Total Literacy Campaigns.* These campaigns launched since 1990–91 have been area-specific, time-bound and participatory. By 1999, 100 million had been targeted for literacy.
(2) *Operations Blackboard in 1987.* This program provided teachers, classrooms and teaching learning material; 310,000 teachers were appointed, and Total Literacy Education (TLE) was provided to 700,000 schools. In addition, 183,000 classrooms were constructed.
(3) *Mahila Samakhya in 1989.* This program for women's empowerment covered 9000 villages.
(4) *Educationally backward areas.* Special projects were set up in educationally backward areas.
(5) *Communities contributions.* Communities contributed land, labour, and material. In all states, in particular, Andhra Pardesh (Rs. 15 million), Mahrashtra (Rs. 75 million), Gujarat (land worth Rs. 10 million), and Himachal (land for 700 schools), support was provided.
(6) *Training.* More than a million teachers were trained every year.
(7) *Teacher training institutes.* Teacher training institutes were set up in 80 per cent of the districts.

5.4. Pakistan

Pakistan claims 47 per cent literacy today. The major cause for the slow progress has been the lack of political will, unlike India, where the top leadership has for the last 25 years given literacy high priority. Pakistan was perhaps one of the first countries to set up a National Commission for Literacy and Mass Education in the year 1981. But political changes and rapid turn around in the office of the chairman of the Commission along with an almost total neglect of adult literacy despite commitment given at Jomtien in 1990 and at New Delhi in 1993, literacy remained until this year a low priority. Considerable attention, however, was paid to primary education and a program for out-of-school children was also launched. However, poor management and inadequate funding stood in the way of achieving the intended results. The drop out rate in the primary schools remained high, around 50 per cent and the quality of education imparted was less than satisfactory. With the formulation of a Plan of Action which includes adult literacy as a follow-up of the Dakar Declaration in 2000 hopes have arisen that the Government will at long last, devote itself seriously to the implementation of the long over-due countrywide program in pursuance of the Dakar goals. Unfortunately, however, with the national literacy commission having been abolished as a part of the economy drive of the Government and implementation of the literacy program having devolved on the new district administration systems, the prospects for an expeditious and smooth management of the complex and daunting tasks involved are not very good. UNESCO perhaps could provide timely and realistic advice to the Government of Pakistan on these problems.

5.5. *Thailand*

Perhaps the most impressive and systematic literacy promotion record has taken place in Thailand. The country had 31.2 per cent literacy in 1938. Under a special law in the period 1943–45, 1.4 million people between the ages of 20 to 45 years became literate. By the year 1980, the illiteracy rate had been reduced to 10.5 per cent This was achieved mostly by expanding primary education, out of school literacy education efforts and work-oriented functional literacy programs, as well as a five-years mass literacy campaign for illiterates between the ages of 14 to 50 years. Special programs for hill tribes in remote areas were also launched. The literacy rate today stands at 97 per cent. The factors responsible for this remarkable achievement are the consistent commitment on the part of the government, large financial allocations, and effective governmental machinery for the planning, management and implementation of programs. This progress was also achieved through the sustained involvement of the communities in the projects undertaken. With an excellent primary education program and with successful population control, it is no surprise that the illiteracy rate was phenomenally lowered over the years. Thailand certainly offers a model for other developing countries and its new *Education Act* needs to be studied by the Education Ministries in other Asian states for inspiration and guidance (Thailand, NEC, 2001).

6. CONCLUSION

In this article, an attempt is made to collect in one place information about the state of adult literacy in the vast and sprawling region of Asia and Pacific where more than 70 per cent of the total world illiterates live. Concepts and definitions of literacy are referred to briefly. Notes about some of the countries are included as illustrations of different settings, experiences and achievements. Reasons and factors relevant to performance, lags, lacks and disparities are cited. Finally lessons drawn from the region-wide experience are culled and summed up for future directions and guidance. Some of the points, which may be stressed at the end of this article are given below.

(1) The population in South Asian Countries needs to be controlled expeditiously.
(2) There is a linkage between adult literacy and primary education. Good programs for both adults and school going children are needed as these complement each other in lowering illiteracy.
(3) Highest priority should be given to adult female literacy.
(4) International contributions to both adult literacy and primary education for developing countries that are deficient in literacy must be enhanced. The contribution should be linked by the commitment of reasonable and adequate allocation of funding by national governments.
(5) There should be a judicious blend of initiatives at the level of central government for planning and coordination and specific programs at the local level.
(6) A post-literacy program is essential to consolidate the initial adult literacy courses that are functionally oriented and relate to learners' day-to-day needs.
(7) Information and communications technology should be used not only for distance education but also for the management of programs, especially for the training of instructors, teachers, and supervisors, and for monitoring and evaluation.

The call for Education for All first came from UNESCO in 1945. The Human Rights Charter in 1948 declared education as a basic human right. The Jomtien Conference set goals in 1990. The Dakar World Forum in the Year 2000 assessed progress and reset the targets. It is now for the countries left behind in the race for literacy to catch up with others. This paper has identified, to some extent, facts and factors relevant to the requirements and guidelines for the formulation and implementation of realistic and forward looking initiatives to achieve the objectives laid down in the Dakar Declaration.

REFERENCES

India (2002). Paper presented by the Indian delegate at the South Asia Forum, Islamabad, March, 2002.
Summers, L. H. (1992). *Investing in All the People*. Washington, DC: World Bank.
Thailand, Office of the National Education Commission (2001). *Thailand's Experience in the Promotion of Literacy*. Bangkok: National Education Commission.
UNESCO (1984). *Towards a Regional Strategy for Eradicating Illiteracy in the Asia and Pacific Region*. Bangkok: UNESCO Regional Office.
UNESCO (2000a). *Synthesis Report of Education for All 2000 Assessment for the Asia-Pacific Region*. Bangkok: UNESCO, PROAP.
UNESCO (2000b). *Global Synthesis: Education for All 2000 Assessment*. Paris: UNESCO.
UNESCO (2000c). *Thematic Studies: Education for All 2000 Assessment*. Paris: UNESCO.
UNESCO (2000d). *Synthesis Report of Education for All 2000 Assessment for East and Southeast Asia Sub-region*. Bangkok: UNESCO, PROAP.

22

Learning Across the Adult Lifespan

ERLINDA PEFIANCO
SEAMEO INNOTECH, Manila, The Philippines

DAVID CURTIS
Centre for Lifelong Learning and Development, Flinders University, Australia

JOHN P. KEEVES
Flinders University Institute of International Education, Australia

1. INTRODUCTION

The past two centuries have not only seen rapid growth in the population of the world, and especially in those countries in the Asia-Pacific region, but they have also seen a marked growth worldwide in the provision for, and participation in, formal education. During the latter half of the nineteenth century the establishment of free and compulsory primary level education was strongly endorsed and in many countries enforced to achieve universal participation. During the first half of the twentieth century secondary education was firmly established. This was commonly in schools that selected students for different types of education, namely, academic, vocational or general. Then, with the growth of secondary education many countries moved towards a more comprehensive type of schooling, with a participation rate of over 80 per cent of each age-cohort remaining at school to the end of the secondary phase. In the latter half of the twentieth century tertiary education was expanded through a marked increase in the number of universities to which students had access, together with a large increase in the number of technical colleges at which students received vocational education and training. Some countries have now achieved levels of participation of around 40 per cent of the age cohort enrolled in universities, and up to 30 per cent of the age cohort enrolled in technical colleges. Within the Asia-Pacific region, wide disparities exist between countries in the extent of student participation in the three phases of education, ranging from very high levels in Japan, the Republic of Korea and Australia to the very low levels found in the countries of South Asia: Afghanistan, Bangladesh, Nepal and Pakistan. Evidence obtained from research studies indicates that, in general, the extent of educational provision is dependent on the wealth of a country and in turn, the extent of provision has an influence on the further increase in wealth of a country (see *Educational Expenditure and Participation in East Asia and Australia, Higher Education and Development, Financing Higher Education in the Asia-Pacific Region*). Countries with low levels of participation face decisions in the expansion of their education systems about whether to give priority to the primary, secondary or tertiary phases.

During the past two centuries, three other very significant changes have occurred worldwide. First, with the mechanisation of many manual tasks, there has been a marked reduction during the twentieth century in the number of hours which it is necessary for people to work outside and inside the home in order to live in a highly satisfactory manner. Second, there has been, and continues to be a remarkable growth in knowledge. Consequently, initial education in primary, secondary and tertiary educational institutions can no longer be considered adequate for people to keep abreast of the new knowledge that they need in their work and daily living. Third, through technology and changing social values and attitudes, women in many countries of the Asia-Pacific region have been set free from many burdensome household and child-rearing tasks, to participate more actively in the workforce and in educational activities.

These changes have, over the last three decades of the twentieth century, led to the emergence of a clearly identifiable fourth phase of educational activity that is now commonly known as 'lifelong learning', 'continuing education' or 'recurrent education'. This phase of education would appear to be catering for people in the age range from 25 to 64 years and beyond, with general recognition that opportunities for further learning should be provided for people throughout life and past the stage of formal employment. Through the expansion of universities and technical colleges, opportunities have been made available for adults in the age range from 25 years upwards to undertake study either for credit towards a qualification, or not for credit, or for general personal enrichment of life. In addition, industry and commerce have been encouraged by governments to provide further educational and training programs for the people they employ. Moreover, there is growing recognition that opportunities for learning must extend beyond the formal provision of education to include nonformal and informal teaching and learning activities. It is becoming apparent that systematic planning must take place to advance and extend educational activity beyond the stages of primary, secondary and tertiary education in order to provide for what may be referred to as a 'quaternary' phase of education, which involves learning across the adult lifespan. Probably the name of this phase should become 'Lifelong Learning and Development' to emphasise, not only the learning that takes place through formal instruction, but also the less formal personal development that is occurring in a variety of ways.

This article draws attention to some of the work being done in the Asia-Pacific region to establish this fourth phase of education in the region, to link it to the three earlier phases, and to provide opportunities for learning by individuals who have not had the opportunity to benefit from education in primary, secondary or tertiary educational institutions. This article also focuses on several developments in the field of adult lifelong learning that are seen to be necessary for the establishment of the fourth phase of education.

2. FORMAL, NONFORMAL AND INFORMAL EDUCATION

During the last three decades, useful distinctions have been drawn between 'formal', 'nonformal' and 'informal' education (Colletta, 1998; Desjardins & Tuijnman, in press). Formal education refers to the purposeful and systematic development of knowledge, skills and attitudes, in educational institutions that are structured in space, time and materials, commonly in order to provide a recognised qualification. Informal education involves the incidental growth of attitudes, knowledge and skills, with an emphasis on attitudes, through very diverse interactions between people in such situations as are provided by the home, the community, and the peer group. Nonformal education involves the deliberate and systematic development of knowledge, attitudes and skills with an emphasis on skills in very flexible arrangements of space, time and materials. For each of these three forms of learning, the organisation of time, space and materials follows very different and culturally relevant patterns in the relationships between the groups of people involved. Where, in the nonformal mode, under apprenticeships, internships and student practica, there has been an emphasis on skills, the advances in information and communications technology and the evolution of the media beyond newsprint and radio has extended the opportunities to develop both knowledge and attitudes as well as skills through the use of television and computer based instruction in nonformal as well as formal modes of educational provision. It is in the field of nonformal education that marked advances are likely to occur, which will enable this mode of education to extend beyond the teaching of skills to include the communication of new knowledge and the development of attitudes and values. The advances in information and communications technology (ICT) will greatly influence learning with the potential of greater cost efficiency. This greater cost efficiency arises from the transmission of interactive learning materials over large distances, as well as the capacity to transfer the costs to the user from the centre of production (Colletta, 1998). However, it should be noted that these developments in distance education and flexible delivery, which now make extensive use of ICT in many countries, challenge the distinction between formal and nonformal education.

Nevertheless, it is the benefits of social interaction between individuals in the learning of knowledge and in the formation of attitudes and values that are sometimes missing in the use of ICT in the provision of learning experiences, unless highly flexible systems, possibly using combinations of both synchronous and asynchronous media, are employed to encourage interaction between the student and teacher and among learners. ICT, like other modes of nonformal education, is very effective in the learning of skills, because appropriate learning experiences can be readily simulated, and students' responses can be rapidly monitored in an interactive way. It would seem that a combination of learning through ICT in interrelationship with social interaction between the individual learner and either a teacher or peers is likely to be the most beneficial mode of learning in the future during the quaternary phase. There is research that shows how some media can contribute to effective interactions of students with materials, of students with teachers, and among students. Such research has been undertaken in Australia (Curtis & Lawson, 2001). However, this research may not be capable of being generalised, because what will work within a particular country depends upon factors such as the uptake of technology by individuals and organisations and upon the ICT infrastructure of that country. Moreover, modes of effective learning may differ at different stages across the lifespan, and for different individuals at different stages. As a consequence, it would appear that no universal approach to learning through formal, nonformal, or informal modes could or should be specified that would be the same across the lifespan, all fields of learning, and in all societies and cultures. Where research is now required is in the identification of combinations of media that together will provide the diversity of interactions, which will lead to optimal learning outcomes in different situations.

3. NEW PROCEDURES FOR CERTIFICATION

New procedures for certification across the four phases of education are emerging in order to assess cognitive and social skills that are developed through learning activities. This section considers the nature of these abilities, skills and developmental tasks as well as their assessment in terms of competencies.

3.1. *Intellectual and Cognitive Development Across the Lifespan*

From the beginning of the twentieth century educational and psychological research workers have been interested in the nature and structure of human intelligence and a most thorough treatment of the problem has been presented by Carroll (1993) who argued for a hierarchical model of intelligence. His study has been further advanced by Spearritt (1996) and Gustafsson (2001), and arising from this work is the view that the cognitive structures developed in an individual during the years of primary, secondary and tertiary education greatly influence the learning experiences sought and attempted later in life.

A different approach to the investigation of the patterns and processes that underlie cognitive development is provided by the work of Piaget and Inhelder (1956, 1974) who have identified stages of cognitive development from the years of childhood to those of late adolescence. An approach to the assessment of student learning and an evaluation of the learning outcomes involved within a Piagetian framework, has been advanced by Biggs and Collis (1982, 1989) who have worked mainly in the Asia-Pacific region. The emerging evidence would appear to indicate that, while students' capacities to perform at the higher levels of cognitive development proposed by Piaget can be enhanced through appropriate educational experiences (Shayer & Adey, 2002), some adults, through lack of such learning experiences at particular stages of their cognitive development, have not formed the capacity to work at the higher levels of operation.

Sweller, (1999), working in Australia, has provided from his research, greater detail on the cognitive structures of working memory, long-term memory, automation, and cognitive load theory, as well as the effects of split attention and redundancy of information. There are clearly some limits to the cognitive processes that some individuals can employ in a particular learning situation as well as some learning conditions that would optimise the learning achieved by certain individuals. Recently, Bransford, Brown and Cocking (1999) reviewed the field of brain research from an educational perspective. However, there is a great deal more that is known than they would appear to have considered and that is relevant to "how people learn" at different periods in their lives. It must be argued by the authors of this article that this knowledge should be taken into consideration in the provision of appropriate learning experiences for different subgroups of adults in different fields of learning. Moreover, it is strongly argued that systematic research into the functioning of the brain at different stages in the lifespan has emerged as a critical field for research in both education and psychology. In addition, it should be noted that research has been undertaken in the United States into the stages of psychosocial development of men and women (Havighurst, 1953), but little work would appear to have been carried out in this field in the Asia-Pacific region. While the developmental tasks formulated in this approach to inquiry into human development provide a framework for the investigation of appropriate programs in the field of adult education, the characteristics of the different stages of development would not appear to have been sufficiently clearly identified for courses to be based on such ideas. Nevertheless, courses proposed for the field of lifelong learning should match the stages that can be clearly identified. Moreover, research should be carried out to test the adequacy of Havighurst's theory of developmental tasks in different cultural settings at a time when globalisation is having a profound impact on the ways in which people live, work, play and study in different cultures and different countries.

4. THE IDEA OF COMPETENCE

As a consequence of the increased number of levels and types of formal education and the emerging strength of nonformal and informal education, with increasing proportions of each age cohort moving through an increased variety of paths in their quest for education, the hallmark standards of a matriculation certificate or an apprenticeship certificate would no longer appear to be very meaningful. In order to facilitate movement from the work place to a training institution and from an educational institution into the workforce in a non-recursive way, some portability of qualifications and credentials across different types of educational and learning organisations is required. Consequently, a system of generic performance indicators has been advanced and referred to as 'key competencies' with their associated levels of 'competence'. German workers in this field have identified two categories of cognitive functioning, (a) the 'mechanics' of the cognitive system, for example, processing speed, reasoning, and working memory capacity, and (b) the 'pragmatics', that involve the application of knowledge gained through education, training and acculturation (Maroske & Smith, 1998). This specification of two categories of cognitive functioning resolves some of the problems that emerge from research in this area.

In Australia in the mid-1980s the Quality of Education Review Committee (QERC) Report (Karmel, 1985) gave some consideration to the idea of competence.

> The Committee has approached the desirable outcomes through the concept of competence, that is the ability to use knowledge and skills effectively to achieve a purpose. This allows the emphasis to be placed on the results of learning, which should be purposeful and have demonstrable effects. It encourages a practical examination of desirable outcomes because it can be used to concentrate attention both on the purposes to be achieved and on the necessary knowledge and the abilities required to apply that knowledge. (Karmel, 1985, p. 70)

QERC identified five so-called 'general competences' as desirable learning outcomes for all students in schools. These competences are given in Table 1. Subsequently, other Australian committees took similar approaches. The Finn Committee (1991) focused on general education and training during the years of post-compulsory education, and the Mayer Committee (1992) identified what it referred to as 'key competencies' which were to provide a bridge between general education and vocational education and training (see Table 1).

At the same time, developments were also occurring in other parts of the world where these ideas were being discussed, and the New Zealand Qualifications Authority (1991) advanced its own version of what were called the 'essential skills' (see Table 1). There are clear similarities between these different proposals. The task of identifying the required or expected standards of performance that were associated with these different sets of skills was envisaged and attempts were made to specify performance levels and standards of performance. However, it became clear that further research was required to identify not only performance levels and indicators of performance, but also the standards of performance and the expected proportions of particular groups of young people who could attain these standards. One of the problems facing advances along these lines was the lack of acceptance of the idea of scales of performance and the lack of acceptance of the statistical and measurement procedures that were necessary to construct such scales and to identify meaningful levels and benchmarks along those scales. The International Adult Literacy

Table 1. Competencies specified in Australia and New Zealand

QERC Competencies (Australia) (1995)	New Zealand Essential Skills
acquiring information	information skills
conveying information	communication skills
applying logical processes	self-managing skills
practical tasks	work and study skills
group tasks	social skills
	numeracy skills
	decision making skills

Finn Committee: Key Areas of Competence (1991) (Australia)	Mayer Committee: Key Competencies (1992) (Australia)
language and communication	collecting, analysing and organising of information
mathematics	communicating ideas and information
scientific and technical understanding	planning and organising information
cultural understanding	working with others and in teams
problem solving	using mathematical ideas and techniques
personal and interpersonal characteristics	solving problems
	using technology

Sources: Karmel (1985), Finn (1991), Mayer Committee (1992).

Study (IALS) (OECD, Statistics Canada, 1995) has developed scales that are related to aspects of communication and computation skills (Tuijnman et al., 1995). However, research workers elsewhere would appear to have been slow to work on the development of measures for the key competencies even in Australia where the use of similar measurement procedures is widely accepted at the primary school level.

The OECD Education Committee and the Employment, Labour and Social Affairs Committee and the Governing Board of the Centre for Educational Research and Innovation have supported the establishment of a DeSeCo Steering Group in collaboration with the Swiss Federal Statistical Office, US National Centre for Educational Statistics, and Statistics Canada. The task of the DeSeCo Group as its name suggests is the 'definition and selection of competencies' and their theoretical and conceptual foundations. A first report by the Steering Group has been published (Rychen & Salganik, 2001), that establishes solid foundations for the further development of statistical indicators of human competencies and has provided references to work for the assessment and interpretation of measured performance relating to general learning and teaching outcomes. This work is complementary to OECD international studies that involve the participation of some Asia-Pacific countries, and in particular, the Programme for International Student Assessment (PISA), the International Adult Literacy Study (IALS) and the Adult Literacy and Lifeskills (ALL) survey. Without the development of these different programs, lifelong learning will continue to be fragmented, unstable, intermittent and unfocused. Furthermore, agreement world-wide on a frame of reference for future assessment activities in the area of key competencies is necessary if portability of qualifications is to be achieved across the world at a time when globalisation is demanding the increased movement of people between countries for both short and long term periods.

5. BARRIERS TO PARTICIPATION IN LIFELONG LEARNING

Among the major problems confronting educational provision in the quaternary phase are the barriers that exist to participation in lifelong learning and development programs. There are many potential learners who may, for a variety of reasons, be excluded from formal, nonformal and informal learning opportunities. It is clear that in each country research is needed to identify these barriers and to investigate ways in which such barriers ought to be broken down.

The Centre for Lifelong Learning and Development in Australia has established a program of research which is built around the framework presented in *Lifelong Learning for All* (OECD, 1996, pp. 92–93) that provides a useful structure for describing the barriers to participation in lifelong learning. The use of this three-level framework as an analytical tool leads to a more complete understanding of the barriers faced by learners. It is able to account for so-called 'failures' in an education and training delivery system and to suggest changes in the system to accommodate the needs of the many different groups of learners. In this work distinctions have been drawn between barriers that operate at the structural or contextual level, at the institutional level and at the individual level. Lack of participation cannot be attributed exclusively to (a) the existence of hostile or inappropriate learning environments, (b) lack of suitable learning opportunities, or (c) lack of an individual's interest and motivation. Lack of participation arises from the barriers constructed by interactions between and contributions from among all of them, as they combine together in any particular situation. Only from a sound understanding of the forces at work that serve to limit participation in lifelong learning, which involves formal, nonformal and informal learning opportunities, would it be possible to identify the underlying barriers to participation and to remove or reduce effectively those barriers that operate in a particular situation.

6. ADULT LEARNING PROGRAMS IN FOUR COUNTRIES

In order to illustrate the emerging nature of lifelong education, and the developments that are occurring in the fields of lifelong learning, this article next considers four major programs that have been introduced in countries that range from one with a low level of economic development to two of the most industrially developed countries in the Asia-Pacific region.

6.1. *Continuing Education Program for Teachers in the Philippines*

New information technologies are allowing people all over the world to communicate, to exchange ideas, and to do business with one another at increasingly faster and more frequent rates. This has resulted in the creation of the new, so-called 'global community' where no nation and no society exist like the proverbial island, but are part of a dynamic, ever-changing whole. In some of the more developed countries their education systems have begun to adapt to this changing world. However, in the case of the developing countries of the Asia-Pacific region, where schools and education systems are still struggling to cope with basic problems, such as the provision and access to quality education, much developmental work needs to be done to prepare the teachers of these countries to face the challenges of the decades ahead. This emphasises the need in the Asia-Pacific region for those teachers, who are at the forefront of educational developments, to be equipped with the competencies that will enable them: (a) to use and manipulate the new technologies, (b) to have a global and progressive outlook, and (c) to learn the skills to become lifelong learners.

It was with this rationale that at the South-East Asian Ministers of Education Organisation (SEAMEO) Centre, INNOTECH in Manila in the Philippines, Project COMPETE was born. This project aims to develop a research-based continuing education program for teachers in the elementary and secondary schools in order to help prepare them for the challenges ahead. The title of this project 'COMPETE', stands for 'Continuing Teacher Education Programme Utilizing Distance Education Technology and Materials'. It is a research and development project that aims to design, develop and trial a competency-based continuing education program for teachers of elementary and secondary school grades. The project is funded by the Canadian International Development Agency (CIDA). Since the project serves the teachers of SEAMEO member countries to help them to provide open and flexible learning environments that will enable their students to become independent and self-directed learners in a technology-enriched setting, it uses distance education as its primary mode of delivery.

The specific objectives of the project are to: (a) develop a shared vision of what basic education will be like in the future; (b) identify the general and specific competencies, namely, knowledge, skills, attitudes and values required for the future; (c) develop a competency chart to guide the design of appropriate learning strategies; (d) develop self-paced and self-instructional learning modules in multimedia formats; and (e) trial the COMPETE learning system and evaluate and refine it.

The products of Project COMPETE as a validated continuing teacher education program consist of:

- self-paced learning print modules, that are the main learning materials;
- video tapes, audio tapes and CDs as supplementary materials to the print modules;

- a distance learning system, using a combination of various media and technologies; and
- facilitator's guides, student support materials and installation handbooks.

The project has built on: (a) a detailed and comprehensive literature review; (b) visioning workshops to provide a vision of the future Philippine society, a vision of basic education in the future, and a vision of a teacher's role in the future; (c) curriculum development workshops; (d) the identification of competencies; (e) the development of learning materials and a learning system; (f) the validation of the learning materials; and (g) the continuing in-service education of teachers through a widespread distance learning system. This project seeks to employ information and communications technology to provide lifelong learning for teachers, by using the methods of teaching that teachers might be expected to employ in the future in their own instructional programs, both in basic education and in adult recurrent education courses.

6.2. Adult Literacy Program in Vietnam

Shortly after Ho Chi Minh announced in 1945 the establishment of the Democratic Republic of Vietnam he launched an 'Appeal to Fight Illiteracy' based on a national romanised script together with the setting up of a Department of Education to plan and conduct the expansion of the school system. In 1945, the literacy rate was 14 per cent and by 1953, a period of only seven years, it had risen to 79 per cent. The success of the campaign was due to the social demand for literacy, and the introduction of the efficient and readily learned romanisation of the Vietnamese language (Wi-vun Taiffalo Chiung, 2002). Although Vietnam was divided into two zones until the end of the Second Indochina War in 1964 to 1975, literacy rates during this period declined only slightly. However, following the reunification of Vietnam and immediately after the termination of the War in 1975, the Vietnamese Government undertook a second mass literacy program in the late 1970s and the early 1980s that focused on the widespread development of adult literacy as well as the expansion of pre-school education and basic education, with a focus on literacy. The program raised the adult literacy rate in a little over ten years from below 75 per cent of the adult population to 86 per cent in 1990 (Bernard & LeTac Can, 1998). The literacy rate has continued to rise to 93 per cent in 2002 through the maintenance of strong national literacy policies and strategies (Vietnam, National Literacy Policies, 2002).

6.3. The Development of a Lifelong Learning System in Japan

A law was formally passed in 1990, which defined measures to develop lifelong learning programs that were planned by local communities. However, a report prepared in 1971 first mentioned the importance of lifelong learning. This imperative was taken up in a further report in 1981 that emphasised the: (a) importance of further education during adult life; (b) opening up of schools, junior colleges, technical colleges, and universities to adults; (c) promotion of so-called 'social education' that included both formal and nonformal educational activities; and (d) improvement of education for the training of workers (Miura, 1998).

In a subsequent report on educational reform in 1985–87, three central elements of further reform were recommended: (a) emphasising the idea of 'individuality' in education; (b) guaranteeing the transformation to a lifelong learning system; and (c) promoting widespread internationalisation and the use of new information media.

In addition, the term 'lifelong education' was changed to 'lifelong learning' to emphasise the idea of individuality and a learner centred approach. By 1990, 28 lifelong learning centres had been set up to develop adult learning programs by the boards of education of the prefectures. The major activities of these 'social education centres', as they were called, using the term 'social education' that was first introduced in 1949 and that implied systematic educational activities for adults and young people who were not in school, were: (a) training leaders who would be responsible for lifelong learning and social education activities in the municipalities; (b) undertaking surveys and research related to lifelong learning activities; (c) providing information and guidance on lifelong learning programs; and (d) providing innovative courses of various types. These lifelong learning centres were able to build on the extensive adult education programs that were linked with schools, colleges and universities, although most of these adult education programs did not give credit towards a qualification, the courses being undertaken for interest and for recreational purposes.

Japan also has an extensive lifelong employment system, with the major responsibility for continuing vocational training of workers resting with the enterprises that employ them. As a consequence, in commerce and industry there is little undertaking of further education for the purpose of obtaining a higher level of qualification and thus being in a position to change employment. Approximately one-third of the labour force is placed in a position each year of being required to participate in a training program. The Japanese Government has a very active role in the specification of training standards, the overseeing of specific vocational courses, providing certificates of qualification, and monitoring the courses through the conferring of qualifications, and the certification of the skills taught (Sako, 1998).

6.4. *A Multimedia Approach to Lifelong Learning in Korea*

In 1972, the Korea Air and Correspondence University was established as part of a lifelong learning system and the Korean Educational Development Institute (KEDI) was made responsible for undertaking research and development work to integrate the use of a variety of media into the education system at all levels. As a consequence of systematic planning and the effective use of multimedia materials, this research institute has been able to help Korea develop an education system that incorporates the use of television as a highly effective device for teaching in the distance mode. Moreover, the Korean education system has been able to overcome the many problems that are encountered in such work, by providing reliable equipment, developing meaningful curricular approaches, employing effective management procedures and using high quality production techniques which are based upon strong research studies, as well as the provision of appropriate feedback to those responsible for the production of multimedia and television materials. The strategy of linking the production of materials to the organisations responsible for curriculum development and the undertaking of research would appear to have yielded substantial benefits to the Korean education system (Se-Ho Shin, 1998).

In 1982, the Korean Government enacted the Adult and Nonformal Education Promotion Law that set out criteria for the recognition of institutes of nonformal education and their programs as holding parity with the formal educational institutions, of schools, colleges and universities. The nonformal and adult education programs have been classified into three kinds: (a) general and liberal education, (b) technical and occupational education, and (c) semiformal or recreational education. The institutions conducting the semiformal programs are referred to as 'para schools' and they do not require full-time and day-long attendance. There is a wide variety of para schools, including civic schools, trade schools, industry attached night schools, school attached night classes, correspondence schools, and open universities. Many of these institutions are privately conducted. In addition, privately run commercial institutes provide general and liberal education programs and occupational training programs as well as courses to assist individuals to make the best use of their leisure time.

7. MONITORING GROWTH OF LIFELONG EDUCATION PROGRAMS

Lifelong education programs are varied in their nature. They involve primarily nonformal and informal education, but also include some formal education courses conducted by both public and private organisations, as well as by employers and government and non-government agencies. In addition, lifelong education employs multimedia based and distance education courses, which involve television programs that make it very difficult to monitor the level of participation in the field. Furthermore, the courses that are conducted are not only part-time or do not provide a qualification, but they are also often short-term and run on an intermittent basis. These types of courses, while having highly desirable flexibility, present very considerable problems for the collection of accurate and meaningful statistics, particularly in large or developing countries such as are found in the Asia-Pacific region.

Initial steps were made during the International Adult Literacy Survey (IALS) (OECD/Statistics Canada, 1995) to collect information on the continuing education and training undertaken by adults. The information collected involved questioning adults on the incidence, duration and nature of their participation in lifelong learning or continuing education programs. The IALS background questionnaire sought information on:

Any participation in education or training that has taken place during the 12 months preceding the survey, specifically any training or education, including courses, private lessons, correspondence courses, workshops, on-the-job training, apprenticeship training, arts, crafts, recreation courses, or any other training or education. (OECD 1996, p. 204)

Three measures are recorded in Table 2. The 'participation rate' is the proportion of the adult population that has been engaged in any continuing education courses during the past 12-month period. The measure given by the 'mean number of hours per participant' relates to the intensity or the quantity of the training received, and is calculated as "the average of the total number of hours spent in the three most recent education courses/programmes taken" (OECD 1998, p. 204). The measure given by the 'mean number of hours per adult' records information on how many hours the typical adult person gives to lifelong education during a 12-month period. This measure is calculated by multiplying the mean number of hours for each participant by the participation rate. The data recorded were collected in the 1994–95 IALS in only two countries in the Asia-Pacific region.

Table 2 records information for Australia and New Zealand and for men and women separately, by four age bands, as well as the complete groups for the three measures: (a) participation rate, (b) mean number of hours per participant, and (c) mean number of hours per adult. In addition, this information is given for: (d) all education and training, and (e) job-related education and training.

The typical Australian person spent 60 hours each year on further education and training, while the typical New Zealand person spent half as much again, or 95 hours per year. On job-related education and training, the typical Australian person spent 45 hours per year, while the typical New Zealander spent nearly twice as much time, namely, 82 hours per year. In general, men spent more time on education and training than did women. Furthermore, in general, it was the youngest age group that spent most time, but women in the 35–44 age band were slightly more likely to engage in further education than younger women in the 25–34 age group, and men in the same 35–44 age band. However, this last relationship did not hold for job-related education and training. Moreover, both men and women in the 35–44 age group spent noticeably less time than their younger counterparts in both countries. As might, perhaps, be expected, the older age groups were less likely to participate in education and training (see *Enterprise Education in Australia and New Zealand*).

Whether such information could be assembled other than by survey methods is uncertain. However, it is clear that this type of information on participation rates in lifelong education programs, if collected systematically over time, would help to provide a greater understanding of the functions fulfilled by such programs, and would assist in the monitoring and growth of the fourth phase of education.

Table 2. Percentage of Australian and New Zealand adults participating in education and training, by age and sex in 1994–1995

		Australia			New Zealand		
		Men	Women	M+W	Men	Women	M+W
All education and training							
Participation rate (%)							
Age in years	25–34	46	38	42	59	47	53
	35–44	40	41	40	50	51	51
	45–54	33	32	32	40	49	45
	55–64	20	20	20	31	25	28
	All	37	34	36	48	45	46
Mean number of hours per participant (hrs)							
Age in years	25–34	201	200	201	307	297	302
	35–44	144	169	156	191	192	192
	45–54	150	160	155	103	108	106
	55–64	129	84	107	118	121	119
	All	165	170	167	212	197	204
Mean number of hours per adult (%)							
Age in years	25–34	93	77	85	182	139	159
	35–44	58	69	63	96	98	97
	45–54	49	51	50	41	53	48
	55–64	26	17	21	37	30	33
	All	61	58	60	102	89	95
Job related education and training							
Participation rate (%)							
Age in years	25–34	43	31	37	52	37	44
	35–44	38	33	36	47	39	43
	45–54	31	23	27	38	43	40
	55–64	17	9	13	24	12	18
	All	34	26	30	43	35	38
Mean number of hours per participant (hrs)							
Age in years	25–34	190	195	192	342	323	334
	35–44	136	133	134	172	204	188
	45–54	127	116	122	107	107	107
	55–64	82	57	74	134	82	115
	All	150	147	149	221	206	214
Mean number of hours per adult (%)							
Age in years	25–34	82	60	71	176	118	146
	35–44	52	44	48	80	79	80
	45–54	39	26	33	41	46	43
	55–64	14	5	10	33	10	21
	All	52	38	45	91	72	82

Source: OECD (1998, p. 204).

8. CONCLUSION

If the fourth phase of education referred to in this article in terms of 'lifelong learning and development' is to advance over the coming half-century, it seems likely that governments will need to pass legislation to promote and support the advances that are to be made. Both Japan and Korea, building on a high level of participation at the upper secondary school level, have made legislative arrangements to support lifelong learning and development as a further phase of education. However, these two countries have worked in different ways to achieve these ends, although both have relied extensively on private support for education. Australia and New Zealand, countries that are similarly placed with respect to levels of participation in education as Japan and Korea, rely heavily on public funding for the support of education and have not moved to pass similar legislation.

Japan has established social education centres to provide a stimulus to advance lifelong education, while Korea has made excellent use of television and distance education to raise levels of participation in nonformal and paraformal education, together with the establishment of para schools. In both countries, there is also evidence that these advances have been supported at least in part by research and development activity. However, it was in Australia and New Zealand that strong data were obtained to provide some measures of levels of participation. It is clear (see *Enterprise Education in Australia and New Zealand*) that both industry and commerce in these two countries are sharing with governmental agencies the tasks involved in providing for lifelong learning and development.

It is noted that there is a clearly evident place for lifelong learning programs in the developing countries as well as the more developed countries. The reports from the Philippines and Vietnam show this actively. However, it is only through research studies that the success of these advances in both the developed and developing countries, together with some monitoring of participation and performance that the fourth phase will develop to the full, to meet the different needs of the different countries in the region. It seems likely that with careful planning, the use of information and communications technology and the interactive use of computers will make a major contribution to advancing lifelong learning and development in the Asia-Pacific region. Nevertheless, it will only be through research and development studies of the highest quality, as the Korean experience has shown, that success in advancing lifelong learning and development will occur.

REFERENCES

Bernard, D. C., & Le Thac Can (1998). Vietnam: System of Education. In T. Husén et al. (Eds.), *Education: The Complete Encyclopedia*. Oxford: Pergamon Elsevier Science (CDROM).

Biggs, J. B., & Collis, K. F. (1982). *Evaluating the Quality of Learning: The SOLO Taxonomy*. New York: Academic Press.

Biggs, J. B., & Collis, K. F. (1989). Towards a model of school-based curriculum devlopment and assessment using the SOLO Taxonomy. *Australian Journal of Education, 33*, 149–161.

Bransford, J. D., Brown, A. L., & Cocking, R. R. (Eds.) (1999). *How People Learn: Brain, Mind, Experience and School.* Washington, DC: National Academy Press.

Carroll, J. B. (1993). *Human Cognitive Abilities.* Cambridge: Cambridge University Press.

Colletta, N. J. (1998). Formal, nonformal and informal education. In T. Husén et al. (Eds.), *Education: The Complete Encyclopedia.* Oxford: Pergamon Elsevier Science (CDROM).

Curtis, D. D., & Lawson, M. J. (2001). Exploring collaborative online learning. *Journal of Asynchronous Learning Networks, 5*(1), 21–34.

Desjardins, R., & Tuijnman, A. (in press). A general approach for using data in the comparative analysis of learning outcomes.

Finn, B. (Chair) (1991). *Young People's Participation in Post-compulsory Education and Training.* Report of the Australian Education Council Review Committee. Canberra: AGPS.

Gustafsson, J. E. (2001). Schooling and intelligence: Effects of lack of study on level and profile of cognitive abilities. *International Education Journal, 2*(4), 166–186.

Harvighurst, R. J. (1953). *Human Development and Education* (revised edition of *Developmental Tasks and Education*). New York: Longman.

Karmel, P. (Chair) (1985). *Quality of Education in Australia.* Report of the Quality of Education Review Committee. Canberra: AGPS.

Maroske, M., & Smith, J. (1998). Development of Competence: Toward a Taxonomy. In T. Husén, et al. (Eds.), *Education: The Complete Encyclopedia.* Oxford: Pergamon, Elsevier Science (CDROM).

Mayer Committee (1992). *Putting General Education to Work: The Key Competencies Report.* Melbourne: The Australian Education Council.

Miura, S. (1998). Japan: Adult education and training. In T. Husén et al. (Eds.), *Education: The Complete Encyclopedia.* Oxford: Pergamon Elsevier Science (CDROM).

New Zealand Qualifications Authority (1991). *A Qualifications Framework for New Zealand.* Wellington: The Authority.

OECD (2002). *Understanding the Brain – Towards a New Learning Science.* Paris: OECD.

OECD/Statistics Canada (1995). *Literacy, Economy and Society. Results of the First International Adult Literacy Survey.* Paris: OECD.

Organisation for Economic Cooperation and Development (OECD) (1996). *Lifelong Learning for All.* Paris: OECD.

Piaget, J., & Inhelder, B. (1956). *The Child's Construction of Space.* London: Routledge and Kegan Paul.

Piaget, J., & Inhelder, B. (1974). *The Child's Construction of Quantities.* London: Routledge and Kegan Paul.

Rychen, D. S., & Salganik, L. H. (Eds.) (2001). *Defining and Selecting Key Competencies.* Göttengen, Germany: Hogrefe and Huber.

Sako, M. (1998). Japan: Vocational education and training. In T. Husén et al. (Eds.), *Education: The Complete Encyclopedia.* Oxford: Pergamon Elsevier Science (CDROM).

Shayer, M., & Adey, P. (2002). *Learning Intelligence: Cognitive Acceleration Across the Curriculum from 5 to 15 Years.* Buckingham: Open University Press.

Se-Ho Shin (1998). Republic of Korea: System of Education. In T. Husén et al. (Eds.), *Education: The Complete Encyclopedia.* Oxford: Pergamon Elsevier Science (CDROM).

Spearritt, D. (1996). Carroll's model of cognitive abilities: Educational implications. *International Journal of Educational Research, 25*(2).

Sweller, J. (1999). *Instructional Design, Australian Educational Review No. 43.* Melbourne: ACER.

Tuijnman, A. C., Kirsch, I., & Wagner, D. A. (Eds.) (1995). *Adult Basic Skills: Advances in Measurement and Policy Analysis.* New York: Hampton Press.

Vietnam (2002). National Literacy Policies (on line). http://www.accu.or.jp/litdbase/policy/vnm/index.htm

Wi-vun Taiffalo Chiung (2002). Language, literacy and power: A Comparative Study of Taiwan and Vietnam (on line). http://ling.uta.edu/~taiffalo/chuliau/lunsoat/english/hansphere/hansphere-v.pdf

23

Workforce Education

DAVID N WILSON
Ontario Institute for Studies in Education, Toronto, Canada

1. INTRODUCTION

Workforce education comprises several different components: (a) initial or pre-employment education and training, (b) on-the-job or in-service education and training, including skill upgrading, and (c) re-training for job change for both employed and unemployed. Some sources include literacy as an adjunct to workplace skills training (Taylor, 1997, p. viii).

The on-the-job training (OJT) components of workforce education differ from pre-employment education in many respects and most research on aspects of workforce education focuses upon issues relating pre-service education and training to labour market requirements. Since workforce education concerns issues of occupational training and re-training, often for new occupations, it also relates to continuing education and lifelong learning. In marked contrast to research on pre-employment education (i.e., elementary, secondary and post-secondary), research on workforce education has been called considerably more 'economicentric'. That is, issues of economic development, return on investment, labour force productivity, and skills training needs have predominated. Moreover, it is unfortunate that much workforce education research has been what is termed 'fugitive literature' because many research reports do not receive widespread circulation. Fugitive literature refers to un-circulated, or limited-circulation publications, such as government documents, reports, research reports, unpublished papers, conference papers and theses.

Workforce education, also referred to as Technical-Vocational Education and Training (TVET) or Vocational Education and Training (VET), is defined as:

> That form of pedagogy that is provided ... by educational institutions, by private business and industry, or by government-sponsored, community-based organizations where the objective is to increase individual opportunity in the labor market or to solve human performance problems in the workplace. (Gray & Herr, 1998, p. 4)

Gray and Herr also note "workforce education differs from general education" because the "outcome goals" of general education "are independent of employment." "Learning to read, for example is general education. Learning how to solve a simple algebraic equation is general education; learning how to use Ohm's law in electrical work is workforce education." (*Ibid.*) That is, workforce education is focused upon the application of learning to the requirements of the workplace.

The terms 'education' and 'training' also require clarification in order to establish the context for this article. The goal of education has been "to create independent problem solvers [with] sufficient depth of understanding." In contrast, the goal of training has traditionally been "to teach people to follow prescribed procedures and to perform in a standardized manner" (Gray & Herr, 1998, p. 159). In the changing world of work it appears that these two, formerly distinct, perspectives are converging (Wilson, 2001, p. 232).

2. GLOBAL INFLUENCES

The importance of workforce education has increased during the past two decades, due to the challenges posed by globalisation and rapid technological change. Workplace change necessitates continuing training, or re-training and information has taken on increasing importance in the workplace. During a person's lifetime, it is projected that occupations and careers will change several times; each change necessitates new learning. Globalisation refers to:

> A process that widens the extent and form of cross-border transactions among peoples' assets, goods and services and that deepens the economic interdependence between and among globalizing entities, which may be private or public institutions or governments. (Lubbers, 1998, p. 1)

Rapid technological change has resulted from the neo-technic revolution, or the conscious creation of new technology through institutional research and development (Mumford, 1970). The changing nature of work, particularly in higher technologies, means that many workers increasingly operate in what is called a 'mechatronic environment' where they work with highly precise mechanical equipment operating under electrical power and controlled by electronic devices, often commanded by means of sophisticated computer programs. The multiple skills and cross-training, or training in more than one skill area, required by this new mechatronic environment have significant implications for the transformation of the workplace and particularly for the skills, attitudes and knowledge required to operate globally (Wilson, 2001, p. 237). Taylor suggests that "as technological change creates new skills and reroutes the flow of information, basic skills training is now being viewed as a critical force in the learning panorama" (Taylor, 1997, p. viii).

Another result of globalisation and technological change has been the upward differentiation of pre-service workforce education from the secondary school to the post-secondary level. In Asia, this trend was first evident in post-war Japan, and led to the growth of upper-secondary Special Training Schools, in agriculture, industry, business, fishery, home economics, nursing, and post-secondary Junior Colleges and Colleges of Technology (Monbusho, 1999, p. 1). As nations like Indonesia and Malaysia achieve development plan targets for the provision of nine years of basic education, enrolment in secondary-level workforce education programs increases proportionately, and this in-turn drives the expansion of post-secondary workforce education programs housed in Polytechnics (Wilson, 1991, p. 216).

3. THE ASIA-PACIFIC REGION

One difficulty facing a survey of research on workforce education in the Asia-Pacific region is the broad variety of constituent nations and the different stages of their cultural, political, economic and educational development. This writer and colleagues faced these dilemmas while producing the first Education Sector Policy document for the Asian Development Bank in 1988. However, what was surprising was the remarkable similarity of workforce education policies and practices among nations with quite diverse political and economic systems (Wilson et al., 1988). These similarities may have been due to the close relationship between workplace education and technology, or possibly to the earlier impact of globalisation.

The World Bank has classified client nations in the region into three groups according to their income level and ranking in the Human Development Report Education Index. These groups are:

(a) very low income countries with poorly educated populations (e.g., Cambodia, and Lao PDR);
(b) poor countries with relatively good educational outcomes (e.g., China, Vietnam, Indonesia and the Philippines);
(c) relatively wealthy countries with comparatively well educated populations (e.g., Thailand, Malaysia and Republic of Korea). (World Bank, 1999, p. 2)

The published research on topics in workforce education is skewed in favour of developed nations. Wonacott (2000, p. 2) observed "comprehensive [vocational education] research programs in the United States, Europe and Australia have different emphases". Further, the majority of published workforce education research has been in the United States, Europe and Australia. However, some studies of workforce education and related topics have been published in Japan, Singapore, Hong Kong, Korea and Taiwan. In addition, The World Bank and The International Labour Organisation (ILO) have made some studies available on their web pages. Many unpublished and limited-circulation studies have been undertaken in India, Indonesia, Thailand, Philippines, Malaysia, and other Asian nations by universities, governments and international organizations. The following brief examination of several research themes provides an indication of previous workforce education research in the region.

4. RESEARCH THEMES

The foremost theme in workforce education research "seeks to answer in one form or another [the] fundamental question: How can we best prepare youth and adults for the workplace?" (Wonacott, 2000, p. 1). "Recurring themes in the United States" examine "what skills workers need for the changing workplace and how vocational education should provide them?" (*Ibid.*). Wonacott also notes "in Europe and Australia, attention is focused more on the impact of research on policy, decision making, and return on investment" (*Ibid.*).

One current Australian study is focused upon the identification of "the capacity of existing data collections to provide nationally comparable information on the cross-sectoral dimensions of post-compulsory education and training" (Pope, 1999, p. 2). Similar problems of comparable cross-national data have long constrained studies in Comparative Education. The contribution of this type of study to comparative studies of workforce education is quite important.

The theme of 'institutional transfer' has been employed to study the transfer and replication of both educational and industrial institutions from developed to developing nations. In an examination of early Colombo Plan aid to workforce education in Singapore and Malaysia, this writer found that the need for trained workers by Singaporean industries validated the effective utilization of TVET institutions developed by Australia, Canada and the United Kingdom from the 1950s under the Colombo Plan. Many innovations and TVET practices transferred by those projects had become part and parcel of training infrastructure by the 1980s (Wilson, 1981).

Similarly, Koike and Inoke studied the transferability of Japanese industry and its training practices to Malaysia and Thailand in 1990. The skill formation systems in the cement, automobile battery, machine tool, and banking industries in Thailand and Malaysia were compared with training systems in Japan. They found similar patterns of skill formation in on-the-job training (OJT) systems, but differences in the breadth and depth of experience and variability in worker productivity. The transferability of Japanese systems to other countries was also examined and it was recommended that OJT be included in programs of technical co-operation and "management techniques to encourage career formation need to be transferred" (Koike & Inoki 1990, p. 30).

Several descriptive comparative studies focused upon themes, including continuity and change, education and political transition in East Asia, have been published by the Comparative Education Research Centre (CERC) at The University of Hong Kong, and include some chapters that concern workforce education. A descriptive chapter on "Education and the Labour Force" in Macau and Hong Kong by Ma (1999) relates workforce development to economic restructuring and human resource development. Another descriptive chapter on 'Democracy, Education and Reform in Mongolia: Transition to a New Order' by Innes-Brown (2001) describes the development of upper-secondary school TVET during the transition from a planned command economy to a market economy.

The Comparative Education Research Centre has also published a joint study with the Asian Development Bank of educational finance in Indonesia. This study includes a valuable comparison of "Indonesia's level of educational expenditure with levels in other Asian nations" (Bray & Thomas, 1998, p. 48). The chapter on 'School-Level Spending' includes a brief section on Vocational Secondary Schools, indicating that "public vocational schools spent three times as much per student as did private schools," which suggests one indicator of workforce education quality.

Economists have produced many rate-of-return (RoR) studies to justify investment in various types of education and training. However, this writer was dismayed that one 1988 RoR study in Indonesia was used to recommend the reversal of the policy to invest in TVET at precisely the point when the STM (*Sekolah Teknik Menengah*) senior secondary technical schools were beginning to make an impact upon the modernizing labour force. An examination found that there had been four previous RoR studies, comparing academic secondary (SMA) to STM graduates, and that the students' lifetime earnings differentials had narrowed to about ten per cent. In view of the likely margin of error for RoR studies, it was suggested that there was little basis for recommendation of such a major policy change (Wilson, 1990). The fact that Indonesian public secondary workforce education in STMs was 50 per cent more expensive than academic secondary education (Dar & Gill, 1999c, p. 2) also biases RoR studies against workforce education.

Hossain provides comparative findings from China indicating "calculations from the 1993 Labor Force Survey data yield very low private rates of return to vocational and technical education, 5 and 9.9 per cent respectively," which he also ascribes "to high unit costs" Hossain (1996, p. 16). On the other hand, research exploring the "social rates of return to planning, or benefits from training, has been understated" (Allen & Kilpatrick, 2001, p. 1).

Employer demand for a skilled and educated workforce has universally formed the basis for manpower surveys in nearly every nation. In most cases, however, such studies are rarely published or circulated. Lewis noted that in Singapore "the demands by employers for more highly skilled labour has meant an expansion of the education system, particularly at the tertiary level, but also increased provision of on-the-job training" (Lewis, 1995, p. 159).

Workforce education development in Singapore has been closely related to economic development policies, beginning with the transition from an *entrepôt* trading economy at independence, to development of import substitution industries in the 1960s, to "increasing export orientation and low value-added manufacturing" in the 1970s, to the development of technology-intensive, high-value-added manufacturing in the 1980s, and then "developing Singapore into an international financial center" in the 1990s (Lewis, 1995, p. 160). This writer noted that Singapore had reformed its education and training systems four times in four decades in concert with its economic development policies (Wilson, 1991). Low (1998) argues that these reforms have given Singapore:

> quite a headstart over other countries (p. 31);
>
> revamping the education system to gear more toward science and technology saw the rapid expansion of new courses and curricula in universities, polytechnics and schools (p28); and
>
> a crucial factor in Singapore's competitiveness lies in its educated and skilled manpower (p. 30).

The Singaporean workforce education experience has been utilised by other Asian and Pacific countries, often in symposia sponsored by the International Labour Organisation. One example of such fugitive reports examined new trends in skill training for employer groups from the region. Pillay indicated that emerging workforce education and training needs included the following skills packages.

> The technical worker's 'skills package' is increasingly perceived by companies as not just for current competence, but for the next and next job.
>
> As productivity becomes the criterion, the 'skills package' itself becomes increasingly composite. One component comprises cognitive skills, attitudes and personal abilities. The second concerns technical knowledge and skills, both generic and company specific. The third component comprises work skills.
>
> To achieve a holistic result, the training of a technical worker has to be personalised. And it has to be 'mentored.' What applied to top management has to be institutionalised for the technical worker as his or her value-added grows. (Pillay, 1992, p. 24)

It needs to be stressed that there are many factors and forces that impact upon workforce education. Among such factors are economic constraints and international agency initiatives. Kioh Jeong explored one such initiative, structural adjustment, in a study of "the harmonious structural adjustment necessary for revitalizing the Korean economy" (Kioh Jeong, 1999, p. 90). The impact of International Monetary Fund structural adjustment policies upon the reform of Korean workforce education was described as a "struggle in the system between market demand and institutionalized practices in education" because "vocational education is always dominated by market motives for change" and this was in conflict "with the institutionalized rules and ideas that form the backbone of the education system" (*Ibid.*, p. 91). It was concluded "the economic crisis in Korea has influenced reform in both positive and negative directions" by strengthening "the motivation to reform vocational education again and weakened the institutionalized constraints on reform" (*Ibid.*, p. 103). It was also concluded that workforce education "appeared to be successful when it served a small percentage of the school-age group to satisfy market forces," but "it began to fail once it became a fundamental part of the universal upper-secondary education" due to workforce education entailing "more profound Western values and approaches than academic education" because workforce education "is a transplant from Western civilization" (*Ibid.*, p. 104).

Many nations have undertaken tracer studies of their secondary and post-secondary TVET graduates in order to document their transition from school to work. Unfortunately, most tracer studies have become fugitive literature when their findings were not widely disseminated. These studies examine the occupational search patterns, employment experience, relationships between training and employment, promotion record and job changes experienced by former graduates. The findings are used to plan reforms of workforce education systems and institutions in order to improve the school-to-work transition for future students. One nationwide tracer study compared employment outcomes of academic and vocational secondary education in Indonesia (Clark, 1983). In a related type of research, Singapore appears to be the only nation to trace its highly-educated emigrants (Lewis, 1995, p. 165).

The World Bank and Asian Development Bank (ADB) have undertaken sector studies in a number of Asian and Pacific countries, but only a few have addressed workforce education issues. Among these are the *Bangladesh: Vocational and Technical Education Review* (World Bank, 1990), and three *Sector Studies* in Indonesia (Wilson et al., 1984, 1989; Wilson, 1992) undertaken by this writer and colleagues. As is useful in a good comparative study, it is essential that a study of workforce education be grounded by a comprehensive description of the entire education system. The World Bank highlighted the "need to do more sector work in order to lay a foundation for future lending and to improve the quality of projects" (World Bank, 1999, p. 8).

The World Bank and the International Labour Organisation (ILO) have undertaken a multi-national study on Constraints and Innovations in the Reform of VET. This meta-research study draws from fugitive studies to evaluate the performance of training institutions. The Malaysia country study included a 1992 tracer study and a 1994 survey of manufacturing enterprises (Dar & Gill, 1999a).

> A 1992 survey of over 4,000 individuals who took trade tests administered by the National Vocational Training Council found that graduates of private institutes are most likely to find work ... [those from] private institutes are likely to get higher starting pay, and are most likely to find jobs in areas in which they were trained.

> A 1994 survey of 2,200 manufacturing firms showed that a high fraction of firms either provide their workers with no training, or rely exclusively on informal on-the-job training.

Most firms either meet their skill needs in-house or through private providers. Public training institutions play a relatively minor role in meeting the in-service training needs of private firms. Of the 21 percent of employers that train formally about an equal proportion use in-house resources as they do external training providers. The most common external sources are private training institutes, skill development centers, and advanced skills training institutes.

A higher proportion of technicians and supervisors (about 30 percent) are trained as compared to production workers (about 15 percent). (Dar & Gill, 1999a, p. 2)

The ILO and World Bank study synthesis of findings indicates that China enrols 52 per cent of the secondary school age cohort and that 55 per cent of these 15.3 million students are enrolled in TVET institutions. Indonesia is noted to enrol 43 per cent of its secondary school age cohort and that 33 per cent of these 4.1 million students are enrolled in TVET institutions. Malaysia is noted to enrol 59 per cent of its secondary school age cohort and that 11 per cent of the 533,000 students are enrolled in TVET institutions. Finally, Korea is noted to enrol 93 per cent of its secondary school age cohort and that 39 per cent of these 2.1 million students are enrolled in TVET institutions (Dar & Gill, 1999b, p. 5).

Haas examined trends in what is termed 'articulation agreements', or pathways allowing graduates of one course of study to progress to another, in TVET in Australia, Indonesia, Malaysia, Philippines, Singapore and Thailand. It was found that "articulation pathways for technical and vocational education course graduates were evident in all countries ... though such provision varied significantly from extensive linkages between TVE and higher education, through to quite limited opportunities for articulation" (Haas, 1998, p. 35). This confirmed earlier findings (Wilson, 1991, p. 216) in Malaysia and Indonesia.

Case studies of three types of secondary workforce education institutions in China examined the relationships among labour market factors, institutional management and employment of graduates (Noah & Middleton, 1988). A rate of return(RoR) study in China indicated that returns to education in centrally-planned command economies were "usually low ... but they tend to increase as market reforms take place" (Jamison & van der Gaag, 1987). A similar examination of RoR in Vietnam (Moock et al., 1998) studied the "early stages of transition" and found that "returns to schooling" were "low by international standards." Among the reasons cited were that secondary and higher education graduates had been assigned employment in the public sector prior to the policy of *Doi Moi*, or economic reform. In addition, "over 80 per cent of the Vietnamese labor force [were] self-employed and many [had] multiple jobs" (Moock et al., 1998, p. 22). The World Bank stressed that "countries in transition from a centrally planned to a market economy present a unique set of challenges" (World Bank, 1999, p. 5).

Needs assessment studies have produced valuable data for the planning of workforce education programs and institutions, but also are of limited circulation. One published study in Taiwan used large-scale survey data to analyse the extent of training in enterprises and identify factors relevant to the training efforts made by those enterprises (San, 1990).

Other important research themes include the 'school-to-work transition', which was studied by Hawley (1997) in Thailand. Although Thailand had no "established formal system of linkages between employers and schools," there were "many experimental programs" which Hawley (1997, p. 7) classified as school-to-work for adults. These included equivalency programs for workers in the garment, toy industry, fish-processing, and food-processing industries sponsored by the Department of Nonformal Education of the Thai Ministry of Education. Hawley also examined "the networks that individuals use to find work." His study found that "the government plays only a small role in structuring the school-to-work linkages for adults" but that "businesses are more active." In addition, although "teachers play no role in helping adults get jobs ... businesses have many informal recruiting mechanisms" and "families and communities play a role in connecting workers and employers." It was also found that "as the number of industry and service sector jobs are increasing, factories are demanding more secondary education graduates." However, since "Thailand has a small percentage of secondary education graduates in its labor force," employers are interested in nonformal programs that upgrade workers' qualifications (Hawley, 1997, p. 7). Finally, an innovative study by Burapharat (2001) examined the transfer of the Western and Japanese concepts of teamwork to Thai industries. She found that team co-operation became grafted upon traditional Thai notions of 'elder brother' and 'little sister.'

5. DESCRIPTIONS AND COMPARISONS OF WORKFORCE EDUCATION SYSTEMS

A considerable number of publications provide descriptions of national workforce education systems and institutions. This writer considers such descriptive studies to constitute comparative studies, since they engender comparisons 'in the mind of the reader' with their own systems and, thus, foster reform, change, and development. For example, the Technical and Vocational Education Research Centre at the National Taiwan Normal University has published reports and articles on secondary school vocational education reforms (Rau et al., 1996, p. 1).

The People's Republic of China produced a study of the development and reform of vocational education for the UNESCO Second International Conference on Technical and Vocational Education in 1999. It was stressed that reform and development has taken place "in parallel with ... reforms in the economic structure." Reforms in workplace education took place at the elementary and secondary levels while "a policy of moderate expansion ... with emphasis

... on the enhancement of quality and effectiveness" took place at the post-secondary level (Sedc, 1999, p. 2).

One exemplary description of the Singapore Institute of Technical Education (ITE), formerly The Vocational and Industrial Training Board (VITB), is included in order to provide the reader with a model worthy of emulation.

> The ITE is an integral part of Singapore's education and training system. As a post-secondary technical institution, its primary function is to provide vocational and technical training for school leavers who have received ten years of general education.
>
> A second primary function of ITE is to provide worker education and training opportunities for working adults through a comprehensive system of Continuing Education and Training (CET) programs.
>
> The CET programs are broadly grouped as Worker Education, Skills Training, and Industry-Based Training. Each category of programming meets different training needs of workers in Singapore.
>
> Worker Education programs allow adults to continue their academic education up to secondary levels. These include the Basic Education for Skills Training (BEST), Worker Improvement through Secondary Education (WISE), and Continuing Education (CE) programs. Skills Training programs provide opportunities for adults to learn new skills or update current skills. The first of these programs offered was the Modular Skills Training (MOST) program. Over the years, ITE has introduced additional Skills Training programs, including the Training Initiative for Mature Employees (TIME) and Adult Cooperative Training Scheme (ACTS), each targeted at different groups of adult workers. ITE launched its latest initiative, the Certified On-the-Job Training Centre (COJTC) System, an Industry-Based Training Program ... to expand training opportunities in the workplace. (Law & Low, 1997, p. 120)

Other writers have focused upon workforce upgrading programs in selected Asian nations, also in a descriptive and analytical manner. One such example is Lee's (1997) study of lifelong learning, workforce development and economic success.

> The shift from a low skilled labour market orientation towards highly skilled knowledge workers is growing at a dramatic rate in many economies. Hong Kong and Chinese Taipei are examples of this trend. Three decades earlier, these economies were characterized by low level technical production and manufacturing. Now, Hong Kong has established itself as a centre for business and finance, developing plants and production activities in the P.R.C. During this same period Chinese Taipei has generated an enviable reputation in the field of information technology, both in manufacturing and research and development. (Lee, 1997, p. 305)

Comparative studies of workforce education in two or more nations are rare, as this writer indicated in *The International Encyclopedia of Education* (Wilson, 1994, p. 6263). Workforce education reform in Malaysia and Indonesia was compared. The two systems were similar in their provision of Universal Primary Education and nine years of Basic Education, as well as providing access to post-secondary TVET by graduates of secondary TVET. However, the systems differed in the proportion of secondary TVET enrolment: 10.3 per cent in STM in Indonesia and only 1.6 per cent in Secondary Vocational School (SVS) in Malaysia and the virtual absence of private institutions. While Malaysian SVS graduates sat the SVPM examination, which is equivalent to the academic examinations, and had access to polytechnics for many years, Indonesia only enabled access to polytechnics by STM graduates in the 1980s (Wilson, 1991, p. 216).

A recent comparative study of adult retraining and re-skilling in Australia and Korea was undertaken by The Australian National Centre for Vocational Education Research (NCVER) and the Korea Research Institute for Vocational Education and Training (KRIVET). While acknowledging the differences between both nations, their similarities were noted to include "responses to economic change," due to changes "in the growth of employment in the service sector and changes in the nature of work." It was concluded that "the vocational education and training systems in both countries need to be responsive to economic change ... [and] ... need to give more attention to adult retraining and reskilling as the proportion of young people in the working age population declines." The study was unique in identifying implications from the experience of both nations and noting areas where they could learn from each other (Ball et al., 2001, p. 88).

6. SUGGESTED FUTURE WORKFORCE EDUCATION RESEARCH

The Australian National Centre for Vocational Education Research (NCVER) examined factors influencing demand for VET courses and identified several areas for further research. While research has identified

> the influence of economic factors, such as income and profit or productivity on demand ... there is no systematic research into the impact of the price of VET on demand by various client groups on particular enterprises and individuals ... Further research is needed into the relative cost of modes of provision, and whether the preferred unit of analysis should be cost per trainee, per module, or per course completed. ... research is needed into the desirable balance between general and job-specific education and training. (Allen & Kilpatrick, 2001, p. 3)

Low found that there was need to investigate

> the missing parameters ... to link jobs, skills and technology include education attainment and skills of workers by more detailed industrial classification, impact of size of firms as affecting skills upgrading, technology content of exports and imports, contribution of technology to productivity. (Low, 1998, p. 32)

World Bank researchers suggest "the first priority on the research agenda ... should be ... studies that evaluate training outcomes in the context of economic and institutional factors." This economicentric approach is taken "to understand the effect on the demand for labor and skills that results from the interactions between different trade, industrial and labor policies on the one hand and technological change on the other." It is also asserted that "policymakers and training managers need to know more about how training institutions acquire and use signals to guide training supply." In addition, "more attention should be given to identifying and estimating training externalities and to evaluating various forms of subsidy programs" (Middleton et al., 1993, p. 293-294).

This brief survey of available workforce education research in Asia-Pacific region has identified salient research themes, suggested research issues and questions, and indicated important research findings. It would be desirable to develop a research agenda that indicates: (a) what is known and generally agreed upon; (b) what is known and not generally agreed upon; and (c) what remains to be learned from future research.

REFERENCES

Allen, K., & Kilpatrick, S. (2001). *Factors Influencing Demand for Vocational Education and Training Courses: Review of Research.* Adelaide: National Centre for Vocational Education Research (NCVER).

Ball, K., Lee, Y.-H., Oanh Phan, & Ra, Y.-S. (2001). *Adult Retraining and Reskilling in Australia and South Korea.* Adelaide: NCVER and Korea Research Institute for Vocational Education and Training (KRIVET).

Bray, M., & Thomas, R. M. (1998). *Financing of Education in Indonesia.* Manila: Asian Development Bank and Comparative Education Research Centre, University of Hong Kong.

Burapharat, Chitrlada (2001). The Importance of Sibling Relationships in Developing an Authentic Setting in Thai Teams, Paper delivered at the Fifth International Workshop on Team Working (IWOT5), Catholic University, Leuven, Belgium, 10 September 2001.

Clark, D. A. (1983). *How Secondary School Graduates Perform in the Labor Market: A Study of Indonesia.* Washington: World Bank Working Paper No. 615.

Dar, A., & Gill, I. (1999a). *Malaysia: Meeting the Demand for Skilled Workers in a Rapidly Growing Economy.* Washington: World Bank and ILO.

Dar, A., & Gill, I. (1999b). *Skills and Change: A Synthesis of Findings of a Multi-Country Study of Vocational Education and Training Reforms.* Washington: World Bank and ILO.

Dar, A., & Gill, I. (1999c). *Vocational Education and Training in Indonesia.* Washington: World Bank and ILO.

Gill, I., & Fluitman, F. (1999). *Skills and Change: Constraints and Innovation in the Reform of Vocational Education and Training.* Washington: World Bank and ILO.

Gray, K. C., & Herr, E. (1998). *Workforce Education: The Basics.* Toronto: Allyn and Bacon.
Haas, A (1998). *Trends in Articulation Arrangements for Technical and Vocational Education in the South East Asian Region.* Melbourne: RMIT and UNEVOC.
Hawley, J. (1997). Finding a Job, Leading a Life: The School to Work Transition in Thailand. Paper presented at the Comparative and International Education Society Conference, Mexico City, Mexico.
Hossain, S. I. (1996). Making an equitable and efficient education: The Chinese experience, In *China: Social Sector Expenditure Review, 1996.* Washington: World Bank.
Innes-Brown, M. (2001). Democracy, education and reform in Mongolia: Transition to a new order. In M. Bray and W. O. Lee (Eds.), *Education and Political Transition: Themes and Experiences in East Asia* (pp. 77–99). Hong Kong: Comparative Education Research Centre, University of Hong Kong.
Jamison, D. T., & van der Gaag, J. (1987). Education and earnings in the People's Republic of China. *Economics of Education Review,* 6(2), 161–166.
Kioh Jeong (1999). Structural adjustment and vocational education in the Republic of Korea: The struggle between markets and the institutionalized system. *Prospects,* 29(1), 89–104.
Koike, K., & Inoki, T. (Eds.) (1990). *Skill Formation in Japan and Southeast Asia.* Tokyo: University of Tokyo Press.
Law, S. S., & Low, S. H. (1997). An empirical framework for implementing lifelong learning systems. In M. I. Hatton (Ed.), *Lifelong Learning: Policies, Practices and Programs.* (pp. 112–127) Toronto: Asia-Pacific Economic Cooperation and Humber College.
Lee, A. (1997). Lifelong learning, workforce development and economic success. In M. I. Hatton, *op. cit.* (pp. 302–315).
Lewis, P. E. T. (1995). Singaporean demand for education. In F. Ferrier & C. Selby Smith (Eds.), *The Economics of Education and Training 1995.* Canberra: Monash University Centre for the Economics of Education and Training.
Low, L. (1998). *Jobs, Technology and Skill Requirements in a Globalized Economy: Country Study on Singapore.* Geneva: ILO Employment and Training Papers, No. 13, www.ilo.org
Ma, H. T. W. (1999). Education and the labour force, In M. Bray & Ramsey Koo (Eds.), *Education and Society in Hong Kong and Macau: Comparative Perspectives on Continuity and Change* (pp. 117–132). Hong Kong: Comparative Education Research Centre, University of Hong Kong.
Middleton, J., Ziderman, A., & van Adams, A. (1993). *Skills for Productivity: Vocational Education and Training in Developing Countries.* New York: Oxford University Press.
Monbusho (Ministry of Education, Science, Sports and Culture) (1999). *An Introduction to Specialized Upper Secondary Schools.* Tokyo: Vocational Education Division, Elementary and Secondary Education Bureau, Monbusho.
Moock, P. R., Patrinos, H. A., & Venkataraman, M. (1998). Education and Earnings in a Transition Economy: The Case of Vietnam. Washington: The World Bank (mimeographed).
Mumford, L. (1970). *The Myth of the Machine: The Pentagon of Power.* New York: Harcourt, Brace, Jovanovich.
Noah, H., & Middleton, J. (1988). *China's Vocational and Technical Training.* Washington: World Bank WPS 18.
Pope, B. (1999). An Analysis of Data on Cross-Sector Student Pathways in Post-Compulsory Education and Training. Canberra: NCVER www.ncver.edu.au
Pillay, G. (1992). *New Trends in Skill Training.* Yogyakarta: South East Asia and Pacific Employers' Symposium.
Rau, D., Lin, T. C., Dai, C. Y., & Hsu, H. G. (1996). The Current Reform of Vocational Education Program for Secondary School in Taiwan. Paper delivered at the Comparative Education Society of Asia Conference, Waseda University, Tokyo, Japan.
San, G. (1990). Enterprise training in Taiwan: Results from the vocational training needs survey. *Economics of Education Review,* 9(4), 411–418.
Singh, Madhu (1998). *School Enterprises: Combining Vocational Learning with Production.* Berlin: UNEVOC.

State Education Commission [Sedc] (1999). *Development and Reform of Vocational Education in the People's Republic of China*. Beijing: Ministry of Education, People's Republic of China

Taylor, M. (1997). *Workplace Education: The Changing Landscape*. Ottawa: Culture Concepts.

Wilson, D. N. (1981). *Education and Occupational Training in Singapore and Malaysia*. Toronto: Ontario Institute for Studies in Education.

Wilson, D. N. (1990). The Deleterious Impact of Rate-of-Return Studies on LDC Education Policies: An Indonesian Case. *Canadian and International Education*, 19(1), 32–49.

Wilson, D. N. (1991). Reform of Technical-Vocational Education in Indonesia and Malaysia. *Comparative Education*, 27(2), 207–221.

Wilson, D. N. (1992). *Indonesia: Sector Study on Education*. Manila: Asian Development Bank.

Wilson, D. N. (1994). Comparative and international studies in technical-vocational education, In T. Husén & T. N. Postlethwaite (Eds.), *International Encyclopedia of Education* (second edition) (Vol. 11, pp. 6261–6266). Oxford: Pergamon Press.

Wilson, D. N. (2001). Technical-vocational education and training, In D., & A. Poonwassie (Eds.), *Fundamentals of Adult Education* (pp. 232–245). Toronto: Thompson Educational Publishing.

Wilson, D. N., & Pernia, E. (1989). *Education and Labor Markets in Indonesia: A Sector Survey*. Manila: Asian Development Bank Economic Staff Paper No. 45.

Wilson, D. N., Teschner, W., & Daroesman, R. (1984). *Indonesia: Sector Study on Education*. Manila: Asian Development Bank.

Wilson, D. N., Teschner, W., & Gorham, A. (1988). *Education and Development in Asia and the Pacific*. Manila: Asian Development Bank.

Wonacott, M. E. (2000). *Vocational Education Research Trends*. Columbus: ERIC Clearinghouse on Adult, Career, and Vocational Education, Trends and Issues Alert, No. 15.

World Bank (1990). *Bangladesh Vocational and Technical Education Review*. Washington: World Bank.

World Bank (1999). *Education and Training in the East Asia and Pacific Region*. Washington: World Bank, Education Sector Unit, East Asia and Pacific Region.

24

Nonformal Education

STEVE WILSON and MONA SHRESTHA
University of Western Sydney, Australia

1. INTRODUCTION

Nonformal education (NFE) has been integral to education in the Asia-Pacific region in the post colonial period. It has been embedded in social development projects, where its practice has been heavily influenced by educational activists such as Freire. NFE currently sits alongside formal education systems within many developing countries, and serves in many cases as the only form of education available to adults and children. This paper examines research in NFE in the Asia Pacific. It examines definitions of NFE employed in the region and overviews the nature of the research field. It reviews the contexts in which NFE exits, and examines some models of NFE. Finally, it examines key issues identified in current NFE literature, including equity in rural education, female participation and empowerment, literacy education, and state priorities and control. It concludes by overviewing possible research directions for the field.

While NFE has a long history of being embedded in emancipatory and social capital projects in the Asia-Pacific region (Ekanayaka, 1978; Guttman & Kosonen, 1994; Haque, 1975; UNESCO, 1981), this paper addresses contemporary (generally post 1995) literature. It does not address work based learning as a component of NFE, as this is treated elsewhere in this volume.

2. DEFINITIONS OF NONFORMAL EDUCATION

Nonformal education is defined in a variety of ways in the research, ranging from instrumental definitions to those which link NFE with deeper social or ideological movements. Robinson (1999) comments that projects and programs implemented under the label of NFE are very diverse. She suggests that defining NFE is problematic, as over time NFE has been described variously as an educational movement, a setting, a process and a system.

An Australian report on adult and community education (ACE), in defining lifelong learning, included NFE as part of its definition:

For the purpose of this paper, the term 'lifelong learning' will be used to refer to the learning that occurs throughout every person's life at intervals appropriate to their needs. It includes:

- *formal education*, as in primary, secondary, tertiary
- *nonformal* education as in much of what happens in the workplace and in ACE
- *informal education*, as in that which is acquired incidentally as a byproduct of life's experiences.

(Campbell & Curtin, 1999, p. 40)

Here 'nonformal education' is distinguished from 'formal education', which is perceived as education provided in traditional education systems run in traditional educational sectors, and from 'informal education', which is regarded as unstructured and often unintended knowledge, skills, attitudes and insights learned from daily experiences and exposure to one's environment. Nonformal education is regarded as having intention and structure. Further, it is generally focused on client groups who live in a particular location or share a common social or educational need. There is general consensus on these so-called 'core' characteristics of NFE, as expressed in the definition provided by Coombs (1985):

Nonformal education is any organized systemic educational activity carried on outside the framework of the formal system to provide selected types of learning to particular subgroups in the population, adults as well as children.
(Coombes, 1985, citing Coombes & Ahmed, 1974, p. 8)

There is often an interchangeable use in the literature of nonformal and informal education. As an example Jilani (1998), writing about conflict resolution among Tamil plantation workers in Sri Lanka, describes NFE as "any knowledge or skills, which the labourers can use to change their present situation in the context of their work and plantation life". The terms also have culturally specific usages which can mask the difference between nonformal and informal education. For example, in Nepal the term '*Anaupacharik Sikshya*' literally means NFE but also includes informal learning as there is no specific term for informal learning in Nepalese culture (Shrestha, 2001).

Definitions of NFE often include reference to the methods employed with an adult education focus. These typically have the needs of learners central to the educational process and increase the capacity of individuals to be informed and active citizens (Campbell & Curtin, 1999; Jones, 1995). While not suggesting that ideology defines NFE, some research claims notions of empowerment and liberation are central to the effectiveness of NFE in the Asia-Pacific region, especially for rural workers in developing countries. This research suggests that NFE must be participatory, action based, and allow participants to research, reflect upon, understand and address traditional power relations within their communities (Jones, 1995; Jones & Ellis, 1995).

3. NATURE OF THE RESEARCH FIELD

Research into NFE in the Asia-Pacific region is marked by a diverse range of materials and sources. Much NFE research is in the form of specific project based evaluation reports and case studies. Accompanying these are a variety of reports and publications relating to the activities of the non-government organisations (NGOs) that usually provide NFE in the region.

These case studies and reports tend to have similar characteristics. They focus on a single project, activity, issue or region. They are usually qualitative studies, providing a good descriptive analysis of the social and educational contexts, rationales, methods, and outcomes of the projects they treat. They do not usually attempt to provide cross-cultural, cross-regional or cross-national analysis. It appears that research into NFE is not highly funded, and that these small, project based case studies will remain the norm for research in the field until this changes. This is despite NFE being of critical importance in the region.

There is little literature exclusively on NFE in the region, and virtually none that theorises the field. Much NFE literature is embedded in broader research and evaluation accounts of community development projects. One paper found to theorise NFE is a paper by Reyner (1999) on NFE in Melanesia, in which she provides a specific analysis of NFE in the South Pacific context. Australian literature is also an exception, where an established adult and community education sector has provided a significant conceptual basis for NFE in adult education through the production of a variety of government sponsored reports (for example, AAACE; 1991; MCEETYA, 1997).

4. CONTEXTS AND MODELS OF NFE

The literature confirms that NFE is practised throughout the Asia-Pacific region, including Australia, Papua New Guinea, Cambodia, Bangladesh, Malaysia, Thailand, India, Nepal, Cambodia, the Philippines, Melanesia, Sri Lanka, Hong Kong, Mongolia and China. NFE occurs in a policy context where many nations, especially developing nations, have prioritised the funding of their formal education systems. This is particularly so in relation to primary school education where, following the Jomtien Conference (Thailand, 1990), the goal of universal primary education was endorsed as a regional priority.

NFE therefore plays different roles in different countries depending upon their national priorities, emphases in the development of formal education, and geographic and economic profiles. In Australia, with well developed formal systems of education and relatively high participation rates among children, NFE tends to be the domain of the adult and community education sector (Campbell & Curtin, 1999). In significantly developed nations such as Malaysia, access to formal education among the young is increasing and it is adults, the elderly and rural dwellers who are the greatest consumers of NFE (Merriam & Mohamad, 2000). In countries which rely on agricultural production and have predominantly rural populations, the provision of formal education is often confined to urban and provincial centres and larger towns. In these countries NFE is an important, and sometimes the only, source of education for adults and children alike, especially for those in rural and remote communities (Bordia, 2000; Unterhalter & Dutt, 2001).

4.1. NFE for Adults

Models of adult NFE vary throughout the region. In Australia, the adult education sector is known as Adult and Community Education (ACE). The sector is governed by a national peak body, the Australian Association of Adult and Community Education, which receives funding from the national government. Nonformal education sits beside a state funded formal education system (schools, technical colleges, and universities) that, at the tertiary level, is accessible on a competitive basis to adults who have required levels of matriculation.

ACE comprises four broad areas of NFE in Australia: adult basic education (literacy, numeracy and communications skills); general or liberal education (personal enrichment, general interest and recreation); occupational education and training (vocational skills, social skills, conflict resolution), and public education (publicly funded museums, and public campaigns on environment and health) (AAACE, 1991). These areas of activity in NFE are replicated throughout the Asia-Pacific region, though in developing countries prominence is given to literacy, health and occupational programs. Presently, ACE in Australia is provided through a diverse range of institutions, including adult and community education centres and colleges, Workers' Educational Associations (WEAs), Technical and Further Education (TAFE) institutes, churches and schools, and community health agencies and aged-care providers (MCEETYA, 1997).

NFE in developing countries does not usually sit beside formal education systems that are readily accessed by adults. Merriam and Mohamad (2000) point out that in Malaysia, the priority has been to develop formal education systems for the young. Adults, and particularly older Malaysians, have little access to formal education and rely on informal learning and NFE. This is a typical pattern in the Asia-Pacific region where, in the last two decades, many developing countries have prioritised the goal of universal primary education. Adults and those in rural areas do not have access to formal education and continue to rely on informal education and NFE as their means of engaging lifelong learning.

A major priority across the region in NFE has been to improve literacy levels amongst adult populations. Other common NFE programs in developing and middle tier countries relate to improving understandings and practices in health care (Gibbon, 1998; Lau, 1998), agriculture (Merriam & Mohamad, 2000; Reyner, 1999) and vocational and craft skills (Baha'i, 2000a; Reyner, 1999; Jones, 1995). Outcomes of literacy projects for adults have often been disappointing due to insufficient funding, local corruption or negligence, or funds being directed to urban rather than rural communities (Rong & Shi, 2001; Unterhalter & Dutt, 2000), although literacy rates are improving amongst children. A successful literacy project is the Total Literacy Project in India, which was funded at the national level and had outstanding results in the state of Kerala (Saini, 2000), which became India's first literate state. This program succeeded because of the critical contribution of over 350,000 volunteers in the program, and because it was designed as a sub component of a broader community education program encompassing health services like eye-testing and provision of eye glasses, which attracted people with health concerns into the literacy program (Saini, 2000).

4.2. NFE for Children

NFE is also important for children, especially in developing countries. In Australia NFE is essentially a non mandatory, supplementary educational activity for children in content areas under-addressed by the formal school curriculum. The NFE child education sector in Australia comprises private providers teaching supplementary private tutoring programs in school curriculum areas, especially literacy and numeracy learning. These are supplemented by hobby and interest courses involving art, music, drama and dance education, and sports tuition (swimming, tennis, martial arts, and gymnastics). Parents pay fees for these courses, so their use is generally, but not exclusively, confined to middle class Australians and those in employment.

Many children in developing countries continue to rely on NFE as their only form of education. Despite priority being given to universal primary school education in developing countries, this goal is yet to be realised. Child participation rates in formal schooling vary, and it is difficult to pin down data in relation to national net participation rates in primary education for the Asia-Pacific region. Reference to UNESCO's Statistical Database on Education (UNESCO, 2002) reveals that many countries do not keep, or do not report to UNESCO, their figures on net participation rates. However some statistics are available. In India, in 1997–98, 98 per cent of boys attended primary school while 81.5 per cent of girls were in primary education (Ministry of Human Resource Development, 2000). In 1995 the primary school net participation rates available for other countries were Indonesia (97% boys, 94% girls), South Korea (92% boys, 94% girls), China (98% boys, 98% girls), Lao Peoples Democratic Republic (74% boys, 66% girls), and Mongolia (78% boys, 81% girls) (UNESCO, 2002). Some research suggests that these reported figures may be overstated (Bordia, 2000; Rong & Shi, 2001).

It is usually children from rural and remote communities who rely on NFE, and girls rather than boys (Rong & Shi, 2001; Sakya, 2001). Often, cultural and economic norms in these communities emphasise family and female participation in agricultural production at the expense of education. Children from rural and remote communities are more likely to miss school, be taken out of school early, or not attend school, when compared to children from larger rural centres or urban areas. The participation in NFE of children in developing countries is often a substitute for participation in primary school education (Bordia, 2000). NFE initiatives for children centre on the provision of basic education by NGO providers who establish schools or pre schools where government schools have not yet been established. These schools are often part of broader community projects which focus on the empowerment of women and their families, and on community literacy projects (Baha'i, 2000b; Unterhalter & Dutt, 2001).

4.3. The Curriculum of NFE

A wide range of courses are reported as the curriculum of NFE. These span vocational and craft training, health, basic literacy and numeracy, environmental education, moral education, women's advancement, critical thinking and problem solving, interpersonal communication skills, personal interest and hobby courses, small business management and small income generation, teacher education, and agricultural management and farming methods management. In developing countries the NFE curriculum is usually provided by NGOs that have government approval to offer services in particular areas, and are funded by private donation, usually from international sources (Rong & Shi, 2001; Wilson, 2000). Funding is sometimes channelled to NGOs through local government agencies. Where NGOs deliver NFE the curriculum reflects a middle path between meeting local needs and enacting the mission of the NGO. This can lead to tension, a feeling of a lack of control within local communities, and a lack of accountability by NGOs to government agencies (Rong & Shi, 2001).

In Australia, the NFE curriculum is provided through various community colleges, private providers and NGOs, often in receipt of government grants. Key initiatives in Australian NFE relate to government funded literacy programs for new, non-English speaking migrants, and a variety of adult education courses in personal growth and development, vocational education and training, general communications skills, and ICT (information and communications technologies) skills. Some programs target youth needs relating to employability, goal setting and life skills. In areas of low socio-economic status (SES), NFE courses are often run by community and religious NGOs, which receive varying amounts of government funding. The sector in Australia is poorly funded in relation to formal education (Senate Standing Committee on Adult and Community Education, 1991).

4.4. NFE and Community Development

NFE often forms the foundation of broad community development projects, where education is seen as a significant tool for social capacity building alongside other forms of economic infrastructure. Such forms of NFE often contain an element of 'conscientization' (Jones, 1995) employing concepts deriving from Freire, in which through NFE communities are made aware of power relations and other factors which impede financial development and democratization. In the past, some programs of this type have met with "brutal and systematic repression" from authoritarian governments in the region (Jones, 1995, p. 122). Nonetheless, there is a significant body of research which argues that in low SES communities, especially rural communities in developing countries, NFE should be participatory, and has a responsibility to engage in raising community awareness and community capacity to influence social and economic issues (Jones, 1993; Jones, 1995; Jones & Ellis, 1995; Reyner, 1999; Stein, 1993).

The literature provides cases of successful community development projects which have had significant social goals beyond the educational project itself, but which were built on NFE. They include the following projects.

Scrap Collectors in Maharastra. This project was set up in Maharastra State, India (Narayan & Chikarmane, 2000) which educated scrap collectors, using participatory methods, to enable them to recognise their economic contribution to the community in solid waste management, and also to have the state recognise this contribution. NFE centres played an important role in providing access for children into formal schooling, and in building trust between the scrap collectors and the broader community.

Pedagogical Practices in a Papua New Guinean Community. This project built on understandings that formal education programs in the region had failed because they were donor-driven projects designed by people who were not part of the community (Nagai, 1999). Imposed Western education models were found to be alienating children from their community. A participatory action research project utilised expatriates as facilitators, and the indigenous people (Maiwala) took responsibility for planning and implementing culturally appropriate classroom practices. This project addressed a range of issues relating to social disengagement and community building through NFE.

Adoption of Computer Based Farming in an Indigenous Thai Community. This project utilised an applied epistemological approach to assist a traditional farming community in adopting computer based technologies into their agricultural practices (Cavallo, 2000). Here NFE built upon local indigenous knowledge embedded in a traditional so-called 'engine culture'. This project enabled the community to adopt and master computer technology, and questioned assumptions that traditional rural communities lack the capacity to use computer based technologies in their farming.

Empowerment of Women in India. Programs such as *Mahila Samakhya* (literally, 'women speaking as equals') in India focused on women's empowerment by establishing local committees of women to oversee community based projects (Bordia, 2000; Unterhalter & Dutt, 2001). The program provided leadership training, funding for committees to seed their own projects, and supporting funding for larger scale community development projects. Women who joined local committees were often illiterate, yet successfully managed the committee and its projects. Common projects initiated by committees included small business seed funding for women, literacy education for women and children, the opening of schools and child care centres, and information courses in social justice issues relating to women and girls.

Distance Education in Mongolia. The Open Distance Education (ODE) program in Mongolia was an NFE program conducted by radio to reach remote communities and assisted the nomadic women of the Gobi desert to become more self-reliant through the provision of information and personal skills (Robinson, 1999). Initially sponsored from international sources, it eventually received funding from the Mongolian government. Poor coordination with local communities was often a drawback of NFE projects. However, this project was successful due to effective collaboration between the project team, provincial and local leaders, and local volunteers. It also succeeded due to culturally appropriate forms of content and support, and the high status attributed to the project by international and local participants (Robinson, 1999).

NFE Education in Refugee Camps in Thailand. In this project, NGOs provided various forms of NFE to the significant number of Burmese citizens in refugee camps in Thailand (Abbey & Phaik-Choo Phuah, 1999; Wilson, 2000). These courses were in teacher education and organisational management, and a few courses operated through distance mode using printed materials and systems of community mentors within each camp. NFE courses were highly regarded by these communities, who saw them, and teacher education programs in particular, as a means of maintaining cultural traditions, increasing community expertise, and empowering young people to be ready for broader social and occupational roles once they left the camps. The NGOs have begun to work collaboratively to build common standards frameworks in their teacher education programs (Wilson, 2000).

Jones (1995) mounts an argument that indigenous NFE activists, well skilled in the integration of NFE into social development projects, should have a role in assisting Western nations in using NFE to achieve broad social goals. The tradition in Western countries is to isolate NFE from both the formal education and community development sectors. Yet, the record of NFE in developing countries indicates that it has the potential to play a significant role in social capacity building in developed countries. An integration of NFE into social capital projects may be an important strategy for developed nations to utilise in pursuing their lifelong learning objectives.

5. KEY ISSUES IN NFE

There are a number of key issues in the Asia-Pacific region that emerge from NFE research. These centre on equity, delivery, and quality assurance issues in NFE in the Asia-Pacific region, particularly in developing countries.

5.1. *Equity in Rural Education*

Rural and remote communities in developing countries have the lowest standards of living and income generation, the lowest standards in literacy and numeracy, and the lowest educational participation rates (particularly the participation of women and girls). These communities also receive the lowest state expenditure on education, and rely most heavily on the NFE sector to provide equity in educational opportunities (Rong & Shi, 2001; Unterhalter & Dutt, 2000). While there are many success stories with NFE in rural areas (Bordia, 2000, Unterhalter & Dutt, 2000) there are also questions about the quality of education provided through rural NFE programs and their accountability to the state. Focusing on rural China, Rong and Shi (2001) argue that the quality of NFE provided in rural communities through NGO or government activity is often problematic:

> The Chinese Government, like governments in many other developing countries, also initiates programs that focus more on nonformal education than on formal schooling and other long-term educational planning. Several recent nonformal educational programs, such as *Xiwang Gongcheng* (Project Hope), *Chenlei Jihua* (Project Spring Flower Bud), and the *Saomang Jihua* (Eliminating Illiteracy Campaign) promoted in rural areas, have usually been substandard, offered only irregularly and based on soft money or donations. Reported achievements of these programs, according to Chinese newspapers, are often held to be questionable. (Rong & Shi, 2001, p. 22)

This scenario is repeated in other literature. NFE often provides the only significant opportunity for education in remote and rural communities, and governments rely upon and promote NFE as a pragmatic alternative to state systems. Thus there can be a lack of quality assurance in NFE in rural communities. The research suggests that if the dramatic economic, social and educational inequalities between urban and rural communities are to be addressed, levels and consistency of funding NFE in rural areas need to improve. It also suggests that quality assurance and accountability to the state in rural NFE programs need to be enhanced.

5.2. *Delivery to Remote Areas*

Remoteness and variations in regional languages are major impediments to the successful implementation of NFE programs in developing countries. Examples include: (a) providing NFE in coastal resource management among the coastal community of Central Visayas region in the Phillippines (Parras, 2001); (b) providing for the nomadic women of Gobi desert (Robinson, 1999); and (c) servicing the disparate and multi-language needs in education and teacher education of Burmese hill tribe and refugee camp communities (Abbey & Phaik-Choo Phuah, 1999; Wilson, 2000). These factors create problems in reaching clients and delivering resources, and imply the need to develop different and specialised forms of delivery and support. While sophisticated technologies have been used to deliver services in some areas and have been found to be liberating where they have been used, they are expensive and are frequently not available to rural dwellers in remote communities.

5.3. Participation and Empowerment of Women

The research identifies gender discrimination in education due to a range of complex factors. Extreme poverty and traditional cultural practices have led to a strong reliance on the economic contribution of children in rural and remote communities. Poverty is the main source of conflict within communities, and gender conflict within households (Bordia, 2000; Gibbon, 1998; Jilani, 1998; Parras, 2001).

Women and female children have the heaviest burden in household and agricultural duties, the lowest participation rates in education, and the lowest literacy levels, both nationally and within their own communities. Rong and Shi (2001), drawing on Chinese women and women from minority groups, observe:

> The vast majority of the illiterate population that lives in these provinces is either female, a member of an ethnic minority, or both ... Minority women residing in the least developed provinces were triply disadvantaged in terms of educational attainment. For example, although four out of 10 minority women were illiterate nationally, the illiteracy rates for the minority female population was 60% in Yunnan and 86% in Tibet. A minority woman residing in Gansu was 24 times more likely to be illiterate than a Han male residing in Beijing (81.5% versus 3.3%, respectively). (Rong & Shi, 2001, p. 119)

Women are also excluded from designing, delivering and participating in programs they need for financial improvement and empowerment. Robinson (1999) identifies how some materials are inappropriately written by urban men for rural women. In the case of the Gobi program for nomadic women, visits by male teachers were often treated by the males like inspection visits. Reyner (1999) shows how agricultural management programs in Melanesia have been developed by men, and it is the men who attend. The women, who do the majority of the rural work and farm management and are in most need of these courses, are excluded from attending.

Unterhalter and Dutt (2001), drawing on NFE in India, argue that some NFE programs for women, while providing additional vocational skills, only serve to increase the oppression of women. They argue this is particularly a characteristic of NFE courses provided by, or heavily influenced by, the state. They argue that it is only through programs such as *Mahila Samakhya*, which focus on establishing women as leaders, which provide women with opportunities to create community projects for women, and which focus on teaching about social justice and acting against inequality, that women can be empowered through NFE.

5.4. Literacy Education

Literacy education is a priority of most governments in their formal education systems, but it is the NFE sector that delivers literacy education in remote and rural communities. The research indicates that literacy education is insufficiently catered for through NFE, which is under funded and inconsistent in its availability to rural communities. It suggests that literacy education needs to be a higher priority in rural areas. While literacy rates for children are rising in many countries in the Asia-Pacific region through significant funding in formal education, literacy rates for adult populations are not improving (Narayan & Chikamarne, 2000) (see *Adult Literacy*).

5.5. State Priorities and Control

The research confirms the commitment in the region to building formal education systems, and the massive levels of investment that have been put into these systems. It also indicates that this investment appears to have advantaged urban communities at the expense of rural communities. Governments rely on NFE to provide many education, health and other services to rural areas. Associated with this trend is a concern that these services are not properly monitored, that the quality of NFE is poor, and that the imbalance of educational outcomes between rural and urban communities is not being addressed (Bordia, 2000).

Some of the research argues that formal education in developing countries is failing (Pradhan, in press; Reyner, 1999) or argues for greater funding for NFE and less funding for formal education (Reyner, 1999). Reyner (1999) argues that, in the context of the Melanesian Pacific countries, the heavy investment in formal education has been misplaced. She argues that formal education ultimately caters for urban elites who access the few jobs available in the government sector (the largest formal labour market employer in the South Pacific region). However, these jobs are not available in proportion to the number of people who come into the labour market each year. She argues that the basis of economies and communities in the South Pacific region is rural production, and that governments should invest far more heavily in NFE as a means of training people to participate effectively in rural industries.

5.6. Best Practice in NFE

Effective NFE is considered to be those models that engage their clients in some form of partnership through which they transcend passive learning. Effective NFE is marked by real gains in basic literacy and numeracy skills and by techniques that use adult learning principles. Effective NFE is also marked by outcomes that empower people to critique and become active participants in their communities, that result in local control, and where real vocational, economic and social improvements are made in communities. Inferior models are those that do not result in real social or economic gains, that impose inappropriate cultural practices on clients, or where learners are positioned as passive recipients.

5.7. Fragmentation and Unreliability in the NFE Sector

This is an issue in developing and developed countries in the Asia-Pacific region. NFE has a characteristic of being subject to the vagaries of transitional and short term funding. It is difficult to plan for the provision of NFE in the longer term, and that is a significant disadvantage to individuals and communities relying on NFE. This is probably a reason for increasing government funding of NFE, or for governments to take more of an interest in negotiating more stable funding environments for NFE. Similarly, it is a general characteristic of the NFE sector that NFE projects are often limited or variable in their application. So-called 'best practice' projects can exist in one region, but are not available in the next. Successful trials can disappear without trace as funding, management expertise or government priorities change. This is possibly why so much NFE literature is case study focused. There appears to be little reason why some NFE projects are in one place and not another, and there appears to be little of the systematic planning and building of the sector that characterises formal education.

6. FUTURE RESEARCH INTO NFE

Research into NFE in the Asia-Pacific region has tended to centre on descriptive and evaluation studies at the project or program level. This research needs to be maintained so that a consolidated literature concerning best practice in methodologies and outcomes in NFE is developed. These studies need to be supplemented by research that theorises the field, and conceptually engages the nature of NFE and the economic, social and educational contribution NFE makes to communities and the state. There is a need to research NFE at the policy level, to consider whether NFE should be given a higher priority among educational objectives and planning, and whether, as in India through the establishment of formal NFE centres (Bordia, 2000), NFE needs to be more formally organised, structured or integrated.

Some research in the Asia-Pacific region indicates that many competencies derived through NFE are equivalent to those learned through formal education (Bordia, 2000; Wilson, 2000). There is a very useful field of research here in measuring the outcomes of NFE, their comparability with those of formal education, and in suggesting potential pathways and articulation arrangements between the two sectors and with employment providers. This research could, through applied projects, assist in upgrading the status and utility of NFE programs.

A third useful area of research relates to the use of new technologies in the provision of NFE, particularly to remote and rural communities. Despite the difficulty these communities have in accessing these technologies, there are accounts of small investments in these technologies having significant impact on such communities. There is a need to document and evaluate the possibilities of information and communications technology (ICT) based NFE programs and to conceptualise the potential of ICT as a tool in NFE in developing countries.

REFERENCES

AAACE (1991). *Celebrate the Difference: Skills Formation Through Community Based Education.* Canberra, Australia: Australian Association of Adult and Community Education and the National Department of Employment, Education and Training.

Abbey, J., & Phaik-Choo, P. (1999). *Survey of Teacher Training and Curriculum Reform Programs in the DEP Target Communities.* Chiang Mai: Distance Education Program of the National Health and Education Committee (NHEC).

Baha'i (2000a). Vocational Training for Rural Women in India Brings Unexpected Dividends. http://bahai.org/article-1-8-1-16.html. Accessed 2/4/02.

Baha'i (2000b). Cambodian Literacy Project Aims to Promote Peace and Empowerment. http://bahai.org/article-1-8-1-8.html. Accessed 2/4/02.

Bordia, A. (2000). Education for gender equity: The Lok Jumbish experience. *Prospects, 30*(3), 313–329.

Campbell, A., & Curtin, P. (1999) (Eds.), *ACE – Some Issues.* Adelaide: National Centre for Vocational Education Research for the Australian National training Authority.

Cavallo, D. (2000). Emergent design and learning environments: Building on indigenous knowledge. *IBM Systems Journal, 39*(3&4). http://www.coop4coop.org/highlight/dasktar/index.htm (Accessed 17/02/02).

Coombs, P. H., & Ahmed, H. (1974). *Attacking Rural Poverty: How Nonformal Education Can Help.* Baltimore: John Hopkins University Press.

Coombs, P. H. (1985). *The World Crisis in Education: The View from the Eighties.* Oxford: Oxford University Press.

Ekanayaka, S. B. (1978). Teacher Education and Community Development Project Organised by the Teachers' College – Hingurakgoda, Sri Lanka. Paper presented at the *UNESCO National Seminar in Education for Rural Development*, Sri Lanka, April 8–13, 1978. ED158919.

Gibbon, M. (1998). The use of formal and informal health care by female adolscents in Eastern Nepal. *Health Care for Women International, 19*, 343–360.

Guttman, C., & Kosonen, K. (1994). *Within Reach: The Story of PROPEL, a Nonformal Education Project for Rural Children in India.* Paris: UNESCO. ED380208.

Haque, M. (1975). *Rural Education in Bangladesh: Problems and Prospects.* IIEP Seminar Paper 23. Paris: UNESCO. ED135535.

Jilani, A. A. (1998). Labouring among conflicts: Challenges for nonformal education on a Tamil tea plantation in Sri Lanka. *Convergence, 31*(3), 50–58.

Jones, A. M. E. (1993). *Educational Planning in a Frontier Zone: Dependence, Domination and Legitimacy.* Aldershot, UK: Averbury.

Jones, A. M. E. (1995). *Control, Community and Change: Asia-Pacific Experiences in Community Development and Adult Education.* Aldershot, UK: Averbury.

Jones, A. M. E., & Ellis, P. (1995). A Carribean – South Pacific perspective on nonformal education and women's empowerment. *Convergence* (Toronto, Ont), *28*(2), 17–27.

Lau, P. (1998). Healthy living promotion to pre-primary and primary school children. *Australian Journal of Nutrition and Dietetics, 55*(1), 47.

MCYEETYA (1997). *National Policy: Adult and Community Education.* Canberra: Ministerial Council on Education, Employment, Training and Youth Affairs.

Merriam, S. B., & Mohamad, M. (2000). How cultural values shape learning in older adulthood: The case of Malaysia. *Adult Education Quarterly, 51*(1), 45–63.

Ministry of Human Resource Development (2000). *Year 2000 Assessment Education for All.* New Delhi: National Institute of Educational Planning and Development.

Nagai, Y. (1999). Developing a community-based vernacular school: A case study of the Maiwala Elementary School in Papua New Guinea. *Language and Education, 13*(3), 194–206.

Narayan, L., & Chikarmane, P. (2000). Beyond literacy: Education for empowerment. In *Lens on Literacy. Proceeding of the Australian Council for Adult Literacy Conference*, 21–23 September. Perth, Western Australia: ACAL. http://cleo.murdoch.edu.au/confs/acal/procs/narayan.html Accessed 13/3/02.

Parras, D. A. (2001). Coastal resources management in the Philippines: A case study in the Central Visayas Region. *Journal of Environment & Development, 10*(1), 80–103.

Pradhan, H. (in press). *Educational Reform for Linking Skill Development with Employment in Nepal.* Paris: UNESCO.

Reyner, C. (1999). Breathing New Life into Education for Life: A Reconceptualisation of Nonformal Education with a Focus on the Melanesian Pacific. Paper presented at the *Joint AARE/NZARE Conference*, Melbourne, November 29 – December 2.

Robinson, B. (1999). Open and distance learning in the Gobi Desert: Nonformal education for Nomadic women. *Distance Education, 20*(2), 181–204.

Rong, X. L., & Shi, T. (2001). Inequality in Chinese education. *Journal of Contemporary China, 10*(26), 107–124.

Saini, A. (2000). Literacy and empowerment: An Indian scenario. *Childhood Education* (International focus issue), 381–384.

Sakya, T. M. (Ed.) (2001). *Literacy Watch Bulletin, June, 2001: No. 22.* Kathmandu, Nepal: National Resource Centre for Nonformal Education and UNESCO.

Senate Standing Committee on Adult and Community Education (1991). *Come in Cinderella: The Emergence of Adult and Community Education.* Canberra: Senate Publications Unit.

Shrestha, S. B. (2001). *Nepalma Anaupcharik Sikshya* (in Nepali) – Nonformal Education in Nepal. Mimeograph, 8 pp.

Stein, R. (1993). Papua New Guinea: Sustainable rainforest cultivation and environmental education. *Adult Education and Development, 40*, 117–126.

UNESCO (1981). *Education of Disadvantaged Groups and Multiple Class Teaching: Studies and Innovative Approaches. Report of a Study Group Meeting (Jakarta, November 17–26, 1980).* Bangkok: UNESCO Regional Office for Education in Asia and the Pacific. ED207732.

UNESCO (2002). *Statistical Database on Education.* http://www.uis.unesco.org/en/stats/statso.htm. Accessed 9/4/02.

Unterhalter, E., & Dutt, S. (2001). Gender, education and women's power: Indian state and civil society intersections in DPEP (District Primary Education Programme) and Mahila Samakhya. *Compare, 31*(1), 57–73.

Wilson, S. (2000). *The Feasibility of an Accredited Course in Teacher Education for Refugee Communities in the Thai/Burma Border Area.* Chiang Mai: Distance Education Program of the Burma National Health and Education Committee (NHEC).

SECTION 3:

LEARNING AND HUMAN DEVELOPMENT

Section Editors – Peter Renshaw and Colin Power

25

The Process of Learning and Human Development

PETER D. RENSHAW
Griffith University, Southport, Australia

COLIN POWER
University of Queensland, St Lucia, Australia

1. INTRODUCTION

Contemporary research on learning and human development is a multi-disciplinary activity that draws on psychology, anthropology, sociology, education and increasingly on cognitive science. As proposed by Bransford, Brown and Cocking (1999) research at the intersection of these disciplines has changed our conception of learning and human development specifically in five related areas: the structure of knowledge and memory; problem solving and reasoning; the early foundations of learning; regulatory processes that govern learning; and the cultural and community context of learning and development. These themes are particularly pertinent to the articles included in this section of the *Handbook* which include consideration of problem solving, metacognition and approaches to learning as well the environmental and community contexts within which learning occurs. Learning outcomes include consideration of cognitive variables such as depth of learning and achievement in specific curriculum domains, as well as social-emotional and attitudinal variables such as levels of self-esteem and endorsement of different values.

Research conducted in the Asia-Pacific region in the past few decades has contributed significantly to the extension of knowledge about learning and human development, principally through the affordances provided by the contrast between the cultural traditions and values of Asia with those of the West. In the introduction to this section of the *Handbook*, we provide specific examples of research from the Asia-Pacific region that have extended and at times transformed an understanding of learning and developmental processes. The key conclusion is that learning and development must be researched as processes embedded within interacting cultural, institutional and social systems. This is in line with Peterson (see *Lifespan Human Development*) who proposes that developmental patterns and plans are shaped by attitudinal factors within cultures, so it is impossible to understand fully the development of any person in isolation. Rather, developmental processes need to be investigated within the cultural milieu of interpersonal and institutional relationships. Below, these issues are explored initially with regard to moral development and values education, and then with regard teaching and learning processes. We conclude the introduction by drawing attention to two lessons derived from the articles that follow. First, researchers need to move beyond their national and cultural boundaries to understand fully, learning and developmental processes. Second, since effectiveness is always determined in relation to specific sets of values that change over time and culture, educational researchers need to adopt the stance of critical participants in analysing and interpreting the processes and outcomes of education.

2. MORAL DEVELOPMENT AND VALUES EDUCATION

Most Asian and Pacific education systems assign a very high priority to moral values and citizenship education. The key objectives of each national education system in the region reflect its particular philosophical, cultural and religious roots, and these in turn help shape programs designed to promote the acquisition of key values, moral development and learning to live together. There is also an emerging literature stemming from studies of the ways in which learning takes place in indigenous cultures and analyses of the discourse and strategies utilized in teaching values and moral judgment development (Ainley et al., 1998; Luke, 1995). But in comparison with research on learning and cognitive development, research on the effectiveness of different methods (cultural transmission, values clarification, moral discourse, conflict resolution, co-operative learning, social action and so on) for promoting the learning of values and moral development is meagre.

Key problems to be confronted include clarifying the meaning in different cultural context of values to be learned, the identification of appropriate methodologies to promote moral development, and the measurement of attitudes and values. For example, considerable debate has been generated on the issue of whether there is a set of distinctively Asian values (or of Pacific Island values) and their place in education and development. Andrich and Luo (see *Measuring Attitudes by Unfolding a Likert-Style Questionnaire*) review recent theoretical research in latent trait theory which seeks to reconcile Thurstone and Likert approaches to the measurement of attitudes, while Masters and Forster (2000) report on progress being made on the development of instruments to assess the moral and ethical outcomes of schooling in Western societies. These projects reflect renewed interest among the nations of the region in the social-emotional and attitudinal outcomes of schooling.

Slee et al. (see *Bullying in Schools*) review research relating to school bullying in Australia, China, Japan, Republic of Korea and New Zealand. Bullying is generally described as repeated intimidation of a physical, verbal or psychological nature by a more powerful person or group of persons. The research indicates that cultural and historical influences appear to shape the way in which bullying is perceived, and that bullying manifests itself differentially in terms of age, gender and causes in the statistics from the countries included in the review. Quisumbing and de Leo (see *Values Education in a Changing World*) review the types of programs being used in the Asia-Pacific region to promote a culture of peace, tolerance, and learning to live together, and the work of Asia-Pacific Network for International Education and Values Education (APNIEVE). The effectiveness of the various elements of the teaching-learning cycle being developed co-operatively through APNIEVE has not been given the attention it deserves from educational researchers. What the little research that has been done in the region suggests is that the proposed school environments, programs and methods can have significant effects on students' moral development, attitudes and values, but that these effects are typically modest in size (Forster & Masters, 2002).

3. TEACHING AND LEARNING PROCESSES IN THE ASIA-PACIFIC REGION

Interest in the educational and socialisation practices of the Asia-Pacific region intensified in recent years due to the outstanding results achieved by many regional countries in international testing programs. Comparisons across countries have provided political leaders with a means to evaluate their own education systems and suggest alternative pathways to reform (Jones, 1999). Market-driven competition for knowledge-intensive industries and the associated requirement for highly skilled and adaptive citizens heightened the importance of such international comparisons during the 1990s. Leaders and policy-makers began to scrutinise international rankings to evaluate in broad terms whether their education systems were effective in ensuring a competitive edge, particularly in terms of mathematics and science learning outcomes. In the early 1990s, the results of the Second International Science Study (Keeves, 1992a,b; Postlethwaite, 1992; Rosier & Keeves, 1991) were published. Recently the results of the Third International Mathematics and Science Study (TIMSS) were published (Gonzales & Miles, 2001). The results confirmed the very high standing of many Asian-Pacific countries in terms of the mathematics and science achievement of their students. In mathematics achievement, countries from this region occupied the first five places (Singapore, Korea, Taiwan, Hong Kong, and Japan) and in science achievement they occupied four of the top five places (Taiwan, Singapore, Hungary, Japan, Korea). Within the TIMSS project itself, the implications for educational practices are being explored through analysis of a series of videotaped lessons across different countries (see *Problem Solving*, for a review of recent relevant studies). At a broader level, the implications are being debated within the research community in order to unravel the factors that have produced such a positive outcome for countries in the region.

3.1. Excellence in Teaching and Learning

The results from TIMSS and the earlier international studies have challenged researchers to reconsider what constitutes teaching and learning excellence. As described by Biggs (1994) four features of excellence can be derived from mainstream Western research, namely: (a) a positive motivational context that supports the students' need to know; (b) a high degree of learner task engagement and reflection on the learning process; (c) interaction with peers and teachers in learning partnerships; and (d) emphasis on the development of a deep, broad and well-structured knowledge base (Biggs, 1994). Similar features of excellence were identified by Newmann and associates (1996), who created the concept of 'authentic pedagogy' to refer to classroom practices which emphasised higher order thinking, substantive conversations between teachers and students, depth of knowledge and understanding, as well as connectedness to the world beyond the classroom. These dimensions were recently adapted by researchers in Australia (Education Queensland, 2001) to form the notion of 'productive pedagogues' which includes (a) intellectual quality, (b) relevance and connectedness, (c) supportive classroom environment, and (d) recognition of difference. It isn't immediately clear that the typical approaches to classroom activities in the Confucian heritage cultures of Asia are consistent with such a view of excellence. Indeed in these countries, classes are typically large, activities are teacher-directed, and study for competitive examinations is emphasised. Until the international testing programs of the 1990s revealed the very high level of achievement of students in these classrooms, Western observers and commentators were prone to criticise rather than to investigate closely what was actually occurring in the Asian classroom (see *Student Learning: A Cross-Cultural Perspective*).

3.2. Excellent Learning Environments in the Asia-Pacific Region

Fraser and Goh (see *Classroom Learning Environments*) document the increased research interest in the Asian classroom. Their review of research on learning environments in various Asian classrooms across the region (Singapore, Korea, Taiwan, Indonesia, as well as Australia) suggests that instruments developed in North America and in Australia to evaluate educational programs, can be successfully adapted to provide valid research results on learning environments in Asian classrooms. The accumulation of research findings across various levels of schooling, curriculum domains and countries, is providing the basis for investigating whether the pattern of associations between classroom environment characteristics and learning outcomes in Asian contexts, mirrors existing findings from research on Western populations. An important aspect of this research is the effort to link different learning environment characteristics with different learning outcomes. Fraser and Goh (see *Classroom Learning Environments*) found with Singapore students, that while actual achievement in national examinations correlated positively with perceptions of cohesiveness among students, other outcomes such as level of self-esteem correlated with teacher support and perceptions of equity. Such research enables practitioners and policy makers to evaluate research findings in relation to different sets of values that are embedded in different outcome measures. In other words, the learning environment research provides evidence to inform decisions about educational policy and practice, but these decisions always involve judgements about what is valued as an outcome from education.

3.3. *Approaches to Study in the Asia-Pacific Region*

Excellence in teaching and learning cannot be analysed in isolation from the values that are privileged in a culture at any particular historical moment (Renshaw, 2002). It also has to be recognised that observation of the practices of one culture through the value-orientations and interpretative lenses of another, can produce distorted understandings. During the 1980s and 1990s the common Western stereotype of Asian teachers and students was challenged (see Stigler & Stevenson, 1991; Renshaw & Volet, 1995; Volet & Renshaw, 1996). Asian teachers had been seen as simply purveyors of information, while their students were characterised as rote learners. Research summarised by Watkins (see *Student Learning: A Cross-Cultural Perspective*) has convincingly challenged such a view. In an overview of research on students' approaches to learning, Watkins concludes that rather than a surface learner, the typical approach to study of students from various Asian countries is adaptive, conscientious and centred on achieving the level of understanding required in the course of study.

In a similar pattern to that reported by Fraser and Goh (see *Classroom Learning Environments*), Watkins chronicles the translation and adoption of British and Australian research instruments measuring students' approaches to learning for use in various Asian countries, notably Hong Kong, China, Japan, and Nepal (see, for example, *Learning Process Questionnaire* (Biggs, 1987)). The use of these instruments in Asia has been guided more explicitly by the goal of determining whether ingrained cultural stereotypes could be challenged by empirical evidence. As the research findings accumulated, many consistent patterns of correlation across cultures and countries were found. Watkins (2000) compared the correlates of a deep approach to learning across various countries in the Asia-Pacific region and found that a deep approach to learning was associated with students' feelings of involvement and perceptions of the teacher as supportive and likeable. In addition, however, there are differences in learning approaches and motivational dispositions that appear to be embedded in long established cultural practices.

Classroom practices in the Asian region draw upon long established traditions of respect for education and teachers. Children enter school with the expectation that they will devote considerable effort to education. The sense of respect and cooperation between children and adults predisposes children to adopt readily, a student role that requires diligence and receptiveness (Hess & Azuma, 1991; Biggs, 1994). Ng and Renshaw (see *Motivation and School Learning*) review research suggesting that ability itself is perceived as a malleable factor that is formed through engagement, effort and persistence. In accord with this perception, learning outcomes are attributed predominantly to internal factors such as immediate and long-term effort rather than to stable factors outside the students' control. Achieving high grades in school is seen a filial duty, a way to bring honour to the family, and also a means to achieve upward social mobility. Institutionally and systemically these values have given rise to an educational ethos where students are expected to be effective and adaptive learners, and where difficulties in learning can be overcome through concerted effort by teachers, parents and the students themselves. In addition, as examined more fully below, specific teaching and learning practices have been identified in various Asian countries that seem to be consistent with a concern for deep understanding. What research in the Asia-Pacific region has demonstrated, therefore, is that educational excellence arises from interlocking systems of values and cultural practices that require systemic analysis in order to unravel and understand.

3.4. Questioning and Understanding

The way that teaching strategies, such as questioning, are deployed in Asian classrooms to achieve particular learning outcomes, was the focus of research in the early 1990s as scholars in the West tried to understand the high academic achievement of Asian students (Stigler & Stevenson, 1991; Hess & Azuma, 1991). The questioning script identified in classrooms throughout the United States and most Western countries, entails an initiation by the teacher, a response by a student, and an immediate evaluation by the teacher – the IRE format (Mehan, 1979; Cazden, 1988). This procedure is used typically to maintain student attention rather than to promote deeper thinking and inquiry. Hess and Azuma (1991) reported contrasting instantiations of questioning techniques in United States and Japanese classrooms. Teachers in the United States were concerned to keep questioning sequences "quick and snappy" in order to maintain student attention and promote lively engagement. In contrast, in the Japanese classrooms, teachers often questioned students at length, lingering over students' responses and probing their suggestions from different perspectives and a variety of conceptual frameworks – a strategy aptly named "sticky probing" (Hess & Azuma, 1991, p. 6). Importantly, the teacher focused on moving students towards a consensus, a specific conclusion approved by the teacher, but this was reached only after extensive consideration of evidence and different viewpoints. Stigler and Hiebert (1999) support the findings summarised above (see also *Problem Solving*). In a comparison of how teachers approached mathematics tasks in United States and Japanese classrooms they found that Japanese teachers spent more time in cooperatively planning key lessons, working on a given problem, and more time helping students to represent the problem. They also chose more challenging problems for their students, focused students' attention on the merits of different solution strategies and were more explicit in drawing connections among the different features of solution methods.

Sticky probing and the kind of focused and thorough approach to problem solving described by Stigler and Hiebert, are not isolated teaching tactics. Rather they reflect a particular relationship between the teacher and students, a specific emphasis in the curriculum, and a distinct form of classroom communication. Students at the centre of sticking probing have their apparently inadequate ideas explored publicly – a strategy which could be regarded as a humiliating experience involving loss of face. However, in the Japanese classrooms studied by Hess and Azuma (1991) students did not show distress during sticky probing, suggesting that a high degree of trust and cooperation existed between the teacher and students. Likewise, the slow and methodical exploration of ideas through questioning indicates that deep conceptual knowledge was the goal of the activity. Students were scaffolded towards this deeper understanding not only by the skilful questioning of the teacher, but also by their own complementary social skills that enabled them to be willing and competent participants in sticky probing. Sticky probing also makes sense as an instructional strategy, only if it is assumed that other students are fully participating by observing and eavesdropping on the conversation. The implicit communicative ground rule is that everyone should listen carefully to the dialogue and vicariously participate in answering the questions. Clearly, we are observing a complex cultural system in operation here, not an isolated teaching technique that might be easily extracted and regrown elsewhere.

3.5. Skill and Creativity

Should exploration and creativity precede or follow skill acquisition? In order to address this question, cross-cultural assumptions about human development and the so-called 'natural' order of learning-related activities need to be considered (see *Lifespan Human Development*). In the individualistic model of development that predominates in the West, the task of parents centres on creating a safe environment where children's creativity, individuality and independence can be fostered (Greenfield & Suzuki, 1997). There is a reluctance to instruct children prior to formal education since learning is seen to arise predominantly from active engagement in free play and creative exploration. In contrast, in the interdependent or collectivistic model that predominates in Asia, children are viewed initially as asocial creatures requiring socialisation into the family and the broader community. The task of parents, therefore, centres on creating a caring environment where children's sense of social connectedness and interdependence can be fostered (Markus & Kitayama, 1991). It is not surprising that specific observations of teaching practices, such as those reported by Gardner (1989), are consistent with these pervasive contrasting models of development. Gardner's observations of Chinese early childhood classrooms where art and music were being taught, revealed a highly directive and imitative regime where children were expected to develop performative skill and fluency at producing a few models. In contrast, the predominant model in early childhood classrooms in the West emphasises the importance of exploration and free expression. Teachers are said to 'follow-in' children's activities, seeking to interpret what they are doing, rather than trying to direct and structure their activities. In contrast, the Asian tradition has provided more explicit scaffolding and greater attention to structuring tasks to ensure children's adoption of specific skills and procedures.

3.6. Cognition and Prior Knowledge

Garton's review of cognition (see *Cognitive Development*) draws our attention to the Piagetian tradition of cross-cultural research where the ages and stages of Piagetian development were compared across different ethnic and cultural groups. These studies were designed to test the universality of Piaget's developmental theory both as a description of major developmental milestones and in terms of the causal mechanisms of developmental change. In particular, Piaget's view that cognitive development did not require access to specific forms of school knowledge provided the instigation for researchers to compare the performance of indigenous children and adolescents with little access to formal schooling, to the performance of students participating in schools. As Garton reports, cross-cultural research in the Piagetian tradition has largely ceased due to the recognition that access to formal schooling plays a large role in the development of the forms of logical thinking tapped by Piagetian cognitive tasks. In place of the universalist and structuralist model of Piaget, a more situated and context-dependent model of cognition has emerged, influenced in part by Vygotsky's sociocultural theory of cognition, as well as by research conducted since the 1980s on background knowledge and expert-novice thinking.

Prior knowledge is widely regarded as the primary predictor of children's future learning. Reading comprehension research (Anderson & Pichert, 1978) and related research on the nature of experts' knowledge (Bransford Brown, & Cocking, 1999) have demonstrated that the richness and accessibility of students' cognitive schemata strongly predict variations in learning outcomes. Experts appear to have task-specific knowledge rather than general problem-solving skills, although recent research has begun to indicate a synergistic interaction between task specific and general skills (see *Problem Solving*). For example, the classic study of expert and novice chess players (Chase & Simon, 1973) demonstrated that the experts' memory for the positioning of chess pieces was superior only when the pattern of pieces resulted from an actual game. When the pattern was randomly generated, novice players were as proficient as the experts in remembering positions. The interpretation of this finding is that experts don't have a better memory for patterns *per se*, but have a rich and accessible schema for patterns of chess pieces that arise from games. It is a context-specific and task-dependent form of expertise that arises from experience. Such a view of cognition highlights the interaction between different cultural practices (the social plane of development as described by Vygotsky) and the kinds of cognitive strategies that can be appropriated by participating in those practices – the individual plane of development as described by Vygotsky (see *Cognitive Development*).

Lawson (see *Problem Solving*) concludes his article, by noting that a focus on situated learning has been one of the major themes of research in this field, and can be expected to continue to be an important issue for researchers interested in problem solving. Drawing on work by Pellegrino, Chudowsky and Glaser (2001), Lawson (see *Problem Solving*) argues that problem solving is a situated activity that is influenced by the cultural context in which the problem situation is embedded, and particularly by the practices and perspectives of the community in which the problem solving is undertaken (Greeno, 1997). Lawson's review of problem-solving research in the Asia-Pacific region includes studies where the influence of the cultural setting on problem representation and strategy choice are clearly demonstrated.

While the initial research on background knowledge was concerned narrowly with cognitive variables such as memories and inferences, current research on prior knowledge includes consideration of personal issues related to race, class, gender, culture and ethnicity. Such considerations extend prior knowledge to include children's self-schemas (see *Motivation and School Learning*) as well as their knowledge of different interactive scripts that influence how they interpret and perform the roles of 'child' or 'student' or 'partner' in schooling contexts. Students bring with them to school a repertoire of practices and expectations that reflect their distinctive cultural and familial backgrounds, and that enable them to interact more or less effectively, more or less confidently, and more or less centrally within the classroom community. Prior knowledge includes consideration of: what the student knows (declarative and procedural knowledge); who the student is (self knowledge and self-appraisal); and the communicative repertoire and social scripts available to the student that are relevant to the specific educational context (social participation scripts). Cross-cultural research conducted partly in this region (see *Cognitive Development, Lifespan Human Development, Problem Solving*) have provided the evidence on which this more culturally-relevant notion of prior knowledge emerged.

3.7. *Mindfulness and automaticity*

In many traditions of learning both in the West and in Asia, repetition has been regarded as crucial to the acquisition of new material. Chanting songs and rhymes in order to learn vocabulary, or repeating the alphabet or the so-called 'times tables' again and again to achieve automatic recall, are well known and reported schooling practices. Such practices came into disrepute during the last century as researchers revealed the importance of mindfulness in the acquisition and transfer of new knowledge (see *Metacognition*). However, rather than being regarded as a low-level and mindless strategy, repetition appears to be a particularly adaptive learning strategy for the kinds of tasks required to be literate within Confucian heritage cultures (Biggs, 1994; Dahlin & Watkins, 1999). In order to master the decoding and production of the thousands of written characters in common usage, children must engage in extended repetitive learning activities, but as Biggs argued, repetition is guided by a multi-modal and meaning focused pattern of enactment using the five organs – "the eyes to see the shape, the ears to hear the sound, the hand to write the shape, the mouth to speak the sound, the mind to think about the meaning" (Biggs, 1994, p. 27). As a strategy beyond early literacy learning, Watkins (2000) argued that repetition is employed in the service of developing deeper understanding. Chinese students in secondary schools in Hong Kong, for example, reported using repetition to develop a deep impression and to discover new meaning, whereas their Western counterparts employed repetition primarily to check their recall of material previously committed to memory. These investigations demonstrate that judgements about the effectiveness of a learning strategy need to be made in relation to the types of cultural skills and knowledge that are being acquired. My so-called 'low road' deployment of repetition may be your 'high road' to deeper engagement and understanding.

3.8. Memorisation and Understanding

Another assumption in the research literature is that understanding should precede rather than follow memorisation. As Bransford Brown and Cocking (1999) contend,

> Humans are viewed as goal-directed agents who actively seek information. They come to formal education with a range of prior knowledge, skills, beliefs, and concepts that significantly influence what they notice about the environment and how they organise and interpret it. This, in turn, affects their abilities to remember, reason, solve problems and acquire new knowledge. (p. 10)

The issue here is not whether different cultural traditions place different values on understanding. The goal of learning in schools across the Asia-Pacific region is to enable students to understand and deploy information and skills in effective and adaptive ways. It is the way understanding is perceived to emerge over time and interact with memory that seems to differ. In studies with Chinese university students, Marton and his colleagues (Marton, Watkins, & Tang, 1997) have shown that the important distinction is not between memorisation and understanding, but between mechanical memorisation and memorisation with understanding. For Chinese learners, Marton et al. (1997) claim, the normal practice is to understand and memorise simultaneously. There is also evidence that Chinese Hong Kong secondary students become more strategic in their use of memory as a tool for understanding. As the quantity of learning material increases, they begin to memorise only the key points and rely on their teachers and discussions with peers to assist them to identify core concepts. Thus, the connection between memory and understanding becomes socially mediated as the amount of material to be remembered and understood increases. This latter observation suggests that variations in cognitive functioning, such as how memorising might be deployed meaningfully or mindlessly, need to be researched as specific practices embedded in interacting cultural and institutional systems. We would suggest that the reliance of the secondary students in Hong Kong on the teacher and more capable peers to identify key points for meaningful memorisation, reflects the interaction of the following factors: (a) the demand on teachers and students to cover substantial curriculum content; (b) the cultural tradition of using examinations to assess student learning; and (c) the disposition of learners within Confucian heritage cultures to accept that learning requires considerable individual effort and persistence, as well as assistance from others. The intriguing research by Marton and associates, and similar research summarised in the chapters that follow in this section of the *Handbook* (see *Motivation and School Learning, Student Learning: A Cross-Cultural Perspective*), reveal only the current systemic interconnections between aspects of cognitive functioning and institutional and cultural practices, not a static or necessarily enduring configuration.

4. CONCLUSION

In concluding, we suggest that there are two general lessons for researchers that arise from reading the chapters in this section of the *Handbook*. First, researchers need to move beyond their national boundaries and cultural comfort zones to reconsider the processes and outcomes of socialisation and education. This introduction has drawn attention to the insights enabled by cross-cultural comparisons of key learning concepts such as memorisation, repetition, study approaches, and creativity. What these processes entail, and how they can be deployed effectively within schools and universities, has been shown to vary across cultures, and we would argue, change across time as new demands and opportunities are created by social, economic and technological change. In the final article in this section Cheung (see *Technology and Learning*) outlines the highly innovative approaches to learning that are being introduced within many of the countries of the region through the use of information and communications technology. These developments that involve embedding education within technology are likely to change the ways in which learning will take place in the future within educational institutions and within different social and cultural contexts.

Second, research conducted in the Asia-Pacific region is providing a catalyst and context for the formation of innovative local theories, and for the reconsideration of key assumptions derived from dominant Western models. We anticipate that this pattern of educational research, focussed on developing local models of pedagogy and exploring local wisdom and practices with regard to socialisation and educational processes, will continue. We hope that collaboration between researchers across nations and cultures will create the conditions for critical reflection on what are valued learning outcomes (cognitive, social-emotional and attitudinal), and critical participation in determining how these outcomes can be enhanced in educational contexts. This work clearly remains significant in optimising the learning and development of individuals, and more generally for fostering cross-cultural understanding and enhancing shared values of tolerance and peace.

REFERENCES

Ainley, J., Batten, M., Collins, C., & Withers, G. (1998). *Schools and the Social Development of Young Australians*. Camberwell, Victoria: Australian Council for Educational Research.

Anderson, R. C., & Pichert, J. W. (1978). Recall of previously unrecallable information following a shift in perspective. *Journal of Verbal Learning and Learning Behavior, 17*, 1–12.

Biggs, J. (1987). *Student approaches to learning and studying*. Hawthorn Victoria: Australian Council for Educational Research,

Biggs, J. (1994). What are effective schools? Lessons from east and west. *The Australian Educational Researcher, 21*, 19–39.

Bransford, J. D., Brown, A. L., & Cocking, R. (1999). *How people learn: Brain mind experience and school*. Washington DC: National Academy Press.

Cazden, C. (1988). *Classroom discourse: The language of teaching and learning*. Portsmouth, NH: Heinemann Press.

Chase, W. G., & Simon, H. A. (1973). Perception in chess. *Cognitive Psychology, 1*, 33–81.

Dahlin, B., & Watkins, D. (1999). The role of repetition in the processes of memorising and understanding. *British Journal of Educational Psychology, 70*, 65–84.

Education Queensland (2001). *Queensland School Reform Longitudinal Study*. Brisbane: Education Queensland.

Forster, M., & Masters, G. (2002). Accepting the challenge: Assessing the moral and ethical outcomes of schooling. In S. Pascoe (Ed.), *Values in Education* (pp. 140–151). Deakin West: Australian College of Education Yearbook.

Gardner, H. (1989). *To Open Minds*. New York: Basic Books.

Gonzales, E., & Miles, J. A. (2001). *TIMSS 1999: User guide for the international database*. Boston, MA.: International Study Center Lynch School of Education, Boston College, and International Association for the Evaluation of Educational Achievement.

Greenfield, P., & Suzuki, L. (1997). Culture and human development: Implications for parenting education pediatrics and mental health. In I. E. Sigel & K. A. Renninger (Eds.), *Handbook of Child Psychology, Vol. 4: Child Psychology in Practice* (pp. 1059–1109). New York: John Wiley & Sons.

Greeno, J. (1997). Theories and practices of thinking and learning to think. *American Journal of Education, 106*, 85–126.

Hess, R. D., & Azuma, H. (1991). Cultural support for schooling: Contrast between Japan and the United States. *Educational Researcher, 20*, 2–8, 12.

Jones, R. (1999). The third international mathematics and science study: Anatomy of this international comparative study in science education. *Australian Science Teachers Journal, 45*(2), 27–37.

Keeves, J. P. (1992a). *The IEA Study of Science III. Changes in Science Education and Achievement: 1970 to 1984*. Oxford: Pergamon.

Keeves, J. P. (1992b). *Learning science in a changing word: Cross-national studies of science achievement, 1970 to 1984*. The Hague: IEA.

Kennedy, K. J. (2001). Searching for values in a globalised world. In Pasoce (op cit).

Luke, A. (1995). Text and discourse in education: An introduction to critical discourse analysis. In M. W. Apple (Ed.), *Review of Research in Education, 21*, pp. 3–48. Washington DC: American Educational Research Association.

Markus, H., & Kitayama, S. (1991). Culture and the self: Implications for cognition emotion and motivation. *Psychological Review, 98*(2), 224–253.

Marton, F., Watkins, D., & Tang, C. (1997). Discontinuities and continuities in the experience of learning: An interview study of high-school students in Hong Kong. *Learning and Instruction, 7*, 21–48.

Masters, G. N., & Forster, M. (2000). *The Assessments We Need*. Melbourne: ACER.

Mehan, H. (1979). *Learning lessons: Social organisation in the classroom.* Cambridge, MA: Harvard University Press.

Newmann, F., & Associates (1996). *Authentic achievement: Restructuring schools for intellectual quality.* San Francisco: Jossey Bass.

Pellegrino, J. W., Chudowsky, N., & Glaser, R. (Eds.) (2001). *Knowing what students know.* Washington, DC: National Academy Press.

Postlethwaite, T. N., & Wiley, D. E. (1992). *The IEA Study of Science II: Science Achievement in Twenty-three Countries* Oxford: Pergamon.

Renshaw, P. D., & Volet, S (1995). South-East Asian students at Australian universities: A reappraisal of their tutorial participation and approaches to study. *Australian Educational Researcher, 22*(2), 85–106.

Renshaw, P. D. (2002). Learning and community. *The Australian Educational Researcher, 29*(2), 1–14.

Rosier, M. J., & Keeves, J. P. (1991). *The IEA Study of Science I: Science Education and Curricula in Twenty-three Countries.* Oxford: Pergamon.

Stevenson, H. W., & Stigler, J. (1992). *The learning gap: Why our students are failing and what we can learn from Japanese and Chinese education.* New York: Summit Books.

Stigler, J., & Stevenson, H. W. (1991). How Asian teachers polish each other to perfection. *American Educator, 15*(1), 12–21 & 43–47.

Stigler, J. W., & Hiebert, J. (1999). *The Teaching Gap.* New York: The Free Press.

Volet, S., & Renshaw, P. (1996). Chinese students at an Australian University: Adaptability and continuity. In J. Biggs & D. Watkins (Eds.) The *Chinese Learner: Cultural, Psychological and Contextual Influences* (pp. 205–220). Hong Kong: Comparative Educational Research Centre University of Hong Kong, and Australian Council of Educational Research.

Watkins, D. (2000). Correlates of approaches to learning: A cross-cultural meta-analysis. In R. Sternberg & L. F. Zhang (Eds.), *Perspectives on Thinking, Learning, and Cognitive Styles* (pp. 165–195). Mahwah, New Jersey: Erlbaum.

26

Cognitive Development

ALISON F. GARTON
Edith Cowan University, Perth, Australia

1. INTRODUCTION TO COGNITIVE DEVELOPMENT

Cognitive development refers to the development of processes that assist humans make sense of and understand their environment. These processes include such things as thinking, learning, memory, perception and attention; they are interconnected and inter-related and enable humans to understand and master their environment.

From infancy, cognitive processes start to develop or to function, with evidence that infants can learn and can remember, from even before birth (for a well-written review of cognitive development in children, see Goswami, 1998). The main questions that researchers ask when studying cognitive development in children are "What develops?" and "How does it develop?" Most studies are concerned with the former and try to chart or describe changes in cognition or cognitive abilities with age, through experimental tasks, tied in to a theoretical or explanatory framework. The latter question is more difficult to answer, and there have been many theoretical shifts in trying to explain how aspects of cognition change and develop over time. At least one contemporary Australian researcher, Halford, has made a substantial contribution to this second question and his work is described later.

This article is concerned with cognitive development in an Asian and Pacific context. It is focused almost exclusively on research that has been conducted in Australia, with Australian populations or by Australian researchers. In describing the contributions of Australians to the study of children's cognitive development, it is possible to look at empirical and theoretical investigations that are being conducted by researchers at Australian universities (technically, some of these people are not Australian by birth but by naturalisation or residency) or on Indigenous populations.

Australian research that examines children's cognitive development does not have its own tradition, and has been dominated by the influence of Piaget. Even the work (to be described later) on the cognitive development of Indigenous

Australians (Aborigines and Torres Strait Islanders) has focused predominantly on the application or relevance of Piagetian theoretical constructs for describing and predicting the cognitive skills and thinking of these people. This chapter describes some of the work that was conducted by Australians to assess the applicability of the theory to non-Western populations, and the more recent critique of this approach to the psychological study of Indigenous people. In addition, the unique theoretical contribution to an understanding of cognitive development by a small number of psychologists is presented.

Asian and Pacific research has, in the same vein, been mainly directed at elaborating theoretical or empirical work conducted in the United States and in Europe, and investigators generally publish their work in internationally recognised journals. Indeed, Dasen and Mishra (2000) comment that the study of human development in general is dominated by a Western perspective. The Japanese psychological community has been the most prolific in terms of contributions to the literature, and includes the work of Hatano and colleagues (for example, recent publications include Harris & Hatano, 1999; Hatano & Inagaki, 1999, 2000). Recent issues of *The Japanese Journal of Developmental Psychology* demonstrate that, during 2001, topics that were being studied included, for example, mother-child relationships (Sugano, 2001), adolescent mental health and the involvement of fathers in families (Hirayama, 2001) and young children's drawings (Taguchi, 2001). These topics are also noted in articles published in Western journals and there is nothing culture-specific about the research or its theoretical underpinnings.

This article is also focused on cognitive development in children, as not only is this the age group who has participated in most of the research, but as it can be argued that cognitive development is life-long (depending on the definition of 'development' employed), a limitation has been set on the age group to be included. Without being too prescriptive, the included research tends to be of approximately four to ten-year-old children, and excludes infants and adolescents.

2. INFLUENCE OF PIAGET

Without a doubt, the single most potent influence, both internationally and in Australia, on modern cognitive development, its study and its theorising, was Piaget. His contribution was to emphasise the development of children's knowledge as exemplified through children's thinking, that is, the active construction of knowledge. Piaget's theory is difficult to encapsulate but essentially he described all cognitive development in terms of three principles: accommodation, assimilation and equilibration, each derived from biology. These three principles manifest themselves as the child moves through three (or, more commonly, four, see below) stages of cognitive development, before attaining an adult, that is, an abstract and scientific, way of thinking. In this way, Piaget's theory was a description of how children progressively achieve more sophisticated thinking as exemplified by Western, educated, adult thought and learning.

The three principles, based as they are on an organic, biological, evolutionary view of human thought, underpin all cognitive development and describe the way in which humans adapt to their environment. It is also important to recognise that Piaget postulated the existence of schemes (or schemas) that were defined as psychological structures that organise experience; otherwise known as mental categories. Schemes are initially based on actions but, after infancy, are based on functional or conceptual relationships. Assimilation refers to the process whereby new experiences are incorporated into existing schemes and accommodation refers to the process where new schemes are modified based on experience. Assimilation and accommodation are usually in balance. If they are not, then disequilibrium results. Finally, equilibration describes the process by which children reorganise their schemes to restore balance, or equilibrium.

The four stages (some of which are further sub-divided in more elaborated versions of the theory) are: the sensory-motor stage, the preoperational stage, the concrete operational stage (in the three stage version, these two are combined and regarded as sub-divisions of one stage), and the formal operational stage. Roughly, these stages correspond to the following ages at which they are attained: 0 to 2 years, 2 to 6 years, 7 to 12 years, and 13 years onwards. The term 'roughly' is used because of cultural, social and educational variations in ages of attainment as well as attainment of the stages being different depending on the domain of thought under investigation. So another important principle underpinning Piaget's stage theory is that development does not occur in all cognitive domains simultaneously, and, for example, a child may demonstrate operational thinking on one task, say conservation (the understanding of identity) and not in another, say classification (the understanding of logical, mathematical ordering). Because Piaget was interested in providing a framework for understanding thinking and reasoning, the domains he used for his investigation tended to be those that reflect scientific concepts.

The sensory-motor stage is characterised by the development of motoric intelligence. The infant's world is dominated by what is referred to as the 'here and now' and it is possible to witness the gradual development of thought and language. In the preoperational stage, logic and imagination are dominated by perception and thinking is characterised by egocentricity, an inability to adopt or take account of the perspectives of others. In the concrete operational stage, children demonstrate the ability to conserve, that is, to understand number, classes and relationships. A major achievement is the development of reversibility in thought. Finally, the formal operational stage is characterised by hypothetico-deductive thinking and scientific abstract thinking.

3. SOCIAL EXPLANATIONS OF COGNITIVE DEVELOPMENT

Vygotsky, born in the same year as Piaget, but working in a different socio-historical culture and a different epistemological framework, has also made a substantial theoretical contribution to the understanding of cognitive development (see Garton & Pratt, 1998).

Vygotsky's theory covered the development of higher mental processes including all forms of intelligence and memory, and sought to "describe and specify the development of those forms of practical intelligence that are specifically human" (Vygotsky, 1978). Vgotsky's theory rests on the premise that cognitive development occurs primarily on the social level, within a particular cultural context. According to this view, children's cognitive development is maximised when it takes place in social settings, from which the culturally appropriate intellectual, cognitive and mental structures and their functions are internalised.

An important distinction made by Vygotsky was between development and learning in children. Learning is best characterised by what goes on in the classroom at school. Distinguishing school learning from development enabled Vygotsky to describe a central tenet to his theory, namely the 'zone of proximal development' (ZPD). This theoretical concept was introduced to explain the distinction between the child's actual cognitive developmental level, as measured by an IQ test for example, and the child's potential developmental level, when working with an adult or more capable peer. The latter level is characterised by what children are capable of achieving, given their socio-cultural development to date.

Vygotsky believed that collaborative functioning was a more useful indicator of a child's cognitive ability than individual performance. In order for a child to learn, tasks slightly in advance of the child's actual cognitive developmental level should be set, and instruction geared to the child's potential cognitive developmental level. Defining instruction as teaching and learning combined, Vygotsky put forward instruction as the mechanism whereby a child can grow intellectually. An adult or more capable peer in collaborating with the child conveys the tools of that society, which the child can pick up and use in interaction and subsequently use alone, independently. Vygotsky's theory has also influenced Australian research, particularly in the areas of cognitive and social development (e.g., Garton & Pratt, 2001; Goodnow, 2001). It is also very highly regarded in educational circles, where the notion of the ZPD has attracted a lot of attention as a teaching and learning mechanism.

4. RECENT THEORETICAL APPROACHES IN COGNITIVE DEVELOPMENT

The publication in 1998 of the updated *Handbook of Child Psychology*, in particular Volume Two (Siegler, 1998), drew attention to the plethora of theoretical frameworks that have been proposed, and supported by evidence, for children's cognitive development. Examples include the study of constraints, information processing, conceptual structures and social accounts. In addition to the vast array of theories, there are new and expanded topics such as cognition as a collaborative process, computer simulation of cognition, and theory-theory approaches to cognitive development. It is noted that these emerging research topics reflect both changes in emphasis as well as different theoretical approaches (Siegler, 1998).

Siegler (1998) notes at least four major trends in the field as follows: (a) increased emphasis on learning; (b) extent and importance of variability in children's thinking and learning; (c) increasing role of formal models; and (d) new metaphors and units of analysis that are shaping current understanding of cognitive development. These four issues are summarised by Siegler but are further fleshed out in the volume, a task that is impossible to do in an article. A comment about the diverse range of approaches, both theoretical and empirical, is warranted and it is worth reminding ourselves of the richness of the area of cognitive development, both as a theoretical or knowledge-building enterprise as well as the personal rewards of working with young children. These various theoretical positions have been adopted by various Australian researchers who conduct their studies of cognitive development within an internationally recognised theoretical framework.

5. COGNITIVE DEVELOPMENT IN INDIGENOUS AUSTRALIANS

In a recently published paper entitled 'Australian psychology has a black history', Garvey, Dudgeon and Kearins (2000) draw attention to two aspects of psychological involvement with Indigenous people. First, the Indigenous people of Australia (specifically Aboriginal and Torres Strait Islander people) were part of early investigations of mental functioning and in particular, of psychological functioning. Indigenous people served as 'subjects', or more accurately as 'objects', for psychological research. Second, they argue, the resultant categorisation of Indigenous people would, in contemporary Australia, be regarded as unethical and inappropriate. Twenty-first century views on Indigenous Australians are tempered not only by the research conducted in its time but by recent reporting and interpretation of history. The focus in this article is on the research conducted on cognitive abilities of mainly Aboriginal children from the 1930s until the 1970s.

Garvey et al. (2000) summarise the bulk of research conducted with Indigenous Australians, beginning from European settlement. Early research was conducted by anthropologists, and then by psychologists, driven by a growing interest in evolutionary origins of life and by the geographical isolation of Australia which seemed to confer on it a scientific advantage as an environment and human habitat untouched by outside influences. The Cambridge Anthropological Expedition in the early twentieth century was specifically undertaken to study Torres Strait Islanders who were regarded as the 'most primitive man'. Assessment was made of their sensorimotor functions such as vision, hearing, reaction times and so on, based on Galton's work which was conducted in the belief that such measures could be used to assess intellect. Comparisons were made with English and educated people, and much to the researchers' surprise, few if any differences were recorded, so there was no evidence to support the view that these people could be said to be 'primitive'.

The first Australian researcher interested in cognitive abilities was Porteus who developed some maze tests to be used for screening purposes in schools, to identify mentally defective students. Garvey et al. (2000) highlight two important contributions that Porteus made to an understanding of the cognitive and intellectual abilities of Indigenous Australians. First, Porteus found that adult Aborigines in the northwestern and central regions of Australia generally performed at lower levels than his norm samples, though with regional variations. Second, instead of categorising the Indigenous groups on a cultural dimension, Porteus developed a so-called 'ladder of development' that provided for an order of performance on his objective measure.

Other pioneers of research with Indigenous Australians, focusing on cognitive development and cognitive abilities include Fowler from the University of Western Australia, and McElwain and Kearney from the University of Queensland (for further discussion of the more general contribution to Australian Psychology of these three scholars, see Cooke, 2000). The development of the Queensland Test (McElwain & Kearney, 1970) led to more extensive assessments of Aboriginal children to determine whether the extent of contact with Western culture (as represented by so-called 'White Australians') had an effect on performance on a range of cognitive tasks. These cognitive tasks, although non-verbal and modified, were still essentially Western both in origin and in content. It was demonstrated that the performance of Indigenous people was inferior to that of comparison groups, to the same degree as the extent of their contact. Thus, McElwain and Kearney claim to have shown that Western cultural experience affects the test performance of Indigenous children. This finding was counter to that claimed by Porteous but it allowed for further research work on cognitive and intellectual development and abilities in Indigenous children.

Most of the work conducted in the 1960s and 1970s was derived from and influenced by Piaget. In the tradition of extending Piaget's theory to determine its generalisability and applicability to children in cultures other than European, many researchers in Africa, the United States and Australia began conducting cross-cultural experiments to examine the conservation abilities of various Indigenous groups. So, in Australia, for example, studies such as those by de Lemos (1973) showed that the development of conservation in Aboriginal children lagged behind that described for Western children. From this it was argued by some that because Piaget's theory described the development of logical thinking, and since conservation (and the underlying cognitive skill of reversibility) was fundamental to this way of thinking, Aboriginal children were somehow deficient and their intellectual development retarded because of this inability.

Garvey et al. (2000) discuss some of the implications of these conclusions, but do note that cross-cultural research in the Piagetian tradition has largely dried up due to the recognition that formal schooling plays a large role in the development of the type of thinking tapped by Piagetian cognitive tasks. These authors are also critical of the research that regarded the skills of Aboriginal children as 'deficient' so they would not benefit from education rather than tailoring the education system to try and foster cognitive skills necessary for functioning in what is now regarded as Western culture.

Two other researchers have been significant in work on cognitive development with Indigenous Australians, namely Seagrim at the Australian National University (see Seagrim & Lendon, 1980) and Kearins (1986) at the University of Western Australia. Seagrim and Lendon (1980) reported the findings of the Hermannsburg project which compared the cognitive performance of children from the Aranda and Loritja people, reared in the isolated Lutheran Mission Station in Central Australia, with other Aboriginal children reared elsewhere and in different circumstances. Cognitive performance was almost exclusively based on Piagetian indices and included tests of conservation, of classification and of seriation. The Hermannsburg project was longitudinal in nature and was conducted between 1965 and 1978, and involved a number of eminent researchers. So as well as the cross-sectional comparative element to the research, some Hermannsburg children were retested over a number of years.

The major aim of the research was to investigate the universality of Piaget's theory, in particular the nature of the causal forces that "propel the child forward through the stages" (Seagrim & Lendon, 1980, p. 2); in other words, to test whether the stages unfolded according to a predetermined pattern or whether they were subject to external pressures. It was claimed that cross-cultural research could begin to answer this question and it was predicted that Aboriginal groups with varying degrees of experience of contact with white culture, would demonstrate differences in cognitive performance and hence of intellectual development.

What Seagrim and Lendon did conclude was that Australian Aboriginal children were as capable as matched white children in the types of thinking identified as the hallmark of epistemology, namely conservation, classification and seriation, at similar ages and with similar educational experiences. However, this was only the case if the children had been totally immersed in the white culture (for a time period and at an age which were still unspecified). Under all the other circumstances studied, Aboriginal children lagged considerably behind or failed to exhibit the types of thinking tested by the Piagetian tasks. Seagrim and Lendon also claimed that schooling has no effect. Their final discussion, entitled "Some speculative conclusions", examined their findings from a theoretical perspective and also called for a recognition that appropriate solutions to the resistance of the Aboriginal students to acculturation must be found.

Kearins (1986) described research that she conducted to solve what she perceived to be a paradox in cognitive differences between human groups, particularly the Australian Aborigines. Starting from the commonly reported finding of cognitive inferiority amongst Australian Aborigines, Kearins noted that Aboriginal people have exceptional knowledge and skills that enable survival in the natural world, hence the paradox. Kearins thus embarked on a research program to identify the survival skills possessed by desert-living Aborigines as examples of cognitive skills. She hypothesised, for the study reported, that Aboriginal desert people would demonstrate high visual-spatial memory skills, since such skills would be necessary for survival. In fact, Kearins was testing a stronger hypothesis, namely that such skills had developed as a result of survival;

that is, there was positive genetic selection for these skills as they resulted from environmental demands. She dismisses this view at the end of the paper.

Reported in the 1986 paper are two experiments examining the spatial location skills and memory of Aboriginal children and adolescents compared with those of metropolitan adolescents. Kearins used a non-verbal version of Kim's Game involving rearranging objects in a grid. On all tasks, Aboriginal adolescents and children performed significantly better than white Australians, even controlling for familiarity with the materials. With the children, a semi-traditional Aboriginal sample was compared both with a white sample as well as a non-traditional Aboriginal sample. Only with the youngest sample, aged around seven and a half years, did the semi-traditional central desert children outperform the non-traditional sample.

Kearins noted that the Aboriginal children sat very still and concentrated on the task, taking their time to relocate objects. White children, by contrast, fidgeted and responded hastily. She infers that the Aboriginal children were using a visual strategy to solve the problem while the white children, as evidenced by their muttering, were using a verbal strategy which she comments was probably not the most efficacious for the materials used in the study. She believes that the similar pattern of results noted in both semi- and non-traditional Aboriginal families may be due to child-rearing practices, reflecting traditional practices and largely unchanged in semi-traditional homes, which lead to different ways of thinking. Kearins concludes that the superior visual spatial memory skills of Aboriginal children are part of a set of wider cognitive skills that are maintained by the culture.

The importance of this work was that it demonstrated that these superior skills shown by Aboriginal children regardless of their upbringing cannot be accounted for simply by speculating about the environment, although she does acknowledge that child-rearing strategies are similar. The studies by Kearins re-ignited the debate in Australia on race and intelligence as her work could be interpreted as showing that different selection processes may be at work to explain the superior visual abilities of young Australian children.

6. CONTEMPORARY AUSTRALIAN CONTRIBUTIONS

Most recently, Australian researchers have examined cultural psychology (e.g., Shweder, Goodnow, Hatano, LaVine, Markus, & Miller, 1998), mental models and relational complexity (e.g., Halford, 1993; Halford, Wilson, & Phillips, 1998), social explanations of theory of mind, with a focus on atypical children (e.g., Peterson, 2001; Peterson & Siegal, 2000), cognitive concomitants of reading difficulties (e.g., McKague, Pratt, & Johnson, 2001), and children's understanding of biology (e.g., Morris, Taplin, & Gelman, 2000). As noted earlier, in general, the contribution of these and other researchers is mainly in extending and elaborating on work that has its origins in the United States or the United Kingdom. This is further highlighted through collaboration with international scholars, often as a result of overseas study trips. While this work is novel and innovative in and of itself, its theoretical underpinnings are generally imported or developed jointly. The research is not a case of seeing if the theories hold for Australian children, it is more a case of testing and extending existing theories and adding to the international literature through publication in American, British and European journals or through international books.

Two volumes, each edited by Davidson (1988, 1994), exemplify the range of research that has been conducted on cognitive development both with Indigenous people and how Australian research has influenced work conducted in the broader Asia-Pacific region. It should be noted however that the latter volume contains very little on cognitive development *per se*; the focus is more on applied psychological research such as counselling and health psychology with multicultural clients; see also Dudgeon, Garvey and Pickett (2000), and the discussion later in this article. Davidson (1988) focuses specifically on cognitive assessment, defined fairly broadly but incorporating psychometric and educational tests. However, many of the issues raised are pertinent to the study of cognitive development in general and to working in a multicultural context in particular. Furthermore, the argument regarding the influence of schooling on cognitive performance (on tests or tasks typically designed to measure learning or intelligence) is placed in a context where it is argued that it may be more important, and more culturally sensitive, to examine cognitive competence that is functional and required for everyday living.

The work of Goodnow was for many years conducted while she worked in the United States. For example, her well-known work with Bruner in the 1950s (Bruner, Goodnow, & Austin, 1956) is a classic study of thinking in adults. However, Goodnow's attention in more recent times has been on the application of cultural psychology to various contexts, cognitive development being one of them. This work has been developed in conjunction with fellow researchers in the United States and Japan. While cultural psychology derives some of its theoretical underpinnings from Vygotsky, it draws more widely from the developmental and social psychological and anthropological literature, where the focus is on people as members of groups.

Cultural psychology acknowledges the role that social context plays in changes in developmental concepts and constructs. It is not new, nor is it concerned specifically with cultural differences. Cultural psychology is the study of how individuals think and act in relation to their particular cultural group. Cultural group is broadly defined as a "symbolic and behavioural inheritance" (Shweder et al., 1998, p. 867), and includes such things as family practices, neighbourhoods, local practices such as demonstrated in legal contexts, as well as the sociohistorical culture. Cultural psychology also uses a range of methodologies and focuses on changes in development. It has applicability across the life span, including children. The individual, according to a cultural perspective, must be an active processor of the cultural and sub-cultural traditions as well as being an active participant in mental life, contributing to maintenance of the inheritance as well to cultural and individual change.

In relation to cognitive development, studies have looked at the impact of others on what are traditionally regarded as solitary activities such as decision making and thinking. These are in addition to studies that have examined the social contexts of the development of theory of mind, the development of various types of cognitive activity such as monitoring and encoding, and the study of the mind as modular or domain-specific. In each of these, there is promise for demonstrating how social and cultural practices are influential (Goodnow, 2001). For example, in relation to the development of theory of mind, the question is how can a cultural view accommodate this theoretical perspective with its emphasis on mind as having an inherent disposition to make certain distinctions and categorisations?

Halford's relational complexity theory (Halford et al., 1998) has been applied to the processing loads associated with various cognitive development tasks (Halford, 2001) such as transitive inference, category induction and class inclusion. Relational complexity is a model or a database that is mathematical in nature. It defines elements or entities in terms of their relationship and roles with one another. By describing these seemingly diverse tasks in relation to their complexity and hence their processing load, Halford and his colleagues are beginning to explain developmental improvements in performance. An example is transitive inference (A is larger than B, B is larger than C, therefore A is larger than C), a problem studied extensively in children. By integrating the two premises ($A > B$ and $B > C$) into one ordered set ($A > B > C$), the processing load is increased and hence it is hypothesised that this is a factor in the difficulty encountered by children when they try and solve transitive inference problems (Halford, 1999). Analysing various cognitive problems in terms of their relational complexity has enabled the development of a framework that can explain and predict cognitive developmental changes.

Halford's unique theoretical contribution to the literature on children's cognitive development is highly regarded and recognised internationally. He highlights the role of higher cognitive processes such as analogy-mapping, relational complexity and neural nets can assist in explanations of how children's thinking develops. In particular, focusing on cognitive processes helps explain the changes in thought such as becoming more explicit, less dependent on content and more flexible, that occur as children get older. Halford's work has been influential internationally as contributing to the debate on how children's cognition develops, how their thinking changes with age and how we can describe the complexity and flexibility of thinking both in children and in adults.

7. FUTURE DIRECTIONS

With increasing globalisation in all aspects of our lives, it is unlikely that a uniquely identifiable Asian-Pacific psychology will emerge. In Australia, there is already a tradition of working with colleagues or theories developed overseas, and coupled with the use of technology such as the Internet and email, there are more opportunities for developmental psychologists to work internationally and collaboratively. However, it is more probable that there will be increasing links with researchers in the immediate Asia-Pacific region, facilitated by the push by some Australian universities to deliver education to students in South-East Asia. Links already established will continue to be fostered. For example, Hatano has presented a keynote address at the past two biennial Australasian Human Development Conferences in 1999 and 2001 and on the second occasion, he brought other Japanese researchers as presenters. China is poised to host the International Congress of Psychology in 2004 and will showcase the research that is currently being conducted. Cognitive development research has been a particular focus since the 1950s and was originally linked to China's cultural and social development. This tradition has continued and there has been a large amount of research on children's mathematical and reading skills and their classroom learning. Opportunities such as conferences and research higher degree studies at Australian universities mean that there is discussion and debate from different cultural perspectives.

In contrast, much contemporary research in places like Thailand, Malaysia and Indonesia has been concerned with the relationship between poverty, in particular malnutrition, and children's cognitive development. This focus has been driven by the World Bank, which has injected large amounts of money into programs that provide food to poor children to protect against the effects of malnutrition. Longer-term goals include the provision of early child development programs and basic education. Research therefore focuses on the development of programs that enhance not only cognitive development but also social and emotional development, and the evaluation of these programs.

However, it may be that, like the cognitive developmentalists in the United Kingdom, an area of interest can be the focus of a high level of research activity, thus ensuring the influence of Australian researchers. Nevertheless, it does have to be acknowledged that any such influence is only recognised through international publication. Halford's relational complexity theory, applied as it is to cognitive developmental problems, and Goodnow's cultural theory would both appear to be promising key areas for Australian research, and ones that can be sustained through research efforts for the foreseeable future.

As noted previously, research on the cognitive development of Indigenous Australians is largely now non-existent. Contemporary psychological work with Indigenous people is more focused on working in culturally sensitive ways, applying different psychological models to counsel, empower and assist Indigenous people and communities (Dudgeon, Garvey, & Pickett, 2000). Most of the psychological work is not research-oriented but attempts to include an indigenous perspective in order to understand better Aboriginal knowledge. This is turn enables the application of more sensitive and appropriate psychological techniques and interventions, ranging from psychometric assessment to community empowerment. Until there is a better understanding of the needs of Indigenous people and a greater awareness of their priorities and knowledge base, then it is unlikely that there will be studies of specific psychological topics such as language or cognitive development.

REFERENCES

Bruner, J. S., Goodnow, J., & Austin, G. (1956). *A Study of Thinking.* New York: Wiley.
Cooke, S. (2000). *A Meeting of Minds: The Australian Psychological Society and Australian Psychologists 1944-1994.* Carlton: The Australian Psychological Society.
Dasen, P. R., & Mishra, R. C. (2000). Cross-cultural views on human development in the third millennium. *International Journal of Behavioural Development, 24*, 428-434.
Davidson, G. R. (Ed.) (1988). *Ethnicity and Cognitive Assessment: Australian Perspectives.* Darwin, NT: Darwin Institute of Technology.
Davidson, G. R. (Ed.) (1994). *Applying Psychology: Lessons from Asia-Oceania.* Carlton: The Australian Psychological Society.
de Lemos, M. (1973). In G. E. Kearney, P. R. de Lacey & G. R. Davidson (Eds.), *The Psychology of Aboriginal Australians* (pp. 71-88). Sydney: John Wiley.
Dudgeon, P., Garvey D., & Pickett, H. (Eds.) (2000). *Working with Indigenous Australians: A Handbook for Psychologists.* Perth: Gunada Press.
Garton, A. F., & Pratt, C. (1998). *Learning to be Literate: The Development of Spoken and Written Language* (2nd Edition). Oxford: Blackwell.
Garton, A. F., & Pratt, C. (2001). Peer assistance in children's problem solving. *British Journal of Developmental Psychology, 19*, 307-318.
Garvey, D., Dudgeon, P., & Kearins, J. (2000). Australian psychology has a black history. In P. Dudgeon, D. Garvey & H. Pickett (Eds.), *Working with Indigenous Australians: A Handbook for Psychologists.* Perth: Gunada Press.
Goodnow, J. (2001, July). Translating cultural perspectives into mainstream developmental research. Keynote address presented at the 12th Biennial Australasian Human Development Conference, Brisbane.
Goswami, U. (1998). *Cognition in Children.* Hove, Sussex: Psychology Press.
Halford, G. S. (1993). *Children's Understanding: The Development of Mental Models.* Hillsdale NJ: Lawrence Erlbaum.
Halford, G. S. (1999). The properties of representations used in higher cognitive processes: Developmental implications. In I. E. Siegel (Ed.), *Development of Mental Representation: Theories and Applications.* Mahwah NJ: Lawrence Erlbaum Associates.
Halford, G. S. (2001, July). Relational complexity and cognitive development. Key Theme Symposium, 12th Biennial Australasian Human Development Conference, Brisbane.
Halford, G. S., Wilson, W. H., & Phillips, S. (1998). Processing capacity defined by relational complexity: Implications for comparative, developmental and cognitive psychology. *Behavioral and Brain Sciences, 21.*
Harris, M., & Hatano, G. (1999). *Learning to Read and Write: A Cross-Linguistic Perspective.* New York: Cambridge University Press.
Hatano, G., & Inagaki, K. (1999). A developmental perspective on informal biology. In D. L. Medin & S. Atran (Eds.), *Folkbiology* (pp. 321-354). Cambridge, MA: MIT Press.
Hatano, G., & Inagaki, K. (2000). Domain-specific constraints of conceptual development. *International Journal of Behavioural Development, 24*, 267-275.
Hirayama, S. (2001). Adolescent mental health and fathers' involvement in families: The incongruent rating of fathers and mothers. *Japanese Journal of Developmental Psychology, 12*, 99-109.
Kearins, J. (1986). Visual spatial memory in Aboriginal and white Australian children. *Australian Journal of Psychology, 38*, 203-214.
McElwain, D., & Kearney, G. E. (1970). *Queensland Test Handbook.* Melbourne: ACER.
McKague, M., Pratt, C., & Johnson, M. B. (2001). The effects of oral vocabulary on reading visually

novel words: A comparison of the dual-route-cascaded and triangle frameworks. *Cognition, 80,* 239–270.

Morris, S. C., Taplin, J. E., & Gelman, S. A. (2000). Vitalism in naïve biological thinking. *Developmental Psychology, 36,* 582–595.

Peterson, C. (2001). Influence of siblings' perspective on theory of mind. *Cognitive Development, 15,* 435–455.

Peterson, C. C., & Siegal, M. (2000). Insights into theory of mind from deafness and autism. *Mind & Language, 15,* 123–145.

Seagrim, G. N., & Lendon, R. J. (1980). *Furnishing the Mind: A Comparative Study of Cognitive Development in Central Australian Aborigines.* Sydney: Academic Press.

Shweder, R. A., Goodnow, J., Hatano, G., LaVine, R. A., Markus, H., & Miller, P. (1998). The cultural psychology of development: One mind, many mentalities. In R. M. Lerner (vol. Ed.), W. Damon (Ed. in chief) *Handbook of Child Psychology Volume 1: Theoretical Models of Human Development* (5th Ed.) (pp. 865–938). New York: Wiley.

Siegler, R. S. (1998). Forward to Volume 2: Cognition, Perception and Language. In D. Kuhn & R. S. Siegler (vol. eds.), W. Damon (ed. in chief), *Handbook of Child Psychology. Volume 2: Cognition, Perception and Language* (5th ed.) (pp. xxi–xxiv). New York: Wiley.

Sugano, Y. (2001). The effect of a mother's negative feelings toward her child on the mother-child relationship. *Japanese Journal of Developmental Psychology, 12,* 12–23.

Taguchi, M. (2001). A developmental study of young children's drawings: Visual realism and amount of information. *Japanese Journal of Developmental Psychology, 12,* 206–215.

Vygotsky, L. (1978). *Mind in Society: The Development of Higher Mental Processes.* Cambridge, MA: Harvard University Press.

27

Lifespan Human Development

CANDIDA C. PETERSON
University of Queensland, Brisbane, Australia

1. INTRODUCTION

This article explores psychological development from a lifespan perspective, with a special focus on the periods of youth, adulthood and old age. These phases, like infancy and childhood before them, are exciting periods of developmental change. As adolescents embark upon mature lives independently, and as adults progress through the successive milestones and turning points of mature life (like marriage, a new baby, a new career, the launching of adult children into independence, retirement from a lifelong career, the birth of a grandchild, or widowhood), new opportunities for psychological growth are continually presented. At the same time, the range of available choices may narrow, losses will arise, and problems and disappointments will almost certainly occur. These adversities, too, will provide the impetus and opportunity for psychological adjustment, and gains in maturity can arise out of successful coping late in life, just as they did during childhood. The lifespan approach to the study of human development seeks to understand these continuities and discontinuities in psychological growth and change over the whole of life.

It is clear that every change in psychological functioning over the course of life has biological underpinnings. Development likewise takes place in a sociocultural context. Throughout life, each person's developmental course draws from hereditary roots in interaction with social and cultural experience. At all ages, psychological growth is nurtured by others and is interwoven with an evolving network of close relationships. At the same time, broader social influences of the surrounding cultural and historical milieux exert an impact upon developing individuals throughout their lives. Furthermore, as Baltes and Staudinger (1996) point out "As one moves into later phases of life, the primary resource for advances in levels and maintenance of functions is not biology but culture" (p. 14).

Some cultural conditions of development are common to most human societies throughout the world and have pervaded many eras in human history (such as nurturance of infants in small family settings, care for weaker young or elderly members of the group by able bodied adults, and parental employment in order to secure the means to feed and support dependent children). Others are unique to a particular cultures and to narrow historical time frames (such as widespread availability of university education for young adults or the norm of 'filial piety' that has shaped attitudes and behaviours towards elderly family members in many countries in the Asia-Pacific region with a Confucian philosophical tradition (Takahashi, 2000). As it takes shape from infancy through old age, the individual life course bears the imprint of all of these specific and general social, cultural and historical influences.

2. A DEFINITION

The lifespan approach to the study of human psychological development seeks a scientific understanding of these varied and continuing patterns of change in human lives from infancy through old age. A core assumption is that human development has an inherent predictability, and is coherently integrated, from conception to death. Thus lifespan researchers view the developmental achievements of newborn infants in the context of the myriad changes that these may lead to throughout the remainder of life, and see old age as the continuing manifestation of patterns that became established decades earlier. Lifespan research thus seeks to piece together the puzzle that links all stages of a human life together across its unique developmental course, and to understand the variations and constancies arising from one culture to another and from one era in history to the next.

As a scientific discipline, 'lifespan human development' came into its own towards the middle of last century along with a number of exciting new scientific breakthroughs (Birren & Birren, 1990). These included: (a) theoretical recognition of the regularities pervading lifelong patterns of age-related psychological change, and of the possibility for genuine growth during mature stages of the lifespan (Erikson, 1950); (b) the implementation of new sequential research designs and methodologies that enabled the integration of cross-sectional and longitudinal assessments of psychological functioning across broad age spans (Baltes & Schaie, 1973); and (c) a divergence of developmental psychology from pediatric and geriatric medicine to promote recognition of the developmental potential that characterises *healthy* psychological ageing, in contrast to elderly sufferers of geriatric illnesses and disabilities (Birren & Birren, 1990). As Birren and Birren explained:

> Development, as scientists have defined it, implies changes in the organization of behaviour from simple to complex forms, from fixed ways of responding to demands and needs to larger repertoires of behaviours that can be strategically chosen. This suggests that development ends at no specific time and that the organism may continue to differentiate behaviours long after

physical maturity, and move toward increasing complexity. (Birren & Birren, 1990, p. 9)

Lifespan developmental psychology emerged out of the union of these three conceptual advances as the scientific discipline that would be devoted to the study of the patterns of continuity and change that punctuate the individual's development course within each domain of psychological functioning beginning at conception and continuing through old age (Goulet & Baltes, 1970). According to Baltes and his colleagues (Baltes, 1989; Baltes, Staudinger, & Lindenberger, 1999), contemporary lifespan developmental research and theory has continued along this promising course by seeking to clarify further, three components of the discipline's knowledge base.

Inter-individual regularities in development. These are the age-related patterns of psychological functioning that apply to most people as they grow up and grow older.

Inter-individual differences in development. These are contrasts in developmental patterns seen among groups of people growing up and growing old in different geographical, historical, cultural, or socio-economic environments, who may also differ on variables like gender, health, temperament, etc.

Intra-individual plasticity in development. This is the extent to which patterns of development are modifiable, both to produce positive developmental gains in psychological capability, and to afford resiliency in offsetting, correcting or minimising loss or damage arising with age.

Scientific research seeking to explore these facets of development over the lifespan is often guided by one or more of the following aims: (a) the goal of *description* of age-related patterns of continuity and change in psychological capacities and functions; (b) the goal of deriving theoretical *explanations* for the causes for these observed regularities over age; and (c) the applied goal of creating and evaluating interventions to *optimise* the individual's lifespan developmental trajectory.

Optimisation research, the most recently emerging of the core research goals of lifespan developmental psychology as a discipline (Baltes & Staudinger, 1996), is arguably the most challenging of the three. The application of developmental science to enhance human psychological wellbeing and effective functioning over the whole of life has been described by Baltes (1989) as including three subgoals: (a) the enrichment of developmental opportunities over the whole lifespan; (b) the prevention of age-linked barriers, difficulties and setbacks that could block the uptake of developmental opportunities; and (c) the alleviation of, or compensation for, age-related losses in psychological capacity and functioning.

The application of these goals to a selection of illustrative research problems is examined throughout the remainder of this article. The next section briefly explores how these scientific concerns of lifespan human development as a research discipline intersect with lay people's conceptions of the life cycle, examining culturally shared beliefs about adult capacities for change, the characteristic features of different age groups and of the problems and potentialities for wellbeing during adult life stages. Wisdom, a culturally shared cognitive construct regarding adult cognition will be examined in some detail, along with some of the insights that empirical studies of wisdom have supplied to assist the understanding of lifespan development more generally. The article concludes with a detailed overview of some of the key scientific findings about the process of lifelong human psychological growth that have emerged from more than half a century of lifespan research guided by the aims and assumptions that have just been outlined.

3. CULTURALLY-SHARED BELIEFS ABOUT LIFESPAN DEVELOPMENT

Long before the emergence of lifespan human development as a scientific discipline of study, popular conceptions have prevailed in most cultures about what kinds of behaviour can reasonably be expected of different age groups (Goodnow, 1996), about the ideal trajectories for development, about the ways people are actually likely to change as they grow up and grow older, and about social standards of appropriate forms of behaviour at various ages. Indeed beliefs about the inevitability of negative cognitive and psychological changes in human ageing are pervasive among cultures throughout the Asia-Pacific region, including Indonesia, Hong Kong, Laos, Korea, the Philipines and Japan, as well as Australia, New Zealand and the USA (Jin, Ryan, & Anas, 2001; Noesjirwan, Gault, & Crawford, 1983; Williams et al., 1997). However, cultures do vary in their popular beliefs about the universality and severity of these anticipated cognitive declines. For example, when Noesjirwan, Gault and Crawford (1983) questioned indigenous Minangkabau inhabitants of western Sumatra and urban Australians in Sydney about the likelihood of forgetfulness in the elderly, they found both groups believed that memory problems would arise in old age, as compared with younger adults. But the Sumatrans were more likely than the Sydneysiders to anticipate severe problems with old people's remembering of trivial information such as the ages of their nieces and nephews or the names of their contemporaries.

Despite some room for variation amongst individuals, however, it does seem that many popular lay beliefs and core philosophies about development are culturally shared (Goodnow, 1996). Even more importantly, recent research into these lay beliefs has shown that they exert important social influences. Indeed, beliefs about development may play a guiding role: (a) in shaping the normative behaviour of members of particular age groups within that culture; (b) in determining how different age cohorts within the culture will interact with one another (e.g., via parental strategies for childrearing, or through adult children's involvement in caring for their elderly parents); and (c) in bolstering or undermining the happiness and emotional wellbeing of individuals, as they act upon beliefs about how the life course should unfold itself, and evaluate their own progress in relation to this culturally-shared framework of developmental ideals. Therefore, as Goodnow and Collins (1990) explained, it is impossible to understand fully the development of any one individual person in isolation. Instead, the cultural milieu must be taken into account, along with all the interconnected and 'intersubjective' (Goodnow, 1996) personal relationships within which every individual lifespan is entwined and embedded. Developmental patterns and plans are shaped by attitudinal factors within the culture, including socially-shared cognitions about how development *does*, and *should* happen. According to Goodnow and Collins "A cultural history of ideas about childhood, parenting and the course of development" (1990, p. 7) underlies each person's progress through the life cycle and is implicit in the decisions we all make as we plan and evaluate our own lives, while exerting direct and indirect influences over the developmental journeys of our own parents, partners, offspring and others around us.

It is rare for these cultural beliefs and expectations about the lifespan to be drawn out into the open, much less to be questioned or challenged in light of scientific research evidence. Yet, without explicit examination, people's belief systems can sometimes block development by proving to be irrationally negative and constraining. Thus it is important to examine objectively how men and women in different cultures conceptualise the life course as a subjective entity. In line with this goal, Byrd and Breuss (1992) conducted a study of impressions of adult life among samples of young, middle-aged and elderly men and women in New Zealand. They examined these adults' beliefs about the chronological age boundaries for different adulthood phases along with these men's and women's subjective evaluations and anticipations about the best and worst phases in the human life cycle.

Specifically, they asked groups of New Zealanders who were themselves either young (in their 20s), middle-aged (in their 30s, 40s and 50s) or elderly (over 60) to name an age in years that depicted: (a) a young man or woman, (b) a middle-aged man or woman and (c) an old man or woman, and also to respond to the subjective probes, (d) "What is the prime of life for a man and for a woman?", (e) "What is the worst time of life for a man and for a woman?". Their results revealed both within-age consistencies and cross-age differences in popular beliefs about the life course. For example, the young New Zealanders considered their own present age, 26 years, to be the ideal stage in life, naming this as the 'prime-of-life' for both sexes, whereas the elderly New Zealand men reported that life's prime arose during the 60s (at a mean of 67 years for a man, and at 63 for a woman). These subjective reports indicate that both actual and anticipated experiences of lifespan development may differ dramatically in New Zealand for men as compared with women, and for younger as compared with older adults. The contrasts between younger and older adults' judgments of life's prime also suggest that the actual experience of living old age in one's own life may be far more positive as a subjective experience than in the cultural stereotype (which is all that the young adults would have had to go on).

However, even if unrealistic, a negative popular stereotype of old age can have adverse social consequences. As Baltes and Staudinger (1996) noted: "Social interactions and transactions involving the elderly often proceed from the very expectation of aging deficits and thereby may contribute to further decline on the part of the elderly" (p. 15). Even worse, younger men and women may avoid old people altogether, owing to their stereotypic perceptions of the sadness and frustration to be encountered were they to involve themselves with people they imagine to be unavoidably depressive, lonely, and gloomy (Smith, 2001).

To what extent are adverse images of old age like these culturally specific? One hypothesis is that norms of filial piety, collectivism and respect for Buddhist teachings and Confucian philosophy (Takahashi, 2000; Williams et al., 1997) may have embued a more positive favour to popular beliefs about old age in China, Japan, Korea, Laos and other parts of Asia-Pacific region than are found in cultures like New Zealand, Australia or the United States with a more strongly European and individualistic cultural heritage. Data relevant to this possibility emerged from a study by Hori (1994) that applied a similar method to that of Byrd and Breuss in Japan. Hori tested a large sample of Japanese adults, grouped by age into: (a) the elderly (195 women and 205 men with a mean age of 69 years), (b) the middle-aged (104 women and 87 men with a mean age of 38 years), and (c) young adults (252 university students with a mean age of 19 years).

There were a number of similarities to the New Zealand data, and a few differences. The elderly Japanese saw the prime of life as occurring in the 40s, whereas the elderly New Zealanders believed it arose after 50. Younger adults in both cultures placed the cut-offs for age periods, and the prime-of-life, at younger ages than their elderly compatriots did. Furthermore, the Japanese students, like their young New Zealand counterparts, seemed to hold bleak impressions of all age periods following the mid-30s. Yet, as in New Zealand, the impressions of adults in Japan who had already reached middle age or old age themselves were much more positive, prompting Hori to conclude: "Better communication and mutual understanding among different generations and possibly redefinition of the human life course are needed. For these reasons, we have to reconsider the role of what we call 'aging education'" (Hori, 1994, p. 447).

At the same time, however, a comparison between the results of these Japanese and New Zealand studies gives no evidence of a beneficial effect of Asian philosophy on subjective views of the final decades of life, as compared with the attitudes of New Zealand adults from an Anglo-European tradition. Indeed, if anything, the New Zealanders held more positive views of old age, especially elderly New Zealand men.

4. THE GETTING OF WISDOM

A lay belief about old age that seems widespread among both Eastern and Western cultures alike, is that the opportunity to become wise may emerge for the first time in old age. In Eastern philosophy (Takahashi, 2000) as in the West (Clayton & Birren, 1980), there has been extensive recognition of the value of old people's advice, based on the wise elder's unique capacity to reason based on accumulated knowledge, wide experience and a lifetime of honing judgmental abilities to their sharpest level.

As Baltes (1993) pointed out, throughout most eras in history, and across many very disparate cultural groups, a popular belief sets intelligent elders apart from intelligent younger people. In particular, in many cultures throughout the Asia-Pacific region, as well as much of the rest of the world, there is general agreement that a certain kind of knowledge, rarely or never seen even in the most quick-witted and erudite of younger adults, emerges for the first time in late middle-age. Labelled as 'wisdom' in English, this cognitive "capstone of the human mind" (Baltes, 1993, p. 385) has its own special name in most other human languages. In addition to being deemed the special purview of the elderly, wisdom, as a culturally shared belief, is seen to have all of the following characteristics (Baltes, 1993).

(1) Wisdom deals with important and difficult matters associated with the conduct of society or individual life and connected with fundamentals of the human condition.
(2) Wisdom provides inarguably more advanced and superior knowledge, judgment and advice than other cognitive processes are capable of producing.
(3) Wisdom consists of knowledge that has unusual depth, scope and balance, and is more pertinent than other kinds of knowledge to the serious everyday problems of life.
(4) Wisdom, when effectively implemented, incorporates and integrates mental or cognitive with emotional/moral elements so that it can be seen as an expression of 'virtue' or 'character' as well as an expression of pure thought.
(5) Wisdom as the culmination of a lengthy developmental process is very difficult to achieve, but somewhat easier to pinpoint and recognize in others.

However, is wisdom defined in this way, a scientifically accessible and reliable phenomenon? Or is it a shared cultural fiction without objective foundation? To test this, Baltes (1993) and his colleagues (see Baltes & Staudinger, 1996; Baltes, Staudinger, & Lindenberger, 1999 for reviews) developed an empirically validated, objective measurement procedure for assessing wisdom in individuals under experimentally controlled conditions. The Berlin Wisdom Paradigm (BWP), currently used extensively in research projects throughout the world, has identified and defined wisdom operationally as "an expert knowledge system in the fundamental pragmatics of life" (Baltes & Staudinger, 1996, p. 280). Research evidence shows that wisdom, defined in this way, is a special cognitive ability psychometrically distinct from general intelligence. It has the following attributes: (a) rich factual and procedural knowledge about life, (b) life-span contextualism, (c) value relativism and (d) tolerance and management of uncertainty. Using this measure, (Baltes, 1993; Staudinger, 1996), among others have shown that wisdom is often found more frequently in older adults than in youths and adolescents, but is by no means universal at any age. As Staudinger explained:

> Age is no guarantee for an actual increase of wisdom-related knowledge and skill. Instead, the accumulation of wisdom-related knowledge may depend on ... a great number of experiences, guidance (having a mentor, i.e., social interaction in dealing with those experiences, and on a certain personality makeup such as the interest in gaining insights into life. (Baltes & Staudinger, 1996, p. 285)

In Australia, a study that similarly measured older adults' wisdom-related knowledge using a different laboratory assessment technique (relativistic operational thought: Sinnott, 1984) likewise revealed the importance of social involvement and active community participation for the maintenance and expression of wise reasoning during old age (Collins, Luszcz, Lawson, & Keeves, 1997).

5. DATA-DRIVEN ASSUMPTIONS ABOUT LIFESPAN DEVELOPMENT

The final section of this article is devoted to a more detailed examination of the nature of contemporary assumptions about development through the lifespan, along with a selection of the theoretical insights and research evidence that has been drawn together in their support (for a more detailed account, see Baltes, 1993; Baltes & Staudinger, 1996).

No age period holds supremacy for growth or loss. The assumption that all periods in life are times for potential development implies the need to investigate change in psychological processes throughout all life phases, looking for patterns of gain and loss in behavioural capacities. Indeed, from conception through old age, losses, as well as gains, are apt to occur in psychological capacity, power and efficiency of functioning (Baltes, 1993), so that from the earliest beginnings of development, not all changes are in a positive direction. Instead, a restriction of some abilities and reserve capacities is likely to accompany dramatic spurts of growth in different directions. Thus, with each new growth gain, something else may be lost and avenues for future development may well be closed off, or at least made more difficult (Johnson & Medinnus, 1968). At the same time, the age-related change in psychological functioning arising during the adult portion of the lifespan is not the unmitigated decline that might be suggested by an over-simplified biological analogy with a withering plant. Human beings may gain psychological strengths well into adult life and old age in such cognitive dimensions as wisdom (Baltes, 1993: and see the previous section of this article), as well as through positively valued emotional attributes like mellowness and breadth of vision or with the acquisition of personality strengths such as creativity, altruism or generativity (Erikson, 1950).

Qualitative and quantitative change. Although lifespan human development as a scientific discipline is concerned with all kinds of changes in behavioural, psychological and social functioning, provided that these can be predicted by chronological age, there is a special focus in the discipline upon changes that have the property of being genuinely developmental. In other words, as outlined above, in addition to being age-related and sometimes quantitative, developmental changes are often qualitative transformations. Genuinely developmental changes also have the properties of being: (a) relatively 'permanent' (as opposed to merely cyclic or temporary changes such as diurnal fluctuations of mood, fatigue or hunger); (b) 'generalisable' across many generational cohorts of people (as opposed to being unique to a particular group developing within a specific time frame in a culture's history); and (c) 'progressively enhancing' of the individual's capacity to function psychologically (as opposed to regressive or degenerative changes).

Multidirectional development. The notion that human psychological development is multidirectional implies a need for consideration of the whole person as a changing, developing organism. For convenience, developmental researchers are likely to focus their investigations on particular psychological processes like memory, mood or conflict resolution within particular domains of psychological functioning like cognition, personality or social relationships. Yet within the context of these specific research studies, the lifespan approach is concerned with regularities and interconnections among age periods and across varied developmental phenomena. Consequently, the complete pattern of development that guides human behaviour from earliest infancy through extreme old age, is best conceived as a coherent, though highly complex, network of growth trajectories that cannot be understood completely in isolation from one another.

The gain-loss balance. Psychological development at all stages in life entails both gains and losses, as noted above. Individuals who grow and change over the lifespan in positive directions do not always simply add greater and greater powers to their psychological repertoires. Instead, many developmental gains entail a narrowing of reserve capacity and a restriction of available avenues for future development. Optimal development can therefore be conceptualised as an effective balancing of gains against losses so that the ratio remains favourable: that is, so that the overall net gain in psychological capacity and power to cope equals, or outweighs, the amount of capacity that has been lost with age (Baltes, 1993).

At later stages in the life span, the rate of gaining new psychological capacities is likely to be slower than during infancy and childhood. Yet new capacities still do continue to emerge. The balance of losses relative to gains is also shifted by declines in physiological processes in late adulthood. For example, biological declines in old age will mean that, provided they live long enough, most older men and women will have weaker visual acuity, less hearing capacity, slower motor speed, and less muscular strength than they had in their youth, and their average performace in these physical domains will probably be below that of an average young adult (Luszcz & Giles, 2001). Health and mobility are likewise subject to decline.

Yet, despite these physical setbacks, psychological development, even in extreme old age reflects a ratio, not an absolutely down-hill course. New problem-solving skills may develop late in life, as noted in the studies of wisdom that were described in the previous section of this article. Older adults will also often have gained an impressive repertoire of social skills and life experiences which can be drawn upon to enrich their relationships with others (Smith, 2001), thus restoring the gain-loss ratio through social and psychological compensations for inevitable physical declines.

Baltes (1993) developed a model known as 'S-O-C' (for 'selective optimisation with compensation') to describe the adult's balancing of developmental losses and gains to achieve optimal cognitive performance. By selecting skills that often remain intact in spite of ageing (such as vocabulary, reading, problem solving), and by compensating with maturational gains (in qualities such as wisdom, mellowness or social experience) for those declines and losses that must inevitably arise (e.g., sensory acuity, reaction speed), the older man or woman can optimise psychological functioning, as when an older piano player chooses slower melodies and practices these more extensively than in youth to achieve an equal level of performance skill on stage. Thus psychological development throughout adulthood and old age can be a highly individualised, fascinatingly complex, and largely the interplay of gains and losses, just as it is at all earlier stages in life. According to Baltes and his colleagues:

> Successful development is defined in this theoretical approach as the conjoint maximization of gains (desirable goals or outcomes) and the minimization of losses (undesirable goals or outcomes). The nature of what constitutes gains and losses, and of the dynamic between gains and losses, is conditioned by cultural and personal factors as well as by the position in the lifetime of an individual. (Baltes et al., 1999, p. 476)

Developmental plasticity. The notion of 'plasticity' in human development implies that human behaviour is always open to change and can take many forms, depending upon the person's life circumstances and developmental history. There is important individual variation in the range of plasticity throughout the life span. Some individuals adapt quickly to change while others of the same age may do so only very slowly, or not at all. For example, Garmezy (1993) discovered a group of so-called 'resilient' children who were unusually flexible in coping with circumstances that might otherwise have blocked their developmental opportunities. Thus many of these children grew up normally, or even came to express above-average levels of talent and psychological adjustment, despite their early exposure to harshly stressful lifestyles, dysfunctional family patterns and extreme poverty. The exceptional plasticity of these children's psychological development in overcoming early environmental adversities appeared to reflect their unique combination of a positive temperament, good coping skills and a close emotional attachment to a nurturant caregiver.

During adulthood and old age, developmental plasticity likewise continues to operate, within defined limits, and two important challenges for lifespan research are: (a) to discover what these limits are in setting upper bounds upon the range of human plasticity in cognitive, personality and social domains at different ages; and (b) to identify individual variability in the plasticity of core developmental processes during late adulthood (for example, in degree recovery of function after a stroke, or in re-establishment social connectedness and emotional well-being after bereavement).

This can often be achieved through applied optimisation research in which, for example, an older learner is given explicit training in mnemonic devices and other deliberate memorization strategies to overcome the forgetfulness that sometimes accompanies old age. As Baltes and his colleagues (1999, p. 476) explained:

The goal is to compress time by providing for high-density developmental experiences; and, by doing so, to identify asymptotes of performance potential (plasticity). These asymptotes, obtained under putatively optimal conditions of support, are expected to estimate the upper range of the age-specific developmental potentiality.

Development is embedded in the social context. As age increases, culture and social attitudes are likely to exert increasingly significant influences over the process of individual psychological development. The younger adult's move out of the family of rearing into the wider world of careers, education, travel and intimate relationships opens new avenues of cultural influence. Over time, each person's varied interactions with the people, culture, and society they are growing up with will come together as mental models of the future lifespan. These implicit notions about development can be compared to a timetable or 'social clock'. According to Neugarten (1979), the 'normative social clock' consists of a set of socially shared beliefs about how milestone events should be timetabled. All age groups come under the jurisdiction of the social clock. Though the injunction 'Act your age!' means something different to a preschooler than to a senior citizen, the prescriptions contained within society's normative clock exert a similar influence in stimulating developmental change for members of all age groups. By calling attention to the social expectations of how to conduct oneself in view of one's age, and to the penalties for violation of age roles (which may range from mild disapproval to social ostracism), the norms embodied in the social clock help to create the regularities in behaviour across all domains of developmental investigation. But norms themselves are apt to fluctuate both from one cultural group to the next and also, within a given culture, according to changing demographic patterns, historical circumstances, the economic climate, and the overall socio-cultural ethos of the times. For example, recent research has shown that the norms embodied in the social clock are far less constraining to contemporary Australian adults than they were in the United States some four decades ago when Neugarten first came up with the concept (Peterson, 1997).

6. MULTIFACETED, MULTIDIRECTIONAL AND MULTIDISCIPLINARY DEVELOPMENT

Though researchers frequently specialise in the study of particular age groups and particular developmental processes from a particular disciplinary perspective (e.g., psychology, health, education, nursing, psychiatry or clinical medicine), the process of lifespan human development itself is an integrated whole that interconnects all age periods in life, is coherent across varied developmental phenomena, and transcends the boundaries of academic research disciplines. Consequently, in order to understand the complete pattern of development that guides human behaviour from earliest infancy through extreme old age, it is necessary to view the person through a range of different practical and methodological lenses, while continuing to keep track of the whole person as a coherent network of growth trajectories. As Levinson explained:

> The study of the life course has presented almost insuperable problems to the human sciences as they are now constituted. Each discipline has claimed as its special domain one aspect of life, such as personality, social role or biological functioning, and has neglected the others. Every discipline has split the life course into disparate segments, such as childhood or old age ... The resulting fragmentation is so great that no discipline or viewpoint conveys the sense of an individual life and its temporal course. (Levinson, 1986, p. 4)

A multidirectional lifespan approach strives to overcome these limitations by attending to the blending of developmental forces acting upon an individual at any given point in time, as well as to their separate lines of influence through decades of time, as people grow up and grow older. As noted above, the multidimensional lifespan approach explores the connections among biological, emotional, social, cultural and cognitive changes within each age period, while following the progress of the individual through a lifetime of psychological growth. Like historians, dramatists, philosophers and biographers who try to make sense of individual human lives, lifespan psychologists seek the underlying coherence in each human life against a backdrop of myriad idiosyncratic personal and temporal experiences.

As an illustration, recall the studies conducted within the Berlin Wisdom Paradigm (Baltes et al., 1995; Baltes & Staudinger, 1996) that were cited in an earlier section of this chapter, as well as the corresponding Australian studies by Collins et al. (1997). The finding that many of the elderly Berlin residents who were nominated by members of their communities as wise had had historically unique, formative experiences as anti-Nazi activists in Hitler's Germany suggests the longterm developmental impact of experiences much earlier in life whereas the contrast in wisdom-related cognitive performance between the Australian women as a function of whether they lived in the community or in an institution suggests intersections between the physical trajectory of age-related change (e.g., an age-linked physical infirmity necessitating institutionalisation) and lines of social and cognitive developmental change.

7. SUMMARY

This article has examined the focus and core assumptions of lifespan developmental psychology as a research discipline, along with a selection of recent research evidence illustrating both current achievements, and the promising future directions, of the lifespan approach. With goals of describing, explaining and optimising human psychological functioning and beneficial developmental change over the whole of life from infancy though old age, the scientific evidence deriving from investigation of human development in the context of the data-driven assumptions listed has already made a substantial contribution to human understanding.

Future research promises to go still further, not only in advancing the science of human behaviour, but also in filling practical needs related to advancing policy, education and social treatment on behalf of all age groups. Indeed, as noted in this chapter, lifespan developmental research evidence can supply the information necessary in order to: (a) assist younger and older adults to overcome their fallacious fears, genuine anxieties and adverse cultural stereotypes about old age (Peterson, 1993, 1996); (b) inform better adult and old-age education (Hori, 1994); (c) improve older people's morale and personal planning; and (d) open informal lines of communication between all age groups so that children and younger adults gain the benefit of older people's wisdom, and older people can be helped to develop greater wisdom and understanding out of social connectedness with younger generations and the collective sharing of problems insights and uniquely subjective, personal experiences of growing up and old (Baltes & Staudinger, 1996; Smith, 2001).

As reviewed in this article, scientific research into the process of human psychological development over the lifespan has surged over the decades following the publication of Goulet and Baltes (1970) seminal volume that inaugurated lifespan developmental psychology as separate research discipline (Baltes, Staudinger, & Lindenberger, 1999). In seeking to understand why some children, adolescents and adults continue to grow and develop psychologically over the whole of life, by continuing to expand on their potential, undertake new challenges, use their experience and gain new capacities to the end of life, whereas others stagnate, vegetate and decline, lifespan research has suggested several key propositions about the essential nature of psychological development as a lifespan phenomenon. As described in and illustrated throughout this article, these include the assumptions that development is: (a) a potential and possibility throughout the whole of life, (b) a process of qualitative as well as quantitative change, (c) a balance of gains against losses in psychological capacity, (d) flexible and plastic, (e) embedded in the historical and cultural context, and (f) multidimensional, multidirectional, multidisciplinary, and multifaceted.

REFERENCES

Baltes, P. B. (1989). The dynamics between growth and decline. *Contemporary Psychology, 34,* 983–984.
Baltes, P. B. (1993). The aging mind: Potential and limits. *The Gerontologist, 33,* 580–594.
Baltes, P. B., & Schaie, K. W. (1973). On life-span developmental research paradigms: Retrospects and prospects. In P. B. Baltes & K. W. Schaie (Eds.), *Life-span developmental psychology: Personality and socialization.* New York: Academic Press.
Baltes, P. B., & Staudinger, U. M. (1996). Introduction. In P. B. Baltes & U. M. Staudinger (Eds.), *Interactive minds.* Cambridge: Cambridge University Press.
Baltes, P. B., Staudinger, U. M., & Lindenberger, U. (1999). Life-span developmental psychology: Theory and application to intellectual functioning. *Annual Review of Psychology, 50,* 471–507.
Baltes, P. B., Staudinger, U. M., Maercker, A., & Smith, J. (1995). People nominated as wise: A comparative study of wisdom-related knowledge. *Psychology and Aging, 10,* 155–166.
Birren, J. E., & Birren, B.A (1990). Concepts, models and examples. In J. E. Birren & K. W. Schaie (Eds.), *Handbook of aging.* San Diego, CA: Academic Press.
Byrd, M., & Breuss, T (1992). Perceptions of sociological and psychological age norms by young, middle-aged, and elderly New Zealanders. *International Journal of Aging and Human Development, 34,* 145–163.
Clayton, V. P., & Birren, J.E (1980). The development of wisdom across the lifespan: A reexamination of an ancient topic. In P. B. Baltes & O. G. Brim (Eds.), *Life-span development and behavior.* New York: Academic Press.
Collins, K. Luszcz, M., Lawson, M. J., & Keeves, J. P. (1997). Everyday problem solving in elderly women: Contributions of residence, perceived control, and age. *The Gerontologist, 37*(3), 293–302.
Erikson, E. H. (1950). *Childhood and society.* New York: W. W. Norton.
Garmezy, N. (1993). Vulnerability and resilience. In D. C. Funder, R. D. Parke, C. Tomlinson-Keasey & K. Widman (Eds.), *Studying Lives Through Time* (pp. 377–398). Washington, DC: American Psychological Association.
Goodnow, J. J. (1996). Collaborative rules. In P. B. Baltes & U. M. Staudinger (Eds.), *Interactive Minds.* Cambridge: Cambridge University Press.
Goodnow, J. J., & Collins, W. A. (1990). *Development according to parents.* Hillsdale, NJ: Erlbaum.
Goulet, L. R., & Baltes, P. B. (1970). *Life-span developmental psychology: Theory and research.* New York: Academic Press.
Hori, S. (1994). Beginnings of old age in Japan and age norms in adulthood. *Educational Gerontology, 20,* 439–451.
Jin, Y. S., Ryan, E. B., & Anas, A. P. (2001). Korean beliefs about everyday memory and aging for self and others. *International Journal of Aging and Human Development, 58,* 103–113.
Johnson, R. C., & Medinnus, G. R. (1968). *Child psychology: Behavior and development.* New York: Wiley.
Levinson, D. (1986). A conception of adult development. *American Psychologist, 41,* 3–13.
Luszcz, M., & Giles, L. (2001). Benefits of close social relationships for health and longevity of older adults. *International Society for the Study of Behavioral Development Newsletter, 41*(1), 15–17.

Neugarten, B. (1979). Time, age, and the life cycle. *American Journal of Psychiatry, 136*, 887–894.
Noesjirwan, J., Gault, U., & Crawford, J. (1983). Beliefs about memory in the aged. *Journal of Cross-Cultural Psychology, 14*, 455–468.
Peterson, C. C. (1993). The accuracy of older and younger Australians' understanding of mental health and aging. *International Journal of Aging and Human Development, 36*, 129–138.
Peterson, C.C (1996). *Looking forward through the lifespan: Developmental psychology.* Sydney: Prentice Hall of Australia.
Peterson, C. C. (1997). The ticking of the social clock: Adults' beliefs about the timing of transition events. *International Journal of Aging and Human Development, 42*, 189–203.
Sinnott, J. D. (1989). A model for solution of ill-structured problems: Implications for everyday and abstract problem solving. In J. D. Sinnott (Ed.), *Everyday problem solving: Theory and applications* (pp. 72–99). New York: Praeger.
Smith, J. (2001). Life contexts and social relationships from age 70 to 100+. *International Society for the Study of Behavioral Development Newsletter, 1/41*, 6–8.
Takahashi, M. (2000). Toward a culturally inclusive understanding of wisdom: Historical roots in the East and West. *International Journal of Aging and Human Development, 57*, 217–230.
Williams, A., Ota, H., Giles, H., Pierson, H. D., Gallois, C., Ng, S. H., Lim, T.-S., Ryan, E. B., Somera, L. B., Maher, J., Cai, D., & Harwood, J. (1997). Young people's beliefs about intergenerational communication: An initial cross-cultural comparison. *Communication Research, 24*, 370–393.

28

Values Education in a Changing World*

LOURDES R. QUISUMBING and JOY DE LEO

Asia Pacific Network for International Education and Values Education in the Philippines and Australia

1. A TIME OF CHANGE

There is a feeling of dissatisfaction with the way we have educated our youth. We have fed them with knowledge and information, to the extent of overloading their minds with more and more data than they can understand, interpret, or much less appreciate. We have enabled them to acquire skills to make them more exact, mechanical, efficient, but not equally effective. We have taught them to be more ambitious and progressive, calculating, materialistic and selfish, but we have not developed their capacity to care for something or someone beyond themselves, and we have stymied their ability to love truly and to share. We make sure that they are informed, but not inspired. The wonderful modern world of progress, of invention, of automation, of information has not been able to solve the most fundamental human problems of poverty, injustice, illiteracy, intolerance, discrimination, hunger, disease, misery, hatred, and violence.

As educators working in the Asia-Pacific region, it falls to us to ensure that the next generation of workers and leaders are prepared for change in the coming decades. Awareness of the responsibility that falls on education systems to develop the human potential towards the building of a more humane and just society, should shock us into questioning our educational philosophies and strategies, and into searching for new and better ways to educate in the context of present-day realities and future scenarios and challenges; to transform the culture of war and violence, of greed and selfishness into a culture of peace and love where true human development can occur. We must educate for peace, for without peace there can be no development, just as without development there can be no lasting peace.

We have to realize that we have not educated the student to become fully

---

* Permission to use sections of an article published by the Australian College of Education and a Sourcebook published by UNESCO, APNIEVE are gratefully acknowledged.

human, we have not tried to develop all the powers and faculties of the human person. Overemphasis on knowledge and skills has led to the neglect of values and attitudes. The product of our education system is an informed and knowledgeable person who may not be mature or emotionally stable, an intelligent and informed individual, a financial wizard who may not behave honestly or ethically, an irresponsible citizen, or even a ruthless criminal. This leads us to the urgency of considering the place and role of values in the holistic education of the total human person.

2. VALUES NEEDED IN A CHANGING WORLD

It is imperative to ask several questions: What are the values needed in a changing world? What can we educators do to transform the culture of war and violence to a culture of peace, where people seek non-violent means to resolve conflict, where negotiation and persuasion, the art of listening and dialogue can be learned and practised, where internationalism and globalism mean the art and skill of learning to live together in peace and harmony? Delors, in his Commission's Report on Education for the Twenty-First century, entitled *Learning: The Treasure Within*, writes that learning throughout life will be a major key to meeting the challenges of the future and that we have to rethink the concept of lifelong education in order to reconcile three dynamic forces which are emerging: *competition*, which provides incentives; *cooperation* which gives strength; and *solidarity*, which can unite peoples and nations into one global village, facing common risks, sharing the same environment and a common human destiny of development or destruction. We have the power to imagine our preferred future and to make it happen.

Lifelong education begins with self-understanding, through an inner voyage whose milestones are knowledge, meditation, and the practice of constructive self-criticism. Learning throughout life requires each individual to learn how to learn, founded on four pillars: learning to know, learning to do, learning to be and learning to live together. Learning to live together in an increasingly complex and fast-changing world is indeed a difficult process, but in the Delors Commission's words: "is a necessary Utopia" pointing to the urgent need for values education. Learning to live and to work together means knowing more about others, about the cultures and ways of life of cultural communities and indigenous peoples. It means developing a greater awareness and deeper understanding of diversity. It consists of carrying out joint projects cooperatively rather than encouraging rivalry, learning to manage conflicts in the spirit of respect for the values of pluralism, mutual understanding and peace. Learning to live and to work together in peace and in harmony, means uniting instead of dividing, empowering us to manage the inevitable conflicts that will arise with the increasing tensions of our generation and the next, in an intelligent and peaceful way.

2.1. Tolerance: A Key Value

Learning to live together implies tolerance, which leads to peace. But what is tolerance and how do we educate for it? The UNESCO *Declaration on the Principles of Tolerance*, adopted and proclaimed during the twenty-eighth General Conference in Paris on Tolerance Day, November 16, 1995, defines, clarifies and underscores the positive and dynamic meaning of tolerance as follows:

> Tolerance is respect, acceptance and appreciation of the rich diversity of our world's cultures, our forms of expression and ways of being human. It is fostered by knowledge, openness, communication, freedom of thought, conscience and belief. Tolerance is harmony in difference. It is not only a moral duty, it is also a political and legal requirement. Tolerance, the virtue that makes peace possible, contributes to the replacement of the culture of war by a culture of peace.

Tolerance is, above all, an active attitude prompted by recognition of the universal human rights and fundamental freedoms of others. Tolerance is responsibility that upholds human rights, pluralism, democracy and the rule of law. It involves the rejection of dogmatism, absolutism and affirms the standards set out in international human rights instruments. It means accepting the fact that naturally diverse human beings, have the right to live in peace and to be as they are. In the modern world, tolerance is more essential than ever before. It is an age marked by the globalisation of the economy and by rapidly increasing mobility, communication, integration and inter-dependence, large-scale migrations and displacement of populations, urbanisation and changing social patterns. Since every part of the world is characterized by diversity, escalating intolerance and strife potentially menaces every region. It is not confined to any country, but is a global threat.

The *Declaration on the Principles of Tolerance* points out the absolute need for tolerance between individuals, at the family, community and global levels, in our modern world of an increasingly-globalized economy, changing social patterns of mobility and diversity. Hence the urgency of promoting and shaping the attitudes of tolerance, openness, mutual listening and understanding, and solidarity in schools and universities, and through nonformal education at home and in the workplace.

The communication media are also in a position to play a constructive role in facilitating free and open dialogue and discussion, disseminating the values of tolerance, and highlighting the dangers of indifference towards the rise in intolerant groups and ideologies. Article 4 on Education of the *Declaration on the Principles of Tolerance*, underscores the importance of education as the principal tool of any change strategy and the most effective means of preventing intolerance. The first step in tolerance education is to teach people what their shared rights and freedoms are, so that they may be respected, and to promote the will to protect those of others.

Education for tolerance should therefore be considered an urgent imperative, that is why it is necessary to promote systematic and rational tolerance through teaching methods that address the cultural, social, economic, political and religious sources of intolerance that are the major roots of violence and exclusion. Education policies and programs should contribute to development of understanding, solidarity and tolerance among individuals as well as among ethnic, social, cultural, religious and linguistic groups and nations.

2.2. *A Culture of Peace*

Learning to live together is a skill, a competence and an art, an attitude and a type of behaviour, a set of values and priorities, a way of life fundamental to meeting the challenges of the twenty-first century, to saving the planet Earth and humanity, to building a sustainable future and empowering the youth to accept their rights and responsibilities, their role and function to transform our culture of violence into a culture of peace. So what is this culture of peace which we hope to build together with and for our youth?

The *Draft Declaration on a Culture of Peace* submitted by UNESCO to the UN General Assembly in preparation for 2000, the International Year of the Culture of Peace, states that:

> a culture of peace is that set of values, attitudes, traditions, modes of behaviour and ways of life, that inspires and espouses respect for life and for all human rights, rejects violence in all its forms, prevents violent conflicts by tackling their root causes through dialogue and negotiation.

A culture of peace is committed: (a) to democratic participation; (b) to equality and partnership between women and men; (c) to the recognition of the rights to freedom of expression, opinion and information; and (d) to the principles of freedom, justice, democracy, tolerance, solidarity, cooperation, pluralism, cultural diversity, dialogue and understanding between nations, between ethnic, religious, cultural and other groups, and between individuals. Indeed, we need an education for a culture of peace, since a culture of peace is a transformational process, which should begin with each individual member of society. Education for a culture of peace should focus on the youth so that their values and attitudes, modes of behaviour and lifestyles will take root in their hearts and minds early in life and become part of their total personality and behaviour. The youth are the leaders and the citizens of the future. It is imperative for us to prepare them for their role and function in becoming peace builders and peacemakers in a just, compassionate and free world where people will learn to live together, and truly love and care for each other.

The key issue for educators is how to do this effectively, while also meeting other educational imperatives. At the fifth session of the UNESCO Advisory Committee on Education for Peace, Human Rights, Democracy, International Understanding and Tolerance, held in Paris in March 2000, the Director-General of UNESCO, Mr. Koichiro Matsuura, emphasised the need for innovative approaches to an integrated concept of education, which would enable UNESCO to revitalise its educational mission and constitutional mandate, so as to respond more effectively to the demands of the twenty-first century. The committee therefore resolved that what was needed for a culture of peace was an:

> integrated, comprehensive education covering human rights, democracy, international understanding, tolerance, non-violence, multiculturalism, and all other values conveyed through the school curriculum ... communicating such values as equality, harmony, solidarity etc. ... at every level in the education system, in which values connected to the culture of peace are to be found.

The Integrated Framework of Action on Education for Peace, Human Rights and Democracy, adopted at the Forty-Fourth Session of the International Conference on Education in Geneva, 1994 and approved by the General Conference of UNESCO in Paris 1995, defines and describes the type and form of education that is required for every individual to be able to live and to work together in peace and harmony.

> The ultimate goal of education for peace, human rights and democracy is the development in every individual of a sense of universal values and types of behaviour on which a culture of peace is predicated. It is possible to identify even in different socio-cultural contexts values that are likely to be universally recognized. (UNESCO, 1995 Article II. Sections 6-12)

3. THE ROLE OF EDUCATION

The Integrated Framework of Action on Education for Peace, Human Rights and Democracy (IFA) states that "Education must develop the ability to value freedom and the skills to meet its challenges." The implications of this for education are that children and young people need to be prepared to become autonomous and responsible citizens, able to make informed choices, cope with difficult and uncertain situations and to join together with others to solve problems for a just, peaceful and democratic community. It is through education also, that children learn to accept diverse cultural values and to communicate, understand, share and co-operate with others, in a spirit of respect. For this, "education must reinforce personal identity, encourage the convergence of ideas and solutions which strengthen peace, friendship and solidarity between individuals and people" (IFA, 1994). This is best approached through the development of inner peace in the minds of students, enabling the qualities of tolerance, compassion, sharing and caring to be firmly established. For balanced and long-term development, equity and solidarity are needed to protect the environment and cultural heritage, and to adopt methods of production and patterns of consumption which lead to sustainable development. Education plays a vital role in developing a global civil society, able to live together in harmony and to use equitably the earth's resources wisely for the benefit of all.

4. APNIEVE

APNIEVE is the acronym for The *Asia-Pacific Network for International Education and Values Education*. It was in response to the 1994 Geneva Declaration of Ministers of Education and the Integrated Framework of Action on Education for Peace, Human Rights and Democracy, that the Asia Pacific Network for International Education and Values Education (APNIEVE) was organized. This network dedicates its efforts to education for peace, human rights, democracy and sustainable development through the sharing of information and experiences, production of teaching-learning materials, and exchange programs of students and teachers to foster international understanding. With recognition of the crucial role of the teacher as a values educator, APNIEVE has produced a sourcebook for tertiary level and teacher-training institutions, entitled *Learning to Live Together in Peace and Harmony*, and has published a second sourcebook, entitled *Learning to Be: A Holistic and Integrated Approach to Human Development*.

These sourcebooks attempt to meet the need to articulate a new educational paradigm, which embraces the totality of the human person, develops the intellectual, emotional and behavioural powers and faculties of the learner. It offers an education of the mind, heart and will; an education that respects the sacredness and the uniqueness of every individual, prepares the student to be a free, responsible, critical and creative, just, peaceful and caring citizen of a nation, and a global citizen of a multi-diverse, multi-ethnic, multi-cultural world. In addition to describing the values for learning to live together and for learning to be, the APNIEVE Sourcebooks emphasise the process by which these values are internalised; a process which may lead to inner peace in the heart and mind and also peace within the family, community, nation, region and ultimately globally. This process is integrated within the teaching and learning context and embedded in the practical modules and lessons that are provided. The valuing process acknowledges that, in order to build international understanding and a culture of peace with others and globally, a person must first find peace within him or herself and must become fully human, with the wisdom, compassion and understanding required for all the roles fulfilled, in order to meet the local and global challenges of the twenty-first century.

5. OTHER UNESCO INITIATIVES

While this need has been acknowledged for some time, progress in implementing the rhetoric has been very slow. In fact it was articulated as far back as 1972 in the Report to UNESCO of the International Commission on the Development of Education, chaired by Faure, entitled *Learning to Be*.

It referred to the role of education in developing all the dimensions of the complete person.

> The physical, intellectual, emotional and ethical integration of the individual into a complete man, is a broad definition of the fundamental aim of education. (Faure, 1972, p. 156)

The 1996 Report to UNESCO of the International Commission on Education for the twenty-first Century, *Learning: The Treasure Within*, picks up on this theme and clearly sets as the fundamental principle that education "must contribute to the all-round development of each individual – mind and body, intelligence, sensitivity, aesthetic sense, personal responsibility and spiritual values" (Delors, 1996, p. 94).

The report describes 'learning to be' as:

> the complete fulfilment of man, in all the richness of his personality, the complexity of his forms of expression and his various commitments – as individual, member of a family and of a community, citizen and producer, inventor of techniques and creative dreamer. (Delors, 1996, p. 95)

The Delors Commission further defines 'learning to be' as:

> a dialectical process which starts with knowing oneself and then opens out to relationships with others. In that sense, education is above-all an inner journey whose stages correspond to those of the continuous maturing personality ... it is thus a very individualized process and at the same time a process of constructing social interaction. (Delors, 1996, p. 95)

More recently, the importance of values for living together was most strongly emphasised at the Forty-Sixth Session of the International Conference of Ministers of Education (ICE) in Geneva on 5 to 8 September 2001, the theme of which was, *Education for All for Learning to Live Together*. As Ministers returned home from the Conference, the tragic events of September 11 in New York seemed to highlight even more the significance of the conference outcomes. A background paper prepared by Lopez for a key session on, *Shared Values, Cultural Diversity and Education: What to learn and how?* states that:

> ... we all share certain characteristics and values as a result of our human condition and the need to establish bridges of dialogue between all the inhabitants of this planet. (This) faces us with urgent decisions regarding the objectives, content and teaching-learning methodologies in education. (Lopez, 2001)

6. VALUES EDUCATION IN THE ASIA PACIFIC REGION

The National Institute for Educational Policy Research of Japan (NIER) in Tokyo, has been conducting regional meetings, consultations and research to foster educational cooperation in the Asia-Pacific region, for more than 30 years. An examination of the topics taken up by the UNESCO-NIER Regional Programme for Educational Development in Asia and the Pacific during the years 1967 to 1996, reveals an initial burst of research activity in the area of moral education in the 1970s, which was not picked up again until the 1990s (NIER, 1997, pp. 67–68). This reflects the trend of the time to focus on the development of the whole person and learning throughout life, as highlighted in the 1972 Faure Report entitled: *Learning to Be*. It is seen again in the four pillars of learning identified in the 1996 Delors Report on Education for the Twenty-First century, *Learning: The Treasure Within*. However in the 1990s, the themes were broadened to include the areas of Education for Humanistic, Ethical/Moral and Cultural Values, later focussed on Peace, Intercultural Understanding, Human Rights, Civics and Democracy, and Sustainable Development. The various NIER reports, produced particularly in the last decade, provide a useful overview of the developments in values education in countries in the region over this period.

Following a regional meeting in September 1991, an analysis of the common issues emerging from country experiences in Humanistic, Ethical/Moral and Cultural Values in Education, concluded that, even though no two countries focused on exactly the same sets of values, the core moral value "caring for others" was identified as the overriding universal value common to all. This value was seen as being connected to "caring for oneself, family, neighbours, community and nation," including "the need to care for other species, for the welfare of one's society and nation, and the liveability of the earth" (NIER, 1991, p. 37). It is useful to note that this synthesis of core, common or universal values, has remained substantially unchanged in subsequent UNESCO, NIER, and APNIEVE priority statements.

Apart from this commonality, approaches to values education in the early 1990s varied significantly. Some countries offered separate courses at the primary and secondary levels. Many countries infused and integrated those in appropriate subjects. A few did a combination of both. The schemes for infusion and integration are by and large unique to each country. However, there are commonalities of issues and problems which could be the focus for regional cooperation, such as:

(a) the changing family structure,
(b) erosion of spirituality,
(c) excessive pursuit of materialism,
(d) the school as a scapegoat for moral decadence, and
(e) declining influence of parents (NIER, 1991).

What has changed since the early 1990s however, is the degree to which:

- values are taught separately as a subject, or are integrated across the curriculum;
- emphasis is placed on content or process in teaching methods;

- values are taught formally and directly or incidentally;
- values are prescribed or drawn from the learner, through dialogue and reasoning about ethical dilemmas;
- the impacts of external influences (e.g., media) on values formation, are acknowledged and addressed, and
- values education involves parents and the whole learning community.

A further development over the past decade, inevitably caused by the process of globalisation, has been the extent to which identified values extend from an individual, family and immediate community or national focus to a broader global focus, for the benefit of all humanity. However, many countries in the region experience a tension between the desire to protect cherished traditional values that are religious or cultural in origin, with the need to compete globally and to manage the threat posed by modernisation, materialism and the proliferation of alternative lifestyles and paradigms, which undermine those values. It is precisely this tension which is the driver for a changing emphasis over time, from the teaching of prescribed traditional moral and ethical values and behaviours, often taught as a separate subject, to the progressive development of thinking and reasoning skills across the curriculum. This would then enable and empower the learner, when confronted by a plethora of paradigm and lifestyle choices, to resolve values conflicts and ethical dilemmas, within a context of shared values, ethical principles and behavioural standards.

The evidence for this trend may be found in the 1994 NIER Report, (NIER, 1994) which stated that values education had been introduced "as an integral part of the school curriculum in each participating country," and that in each case, the values emphasised, "vary with the respective cultural and historic traditions, as well as technological changes and the impact of social, economic and political challenges." However, despite the universal intention to transmit deeply held humanistic values, as expressed explicitly in the educational goals of each country in the region, and the variety of forms utilised to convey this, "the values are often presented in a diffused and uncoordinated fashion and students are rarely exposed to the range of moral dilemmas that arise in the application of these values to real life situations" (NIER, 1991, p. 42).

While there is evidence that this situation has improved in the last decade, the success of values education still depends largely on the interest and skill of individual teachers, in the absence of a systematic and coordinated values-based curriculum framework, accompanied by an appropriate teaching-learning process, and comprehensive teacher training and community involvement.

A notable exception is the case provided by the Philippine Department of Education, Culture and Sports (DECS), Conceptual Framework for Values Education, which was introduced in 1988 throughout the entire education system of the country. The Framework facilitated the teaching of values as a separate subject in the secondary school and integration of values in the various subjects of the elementary curriculum, with a deliberate emphasis on the valuing process. This was accompanied by a comprehensive teacher training program and the production of instructional materials and implemented nationwide. An evaluation of the program in the National Capital Region of Manila and surrounding cities, carried out after five years of the program, showed considerable success. The efforts of the Philippine Department of Education were underscored by the 1993 Kuala Lumpar Declaration of the Ministries of Education and Development of the Asia Pacific Region (MINEDAP VI) which gave emphasis to the overarching concern and importance of values, ethics and culture in education.

Another area of values education, which was highlighted a decade ago as being important and problematic and remains so, is the area of assessment and evaluation. The key questions remain, how to monitor learner progress in reasoning and valuing skills, and how to evaluate the effectiveness of the teaching-learning process, methods and materials used. While there have been many attempts since then to develop strategies and approaches for values assessment and evaluation, the challenge now faced is to integrate these approaches into a values-based curriculum framework with assessable outcomes and standards.

It is stated in the 1991 NIER Report that assessment and evaluation of values education should ideally encompass the cognitive, affective and psychomotor domains, and that while traditional forms of assessment address the former and the latter domains, the affective realm is relatively unchartered territory. While there is considerably more awareness now about the important role that emotions play in the learning process, and increasing numbers of teachers in the region are exploring the affective in their teaching practice, sporadic attempts are yet to succeed on a larger scale. The 1991 NIER Report further states that, for values education to become a systematic and coordinated part of an assessable curriculum, there are also significant implications for teacher training approaches, both pre-service and in-service, which should also seek to address the affective, not only for the student as learner, but also for the prospective teacher as a continuous learner throughout life. It is encouraging to note that developments are occurring in teacher training institutions in the region, but there is much to be done.

The 1994 NIER Report closely connects values education with education for peace and international understanding, a link not made in the earlier 1991 report, attesting to the growing trend to synthesise diverse values groupings, and to apply them universally to the broader global context, beyond the local and national. The 1994 Report again picks up on some of the areas identified in 1991 as needing further development, as follows:

- a lack of teacher competence and training,
- the difficulty in formally assessing values,
- reflecting values in school practices and policies,
- programs fragmented across subjects, and
- students not considering values as significant or perceived as policy instruments of the government.

The evidence for the significant developments made in the field of values education some five years later, may be found in the 1999 NIER *Report on Teacher Education for Peace and International Understanding* (NIER, 1999). This report clearly articulates the need for a greater emphasis on pedagogy, appropriate teaching and assessment methods, organising the classroom to reflect the values conveyed, the need for a holistic approach across the curriculum, for the development of the whole person and the central importance of teacher training.

Of particular note in this report is the article: *Teaching for Peace and International Understanding: A process approach* (Teasdale & Teasdale, 1999), which explores new ways of thinking and knowing and encompasses the reality of the spiritual and our connection with the environment, focused on a holistic view of knowledge and learning, that emphasises the essential one-ness of humanity and nature. This necessarily has implications for a teaching-learning process that is more reflective and learner-centred in its approach, and which contextualises learning, to make it more meaningful and relevant, according to the personal, social, cultural, environmental and spiritual needs of the learner. The article further explores the critical role of the educator as co-learner and facilitator of a dynamic two-way teaching and learning process, that is both cooperative and collaborative, and where learners are in control of and take responsibility for their own learning.

While there remain considerable differences in the region in approaches taken to values education, we also find consistent trends. This is undoubtedly a result of ongoing regional dialogue and collaboration, such as the integration of values within school curricula, policies and practices, increased teacher training and greater emphasis on the teaching and learning process towards new models for learning which include the affective for the development of the whole person.

7. VALUES EDUCATION IN THE FUTURE

The Advisory Committee on Education for Peace, Human Rights, Democracy, International Understanding and Tolerance at its March 2000 meeting, stated that, in addition to the principles of human rights,

> ethical values are at the very core of any strategy for a culture of peace. It is (however) not enough merely to list or learn them (i.e. values): it is everyday, practical application that makes those values a reality, soundly anchored in society.

The Advisory Committee further stated that education should be "a participatory and interactive process of instruction and learning, comprising the total sum of values and knowledge transmitted" (i.e. the valuing process). The valuing process described in the APNIEVE sourcebook, *Learning to Be*, offers a way for the practical application of values in the learning and educational context to become a living reality, through the active participation of learners in the formation, identification and internalisation of values. The valuing process is also an integral part of the holistic and integrated approach to teaching and learning which takes into consideration the cognitive, affective and behavioural powers of the learner. The teaching-learning cycle starts with knowing and understanding oneself and others, leading to the formation of a positive self-concept, a sense of identity, self-esteem, self-worth and self-confidence, as well as a genuine respect for diversity. It proceeds to valuing, reflecting, choosing, accepting, appreciating, and acquiring needed skills, such as communication, decision-making, and finally results in action. Figure 1 presents in diagrammatic form, the Teaching-Learning Cycle which seeks an integration of the learner's knowledge, values and attitudes, abilities and skills to bring about his or her full development.

Finally, in addition to including values within educational curricula in an integrated way, and by the application of valuing and appreciating to the learning process, it is necessary to give attention to the nature of the learning environment. It is often said that values are more likely caught than taught, which leads educators to examine the values behind their words, actions and daily interactions with students and the values underpinning their policies, guidelines and decision making processes. Let schools be laboratories where tolerance is learned, where acceptance of the other is cherished, where a culture of peace prevails in the campus atmosphere, because it is found in the relationships between school and community, administration and faculty, teaching and non-teaching personnel, parents and teachers, teachers and students, and among the students themselves. Let every school be a zone of peace where values taught in the curriculum

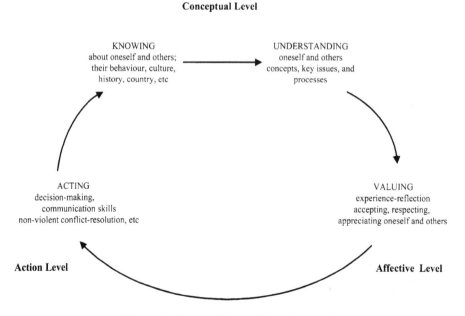

Figure 1. The teaching and learning cycle.

find their way into the student's daily life and behaviour, where the dignity of each individual is held sacred, where true democracy and genuine freedom are deeply cherished.

Let us all together in the region of Asia and the Pacific draw wisdom and strength from our distinctive cultures and traditions, from our own wealth and uniqueness to find our distinctive way, our understanding of tolerance, our own adaptation to modernity. Let us look and discover deep within ourselves those positive and constructive values that give us strength and anchor in the turbulent seas of change, to reinforce them and promote them in our children. Let us develop those that are dynamic, and can give us the wings with which to face the future with confidence, such as: initiative, determination, critical thinking and creativity, openness to innovation, regularity and flexibility, and punctuality and order, accountability and justice, honesty, freedom and responsibility, self-discipline and self-regulation, courage to change for a better future, knowledge and acceptance of one's self, one's strengths and limitations, acceptance and respect of the other. Let us learn how to harness the very best that is inherent within all of us to meet the challenges of the twenty-first century. Let us promote respect for human rights, cultural and religious diversity, democracy, and a form of development, which is humanistic, holistic and sustainable. Let us learn and teach others how to live together in peace and in harmony, respecting each other's uniqueness and diversity and building on our shared values.

REFERENCES

Delors, J. (1996). *Learning: The Treasure Within*. Report to UNESCO of the International Commission on the Development of Education (J. Delors, chair). Paris: UNESCO.

Faure, E. (1972). *Learning to Be*. Report to UNESCO of the International Commission on the Development of Education (E.Faure, chair). Paris: UNESCO.

Lenour, N. (1995). Spring of ethics. *Spotlight on Ethics*, 1.

Lopez, L. E. (2001). Shared values, cultural diversity and education: What to learn and how? In UNESCO-ICE Geneva (2001). *Education for All for Learning to Live Together*. Geneva: UNESCO-ICE September.

Mayor, F. (1995). *The New Page*. Paris: UNESCO.

Mayor, F. (1995). The Teaching of Tolerance, Paper presented in Carthage, 21 April, 1995.

National Institute for Educational Research of Japan (NIER) (1991). *Education for Humanistic Ethical/Moral and Cultural Values*. Tokyo: NIER.

National Institute for Educational Research of Japan (NIER) (1994). *Enhancing Humanistic, Ethical, Cultural and International Dimensions of Education in Asia and the Pacific*. Tokyo: NIER.

National Institute for Educational Policy Research of Japan (NIER) (1999). *Teacher Eucation for Peace and International Understanding*. Tokyo: NIER.

Quisumbing, L. R. (1998). Values in a changing world. In UNESCO, APNIEVE (1998). *Learning to Live Together in Peace and Harmony*. Bangkok: UNESCO, APNIEVE.

Teasdale, G. R., & Teasdale, J. (1999). Teaching for peace and international understanding: A process approach. In NIER (1999). *Teacher Education for Peace and International Understanding* (pp. 10–25). Tokyo: NIER

UNESCO (1995). Declaration of Principles of Tolerance. Paris: UNESCO.

UNESCO (1995). What education for what citizenship. *Innovation*, March, 1995.

29

Measuring Attitudes by Unfolding a Likert-Style Questionnaire

DAVID ANDRICH
Murdoch University, Perth, Australia

GUANZHONG LUO
National Institute of Education, Singapore, South China Normal University, China, and Murdoch University, Perth, Australia

1. INTRODUCTION

Thurstone (1928) provided a rigorous model and methodology in demonstrating that attitudes could be measured. Since then, the measurement of attitude has become pervasive in education and other social sciences. It is used in particular for the assessment and evaluation of affect, and in particular attitudes to some construct or entity. Thurstone used two stages to measure attitudes: in the first he constructed a scale and operationalised a variable; in the second he used the scale to measure attitudes. To construct the scale, he required judges to compare statements for their intensity with respect to some construct and then used his law of comparative judgment to analyse the judgments in order to locate the statements on a continuum. This operationalised the variable. To measure the attitude, a person simply agreed or disagreed with the statements and the mean or median of the scale of values of the statements agreed to was taken as the attitude measure.

Most questionnaires that survey attitudes now, however, have a Likert-style response format of Strongly Agree (SA), Agree (A), Disagree (D), Strongly Disagree (SD) in which the categories are scored with successive integers and which a person's measure is simply the sum of the scores to the statements. These questionnaires were introduced by Likert (1932) explicitly to overcome the relatively time consuming procedure for constructing a scale introduced by Thurstone. Though eminently practical, and with more than two categories of response potentially more precise, Likert's procedure is neither as rigorous as Thurstone's nor does it operationalise the variable by locating the statements on the continuum. This article summarises relatively recent theoretical research in latent trait theory which has reconciled these approaches and in which Likert-style responses can be used with a Thurstone-style scale. It provides an illustrative example in which attitudes to capital punishment were measured with convenient samples of university students in Australia, Japan and Singapore.

2. THURSTONE SCALES

The pair-comparison design, in which judges compare statements for their intensity on the attitude continuum irrespective of their own attitude, is the basic design for constructing a Thurstone attitude scale. The implied response function of the law of comparative judgment (LCJ) with which these data are analysed is monotonic – the greater the difference between the locations δ_1 and δ_2 of statements 1 and 2 respectively, the greater the probability that any judge will declare that $\delta_1 > \delta_2$ (Thurstone, 1927). Figure 1 shows such a probability response function.

When persons whose attitudes are to be measured agree or disagree with a statement, the implied response function for this response process is single-peaked in that it is expected that a person will agree with the statements that are close to the person's own attitude, and disagree to those statements that are far from the person's location in either direction. Coombs (1964) developed this implied response process within a deterministic framework, and established methods for locating the statements and the persons simultaneously from the agree/disagree responses of the persons to the statements. This obviated the need for Thurstone's two steps in the measurement of attitude. Although Coombs' procedure did not involve two steps, the procedure was also extremely cumbersome for more than four statements and therefore did not challenge the Likert approach as the favoured practical procedure. Coombs coined the term 'unfolding' for the simultaneous process of locating persons and items on a scale from the agree/disagree responses, and this term continues to be used in the literature. Coombs also referred to the person's location as the ideal point, reflecting the assumption that the a person would tend to agree with statements that were close to this point for the person, and tend to disagree with statements that were further away in either direction.

Figure 2 shows the deterministic single-peaked response function as well as a probabilistic counterpart to be considered shortly. In each of these functions, the response is dichotomous. The distance ρ_i is the latitude of acceptance with respect to the statement – it is the range in which the probability of an Agree (A) response is greater than the probability of a Disagree (D) response. In the deterministic model of Coombs, the former is always 1 and the latter is 0. Van Schuur (1989, 1997), Hoijtink (1990) and others, have constructed and applied models for unfolding with the work of Hoijtink being explicitly a probabilistic model.

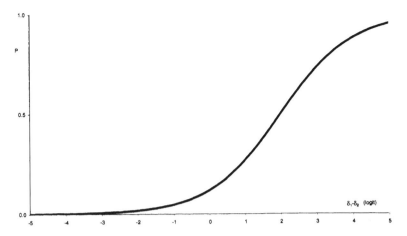

Figure 1. The implied response function in Thurstone's law of comparative judgment (LCJ).

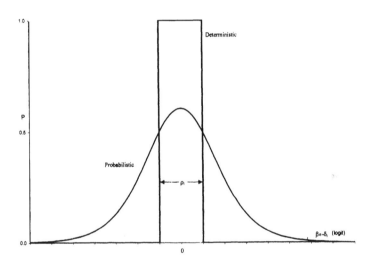

Figure 2. Response function for dichotomous unfolding: Deterministic vs. Probabilistic.

3. LIKERT SCALES

The implied response process in the Likert scales in which successive categories are scored with successive integers is monotonic in that the greater the person's attitude, the greater the score of the response. Figure 3 shows the expected value function, $E[X]$, for an item with four ordered categories, SD, D, A, and SA, which are scored by successive integers beginning with 0: $X = x \in \{0, 1, 2, 3\}$. This relationship permitted checking the internal consistency of statements using statement by total-score correlations within the framework of traditional test theory (Gulliksen, 1950). Van Schuur and Kiers (1994) have considered the structure of the responses and compared the results of analysing questionnaires with cumulative models and traditional methods of analysis and those using models for unfolding.

Studies have been conducted to compare Thurstone's and Likert's approaches to attitude measurement. The major observation that appears when Likert's statements are scaled using Thurstone' LCJ is that they appear at two ends of the continuum with a gap in the middle (Ferguson, 1941). This gap is a symptom of the process of scoring that Likert adopted. For negatively oriented statements, Likert simply reversed the scoring. However, that required that the statements were clearly either positively or negatively oriented in order that it could be decided how to score the statements. Statements that represented an ambivalent attitude could not be used. The example below makes this observation concrete.

Consider the three statements in Table 1 which form a Thurstone scale for measuring attitudes to capital punishment. The first statement is clearly against capital punishment, and in this Table, the statement is scored so that the greater the score, the stronger the attitude against capital punishment. The second statement is for capital punishment, and to make the scoring consistent with that of the first statement, its scoring is reversed. The third statement, however, is ambivalent towards capital punishment, and it is difficult to decide in which direction to score this statement. As a result, this kind of statement, present in Thurstone scales, is absent in Likert scales. Andrich (1996) reconciled the Thurstone and Likert procedures of attitude measurement within the framework of Rasch models for ordered categories.

4. THE HYPERBOLIC COSINE MODEL (HCM) FOR UNFOLDING DICHOTOMOUS RESPONSES

The model in which a Likert response format can be used with a Thurstone scale originates with the HCM unfolding model for dichotomous responses. This model was derived from the Rasch model for ordered categories (Rasch, 1961; Andersen, 1977; Andrich, 1978, 1982), in which the number of categories was

Table 1. Three statements from a Thurstone-type scale for measuring attitude to capital punishment

	Statement		Response		
1	Capital punishment does not stop serious crime *(Against capital punishment – forward scored) (Score)*	SD *(0)*	D *(1)*	A *(2)*	SA *(3)*
2	Until we find a way to prevent serious crime, we need capital punishment *(For capital punishment – reverse scored) (Score)*	SD *(3)*	D *(2)*	A *(1)*	SA *(0)*
3	I do not believe in capital punishment but maybe it is justified *(Ambivalent towards capital punishment) (Cannot score)*	SD *(?)*	D *(?)*	A *(?)*	SA *(?)*

taken as three. The middle category was taken to reflect the probability of the Agree (A) response because the person's ideal point was close to that of the statement and termed Agree Close (AC). The other two categories were taken as the *two resolved latent* responses of the one *observed* Disagree (D) response. One of the latent D responses was taken to occur when the person's ideal point was below that of the statement, termed Disagree Below (DB), and the other was taken to occur when the person's ideal point was above that of the statement, termed Disagree Above (DA). Figure 4 shows the construction of the HCM in which $AC \rightarrow X_{ni} = 1$ and $(DB + DA) \rightarrow X_{ni} = 0$. The same model, expressed differently, was derived independently by Verhelst and Vestralen (1993).

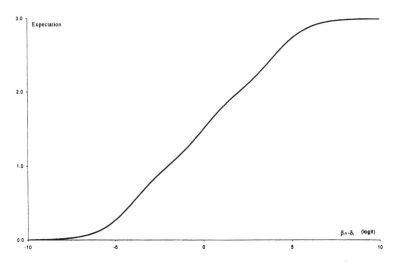

Figure 3. The implied response function in the Likert scales.

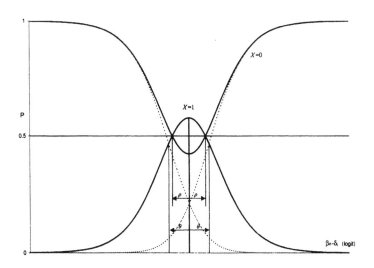

Figure 4. The construction of the Hyperbolic Cosine Model.

Figure 4 shows the relevant details of the construction of the HCM which takes the form (Andrich & Luo, 1993)

$$P\{X_{ni} = 1\} = \frac{\exp(\theta_i)}{\exp(\theta_i) + 2\cosh(\beta_n - \delta_i)} \quad (1)$$

where β_n and δ_i are the locations of the persons and the items respectively, and θ_i is the half distance between the thresholds defining the region in which the Agree response is more likely than the Disagree response because the person is below as well as the Disagree response because the person is above the location of the item.

The HCM can be simplified to the form (Luo, 1998)

$$P\{X_{ni} = 1\} = \frac{\cosh(\rho_i)}{\cosh(\rho_i) + \cosh(\beta_n - \delta_i)} \quad (2)$$

in which $\cosh(\rho_i) = 2\exp(\theta_i)$, ρ_i is the latitude of acceptance with respect to the statement and in which the probability of an Agree response is more likely than the single manifest Disagree response. This is the structure of the probabilistic response function of Figure 2.

4.1. A General Form for Polytomous Unfolding Models

The model for ordered categories, which is a direct extension of the procedure for deriving the model for dichotomous responses, can be derived in two ways. The first is derived in Andrich (1995) and a parallel derivation in a slightly different form is given by Roberts and Laughlin (1996) and developed further by Roberts, Donoghue and Laughlin (2000). Luo (2001a) provides a related derivation which begins with the construction of the Rasch model for ordered categories itself (Andrich, 1978), but that exposition is beyond the scope of this article.

Consider again the four ordered categories SD, D, A and SA. If person X responds SA to a statement then it is taken that the person perceives the statement to be close to his or her ideal point. If person Y responds A to the same statement, then it is taken that person Y perceives his or her location close to that of the statement, but not as close as person X. However, person Y may be further away from the location of the statement than person X in either direction. Thus the A response must be resolved into two latent responses. Similarly for the D and the SD responses.

Table 2 shows the resolution of the four manifest responses of SD, D, A and SA, and their resolution into seven latent responses.

The response functions for the manifest categories are shown in Figure 5. It is evident that the response function for category SA is unimodal, that for each of A and D it is bimodal, and that it tends to 1.0 for SD as the person's location deviates from that of the statement in either direction. The equation of this model, which is a special symmetric case of the most general form (Andrich,

Table 2. Resolution of four manifest Likert-style responses into seven latent responses

Manifest response	SD	D	A	SA			
Score	0	1	2	3			
Latent response	SD	D	A	SA	A	D	SD
Latent score	0	1	2	3	4	5	6

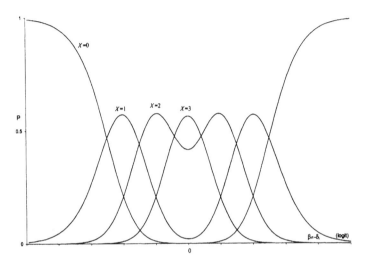

Figure 5. The general Hyperbolic Cosine model for polytomous unfolding.

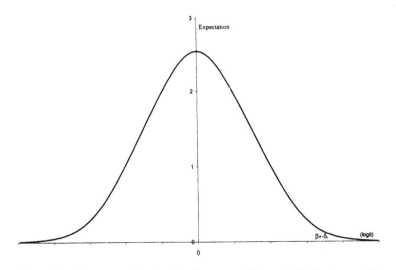

Figure 6. The expected value for the general Hyperbolic Cosine model.

1996), takes the form

$$P\{X_{ni} = x; x < m\} = \frac{1}{\gamma_{ni}} \exp[x((2x-m)\theta_i)2\cosh((m-x)\beta_n - \delta_i))]$$

$$P\{X_{ni} = x; x = m\} = \frac{1}{\gamma_{ni}} \exp[x(2x-m)\theta_i]$$

(3)

The model of equation (3) is termed the general HCM (GHCM).

The expected value function of this model is shown in Figure 6. It is evident that, unlike the expected value function in Figure 3, that the expected value function in Figure 6 is single peaked.

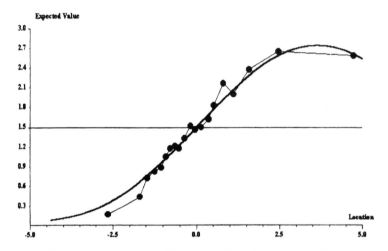

Figure 7. Expected value curve with means of 20 class intervals for statement 9.

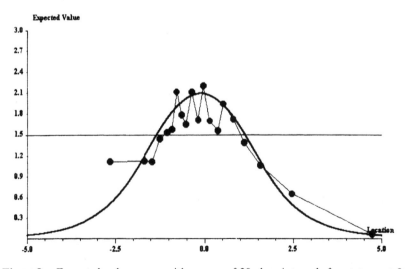

Figure 8. Expected value curve with means of 20 class intervals for statement 8.

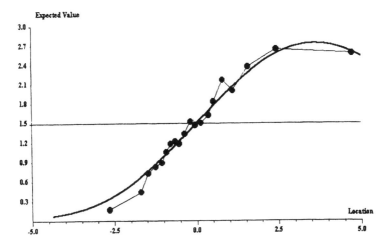

Figure 9. Expected value curve with means of 20 class intervals for statement 10.

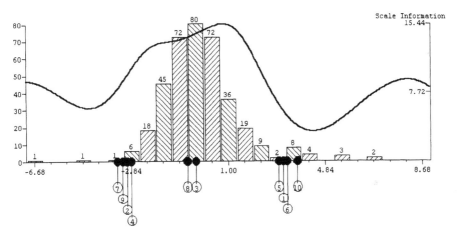

Figure 10. Distribution of the persons and the information function in relation to the location of the statements.

The method of estimation applied for the GHCM is not repeated here. It is a generalisation of the equations for the dichotomous model (Andrich & Luo, 1993; Luo, 2000) and summarised in Luo, Andrich and Styles (1998). The method involves the joint maximum likelihood procedure in which the person and item parameters are estimated simultaneously. This requires a correction factor in order to overcome the inconsistency in the estimation. It also requires that a general common latitude of acceptance parameter, which is not arbitrary but a property of the data (Andrich, 1995), is estimated first from the data. In addition it requires that the individual latitudes of acceptance for the different statements are estimated as deviations from this common estimate. The method of estimation is described in Luo (2001b). The test of fit at this stage is a general graphical comparison between the mean response of persons in a short class interval and their expected value according to the model. The model of any data analysis can be constrained to have a common latitude of acceptance across statements, or to have them different. The model of analysis used in this article is one in which the statements have a different latitude of acceptance parameter.

4.2. *The Information Function*

Precision of the estimates of the parameters is obtained in the process of estimation of the parameters. The focus here is on the precision of the estimates of the person parameters – the precision of the estimates of the items is analogous. The standard error of each person parameter estimate is taken as the expected value of the negative inverse of the second derivative of the log likelihood function. The information function is simply the negative of the expected value of the second derivative (Samejima, 1969), and is given by

$$I_n = -E\left[\sum_{i=1}^{I} \frac{\partial^2 L}{\partial \beta_n^2}\right]. \qquad (4)$$

In anticipation of the results in the example, it is noted (Andrich, 1988; Andrich & Luo, 1993) that the maximum information on the estimate of the location of a person relative to the location of a statement does not occur when the person and statement locations are close, but at some distance between the two. Indeed, the location of the information when the person and statement locations are the same in the unfolding model considered here is a minimum. This has implications for the precision of estimates of the locations of persons which will be investigated with the example. In the general form of the polytomous model, the first derivative of the log-likelihood function for the person parameter, given the item parameters, is given by

$$\varphi_{\beta_n} = \frac{\partial L}{\partial \beta_n} = -\sum_{i=1}^{I} \{x_{ni} - E[X_{ni}]\} \frac{\partial \log \Psi(\beta_n - \delta_i)}{\partial \beta_n}; \qquad (5)$$

and the negative of the expected value of the second derivative is given by

$$I_n = -E\left[\frac{\partial \varphi_{\beta_n}}{\partial \beta_n}\right]$$

$$= -\sum_{i=1}^{I} (\beta_n - \delta_i) \cdot \frac{\partial \log \Psi(\beta_n - \delta_i)}{\partial \beta_n}$$

$$\times \left\{\left[\sum_{k=0}^{m_i} k^2 \Pr\{X_{ni} = k\}\right] - \left[\sum_{k=0}^{m_i} k \Pr\{X_{ni} = k\}\right]^2\right\} \qquad (6)$$

where in the case of the GHCM,

$$\Psi(\beta_n - \delta_i) = \cosh(\beta_n - \delta_i). \qquad (7)$$

Equation (6) is a generalisation of the equation for the dichotomous case of the general form of unfolding models, which is studied in detail in Luo and Andrich

(2000). The shape of this function is shown in Figure 10 in conjunction with the distribution of person and item locations in the sample.

5. THE EXAMPLE

The example involves responses of university students to an attitude questionnaire regarding capital punishment. The statements on which the questionnaire is based was originally published in Thurstone (1932), reproduced in Shaw and Wright (1967), and was also the basis of the one used by Roberts and Laughlin (1996). The questionnaire contains ten statements, of which six were used in Andrich (1988) and Andrich and Luo (1993). Four further statements have been incorporated with the wording in some questions modified slightly to make them easier to read (e.g., a triple negative was removed from one statement). The questionnaire, with statements ordered according to their empirical locations, is shown in Table 3. This was not the order of statements in the questionnaire administered.

The students who responded to the questionnaire came from universities in Australia, Japan and Singapore. The students in all countries could read the statements in English, but in addition, the students in Japan had the statements interpreted orally in Japanese by the supervisor. They were convenient samples involved in classes and cannot be considered representative of the population in these countries. The students were asked to give their gender, but not their name. Moreover they were assured that their responses would be treated confidentially, and they were asked to give an honest response.

5.1. Locations and the Latitude of Acceptance of the Statements

Table 3 shows the locations and the magnitudes of the latitude of acceptance for each statement. The locations have an arbitrary origin of 0.0 but the value of the latitude of acceptance has no arbitrary constraint.

It is clear that the empirical locations of the statements are consistent with the idea of a continuum, ranging from those statements which reflect a positive attitude, through to those which reflect an ambivalent attitude, to those which reflect a negative attitude towards capital punishment. Two statements that might have been considered more extreme, Statement 4 supporting capital punishment and Statement 6 rejecting capital punishment did not turn out to be totally extreme, but they are in the correct part of the continuum. This may result in part because of the interaction between the estimates of the locations of the statements and their latitudes of acceptance. The two statements which reflect a relatively ambivalent attitude towards capital punishment, 8. "Capital punishment is necessary but I wish it were not" and 3. "I do not believe in capital punishment but maybe it is justified", and which would be difficult to score in a Likert-type scale, are in the middle of the continuum and in a consistent ordering with the other statements.

Table 3. Locations and latitude of acceptance parameter values for 10 statements

Statement	Location (SE)	Lat. Acceptance (SE)
7. Capital punishment is justified because it stops serious crime	−3.384 (0.037)	1.625 (0.018)
9. Capital punishment is just and necessary	−3.172 (0.037)	1.582 (0.018)
2. Until we find a way to prevent serious crime, we need capital punishment	−2.997 (0.038)	1.594 (0.019)
4. Capital punishment gives criminals exactly what they deserve	−2.815 (0.037)	1.455 (0.019)
8. Capital punishment is necessary but I wish it were not	−0.601 (0.042)	0.637 (0.017)
3. I do not believe in capital punishment but it may be justified	−0.266 (0.045)	0.667 (0.017)
5. The state cannot teach that human life is sacred by destroying it	2.996 (0.039)	1.874 (0.020)
1. Capital punishment does not stop serious crime	3.173 (0.038)	1.841 (0.019)
6. Capital punishment is one of the most hideous practices in our society	3.325 (0.037)	1.727 (0.018)
10. Capital punishment is never really justified	3.741 (0.038)	1.883 (0.018)

5.2. Graphical Tests of Fit Illustrated with Three Items

As indicated earlier, the expected value of the response as a function of the locations of the persons is single peaked. Figures 7, 8, and 9 show the estimated response functions for statements 9, 8 and 10 respectively, where statement 9 is positive, statement 8 is ambivalent, and statement 10 is negative, towards capital punishment. On the curves are shown the mean values of persons in 20 class intervals, and it is evident that these follow the expected value curves reasonably well. In particular, for statement 8 which is ambivalent, it is evident that the persons close to the statement tend to have the highest mean, representing a score of 3 and the response of SA, and that persons located in either direction of the location of the statement, tend to have lower scores.

5.3. The Person Distribution in Relation to the Locations of Statements and the Information

An important aspect of scaling when using the principle of unfolding is to have the statements span the entire continuum, ranging from positive to ambivalent, to negative with respect to some issue. Figure 10 shows the distribution of persons in relation to the location of statements. It is evident from this figure that the locations of the persons is relatively normal though perhaps positively skewed, that there are people who are against and those who are for capital punishment (the right side of the continuum reflects an attitude against capital punishment), and that the items fit essentially into three groupings – those for capital punishment, those ambivalent to capital punishment, and those against capital punishment. The persons are located mostly over the two statements that reflect ambivalence to capital punishments, statements 8 and 3.

However, equally impressive aspects of Figure 10 is the shape of the information function relative to the locations of the persons. As indicated earlier, the information in unfolding models is at a minimum when the person is located at the statement. This is reflected in Figure 10 where the middle of the continuum, which has only two statements, has greater information than in the regions where there are four statements. However, although the region in the middle of the continuum has the least number of statements, this is the region in which, in this data set, most persons are located, and it is also exactly the region which has the maximum information. If the distribution of the statements had been more uniform, then the information function would have also been more uniform. If the distribution of persons had also been wider so that it had more persons where there are statements at present, then it would have been useful to have more statements where there is now a gap. This is desirable, because of the feature that statements provide maximum information away from their location in either direction. To consolidate this point, the peak in the middle of the continuum is greater than the one on the right because statements at both ends of the continuum contribute to this information, whereas the peak on the right is not as high because the main information is provided only by statements that are on the right of the continuum. It seems that the relationship between empirical person distributions, locations of statements, and the information function should be considered routinely in data analyses, together with the estimates and fit.

5.4. Comparison Among Samples

For completeness, Table 4 shows the means, standard deviations, and the separation indices for each of the three samples of students together with an analysis of variance among their means. The separation index for a sample is analogous in calculation to that of the traditional reliability index of internal consistency in that it is the ratio of the estimated true variance among the persons relative to the observed variance, where the former is estimated by subtracting the

Table 4. Locations and analysis of variance for comparisons among students from the three countries

Group	Country	Number	Mean	Standard Deviation	Separation Index	ANOVA F Ratio	P <
1	Australia	135	0.765	2.044	0.930		
2	Japan	127	−0.478	1.038	0.830		
3	Singapore	118	−0.592	1.117	0.844		
Total		380	−0.072	1.618	0.911	32.769	0.00000

average error of measurement variance from the observed variance. It is evident that this is large for all samples and for the group as a whole. It is also evident that there is a significant difference in attitude between the samples. However, here the locations of the individuals on the continuum in relation to the locations of the statements is very informative. Australian students on the average (mean = 0.765) are located most closely to statement 3, "I do not believe in capital punishment but it may be justified", and the Japanese and Singapore students (means of -0.478 and -0.592 respectively) are located most closely to statement 8, "*Capital punishment is necessary but I wish it were not*" ... Thus although there is a statistically significant difference in the locations, and the Australian students tend to be more against capital punishment than the students from Singapore and Japan, the majority of students in all countries tend to be mostly ambivalent in their attitude. It is the case that in all countries, there is a wide range of opinion, and it is stressed that the samples are convenient samples of students where the data are analysed for the purpose of illustrating a method of attitude measurement that combines the rigour of Thurstone's construction of scales and response principles, and the more practical and popular approach introduced by Likert.

6. CONCLUSION

Likert introduced his form of measuring attitudes explicitly to avoid the rigorous and time consuming procedures for scaling that were introduced by Thurstone to measure attitudes. The reason Likert-style scales are easier to work with than Thurstone scales is that they make the response process cumulative, which implies that scores can be summed in order to obtain a summary index. However, in order to work as cumulative scales, many Likert-style questionnaires require that the statements are polarized – that they are very much for or very much against the issue in question. This is necessary in order that it is known how to score the questions, either directly or by reversing the scoring. However, in this way it is not possible to gain very much information regarding the location of the statements themselves and the meaningfulness of the continuum – the statements are located at two extremes of the continuum. By using Thurstone's original response process, but applied to the Likert response format, it is possible to have statements that span the whole continuum, with the location of the statements operationalising the continuum. This article describes and applies a model of modern test theory in providing an example of using Thurstone's response process to statements with a Likert-style response format in which statements do not have to be at extremes of the continuum.

REFERENCES

Andersen, E. B. (1977). Sufficient statistics and latent trait models. *Psychometrika, 42,* 69–81.
Andrich, D. (1978). A rating formulation for ordered response categories. *Psychometrika, 43,* 561–574.

Andrich, D. (1988). The application of an unfolding model of the PIRT type for the measurement of attitude. *Applied Psychological Measurement, 12*, 33–51.

Andrich, D. (1995). Hyperbolic cosine latent trait models for unfolding direct-responses and pairwise preferences. *Applied Psychological Measurement, 19*, 269–290.

Andrich, D. (1996). A hyperbolic cosine latent trait model for unfolding polytomous responses: Reconciling Thurstone and Likert methodologies. *British Journal of Mathematical and Statistical Psychology, 49*, 347–365.

Andrich, D., & Luo, G. (1993). A hyperbolic cosine latent trait model for unfolding dichotomous single-stimulus responses. *Applied Psychological Measurement, 17*, 253–276.

Coombs, C. H. (1964). *A Theory of Data*. New York: Wiley.

Cronbach, L. J. (1951). Coefficient alpha and the internal structure of tests. *Psychometrika, 16*, 297–334.

DeSarbo, W. A., & Hoffman, D. L. (1986). Simple and weighted thresholds model for the spatial representation of binary choice data. *Applied Psychological Measurement, 10*, 247–264.

Ferguson, L. W. (1941). A study of the Likert technique of attitude scale construction. *Journal of Social Psychology, 13*, 51–57.

Gulliksen, H. (1950). *Theory of Mental Tests*. New York: Wiley

Hoitjink, H. (1990). A latent trait model for dichotomous choice data. *Psychometrika, 55*, 641–656.

Likert, R. (1932). A technique for the measurement of attitudes. *Archives of Psychology*, No. 140.

Luo, G. (1998). A general formulation for unidimensional. unfolding and pairwise preference models: Making explicit the latitude of acceptance. *Journal of Mathematical Psychology, 42*, 400–417.

Luo, G. (2000). The JML estimation procedure of the HCM for single stimulus responses. *Applied Psychological Measurement, 24*, 33–49.

Luo, G. (2001a). A class of probabilistic unfolding models for polytomous responses. *Journal of Mathematical Psychology, 45*, 224–248.

Luo, G. (2001b). Estimating parameters with JML in a class of probabilistic unfolding models for polytomous responses. Unpublished manuscript under revision.

Luo, G., Andrich, D., & Styles, I. M. (1998). The JML estimation of the generalised unfolding model incorporating the latitude of acceptance parameter. *Australian Journal of Psychology, 50*(3), 187–198.

Luo, G., & Andrich, D. (2000). Item information functions of the general unfolding models. Invited presentation on the Fifth International Conference on Logic and Methodology, Cologne, Germany, October 2000.

Rasch, G. (1961). On general laws and the meaning of measurement in psychology. In J. Neyman (Ed.), *Proceedings of the Fourth Berkeley Symposium on Mathematical Statistics and Probability. IV* (pp. 321–334). Berkeley CA: University of California Press.

Roberts, J. S., & Laughlin, J. E. (1996). A unidimensional model for unfolding responses from a graded disagree-agree response scale. *Applied Psychological Measurement, 20*, 231–255.

Roberts, J. S, Donoghue, J. R., & Laughlin, J. E. (2000). A general item response theory model for unfolding unidimensional polytomous responses. *Applied Psychological Measurement, 24*(1), 3–32.

Rost, J., & Luo, G. (1997). An application of a Rasch-based unfolding model of a questionnaire on adolescent centrism. In J. Rost & R. Langeheine (Eds.), *Applications of Latent Trait and Latent Class Models in the Social Sciences* (pp. 278–286). Münster and New York: Waxmann Verlag GMBH.

Samejima, F. (1969). Estimation of latent ability using a response pattern of graded scores. *Psychometrika Monograph, 34* (4, Part 2).

Shaw, M. E., & Wright, J. M. (1967). *Scales for the measurement of attitudes*. New York, NY: McGraw-Hill.

Thurstone, L. L. (1927). A law of comparative judgement. *Psychological Review, 34*, 278–286.

Thurstone, L. L. (1928). Attitudes can be measured. *American Journal of Sociology, 33*, 529–554.

Thurstone, L. L. (1932). *Motion pictures and attitudes of children*. Chicago, IL: University of Chicago Press.

Van Schuur, W. H., & Kiers, H. A. L. (1994). Why factor analysis is often the wrong model for analyzing bipolar concepts and what model to use instead. *Applied Psychological Measurement, 18,* 97–110.

Van Schuur (1997). Intrinsic and extrinsic work values as a single unfolding scale. In J. Rost & R. Langeheine (Eds.), *Applications of Latent Trait and Latent Class Models in the Social Sciences.* (pp. 163–171). Münster and New York: Waxmann Verlag GMBH.

Van Schuur, W. H. (1989). Unfolding German political parties: A description and application of multiple unidimensional unfolding. In G. de Soete, H. Ferger & K. C. Klauer (Eds.), *New Developments in Psychological Choice Modelling* (pp. 259–277). Amsterdam: North Holland.

Verhelst, N. D., & Verstralen, H. H. F. M. (1993). A stochastic unfolding model derived from the partial credit model. *Kwantitative Methoden, 42,* 73–92.

30

Bullying in Schools

PHILLIP T. SLEE[1], LANG MA[2], HEE-OG SIM[3], KEITH SULLIVAN[4], MITSURU TAKI[5]

1. INTRODUCTION

There is no doubt that the issue of school bullying is now well and truly on the agenda for educationalists and employers on a global scale (Graham & Juvonen, 2001; Ohsako, 1997). In the Asia-Pacific region countries significant cross-cultural research into the issue has been conducted by Rigby and Slee (1999), Morita et al. (1985, 2001), and Sullivan (2000a). These researchers have addressed the issue of bullying within their individual countries including Australia (Slee, 2001);China (Lang Ma & Zhang, 2002); Japan (Taki, 2001); Korea (Sim, 2001); and New Zealand (Sullivan, 2000a) The present article draws together for the first time a summary of research relating to school bullying from these five countries.

2. AUSTRALIA

2.1. Historical, Cultural and Social Factors Related to School Bullying

While bullying at school has long been recognised as existing in Australian literature (e.g., Blacklock, 1995) the empirical study of the phenomenon really did not begin until 1989–90. The interesting question concerns just why school bullying has become the focus of so much research in Australia? Part of the answer to this question is the impetus that international research (e.g., Olweus, 1993; Smith & Sharp, 1996) has given to the research. Further momentum arose from the 1994 Federal Government inquiry into violence in Australian schools which concluded that while violence was not a major problem in Australian

---

[1] *Flinders University, Adelaide, Australia.*
[2] *Sichuan University, China.*
[3] *Kunsan National University, Seoul, Korea.*
[4] *University of Wellington, New Zealand.*
[5] *National Institute for Educational Policy Research of Japan, Tokyo, Japan.*

schools, bullying was. A recommendation of the inquiry was for the development of intervention programs to reduce school bullying.

2.2. Major Understandings Regarding the Nature of School Bullying

Bullying is generally described as: "Repeated intimidation, over time, of a physical, verbal or psychological nature of a less powerful person by a more powerful person or group of persons" (Slee, 2001). Bullying is now widely accepted to be a sub-set of aggressive behaviour that has its own defining characteristics.

The following information regarding the extent of bullying in Australia is based on research involving approximately 25,500 primary and secondary students from over 60 Catholic, Independent and public schools around Australia. The data have been collected using the *Peer Relations Questionnaire* (PRQ) which has been developed by Rigby and Slee (1995) in response to teacher's requests for a standardised method for assessing the nature and extent of school bullying. In gathering data anonymously care was taken to differentiate between bullying in which there was a perceived imbalance of power, and other aggressive acts such as fighting and quarrelling between equals.

Frequency of bullying data are recorded in Table 1 from over 25,500 Australian students across more than 60 schools and provide the basis for the following broad conclusions regarding bullying.

Overall, between one in five and one in seven students reported being bullied several times a week or more. It is shown in Table 1 that bullying is more frequently reported by younger students, and girls generally report less bullying than boys. In secondary school the amount of bullying is highest in Years 8 and 9. The pattern of results found in the national data provides a basis for the development of school intervention programs.

Table 1. Incidence of victimisation according to age; students reporting being bullied 'at least once a week' in co-educational schools in Australia

Age in years	Boys (N = 13,977) Schools	%	Students	Girls = (N = 10,560) Schools	%	Students
8	7	50.0	110	7	35.3	116
9	10	30.3	185	11	31.1	212
10	12	25.4	232	12	28.4	271
11	26	22.6	336	25	23.2	388
12	42	27.8	1193	42	22.1	1055
13	39	25.5	1807	40	20.9	1658
14	36	22.7	1675	35	13.2	1600
15	33	16.6	1510	32	12.2	1390
16	31	11.8	906	31	9.9	878
17	24	10.6	462	23	7.0	474
18	19	7.5	80	17	14.5	69

Duration of bullying. The research has shown that while most bullying lasts for a day or two, for a disturbingly high percentage of students it lasts weeks or more. Research now leaves little doubt regarding the cumulative negative effects of being subject to repetitive acts of violence (Rigby, 1997; Slee, 1997).

Safety from bullying. We asked students in the large scale sample if school was a safe place for "young people who find it hard to defend themselves from attack from other students?" Among both males and females less than 20 per cent see school as a safe place for vulnerable students. Of the students who report being bullied at school over nine per cent report that they have truanted and over 15 per cent report thinking about staying away from school (Slee, 1997). School bullying then raises the question of equity and access for some students in relation to education.

Types of bullying. Bullying may be physical, verbal or psychological. Physical bullying occurs more with boys. The Australian research of Owens, Slee and Shute (2001) has provided new insight into the nature of girl's aggression and to the damaging effects of indirect or relational aggression in peer relationships.

The effects of bullying. Generally, the findings (Slee, 2001) confirm that bullying is a physically harmful, psychologically damaging and socially isolating aspect of an unnecessarily large number of Australian children's school experience. The damaging physical effects have been highlighted in Australian studies linking poor health, depression and suicidal ideation with bullying. Psychological well-being (eg. self esteem and happiness) have been shown to suffer with bullying while loneliness and alienation from peers is also linked with victimisation. Research has clearly linked victimisation with poor school adjustment and suicidal ideation (Slee, 1998a,b; Rigby & Slee, 1999).

2.3. Suggestions for Intervention

In order to help understand what Australian students think should be done 25,000 students were questioned regarding their opinion about school interventions (Rigby & Slee, 1999). Australian students are strongly of the opinion that the school community should act to stop bullying, although responsibility for stopping it is largely attributed to teachers. Research similarly documents a strong desire by teachers and parents for action to reduce school bullying (Slee, 2001).

An increasing number of Australian schools are now taking action to address the issue of bullying. Unfortunately in the last five years in Australia, the push for quick solutions to school bullying has had some negative outcomes including undue pathologising of the individual. The task facing Australian schools is to resist the temptation to solve the bullying problem by simply focusing on problem students' behaviour. Interestingly, in the last year a number of school communities have taken up the challenge and begun to examine bullying in a broader systemic sense (Slee, 2001). This has involved reaching out to the broader community and engaging agencies such as welfare, parent organisations and the police and involving them in the development of community based anti-bullying programs. Schools are challenged to examine carefully their ethos and culture in the context of a socially critical curriculum as a means for reducing bullying.

3. CHINA

China is one of the countries that take great pride in its long recorded histories of civilization. It is the third largest country in the world in terms of size (9,600,000 square kilometres), and it is the most populous country with a population of nearly 1.3 billion. There are about 0.2 billion children and adolescents studying in primary and secondary schools. Chinese culture is highly diverse with 56 ethnic groups, among which the Han is the largest that takes up more than 90 per cent of the population.

3.1. *Historical, Cultural and Social Factors Related to Bullying*

The following speculations may call attention of other researchers to some similar factors in their own countries. According to Chinese tradition, parents and teachers are absolute authorities and it is normal for them to discipline children in whatever way they like. At the same time, children are expected to obey them in every way. It can be understood that the more powerful are entitled to command the less powerful. This can serve as a model in peer relationships, as an imbalance of power is proved to be at the heart of the bullying dynamic. The educators, the education administrations, and the public have come to recognise that children have long been unreasonably pressed to be academically successful, and efforts are being made to improve the situation (Li, Chen, Xu, Wang, & Lin, 2001). There are reports that some children are punished physically or verbally by teachers for poor academic performances and some teachers even order peers of the so-called 'bad students' to participate actively in these punishments (Li, Chen, Xu, Wang, & Lin, 2001; Li, 2001). According to Social Learning Theory, such punishments may play a role in the development of bullying behaviours among children. In addition, there are virtually no facilities that can help to prevent or to deal with bullying effectively in China. There are few school psychologists and hardly any intervention programs, and social skills are rarely integrated as a part of education. Moreover, anti-bullying is not included in pre-service or in-service training for teachers.

3.2. *Major Understandings Regarding the Nature of School Bullying*

Bullying is called '*qifu*' or '*qiwu*' in Chinese and it means much the same as in Western culture. Some children simply call it '*da-qi-xiao*', an incident in which the senior students bully the junior students. It is described as aggressive behaviours that some students treat other students wrongly (slap, punch, hit, threaten, extort, isolate, mock, call bad names, and so on) in order to upset or hurt. Bullying studies began in the middle of 1980s in China. However, this theme is infrequently addressed in research, and no national data are available yet.

Studies have revealed that the prevalence estimates of being bullied ranged from 6.7 per cent to 23.6 per cent (Ekblad, 1990; Ma & Zhang, 2002; Zhang, Gu, Wang, Wang, & Jones, 2000). As the methods used in these studies are different, it seems improper to compare the results directly. Nevertheless, the authors agree that bullying occurs frequently in primary and secondary schools in China. Some studies suggested that there was no difference in prevalence between genders (Ma & Zhang, 2002; Zhang, Gu, Wang, Wang, & Jones, 2000), while some other studies implied that boys were more likely to be bullied than girls (Ekblad, 1990). Findings indicated that the younger students seemed to be more likely to be bullied (Ma, Zhang, Wei, & Shen, 2001).

There seem to be three types of bullying among school teenagers: physical (slapping, punching, hitting, and so on), verbal (mocking, bad names, cruel teasing, rumours, and so on), and threatening (extorting, and so on) (Ma, Zhang, Zou, Wei, & Shen, 2001). Among the three types, verbal bullying seems to be the most frequent. One study showed that 7.8 per cent, 9.9 per cent, and 17.3 per cent of school teenagers reported being bullied physically, being threatened, and being bullied verbally respectively in the last year (Ma, & Zhang, 2002). However, the prevalence estimates between genders were not significantly different for any of the three types (Ma & Zhang, 2002).

Poor emotional adjustment, poor conflict resolution skills, loneliness, depression, and suicidal ideation were found to be linked with being bullied (Chen, 2001; Ekblad, 1990; Ma, Zhang, Wei, & Shen, 2001; Ma, Zhang, Wei, Shen, Xiao, Liu et al., 2000). Boys being bullied physically and being threatened with physical harm were more likely to think about killing themselves, while being bullied verbally was associated with suicidal ideation in girls (Ma & Zhang, 2002).

3.3. *Suggestions for Possible Lines of Research into School Bullying*

Longitudinal studies are needed to understand better the nature, causes, and outcomes of bullying at different stages of development. Also, it could be meaningful to understand bullying from a contextual perspective by exploring how school policy, teachers, peers, parents, and community, influence the development of bullying behaviours. Thus effective anti-bullying intervention can be developed and delivered on the basis of such understanding. Collaborating in cross-cultural studies with researchers from other countries can be of great value, for bullying is a matter of common concern despite socio-cultural differences. Sharing information and exchanging ideas equally can help to understand bullying in different backgrounds and can help to improve intervention in all the countries involved.

4. JAPAN

In reviewing and theorizing Japanese research in relation to school bullying, it is argued that Japanese understanding of bullying is a little different from that in many other countries, especially European ones. Consideration is given here to drawing out some of these differences.

4.1. An Overview of Historical, Cultural and Social Factors Related to Bullying

In the late 1970s, Japan had a serious problem with school violence (*kounai bouryoku*) in lower and upper secondary schools. This involved physical violence among peers, against teachers and vandalism, and was recognised as largely a problem associated with boys' physically aggressive behaviour. Although most educators and researchers focused on such school violence in this period, a small number of them had discovered a new type of aggression unlike physical violence. It was labelled '*ijime*' or '*yowaimono ijime*' which translated means to 'ill-treat', 'treat someone harshly', 'be insensitively cold to someone', 'be cruel to someone', 'tease', 'annoy' and so on. Some researchers in Gekkan Seitosidou (1980) noted that *ijime* had three characteristic features, namely; (a) it involves group behaviour, (b) is of long duration, and (c) is invisible (artful, guileful or tricky). It was noted that while *ijime* was less violent than *kounai bouryoku* it was none-the-less harmful.

Although the word '*ijime*' is recognized as generally equivalent to the Western word 'bullying', it is necessary to emphasise that the concept of '*ijime*' is less physical and less violent than bullying. Japanese researchers use the word '*ijime*' deliberately in order to distinguish it from the usual physical violence, *kounai bouryoku*. '*Ijime*' is the word considered typical of girlish aggression but is not red-blooded aggression. It stands in contrast to the Western word 'bullying', which is typically associated with overt physical aggression.

In the mid 1980s, a tragic chain of suicides caused by *ijime* made educators recognize it as a serious problem in Japan. *Ijime* became one of the biggest social issues featured through mass media. Morita (1985) was the pioneer of *ijime* studies utilizing a self-report anonymous questionnaire that clearly identified its frequency of occurrence. A definition of '*ijime*' is as follows:

> A type of aggressive behaviour by (which) someone who holds a dominant position in a group-interaction process, by intentional or collective acts, causes mental and/or physical suffering to another inside a group.

Although it appears similar in many respects to European definitions, it is necessary to emphasize two points. First, it incorporates the idea of 'a dominant position' that is determined by an in-group interaction process. It does not mean only 'physical power' nor an 'imbalance of power'. It suggests that the victim interacts with bullies, often in the same group or classroom, and is forced into an unequal power relation with the bullies. Secondly, it emphasises mental or emotional anguish over physical force that arises out of group processes and interactions. Most bullying research in the West is based on the work of Olweus (1993), that drew on his preceding research on boys' aggressive behaviour. This research overlooked mental or emotional anguish and girlish aggression in unintentionally focussing on physical violence among boys. The word '*ijime*', however, was used originally for both mental and physical aggression, and for both of girls' and boys' behaviour.

In the 1990s, it was noticed that bullying was not only a particular Japanese problem but also occurred in most societies. In 1996, NIER and the Ministry of Education of Japan held an International Symposium on the Problem of Bullying inviting researchers from the United Kingdom, Norway, the Netherlands and Australia. In 1997, Morita (2001) and his research group conducted a comparative survey on bullying with the cooperation of foreign researchers that used a self-report anonymous questionnaire based on Olweus' research. This symposium and research showed not only the similarities between bullying in Japan (*ijime*) and bullying in the West, but also highlighted the differences. Morita (2001) shows that bullying occurs in both the classroom and the playground among Japanese, English, Dutch, and Norwegian students. On the other hand, it clearly happens more in the classroom than in the playground in Japan but clearly less in the classroom than in the playground in Norway. In the United Kingdom and the Netherlands, it occurs to the same degree in the classroom as in the playground.

4.2. *An Examination of Major Understandings Regarding the Nature of School Bullying*

From further research on bullying in Japanese schools, Japanese authorities reached a consensus. It was expressed as a part of the *Emergency Appeal* enacted by the Minister of Education:

> It is possible that serious bullying incidents may happen at any classroom, at any school and among any children. (*Emergency Appeal*, 1996, Jan. 30)

This was interpreted to mean that *ijime* is considered not as a specific behaviour conducted by an extraordinary child with a problematic background, but as behaviour that can be carried out by an ordinary child.

Taki (2001b) has clearly demonstrated the characteristics of Japanese bullying using longitudinal survey comparative data between Japan and Australia. There are three key findings.

(1) Almost eight per cent of Japanese lower secondary school students bullied someone (in each term) and six per cent were bullied by someone (in each term) between 1998 and 2000.
(2) There was little evidence among Japanese students to suggest that extraordinary bullies or victims were identifiable in terms of any stable tendency to bully others or be victimised from one school term to the next, as very little continuity was found in either bullying or victimised behaviour from one time to another.
(3) One of the main determinants of bullying among Japanese students was

stress. The correlation between stress and bullying others was also the same for girls' bullying in Australia but not for boys' bullying.

Many Western researchers seem to believe that aggressive character and culture causes bullying. This may be so if they mainly focussed on boys' bullying, but may not hold true for girls' bullying.

4.3. Possible Lines of Research Into School Bullying

Taki (2001b) also has shown that Japanese children feel a great deal of stress in terms of peer relationships. If children can develop their interactive ability with peers and become less stressed, *ijime* and also other problematic behaviours may be reduced. Taki (2001a) suggested that the program of whole school involvement called 'Japanese Peer Support Program (JPSP)' may help children to develop those abilities.

Japanese schools have had many traditional activities for helping others and children receive a sense of affirmation from others through the activities. However, this tradition has lost its focus recently, because children have become less concerned about others. As children are losing their peer group experiences in communities, they do not learn how to interact successfully, nor develop their social skills through playing with peers. As a result, children are reluctant to join the traditional activities voluntarily because of their lack of social skills. These activities are not available to help them to receive a sense of affirmation from others, so we find an increase in problematic behaviours among students.

In order to reduce recent problematic behaviours, JPSP was developed to: (a) compensate the missing peer group experience with the so called social skill training as the first part; and (b) reconstruct Japanese traditional activities for children to receive a sense of affirmation from others in the second part. The training in the first part is the preparation or warming up for the second part. JPSP does not aim to change children solely by skill training but by the combination of basic social skill training and activities in helping others. Through the two parts in combination, children develop their motivation and an ability to engage in rewarding with interactive relationships with others and not engage in *ijime*.

5. REPUBLIC OF KOREA

5.1. Historical, Cultural and Social Factors Related to Bullying

A number of documented suicides linked to bullying in Korea have resulted in school bullying becoming a social issue. Various research papers (Kim & Kim, 1999; Kim & Park, 1997; Ku, 1997; Kwon, 1999; Lee, 2000; Lee & Kwak, 2000; Park, Sohn, & Song, 1998) published since 1997 have attempted to understand the phenomenon of bullying from various perspectives. Figure 1 highlights the factors that have been examined as a means for understanding the issue of bullying.

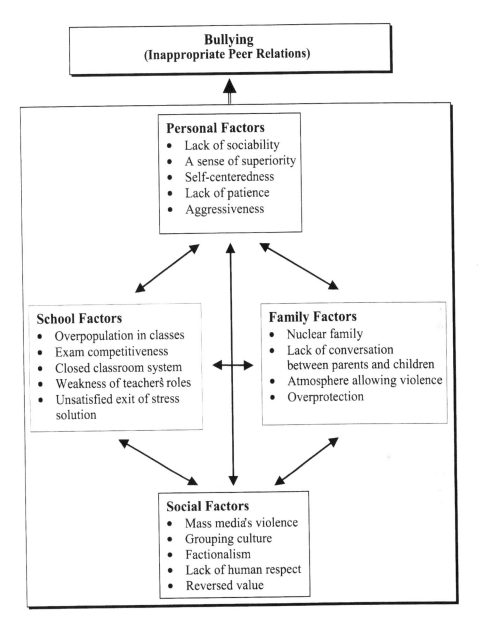

Figure 1. Factors influencing bullying in schools.

In Korea 'wangtta' is the most popular word coined to enable a better understanding of student peer difficulties and problems. *Wang* means 'entirety', 'all', 'largeness', 'many', or 'seriousness' and *tta* means 'to make outcast from peers or class'. That is, *wangtta* indicates total outcasting and rejection, or the highest or worst level of bullying. There are several words among children to describe the various conditions of peer difficulties. *Euntta* means 'bullying secretly', *youngtta* means 'bullying permanently', *kabtta* means 'bullying suddenly', and *jeontta* means 'bullying of the whole class'.

5.2. Major Understandings Regarding the Nature of School Bullying

National organizations such as the Korean Educational Development Institute, Korea Youth Counseling Institute, and Seoul Metropolitan Counseling Center for Youth have conducted research on bullying and have tried to develop programs with concerns about adolescents' lives from the national viewpoint. In Korea, bullying is understood as one type of school violence that is getting worse among adolescents. Similar to Western countries, bullying is defined as verbal and physical behaviours of more than two persons who make a group and outcast a specific person and disgrace and hurt him or her secretly, so that this person cannot fulfil his or her role as a group member (Ku, 1997). Since *wangtta* is a group or whole class phenomenon, some researchers see it as more similar to bullying in Japan than that in Western cultures.

5.3. Major Research Findings Regarding Bullying

Although research regarding bullying keeps accumulating, the results from just a few organizations that have done nation-wide research on the condition of bullying in Korea are presented here. Mostly the research focuses on students above fifth grade.

Kim and Park (1997) reported that among 1624 nation-wide students from fifth grade to high school, 48 per cent had generally experienced bullying (males: 41%, females: 53%). More specifically, the frequency of bullying during the last six months was 81 per cent (1–2 times), 12 per cent (3–5 times), and four per cent (almost every day). Also, 30 per cent of the subjects reported being victimized (males: 26%, females: 32%), the frequency of being bullied during the past six months was 73 per cent (1–2 times), 15 per cent (3–5 times), and five per cent (almost every day). In addition, 22 per cent of the subjects were bully-victims in this study. Bullying happened more among elementary school students. Victim's characteristics were boasting and ignoring of others (71%), tattling to teachers (35%), only studying and pretending to be smart (32%), teasing (31%), looking stupid (29%), tattling to mothers (25%), and sneaking (25%).

Park, Sohn, and Song (1998) showed that among 6893 students from fourth grade to high school, 24 per cent experienced bullying during the past year. Middle (27%), elementary (25%), high school students (21%), males (28%), and females (20%) had this experience. From a regional viewpoint, country areas were worst (30%), followed by small and middle-size cities (24%), the largest city, Seoul (24%), and finally, large cities (23%).

Kim and Kim (1999) showed that among 2746 students from fifth grade to high school the number of victims in a classroom was 43 per cent (1–2 persons), seven per cent (3–4 persons), one per cent (5–6 persons), and one per cent (more than 7). What would help victims to avoid being bullied were correcting weak personality (27%), learning to express their own ideas (20%), being in the company with victims as friends (16%), and refusing unjust requests (10%).

Even though it is not nation-wide, Lee and Kwak (2000) reported that out of 1340 students from fourth grade to middle school, 471 students could be divided into four groups of bullies, victims, bully-victims and not involved students. The research showed that bullies had a higher level of social acceptance than victims and bully-victims, and that male bullies were highest in athletic competence and that bullies as well as those not involved had high global self-worth. Also bullies reported higher social support than victims. Bully-victim students showed the highest level of depression.

Since researchers use different methods, it is difficult to compare results. Overall, Korean research indicates that between 18 and 30 per cent of school students experience bullying, and between 2 and 3 per cent are seriously victimised. Overall, females seem to be more victimised, especially in elementary schools (Lee & Kwak, 2000).

5.4. *Suggestions for Possible Lines of Research into School Bullying*

First, it is necessary to study bullying amongst preschoolers and lower grades of elementary students. Since adolescent-related government organizations have conducted research on school bullying, most studies have focused on the years above middle childhood. Second, longitudinal studies should be conducted locally and nation-wide. Since most studies have been cross-sectional and dealt mostly with the conditions of bullying, they did not reveal the cause and effect factors related to school bullying. Third, cross-cultural studies are required in order to compare definitions, types of bullying, and coping with bullying among cultures. Finally, programs that operate on a regular daily life basis in schools and families for prevention and cure of bullies and victims are urgently needed.

6. NEW ZEALAND

6.1. *Historical, Cultural and Social Factors Related to Bullying*

As no major study of bullying in New Zealand has been done, linking school bullying to historical, cultural and social factors can only be speculative. Having said this, there is within New Zealand society a considerable macho male ethos which values success on the sports field and gives scant recognition to academic achievement or the arts.

Bullying receives only cursory public notice except in exceptional circumstances when boys who do not fit in are abused by a group of more powerful boys. In recent years, a number of such bullying incidents have been highlighted in the news. The latest of these, which has clearly moved beyond bullying is in the area of sexual violation and assault. A criminal case is currently before the courts, and the past ten years have produced a number of similar cases, including several resulting in suicide.

While New Zealand is often lauded as a great place to bring up children, in recent years the increasing amount of child abuse that has been identified challenges this pristine image. Throughout 2001, child welfare groups campaigned to overturn Section 59 of the Crimes Act. Section 59 provides a defence for parents charged with assault against their children. Under Section 59, every parent of a child (and every person in the place of a parent of a child) is justified in using force by way of correction towards the child, if the force is reasonable in the circumstances (Carswell, 2001, p. xi). It is sometimes agreed that support for physical punishment can create an insidious acceptance of physical violence in society. By not choosing to change Section 59, it is clear that an attitude of indifference is more important for our current government than children's rights.

6.2. Major Understandings Regarding the Nature of Bullying

In New Zealand, bullying is usually associated with boys' physical bullying, and tends to be interpreted according to its presentation in the news. However, bullying is a complex and non-gendered phenomenon. Although understanding about and approaches to dealing with bullying are variable (see Sullivan, 1999; 2000a, pp. 52–67), there is a stubborn myopia in society's willingness to confront the dynamics, range and reality of bullying.

Bullying involves physical, psychological and social behaviour; varying dynamics including individual, paired and group bullying; and a wide range of actions and tactics. Many types and ages of children are involved, and it occurs throughout the educational spectrum. It is tackled on a piecemeal basis in many settings, ignored and said not to exist in others, and confronted fully by a few.

There have been several viable attempts to recognise fully the extent and negative consequences of bullying which try to redress the apathy about and denial of its virulence and harmfulness throughout society (eg, *Kia Kaha*; *Cool Schools* program). Other organisations such as the Office of the Commissioner for Children have been vociferous in their condemnation of bullying. Some individual schools have attempted to introduce and develop anti-bullying programs. In 1999, the Minister of Education allocated NZ $1.299 million to be spent over three years on the Specialist Education Services' Eliminating Violence program, which raises awareness about violence but is not a practical program. Although this allocation was well-intended, it was an *ad hoc* response and lacked follow through. It was designed to cater for 40 schools per year for three years accounting for 4.6 per cent of all New Zealand's schools. Such money would have been better spent creating a unified and more substantial national approach to bullying.

6.3. Major Research Findings Regarding Bullying in New Zealand

Adair et al.'s (2000) study of 2066 secondary schools students found that, according to their own definition of bullying, 58 per cent, and, with reference to a list of bullying behaviours, 75 per cent of respondents reported having been victims of bullying. Forty-four per cent said that they had bullied others at some time during their schooling; 76 per cent of reported incidents involved boys.

When they had observed a bullying incident (81% reported having been a witness to bullying), only 21 per cent had reported it to an adult. Nearly half of the students stated they were as likely to ignore a bullying incident as to take action. Nearly half said that they neither believed bullying could be stopped nor had any strategies to deal with it.

Maxwell and Carroll-Lind (1997) reported that being physically or emotionally bullied by other children was listed among the four worst things that had happened to children. Someone chose dying as the only experience that was felt to be worse. Sullivan (1998) has found that while bullying clearly exists in its stereotypical form, it can also be psychological, subtle and carried out by girls. Cleary (2001) has shown that peer group pressure and low levels of awareness among adults can be such that, even in a secondary school with a major anti-bullying initiative, adolescents can create a bullying dynamic that is destructive and can go undetected.

6.4. *Possible Lines of Research into School Bullying in New Zealand*

The major issue for New Zealand schools is how to use national and international understandings regarding bullying in the school-age society. In their evaluation of the Eliminating Violence program in South Auckland, Moore et al. (1997) identified the existence of extensive racist bullying (see also Sullivan, 2000b).

7. SUMMARY

A number of common elements have emerged from this opportunity for cross-cultural discussion of the emerging issue of school bullying. The issue of how best to define or describe bullying was a key element readily identified as a point warranting further discussion. Cultural and historical influences appear to shape significantly how bullying is viewed and the Chinese, Japanese and Korean authors drew attention to the language used to define the concept. It also appeared that bullying manifested itself differently in terms of age and gender as the statistics from all countries highlighted. The country reports also highlighted that different causes were linked to school bullying, for example, the Japanese report has strongly linked bullying to stress. A significant need identified by most countries was for the development of a more comprehensive data base to understand better the issue. A strong call was made for longitudinal and cross-cultural research.

REFERENCES

Adair, V. A., Dixon, R. S., Moore, D. W., & Sutherland, C. M. (2000). Ask your mother not to make yummy sandwiches: Bullying in New Zealand secondary schools, *New Zealand Journal of Educational Studies, 35*(2), 207–221.

Blacklock, D. (1995). *Comet Vomit.* Sydney: Allen & Unwin.

Carswell, S. (2001). *Survey on Public Attitudes towards the Physical Discipline of Children.* Wellington: Ministry of Justice.

Chen, S. (2001). Relationships between interpersonal conflict resolution strategy and bullying behaviours among school children. *Psychological Science, 24*, 234–235.

Cleary, M. (2001). *Bullying Behaviour in Schools: Towards better understanding and practice.* Unpublished MA thesis, Victoria University of Wellington.

Ekblad S. (1990). Bullying behaviours and incidence of being bullied among primary school children in China. *Chinese Mental Health Journal., 4*, 247–249.

Emergency Appeal (1996). Japanese Minister of Education. Jan. 30th.

Gekkan Seitosidou (1980). *Gekkan Seitosidou* (Japanese) [Monthly Guidance and Counselling]. Tokyo: Gakuji Syuppan.

Graham, S., & Juvonen, T. (Eds.) (2001). *Peer Harassment in School. The Plight of the Vulnerable and Victimized.* New York: Guilford Publications.

House of Representatives Standing Committee on Employment, Education and Training (1994). *'Sticks and Stones' – Report on Violence in Australian Schools.* Canberra: AGPS.

Kim, T., & Kim, I. (1999). The survey on peer relations among adolescents. The 21st Adolescents Problem Discussion in Korea Youth Counseling Institute. *Youth Counselling Problem Study Report, 31.*

Kim, Y., & Park, H. (1997). The survey on bullying among adolescents. Korean Youth Counseling Institute. *Youth Counseling Problem Study Report, 29.*

Ku, B. (1997). The cause and guidance of on bullying among adolescents. Korean Youth Counseling Institute. *Youth Counseling Problem Study Report, 29.*

Kwon, J. (1999). *Methodological Study on School Violence (bullying).* Symposium of Korean Psychological Association.

Lee, C., & Kwak, K. (2000). *Bullying at School: Actual Condition and Characteristics.* Seoul: Gibmoondang.

Lee, H. (2000). *A School Model for Bullying Solution.* Research materials from Seoul Metropolitan Counseling Center for Youth.

Li, H. (2001). Violence interview: In *School Psychological Damage Records and Coping Strategies* (pp. 33–103). Beijing: Writer Press. (Chinese)

Li, P., Chen, L., Xu J., Wang, J., & Lin, Y. (2001). *The Urgent Task of Quality Education: An Relieving Children of Academic Burden and on Reform.* Beijing: Xinhua Press.

Ma, L., & Zhang, J. (in press). Suicidal ideation and experiences of being bullied among school teenagers in China. *Chinese Journal of School Health.*

Ma, L., Zhang, J., Wei, S., & Shen, L. (2001). Correlates of being bullied among school teenagers in China. *Chinese Journal of School Health., 22*, 249–250.

Ma, L., Zhang, J., Wei, S., Shen, L., Xiao, C., Liu, Y. et al. (2000). A study on factors related to suicidal ideation among urban middle school students in China. *China Public Health, 16* (Suppl. 6–8).

Ma, L., Zhang, J., Zou, Y., Wei, S., & Shen, L. (2001). A preliminary revision study on Teen Life Survey. *Modern Preventive Medicine, 28*, 279–282.

Maxwell, G., & J. Carroll-Lind (1997). *The Impact of Bullying on Children.* Wellington: Office of the Commissioner for Children, Occasional Paper No. 6.

Ministry of Education (2001). *Education Statistics of New Zealand for 2000.* Wellington: Data Management and Analysis Division, Ministry of Education.

Ministry of Education (1996). *Te Whāriki: He Whāriki matauranga mo nga mokopuna o Aotearoa.* Early childhood curriculum. Wellington: Learning Media.

Moore, D., Adair, V., Lysaght, K., & Kruiswijk, J. (1997). *Eliminating Violence from Schools Evaluation Project.* Auckland: Education Department, University of Auckland.

Morita, Y. (Eds.) (1985). *Ijime Syuudan no Kouzou nikansuru Syakaigakuteki Kenkyu* (Japanese) [Sociological Study on the structure of Ijime Group]. Osaka: City College Sociology Study.

Morita, Y. (Eds.) (2001). *Ijime no Kokusai Hikaku Kenkyu* (Japanese) [The Comparative Study on Bullying in four countries]. Tokyo: Kaneko Shobo.

Ohsako, T. (Ed.) (1997). *Violence at School: Global Issues and Interventions.* Paris: International Bureau of Education.

Olweus, D. (1993). Bullying in schools. In *What We Know and What We Can Do*. Oxford: Blackwell.
Owens, L., Slee, P., & Shute, R. (2001). Victimization among teenage girls. What can be done about indirect harassment? In J. Juvonen & S. Graham (Eds.), *Peer Harassment in School: The Plight of the Vulnerable and Victimized* (pp. 215–241). New York: Guilford Publications.
Park, K., Sohn, H., & Song, H. (1998). Bullying in elementary, middle, and high schools. *Korean Educational Development Institute, Research Report*, 98.
Rigby, K & Slee, P. T. (1995). *The Peer Relations Questionnaire*. Adelaide: University of South Australia.
Rigby, K. (1997). What children tell us about bullying in schools. *Children Australia*, 22, 28–34.
Rigby, K., & and Slee, P. T. (1999). Suicidal ideation among adolescent school children's involvement in bully/victim problems and perceived low social support. *Suicide & Life-threatening Behaviour*, 29, 119–130.
Sim, H. (2001). Children coping with peer conflict: Cross-sectional and longitudinal correlates of bullying, victim, and prosocial behavior. *Korean Journal of Child Studies*, 22(3), 49–61.
Slee, P. T. (1998a). Bullying in Australian primary schools. Some barriers to help seeking and links with socio-metric status. In P. Slee & K. Rigby (Eds.), *Children's Peer Relations* (pp. 205–215). London: Routledge.
Slee, P. T. (1998b). *Bullying Amongst Australian Students: An International Perspective*. A paper presented at the International, Society for the Study of Human Development Conference, Berne, June.
Slee, P. T. (2001) (3rd. ed.). *The P.E.A.C.E. Pack: A Programme for Reducing Bullying in Our Schools*. Adelaide: Flinders University.
Smith, P., & Sharp, S. (1994). *School Bullying: Insights and Perspectives*. London: Routledge.
Sullivan, K. (1998). Isolated children, bullying and peer group relations. In P. T. Slee & K. Rigby (Eds.), *Children's Peer Relations* (International Library of Psychology Series) (pp. 144–162). London and New York: Routledge.
Sullivan, K. (1999). 'Aotearoa/New Zealand'. In P. K. Smith, Y. Morita, J. Junger-Tas, D. Olweus, R. F. Catalano & P. Slee (Eds.), *The Nature of School Bullying: A Cross-National Perspective* (pp. 340–356),.London and New York: Routledge.
Sullivan, K. (2000a). *The Anti-Bullying Handbook*. Auckland: Oxford University Press.
Sullivan, K. (2000b). Racist bullying: Creating understanding and strategies for teachers. In M. Leicester, C. Modgil & S. Modgil (Eds.), *Education, Culture and Values – Volume II. Institutional Issues: Pupils, Schools and Teacher Education* (pp. 80–90). London and New York: Falmer Press.
Taki, M. (2001a). Japanese School Bullying: *Ijime* – A survey analysis and an intervention program in school. A paper presented at the conference of Understanding and Preventing Bullying: An International Perspective, at Queen's University in Canada.
Taki, M. (2001b). Relation among bullying, stress and stressor: A follow-up survey using panel data and a comparative survey between Japan and Australia. *Japanese Society*, 5.
Zhang, W., Gu, C., Wang, M., Wang, Y., & Jones, K. (2000). A study on the gender differences in school bullying. *Psychological Science*, 23, 435–439.

31

Student Learning: A Cross-Cultural Perspective

DAVID N. WATKINS
University of Hong Kong, Hong Kong

1. INTRODUCTION

The area of student learning is one in which researchers in the Asia-Pacific region have been at the forefront of research and theoretical developments for the last 30 years. At first much of this work focused on Australian school and university students but in the last ten years this focus has spread particularly to so-called Confucian heritage countries in South-East Asia such as Japan and Hong Kong. The impetus for this latter focus has been the excellent performance of students from such countries in international comparisons of educational progress. The question has been raised of cultural differences in student learning and a controversy has arisen about the very existence and the likely explanation of such differences. Other countries in the region, like elsewhere in the world, have recognised the importance of the quality of learning outcomes for economic development (Altbach & Selvaratnam, 1989). Consequently such research has been widely replicated in this region and so much is now known about how and why its students learn and the likely impact on the outcomes achieved. The great majority of this work has been based on Western concepts and theorising. This review focuses on the issue of the relevance of these imported ideas for non-Western countries through both a conceptual analysis and a cross-cultural meta-analysis involving 12 countries in the region. Issues such as cross-cultural differences and factors that particularly impact on student learning in the region are also briefly addressed.

2. APPROACHES TO LEARNING

Research into student learning in recent years has been based primarily on two overlapping but distinct theoretical positions. In North America the concepts of goal theory and self-regulated learning have dominated. In Europe and indeed in the Asia-Pacific region research has been influenced by what has become known as the Student Approaches to Learning (SAL) position.

The impetus for the SAL approach was a paper by Marton and Saljö (1976), one of the most widely cited sources in the entire literature of educational psychology. That paper described a study where Swedish university students were asked to read an academic article and then explain what they had learned and how they had achieved that learning. These students generally expressed two major ways of tackling this task. Some tried to memorize details or key terms in order to be able to answer subsequent questions. They tended to focus on the reading at word or sentence level. Most of the other subjects tried to understand the message that the passage was trying to impart. They tended to focus on the themes and main ideas and generally tried to process the reading for meaning. These intentions and their associated reading strategies were called 'surface' and 'deep' approaches, respectively. The researchers reported qualitative differences in learning outcomes depending on the approach to reading that had been utilized. Students who had adopted a surface approach typically could not explain the authors' message and could only recall isolated factual fragments of the passage. Those adopting a deep approach were able to provide a more sophisticated overview of the authors' intentions and frequently used extracts from the reading to support their reasoning.

At this point the SAL literature proceeded in two contrasting but not incompatible directions. The Swedish researchers developed a qualitative approach to research which they called 'phenomenography' (Marton, 1981). The aim of this approach was to understand how students perceived the content and process (the 'what' and 'how') of learning. The underlying rationale was the phenomenological notion that people act according to their interpretation of a situation rather than to objective reality.

The basic principle of the phenomenographic view of learning is that "learning should be seen as a qualitative change in a person's way of seeing, experiencing, understanding, conceptualizing something in the real world" (Marton & Ramsden, 1988, p. 271). From this perspective there is no point trying to derive general principles of learning independently of the context and content of learning. The ways students learn is a function of how they perceive the learning task and the learning environment. Although phenomenography itself is seen as descriptive, rather than prescriptive, principles based on this approach, have been shown to lead to a higher quality of teaching and learning. In particular, it is emphasized that the focus of learning is conceptual change and that teachers need to understand their students' conceptions of learning and how they can facilitate conceptual change (Bowden, 1988; Ramsden, 1992).

The quantitative SAL approach was founded by the work of Biggs in Australia and Entwistle in the United Kingdom. Both researchers developed, relatively independently, learning process inventories which owe a debt to the paper of Marton and Saljö (1976) and later phenomenographic writing by adopting the 'surface/deep' and 'approaches to learning' terminology.

Biggs (1987), in developing his *Learning Process Questionnaire* (LPQ) and its tertiary counterpart, the *Student Process Questionnaire* (SPQ), and Entwistle and Ramsden (1983) in developing their *Approaches to Studying Inventory* (ASI) added a third approach, 'achieving'. Students adopting this approach tried to achieve the highest possible grades by such strategies as working hard and efficiently, and being cue conscious. They would use any strategy, be it rote memorizing lots of facts, or understanding basic principles that they perceived would maximize their chances of academic success.

Biggs' instruments are based on a neat 'motive/strategy' model of learning. He operationalizes the constructs of approach to learning in terms of this motive/strategy combination. Factor analyses of responses to the SPQ, LPQ, and ASI have generally supported the underlying structure of surface, deep, and achieving approaches to learning for Western students (Biggs, 1993). Biggs emphasizes that the motive/strategy model is related to the students' intentions and their perceptions of the learning context, and is therefore only meaningful in context. He has adapted a model of teaching proposed by Dunkin and Biddle (1974) to capture the relationships between characteristics of the learner and the learning context (Presage), student approaches to a particular learning task (Process), and outcomes of learning (Product) in his 3P model of learning. He emphasizes the systemic nature of this model. The variables involved in the 3P model do not form a simple linear path from presage to process to product. Rather each component of the system interacts with all other components until equilibrium is reached. Inspection of this model indicates why both simple general laws of learning have not been possible to validate, and attempts to improve learning outcomes based on the so-called 'deficit' model are ineffective. To explain student learning requires an appreciation of the interactive, multi-dimensional nature of the swamp of real life learning. General laws, which focus on just one aspect of the learning situation, such as reinforcement, cannot achieve this.

2.1. Strategies or Styles: The State-trait Debate

One of the longest running war of words in the psychological literature has been over what is known as the state-trait debate: the degree to which our constructs are stable properties of an individual or can vary according to the situation. In the learning area this debate is over the strategy-style distinction. The basic issue is whether learners are relatively consistent in their way of learning or whether they vary their approach according to the learning task and content. The phenomenographic approach emphasises that an approach to learning is context specific and that a conception of learning is a relation between the learner and the task (Marton, Hounsell, & Entwistle, 1984). However, subsequent research showed much evidence of individual consistency at least in conceptions of learning (Marton, Dall'Alba, & Beaty, 1993).

Questionnaires such as the SPQ and LPQ are used to assess how a student would usually go about their learning tasks in general, although instructions can be changed to ask respondents to focus on a particular course rather than their learning in general. The elements of the state or trait issue are portrayed in the 3P model of learning (Biggs, 1987) where the Presage stage which includes both personality and situational elements in turn affects the Process and Product of learning.

2.2. Cross-cultural Equivalence

Before utilising any instrument in cross-cultural research its cross-cultural validity needs to be demonstrated. The central notion that needs to be understood here is that of 'equivalent usage'. There is a hierarchy of possible uses to which an instrument can be put, each level of which requires the demonstration of a corresponding hierarchy of assumptions (Hui & Triandis, 1985). The lowest level involves conceptual equivalence and the highest, metric (or scalar) equivalence. In this section it is first asked whether the constructs of conceptions of and approaches to learning at the heart of the Student Approaches to Learning position which is the theoretical basis for instruments such as the SPQ (and ASI) are relevant to non-Western cultures in the Asia-Pacific region as well as Australia where much of the basic research took place. If so, are responses to such instruments reliable and do they have the hypothesized underlying factor structure in such cultures? As we are not concerned at this stage with comparing scores of students in different cultures we do not need to demonstrate metric equivalence, that is the equivalence of raw scores.

2.3. Conceptual Equivalence

The notions of conceptual equivalence and 'etic' and 'emic' approaches to research are closely associated (Berry, 1989). The former approach seeks to compare cultures on what are thought to be universal categories. By way of contrast, the latter approach uses only concepts that emerge from within a particular culture and is associated with the traditions of Anthropology but also more recently those of Indigenous Psychology (Kim & Berry, 1993). Triandis (1972) has pointed to the dangers of so-called 'pseudoetic' research that involves the imposition of the concepts of one culture upon another as if they were universal without any prior research into the veracity of this assumption.

In order to assess the conceptual equivalence of the constructs underlying the SAL position and learning instruments such as the SPQ requires qualitative analysis. To date such studies have, to the author's knowledge been conducted in the Asia-Pacific region with students in China, Hong Kong, Japan, and Nepal, and from the University of the South Pacific. There have also been a number of recent qualitative investigations of the learning approaches and conceptions of Chinese learners in Hong Kong and China (Kember, 1996; Kember & Gow, 1991; Watkins & Biggs, 1996) and students from a number of Pacific Island countries at the University of the South Pacific (Mugler & Landbeck, 1998). These studies have partially supported the conceptual validity of the constructs of deep and surface approaches underlying the SAL position for students. However, this research has also concluded that Chinese students tend to view memorization as relevant to both approaches whereas Western students and educators are more likely to view memorization as characteristic of a surface approach. Relative to Western students Chinese students tend to view understanding as a slow process requiring considerable effort and cognitively-engaging repetition (Dahlin & Watkins, 1999). Research in Nepal (Watkins & Regmi, 1992, 1995; Dahlin & Regmi, 1997) concluded that while deep and surface approaches were relevant for these students, the concept of learning as 'character development' emerged at a lower cognitive level than in Western studies. So it may be fair to conclude that while the constructs of deep and surface approaches to learning are relevant to non-Western cultures, culturally specific aspects of these constructs are also likely.

2.4. Reliability

The responses to any measuring instrument need to be assessed for reliability in any culture where the questionnaire is to be used. Watkins (1998) reported the internal consistency reliability estimates coefficient α for responses to the SPQ scales by 14 independent samples of 6500 university students from 10 countries, including six from the Asia-Pacific region. The α coefficients ranged as follows: Surface Motivation 0.37 to 0.67 (median 0.55); Surface Strategy 0.25 to 0.66 (median 0.55); Deep Motivation 0.44 to 0.70 (median 0.64); Deep Strategy 0.47 to 0.76 (median 0.69); Achieving Motivation 0.48 to 0.77 (median 0.68); and Achieving Strategy 0.56 to 0.77 (median 0.72). All but 13 of the 84 alpha coefficients exceeded 0.50: a magnitude that is considered to be acceptable for a research instrument used for group comparisons but well below the level required for important academic decisions about an individual student (Nunnally, 1978). Not surprisingly, the reliability estimates were slightly higher for Australian students for whom it was developed and particularly low for the Nepalese for whom the concepts might not have been as relevant and whose level of English competence was relatively low. Research has also supported, often even more clearly, the internal consistency of responses to the other instruments used in this meta-analysis for the participants whose data are reported.

2.5. Within-construct Validity

The within-construct validity of the LPQ and SPQ have been examined by comparing the results of internal factor analysis of responses to the LPQ and SPQ scales for different cultures both with each other and the theoretical model expected. Moreover, correlations between scales of inventories supposed to be tapping the same constructs should be statistically significant and of a magnitude indicative of convergent validity.

Watkins (1998) reported the factor loadings of the SPQ scales based on two factor solutions (which typically explained 65 per cent of the variance) obtained after principal axis factor analysis followed by rotation to oblique simple structure using the Oblimin procedure for samples of university students from eight countries. In all eight samples the results were clear-cut with distinct surface and deep approach factors. The achieving scales as explained earlier were not expected to load consistently on one or other of the factors but rather be associated with the approach which was more likely to succeed in that context. Thus, the Hong Kong students sampled clearly associated both the achieving approach scales with a deep approach to learning. Interestingly, there was a tendency in the remaining countries for achieving strategies to be strongly associated with a deep approach, but this trend was weaker for the corresponding motivation scale whose loadings tended to be divided between the two factors. Confirmatory factor analysis of responses to the LPQ, which shares the same underlying motive and strategy model as the SPQ, for ten samples of school students from six different countries also confirmed the two basic factors of deep and surface approach (Wong, Lin, & Watkins, 1996). A review of the factor analytic studies of the ASI by Richardson (1994) also supported the cross-cultural validity of underlying deep and surface approaches.

3. CROSS-CULTURAL META-ANALYSIS

The main aim of this analysis was to use quantitative synthesis in the meta-analytic tradition, to test the relevance for countries in the Asia-Pacific region of variables proposed in SAL theory to be significantly correlated with surface, deep, and achieving approaches to learning. According to Biggs (1987) how a student learns depends on presage factors related both to the person and the learning environment. In particular, the following relationships are examined from a cross-cultural perspective.

Correlates with self-concept and locus of control. Students who are more self-confident, particularly with their academic abilities and who accept greater responsibility for their own learning outcomes are more likely to adopt deeper, more achieving approaches to learning which require them to rely more on their own understanding of the course materials rather than being overly-dependent on the teacher or text-book (Biggs, 1987; Schmeck, 1988).

Correlates with academic grades. It would be expected that the students' approaches to learning influence their academic performance. In particular, it is predicted that in any culture a surface approach would be significantly negatively correlated with academic achievement. It is further predicted that deep and achieving approaches will be positively associated with grades (Biggs, 1987; Schmeck, 1988). However, it is also recognised that these relationships also assume that higher quality learning outcomes are rewarded by the assessment system. Unfortunately this is not always the case.

Correlates with learning environment. A number of studies, mainly from the Asia-Pacific region, have shown that the classroom environment as perceived by pupils influences their learning outcomes (Fraser, 1986). (See *Classroom Learning Environments*). Classrooms perceived as orderly, organised, cohesive, and goal directed are theoretically predicted and consistently found to be associated with better achievement. At least in Western research, deeper level approaches to learning are likely to be encouraged by a warm classroom climate, an appropriate workload, interaction with others, and a well planned and resourced learning environment (Biggs & Watkins, 1995).

3.1. Method

The first stage of any meta-analysis is to select the studies to be quantitatively synthesised. A decision which has to be made at this stage is whether only studies satisfying some predetermined quality criteria should be included and, of course, what such criteria should be (for example, see Slavin, 1987, for a discussion of this issue).

In this article all studies based on students in the Asia-Pacific region found which reported correlates of at least one approach to learning and measures of self-esteem, locus of control, learning environment, and academic achievement were considered. Where it was possible to estimate statistically such correlations from the data provided, they were included, provided responses to the scales showed a reasonable level of internal consistency (alphas of at least 0.50) for the culture being studied. This led to the dropping of four studies. The studies were obtained both by formal searches of established research data bases and by more informal means such as hands-on search of the extensive journal collection in the Hong Kong University library and requests for relevant published and unpublished material at international conferences and letter and e-mail appeals to established researchers in the area.

Another issue in this type of meta-analysis is whether scales from different instruments are really measuring the same variables and so can be combined. In this article a number of different learning process instruments are each assumed to be assessing a student's approach to learning. In addition, different measures of self-esteem such as the *Self Description Questionnaire* (Marsh, 1990), locus of control such as the *Causal Dimension Scale* (Russell, 1982), and academic achievement (as measured by school tests, grade point average, standardized achievement tests, etc.) are assumed to be measuring the same variable.

Once all the studies to be included were identified and the relevant correlations obtained, average correlations were then calculated (in this article for simplicity the size of the sample will not be considered and each correlation will be given equal weight; see Hedges and Olkin (1985), for a discussion of weighting in meta-analysis). The relationships between approaches to learning and the other variables of interest are also examined separately at school and university level.

3.2. Results

The correlations found and the characteristics of the studies from which they are taken are shown in Appendices 1, 2 and 3 for the relationships between approaches to learning and self-esteem, internal locus of control and academic achievement, respectively. While the relevant average correlations for the overall Asia-Pacific region and at school and university level are shown in Table 1.

Table 1. Average correlations between learning approach scales and self-esteem, locus of control, and academic achievement at school and university level

Correlated variable	Sample size	Surface approach	Deep approach	Achieving approach
Self-esteem				
School level	3752	0.02	0.30	0.33
University level	2436	−0.08	0.34	0.26
Total	6188	−0.01	0.31	0.31
Locus of control				
School level	8964	−0.24	0.11	0.14
University level	2028	−0.16	0.12	0.17
Total	10992	−0.23	0.11	0.15
Academic achievement				
School level	16110	−0.14	0.18	0.21
University level	6407	−0.11	0.16	0.17
Total	22517	−0.13	0.17	0.20

Approaches to learning and self-esteem. From Table 1 and Appendix 1 it can be seen that, based on 6188 respondents from eight countries, the average correlation between self-esteem and surface, deep, and achieving approaches to learning were −0.01, 0.31, and 0.31, respectively. The correlations were slightly higher at the university level than at the school level for the deep approach and slightly higher at the school level that at the university level for the achieving approach.

Approaches to learning and academic achievement. From Table 1 and Appendix 2 it can be seen that the average correlation, based on 22,517 students from eight countries, with surface, deep, and achieving approaches to learning were −0.13, 0.17, and 0.20, respectively. These relationships were slightly greater at the school than at the university level.

Approaches to learning locus of control. From Table 1 and Appendix 3 it can be seen that the average correlation based on 10,992 students from seven countries between internal locus of control and surface, deep, and achieving approaches to learning were −0.23, 0.11, and 0.15, respectively. The relation with surface approach was much larger at the school (−0.24) than at the university (−0.16) level.

Approaches to learning and the learning environment. Due to the diverse instruments assessing rather different dimensions of the learning environment it is difficult to synthesise quantitatively findings about their impact on student learning. However, Watkins (2000) reviewed seven studies involving some 4,000 school students in four countries including Australia (two studies) and Hong Kong (three studies) and five studies involving over 4,000 university students from three countries (including three Australian and one Hong Kong). It was concluded that in each study a deep approach to learning is encouraged in school classrooms where the students feel involved and perceive the teacher to be supportive and likeable. At university level a surface approach was associated with student perceptions of too heavy a workload and inappropriate assessment. As in the school research, supportive teaching was typically associated with a deep approach to learning by university students. Research in Singapore (Hoi, Mau, Kai, & Seng, 1999) and at the University of the South Pacific (Mugler & Landbeck, 1998) reached similar conclusions.

4. CULTURAL DIFFERENCES IN STUDENT LEARNING

The meta-analysis reported above found considerable similarity between personality and contextual correlates of approaches to learning across a range of countries in the Asia-Pacific region. But how similar are the students' actual learning strategies? Findings on this issue while always of interest must be treated skeptically as they typically involve the comparison of questionnaire raw scores across cultures or inferences from observational or qualitative studies. As discussed in Section 2.2 above, inferences from such quantitative data are of doubtful validity and the other types of data are hardly better in this respect.

4.1. *America versus Japan*

Due to the poor performance of United States students, particularly relative to Japanese and Singapore students, in comparisons of educational achievement such as the IEA studies (See *Comparative Educational Achievement Studies*) United States researchers have been trying to pinpoint why such differences occur. While there is some rather dubious evidence of racial differences in intelligence favouring some Asian cultures most effort has focused on identifying differences in cultural beliefs and practices of teaching and learning which may bring about such differences in learning outcomes. The series of studies by Stevenson and Stigler and their associates has been particularly influential in this regard but rather controversial (Stevenson & Stigler, 1992; Stigler & Stevenson, 1991). The latter study compared elementary classrooms in China, Taiwan, Japan, and mid-West United States and concluded (p. 43):

> A common Western stereotype is that the Asian teacher is an authoritarian purveyor of information, one who expects students to listen and memorise correct answers and procedures rather than to construct knowledge themselves. This does not describe the dozens of elementary school teachers that we have observed.

In like vein, Purdie, Hattie, and Douglas (1996) found that, relative to Australian peers, Japanese secondary school children were more likely to view learning as personal fulfilment rather than memorising and reproducing.

4.2. The Paradox of the Chinese Learner

A number of researchers based at Asian universities and utilising both quantitative and qualitative methods have focused much attention on explaining a seeming paradox: the good performance of Chinese students despite what to Western educators seems the over-dependence of such students on the use of rote learning and poor teaching conditions such as large class sizes, harsh teacher-student relationships, undue emphasis on assessment, and teacher-centred teaching. Moreover when responding to self-report instruments such as the SPQ students from a range of Asian countries such as China, Hong Kong, Singapore, Vietnam, and Malaysia report greater use of deeper learning strategies than do their Australian peers. While much of the good performance is undoubtedly due as in Japan to cultural beliefs emphasing the value of hard work and effort backed up by intense family pressure for success, this seems only part of the answer.

These issues have been addressed in two recent books (Watkins & Biggs, 1996, 2001) and there is only room here to summarise their conclusions. It seems that a number of well accepted Western dichotomies, such as intrinsic *versus* extrinsic motivation, student-centred *versus* teacher-centred teaching, and memorisation *versus* understanding, lack cross-cultural validity. While virtually all Chinese students are trained to utilise memorisation and can produce model answers if required, many of the better such students combine the processes of memorising and understanding to produce what are often higher quality learning outcomes than their Western peers. However, they seem to their Western teachers to be 'mere rote learners' and examiners observe the frequent use of memorised model answers. However, if the assessment system is perceived by these better students as rewarding higher order outcomes, they are able to perform at very high levels. The hopeful point here is that most Chinese students are very cue-conscious so changes to the assessment system can be used to improve student learning. As far as teaching goes it seems that the better Chinese teachers are able cognitively to engage students even when using whole-group teaching with classes of over 50 pupils. It seems that this approach may not transfer to classes in other cultures as it does depend on what Cortazzi and Jin (2001) refer to as 'learner-trained learners' who are eager to learn by observing others.

While some differences between students from different cultures have been identified to what extent they are due to cultural differences is another matter. Thus this writer has been told by his teacher education students on a number of occasions that any attempt to introduce greater use of collaborative learning in Hong Kong was contrary to Chinese values. Of course, it was pointed out to these students that Chinese culture was supposed to be collectivist in nature so social learning should be appropriate. What these students meant was that they like most others in Hong Kong had not come across collaborative learning in their schooling so it was something that seemed foreign to them. This leads to the point that many of the Japanese and Chinese cultural values based on Confucian principles have in fact been translated into practice rather differently in places such as Singapore and Hong Kong, despite their also sharing a strong British influence on schooling, let alone in mainland China where the Cultural Revolution swept aside many of the former beliefs, some of which have not been reinstated as yet. Moreover, the data of Smith (2001) indicates that Chinese students in Malaysia, Hong Kong, and Singapore may well have rather different approaches to learning.

4.3. International Students

Much recent research has focused on the way students from Asian countries cope with being students in countries such as the United States and Australia. In most of these studies it is common to lump together not only students from Confucian heritage countries, not necessarily very similar in their approaches to studying as Smith (2001) makes clear, but also students from countries with very different cultures and education systems such as Indonesia and the Philippines. Despite such limitations the United States studies seem to identify clearly differences between the performance, motivation, and strategies of typical Asian- and Euro-American students. Such differences seem to hold up at least for the first generation of migrants from Asia. Interestingly in this regard Volet and Renshaw (1996) report how many Singapore students in Australia are able to adapt to the learning requirements of tertiary courses often better than local students.

4.4. Indigenous Students

In countries such as Australia and New Zealand the indigenous peoples tend to perform well below the national averages in their schooling. It has been claimed that this may at least in part be due to cultural differences. Hughes (1987) reported, for instance, that Aboriginal students not only come from a collectivist culture so had difficulty adjusting to the individualism encouraged in Australian school systems, but also their traditional learning approach relies on repetition and listening as opposed to the formal school system which needs learning to be structured, enquiry oriented, and verbalised. Boulton-Lewis, Wilss, and Lewis (2001) in an in-depth longitudinal study of the conceptions of learning of Aboriginal and Torres Strait Islander students found that most in their first year of study espoused quantitative views of learning that depended on the acquisition of information primarily by repetitive processes. Rather low level learning outcomes are likely from such processes. However, as their studies progressed many developed a greater awareness of what learning methods were appropriate for tertiary study. Hemara (2001) investigated traditional and contemporary non-Maori and Maori pedagogies by reviewing a range of written records and publications. She concluded that there was an educational gap between these ethnic groups in terms of world views and methods of instruction, which led to tensions and the under-performance of Maoris in a Pakeha-based education system.

5. FACTORS AFFECTING LEARNING

There are several factors, which particularly affect learning in this region. Two of these are discussed briefly below.

5.1. *Assessment*

It has long been recognised that assessment is the factor, which most strongly influences student learning. China, in particular, has had a long history of civil service entry examinations, which allowed talented but poor students to raise a family's social status. So in Confucian heritage cultures such as Japan, Korea, Singapore, Hong Kong, China, and Taiwan there is a great belief in the value of schooling and great pressure for children to succeed academically. Educational reformers in such countries have questioned the emphasis placed on both public examinations and frequent classroom testing. It is now recognised that these practices have too often led to social problems such as student suicide and over reliance on rote learning methods.

5.2. *Medium of Instruction*

In many countries of this region students are forced to learn in a language other than their mother-tongue. Not surprisingly this can have detrimental effects on the quality of learning, particularly in cases where neither teachers nor students have an adequate mastery of the language of instruction. The language adopted often seems to have more to do with political rather than educational considerations. Hong Kong has been a prime example of this. During the British colonial era the medium of instruction at secondary school level was English. All too often this encouraged rote learning and anxiety. After the handback to China, the Hong Kong government ordered most secondary schools to switch to Cantonese, the mother tongue of 95 per cent of the population. Cantonese medium has been shown to be greatly beneficial in terms of both learning outcomes and self-esteem (see Watkins & Biggs, 1996, 2001). Now, however, pressure is being applied to switch to English and Putonghua (the national language of the People's Republic of China) as the medium of instructions within ten years. It has to be hoped that in the interest of both the psychological health of Hong Kong students and teachers and the quality of learning outcomes that this pressure will be resisted.

6. CONCLUSIONS

It would seem that Western notions of conceptions and approaches to learning established in previous research studies have considerable cross-cultural relevance but may take on slightly different forms in non-Western cultures, such as those of South-East Asia. Moreover, the cross-cultural meta-analysis reported here based on data from 12 countries in the Asia-Pacific region indicates that the correlates of approaches to learning also are relatively consistent across cultures. In particular, it seems that personality characteristics of the students, such as self-esteem and locus of control are relatively significant correlates of approaches to learning. However, self-esteem seems to be more closely related to the student adopting learning strategies appropriate for developing an understanding while an external locus of control seems to be related to the adoption of superficial learning strategies. However, as in the Biggs 3P model, characteristics of the learning environment are also associated with approaches to learning. In particular, an unsupportive classroom where the workload is excessive and the assessment is perceived as rewarding reproduction of facts is likely to be associated with superficial learning strategies. Thus these findings support the view that while there is consistency in how students learn (learning styles) they also adapt their study methods to the learning context (learning strategies).

The research studies reviewed here also point to a number of possible future directions of applied research in the Asia-Pacific region that may tell us much more about how to improve learning in this region.

6.1. *Improving Learning*

While the results summarised above must be treated with caution as they are correlational and not causal in nature, it does seem that to improve learning outcomes we may have to consider both the students and the learning environment. In the first respect it may be necessary to bolster students' self-esteem and help them develop a more internal locus of control through attributional retraining. Methods for enhancing both these aspects of personality are well established in Western research (see, for instance, Hattie, 1992) but their appropriateness for non-Western cultures needs to be established. The meta-analysis of Hattie, Biggs, and Purdie (1996) indicates that to improve study skills the focus should be more on conceptual rather than 'how to do it' issues. But again the validity of these claims for non-Western cultures has yet to be put to the test. Hattie et al's review also suggests that for low achieving students a 'whole-school' rather than an 'individualised' learning environment may be better. Perhaps, in this regard, the value of trying to utilise a more culturally appropriate pedagogy for indigenous people such as the Maoris may be worth evaluating.

This review has also highlighted the effects of educational policies involving assessment and the medium of instruction on student learning. As a number of countries in this region are currently undergoing such reforms an opportunity for real-world testing of the effects of these policy-led changes would be a pity to miss. More in-depth ethnographic studies such as those conducted in rural schools of India and China by Rao and Cheng (2001) are also necessary if we are to understand how and why students go about their learning in non-Western countries of the region.

REFERENCES

Altbach, P., & Selvaratnam, V. (Eds.) (1989). *From dependence to autonomy: The development of Asian universities.* Dordrecht: Kluwer.

Beckwith, J. (1991). Approaches to learning, their context and relationship to assessment performance. *Higher Education, 22*, 17–30.

Berry, J. (1989). Imposed emics-derived etics. The operationalisation of a compelling idea. *International Journal of Psychology, 24*, 721–735.

Biggs, J. B. (1987). *Student approaches to learning and studying.* Melbourne: Australian Council for Educational Research.

Biggs, J. B. (1992). *Why and how do Hong Kong students learn?* Hong Kong; Faculty of Education, University of Hong Kong.

Biggs, J. B. (1993). What do inventories of students' learning processes really measure? A theoretical review and clarification. *British Journal of Educational Psychology, 63*, 3–19.

Biggs, J. B., & Watkins, D. (Ed.) (1995). *Classroom learning: Educational psychology for the Asian teacher.* Singapore: Prentice Hall.

Boulton-Lewis, G. M., Wilss, L., & Lewis, D. C. (2001). Changes in conceptions of learning for Indigenous Australian university students. *British Journal of Educational Psychology, 71*, 327–342.

Bowden, J. (1988). Achieving change in teaching practice. In Ramsden, P. (Ed.), *Improving Learning: New Perspectives.* London: Kogan Page.

Chan, I. (1990). The relationship between motives, learning strategies, attributions for success and failure and level of achievement among secondary school students in Hong Kong. Unpublished M.Soc.S. dissertation, University of Hong Kong.

Cortazzi, M., & Jin, L. (2001). Large classes in China: 'good' teachers and interaction. In D. Watkins & J. Biggs (Eds.), *Teaching the Chinese Learner: Psychological and Pedagogical Perspectives* (pp. 115–134). Hong Kong/Melbourne: Comparative Education Research Centre/Australian Council for Educational Research.

Dahlin, B., & Watkins, D. (1999). The role of repetition in the processes of memorising and understanding. *British Journal of Educational Psychology, 70*, 65–84.

Drew, P-Y. (1998). Towards a model of learning outcomes for Hong Kong tertiary students. Unpublished Ph.D. thesis, University of Hong Kong.

Drew, P-Y., & Watkins, D. (1998). Affective variables, learning approaches and academic achievement: A casual modeling investigation with Hong Kong Chinese tertiary students. *British Journal of Educational Psychology, 68*, 173–188.

Dunkin, M. J., & Biddle, B. J. (1974). *The study of teaching.* New York: Holt, Rinehart, & Winston.

Eley, M. (1992). Differential adoption of study approaches within individual students. *Higher Education, 23*, 231–254.

Entwistle, N. J., & Ramsden, P. (1983). *Understanding student learning.* London: Croom Helm.

Fogarty, G. J., & Taylor, J. A. (1997). Learning styles among mature-age students: Some comments on the Approaches to Studying Inventory (ASI-S). *Higher Education Research & Development, 16*, 321–330.

Fraser, B. J. (1986). *Classroom environment.* London: Croom Helm.

Gao, L. B. (1998). Conceptions of teaching held by school physics teachers in Guangdong, China and their relations to student learning. Unpublished Ph.D. thesis, University of Hong Kong.

Gordon, C., Lim, L., McKinnon, D., & Nkala, F. (1996). Learning approach control orientation, and self-efficacy of beginning teacher education students. Conference of Australian Association for Educational Research, Melbourne.

Hattie, J. (1992). *The self-concept.* Hillsdale, New Jersey: Erlbaum.

Hattie, J. Biggs, J., & Purdie, N. (1996). Effects of learning skills intervention on student learning: A meta-analysis. *Review of Educational Research, 66*, 99–136.

Hedges, L. V., & Olkin, I. (1985). *Statistical methods for meta-analysis.* San Diego, CA: Sage.

Hemara, W. (2001). Maori pedagogies: A view from the literature. *In Annual Report of the New Zealand Council for Educational Research*, Wellington.

Ho, I. T. (1992). Unpublished Master's thesis, University of Hong Kong.

Ho, I. T., Salili, F., Biggs, J. B., & Hau, K. T. (1999). The relationship among causal attributions, learning strategies and level of achievement: A Hong Kong Chinese study. *Asia Pacific Journal of Education, 19*, 44–58.

Hoi, P. Mau, R., Cheng, Y., Kai, Y. Y., & Seng, Q. K. (1999). The learning and study approach of

NIE students: A longitudinal study. In M. Waas (Ed.), *Enhancing learning* (pp. 390–401). Singapore: Educational Research Association.

Hughes, P. (1987). *Aboriginal culture and learning styles – A challenge for academics in higher educational institutions*. Publications Office: University of New England.

Hui, C. H., & Triandis, H. C. (1985). Measurement in cross-cultural psychology: A review and comparison of strategies. *Journal of Cross-Cultural Psychology, 16,* 131–152.

Kember, D. (1996). The intention to both memorise and understand: Another approach to learning? *Higher Education, 31,* 341–354.

Kember, D., & Gow, L. (1991). A challenge to the anecdotal stereotype of Asian students. *Studies in Higher Education, 16,* 117–128.

Kim, V., & Berry, J. W. (Eds.) (1993). *Indigenous psychologies: Research and experience in cultural context*. London: Sage.

Ma, K. H. (1994). The relationship between achievement in and attitude towards science, approach to learning and classroom environment. Unpublished M.Ed. dissertation, University of Hong Kong.

Marsh, H. W. (1990). *Self-Description Questionnaire 1 manual*. University of Western Sydney, Macarthur.

Marton, F. (1981). Phenomenography: Describing conceptions of the world around us. *Instructional Science, 10,* 177–200.

Marton, F., Dall'Alba, G., & Beaty, E. (1993). Conceptions of learning. *International Journal of Educational Research, 19,* 277–300.

Marton, F., Hounsell, D., & Entwistle, N. J. (Eds.) (1984). *The experience of learning*. Edinburgh: Scottish Academic Press.

Marton, F., & Ramsden, P. (1988). What does it take to improve learning? In Ramsden, P. (Ed.), *Improving Learning: New Perspectives*. London: Kogan Page.

Marton, F., & Säljö, R. (1976). On qualitative differences in learning – I: Outcome and process. *British Journal of Educational Psychology, 46,* 4–11.

Mugler, F., & Landbeck, R. (1998). 'It's just you and the books': Learning conditions and study strategies of distance learners at the University of the South Pacific. In J. F. Forest (Ed.), *University teaching: International perspectives* (pp. 113–135). New York: Garland.

Murray-Harvey, R., & Keeves, J. (1994). *Student learning processes and progress in higher education*. Paper presented at the annual meeting of the American Educational Research Association, New Orleans.

Nunnally, J. C. (1978). *Psychometric theory* (2nd ed.). New York: McGraw Hill.

Provost, S., & Bond, N. (1997). Approaches to studying and academic performance in a traditional Psychology course. *Higher Education Research & Development, 16,* 309–320.

Purdie, N., Hattie, J., & Douglas, G. (1996). Student conceptions of learning and their use of self-regulated learning strategies: A cross-cultural comparison. *Journal of Educational Psychology, 88,* 87–100.

Ramsden, P. (1992). *Learning to teach in higher education*. London: Routledge.

Rao, N., & Cheng, K. M. (2001). Sociocontextual influences on teaching mathematics. Paper presented at the World Congress of Comparative Education Societies, July 2–6, Chungbuk, South Korea.

Rao, N., Moely, B. E., & Sachs, J. (2000). Motivational beliefs, study strategies and mathematics attainment in high- and low-achieving Chinese secondary school students. *Contemporary Educational Psychology, 25,* 287–316.

Richardson, J. T. E. (1994). Cultural specify of approaches to studying in higher education: A literature survey. *Higher Education, 27,* 449–468.

Richardson, J., Landbeck, R., & Mugler, F. (1995). Approaches to study in higher education: A comparison study in the South Pacific. *Educational Psychology, 15,* 417–431.

Russell, D. (1982). The Causal Dimensional Scale: A measure of how individuals perceive causes. *Journal of Personality and Social Psychology, 42,* 1137–1145.

Schmeck, R. (Ed.) (1988). *Learning strategies and learning styles*. New York: Plenum.

Slavin, R. E. (1987). Ability grouping and student achievement in elementary schools: A best-evidence synthesis. *Review of Educational Research, 57*, 293–336.

Smith, I. D., & Chang, A. S. C. (1999). Self-regulated learning in Singaporean and Australian tertiary students. In M. Waas (Ed.), *Enhancing learning* (pp. 342–349). Singapore: Educational Research Association.

Smith, S. N. (2001). Approaches to study of three Chinese national groups. *British Journal of Educational Psychology, 71*, 429–442.

Stevenson, H. W., & Stigler, J. (1992). *The learning gap: Why our students are failing and what we can learn from Japanese and Chinese education.* New York: Summit Books.

Stigler, J., & Stevenson, H. W. (1991). How Asian teachers polish each other to perfection. *American Educator, 15*(1), 12–21 & 43–47.

Thomas, T. A. (1984). An investigation into the influence of anxiety and the effectiveness of treatments involving positive coping skills. Unpublished bachelor's honor's thesis, University of Sydney.

Triandis, H. C. (1972). *The analysis of subjective culture.* New York: John Wiley.

Trigwell, K., & Prosser, M. (1991). Improving the quality of student learning: The influence of learning context and approaches to learning on learning outcomes. *Higher Education, 22*, 251–266.

Watkins, D. (1982). Identifying the study process dimensions of Australian university students. *Australian Journal of Educational Research, 26*, 76–85.

Watkins, D. (1987). Academic locus of control: A relevant variable at tertiary level? *Higher Education, 16*, 221–229.

Watkins, D. (1998). Assessing approaches to learning: A cross-cultural perspective. In B. Dart & G. Boulton-Lewis (Eds.), *Teaching and learning in higher education.* Melbourne: Australia Council for Educational Research.

Watkins, D. (2000). Correlates of approaches to learning: A cross-cultural meta-analysis. In R. Sternberg & L. F. Zhang (Eds.), *Perspectives on Thinking, Learning, and Cognitive Styles* (pp. 165–195). Mahwah, New Jersey: Erlbaum.

Watkins, D., & Biggs, J. (Eds.) (1996). *The Chinese learner: Cultural, psychological, and contextual influences.* Hong Kong/Melbourne: Comparative Education Research Centre/Australian Council for Educational Research.

Watkins, D., & Biggs, J. (2001). *Teaching the Chinese learner: Psychological and pedagogical perspectives.* Hong Kong/Melbourne: Comparative Education Research Centre/Australian Council for Educational Research.

Watkins, D., & Hattie, J. (1981). The learning processes of Australian university students: Investigations of contextual and personological factors. *British Journal of Educational Psychology, 51*, 384–393.

Watkins, D., & Hattie, J. (1990). Individual and contextual differences in the approaches to learning of Australian secondary school students. *Educational Psychology, 10*, 333–342.

Watkins, D., Hattie, J., & Astilla, E. (1986). Approaches to studying by Filipino students: A longitudinal investigation. *British Journal of Educational Psychology, 56*, 357–362.

Watkins, D., & Ismail, M. (1994). Is the Asian learner a rote learner? A Malaysian perspective. *Contemporary Educational Psychology, 19*, 483–488.

Watkins, D., & Regmi, M. (1990). An investigation of the approach to learning of Nepalese tertiary students. *Higher Education, 29*, 459–469.

Watkins, D., & Regmi, M. (1992). How universal are student conceptions of learning? A Nepalese investigation. *Psychologia, 35*, 101–110.

Watkins, D., & Regmi, M. (1995). Assessing approaches to learning in non-Western cultures: A Nepalese conceptual validity study. *Assessment and Evaluation in Higher Education, 20*, 203–212.

Watkins, D., Regmi, M., & Astilla, E. (1991). The Asian-learner-as-a-rote-learner stereotype: Myth or reality? *Educational Psychology, 11*, 21–34.

Wong, M. (1998). Self-concept and approach to learning among high and low ability-grouped Hong Kong students. Unpublished master's thesis, University of Hong Kong.

Wong, N. Y. (1995). The relationship between Hong Kong students' perception of their mathematics classroom environment and approaches to learning. Unpublished doctoral dissertation, University of Hong Kong.

Wong, N. Y., Lin, W. Y., & Watkins, D. (1996). Cross-cultural validation of models of approaches to learning: An application of confirmatory factor analysis. *Educational Psychology, 16*, 317-327.

APPENDICES

NOTES

The source reference for the data reported in Appendices 1 to 3 and from which further details can be obtained are as follows.

Appendix 1 (Correlations with self-esteem)

Australia (a) (Murray-Harvey, personal communication); Australia (b) (Watkins & Hattie 1990); Australia (c) (Thomas, 1984); Australia (d) (Gordon et al., 1996); Australia (e); Hong Kong (a) (Drew & Watkins, 1998); Hong Kong (b) (Wong, 1998); Hong Kong (c) (Drew, 1998); Hong Kong (d) (Rao, Moely, & Sachs, 2000); Malaysia (Watkins & Ismail, 1994); Nepal (a), (b) (Watkins & Regmi, 1990, and unpublished research); Philippines (a); Philippines (b) and (d) (Watkins et al., 1991); Philippines (c) (Watkins et al., 1986); Singapore, Vietnam (Helmke & Vo, unpublished data).

Appendix 2 (Correlations with achievement)

Australia (a) and (b) (Biggs, 1987); Australia (c) (Murray-Harvey & Keeves, 1994); Australia (d) (Watkins, 1982); Australia (e) (Watkins & Hattie, 1981); Australia (f) (Provost & Bond, 1997); Australia (g) (Fogarty & Taylor, 1997); Australia (h) (Biggs, 1987); Australia (i) (Watkins & Hattie, 1990); Australia (j); Australia (k) and (l) (Trigwell & Prosser, 1991); Australia (m) (Beckwith, 1991); (Eley, 1992); Fiji (Richardson et al., 1995); China (a) and (c) Gao, 1998); China (b), Hong Kong (e) and USA (c) (Zhang, personal communication); China (d) (Gao, personal communication); Hong Kong (a) (Drew & Watkins, 1998); Hong Kong (b) (Biggs, 1992); Hong Kong (c) and (d) (Wong, 1995); Hong Kong (f) (Kember et al., 1995); Hong Kong (g) (Drew, 1998); Hong Kong (h) and Hong Kong (i) (Ma, 1994); Hong Kong (j) (Ho, 1992); India (Watkins & Dhawan, unpublished data); Japan (a) and (b) (Stribling, personal communication); Nepal (a) (Watkins & Regmi, 1990); Nepal (b) and (c) and Philippines (a) (Watkins et al., 1991); Philippines (a) (Watkins et al., 1986); Philippines (b) (Watkins & Hattie, 1981).

Appendix 3 (Correlations with locus of control)

Australia (a) (Gordon et al., 1996); Australia (b) (Murray-Harvey personal communication); Australia (c) (Watkins, 1987); Australia (d) and (e) (Biggs, 1987); Hong Kong (a) Drew & Watkins, 1998); Hong Kong (b) (Chan, 1990); Hong Kong (c) (Wong, 1995); Hong Kong (d) (Drew, 1998); Hong Kong (e) (Biggs, 1992); Hong Kong (f) (Ho, Salili, Biggs & Hau, 1999); India (Watkins &

Dhawan, unpublished data); Indonesia (Hotma Ria, 1993, personal communication); Malaysia (a), (b) (Watkins & Ismail, 1994); Nepal (a), (b) (Watkins & Regmi, 1990, and unpublished data); Nepal (c) (Watkins et al., 1991); Philippines (a) (Watkins et al., 1991); Philippines (b) (Watkins et al., 1986).

Learning Questionnaires were ASI = Approaches to Studying Inventory; ASI (S) = Short version of ASI; ASI (R) = revised ASI; CSI = Cognitive Skills Inventory; HIS = How I Study Inventory; ILP = Inventory of Learning Processes; LPQ = Learning Process Questionnaire; SPQ = Study Process Questionnaire; LSI = Learning Styles Inventory: MSLQ = Motivated Strategies for Learning Questionnaire.

Appendix 1 Summary of research reporting correlations between learning approach scales and self-esteem

	Country	Learning questionnaire	Participants	Surface approach	Deep approach	Achieving approach
(1)	Australia (a)	SPQ	386 university students	0.01	0.20*	0.32*
(2)	Australia (b)	HIS	1274 secondary school students	0.18	0.33*	0.34*
(3)	Australia (c)	LPQ	130 secondary school students	−0.10	0.35*	0.52*
(4)	Australia (d)	SPQ	65 university students	0.09	0.36*	0.29*
(5)	Australia (e)	LPQ	355 secondary school students	−0.12	0.37*	0.44*
(6)	Hong Kong (a)	SPQ	162 university students	−0.13	0.25*	0.22*
(7)	Hong Kong (b)	LPQ	240 secondary school students	−0.09	0.26*	0.32*
(8)	Hong Kong (c)	SPQ	417 university students	−0.16*	0.14*	0.14*
(9)	Hong Kong (d)	MSLQ	94 secondary school students	—	—	0.57*
(10)	India	LPQ	250 secondary school students	−0.10	0.32*	0.34*
(11)	Malaysia	LPQ	301 secondary school students	−0.03	0.26*	0.38*
(12)	Nepal (a)	ASI	302 university students	−0.15*	0.29*	—
(13)	Nepal (b)	LPQ	398 university students	−0.02	0.54*	0.30*
(14)	Philippines (a)	SPQ	218 secondary school students	−0.04	0.35*	0.29*
(15)	Philippines (b)	LPQ	261 secondary school students	−0.11	0.22*	0.18*
(16)	Philippines (c)	ASI(S)	445 secondary school students	−0.12*	0.12*	0.16*
(17)	Philippines (d)	HIS	184 secondary school students	0.16	0.42*	0.31*
(18)	Singapore	MSLQ	249 university students	—	0.30*	0.35*
(19)	Vietnam	MSLQ	457 university students	—	0.56*	—

*Correlation is significantly different from zero at 0.05 level.

Appendix 2 Summary of research reporting correlations between learning approach scales and academic achievement

	Country	Learning questionnaire	Participants	Surface approach	Deep approach	Achieving approach
(1)	Australia[a] (a)	SPQ	815 university students	−0.18*	0.22*	0.23*
(2)	Australia[a] (b)	SPQ	1550 university students	−0.10*	0.22*	0.21*
(3)	Australia (c)	SPQ	278 university students	−0.03	0.12*	0.25*
(4)	Australia (d)	SPQ	249 university students	−0.25*	0.24*	0.18*
(5)	Australia (e)	ILP	249 university students	−0.19*	0.31*	0.35*
(6)	Australia (f)	ASI (S)	175 university students	−0.14	0.16*	—
(7)	Australia (g)	ASI (S)	503 mature age university students	−0.19*	0.01	0.03
(8)	Australia[a] (h)	LPQ	1352 secondary school students	−0.13*	0.18*	0.22*
(9)	Australia (i)	HIS	1274 secondary school students	−0.14*	0.23*	0.25*
(10)	Australia (j)	SPQ	152 university students	−0.23*	0.22*	0.35*
(11)	Australia (k)	ASI	74 university students	−0.07	0.14	—
(12)	Australia (l)	ASI	143 university students	−0.07	0.15	—
(13)	Australia (m)	SPQ	105 university students	−0.07	−0.02	0.00
(14)	China (a)	LPQ	130 university students	−0.08*	0.10*	0.08
(15)	China (b)	SPQ	215 university students	−0.20*	0.13	0.13
(16)	China (c)	LPQ	915 secondary school students	−0.08*	0.10*	0.08
(17)	China (d)	LPQ	5400 secondary school students	−0.18*	0.28*	0.33*
(18)	Fiji	ASI (S)	918 secondary school students	−0.20*	−0.11	−0.08
(19)	Hong Kong (a)	SPQ	162 university students	−0.23*	0.20*	0.23*
(20)	Hong Kong[a] (b)	LPQ	3770 secondary school students	−0.09*	0.11*	0.16*
(21)	Hong Kong (c)	LPQ	127 secondary school students	−0.12	0.13	0.25*
(22)	Hong Kong (d)	LPQ	314 secondary school students	−0.10	0.14*	0.06
(23)	Hong Kong (e)	SPQ	326 university students	0.09	0.13*	0.12
(24)	Hong Kong (f)	SPQ	34 university students	0.15	0.23	0.18

(Continued)

Appendix 2 (Continued)

(25)	Hong Kong (g)	SPQ	417 university students	−0.06	0.10	0.16*
(26)	Hong Kong (h)	ASI (R)	183 university students	−0.02	0.07	0.08
(27)	Hong Kong (i)	LPQ (S)	115 secondary school students	—	—	0.24*
(28)	Hong Kong (j)	LPQ	237 secondary school students	−0.20*	0.18*	0.42*
(29)	Hong Kong (k)	MSLQ	94 secondary school students	—	—	0.04
(30)	India	LPQ	250 secondary school students	−0.23*	0.08	0.07
(31)	Japan (a)	SPQ	182 university students	−0.15*	−0.07	−0.05
(32)	Japan (b)	LPQ	41 secondary school students	−0.19	−0.14	0.09
(33)	Nepal (a)	SPQ	342 university students	−0.10*	0.06	0.06
(34)	Nepal (b)	LPQ	509 secondary school students	−0.14*	0.09	0.09
(35)	Nepal (c)	HIS	202 secondary school students	−0.11	0.21*	0.29*
(36)	Philippines (a)	LPQ	147 secondary school students	−0.14*	0.29*	0.27*
(37)	Philippines (b)	ASI (S)	445 secondary school students	−0.14*	0.28*	0.13*
(38)	Philippines (c)	ILP	123 university students	0.16	0.30*	0.10

* Correlation is significantly different from zero at 0.05 level.
[a] These correlations are based on self-estimates of academic achievement.

Appendix 3 Summary of research reporting correlations between measures of learning approach scales and internal locus of control

	Country	Learning questionnaire	Participants	Surface approach	Deep approach	Achieving approach
(1)	Australia (a)	SPQ	65 university students	0.23	0.33*	0.39*
(2)	Australia (b)	SPQ	83 university students	−0.18	0.22*	0.18
(3)	Australia (c)	ASI	741 university students	−0.21*	0.11*	0.23*
(4)	Australia (d)	LPQ	1353 secondary school students	−0.18*	0.12*	0.17*
(5)	Australia (e)	LPQ	979 secondary school students	−0.22*	0.13*	0.22*
(6)	Hong Kong (a)	SPQ	162 university students	−0.34*	0.00	0.24*
(7)	Hong Kong (b)	LPQ	244 secondary school students	0.06	0.23*	0.27*
(8)	Hong Kong (c)	LPQ	314 secondary school students	−0.24*	0.09	0.08
(9)	Hong Kong (d)	SPQ	417 university students	−0.11	0.05	−0.03
(10)	Hong Kong (e)	LPQ	3770 secondary school students	−0.28*	0.09*	0.12*
(11)	Hong Kong (f)	LPQ	237 secondary school students	−0.27*	0.22*	0.33*
(12)	India	LPQ	250 secondary school students	−0.46*	0.05	0.10
(13)	Indonesia	SPQ	90 university students	−0.18	0.16	0.15
(14)	Malaysia (a)	LPQ	301 secondary students	−0.19*	0.02	0.17*
(15)	Malaysia (b)	LPQ	301 secondary students	−0.49*	−0.16	−0.18
(16)	Nepal (a)	SPQ	128 university students	−0.18*	0.10	0.20*
(17)	Nepal (b)	SPQ	342 university students	−0.10*	0.24*	0.21*
(18)	Nepal (c)	LPQ	509 secondary school students	−0.32*	0.19*	0.17*
(19)	Philippines (a)	LPQ	261 secondary school students	−0.07	0.21*	0.16*
(20)	Philippines (b)	ASI(S)	445 secondary school students	−0.08	0.21*	0.10

* Correlation is significantly different from zero at 0.05 level.

32

Classroom Learning Environments

BARRY J. FRASER
Curtin University of Technology, Perth, Australia

SWEE CHIEW GOH
Nanyang Technological University, Singapore

1. INTRODUCTION

The study of learning environments has gained much recognition internationally in the last 30 years as a significant field of educational research (Fraser, 1998a). This trend is also evident in Asia, where this field has attracted the attention of educational researchers especially over the previous decade. The way in which studies in various Asian countries covering different types of learning environments have gained momentum in the last decade is illustrated in Goh and Khine's (2002) book. With the ensuing enthusiasm in learning environment research, studies began to emerge in countries such as Singapore, Korea, Taiwan and Indonesia, some of which can be regarded as pioneering in the field. Those studies focussed on students' and teachers' perceptions of classroom learning environments and science laboratory classes. Overall, much progress has been achieved in the conceptualisation, assessment and investigations of learning environment (Fraser, 1994, 1998a).

From a survey of studies on learning environments (Fraser, 1998a), the following lines of research are discernible. First, one main focus is associations between the classroom environment and learning outcomes, both cognitive and affective. Second, another important focus involves the use of classroom environment measures as criteria of effectiveness in the evaluation of educational programs. Third, there is also evidence of gender differences. Fourth, cross-cultural or cross-national studies involve the validation and use of learning environment questionnaires in other countries, with evidence of similarities and differences between the views of students in different countries. Fifth, a recent focus has been the translation and validation of learning environment questionnaires in local languages and their use for research purposes. This article highlights these five trends in learning environment research and draws examples particularly from the Asia-Pacific region.

These five research thrusts are discussed in turn in Sections 3–7 below, after a historical perspective is provided in Section 2. This article ends with a consideration of desirable future research directions.

2. HISTORICAL PERSPECTIVE

The first classroom learning environment questionnaires were developed in the United States in the early 1960s, with scales measuring the views of students being employed in the First IAE Mathematics Study (Husen, 1967). Following this work, Walberg and Anderson (1968) developed the *Learning Environment Inventory* (LEI) in conjunction with research and evaluation related to Harvard Project Physics, and later this was simplified to form the *My Class Inventory* (MCI) for use with younger students. Simultaneously, Moos and Trickett (1974) developed the *Classroom Environment Scale* (CES) as part of a more comprehensive research program involving a range of human environments.

Although these early questionnaires have seldom been used in Asia, there are some notable exceptions. Walberg, Singh and Rasher (1977) used the LEI with 3000 tenth grade students in India. The MCI has been used with a sample of 1512 primary mathematics students in Singapore (Goh, Young, & Fraser, 1995) and with 1565 secondary mathematics students in Brunei Darussalam (Majeed, Fraser, & Aldridge, 2002). The CES was used in an early study in Indonesia (Paige, 1979), while Hirata and Sako (1998) recently used a modified version of the CES in Japan.

Whereas the LEI, CES and MCI were designed for teacher-centred classrooms, the *Individualised Classroom Environment Questionnaire* (ICEQ) was designed in Australia in 1980s to assess dimensions which distinguish individualised classrooms from conventional ones (Fraser, 1990). The ICEQ appears to have been used very little in the Asian context, with the exception of Asghar and Fraser (1995) in Brunei Darussalam.

In research, which originated in The Netherlands in the 1980s, researchers focussed on the nature and quality of interpersonal relationships between teachers and students (Wubbels & Brekelmans, 1998; Wubbels & Levy, 1993). Drawing upon a theoretical model of proximity (cooperation-opposition) and influence (dominance-submission), the *Questionnaire of Teacher Interaction* (QTI) was developed to assess student perceptions of eight behavioural aspects (Leadership, Helpful/Friendly, Understanding, Student Responsibility/Freedom, Uncertain, Dissastisfied, Admonishing and Strict). As discussed later in this chapter, the QTI has been used in a range of significant studies in Asia.

Most of the more recent classroom environment questionnaires were developed in Australia, which is now the world centre for learning environments research (Fraser, 1998b). In particular, these include the *Science Laboratory Environment Inventory* (SLEI), *Constructivist Learning Environment Survey* (CLES) and *What is Happening in this Class?* (WIHIC) questionnaire. The comprehensive research programs involving the use of these questionnaires in Australia and Asia are considered in detail in other parts of this article.

3. CLASSROOM ENVIRONMENT AND LEARNING OUTCOMES

Investigating relationships between the classroom environment and learning outcomes constitutes one major focus in the study of learning environments (Fraser, 1994). Many studies examined this environment-outcome relationship partly because one prime concern of the teaching-learning process has been the academic performance or achievement of students. In most Asian countries, scholastic achievement is regarded as one measure of excellence and learning environment research inevitably encompasses consideration of student outcomes. There is also a belief that a positive classroom environment promotes and motivates student interest in learning, hence leading to better cognitive and affective outcomes.

Most of the learning environment studies undertaken in Singapore have included the investigation of outcome-environment relationships. The list of Singaporean studies include primary mathematics classroom environments (Goh & Fraser, 2000), secondary geography classrooms using computer-mediated methods (Teh & Fraser, 1994), secondary geography and mathematics classrooms (Fraser & Chionh, 2000), secondary science laboratory classroom environments (Wong & Fraser, 1996), secondary science gifted education classrooms (Quek, Fraser, & Wong, 2001), adult education classrooms (Khoo & Fraser, 1998) and junior college General Paper (English) classroom environments (Wilks, 2000). The findings from these studies all point to statistically significant relationships between classroom environment and student outcomes.

Furthermore, educational researchers in other Asian countries – for instance, Brunei (Khine & Fisher, 2001, 2002; Majeed, Fraser & Aldridge, 2002; Riah & Fraser, 1998; Scott & Fisher, 2001), Taiwan (Aldridge & Fraser, 2000), Indonesia (Margianti, Fraser, & Aldridge, 2002; Soerjaningsih, Fraser, & Aldridge, 2001) and Korea (Kim, Fisher, & Fraser, 1999, 2000; Lee & Fraser, 2001, 2002) – have also studied outcome-environment associations in their research into learning environment in the respective countries. The findings from this range of Asian countries reinforce the existence of strong associations between classroom environment and learning outcomes. That is, a more positive classroom environment is most likely to promote better student achievement and more favourable student attitudes towards learning.

In view of the number of studies investigating environment-outcome associations, one specific study by Chionh and Fraser is discussed in this article to illustrate the details and highlight the significance of this aspect of learning environment research (Fraser & Chionh, 2000). The research involved the use of the instrument entitled *What Is Happening In This Class?* (WIHIC) with a large sample of over 2000 secondary students in Singapore to assess their actual and preferred perceptions of two different school subjects, namely, geography and mathematics. Three types of student outcomes were measured: attitudes, self-esteem and achievement in national examinations (the Singapore-Cambridge General Certificate of Education Ordinary [GCE 'O'] Level Examination). In addition, the study also aimed to validate the WIHIC questionnaire in the

Singapore context to explore differences between students' perceptions of their geography and mathematics classrooms. In terms of student outcomes, better examination scores were found in classrooms with more student cohesiveness, whereas self-esteem and attitudes were more favourable in classes with more teacher support, task orientation and equity. In terms of the WIHIC questionnaire, data analyses supported each scale's factorial validity, internal consistency reliability and ability to differentiate between classrooms. Generally, students perceived their geography and mathematics classrooms in a relatively similar manner, although there were small but statistically significant differences for some scales.

While many past learning environment studies have employed techniques such as multiple regression analysis, few have used multilevel analysis (Bryk & Raudenbush, 1992), which takes cognisance of the hierarchical nature of classroom settings. However, two studies in Singapore compared the results from multiple regression analysis with those from an analysis involving the hierarchical linear model. In Wong, Young, and Fraser's (1997) study involving 1592 Grade 10 students in 56 chemistry classes, associations were investigated between three student attitude measures and a modified version of the SLEI. In Goh's study with 1512 Grade 5 mathematics students in 39 classes, scores on modified versions of the MCI and QTI were related to student achievement and attitude. Most of the statistically significant results from the multiple regression analyses were replicated in the HLM analyses, as well as being consistent in direction (Goh, Young, & Fraser, 1995; Goh & Fraser, 1998).

4. EVALUATION OF EDUCATIONAL PROGRAM

A second important focus of learning environment research is the evaluation of educational programs. In Australia, a pioneering study included learning environment dimensions among a range of criteria in an evaluation of the Australian Science Education Project (Fraser, 1979).

Learning environment research is comparatively new in Korea, with 1993 marking the beginning of the field in that country (Yoon, 1993). Much of the Korean research is linked to the curriculum development in science and technology education that formed the pivot of the Korean education system's attempt to keep abreast with economic and technological development. Within a span of just ten years, learning environment research has captured the imagination and interest of educators and researchers in Korea. Studies have been undertaken in science laboratory classrooms at different levels (primary, junior high, senior high and university) and in different streams (science-independent, science-oriented and humanities). Several learning environment questionnaires were carefully translated into the Korean language. Reflective of this research zeal are the studies carried out by Lee (Lee & Fraser, 2001, 2002), Kim (Kim, Fisher, & Fraser, 1999, 2000) and Son (1999). Noh and Kang (1997) have documented their research efforts in the Korean language. All of these efforts are related to major curriculum changes in Korean education, namely, the Sixth and Seventh Science Curricula. Simultaneously, the *Constructivist Learning Environment Survey* (CLES), the *Science Laboratory Environment Inventory* (SLEI) and the *Questionnaire on Teacher Interaction* (QTI) were translated into the Korean language for research purposes. The findings confirmed that students had very positive perceptions about their science classroom and laboratory environments and that they showed highly positive attitudes towards the learning of science. The gap between the actual and the preferred perceptions of students narrowed, indicating a shift for the better.

Despite the potential value of evaluating educational innovations and new curricula in terms of their impact on transforming the classroom learning environment, only a relatively small number of such studies have been carried out in Asian countries. However, in Singapore, Teh used his own classroom environment instrument (the *Geography Classroom Environment Inventory*) as a source of dependent variables in evaluating computer-assisted learning (Teh & Fraser, 1994). Compared with a control group, a group of students using micro-PROLOG-based computer-assisted learning had much higher scores for achievement (es = 3.5), attitudes (es = 1.4) and classroom environment (es = 1.0 to 1.9). Khoo and Fraser (1998) used the WIHIC in evaluating adult computer application courses in Singapore with a sample of 250 students in 23 classes. Generally students perceived their computing classes as being relatively high in involvement, teacher support, task orientation and equity, but the course was differentially effective for students of different sexes and ages.

5. GENDER DIFFERENCES

The study of gender differences is another strand of learning environment research that has attracted attention from educational researchers eager to find out whether gender makes a difference in the learning process. The importance of this aspect is seen in the fact that many studies of learning environment include as one of their objectives an examination of gender differences. Several studies have established a pattern in which females generally have more favourable perceptions of their classroom environment than do males (Fraser, 1998a). Two Asian studies below illustrate this line of research.

A study in primary mathematics classrooms in Singapore investigated, among other questions, whether there were gender differences in students' achievement, attitudes and perceptions of the classroom environment (Goh & Fraser, 1998). Although there were no differences in the attitudes of boys and girls towards the subject of mathematics, boys showed better mathematics achievement than did girls. There was a small but significant gender difference in mathematics achievement in favour of boys. With regard to perceptions of the classroom environment, namely, interpersonal teacher behaviour and classroom climate, significant differences were detected. In relation to interpersonal teacher behaviour, girls perceived that their teachers exhibited significantly more positive interactional qualities in terms of being more helpful, friendly and understanding and displaying significantly less negative interactional qualities in terms of being uncertain, dissatisfied and admonishing, than did boys. Although the magnitudes of the significant gender differences generally were small, Singaporean girls consistently perceived teacher interactional behaviour more favourably than did boys. With regard to perceptions of the classroom climate, boys considered their classrooms more competitive than did girls, whereas girls perceived that their classrooms were more cohesive and task-oriented and had less competition and friction. Such gender differences seem to suggest that girls tend to be better behaved and more task-oriented and to view their teachers more favourably.

Khine's study of secondary science learning environments in Brunei Darussalam also identified gender differences. First, Khine and Fisher (2002) reported gender differences in terms of students' perceptions of interpersonal teacher behaviour in the science classrooms, with female students perceiving that their teachers displayed a greater degree of leadership and were more understanding, helpful and friendly. On the other hand, male students perceived that their teachers were more dissatisfied, uncertain and admonishing in their behaviour. Female students perceived their interactions with teachers more favourably than did males and these differences are similar to the results reported by Riah and Fraser (1998) in a similar context in Brunei.

Second, in terms of classroom climate, Khine and Fisher's (2001) study revealed that female students perceived their classroom learning environment more favourably than did the male students. Female students perceived significantly higher levels of task orientation, cooperation and equity than did male students. The fact that female and male students perceived their classrooms differently suggests that students might not have equal learning opportunities in their classes.

6. CROSS-NATIONAL STUDIES

Following the use of school and classroom environment measures in the studies conducted by the International Association for the Evaluation of Educational Achievement in Mathematics in 1964 (Husen, 1967), Science in 1970–1971 (Comber & Keeves, 1973) and again in Science in 1983–1984 (Keeves, 1992), much effort in learning environment research has also been directed to cross-national studies. Noteworthy studies include collaboration between Australian and Singaporean researchers and between Australian and Taiwanese researchers.

6.1. *Australia-Singapore Collaboration*

In 1997, a group of researchers from Australia and Singapore carried out a cross-national study of secondary science classes (Fisher, Goh, Wong, & Rickards, 1997). Three versions of the *Questionnaire on Teacher Interaction* (QTI) were administered to both students and teachers. All students completed the student version of the QTI to describe teacher-student interpersonal behaviours in their classrooms. Teachers completed the actual version of the QTI to indicate their perceptions of their own behaviours with their students and the preferred version for their perceptions of an ideal science teacher. Data were gathered from a sample of 20 classes from 10 secondary schools in both Australia and Singapore. Overall, attitude scores were higher in classrooms in which students perceived greater leadership and helping and friendly behaviours in their teachers. These were crucial interpersonal teacher behaviours that most likely encourage student learning.

Notable differences were found between student perceptions of their respective science teachers in Singapore and Australia. One major difference was that Australian teachers were perceived as giving more responsibility and freedom to their students than was the case for the Singapore sample. Another important difference was that the teachers in Singapore were perceived as being stricter than their Australian counterparts. Given the different cultural backgrounds and education systems in the two countries, these differences are not surprising. This collaborative effort also resulted in the validation of the QTI for use in secondary science classrooms in Australia and Singapore.

6.2. Australia-Taiwan Collaboration

A group of researchers from Australia and Taiwan completed a cross-national study of secondary science classes (Aldridge, Fraser & Huang, 1999; Aldridge, Fraser, Taylor, & Chen, 2000). Painstaking efforts were expended in developing, modifying, translating and validating the *What Is Happening In This Class?* (WIHIC) questionnaire and *Constructivist Learning Environment Survey* (CLES) in two languages (English and Chinese). This could be regarded as among the first major attempts at studying the nature of science classroom environments in Taiwan. Quantitative data were obtained from the WIHIC and CLES, while observations of classrooms and interviews with students and teachers provided the rich qualitative data. The multimethod approach allowed triangulation of data. Also, data from the questionnaires guided the qualitative data-collection, with classrooms being selected for observation based partly on questionnaire results. Qualitative information provided valuable insights into the perceptions of students in each of the countries, as well as helping to explain some of the differences in scale scores between countries.

7. TRANSLATION OF LEARNING ENVIRONMENT QUESTIONNAIRES

Studies of learning environments undertaken in Indonesia, Korea, Taiwan and Brunei required the translation of the instruments from the English language into the Indonesian, Korean, Chinese and Malay languages. The instruments were developed originally in English-speaking countries. The process of translation was tedious and time-consuming as it must be ensured that the items have not changed in meaning during translation.

The WIHIC has been translated into Indonesian, Korean and Chinese languages and used to provide valuable data about the status of learning environment research in the countries concerned. An Indonesian version of the WIHIC has been used in two studies of the learning environments in computing courses at the university level (Margianti, Fraser, & Aldridge, 2002; Soerjaningsih, Fraser, & Aldridge, 2001). A Chinese version of WIHIC was developed for research in secondary science classrooms in Taiwan (Aldridge & Fraser, 2000; Aldridge, Fraser, & Huang, 1999).

In Korea, research into learning environments is intertwined with curriculum development, especially in science and technology education. Questionnaires used in learning environment research have been translated into the Korean language to ensure that the data are meaningful not only for teachers and researchers, but also for administrators and educational officers. Among these efforts was the translation of the *Science Laboratory Environment Inventory* (SLEI) by Kim and her colleagues in 1995, 1996 and 1997, the information about which is documented in Korean-language publications. Lee and Fraser also undertook research with a Korean-language version of the QTI and SLEI (Lee & Fraser, 2001, 2002). Kim, Fisher and Fraser (1999, 2000) worked on the translation of the *Constructivist Learning Environment Survey* (CLES), *Questionnaire on Teacher Interaction* (QTI) and *What is Happening in this Class?* (WIHIC) questionnaire for use with secondary science students. These developments are momentous and speak volumes about the importance of learning environment and its impact on students' achievement and attitudes to learning.

In Brunei, Scott and Fisher (2001) developed a Malay version of the QTI and validated it with a sample of 3104 students in 136 classes.

8. DIRECTIONS AND PROSPECTS

Currently, the field of learning environment research commands much interest among educators and researchers. Its study also reveals significant impact on the educational scene in the Asia-Pacific zone in terms of the associations found between the learning environment and student outcomes, particularly in the cognitive and affective spheres. This field of study has also reached a high level of robustness and the following sections explore its future directions and prospects.

8.1. *Combining Qualitative and Quantitative Methods*

Research on learning environments in the Asia-Pacific region mostly involved obtaining data from perceptions of both teachers and students generated using paper-and-pencil questionnaires. In recent years, more studies have included a qualitative element, thus combining quantitative and qualitative methods of inquiry (Tobin & Fraser, 1998). The mixing of quantitative and qualitative methods probably was prompted by the realisation that the information gained would be more holistic and that thick and rich qualitative data could provide greater substantiation of information gained through quantitative measures.

The latest research in Singapore done by Wilks (2000) has shown the way in this direction. This study examined the classroom environment of the English subject called General Paper taught at Junior College level. It encompassed a sizeable qualitative component in addition to strong quantitative elements. The instrument used was the *General Paper Constructivist Learning Environment Survey* (GPCLES), an adapted version of the *Constructivist Learning Environment Survey* (Taylor, Fraser, & Fisher 1997), to meet the needs of this subject. This provided quantitative data, while the qualitative part included classroom observations, interviews with teachers and students, specific case studies and a personal journal kept by the researcher. The triangulation of data further enhanced the findings. This study could well provide another meaningful reference for the conduct of further learning environment research.

8.2. Developing On-line Questionnaires

With increasing availability and use of technology in education, e-learning has become an integral part of the educational scene worldwide. It can be envisaged that completing questionnaires on-line will be possible sooner than expected. The traditional paper-and-pencil instruments could become obsolete with the widespread and integrated use of computers in classrooms. Currently in Singapore, at the National Institute of Education, graduate teacher trainees (in the Postgraduate Diploma in Education Programme) self-evaluate their interpersonal teacher behaviour on-line using the *Questionnaire on Teacher Interaction* (QTI; Wubbels & Levy, 1993). In this pilot effort, the teacher trainees could see their interactional pattern with their students once they complete the QTI on-line. Further efforts could be made in this direction to develop on-line learning environment questionnaires in line with the progress of e-learning. Teachers, students and researchers could then obtain the results almost instantly for self-evaluation or research purposes. This would be economical in terms of time, effort and resources.

8.3. Developing Custom-made Research Instruments

From past research practices, it is clear that learning environment instruments or questionnaires were initially developed and validated for use by educational researchers in their countries in the English language. In the course of the last ten years, with the spread of learning environment research into Asian countries, such questionnaires have been translated into Asian languages as discussed in earlier sections of this chapter. For instance, in Korea, translations of research questionnaires provide an immediate solution to the lack of suitable local instruments. Moreover, Noh and Kang (1997) constructed their own instruments by selecting several items from several existing instruments, namely, the *Individualised Classroom Environment Questionnaire, Science Laboratory Environment Inventory* and *Classroom Environment Survey*. The idea was to have an instrument that measured what the researchers sought. Researchers could then consider developing instruments suited to their social and cultural context, rather than mixing and matching or translating existing instruments into their own language of instruction. The process of developing and validating their own instruments in their own language would make it easier to capture local nuances rooted in social and cultural practices, which would not be possible with a translated version that required keeping to the original meanings and intentions of the items developed for a different setting. This could be another step forward in ensuring that research in learning environments remains relevant and meets the contemporary needs of varying learning environments.

8.4. Practical Attempts to Improve Classroom Environments

Feedback information based on students' perceptions of actual and preferred environment has been employed in Western countries in a five-step procedure as a basis for reflection upon, discussion of, and systematic attempts to improve classroom environments (Fraser, Sinclair, & Ledbetter, 2001; Thorp, Burden, & Fraser, 1994). Yarrow, Millwater, and Fraser (1997) reported a study in which 117 preservice education teachers were introduced to the field of learning environment through being involved in action research aimed at improving their university teacher education classes and their 117 primary school classes during teaching practice. Surprisingly, this important practical benefit has not yet been realised in Asia as no published article could be located that reported teachers' attempts to use learning environment assessments to guide improvements in their classroom environments.

8.5. Transition from Primary to Secondary Schooling

There is considerable interest in the effects on early adolescents of the transition from primary schools to the larger, less personal environment of the junior high school. Ferguson and Fraser's (1998) study of 1040 Australian students from 47 feeder primary schools and 16 linked high schools indicated that students perceived their high school classroom environments less favourably than their primary school classroom environments, but the transition experience was different for boys and girls and for different school size 'pathways'. Furthermore, also in Australia, Hine and Fraser (2002) reported a similar decline in scores. Because it appears that research into transition between schools levels has not been reported for Asian countries from a learning environments perspective, this provides another desirable direction for future research.

REFERENCES

Aldridge, J. M., & Fraser, B. J. (2000). A cross-cultural study of classroom learning environments in Australia and Taiwan. *Learning Environments Research, 3*, 101–134.

Aldridge, J. M., Fraser, B. J., & Huang, T.-C. I. (1999). Investigating classroom environments in Taiwan and Australia with multiple research methods. *Journal of Educational Research, 93*, 48–62.

Aldridge, J. M., & Fraser, B. J., Taylor, P. C., & Chen, C. C. (2000). Constructivist learning environments in a cross-national study in Taiwan and Australia. *International Journal of Science Education, 22*, 37–55.

Asghar, M., & Fraser, B. (1995). Classroom environment and attitudes to science in Brunei Darussalam. *Journal of Science and Mathematics Education in Southeast Asia, XVIII*(2), 41–47.

Comber, L. C., & Keeves, J. P. (1973). *Science education in nineteen countries: An empirical study* (International Studies in Evaluation). Stockholm: Almqvist and Widsell.

Bryk, A. S., & Raudenbush, S. W. (1992). *Hierarchical linear models: Applications and data analysis methods.* Newbury Park, CA: Sage.

Ferguson, P. D., & Fraser, B. J. (1998). Changes in learning environment during the transition from primary to secondary school. *Learning Environments Research, 1*, 369–383.

Fisher, D. L., Goh, S. C., Wong, A. F. L., & Rickards, T. W. (1997). Perceptions of interpersonal teacher behviour in secondary science classrooms in Singapore and Australia. *Journal of Applied Research in Education, 1*(2), 2–13.

Fraser, B. J. (1979). Evaluation of a science-based curriculum. In H. J. Walberg (Ed.), *Educational Environments and Effects: Evaluation, Policy, and Productivity* (pp. 218–234). Berkeley, CA: McCutchan.

Fraser, B. J. (1990). *Individualised Classroom Environment Questionnaire.* Melbourne, Australia: Australian Council for educational Research.

Fraser, B. J. (1994). Research on classroom and school climate. In D. Gabel (Ed.), *Handbook of Research on Science Teaching and Learning* (pp. 493–541). New York: Macmillan.

Fraser, B. J. (1998a). Science learning environments: Assessment, effects and determinants. In B. J. Fraser & K. G. Tobin (Eds.), *The International Handbook of Science Education* (pp. 527–564). Dordrecht, The Netherlands: Kluwer.

Fraser, B. J. (1998b). Classroom environment instruments: Development, validity and applications. *Learning Environments Research, 1*, 7–33.

Fraser, B. J., & Chionh, Y. H. (2000, April). *Classroom environment, self-esteem, achievement, and attitudes in geography and mathematics in Singapore.* Paper presented at the annual meeting of the American Educational Research Association, New Orleans, LA.

Fraser, B., Sinclair, B. J., & Ledbetter, C. (2001, December). *Assessing and changing classroom environments in urban middle schools in Texas.* Paper presented at the annual conference of the Australian Association for Research in Education, Fremantle, Australia.

Goh, S. C., & Fraser, B. J. (1998). Teacher interpersonal behaviour, classroom environment and student outcomes in primary mathematics in Singapore. *Learning Environments Research, 1*, 199–229.

Goh, S. C., & Fraser, B. J. (2000). Teacher interpersonal behaviour and elementary student outcomes. *Journal of Research in Childhood Education, 14*, 216–231.

Goh, S. C., & Khine, M. S. (Eds.) (2002). *Studies in educational learning environments: An international perspective.* Singapore: World Scientific.

Goh, S. C., Young, D. J., & Fraser, B. J. (1995). Psychosocial climate and student outcomes in elementary mathematics classrooms: A multilevel analysis. *Journal of Experimental Education, 64*, 29–40.

Hine, P., & Fraser, B. J. (2002, April). *Combining qualitative and quantitative methods in a study of Australian students' transition from elementary to high school.* Paper presented at the annual meeting of the American Educational Research Association, New Orleans, LA.

Hirata, S., & Sako, T. (1998). Perceptions of school environment among Japanese junior high school, non-attendant, and juvenile delinquent students. *Learning Environments Research, 1*, 321–331.

Husen, T. (1967). *International study of achievement in mathematics* (2 volumes). Stockholm: Almqvist and Wiksell.

Keeves, J. P. (Ed.) (1992). *The IEA study of science III: Changes in science education and achievement: 1970 to 1984.* Oxford, England: Pergamon Press.

Khine, M. S., & Fisher, D. L. (2001, December). *Classroom environment and teachers' cultural background in secondary science classes in an Asian context.* Paper presented at the annual meeting of the Australian Association for Research in Education, Perth, Australia.

Khine, M. S., & Fisher, D. L. (2002, April). *Analysing interpersonal behaviour in science classrooms: Associations between students' perceptions and teachers' cultural background*. Paper presented at the annual meeting of the National Association for Research in Science Teaching, New Orleans, LA.

Kim, H. B., Fisher, D. L., & Fraser, B. J. (1999). Assessment and investigation of constructivist science learning environments in Korea. *Research in Science and Technological Education, 17*, 239–249.

Kim, H. B., Fisher, D. L., & Fraser, B. J. (2000). Classroom environment and teacher interpersonal behaviour in secondary school classes in Korea. *Evaluation and Research in Education, 14*, 3–22.

Khoo, H. S., & Fraser, B. J. (1998, April). *Using classroom environment dimensions in the evaluation of adult computer courses*. Paper presented at the annual meeting of the American Educational Research Association, San Diego, CA.

Lee, S. S. U., & Fraser, B. J. (2001, March). *High school science classroom learning environments in Korea*. Paper presented at the annual meeting of the National Association for Research in Science Teaching, St. Louis, MO.

Lee, S., & Fraser, B. J. (2002, April). *High school science classroom learning environments in Korea*. Paper presented at the annual meeting of the American Educational Research Association, New Orleans, LA.

Majeed, A., Fraser, B. J., & Aldridge, J. M. (2002). Learning environment and its associations with student satisfaction among mathematics students in Brunei Darussalam. *Learning Environments Research, 5*, 203–226.

Margianti, E. S., Fraser, B. J., & Aldridge, J. M. (2002, April). *Learning environment, attitudes and achievement: Assessing the perceptions of Indonesian university students*. Paper presented at the annual meeting of the American Educational Research Association, New Orleans, LA.

Moos, R. H., & Trickett, E. J. (1974). *Classroom Environment Scale manual*. Palo Alto, CA: Consulting Psychologists Press.

Noh, T. H., & Kang, S. J. (1997). The effect of the general science course on the students' views about science-technology-society relationships and their perceptions of science classroom environment. *Journal of the Korean Association for Research in Science Education, 17*(3), 95–403 (in Korean).

Paige, R. M. (1979). The learning of modern culture: Formal education and psychosocial modernity in East Java, Indonesia. *International Journal of Intercultural Relations, 3*, 333–364.

Quek, C. L., Fraser, B. J., & Wong, A. F. L. (2001, December). *Determinants and effects of perceptions of chemistry classroom learning environments in secondary school gifted education classes in Singapore*. Paper presented at the annual conference of the Australian Association for Research in Education, Fremantle, Western Australia.

Riah, H., & Fraser, B. J. (1998, April). *The learning environment of high school chemistry classes*. Paper presented at the annual meeting of the American Educational Research Association, San Diego, CA.

Scott, R., & Fisher, D. (2001, December). *The impact of teachers' interpersonal behaviour on examination results in Brunei*. Paper presented at the Annual conference of the Australian Association for Research in Education, Fremantle, Australia.

Soerjaningsih, W., Fraser, B. J., & Aldridge, J. M. (2001, April). *Achievement, satisfaction and learning environment among Indonesian computing students at the university level*. Paper presented at the annual meeting of the American Educational Research Association, Seattle.

Son, S. N. (1999). *Effects of portfolio system on socio-psychological classroom environment in elementary science class*. Unpublished Master project. Teachers' College. ChungJu University. ChungJu, Korea.

Taylor, P. C., Fraser, B. J., & Fisher, D. L. (1997). Monitoring constructivist classroom learning environments. *International Journal of Educational Research, 27*, 293–302.

Teh, G., & Fraser, B. J. (1994). An evaluation of computer-assisted learning in terms of achievement, attitudes and classroom environment. *Evaluation and Research in Education, 8*, 147–161.

Thorp, H., Burden, R. L., & Fraser, B. J. (1994). Assessing and improving classroom environment. *School Science Review, 75*, 107–113.

Tobin, K., & Fraser, B. J. (1998). Qualitative and quantitative landscapes of classroom learning environments. In B. J. Fraser & K. G. Tobin (Eds.), *International Handbook of Science Education* (pp. 623–640). Dordrecht, The Netherlands: Kluwer.

Walberg, H. J., & Anderson, G. J. (1968). Classroom climate and individual learning. *Journal of Educational Psychology, 59,* 414–419.

Walberg, H. J., Singh, R., & Rasher, S. P. (1977). Predictive validity or student perceptions: A cross-cultural replication. *American Educational Research Journal, 14,* 45–49.

Wilks, D. R. (2000). *An evaluation of classroom learning environments using critical constructivist perspectives as a reference for reform.* Unpublished Doctoral Thesis, Curtin University of Technology.

Wong, A. F. L., & Fraser, B. J. (1996). Environment-attitude associations in the chemistry laboratory classroom. *Research in Science and Technological Education, 64,* 29–40.

Wong, A. F. L., Young, D. J., & Fraser, B. J. (1997). A multilevel analysis of learning environments and student attitudes. *Educational Psychology, 17,* 449–468.

Wubbels, Th., & Brekelmans, M. (1998). The teacher factor in the social climate of the classroom. In B. J. Fraser & K. G. Tobin (Eds.), *International Handbook of Science Education* (pp. 565–580). Dordrecht, The Netherlands: Kluwer.

Wubbels, Th., & Levy, J. (Eds.). (1993). *Do you know what you look like?: Interpersonal relationships in education.* London: Falmer Press.

Yarrow, A., Millwater, J., & Fraser, B. J. (1997). Improving university and primary school classroom environments through preservice teachers' action research. *International Journal of Practical Experiences in Professional Education, 1*(1), 68–93.

Yoon, H. K. (1993). *The investigation on the relationship between psychological environment of science laboratory and learning outcomes.* Unpublished Masters Project, Seoul National University, Seoul. Korea.

33

Metacognition

CHRISTA E. VAN KRAAYENOORD and MERRILYN GOOS
University of Queensland, Brisbane, Australia

1. INTRODUCTION

Metacognition is primarily concerned with the human reasoning processes that are necessary to solve problems across many domains and can be applied in a wide range of learning situations, for example, solving a mathematical problem, reading for meaning and memorising a prose passage. Whereas cognition is concerned with what people know and think, metacognition refers to how people think about their own thinking. Metacognition is generally considered to have two components, knowledge or awareness about one's own cognitive processes, and control or self-regulation of these processes in order to achieve a particular goal (Brown, Bransford, Ferrara, & Campione, 1983; Flavell, 1976).

In this article we focus on two issues of relevance to research and practice: the nature of metacognitive awareness and self-regulation within specific knowledge domains such as mathematics, science, and literacy; and teaching approaches that promise to improve students' metacognitive capabilities within these domains. The international literature on metacognition is used to begin mapping out this territory in general terms. The article then moves on to review key studies conducted within the Asia-Pacific region in order to highlight different methodological and theoretical approaches that have been taken.

2. METACOGNITIVE AWARENESS AND SELF-REGULATION

Metacognitive awareness refers to knowledge about factors or variables that affect performance. According to Flavell (1979) these include person, task, and strategy variables. Person variables include what individuals know about their own and other's cognitive processes and what they understand about the properties of cognition, for example, that there are various kinds and degrees of understanding, such as attending or remembering. Task variables include knowledge about the task (e.g., quantity, quality, familiarity of the task), as well as an understanding of the implications that these differences in the task may have for performance. Further, task variables include awareness about the nature of the task demands. Strategy variables are concerned with awareness about what strategies are available and when and where these strategies are best employed. This also includes knowing when strategy change is required. The three variables (person, task and strategy) may also work in combination and interact with the other variables.

Regulation of cognition involves such activities as planning an overall course of action, selecting specific strategies, monitoring progress, assessing results, and revising plans and strategies if necessary. Schoenfeld (1985, 1992) frames these activities in terms of resource allocation, and identifies two broad types of metacognitive self-regulation decisions that can influence problem solving outcomes. He argues that success is favoured if students (a) exploit their knowledge to act on potentially useful information, and (b) discontinue inappropriate and unproductive strategies.

However, success cannot be attributed to metacognitive awareness and self-regulation alone. Paris and Winograd (1990) argue that metacognition should accommodate motivational and affective aspects of thinking. These include attributions for past successes and failures, which in turn create expectations regarding future outcomes (Borkowski, Carr, Rellinger, & Pressley, 1990; Dweck, 1986). A number of other authors have also pointed to the links between motivation, affect, and beliefs (Pintrich & De Groot, 1990), between will and skill (McCombs & Marzano, 1990), and the role of self-efficacy in developing positive metacognitive dispositions.

2.1. Is Metacognition Teachable?

Research from the 1980s demonstrated that children's metacognitive awareness developed with age; that is, young children are not good at recognising inconsistencies in a narrative, or recognising preferred approaches to learning (Brown et al., 1983). Other authors have suggested that metacognitive regulation strategies can be taught (van Kraayenoord & Paris, 1997), for example, through teaching children to use self-appraisal and self-management. One of the implicit goals of education is to promote students' self-assessment of their knowledge and skills, and developmental progress. As students mature they learn to monitor and interpret their actions and to assess their behaviour with more insight about possible causes of success and failure. They also gain insight and more accuracy about their progress relative to their past achievements. The reflection and evaluation process helps to develop feelings of ownership and responsibility for learning.

Efforts to teach explicitly metacognitive strategies have historically taken an experimental approach in the form of training studies, often involving students with learning difficulties and intellectual disabilities (Wong, 1986). Despite achieving some positive results in helping students to acquire and apply strategies, it seems that this form of short-term intervention has not produced the hoped for results in the spontaneous use of cognitive and metacognitive strategies in unfamiliar situations (Montague, 1997).

More recently there has been a move towards classroom based research, in order to acknowledge the role in which a number of variables within the classroom affects metacognitive awareness and regulation. These include motivation, affect, student and teacher beliefs, teaching practices, and the classroom culture. Perhaps the earliest and best known of these studies was the work of Palincsar and Brown (Brown & Palincsar, 1987; Palincsar & Brown, 1984) in developing the reciprocal teaching approach for fostering comprehension before reading and monitoring strategies during and after reading. This approach involves the process of teaching the acquisition and application of cognitive strategies by teacher modelling of a dialogic structure that focuses on the strategies of predicting, clarifying, questioning, and summarising. Teachers initially take the greater responsibility for leading the discussion, but gradually relinquish control to the students. This framework or scaffolding enables learners to carry out a reading task which would otherwise be beyond their unassisted efforts, thus locating instruction within the learner's zone of proximal development (Vygotsky, 1978).

Schoenfeld's (1985) highly successful work with college students provides another example of teacher scaffolding, this time in the mathematics classroom with the teacher acting as both a model and intellectual coach. Scaffolding occurs not only through the teacher's orchestration of whole class debriefing sessions where strategies and metacognitive decisions are dissected, but also through questions posed to students as they work on problems in small groups. Other researchers have extended this concept of scaffolding between teacher as expert and student to interactions between learners of roughly equal expertise. Central to these studies is the notion of collaboration involving processes of jointly constructing understanding, exploiting the collective knowledge of the peer group, and challenging as well as building on each other's ideas (Mercer, 1995; Renshaw, 1996; Renshaw & Brown, 1997).

3. METACOGNITIVE RESEARCH IN THE ASIA-PACIFIC REGION

The number of studies relating to metacognition carried out in the Asia-Pacific region is evidence of substantial interest in this field. Empirical research has been carried out in domains such as mathematics, science, and literacy, with participants including students and teachers in primary and secondary schools as well as tertiary settings. The review that follows is not intended to be encyclopaedic; instead, studies have been selected to be representative in each knowledge domain that relate to the two issues identified at the start of this article, the nature of metacognition and its teachability.

3.1. *Metacognition and Mathematical Problem Solving*

Research on the role of metacognition in mathematical problem solving includes studies that set out to describe the extent of students' metacognitive awareness and use of regulatory strategies, and others that have attempted to improve students' metacognitive abilities or identify instructional approaches that facilitate metacognitive development. As well as yielding useful insights into the nature and quality of metacognition, descriptive studies add to an understanding of how these processes might be investigated. The most commonly used methods include questionnaires, observation of problem solving behaviour, clinical interviews, and analysis of verbal protocols obtained from thinking aloud while solving a problem (see Goos & Galbraith, 1996, for a review of these methods and of the difficulties inherent in gathering data on covert metacognitive processes).

A series of descriptive studies carried out by Yeap and colleagues in Singapore is typical of research that provides evidence of the nature of students' metacognitive activity during mathematical problem solving (Yeap & Menon, 1996; Yeap, 1998; see also Wilson, 1998, for an Australian study). Here, metacognition was defined as metacognitive knowledge, metacognitive experiences (conscious experiences related to any aspect of a cognitive enterprise), and the interaction between these. A mixed ability group of ten Year 7 students was selected from an intact class, trained in the think aloud method, and then asked to verbalise their thinking while attempting to solve three new problems. The resulting transcripts were supplemented by adding information from the researcher's observational field notes, the students' written work, and a post-task interview. Yeap analysed these protocols using two complementary methods. The first method involved segmenting the protocols into episodes representing consistent problem solving behaviours, by adapting a classification scheme originally developed by Foong (1993). Thus behaviours were categorised as problem orientation, heuristic, domain-specific, affective, or metacognitive. The latter category is particularly useful, as it provides a catalogue of observable metacognitive behaviours that teachers could use to design activities to promote, and assess, the development of metacognition. These behaviours include: starting a plan, clarifying task requirements, reviewing progress, recognising an error, and detecting new developments. In the second analysis method, derived from Flavell's (1981) model of cognitive monitoring, cognitive-metacognitive maps were generated to show inter-relationships between cognitive goals, cognitive actions, metacognitive experiences, and metacognitive knowledge.

Rather than asking individual students to think aloud while working on problems, Goos adapted Schoenfeld's (1985) paired problem solving method to investigate Australian students' monitoring and regulatory strategies as they worked together on problems in applied mathematics in a senior secondary school setting (Goos & Galbraith, 1996). Although the two students generally benefited from adopting complementary metacognitive roles (one was described as the idea generator and calculation checker, while the other acted as a procedural assessor), unhelpful social interactions sometimes impeded progress. These findings prompted a larger, three year study of collaborative metacognitive activity in senior secondary school mathematics classrooms (Goos, 2000). In this later study, metacognition was conceptualised not only in terms of awareness and regulation, but also as a disposition towards making sense of mathematics in the context of particular classroom environments. Consequently, the study applied sociocultural theories of learning to identify patterns of social interaction associated with successful and unsuccessful metacognitive activity and to examine the teacher's role in creating a classroom culture that supported students' mathematical thinking.

Evidence of metacognitive strategy use came from transcripts of interviews and videotaped lesson segments in which students worked on problems or read explanations and examples in mathematical text. Unsuccessful problem solving outcomes were characterised by poor metacognitive decisions exacerbated by lack of critical engagement with each other's thinking. In practice this was observed when students passively accepted unhelpful or misleading ideas and ignored potentially useful strategies suggested by peers. In contrast, successful problem solving was favoured if students challenged and subsequently discarded unhelpful ideas and actively endorsed fruitful strategies (Goos, Galbraith, & Renshaw, 2002). When students interrogated mathematical text, their collaborative metacognitive activity was structured by cycles of comprehension monitoring and jointly constructed explanations (Goos, 1999a). These findings shed some light on how a collaborative zone of proximal development can be created through interaction between students of comparable expertise in the course of monitoring and regulating their own and each other's thinking. Analysis of classroom field notes, lesson videotapes, and interviews with students and teacher also showed how the teacher scaffolded the processes of mathematical inquiry, which included metacognitive strategies for tackling unfamiliar problems and reading mathematical text (Goos, 1999b; Goos, Galbraith, & Renshaw, 1999).

While studies such as those referred to above have clear implications for teaching, research may also be explicitly designed to intervene in students' learning so as to develop or improve metacognition. Curriculum reform often provides the impetus for such research; for example, mathematics curricula introduced in Australia and Singapore during the last decade or so have a new emphasis on problem solving and mathematical reasoning or "working mathematically" (Australian Education Council, 1991; Ministry of Education, Singapore, 2000). Research of this type has been conducted in both primary and secondary school mathematics classrooms, using a variety of methods.

Adibnia (Adibnia, 1996; Adibnia & Putt, 1998) adopted a quasi-experimental design in order to evaluate the effectiveness of instruction intended to improve problem solving performance in Australian classrooms. Three Year 6 classes participated in the study, one experimental and two control classes taught by their regular teachers. The cognitive-metacognitive framework developed by Garofalo and Lester (1985) formed the basis for the instructional intervention, which lasted for 14 lessons of 90 minutes duration over a period of ten weeks. Data were gathered on students' problem solving performance (through commercial and researcher designed tests), their problem solving beliefs and attitudes, and cognitive and metacognitive activity while working on problems (using questionnaires and clinical interviews). Students in the experimental class made significantly greater gains in problem solving performance than those in the control classes, and the experimental group also demonstrated significant gains in relation to beliefs and attitudes.

Low achieving students have been targeted by research on problem solving in Singapore secondary schools. In order to assist weaker students to monitor their comprehension of word problems and regulate their use of resources, Chang, Yeap and Lee (2000) devised a 'problem wheel' that acted as a structural support for metacognitive activity during problem solving. At the centre of the wheel was the problem itself, which was connected through spokes to five problem solving elements – Given (what is known), Find (unknown), Picture (as a means of translating information into a representation of the problem), Topic and Formula (selection of mathematical concepts and skills). Four students identified as low achievers met for a weekly remedial tutorial over a 12-week period. The problem wheel was used as a framework to support instruction based on questioning and pair problem solving. Students completed a problem solving pre- and post-test, and after attempting each problem answered questions designed to probe the thinking processes they had used. Test results showed improved achievement in problem solving performance, while qualitative analysis of students' responses to post-task questions also suggested that the metacognitive teaching approach had been effective in helping students comprehend the problem posed.

Longer term approaches involving action research have also been successful in developing students' metacognitive knowledge and strategies for independent learning. In Australia, Nothdurft (2000) designed a new teaching approach that emphasised metacognition, collaborative learning, and inquiry methods to help her Year 12 mathematics students become autonomous learners. She documented her work, and the students' responses, over a period of two years through questionnaires and interviews, classroom observations, student journals and work samples. While some students did not respond favourably to the changed teaching approach, remaining passive participants who tended not to contribute to class or small group discussions, on the whole the class did move from dependence towards autonomy. In addition, students benefited in terms of their achievement in mathematics assessment tasks, their perceptions of themselves as autonomous learners, and their beliefs about mathematics and how it should be taught. Nothdurft also identified aspects of her practice that proved difficult to change, citing as reasons her guilt about 'letting go', the students' discomfort with moving towards self-regulation, and the possible conflict between mastery and performance goals necessitated by high stakes assessment in the final year of secondary school.

The work of both Nothdurft and Goos highlights the significance of the classroom culture involving assumptions about the nature of mathematics and how mathematics should be learned in helping students develop metacognitive habits of mind. However, the term 'culture' can also be interpreted in a broader sense. In particular, Ng (2001) argues that students from diverse ethnic backgrounds constantly draw on their own culture in devising plans and frames for thinking, feeling, acting, and interacting. In a study carried out in Australia, Ng investigated issues relating to motivation, learning and achievement for four different ethnic groups of Year 10 mathematics students: white Australians, Chinese, Southeast Asians (including Malaysians, Thais, Filipinos), and Europeans (including Italians, Greeks, Yugoslavians). Amongst the measures used by Ng was a survey that gathered information on students' achievement goals (e.g., mastery, performance, social solidarity), approaches to learning mathematics (based on Biggs's, 1987, conceptualisation of deep, achieving, and surface approaches), and self-regulated learning strategies (planning, monitoring, and self-regulatory behaviours in finishing mathematics assignments). Distinctive differences were found between Australian students on the one hand, and Chinese and Southeast Asians on the other. The latter group displayed a learning engagement pattern characterised by employment of mastery and social solidarity goals, a deep learning approach, and self-regulating strategies. In contrast, Australian students held relatively weak mastery goals, and reported less use of a deep learning approach and self-regulating strategies. Nevertheless, within-group variations in goals and learning patterns showed how individuals could divert from their cultural value schema to suit their personal situation. Thus the construction of motivation and learning strategies is not determined solely by cultural values, but is also influenced by the immediate sociocultural environment in which students find themselves. This observation is especially relevant to multicultural education involving migrant students.

3.2. Metacognition and Conceptual Change in the Learning of Science

Whereas metacognitive research in mathematics education has mostly been concerned with the nature of self-regulatory strategies in problem solving, in science education the focus has been on facilitating conceptual change through increasing metacognitive awareness. Students' intuitive conceptions of phenomena in the physical world are often at odds with accepted scientific explanations, and these so-called 'alternative conceptions' have been shown to be highly resistant to change. A common approach to bringing about conceptual change, based on the Piagetian notion of cognitive disequilibrium, involves confronting prior conceptions with contradictory information. However, there is increasing evidence that this approach is of limited use on its own, since students can ignore or distort scientific concepts that conflict with their naive understanding. Students additionally need to be consciously aware of the conflict between their existing conception and the new information if conceptual change is to occur. Science learning involves treating knowledge as the object of inquiry, thus metaconceptual awareness is vital in evaluating the status of one's beliefs and the evidence that supports them.

A series of Hong Kong based research studies has examined instructional implications of this metacognitively-oriented conceptual change model. Chan and Chong (2000) conducted a short term quasi-experimental study involving two Grade 10 Science classes learning particle theory concepts. In eight sessions over two weeks, the experimental class experienced an instructional program adapted from the predict-observe-explain framework, where students performed experiments that often produced puzzling results. Explanations were generated and tested in small group and whole class discussions, and students additionally kept learning diaries with responses structured by metacognitive prompts provided by the teacher. A comparison class covered the same science content with the regular teaching approach, which relied heavily on teacher and textbook explanations. The experimental class demonstrated greater improvement than the comparison class on open-ended questions designed to measure conceptual understanding. Analysis of learning diaries sought evidence of metacognitive awareness, and revealed that students who gave more reflective responses achieved greater conceptual change. While these findings support the value of metacognition in developing scientific reasoning, they should nevertheless be treated with some caution due to the very brief duration of the intervention.

In a related study, Chan and Chui (1999) investigated the effects of self-explanations and self-questioning on students' conceptual understanding of ecology. Self-questioning is a means of monitoring one's understanding, while the related activity of self-explanation is aimed at improving understanding by repairing one's mental model of a concept. Thus these two knowledge construction activities may assist learners to resolve conflicts between new information and their existing conceptual models. A group of 14 Year 10 science students was provided with three training workshops, each of 1.5 hours duration, where they were taught to self-question and self-explain in conjunction with reading text passages. A comparison group of nine students simply read the text on their own. Both groups then read a new text passage, with students in the instructional group encouraged to think aloud after reading each text segment, after which all students responded to written and interview questions designed to assess their understanding of ecology. The instructional group outperformed the comparison group on both measures of conceptual understanding. Within this group, students with the greatest conceptual gains also produced the greatest number of self-directed, so-called 'learning questions' and the most self-explanations that integrated the text and their prior knowledge. It remains to be seen as to whether the instructional approaches tested in these two studies can be successfully implemented in classrooms over an extended period of time. Perhaps the most significant implication of these studies lies in the way they challenge the cultural stereotyping of Chinese learners as passive, reluctant to ask questions, and dependent on the teacher for explanations of new concepts. Instead, the participants benefited from instruction that encouraged them to view knowledge as problematic and to take control of their own learning.

A longer term study carried out in an intact Year 11 Chemistry classroom highlights once again the different methodological and theoretical assumptions underlying research on metacognition. Thomas and McRobbie (2001) reported an Australian study that used an interpretive, rather than experimental, method, to investigate the effect of the metaphor of 'learning as constructing' on students' metacognitive awareness and learning processes. Like Chan and her colleagues, Thomas and McRobbie argued that metacognition is necessary for facilitating conceptual change. However, they were more explicit in pointing out that this also required students to change their conceptions of learning from passive reception of content to active inquiry and construction of personal understanding. Thus their study focused on using metaphor to develop a shared language of learning in a classroom where the first author was also the teacher. About one third of the students in the class ($n = 24$) showed evidence (from questionnaires, journals, interviews) of increased metacognition, as the result of a teaching intervention that emphasised learning as construction of richly connected knowledge networks. However, around half the class demonstrated no improvement to their initial low levels of metacognitive awareness, and resisted changing their approach to learning. In fact, most students commented on how difficult it was to change the way they thought about learning at this late stage of their schooling. They were accustomed to being told by their teachers what to do and think, and had previously been rewarded for passive learning in Science by assessment tasks that did not require higher order thinking. Thomas and McRobbie concluded that the cultural values and norms reflected in educational practices have an influence on students' motivation to become more metacognitively aware.

Nuthall (1999) goes even further to claim that metacognitive awareness is culturally acquired through participation in classroom activities. Using examples from several studies of science and social studies learning in New Zealand classrooms, he presents evidence of students' emerging awareness of their own thinking in the self-talk and semi-private talk occurring during small group activities. Culture-specific knowledge structures shape metacognitive awareness in different ways. For example, students' judgments of the state of their knowledge could exclude them from class discussion of scientific concepts if they incorrectly believed that their everyday understanding of physical phenomena, acquired within their home culture, was adequate.

This view that metacognition is inseparable from the classroom context is consistent with the approach taken by the PEEL (Project for Enhancing Effective Learning) Project (Baird & Mitchell, 1986; Baird & Northfield, 1992). The impetus for this Australian action research project came from related research that found science students who appeared to be successful learners in terms of their examination results showed very little understanding of the concepts that they had been taught. In particular, poor learning was claimed to be related to students' lack of awareness and inadequate monitoring of their own understanding. The PEEL Project was initially established in a single school, and involved teachers across a range of subject areas in implementing a program for fostering students' independent learning through training for enhanced metacognition. Effective teaching strategies included engaging students in interpretive discussions, encouraging 'what if?' questions, and using concept maps to link different topics that had been studied. One of the most significant outcomes of the project was the change in teacher attitudes, beliefs, and actions to ones that promoted independent learning and purposeful inquiry.

3.3. Metacognition and Literacy

In the literacy domain studies in metacognition in the Asia-Pacific region have been in reading, writing, listening, and English as a second language. Research in this area was initially dominated by descriptive studies, which later led to experimental work designed to improve metacognitive abilities. Much of this intervention research involved explicit instruction in metacognitive processes and strategies, particularly aimed at special populations such as students with learning difficulties, poor readers and the gifted.

Perhaps the most well-known studies of metacognition in reading in the Asia-Pacific region have examined the role of metalinguistics in early reading achievement. The work of Tunmer and Nesdale (Nesdale, Herriman, & Tunmer, 1980; Tunmer, Herriman, & Nesdale, 1988) was among the earliest in Australia to focus on the role of phonological awareness in beginning reading. This research found that phonological awareness, especially recoding, was necessary for students to identify unfamiliar words. Bowey's research in Australia (e.g., 1996a, 1996b) also examined aspects of phonological awareness in the acquisition of reading and found support for Tunmer's contention that phonological recoding is the main skill acquired in learning to read English orthography and that this variable influences reading achievement. Tunmer and his colleagues also undertook intervention research which suggested that a metacognitive approach to decoding instruction was effective with students with difficulties in reading (Tunmer & Hoover, 1993; Tunmer & Chapman, 1998). Greaney, Tunmer, and Chapman (1997), for example, found a positive effect of strategy training (of rime analogies) on reading performance of children with reading difficulties. Byrne and his Australian colleagues also focused on phonemic awareness in the acquisition of reading and the effects of phonemic awareness instruction on later reading achievement (Byrne, 1992; Byrne & Fielding-Barnsley, 1993, 1995; Byrne, Freebody, & Gates, 1992). Byrne, Fielding-Barnsley, and Ashley (2000) found that preschool instruction in phonemic awareness affected later reading achievement. However, children who had problems with this metacognitive ability as preschoolers often continued to have difficulty with reading.

Other researchers have also looked at metacognition at the word level but with older students and Spedding (1991) and Spedding and Chan (1993, 1994) found that Grade 5 students identified as poor readers were inferior in their metacognitive abilities in word identification, phonemic awareness and in word identification skills, with the first two mentioned variables affecting reading comprehension both directly and indirectly through the mediating variable of word identification skills.

In contrast to the studies above which focused on examining metacognitive and metalinguistic skills at the word level, a number of other researchers have undertaken descriptive studies to document the metacognitive awareness of person, task and strategy variables in reading. Moore and colleagues (Moore, 1983; Moore & Kirby, 1981), for example, investigated children's metacognitive knowledge about reading and its relationship to reading performance in the

Australian context. These studies demonstrated developmental differences, with younger children having a more mechanistic view of reading than older readers. A stronger relationship between metacognitive knowledge and reading achievement was found in older readers when compared to younger readers. Applying aspects of this work to English as second language learners in Singapore, Wong and Chang (2002) and Zhang (1999, 2000) found significant differences in metacognitive knowledge of good and poor readers. However, there were no differences between students at the different grade levels in terms of use of strategies (Wong & Chang, 2002).

In the area of writing, Martello (1999, 2001) examined Year 1 children's perceptions of learning to write. The children reported the use of strategies to assist with writing, in particular copying and practising and made reference to those who helped them. Significant differences were found in the children's ability to use language to talk about writing (a metalinguistic ability). Taking a more task-specific approach, van Kraayenoord and Paris (1997) examined students' abilities to self-appraise their literacy-related work samples. A developmental trend was found here, as well as gender effects with girls providing more elaborated comments related to improvement of their work and future expectations. However, teacher practices in particular classrooms were also influential, demonstrating the effects of teaching emphases on students' abilities to self-assess their work. In a larger longitudinal study Paris and van Kraayenoord (1998) used tasks thought to be useful for assessing metacognitive aspects of literacy (e.g., The Book Selection Task, Kemp, 1990; Think Along Passages, Paris, 1991) with primary school children, 75 per cent of whom participated in a two year follow up. The metacognitive tasks correlated with reading comprehension tasks and had good predictive validity over a two-year period. The authors suggested that the tasks were suitable for classroom teachers who wanted to use more authentic measures of literacy learning.

Rather than seeking information directly from students about their knowledge and use of reading strategies, Arabsolghar and Elkins (2001) investigated Australian teachers' expectations about students' use of reading strategies. In this study, 45 Grade 3, 5, and 7 teachers were asked to make judgements about whether or not students of high, average and low ability levels in their classes would demonstrate the nominated reading skills grouped according to the components of strategies, knowledge and behaviour. Results indicated a significant ability and component interaction. Specifically there was much greater variability in the three components for the low and average students than for those with high ability. There was also a significant effect for ability with teachers having the highest expectations for the most able students. While the teachers held equivalent performance expectations for the high ability students with respect to the components of strategies, knowledge and behaviour, they had higher expectations for the average and low ability students for knowledge than for strategies and behaviours. In similar studies, these researchers compared expectations of teachers and parents of students with learning difficulties and intellectual disabilities (Arabsolghar & Elkins, 2000).

De Carvalho-Filho and Yuzawa (2001) examined the twin components of knowledge and regulation of cognition of 77 undergraduates at Hiroshima University. The study revealed that individuals with high knowledge of cognition performed better and were more confident in their test answers than individuals with low knowledge, and high regulators also performed significantly better than low regulators. According to the authors, these findings suggested that these two aspects of cognition are independent but related constructs. Knowledge of cognition also appeared to be a good predictor of performance and level of confidence, while regulation of cognition was a good predictor of performance and global accuracy. Goh's (1997) study found that high-ability listeners had twice as much metacognitive knowledge about listening as low-ability listeners. Goh (1998) also found that students described as high-ability listeners employed more varied strategies and tactics than low ability listeners, with prior knowledge acting as a powerful influence on comprehension.

The relationship between metacognition and motivational characteristics in literacy has been one area within the research of the Asia-Pacific region that has received considerable attention. For example, van Kraayenoord (1986) investigated metacognitive knowledge, oral reading behaviour, comprehension monitoring, self-perceptions of reading ability, and reading-related causal attributions in 11 and 12-year-old students with learning disabilities (LD) and their peers in New Zealand. The results showed that the LD readers were similar to the non-LD students (NLD) in their metacognitive knowledge of positive strategies for gaining meaning from a story and decoding an unknown word, and in their self-reports of regulatory behaviours during oral reading. Differences between the two groups emerged in the reading behaviour and comprehension monitoring on their individual difficult passages, with LD students showing less proficiency. Van Kraayenoord noted that while many similarities were found in the study between LD and NLD readers in terms of metacognition, reading and causal attributions, the findings suggested that students with LD need assistance in particular aspects of their reading and help in building a more positive self image. Chan (1994) similarly studied the relationship between motivation, strategic learning and reading achievement in students with and without learning difficulties in Grades 5, 7 and 9 in Australia. She found a strong relationship between strategic learning and motivational variables (e.g., attributional beliefs) (see also Chan 1996a). Wey (1998) undertook a study of goal orientations, self-efficacy, effort, metacognition and writing achievement in a sample of Grade 11 students in Taiwan. Outcomes from structural equation modelling revealed learning goal orientation had stronger effects on metacognition, self-efficacy and effort than performance goal orientation. Self-efficacy had positive and significant effects on metacognition and effort, metacognition had a significant effect on effort, while self-efficacy and effort had a direct and significant impact on writing achievement and metacognition had an indirect effect on writing achievement through the effect of effort. Liang (1997) studied cognitive, metacognitive and motivational strategies in curricular and non-curricular reading of undergraduate students in English in Guangzhou, China. The author reported that reading context, metacognition and motivation affected online strategy use, with strategy use changing, but depending on context. The author suggested that metacognitive knowledge and regulation contributed to the differences found in the study rather than the ability of the readers.

Several authors have also explored the question of whether metacognition in literacy is teachable. Cullen (1985) suggested that metacognitive instruction should include self-appraisal and self-management of affective and motivational elements of learning. Consistent with this view, Chan (1996b) used a combination of strategy and attributional training with average and poor readers in Grade 7. The study showed that instruction in strategy use coupled with convincing students that their reading performance was attributable to their use of effective strategies improved comprehension performance and increased the use of reading strategies, as well as reduced the perceptions of learned helplessness in poor readers. This work represents a substantial advance on Chan's earlier research, which concentrated largely on strategy training (Chan, 1991; Chan & Cole, 1986; Chan, Cole, & Barfett, 1987).

Building on notions of scaffolding and Palincsar and Brown's work on reciprocal teaching, Bruce (1998) and Bruce and Chan (1991) carried out three intervention studies in which word identification strategies were taught. Results in these studies suggested that reciprocal teaching procedures could be used successfully to teach word identification and improve reading comprehension of poor readers. Scaffolding of higher order thinking was investigated in a case study of a gifted Grade 1 student. Lowrie (1998) illustrated how a teacher used a series of questions which challenged students to reflect on their own thinking and take the perspective of another person. This activity allowed the student to demonstrate story comprehension at increasingly higher levels through verbal description and drawing. The prompts activated metacognitive skills such as predicting and hypothesizing in so-called 'what if' situations.

4. CONCLUSION

In this article we have considered two issues related to research and practice in metacognition. The nature of metacognition has been studied from the perspectives of awareness and self-regulation, but with different emphases in different knowledge domains. The significance of metacognition was first recognised in the field of literacy, especially with respect to the influence of students' awareness of cognitive processes on literacy performance. In science education, the emphasis has been on the role of students' awareness in facilitating conceptual change, whereas self-regulatory strategies in problem solving have been the subject of most metacognitive research in mathematics education.

The second issue concerns the effectiveness of different approaches to teaching metacognitive strategies and improving metacognitive awareness. In the domain of literacy this has often involved explicit strategy training, sometimes coupled with intervention in motivational aspects of learning such as attribution training.

This reflects the interest in enhancing the performance of students with problems and difficulties in literacy learning. However, in science and mathematics education there has been a trend towards research on teaching approaches within classroom settings. Often this research has been quasi-experimental, involving intervention and comparison classes. More recently, classroom-based studies have taken an action research or interpretive approach. These have given attention to contextual factors such as students' motivation and beliefs, and the roles of teachers in bringing about lasting change in students' approaches to learning.

Metacognitive research in the Asia-Pacific region has made an important contribution to an understanding of the nature of metacognition, and of teaching approaches that may prove beneficial for students with diverse characteristics in a variety of settings. However, it is suggested that the metacognitive research agenda needs to move further in the direction of long term, classroom-based studies. These studies should be located within the teaching and learning contexts in which metacognitive knowledge is developed, monitoring and regulatory strategies are practised, and the beliefs and values which support such modes of thinking are instantiated.

REFERENCES

Adibnia, A. (1996). *An exploration of the effects of a teaching method on Year 6 students with different ability levels in mathematical problem solving based on Garofalo and Lester's cognitive-metacognitive framework.* Unpublished doctoral thesis, James Cook University, Townsville, Qld.

Adibnia, A., & Putt, I. (1998). Teaching problem solving to Year 6 students: A new approach. *Mathematics Education Research Journal, 10*(3), 42–58.

Arabsolghar, F., & Elkins, J. (2000). Comparative expectations of teachers and parents with regard to memory skills in children with intellectual disabilities. *Journal of Intellectual Disability, 25*(3), 169–179.

Arabsolghar, F., & Elkins, J. (2001). Teachers' expectations about students' use of reading strategies, knowledge and behaviour in Grades 3, 5 and 7. *Journal of Research in Reading, 24*(2), 154–162.

Australian Education Council (1991). *A national statement on mathematics for Australian schools.* Melbourne: Australian Education Council and Curriculum Corporation.

Baird, J., & Mitchell, I. (1986). *Improving the quality of teaching and learning: An Australian case study – The PEEL project.* Melbourne: Monash University.

Baird, J., & Northfield, J. (1992). *Learning from the PEEL experience.* Melbourne: Monash University.

Biggs, J. (1987). *Student approaches to learning and studying.* Melbourne: Australian Council for Educational Research.

Borkowski, J., Carr, M., Rellinger, E., & Pressley, M. (1990). Self-regulated cognition: Interdependence of metacognition, attributions, and self-esteem. In B. F. Jones & L. Idol (Eds.), *Dimensions of Thinking and Cognitive Instruction* (pp. 53–92). Hillsdale, NJ: Erlbaum.

Bowey, J. A. (1996a). Phonological recoding of nonword orthographic rime primes. *Journal of Experimental Psychology: Learning, Memory, and Cognition, 122*(1), 117–131.

Bowey, J. A. (1996b). Phonological sensitivity as a proximal contributor to phonological recoding skills in children's reading. *Australian Journal of Psychology, 148*(3), 113–118.

Brown, A., Bransford, J., Ferrara, R., & Campione, J. (1983). Learning, remembering, and understanding. In P. H. Mussen (Ed.), *Handbook of Child Psychology, Vol. 3* (4th ed., pp. 77–166). New York: Wiley.

Brown, A. L., & Palincsar, A. S. (1987). Reciprocal teaching of comprehension strategies: A natural history of one program for enhancing learning. In J. Borkowski & J. D. Day (Eds.), *Intelligence and Cognition in Special Children* (pp. 81–132). New York: Ablex.

Bruce, M. (1998). *A metacognitive program for improving the word identification and reading comprehension skills of upper primary poor readers.* Unpublished doctoral dissertation, University of Newcastle, Newcastle, Australia.

Bruce, M. E., & Chan, L. K. (1991). Reciprocal teaching and transenvironmental programming: A program to facilitate the reading comprehension of students with reading difficulties. *Remedial and Special Education, 12*(5), 44–54.

Byrne, B. (1992). Studies in the acquisition procedure for reading: Rationale, hypotheses, and data. In P. B. Gough (Ed.), *Reading Acquisition* (pp. 1–34). Hillsdale, NJ: Erlbaum.

Byrne, B., & Fielding-Barnsley, R. (1993). Evaluation of a program to teach phonemic awareness to young children: A 1-year follow-up. *Journal of Educational Psychology, 85*(1), 104–111.

Byrne, B., & Fielding-Barnsley, R. (1995). Evaluation of a program to teach phonemic awareness to young children: A 2- and 3-year follow-up and a new preschool trial. *Journal of Educational Psychology, 87*(3), 488–503.

Byrne, B., Fielding-Barnsley, R., & Ashley, L. (2000). Effects of preschool phoneme identity training after six years: Outcome level distinguished from rate of response. *Journal of Educational Psychology, 92*(4), 659–667.

Byrne, B., Freebody, P., & Gates, A. (1992). Longitudinal data on the relations of word-reading strategies to comprehension, reading time, and phonemic awareness. *Reading Research Quarterly, 27*(2), 140–151.

Chan, C., & Chong, Y. (2000). *Fostering conceptual change through cognitive conflict and metacognition.* Paper presented at the annual meeting of the American Educational Research Association, New Orleans.

Chan, C., & Chui, H. (1999). *Fostering conceptual change through self-questioning and self-explanation.* Paper presented at the annual meeting of the American Educational Research Association, Montreal.

Chan, L. K. (1991). Promoting strategy generalisation through self-instructional training in students with reading disabilities. *Journal of Learning Disabilities, 24*(7), 427–433.

Chan, L. K. S. (1994). Relationship of motivation, strategic learning, and reading achievement in Grades 5, 7 and 9. *Journal of Experimental Education, 62*(4), 319–339.

Chan, L. K. S. (1996a). Motivational orientations and metacognitive abilities of intellectually gifted students. *Gifted Child Quarterly, 40*(4), 184–193.

Chan, L. K. S. (1996b). Combined strategy and attributional training for seventh grade average and poor readers. *Journal of Research in Reading, 19*(2), 111–127.

Chan, L. K., & Cole, P. G. (1986). The effects of comprehension monitoring on the reading competence of learning disabled and regular class students. *Remedial and Special Education, 7*(4), 33–40.

Chan, L. K., Cole, P. G., & Barfett, S. (1987). Comprehension monitoring: Detection and identification of text inconsistencies by LD and normal students. *Learning Disability Quarterly, 10*(2), 114–124.

Chang, S., Yeap, B., & Lee, N. (2000). *Infusing thinking skills through the use of graphic organisers in primary mathematics to enhance weak pupils' learning.* Paper presented at the ERA-AME-AMIC Joint Conference 2000, Singapore.

Cullen, J. L. (1985). Children's ability to cope with failure: Implications of a metacognitive approach for the classroom. In D. L. Pressley, G. E. McKinnon & T. G. Waller (Eds.), *Metacognition, Cognition and Human Performance: Vol. 2, Instructional Practices* (pp. 267–300). Orlando, FL: Academic.

de Carvalho Filho, M. K., & Yuzawa, M. (2001).The effects of social cues on confidence judgements mediated by knowledge and regulation of cognition. *The Journal of Experimental Education, 69*(4), 325–343.

Dweck, C. (1986). Motivational processes affecting leaning. *American Psychologist, 41,* 1040–1048.

Flavell, J. (1976). Metacognitive aspects of problem solving. In L. R. Resnick (Ed.), *The Nature of Intelligence* (pp. 231–235). Hillsdale, NJ: Erlbaum.

Flavell, J. H. (1979). Metacognition and cognitive monitoring: A new area of cognitive-developmental inquiry. *American Psychologist, 34*, 906–911.

Flavell, J. (1981). Cognitive monitoring. In W. Dickson (Ed.), *Children's Oral Communication Skills* (pp. 35–60). New York: Academic Press.

Foong, P. (1993). Development of a framework for analysing mathematical problem solving behaviours. *Singapore Journal of Education, 13*(1), 61–75.

Garofalo, J., & Lester, F. K., Jr. (1985). Metacognition, cognitive monitoring, and mathematical performance. *Journal for Research in Mathematics Education, 16*, 163–176.

Goh, C. (1997). Metacognitive awareness and second language listeners. *ELT Journal, 51*(4), 361–369.

Goh, C. (1998). How ESL learners with different listening abilities use comprehension strategies and tactics. *Language Teaching Research, 2*(2), 124–147.

Goos, M. (1999). Understanding mathematical text through peer explanations. In J. Truran & K. Truran (Eds.), *Making the Difference* (Proceedings of the 22nd annual conference of the Mathematics Education Research Group of Australasia, Adelaide, pp. 238–245). Sydney: MERGA.

Goos, M. (1999b). Scaffolds for learning: A sociocultural approach to reforming mathematics teaching and teacher education. *Mathematics Teacher Education and Development, 1*, 4–21.

Goos, M. (2000). Metacognition in context: A study of metacognitive activity in a classroom community of mathematical inquiry, Unpublished PhD dissertation. The University of Queensland.

Goos, M., & Galbraith, P. (1996). Do it this way! Metacognitive strategies in collaborative mathematical problem solving. *Educational Studies in Mathematics, 30*, 229–260.

Goos, M., Galbraith, P., & Renshaw, P. (1999). Establishing a community of practice in a secondary mathematics classroom. In L. Burton (Ed.), *Learning Mathematics: From Hierarchies to Networks* (pp. 36–61). London: Falmer Press.

Goos, M., Galbraith, P., & Renshaw, P. (2002). Socially mediated metacognition: Creating collaborative zones of proximal development in small group problem solving. *Educational Studies in Mathematics, 149*, 193–223.

Greaney, K. T., Tunmer, W. E., & Chapman, J. W. (1997). Effects of rime-based orthographic analogy training on the word recognition skills of children with reading disability. *Journal of Educational Psychology, 89*(4), 645–651.

Kemp, M. (1990). *Watching children read and write*. Portsmouth, NH: Heinemann.

Liang, J. (1997). *How college EFL students regulate their cognition and motivation to deal with difficulties in reading comprehension: A case study of Chinese EFL learners' reading strategy use*. Unpublished doctoral dissertation, University of Texas at Austin, TX.

Lowrie, T. (1998). Developing metacognitve thinking in young children: A case study. *Gifted Educational International, 13*, 23–27.

Martello, J. (1999). In their own words: Children's perceptions of learning to write. *Australian Journal of Early Childhood, 24*(3), 32–37.

Martello, J. (2001). Talk about writing: Metalinguistic awareness in beginning writers. *Australian Journal of Language and Literacy, 24*(2), 101–111.

McCombs, B., & Marzano, R. (1990). Putting the self in self-regulated learning: The self as agent in integrating will and skill. *Educational Psychologist, 25*, 51–69.

Mercer, N. (1995). *The guided construction of knowledge*. Clevedon: Multilingual Matters.

Ministry of Education, Singapore (2000). *Ministry of Education 2001 – Mathematics syllabus (primary)*. Singapore: Ministry of Education.

Montague, M. (1997). Cognitive strategy instruction in mathematics for students with learning disabilities. *Journal of Learning Disabilities, 30*, 164–177.

Moore, P. J. (1983). Aspects of metacognitive knowledge about reading. *Journal of Research in Reading, 6*(2), 87–102.

Moore, P., & Kirby, J. (1981). Metacognition and reading performance: A replication and extension of Myers and Paris in an Australian context. *Educational Enquiry, 4*(1), 18–29.

Nesdale, A. R., Herriman, M. L., & Tunmer, W. E. (1980). The development of phonological awareness. *Education Research and Perspectives, 7*(1), 52–76.

Ng, C. (2001). Students as cultural beings: Motivation, learning and achievement among students of diverse ethnic backgrounds in Australia. In F. Salili & R. Housain (Eds.), *Research in Multicultural Education and International Perspectives Vol. 1* (pp. 87–124). Greenwich: IAP Inc.

Nothdurft, L. (2000). *Teaching for autonomy in senior secondary mathematics*. Unpublished EdD thesis. Queensland University of Technology, Brisbane.

Nuthall, G. (1999). Learning how to learn: The evolution of students' minds through the social processes and culture of the classroom. *International Journal of Educational Research, 31*, 141–256.

Palincsar, A. S., & Brown, A. L. (1984). Reciprocal teaching of comprehension-fostering and comprehension-monitoring activities. *Cognition and Instruction, 1*, 117–175.

Paris, S. G. (1991). Assessment and remediation of of metacognitive aspects reading comprehension. *Topics in Language Disorders, 12*, 32–50.

Paris, S. G., & van Kraayenoord, C. E. (1998). Assessing young children's literacy strategies and development. In S. G. Paris & H. M. Wellman (Eds.), *Global Prospects for Education: Development, Culture and Schooling* (pp. 193–227). Washington, DC: American Psychological Association.

Paris, S., & Winograd, P. (1990). How metacognition can promote academic learning and instruction. In B. F. Jones & L. Idol (Eds.), *Dimensions of Thinking and Cognitive Instruction* (pp. 15–51). Hillsdale, NJ: Erlbaum.

Pintrich, P., & De Groot, E. (1990). Motivational and self-regulated learning components of classroom academic performance. *Journal of Educational Psychology, 82*, 33–40.

Renshaw, P. (1996). A sociocultural view of the mathematics education of young children. In H. Mansfield, N. Pateman & N. Bednarz (Eds.), *Mathematics for Tomorrow's Young Children* (pp. 59–78). Dordrecht: Kluwer Academic Publishers.

Renshaw, P., & Brown, R. (1997). Learning partnerships: The role of teachers in a community of learners. In L. Logan & J. Sachs (Eds.), *Meeting the Challenges of Primary Schools* (pp. 200–211). London: Routledge.

Schoenfeld, A. (1985). *Mathematical problem solving*. Orlando: Academic Press.

Schoenfeld, A. (1992). Learning to think mathematically: Problem solving, metacognition and sense making in mathematics. In D. A. Grouws (Ed.), *Handbook of Research on Mathematics Teaching and Learning* (pp. 334–370). New York: Macmillan.

Spedding, S. F. (1991). *Metacognitive abilities in word identification and its relationship with reading competence*. Unpublished masters thesis, University of Newcastle, Newcastle, Australia.

Spedding, S., & Chan, L. K. (1993). Metacognition, word identification, and reading competence. *Contemporary Educational Psychology, 18*(1), 91–100.

Spedding, S., & Chan, L. K. S. (1994). Metacognitive abilities in word identification: Assessment and instruction. *Australian Journal of Remedial Reading, 26*(3), 8–12.

Thomas, G., & McRobbie, C. (2001). Using a metaphor for learning to improve students' metacognition in the chemistry classroom. *Journal of Research in Science Teaching, 38*(2), 222–259.

Tunmer, W. E., & Chapman, J. W. (1998). Implicit and explicit processes in reading acquisition. In K. Kirsner, C. Speelman, M. Maybery, A. M. O'Brien, M. Anderson & C. MacLeod (Eds.), *Implicit and Explicit Mental Processes* (pp. 357–370). Mahwah, NJ: Lawrence Erlbaum.

Tunmer, W. E., Herriman, M. L., & Nesdale, A. R. (1988). Metalinguistics abilities and beginning reading. *Reading Research Quarterly, 23*, 134–158.

Tunmer, W. E., & Hoover, W. A. (1993). Phonological recoding skill and beginning reading. *Reading and Writing, 5*(2), 161–179.

van Kraayenoord, C. E. (1986). *Metacognition, reading and causal attributions: A comparison of learning disabled and non learning disabled intermediate school children*. Unpublished doctoral dissertation, Massey University, Palmerston North, New Zealand.

van Kraayenoord, C. E., & Paris, S. G. (1997). Australian students' self-appraisal of their work samples and academic progress. *The Elementary School Journal, 97*(5), 523–537.

Vygotsky, L. (1978). *Mind in society*. Cambridge, MA: Harvard University Press.

Wey, S-C. (1998). *The effects of goal orientations, metacognition, self-efficacy and effort on writing achievement (Taiwan, China)*. Unpublished doctoral dissertation, University of Southern California, Los Angeles.

Wilson, J. (1998). Metacognition within mathematics: A new and practical multi-method approach. In C. Kanes, M. Goos, & E. Warren (Eds.), *Teaching Mathematics in New Times* (Proceedings of the 21st annual conference of the Mathematics Education Research Group of Australasia, Gold Coast, pp. 693–700). Brisbane: MERGA.

Wong, B. Y. L. (1986). Metacognition and special education. *Journal of Special Education, 20*(1), 9–29.

Wong, M. Y., & Chang, S. C. A *Knowledge and use of metacognitive strategies.* Paper presented at the Annual Conference of the Australian Association for Research in Education, Adelaide. [on line] Available on http://www.aare.edu.au/01pap/won01419.htm

Yeap, B. (1998). *Metacognition and mathematical problem solving.* Paper presented at the Annual Conference of the Australian Association for Research in Education, Adelaide. [on line] Available http://www.aare.edu.au/98pap/yea98408.htm.

Yeap, B., & Menon, R. (1996). Metacognition during mathematical problem solving. Paper presented at the joint conference of Educational Research Association, Singapore and Australian Association for Research in Education.

Zhang, L. J. (1999). *Metacognition. cognition and L2 reading.* Unpublished doctorial dissertation, ELAL, Nanyang Technological University.

Zhang, L. J. (2000). Research on metacognition and reading in a second language. *Review of Educational Research and Advances for Classroom Teachers, 1,* 21–27.

34

Motivation and School Learning

CHI-HUNG NG
Open University of Hong Kong, Hong Kong

PETER RENSHAW
Griffith University, Southport, Australia

1. INTRODUCTION

Research regarding motivation and learning in the Asia-Pacific region in the past four decades has been characterized by the search for similarities and differences across cultures, and by the search for models of motivation that reflect the distinctive cultural values of the region. In general, the research literature on motivation has followed recent theoretical shifts towards more cognitive, contextualized and culturally sensitive models of human development and learning. In addition, researchers are increasingly aware that motivation to learn and participate in educational processes is related to: (a) historical conditions such as the changing nature of the economy and employment opportunities, (b) cultural variations in values and traditions, and (c) intercultural exchanges associated with increasing mobility, migration and communication across national boundaries. These dynamic and interacting factors need to be considered when reviewing research on motivation.

2. THE PRELUDE

Following the pioneering work of Murray (1938) on human needs, McClelland (1963, 1985) conceptualized motivation as a need for achievement, that is, as a need to do something better, to overcome obstacles and difficulties, and to strive for success (Franken, 1998). Need for achievement was regarded as an inherent personal attribute that emerged as a product of socialisation. Need for achievement within individuals in a particular society was seen by McClelland (1987) as related primarily to variations in early socialisation practices. During the 1960s and 1970s, research using McClelland's model of motivation was conducted in Australia and New Zealand (e.g., Campbell, 1967; Hines, 1973, 1974).

His measurement procedure was validated cross-culturally by a number of researchers (e.g., Chu, 1968; Han, 1965; Ni, 1962; Yang & Liang, 1973). However, the prediction derived from the model that independence and mastery training by parents produced a high need for achievement was not supported with Asian populations, for example in research with Japanese (e.g., DeVos, 1968, 1973; Hayashi & Yamauchi, 1964), Taiwanese (e.g., Olsen, 1971; Yu, 1991) and Hong Kong Chinese samples (e.g., Li, 1974). In particular, the expectation of lower levels of achievement motivation among Japanese and Chinese populations based on their traditions of child-rearing practices was not supported (DeVos, 1968, 1973; Yu, 1991). There was increasing critical awareness that McClelland's model reflected Western traditions of individualistic achievement rather than conceptions of achievement related to the collectivist values of many Asian cultures (Yu, 1980; Yu & Yang, 1987). These criticisms of McClelland's model of achievement motivation set the stage for the development of research into motivation and learning by Asia-Pacific researchers.

3. THE COGNITIVE PHASE

Cognitive theories of motivation have been proposed from a variety of theoretical perspectives, but have in common the assumption that achievement-related behaviours such as participation and persistence are mediated by mental activities related to perceptions, interpretations and expectations. Extending McClelland's theory, for example, Atkinson (1957) argued that motivation was the result of the perceived probability of success or failure multiplied by the personal value attached to achieving success or avoiding failure. This 'expectancy by value' model of motivation placed cognitive activities in a central mediating role. Other cognitive theories have focussed on the individual's perceived locus of control, and how success and failure are attributed to different causes (Heider, 1958; Weiner, 1972).

Events that are perceived as within the control of an individual are categorised as internal, whereas events that are perceived beyond the control of an individual are external. With regard to research on perceived locus of control, researchers (Chan, 1989; Lao, Chuang, & Yang, 1977; Wang, 1991) have validated versions of established instruments like Rotter's Internal-External Locus of Control Scale for Chinese populations. Certain cross-cultural differences in locus of control have also been found. For example, McGinnes, Nordholm, Ward, and Bhanthumnavin (1974) found that Japanese students were more external in their locus of control compared with American students, while no difference was found between students from Australia, New Zealand and the United States. Other research comparing Western and Asian groups of students have produced inconsistent results. Hung (1974) demonstrated that Taiwan Chinese students did not differ from American students in their externality of control. However, Hamid (1994) showed that Chinese students had stronger external perceived control than New Zealand students.

Differences between cultural groups in locus of control are difficult to interpret at face value. Leung (1996) challenged the characterisation of Chinese students as orienting towards externality by arguing that the Chinese norm of humility may have contributed to their attribution of outcomes to external factors. Other studies draw attention to the effect on locus of control of relevant contributing variables like domain specificity (Ang & Chang, 1999) and important individual attributes like gender (Wu, 1975), age (Hwang, 1979) and achievement level (Chyn, 1992). For example, Chan (1989) demonstrated that Hong Kong undergraduate students showed internal control only in the specific domains of achievement and interpersonal relationships. Moreover, Park and Kim (1998) demonstrated that Korean high achievers tended to have internal locus of control while low achievers oriented more towards external locus of control. In addition, Chia, Cheng and Chuang (1998) showed that sources of internal control among Chinese college students in Taiwan were perceived to originate not just from the self but also from other in-group members, who were perceived as extensions of the self rather than as external sources of support. This is consistent with the view that contrasting cultural values, such as a collectivist versus individualist values, influence how control is perceived. Further research certainly is needed to investigate the internal versus external locus of control of Asian students, and special attention should be given to the effects of cultural values like humility versus self-promotion, and collectivism versus individualism. In addition, the relationships between locus of control, learning behaviours and achievement level are not clear. How these variables link with each other in different cultural groups in the region requires more attention.

Weiner's attribution model (1972, 1985) has attracted much interest among educational researchers in the region. In Weiner's model of motivation, attributions are defined as the perceived reasons for academic success or failure. They are related in predictable patterns to different affective states such as pride or shame, and to achievement related behaviours such as persistence. This complex model linking motivational constructs with different learning related variables provides a clear conceptual framework for studying motivation, learning and their relationships. Using different cultural groups including Filipinos, Australians and Chinese, various researchers have shown that different attributional patterns are associated with individual attributes like self-esteem (Watkins & Astilla, 1980b), giftedness (Chan, 1996a), and achievement level (Hau & Salili, 1989). Aside from individual differences in attributions, cultural differences have been reported and interest in exploring these differences has produced a burgeoning research literature.

Initial attributional research with white North American students (Euro-American students) found that they were more likely to attribute success to ability rather than to effort, and to regard ability as the major factor in determining achievement (e.g., Covington & Omelich, 1979; Nicholls, 1989). Ability in turn was considered as a rather stable construct (Weiner, 1985). However, this attributional pattern has not been consistently found in students from other Western societies. For example, New Zealanders rated effort followed by ability as the predominant causes for both success and failure outcomes (Ng, McClure, Walkey, & Hunt, 1995). In an Australian study, it was found that children attributed achievement outcomes to effort while their parents made more ability attributions (Cashmore & Goodnow, 1986).

The major contrast in attributional patterns, however, that is found between Euro-Americans and Asians. Chinese (e.g., Hau & Salili, 1989), Japanese (e.g., Hayamizu & Hasegawa, 1979, Ichikawa, 1986; Yamauchi, 1988), Koreans (Grant & Dweck, 2001; Park & Kim, 1998), and Filipinos (e.g., Watkins & Astilla, 1980a, 1980b) tends to emphasize effort and usually attributes success or failure to internal controllable causes. Effort and hard work are perceived to be the major means for achievement, and are reinforced in socialisation practices (e.g., Hau & Salili, 1989; Hess, Chang, & McDevitt, 1987). In addition, various studies have shown that effort and ability attributions are positively related (Hau & Salili, 1989, 1990; Salili & Hau, 1994). Effort was found to be an increasingly more important determinant of reward or punishment with age (Salili & Hau, 1994). Among Chinese samples, achieving through effort and attempting difficult tasks beyond one's ability are considered virtuous, which provides a cultural explanation for the close relationship between feelings of guilt and attributions to a lack of effort (Hong, 2001; Yang, 1982), and for the adaptive effort-related attributional pattern found among Chinese and Japanese underachievers at different educational levels (Lau & Chan, 2001; Tuss, Zimmer, & Ho, 1995). Recently, Salili (1997) also showed that various attributional patterns are associated with different approaches to learning, which in turn affect achievement level.

Hau, Fung, Tang and Cheung (1990) found that Hong Kong primary school students perceived ability as modifiable through effort and persistence. This malleable interpretation of ability is similar to the incremental view of intelligence studied by Dweck and her colleagues in North American samples (Dweck, 1991; Dweck & Leggett, 1988). Dweck distinguished between an entity view of intelligence where individual competence is seen as stable and fixed, with an incremental view where competence is seen as modifiable through the acquisition of new skills and knowledge. The research by Hau and his colleagues (1990) suggests that the incremental interpretation may be more widespread and more strongly endorsed in Asian countries, but it is also widely endorsed in North American samples as well.

The differences in attributional patterns between Western and Asian students highlight the impact of cultural values on the interpretation of learning and achievement. Especially among Chinese populations, effort is regarded as both virtuous and essential to learning. On the positive side, the implication that failures and difficulties can be overcome by renewed or increased effort, functions to protect self-esteem and guards against feelings of helplessness. However, learning with effort is expected of Chinese students, and those who fail to perform according to this norm are negatively evaluated. Chinese students seldom receive or rely on praise for motivation but on social resources originating from the consistently high teacher and parental expectations for academic success (Salili, 1996).

The adaptive nature of effort attributions has been demonstrated cross-culturally in some attribution retraining programs. For example, positive results on future motivation were shown with Australian underachievers who were induced to adopt effort attributions (Ho & McMurtrie, 1991). In another study, Chan (1996b) found that poor Australian readers could be trained to attribute their success to the use of effective reading strategies, which in turn raised their reading performance and reduced maladaptive attributional patterns. Nevertheless, there may be a limitation associated with effort attribution. Several researchers (e.g., Ho et al., 1999, Hong, 2001) have argued that effort attribution, if carried to an extreme, may arouse excessive anxiety and may have detrimental effects on students' self-esteem. Future studies should therefore investigate the problems associated with effort attribution and to test the suitability of promoting it in different cultural groups.

4. CURRENT SCENE

While attribution theory still remains part of the research agenda, motivation conceptualised as goal-directed behaviours is receiving increased attention. This development is associated with the conceptualization of students as individuals with specific capability, values, beliefs and purposes for learning. Various important cognitive or sociocognitive constructs are associated with this viewpoint, including, self-efficacy, intrinsic versus extrinsic motivation, values and interests, as well as achievement goals. Asia-Pacific researchers have studied the close links between these variables. For example, Rao, Moely and Sachs (2000) showed that students with different achievement levels in learning mathematics differed in self-efficacy beliefs, perceived values of mathematics learning, test anxiety, strategy use, and achievement goals. In addition, Asia-Pacific researchers also demonstrated the cross-cultural differences in these major motivational constructs. For example, Watkins and Ismail (1994) compared 14- to 15-year-old Malaysians, Hong Kong Chinese and Australians students and found that the Asian groups used less extrinsic motivation, had a lower level of failure anxiety and used less superficial learning strategies than did the Australians. Inter-ethnic differences in self-efficacy test anxiety and preferred learning strategies were also reported among different cultural groups in New Zealand (Beaver & Tuck, 1998).

Among these different socio-cognitive constructs, achievement goals have attracted the most attention. Achievement goal theory provides an integrative framework for conceptualizing goal directed behaviours, and linking different important cognitive as well as affective variables together. Achievement goals defined as perceived purposes for achievement and learning are considered as having effects on learning related cognitions, perceptions, strategies, affect and different outcomes indicators. It is proposed that achievement goals affect why and how students learn.

Following the lead of North American researchers, two important categories of achievement goals, namely mastery and performance goals, have been extensively tested in the Asia-Pacific region. Consistent with the Western studies, Asia-Pacific researchers (Dowson & McInerney, 1997; Kong & Hau, 1996; Ng, 2000, 2001; Ng & Renshaw, 2002; Salili, Chiu & Lai, 2001; Smith, Sinclair and Chapman, 2002; Tao & Hong, 2000; Volet, 1999; Yip, 1992; c.f. Watkins et al., 2002) found that mastery goals are generally associated with engagement patterns and strategies consistent with deep learning and comprehension, and therefore, usually yield better achievement. In contrast, performance goals are usually associated with strategies and engagement patterns orienting students towards a surface level of learning, yielding therefore a comparatively lower achievement level. However, it was found that these detrimental effects of performance goals are confined to the avoidance orientation. As for performance goals with an approach orientation such as demonstrating one's ability, positive effects are found on learning outcomes (Chen, 2001; Ng, 2000, 2001).

While the model of motivation and learning as specified in the achievement goal theory has generally been validated and similarities have been found using culturally different samples in the region (e.g., Maehr, Kan, Kaplan, & Wang, 1999; Volet, 1999), some important observations related to the effects and operation of the achievement goals need further elaboration. First, Western researchers generally consider mastery and performance goals as two discrete sets of orientations, and empirical evidence from Western samples has supported this assumption (Ames & Archer, 1988). However, studies of achievement goals among Asian students in China, Hong Kong, Taiwan and Singapore (Kong & Hau, 1996; Ng, 2000; Salili et al., 2001; Shi et al., 2001), as well as other cultural groups like Australian Aborigines (McInerney, 1995) have shown that mastery and performance goals are not unrelated. Tao and Hong (2000) found that performance goals are in fact related to mastery goals for the fulfilment of social obligations, like filial piety and family honour among Chinese in Hong Kong. Chang, Wong, & Teo (2000) focusing on a Singaporean sample and Ng (2000) focussing on a group of Hong Kong students, also showed a positive relationship between performance goals and mastery goals as well as other social goals. To explain this complex interrelationship, researchers have begun to draw attention to important cultural or contextual factors. For example, Shi and colleagues (2001) suggested that the positive relationship between these two categories of goals might be attributed to the importance of social comparison and approval within the Chinese collectivistic society. Collectivistic values might have turned performance goals into legitimate means for achievement and learning. In other words, cultural values might have mediated the meaning of achievement and influenced the means of achievement.

Many researchers are now viewing students' stated learning goals as reflecting the institutional context of their learning. For example, the widespread endorsement of performance goals across various cultural groups of students (Ng, 2000; 2001; Ng & Renshaw, 2002; Salili et al., 2001) suggests that summative assessment processes and the competitive nature of learning within schools are major determinants of the performance goal orientation (McInerney, 1991; McInerney,

Roche, McInerney, & Marsh, 1997; Ng & Renshaw, 2002). Smith, Sinclair and Chapman (2002) provided strong evidence regarding the influences of summative assessment on achievement goals and other important learning variables. They studied a group of Australian students in the final year of their secondary education, during which these students were assessed continually, competing for limited university places. Over the academic year, they showed significant increases in negative affect, the use of performance avoidance goals and self-handicapping strategies, and decreases in performance approaching goals and academic self-efficacy.

Aside from the studies of mastery and performance goals, Asia-Pacific researchers have begun to study different types of social goals. Dowson and McInerney (1997) examined the relationships between different social goals, cognitive strategies and achievement levels among Australian high school students. Ng (2001) showed that various ethnic groups studying in Australia differed from each other in terms of social solidarity goals. He found as expected, that Asian students – Chinese, Malaysians, Thais and Filipinos held stronger social solidarity goals than did White Australians and other European migrants. Using a goal web framework, Ng (2001) also demonstrated how social goals had come into play with other achievement goals affecting their learning. Furthermore, using an inductive method, Dowson and McInerney (2001) established the parameters of different types of social goals, providing a working framework for assessing their effects. At the more general level, Yu (Yu, 1991, 1994, 1996; Yu & Yang, 1987) advanced the study of social goals of Chinese students by distinguishing between social-oriented versus individual-oriented motivation. For socially-oriented achievement motivation, significant others, social groups and perceptions of broader societal values, set the achievement goals and standard of excellence, approve the means for their attainment, evaluate the outcomes against the standards of the groups, and give positive or negative reinforcements as a result of the outcome evaluation. Overall, socially oriented motivation is high in social instrumentality. In contrast, individuals set their own achievement goals and standards of excellence for individual oriented achievement motivation. In addition, individuals also select and determine their own achievement behaviours and means, make evaluation of their outcomes mainly against their own goals and standards, and provide positive or negative reinforcement after their own evaluation. In short, individual oriented achievement motivation is high in self-instrumentality. To sum up, the major differences between these two forms of achievement motivation lie in whose standard one wants to meet and who is going to make the judgment.

Yu (1991) found that Taiwanese parents who trained children in reliance on others led to the development of the socially oriented motivation while training of independence was related more to individualistic motivation. In an experimental study, Yu (1994) showed that Taiwanese university students with high socially-oriented achievement motivation sought more help and feedback, and showed a greater level of persistence and completion rate on the experimental tasks than did the low socially-oriented achievement motivated group. However, no differences were found between students with high or low individualistic achievement motivation. Yu took these findings as an indication of the importance of social comparative information in arousing learning and achievement behaviours among students of high or low socially oriented achievement motivation. Recently, Yu's conceptualization and measures of social and individual achievement motivation have been applied to other Chinese groups. Using a Hong Kong sample, Tao and Hong (2000) demonstrated the close relationship between socially oriented achievement motivation and the use of performance goals, which was explained by the fact that performing well publicly serves to fulfil parental expectations. In contrast, individual oriented achievement motivation was related to both learning and performance goals, which was related to personal experiences of learning and the need to show one's mastery of learning publicly. Chang, Wong and Teo (2000) studied the Singaporean Chinese and demonstrated that socially oriented motivation with its concern about the standards and judgement of significant others, was closely linked with competition while individual oriented achievement motivation was linked with mastery and work ethics. These findings suggest that social and individualistic orientations were two alternative adaptive types of paths for achievement and learning among Chinese.

Another major trend in the study of motivation and learning takes a wider perspective and focuses on contextual variables such as age, gender, as well as family and school factors. For example, Yang and Liang (1973) showed that gender was an important factor in the individual context for understanding motivation and achievement among Taiwan Chinese. Shi and his colleagues (2001) showed that age, gender, family and school factors affected Chinese students' adoption of achievement goals. Salili (1994) demonstrated that students' need for achievement differed with age, sex and culture. Archer and Scevak (1998) showed that the climate of university classrooms and the design of the major assignment influenced Australian students' adoption of mastery goals and adaptive learning behaviours. The list of contextual factors seems endless. Important ones like classroom goals (Chen, 2001), teacher effects (Salili & Hau, 1994) and parental influences (Choo & Tan, 2001) have been studied in the region. Asia-Pacific researchers therefore have begun to shift from a concern with individual differences per se, to the study of contextual variables and variations between and within different demographic groups.

Closely linked with the study of context is the concern with cultural contact and associated cultural change. Increased student mobility across countries within the region has enabled the investigation of the effects of changing study context. The studies of newly arrived mainland children in Hong Kong schools (e.g., Hong Kong Government, 2000; Rao & Yuen, 2001) and international students from China studying in Singapore (Tsang, 2001) are recent examples of this line of research. A concerted research effort on the impact of novel study context was conducted by Australian researchers, Volet and Renshaw (1995, 1996) who found that SE Asian undergraduate students adopted the learning approaches of local students after one semester of study in Australia. Purdie and Hattie (1996) found that Japanese students studying in Australia resembled Australian students' use of strategies more than their Japanese counterparts at home. Similarly, Ramburuth and McCormick (2001) found no significant difference between Asian international students and Australian students in the use of approaches to learning after the former group has been studying in Australia. In addition, McInerney and his colleagues (1997) found that after prolonged socialization in Western school systems, Aboriginal Australians showed more similarities than differences with other Australians in learning goals, strategies and other important self-beliefs. All these studies consistently show that the demands and characteristics of the new learning environment affect students' motivational and learning patterns.

Cultural exposure, contact and hybrid socialization practices certainly have effects on students' motivation and learning. Nevertheless, alternative explanations should be considered for the change of motivational and learning behaviours in a novel environment. Assuming a cognitive paradigm, Volet (2001a) suggested that students undergo cognitive appraisal of each learning situation and make appropriate adaptations and changes. Similarly, when discussing the change of learning strategies of migrant Chinese in Australia, Ng (2001) suggested that Chinese students might have applied the cultural logic of being adaptable, that is to select strategically appropriate motivational and learning strategies to fit into the demands while maintaining cultural particularities of the Chinese model of motivation and learning. Future studies of international and migrant students need to take into consideration their adaptive strategies in the new learning environment, and greater emphasis should be placed on the dynamic interplay of personal, contextual and cultural factors in affecting motivation and learning. The cognitive-situative framework for understanding learning and motivation proposed by Volet (2001b) provides a useful conceptual tool for theorising and researching learning and motivation in context. Based on the learning experiences of international students across different cultural-educational contexts, Volet showed the significance of situating students' learning and motivation in the dynamic interface of different levels of specificity involving different personal and contextual dimensions.

5. EMERGING HORIZONS

Motivation for academic learning has been researched within several different paradigms and currently there is a movement from predominantly 'etic' towards more 'emic' approaches (McInerney, 1991; McInerney & Van Etten, 2001, 2002). The purpose of the 'emic' approach is to move beyond simply revealing similarities and differences between students of diverse cultural origins, to researching specific sociocultural contexts in order to understand how particular motivational goals and states arise and are sustained. It is not surprising, therefore, to note that sociocultural theories and concepts have been given more emphasis.

For example, using sociocultural notions of canalisation, zone of proximal development (ZPD), and communities of practices, Pressick-Kilborn and Walker (2002) explored how personal interest, as a motivational construct was co-created in the context of classroom social interaction. MacCallum (2001) reported ten case studies of Australian students in transition from primary to secondary school, showing how their motivational goals drew them to attend to different aspects of the context and thereby created diverse overlapping learning environments. Volet's multi-context model of motivation and learning (2001), and Archer's (2001) proposal that Australian cultural values like mateship and group solidarity influence students' attributional processes, are other recent attempts to incorporate sociocultural perspectives in the study of motivation. We expect that more studies in this vein will enrich our understanding of motivation as a social and evolving process situated within a particular sociocultural setting. In addition, researchers in different locales within the region have already addressed how culture, ethnicity and other socio-cultural factors influence how motivation and learning are conceptualised. With more persistent research effort on the cultural and contextual influences on motivation and learning, we consider that insightful cultural models of motivation and learning will emerge within the region to challenge the dominant models derived from established Western traditions.

While there is much promise in cultural models of motivation and learning, the trap of cultural reductionism has to be avoided. The comparison of groups across cultures, where culture is regarded as static, uniform, and pervasive across all sections of a society, cannot capture the evolving nature of culture itself, nor the dynamic aspects of motivation and learning. Recent research studies on the adaptation of specific cultural groups to new contexts (e.g., Volet and Renshaw, 1995, 1996) highlight the importance of research designs capable of capturing dynamic variation and uncertainty at the individual and group levels. In addition, it is suggested that research on student motivation needs to be contextualised in terms of contemporary developments in educational policies and practices, as well as in terms of contemporary social and cultural changes.

6. CONCLUSIONS

The pioneering scholarship of McClelland examined the relationship between culture, motivation and learning, albeit within the intellectual framework and history of the west. His proposed link between socialization, personality traits and achievement can be taken as the forerunner of the emerging contextual and sociocultural models of motivation and learning among Asia-Pacific researchers (e.g., Volet, 2001b). With persistent effort (e.g., Yu, 1991, 1994, 1996) indigenous models of motivation and learning are being developed by Asia-Pacific researchers that take specific sociocultural characteristics into account.

REFERENCES

Ames, C., & Archer, J. (1988). Achievement goals in the classroom: Students' learning strategies and motivational processes. *Journal of Educational Psychology, 80*(3), 260–267.
Ang, R. P., & Chang, W. C. (1999). Impact of domain-specific locus of control on need for achievement and affiliation. *Journal of Social Psychology, 139*(4), 527–529.
Archer, J. (2001). *Achievement motivation: Defining Australian characteristics.* Paper presented at the Annual Conference of Australian Association for Research in Education, Fremantle, Western Australia.
Archer, J., & Scevak, J. J. (1998). Enhancing students' motivation to learn: Achievement goals in university classrooms. *Educational Psychology, 18*(2), 205–223.
Atkinson, J. W. (1957). Motivational determinants of risk-taking behavior. *Psychological Review, 64,* 359–372.
Beaver, B., & Tuck, B. (1998). The adjustment of overseas students at a tertiary institution in New Zealand. *New Zealand Journal of Educational Studies, 33*(2), 167–179.
Campbell, W. J. (1967). Excellence or fear of failure: The teacher's role in the motivation of learners. *The Australian Journal of Education, 11*(1), 1–12.
Cashmore, J. A., & Goodnow, J. J. (1986). Parent-child agreement on attributional beliefs. *International Journal of Behavioral Development, 9*(2), 191–204.
Chan, D. W. (1989). Dimensionality and adjustment correlates of locus of control among Hong Kong Chinese. *Journal of Personality Assessment, 53*(1), 145–160.
Chan, L. K. S. (1996a). Motivational orientations and metacognitive abilities of intellectually gifted students. *Gifted Child Quarterly, 40*(4), 184–193.
Chan, L. K. S. (1996b). Combined strategy and attributional training for seventh grade average and poor readers. *Journal of Research in Reading, 19*(2), 111–127.
Chang, W. C., Wong, W. K., & Teo, G. (2000). The socially oriented and individually oriented motivation of Singaporean Chinese students. *Journal of Psychology in Chinese Societies, 1*(2), 39–65.
Chen, C. C. (2001). The relationship among achievement goal orientation, perception of motivational climate and learning behavior pattern of high school students (Chinese). *Journal of Education and Psychology, 24,* 167–190.
Chia, R. C., Cheng, B. S., & Chuang, C. J. (1998). Differentiation in the source of internal control for Chinese. *Journal of Social Behavior & Personality, 13*(4), 565–578.
Choo, O. A., & Tan, E. (2001). Fathers' role in the school success of adolescents: A Singapore study. In D. McInerney & S. Van Etten (Eds.), *Research on Sociocultural Influences on Motivation and Learning.* (Vol. 1, pp. 183–203). Greenwich, CT: IAP.
Chu, C. P. (1968). The remodification of TAT adapted to Chinese primary school children: I. Remodification of the pictures and setting up the objective scoring methods. *Acta Psychologica Taiwanica, 10,* 59–73.
Chyn, M. C. (1992). Pupil control ideology, locus of control effects in students' study habits and attitudes (Chinese). *Journal of Education and Psychology, 15,* 129–172.
Covington, M. V., & Omelich, C. L. (1979). It is best to be able and virtuous too: Student and teacher evaluative response to successful effort. *Journal of Educational Psychology, 71,* 688–700.
De Vos, G. A. (1968). Achievement and innovation in culture and personality. In T. Norbeck, D. Price-Williams & W. M. McCord (Eds.), *The Study of Personality: An Interdisciplinary Approach* (pp. 348–370). New York: Holt, Rinehart and Winston.
De Vos, G. A. (1973). *Socialization for achievement: Essays on the cultural psychology of the Japanese.* Berkeley, CA: University of California Press.
Dowson, M., & McInerney, D. M. (1997). *Relations between students' motivational orientations, cognitive processes, and academic achievement.* Paper presented at the Annual Conference of the Australian Association for Research in Education, Brisbane.
Dowson, M., & McInerney, D. M. (2001). Psychological parameters of students' social and work avoidance goals: A qualitative investigation. *Journal of Educational Psychology, 93*(1), 35–42.

Dweck, C. S. (1991). Self-theories and goals: The role in motivation, personality, and development. In R. Dienstbier (Ed.), *Nebraska Symposium on Motivation: Perspectives on Motivation* (Vol. 38, pp. 199–235). Lincoln, NE: University of Nebraska Press.

Dweck, C. S., & Leggett, E. L. (1988). A social-cognitive approach to motivation and personality. *Psychological Review, 95,* 256–273.

Franken, R. E. (1998). *Human Motivation.* Pacific Grove, California: Brooks/Cole.

Grant, H., & Dweck, C. S. (2001). Cross-cultural response to failure: Considering outcome attributions with different goals. In F. Salili, C. Y. Chiu & Y. Y. Hong (Eds.), *Student Motivation: The Cultural and Context of Learning* (pp. 203–219). New York: Kluwer Academic/Plenum Publishers.

Hamid, P. N. (1994). Self-monitoring, locus of control, and social encounters of Chinese and New Zealand students. *Journal of Cross-cultural Psychology, 25*(3), 353–368.

Han, Y. H. (1965). Responses of Chinese university students to the Thematic Appreciation Test. *Psychological Testing (TaiWan), 12,* 52–70.

Hau, K. T., Fung, K. C., Tang, M. S., & Cheung, C. H. (1990). Concepts of intelligence of Hong Kong primary students (Chinese). *Educational Research Journal, 5,* 113–117.

Hau, K. T., & Salili, F. (1989). Attribution of examination result – Chinese primary school students in Hong Kong. *Psychologia, 32,* 163–171.

Hau, K. T., & Salili, F. (1990). Examination result attribution, expectancy and achievement goals among Chinese students in Hong Kong. *Educational Studies, 16*(1), 17–31.

Hayamizu, T., & Hasegawa, T. (1979). Causal attribution of academic achievements (Japanese). *Japanese Journal of Educational Psychology, 27*(3), 197–205.

Hayashi, T., & Yamauchi, K. (1964). The relation of children's need for achievement to parents' home discipline in regard to independence and mastery. *Bulletin Kyoto Gaugei University, Series A, 25,* 31–40.

Heider, F. (1958). *The psychology of interpersonal relations.* New York: Wiley.

Hess, R. D., Chang, C. M., & McDevitt, T. M. (1987). Cultural variations in family beliefs about children's performance in mathematics: Comparisons among People's Republic of China, Chinese-American, and Caucasian-American families. *Journal of Educational Psychology, 79*(2), 179–188.

Hines, G. (1973). Achievement motivation and conservatism factors in the emigration of New Zealand university graduates. *New Zealand Journal of Educational Studies, 8*(1), 19–24.

Hines, G. (1974). Achievement motivation levels of immigrants in New Zealand. *Journal of Cross-cultural Psychology, 5*(1), 37–47.

Ho, I. T., Salili, F., Biggs, J. B., & Hau, K. T. (1999). The relationship among causal attributions, learning strategies and level of achievement: A Hong Kong Chinese study. *Asia Pacific Journal of Education, 19*(1), 44–58.

Ho, R., & McMurtrie, J. (1991). Attributional feedback and underachieving children: Differential effects on causal attributions, success expectancies, and learning processes. *Australian Journal of Psychology, 43*(2), 93–100.

Hong Kong Government. (2000). *Survey on immigrant children newly admitted to schools October 1998 – September 1999.* Hong Kong: Government Printer.

Hong, Y. Y. (2001). Chinese students' and teachers' inferences of effort and ability. In F. Salili, C. Y. Chiu & Y. Y. Hong (Eds.), *Student Motivation: The Culture and Context of Learning* (pp. 105–120). New York: Kluwer Academic/Plenum Publishers.

Hung, Y. Y. (1974). Sociocultural environment and locus of control (Chinese). *Acta Psychologica Taiwanica, 16,* 187–198.

Hwang, C. H. (1979). A study of internal-external control of Chinese school pupils (Chinese). *Bulletin of Educational Psychology, 12,* 1–14.

Ichikawa, F. V. (1986). Japanese parents' and children's causal beliefs about academic achievement. *Asian American Psychological Association Journal, 22*–25.

Kong, C. K., & Hau, K. T. (1996). Students' achievement goals and approaches to learning: The relationship between emphasis on self-improvement and thorough understanding. *Research in Education, 55,* 74–85.

Lao, R. C., Chuang, C. J., & Yang, K. S. (1977). Locus of control and Chinese college students. *Journal of Cross-cultural Psychology, 8*(3), 299–313.

Lau, K. L., & Chan, D. W. (2001). Motivational characteristics of under-achievers in Hong Kong. *Educational Psychology, 21*(4), 417–430.

Leung, K. (1996). The role of beliefs in Chinese culture. In M. H. Bond (Ed.), *The Handbook of Chinese Psychology* (pp. 247–262). New York: Oxford University Press.

Li, A. K. F. (1974). Parental attitudes, test anxiety, and achievement motivation: A Hong Kong study. *Journal of Social Psychology, 93*, 3–11.

MacCallum, J. (2001). The contexts of individual motivation change. In D. McInerney & S. Van Etten (Eds.), *Research on Sociocultural Influences on Motivation and Learning* (Vol. 1, pp. 61–97). Greenwich, CT: IAP.

Maehr, M. L., Kan, S., Kaplan, A., & Wang, P. (1999). Culture, motivation and achievement: Towards meeting the new challenge. *Asia Pacific Journal of Education, 19*(2), 15–29.

McClelland, D. C. (1963). *The achieving societies*. Princeton, NJ: Van Nostrand.

McClelland, D. C. (1985). How motives, skills, and values determine what People do. *American Psychologist, 40*(7), 812–825.

McClelland, D. C. (1987). *Human motivation*. New York: Cambridge University Press.

McGinnes, E., Nordholm, L. A., Ward, C. D., & Bhanthumnavin, D. L. (1974). Sex and cultural differences in perceived locus of control among students in five countries. *Journal of Consulting & Clinical Psychology, 42*(3), 451–455.

McInerney, D. M. (1991). Key determinants of motivation of urban and rural non-traditional aboriginal students in school settings: Recommendations for educational change. *Australian Journal of Education, 35*, 154–174.

McInerney, D. M. (1995). Goal theory and indigenous minority school motivation: Relevance and application. In M. L. Maehr & R. P. Pintrech (Eds.), *Advances in Motivation and Achievement* (Vol. 9, pp. 153–181). Greenwich, CT: JAI Press.

McInerney, D. M., Roche, L. A., McInerney, V., & Marsh, H. W. (1997). Cultural perspectives on school motivation: The relevance and application of goal theory. *American Educational Research Journal, 34*(1), 207–236.

McInerney, D. M., & Van Etten, S. (Eds.) (2001). *Research on sociocultural influences on motivation and learning* (Vol. 1). Greenwich, CT: IAP.

McInerney, D. M., & Van Etten, S. (Eds.) (2002). *Research on sociocultural influences on motivation and learning* (Vol. 2). Greenwich, CT: IAP.

Murray, H. A. (1938). *Explorations in personality*. New York: Oxford University Press.

Ng, C. H. (2000). A path analysis of self-schemas, goal orientations, learning approaches, and performance. *Journal of Psychology for Chinese Societies, 1*(2), 93–121.

Ng, C. H. (2001). Students as cultural beings: Motivation, learning and achievement among students of diverse ethnical backgrounds in Australia. In F. Salili & R. Hoosain (Eds.), *Research in Multicultural Education and International Perspectives* (Vol. 1, pp. 87–124). Greenwich CT: Information Age Publishing Inc.

Ng, C. H., & Renshaw, P. D. (2002). Self-schema, motivation and learning: A cross-cultural comparison. In D. McInerney & S. Van Etten (Eds.), *Research on Sociocultural Influences on Motivation and Learning* (Vol. 2, pp. 55–87). Greenwich, CT: IAP.

Ng, D., McClure, J., Walkey, F., & Hunt, M. (1995). New Zealand and Singaporean attributions and achievement perceptions. *Journal of Cross-cultural Psychology, 26*(3), 276–297.

Ni, L. (1962). Study of the causes of maladjustment of adolescents through the use of projective test. *Acta Psychologica Taiwanica, 4*, 32–52.

Nicholls, J. G. (1989). *The competitive ethos and democratic education*. Cambridge, MA: Harvard University Press.

Olsen, N. J. (1971). Sex differences in child training antecedents of achievement motivation among Chinese children. *Journal of Social Psychology, 83*, 303–304.

Park, Y. S., & Kim, U. (1998). Locus of control, attributional style, and academic achievement: Comparative analysis of Korean, Korean-Chinese, and Chinese students. *Asian Journal of Social Psychology, 1*(2), 191–208.

Pressick-Kilborn, K., & Walker, R. (2002). The social construction of interest in a learning community. In D. McInerney & S. Van Etten (Eds.), *Research on Sociocultural Influences on Motivation and Learning* (Vol. 2, pp. 153–182). Greenwich, CT: IVP.

Purdie, N., & Hattie, J. (1996). Cultural differences in the use of strategies for self-regulated learning. *American Educational Research Journal, 33*(4), 845–871.

Ramburuth, P., & McCormick, J. (2001). Learning diversity in higher education: A comparative study of Asian international and Australian students. *Higher Education, 42*(3), 333–350.

Rao, N., Moely, B. E., & Sachs, J. (2000). Motivational beliefs, study strategies, and mathematics attainment in high- and low-achieving Chinese secondary students. *Contemporary Educational Psychology, 25*, 287–316.

Rao, N., & Yuen, M. T. (2001). Accommodations for assimilation: Supporting newly arrived children from the Chinese Mainland to Hong Kong. *Childhood Education, 77*(5), 313–318.

Salili, F. (1994). Age, sex, and cultural differences in the meaning and dimensions of achievement. *Personality and Social Psychology Bulletin, 20*(6), 648–661.

Salili, F. (1996). Accepting personal responsibility for learning. In D. Watkins & J. B. Biggs (Eds.), *The Chinese Learner: Cultural, Psychological and Contextual Influences* (pp. 85–105). Hong Kong: CERC & ACER.

Salili, F. (1997). Explaining Chinese students' motivation and achievement: A sociocultural analysis. In M. L. Maehr & P. R. Pintrich (Eds.), *Advances in Motivation and Achievement* (Vol. 9, pp. 73–118). Greenwich, CT: JAI Press.

Salili, F., Chiu, C. Y., & Lai, S. (2001). The influence of culture and context on students' motivational orientation and performance. In F. Salili, C. Y. Chiu & Y. Y. Hong (Eds.), *Student Motivation: The Culture and Context of Learning* (pp. 221–247). New York: Kluwer Academic/Plenum Publishers.

Salili, F., & Hau, K. T. (1994). The effects of teachers' evaluative feedback on Chinese students' perception of ability: A cultural and situational analysis. *Educational Studies, 20*(2), 223–235.

Shi, K., Wang, P., Wang, W., Zuo, Y., Liu, D., Maehr, M. L., Mu, X., Linnenbrink, L., & Hruda, L. (2001). Goals and motivation of Chinese students – Testing the adaptive learning model. In F. Salili (Ed.), *Student Motivation: The Culture and Context of Learning* (pp. 249–270). New York: Kluwer Academic/Plenum Publishers.

Smith, L., Sinclair, K. E., & Chapman, E. S. (2002). Students' goals, self-efficacy, self-handicapping, and negative affective responses: An Australian senior school student study. *Contemporary Educational Psychology, 27*, 471–485.

Tao, V., & Hong, Y. Y. (2000). A meaning system approach to Chinese students' achievement goals. *Jounral of Psychology in Chinese Societies, 1*(2), 13–38.

Tsang, E. W. K. (2001). Adjustment of mainland Chinese academics and students to Singapore. *International Journal of Intercultural Relations, 25*(4), 347–372.

Tuss, P., Zimmer, J., & Ho, H. Z. (1995). Causal attributions of underachieving fourth-grade students in China, Japan, and the United States. *Journal of Cross-cultural psychology, 26*(4), 408–425.

Volet, S. (1999). Cultural and multicultural perspectives on learning and motivation. *Asia Pacific Journal of Education, 19*(2), 10–14.

Volet, S. (2001a). Significance of cultural and motivation variables on students' attitudes towards group work. In F. Salili, C. Y. Chiu & Y. Y. Hong (Eds.), *Student Motivation: The Culture and Context of Learning* (pp. 309–333). New York: Kluwer Academic/Plenum.

Volet, S. (2001b). Understanding learning and motivation in context: A multi-dimensional and multi-level cognitive-situative perspective. In S. Volet & S. Järvelä (Eds.), *Motivation in Learning Context: Theoretical Advances and Methodological Implications* (pp. 57–84). Amsterdam: Pergamon.

Volet, S. E., & Renshaw, P. D. (1995). Cross-cultural differences in university students' goals and perceptions of study settings for achieving goals. *Higher Education, 30*(4), 407–433.

Volet, S. E., & Renshaw, P. D. (1996). Chinese students at an Australian university: Adaptability and continuity. In D. Watkins & J. Biggs (Eds.), *The Chinese Learner: Cultural, Psychological and Contextual Influences* (pp. 205–220). Hong Kong: CERC & ACER.

Wang, D. (1991). A norming study of a Chinese version of Rotter's Internal-External Locus of Control Scale with Chinese college students (Chinese). *Acta Psychologica Sinica, 23*(3), 292–298.

Watkins, D., & Astilla, E. (1980a). Causal attribution for success and failure at university examination. *Higher Education, 9*, 443–451.

Watkins, D., & Astilla, E. (1980b). Self-esteem and causal attribution of achievement: A Filipino investigation. *Australian Psychologist, 15*, 219–225.

Watkins, D., & Ismail, M. (1994). Is the Asian learner a rote learner? A Malaysian perspective. *Contemporary Educational Psychology, 19*, 483–488.

Watkins, D., McInerney, D., Lee, C., Akane, A., & Regmi, M. (2002). Motivation and learning strategies: A cross-cultural perspective. In D. M. McInerney & S. Van Etten (Eds.), *Research on Sociocultural Influences on Motivation and Learning* (Vol. 2, pp. 329–343). Greenwich, CT: IAP.

Weiner, B. (1972). *Theories of motivation: From mechanism to cognition.* Chicago: Rand-McNally.

Weiner, B. (1985). An attribution theory of achievement motivation and emotion. *Psychological Review, 92*(4), 548–573.

Wu, W. T. (1975). Children's sex. locus of control, and academic achievement. *Bulletin of Educational Psychology, 8*, 107–114.

Yamauchi, H. (1988). Relationships of achievement-related motives to causal attributions, affects, and expectancy for success and failure under male-female competitive situation. *Psychologia, 31*, 187–197.

Yang, K. S. (1982). Causal attributions of academic success and failure and their affective consequences (Chinese). *Acta Psychologia Taiwanica, 24*(2), 65–83.

Yang, K. S., & Liang, W. H. (1973). Some correlates of achievement motivation among Chinese high-school boys. *Acta Psychologica Taiwanica, 15*, 59–67.

Yip, K. (1992). Goal orientation and its impact on student affect: Some findings from a Singapore sample. *Singapore Journal of Education, 12*(2), 88–92.

Yu, A. B. (1991). Socialization factors of individual's achievement motivation in family (Chinese). *Bulletin of the Institute of Ethnology Academic Sinica, 71*, 87–132.

Yu, A. B. (1994). Is social-oriented achievement motivation (SOAM) different from individual-oriented achievement motivation (IOAM)? Further discussion of the relationship between motivation and behaviour (Chinese). *Bulletin of the Institute of Ethnology, 76*, 197–224.

Yu, A. B. (1996). Ultimate life concerns, self, and Chinese achievement motivation. In M. H. Bond (Ed.), *The Handbook of Chinese Psychology* (pp. 227–246). New York: Oxford University Press.

Yu, A. B., & Yang, K. S. (1987). Social oriented and individual oriented achievement motivation: A conceptual and empirical analysis (Chinese). *Bulletin of the Institute of Ethnology, 64*, 51–98.

Yu, E. S. H. (1980). Chinese collective orientation and need for achievement. *International Journal of Social Psychiatry, 26*, 184–189.

35

Problem Solving

MICHAEL J. LAWSON
Flinders University, Adelaide, Australia

1. INTRODUCTION

It is an exciting time to be considering research on problem solving in the Asia-Pacific region. This topic has attracted attention from a large group of researchers in this region and the findings from this research have had an important influence on the way that problem solving is being conceptualised in the wider educational research community. Perhaps because the topic of problem solving has a quite wide field of reference there is a growing body of research publication throughout the region. In addition, one of the few journals devoted explicitly to problem solving, the *Korean Journal of Thinking and Problem Solving*, is located in this region and it has published reports from some of the major research groups in other regions of the world. The major focus in this article is a report on recent research activity on problem solving in countries in the Asian part of the region, though work from Australia is also discussed. Rowe (1999) has recently completed a comprehensive review of Australian research which covers problem solving and related fields. Readers are referred to that source.

Two further delimitations of the article need to be noted. First, it is concerned with a selection of research that has been published since 1995. The selection is intended to provide an outline of the developments in research on problem solving. Second, this review does not treat the topic of creativity at length, though some sources of concern for creativity and problem solving are noted.

In this review the term 'problem solving' has been interpreted broadly to refer to complex mental action that includes topics sometimes labelled as 'higher order thinking.' In published research the overlap between the two terms is quite considerable, with some researchers using the terms as synonyms, and problem solving is used as the label of choice here. Hence the research reviewed in this article refers to the problem solving situation, activities involved in preparation for problem solving, judgements made during problem solving and reflective activities arising from a solution attempt. Problem solving is a broadband issue for education because one of the major aims of all education systems is to help students to improve their capabilities to solve the problems they and their societies will face.

2. A FRAMEWORK FOR CONSIDERING PROBLEM SOLVING

2.1. *The Problem Situation*

A problem situation is one where an individual has no readily available procedure that will allow him or her to reach a desired goal. Although an effective procedure may eventually be developed or remembered, at the time of the problem such a procedure is not at hand and so the individual must set about the process of developing the procedure or accessing one that has already been developed. The broad label given to these processes is problem solving.

Much of social-cognitive activity is characterised by the above description of problem solving. Organising the first meal of the day might present a problem if milk is a necessary ingredient and there is none in the house and the car battery is found to have been drained by a drop in temperature overnight. Communication with a fellow student might create a problem when it is discovered that the student has a severe hearing loss. Each of these situations is likely to require the development of a new procedure to enable the individual to achieve the desired goal. At a broad level each of these situations imposes on the individual a set of demands that have a similar character to that imposed by the presentation of a difficult mathematical task, or the interpretation of a set of documents in a history class. In all these cases the individual must do some work before the situation can be satisfactorily resolved. Such 'work' is another name for problem solving.

Most tasks or situations will be problems in varying degrees. The degree to which the task is a problem will depend upon the nature of the problem and on the resources available to those attempting a solution. Resources for problem solving include the individual's or group's background knowledge and experience in the area, the physical resources available at the time, and the nature of the situation in which the task must be completed. Communication with the deaf student might be easily organised if he has a laptop computer operating at the time you wish to interact with him. Obtaining milk for breakfast is more difficult if the drop in temperature was associated with a heavy fall of snow.

Problems also differ in nature (Hayes, 1988). Well-defined problems have a clear structure, provide necessary information and generally have a single solution. Ill-defined problems are less clearly structured, may have no single agreed solution and may not be presented with all the relevant information. For this latter class of problems there may only be better or worse solutions. Many social, political and economic situations that occur in daily life are of this nature, but so are situations that arise in classroom tasks, in work, and in some examinations.

2.2. The Problem Solving Process

The dominant perspective on problem solving in the last three decades has been one stimulated by the original work of Newell and Simon (1972). This represented problem solving as a multistage process in which a path was developed through a problem space. The problem space circumscribed a number of the possible states of the problem. Two obvious problem states are the initial state, what exists at the moment, and the goal state, which is the desired goal. In this framework problem solvers are seen to generate a path, or a set of moves, that is designed to take them from the initial state to the goal state.

Sitting alongside this problem-space framework has been a description of problem solving in terms of stages of cognitive activity. There have been many such descriptions generated over a long period of time, with a representative model being provided by Bransford and Stein (1984). The model proposes five stages of problem solving: identifying the problem; defining the problem; exploring alternative approaches to produce a plan for action; acting on the plan; and looking back or reviewing the outcome.

These two different perspectives have served different purposes in research on problem solving. The former has been most influential in driving analyses of simulations of problem solving behaviour. The latter has provided a more general descriptive framework that has been particularly influential in educational research. Framing problem solving in this way draws attention to the intimate link between problem solving and learning. Generation of a solution to a problem implies that some learning has occurred, that an existing knowledge schema has been modified or a new knowledge schema established. This learning can occur in different stages of the problem solving process: a new path through the solution space might be discovered, or a new feature of an object or situation might be identified, or a new relationship between features of a situation could be established. Learning might occur even if the problem is not solved. Recognition of this role of learning during problem solving underlies the design of problem-based learning (Evensen, Salisbury-Glennon, & Glenn, 2001).

2.3. Situating Problem Solving

In large part descriptions of the cognitive activity noted above have been substantiated by recent research. Yet problem solving activity is not just concerned with **cold**, individual, cognitive processing events. The concern to understand other features of problem solving is represented in three major streams of contemporary research in psychology and education. The first focuses on the affective and motivational states of problem solvers and draws attention to the crucial influences of these states on the outcomes of problem solving. This stream can be represented by the self-regulation framework developed by work such as that of Schunk and Zimmerman (1997) and the social-cognitive framework advanced by Bandura (1997). A second, and related, stream of recent research has argued for recognition of influences on problem solving that come from beyond the individual, through social interaction and group activity (Palincsar, 1998).

More broadly it has been argued that problem solving needs to be represented as a **situated** activity, an activity that is influenced by the features of the situation in which it is undertaken (Pellegrino, Chudowsky, & Glaser, 2001). At the broadest level these features include the cultural context in which the problem situation is embedded. In the situative perspective it is argued that the learning that occurs during problem solving is also influenced by the practices and perspectives of the community in which the problem solving is undertaken (Greeno, 1997). Concern for the impact of social interaction and group activity, and the influence of cultural setting, have a particular pertinence in this review because it can be argued that some of the strength of argument about these two sets of influences has come from research carried out in the Asia-Pacific region.

3. SITUATIONAL INFLUENCES

3.1. *Cultural Approaches to Problem Solving*

The issue of cultural influences on broad approaches to problem solving has been illustrated by Hong (2000). The context for Hong's analysis was assembly-line work in the manufacturing industry in South China. He considered differences in the way that managers in a local Chinese and Western company proceed when a problem arises in such a worksite. Hong argued that the value placed by Chinese workers and managers on the cultural factors of *guanxi* and 'face' would lead them to adopt quite a different approach to that of many Western managers. The influence of these ways of understanding interpersonal relationships were argued to encourage the Chinese workers to view the problem situation in a more internal manner. In Hong's view consideration of these cultural factors by these workers acts to limit the extent to which the problem might be dealt with in an open manner. Thus the Chinese workers would be inclined to take the major responsibility for the problem and to be sensitive to the effect of the problem on the interpersonal relationships among the individuals involved. This approach stood in contrast to the more direct and linear cause and effect approach observed in the approaches used by Western managers. For Hong, the challenge for the problem solvers in these situations was, first to understand the nature of the broad differences in representation of the problem situations, and then to consider ways in which staff using these different approaches can interact effectively.

The description of these as broad approaches is meant to suggest that these approaches are likely to exercise influence over a wide range of the activity occurring during problem solving. This implies that these approaches need to be given some priority in consideration if other parts of problem solving are to be undertaken successfully.

3.2. *Collaborative Activity*

Another perspective on collaborative social activity among Chinese learners has been examined in the work assembled by Watkins and Biggs (1996). Biggs (1996) argued that the representation of Confucian heritage learning cultures (CHC) in many Western sources was not accurate. This representation, which emphasised the combined influence of large class sizes, an apparent focus on memorisation and teacher-directed activity, implied that the learning in CHC classrooms was unlikely to be characterised as **deep** learning. However, Biggs noted that observation of classroom activity in these classrooms suggested that this was a caricature. The classrooms observed showed a high degree of cooperative group activity in problem solving, this being fostered by the supportive climate established by the teacher, in the face of the demands of a competitive examination system. Biggs' view is supported by the research of Sallili (1996) and Tang (1996). Tang's observation of CHC classrooms showed evidence of spontaneous collaborative activity that had an effect on the way that students learned in preparation for class assignments. Sallili (1996) proposed that this cultural emphasis on collective behaviour in CHC classrooms also had an effect on the extent to which ability was seen as controllable. This suggests that students in these classrooms would react to a problem situation in an adaptive way, giving emphasis to increased effort. Support is given to this position by Jehng's (1998) comparison of the effects of collaborative and individual learning in computer programming tasks, which showed that the students in a collaborative group had superior problem solving performance.

4. PHASES OF PROBLEM SOLVING

The broad phase descriptions of problem solving provide a useful framework for organising research. This section starts with a focus on the problem solver's dispositional state and moves on to consideration of how activity involved in transformation and use of knowledge during problem solving has been examined.

4.1. *Motivation and Affect*

Sallili's (1996) work, noted above, drew attention to the role of attributional influences on problem solving. The impact of causal attributions emerged in the analysis of Weiner. In an interview in the *Korean Journal of Thinking and Problem Solving* (Shaughnessy, 2000) Weiner suggested that attributional analysis provides a key source of motivational knowledge that is relevant in problem solving. Patterns of attribution for failure and success adopted by students may be adaptive or maladaptive. A maladaptive attribution of cause for failure might, for example, result in the lowering of a student's expectation of success in a future problem solving episode that would be manifested in lack of persistence with the task. Weiner supports Sallili's analysis suggesting that attribution of cause is more likely to be assigned to individual traits in individualistic cultures than is the case in more collective cultures.

The role of affect in problem solving has been the focus of the cross-national research on mathematics anxiety of Ho, Senturk, Lam, Zimmer, Hong, Okamoto, Chiu, Nakazawa, & Wang (2000). In their study of mathematics anxiety of sixth grade students in China, Taiwan and the United States this group have focussed on examining the influence of two dimensions of mathematics anxiety. Initially they examined the structure of mathematics anxiety and found evidence of affective and cognitive components of anxiety in each of their national samples. The affective factor, concerned with emotional reactions to mathematics, showed similar substantial negative relationships with achievement in each sample. The relationships between performance and scores on the cognitive factor that encompassed such feelings as negative expectations, were not consistent in the three sixth grade samples. The factors contributing to the development of affective anxiety and the reasons for the different relationships between the cognitive component and achievement of boys and girls in different samples are areas that can be followed up in future research.

4.2. *Cognitive Load*

A major concern in the design of any instructional procedure is that it is sensitive to the current state of the student. In cognitive load theory, which has been developed largely through the work of Sweller and his colleagues, it is the limitation of the student to handle an amount of information at a given time that is considered (Sweller, 1994). In cognitive load theory it is assumed that students have a limitation in working memory and that the design of the instruction has an impact on the load that is placed on that working memory. Sweller and his colleagues have examined many of the implications of cognitive load theory for instructional design and have drawn attention to the practical implications of the theory for the design of instructional text, for schema acquisition and automation of rules (Sweller, 1999).

4.3. *Problem Representation*

Each problem situation must be understood, or represented. The stage of problem representation is crucial, because the outcome of this process will direct the subsequent problem solving activity. Fu (1995) demonstrated, in his study of solitaire chess, that the different problem solution strategies that he observed in his study with Chinese college students were quite strongly linked to the different types of problem representations developed by the students. The more awareness of problem structure shown in the problem representation, the more effective the solution strategy.

In his analysis of strategy change during solution of proportional reasoning problems by Japanese students, Fujimura (2001) argued that generation of new problem representation is the initial stage in strategy change. Once a new representation is available it can be examined by the student and then applied. Fujimura used this model of strategy change to generate designs of educational interventions for challenging concepts such as ratio and proportion, designs that build on the children's intuitive knowledge.

4.4. Knowledge Transforming Strategies

Strategy instruction is of central interest in problem solving research. The procedures applied to transform knowledge once the problem has been represented have a powerful impact on the outcome of the solution attempt. Wong, Lawson and Keeves (2002) investigated the influence on problem solving of Australian students' use of a self-explanation strategy during learning of a new theorem in Grade 9 geometry. The purpose of this strategy was to scaffold the development of an elaborated theorem schema. Students were trained to use questions to prompt detailed analysis of new material, the development of links to their prior knowledge, and evaluation of their current understanding. The results of the study showed that the self-explanation training had a substantial positive effect on transfer of knowledge to more difficult problems. Wong et al. also demonstrated an effect of knowledge access and knowledge generation procedures that were argued to mediate the impact of the training on performance.

The impact of strategy use on schema acquisition was also the subject of the study of Filipino high school students carried out by Bernardo (2001). In this case the strategy used by the student was prompted by the method of presentation of principles in the study of probability. Bernardo compared the effect of provision of the principle with use of worked examples illustrating use of the principle. The instruction was then followed either by examination of analogous situations or constructions by the students of their own problem analogues. Bernado found that, contrary to previous research, the impact of the instructional method on problem solving transfer depended on whether the students had used an analogy or had constructed their own problem analogues. The patterns of findings in this study reinforce the arguments made about the situated nature of learning, and provide a reminder of the need to focus on more than the initial method of presentation of material in a teaching situation.

4.5. Knowledge Organisation

The patterns students use to establish memory schema were examined by Chang and McDaniel (1995). Of interest in this study were the ways which students devised to study material in a Hypercard stack format. Chang and McDaniel identified four different ways that students used to develop an understanding. The group classified as 'aimless wanderers' worked through the material in a haphazard manner. The other students used more directed strategies. The 'fact retrievers' developed sets of questions and searched for answers to these questions, though there was no explicit theme guiding the generation of questions. The questions developed by the 'casual investigators' showed evidence of questions to develop a more directed search of the study material. However, this group did not attempt to develop relationships among the outcomes of the search process. Such integration of findings and clear direction in search was evident in the strategies used by the group of students that Chang and McDaniel labelled the 'integrative analysts'. The objective of this final group was to develop a more coherent understanding of the material.

Coherence of understanding was also a focus of a study by Lawson and Chinnappan (2000) that examined the relationship between problem solving performance and the quality of knowledge connectedness. When the performance of high-achieving and low-achieving high school mathematics students was compared it was found that the high achieving students were able to access more problem relevant knowledge, could do this more quickly and with less assistance, and also could establish more links among knowledge schemas relevant to the geometry problems that they were trying to solve.

4.6. Monitoring Skills

The final phase of problem solving to be considered here is the monitoring of problem solving activity. The discussion of monitoring at this point in the discussion of phases of problem solving is not meant to imply that this occurs only at the end of a solution attempt. As is made explicit in models of self-regulation, monitoring is a key activity throughout any instance of problem solving. Lee and Thompson (1997) investigated the use of cognitive monitoring strategies while college students were undertaking a Logo programming exercise. The provision of teacher guidance of students in cognitive monitoring and students' subsequent use of these skills led to improvements in both the students' identification of errors in programs and their debugging of the programs. In each of these areas the students receiving training outperformed students in a no-training control group. The findings in this study provide an explicit example of one form of regulatory activity that is central to the self-regulatory view of learning discussed earlier. This is one way in which teacher guidance can impact on the development by students of more powerful procedures for problem solving. Further research on teaching is reviewed in the following section.

5. TEACHING AND PROBLEM SOLVING

The ways in which teaching procedures affect students' problem solving is a very active area of research in the Asia-Pacific region. One stream of research in this field is concerned with teaching about the phases of problem solving discussed above. A second, related, stream has been associated with the interest in teaching in the Asia-Pacific region generated by the findings of cross-national studies of school performance.

5.1. Asian Approaches to Teaching

A very large body of literature on the topic of teaching and learning has been generated by the superior performance of Asian students in international studies of educational evaluation. Only some of the literature relevant to problem solving can be discussed here.

A major research effort has developed around the study of teaching in mathematics classes in Asian, American and other countries. Stigler and Hiebert (1999) have reported on the outcomes of analysis of videotapes of mathematics teaching in the United States, Japan and Germany. Stigler and Hiebert draw attention to a major difference in approach to the treatment of mathematical problems in the United States and Japanese classrooms. Compared with their United States counterparts, Japanese teachers spend more time in cooperatively planning key lessons, spend more time on helping students to work on the problem representation process and more time working on a given problem. The Japanese teachers observed chose more challenging problems for their students, focussed students' attention on the merits of different solution strategies and were more explicit in drawing connections among the different features of solution methods.

The Stigler and Hiebert report is provocative in the way that it challenges mathematics educators to consider the nature of teaching for problem solving. It makes clear the cultural embeddedness of teaching approaches, but also poses important questions for education systems, curriculum designers and researchers. One such question is whether the Japanese teachers' emphasis on spending more time on deeper analysis of a narrower range of problems should be mirrored in classrooms in other countries.

5.2. *Follow-up Cross-national Comparisons of Teaching and Learning*

The cross-national comparisons of performance have also generated studies of specific features of problem solving. Brenner, Herman, Ho and Zimmer (1999) examined the nature of problem representation in mathematics among samples of Grade 6 students from the United States, China and Taiwan and Japan. Three aspects of the representation process were considered: (a) transformations within the written and symbol systems; (b) translations among different written representations; and (c) written representations and translation between visual and written representations. The students in the Asian samples showed evidence of both stronger basic skills and stronger representational skills that resulted in better performance in judging the appropriateness of different representations. There were, however, differences among the performances of the Asian samples, with the Japanese group performing at a level between the American and Chinese groups. Additionally there were specific weaknesses in each of the four groups, with the Chinese students being the lowest scoring group on items involving visual representations. The authors speculate that the relative performance of the United States and Chinese groups on these items is related to the format of the texts used in the different school systems.

The existence of specific differences in mathematical problem solving profiles of national groups also emerged in the research of Cai (2000). Cai focussed on United States and Chinese students' problem solving performance and their explanations of solution paths in two different types of problems. One type, called 'process-constrained' problems, limited the range of procedures that would generate a solution, and could mostly be solved by use of a standard algorithm. The other type, called 'process-open' problems, usually could not be solved by use of a standard algorithm, but required exploration of the problem situation and choice among a number of acceptable alternative solution strategies. Although the Chinese students outperformed the United States' students overall, the patterns of performance on the two different problem types were different. On the process-constrained problems the level of performance of the Chinese students was higher. The pattern was reversed for the process-open problems on which the United States' students achieved higher scores. Again problem-representation differences between the groups were observed on the different types of problems. Cai (2000) pointed to the likelihood of differences in instructional practice being associated with ways that students represented the problems, with the earlier contact with variables and equations in Chinese classrooms being a possible influence on the different ways that the groups approached the process-constrained problems.

5.3. Teaching About Problem Solving

The program devised and evaluated by English (1997) was directed at improving the flexibility of thinking during problem solving by engaging the students in problem-posing activities. In this study with Australian Grade 5 students the objectives set for students were to generate new problems and questions during exploration of a mathematical problem situation and to consider the need to re-formulate a problem during the process of a solution attempt. English argued that these activities focus students' attention on the problem structure and allow them to represent mathematical situations in diverse ways. Following a ten-week teaching program the students who had received instruction in problem-posing activities showed improvement in recognition of problem structures and in creation of complex and diverse problems that could be associated with a given situation. English (1997) argued that activities such as these enable students to develop knowledge of problem structures that is independent of their understanding of the problem situation. In this respect the problem-posing activities have the potential to move the students toward the identification of deep structure that is characteristic of more expert performance (Pellegrino et al., 2001).

5.4. Teaching Through Problem Solving

This approach is compatible with the approach toward teaching described by Sawada (1999). In his observation of Japanese elementary classroom mathematics teaching, Sawada argued that the teacher was teaching through problem solving. Students were not only examining the mathematical features of a problem situation, but they were also learning about how they could use errors to develop more elaborate understanding of the situation and of the mathematical concept. Sawada's observations about the willingness of Japanese teachers to spend longer periods of time in consideration of a single problem situation are in accord with those of Stigler and Hiebert (1999). Again the question of instructional methods and textbook design emerge as areas for further study. Sawada suggests that the typical American lesson mostly finishes with students working from textbooks at their desks, whereas many of the Japanese lessons ended in discussion. In Sawada's view this latter situation increases the likelihood that the medium of problem solving becomes a subject of students' knowledge development.

Son and VanSickle (2000) also investigated teaching through problem solving. The authors devised a program for teaching through problem solving in high school economics and compared the effects of this with the outcomes generated from an expository teacher-directed approach. The major elements of the problem solving approach in this study were exploration of the problem situation, activation of relevant prior knowledge, clarification of terms and concepts in new material through group discussion, examination of ways to represent the problem, and the summarising of main ideas. When students' performance was examined after the training, the problem solving group showed superior knowledge of the details of the topic and maintained this advantage over a four-week period. There were no differences in the knowledge structuring scores for the two groups.

Not all teachers show the same enthusiasm for use of a problem solving approach to teaching or for a focus on problem solving activity. In a survey of elementary science teachers in Singapore, Lee, Tan, Goh, Chia and Chin (2000) found that only about a third of these teachers had a regular focus on problem solving activity in their classrooms. In this relatively large sample of teachers most felt that they were under a strong pressure to cover the science content that would be examined in the national examination at the end of Grade 6. The pressure to cover this content seemed to divert teachers away from teaching through problem solving.

The views of these elementary teachers stand in contrast to the principles of teaching highlighted by Sawada and the approach to design of the teaching sessions adopted by Son and VanSickle (2000), which are closely related to the problem-based learning procedures (PBL) described by Evensen et al. (2001). In PBL a problem solving framework is used as the basis for the structuring of the total learning experience for the student and the role of the teacher is more facilitative than expository. However, the basic elements of the Son and VanSickle problem solving instruction are also central to PBL and it may be that the use of this approach in high-status areas of teaching such as medicine will encourage a re-assessment of its use in secondary and elementary schooling. What is clear from the PBL and Son and VanSickle research is that the use of a problem solving framework for the design of teaching can result in the establishment of powerful schemas for domain-specific knowledge. More controversial is the effect of instruction in the use of general problem solving procedures. This is one of a number of issues associated with problem solving that continue to attract the attention of researchers in this region.

6. PROBLEM SOLVING ISSUES OLD AND NEW

6.1. *The Teaching of General Strategies*

The study of expert behaviour in a domain has been a focus of educational research in the last two decades. A continuing concern of this research has been the relative importance to expert performance of domain-specific content knowledge and the use of general problem solving procedures. In the mid 1980s a strong view noted in Pellegrino et al. (2001) was that the major dimension of difference between novice and expert was in domain-specific knowledge. Yet studies of expertise, such as that of Dhillon (1998), have shown that differences in domain-specific knowledge are associated with differences in use of some general problem solving procedures. In Dhillon's study of experts and novices in physics, expert problem solvers were more likely to use working-forward and problem decomposition procedures and novices more likely to use generate-and-test and means-end analysis procedures. Rather than seeing the domain-specific and general procedure components of the performance differences as unrelated, Dhillon suggested that they are complementary, so that the general procedures used by experts are chosen because the experts have access to large and well organised domain-specific schemas.

The results of a study with chemistry undergraduates in Singapore also support the interaction of problem-related knowledge and general procedure use (Lee, Goh, Chia & Chin, 1996). Lee at al. (1996) found that the most important predictor of success on electrochemistry problems was problem-translating skill. Problem translating in this study referred to skills that encompass both content-related and general procedures. Effective problem translating required that students could use their content knowledge to understand the problem, but also drew on skill in carrying out a systematic and complete analysis of the given information. This latter component of problem translation is not part of domain-specific knowledge in chemistry. Rather it is a general procedure that is part of the student's knowledge of how to act in a problem situation. Indeed this skill in analysis is seen as a key component of creative problem solving (Dung, 2000).

6.2. New Technologies and Problem Solving

The impact of new information and communication technologies for learning and teaching is discussed at length in the articles on *New Technologies in Education* and *Technology and Learning*, but is also a topic of growing importance in research on problem solving. Chang (2001) examined the effect of a problem solving based computer-assisted tutorial system (PSCAT) on the performance of Grade 10 earth science students in Taiwan. In this system the students had access to a number of virtual facilities, such as a virtual office and a virtual field trip in which they could carry out investigations. When compared on achievement and attitude measures with a classroom based lecture-discussion approach, the PSCAT system emerged as a viable alternative instructional system for students and teachers in this area of the science curriculum. The evidence from studies such as that of Chang shows that students are unlikely to suffer any disadvantage in using such new resources and there is clearly a high potential for such systems to be able to add capabilities that are not easily accessible in most classrooms.

7. CONCLUSION

The breadth of research on problem solving in the countries of the Asia-Pacific is impressive. Within the limited sample of studies noted in this review it is evident that the questions pursued by researchers in this region are distributed across areas of both practical and theoretical importance. The general concern with the situated nature of learning that has been one of the major themes of research in this region can be expected to continue to be an important issue for other researchers interested in problem solving. The research on this topic has had major impact on models of problem solving and on analyses of the classroom actions of both teachers and students. The knowledge about problem solving developed by these groups will also become a focus of further research and this in turn can be expected to influence research on problem solving processes.

REFERENCES

Bandura, A. (1997). *Self efficacy: The exercise of control.* New York: W. H. Freeman.
Bernardo, A. B. I. (2001). Principle explanation and strategic schema abstraction in problem solving. *Memory and Cognition, 29,* 627–633.
Biggs, J. B. (1996). Western perceptions of the Confusion-heritage learning culture. In D. Watkins & J. B. Biggs (Eds.), *The Chinese Learner* (pp. 45–67). Melbourne: CERC and ACER.
Bransford, J. D., & Stein, B. S. (1984). *The ideal problem solver.* New York: W. H. Freeman.
Brenner, M. E., Herman, S., Ho, H. Z., & Zimmer, J. M. (1999). Cross-national comparison of representational competence. *Journal for Research in Mathematics Education, 30,* 541–557.
Cai, J. (2000). Mathematical thinking involved in U.S., & Chines students solving of process-constrained and process-open problems. *Mathematical Thinking and Learning., 2,* 309–340.
Chang, C. Y. (2001). A problem solving based computer-assisted tutorial for earth sciences. *Journal of Computer Assisted learning, 17,* 263–274.
Chang, C. K., & McDaniel, E. (1995). Information search strategies in loosely structured settings. *Journal of Educational Computing Research, 12,* 95–107.
Dhillon, A. S. (1998). Individual differences with problem solving strategies used in physics. *Science Education, 82,* 379–405.
Dung, P. (2000). Dialectical systems thinking for problem solving and decision making. *Korean Journal of Thinking and Problem Solving, 10,* 49–67.
English, L. D. (1997). The development of 5th grade problem-posing abilities. *Educational Studies in Mathematics, 34,* 183–217.
Evensen, D., Salisbury-Glennon, J. D., & Glenn, J. (2001). A qualitative study of six medical students in a problem-based curriculum: Toward a situated model of cognition. *Journal of Educational Psychology, 93,* 659–676.
Greeno, J. (1997). Theories and practices of thinking and learning to think. *American Journal of Education, 106,* 85–126.
Fu, X. (1995). Problem representation and solution strategies in solitaire chess. *European Journal of Cognitive Psychology, 7,* 261–281.
Fujimura, N. (2001). Facilitating children's proportional reasoning: A model of reasoning processes and effects of intervention on strategy change. *Journal of Educational Psychology, 93,* 589–603.
Hayes, J. (1988). *The complete problem solver* (2nd ed.). Mahwah, NJ: Erlbaum Associates.
Ho, H. Z., Senturk, D., Lam, A. G., Zimmer, J. M., Hong, S., Okamoto, Y., Chiu, S. Y., Nakazawa, Y., & Wang, C. P. (2000). The affective and cognitive dimensions of math anxiety: A cross-national study. *Journal for Research in Mathematics Education, 31,* 362–379.

Hong, J. (2000). Change as challenge for shop-floor learning: The case of Western and local manufacturing companies in South China. *International Review of Education, 46,* 581–597.

Jehng, J. C. J. (1998). The psycho-social and cognitive effects of peer-based collaborative interactions with computer. *Journal of Educational Computing Research, 17,* 19–46.

Lawson, M. J., & Chinnappan, M. (2000). Knowedge connectedness in geometry problem solving. *Journal for Research in Mathematics Education, 31,* 26–43.

Lee, K-W. L., Goh, N-K., Chia, L-S., & Chin, C. (1996). Cognitive variables in problem solving in chemistry: A revisited study. *Science Education, 80,* 691–710.

Lee, K-W. L., Tan, L-L, Goh, N-K., Chia, L-S., & Chin, C. (2000). Science teachers and problem solving in elementary schools in Singapore. *Research in Science and Technological Education, 2000, 18,* 113–126.

Lee, M. O. C., & Thompson, A. (1997). Guided instruction in Logo programming and the development of cognitive monitoring strategies among college students. *Journal of Educational Computing Research, 16,* 125–144.

Newell, A., & Simon, H. (1972). *Human problem solving.* Upper Saddle River, NJ: Prentice Hall.

Palincsar, A. S. (1998). Social constructivist perspectives on teaching and learning. *Annual Review of Psychology, 49,* 345–375.

Pellegrino, J. W., Chudowsky, N., & Glaser, R. (Eds.) (2001). *Knowing what students know.* Washington, DC, US: National Academy Press.

Rowe, H. (1999). Cognition and instruction. In J. Keeves & K. Marjoribanks (Eds.), *Australian Education: Review of Research 1965–1998* (pp. 59–82) Melbourne: ACER.

Sallili, F. (1996). Accepting personal responsibility for learning. In D. Watkins & J. B. Biggs (Eds.), *The Chinese Learner* (pp. 85–105). Melbourne: CERC and ACER.

Sawada, D. (1999). Mathematics as problem solving: A Japanese way. *Teaching Children Mathematics, 6,* 54–58.

Schunk, D. H., & Zimmerman, B. J. (1997). Social organisation of self-regulatory competence. *Educational Psychologist, 32,* 195–208.

Shaughnessy, M. F. (2000). An interview with Bernie Weiner: About attribution, problem solving and thinking. *Korean Journal of Thinking and Problem Solving, 10,* 61–65.

Son, B., & VanSickle, R. L. (2000). Problem solving instruction and students' acquisition, retention and structuring of economics knowledge. *Journal of Research and Development in Education, 33,* 95–105.

Sweller, J. (1994). Cognitive load theory, learning difficulty and instructional design. *Learning and Instruction, 4,* 295–312.

Sweller, J. (1999). *Instructional designs in technical areas.* Melbourne: ACER Press.

Stigler, J. W., & Hiebert, J. (1999). *The teaching gap.* New York: The Free Press.

Tang, C. (1996). Collaborative learning: The latent dimension in Chinese students' learning. In D. Watkins & J. B. Biggs (Eds.), *The Chinese Learner* (pp. 183–204). Melbourne: CERC and ACER.

Watkins, D., & Biggs, J. B. (1996) (Eds.), *The Chinese Learner.* Melbourne: CERC and ACER.

Wong, R., Lawson, M. J., & Keeves, J. P. (2002). The effects of self-explanation training on students' problem solving in high school mathematics. *Learning and Instruction, 12,* 233–262.

36

Technology and Learning

KWOK-CHEUNG CHEUNG
University of Macau, Macao, SAR China

1. INTRODUCTION

Students nowadays are required not only to learn about technology, but also to learn through technology. Hence, the term 'technology', when used in the teaching and learning contexts, refers to the application of contemporary educational theories and tools to design environments to carry out reliable and effective modes of teaching and learning. Ever since Skinner's Reinforcement Theory in the 1950s and Keller's Personalized System of Instruction in the 1960s, the psychological foundation of learning has shifted from the behavioural to cognitive and social-psychological paradigms. Soft technology, as opposed to the hardware aspect known as hard technology, has changed from those emphasizing reinforcement and feedback, and personal learning rates, to authentic problem-based learning contexts, cooperative learning, as well as computer or internet-based learning (Heinich, Molenda, & Russell, 1993). During the past decades, educators have actively investigated the use of the latest or the most affordable technology in their teaching experiments and everyday practices. In the information era, it is therefore not surprising to witness that most countries in the Asia-Pacific region are eagerly experimenting on how to reap the benefits of information and communication technologies, in the hope of achieving the goals of building a knowledge-based society.

The organization of the article is as follows. A first section seeks to provide an overview of the state-of-the-art learning technologies in the Asia-Pacific countries. The exemplary projects described in 13 countries and systems are by no means totally representative of what has been going on in the country or region under discussion. Instead, the intention is to depict some of the most promising or mature learning technologies under investigation and development that may in the future have an immense impact on the educational community locally or worldwide. A second section introduces two commercial learning technology products originally developed in Western countries but available worldwide. These high technology learning tools, among others, are also gaining popularity in primary and secondary science and technology classrooms. A final section concludes that learning technology will continue to develop in accordance with emerging perspectives of pedagogy, and adoption of developed learning technology relies upon its integration with the school curricula and the availability of re-skilled teaching professionals.

2. EXEMPLARY LEARNING TECHNOLOGY DEVELOPMENTS

2.1. *China*

In 1994, China started a national educational research project to examine how the four dimensions of Chinese language learning can be integrated, namely, literacy teaching, reading comprehension, composition writing, and computer utilization. Around 700 primary and secondary schools and teacher education colleges in 26 provinces or cities participated in order to investigate how information and communication technology (ICT), combined with modern educational and cognitive theories of learning (for example, constructivism, together with problem-based, cooperative and situated learning), contribute to innovative and creative language pedagogy. A range of learning infrastructures and environments is examined and developed, including a multimedia teacher-control platform for classroom language instruction, multimedia electronic libraries, and an internet-linked campus network. Educational courseware, training packages, individual tutoring systems, as well as web-based resources have been located, organized and developed. Among the various instructional modes investigated, the six-stage ICT-based Chinese language classroom mode of instruction is exemplary in the approach adopted that involves the following: (a) creation of problem context, (b) guidance on analytical thinking, (c) formation of creative ideas, (d) engagement on genuine explorations, (e) construction of meanings, and (f) consolidation and self-evaluation. It is noteworthy that by deploying a multimedia Chinese encoding tutoring system, students are initiated into what is called the 'see-listen-talk-write-type-imagine' mode of literacy teaching with desirable educational results (Li, 2000).

From its beginnings in October 2000, the Modern Educational Technology Research Center of Beijing Normal University maintains an on-line scholarly magazine *Educational Technology Communication* to introduce the latest developments in learning technology to educational professionals in the Chinese-speaking regions. The main contents of the magazine, among others, include: (a) key articles featuring the state-of-the-art of learning technology, (b) exemplary theory and practice around the world today, (c) introduction of famous scholars and academics, (d) forthcoming events and activities, (e) new horizons and latest developments in the various foundations of education, (f) resources and products related to learning technology, and (g) provision of a forum for scholarly exchanges. The most important articles that have gone through review are being published in the new academic journal *Journal of Educational Technology* that is published in China.

2.2. Hong Kong

After nearly two decades of active research on computer-assisted Chinese language learning, the Department of Curriculum Studies of the University of Hong Kong released the *Dragonwise* software series for primary and preprimary school children to learn Chinese characters interactively through fun. The difficult task of learning the several thousand commonly used characters is then greatly alleviated when children are able to grasp the rules of composition of the much fewer phonetic and semantic components applied in everyday and cultural contexts. This software further introduces to children the genesis of words, character stroke sequence, rules for composing words using the phonetic and semantic components, as well as characteristics of various groupings of words. In line with contemporary theories, learning is conceptualized to occur in familiar, meaningful cultural contexts in the form of songs, stories and computer games.

At the Center for Information Technology in School and Teacher Education, at the University of Hong Kong, a group of researchers is experimenting with the use of *Worldmaker* to construct computer-based iconic models to simulate objects and events. The main idea is that simple rules governing local interactions in discrete units of space and time in nature often give rise to predictable trends and observations. Therefore, simulations of scientific phenomena (such as hill fires, ecological systems, molecular interactions and genetic inheritance) can be explored and hypotheses tested when these phenomena are considered as the results of simple interactions of entities with their immediate neighbours. Hong Kong students, like those in the United Kingdom, are taught to use *Worldmaker* to build computational models to support their work in theorizing, and deeper understanding of the nature of science is achieved as an outcome. This simulation tool is particularly powerful for models that involve unobservable entities, such as genes and ions in the biological and chemical sciences.

2.3. Macao

At the turn of the century, Macao schools undertook teaching experiments on individually configured education based on Gardner's Theory of Multiple Intelligences. Using a common action research strategy, principals and teachers conducted action research to assess children's spectra of multiple intelligences for the purposes of teacher professional development (Cheung, 2000). In order to help teachers validate the school-based intelligence scales, the researchers at the University of Macau developed the SMILES (*School-based Multiple Intelligences Learning Evaluation System*) software (Cheung, Wai, & Chiu, 2000). Apart from scale analysis and validation, this system produces criterion-referenced profiles of multiple intelligences (called MI-Spectrum) to supplement the regular academic reports. This project, commonly known as SMILES has subsequently spread to Hong Kong, Taiwan and Mainland China.

Another noteworthy ICT development is one in which a scientific and technological enterprise in Macao works with a group of academics and scientists from China's Academy of Science to investigate ways of teaching secondary mathematics dynamically using multimedia computers. Automated theorem proving in plane geometry and analytical geometry is one of the main features of the research program. In 2001, the research product $Z + Z$ *Intelligent Education Platform* was formally introduced for classroom use in Macao, Hong Kong, Taiwan and Mainland China. This software supports fully the secondary mathematics curricula in Mainland China and is stipulated by the Chinese government as essential geometry teaching material in all secondary schools. According to the research team, other topics under research and development include trigonometry, three-dimensional geometry, algebra, physics and chemistry at both the junior and secondary grade levels.

2.4. *Taiwan*

ICT-based research is extremely active in Taiwan. One pioneering project is the development of a web-based learning portfolio (WBLP) system (Chang & Tung, 2000). This system assists teachers to document, organize, search, and analyze quantitative and qualitative data pertaining to the learning processes and resulting learning outcomes. It supports non-conventional types of testing practices, such as authentic, performance and portfolio assessment. It provides opportunities for teachers, students and peers to review learning progress, (such as, reflection on learning goals and classroom processes) and to evaluate learning products representative of students' achievement and potential, (such as, assignments, projects and personal web pages). This system, developed originally for use by computer majors at the university level, is now being extended to the preprimary, primary and secondary levels for both subject-based and interdisciplinary areas of study. This project will have immense implications for Taiwan's nine-year basic education curriculum reform commenced at the turn of the twenty-first century.

Another successful project is being carried out at National Hsin-Chu Teachers College. Researchers are using network and virtual reality technologies to build an internet virtual marine museum consisting of three exhibition halls. Through the provision of three-dimensional visual effects and an interactive interface, an audience can enter the virtual museum to experience wonders and thrills. They can travel through an under-sea tunnel to view sharks swimming around the coral reefs. They can also choose to raise fish in an aquarium to help them understand ocean ecology and environmental protection. Within this virtual environment, organisms of different species in both fresh water and oceans can be observed as if in real life situations. Care has been taken to create three-dimensional models of various kinds of fish and marine creatures, and to imitate their habits and behaviours as authentically as possible. No admission fee is charged. The museum is open 24 hours a day so that education-on-demand becomes a reality in everyday science learning.

Strongly supported by the Government, Taiwan is keen on developing large-scale autonomously managed web-based virtual learning communities that assist people to engage in social exchanges and lifelong learning. Administered by the Learning Technology Center of the National Central University and sponsored by the National Science Council of the Taiwan Government, EduCities claims itself to be the world's first educational city in cyberspace. All students in Taiwan are by design EduCities's major citizens, and their teachers, parents and others who are interested in collaborative life-long learning are also welcome. As this virtual city is modelled against a real Taiwanese city, its citizens are readily introduced to this new type of web-based learning and all strive hard to become good 'netizens' – citizens living on the net. One key characteristic of this project is that there is an open web-based educational platform for every citizen in EduCities to enter courses free of charge. There is no limitation on tutor requirements as long as there are others who are willing to learn. One ambitious aim of this project is to achieve the ideal of 'School for all, School by all, and School of All'.

2.5. Japan

Japan is also expert in ICT education. For example, research on artificial intelligence has changed from building stand-alone machines that try to solve problems entirely by themselves to building partners that augment human capability in problem solving. This is in line with the modern view of intelligence that it is distributional in nature (Sison & Shimura, 1998). Ontology theory and technology, which pay equal attention to both form and content of knowledge, have been advanced as essential building blocks of next-generation intelligent educational systems, such as Computer Supported Collaborative Learning (CSCL) and Intelligent Tutoring/Training Systems (ITS). It is argued that there is a need in CSCL to design a good ontology to represent the domain knowledge, the communication model, and the learning process model from an educational point of view. The Framework for ITS (FITS), which seeks to enumerate computational agents needed for implementing reactive behaviours of tutoring systems, can be domain-independent in terms of tutoring strategies at the symbol level but task-dependent in terms of vocabulary at the knowledge level (Ikeda & Mizoguchi, 1994).

Another interesting project is being undertaken at the Hokkaido University of Education. Researchers have developed a system that brings real-time ground-based weather data (for example, temperature, atmospheric pressure, wind direction and speed, rainfall amounts, humidity) and geo-stationary weather satellite images (for example, infrared and visible pictures of Japan and various zones of the globe) to classrooms through the internet. Students at the K-12 levels can experiment with the data and the images (for example, display of cloud-top temperature, changes of weather conditions over the past 24 hours) to increase scientific literacy in their everyday lives. These images can be animated so that students can intuitively understand the types and movement of clouds associated with particular weather conditions, such as those during the various stages of a front, cyclone or typhoon. In order to facilitate this type of teaching, teachers are trained in workshops before students are introduced to topics of weather forecasting from a global perspective (Takahashi et al., 1999).

2.6. *Korea*

Korea, similar to Japan, is one of the leading countries in ICT development. One weakness of existing web-based learning environments identified by The Electronics and Telecommunications Research Institute in Korea, is that present hyperlink chain structures which bind static resources together cannot point to dynamic human resources. There is no mechanism to support awareness of who is actually engaged on the web. This weakness, if overcome, allows students to a web page to connect to their teachers or other human resources and ask questions just by clicking the required links. In order to meet this end, the Institute develops the *PageTogether* plug-in software, a web-based cooperative work system using a multi-protocol interface, to allow students and teachers during distance education to exchange information and resources with each other even though they are in the web simultaneously. Teachers of various subjects can put the hyperlinks pointing towards themselves in their web pages where through *PageTogether* collaborative browsing, multimedia and data conferencing are conducted simultaneously. This is done even though they are communicating among themselves using different internet standard protocols. It is anticipated that this invention will revolutionize future learning technology in web-based learning environments.

2.7. *Singapore*

Singapore is widely applauded for its ambitious plan to build up a thinking nation to keep abreast of the information era. *SpaceALIVE!*, a multi-user real-time collaborative web-based learning environment, was designed and released for use by the Kent Ridge Digital Labs in 1996. It provides users simultaneous online control and viewing of shared documents and applications. It has been used by students in Singapore, Hong Kong and other South East Asian Countries (such as Brunei, Indonesia, Malaysia, Philippines and Thailand) to collaborate on interdisciplinary projects in both real and virtual learning environments. *SpaceALIVE!* is a kind of MUD/MOO virtual reality that allows students to participate in the form of knowledge-building communities and this mode of learning is guided by educational principles rooted in constructivism, as well as cooperative, situated learning. There are projects on future homes, aromatherapy, acid rain, natural paint, transportation, e-commerce, e-education, health and environment, fashion and entertainment. As all such projects are mainly led by researchers in Singapore, the research and development strategies and methods are in line with the four dimensions of Singapore's national goals for information technology in education, namely, curriculum and assessment, content and learning resources, physical and technological infrastructure, and human resource development. Project SUCCESS, conducted by the Instructional Science Academic Group of the National Institute of Education, Singapore is one of such exemplary *SpaceALIVE!* Projects that seek to achieve quality ICT-integrated learning (Chen, 2001).

Another very interesting project is being carried out at the National University of Singapore. Researchers work within the constructivist paradigm with a system that creates extensible simulation-oriented virtual collaborative learning environments (Yam & Yong, 2000). Within such environments, students can steer ancient battleships and fire cannon balls at each other to explore concepts of relative velocities and projectiles. Likewise, students can mix and test chemical reactions in chemistry lessons in the safety of a virtual chemistry laboratory. Similar to other virtual reality environments, there are avatars to represent the users' presence and to increase their sensations and interactions through direct manipulation of virtual objects. Multiple views from a two- or three-dimensional perspective are available to aid navigation through large virtual worlds. Future developments will include letting students see the actions and gestures so that less time and effort are spent on online discussion using text-chat.

2.8. *Australia*

Equipping teachers and schools to meet teaching and learning needs is of paramount importance in implementing ICT education. In keeping with Australia's Northern Territory Department of Education government standards, the Learning and Technology in Schools (LATIS) project allocates project-based resources across schools to improve student access to information technology in the classrooms. It seeks to increase learning outcomes by transforming, enhancing, and enabling education programs through the use of information communication technology. Specifically, LATIS provides support for digital materials and multimedia curricula, and assists in the purchase and sharing of software and courseware. It also seeks to ensure that schools have flexible options and choices for workstations, local area networks and internet services. With a huge funding commitment from the government in the coming years, LATIS is dedicated to support teacher professional development workshops to transform teachers' roles and relationships, classroom spaces and interactions to technology-enabled approaches that are student-centred, and collaborative.

In a similar vein, the Teaching and Learning Strategy and the Information Technology Alignment Project at The Royal Melbourne Institute of Technology moves learning away from the teacher-centred classroom by flexible delivery of student-centred programs in all subjects and courses. This flexible teaching and learning model, which emphasizes shared responsibility of learning, is based on a hypertext site consisting of seven module areas: subject guide, study program, assessment, student projects, resource kit, contacts and help. Every subject homepage is further linked to communication and collaboration tools, such as threaded discussion, real time chat session, electronic whiteboard, file transfer and collaborative group workspaces. Subject resources are presented in a number of ways in the form of hypertext pages, such as scanned articles and documents, compressed slides and videos, online databases and case studies. Student-based assessment is possible since students can evaluate themselves or participate in peer assessment activities. This mode of learning is particularly useful for part-time and rural students although optional face-to-face sessions are also arranged during most weeks in the early part of the semester.

Competitions and awards are valued means of mobilising schools to deploy ICT in their programs. For instance, the National Assessment Award for Classroom/School, a result of collaboration between the Assessment Research Centre of the University of Melbourne and the schools, encourages excellence in assessment practices that are exemplary in local schooling contexts. The Year 2000 winner was Thomastown East Primary School, Victoria for its Digital Portfolio Project. The project has enabled exemplary practice in student assessment with learning technology while at the same time providing an alternative to the commercially produced *KIDMAP* software program in charting profiles of student learning. Students, parents and teachers work together to provide a digital portfolio so that when the students leave the school they take with them a computer diskette that contains the report and samples of their work to illustrate the skills and knowledge that they have acquired (Assessment Research Centre, 2000).

2.9. New Zealand

Like many countries in the region, New Zealand organizes projects to encourage school children to communicate and collaborate with others on the other side or hemisphere of the globe in order to explore and appreciate the richness and diversity of human culture. The Schools InterLink Project, initiated by the British Council in 1997, paired schools in New Zealand and Britain to communicate and share their discoveries in activities and projects with each other through e-mail and the World Wide Web. The projects are related not only to contemporary themes of common interest, but also to their communities and some of the past historical links that exist between the two countries. The themes are intended to be curriculum-based, reflecting the aims and objectives of a number of key curriculum areas, including English, Social Studies, Science, Technology and Environment. The completed projects are showcased on an internet site for public viewing by the national and global audience. One observation is that participating students develop appreciably in communication, team building and problem solving capacities. They are found conversant with research skills through their engagement in projects and activities.

2.10. Philippines

The power of ICT can be seen in the following manpower-training example. Out of the 40,000 libraries in the Philippines, there are only a handful of librarians knowledgeable in accessing, retrieving and delivering information. In this regard, The University of San Carlos, Philippines applies funding from UNESCO to operate the Certificate Course in Information Technology to be delivered through distance learning modes, including audio and videotapes, the internet, and visits from affiliated lecturers and tutors. Cafes are set up throughout the country to facilitate those librarians who do not have an easy access to the internet within their libraries. This project retrains the librarians in a short time, since the annual rate of graduation from the many library schools in the country amounts only to several hundred people counted at both the undergraduate and graduate levels. This course is considered to be of great help to those librarians who cannot afford to leave their workplace for an extended period of time.

Another hot area of ICT-based learning comes from De La Salle University, Manila where there has been active research into the modelling of a tutoring agent using reinforcement learning. It is hoped that the Intelligent Tutoring System paradigm within the field of artificial intelligence can qualitatively model the knowledge of individual students so as to provide immediate remedial instruction for them (Sison & Shimura, 1998). In essence, the system identifies the best teaching interaction sequence for a particular group of students, and at the same time the system learns from the tutoring experiences through a reward or penalty mechanism for subsequent generalizations in on-line, real-time learning. The tutor receives a positive reward when the teaching goal is reached; otherwise, it is negatively reinforced. In this way, the tutor model is constantly updated in line with pre-determined tutoring policies for students of a particular classification, and as a result of reinforcement learning the system provides teaching tasks in a domain that is customized to individual learners.

2.11. Thailand

Thailand is a fast developing country with good communications to other places in the Asia-Pacific region. The Asia-Pacific Distance and Multimedia Education Network (APDMEN), cosponsored by the Association of Universities of Asia and the Pacific (AUAP) and the Bunkyo University of Tokyo, was formally organized at its founding conference in Thailand in 1998. In collaboration with Nippon Telegragh and Telecommunications (NTT), APDMEN runs a distance learning system in Asia to be broadcast from Tokyo to core member universities in Indonesia, Japan, Malaysia, Philippines and Thailand. Under the auspices of AUAP, APDMEN pools resources to develop multimedia courseware in various fields and exchanges data and learning materials. Participating universities can be networked to form virtual universities and web classrooms, to undertake joint research, and promote digitization of libraries. Recognizing the constraints of qualified courseware production personnel, Suranaree University of Technology (SUT), Thailand is working on a project called 'Border-less Education in Thailand' to initiate the formation of a core of trained personnel and its successful experiences will be shared with core member universities of APDMEN.

2.12. Malaysia

Some ASEAN countries, like Malaysia, are finding ways to implement low cost learning technology as not all schools can afford expensive learning equipment. At the Universiti Malaysia, Sarawak, researchers are examining the viability of developing affordable virtual reality technology for use in constructivist learning environments. As classroom uses of immersion virtual reality are still limited, the relatively low cost desktop virtual reality systems provide an alternative in order to use constructivist learning environments, within which students interact in real time with computer-generated images on a normal computer monitor. Users can wear stereo glasses to view two-dimensional perspectives of three-dimensional virtual objects, or in a reverse manner to reconstruct three-dimensional stimuli from two-dimensional displays mentally. In line with the philosophy of constructivism, this learning technology supports in a virtual sense construction of multiple perspectives or interpretations of reality in contextual and experiential learning situations. Navigation through these virtual environments allows students to articulate solutions to problems by direct manipulation and interaction with the virtual objects.

2.13. Indonesia

Indonesia is a huge country with spacious and remote rural areas and the government has been trying to improve basic science education in public primary and secondary schools in the whole country using information and communication technology. The Center for Scientific Documentation Information, Indonesian Institute of Sciences seeks to establish schools and libraries that can serve as gateways for information access in rural and community development programs. The Center will make available science teaching and learning modules to teachers in both printed and electronic forms through domestic electronic networks and the internet. This project, if achieved, will prepare students for higher education opportunities in science and engineering colleges, as well as for jobs in science-based industries. The goal is that students, whether urban or rural, can have a deeper understanding of science concepts for everyday decision-making.

3. EXAMPLES OF COMMERCIAL LEARNING TECHNOLOGY PRODUCTS

The world becomes a global village in the information age. ICT developments in Western countries are also having this impact everywhere. Although not originally developed by scholars and researchers in the Asia-Pacific countries, there are cases of expensive learning technologies actively being advertised for use in those primary and secondary classrooms that can afford them. These products may have less appeal to those developing or underdeveloped countries that are in favour of seeking low cost learning technologies. Also, teachers feel less threatened when schools undertake technology reform slowly and progressively because their teaching competence need not be re-skilled rapidly and frequently.

3.1. *Electronic Measurement*

In the area of electronic measurement, there are now commercial products (for example, *PASCO Science Workshop*) that integrate computer technology into science classrooms. Students engage in hands-on and mind-on activities outdoors or in laboratories by using various kinds of sensors and data logging devices to collect and analyze data while scientific experiments are performed in real time. Hundreds of experiments in the area of general science, physics, biology, earth science, and mathematics can be performed. For instance, students can actually see the results of plant transpiration as it happens when a leaf is placed in a sunny window or into a breeze. Consequently, students spend less time on the setting up of an experiment and data recording and more time in asking the 'what-if' questions in the exploration and testing of ideas and concepts. Data displays can be transferred instantly to printers, spreadsheets and the World Wide Web for presentations.

3.2. *ROBOLAB*

In 1980, American scholar Papert invented LOGO to help children construct geometrical knowledge by clarifying and testing ideas (Papert, 1980). LOGO, commonly known as *Turtle Geometry*, is not only a programming language, but also a carefully designed computer-based learning environment where microworlds constructed by children can be manipulated by connecting abstract mathematical concepts to concrete geometrical lines and shapes displayed visually on computer screens. About 20 years later, Tufts University and National Instruments in the United States combined their efforts with LEGO DACTA in Denmark to develop ROBOLAB that follows the learning principles of LOGO (Martha, 1998). Specifically, ROBOLAB is an icon-based programming tool that allows children to control movements of the robots built by them (for example, a bumping car) using LEGO bricks, motors, light and pressure sensors, and an infra-red controlled RCX brick (that is, main body of robot in the form of a LEGO brick containing a microprocessor). After programming the movements of the robots using a template, instructions for moving the robot around are downloaded to the RCX brick through infrared transmission. The robot can then be activated and children see whether their ideas can be tested and compared in authentic learning situations. Some schools are now using ROBOLAB in the inculcation of problem solving ability and creativity.

4. CONCLUSIONS

Several decades ago, scientists and educators dreamt of seeking various kinds of information and resources instantaneously and in whatever media format they might appear. Now research into multimedia digitization and hypertext links makes this dream a reality. Various kinds of research are being actively conducted in the region to explore how ICT can revolutionize teaching and learning. Countries are busy setting curriculum standards despite the danger of rapid revisions due to the galloping advances in this area. At the teacher education level, there is an immediate urgency to educate teachers so that students can learn about ICT, learn through ICT, and to learn for ICT. Schools are faced with financial problems of equipping classrooms and laboratories choosing between low-cost and high-cost learning technologies. The irony is that ICT curricula and equipment often become outdated not long after the programs start. On the other hand, educators are concerned with how ICT can tie in well with contemporary theories of teaching and learning, such as constructivism, problem-based learning, situated learning, simulation-based learning, cooperative learning, as well as learning approaches related to activity theory and theory of multiple intelligences. The examples presented in this article are cases in point. Finally, there are fervent calls to set up minimum standards for teachers with respect to knowledge and skills in using learning technology. Given that changes are so rapid there is clearly a need to conduct another review in a few years time when the scenarios are hopefully more or less settled.

REFERENCES

Assessment Research Centre (2000). *2000 Annual Report.* Melbourne: University of Melbourne.

Chang, K. S., & Tung, Y. W. (2000). Construction and evaluation of a web-based learning portfolio system. In G. K. Yeo (Ed.), *Teaching and Learning in the New Millennium – GCCCE 2000 Proceedings* (Vol. 1, pp. 512–519). Singapore (Paper written in Chinese).

Chen, A. Y. (2001). *Project SUCCESS – Strategic Use of Computers in Constructing Effective Studies.* Singapore: Nanyang Technological University.

Cheung, K. C. (2000). Action research proposal for teacher professional development: Design of school-based multiple intelligences learning evaluation system. *New Horizons in Education, 42,* 11–17.

Cheung, K. C., Wai, F. L., & Chiu, K. H. (2000). *School-based Multiple Intelligences Learning Evaluation System (User Manual and Software).* Hong Kong: Crystal Publications.

Heinich, R., Molenda, M., & Russell, J. D. (1993). *Instructional Media and the New Technologies of Instruction.* New York: Macmillan.

Ikeda, M., & Mizoguchi, R. (1994). FITS: A framework for ITS – A computational model of tutoring. *Journal of AI in Education, 5*(3), 319–384.

Li, K. D. (2000). Application of information technology in Chinese teaching reform. In G. K. Yeo (Ed.), *Teaching and Learning in the New Millennium – GCCCE 2000 Proceedings* (Vol. 1, pp. 7–11), Singapore (Paper written in Chinese).

Martha, N. (1998). *ROBOLAB – Getting Started.* Copenhagen: LEGO DACTA.

Papert, S. (1980). *Mind-storms – Children, Computers, and Powerful Ideas.* New York: Basic Books.

Sison, R., & Shimura, M. (1998). Student modeling and machine learning. *International Journal of Artificial Intelligence in Education, 9*(1–2), 128–158.

Takahashi, T., Suzuki, H., Tsuchida, M., & Hirono, T. (1999). Atmospheric and environmental phenomena read from a CD-ROM of annual weather satellite images. *Proceedings of Fifth International Conference on School and Popular Meteorological and Oceanographic Education* (pp. 140–141). Ballarat and Melbourne, Australia.

Yam, S. C., & Yong, B. K. (2000). Designing extensible simulation-oriented collaborative virtual learning environments. In S. S. Young, J. Greer, H. Maurer & S. C. Yam (Eds.), *Learning Societies in the New Millennium: Creativity, Caring & Commitment – Proceedings of Eighth International Conference on Computers in Education/International Conference on Computer-Assisted Instruction* (pp. 222–230). Taipei, Taiwan.

SECTION 4:

CURRICULUM AND TECHNICAL EDUCATION
Section Editor – Robyn Baker

Curricula of the Schools

37

Change in the School Curriculum: Looking to the Future

ROBYN BAKER
New Zealand Council for Educational Research, Wellington, New Zealand

ANDY BEGG
Formerly University of Waikato, New Zealand

1. INTRODUCTION

Curriculum has been conceptualised in many ways. In *Understanding Curriculum* (Pinar, Reynolds, Slattery, & Taubman, 1995) it is analysed as historical, political, racial, gender, phenomenological, post-modern, biographical, aesthetic, theological, institutionalised, and international text. While each of these adds to an understanding of curriculum, for an educational authority the curriculum is a policy document, and for teachers it is simply an outline of some form, that frames "all planned activity for the classroom", whether it be at school or part of technical education.

Historically what has been taught has depended on the perceived purpose of education and the students who were to be taught. The changes over the last two millennia were summarised by Lundgren (1983, in Kemmis, 1986, pp. 31, 32) when he wrote about the idea of the 'code' that underpins curriculum.

The classical code (of the Greeks and Romans) involved a balance of intellectual, physical and aesthetic education ... (this) was then challenged and transformed at the time of the Renaissance with ... the 'realistic' code, according to which knowledge through the senses and scientific knowledge were emphasised. ... the realistic code developed to offer a more useful education to the emerging middle class. This code was associated with a broadening of access to schooling, and with the rise of merchant and administrative classes. ... (it was) overtaken by the 'moral' curriculum code ... in the late eighteenth and early nineteenth centuries, in response to the needs of new nation-states for a committed citizenry ... The moral code was associated with the rise of mass education. The 'rational' curriculum code followed ... training citizens ... instilling the values of liberalism ... The rational code was built on a pragmatist philosophical base, an interest in the individual, and an interest in science as the basis for the rational organisation of society. ... the curriculum code of the present ... the invisible curriculum code – a code in which the explicit ideals and aspirations of earlier curriculum codes have become implicit, in which state control of education and curriculum development is sufficiently well advanced that the key value questions of education are now the responsibility of technologists of curriculum ... leaving teachers and students with a curriculum whose values have been predigested, and where curricula appear ... relatively value-neutral.

While such assumptions reflect a Euro-centric view, they are similar to those that underpin curriculum in many countries that have been past colonies of Britain, Europe or the United States or have been heavily influenced by these countries.

Since the 1930s education has become available for an increasing number of students. This increasing participation in education was summarised by the slogan 'education for all'. At the same time, a gradual breaking down of the barriers between academic, technical, and general education happened which reflected a social concern for democratic and equitable education. These two aspects of education – increased participation, and access to the same forms of education for all – have been accompanied in many countries by governments at local, regional or national levels assuming an increased responsibility for education. As this has occurred we have witnessed the emergence of specialist groups or agencies with concerns about curriculum, assessment, research, and other associated topics. Thus, our concerns related to curriculum have arisen in the last half of the twentieth century. During the last 50 years, there have been a number of major swings in curriculum in countries in the Asia-Pacific region. First, in the 1950s, many countries were influenced by Anglo-American curriculum and educational theory, and they accepted the assumptions of behaviourism. These assumptions included the analysis of subjects into specific objectives for teaching purposes. Next, in the post-sputnik era, a number of curriculum projects, in particular in science and mathematics, were developed by subject specialists: these focused on subject content rather than pedagogy. Then, in the 1980s, curriculum became more child-centred, and constructivism began to replace behaviourism as the underpinning learning theory, although many subject curricula still remained constrained by the perceived demands of tertiary education requirements. In the late 1980s some subjects were beginning to be redefined by their curriculum and take into account what the subject specialists did, as well as what they knew, that is the subject processes as well as the content. Finally, in the 1990s, managerial policies (Mahony & Hextall, 2000) within education, focussing on effectiveness, accountability, and assessment began to influence the curriculum in the Anglo-American world. Judging from the past, such influences are likely to have a flow-on effect in many countries in the region.

2. LEVELS OF CURRICULUM

The term curriculum can have a multitude of meanings and teachers, educators, and people from different countries often use the word curriculum differently.

According to Goodson (1989), the word originally meant 'chariot race' and from this we obtain the idea of 'sequencing in schooling'. Many terms may be used – curriculum, course of study, school schemes, lesson plans, syllabus, program, prescription, and standards – but these are usually linked with specific school subjects. In some countries they are also linked with assessment requirements.

In most countries in the Asia-Pacific region the word curriculum is used to describe the national or regional document or the 'official' curriculum, but the word has other meanings and the official curriculum needs to be seen in relationship to other forms of curriculum which are presented in Figure 1.

The level of curriculum that is of prime importance in this section of this *Handbook* is the official national or regional curriculum that in many countries in the Asia-Pacific region is the compulsory curriculum. This is usually interpreted at school level to suit local conditions and then interpreted even further as teachers plan their lessons.

3. CURRICULUM AIMS

The school curriculum, as expressed at the national level, is a key vehicle for countries to convey the goals of the education system. In a comparative study of school curriculum that included 15 countries from the Asia-Pacific region, priorities for national curriculum included encouraging social cohesion and national identity, preserving cultural heritage, imparting cultural, ethical and moral values, supporting economic well-being and international competitiveness, promoting education for all, and raising achievement for all students (National Institute for Educational Research, 1999). These priorities are then used to guide the curriculum specifications. Singapore, for example, to achieve its aims of

the ideal curriculum (sometimes, the international curriculum)
the curriculum framework
the official (national) curriculum (including regulations etc)
    regional or local curriculum
        the school curriculum
        a subject or departments program
        individual teachers' intended curriculum (work book and lesson plans)
            the schools textbooks (and other resources)
            the taught curriculum
            the assessed curriculum
            the learnt curriculum
            the remembered curriculum

---

and   the hidden curriculum (the class/culture curriculum)
            the out-of-school curriculum
            the peer curriculum
            the home curriculum

Figure 1. Levels of curriculum.

supporting economic growth and promoting social harmony, has a curriculum which focuses on building core competencies including literacy, numeracy and quantitative reasoning, nurturing positive attitudes towards change and lifelong learning, and fostering teamwork and collaboration (Lee, 2002).

The perceived aims of the national curriculum, and the assumptions underlying curriculum construction, can lead to very different understandings of curriculum and hence to quite different approaches to implementation and subsequent outcomes for students. For example, curriculum could aim to reproduce society and educate children to fit in as good citizens, or it could take a more critical view and aim to prepare children to make changes as citizens and thus transform society. The structure of the curriculum may also have a fundamental impact on educational practice. It may be a visionary document that provides a sense of direction for teachers or it may be constructed as a practical guide to be used to support daily practice. The latter form of curriculum could be thought of as a way of operationalising the aims of education, but the purpose of such an approach could be viewed as an assistance to teachers, to support teachers' professional growth, or to deprofessionalise them by taking away their decision-making power. These issues are important and not commonly debated by the educational community. As a result there may not be a shared understanding of reasons for having a national curriculum nor for its structure.

4. INFLUENCES ON CURRICULUM

At the level of curriculum policy there are two seemingly opposing current influences on curriculum. The first is that of internationalisation and globalisation. While many definitions exist, Clarkson and Atweh (2001) talk of internationalisation as the integration of an international dimension in curriculum and research, including activities that promote inter-country collaborations. They use globalisation to refer to the phenomenon of knowledge, values, principles and curricula developed in a local context gaining a global adherence. Both these trends are evident in the curricula of many countries and while these developments are understandable it means that untried and sometimes problematic trends, such as outcomes-based documents, can rapidly become the accepted rhetoric.

The curriculum in the Asia-Pacific region has long been influenced by other countries as European (in particular British) colonialists influenced schooling, and more recently the United States, Australia and countries involved in aid projects have been influential. The acceptance of the Western partitioning of knowledge into school subjects is just one example of how international pressures have influenced schools. On the other hand, maybe as a reaction to globalisation, the second major influence is the curriculum focus on issues of national identity and a valuing of the local culture. India, for example, views the curriculum as a whole as promoting a "profound sense of patriotism" (National Institute for Educational Research, 1999, p. 202), Thailand requires curricula with "high privilege given to Thai tradition and local culture" (p. 432), and Lao P.D.R. requires an awareness of the "national and revolutionary tradition and the spirit of patriotism and love of people's democratic society" (p. 275). One major difference between countries in the region is the existence of religious goals with countries such as Indonesia and Malaysia, maybe partly a consequence of the significant involvement of religious groups in schooling, placing considerable emphasis on such goals and others, including Australia and New Zealand, being secular in their public education systems (National Institute for Educational Research, 1999).

The focus of curriculum in terms of content and process also changes, and common influences include: (a) new subject knowledge, (b) new educational theories, and (c) assessment.

New subject knowledge. Most subjects continually develop with new knowledge becoming known and from time to time some is judged as more suitable for the school curriculum than other knowledge. This occurs not only from the subject itself, but also from within education in terms of the specific subject context. An example of the latter is the promotion of the life sciences in the school curriculum of Singapore because of the perceived importance of these sciences for the country's economic developments and so the need for students to have the knowledge and tools to understand the development and to make informed decisions (Lee, 2002). Another influence in some subjects is information technology that redefines what is possible within the subject. With such technology increasingly available in schools in some countries, this impacts on what is possible in the school curriculum.

Constructivism. Constructivism has become accepted in many countries in the Asia-Pacific region as the dominant theory about learning. This acceptance is influencing the rhetoric of educators although it is not always so evident in the region's classrooms. It involves a subjective rather than an objective view of knowledge, and with every subject the focus becomes 'making sense of one's world' from the perspective of that subject. While subject knowledge is seen as being personally and socially constructed, there is a need for people to share common understandings about their worlds, otherwise communication would become impossible. Constructivism has influenced the curriculum by putting more emphasis on starting with the learners' experiences, and by stressing the need to consider the alternative conceptions that learners bring to classrooms. This has resulted in curriculum being influenced by placing emphasis on the big ideas of the subject rather than on specific behavioural objectives, and on making connections as a way of extending and linking knowledge.

Assessment. While constructivism has influenced the curriculum in one way, assessment has largely acted as a conservative influence. Assessment is primarily based on behavioural thinking with a hierarchy of behavioural objectives assuming notions of progression and levels of attainment. From this perspective knowledge can be seen as an objective body of facts that can be taught, learned, and assessed with little consideration of local situations.

The relative success of some countries in the region, such as the Republic of Korea, Japan and Singapore, in international assessment studies however, has not limited critique of their national systems as they seek new outcomes from schooling in the future. The Republic of Korea, for example, is concerned about the emphasis on rote memorisation in its education system and the way this limits the development of students' creativity and critical thinking. Moreover, Singapore has identified character development, values education, information and thinking skills, and communication and cooperative skills as key drivers for future success. In an attempt to ensure that there will be time to achieve quality educational outcomes, both Japan and Korea have reduced curriculum content by 30 per cent in the belief that students need more time to develop their own interests, and that innovative and creative people need to be more self-directed. The challenge will be to achieve change not by scrutinising education through a Western lens but by building on existing practice as there is considerable evidence (such as Stigler & Hiebert, 1999) that countries outside Asian have much to learn from the East.

The curricula in many countries, such as Malaysia and Vietnam, are also changing to ensure that they are more relevant to the students and their everyday experience. In addition, there is a growing emphasis on the inclusion of indigenous knowledge, as evident in movements such as ethno-science and ethno-mathematics, but as yet little appears to be done in adapting curriculum to fit cultures that are not predominantly Anglo-American.

As subjects and curricula have changed in terms of content, the structure of the documents has also changed. Curriculum framework documents are emerging in some countries (e.g., New Zealand) as a way of bringing together the different school subjects within a more unified philosophy and (presumably) to emphasise to teachers the need to make connections across subject boundaries. In some countries these framework documents seem to have had little influence on subject curricula, but as they are a newly emerging development perhaps this is to be expected. There is also a tendency for curriculum documents to be more comprehensive and with the increasing size and the way that small chunks of knowledge are seen as appropriate for various levels of students, the subjects may become more fragmented. Such a view is appropriate with a behavioural view of learning that requires the analysis of subjects into objectives. However, it is inappropriate with views about the nature of knowledge that suggest that knowledge is primarily concerned with synthesis and the analytic approach implied in the objectives model readily trivializes it (Stenhouse 1975). There is a need to consider how a curriculum can be presented based on broad learning areas which will provide direction, allow for flexibility and negotiation, but allow teachers to control the main thrust of their lessons. Such an approach will probably use a curriculum document as a check-sheet after teaching, rather than as a planning document before teaching. This usage would fit better with the concept of problem-centred teaching, rich learning activities, and the open-ended approaches that have been discussed by teachers over the years and in specific contexts such as mathematics in Japan by Becker and Shimada (1997).

Another structural aspect of curriculum documents is their relationship to teacher guides and textbooks. While the curriculum in many countries is compulsory, teachers' guides have been optional, but where the two documents have merged there seems to be an assumption of increased control of how things are taught as well as what is taught. When textbooks are used a number of possibilities emerge depending on government policy. Five main alternatives seem to occur, some countries:

(a) supply one textbook for each student at each class level;
(b) approve a small number of textbooks and allow schools to select;
(c) allow schools to select a textbook without restriction;
(d) encourage schools to purchase a variety of resources; and
(e) have virtually no funds for textbooks and most students can not afford them.

With (a), (b) and (c) the text often becomes the *de facto* curriculum, and in (d) the teachers' textbook serves much the same purpose. It is only in case (e) or in situations where the teachers do not rely heavily on textbooks that their interpretation of the curriculum is not overly influenced by textbooks. In the first case the development of the textbook is often assumed to be curriculum development. In one of the worst scenarios with aid money but lack of time, or because of pressure from overseas consultants who are not sympathetic enough to local needs, textbooks (and curriculum) from other countries can be imposed.

5. CURRICULUM DEVELOPMENT

The official curriculum in most countries changes, not on a regular basis with periodic reviews and updates, but from time to time usually driven by a political agenda. These decisions, even when political, are commonly based on the emergence of new aims for education, a new purpose for curriculum, the development of new subject knowledge or a new (or redefined) subject, advances in pedagogy, new assessment initiatives, general dissatisfaction with the current curriculum and international pressures. At tertiary level the reasons are often linked to changing vocational needs and economic growth.

Most curriculum development groups between the 1950s and the late 1980s used a research-development-dissemination model (RDD) for curriculum development. It was assumed that research informed development that in turn informed the dissemination process, and that these three stages were performed by different groups of people. The model was also used in policy development and within other sectors of society and was assumed to be appropriate. After the research and development were completed the dissemination process began

– typically involving the production of textbooks or teachers guides, and some teacher development activities. In many countries when financial resources were limited, the research and dissemination components were also often limited.

While the RDD model has been used in the past, there is a growing acceptance that the curriculum development or change process in education is complex, and that a multiplicity of influential activities need to be acknowledged. From this perspective the influential activities are seen to be emerging together, mutually interactive, and unable to be separated (Begg, Davis, & Bramald, 2003). These activities include researching, theorizing, reflecting on practice, developing policy, growing professionally, developing assessment, developing resources, and developing curriculum, and are illustrated in Figure 2.

In this model the eight activities can occur at three or more levels (individual teacher, school, and education system), and can be stimulated further by outside sources. Thus, while the 28 links between the activities already suggest a complex model, this complexity is increased as one thinks of it at three levels and with additional external influences.

It is interesting to compare the processes used for curriculum development for schools and for technical education at tertiary level. The curriculum for technical education has traditionally not been influenced to the same extent by politics as the school curriculum, but instead, by the sectors of industry for whom the students are being prepared. This leaves control of the curriculum more with the teachers who are assumed either to have had recent experience

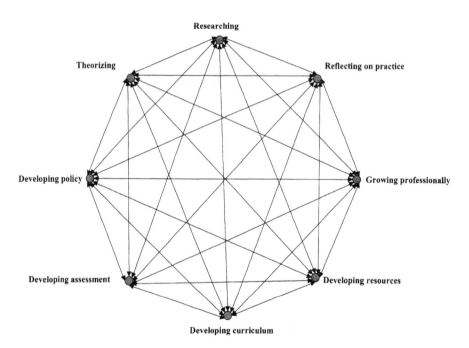

Figure 2. The eight co-emerging activities in the educational change process.

in the industry or to maintain a close liaison with industry partners. In terms of Figure 2 this puts a greater emphasis on the activity of 'reflecting on practice' and this different emphasis is likely to be looked at with envy by some teachers in schools.

6. CURRICULUM RESEARCH

With the alternative model for change (Figure 2), one can imagine traditional curriculum research occurring under the heading 'researching'. At the same time allied activities that some might call research are occurring at the other nodes of the model. This suggests a need to consider extending what might be regarded as curriculum research. In doing this it is interesting to consider what others call research. Boyer (1990) discusses four scholarships which are:

- the scholarship of discovering (original research and the advancement of knowledge)
- the scholarship of integration (connecting ideas and synthesis across discipline boundaries)
- the scholarship of application (assembling knowledge through the interaction between intellectual and 'real world' problems of practice)
- the scholarship of teaching (transforming knowledge through bridging the gap between the teacher's understanding and the student's learning).

The New Zealand Qualifications Authority (1995) wrote a policy statement stating that there were five (not mutually exclusive) kinds of research, and two activities that might be equivalent to research.

(1) *Basic or fundamental research:* experimental or theoretical work undertaken primarily to acquire new knowledge without any particular application or use in view.
(2) *Strategic research:* work which is intended to generate new knowledge in an area which has not yet advanced sufficiently to enable specific applications to be identified.
(3) *Applied research:* work which develops or tests existing knowledge and is primarily directed towards either specific practical objectives or towards the evaluation of policies or practices. Work which involves the routine application of established techniques on routine problems is unlikely to constitute research.
(4) *Scholarship:* work which is intended to expand the boundaries of knowledge and understanding within and across disciplines by the analysis, synthesis and interpretation of ideas and information, making use of a rigorous methodology.
(5) *Creative work:* the invention and generation of ideas, hypotheses, images, performances or artifacts, including design, in any field of knowledge, leading to the development of new knowledge, understanding or expertise.

In addition, there are two activities that may be considered to be equivalent to research.

(6) *Consultancy:* which involves the deployment of existing knowledge and the application of analytical and investigative skills to the resolution of problems presented by a client, usually in the industrial, commercial or professional context.
(7) *Professional practice:* some of which overlaps with consultancy when conducted at an advanced level. In certain subject areas and professions the theorisation and effectiveness of professional practice are advanced by academic staff who practise and participate in it.

From the model, and from these two categorisations it can be assumed that the following can all influence curriculum and could be considered as forms of research:

(a) exploratory studies, small studies by teachers to explore ideas and strategies to inform development;
(b) informal teacher research, minor research activities that are often not written up formally;
(c) reflection-on-practice, cognitive consideration of current and past practice;
(d) practitioner hunches, unformulated or intuitive ideas based on experience;
(e) action research, problem solving cycle research;
(f) development research, trialling and experimenting with resources etc before production;
(g) teaching experiments, trialling alternative teaching strategies and learning activities;
(h) evaluatory research, process of evaluating textbooks, resources, and lessons;
(i) creative work, original and inventive notions related to possible practice;
(j) scholarship, study, teachers' professional reading, and/or theory building, consideration of overseas trends.

These different forms of research together with the other activities from Figure 2 indicate a participatory way of going about curriculum development. Researchers, policy makers, and teachers are all seen as partners in the curriculum development enterprise.

7. CURRICULUM – FUTURE POSSIBILITIES

Internationally, debate continues on the future of curriculum with two current areas being the use of standards and the notion that 'curriculum development' is dead. In spite of these debates, teachers going into classes have lessons in mind, and many feel a need for guidelines on teaching rather than assessment, so it is likely that some middle ground will be found.

The countries preferring national standards suggest that standards will ensure that students are taught the curriculum and this will give a basis for national assessment. Unfortunately such standards often emphasise what can be measured at the expense of the immeasurable (Broadfoot, 1999). In addition, nationally prescribed standards, in particular those intended for national assessment, tend to ignore social and cultural contexts rather than demonstrating a commitment to the social and multicultural mix that often exists. Further, they often emphasise independent rather than collaborative learning, and ignore attributes such as enabling students to become reflective, creative and critical thinkers, and facilitating social justice (Ainsworth and Johnson 2000). Often the justification for having national standards is to raise the educational level for economic reasons, although, as Budge (1997, p. 17) has shown, there is no direct and causal link between pedagogy, attainment in literacy and national economic competitiveness.

An alternative viewpoint is that "curriculum development is dead," and that "curriculum understanding is what is needed" (Pinar et al., 1995). This fits with a phenomenological approach to curriculum, and to the notion that all teachers are professionals and need to constantly plan curricula in a flexible way to build on the students' interests and background. However, the curriculum understanding that is explicit in this notion is itself a form of curriculum in that teachers are planning curricula at a classroom rather than a national level.

The middle ground might be to have curriculum guidelines that would give teachers both guidance and flexibility. Such flexibility has been available in some countries in Europe where at least one country suggests that a fraction of the curriculum (about 25%) should be adjusted to suit local needs, while another has a national curriculum that it is not compulsory. Similarly, Singapore is aiming to reduce the current curriculum content by 30 per cent to enable the introduction of new knowledge as well as to give "schools more latitude in deciding how teaching and learning can take place based on the implementation guidelines provided" (Lee, 2002, p. 5). It is argued that this will ensure that the curriculum more effectively meets student needs and that it will be based on what teachers can deliver. Whether such a curriculum emerges depends on political decisions and as Brown (1992) said, "the greatest enemy of pedagogical tactfulness is the hegemony or desire for control" (p. 57).

Recent work in curriculum studies has attempted to reconceptualize the field. As Miller (1998) wrote,

> ... many associated with the reconceptualizing of the curriculum field have worked, for more than 20 years, to move the field from its long-standing managerial, technocratic, and positivist orientation, and towards multivocal, multiperspectival theorizing of curriculum. (pp. 498–499)

As part of this reconceptualizing, Applebee (1996) has argued that what educators consider most worth knowing reflects a fundamental misconception about the nature of knowledge and learning. He claims that it strips knowledge of the context that gives it meaning and vitality. Instead, he emphasises knowledge-in-action, such knowledge arising from participation in ongoing conversations about things that matter. Such notions reflect the view of Pinar et al. (1995) that curriculum (in its traditional sense) is dead. This reconceptualizing puts responsibility back on the professional teacher, it requires less political control of education, and it throws up challenges to curriculum developers and teachers – what might be the form of a future curriculum document and how might it be used in schools? While this reconceptualization moves control of curriculum from central agencies to teachers, and many teachers may be glad of this, one concern is how might it be accomplished in practice.

8. CURRICULA OF THE SCHOOLS: SPECIFIC SUBJECT AREAS

The following seven articles in this subsection of the *Handbook* are concerned with particular curriculum areas in schools. While many common influences impact on all school subjects, for example, the aims of education, dominant learning theories, assessment, culture, and the development process, each subject curriculum also has some unique features. One or two of the unique features from each article are briefly summarised here.

The curriculum part of this section begins with an article on *Civics and Citizenship* where the issues of its scope and status within the school curriculum are of particular interest. In the article on *Environmental Education and Education for Sustainable Development* the unique aspects that are highlighted relate to the lack of synchronicity between real world concerns and official curriculum documents. The next article focuses on *Literacy and Reading* and here the influence of a range of pedagogical models on reading literacy is considered. The following article, the *Mathematics Curricula*, discusses the influence of research and stresses the shift in emphasis from content to processes or from what mathematicians know to what they do. In the article on the *Science Curricula* the main points are about the tension in achieving the multiple purposes of learning science and the impact on policy and practice emerging from research, particularly research related to learning in science. The next article is concerned with *Supporting Curriculum Initiatives in Second Language Learning* and the issues here include the roles of assessment research. The final curriculum article is on *Education for Peace and International Understanding* and the message from this article is about how to live a peaceful life together in the Asia-Pacific region.

There are many other aspects of school subjects that could be discussed, and other school subjects are taught in many countries including technical (or technology) subjects, commercial subjects, health and physical education, religious and values education. The choice of the seven specific subjects is based partly on their importance in the region, and partly because the issues that arise within these subjects are similar to those that arise in subjects that have not been selected for specific attention.

9. BEYOND THE CURRICULA OF THE SCHOOLS

The programs provided by the schools serve as preparation for a life of work, leisure and further education. For most people in the Asia-Pacific region the completion of schooling, that unfortunately for some is all too brief and inadequate, leads directly to the world of work. The second subsection of this section on *Curriculum and Technical Education*, involves *Education and the World of Work*. The opening article in this subsection is concerned with planning of educational services that relate directly to the labour market (see *Planning Technical and Vocational Education and Training*) and addresses issues of supply and demand and the methods employed in human resource development planning in the Asia-Pacific region. The article that follows is concerned with *Vocational Education and Training in Asia*, and with the relative emphases on 'general human capital' through general education and 'specific human capital' through the provision of vocational and technical education. While both general and specific human capital contribute to economic growth, a balance must be maintained between general education and vocational education. The Pacific Island countries, however, face the problem that population growth exceeds the capacity of their education systems to provide adequate technical and vocational educational services to fill the key positions in both the government and private sectors (see *Pacific Island Issues in Vocational Education and Training*). The problems in the region are accentuated by the growing numbers of drop-outs who do not complete secondary schooling, while many who have gained higher levels of skill move from their home countries to obtain more lucrative employment in other lands. The problems of youth unemployment are addressed in the article that follows (see *Transition from School to Work in East Asia*). These problems have greatly increased during recent years as a consequence of the East Asian economic crisis of 1997–98. However, these problems cannot be solved by economic expansion alone, and both the public and private education systems must make contributions towards their resolution. Of particular significance is the contribution that can be made by employers in commercial and industrial enterprises making provision for the development of knowledge and skills through the conduct of courses within their organisations or by assisting employees through time-release and financial support to undertake further education and training (see *Enterprise Education in Australia and New Zealand*). While this concluding article to the section focuses on only two countries in the region, these countries are among the leading nations in the provision of lifelong educational programs and the article indicates the directions in which other nations might be expected to follow in future decades.

REFERENCES

Ainsworth, S., & Johnson, A. (2000). The TTA consultation documents on ITT: What no values? In D. Lawton, J. Cairn & R. Gardener (Eds.), *Education for Values: Morals, Ethics and Citizenship in*

Contemporary Teaching. London: Kogan Paul (forthcoming). (Cited in Mahony & Hextall, 2000, p. 51.)

Applebee, A. N. (1996). *Curriculum as Conversation: Transforming traditions of teaching and learning.* Chicago: University of Chicago Press.

Becker, J. P., & Shimada, S. (Eds.) (1997). *The Open-Ended Approach: A New Proposal for Teaching Mathematics.* Reston, VA: National Council of Teachers of Mathematics.

Begg, A., Davis, B., & Bramald, R. (2003). Obstacles to the dissemination of mathematics education research. In A. J. Bishop, M. A. Clements, C. Keital, J. Kilpatrick, and F. K. S. Leung (Eds.), *Second International Handbook of Mathematics Education.* Dordrecht: Kluwer Academic Publishers.

Boyer, E. L. (1990). *Scholarship Reconsidered: Priorities of the Professoriate.* Princeton, NJ: Carnegie Foundation for the Advancement of Teaching.

Broadfoot, P. (1999). *Assessment and Lifelong Learning.* Paper presented to British Education Research Association Annual Conference, University of Sussex. (Cited in Mahony & Hextall, 2000, p. 32.)

Brown, R. K. (1992). Max van Manen and pedagogical human science research. In W. F. Pinar & W. M. Reynolds (Eds.), *Understanding Curriculum as Phenomenolgical and Deconstructed Text* (pp. 44–63). New York: Teachers College Press.

Budge, D. (1997). In search of foreign correspondences. *Times Educational Supplement,* 5 December, p. 17 (Cited in Mahony & Hextall, 2000, p. 9.)

Clarkson, P., & Atweh, B (2001). Internationalisation and globalisation of mathematics education in higher education. In: M. A. Clements, H. H. Tairab & K. Y. Wong (Eds.), *Energising Science, Mathematics and Technical Education for All.* Brunei: Universiti Brunei Darussalam.

Goodson, I. (1989). 'Chariots of fire': Etymologies, epistemologies and the emergence of curriculum. In G. Milburn, I. Goodson & R. J. Clark (Eds.), *Re-Interpeting Curriculum Research: Images and Arguments* (pp. 13–25). East Sussex/London, ont: Falmer Press/Althouse Press.

Kemmis, S., with Fitzclarence, L. (1986). *Curriculum Theorising: Beyond Reproduction Theory.* Geelong vic: Deakin University.

Lee, K. C. (2002). *Knowledge for the New Century: How to Deal with its Challenge in the School Curriculum – the Singapore Approach.* Paper presented to International Symposium on Creation of Schools for the 21st century, National Institute for Educational Research, Tokyo 12 March 2002.

Lundgren, U. P. (1983). *Between Hope and Happening: Text and Context in Curriculum.* Geelong vic: Deakin University (Cited in Kemmis, 1986.)

Mahony, P., & Hextall, I. (2000). *Reconstructing Teaching.* London: Routledge/Falmer.

Miller, J. L. (1998). Curriculum reconceptualized: A personal and partial history. In W. F. Pinar (Ed.) (1999). *Contemporary Curriculum Discourses: Twenty Years of JCT* (pp. 498–499). New York: Peter Lang.

National Institute for Educational Research (1999). *An International Comparative Study of School Curriculum.* Tokyo: National Institute for Educational Research.

New Zealand Qualifications Authority (1995). *Quality Assurance for Degrees and Related Qualifications.* Wellington: New Zealand Qualifications Authority.

Pinar, W. F., Reynolds, W. M., Slattery, P., & Taubman, P. M. (1995). *Understanding Curriculum: An Introduction to the Study of Historical and Contemporary Curriculum Discourses.* New York: Counterpoints/Peter Lang.

Stenhouse, L. (1975). *An Introduction to Curriculum Research and Development.* London: Heinemann.

Stigler, J. W., & Hiebert, J. (1999). *The Teaching Gap: Best Ideas from the World's Teachers for Improving Education in the Classroom.* New York: The Free Press.

38

Civics and Citizenship

THOMAS KWAN-CHOI TSE
The Chinese University of Hong Kong, Hong Kong

1. INTRODUCTION

Civics and citizenship education, as their names suggest, is the cultural transmission and acquisition with regard to the notions of citizen and citizenship which take place within schools. Citizenship education can be viewed as a part of a broader phenomenon of political learning and political socialisation which is about the transmission and learning of political knowledge, attitudes, sociopolitical norms and values for the members of a political community. Citizenship, often taught as a component of the school curriculum, is distinctive in its deliberate, planned, and institutionalized form in the early stages of the education of the younger generation in a modern nation-state.

After outlining the basic concepts of citizenship education, this article aims to describe the pattern and development of the citizenship curricula in the Asia Pacific region in the post World War II era. The major focus is put on the changes in the 1990s. Some general trends are presented and key issues observed. These are illustrated with case studies and summaries of major research findings that had been conducted in the region. Finally, consideration will be given to issues for further studies and the future of citizenship education in the Asia-Pacific region.

2. SIGNIFICANCE OF CITIZENSHIP CURRICULUM STUDIES

Schools in all societies are educational as well as political establishments. The socialisation function of schools has been recognized by many scholars and educators, either in their discussion on the role of education in political development or in their studies of school curriculum. Citizenship education is generally treated as effective transmission of officially legitimate knowledge to school students. With the establishment of modern school system worldwide, every nation-state or government sought to convey its ideal of citizenship and nationhood within the school curricula. The content and orientation of citizenship education varies in time and space, depending on the features a particular political system. It could be about an obedient passive subject in a totalitarian state or an active participating citizen in a democratic polity. The role of citizenship curriculum as an effective medium of political culture transmission or political indoctrination remains debatable, but undoubtedly the curriculum is a manifestation of official political ideologies. Therefore, an inquiry of the citizenship curriculum could shed light on an understanding of the ideal or desirable nationhood and citizenship, as well as the relations between the individual and political community as defined by the concerned authorities. It is also interesting to see the divergent discourses and representations of citizenship and nationhood as revealed in different counties or education systems in the region.

The citizenship curriculum, in the form of syllabi, guidelines and textbooks, covers and defines the objectives, goals and topics for teaching and learning, and underscores the basic orientation of political culture. The syllabuses and textbooks not only provide political knowledge, but also define the normative expectations, appropriate attitudes, values and behaviour of an ideal citizen. As such, the treatment of topics and contents in the syllabuses and textbooks can be viewed as the expression of these political and cultural norms. From a critical perspective, the curricula and textbooks can be used as central objects of an ideological critique (Tse, 2000).

To a certain extent, change in citizenship curriculum and policy can be viewed as an indicator for tracking socio-political transition of a particular country. The introduction of new curricula and textbooks and change in citizenship education often imply a re-evaluation or rejection of the past, a replacement of old political and social ideologies, and a re-framing of the national problem. This makes citizenship education a fascinating field for studying the relations between education and politics, as well as the change of political ideologies. Such study can be used to illustrate how education in transition mirrors a nation in transition. For example, in Mongolia, education in socialist times mainly facilitated conformity, and in turn, ensured the achievements of national goals in a centrally-planned system (Innes-Brown, 2001). Within the region there has been a shift from collectivism to individualism in recent years. Now more emphasis is put on enabling individuals to achieve personal goals. Also, for many educators and government officials, how to prepare students for citizenship and make citizenship education relevant to political transitions and reforms in their countries are significant educational and political concerns.

3. CONTENTS, CONTEXTS AND DEVELOPMENT

3.1. *Multidimensionality of Citizenship*

At the core of citizenship education is the idea of 'citizenship'. Citizenship basically refers to the legal status of a full membership of a modern nation-state and the associated rights and obligations (Heater, 1990). Such membership confers equal status, with respect to rights and duties, with all other members of the state. In addition, citizenship also signifies both an identity and a virtue (i.e. character traits or desirable qualities of a person). In educational terms, therefore, it requires cognitive, affective and skills learning leading each individual student to understand and use the status, and to behave in citizenly manner. Generally speaking, the content of citizenship education is very wide-ranging, spanning from interpersonal to international relations. With the aims of imparting the knowledge, values, attitudes, and group identifications necessary for a political community as well as its members, it usually includes (a) knowledge of the history and structure of political institutions at both the national and local levels, (b) positive attitudes toward the nation and political authority, (c) fundamental socio-political beliefs and values, (d) obedience to laws and social norms, as well as (e) a sense of political efficacy and both interest in and skills concerning political participation. In recent years, new emphases are on human rights, multiculturalism, and global citizenship or education for international understanding. Divergent conceptions of citizenship push toward a more diffused and ever-expanding scope of citizenship education, thus making the civics curriculum almost like a hotchpotch.

3.2. Changing Contexts of Citizenship Education in the Asia-Pacific Region

The expansion of nation-states over the past several centuries has led to an emphasis on public education and citizenship education worldwide (Meyer, Kamens, & Benavot, 1992). Citizenship is increasingly expected to be taught in formal lessons and has become an increasingly significant part of the school curriculum. States around the world have focused attention on using the school curriculum as a medium for transmitting political culture to the younger generation, with the social subjects like History, Civics and Social Studies officially designed to acquaint students with nationalistic values and particular political ideologies. The appearance of citizenship education in the Asia-Pacific region is a very recent phenomenon, mainly an outcome of colonialism which brought the Western education system as well as nationalism into the region.

In the former colonial period, citizenship education in the region was characterised by alienation and depoliticisation (Carnoy, 1974; Altbach & Kelly, 1991). Colonial education, including its curriculum, is accused of disseminating cultural imperialism and sustaining the colonial rule over indigenous people. For example, civic education in Hong Kong and Macau from the 1950s to early 1980s was in a state of poverty and barely visible, exhibiting strong a-political and a-nationalistic features (Tse, 1999).

For many places in the region, the second period of civic education was triggered by decolonisation and nation independence. With the retreat of colonialism, many former colonies inherited a modernized polity as well as a plural society which was ethnically divisive in terms of religion, languages, political loyalty and ideological orientations. These circumstances prompted the need for establishing a national education system and the adoption and development of nationalistic education – a common concern to many new nation-states.

Citizenship education thus becomes the social cement of national identity to foster unity and commonalities among a population undermined by economic, ethnic and political cleavages.

With the advent of the third wave of democratisation since the 1970s, and the accelerated globalisation in the 1980s, civic education has become a hot topic and elevated over the last decade to the academic and official agenda of many countries. Accordingly many education systems have striven to develop educational policies and school curricula to promote citizenship. This has been achieved through either revising the existing syllabi or introducing new civic subjects. The increased focus on the promotion of citizenship has been paralleled with a remarkable resurgence in academic discussion and research regarding citizenship education in the region, notably by the works found in Kennedy (1997), Ichilov (1998), Cogan and Derricott (1998), and Torney-Purta et al. (1999), as well as some special issues on civics and values education in the region published by *The International Journal of Social Education* (1999), *Asia Pacific Journal of Education* (2000), and *International Journal of Educational Research* (2001). Also, regional research centres have been set up in various tertiary institutions in the region, most notably the Centre for Citizenship Education at Hong Kong Institute of Education in Hong Kong, and the Centre for Research and Teaching in Civics, University of Sydney in Australia. Besides, the Asia-Pacific experiences have captured the attention and interests of some Western countries. For example, since 1996, the Qualifications and Curriculum Authority in England has undertaken an international review of curriculum and assessment frameworks (known as *INCA*) (Kerr, 1999), which currently includes national archives of 18 education systems in the developed countries, among them five countries are in the Asia-Pacific Rim (Australia, Japan, Republic of Korea, New Zealand and Singapore).

3.3. *The Development of Civics and Social Studies Curricula*

Adopting a neo-institutionalist perspective and through a series of cross-national and longitudinal studies, Meyer and his colleagues (Cha, et al., 1988; Wong, 1989, 1991; Meyer, Kamens, & Benavot, 1992) examine how social science and civics instruction has evolved in public education. They find that countries frequently adopt social science curricula at primary level independent of local conditions, hence producing a homogeneity of curricula over time and national boundaries. This trend was particularly evident after World War II when there was a shift from traditional subjects like history and geography to a new integrated subject called 'social studies'. Under the extensive influence of the American social studies movement, the American invention of social studies in 1916 became the dominant form of social studies and citizenship education in other regions afterwards. It is noted that instruction in history, geography and civics have declined while social studies has increased over the period between 1945–1986. While the overall proportion of the social science curriculum area remains constant over time, individual subject components within this area have evolved quite differently from one another. As for the Asian countries, the overall social science curriculum area has tended to occupy 8.75 per cent of the total instruction time for the aforementioned period. While there was a dramatic decline in the teaching of history and geography, the proportions for civics and social studies have increased in the later period. Another striking feature was that from 1945 to 1986, there was a decline in the instruction time for civics worldwide but not in Asia. With a shift to the teaching of civics as an integrated subject at primary level, the Asian school curricula also reflect a similar conception of individual and society as the American model.

On the other hand, inheriting the British legacy and more latterly influenced by the United States, the Australasian education systems have taken a different path from their Asian counterparts.

4. KEY ISSUES

Since civic education embodies elements such as membership, entitlements, identity and virtues, this multi-dimensionality and complexity gives rise to a wide range of issues.

4.1. Nationalism and its Challenges

A key dimension of citizenship education is its geographic level or scope of community. Although nation-state is the backdrop of citizenship and nationalism is the basis of citizenship education, there is an immanent tension between localism, nationalism, and trans-nationalism (Bray & Lee, 2001). It is a thorny issue for many multi-national states or multi-ethnic nations, particularly those new-born nation-states in the region in the post-colonial period.

In order to maintain a unified nation-state, some core values, national heritage and cultural traditions were defined, selected and invented to present an imagined community. For many nations, their citizenship education curricula exhibit a strong nationalist flavour. An overriding emphasis is put on an understanding and appreciation of the country's history and efforts of building a common national identity, inculcating a spirit of patriotism, national consciousness and love towards the country, and feeling of pride in being a member of the nation or state. With the tendency to override localism in favour of the promotion of nationalistic education, these cultural, historical and ethnic commonalities were often achieved at the expense of the subordination of minorities and ethnic groups. For example, in Taiwan, traditional school curricula and textbooks legitimized the dominant national Chinese cultural identity and unity without considering specific perspectives and voices of different gender, cultural and ethnic groups.

But the tension between nationalism versus localism is now salient for those nations that are experiencing liberalisation and democratisation. In recent years, with the notion of multiculturalism, more ethnic groups within the nation are becoming active to assert their own identities. As a result state governments are facing a dilemma of how to recognize and accommodate differences and diversity as well as to maintain unity and identity.

Furthermore, nationalistic education is now encountering another challenging force – globalisation. Increasing global interdependence and international exchange require the national curriculum to foster the essential abilities and skills necessary for living in a global village, for example, addressing the environmental and economic concerns at a global level. Many countries put more curricular emphasis on developing in children an attitude of respect for the cultures and histories of other countries, as well as an increased understanding of the international community. In a study of the changing content of civic education throughout the world from 1955 to 1995, Rauner (1998, 1999) shows that there has been a shift of emphasis of topical coverage from national citizenship to global citizenship in that period. The study also found that wealthy countries such as Hong Kong, Japan, New Zealand, and Singapore were more likely to emphasise global civics content.

Nowadays, the most powerful challenges to nationality education are multi-culturalism and global citizenship and the issues of post-national or trans-national identity arise. With the advent of increasing internationalisation or globalisation, a dilemma for many governments is how to maintain their own identity in the tide of globalisation. There are worries about loss of Asian values such as collectivism and family values and of a person's distinctive identity. Paradoxically, an increase in global citizenship has developed hand in hand with an emphasis on national culture and traditions. When facing globalisation and international competition, many states advocate for an increase in international understanding on the one hand, and reinforce nationality education on the other hand. Countries like Japan, South Korea, Singapore and Thailand, for example, have all tried to preserve their distinct cultural heritage and traditions to counter the tide of globalisation (*The International Journal of Social Education*, 1999). However, balancing national and international identities, while at the same time reconciling identity and differences, remains a thorny issue for many states.

4.2. The Status Problem: Opportunities and Threats

As mentioned in Section 3.3, social science instruction in the modern school curriculum has been institutionalized since the beginning of the twentieth century. Even for Islamic counties with a strong religious tradition, the latest addition of citizenship in the curriculum also reflects the perceptions of its increased importance. For example, in Malaysia, along with Islamic religious studies, the government has introduced moral education to non-Muslim pupils.

Despite the fact that citizenship is highly institutionalized in the school curricula of many places and the claims made by many governments in recent years of its overriding importance, the subject itself still experiences a problematic subject identity and it is struggling to attain independence and a legitimate place within the curriculum. The marginal status and ambivalent position of citizenship in the school curricula remain a problem unsolved. Unlike other well-established subject areas like languages and mathematics, citizenship education suffers from more diffuse, uncertain, and ever-changing boundaries. In many countries, citizenship is still taught together with moral education and religious education. For the countries that are not fully secularized, religious doctrine is a still vital part of citizenship education. Many governments like Hong Kong and Macau also define civic education in the broadest sense, and treat it as a mixture of moral, political and lifeskills education (Tse, 1999).

Further, citizenship education is often constrained by an over-crowded curriculum which make its struggles for status even more difficult. In most instances, citizenship is not an independent subject within the school curriculum but is embedded within existing humanistic subjects or integrated social subjects. History, for example, is still a common vehicle for teaching civics within the existing school curriculum. At higher levels of schooling, citizenship education is usually an optional subject rather than a compulsory component of the curriculum.

The over-crowded curriculum, and the competing priorities of many subjects, has not helped to improve the perceived value of learning civics. School administrators, teachers and students accord citizenship a low priority in teaching and learning in a highly academic and competitive education system because it is a non-examination subject. The problem of scholarship versus citizenship is quite common in many examination-oriented countries in East Asia, particularly when teaching and learning is led by the university entrance examinations. Teachers and students, anxious about the upcoming university entrance examinations, tend to focus only on those subjects that compose the main part of the examinations. It is also not uncommon to find that in the region, teachers receive little training, either in their pre-service or in-service programs to deal with the content related to citizenship. Even more, many teachers currently do not adequately teach civics and citizenship in their classrooms.

The recent large-scale curriculum reforms in the region have significant implications for the future status of citizenship education, especially with measures such as a further integration of subjects (subject re-groupings), a reduction of instructional hours, and making civic education more school-based, inter-disciplinary, and comprehensive. For example, countries like Australia, New Zealand, Taiwan and Hong Kong have subsequently re-classified the existing subjects into certain key learning areas (*Asia Pacific Journal of Education*, 2000). With the redrawing of the subject boundaries, it is uncertain whether it will in effect weaken or elevate the status of citizenship education.

4.3. *Recent Reforms in Pedagogy and Assessment*

Another salient trend of curriculum reform in citizenship education lies in changes of pedagogy and assessment. With the influence of child-centred educational philosophies and the Piagetian-Kohlbergian theory of cognitive and moral development curriculum planners in the region are attaching more importance to the nature of children's capacities as well as to their natural creativity. They also are placing more emphasis on stimulating children's willingness to learn, and enabling each child to give full play to his or her individuality. Starting from the early 1980s, there has been a promotion of a wide variety of new teaching strategies similar to those emphasized in American schools: experiential learning, individualised instruction, and child-centered approaches.

Educators also are trying to bridge the gap between cognition and action. With the changing curricular emphasis on developing the desirable attitudes and competencies of citizenry like democratic-minded, open-minded, tolerance, critical thinking, inquiry-minded, and action-oriented, there has also been changing emphases in teaching and assessment, most notably a switch from knowledge-based towards value-oriented and skills-based.

Accordingly, a more progressive vision of citizenship education is witnessed in many recent curriculum reform initiatives: the most remarkable is the introduction of an issue-based approach and discussion of controversial issues. This is to suggest that citizenship education is an exploration of issues together with the students rather than a one-way transmission of knowledge and values. The aim of such an approach is to enhance students' abilities to discuss, reason, make decisions and think critically; so that they can approach an issue from different perspectives, and reflect on their own values and beliefs. Students are also encouraged to be actively involved in handling information in response to the issues discussed. In addition, to reduce the widespread practices of textbook-centred instruction, participation is highlighted as another important element in civic education. Participatory learning activities include activities such as preparing newspaper cuttings, analysis of current affairs, role plays, field visits and case studies.

More attention is also paid to the classroom environment which is intended to provide direct civics experiences to students and so contribute to the more effective implementation of civic education. Hence, teachers are advised to build up an open and supportive atmosphere of mutual respect and a democratic environment for teaching controversial issues and for conducting a variety of learning activities. In addition, extra-curricular activities are highlighted as a significant complement to classroom teaching. Most common suggestions are volunteering and participation in social services and affairs to enhance civic learning.

With respect to assessment, more and more syllabi assert the importance of formative and diversified assessment which includes the evaluation of values and attitudes. The main objectives of school civic education today are not just to inculcate knowledge but also to help students in the development of attitudes, values and competence, as well as their participation in relevant activities. It is argued that the evaluation of students' learning outcomes needs to be a continuing process. In addition to traditional objective tests used to assess students' learning outcomes in terms of knowledge acquired, a number of evaluation instruments aiming at assessing students' attitudes and skills have been developed, for example, personal portfolios, projects and essay writing.

4.4. *Local, National and International Influences on Curriculum*

Curricular change is the complex interaction of endogenous and exogenous forces at many levels. One salient trend observed in the region is that curricular changes often follow societal changes at large. The most eye-catching cases are the post-communist transitions brought by liberalisation and democratisation since 1991 (e.g., Russia, five newly independent central Asian countries and Mongolia, see Torney-Purta et al., 1999; Fägerlind & Kanaev, 2000; Innes-Brown, 2001), and the post-colonial transitions and change of sovereignty (e.g., Hong Kong and Macau in the late-1990s, see Tse, 1999). Also, curricular change is under the influence of political leadership (e.g., the promotion of democratic citizenship education in Australia, see Print, 2000).

A curriculum is a selection of culture, which is heavily affected by the cultural context in which it is embedded. The distinct cultural and historical contexts in the region in which there are strong traditions of moral education or religious influence mean that, many societies are not as fully secularised as the ones in the West. Further, there exist close and sometimes competing relations among civics, moral education, and religious education in most countries in the region. For example, countries in the Confucian heritage culture highlight moral education whereas Islamic societies place more emphasis on religious education (Cha et al., 1988). Similarly, in Indonesia, Islamic ideals dominate much of the Indonesian curriculum and its instruction. Also, the strong tradition of collectivism evident in the civic curricula may come from either religion (Islam), cultural tradition (Confucian and familial ethics), or political ideologies (Marxism-Leninism). In many Asian countries, the goals and objectives of civic curricula are heavily derived from the principles of constitution, national philosophies or cultural traditions (for example, *RUKUNEGARA* in Malaysia, the *Pancasila* (the five basic principles of Indonesian society) in Indonesia, Mao Ze-dong's Thought and Deng Xiao-ping's ideas in mainland China, and Dr Sun Yat-sen's three principles of people in Taiwan).

Apart from macro socio-political change as a catalyst, and the crucial influence of cultural traditions, the process of curricular change is also mediated by the state-society relations embedded in a particular historical context. For example, in Singapore, the so called 'strong state-weak civil society relation' is also fully reflected in its citizenship education program. The values espoused by the state reinforce the paternalistic relations between government and people. As for the case of Macau, the role of the state in citizenship education is not only influenced by the external factors of decolonisation and national reintegration, but is also conditioned and constrained by the state capacity, autonomy and initiative vis-à-vis the civil society. Hence, the official curriculum did not appear until 1995, and it is still out of reach to the large private school sector in the territory. Macau as a weak state demonstrates the significance of state strength in constructing its citizenship education program (Tse, 2001).

The disputes over the civics curriculum in Taiwan are vivid examples of the power dynamics of local groups. Beginning from 1987 onwards, Taiwan faced the challenge of shifting from being an authoritarian state to a democratic one. Following the changes in social conditions has been a radical curriculum reform and a transformation of the citizenship curriculum. However, in the process of constructing Taiwanese identity through indigenisation, the so called 'identity politics' flourished and different groups fought over the representation of the curriculum. Ethnic culture, gender issues and indigenous culture were politically and culturally subtle factors in the process of identity construction (Mao, 1997).

Another significant change in recent years is the method of curriculum planning. Many nations have relaxed the central control of curriculum and instructional materials. For the large education systems like China and Russia, there has been a call for decentralisation and regionalisation of curriculum development and no longer is one single curriculum with textbook used for the entire country. The advocacy of school-based curricula and the decentralisation of curriculum decision-making means more discretion is allowed to schools and frontline teachers. So the practices of civics curriculum within a single country is becoming more diverse and uncertain in the future.

Curricular change is also complicated by external forces. The constant influence of external forces is evident in the academic exchanges and fertilisation of curriculum reforms across the countries within the region. In the post World War II era, two international organisations: the civics education community in the United States and UNESCO, have been central to the worldwide development and dissemination of citizenship education (Rauner, 1998, 1999). As an early citizenship education leader, the United States was more influential from 1955 to 1965, and UNESCO more influential from 1985 to 1995. Their influence was exercised through their organisational linkages in the first place and the establishment of worldwide norms afterwards. In the earlier period, with the cold war configuration and the establishment of American hegemony in the region, many countries modelled on the United States pattern and introduced social studies into their primary schools.

External forces still play an important part in the civics curriculum today. For example, CIVITAS, an international consortium for civic education based in the United States, was set up in 1995 with the aims to strengthen informed and responsible citizenship education in new and established democracies around the world. Under CIVITAS, an international curriculum development project called Comparative Lessons For Democracy (CLD) has been developed for educators in several post-communist countries to implement effective civic education. This project offers civic education leaders from these places opportunities to learn from, and assist each other, in improving education for democracy in their respective nations. In addition, CIVITAS organised the first major conference on civic education in the Asia-Pacific region in Kuala Lumpur in 1998. With 120 attendees from 15 countries in the region, together with over a dozen of their counterparts from around the world, the conference provided an occasion for civic educators, government officials and representatives of non-governmental organisations in the region to exchange ideas and experiences with one another, and to establish a regional network of civic educators.

5. KEY RESEARCH QUESTIONS

Probably due to language barriers and an uneven development of academic enterprises in the region, there is limited shared knowledge about citizenship education (available in English) accumulated in the different parts of the region. In particular, there is relatively little knowledge about many Islamic countries and the countries that emerged from the former Soviet Union (a recent review can be found in Fägerlind & Kanaev, 2000), let alone many small states in the Pacific Ocean.

Over the years, the major focus of civics curriculum research studies has been on the content of the curriculum, but this has left the questions of origins, processes and effects of the civics curriculum relatively unexplored. In the future, there are a number of key issues for further research (see also, Meyer & Kamens, 1992). There is a need to complement case studies of specific places and periods with comparative studies. The issues of curricular change and stability over time was well-addressed with a longitudinal and cross-national approach launched by Meyer's research group. This valuable series of studies provided a very good overview of the patterns of change over time, and the general variations across countries, as well as suggesting some telling explanations for these patterns. These studies also serve to correct the conclusion of previous single case studies which were less sensitive to variations between countries and types of countries. Furthermore, when sketching the big picture, Meyer's group brought the external forces and international factors into focus, which have long been neglected.

However, with a focus on the worldwide and homogenous character of the curriculum, this approach placed an undue emphasis on the role of the wider world environment in structuring national curricula. In order to describe and explain the pattern of curriculum and the causes of these changes, equal attention needs to be paid to both external and local factors at work at several levels. Such a comparative study would need to draw attention to both local diversity and generalised patterns. It is crucial and interesting to exhibit the common as well as peculiar interpretations of citizenship and nationhood in different countries. Also, when explaining the patterns of internationalisation and standardisation, that is, how do worldwide changes reach into national curricular policy, there is a need for substantial case studies to illustrate the dynamics of external forces in the creation of national curricula, particularly curricular decision making in those countries responding to developments in countries which are initiating change. Overall, the mechanisms of curricular planning and development in many countries remains a black box yet to be opened.

Another line of research worth taking is the issue of implementation of civics curriculum at school and classroom levels. The civics courses in many countries within Asia are taught primarily in a rote learning style, a method designed to prepare students for high school and university entrance examinations. This is in contrast to the stated purpose of civics education, which is to encourage adolescent students to think in a systemic and critical way, as well as to encourage participation in public life and develop a sense of global awareness. Accordingly, reforms in curriculum, pedagogy and assessment have been endeavouring to improve a currently ill-informed citizenry. However, whether these measures can produce any effect remains questionable. A common observation is that classroom teaching has changed little despite advocacy for years (Morris & Cogan, 2001). That is, there appear to be big contrasts between the intended curriculum and the actual one implemented in classrooms. To understand how curricular policy is translated into practices across countries, detailed studies of the linkages between official curricula and classroom practice are needed. Recently, increasing attention has been paid to the nature and impact of the implemented curriculum (*International Journal of Educational Research*, 2001). More such studies are needed to explore the dynamics of classroom teaching and students' learning of civics in future.

Finally, there are on-going controversies, debates and changes in citizenship and nationalism within the political realm and the academic circle. The forms and substances of citizenship in general, and civics in particular, are subject to greater changes in the days to come. These changes will open many new issues for further studies, such as, for example, the balance between rights and duties, global citizenship, human rights, multi-culturalism, and Asian values.

6. THE LIMITS AND POSSIBILITIES OF THE CURRICULUM

For years, citizenship education has been assigned with high expectations with respect to a wide variety of political objectives. In many countries in the region, citizenship education is now treated as the vehicle of democratic transformation or consolidation. Obviously civics curriculum can not do it alone. A truly democratic citizenship education is not possible without a corresponding change in the social milieu. In fact, given the prevalence of non-democratic polities in many parts of the Region, the political realities dictate that most citizenship education is oriented towards a good and compliant citizen, instead of education for genuine democracy and social transformation. Another potential danger of citizenship education is that it becomes very utilitarian and instrumental, either in terms of political goals or economic considerations (e.g., disseminating national propaganda and developing human resources in a global competitive world), and so runs the risk of fulfilling the political and economic imperatives instead of human needs. Most important, the major approach to citizenship education in many countries is still in the mode of citizenship transmission (Giroux, 1983). Civics instruction remains primarily teacher-centered and the content easily becomes irrelevant and boring to many students. Despite the current interest in reforming citizenship education, whether it will be successfully adopted and institutionalised within classroom practices, and in turn, contributes to a fully-developed citizenry, remains to be seen.

REFERENCES

Altbach, P. G., & Kelly, G. P. (Eds.) (1991). *Education and the colonial experience* (2nd revised ed). New York: Advent Books.

The Archive of the International Review of Curriculum and Assessment Frameworks Project (INCA). England: Qualifications and Curriculum Authority and the National Foundation for Educational Research. Available at http://www.inca.org.uk/

Asia Pacific Journal of Education (2000), *20*(1), 7–104.

Bray, M., & Lee, W. O. (2001). Education and political transitions in East Asia: Diversity and commonality. In M. Bray & W. O. Lee (Eds.), *Education and Political Transition: Themes and Experiences in East Asia.* (2nd ed., pp. 1–18). Hong Kong: Comparative Education Research Centre, The University of Hong Kong.

Carnoy, M. (1974). *Education as Cultural Imperialism.* New York: David McKay.

Cha, Y. K., Wong, S. Y., & Meyer, J. (1988). Values education in the curriculum: Some comparative empirical data. In W. K. Cummings, S. Gopinathan & Y. Tomoda (Eds.), *The Revival of Values Education in Asia and the West* (pp. 11–28). London: Pergamon Press.

Cogan, J., & Derricott, R. (Eds.) (1998). *Citizenship for the 21st century: An International Perspective on Education.* London: Kogan Page.

Fägerlind, I. E., & Kanaev, A. (2000). Redefining citizenship education in the Central Asian countries. *Educational Practice and Theory, 22*(1), 95–113.

Giroux, H. (1983). *Theory and Resistance in Education: A Pedagogy for the Politics of the Opposition.* New York: Bergin & Garvey.

Heater, D. B. (1990). *Citizenship: The Civic Ideal in World History, Politics, and Education.* London: Longman.

Ichilov, O. (Ed.), *Citizenship and Citizenship Education in a Changing World.* London: Woburn Press.

Innes-Brown, M. (2001). Democracy, education and reform in Mongolia: Transition to a new order. In M. Bray & W. O. Lee (Eds.), *Education and Political Transition: Themes and Experiences in East Asia* (2nd ed., pp. 77–99). Hong Kong: Comparative Education Research Centre, The University of Hong Kong.

International Journal of Educational Research (2001). *35*(1), 1–123.

The International Journal of Social Education (1999). *14*(1), 1–79.

Kennedy, K. (Ed.) (1997). *Citizenship Education and the Modern State.* London: Falmer Press.

Kerr, D. (1999). *Citizenship Education: An International Perspective.* London: Qualifications and Curriculum Authority.

Mao, C. J. (1997). *Constructing a Taiwanese Identity: The Making and Practice of Indigenization Curriculum.* Unpublished doctoral dissertation, University of Wisconsin (Madison).

Meyer, J. W., Kamens, D. H., & Benavot, A. (1992). *School Knowledge for the Masses: World Models and National Primary Curricular Categories in the Twentieth Century.* London: Falmer Press.

Meyer, J., & Kamens, D. H. (1992). Conclusion: Accounting for a world curriculum, In J. W. Meyer et al. (Eds.), *School Knowledge for the Masses: World Models and National Primary Curricular Categories in the Twentieth Century* (pp. 176–179). London: Falmer Press.

Morris, P., & Cogan, J. (2001). A comparative overview: Civic education across six societies. *International Journal of Educational Research, 35*(1), 109–123.

Print, M. (2000). Curriculum policy, values and changes in civics education in Australia. *Asia Pacific Journal of Education, 20*(1), 21–35.

Rauner, M. H. (1998). *The Worldwide Globalization of Civics Education Topics from 1955 to 1995.* Unpublished doctoral dissertation, Stanford University.

Rauner, M. H. (1999). UNESCO as an organizational carrier of civics education information. *International Journal of Educational Development, 19*(1), 91–100.

Torney-Purta, J. V., Schwille, J., & Amadeo, J.-A. (1999). *Civic Education Across Countries: Twenty-four National Case Studies from the IEA Civic Education Project.* Amsterdam: IEA Secretariat.

Tse, K. C. (1999). Civic and political education. In M. Bray & R. Koo (Eds.), *Education and Society in Hong Kong and Macau: Comparative Perspectives on Continuity and Change* (pp. 151–169). Hong Kong: Comparative Education Research Centre, The University of Hong Kong.

Tse, K. C. (2000). Deformed citizenship: A critique of the junior secondary economic and public affairs syllabus and textbooks in Hong Kong. *Pedagogy, Culture and Society, 8*(1), 93–110.

Tse, K. C. (2001). Society and citizenship education in transition: The case of Macau. *International Journal of Educational Development, 21*(4), 305–314.

Wong, S. Y. (1989). *The Evolution and Organization of the Social Science Curriculum: A Cross-national Study, 1900–1986.* Unpublished doctoral dissertation, Stanford University.

Wong, S. Y. (1991). The evolution of Social Science instruction, 1900–86: A cross-national study. *Sociology of Education, 64*(1), 33–47.

39

Environmental Education and Education for Sustainable Development*

JOHN FIEN and DEBBIE HECK
Griffith University, Brisbane, Australia

1. INTRODUCTION

This article outlines trends towards education for a sustainable future in the Asia-Pacific region. The paper begins with an overview of the present state of the natural and social environment in the Asia-Pacific region. This is followed by an account and examples of educational responses to the challenges of sustainable development. The main theme developed here is that countries and organisations in the region responded well to the first phase of challenges of sustainable development. Examples of innovative ways in which this has been done are provided to illustrate this. However, the analysis of these trends, which is presented in the next section of the article, indicates that these innovations may represent a case of 'innovation without change' as there is little evidence in the region of meaningful change in young people's lives or in the broad reorientation of education practices, systems and structures that is necessary for education to support the processes of sustainable development at national or regional levels. In this article, this wider reorientation of education is called the second phase of education for a sustainable future. The article concludes with a brief case study of one project in the region which is using teacher education as a starting point to provide the necessary capacity development needed to support this second phase of educational reform.

2. THE STATE OF THE REGION

Despite the formulation of many international and national policies for sustainable development in recent years, the global picture is not encouraging. The state

---

* Professor Osamu Abe (University of Saitama and Director of the Environmental Education Project of the Institute of Global Environmental Strategies) and Dr Bishnu Bhandari, (Research Officer, Environmental Education Project of the Institute of Global Environmental Strategies) provided valuable assistance on an earlier draft of this chapter.

of the planet and the lives of the people who call it home have been exhaustively documented by such bodies as the United Nations Development Programme (2000), the United Nations Environment Program (UNEP, 1999), the World Bank (2000), the World Resources Institute (2000), the World Watch Institute (1999), and the World Wide Fund for Nature (1999). Conditions in Asia and the Pacific are also becoming increasingly well-documented, as seen in reports of the World Bank (1993) and the Asian Development Bank (1997). These publications paint a generally bleak picture of a descending spiral of unsustainable development.

The social and economic costs of environmental degradation in the region are very high. This descending spiral of environmental decline and lost social and economic opportunities is reflected in the broad patterns of living conditions in the Asia-Pacific region. Despite being home to some of the world's largest and fastest growing economies, the Asia-Pacific region is also one of great poverty. The acute impact of the 1997 economic collapse in the region is evidence of the precarious nature of the last three decades of development efforts. Thus, the Asia-Pacific region is home to over two-thirds of the world's poor and an equal percentage lack basic literacy. Population figures have doubled over the past 40 years and are still on the increase, and the environmental and social effects of such numbers are beginning to take their toll.

3. EDUCATIONAL RESPONSES

Education has been identified as a critical way of addressing this range of concerns in the Asia-Pacific region. Thus, many countries in the region can point to ways in which their education systems have been responding to the challenges posed by the descending spiral of unsustainable development. Many of their initiatives preceded the Earth Summit and are the result of the active International Environmental Education Programme led by UNESCO and the United Nations Environment Programme (UNEP) in the region. After the 1977 Inter-governmental Conference on Environmental Education in Tbilisi, follow-up workshops were held in Asia in 1980 and 1997. These provided for a range of catalytic activities, including: the exchange of information among institutions, the collection and dissemination of information, publication of materials for use in curriculum development and teacher education, study-visits and attachment programs, demonstration projects, and the development of a pool of experienced resource persons to provide consultancy services to the member countries (Gregario, 1993). The impacts of this and related programs may be seen in the relatively high adoption of forms of environmental education in schools across the region. These include: (a) the development of curriculum guidelines and new teaching materials, (b) the revision of syllabuses to infuse an environmental perspective, (c) the adoption of whole-school approaches to curriculum planning for environmental education, and (d) the establishment of specialised environmental education centres.

During the 1990s, efforts were made to integrate the concept of sustainable development into these initiatives. The basic thrust for this began with the Earth Summit and was further encouraged by the Third Ministerial Conference on Environment and Development in Asia and the Pacific that was held in 1995 under the auspices of United Nations Economic and Social Commission for Asia and the Pacific (ESCAP). This meeting decided upon a five year regional Action Programme for environmentally sound and sustainable development in the region and subsequently a number of initiatives were introduced. For example, the UNESCO Asia-Pacific Programme of Education for All (APPEAL) focuses on primary education and eradicating illiteracy in the region as a foundation for social and economic development. UNICEF also plays a major role in this goal. The UNESCO Asia-Pacific Programme of Educational Innovation for Development (APEiD) is active in the areas of secondary education reform, education for girls, pavement dwellers and refugees, vocational education and higher education, including teacher education. These important elements in the reorientation of mainstream education towards a sustainable future were synthesised at a UNESCO-ACEID conference on Educational Innovation for Sustainable Development which further developed this important area of the curriculum (Maclean, 1997). UNEP supports the development of capacity to prepare and teach courses on sustainable development issues in the region's universities through its Network for Environmental Training at Tertiary Level in Asia (NETTLAP).

The Association for South East Asian Nations (ASEAN) and the Asia Pacific Economic Cooperation (APEC) have small information, training, and network programs to support member countries while the South Pacific Regional Environment Programme (SPREP) has prepared a draft *Action Strategy for Environmental Education and Training in the Pacific Region 1999–2003* (SPREP, 1998). Several international NGOs are also active in supporting education strategies for sustainable development in the region. For example, IUCN supports the South and South-east Asia Network for Environmental Education (SASEANEE) while World Wide Fund for Nature has initiated a *South Asia regional Cooperation Programme Framework* as part of the WWF Global Priorities to capacity building for managing natural resources. The Asia-Pacific Bureau of Adult Education (ASPBAE) has developed a framework for environmental adult education in the region in order to promote the principles of the *Treaty on Environmental Education for Sustainable Societies and Global Responsibility* endorsed at the NGO Global Forum at the Earth Summit in 1992. Regional conferences of the Asia Environmental Council (AEC) and the Asia-Pacific NGO Environmental Conference (APNEC) have also emphasised the importance of education in creating sustainable societies. The Environment Agency of Japan and the newly formed Institute for Global Environmental Strategies (IGES) are also supporting cooperative regional efforts to promote sustainable development through education. As a result of inititatives such as these, many examples of innovative practice may be found across the region.

The examples in Table 1 are presented in alphabetical order of country name and illustrate the range of innovations that may be found in the region.

4. AN ANALYSIS

This overview of region-wide efforts to promote sustainable development through education indicates that the emphasis thus far has been upon what might be described as the first phase of educational reform that followed the Earth Summit, namely, the reformulation of environmental education to include issues of sustainable development. This was not a difficult task as the concept of 'environment' in the region has always included the human element. In many cultures, nature is seen as a mother or as a teacher and, as life in most Asian societies remains predominantly rural and organised around the seasons, people can easily see that the quality of their lives is related to the sustainability of the natural world. With air and water pollution being the major causes of infant mortality in the region, environmental education guidelines could readily integrate the rhetoric of sustainable development. However, the wider reorientation of educational practices, systems and structures to support sustainability that is emerging as the second phase of educational reform since the Earth Summit is yet to be seen in the region.

As a result, several outstanding issues and problems remain. In most countries in the region, for example, most initiatives have remained embedded within pre-Earth Summit conceptions of environmental education. These tend to favour nature conservation, especially through the study of science and geography, rather than the multi-disciplinary bases of sustainable development and the holistic imperatives that are served by the emerging concept of education for sustainable futures. Consequently, most initiatives to promote environmental education in the Asia-Pacific have tended to come from Ministries of Environment, Agriculture or Natural Resources rather than Ministries of Education. While welcome, the efforts of such ministries tend to be directed to specific environmental issues rather than a whole-of-government commitment to sustainability. They also tend to concentrate upon information and awareness-raising campaigns directed at individual behavioural change rather than broader educational or sustainability goals. Indeed, sustainable development is not well understood as a concept outside of limited environmental circles in most countries Several countries in the region also still lack national policies or guidelines for environmental education. The result of this set of problems has been a lack of coherence and long term planning for educational approaches to sustainable development. Indeed, even in those countries that do have environmental education policies, very few have been revised to incorporate the broad social, economic and political, as well as conservation, aspects of sustainable development.

The general lack of interest in matters of sustainability by Ministries of Education has tended to marginalise environmental education from mainstream education policy. Most countries therefore lack a coherent plan for progression

Table 1. Examples of innovative practices in the Asia-Pacific region

Australia	• A tradition of school based curriculum development within broad framework syllabuses which encourages local innovation and across-the-curriculum support for environmental education. • A series of state policies, curriculum guidelines and support materials for environmental education. • Integration of professional development with curriculum development in Landcare Education programs.
People's Republic of China	• Environmental protection is a basic state policy. • Chaozhou City was named by UNEP as one of the "500 Best cities in the World" for its achievements in environmental education where 200,000 students in over 1,000 schools underwent an environmental education program, which combined in-school and out-of-classroom activities. • Teacher education for sustainability project sponsored by WWF.
India	• The National Policy on Education of 1968 and 1986 made environmental themes integral aspects of the curriculum. • The National Council of Educational Research and Training (NCERT) has produced model national textbooks for Years 3–5 on environmental studies. Beyond Year 6, texts of all subjects are to include environmental education. • The Supreme Court of India has made a court order to ensure all education systems promote environmental education. • Environmental themes integral to adult and nonformal education.
Indonesia	• A network of Environmental Study Centres in universities and incorporation of environmental education into national policies on environmental management. • A system of non-degree training programs in environmental impact assessment and other topics. • Widespread co-operation between schools, universities and communities in local action projects such as Clean River Campaigns.
Japan	• Comprehensive attention to environmental topics in a wide range of primary and secondary school subjects. • Identification of issues concerning the promotion of environmental education. For example: – the need to relate environmental education to pupils' lives to improve quality of life, and – the development of teaching materials, especially on the local environment covering the full range of environmental education approaches.

(Continued)

Table 1. (Continued)

	• Development of links between schools and administrative agencies, eg Ministry of Environment and Ministry of Education, to produce guidance notes and supplementary readers for primary and lower secondary schools, and to coordinate in-service education.
Malaysia	• "Man and Environment" topics integrated into five subjects in primary school; Social Science, Health Education, Civics, History and Geography. • A wide range of co-curricula activities, eg. nature clubs, Environment Week, camping, "School in the Garden", and environmental education projects. • Government agencies, NGOs and media support environmental education.
New Zealand	• Involvement of the NGO sector in environmental education is strong, eg. New Zealand Natural Heritage Foundation and Environmental Education Centre of New Zealand. • School/University links provide special programs for teachers and students through programs such as Eco-school and Enviro-school.
Philippines	• Environmental concepts and skills integrated into National Minimum Learning Competencies for elementary schools and Desired Learning Competencies for secondary schools. • A national environmental education review gave strong support for formal and non formal environmental education. • A strong curriculum materials and professional development program in environmental education for teachers.
Republic of Korea	• Environmental Conservation Model School program to provide examples of environmental education across-the-curriculum. • Environmental education is central in the new Sixth Curriculum from 1995. At the secondary school level it will be a separate subject.
Singapore	• Environmental Education is central in the government's plan to become a Model Environmental City by 2000. • There are at least 15 different governmental and non-governmental institutions that are actively involved in promoting environmental awareness and action nation-wide. • Successful 'Clean River' campaign and the promotion of the annual 'Clean and Green Week'. • Environmental education is already incorporated in the academic and curriculum studies in the pre-service teacher education.
Sri Lanka	• A strong connection between culture and religion and the philosophy of environmental education.

(Continued)

Table 1. (Continued)

	• National Education Commission requires schools to contribute to the evolution of a sustainable pattern of living. • Strong integration of environmental topics into primary and secondary curriculum, and the setting up of Environmental Pioneer Brigades and Environmental Clubs in some schools. • Active NGO involvement in environmental education.
Thailand	• Environmental education is integral to the issues of quality of life and health. • Environmental education is integrated into three units in the Life Experiences curriculum in elementary schools. Life Experience integrates Science, Social Studies, Health and Moral Education. • Community development electives in junior secondary social studies provide wide opportunities for student participation in working to solve local environmental problems. • There is a goal to have an accredited environmental park and community resource centre in every village.
Vietnam	• Environmental education is integral to the 1991 National Plan on Environment and Sustainable Development. • Incorporation of environmental education into three subjects in primary school (Finding Nature and Society, Health Education and Moral Education) and three in secondary school (geography, biology and moral/civic education). • Incorporation of National Festival of Growing Plants directly into the curriculum with inter-Ministry cooperation.

Source: (Fien & Tilbury, 1996).

in environmental education from kindergarten to college level. As a result, it is often not a priority, especially where the curriculum is over-crowded. In addition, the low profile of environmental education and sustainable development in external examination subjects contributes to a lack of status for this area of learning. Therefore, it is not surprising to find that many teachers, students and parents do not perceive it as a curriculum priority. In some countries the innovative teaching methods of environmental education conflict with the traditional culture of schooling. This problem is particularly acute in countries where the curriculum emphasises the recall of content and external examination performance rather than the development of thinking and problem solving skills. Such problems are intensified by a general lack of awareness and support for environmental education from many education policy makers, school administrators and academics in teacher education institutions. This makes the introduction of both in-service and pre-service teacher education for sustainability difficult and, unfortunately, when in-service courses are provided, they tend to be attended by teachers who are already committed to environmental education. As a result, the official as well as the hidden curricula of schools are often not sympathetic to the social vision of education for a sustainable future. Indeed, while the official curriculum is often deficient in these matters, the hidden curriculum is often an even greater barrier to sustainable development.

The effects of this pattern may be seen in the results of an international project that investigated the environmental knowledge, attitude and actions of over 10,000 students, aged 16 to 17 years in 11 countries in the region. The research involved a study of the cultural background and education system in each country, questionnaire surveys and focus group interviews in each country and a meta-analysis of the national studies (Yencken, Fien and Sykes, 2000). Three key findings of the study indicate that much remains to be done to ensure that education, especially in secondary schools, is reoriented towards sustainability. These relate to: (a) levels of student awareness and interest, (b) the learning of appropriate concepts, and (c) the willingness and ability of students to adopt sustainable lifestyles behaviours and to share civic responsibility for sustainable development activities.

4.1. *Levels of Student Interest in the Environment*

Several findings from the research indicate that young people in the Asia-Pacific region have a strong interest in learning much more about environmental matters than they are currently doing. For example, Table 2 shows that students in only one country (Singapore) wanted less frequent regular discussion of environmental matters in class. Similarly, in the focus group interviews, students from several countries reported that they had "learnt hardly anything at all about the environment since primary school" and did not believe that it was fair for these sort of topics to be taught only to those students who study biology or geography.

Table 2. Current frequency of regular discussion of environmental matters in class versus the percentage of students who say that they would prefer to do this regularly in selected Asia-Pacific cities and countries (Yencken, Fien & Sykes, 2000)

	Current frequency	*Desired frequency*
Australia	30	52
Indonesia	44	88
Brunei	33	59
China – Guangzhou	11	38
China – Hong Kong	19	41
India	54	79
Japan	16	27
New Zealand	19	38
Singapore	18	3
Thailand	14	65

4.2. Learning of Appropriate Concepts

The students in the survey were asked to indicate whether they were familiar with a set of 11 concepts and then to define them. Tables 3 and 4 show that the concepts which students are presently learning about in school are limited to traditional concepts from biology and geography, such as renewable resources, ecology, interdependence and carbon cycle, and the two major climate change issues of ozone layer depletion and the greenhouse effect. Students reported that they were partially familiar with the concept of sustainable development but that they were not familiar at all with the related concepts of biodiversity, carrying capacity, precautionary principle, and intergenerational equity. When students were asked to define this set of concepts, their knowledge scores were very disappointing. This situation points to the urgent need to integrate such concepts into syllabuses in the region so that students can begin to develop an understanding of concepts central to sustainable development. While only five such concepts were used in the survey, many others from the fields of political ecology and ecological economics could have been used. These include: ecological footprint, ecospace, natural resource accounting, life-cycle analysis, environmental assessment, eco-efficiency, sustainable consumption and so on (OECD, 1997).

4.3. The Willingness and Ability of Students to Practise Civic Responsibility

The third and, perhaps, most disheartening finding of the research was the ambivalence that the young people showed towards making life style changes and practising civic responsibility in accord with their high levels of expressed concern for the environment. While the young people in every country expressed a strong desire to improve the environment, few reported a past record of active environmental citizenship or a willingness to work for environmental protection in the future. Recycling and reusing, choosing household products that are better for the environment, and reducing water consumption were cited as regular activities by some students and some also said that they had taken part in tree planting and clean-up campaigns. However, only a very small minority of young people in any of the countries said that they had written letters, signed petitions, attended meetings or made formal complaints. These political actions are also the actions that most said that that they would not consider taking in the future. This is despite the fact that a large majority of respondents (between 70% and 94%) in all countries reported that they felt 'positive' or 'really good' when they took pro-environmental actions and that they generally experienced positive reactions and strong support from others involved, their teachers and their immediate families.

This paradox cannot be easily explained. There are many cultural and political barriers to Western styles of active citizenship in several counties in the Asia-Pacific region. However, there is a strong indication in the survey findings that the nature of common educational experiences also plays an influential role. For example, most young people said that they had poor skills and knowledge for bringing about environmental improvements, even if in only a small way. When

Table 3. Group 1 Concepts: Relatively high level of awareness and knowledge

	Greenhouse effect	Ozone layer	Renewable resources	Ecology	Carbon cycle	Interdependence
Australia – Brisbane						
– Heard of	99	99	94	88	53	60
– Discussed in class	81	81	59	44	20	18
– Correct	24	39	59	35	44	77
Australia – Melbourne						
– Heard of	98	99	94	94	74	70
– Discussed in class	81	81	61	67	41	26
– Correct	68	36	61	50	47	–
Bali						
– Heard of	–	–	–	–	–	–
– Discussed in class	74	76	92	88	81	–
– Correct	27	47	85	80	44	–
Brunei						
– Heard of	98	99	98	90	91	71
– Discussed in class	58	57	58	51	73	20
– Correct	63	37	–	44	60	–
China – Guangzhou						
– Heard of	92	97	98	94	56	94
– Discussed in class	46	49	67	46	26	33
– Correct	7	54	70	44	40	–
China – Hong Kong						
– Heard of	98	96	98	72	47	78
– Discussed in class	59	47	56	35	18	25
– Correct	11	25	42	55	40	–
Fiji						
– Heard of	–	–	–	–	–	–
– Discussed in class	–	–	–	–	–	–
– Correct	29	45	43	42	36	–
India						
– Heard of	100	97	99	100	99	97
– Discussed in class	95	93	95	73	95	85
– Correct	67	57	51	73	50	–
Japan						
– Heard of	86	92	32	92	52	50
– Discussed in class	33	58	6	18	18	8
– Correct	48	82	10	14	26	–
Korea						
– Heard of	–	–	–	–	–	–
– Discussed in class	–	–	–	–	–	–
– Correct	61	70	29	19	23	–
New Zealand						
– Heard of	95	97	91	78	75	79
– Discussed in class	64	67	60	38	50	45
– Correct	55	32	49	24	48	–
Singapore						
– Heard of	99	99	99	97	91	84
– Discussed in class	91	88	77	71	73	45
– Correct	94	75	57	59	78	–
Thailand						
– Heard of	99	99	87	99	70	98
– Discussed in class	70	69	36	69	27	32
– Correct	15	39	61	82	16	–

Source: Yencken, Fien and Sykes (2000).

Table 4. Group 2 Concepts: Relatively low level of awareness and knowledge

	Sustainable development	Carrying capacity	Biodiversity	Intergen'al equity	Precautionary principle
Australia – Brisbane					
– Heard of	51	43	49	52	21
– Discussed in class	12	10	12	4	3
– Correct	26	77	82	66	21
Australia – Melbourne					
– Heard of	57	55	49	48	23
– Discussed in class	20	22	18	8	3
– Correct	26	79	79	63	19
Bali					
– Heard of	–	–	–	–	–
– Discussed in class	31	28	93	35	26
– Correct	70	64	37	82	61
Brunei					
– Heard of	54	50	57	25	37
– Discussed in class	7	9	33	3	3
– Correct	9	40	69	50	25
China – Guangzhou					
– Heard of	87	72	90	62	66
– Discussed in class	11	22	43	11	15
– Correct	53	65	50	73	55
China – Hong Kong					
– Heard of	48	52	41	44	38
– Discussed in class	9	16	12	9	8
– Correct	24	66	52	59	25
Fiji					
– Heard of	–	–	–	–	–
– Discussed in class	–	–	–	–	–
– Correct	34	49	41	46	25
India					
– Heard of	68	48	86	35	26
– Discussed in class	38	26	72	17	14
– Correct	25	39	46	71	19
Japan					
– Heard of	43	43	67	36	26
– Discussed in class	13	10	12	4	3
– Correct	49	55	24	39	20
Korea					
– Heard of	–	–	–	–	–
– Discussed in class	–	–	–	–	–
– Correct	54	–	55	60	63
New Zealand					
– Heard of	47	54	50	40	31
– Discussed in class	12	13	15	8	6
– Correct	20	58	58	53	49
Singapore					
– Heard of	45	62	53	30	28
– Discussed in class	10	25	19	4	4
– Correct	19	22	86	66	32
Thailand					
– Heard of	34	95	90	94	96
– Discussed in class	6	55	39	25	25
– Correct	60	70	68	64	14

Source: Yencken, Fien and Sykes (2000).

they were asked to rate their knowledge and skills in this area, the highest response in all countries was only a medium ranking. Indeed, students in all the countries studied said that the two most common reasons for not acting in an environmentally-friendly way were beliefs that: (a) their actions would not make a difference; and (b) that there was no practical alternative even when they knew that what they did was wrong. This reflects not only a lack of knowledge of possible alternatives but also a failure of schools to provide students with experiences that teach such knowledge and skills. It also indicates that students have rarely had the opportunity to work with others on practical environmental projects and develop confidence in their individual and collective abilities to bring about change successfully.

A reaffirmation of the contribution of education to active citizenship would mean that one of the central goals of education would be to help students learn how to identify elements of unsustainable development that concerned them and to address these problems. This would involve students learning to reflect critically on their place in the world and considering what sustainability meant to them and their communities. It would also involve practice in envisioning alternative ways of development and living, evaluating alternative visions, learning how to negotiate and justify choices between visions, making plans for achieving desired ones, and participating in community actions to bring such visions into effect. These are the abilities that Jensen and Schnack (1997) describe as 'action competence'. Democratic action competence is the opposite of predetermined behavioural change as a goal for education and aligns education for sustainability as part of the process of building an informed, concerned and active civil society. In this way, education for sustainability can contribute to education for democracy.

5. THE ROLE OF TEACHER EDUCATION

This situation indicates the need for a revision of the objectives and content themes of school curricula in the region so that sustainability is a central concern, and teaching and learning processes emphasise appropriate concepts, learning how to learn, civic mindedness, and the motivation and abilities to work with others to help build a sustainable future. This is not a small task for, as Smyth (1995, p. 18) has remarked, "It is difficult to avoid the conclusion that many have reached that education should be largely recast" when the wide scope of the task of reorienting education towards sustainability is considered. This will require a realignment of the major foci of education. Schools have the role of both empowering students to play an informed and active role as members of society and encouraging the politically endorsed (and mostly economically motivated) values, practices and institutions of the existing social order. These are not mutually exclusive roles, and education is designed to promote both. However, without a whole-of-government commitment to sustainable development in most countries, schools have tended to reproduce an unsustainable culture that intensifies environment and development problems rather than one that empowers citizens to work towards their solution. This situation of unbalanced priorities calls for a reaffirmation of the role of education in building civil society by helping students: (a) develop criteria for determining what is best to conserve in their cultural, economic and natural heritage; (b) discern values and strategies for creating sustainability in their local communities; and (c) work with others to build sustainability outwards to include national and global contexts. This is not to say that the economic imperatives that underlie the reproductive functions of formal education are to be ignored. Economically sound, ecologically sustainable and socially just forms of development are to be encouraged; indeed, appropriate development is a core principle of a sustainable society. However, a reorientation of education towards sustainability calls attention to the problematical effects of inappropriate development and unfettered economic growth, and also to the ways that these are perpetuated through dominant patterns of schooling and the narrow and limited range of knowledge, attitudes and skills students tend to learn as a result.

The curriculum reforms that flow from a reorientation of education towards sustainability need to be supported by reforms to many current patterns of curriculum development and assessment in the Asia-Pacific region. For example, the centralised control of teaching and learning through nationally mandated syllabuses, textbooks and assessment in many countries does not readily support the localisation of curriculum themes or encourage student participation in local community projects. These reforms also require new attitudes and skills among teachers. This makes teacher education an especially important area for action.

Our Common Future, the Report of the World Commission on Environment and Development (1987, p. xiv) states that "the world's teachers ... have a crucial role to play" in helping to bring about "the extensive social changes" needed along the pathway towards a sustainable future. Thus, teacher education for sustainability has been the theme of a major UNESCO project in the Asia-Pacific region.

5.1. *Learning for a Sustainable Environment – Innovations in Teacher Education Project*

This project began in 1994 to assist teacher educators in the region to include the principles and innovative teaching and learning strategies of education for sustainability in their programs. regional and subregional meetings in 1993 and 1994, which had been convened by UNESCO and the South East Asia Ministers of Education Organisation, provided the necessary needs analysis and direction for the project. These indicated that the project should focus on the personal and professional development of teacher educators, rather than on the production of resources, in order to encourage appropriate pedagogical practice in teacher education which could have multiplier effects with teachers and their students.

Thus, the primary aim of the project was to support teacher educators in the

Asia-Pacific region as they developed locally relevant ways of rethinking their courses and make plans to reorient teacher education in their colleges and countries towards sustainability. The project developed an action research network of teacher educators across 20 countries in the region. The purpose of the network was, and remains, to support teacher educators who wished to share in writing carefully-researched, evaluated and culturally-sensitive modules for use in initial pre-service and continuing in-service programs in teacher education.

Evaluation reports indicate that the major outcome of the network has been the professional development of those involved and a series of national workshops and networks in many countries in the region (NIER, 1996). An attractive professional development guide has also been published (Fien, Heck, Ferreira, 1997). Containing edited selections from the most interesting and innovative work completed by the network, the modules in this guide are not seen as a finished product but as inspirations for further adaptation in different countries. Some evidence of the success of this project includes:

- the development of an action research network of over 70 teachers' colleges which operates in Karnataka state in India and which is presently being replicated in the neighbouring state of Kerala;
- the establishment of a national environmental education resource centre in Vietnam;
- revision of the teacher education degree curriculum in several participating institutions to include either a compulsory study of environmental education, issues of sustainable development, or a specialised curriculum stream in environmental education;
- shared course materials and joint degree programs between institutions to promote postgraduate studies and research in environmental education in several countries, including international joint degrees;
- the publication of a set of workshop modules, the action research guide and several sample action research case studies as a book called *Learning for a Sustainable Environment: A Professional Development Guide for Teacher Educators* (Fien, Heck, & Ferreira, 1997) and as an internet site (http://www.gu.edu.au/ciree/lse/index.html);
- the revision of many of the modules into national training manuals and teacher education guides, (e.g., in India, Fiji and Vietnam);
- the development of a self-study internet site and CD-ROM called *Teaching and Learning for a Sustainable Future* (http://www.unesco.org/education/tlsf);
- the adoption of the action research network process by the York University UNESCO Chair Network on Teacher Education for Sustainability to facilitate professional development and curriculum change in colleges and universities in 34 countries; and
- the development of research expertise of project members such that many went on to participate in a survey and focus group study of factors influencing youth environmental attitudes in the region (Yencken, Fien, & Sykes, 2000).

6. CONCLUSION

The widespread reorientation of educational practices, systems and structures is not common in the Asia-Pacific region. Hence, the Asia-Pacific region is only beginning its entry into the second phase of education for a sustainable future. This shift is a very large undertaking and one that the economically wealthy regions of the world have yet to make. Therefore it is not surprising that some of the world's economically poorer countries are yet to enact such reforms. However, there is sufficient leadership in the region, in the form of international and regional agencies and active NGOs, to indicate that if member states can be convinced that a whole-of-government approach to sustainable development is desirable, then the teacher educators, curriculum development officials and teachers of the region will have the necessary support to make the necessary reforms.

REFERENCES

Asian Development Bank (1997). *Emerging Asia: Changes and Challenges.* Manila: Asian Development Bank.
Fien, J., Heck, D., & Ferreira, J. (Eds.) (1997). *Learning for a Sustainable Environment: A Professional Development Manual for Teacher Educators.* Bangkok: UNESCO Asia-Pacific Programme of Educational Innovation for Development (ACEID).
Fien, J., & Tilbury, D. (1996). *Learning for a Sustainable Environment: An Agenda for Teacher Education in Asia and the Pacific.* Bangkok: UNESCO Asia-Pacific Programme of Educational Innovation for Development (ACEID).
Gregario, L. (1993). UNESCO initiatives in environmental education for Asia and the Pacific, unpublished briefing paper for International Experts Meeting on Overcoming the barriers to Environmental Education through Teacher Education, Griffith University.
Jensen, B. B., & Schnack, K. (1997). The action competence approach in environmental education, *Environmental Education Research*, 3(2), 163–178.
Maclean, R. (1997). *Educational Innovation for Sustainable Development.* Bangkok: UNESCO-ACEID.
National Institute for Educational Research (NIER) (1996). *Learning for a Sustainable Environment: Environmental Education and Teacher Education in Asia and the Pacific.* Tokyo: NIER.
OECD (1997). *Sustainable Consumption and Production.* Paris: OECD.
O'Riordan, T. (1994). Education for the sustainability transition. *Annual Review of Environmental Education*, 8.
Smyth, J. (1995). Environment and education: A view of a changing scene, *Environmental Education Research*, 1(1), 3–20.
South Pacific Regional Environment Programme (SPREP) (1998). *Action Strategy for Environmental Education and Training in the Pacific Region 1999–2003.* Apia: SPREP.
United Nations Development Programme (2000). *Human Development Report 2000.* New York: Oxford University Press.
United Nations Environment Programme (1999). *Global Environmental Outlook – 2000.* New York: Oxford University Press.
UNESCO-PROAP (1996). *Celebrating Diversity, Cultivating Development, Creating Our Future Together: UNESCO in Asia and the Pacific.* Bangkok: UNESCO.
World Bank (1993). *Toward an Environmental Strategy for Asia.* World Bank Discussion Paper No. 224, Washington DC.: World Bank.

World Bank (2000). *World Development Report 2000.* New York: Oxford University Press.
World Resources Institute (2000). *World Resources – 2001* New York: Oxford University Press.
World Watch Institute (1999). *State of the World 1999: The Millennium Edition.* New York: W. W. Norton & Company.
World Wide Fund for Nature (1999). *Living Planet.* http://panda.org/livingplanet/lpr/index.htm
World Commission on Environment and Development (1987). *Our Common Future.* New York: Oxford University Press.
Yencken, Fien, J., & Sykes (2000). *Environment, Education and Society in the Asia-Pacific: Local Traditions and Global Discourses.* London: Routledge.

40

Literacy and Reading

WARWICK B. ELLEY
University of Canterbury, New Zealand

HO WAH KAM
Singapore Association for Applied Linguistics, Singapore

1. INTRODUCTION

This article summarises the research conducted on children's reading, in the Asia-Pacific region. The article is organised around a series of themes, which are common to a number of countries in the region. Judgements about the priority of researchable literacy problems are made somewhat tentatively, in view of the extraordinary diversity found in these countries – diversity in size, wealth, culture, literacy levels, research traditions, school resources, mother tongues and languages of instruction, to list a few of the more obvious differences. Thus, problems that are seen as pressing matters in one country, may be perceived as of marginal significance in others.

Nevertheless, all countries share a common goal of seeking to teach their pupils to read as well as possible, in at least one language. Therefore, policy makers and teachers in all countries should be interested in research on reading acquisition, on reading assessment procedures, on current standards of reading in the schools, and on the impact of programs which assist those who are at risk. As large numbers of children in the region are expected to learn to read in a non-native tongue, (usually English) it is also necessary to give priority to bilingual research. All these themes deserve a place in this article, and all are addressed.

2. WHAT IS MEANT BY READING-LITERACY?

The concept of literacy has a long and contentious history, and there is continuing debate about the meaning and significance of basic literacy, functional literacy, workplace literacy, cultural literacy, computer literacy and multiple literacies, to name a few (Luke, 1994; Roberts, 1995). In order to make the task manageable, we propose to limit our coverage to reading skills acquired up to and during the school years, which excludes some of the more debatable issues associated with adult literacy for the workplace, or for escaping from political oppression. However, we must recognise and try to allow for the enormous diversity of reading tasks faced by children brought up in different ways, under different curricula and taught in different tongues and orthographies.

In order to incorporate findings of international studies of reading-literacy, there is merit in embracing the definition proposed for the cross-national IEA study of reading in 32 education systems (Elley, 1994) and adopted again by the next major international study (Campbell et al., 2001).

> Reading-literacy is the ability to understand and use those written language forms that are required by society and/or valued by the individual. (Elley 1994, p. 5; Campbell et al., 2001, p. 3)

Such a definition allows for the inclusion of studies in which reading is required for reading textbooks, public notices, directions, tables, advertisements, newspapers, computer manuals, and other language forms which children are expected to master at school.

3. HOW DO CHILDREN LEARN TO READ?

This section deals with the various ways in which children acquire reading skill, at home, in primary school and in the middle and upper school.

3.1. *Emergent Literacy*

The development of reading ability has its roots in the child's first encounters with language in the home. Researchers in several countries in the region have studied the ways in which young children are socialised into reading in the preschool years. Traditions of bedside reading to young children are strong in New Zealand and Australia, and several observational studies in the 1970s focussed on their beneficial effects (Clay, 1972; Holdaway, 1979). In Holdaway's developmental model, frequently read-to children were found to develop a literacy set. They became aware of the pleasures of reading, they acquired book language, they learned such operations as the ability to predict the story, and to visualise the events without picture support, and they learned many of the concepts and conventions of print (Holdaway, 1979). Such benefits are found to enable these children to move easily into traditional reading instruction at school (Gibbons, 1981, Ritchie, 1978). Such research has had a strong influence on home and preschool practice in New Zealand.

Some recent sociological research has focused on the mismatch between the typical middle-class literacy environment of the school and the home literacy practices of many working class children in New Zealand (Berwick-Emms 1989), and Australia (Breen et al., 1995; Freebody, 1997); of Pacific Islands children in

New Zealand (McNaughton, 1995) and Aboriginal children in Australia (Clayton et al., 1996). The need for teachers to become familiar with the cultural values and the nature of the early literacy experiences of their indigenous and minority pupils is underlined by such studies. To help address these problems, McNaughton (1995) has developed a 'Co-Construction' theory, which explicates the nature of the family expectations and actions when young children from various cultural backgrounds encounter print in the early years.

In Singapore, large-scale studies of pre-schoolers showed that over 50 per cent of four year-olds were already equipped with pre-reading skills in English (Ko & Ho, 1992). In Hong Kong, Ng (1999) has developed a child-centered approach to learning English in pre-school, using oral-aural methods and high-interest stories and songs, with strong benefits, when compared with the effects of traditional rote learning approaches.

3.2. Teaching and Learning in the Primary Years

Age of Beginning Instruction. Considerable variation exists in the age of beginning instruction at school. The British tradition, followed in Australia and New Zealand, sees children beginning instruction, in their mother tongue, at five years, while most Asian and Pacific countries delay the start until six years, or later. While many children may benefit from an early start in reading, there is some international research which suggests that when children start too early, before they are mature enough, and struggle in the early stages, they may have recurring problems (Smith & Elley, 1997). Australian researchers have pointed to the dangers of assessing children too early, and labelling them as at risk, when they may merely lack experience with the kinds of literacy practices typical of the western school (Hill et al., 1998).

Methods of Instruction. Again, diversity is the keynote. At one extreme, New Zealand teachers, with government support, have adopted a distinctive child-centred, whole language or natural language style of instruction, with strong emphasis on language experience (Ashton-Warner, 1963), shared reading (Holdaway, 1979), story reading from good literature, and regular free writing. The teaching of phonics, taught as isolated word-sound associations, has been downplayed, (although it is encouraged as a skill to be taught in context.). By contrast, Chinese children are taught by formal methods, to memorise the *Hanyu Pinyin* alphabet by phonic teaching, and then go on to learn about 2000–3000 Chinese characters in the primary school, using predominantly rote methods (Ingulsrud & Allen, 1999). Most countries fall between these extremes. Singaporean children, for instance, enjoy a literature-based approach, with frequent writing, but with more directed instruction and assessment than in New Zealand.

One important issue for Asian educators is the nature of the challenge presented by the ideographic script. While the memory load in acquiring the characters is notable, it does not appear to hamper most Chinese children unduly. In a large carefully matched, comparative study of first grade children in Taipei and Minneapolis, the Chinese children surpassed their American counterparts in most aspects of reading skill (Lee et al., 1988). The researchers concluded, as have others (Duke, 1986), that Asian children work harder and longer at their learning, at school and at home, and receive more support from parents. The nature of the initial learning task was of minor significance in drawing comparisons. More research is needed on the importance of the script for early acquisition of reading.

Australia and New Zealand. Heated debates about literacy standards and the best methods of instruction are common in Australia and New Zealand (Dawkins, 1990; Wilkinson et al., 2000). In Australia, Cambourne (1988), has developed a 'whole language' model of how children became literate naturally, through immersion in good quality print. His research and liberal philosophy have influenced many teachers in the region, and drawn criticism from others. Many Australian teachers, "still regard phonics instruction as important in the teaching of reading" (Kidston & Elkins, 1992), although there is a growing place for more child-centred approaches using language experience, shared reading with so-called 'Big Books', and regular silent reading of literature (Saxby, 1993; van Kraayenoord et al., 1994). Phonic-based instruction has received a boost from empirical research on the benefits of teaching phonemic awareness directly from the outset (Byrne & Fielding-Barnsley, 1995; Bowey, 1996), but experimental attempts to duplicate such work in New Zealand whole language classes have met with mixed success (Nicholson, 1998).

Early literacy instruction in New Zealand schools has been much influenced by the research of Clay (1972, 1991) and of Holdaway (1979). In her early research, Clay observed closely, the development of 100 five year-olds over 12 months, as they came to grips with print. Her observations led her to see children as "constructive, problem-solving doers and thinkers" (Clay, 1998, p. 3) as they learned to coordinate the many cues that helped them arrive at the meaning of a message. Teaching the components of reading separately and trying to coordinate them later (as in systematic phonics) was not encouraged by this research. Her work did promote the benefits for teachers, of close observation of children, of systematic diagnosis as they read aloud, of building on each child's individual strengths, rather than teaching to their weakness. She developed a number of useful diagnostic tools, including the popular 'running record', and her research has resulted in the development of the widely adopted Reading Recovery program (Clay, 1972).

Holdaway (1979) has also had a powerful influence on the literature-based approach to reading found in New Zealand schools, and increasingly throughout the region. From his observational studies, he developed the shared-book (or shared reading) method of sharing a suitable story with a class, several times, with enjoyable activities, until children become familiar with the language of the book. For older children he promoted Guided Silent Reading, in groups, and individualised silent reading. These procedures were promoted with novel in-service training packages (ERIC and LARIC) and are now commonly used in many countries.

Ashton-Warner (1963) was another influential New Zealand teacher, renowned for her development of the Language Experience approach. In place of the insipid reading texts of her day she arranged for her children to have real life experiences, which they naturally talked about, then drew, then wrote captions for, and finally read aloud to peers, parents or teachers. The method became very popular among teachers and is extensively used in New Zealand, Australia, Singapore, and North America.

Several researchers have challenged the child-centered, literature-based approach to reading instruction of New Zealand schools (Tunmer & Chapman, 1999; Nicholson, 1999) but it is still firmly supported by the Ministry of Education, the Colleges of Education, and most primary schools. It has been boosted by evidence of its apparent success, drawn from international studies (Thorndike, 1973; Wagemaker, 1993), and from a series of evaluations of the approach when transferred to a variety of Pacific and Asian countries (Elley, 2001).

The Asian Scene. In Singapore, children start instruction in English and their mother tongue simultaneously in Grade 1. Changes in the pattern of teaching in reading classes have been documented in Singapore schools by Ng (1984). Observing 72 junior classes, the researchers found low achievement levels, poor word attack skills and a predominantly authoritarian style of teaching, with little child activity, or story reading by the teacher. These findings prompted the development of a new literature-based program, the Reading and English Acquisition Program (REAP), using language experience and shared reading in the early years. Introduced in 1985, REAP brought about systematic changes in teacher behaviour and attitudes, and produced consistent benefits in children's reading and writing (Ng & Sullivan, 2001). A similar program designed for the primary schools of Brunei Darussalam has also shown strong positive gains (Ng, 2001). In both these countries large numbers of children are growing up biliterate, with positive attitudes towards reading, a situation which others would like to emulate.

Parallel research in the mother tongue include studies by Walker et al. (1992) in Thailand and by Gaffney (2001) in China, Walker used shared reading with a small number of 'starter books' to give Thai pupils a 'concentrated language encounter' which led to a powerful impact on children's reading, writing, and dictation.

In a ground-breaking study in Beijing, United States and Chinese researchers used the shared book approach with so-called 'Big Books' with Grade 1 children learning in the Chinese language. Initial findings show promising benefits in the amount of text read and in several tests of characters and words learned (Gaffney, 2001).

South Pacific. Over the past two decades, a considerable volume of research has been conducted on reading instruction methods in the South Pacific Islands.

For many years, children in most of the English-speaking nations, learned to speak and read in English, using the audio-lingual, structured Tate Program (Tate, 1971). Instruction in English as the medium, typically takes place after three or four years at school. Surveys of children's reading showed relatively low levels of reading skill in English, by the end of primary school throughout Fiji. An alternative program, developed at the University of the South Pacific, using a 'Book Flood' of high-interest illustrated story books, and shared reading methods, produced dramatic improvements in literacy (Elley & Mangubhai, 1983). Following this work, a Literacy Centre was established at the University, to stimulate the writing and publication of literature for children in the region, and a new reading in-service program for teachers (South Pacific Literacy Education Course – SPLEC) was developed at the University of the South Pacific, following the pattern of a New Zealand whole language, literature-based philosophy. Such developments have changed the character of reading instruction in many South Pacific schools, with consistently positive results (see Elley, 2001), and lessons for educators in many developing countries. The need for suitable books to support such methods still hampers further progress.

Similar studies of the benefits of shared reading with good books have been conducted in the island of Niue (De'Ath, 2001) and the Solomon Islands and Vanuatu (Singh, 2001), and in Samoa. (Elley et al., 1999). In related research, Ricketts (1983), demonstrated the literacy benefits of daily story reading aloud to Fijian primary school children, and Elley (1989) showed how repeated story reading enhances the vocabulary of children in Fiji and Kiribati schools.

Further north, Au's Hawaiian literacy research on the Kamehameha Elementary Education Program (KEEP) over 30 years deserves special mention (Au & Asam, 1997). The program is designed to help young native Hawaiian children from disadvantaged backgrounds. After initial studies in the 1970s, with a behavioural mastery-learning approach, the direction shifted in 1989 to a holistic program, with a social constructivist approach to reading. Prominent features are an emphasis on student ownership, process writing, reading for meaning, voluntary reading and portfolio assessment in relation to clear benchmarks. Regular evaluation studies have led to progressive changes in approach, improved teacher training, and many positive benefits for Hawaiian students on three of the islands.

3.3 Reading in the Middle and Upper School

Once children learn to read independently, the emphasis shifts to reading to learn. As in other countries, numerous researchers have explored the benefits of reciprocal teaching in New Zealand (Gilroy & Moore, 1988; Kelly et al., 1994).

Extensive Reading. Extensive Reading (ER) has been widely used in many countries of the region as a way of boosting interest, vocabulary and reading skill. Elley and Mangubhai (1983) found experimental support for daily silent reading in Fiji and Lituanas et al. (2001) produced strong effects for an extensive reading program in a Philippines secondary school. Yu (1999) found beneficial effects for ER in a Hong Kong study, while Jacobs et al. (1997) at the SEAMEO Regional Language Centre (RELC) in Singapore have reviewed several other small-scale Asian studies in this field. In New Zealand the daily silent reading session is almost universal, although some researchers remain sceptical of its benefits (Nicholson, 1999). Pluck et al. (1984) found stronger effects on weak readers when the teacher modelled the reading process during extensive reading.

Vocabulary Acquisition. Another common theme for research has been vocabulary acquisition. Elley (1989) explored how children acquired new vocabulary from listening to stories read aloud, in first and second language settings. Nation (1988) has assessed the numbers of words known by mature native speakers and overseas students, and shown how students acquire new vocabulary readily, from context, when reading an interesting novel (Saragi et al., 1978). Numerous word lists have been developed in the region, and become the basis for direct teaching, for preparing tests, and for grading passages for readability (Elley & Croft, 1989; Campion, 1970; Nation, 1988). In China, Shu et al. (1995) have found that Chinese students learn new Chinese vocabulary, from context while reading, in much the same way as English speakers do, suggesting that the phenomenon could be universal.

Systemic Grammar. An influential instructional model for enhancing literacy, developed in Australia, is the systemic functional grammar approach, based on the linguistic research of Halliday (1975). What children learn from their science or social studies texts depends on their grasp of the language forms and structures, as well as the specialist vocabulary of each discipline. Therefore, teachers need to teach children these special forms, or genres, to enhance their understanding and assist their writing in different content areas.

4. CHILDREN WITH READING DIFFICULTIES

In the best of reading programs there are always some who struggle to master the process. This is a recurring problem in most parts of the region. Estimates of the number of failing readers vary from time to time and country to country, depending on the criteria used for selection, as well as the quality and the style of teaching. For instance, Japanese researchers put the number of their failing readers at less than one per cent (Sakamoto, 1992) but Stevenson and Stigler (1992) in a cross-cultural study of children from Japan, Taiwan and United States, using other criteria, estimated the figure at eight per cent. The same study found much more variability in achievement within each grade for American children. The ability of English speaking children to read well above grade level was attributed partly to the difference in scripts. United States students were able to sound out unfamiliar words, but this factor could not account for the slow progress of readers in this United States sample. In Stevenson's study,

American schools had far more at risk students than the Taiwanese. The cross-national differences were explained largely in terms of time on task. American students spent less time reading or studying.

A large cross-national survey (Elley, 1994) which included six countries in the region, found very few failing readers in New Zealand, Hong Kong and Singapore, on common tests of reading literacy, but considerably more in Indonesia, Thailand, and the Philippines. Other surveys of literacy in the South Pacific, on the common Pacific Islands Literacy Levels (PILL) Test (Withers, 1991) show large variations, from one island nation to the next, in vernacular and English languages. Ho and Wong (2000) also report large variations in literacy levels in East Asian countries. Such surveys have been used by participating nations to investigate and address their problems, but the research has been sporadic.

4.1. Reading Recovery

One of the outstanding contributions of reading research in the region has been the development and spread of the Reading Recovery program. On the basis of her Auckland studies of at risk five year-old readers, Clay (1972, 1985) developed a widely respected tutorial program for assisting children who were having difficulty learning to read after one year at school. The pupils' regular reading program is supplemented with daily one-to-one 30 minute lessons for 12 to 20 weeks with a specially trained Reading Recovery teacher. The teacher studies each individual child's strategies, and builds on them with a specially tailored program, designed to improve those strategies. The program has been exported to Australia, North America and Britain, with many positive evaluations by researchers (e.g., Lyons et al., 1993; Wade & Moore, 1998), and enthusiastic testaments from teachers and parents. For instance, approximately 600,000 children in 48 states of the United States have benefited from Reading Recovery since its introduction in 1985.

There is little question of its short-term benefits and the New Zealand Ministry of Education has consistently supported the program, and funded implementation in most schools. However, criticisms of the program based on studies by Chapman and Tunmer (1991) in New Zealand, and by Center et al. (1995) in Australia have raised questions about the long-term effectiveness of the approach, and prompted the Ministry to call for more independent research within New Zealand on Reading Recovery in its current form.

For the few children who are not helped by Reading Recovery, recent research by Phillips and Smith (1997) has shown how a so-called 'third wave' intervention at age seven years, can be profitable.

4.2. Pause, Prompt and Praise Methods

Another style of remedial reading program, based on behavioural principles, has been developed, by Glynn and his colleagues in New Zealand schools (Wheldhall & Glynn, 1989). The approach makes use of parents or peers who act as tutors in a one-to-one situation, for ten minute sessions, two or three times a week. The child reads aloud to the tutor, who follows a specific set of procedures. If the child makes an error, the tutor pauses for five seconds. If the child does not correct the error, the tutor prompts – using either meaning cues or the way the word looks and sounds. Finally, praise is offered for genuine attempts to correct errors. An advantage of this procedure is that it requires less training to be effective than some methods.

Wheldhall and Glynn (1989) report several studies of the effectiveness of the method. Other researchers have found positive benefits from peer tutoring, using the same principles, and the method has been translated and successfully used in Maori language classes (see Smith & Elley, 1997).

4.3. Taped Read-Along Stories

Taped stories have been used successfully in New Zealand as a way of helping older children with reading problems. The Rainbow Reading Program, developed by Pluck (1995) has children first, listen to audio-tapes of high-interest stories as they read along silently from the taped text. Then they read the text without the tape and have a conference with the teacher. Research shows encouraging gains for many slow readers.

5. THE IMPACT OF TECHNOLOGY

Many claims have been made about the potential benefits of new technologies in promoting literacy, but inadequate resources in many countries of the region, and a lack of research support mean that progress has been slow in realising that potential.

In New Zealand and Australia, a few studies have addressed the potential of videos in teaching young children to read. One program with good research support is *The Magic Box*, which consists of a series of 25-minute videos designed to teach five year olds to read. It was produced by Pye (1993) and shown on television networks in several countries. The videos present short stories based on the popular *Sunshine* series for beginning readers, with automatic page turning, verbal commentary, appealing sound effects, highlighting of words and letters in the books and other devices suited to television. Children show unusually high levels of concentration. Evaluations in four different studies have shown powerful effects on reading growth (Elley & Cowie, 1999). Videos have also been used effectively in training packages for teachers.

6. ASSESSMENT OF LITERACY

Standardised tests of reading, measuring word recognition, vocabulary and comprehension skills, have been developed and widely used on a voluntary basis by teachers in Australia and New Zealand for many years. Some innovative assessments developed in the region are the running records and *Concepts about Print* (Clay, 1985), both part of a battery of tests used to assess beginning readers; the *Progressive Achievement Tests of Reading* (Reid & Elley, 1990) which report both norm referenced and criterion referenced scores, and the innovative cloze-type *TORCH Reading Tests* are widely used in Australia. Other recent Australian developments are the introduction of nation-wide and state-wide reading tests, which report results using Rasch scaling rather than traditional norms (Masters & Forster, 1997). Portfolio assessment has been evaluated by van Kraayenoord (1997), and there is more attention devoted to benchmark assessment.

In New Zealand, Crooks and Flockton have developed some novel approaches to assessing reading, writing and attitudes through the National Educational Monitoring Project (NEMP, 1997) and the New Zealand Council for Educational Research is pioneering a computer-based series of Assessment Resource Banks which enable teachers to access assessment tasks of appropriate difficulty and content from a national bank of pre-tested tasks.

7. CONCLUSION

While there is much distinctive research to report about the way children acquire literacy in their first language in New Zealand and Australia, it is fair to say that there is much more to be learned about the way that Asian and South Pacific children learn to read and write in their mother tongue. In view of the fact that English is fast becoming a global language (Ho & Ward, 2000), it is heartening to know that considerable progress has been made in studies of the learning of English as a second language in the region. However, it is a matter of concern that levels of literacy in much of the region are still relatively low, largely due to lack of resources, and well trained teachers.

One serious omission is the dearth of evaluative research on the impact of technology on children's literacy development. Computers are widely used in the classrooms of several countries, but empirical studies of the costs and benefits of the diverse range of software programs on reading achievement and attitudes are sorely needed.

REFERENCES

Ashton-Warner, S. (1963). *Teacher.* New York: Bantem Books.
Au, K., & Asam C. (1997). Effective literacy instruction: Findings of the Kamehameha Elementary Education Program. In J. Flood, S. B. Heath & D. Lapp (Eds.), *Research on Teaching Literacy through the Communicative and Visual Arts.* New York: Macmillan.
Berwick-Emms, P. (1989). Classroom patterns of interaction and their underlying structure: Unpublished PhD Thesis, Christchurch: University of Canterbury.
Bowey, J. A. (1996). Phonological sensitivity as a proximal contributor to phonological recoding skills in children's reading. *Australian Journal of Psychology, 48,* 113–118.
Breen, M., Louden, W., Barratt-Pugh, C., Rivalland, J., Rohl, M., Rhydwen, M., Lloyd, S., & Carr, T.

(1995). *Literacy in its Place: Literacy Practices in Urban and Rural Communities.* Report to the Commonwealth Department of Employment, Education and Training, Canberra. Perth: Edith Cowan University.

Byrne, B., & Feilding-Barnsley (1995). Evaluation of a program to teach phonemic awareness to young children. A 2- and 3-year follow-up and a new preschool trial. *Journal of Educational Psychology, 87*, 488–503.

Cambourne, B. (1988). *The Whole Story: Natural Learning and the Acquisition of Literacy in the Classroom.* New York: Ashton Scholastic.

Campbell, J. R., Kelly, D. L., Mullis, I. V. S., Martin, M. O., & Sainsbury, M. (2001). *Framework and Specifications for PIRLS Assessment 2001* (2nd edition). Boston: International Study Centre, IEA, Boston College.

Campion, M. (1970). *An Academic Word List.* Wellington: NZ Council for Educational Research

Center, Y., Wheldhall, K., Freeman, L., Outhred, L., & McNaught, M. (1995). An evaluation of reading recovery. *Reading Research Quarterly, 30*, 240–263.

Chapman, J. W., & Tunmer, W. E. (1991). Recovering 'reading recovery'. *Australia and New Zealand Journal of Developmental Disabilities, 17*, 59–71.

Clay, M. M. (1972). *Reading: The Patterning of Complex Behaviour.* Auckland: Heinemann.

Clay, M. M. (1991). *Becoming Literate: The Construction of Inner Control.* Auckland: Heinemann.

Clay, M. M. (1993). *An Observational Study of Early Literacy Achievement.* Auckland: Heinemann.

Clay, M. M. (1998). *By Different Paths to Common Outcomes.* York, Maine: Stenhouse Publishers.

Clayton, J., Barnett, J., Kemelfield, G., & Mulhauser, P. (1996). *Desert Schools: An Investigation of English Language and Literacy Among Young Aboriginal People in Seven Communities.* Report to the Department of Employment, Education and Training, Canberra: AGPS.

Dawkins, J. (1990). *Australian Literacy and Language Policy.* Canberra: Australian Government Publishing Service.

De'Ath, P. (2001). The Niue literacy experiment. *International Journal of Educational Research, 35*, 137–146.

Duke, B. (1986). *The Japanese School: Lessons for Industrial America.* New York: Praeger

Elley, W. B. (1989). Vocabulary acquisition from listening to stories. *Reading Research Quarterly, 24*(2), 176–186.

Elley, W. B. (Ed.) (1994). *The IEA Study of Reading-Literacy: Achievement and Instruction in Thirty-Two School Systems.* Oxford: Pergamon.

Elley, W. B. (Ed.) (2001). Book-based approaches to raising literacy levels in developing countries. *International Journal of Educational Research, 2*, 127–246.

Elley, W. B., & Cowie, C. R. (1999). *Evaluation of the Magic Box Program in Northland Schools.* Auckland: Wendy Pye.

Elley, W. B., & Croft, A. C. (1989). *Assessing the Difficulty of Reading Materials: The Noun Frequency Method.* Wellington: NZ Council for Educational Research.

Elley W. B., & Mangubhai, F. (1983). The impact of reading on second language learning. *Reading Research Quarterly, 9*(1), 53–67.

Elley, W. B., Singh, G., & Lumelume, S. (1999). *Report of an Evaluation of Samoa Literacy Program in Primary Schools.* Suva: Institute of Education, University of the South Pacific.

Freebody, P. (1997). Cautionary notes on the home-school interface in early literacy learning. *Set Special 1997, No. 8.* Wellington: NZ Council for Educational Research.

Gaffney, J. S. (2001). Shared book reading in China. In Wenling Li, J. Gaffney & J. L. Packard (Eds.), *Chinese Children's Reading Acquisition: Theoretical and Pedagogical Issues.* Dordrecht, Netherlands: Kluwer Academic Publishers.

Gibbons, J. (1981). The benefits of early book experience on children's responses to text. Unpublished M.Ed. Thesis. Hamilton: University of Waikato.

Gilroy, A., & Moore, D. (1988). Reciprocal teaching of comprehension-fostering and comprehension-monitoring activities. *Educational Psychology, 8*, 41–49.

Halliday, M. (1975). *Learning How to Mean: Explorations in the Development of Language.* London: Edward Arnold.

Hill, S., Comber, B., Louden, W., Rivalland, J., & Reid, J. (1998). *100 Children Go to School: Connections and Disconnections in Literacy Development in the First Year of School.* Report to the Commonwealth Department of Employment, Education and Training, Canberra: AGPS.

Ho Wah Kam & Wong Ruth Y. L. (2000). *Language Policies and Language Education.* Singapore: Times Academic Press.

Ho Wah Kam & Ward, C. (2000). *Language in the Global Context: Implications for the Classroom.* Singapore: Regional Language Centre.

Holdaway, D. (1979). *Foundations of Literacy.* Auckland: Ashton Scholastic.

Hua, S. H., Anderson, R. C., & Houcan Zhang (1995). Incidental learning of word meanings while reading: A Chinese and American cross-cultural study. *Reading Research Quarterly, 30*(1), 76–95.

Ingulsrud, J. E., & Allen, K. (1999). *Learning to Read in China: Sociolinguistic Perspectives on the Acquisition of Literacy.* New York: Edwin Mellen Press.

Jacobs, G. M., Davis, C., & Renandya, W. A. (1997). *Successful Strategies for Extensive Reading..* Singapore: Regional Language Centre.

Kelly, M., Moore, D., & Tuck, B. F. (1994). Reciprocal teaching in a regular primary school. *Journal of Educational Research, 88*, 53–61.

Kidston, P., & Elkins, J. (1992). Australia. In J. Hladczuk & W. Eller (Eds.), *International Handbook of Reading Education.* London: Greenwood Press.

Ko Peng Sim & Ho Wah Kam (Eds.) (1992). *Growing Up in Singapore: The Pre-School Years.* Singapore: Longman.

Lee S-Y, Stigler, J. W., & Stevenson, H. W. (1988). Beginning reading in Chinese and English. In B. R. Foorman & A. W. Sieger (Eds.), *Acquisition of Reading Skills: Cultural Constraints and Cognitive Universals.* Hillsdale, NJ.: Lawrence Erlbaum.

Lituanas, P. M., Jacobs, G. M., & Renandya, W. A. (2001). An investigation of extensive reading in a Philippines secondary school. *International Journal of Educational Research, 35*, 217–225.

Luke, A. (1994). *The Social Construction of Literacy in the Primary School.* South Melbourne: Macmillan Education Australia.

Lyons, C. A., Pinnell, G. S., & De Ford, D. E. (1993). *Partners in Learning: Teachers and Children in Reading Recovery.* New York: Teachers College Press.

Masters, G., & Foster, M. (1997). *Mapping Literacy Achievement: Results of the 1996 National English Literacy Survey.* Canberra: Department of Education, Training and Youth Affairs.

McNaughton, S. (1995). *Patterns of Emergent Literacy.* Auckland: Oxford University Press.

Nation, P. (1988). *Teaching and Learning Vocabulary.* Wellington: English Language Institute, Victoria University of Wellington.

NEMP, (1997). *National Education Monitoring Project: Reading.* Wellington: Ministry of Education.

Nicholson, T. (1989). A comment on reading recovery. *New Zealand Journal of Educational Studies, 24*(1), 95–99.

Nicholson, T. (1998). Fragile phonics gains made. *NZ Education Review*, Feb 4, 1998.

Nicholson, T. (1999). Literacy in the family and society. In G. B. Thompson & T. Nicholson (Eds.), *Learning to Read: Beyond Phonics and Whole Language.* New York: Teachers College Press.

Ng, S. M. (1984). Reading acquisition in Singapore. *Singapore Journal of Education, 6*(2), 15–20.

Ng, S. M. (1999). Learning English in Hong Kong preschool centres: A research project. In Cheah Yin Mee & Ng Seok Moi (Eds.), *Language Instructional Issues in Asian Classrooms.* Newark, DE: International Reading Association.

Ng, S. M. (2001). The Brunei Reading and English Acquisition Project. *International Journal of Educational Research, 35*, 169–179.

Ng, S. M., & Sullivan, C. (2001). The Singapore Reading and English Acquisition Program. *International Journal of Educational Research, 35*, 157–167.

Phillips, G., & Smith, P. (1999). *Closing the Gaps: Literacy for the Hardest-to-Teach.* Wellington: NZ Council for Educational Research.

Pluck, M. (1995). Rainbow reading program: Using taped stories. *Reading Forum, NZ, 1*, 25–30.

Pluck, M. L., Ghafari, E., Glynn, T., & McNaughton, S. (1984). Teacher and parent modelling of recreational reading. *NZ Journal of Educational Studies, 19*(2), 114–123.

Pye, W. (1993). *The Magic Box.* Video. Auckland: Wendy Pye, Ltd.

Reid, N. A., & Elley, W. B. (1991). *Progressive Achievement Tests of Reading*. Wellington: NZ Council for Educational Research.

Ritchie, J. (1978). *Chance to be Equal*. Picton, NZ: Cape Catley.

Roberts, P. (1995). Literacy studies: A review of the literature, with signposts for future research. *NZ Journal of Educational Studies, 30*(2), 189–205.

Saragi, T. Nation, I. S. P., & Meister, G. F. (1978). Vocabulary learning and reading. *System, 6*(2), 72–78.

Sakamoto, T. (1992). Japan. In J. Hladczuk & W. Eller. *International Handbook of Reading Education*. London: Greenwood Press.

Saxby (1993). Children's literature: What to look for in a primary school program. In L. Unsworth (Ed.), *Literacy Learning and Teaching*. Sydney: MacMillan.

Singh, G. (2001). Literacy impact studies in Solomon Islands and Vanuatu. *International Journal of Educational Research, 2*, 227–236.

Smith, J. W. A., & Elley, W. B. (1997). *How Children Learn to Read*. Auckland: Addison Wesley Longman.

Stevenson, H. W., & Stigler, J. W. (1992). *The Learning Gap*. New York: Summit Books.

Tate, G. (1971). *Oral English Handbook*. Wellington: Reed Education.

Thorndike, R. L. (1973). *Reading Comprehension Education in Fifteen Countries*. Stockholm: Almquist & Wiksell.

Tunmer, W. E., & Chapman, J. W. (1999). Teaching strategies for word identification. In G. B. Thompson & T. Nicholson (Eds.), *Learning to Read: Beyond Phonics and Whole Language* (p. 4). New York: Teachers College Press.

van Kraayenoord, C. E. (1997). Children's self-appraisal of their work samples and academic progress. *Elementary School Journal, 97*, 5.

van Kraayenoord, C. E., & Paris, S. G. (1994). Literacy instruction in Australian primary schools. *The Reading Teacher, 48*(3), 210–217.

Wade, B., & Moore, M. (1998). Attitudes to reading: A longitudinal study of the effectiveness of reading recovery. *NZ Journal of Educational Studies, 33*(1), 95–106.

Wagemaker, H. (Ed.) (1993). *Achievement in Reading Literacy: New Zealand's Performance in a National and International Context*. Wellington: Ministry of Education.

Walker, R, Rattanavitch, S, & Oller, J. (1992). *Teaching All the Children to Read*. Buckingham, UK: Open University Press.

Wheldhall, K., & Glynn, T. (1989). *Effective Classroom Learning*. Oxford: Basil Blackwell.

Wilkinson, I. A. G., Freebody, P., & Elkins, J. (2000). Reading research in Australia and Aotearoa/New Zealand. In M. L. Kamil, P. B. Mosenthal, P. D. Pearson & R. Barr. (Eds.), *Handbook of Reading Research*, Vol III. Mahwah, New Jersey: Lawrence Erlbaum.

Withers, G. (1991). *Pacific Islands Literacy Levels*. Suva: South Pacific Board of Educational Assessment.

Yu, Wai Sze (1999). Promoting second language development and reading habits through an extensive reading program. In Cheah Yin Mee & Ng Seok Moi (Eds.), *Language Instructional Issues in Asian Classrooms*. Newark, DE: International Reading Association

41

Mathematics Curricula

ANDY BEGG
Open University, United Kingdom

1. MATHEMATICS IN THE CURRICULUM

School subjects can be said to provide ways of making sense of one's world. In mathematics these include quantifying with number, measurement, and statistics; describing and linking shapes with geometry and trigonometry; and generalising with arithmetic, algebra, and calculus. These ways are both descriptive (conceptual) and concerned with relationships (including applications). These ways also allow people to solve problems, explain and prove results, and communicate – that is, to think mathematically.

One aim of education is to prepare people for work, and because of this, the place of mathematics in the curriculum is assumed. However, with emerging technology, is mathematics needed for work? Some people argue that while society becomes more technological and while technology depends on mathematics, the level of mathematics required by users is decreasing. I argue that while the procedural mathematics required might be reduced, the level of technology use and the ability to understand and apply concepts appropriately is increased. However, Aoki (1987), writing in terms of computer applications in mathematics education, cites Gadamer (1975) who sees applications as important for understanding.

> ... application is not a subsequent nor a merely occasional part of understanding but codetermines it as a whole from the beginning ... application is not the mere relating of some pregiven generalized notion of the particular situation. (Aoki, 1987, p. 67)

If education is to prepare people for work then should mathematics be for everyone or only for those who choose it? Since the 1960s, most countries have accepted the UNESCO call 'mathematics for all'. Thus, as education becomes universal more children learn mathematics, and regardless of whether it is appropriate mathematics, its place in the curriculum is not questioned.

2. THE CURRICULUM

Curriculum in this article means 'all planned activity for the mathematics classroom'. As such it could be a noun, a product or a process. As a product it is usually documents: framework documents, subject syllabi, assessment schemes, textbooks, school programs, and lesson plans. One important document is often the textbook, this means that the authors interpret the curriculum for teachers because publishers rarely allow for pre-publication trialling or feedback from teachers. Adopted textbooks often become the *de facto* curriculum, and there is rarely any incentive for teachers to adapt them to fit local situations.

Curriculum is also a development process at both the regional and local level. It includes the continuous process of adapting lesson plans as students and teachers interact, as needs and interests are revealed, and as external events become relevant. Thus, curriculum means responding to students, context, practice, and theory. This process involves planning with flexibility so that changes are possible to build on questions, contexts, and student needs.

3. CURRICULUM CHANGE

In the last 50 years many changes have occurred in school mathematics; some of these are listed in Table 1.

Mathematicians, statisticians, or teachers initiated most of these changes. Few

Table 1. Five decades of change in mathematics

1950s	mathematics made compulsory
	calculus and co-ordinate geometry introduced for senior classes
1960s	'new' mathematics introduced (focus on sets, logic, and structure)
	transformation and/or vector geometry introduced (in some countries)
	(some) countries decimalised currency
1970s	(many) countries introduced metric system
	applied mathematics (in particular, mechanics) reconsidered
	statistics 'mainstreamed' (in some countries)
	interest in calculators and computers
1980s	a swing from the excesses of 'new mathematics'
	project work considered (in a few countries)
	internationalisation ICME, Cockcroft, NCTM Standards
	alternative learning/teaching strategies considered (practical work and discussion)
	constructivism in the debates
1990s	increased emphasis on the mathematical processes
	statistics gaining international recognition
	culture recognized in the Asia-Pacific region (ethnomathematics)
	increased use of technology, in particular, graphics calculators

had a traditional research base and the important influence was what was happening elsewhere. The six main changes have been: new mathematics, alternative teaching and learning strategies, statistics, mathematical processes, mathematics replacing arithmetic in primary schools, and the use of technology.

4. MATHEMATICAL PROCESSES

Holton (1993) wrote about what mathematicians do as distinct from what they know, and the relevance of this to the classroom. He emphasised problem solving – experimenting, conjecturing, proof (or counter-example), generalisation and extension, and publication. These reflect the processes from the United States (NCTM, 1989) and from curricula in some countries in the Asia-Pacific region. The processes include: problem solving, logical reasoning, communicating, making connections, and using technology. They are interrelated and could be integrated with the content knowledge of mathematics. Teachers often treat them separately because of the structure of curriculum documents, because professional development focusing on understanding these processes has been inadequate, or because processes are usually separated from content knowledge in assessment.

Related to the process of problem solving is mathematical modelling as shown in Figure 1.

In the past school mathematics was concerned with Step 2. Now the four steps are seen as mathematics, and Step 2 can often be done using technology. Real world problem solving together with making connections, suggests that contexts warrant attention. The real world for learners depends on their interests; it does not always mean the world outside the classroom. For some students the context is pure mathematics, for others it may involve mathematical puzzles, or other school subjects, or depend on interests outside school. Students construct meaningful contexts from activities in which they develop interest, and by carefully choosing learning activities, teachers can extend the contexts that learners find and call 'real'.

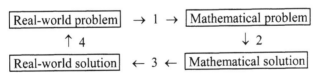

Figure 1. Problem solving process.

Step 1 is modelling or translating the real problem into mathematics. Step 2 is solving the mathematical problem. Step 3 is translating the mathematical solution back to the real situation. Step 4 is checking the reasonableness of the answer.

5. TECHNOLOGY

Engelbrecht and Harding (2001) summarized the influence of technology when they said that:

- some mathematics becomes more important because technology requires it;
- some mathematics becomes less important because technology replaces it;
- some mathematics becomes possible because technology allows it; and
- some mathematics can be taught using technology.

While these four statements all have curriculum implications, the acceptance of calculators (four-function, scientific, graphics, and symbol-manipulation) and computers in mathematics introduces issues related to cost, equity, assessment, and teacher development, that must be faced. This may suggest a need for more research on technology but such research has often been criticised when it is done by people who are familiar with technology and who are convinced of its worth even before they begin to research. These researchers can be reluctant to report failure, they work hard to ensure their interests are portrayed positively, and their industriousness as researchers and innovators in the classrooms is not usually replicated by other teachers later. Yet, this recognised and so-called 'Hawthorne' effect is generally ignored. Of course this criticism is also true about other research but perhaps to a lesser extent.

6. CURRICULUM RESEARCH

While various forms of research impinge on curriculum change, research is only one influence and curriculum change also influences research (see *Change in the School Curriculum; Looking to the Future*). In looking at the six main changes over the last 50 years it is interesting to consider the related research.

6.1. New Mathematics

New mathematics was a revolution in mathematics curriculum that occurred in the 1960s. New topics were introduced and one focus seemed to be to make school mathematics into a rigorous introduction to pure mathematics. With the new mathematics the initial research was in curriculum and textbook development. It involved mathematicians and the emphasis was logical rather than psychological. The work began mainly in the United States, the United Kingdom and Europe, with countries in the Asia-Pacific region adopting or adapting the ideas. The main research in the region was informal evaluations by teachers following implementation, which led to a gradual swing from the extremes of this initiative.

6.2. Alternative Teaching and Learning Strategies

In the 1980s, three main influences led to changes in mathematics teaching and learning. First, teacher dissatisfaction with traditional methods that arose from reflection-on-practice and led teachers to experiment with other methods. Articles in teacher journals sometimes stimulated these experiments but few of the articles were formal research reports. Second, the *Cockcroft Report* (DESWO, 1982) was a focus for many papers at Adelaide at the International Congress on Mathematics Education in 1984. It involved research and was concerned about how mathematics was and should be taught. Third, constructivism was researched in the Asia-Pacific region in science education both in New Zealand (Osborne & Freyberg, 1985) and Australia (White & Gunstone, 1992). The ideas become known to mathematics teachers, but a bigger influence in the 1990s was the writings from the United States on radical constructivism (von Glasersfeld, 1995), social constructivism (Cobb, 1994), and situated cognition (Lave & Wenger, 1991). Constructivism built on the work of Piaget and Vygotsky, it was interpreted in many different ways, and it emphasised alternative teaching ideas including: (a) building on students prior knowledge; (b) considering alternative conceptions; (c) problem-centred teaching, (d) discussion and practical work (DESWO, 1982), (e) rich mathematical activities (Ahmed, 1987), and (f) open-ended approaches (Becker & Shimada, 1997).

6.3. Statistics

In universities statistics has grown and often separated from mathematics. In schools this separation has not happened, statistics represents a redefining of school mathematics. The push for statistics came from statisticians, but teachers knew that other subjects need statistics, they thought that it was practical, they believed that it appealed to students, and many had studied it at university. The preliminary research was associated with curriculum and resource development. Australia and New Zealand were involved at an early stage, and considerable research in the area has occurred in Australia since the introduction of the subject (e.g., Watson, 1998). Statistics involved a change in content rather than in pedagogy (which is usually less threatening to teachers). Within the Asia-Pacific region there are many countries, in particular some of the less developed ones and those where the curriculum influence rests mainly with pure mathematicians, that have not yet included statistics in their curricula. For others such as Australia and New Zealand, it is taught at all class levels.

6.4. Mathematical Processes

The introduction of mathematical processes within Asia-Pacific countries followed Anglo-American precedents. Polya's (1957) work on problem solving had stimulated some of this. While reasoning and problem solving, traditionally in Euclidean geometry and applications, had always been part of mathematics, they were emphasised less in the 1970s and 1980s. But, mathematicians saw processes as important (for example, Holton, 1993), and many teachers believed that they would help make mathematics more relevant. Such thinking helped redefine school mathematics and these processes of problem solving, logical reasoning, communicating, making connections, and using tools, are now included in many curriculum documents. The research on processes in the region tends to have followed their introduction into the curriculum because of the comparatively speedy way that these influences impacted on curriculum design.

6.5. Mathematics in Elementary School

The notion that elementary school children should learn mathematics rather than arithmetic originated with the introduction of decimal currency and measures and the substantial saving of teaching time. These changes heralded the introduction of calculators and computers and the need for children to understand the underlying mathematical processes.

6.6. Technology

Technology has been introduced over a considerable time span and this has allowed time for research. Technology changes how mathematicians work, and how children can do and can learn mathematics. The work of Shuard and her colleagues in the United Kingdom with calculators for young children has been influential (Prime Project, 1989), and has been replicated in Australia (Groves & Stacey, 1998).

7. TYPES OF RESEARCH

In this article six forms of research in mathematics are discussed.

7.1. Basic Research

Basic research is concerned with curriculum, assessment, learning, teaching, aspects of development, and the nature of mathematics. Research on these has occurred although usually in a general educational context, however such research influences all school subjects and many teachers of mathematics teach other subjects. Curriculum developers do not usually initiate such research as it tends to be long-term, and, while it could inform policy, it could make it harder for politicians to push changes they want to impose. Thus, basic research is more often undertaken by academics and is often not well publicised or easily accessible. For example, Neyland's (2001) research critiques the technocratic assumptions that underpin many developments, but such critiques imply reconsideration and reconceptualisation of assumptions, and curriculum offices are usually concerned with producing documents and change within short political timelines. Neyland's argument fits with that of enactivism but is based on philosophy rather than on learning theory. He identified the need for us to reconsider education in general, and the assumptions that underpin the curriculum in particular. He writes of the need for an ethical philosophy that recognises the professionalism of teachers.

Basic research about the nature of mathematics asks, what is mathematics, what is mathematical knowledge, what do we mean by 'doing mathematics', and what is mathematics education? People including Lakatos (1976), Davis and Hersch (1981), Freudenthal (1973), and Skemp (1989) have researched these, but this type of research within the Asia-Pacific region seems to focus more on specific topics such as number, geometry, algebra and statistics and on aspects such as problem solving.

7.2. Research Regarding Particular Topics

A number of research studies that inform specific aspects of mathematics education (content, processes, technology, affective domain) have been undertaken and are available through journals and conference proceedings. Because of their specificity they do not have immediate implications for curriculum. Research syntheses that bring associated papers together and provide an overview of the different aspects are a useful way that such research is presented to people involved with curriculum although in this area there is often a reliance on overseas publications such as Grouws (1992).

7.3. Comparative Research

Two types of comparative research impact on curriculum development. The first is research such as the Third International Mathematics and Science Study (see Beaton, Mullis, Martin, Gonzales, Kelly, & Smith, 1996; Mullis, Martin, Beaton, Gonzales, Kelly, & Smith, 1996). Kaiser, Luna and Huntley (1999) have critiqued these studies and their work needs to be considered alongside the project reports. TIMSS highlighted differences (and therefore possibilities) between education systems and curriculum, and focused on many aspects of school mathematics. For example, some highly successful Asian countries know that they emphasise procedures and routine examples, and are considering putting more emphasis into creative approaches and focussing more on the mathematical processes.

The second type of comparative research involves the sharing curriculum documents from other countries. This sharing is usually from neighbouring countries, and from more developed countries with ties (through colonialism, similar languages, examination boards, aid projects, or international status). One danger exists with such document sharing, most curriculum projects are politically driven, and sometimes a curriculum can be accepted at surface level without an exploration of, or an agreement with, the underpinning assumptions and their related implications.

7.4. Evaluatory Research

Many countries undertake an evaluation of existing curriculum before commencing new development projects but the depth of analysis and the search for explanations varies considerably. Evaluation may also be carried out during a development project to get feedback on draft documents. This feedback has been criticised on two counts – the draft is based on assumptions, which appear non-debatable; and the time to comment does not allow for trialling, thus, while responses are usually well argued, they are not always supported by evidence. Finally, it is possible to evaluate a new curriculum some time after it has been implemented and then modify it, or to evaluate annually and review it but there is no evidence of systematic reviews in the region.

7.5. Teacher Research

Teacher research may be completed as part of their professional development, or as part of a qualification upgrading, but more often it is informal. It may be based on explorations by teachers, professional discussions with colleagues, consideration of ideas from the literature, or reflections-on-practice. Researchers such as Schön (1983) have no doubt influenced the use of reflection, but more often teachers simply take a thoughtful and professional approach to their work. While reflection starts by being descriptive, it becomes interpretative as teachers consider alternatives, and critical as they question the underpinning assumptions. Unfortunately teacher research is rarely written up or shared beyond immediate colleagues. However, it influences teachers when lobbying for curriculum change, responding to drafts, adapting official curricula to suit specific situations, and more importantly, it informs practice and helps those involved to evolve continually and improve their work. With teacher research two gaps emerge – academics and researchers see a theory and research-to-practice gap, teachers see a practice-to-theory gap, both exist, and need to be minimised.

7.6. Scholarship

Within all the above forms of research scholarship plays a very significant part. It is often through the reading, thinking, theory building, and formulation of new ideas and new links from one's experiences as well as from the research of others that leads to better syntheses of ideas and more coherent literature reviews and summaries of research being presented.

8. RESEARCH IN THE REGION

As part of writing this article a questionnaire was sent out to colleagues and curriculum officers in just over 50 countries in the region. Responses were received from nearly half the countries. The response rate was encouraging although the responses were, perhaps naturally, somewhat biased towards countries where English language dominates, where research is either being conducted or where considerable notice is taken of research, and where national economies are comparatively well developed. Many respondents reported that their "curriculum was not research based" although virtually all of them talked of analysing curricula from other countries and surveying opinion about draft versions of documents.

All but one of the countries said that they had been influenced by curriculum documents from other countries, these countries being the United States, the United Kingdom, neighbouring countries, and countries with the same language of instruction; although France, Russia, Canada and The Netherlands were each mentioned once. Most of the countries had done some research or evaluation projects within their own country. The other influences varied considerably and included studying research on numeracy, information technology, calculators, thinking, algebra, statistics, arithmetic meaning, children's ideas, open-ended questioning, modelling, assessment, professional development, and the nature of mathematics.

What might have appeared at first to be a paucity of curriculum-focussed research in some of the countries from the region is understandable because their priorities are to expand access rather than quality, and because of their limited resources for research. In addition, some countries may have been doing curriculum research that was not specific to mathematics, but the survey for this article had not requested information about such projects.

9. CURRICULUM DEVELOPMENT

Traditionally curriculum development has used the research-development-dissemination (RDD) model, but the suggested model with eight emerging activities that has been considered in the article on *Change in the School Curriculum: Looking to the Future*, offers an alternative. While development is usually thought of at the regional and national levels, it also occurs at the micro level as teachers work to improve their lessons. Ideally there is a rich dialogue between the micro and the macro levels so that a sense of ownership of the curriculum change process emerges, and so that regional documents are influenced by practising teachers who in turn will then adopt rather than adapt the changes. This continuous dialogic process between teachers and developers should not be envisaged as a stop-start process during the dissemination phase of an initiative, but rather as ongoing. Such development activities are also influenced by theoretical considerations that impinge on the teachers.

While teachers plan for their classrooms, and teachers and developers maintain a dialogue, another question is: whose voices should be heard in official curriculum projects? Being called 'official', the documents are government policy statements with central agencies involved. Other possible involved people are mathematicians (professional and practising pure and applied mathematicians and statisticians), mathematics educators and general educators, teachers unions and associations, parents, and students. The challenge is to take these peoples ideas into account in a continuing development process.

10. EDUCATIONAL THEORIES

Many theories influence mathematics education, these include theories about the nature of mathematics (e.g., the process/content debate), assessment (e.g., outcomes-based), teaching, and learning. Perhaps the most influential theories impacting on mathematics curricula are to do with learning. Such theories are not right or wrong, they are ways of making sense of learning, and each has contributions to make.

Until 1980, the dominant Western theories about education involved direct instruction, associationism, and behaviourism. These assumed a causal link between what the teacher did (the stimulus) and what the student learnt (the response). These theories were interpreted in different ways, some people assumed that drill and practice led to rote memorisation, others worked towards memorisation with understanding. The theories were often considered simplistically without accepting that multiple stimuli could influence the learner, and the objectives were often ordered rigidly with the final one (synthesis) omitted. During this period other theories (from Dewey, Steiner, Montessori, Neill, Rogers and others) had a minor influence. Behaviourism and direct instruction are still dominant in some developing countries in the region and where teachers are authoritarian.

More recently constructivism in various forms has become dominant (Steffe, Nesher, Cobb, Goldin, & Greer, 1996). Constructivism differs from earlier theories by seeing teaching and learning as being interactive and not causal (in a Newtonian sense). It assumes that learners or groups of learners create knowledge and that prior experience and alternative conceptions are important. It favours broad learning objectives rather than specific behavioural objectives, and involves the teacher trying to 'get inside the learner's head' rather than only considering and measuring, behaviours.

Curriculum documents still tend to be structured in terms of aims and objectives. With behaviourism the objectives are described as behavioural or specific because they specify the behaviours that are to result. With constructivism they are sometimes called learning objectives and they tend to be somewhat broader. In both cases an ordering of objectives is implicit although with constructivism teachers think much more of the 'construction of a schema' rather than a 'linear sequence of objectives'.

Unfortunately, when assessment is important, the objectives become assessment objectives, and focus on what is easy to measure. They often fragment the subject, and tend to be unidimensional rather than assume that the mathematics teacher is also a teacher of language, values, social behaviour, and so on. Related to assessment is the notion of progression. This was assumed by behaviourism when subjects were analysed into specific objectives that were ordered for the curriculum. Progression was reinforced in the 1960s by the new mathematics with order being logical rather than psychological. Although constructivism emphasises children's prior knowledge, the curriculum continues to be based on a behavioural-type analysis reinforced by teacher-accountability measures and by external assessment. Teachers and developers have socially constructed progression; it has become a self-fulfilling prophecy, but is now being questioned by people who see knowledge differently. Block puts it nicely,

> The establishment of prerequisites is an exclusionary device which prevents the development of natural curiosities and interests even as it tantalizes the learner with golden apples which are made to recede even as they are grasped at by eager minds. (Block, 1988, p. 40)

Living without progression will be a challenge in the future.

In the 1990s, another new learning theory began to emerge. It is known as enactivism. The theory originated with the biologists Maturana and Varela (see Maturana & Varela, 1987; Varela, Thompson, & Rosch, 1991). Davis (1996) has interpreted enactivism into the context of mathematics, and with colleagues, into more general contexts (Davis, Sumara, & Luce-Kapler, 2000). This work has stimulated interest amongst some mathematics educators in New Zealand and Australia. Enactivism can be considered as an elaboration of constructivism. It enlarges the notion of what we consider as a learning system, it takes into consideration forms of knowing other than the logical or rational and the motor or sensory, and it conflates knowledge, activity and identity. In addition, knowledge is seen not as independent of individuals and their environments, or as something that can be tested or matched against external standards, but rather as embodied. From a curriculum perspective the enactivist teacher is said to be more concerned with what can be called 'curriculum occasioning' and 'curriculum anticipating' in response to students in the class. That is, with how to choose good learning activities to extend the basic ideas from a curriculum to involve all the students, and how to anticipate how the lesson might flow for different class members and prepare for students who go off in unexpected directions. These activities are similar to what many good teachers do and what has been reported from Japanese lesson planning.

11. CULTURE AND ETHNOMATHEMATICS

Just as the West has dominated learning theories, so mathematics has been regarded as mainly Western though culture free. This is surprising. The number system owes much to India, algebra is from the Arab world, and calculus was developed in Japan at the same time as in Europe. Unfortunately, colonisation, post-war occupation, and aid projects, have reinforced the Western perspective.

The Western emphasis began to change when D'Ambrosio (1984) spoke at the International Congress on Mathematics Education about ethnomathematics in his plenary address, and even more so four years later, when a whole day was devoted to the subject at the next congress. The work of Lean (1988), Bishop (1988), and others in Papua New Guinea was critical in the Asia-Pacific region and has resulted in a research centre being established at the University at Goroka. Such activities stimulated initiatives including UNESCO conference that was held in 1991 to consider Polynesian language issues in mathematics (Begg, 1992).

In terms of mathematics curriculum for indigenous people, New Zealand produced a document (Ministry of Education, 1994) and others in the region are working to develop suitable resources for local communities. Unfortunately, this work focuses on making Western mathematics acceptable to others, and does not address cultural issues, in particular issues to do with different ways of thinking. For example, mathematics is not seen as a separate subject in some Oceanic countries (where subjects are seen as a Western partitioning of knowledge), and mathematics in India is more concerned with answers than proof and has a recreational dimension. Such differences would be expected to influence what happens in the curriculum documents in those countries.

From the recommendations of the Australian Human Rights and Equal Opportunity Commission (2000) I see three important curriculum needs enunciated for indigenous people, and for students living in remote areas. These needs are indicative of similar problems emerging in numerous countries. The first related to the provision of curricula that are culturally appropriate. The second, to the language of instruction. The third, to the desirability of providing local and regional content while still achieving established learning outcomes. These present a major challenge for the future.

12. ASSESSMENT

Assessment is intended to help teachers monitor students' progress, make instructional decisions, assess student achievement, and evaluate programs. The first two of these are formative assessment, the third is summative, and the fourth is evaluative. With good teaching formative assessment occurs continuously and informally as part of the teacher-learner interactions and is part of teaching rather than assessment. The third is given considerable emphasis in many countries. It may mean annual examinations that result in holding students back a year or terminating their formal education. Such assessment often dictates school programs, and this is paralleled when national, or state-wide, assessment schemes are promulgated for a specific age group and the demands of assessment tend to overshadow curricula intentions.

In debating assessment, Firsov (1996) suggested an alternative form of assessment. His form assumes:

(a) we hardly ever know a subject until some time after we were first taught it;
(b) success is the critical motivating factor;
(c) students should be able to achieve with assessment tasks;
(d) assessment should be related to the students' right to choose (because of their prior knowledge and interests) and choice should exist within mathematics;
(e) assessment often confirms failure rather than success;
(f) a two-level curriculum is needed, the top being what learning tasks aim at, the lower being for assessment;
(g) assessment should be based on the parts of the curriculum that all students must know and do and that teachers can assume they can do;
(h) the taught curriculum should provide opportunities for students to be extended to follow their interests, and to negotiate their learning;
(i) assessment in mathematics should not use multi-choice formats; and
(j) students will show all working in their books, so there is no need for portfolios.

Firsov believes that students need success in every lesson and suggests that teachers should change from a pedagogy of subtraction (taking marks off) to one of addition. That is, assessment should be based on strengths rather than deficits, or as Cockcroft said (DESWO, 1982), we should assess what students know, not what they do not know.

13. WIDER THAN MATHEMATICS

Many issues that influence school mathematics also impact on other subjects and decisions on these can not be made unilaterally by mathematics teachers. These include cross curriculum initiatives, educational aims, pre-service teacher education, the question of whose voice should be heard in curriculum development, and the structure of the curriculum itself.

The making of connections from mathematics fits with curriculum frameworks that link subjects. The mathematics curriculum is a subset of the school curriculum and mathematics has a service role in many subjects and this could provide an opportunity for cross curriculum education. As part of developing an official framework, the aims of education need to be considered, and then operationalised in all school subjects including mathematics. The aims imply discussion regarding such things as transforming or preserving society, focusing on individual or societal needs, defining national development, clarifying values (e.g., moral, caring, political, or religious values). Such debates are occurring to some extent, one example is a project on values in mathematics education which is currently involving colleagues in Australia and Taiwan (Clarkson & Bishop, 2000). Such debates are likely to be easy for teachers who teach many subjects, but mathematics specialist teachers need to be involved to avoid being marginalised.

An aim in education that is sometimes overlooked is to help students become autonomous learners so that their learning in all areas is enhanced and will continue as they face future needs in life and work. While autonomous learning is often a curriculum aim, it raises issues of responsibility for learning and choice in the classroom that many mathematics teachers have not considered, yet these values may have more influence on students than the content they are taught.

The role of professional development for teachers has been referred to as part of the ongoing curriculum development process. The other aspect of teacher education is pre-service education. Currently, in many countries, there is a shortage of well-qualified mathematics teachers to teach in high schools. Many generalist teachers have an inadequate background in mathematics, and there is a shortage of mathematics educators with a background in both mathematics and education. Addressing these shortages is a challenge.

14. FUTURE CHALLENGES

The future requires a reconceptualization of curriculum. According to Davis and Sumara there are two views of curriculum:

> ... on one hand curriculum is seen as a straightforward project of selecting

outcomes and parsing those outcomes into incremental learning trajectories. ... On the other hand ... highlight the complexities of the classroom situation, its possibilities for surprise, its dependence on the particularities and diversities represented, its propensities for reflecting and re-enacting broader social dynamics, and so on – in brief, the scale independence and the specificity of the moment of teaching. (pp. 839–840)

... the product of curriculum engagement cannot be predicted or controlled – but that does not mean that it defies comprehension. It just means that the structure that emerges or the path that unfolds has to be lived through for its endpoint to be realized. Rather than thinking in terms of a pre-specified structure, one might think of a myriad of potentialities, one of which will be pulled into existence – but only by living through the event. (Davis & Sumara, 2000, pp. 841–842)

If the first view is preferred, there is a need to ask whether a global curriculum or local ones are preferred? How much flexibility is required for good teaching? Can learning take precedence over assessment? How can teachers be involved in official curriculum projects, and how can their work with planning for classes be fostered and valued? Can approaches be designed so that curriculum, teacher, resource, and assessment development are integrated and ongoing? How can the mathematics classroom be improved so that it better reinforces the general aims of education? If the second view is preferred then the challenge is greater.

The slogans 'small is beautiful' and 'think globally, act locally' are worth remembering. Small changes continue to be made in classrooms where teachers and students share responsibility, and although we would like to change the world, we cannot change others, we can only change ourselves.

Our aim in mathematics education and in curriculum design must be to change mathematics so that it provides a gateway for students and ceases to be the gatekeeper.

REFERENCES

Ahmed, A. (1987). *Better Mathematics (A Curriculum Development Study based on LAMP)*. London: Her Majesty's Stationery Office.

Aoki, T. (1987). Towards understanding 'computer application'. *The Journal of Curriculum Theorizing*, 7(2), 61–71. (Reprinted In W. Pinar (Ed.) (1999), *Contemporary Curriculum Discourses: Twenty years of JCT* (pp. 168–176.) New York: Peter Lang Publishing).

Australian Human Rights and Equal Opportunity Commission (2000). *Recommendations: National Inquiry into Rural and Remote Education*. Sydney: Human Rights and Equal Opportunity Commission.

Beaton, A., Mullis, I., Martin, O., Gonzales, E., Kelly, D., & Smith, T. (1996). *Mathematics Achievement in the Middle School Years*. Boston: CSTEEP Boston College (TIMSS).

Becker, J., & Shimada, S. (Eds.) (1997). *The Open-Ended Approach: A New Proposal for Teaching Mathematics*. Reston VA: National Council of Teachers of Mathematics.

Begg, A. (Ed.) (1992). *Mathematika Pasefika – Vocabulary Database* (version 2.0) (unesco conference). Hamilton, University of Waikato.

Bishop, A. (1988). *Mathematical enculturation: A cultural perspective on mathematics education.* Dordrecht: Kluwer Academic Publishers.

Block, A. (1988). The Answer is Blowin' in the Wind: A deconstructive reading of the school text. *The Journal of Curriculum Theorizing, 8*(4), 23–52. (Reprinted in, W. Pinar (Ed.) (1999), *Contemporary Curriculum Discourses: Twenty years of JCT* (pp. 177–198.). New York: Peter Lang Publishing).

Clarkson, P., & Bishop, A. (2000). Values and mathematics education. In A. Ahmed, H. Williams, & J. Kraemer (Eds.), *Cultural Diversity in Mathematics Education* (pp. 239–244). Chichester UK: Horwood Publishing.

Cobb, P. (1994). Where is the mind? constructivist and sociocultural perspectives on mathematics development. *Educational Researcher, 23*(7), 13–20.

D'Ambrosio, U. (1984). Socio-cultural bases for mathematical education. In, M. Carss (Ed.), *Proceedings of the Fifth International Congress on Mathematical Education* (pp. 1–6). Boston: Birkhäuser.

Davis, B. (1996). *Teaching mathematics: Towards a sound alternative.* New York: Garland Publishing.

Davis, B., & Sumara, D. (2000). Curriculum forms: An the assumed shapes of knowing and knowledge, *Journal of Curriculum Studies, 32*(6), 821–845.

Davis, B., Sumara, D., & Luce-Kapler, R. (2000). *Engaging Minds: Learning and Teaching in a Complex World.* Lawrence Erlbaum Associates.

Davis, P., & Hersch, R. (1981). *The Mathematical Experience.* Boston: Birkhauser.

Department of Education and Science and the Welsh Office DESWO (1982). *Mathematics Counts* (Report of the Committee of Inquiry into the Teaching of Mathematics in Schools under the Chairmanship of Dr W. H. Cockcroft). London: Her Majesty's Stationery Office.

Engelbrecht, J., & Harding, A. (2001). *Mathematics is not got grown ups.* Seminar presented at the Mathematics Education Unit of the University of Auckland.

Firsov, V. (1996). *Russian standards: Concepts and decisions.* Paper presented at the 8th International Congress on Mathematics Education, Seville Spain.

Freudenthal, H. (1973). *Mathematics as an Educational Task.* Dordrecht: Reidel.

Gadamer, H.-G. (1975). *Truth and Method.* New York: Seabury Press.

Grouws, D. A. (Ed.) (1992). *Handbook of Research on Mathematics Teaching and Learning.* New York: Macmillan Publishing (with the National Council of Teachers of Mathematics).

Groves, S., & Stacey, K. (1998). Calculators in primary mathematics: Exploring number before teaching algorithms. In L. Morrow & M. Kenny (Eds.), *The Teaching and Learning of Algorithms in School Mathematics: 1998 Yearbook of the National Council of Teachers of Mathematics* (pp. 120–129). Reston VA: National Council of Teachers of Mathematics.

Holton, D. (1993). What mathematicians do and why it is important in the classroom, *Set (Research Information for Teachers), 1,* Item 10, (1–6).

Kaiser, G., Luna, E., & Huntley, I. (Eds.) (1999). *International Comparisons in Mathematics Education.* London/Philadelphia: Falmer Press.

Lakatos, I. (1976). *Proofs and Refutations.* Cambridge: Cambridge University Press.

Lave, J., & Wenger, E. (1991). *Situated learning: Legitimate peripheral participation.* New York: Cambridge University Press.

Lean, G. (1988). *Counting Systems of Papua New Guinea,* Vols 1–17. Lae: Papua New Guinea University of Technology.

Maturana, H., & Varela, F. (1987). *The tree of knowledge: The biological roots of human understanding.* Boston MA: Shambala Press.

Ministry of Education (1994). *Pangarau: Te Taua ki Marautanga [He Tauira].* Wellington: Learning Media, Ministry of Education.

Mullis, I., Martin, O., Beaton, A., Gonzales, E., Kelly.D., & Smith, T. (1996). *Mathematics Achievement in the Primary School Years.* Boston: CSTEEP Boston College (TIMSS).

National Council of Teachers of Mathematics (1989). *Curriculum and Evaluation Standards for School Mathematics.* Reston VA: NCTM.

Neyland, J. (2001). *An Ethical Critique of Technocratic Mathematics Education: Towards an Ethical Philosophy of Mathematics Education.* Unpublished PhD thesis, Victoria University of Wellington.

Osborne, R., & Freyberg, P. (Eds.) (1985). *Learning in Science: The implications of children's science.* Auckland: Heinemann.

Polya, G. (1957). *How to solve it: A new aspect of mathematical method.* New York: Doubleday.

Prime Project (1989). *The Second Year of CAN (Calculator Aware Number, part of the primary initiatives in Mathematics Education).* Cambridge: Prime.

Schön, D. (1983). *The reflective practitioner: How professionals think in action.* New York: Basic Books.

Skemp, R. (1989). *Mathematics in the Primary School.* London: Routledge.

Steffe, L., Nesher, P., Cobb, P., Goldin, G., & Greer, B. (Eds.) (1996). *Theories of Mathematical Learning.* Mahwah NJ: Lawrence Erlbaum Associates.

Varela, F., Thompson, E., & Rosch, E. (1991). *The embodied mind: Cognitive science and human experience.* Cambridge MA: Massachusetts Institute of Technology Press.

von Glasersfeld, E. (1995). *Radical constructivism: A way of knowing and learning.* London: Falmer Press.

Watson, J. (1998). Professional development for teachers of probability and statistics: Into the era of technology. *International Statistical Review, 66,* 271–289.

White, R., & Gunstone, R. (1992). *Probing Understanding.* London: Falmer Press.

42

Science Curricula

ROBYN BAKER and ROSEMARY HIPKINS
New Zealand Council for Educational Research, Wellington, New Zealand

1. INTRODUCTION

Science is commonly viewed as fundamental to the education of all students, with 'scientific literacy', being seen as a key curriculum goal. During their school science learning, students are generally expected to come to an understanding of three interrelated aspects of science: science content knowledge, practical work, and nature of science or science and society areas respectively. Students are also typically expected to develop positive attitudes towards science and technology as a result of their school learning experiences.

The translation of these broad goals into specific school curricula is complex and is underpinned by varying assumptions about learning, teaching, content and purposes. Cheung and Ng (2000) identify five distinct curriculum orientations that can result from the relative emphases given to these different goals. An academic orientation privileges accurate learning of a body of science discipline knowledge – content acquisition is the primary goal. A cognitive processes orientation emphasises learning about the methods of science and the development of investigative skill. A society-centred orientation focuses on the goal of democratic participation in adult life. A humanistic orientation emphasises the role of science knowledge in personal development, intellectual growth, and opportunities for higher education, allied with enhancement of opportunities for personal prosperity. A technological orientation focuses on technological aspects of science, as the name suggests. Cheung and Ng point out that national curricula, that is, the *intended* curriculum, are usually a mix of these orientations, and that local school and teacher decision making for the *implemented* curriculum is context dependent and probably influenced by culture.

While Cheung and Ng direct one level of their analysis to the intended curriculum for Hong Kong, they also note that the culture of different science subject disciplines, for example physics, appears to have an influence on curriculum orientation, and hence on the implemented curriculum. They also make the observation that many Hong Kong teachers appear to move closer to a cognitive orientation as their years of teaching experience increase. Such within-nation variation has also been described by Wallace and Chou (2001), for Taiwanese and Australian teachers, albeit in the context of pedagogical practice rather than curriculum orientation. Findings such as these serve as reminders that curricula are complex and dynamic, and it is important not to make essentialist assumptions that the nature of science teaching in one country is a feature of national culture alone. Nevertheless there are broad patterns of similarities and differences in national science curricula in the Asia-Pacific region, and these are outlined in the first section of this article. The second part of the article reviews the role of key research areas in influencing curriculum decision making within the Asia-Pacific region, at both intended and implemented levels.

2. THE ORGANISATION OF SCIENCE IN THE CURRICULUM

In the Asia-Pacific region, science is included in the school curriculum from Year 1 (e.g., in Australia and New Zealand); from Year 3 (e.g., in Indonesia and the Republic of Korea) and from Year 4 (e.g., in Vietnam and Lao). Most countries offer science as a separate subject but variations on this include the Philippines that begin with science and health (Years 1-6) and then offer science and technology as a compulsory subject in Years 7-10. Similarly, Sri Lanka begins with environmental studies (Years 1-6) before introducing Science and Technology (Years 7-9). The integration of science into a general science curriculum is continued into the junior high school in a number of countries (such as Japan, Korea, Thailand and Australia) but others by Year 8 are teaching earth science, biology, physics and chemistry as separate subjects (e.g., Taiwan and Indonesia). However, even within the integrated science courses there is a considerable range of subject areas included. In New Zealand, for example, the general science curriculum includes biology, physics, chemistry, astronomy and earth science, while in the People's Republic of China it includes nature, mathematics, physics, chemistry, biology, hygiene and environmental protection.

While school science and technology curricula are frequently linked there are many ways in which this relationship is translated into a specific curriculum structure. In Australia and New Zealand the science and technology curricula are separate. In some countries they are linked within the one curriculum, science and technology, and in China, for example, science, technology and cultural studies are all linked within the same curriculum area. Despite these differences in curriculum structure, there is a common expectation that science education should provide "some understanding of the principles underlying the technological developments which have been influential on our lifestyle and develop some appreciation of their impact on the way we live" (Millar and Osborne, 1998, p. 18).

At the upper secondary level the traditional school science subjects of biology, physics and chemistry are commonly offered and there is a growing diversity of other science courses. In Japan, for example, students in the tenth grade need to select one of three courses. Two of these are labelled as Comprehensive Science (one covering biological diversity and environments and the other matter and energy) and the third as Fundamental Science (*Riko-Kiso*), which places the focus on learning science through case studies of famous events and stories from the history of science (Ogawa, 2001). Similarly, in Malaysia the traditional science courses are complemented by Additional Science, which encompasses physics, chemistry, biology, earth science, agriculture, oceanography and space science.

3. THE INTENDED SCIENCE CURRICULUM

Cogan, Wang and Schmidt (2001) carried out a comparative analysis of the science content taught within the eighth grade curricula of countries participating in the Third International Mathematics and Science Study (TIMSS). The analysis suggested that in different countries "what constitutes school science – how subjects are grouped together for study at specific grade levels, the sequence of topics studied from grade to grade, and how much emphasis each receives in any one year – all appear to reflect culturally or nationally specific patterns of choices" (p. 106). However, while there is diversity in the composition of school science courses in the region, the stated aims and intended outcomes of school science education commonly encompass the four key areas that have already been identified in the introduction to this article: (a) knowing basic science facts and understanding science concepts; (b) experiencing the doing of science through practical investigations; (c) understanding something of the nature of scientific inquiry; and (d) developing positive attitudes to science and learning science.

Cogan et al.'s analysis of the intended curriculum for eighth grade students in the participating TIMSS nations indicated that understanding the concepts of science received a major emphasis in all the participating countries of the region. While few of the countries involved in the study gave a major emphasis to using laboratory equipment and performing science experiments, many of those that did were from the Asia-Pacific region, including Hong Kong, Japan, Korea, Malaysia and Singapore (Martin et al., 2000). There was, however, much less emphasis in the region on designing and conducting scientific investigations, activities that are arguably more likely to lead towards an understanding of the nature of science – that is, how new scientific knowledge is produced, validated, and applied within and beyond the community of working scientists. There were also quite diverse findings with respect to students' attitudes to science, with students in Malaysia and the Philippines indicating very positive attitudes and those in Hong Kong, Korea and Japan recording the least positive attitudes. While there was a clear positive association between students' attitudes towards science and science achievement, it may be that the demanding science curriculum of the latter countries leads to high achievement but little enthusiasm for the subject matter (Martin et al., 2000).

The science curriculum, as implemented within classrooms, needs to achieve some balance between these four sets of science aims or outcomes. The way this is achieved in practice is influenced by what is perceived to be the overall purpose of learning science at school.

4. PURPOSES FOR LEARNING SCIENCE

School science education can be viewed as either an education for future scientists and science-related professionals, or as aiming for a type of scientific literacy where people "are comfortable, competent and confident with scientific and technical matters and artefacts" (Millar & Osborne, 1998, p. 9). These purposes may be interpreted as being mutually exclusive, although a number of curriculum commentators have pointed out that future scientists are also future citizens and so they should not be exempted from the need to become broadly literate in all areas of science (Goodrum, Hackling & Rennie, 2000). The former purpose may lead to a disproportionate focus on content delivery and abstract scientific principles – that is, a relatively academic orientation to curriculum (Cheung & Ng, 2000). The scientific literacy purpose places the emphasis on learning key science principles, together with broad understandings about science, to enable informed decision-making about science-related issues in everyday life.

In practice, despite broader aims in the intended curriculum, science education is often experienced by students as an overwhelming body of content to be learned. Goodrum et al. (2000) suggest that this happens because upper secondary science courses have been designed to select and prepare students for the further study of science. The approach taken to such courses often "cascades down to lower secondary school, resulting in irrelevant, content-laden curriculum which lack meaning and relevance to most of the students who study them" (Goodrum et al., 2000, p. 8). They suggest that the conflict can be resolved by maintaining a focus on scientific literacy during the compulsory years of schooling and providing a diversity of science courses to cater for the range of needs of students in the post-compulsory years.

Many science educators have been advocating for such an approach for some time and there is a growing empathy with this position from policy makers. This is demonstrated, for example, by the countries that have opted to participate in the OECD's Programme for International Student Assessment (PISA) which focuses on the assessment of scientific literacy of 15 year-old students, that is, how students' education is preparing them to engage with science in their adult lives.

Despite this OECD initiative, the relative emphasis given to the dual purposes of school science is still a contentious issue and one that will be difficult to resolve. Criticism of science education from scientists, politicians and the media often focuses on the failure to ground students in the basic knowledge of science, on the so-called 'dumbing down' of courses by relating science to broader social issues and on the way it limits the opportunities for potential scientists. The essence of the tension is outlined by Ogawa (2001) as he describes the new

Japanese science elective system in Grades 10 to 12. He suggests that this initiative is good for the general science literacy purposes but that it does not allow future tertiary science students to complete every science course in the upper secondary school. The importance of science, particularly the life sciences, for on-going economic development has been an explicit driver of curriculum change in Singapore. In this case, a two-tiered approach has been taken, one aiming for literacy for the general student population and the other for students interested in pursuing their studies in the life sciences.

5. ISSUES IN THE IMPETUS FOR CURRICULUM CHANGE

While recent impetus for curriculum change in science has come from the development of new knowledge, such as in the case of the life sciences, there has also been a desire to improve achievement in science through curriculum change. Over the last two decades, concerns about the impact of the implemented science curriculum on attitudes to science have focused on particular groups of students, including girls and students from other than white Western family backgrounds.

While in general the achievement of girls in science is similar to that of boys, there are differences in their participation in science courses in post-compulsory schooling. Girls tend to have less positive attitudes to science and lower levels of confidence about their abilities in science. They commonly have different interests both in the areas of science and in the content within the science areas. In some countries in the region the gender-imbalanced participation rates in upper secondary science courses reflect individual student choice. However, in other countries, particularly those with relatively low incomes, girls are less likely than boys to be still at school as well as less likely to be involved in science courses. This is evident in many of the Pacific Island countries such as the Solomon Islands, Fiji and Papua New Guinea.

Efforts to promote the participation of girls in science in countries such as New Zealand and Australia have focused on attempting to address issues relating to attitude and confidence. Rennie (2000) suggests that similar approaches may be needed in Taiwan in an attempt to address the low numbers of female students in tertiary science courses. Rennie cites earlier research by She who found that Taiwanese school students held sex-stereotyped views about science and scientists that were influenced by their peers, parents, their science textbooks and the media. While older students had more realistic views and girls were more willing than boys to consider scientists as female, they were more reluctant to consider a science career for themselves.

While the participation of girls in science remains a concern in the region, in recent years the science education outcomes attained by different cultural and social groups have received increasing attention. In New Zealand, for example, the national and international monitoring of student achievement in science has indicated that the achievement of many Maori, the indigenous people of the country, is relatively low. So is that of Pacific Island students who attend New

Zealand schools. There is a dearth of actual classroom research that might shed some substantive light on this issue (McKinley, 1999). Concern about these achievement gaps led to a recent Government-commissioned review aimed at providing evidence of pedagogy that might have a positive impact on student achievement in science education for the diversity of students in New Zealand (Hipkins et al., 2002).

It is not just achievement *per se* that is of concern to educators in the Asia-Pacific region. Countries such as Japan, Korea and Singapore, all of which are renowned for their achievement in science, are seeking to develop greater creativity, more sophisticated thinking and problem-solving skills, and a focus on original investigation. These changes are to be effected by reducing curriculum content and, in the case of Singapore, by introducing the teaching of thinking skills.

Within the region, as is the case worldwide, response to these pressures has led to science curricula that tend to be more practical and more directly related to students' everyday lives. In nations such as Japan the science curriculum is changing to take account of the needs and interests of students in the belief that this will promote better learning as well as ensure more equitable access to, and participation in, science (Ogawa, 2001).

These developments in science education have mostly been informed by research rather than led by research. It is often the case that a curriculum-policy response to one area of research may create tensions in other areas. The next section details some of the significant areas of research that have influenced curriculum in the Asia-Pacific region at both policy and practice levels, with their attendant tensions.

6. THE IMPACT OF RESEARCH IN SCIENCE EDUCATION ON CURRICULUM

Research in science education is a relatively recent phenomenon in many parts of the world, although it has a longer history in North America and, like most new research fields, is characterised by a diversity of approaches and concerns (Jenkins, 2001). In the Asia-Pacific region, as elsewhere, science education research has gathered momentum during the second half of the twentieth century.

Much research in the region has concentrated on identifying challenges for, or features of, effective teaching and learning of science content, an approach that is congruent with content-dominated curricula. The growth of a science education research tradition throughout the Asia-Pacific region coincided with the discovery that the learning of science is more problematic than had been acknowledged when earlier, (predominantly American) research agendas were largely empiricist, with significant credibility gaps between the research community and teachers (Jenkins, 2001). Differences between meanings and understandings constructed by students during their learning and those intended by their teachers triggered a wave of new research that gained the attention of teachers because they could, at least initially, see direct implications for their classroom practice (White, 1992; Jenkins, 2001).

6.1. *The Impact of Alternative Conceptions Research on Curriculum*

Australian and New Zealand researchers have been at the forefront of alternative conceptions research into student learning. The Learning in Science Projects (LISP) that were undertaken in New Zealand from 1979–1996 focused on learners' everyday views about scientific ideas and demonstrated that these understandings are unlikely to change when students are confronted with scientific explanations that are inconsistent with their personally-held views. This research tradition has continued throughout the region, adding to the ongoing compilation of a bibliography of international studies that have identified the common alternative conceptions and misconceptions involved in children's science ideas in many different areas of science content (Pfundt & Duit, 2000).

The worldwide response to this veritable avalanche of research has been "overwhelmingly pedagogical" (Fensham, 1999). The constructivist teaching approaches that were developed at this time have been the subject of on-going, sometimes "intemperate debate" (Jenkins, 2001, p. 20) and in any case, have so far not delivered on their early promise of providing helpful guidance for making teaching more effective. Shifting student thinking from everyday conceptions to scientific ones is easier said than done, not least because everyday ideas serve people perfectly well in the everyday world (White, 1992; Jenkins, 2001) and they are accordingly, very resistant to change.

Fensham (1999) argues that most of the alternative conceptions research was carried out on traditional content because researchers could gain easy access to classrooms where such content was already being taught. The difficulties in learning that were uncovered by this research then led to a push for expanded opportunities to learn the traditional content, including beginning teaching some science content at an earlier age. Thus, the opportunity to respond to the research by critically reviewing curriculum content was not taken up. Fensham (1999) questions what the influence on curriculum might have been had the research also focused on students' learning of concepts associated with the environmental, technological, and socio-scientific content, as was beginning to be tried in the science technology and society (STS) types of science curricula in the 1980s.

Some early alternative conceptions research in the Asia-Pacific region did focus on problems associated with practical work in science. In New Zealand, for example, LISP research conducted in more than 40 classrooms found that the teachers and students had very different views of the purposes for undertaking practical activities, and the subsequent impact of the practical experiences on students' existing ideas was often quite different to that intended by the teacher (Tasker & Freyberg, 1985). Again however, the opportunity to question the place and role of practical work in the overall curriculum tended to be sidelined by the overwhelming volume of content research. This area of concern has only recently begun to be re-addressed within the region (see, for example, Toh, Boo and Yeo, 1997; Tsai, 1999; Hipkins et al., 2002).

6.2. The Intersection of Alternative Conceptions Research and Equity Concerns

Some systems in the Asia-Pacific region have tried to forge a curriculum that will accommodate comprehensive content coverage, constructivist pedagogical approaches, and the development of more positive attitudes to science as an outcome for a diverse range of the student population. This accommodation has typically been achieved by specifying broad areas of content to be covered while advocating flexibility of interpretation at the local school level, as illustrated for example by the national curriculum documents of New Zealand and Australia. The latter undergoes two levels of interpretation, with different states modifying the national statement to different degrees in their own state curricula (Goodrum et al., 2000) before these are again interpreted at the school and classroom level.

Goodrum et al. (2000) point out that "having common outcomes at the end of schooling does not imply there must be a common curriculum. In fact, because students are different, and develop at different rates, it is almost essential that there is an uncommon curriculum" (p. 33). This ideal has, however, created a number of curriculum tensions, not least of which is the tightrope act required of teachers as they judge how to balance the diverse learning needs of their particular student group with the imperative of success in national assessments, which remain largely content-focused. Finding the point of balance between transmission of essential content and the promotion of personal understanding has to be determined by each teacher, for every topic in the curriculum – an act which calls for the exercise of great judgement (White, 1992). In any case, should they so choose, teachers can respond to deliberately flexible curricula by simply continuing to teach in traditional ways.

Towards the end of the twentieth century, learning came to be more widely viewed as socially as well as personally constructed. At the most basic level, the curriculum response was to specify that learning should be set in contexts of local relevance to students. This implies a degree of sub-discipline integration, so that contextual topics (e.g., cooking; toys) rather than more traditional discipline based topics (e.g., chemical reactions; force and motion) determine the order and sequencing of curriculum content.

A somewhat more demanding curriculum interpretation may require teachers to take account of students' traditional worldviews and considerable research effort in different parts of the Asia-Pacific region has been expended on comparing and contrasting local beliefs to science views of the same phenomena. For example Tsai (2000) has found that Taiwanese students commonly hold everyday views of earthquakes that include perceptions of supernatural forces and myths. Such myths are a feature of traditional worldviews for many different cultures in the region, including those of Australian Aborigines (Michie and Linkson, 1999) and of New Zealand Maori (McKinley et al., 1992). Similarly, Loo (2001) illustrates the complexity of relationships between the culture of science and other types of cultural views with reference to the impact of Islamic thinking on the national curriculum of Malaysia.

Notwithstanding the equity intentions of this type of curriculum development, epistemological and ethical challenges have now become apparent. Attempts simply to juxtapose science and other worldview ideas without making any attempt to relate them to each other may be advocated as a means of sidestepping problems of comparison, as in Linkson (1999). However, if students are not to be left with relativist impressions about the status of science theories, comparisons between science and other worldviews are inevitable.

In his research, Tsai (2000) found that students employed three major approaches to resolve differences between indigenous and scientific worldviews. Some accepted the science view, abandoning their original worldview, a process that Aikenhead (2001) describes as 'assimilation'. Some tried to grasp the science view while maintaining an unchanged indigenous view; and others simply ignored the science view. One response to the recognition of this range of possible outcomes has been advocacy for a cross-cultural approach, in which students come to learn about different types of knowledge construction, and how and why views of the same phenomenon can be so different. The implementation of such an approach could hold promise for the Asia-Pacific region, where a diversity of local cultures exist, but it would require considerable debate and subsequent curriculum revision, which does not yet appear to have begun in the region. It would also require many science teachers to develop much more explicit understandings of the unique epistemological features of science than they currently appear to hold.

6.3. *The Impact of Situated Cognition on Science Curriculum*

The socio-cultural tradition has provided another focus for science education research, drawing on ideas of 'situated cognition'. In this view authenticity is favoured for student learning, which may be seen as a form of student apprenticeship into science ways of investigating. However, such approaches appear to have had little impact on curriculum content at the national level in the Asia-Pacific region. In spite of this, there has been a significant research focus on, and considerable local advocacy for, the inclusion of more open investigation in place of traditional practical work: such as in Australia (Goodrum et al., 2000); in Singapore (Toh et al., 1997); and in Taiwan (Tsai, 1999).

Mayer and Kumano (1999) argue for situated learning, from a different initial perspective. They critique school curricula that typically favour traditional physical science disciplines, where reductionist approaches to inquiry are more likely. They advocate for the inclusion of systems orientated science methods and content, so that students can come to appreciate better the impact of human interventions that have led to "global changes in our environment and society" (p. 87). They argue that an appreciation of the complexity and wholeness of such systems should be gained through field activities, where students can "examine large systems as they normally function in nature" (p. 87). They assert that direct student participation in this type of 'system science' is the best preparation for taking a critical and informed stance to future socio-scientific issues.

Advocacy for cross-subject curriculum integration at the secondary level is also congruent with authentic inquiry approaches. As a result of extensive research on curriculum integration in Australia, Venville et al. (2002) have come to the realisation that sustained implementation of such curriculum initiatives requires teachers to step outside subject-bounded views of curriculum. This is a challenging paradigm shift when powerful within-subject loyalties are built during initial within-subject tertiary education. Their argument serves an apt reminder that the implemented curriculum is ultimately reliant on teacher decision-making, no matter what is mandated.

6.4. Metacognition and Curriculum Decision Making

While teacher learning and teacher beliefs are undoubtedly an important aspect of curriculum change, student expectations also exert considerable influence on the implemented curriculum (White, Russell, and Gunstone, 2002). The move to link students' personal understanding of purposes and progress in their own learning to increased levels of motivation and achievement in science has been strongly influenced by Australian-based research that began in the 1980s. Early research in metacognition linked alternative conceptions research to a growing recognition that students lacked control over their own learning. Whether learners were unable to direct their own learning because they had not learned how, because they were not allowed to, or because they did not want to, it was believed that training in metacognition might overcome these impediments. This belief resonated with a personal constructivist view that adequate metacognition empowers and motivates the learner to undertake the demanding process of recognition, evaluation, and revision of personal views (White and Mitchell, 1994).

The Project for Enhancing Effective Learning (PEEL) which began in 1985 with 10 teachers in one secondary school, and has spread to over 20 schools in Australia and other countries (White & Mitchell, 1994), aimed to support teachers to use a variety of strategies to encourage student engagement and thinking. Examples of this type of research within the Asia-Pacific region illustrate its potential for helping to adapt the implemented curriculum to accommodate students' expectations and cultural viewpoints. For example, working with 13-year-old students in Singapore, Toh, Boo and Yeo (1997) found that students' beliefs about the nature and characteristics of scientific inquiry shape their actual learning in open-ended practical situations. Tsai (1999) similarly found Taiwanese students who were more orientated to a constructivist view of science tended to focus more on negotiating the meanings of experiments with their peers than did students whose views were more in line with empiricist views of science. In the People's Republic of China, Wang et al. (1996) suggest that problems arise for developing students' expertise in practical science where cultural respect for scholarship means that people place more value on the learning of theory and look down on practical experimental skills (p. 216). There are clear metacognitive challenges for teachers when addressing this assumption.

The PEEL initiative represents a rare case of teachers and researchers working in a sustained close collaboration (Jenkins, 2001) and has highlighted the necessity for a flexible curriculum that allows room for the teacher to exercise personal judgement (White, 1992). However, just as the whole alternative conceptions research movement faces new questions that have arisen from socio-cultural views of learning, so ongoing metacognitive research such as PEEL also now faces new questions and research directions. For example White et al. (2002) challenge traditionally sequential relationships between thinking and experience, questioning how students (or indeed teachers facing change in their teaching practice) can be expected to address "the answers to questions they have not yet learned to ask" (p. 237). They suggest that experience necessarily precedes understanding, and that both teachers and students need to rethink their roles, with students taking significant responsibility for their own learning, and both teachers and students being prepared to take more risks as they experiment with change.

When viewed from this perspective, it seems scarcely surprising that researchers have found a wide gap between the actual and the ideal in current classroom teaching in Australia (Goodrum et al., 2000). Firmly established traditional expectations of student and teacher roles, and of the nature of appropriate content, are further reinforced by the influence of high-stakes, summative assessment in examination-driven systems. It is difficult to change a curriculum emphasis unless a similar change is made in the corresponding assessment regime.

7. NEW CHALLENGES FOR THE FUTURE

The challenges that exist for teachers when addressing curriculum content in new ways will be multiplied considerably if advocacy for a greater curriculum focus on the nature of science, and on the exploration of socio-scientific issues, is successful. There is a growing impetus for this substantial redirection of curriculum emphasis, with its associated implications for content change. Recent research in the United Kingdom has addressed philosophically-based differences of opinion about what should be included in such a curriculum (Ratcliffe et al., 2001) providing a sound basis for further debate.

Widespread student disenchantment with science, as identified in the large-scale review of teaching and learning in Australian schools (Goodrum et al., 2000) presents a serious challenge to currently accepted practice. Curriculum reform would appear to be long overdue. Ogawa (2001) further suggests that the issue of curriculum reform goes beyond science education into the heart of schooling itself:

> Does 'school' as a kind of social instruction continue to take the same social role, function, and responsibility that it did in the present or past? Should science be taught in school contexts alone? Should or can science teachers take a specific role, function, and responsibility on scientific and technological literacy education among the general public? We cannot avoid asking

such fundamental questions if we want to look to the future of science education. What is really needed right now may be an effort to search for a new rationale for science education policymaking, curriculum development policymaking, and science teacher education policymaking in this unknown and chaotic future society. (Ogawa, 2001, p. 604)

If science is to continue to justify its current place in the overall school curriculum, it seems that national curriculum developers will also need to be prepared to take risks. Shifting learning responsibility, with appropriate support, to teachers and their students, and maybe even out into the wider community, will be necessary if momentum in science curriculum research is to be sustained in directions that address the issues raised in this chapter.

REFERENCES

Aikenhead, G. (2001). Renegotiating the culture of school science. In R. Millar, J. Leach & J. Osborne (Eds.), *Improving Science Education – The Contribution of Research* (pp. 245–264). Buckingham: Open University Press.

Cheung, D., & Ng, P. (2000). Science teachers' beliefs about curriculum design. *Research in Science Education, 30*(4), 357–375.

Cogan, L., Wang, H., & Schmidt, W. H. (2001). Culturally specific patterns in the conceptualisation of the school science curriculum: Insights from TIMSS. *Studies in Science Education, 36*, 105–134.

Fensham, P. (1999). Science content as problematic: Issues for research. In H. Behrendt & H. Dahnke (Eds.), *Research in Science Education – Past, Present and Future*. Dordrecht: Kluwer.

Goodrum, D., Hackling, M., & Rennie, L. (2000). The *Status and Quality of Teaching and Learning of Science in Australian Schools*. Research Report prepared for the Department of Education, Training and Youth Affairs: Canberra.

Hipkins, R., Bolstad, R., Baker, R., Jones, A., Barker, M., Bell, B., Coll, R., Cooper, B., Forret, M., France, B., Haigh, M., Harlow, A., & Taylor, I. (2002). Curriculum learning and effective pedagogy: A literature review in science education. Wellington: Ministry of Education.

Jenkins, E. (2001). Research in science education in Europe: Retrospect and prospect. In H. Behrendt & H. Danke (Eds.), *Research in Science Education – Past, Present, and Future* (pp. 17–26). Dordrecht: Kluwer.

Linkson, M. (1999). Some issues in providing culturally appropriate science curriculum support for indigenous students. *Australian Science Teachers' Journal, 45*(1), 41–48.

Loo, S. (2001). Islam, science and science education: Conflict or concord. *Studies in Science Education, 36*, 45–77.

Martin, M., Mullis, I., Gonzalez, E., Gregory, K., Smith, T., Chrostowski, S., Garden, R., & O'Connor, K. (2000). *TIMSS 1999 International Science Report: Findings from IEA's Repeat of the Third International Mathematics and Science Study at the Eight Grade*. Chestnut Hill MA: International Study Centre, Boston College.

Mayer, V., & Kumano, Y. (1999). The role of system science in future school science curricula. *Studies in Science Education, 34*, 71–91.

McKinley, E., McPherson Waiti, P., & Bell, B. (1992). Language, culture and science education. *International Journal of Science Education, 14*(5), 579–595.

Michie, M., & Linkson, M. (1999) Interfacing Western science and indigenous knowledge: A Northern Territory perspective. 30th Australasian Science Education Research Association Conference. Rotorua, July.

Millar, R., & Osborne, J. F. (Eds.) (1998). *Beyond 2000: Science Education for the Future*. London: Kings College.

Ogawa, M. (2001). Reform Japanese style: Voyage into an unknown and chaotic future. *Science Education*, 85(5), 586–606.

Pfundt, H., & Duit, R. (2000). *Bibliography: Students' Alternative Frameworks and Science Education* (5th ed.). Kiel: Institute for Science Education at the University of Kiel.

Ratcliffe, M., Osborne, J., Collins, S., Millar, R., & Duschl, R. (2001) Evidence-based practice in Science Education (EPSE). Teaching pupils 'ideas-about-science': Clarifying learning goals and improving pupil performance. *Third Conference of the European Science Education Research Association (ESERA)*. Thessaloniki, Greece, 21–25 August 2001.

Rennie, L. (2000). Gender and science, technology and vocational education in Asia and the Pacific. In E. Jenkins (Ed.), *Innovations in Science and Technology Education* (pp. 99–142). Paris: Falmer UNESCO.

Tasker, R., & Freyberg, P. (1985). Facing mismatches in the classroom. In R. Osborne & P. Freyberg (Eds.), *Learning in Science: The Implications of Children's science*. Auckland: Heinemann.

Toh, K., Boo, H., & Yeo, H. (1997). Open-ended investigation: Performance and effects of pre-training. *Research in Science Education*, 27(1), 131–140.

Tsai, C. (1999). Laboratory exercises help me memorise scientific truths: A study of eight graders' scientific epistemological views and learning of laboratory activities. *Science Education*, 83(6), 654–674.

Tsai, C. (2000). Ideas about earthquakes after experiencing a natural disaster in Taiwan: An analysis of students' worldviews. International. *Journal of Science Education*, 23(10), 1007–1016.

Venville, G., Wallace, J., Rennie, L., & Malone, J. (2002). Curriculum integration: Eroding the high ground of science as a school subject. *Studies in Science Education*, 37, 43–84.

Wallace, J., & Chou, C. (2001). Similarity and difference: Student cooperation in Taiwanese and Australian science classrooms. *Science Education*, 85, 694–711.

Wang, W., Wang, J., Zhang, G., Lang, Y., & Mayer, V. (1996). Science education in the People's Republic of China. *Science Education*, 80(2), 203–222.

White, G., Russell, T., & Gunstone, R. (2002). Curriculum change. In J. Wallace & W. Louden (Eds.), *Dilemmas of Science Teaching: Perspectives on Problems of Practice* (pp. 231–244). London: Routledge Falmer.

White, R. (1992). Implications of recent research on learning for curriculum and assessment. *Journal of Curriculum Studies*, 24(2), 153–164.

White, R., & Mitchell, I. (1994). Metacognition and the quality of learning. *Studies in Science Education*, 23, 21–37.

43

Assessment Research in Second Language Curriculum Initiatives

KATHRYN HILL and TIM McNAMARA
Language Testing Research Centre, The University of Melbourne, Australia

1. INTRODUCTION

This paper considers the development of second and foreign language education in schools in the Asia-Pacific region from the point of view of assessment. It will be argued that assessment research can play a diverse range of roles in language policy formulation and implementation within education systems.

In the Asia-Pacific region, as in the rest of the world, globalisation has led to an increased focus on the teaching and learning of English as the global language. This has been reflected in policy developments in a number of countries, particularly the introduction of English language teaching in the elementary school. The adoption of such a policy involves painful issues of cultural identity, as the global language and culture will be introduced at the same time as the socialisation of the children in the language and culture of the mother tongue. In addition, very practical resourcing questions are raised, particularly the supply of teachers with sufficient proficiency in the language being taught. This issue is made more acute in cases where education systems cannot afford to employ specialist English teachers for work with elementary classes, and home room teachers, who are responsible for delivering the majority of the curriculum, are the ones responsible for teaching English.

Globalisation has also led to a further shift, namely in the priorities of foreign language study. Greater emphasis is given to the teaching of the languages and cultures of major trading partners in the region at the expense of traditional school languages, particularly European languages such as French and German. Nowhere has this been more notable than in Australia, where a number of circumstances have together conspired to achieve remarkable changes in the policy and practice of language teaching in schools. Japanese and Indonesian have long rivalled traditional European languages such as French and German as the most popular languages learned in school, and there is an increasing demand from families for their children to learn Chinese. The concomitant advances in the teaching of these languages in Australia, in terms of curriculum, materials and assessment tools, are important for the rest of the English speaking world, where they are often designated as 'less commonly taught languages' and accorded relatively scant policy and research attention. The Australian context for research on foreign and second language learning is favoured by the fact that the field of applied linguistics in Australia is particularly strong, and government support for research on the teaching and learning of regional languages in schools has had a 15-year period of relatively generous support since the adoption of the National Policy on Languages (Lo Bianco, 1987), although this support is currently weakening. One area of applied linguistics research which has prospered unusually well is research on language testing. Government support under the National Policy on Languages saw the establishment of a network of research centres, including two specialising in language testing. The same period saw the establishment of a research centre to support the English language education of adult and child immigrants. The net result is that Australia is now endowed with what is by world standards an unusually strong base of expertise in language testing research, and this has begun to operate as a regional resource. Given the strength of assessment research in Australia, and the affiliation and research experience of the authors, often within the context of policy developments on the teaching of regional languages, it seemed appropriate in this paper to use assessment as a perspective from which to view curriculum developments in language teaching in the region.

In what follows, a number of assessment research projects supportive of policy developments in second and foreign language teaching and learning are presented. The languages involved are English, Indonesian, Japanese, Chinese, Italian and French, as taught in Australia, Indonesia and the Republic of Korea. The paper illustrates the multiple roles that assessment may play in support of curriculum initiatives in school foreign language learning. While this is not a comprehensive survey of current research activity in language learning in the region, it presents cutting-edge research in relation to a number of languages in different national contexts.

2. IMPLEMENTING STANDARDS-BASED SECOND LANGUAGE CURRICULUM INITIATIVES

Current thinking on communicative approaches to language learning and teaching continues to focus on actual performance in the languages concerned, with special emphasis given to communication in the spoken and written language. Increasingly, curriculum goals are specified in terms of expected practical communicative skills in a number of aspects of communicative competence in the languages concerned. These specifications typically take the form of a framework describing outcomes at different levels in each of the macroskills (speaking, listening, reading, writing, in various combinations). This framework is used as a frame of reference to map expected paths of development, with defined stages of growth. A recent and extremely influential example of this is the *Common European Framework of Reference for Languages: Learning, Teaching and Assessment of Modern Languages* (Council of Europe, 2001). In line with developments elsewhere, regional education authorities in the Asia-Pacific region have developed a number of curriculum projects in modern languages involving frameworks and standards. Building on work by Clark and his colleagues in Hong Kong, Australian researchers have been active in the development of these frameworks, particularly the Australian Language Levels (ALL) project in the late 1980s, whose influence has been evident in subsequent projects (see below). As these frameworks define target performance at each level, they constitute a definition of the domain or construct in terms of which assessment of individual achievement can be carried out. The curricula thus offer a strong basis for the integration of curriculum and assessment, if assessment is constructed in terms of performance against these statements of standards at each level and in each skill area. A distinctive feature of the best of this work has been the detailed attention given to assessment, often in the form of specific guides to assessment practice for teachers, for example in the excellent materials accompanying the Victorian Curriculum and Standards Framework for ESL (see Section 2.1).

An important task in the introduction of such frameworks, which are necessarily general and rather abstract in their formulations, is to introduce teachers to the detailed practical interpretation of the frameworks in guiding their work. In this context, assessment research can function in helping teachers understand in concrete terms what the statements of standards mean in terms of actual student performance. As an example of the issues and possibilities raised here, one such research project is described below.

2.1. *Curriculum and Standards Framework, Victoria: Annotated Student Work Samples Project (Chinese, Indonesian and French)*

The *National Languages Other than English (LOTE) Profiles and Standards* framework (Curriculum Corporation, 1994a, 1994b), a national initiative, represents an attempt to describe progress in language learning in Australian schools from the beginning of school to the end of Grade 10.[1] Such a national initiative in education is potentially somewhat problematic in Australia, as under Australia's federal system of government, education falls under the jurisdiction of the States (Victoria, New South Wales, Tasmania, South Australia, Queensland and Western Australia) and Territories (Australian Capital Territory, Northern Territory), rather than under federal jurisdiction. States tend to be somewhat wary of federal initiatives in this area, on the grounds of preserving the rights of the States in the face of the encroachment of federal government powers. Nevertheless, most States have responded to the national initiative by using it as a starting point for producing their own language frameworks. One such framework is the *Curriculum and Standards Framework* (CSF, recently revised and now known as CSF II), produced by the Department of Education, Victoria.

According to Scarino, the appearance of these frameworks represents an important development for foreign language education in Australia to the extent that it has required teachers to "think of language learning beyond the one-off episode ... [and to reflect more] deeply on issues related to long-term progress in language learning" (Scarino, 1995, p. 40). Moreover, they embody a commitment to practical performance outcomes in language education. However, such frameworks have in general been criticised for lacking a clear definition of what constitutes an acceptable level of performance and for providing insufficient guidance about how to assess learners against the specified standards (Pollitt, 1991, pp. 87–88). Davies (1995) also draws attention to the gap between generalised reporting frameworks and the evaluation of individual instances of performance.

In recognition of this problem, the *Victorian Curriculum and Standards Framework* (CSF II) is accompanied by annotated student work samples for (to date) three languages: Chinese, Indonesian and French.[2] These work samples are intended to illustrate sound achievement of selected learning outcomes for each of the *Strands* (reading, speaking, writing, listening), *Pathways* (K-10 or Years 7–10) and *Levels* (1–6) included in the framework. The effectiveness of work samples as an elaboration of frameworks and profiles of achievement is discussed by McKay (2000).

Development of the annotated work samples involved a number of stages.[3] First, assessment tasks were designed to meet some or all of the level outcome descriptors for the nominated level and strand. These tasks were then used to elicit work samples from students in so-called 'best practice' schools. Finally, a selection of the work samples was annotated to explain why each one was considered to represent 'sound achievement' of the relevant standard. Detailed input from experienced teachers of the languages concerned was involved at each stage of the process.

The work samples are not intended to show the full range of student achievement or achievement of all outcomes at a particular level. Rather, the samples provide a reference for teachers assessing students' performance on a range of tasks over time.

The annotated samples have recently been published on CD-ROM. Eventually, it is intended that the materials will also be published on-line.[4]

3. RESOURCING CURRICULUM INITIATIVES

Initiatives in language curriculum inevitably carry resource implications. A primary example of this is the provision of sufficient teachers with adequate proficiency in the languages being taught to implement the policy. Assessment research can support initiatives in language curriculum in this case by determining the second language proficiency of teachers of the language in question, both in order to determine need, and to provide certification. Language testing in this context can be a delicate matter as policies often run ahead of the capacity of the system to deliver, and assessments have the potential to expose weaknesses in a way that the system cannot bear. On the other hand, planning for the implementation of policies requires realistic data on the proficiency of teachers, in order to plan for supplementary language training of the teachers in question. Assessment leading to certification can be motivating where resources for training are provided for teachers wishing to improve their language proficiency, and for courses leading to certification assessment of teacher proficiency is a natural culmination of effort. In other circumstances, where proficiency is often low and where resources for teacher re-training are not readily available, assessment will have a very different purpose and needs to be reconceptualised in order to provide a supportive role. Three examples are given of contexts in which this issue has been addressed, in Indonesia, Australia and Korea.

3.1. *English Proficiency Test for Indonesia (EPTI)*

The spread of English as an international language in Asia is reflected in changes to school curricula in the region. For example, in Indonesia, the *School Curriculum Policy* (1994) stipulates that English should be taught for four 45-minute periods per week in Lower Secondary School (SLTP) and for up to 11 hours per week at senior secondary level (SMU).[5] Since 1992, English has also been taught to students in Grades 5 and 6 in a small number of primary schools and this is expected eventually to become the norm throughout Indonesia.

The increased demand for teachers of English together with the greater emphasis given to speaking skills in the new syllabus has highlighted the need to improve the level of teacher qualifications (Huda, 1999) and for some means of assessing teachers' English language proficiency. The *English Proficiency Test for Indonesia* (EPTI)[6] is a specific purpose test designed to assess the English language proficiency of classroom teachers. Its purpose is to assess teachers at the end of training and to determine eligibility for in-service training for practising teachers. However, it is also anticipated that the communicative orientation[7] of the test will have a positive influence on the way these teachers are trained and provide a model of tasks and activities appropriate for use in the communicative classroom. Accounts of the development of the test and issues arising in its implementation, particularly the use of non-native speakers as raters, are discussed in Brown and Lumley (1994, 1998) and Hill (1996).

EPTI comprises two integrated tests, Reading/Writing and Listening/Speaking, and is designed to assess the ability to use English in relation to classroom activities. It is called a 'local' test: test content is drawn from topics and situations relevant and familiar to Indonesians and others in the ASEAN region. As local teachers will rarely achieve so-called 'native-like' proficiency and because students are more likely to use English to communicate with other Asians than with native speakers (Kachru, 1994, p. 5), the test is designed to measure English as it is used in the region. The test is designed to be rated *in situ* by trained English-speaking Indonesians (e.g., from teacher training institutions) both for practical reasons and because it was considered that only local raters could define an acceptable level of performance on the test for its purposes.

3.2. *Language Teacher Proficiency Tests – Italian, Japanese, Indonesian*

Initiatives to increase enrolments in foreign languages, particularly Asian languages, in Australia have raised similar concerns about teacher quality and supply to meet increasing demand[8].

The *Languages Other Than English (LOTE) Teacher Proficiency Tests* have been developed to ensure appropriate standards of language proficiency for teachers of Indonesian, Italian and Japanese respectively in Australian schools. The purpose of the tests is to establish whether a candidate's level of proficiency will enable them to function effectively as teachers, both linguistically and pedagogically. As with EPTI, the tests are suitable for teacher accreditation purposes, to indicate readiness for teacher-training courses, or as a means of identifying pre- or in-service training needs.

The tests cover reading, listening, writing and speaking skills. Like EPTI, the tests have been designed to assess the ability to use the target language in relation to classroom activities. Tasks were based on Elder's framework (1994) of language or language-related ability considered central to the role of language teachers. This includes the ability to:

- use the target language both as the medium and the object of instruction,
- modify target language input to render it comprehensible to learners,
- produce well-formed input for learners, and
- draw learner's attention to the formal features of the target language.

The tasks derived from a job analysis of the roles language teachers play in class and in the school environment. The job analysis was used to develop simulated tasks – for example, setting up an activity in the classroom, presenting a narrative from pictures, explaining points of language – which are presented to candidates in a role-play format with the examiner adopting an appropriate complementary role. Each test assumes knowledge of the language approximately equivalent to three years post-secondary standard, which is the minimum required for teaching languages other than English in most Australian States. Test reports profile each candidate's skills in relation to the nominated teaching abilities.[9] Examples of the Italian test in action, and discussion of the stages of its development, can be seen as part of the video-taped series on language assessment *Mark My Words* (Stow, 1996).

3.3. *Classroom Communicative Competence Project, Korea*

The Korean education system is undergoing major structural reform and a significant component of the reform agenda has been the introduction of the study of English into the elementary school. A major issue facing the system has been the development of the classroom communicative competence of the Korean teachers responsible for the implementation of the English curriculum. In Korea, school curricula are revised every few years. The new policy on English was introduced as part of the curriculum revisions implemented in 1996, in a period of considerable prosperity, and native speakers of English were used to support the work of regular teachers in delivering the lessons. Since the financial crisis of the late 1990s, however, the burden of responsibility for the delivery of the new curriculum has fallen on homeroom teachers, many of whom have limited proficiency in English. In order to supplement their work, relatively self-contained audiovisual materials delivered on CD ROM and shown on large screens in classrooms have been provided. In a subsequent revision of the curriculum these materials have also been revised.

What role might assessment play in such a setting? One possible answer would be the development of a proficiency test to establish levels of competence among the teachers, in order to allow planning of professional development, as in the previous contexts. It was considered, however, that the impact of such a test might be negative in this context, in that it would highlight the existing deficiencies in competence of which the teachers (and indeed the system) were all too well aware. Instead, it was decided to explore the potential of assessment to play a more constructive role in language teacher development. A joint Korean-Australian project[10] was initiated to construct such an assessment (Jin et al., 2001). The aim of the project was the development of peer and self assessment tools to be used by elementary school English teachers to raise their awareness of the patterns of language and interaction used by both teachers and students in elementary English classes. It was considered that heightened awareness of current and potential classroom behaviour would help teachers in the formulation of personal goals for improvement in their own classroom communicative competence. Using assessment techniques in this formative and supportive way, rather than developing a formal proficiency test which might be used merely to expose deficiencies in teacher proficiency in English, was felt to be a constructive approach to the issue of furthering the goals of English language education in the Korean elementary school.

The project involved the development of video materials of teachers working with the new curriculum materials, and accompanying self- and peer-assessment worksheets to help teachers focus on aspects of communicative interaction in the lessons. The following areas were addressed:

(a) familiarity with activities in new curriculum materials (recognition of lesson stages, identification of types of activity, identification of lesson goals);
(b) focus on the teacher (classroom management, rapport, specification of learning objectives);
(c) focus on the learner (identification of opportunities for learners to use the various language macroskills, to seek clarification, and to engage in meaningful communication in English);
(d) focus on communication (identification of features of the teacher's modelling

of language, provision of feedback to learners, control of metalinguistic skills); and
(e) focus on interaction (identification of patterns of interaction between teacher and students and among students in the lesson).

For each area, the worksheets focussed on an awareness of both lesson structure and teacher skills and an awareness of teacher language use (Korean or English). Teachers were encouraged to identify specific priorities for change in each aspect. The materials were piloted at a five-day workshop involving 25 teachers from all over Korea, who were asked to bring videotape materials of their own teaching. The aim of the workshop was to train the teachers in various areas of awareness and then to apply that awareness to their own lessons. Following the workshop, the materials were revised and made less complex to use and then made available to teachers throughout the country in CD ROM format.

While self-assessment and peer-assessment were thus the primary assessment focus of this project, assessment played an additional role, as a way of evaluating change in awareness among teachers before and after participation in the workshop. For this purpose, a number of episodes of teaching were seen early and late in the workshop, and teachers carried out a task each time which was designed to elicit their awareness of lesson structure and teacher and learner language use. A comparison of responses before and after exposure to the workshop materials revealed modest but real gains in awareness over the period of the workshop, particularly in relation to more complex classroom activities.

A further stage of this work is currently being conducted, to support the work of middle school teachers of English, who differ from their colleagues in the elementary school in that they are required to have specialist training as English teachers.

4. EVALUATING CURRICULUM INITIATIVES AND INFORMING NEW POLICY

A final role for assessment research in the development and implementation of policies for school language learning is in the area of the monitoring of learner achievement as part of the evaluation of new policy outcomes. In Australia, as elsewhere, demand for accountability has been increasing in all areas of government, including education. However, a review published in 1998 found that the quality of nationwide data about the status of foreign language teaching and learning was inadequate (Australian National University, 1998). One particular source of difficulty is the absence of a common framework for collecting data on student learning outcomes.

There are a number of reasons why the types of curriculum and standards frameworks described in the first part of this paper are inappropriate for this purpose. First, these documents are intended as a guide for classroom based assessment and, therefore, do not lend themselves well to system-wide reporting.

With the exception of Tasmania, there is currently no formal process for moderation of either tasks or assessments beyond the individual school level, which increases the likelihood that the interpretation and reporting of standards will vary from one school to another. In an attempt to overcome this problem individual States have been attempting to monitor outcomes in more and less comprehensive ways. For example, Western Australia has been conducting a program of formal testing to enable a statewide audit of learning outcomes against the specified standards. New South Wales has also started this process (in a less formal way) for French and Indonesian programs in Grades 6 and 7 using a listening test comprising multiple choice questions.

However, even if this process were to be repeated in other States, it would still be difficult to provide data in a comparable form. Not only do the duration and intensity of foreign language programs vary significantly from State to State, but individual frameworks also differ on a number of key dimensions. For example, some frameworks are language-specific, while others are generic across languages. Frameworks also differ in the number of levels described, the organization of macro skills (e.g., discrete or integrated), whether criteria are specified or teacher-derived, and whether they distinguish between learners continuing the target language from primary level and those who have commenced the language in high school.

A *Longitudinal and Comparative Study: The Attainment of Language*[11] (Brown et al., 2000a, 2000b; Hill, 2000) represented an attempt to explore some of the issues involved in the development of comparable nation-wide assessments. The main objectives of this study were to investigate how long it takes to learn a language at school[12] and whether some languages are more difficult to learn than others. The languages investigated were French, Indonesian, Italian and Japanese[13]. Following a review of the various curriculum and syllabus documents, tests of Speaking, Writing, Reading and Listening were developed for administration to students at the end of Grade 8. The requirement to produce evidence on the relative difficulty of the respective languages meant that it was necessary to design tests with the same content (texts and questions) for each language. The tests were administered to 2,745 Grade 8 students in four States. The study found significant differences in levels of achievement in the respective languages, with students of Japanese performing at consistently lower levels across all skills. Large-scale formal assessment along the lines of the Western Australian model has been considered again more recently (Erebus Consulting Partners, 2001), but the use of standardised tests with limited substantial teacher input remains problematic on policy and other grounds. A trial national project to establish what possible measures could be used to establish achievement in Indonesian and Japanese at key exit points from the system is currently under way.

One interesting finding in the study just discussed illustrates the specific way in which assessment research may influence policy. It was found that the performance on the Grade 8 tests did not differ between students who had and who had not studied the language concerned at primary school (in Australia, primary school finishes at the end of Grade 6) (Hill, 2001). That is, the language proficiency gains from learning languages at primary school appeared to have disappeared after a further two years of study. Whether this is because the needs of this cohort of learners are being neglected in the years of language learning subsequent to primary school, and whether this lack can be remedied, are matters requiring further research. But the finding has already impacted on the ongoing debate within Australia on the effectiveness of expending significant levels of educational resources on efforts to teach languages in the early years of schooling. This issue remains the subject of widespread discussion and experimentation throughout the region, not least in Japan, which has been grappling with the wisdom of introducing English into the elementary school curriculum for many years, to date without any clear resolution.

5. CONCLUSION

This article has demonstrated the variety of roles that assessment research can play in the development and implementation of policies affecting the learning of second and foreign languages in schools. Using examples involving English, Indonesian, Japanese, Chinese, Italian and French, it has shown that assessment research can have the following functions: helping teachers understand newly introduced curriculum and assessment frameworks for languages; providing information to policy makers on the resource implications of the introduction of new policies, particularly the issue of the adequacy of teachers' proficiency in the languages they are teaching; helping teachers define specific targets for the ongoing development of their own classroom communicative competence; and monitoring learner achievement in languages in response to policy initiatives, to further inform policy developments. The forces of globalisation are enhancing attention to languages of wider communication in the Asia-Pacific region, and the regional strength in assessment research can assist in better understanding the implications of the policy initiatives currently under way.

ENDNOTES

[1.] The particular issue of regional languages is dealt with in Australian national policy through the National Asian Languages and Studies in Australian Schools (NALSAS) Strategy and contains two language elements: Community Languages (languages represented within the Australian community, particularly languages of immigrant communities), and Priority Languages (languages important for Australia's international relations and trade).

[2.] Annotated student work samples for further languages will follow subject to the availability of funding.

[3.] The research was carried out at the Language Testing Research Centre, The University of Melbourne.

[4.] Further information on the work samples can be found at <http://www.vcaa.vic.edu.au/csf/WorkSamples/websiteinfo.htm>

[5.] The number of hours depends on the area of specialisation.

[6.] The test was developed by the Language Testing Research Centre, University of Melbourne, in collaboration with the South East Asian Ministers of Education Regional Language Centre

(SEAMEO-RELC) and a number of state teacher training institutions (IKIP) in Indonesia with funding from the Australian government through its AusAid program

7. This test is 'communicative' in that it includes authentic texts as well as writing and speaking components and emphasises the effectiveness of the performance. This is in contrast to the focus on grammar and mechanics typical of language classrooms in Indonesia.

8. The most recent of these, *Asian Languages and Australia's Economic Future* (Council of Australian Governments, 1994) set the following targets for school enrolments in LOTE: 60 per cent Grades 3–10 in Asian languages; 40 per cent Grades 3–10 in non-Asian languages; 15 per cent Grades 12 in any LOTE; 100 per cent Grades 3–10 in Asian studies.

9. As part of the project requirements, results on the Indonesian test are reported using the ISLPR – Version for Indonesian Teachers (Wylie & Ingram, 1996)

10. The project was jointly funded by the Korean Institute of Curriculum and Evaluation (KICE) and the Department of Education, Science and Training of the Australian Government. The work was carried out jointly by researchers from KICE and from the Language Testing Research Centre at The University of Melbourne.

11. This project was funded by the Australian Government Department of Education, Training and Youth Affairs (DETYA).

12. As funding was only provided for once year, only one set of data collection (Grade 8) was completed.

13. The languages were selected on the following basis: one language (French) is already well researched and documented which allows for contrastive analysis with the other languages; one language (Italian) enabled the native speaker issues associated with second language learning to be considered; Asian languages that have not been well researched in a longitudinal and comparative manner and with few background speakers (Japanese and Indonesian) were included given the emphasis in school language programs on teaching Asian languages, and to provide a comparison to the well researched and background spoken languages; and the languages chosen all had a cohort large enough to enable a viable cohort in Grade 12 (five years later) assuming a 90 per cent drop-off rate.

REFERENCES

Advancing Australia's Languages: Overview report. Evaluation of the Commonwealth School Languages Program. Faculty of Asian Studies, Australian National University (1998).

Brown, A., Hill, K. & Iwashita, N. (2000a). A longitudinal and comparative study: the attainment of language proficiency. *Melbourne Papers in Language Testing*, **9**(1), 1–28.

Brown, A., Hill, K. & Iwashita, N. (2000b). Is learner progress in LOTE learning comparable across languages? *Australian Review of Applied Linguistics*, **23**(2), 35–60.

Brown, A. & Lumley, T. (1994). How can English proficiency tests be made more culturally appropriate? A case study: The assessment of English teacher proficiency. *Proceedings of International English Language Education Conference (INTELEC)* (pp. 122–128). Kuala Lumpur: Language Centre Universitas Kebangsaan Malaysia.

Brown, A. & Lumley, T. (1998). Linguistic and cultural norms in language testing: A case study. *Melbourne Papers in Language Testing*, **7**(1), 80–96.

Council of Australian Governments (1994). *Asian languages and Australia's economic future*. Brisbane: Queensland Government Printer.

Council of Europe (2001). *Common European Framework of Reference for Languages: Learning, Teaching and Assessment*. Cambridge: Cambridge University Press.

Curriculum Corporation of Australia (1994a). *Languages other than English – a curriculum profile for Australian Schools*. Melbourne: Curriculum Corporation.

Curriculum Corporation of Australia (1994b). *A statement on languages other than English for Australian Schools*. Melbourne: Curriculum Corporation.

Davies, A. (1995). Introduction: Measures and Reports. *Melbourne Papers in Language Testing*, **4**(2), 1–11.

Elder, C. (1994). Performance testing as a benchmark for LOTE Teacher Education. *Melbourne Papers in Language Testing*, 3(1), 1–27.

Erebus Consulting Partners (2001). Further Options for an Outcomes Framework for Reporting Purposes for the National Asian Languages and Studies in Australian Schools (NALSAS). Strategy Paper prepared for the NALSAS taskforce. Adelaide, SA: Erebus Consulting Partners.

Hill, K. (1996). Who should be the judge? The use of non-native speakers as raters on a test of English as an international language. *Melbourne Papers in Language Testing*, 5(2), 29–50.

Hill, K. (2000). Testing comparability across languages – equal but different? Paper presented at the American Association for Applied Linguistics annual conference, Vancouver, Canada, 11–14 March.

Hill, K. (2001). Between the cracks: The transition from primary to secondary school foreign language study. Asia Pacific Applied Linguistics: The Next 25 Years. *Proceedings of the 2001 ALAA National Congress*. http://www.slie.canberra.edu.au/alaa

Huda, H. (1999). *Language Learning and Teaching: Issues and Trends*. Malang, Indonesia: IKIP Malang Publisher.

Jin, K., Kim, M., McNamara, T., Brown, A. & Lee, W. (2001). *Developing a diagnostic assessment framework for Elementary English teaching*. Seoul: Korea Institute of Curriculum and Evaluation.

Kachru, B. B. (1994). Teaching World Englishes without myths. *Proceedings of International English Language Education Conference (INTELEC)* (pp. 1–19). Kuala Lumpur: Language Centre Universitas Kebangsaan Malaysia.

Lo Bianco, J. (1987). *National Policy on Languages*. Canberra: Australian Government Publishing Service.

McKay, P. (2000). The effectiveness of work samples as an elaboration of profiles. *Babel*, 34(3), 21–25.

Pollitt, A. (1991). Response to Alderson, 'Bands and scores'. In J. C. Alderson & B. North (Eds.), *Language Testing in the 1990s*. London: Modern English Publications/British Council/Macmillan.

Scarino, A. (1995). Language scales and language tests: developments in languages other than English. *Melbourne Papers in Language Testing*, 4(2), 30–42.

Stow, H. (1996). *Mark My Words: Assessing second and foreign language skills* [video series]. Parkville, Victoria: Language Testing Research Centre and Multimedia Education Unit, The University of Melbourne.

Wylie, E. & Ingram, D. (1996). *International Second Language Proficiency Ratings (ISLPR) – Version for Indonesian Teachers*. Nathan, Queensland: Centre for Applied Language Learning, Griffith University.

44

Education for Peace and International Understanding

YOSHIYUKI NAGATA
National Institute for Educational Policy Research of Japan, Tokyo, Japan

G.R. (BOB) TEASDALE
Flinders University Institute of International Education, Australia

1. INTRODUCTION

The interrelated areas of education for peace and education for international understanding are subsets of the broader area of values education (see *Values Education in A Changing World*), alongside other subsets such as, moral education; education for justice, equity and freedom; civics and citizenship education; education for democracy and human rights; and education for conflict resolution. Education for peace links closely with another area of educational inquiry, that of school violence and bullying (see *Bullying in Schools*). The two share a number of common goals and teaching strategies, including peace building through peer mediation, conflict resolution and the development of interpersonal harmony. Education for international understanding links closely with education for cross- or inter-cultural understanding. While both focus on the exploration of social, political and cultural differences between nations, the latter also can include the study of cultural and social differences within a nation state, with the aim of building national harmony and cohesion. The interrelations between education for peace and education for international understanding require clarification. The former is a broader concept that encompasses the latter. Most writers assume that education for international or cross-cultural understanding is one of the key avenues for the promotion of peace. While this seems a logical assumption we are not aware of any empirical evidence to support it, at least in the Asia-Pacific region. Nevertheless we will accept the assumption, and from here on use 'peace education' as an inclusive term that includes education for international understanding.

In reviewing research findings in the field of peace education in the Asia-Pacific region we have amassed a substantial collection of scholarly articles, conference papers, reports and teaching programs. In overviewing this collection it is immediately apparent that Western approaches to educational research, measurement and evaluation have seldom been used, thus compelling us to question the meaning and methods of research in Asian and Pacific contexts. It appears to us that the knowledge traditions of the region, many of which predate those of the West by many millennia, have shaped a fundamentally different research ethos, at least in the field of peace education. The analytical, objective and quantitative research paradigms of the West are little in evidence in the writings we have reviewed. Rather, Asian and Pacific scholars are using research approaches that are more holistic, reflective, contextualised and at times subjective, approaches that some Western scholars may not even recognise as 'research'.

While Western research methods have been profoundly influenced by the rise of modern science and the industrial revolution, those of Asia and the Pacific have much deeper roots in the value systems and religious traditions of the East, and in indigenous spiritualities. The writings of Asian scholars on peace education draw deeply on Buddhist, Shinto, Islamic, Confucian, Daoist, Hindu and other religious texts, and research in this context is a reflective process of reinterpretation of textual material and its application to the contemporary world. Likewise, in the Asian and Pacific region indigenous scholars are drawing on remaining sources of oral literature to reflect on the implications for peace education of their own wisdoms and spiritualities.

There is a further challenge in reviewing research and scholarship in the Asia-Pacific region. The material we have gathered reflects the fact that between us we can read and write in only two of the several thousand languages of the region, namely Japanese and English. We have not collected writings in any of the other languages. What we are reviewing therefore is only a tiny proportion of the whole. We are aware, for example, that eminent Chinese scholars have been researching Confucian writings with renewed vigour, seeking to interpret their significance for contemporary Chinese education, especially from the perspectives of values and peace. But the products of this research are largely recorded in the Chinese (Mandarin) language, and at this stage we have only fleeting glimpses of the outcomes in the few papers produced in English. By way of example, we are aware that a former Vice-President of the China National Institute for Educational Research, Zhou Nanzhou, has written several texts in Chinese based on his analyses of Confucian philosophies, his epilogue in the Delors report giving an all too brief summary in English of his findings (Zhou, 1996). We look forward to the day when these and similar materials can be translated into our own languages so that they are accessible to us.

It is our intention in this article (a) to review peace education research in a selection of countries in the Asia-Pacific region, including China, India, Japan, the Philippines and Thailand, (b) to overview the findings of an action-research study, the UNESCO Teacher Education for Peace Project and (c) to examine the results of a questionnaire-based survey on peace and international understanding education in the Asia-Pacific region.

2. REVIEW OF PEACE EDUCATION RESEARCH

2.1. *China*

China is a country with a rich cultural tradition inherited from great thinkers and philosophers. Hundreds and even thousands of years ago the ancient Chinese elucidated the moral visions of truth, beauty, justice and liberty and eminent scholars have documented their teachings. It is not difficult to find universal values such as benevolence, mercy, a spirit of caring and a respect for nature, the major religious teachings or ancient philosophies. In particular, some of the humanistic values advocated by the teachings of Confucius are well known. Zhou (1996), one of the members of the International Commission on Education for the Twenty-first Century of UNESCO, stressed the importance of such Chinese traditional virtues and their significance in our present-day lives as follows.

> (...), the spirit of 'caring' was embedded in the Confucian 'benevolence', the Mohist 'concurrent loving' and the Buddhist 'mercy'. The sensitivity to environmental protection was expressed in ancient China by the concern of the Taoists about the destructive consequences of technical advances to natural resources and their advocacy of 'return to Nature'. (...) Humanity in the next century may find elements of wisdom of Confucianism as relevant as it was long ago. (Zhou, 1996, p. 245)

Chinese people have inherited these virtues, qualities that can be closely linked with notions of public good in the contemporary world. As Zhou (1998 p. 63) pointed out, this is why one of the learning pillars of the Delors report, "learning to live together or learning to care and share", has been readily accepted in Chinese schools.

In the current Chinese education system, teacher education has attached great importance to peace and values education (Zheng Xin-rong & Shi Yuntal, 1999). Based on the traditional moral values, as part of the educational reform, many efforts have been made to nurture teachers' democratic spirit and the acceptance of diversity, and to enlarge their multi-cultural knowledge. These efforts may lead China to be one of the countries that incorporates modern humanistic values with traditional virtues, as described in Confucius' teachings, and so form a new ethical values system in the future.

Evidence of the potentialities for further development of peace education in contemporary China is provided by the International Association for the Evaluation of Educational Achievement (IEA) Civic Education Project in Hong Kong. The IEA Civic Education Study conducted in Hong Kong shows the students' civic knowledge there is highly ranked (fifth among the 28 participating countries), having similar scores to Poland, Finland, Cyprus, the United States and significantly higher than the international mean. However, it was revealed that the scores on the importance of 'social movement-related activities for citizenship' and 'confidence in participation at school' are significantly lower than the international mean (Wing On Lee, 2001). When it comes to identifying strengths and weaknesses of humanistic values formation in non-Western countries, these data may provide useful guidance for the future development of Chinese education for peace and international understanding.

2.2. *India*

Peace education research in India is also deeply rooted in the nation's history and religious traditions, and reflects the rich diversity and complexity of Indian cultures. As Pandey (1999, p. 143) so eloquently notes:

> Indian society is plural and heterogeneous with an underlying current of unity, which is unparalleled in the world. Equal respect for all religions (*Sarva Dharma Sambhav*) and world as a family (*Vasudhaiva kutumbakam*) was India's message to the world at a time when most of the world civilizations were in their infancy, and it continues to be its message even today.

An extensive network of research institutes, foundations and programs maintains an active focus on all matters to do with peace, values and education. While some are university-based and take a secular focus, others are sponsored by religious and political organisations. A review of their publications suggests that peace education in India has at least three interrelated strands.

Textual and linguistic analysis. Many researchers have explored the diverse religious traditions and writings of India, reviewing their relevance for the teaching of peace. Ancient religious texts have been a particularly rich source of data. Linked with this has been linguistic analysis of key concepts. Kunnunkal (2001, p. 7), for example, reviews the significance of *Dharma*, a central concept in Indian and especially Hindu thought. He notes that the root meaning is "to hold together, to unite, to integrate or bond", suggesting that "unity in diversity" is at the heart of *Dharma*. He then goes on to explore ways of promoting a deeper understanding and application of *Dharma* in everyday life, and the role of education in facilitating this. *Dharma Bharathi*, the National Institute of Peace and Values Education in Andhra Pradesh, under the leadership of its President and Director, Professor M. Abel, likewise has developed new ways to teach peace using a multicultural and pluralistic approach based on its research into "the values embedded in the cultural and spiritual heritage of India" (Abel, 2001, p. 6). The Institute advocates the teaching of meditation techniques, beginning with "one of the oldest and simplest spiritual exercises of India", that of *Namajapa*, and going on to *Shanti Yagna*, a form of meditation that promotes reconciliation and peace in one's own life (Abel, 2001, p. 7). This emphasis on "peace within" is seen to help the development of "inner power" and "a reflective and peace-loving nature" (Abel, 2001, p. 7–8).

Historical analysis. A second strand of research is based on analysis of the life, work and teachings of Mahatma Gandhi, and of other Indian prophets and gurus, and their relevance to peace education. The Centre for Gandhian Studies and Peace Research at the University of Delhi plays a key role here. Rajput and Walia (2001, p. 325) refer to the impact of the Gandhian school of thought on education in India: "Its comprehensive approach was built upon an understanding of Indian ethos, culture and traditions, and an appreciation for its diversity, plurality and inherent trend to unity". At the core of the Gandhian approach to peace education is the concept of non-violence, not just as a personal but as a social virtue where "society is largely regulated by the expression of nonviolence in its mutual dealings" (Bose, 1994, p. 8). Pandey (1999) offers a systematic analysis of the role of peace education in the National Curriculum Framework (NCF) for primary and secondary schools developed by the National Council for Educational Research and Training in 1988. She notes: "Indian history is replete with examples of apostles of peace, harmony, human rights, universal brotherhood and understanding. Mahatma Gandhi even sacrificed his life for the cause of tolerance, peace and non-violence" (Pandey, 1999, p143). It is clear from her subsequent analysis that Gandhian thought has had a profound influence on the NCF, and on the later development of a curriculum framework for teacher education.

Political analysis. A third key avenue of research is analysis of the political foundations of modern India, beginning with a study of its Constitution of 1950. Rajput and Walia (2001), in a particularly cogent analysis, explore the implications of the Constitution of India for peace education and more broadly for values education in contemporary India, concluding that the role of the teacher is critical: "In order for them to be the transmitters of social cohesion and harmony, their role has to be reformulated and effectively internalized so they can inculcate faith in democratic procedures and in the values of justice, liberty and freedom" (Rajput & Walia, 2001, p. 326). Building on an analysis of the Constitution of India, Pandey (1999) goes on to research the National Policies on Education (NPE) of 1968 and 1986, and their advocacy of peace education. She notes especially paragraph 3.5(1) of the 1986 NPE:

> India has always worked for peace and understanding between nations, treating the whole world as one family. True to this tradition, education has to strengthen this worldview and motivate the younger generations for international cooperation and peaceful co-existence.

Pandey then draws on her analyses to trace the impact of the Constitution of India, and of the National Policies on Education, on the NCF of 1988 and the later curriculum framework for teacher education, noting the extent to which peace education and values education are integrated into the fabric of the various curricula and the textbooks developed from them.

2.3. *Japan*

It can be argued that Japanese peace education in the contemporary period started with the tragedy of the A-bomb attacks in Hiroshima and Nagasaki.

Since then, formal education has taken responsibility for promoting peace awareness among students through initiatives such as classroom-based lessons, school study tours to both cities and action-research by students in their own local towns. As part of nonformal education Non-Governmental Organizations (NGOs) have implemented a variety of peace-related activities such as study tours and international understanding programs in and outside the country.

With regard to research on education for peace and international understanding, activities or programs of the Japan Association for International Education play a key role. It is one of the academic associations dealing mainly with international understanding education and inter-cultural communication. Its members are researchers, teachers and students at primary, secondary and tertiary levels who are actively engaged in various programs of peace and international understanding education. Members of the association are also concerned with developing learning materials on international understanding. One of the most significant efforts recently undertaken in this area was by Professor A. Chiba (2001) and his university students. Under the auspices of the AIEJ/UNESCO Funds-in-Trust and Promotion of International Cooperation and Mutual Understanding University Students Exchange Programme, Professor Chiba and a group of UNESCO Club students organised a study tour to India and produced their own learning textbook in Japanese and English. This experimental program illustrates the potential for university students to be involved in developing materials for international understanding.

As mentioned in the later part of this article, the National Institute for Educational Policy Research of Japan (NIER) has been an active organisation that has long undertaken research on peace and values education in collaboration with UNESCO. NIER has committed itself to the promotion of peace and international understanding education by organising regional programs on values, ethical and moral education in Asia and the Pacific from the 1970s.

Also, apart from these activities on the government side, Non-Government Organizations (NGOs) have recently implemented various programs by organising work camps or seminars on related topics of peace education. The National Federation of UNESCO Associations in Japan (NFUAJ) is one of the organisations that has a long history of citizens' movements for peace through education. It has produced qualitative learning materials for international understanding and organised study tours for students in collaboration with local NGOs in developing countries.

Last but not least, recent educational reform should be referred to in connection with education for international understanding. As a result of a newly introduced subject named 'Comprehensive Learning Hours' being introduced from 2002 into the school curriculum, international education is expected to be one of the study areas that many teachers will take up. A variety of practices in the field of education for international understanding by teachers and students at primary and secondary levels will take place, and action research or case studies on these voluntary efforts will contribute to the promotion of education for peace and international understanding.

2.4. Philippines

Educators in the Philippines have played a particularly active role in promoting peace education, mainly within the context of values education. Unlike most other countries in Asia, their approach has its foundations predominantly in the Christian faith, and in particular in the teachings of the Roman Catholic Church. They also have borrowed more from the models and theories of Western educators than many of their Asian neighbours. A key figure in the promotion of peace education and values education in the Philippines is Dr Lourdes Quisumbing, who served as Secretary of Education, Culture and Sports during the presidency of Corazon Aquino from 1986 to 1990. Dr Quisumbing pioneered the introduction of values education as an integral part of the school curriculum, a major Program Framework being developed in 1988 to serve education at all levels: elementary, secondary and tertiary (Punsalan & Cruz, 1999). Following her departure from public office, Dr Quisumbing was instrumental in establishing the UNESCO Asia Pacific Network for International Education and Values Education (APNIEVE). She continues to serve as Founding President of APNIEVE, and has had a profound influence on the development of values education and peace education within the region (see *Values Education in a Changing World*).

While educators in the Philippines have been very active in building conceptual frameworks and curricula for peace education and values education, and in the training of teachers, research has been largely confined to evaluative studies. In the summer of 1991, for example, an evaluation team:

> ... went around the country to observe the implementation of the Values Education Program particularly in the classroom level. The research reported that the teachers observed in their classrooms very satisfactorily and effectively displayed skills in employing the ... varied experiential strategies they learned in the previous mass training programs for teachers. The data indicated the usefulness and effectiveness of the methodology in the conduct of values lessons. (Punsalan & Cruz, 1999, p. 207)

Punsalan (1992) subsequently undertook a study of 204 teachers, sampled across eight regions, reaching similar findings. Pantaleon (cited by Punsalan & Cruz, 1999) studied the cognitive and affective learnings of secondary students following a one semester values education course, and among other things noted a stronger sense of social responsibility, greater valuing of friendship, and a commitment to helping families in need.

The UNESCO National Commission of the Philippines, under the leadership of its then Secretary General, Dr Quisumbing, undertook a major ten-year review and evaluation of the 1988 Program Framework, leading to a substantially revised version which emphasised seven core values within a more holistic and unified approach. The core values included 'health and harmony with nature' and 'peace and justice'. Punsalan and Cruz (1999) report several other evaluation studies, all of which have led to continuing development and refinement of the national values education curriculum.

One significant inclusion in the revised Philippines curriculum is the 'health and harmony with nature' core value, thus implying that human values and environmental values cannot be separated, and that we cannot have peace between peoples unless we build peaceful relationships with the natural world. This idea has been comprehensively researched in the context of the Philippines by Gicain (2001). She argues that there is an essential interconnectedness between human and environmental values, and that both need to be taught in an integrated way, not only in schools but also in programs of lifelong learning. Drawing on a detailed case study of her own home island of Manicani in the eastern Philippines, Gicain (2001) demonstrated how a community education program with a focus on values education and peace education could be used to restore harmony both with the environment and among the people of her island.

2.5. *Thailand*

Peace education research in Thailand has focused largely on analysis and review of Buddhist textual material, and on the role of meditation in creating inner peace leading to more peaceful relations with others. Laksana (1999, pp. 170–171), for example, describes the work of the Venerable Prayudh Payutto, Abbot of Wat Nyanavesakawan, in developing a "... theoretical framework in the essence of peace, democracy, ethics, morality, and Buddhist ways of teaching and learning" that has been used as a major resource for teacher education curricula in Thailand.

Ma Rhea (1996, 2000) conducted a major study of the role of traditional Thai knowledge and Buddhist religious practices in contemporary higher education in Thailand. Notwithstanding the impact of globalisation, she found evidence that traditional knowledge and wisdom still played a significant role in university teaching and learning, contributing to a greater sense of harmony and peace both within and between individuals. In particular, she found that the reintroduction of Buddhist meditation practices into the teaching and learning environment of some rural universities helped develop a more peaceful ethos. Bunruangrod and Waiyawudh (1999) provide a detailed account of the incorporation of peace education into both the school and teacher education curricula in Thailand. They note in particular the pilot projects currently being implemented in teacher education programs at selected Rajabhat Institutes, and the place of peace education in the new basic education curriculum for primary schools. It is obvious from their account that these developments are based on significant research and theorising, especially within the context of traditional Buddhist values and perspectives.

3. THE UNESCO TEACHER EDUCATION FOR PEACE PROJECT

This major international research project was launched in the Asia-Pacific region in 1998. Using a Participatory Action Research (PAR) model, the project sought to facilitate the development of in-country programs throughout the Asia-Pacific region. A two-week workshop in September and October 1999, funded by the Government of Japan through the National Institute for Educational Policy Research (NIER), brought together two senior teacher education personnel from each of 12 Asia-Pacific countries to develop and plan implementation of the project in their particular settings. In some cases the country dyads chose to develop an exemplary project in one institution, in other cases national action plans were developed. NIER, in collaboration with UNESCO, is committed to bringing the group together during 2003 for a follow-up seminar when each dyad will report on project outcomes and achievements, and dissemination activities will be planned.

The project is based on two assumptions: (a) that effective teaching for peace must first target teachers themselves, together with those who train them; and (b) that, to be truly effective, peace education must infuse the entire curriculum and not just be a separate entity, taught in isolation. From this perspective peace education becomes the responsibility of every teacher in an educational institution. In further theorising the foundations of the project, the coordinators argue that the curriculum process is equally as important as the curriculum content: "... we believe that processes of teaching and learning, and processes of thinking and knowing, are equally as important as curriculum content" (Teasdale & Teasdale, 1999, p. 11).

4. THE PRESENT SITUATION OF EDUCATION FOR PEACE AND INTERNATIONAL UNDERSTANDING

The nature of education for peace and international understanding in the region differs from one country to another. These characteristics reflect the variety of historical, cultural, political and social backgrounds within the countries of the region. However, in order to get a picture of the present situation on peace education at the research level, the present authors conducted a small and modest survey in 2001. A two-page questionnaire composed of several basic questions on education for peace and international understanding was sent to all the National Commissions for UNESCO in the member states of the region and also to government officials or researchers working as specialists in the field. Questionnaires were returned from 41 institutions and eight countries; India, Japan, Laos, Malaysia, the Philippines, Republic of Korea, Thailand and Vietnam. The following summarises the major findings from the survey.

First, in the questionnaire we asked about the nature of research in the field of peace education in each country. Among the answers to the question there was only one country that replied 'non-existent'. Most countries answered "individual scholars are working in the field, but with limited funding" (e.g., India, Malaysia, Thailand) or "There is an effective network of scholars working in the field with adequate funding, but with minimal impact on educational policy" (e.g., Japan, Philippines). There were no countries that chose "research is well developed with a number of projects although the impact on educational policy is modest" or "research is very well developed with a number of substantial projects that are having a direct impact on educational policy". It is apparent that in many countries in the region there are individual scholars or specialists devoting themselves to education for peace and international understanding, but they are working in rather isolated situations or within effective networks but having very little impact on policy-making.

Second, in an attempt to elicit information about the current status of peace education we asked about "the nature and scope of publications in the field of international understanding or peace education in each country". The results for this question are given in Table 1.

From those findings the characteristics of education for peace and international understanding in the region can be identified as follows.

Many actions for peace, but not much action-based research is being undertaken. Nowadays, it is known that there are many NGOs in the region actively engaged in the promotion of peace through initiating innovative educational programs. As shown in Table 1, however, there are some countries with a limited number of case studies designed to investigate the quantity of these programs. It is recommended that action research that has strong linkage with citizens' activities on peace education should be even more strongly encouraged.

Table 1. The nature and scope of publications on peace education

Category of publication	None	A few	Some	Many
Impressionistic/reflective papers that are not research based	LAO	MAL, PHI, VTM	JPN, ROK, THA	IND
Case studies of innovative programs and curricula	LAO	IND, MAL, THA	JPN, PHI, ROK, THA	VTM
Research reports and academic papers (non-refereed)	LAO	N/A	IND, JPN, MAL, PHI, ROK, THA, VTM	N/A
Academic research papers in national refereed journals	LAO, MAL	IND, JPN, PHI, THA, ROK	N/A	VTM
Academic research papers in international refereed (English language) journals	JPN, LAO, MAL, THA, ROK	IND, PHI, VTM	N/A	N/A

* The abbreviations listed above are: IND: India, JPN: Japan, LAO: Laos, MAL: Malaysia, PHI: Philippines, ROK: Republic of Korea, THA: Thailand, VTM: Vietnam.

Many texts in local languages on peace education, but little documentation. It is inferred from the findings on the question asked that there are very few documents on peace education available in English. Generally speaking our accessibility not only to academic journals, but also to non-academic articles on peace education in English is very limited. In order to promote peace education in the region, more opportunities for sharing ideas and information between countries in the region must be given. In addition, the translation of Asian philosophies or thoughts for peace into English and other languages should also be encouraged. Many thinkers and religious leaders have advocated the importance of tolerance, freedom and equality in Asia from ancient times to the contemporary age. For example, Sen (1999, pp. 235–240) refers to important leaders who emphasised freedom and tolerance. Among them were Emperor Ashoka in the third century in India and the great Monghul emperor Akbar in the sixteenth to seventeenth centuries. Both were practitioners of tolerance of diversity and both stressed the acceptability of diverse forms of social and religious behaviour. Such information in English would give a more comprehensive and accessible portrait of Asian civilisations, and so contribute to the promotion of peace education in the region.

Many impressionistic or descriptive writings on peace education. One of the most notable features with respect to peace education in the region is that there are quite a few publications of an impressionistic and reflective nature (e.g., Japan, Korea and Thailand) and India has produced many non-academic papers on peace education. Few countries have academic papers in nationally refereed or internationally refereed journals, although so-called 'English-speaking countries' such as the Philippines or India replied that there were a few internationally refereed papers. This suggests that there are very few quantitative research publications compared to the number of impressionistic writings. In order for actions and movements for peace to be sustainable, there is a need for more quantitative as well as qualitative research-based writings. However, this does not necessarily deny the ethos or the research methods of Asian scholars. As mentioned in the earlier part of this article, the holistic and reflective research approaches of the Asia-Pacific region should also be cherished as well as re-examined.

5. CONCLUSION

Last but not the least, it should be stressed that with regard to peace education research we should avoid falling into a trap of dichotomous ways of thinking, such as emphasising that scientific and objective research is superior to artistic and subjective research. It is true that our survey may confirm a general impression that research on peace education in Asia and the Pacific relies largely on qualitative and not quantitative methods. However, these unique features of the Asian research ethos with an emphasis on holistic and reflective perspectives should be further investigated. Especially in the new post-September 11 era, such non-Western ways of thought or behaviour may serve as the basis for a new social order. In the context of education for international understanding, the tragedy on September 11, 2001 seems to highlight the limitations of our ways of understanding others in our modernised world. One of the difficulties of education for international understanding today probably lies here, because the education provided usually makes a premise that we can or must understand others, and the premise itself is a parallel to the ethos of colonialism that regards others as an extension of the self. In this regard in the Asia-Pacific region the ways of understanding others have long been diversified to include ancestral wisdom on how to live together with others whom we may never fully understand, and how to accept others as they are, with respectful and caring distance in relationships. Fortunately the Asia-Pacific region has ample living examples on how to live a peaceful life, leaving the region entrusted with a mission of using the wisdom embedded in its own legacies to undertake investigations which contribute to effective education for peace and international understanding for the future.

REFERENCES

Abel, M. (2001). Peace education and its three dimensions. Paper presented at a National Conference on Peace and Value Education for Schools, Osmania University, Hyderabad, 14–15 December.

Bose, A. (1994). Peace education: An imperative in India's academia today. *University News* (New Delhi), *21*, 8–10.

Bunruangrod, D., & Waiyawud, S. (1999). Country report: Thailand. In *Teacher Education for Peace and International Understanding* (pp. 237–247). Tokyo: National Institute for Educational Research of Japan.

Gicain, M. S. (2001). Education for peace in the Philippines: A study of developmental aggression and cultural traits in Manicani. Unpublished MA thesis, Flinders University, Adelaide.

Kunnunkal, T. V. (2001). Value education for a culture of peace and non-violence. *Journal of Value Education* (India), *1*(1), 6–24.

Laksana, S. (1999). Education for international understanding and peace: Thai experience. In *Education for International Understanding and Peace in Asia and the Pacific* (pp. 167–172). Seoul: Korean National Commission for UNESCO.

Lee, Wing On (2001). Citizenship education in Hong Kong: Development and challenges. In *Redefining the Democratic Citizenship Education in the Globalized Society: The Proceedings of the International Forum of Democratic Citizenship Education in the Asia-Pacific Region* (pp. 87–112). Seoul: KEDI.

Ma Rhea, Z. (1996). Universities and wise futures. Unpublished PhD thesis, Flinders University, Adelaide.

Ma Rhea, Z. (2000). Contemporary knowledge production and reproduction in Thai universities: Processes of adaptive balancing. In G. R. Teasdale & Z. Ma Rhea (Eds.), *Local Knowledge and Wisdom in Higher Education*. Oxford: Pergamon.

Pandey, S. (1999). Country report: India. In *Teacher Education for Peace and International Understanding* (pp. 143–152). Tokyo: National Institute for Educational Research of Japan.

Punsalan, T. G. (1992). The Values Education Program as perceived by the values education teachers in eight regions of the country. *Philippines Normal University Research Series* No. 24.

Punsalan, T. G., & Cruz, T. M. (1999). Country report: Philippines. In *Teacher Education for Peace and International Understanding* (pp. 204–214). Tokyo: National Institute for Educational Research of Japan.

Quisumbing, L., & de Leo, J. (2002). Values education on a changing world: Some UNESCO perspectives and initiatives. In S. Pascoe (Ed.), *Values in Education* (pp. 164–172). Canberra: Australian College of Educators.

Rajput, J. S., & Walia, K. (2001). Teacher education for social cohesion: The Indian context. *Prospects: UNESCO Quarterly Review of Comparative Education, 31*(3), 325–332.

Sen, A. (1999). *Development as Freedom* (pp. 227–248). New York: Alfred A. Knopf.

Teasdale, G. R., & Teasdale, J. I. (1999). Teaching for peace and international understanding: A process approach. In *Teacher Education for Peace and International Understanding* (pp. 10–25). Tokyo: National Institute for Educational Research of Japan.

Zheng Xin-rong & Shi Yuntao (1999). Country report: China. In *Teacher Education for Peace and International Understanding* (pp. 133–142). Tokyo: National Institute for Educational Research of Japan.

Zhou, N. (1996). Interactions of education and culture for economic and human development: An Asian perspective. In J. Delors (chair), *Learning: The Treasure Within* (pp. 239–246). Report to UNESCO of the International Commission on Education for the Twenty-first Century. Paris: UNESCO.

Zhou, N. (1998). Learning to live together. An imperative for human development and world peace in the 21st century. In G. W. Haw & P. W. Hughes (Eds.), *Education for the 21st Century in the Asia-Pacific Region: Report on the Melbourne UNESCO Conference*, 1998 (pp. 61–70). Canberra: Australian National Commission for UNESCO.

Education of the World of Work

45

Planning Technical and Vocational Education and Training in Asia

DAVID N. WILSON
Ontario Institute for Studies in Education, Toronto, Canada

1. INTRODUCTION

The planning of Technical and Vocational Education and Training (TVET) is a sub-set of both educational and Human Resource Development (HRD) planning. Several government ministries normally perform these functions; for example, Educational and TVET Planning are performed by Ministries of Education and Training, or the latter by Ministries of Labour, while HRD planning is performed by Ministries of Human Resource Development or Economic Development.

Finch and Crunkilton (1999) assert "projecting labor supply and demand" is "one of the crucial stages in the development of relevant vocational programs." Since "the major thrust of vocational education is to prepare individuals for employment," planners must be knowledgeable about "the occupations most closely related to" employment opportunities "that actually exist."

Antecedents of TVET and HRD planning are traceable to military logistics with roots in both Europe and Asia. European roots stem from von Clausewitz's *On War* (1832) while Asian roots are attributed to Sun Tsu's *The Art of Warfare* (512 BC) (Mintzberg, 1998). The earliest manifestations of TVET and HRD planning originated in so-called 'command economies', for example, the former U.S.S.R. and the Peoples' Republic of China (Carlson and Awkerman, 1991; Bertrand, 1992). Application of the concept of HRD planning to exchange economies commenced with the Organisation for Economic Co-operation and Development (OECD) Mediterranean Regional Project in 1962. OECD planning methods were adopted by many developing nations and international organisations from the 1960s onward (Parnes, 1962). Bertrand (1992) notes India and Pakistan were the first Asia-Pacific nations to adopt manpower planning in the mid-1960s.

HRD planning was formerly known as 'manpower planning', but this term is said to be 'politically incorrect.' Ironically, the term is not problematic in, for example., French [*planification de main d'oeuvre*] or Spanish [*planificaciòn de mano de obra*] which both refer to 'hand work.' However, in the Information Age, the restructuring of work concerns less manual labour and increasingly the education of knowledge workers, required to use "logical-abstract thinking to diagnose problems, research and apply knowledge, propose solutions, and design and implement those solutions, often as a member of a team" (Wilson, 2001a).

Finch and Crunkilton (1999) identify "four approaches" to assess labour market demand: "employer surveys, extrapolation, labor market signalling and job vacancy." They note that "employer surveys" are "probably the most widely used approach in assessing labor demand." They indicate, "extrapolation ... is based on the assumption that past and current trends will give an indication as to what will happen in the future." They also note "a new approach ... to educational planners for labor forecasting is called labor market signalling," a concept "based on the premise that as shifts occur in the labor market supply and demand, certain signs become evident to the observer that can be used to understand the change underway." "These changes can then be analyzed to determine the impact on the labor demand and supply." The "job vacancy ... approach to labor demand forecasting is based on current job vacancies existing for thirty days or more."

The process of TVET planning normally commences with a survey of Human Resource needs, or requirements, for a defined future period. HRD surveys constitute applied research endeavours, often lacking the rigour normally associated with pure research. These surveys can range from basic needs assessments to the derivation of HRD requirements from more sophisticated economic, and econometric, analyses. The latter usually are prone to errors associated with the linear projection of current labour market conditions into the future. Since development is rarely linear, and usually is widely divergent, the findings from such studies should be treated with caution. Moreover, analyses of actual economic and labour force development suggest that few projective studies are able to account for new economic and occupational fields.

The findings from these various types of HRD studies are, then, utilised for planning future expansion, reform and changes in the existing TVET infrastructure. These changes can include curriculum modernisation, structural change, training facility re-design, technical teacher training and re-training. Poignant (1967) notes "estimated manpower needs are subsequently converted into training plans, and it will be mainly – but not entirely – the responsibility of training establishments to put them into effect." This article summarises the research methods normally used to conduct TVET and HRD planning and then examines several representative studies from the Asia-Pacific region.

2. TVET AND HRD PLANNING METHODS

There is no generally accepted method for estimating future HRD requirements. There is also no clear conception of the meaning of 'future requirements.' The terms used include: 'forecasting', 'predicting', 'projecting' and 'forward target-setting'. Bertrand (1992) defines a 'projection' as "the protraction in the future of a past trend in accordance with certain assumptions of extrapolation or deviation." He also notes a "projection is not a forecast unless it involves a probability." A 'forecast' "is defined as the assessment, made with a certain degree of confidence in its probability, of what will happen between now and a given future date."

The so-called 'Manpower Requirements Approach' estimates the needed trained human resources from a set of projections of economic growth, which basically comprise forecasts of required skills to set targets for planning of TVET. These targets are used to determine the required output from training institutions to produce the skills required in the labour force. A tabular distribution of required skills is disaggregated by occupational area, using Occupational Classification systems. Then, assumptions about the levels of formal education required for each occupation are developed. Estimates of the required human resources for each occupation are produced and then compared with the existing stock of human resources. This planning exercise determines expected HRD requirements; required replacements in the existing labour force, and new net HRD requirements (see Middleton, Ziderman, & van Adams, 1993).

The approach is designed to balance demand for HRD with supply from training institutions. This identifies requirements for and imbalances in future labour availability. Projections are used to develop a supply-demand equation and the identified imbalances are used as input to TVET planning. Parnes (1962) wrote that the term 'manpower requirements' referred to the occupational configuration of the labour force that will be necessary if certain social and economic targets are to be achieved.

Another HRD planning mechanism, favoured by The World Bank, is 'Labour Market Signalling'. This approach tracks movements in employment data and wages and salaries to determine changes in the demand and supply of specific occupations and skills. The identification of labour market trends is then used to identify shortages or over-supplies of particular occupations and these findings are used in planning for the expansion, or contraction, of TVET. While this approach requires TVET planners "to focus on education and training qualifications rather than occupational classifications," due to the poor quality of occupational statistics, "the effect of technology on the concept of an occupation, and the practical link between academic specialization and occupational placements" mitigates some of the problems found in other HRD planning approaches. It is noted that in Japan, "workers' roles are rapidly changed as needs arise" because "skills, rather than occupations, become the central issue in this context" (Middleton, Ziderman, & van Adams, 1993).

One of the pioneers of manpower planning, Harbison (1967) noted "the manpower analyst ... is particularly interested in the present and future size of the labour force, its growth rates in both the traditional and modern sectors, and the factors which determine labour force participation of various groups."

The simplest HRD planning method is to ask existing establishments to estimate their future HRD requirements. This method is limited because it only provides short-term requirements and is unreliable for long-term estimates.

Further, establishments may go out of business, and new fields and enterprises will be developed. A major difficulty is that many employers are either unable or unwilling to estimate future employment requirements, often fearing that their competitors may use the information. Harbison (1967) writes "in setting targets for education and training programmes, the analyst is concerned with two related but distinct concepts – manpower requirements and absorptive capacity." He defined manpower requirements as "clearly evident needs for persons with particular education, training and experience." He noted that absorptive capacity "is a looser term which refers to a country's capacity to provide some kind of useful employment for persons with certain educational qualifications." This introduces the important element of balancing HRD supply with HRD demand, since imbalance can exacerbate under- and un-employment.

Planning methodologies mirror the macro and micro economic approach to the study of economic systems. Macro-economics is the study of the overall averages and aggregates of an entire economic system. In contrast, micro-economics is the study of particular enterprises in terms of their market behaviour, interactions with their environment and forces that determine relative prices. The objective is to anticipate and avoid shortages, or surpluses, in human resources in various occupations.

Gray and Herr (1998) note, "demand data are a projection of job openings and can be listed by industry, region, or occupation." They further indicate, "demand projections attempt to predict growth or decline of employment" and "also take into account the average age of workers and the number of those retiring who will need to be replaced." Poignant (1967) suggests that "the drawing up of good forecasts of manpower needs for use in planning educational expansion would require a tremendous amount or preparatory work."

Analyses of past trends can be used to estimate future HRD requirements. This has been used successfully to estimate required numbers of engineers, scientists, teachers, medical personnel, technologists and technicians. However, the linear extrapolation of past trends can be misleading and inaccurate. This is because linear projective methods merely project the past into the future. Such planning methods ignore changes in worker productivity, do not take account of technological change, and the fact that many contemporary occupations, and even industries, did not exist ten or 20 years ago.

The method of estimating changes in productivity commences with a HRD inventory, preferably by economic sectors. The output patterns for each sector are then projected and employment within sectors is allocated, or attributed, among various occupations. The supply of qualified personnel is estimated and examined comparatively in the light of estimated outputs of education and training institutions. The gaps between supply and demand are then calculated.

The advantages of the productivity change forecasting method are that it appeals to economic development planners. This method was developed by the OECD Mediterranean Regional Project and links HRD requirements to worker productivity to identify high-level human resource bottlenecks which may affect production. The method logically relates human resource needs to economic requirements (Parnes, 1962).

According to Middleton, Ziderman and van Adams, (1993) "identifying and deciphering labor market signals requires a basic understanding of demand and supply analysis as applied to labor markets." They further state that:

> To develop and analyze these signals, manpower planners need to be firmly grounded in analytical techniques such as multiple regression analysis, survey research methods, and basic inferential statistics. The planners' job will be easier if an infrastructure of labor market information exists.

Another HRD forecasting and planning method was advocated by Harbison and Myers (1964). They analysed human resource structures in a sample of nations and devised indices that they then applied to developing nations. This method was critiqued as applying correlations calculated in sampled economies to economies that may have no comparable structure and HRD dynamics. This method has not been used in many years.

Finch and Crunkilton (1999) claim the strength of the extrapolation method "is that it is relatively easy to perform and can be done in a short time," and note, "the cost of extrapolating is quite low." They also claim the strength of the job vacancy approach "is that immediate needs of an area can be quickly ascertained." This approach may be more useful for forecasting at the micro, or enterprise, level.

At the micro, or enterprise, level planning methods project future HRD requirements for the organisation. These estimated future requirements are then compared with existing internal labour supply. Micro-level HRD planning may only pertain to a few key occupations, since most medium and small-scale enterprises do not require such planning. Planning methods may range from the simple examination of personnel records to the use of sophisticated computer-based calculations. Once future labour requirements have been determined, either training (or re-training) of existing personnel, or recruitment of new personnel with the desired skills, can be undertaken. Training or retraining can either be undertaken in-house, by means of on-the-job training (OJT) or in TVET institutions on a contracted training basis. Both systems require careful planning and evaluation.

Gray and Herr (1998) note, "the small-firm labor market is typically informal in nature and difficult to access." They also indicate "small firms are significantly less likely to provide formal training because they cannot afford the associated costs." Harbison (1967) cautioned "the educational planner must never be confused by statistics which show a great need for a particular category of manpower if prevailing social and material incentives make people unwilling to enter into that category."

It is instructive for planners in other nations that The American Society for Training and Development (ASTD) "study of skills training in the United States found that small firms were much more likely to expect employees to bear the cost of training" (cited in Gray and Herr, 1998). Middleton, Ziderman and van Adams (1993) indicate the "key data sources for manpower planning" are as shown in Table 1.

HRD forecasting techniques are mainly external to the TVET planning process, which is an internal function of a Ministry of Education and Training. TVET planners are consumers of HRD data that they use in the preparation of their plans. TVET planning can include enrolment forecasting, facility planning, TVET teacher and instructor training, curriculum planning, and can be a significant component of education system reform. The planning of TVET facilities and equipment is significantly more complex, and expensive, than planning for the expansion or reform of more academic programs. TVET planning must also pay considerably greater attention to routine and preventive maintenance of both equipment and facilities, due to heavy capital investment.

Table 1. Key data sources for manpower planning

Data source	Type of data	Purpose
National Household Survey	Population Labour force activity Unemployment Unemployment Incomes and wages Education and training Other demographic Characteristics	Rate-of-return studies Wage and employment trends Labour market analysis
National Establishment Survey	Employment Industry Earnings Firm Size Value Added	Wage and employment trends Productivity and labour market analyses
Social Insurance Administrative Data	Employment Unemployment Earnings Industry	Wage and employment trends
Tracer Studies	Employment Unemployment Earnings Occupation	Rate-of-return studies (benefits)
Cost Studies	Capital costs Recurrent costs Enrolments Training capacity	Rate-of-return studies (costs)

Source: Middleton, Ziderman and van Adams (1993, p. 152).

3. SHORTCOMINGS OF HRD PLANNING METHODS

Psacharopoulos and Woodhall (1985) introduced the distinction between "manpower planning as a continuous process rather than a technique, whereas the latter is engaged primarily in preparing quantitative projections for the overall development plan." They suggest, "less emphasis should be placed on planning *techniques* and more on the concept of planning as a *continuous process.*" They cite labour market studies undertaken by the UNESCO International Institute for Educational Planning (IIEP) in 1980, which found that:

> Even when we have gained a more thorough knowledge of the social context and, in particular, of the interactions between education and employment, even when the objectives of the educational and productive systems have been fixed, and even when society's needs for skilled manpower have been estimated with the greatest possible precision, we will still have to accept discontinuities between future projections and real events.

Psacharopoulos and Woodhall (1985) concluded,

> this comment suggests a continuing but limited role for forecasting. If manpower forecasting is to play a more subsidiary role, however, manpower analysis in the wider sense ... will still be a necessary ingredient of investment decisions. Such manpower analysis may include forecasts for particular occupations, which experience has shown may be more accurate than for the economy as a whole.

Bertrand (1992) describes an evaluation of Indian experience with manpower planning in the 1960s and 1970s that revealed:

> Most forecasts of manpower needs have been over-estimates, firstly because estimates of economic growth have themselves been over-optimistic, and secondly because specialists tended to boost manpower requirements in their own fields.

> Furthermore, jobs, which, according to the planners, should have been filled by skilled personnel, have actually been filled by personnel who do not possess the skills theoretically required but who are less highly paid. This is the consequence of not taking remuneration into account in planning.

The 'productivity' criterion is not appropriate for all economic sectors. While it is effective in predicting human resource needs in the mining, transportation, construction and manufacturing sectors, it is less effective in service occupations, health occupations and government. The indices devised by Harbison (1965) were also inappropriate for application in other countries and were, in fact, critiqued as being unscientific.

Problems inherent in HRD planning include the lack of empirical data, which makes it difficult to estimate increases in productivity; namely, output per worker. The incorrect assumption that productivity remains constant is a major methodological problem. Therefore, it is only possible to generate general assumptions. The arbitrary determination of educational requirements for many occupations ignores the reality whereby individuals with various levels of education and experience gain entry to these occupations. Therefore, there are few binding relationships between jobs and educational attainment. Since this assumption underlies most HRD planning methods, this constitutes a fundamental problem. Further, there are no available mechanisms to specify the responses of wages and salaries to changes in supply and demand. Moreover, at the level of a TVET system such over-production of un-needed human resources can be very expensive.

Poignant (1967) writes, "forecasting requires a minimum amount of basic information concerning fields which frequently have not yet been properly explored." He also asserts "the factor which is likely to change the job/skill equation most directly and rapidly ... is actually the expansion of further education."

The job vacancy approach is noted to have several limitations. First, it is unclear whether "the jobs listed" are "permanent jobs or seasonal jobs." Second, it is difficult "to ascertain whether the actual job entry qualifications are similar to traditional competencies required for that specific occupation." Third, "if one vacancy [is] filled, it might lead to three other vacancies or jobs becoming available that complement the original vacancy" (Finch & Crunkilton, 1999).

As a result, available methods can only project needs or targets for the assumed desirable output of educational and training institutions. This is quite different from effective demand for trained human resources. Finch and Crunkilton (1999) confirm "accurate and guaranteed approaches to use in projecting precise labor demands do not exist." Moreover, they note "labor demands projected beyond four years are often inaccurate." Poignant (1967) supports this scepticism by noting that "the present economic systems in the developing countries, and the uncertainty regarding their development ... do not allow us simply to use the methods already employed in the industrialized countries" where "surveys which show current deficits and short-term needs are generally all that is required to produce a valid plan for training."

Wilson (2001b) addressed TVET implications of the changing workplace influenced by technological innovation, empowerment of workers when levels of management are said to 'flatten,' and the changing notion of work as we move from an Industrial Age to an Information (or Post-Fordist) Age.

In many countries, problems with data collection and analysis prove to be insurmountable. In addition, many HRD plans are out-of-date before they are even completed. Further, policy-makers often ignore plans. Some economists assert that *Say's Law* 'supply creates its own demand' is often used by policy-makers to justify expansion of their educational and training system (Blaug, 1968).

Middleton, Ziderman and van Adams (1993) assess the popularity of the manpower requirements approach used in TVET planning in spite of its shortcomings, noting:

> Despite abundant evidence of the technique's failure to forecast accurately the need for skills training, the technique has remained popular for a number of reasons. The methodology is transparent and appeals to common sense. The technique is straightforward, its data requirements and assumptions easily grasped. The concept that economic growth creates a demand for skilled labor that can be balanced with the supply of this labor is intuitively logical on the surface. People like the precise numbers produced and the appearance of certainty over uncertainty. Moreover, most countries that use the technique do not have a system of accountability for failure. The political process in these countries pays little attention to yesterday's decisions and errors.

Wilson (1990) critiqued one aspect of the Labour Market Signals approach, used in Indonesia, because of its heavy reliance upon rate-of-return analysis to generate labour market signals. In particular, policy advice suggesting that Indonesia should reduce investment in technical secondary schools (*Sekolah Teknik Menengah* – STM) because of lower rates-of-return accruing from their studies, as compared with academic secondary education (*Sekolah Menengah Atas* – SMA), was noted to contain methodological inaccuracies. He discovered that a sequence of five rate-of-return studies had been conducted in Indonesia over a ten-year period and pointed out that the lifetime earnings differentials between academic and technical secondary graduates had declined to a difference of 13 per cent. It was suggested that rate-of-return analysis might have a ten per cent margin of error, which would further suggest that the remaining percentage difference was not a sound justification for such a sweeping policy prescription.

It is also apparent that, once education and training have been completed, there is no guarantee that those who have received training will enter those occupations for which they have been trained. A major difference between command economies and free-market economies has been the allocation of trained human resources to defined workplaces. The modernisation of former command economies has faced difficulty in re-orienting such human resource allocation mechanisms to a free-market system.

Finally, Gray and Herr (1998) caution that "because labor market demand is so highly influenced by changes in technology, the business cycle and international competition, reliability is often suspect."

4. HRD PLANNING RESEARCH IN THE ASIA-PACIFIC REGION

Unfortunately, much of the applied research undertaken by governments, and even by international agencies, has not been widely disseminated. The lack of dissemination by means of publication is referred to as 'fugitive literature'. While there is a great deal of published material on HRD and TVET planning in developed nations, there is a dearth of material concerning developing nations, particularly in the Asia-Pacific region. In this context, published HRD and TVET research in Australia, Japan and Singapore overshadows research and publication in other regional nations.

By way of example, Wilson (1976) undertook an Industrial Manpower Survey in Eastern Nepal for The Asian Development Bank (ADB) in 1975. The survey report was used by ADB as the basis for the preparation of a project to finance the Eastern Regional Campus of Tribhuvan I University Institute of Engineering. None of these project-related documents have been placed in the public domain and, as such, constitute fugitive literature.

This study is important because it was found that graduate-level engineers were underemployed in the Eastern Development Region of Nepal; therefore, a skilled trades, technician and technologist-level training institution was developed, rather than an engineering faculty. In this instance, manpower research directly influenced both TVET policy and planning.

The survey situated industry in the region along a continuum, ranging from a completely labour-intensive *biri* (cigarette) enterprise at the low-end to a fully-automated biscuit and confectionery enterprise at the capital-intensive high-end. The provision of training was targeted to the realities observed in the labour market and the likely expansion of the regional economy and labour force that would result from projects under development. Wilson (1985) also undertook the end-of-project summative evaluation of this project for ADB. One finding was that the TVET planning which underlay the project was both realistic and effective. Lamentably, this report also constitutes fugitive literature.

Some government documents on TVET research and planning have been made available through the Educational Resources Information Center (ERIC) Clearinghouse. One such document is a two-volume report on HRD and educational planning for human resource development in Thailand that was undertaken by a joint Thai-U.S. Task Force on Human Resource Development in 1962.

Since the 1970s, The UNESCO International Institute for Educational Planning (IIEP) has commissioned publications on HRD and TVET planning, of which several are concerned with the Asia-Pacific region. For example, Khan (1979) examined the growth of higher education in India between 1947 and 1977 from the perspective of manpower planning. Khan suggested guidelines for the integration of manpower planning and educational planning in the light of Indian experience. In particular, he described the mismatch between employer requirements and employee qualifications. He advocates that manpower planning should be balanced with students' aspirations in order to make planning more realistic.

In recent years, the dearth of project-related research and development insights that was reflected in the fugitive literature situation has been alleviated as multilateral agencies, such as The World Bank, International Labour Organisation, Asian Development Bank, UNESCO and The United Nations Development

Programme (UNDP) have begun to publish, or reference, such previously-unavailable materials. The citation of such fugitive literature in publications by these agencies is a welcome development.

A review by Amjad for the ILO (cited by Middleton, Ziderman and van Adams, 1993) indicated, "seven out of ten market economies in Asia used manpower requirements forecasting." The Middleton, Ziderman and van Adams book, which resulted from an internal World Bank study, also contains a great deal of previously unpublished material. The "weak link between skill specialization and occupational placement," noted above, was validated in a Philippine study by Arcelo and Sanyal (1987) that found, "among those employed, only 73 per cent of the recent graduates in applied science and 47 per cent of the liberal arts graduates were actually working in their field of academic specialisation" (Cited by Middleton, Ziderman, & van Adams, 1993).

Although not stated by its authors, one conclusion suggested by the meta-analyses of HRD and TVET planning studies by Middleton, Ziderman and van Adams (1993) is that the planning methods used should be commensurate with the level of development in those nations. The Asia-Pacific examples cited in their chapter on "Establishing Market-Oriented Educational Planning" range from Laos to Korea. The authors note that The Peoples' Democratic Republic of Laos "began economic reforms in 1986 in an effort to move from a centrally planned to a market economy." In the absence of information on labour force activity and employment, the UNDP "funded several small-scale studies to aid the government in assessing retraining needs" and "a survey of public training institutions was planned to assess the training capacity and performance of these institutions."

The section describing the "integration of economic development and manpower planning in the Republic of Korea" noted "since the early 1960s Korea has been among the fastest growing countries in the world." They indicated "Korea's first economic plan was prepared in 1962" with an industrial development strategy that "linked increasing technological sophistication in production with expanded levels of education and training." They concluded, "the integration of economic development and manpower planning ... was instrumental to the country's growth."

Ritzen and Balderston (1975) undertook one of the most comprehensive case studies of TVET planning in the Asia-Pacific region in 1969 and 1970. Their study, *Methodology for Planning Technical Education* continues to be a model available to other developing countries in the region, even though the data they used is obsolete. The authors' prescience even predates subsequent research and practice on TVET evaluation and issues of sustainability. For example, they note that:

Little attention has been given to the continuing planning, control, and monitoring of technical schools once they are set up.

Foreign assistance programs are heavily biased toward the provision of capital outlay and foreign consultants but leave much of the ensuing administration to the receiving country's government. These governments suffer from a shortage of qualified analysts and planners; often they are totally unprepared to cope with the large size and complexity of the newly emerged structure of technical education.

These comments presage the subsequent development of project evaluation and monitoring methods and also introduce notions of sustainability, which is a current theme in TVET development. It is noteworthy that few HRD and TVET planning studies of the magnitude undertaken by Ritzen and Balderston (1975) have been undertaken during the past quarter century. Instead, the available literature indicates that small-scale and sectoral studies predominate.

The first monograph published on the topic was a comparative study of TVET in 16 nations, undertaken by UNESCO in 1982 (UNESCO, 1984) including case studies of Australia, India, Indonesia and Sri Lanka, representing the Asia-Pacific region. This study examined policy, planning and administration of TVET in case studies prepared by representatives for a UNESCO conference.

An unpublished conference paper by Basu (1996) called for increased international and regional co-operation, particularly in the Asia-Pacific region, to strengthen TVET for human development. Basu noted that in spite of the region's great geographic, economic and demographic diversity, Asia-Pacific countries share many common challenges and issues fundamental to the improvement of the quality and relevance of TVET as a means of human resource development. He identifies critical issues, which must be considered in TVET planning as: population growth, urbanisation, poverty, the lack of income-generating capacity, increasing demands for literacy and secondary and technical education and pollution and environmental degradation. Basu recommends replacing traditional TVET curricula and delivery systems with a broader-based, flexible multi-dimensional approach, incorporation of new education and training technologies into TVET programs, and increased regional co-operation.

Although focused upon the topics of structural adjustment and educational reform, rather than planning of TVET, an article by Kioh (1999) equates rapid industrial development with the upward differentiation of TVET from vocational high schools to community colleges. This trend has also been salient in Japan, Taiwan and Singapore and may be beginning in Thailand and the Philippines. Kioh noted:

After the beginning of the 1980s vocational high schools could no longer be seen as a competitive institutional sector in the educational system as a whole. Instead, enrolments in junior colleges increased sharply.

The industrial manpower outlook for 1998, forecast by the Korea Research Institute for Vocational Education and Training (KRIVET), described the national skill profile as having an "overflow of low skills and a shortage of high skills."

The Australian National Centre for Vocational Education Research (NCVER) has sponsored considerable research on topics concerned with TVET planning. Selby-Smith (2001) published 17 case studies on the impact of research and development on decision-making in Australian TVET, Technical and Further Education (TAFE) and Adult and Community Education (ACE). In a subsequent paper, Selby-Smith concludes that there is "evidence that R&D does have an impact on decision-making by policy-makers and practitioners." He also finds that "the research enterprise is cumulative," and therefore "over time" may influence policy decisions. Further, he notes, "the extent to which research is used and has influence on decision-making can be *enhanced* by the actions of the stakeholders."

Saunders (2001) used training indicators to improve planning for TVET in Australia based upon research undertaken for NCVER. His training indicators and derived measures to compare demand to supply are presented in tabular form in Table 2.

5. CONCLUSION: A TVET RESEARCH AND PLANNING AGENDA

Atchoarena (2001) cites the UNESCO Second International Congress on Technical and Vocational Education and Training, held in Korea in 1999, as having 'renewed interest' in TVET "motivated by the necessity to address new economic challenges." He asserts that the emerging policy and research agenda includes three key areas:

(1) The transition from school to work, including the need to make TVET institutions more responsive to the needs of the labour market. This concern motivates the global interest for apprenticeship schemes and work experience programs.
(2) Reforming the institutional framework to finance and govern TVET – a key principle being partnership with industry. The establishment of National Training Boards and of National Training Funds represents an important trend in this effort.
(3) Promoting competency-based training and establishing national qualification frameworks is also a significant trend in an increasing number of developing countries in Africa, Asia and Latin America.

Atchoarena (2001) also calls for strengthened links between research and policy, including the training of 'TVET planners, managers, and policy-makers' and the 'dissemination and access to research results.' He notes that "the newly-established agreement between the [Australian] NCVER and UNESCO to make the NCVER database available to an international audience ... will constitute a very useful step towards increasing the access to TVET research findings."

The foundation for Asia-Pacific regional co-operation has existed for decades and includes the South-East Asia Ministers of Education Organisation

Table 2. Training demand and supply indicators

Training demand indicators	Training supply indicators
Output and productivity, growth forecasts	VET funding and trends
Employment, recent employment change, growth forecast	Training providers (numbers, types, locations and trends)
Assessment of 'strategic importance' (of an industry to the economy)	Training activity and trends – Students, enrolments, hours and trends
Industry characteristics (size and distribution of firms)	Training trends in detail – Course enrolments, levels, completions and trends
Industry training needs (emerging or contracting skills demands)	– Enrolments by package (competencies) and trends
Replacement demand levels	– Contracts of training, completions, and trends
VET graduate employment and salaries and trends	– Module enrolments, completions and trends
Employer and student satisfaction, and trends	Shares of training market (by provider, by pathway, by level)
Job market trends (wages and conditions) (regional) demographics	Other supply sources (existing workers, retraining, migration) (Regional) enrolment demographics

Derived measures (comparing demand to supply)

Output or strategic importance (of an industry in the economy versus VET funding levels
Employment levels versus VET funding levels
Employment levels versus levels of training hours
Employment levels and trends versus enrolments, contracts or training, completions
Growth and replacement needs versus training completions
Regional demographics versus regional enrolment demographics
Industry market needs versus training trends and training market shares
Suggested direction of training effort (+, 0, −)
Suggested training gaps and (purchasing) opportunities

Source: Saunders (2001).

(SEAMEO) Centre in Brunei Dar-es-Salaam, TVET research institutes in Australia, Korea, Singapore, and Taiwan and national training boards in many regional nations. International co-ordination of TVET activity has been provided since 1990 by the UNESCO UNEVOC Project which is now a component of the UNESCO International Centre for Technical and Vocational Education and Training in Bonn, Germany, serving national UNEVOC Centres in many Asia-Pacific countries.

REFERENCES

Basu, C. K. (1996). Asia-Pacific Partnership for Human Development Through TVET, Paper presented at the Annual Meeting of the International Vocational Education and Training Association (IVETA) and the American Vocational Association (AVA), Cincinnati, Ohio, December 1996.

Bertrand, O. (1992). *Planning Human Resources: Methods, Experiences and Practices*. Paris: UNESCO International Institute for Educational Planning.

Blaug, M. (Ed.) (1968). *Economics of Education*. London: Penguin.

Calkins, M. A. (1984). Policy, planning and management in technical and vocational education: A comparative study. *Trends and Issues in Technical and Vocational Education, 3*.

Carlson, R. V., & Awkerman, G. (Eds.) (1991). *Educational Planning: Concepts, Strategies, Practices*. New York: Longman.

Finch, C. R., & Crunkilton, J. R. (1999). *Curriculum Development in Vocational and Technical Education: Planning, Content, and Implementation*. Boston: Allyn and Bacon.

Gray, K. C., & Herr E. L. (1998). *Workforce Education: The Basics*. London: Allyn and Bacon.

Harbison, F. (1965). *Educational Planning and Human Resource Development*. Paris: UNESCO International Institute for Educational Planning.

Harbison, F., & Myers, C. A. (1964). *Education, Manpower and Economic Growth: Strategies of Human Resource Development*. New York: McGraw-Hill.

Khan, Qamar Uddin, (1979). *Manpower Aspects of Higher Education in India*. Paris: UNESCO International Institute for Educational Planning.

Kioh, Jeong (1999). Structural adjustment and vocational education in the Republic of Korea: The struggle between markets and the institutionalized system. *Prospects, 291*, 89–104.

Middleton, J., Ziderman, A., & van Adams, A. (1993). *Skills for Productivity: Vocational Education and Training in Developing Countries*. New York: Oxford University Press for The World Bank.

Mintzberg, M., Ahlstrand, B., & Lampel, J. (1998). *The Positioning School*. New York: Free Press.

Palakawongsa, Nai Nob et al. (1963). *Preliminary Assessment of Education and Human Resources in Thailand*. Bangkok: Ministry of Education.

Parnes, H. S. (1962). *Forecasting Educational Needs for Economic and Social Development*. Paris: OECD.

Poignant, R. (1967). *The Relation of Educational Plans to Economic and Social Planning*. Paris: UNESCO International Institute for Educational Planning.

Ritzen, J. M., & Balderston, J. B. (1975). *Methodology for Planning Technical Education with a Case Study of Polytechnics in Bangladesh*. New York: Praeger.

Saunders, S. (2001). Using Training Indicators to Improve Planning for Vocational Education and Training. Paper delivered at the 2001 Australian Vocational Education and Training Research Association (AVETRA) Conference.

Selby-Smith, C. (1999). *The Impact of Research and Development on VET Decision Making: A Range of Case Studies*. Adelaide: National Centre for Vocational Education Research.

Selby-Smith, C. (2001). The Impact of Research on Decision-Making by Practitioners and Managers. Paper delivered at the 2001 AVETRA Conference.

Wilson, D. N. (1976). *Report of the Industrial Manpower Consultant on the Feasibility of Loan Financing of the Eastern Regional Campus of the Institute of Engineering, Tribhuvan I University, Nepal*. Manila: Asian Development Bank.

Wilson, D. N. (1990). The deleterious impact of premature rate-of-return studies on LDC education policies: An Indonesian case. *Canadian and International Education, 19*(1), 32–49.

Wilson, D. N. (2001a). Technical-vocational education and training In D. & A. Poonwassie (Eds.), *Fundamentals of Adult Education*. Toronto: Thompson.

Wilson, D. N. (2001b). Reform of TVET for the changing world of work. *Prospects, XXXI*(1), 21–37.

Wilson, D. N., & Mummery, D. (1985). *Project Completion Report on The Vocational Education Project (Loan No. 315-NEP(SF) Eastern Region of Nepal*. Manila: Asian Development Bank.

46

Vocational Education and Training in Asia

JANDHYALA B.G. TILAK
National Institute of Educational Planning and Administration, New Delhi, India

1. INTRODUCTION

General or vocational education? This is a 'tough choice' in many developing countries (Yang, 1998, p. 289). In the human capital framework, general education is said to create 'general human capital' and vocational and technical education 'specific human capital' (Becker, 1964). The former is portable across one's life and from job to job, while the latter is not and hence many advocate general education, as more suitable for a flexible labour force that can change task and even the type of work; but the latter has an advantage, imbibing specific job-relevant skills, that can make the worker more readily suitable for a given job and would make him or her thus more productive. Hence both are important, and education systems in many countries therefore include both general and vocational streams of education in varying proportions.

Countries in the Asian region have placed varying emphases on general and vocational education, depending upon several historical, social, economic and political considerations. While general secondary education is somewhat of a homogenous nature, there is a diverse pattern of provision of vocational and technical education and training (abbreviated hereafter simply as VET) in many countries. It includes at least two major forms: vocational and technical education in formal education systems (lower and senior secondary schools, post-senior secondary but below college level institutions like polytechnics, and colleges at tertiary level), and training outside a formal system of education (pre-employment training and on-the-job-training). The latter kind also includes apprenticeship training systems, nonformal training centres and enterprise based training. Polytechnics in many countries, industrial training institutes in India, and technical colleges in Sri Lanka belong to the post-secondary level (below tertiary level). Vocational and technical education has been an important part of senior secondary education, but it was also introduced in the tertiary level colleges in India in recent years. Most countries have both exclusive vocational schools and diversified secondary schools with general academic as well as vocational courses. In several East Asian countries, the emphasis was not on formal vocational and technical secondary schools, but on training institutions and on-the-job training. In many of the countries of the region, employers are also responsible for specific skill training.

With rapid transformation of societies in social, political, economic, technological, and education spheres, there has been a change in the perspectives on the need for and nature of VET. New challenges have begun to emerge, and old ones to re-emerge. This article provides a brief account of the progress made by countries in the Asian region in VET, and discusses a few important emerging issues of serious concern.

2. WHY AND WHY NOT VET?

The issue of VET has been a matter of concern of many countries for a long time. In India, back in the British days of the Wood's Dispatch (1854), there was a cry for the introduction of occupational education. Several commissions and committees of the British India suggested the introduction of two streams of education, academic and technical. These arguments by the colonial rulers in India and other developing countries were viewed as measures "to stabilize traditional agricultural life and to curb educational 'over-production', the tendency of individuals from rural areas to continue in school past the capacity of labour markets to absorb them" (Grubb, 1985, pp. 527–528). During the post-independence era also arguments have been advanced in favour of VET in developing countries; leaders such as Mahatma Gandhi, Mao and Julius Nyerere have been quoted in support of such educational reforms.

Leading social scientists have lent strong support for vocational education. For instance, Balogh (1969, p. 262) was emphatic in arguing: "As a purposive factor for rural socio-economic prosperity and progress, education must be technical, vocational and democratic." He in fact suggested that even "elementary education must impart technical knowledge to rural youth in an eminently practical way ..." (p. 265). The case for VET received much support in the context of the global educational crisis. VET was viewed as the solution to the educational problems in the developing economies. It was believed that many educational problems could be solved by diversifying the secondary education curriculum. The unbridled demand for higher education could be controlled. The financial crisis in education would be eased by reducing pressures on higher education budgets, and unemployment among college and secondary school graduates would be reduced. All this was based on the following assumptions.

- Differentiation of occupation in the developing economies requires secondary school graduates with varied skills. Because of changes in production processes resulting from technological advances, the nature of the demand for skills, both in terms of quantity and quality, changes. Modern technology requires fewer highly qualified middle and lower level skilled personnel. Vocational education can produce exactly this kind of manpower.

- Vocational education would contribute to such progress, both by reducing unemployment, through creating employment in the fields of pre-vocational specialisation and self-employment, and by engendering a higher propensity for labour force participation at the end of secondary schooling, improving productivity, and correspondingly resulting in higher graduate earnings. Vocational and technical secondary education can establish a closer relationship between school and work.
- Vocational education is also seen as an equity measure. As an antidote to urban-biased elite education, vocational education will promote equity with a rural bias and serve the needs of relatively poor people. Also as Grubb (1985, p. 527) states, vocational education has been seen as the answer to an enrolment problem. The tendency of some students (especially lower class students) to drop out of schools without occupational skills is a problem that vocational education promises to resolve by providing a more interesting and job-relevant curriculum. More specifically, it is believed to be an effective education strategy to solve: (a) rural problems, (b) alleviate unemployment, (c) reorient student attitudes towards rural society, (d) halt urban migration, and (e) transmit skills and attitudes useful in employment (Lillis & Hogan, 1983). In addition, it is an important measure of development for disadvantaged youth in rural and urban areas.
- Further, vocational education is considered helpful in developing what can be termed as 'skill-culture' and attitude towards manual work, in contrast to pure academic culture and preference for white collar jobs; and to serve simultaneously the 'hand' and the 'mind', the practical and the abstract, the vocational and the academic" (Grubb, 1985, p. 548).

Vocational and technical education is not necessarily favoured by all. There are strong opponents as well. In a seminal oft-quoted work, Foster (1965) exploded the vocational school myth and called it the 'vocational school fallacy.' Foster and later Blaug (1973) clearly argued that vocationalisation cannot be a remedy for educated unemployment: it cannot prepare students for specific occupations and reduce mismatches between education and the labour market. Academic streams promise higher wages than vocational streams and accordingly the demand for vocational education might not exist, and Say's law that supply creates its own demand might not work. Furthermore, vocational schooling may create "a sense of second class citizenship among both teachers and taught which militates against effective learning" (Blaug, 1973, p. 22).

With the succinct, clear and powerful arguments of Foster, Blaug and others, it was hoped that the issue was buried. But it refuses to stay buried. Few countries have given up their efforts to develop elaborate systems of VET. After all, it has inherently a powerful appeal. Many countries have set ambitious targets as well. For example, China had a goal of expanding vocational education so that at least 50 per cent of the enrolments in secondary education would be in vocational education in the near future. India has a similar target of reaching 25 per cent; and Bangladesh 20 per cent. As Psacharopoulos (1987, p. 203) aptly stated, "because of the inherently logical and simplistic appeal, vocationalism will be with us for years to come, and more countries will attempt (...) to tune their formal educational systems to the world of work."

Organisations such as UNESCO and the World Bank have played a leading role in reviving and furthering the cause of vocational or diversified secondary education. UNESCO adopted in 1974 an important detailed recommendation concerning technical and vocational education, and argued for provision of technical and vocational education as "an integral part of general education," as "a means of preparing for an occupational field," and as an instrument to reduce the mismatches between education and employment and between school and society at large. The World Bank's sector policy paper on education (World Bank, 1974) attacked school curricula as excessively theoretical and abstract, insufficiently oriented to local conditions, and insufficiently concerned with attitudes and with manual, social and leadership skills; and accordingly the Bank also suggested increasing vocationalisation of the curricula of academic schools.

3. ACHIEVEMENTS AND FAILURES

The question to vocationalise or not to vocationalise? (Psacharopoulos, 1987), is no more a dilemma. The question rather, is how much of the education system should be vocational and how much should be general in character. To strike a balance between the two is indeed a challenge. Several developing countries, including countries in the Asian region have a long history of vocational and technical education and training, and they have vocational or diversified secondary education systems. India has had a diversified secondary education system for a long time. Even in the nineteenth century in India, there was a reasonably good vocational and technical system (see Crane, 1965). However, after its slow demise during the colonial period, India has had to start afresh on vocationalisation since independence. It is more or less the same situation in the other developing countries of the region, many of them having had a long colonial and feudal rule. Only after independence, and particularly since the 1950s, has increasing attention been given to vocational education. Initial efforts at vocationalisation in Sri Lanka date back to the 1930s and in Philippines to 1920s. A *Vocational Education Act* was passed in 1927 in Philippines stating that the "controlling purpose of vocational education is to fit pupils (persons) for useful employment" (UNESCO, 1984, Philippines, p. 11). Malaysia established its first technical college in 1906. South Korea and Taiwan placed high priority on special vocational education at an early stage of the industrialisation process in the respective countries. The very first educational development plan of Pakistan envisaged technical and commercial education as an integral part of general education, with diversification of the secondary education curriculum. The National Education Commission in Bangladesh, appointed immediately after independence, recommended in 1972 the diversification of secondary education from Grade 9 onwards. China had long emphasised vocational education in its school curriculum. After 1978, quite a number of government senior secondary schools were converted into vocational schools. Polytechnic institutions, vocational schools, institutes of technical education, and technical colleges figure prominently in the education systems in Japan, Korea, Taiwan, Singapore and India. Vocational and technical schools received serious attention in Japan even during the nineteenth century (Yamamoto, 1994). The so-called 'Taiwan miracle' is indebted to its system of VET (Boyd & Lee, 1995, p. 195). In several countries of the region many academic secondary schools that concentrated for a long period on preparing students for university entry, tried to become multi-purpose institutions to serve a broad spectrum of students and needs, including specific types of occupational training. In addition, various types and models of specialised secondary training institutions have been created in several countries to meet different middle level manpower needs.

All countries in the Asian region have, however, not accorded equal degree of attention to VET. As a result, they are at various levels of development of vocational education. As the Asian Development Bank (1991, pp. 53–55) categorised several Asian countries: (a) Korea as 'a leading example' of how governments can promote an extensive school-based VET; (b) Singapore has developed a 'comprehensive vocational training infrastructure,' forging strong linkages between education institutions and training agencies; (c) Indonesia, Malaysia, Philippines, Thailand and Sri Lanka have 'fairly developed' vocational and technical education systems – both in public and private schools; (d) the agrarian economies of Bangladesh, Nepal, Pakistan and Myanmar have 'patchy' systems of vocational and technical education; and (e) India and China, the two big countries on the globe, suffer from 'prejudice against manual work' and hence have 'lopsided' education development structures including VET. On the other extreme, Japan has the 'most developed and well-established infrastructure' providing school based as well as enterprise based VET.

The nature of VET also differs between several countries. Vocational education in many countries generally refers to the inculcation of vocational and technical skills relevant for specific occupations. In a few countries, vocational education is also general in curriculum. For example, vocational education in Japan and Korea is fairly general in character. General skills, broad attitudes and discipline are more valued than vocational skills *per se* in the labour market. Accordingly schools, even vocational schools emphasise, for example, in Korea, moral education and discipline (Green, 1997, p. 50).

The current status with respect to VET in several Asian countries as it developed over the last three decades is presented in Table 1.

In general, more than 70 per cent of the enrolments in secondary education are in general education and in some counties vocational education accounts for less than one per cent. Some countries have expanded their vocational education systems fast, and many have not. Korea has expanded its vocational educational system considerably, the enrolments in vocational education forming more than 20 per cent of the enrolments in secondary education. Countries in East Asia like Thailand, Japan, China, and Indonesia have also high enrolments

Table 1. Enrolment in vocational education as a proportion of total enrolments in secondary education in Asia (per cent)

	1970–71	1980–81	Latest year	Change 1980–81 to 1970–71	LY to 1980–81	LY to 1970–71
Bangladesh	–	1.0	0.7	–	−0.3	–
Brunei	1.1	3.6	5.7	2.5	2.1	4.6
Cambodia	3.5	–	1.6	–	–	−1.9
China	0.1	2.1	15.0	2.0	12.9	14.9
Hong Kong	6.1	6.6	2.9	0.5	−3.7	−3.2
India	1.0	1.2	1.1	0.3	−0.1	0.2
Indonesia	22.1	10.7	12.6	−11.4	1.9	−9.6
Iran	2.9	7.4	4.5	4.5	−2.9	1.6
Japan	18.7	14.8	14.5	−3.9	−0.3	−4.1
Korea, South	14.3	20.6	20.4	6.3	−0.2	6.1
Lao	13.9	2.2	3.3	−11.7	1.1	−10.5
Malaysia	2.9	1.7	2.6	−1.2	0.9	−0.2
Mongolia	11.0	7.6	5.8	−3.4	−1.8	−5.2
Myanmar	0.0	1.4	0.3	1.3	−1.0	0.3
Pakistan	1.5	1.5	1.1	0.0	−0.4	−0.4
Papua New Guinea	19.4	16.2	10.1	−3.2	−6.1	−9.2
Singapore	8.3	7.4	3.8	−0.9	−3.6	−4.5
Thailand	22.3	15.5	18.0	−6.8	2.5	−4.2
Vietnam	–	5.7	3.2	–	−2.5	–

–: Not available; LY: latest year.
Latest year: data available in UNESCO (1999) mostly relating to mid/late 1990s.
Source: Calculated by the author, based on UNESCO (1999).

in vocational education. But on the other side, countries in South Asia like Bangladesh, India, and Pakistan have very tiny vocational secondary education systems (Table 2).

Some countries have placed an emphasis on vocational education for a fairly

Table 2. Countries classified by level of enrolment in vocational education (latest year) (enrolment in vocational education as % of total enrolment in secondary education)

<2%	2–5%	5–10%	10–15%	>15%
Myanmar	Malaysia	Brunei	Papua New Guinea	Thailand
Bangladesh	Hong Kong	Mongolia	Indonesia	Korea, South
India	Vietnam		Japan	
Pakistan	Lao		China	
Cambodia	Singapore			
	Iran			

Source: Based on Table 1.

long period. For example, as shown in Table 3, Indonesia, Japan, South Korea, Papua New Guinea, and Thailand, had maintained their enrolments in secondary education at above the ten per cent level during the last three decades. On the other hand, countries like Bangladesh, India, Myanmar, Pakistan, Malaysia, have never accorded a high place to vocational education. Negative attitudes to manual work on one side, and the less diversified economic structure on the other, are the demand side factors responsible for the low level of enrolment in vocational education in South Asian countries. Only a few countries, for example, China, have made special efforts to expand vocational education rapidly. China stands as a special case that had made significant improvement in vocational education since 1970–71. It is also note-worthy that it also experienced very rapid economic growth during this period.

All the countries that progressed well in vocational education, could not maintain consistently high levels of enrolment in vocational education. For example, in Korea the enrolments in vocational education as a proportion of total enrolments in secondary education declined from 44 per cent in 1955 to 20 per cent in 1996–97; in Indonesia it declined from 22 per cent in 1970–71 to 13 per cent in 1996–97, in Mongolia from 11 per cent to six per cent, in Hong Kong from six per cent to three per cent, in Lao from 14 per cent to three per cent, and so on during this period. On the whole, of the countries considered in Table 1, many countries have experienced a decline in the relative size of vocational education over the years, and only a few countries have registered improvement.

The data on enrolments in Tables 1 through 3 drawn from UNESCO, refer

Table 3. Performance of the Asian countries in vocational education (1970 to 1990s) (based on enrolment in vocational education as % of total enrolments in secondary education)

Ignored vocational education throughout (less than 3%)	Maintained reasonably high levels of enrolment throughout (above 10%)
Bangladesh	Indonesia
India	Japan
Myanmar	South Korea
Pakistan	Papua New Guinea
Malaysia	Thailand

Progressed significantly*	Fared badly**
China	Hong Kong
	Lao

* Increase by at least five percent points.
** Base/current levels are less than 3 per cent and experienced decline over the years; countries with high enrolments, but experienced decline over the years are not included here.

Source: Based on Table 1.

to enrolments in vocational education as a proportion of total enrolments in secondary education. However, in quite a few countries, vocational education is an important segment, not at secondary, but at the upper secondary level. It may, in fact, be non-existent at the lower secondary level in many countries. The enrolments in vocational education as a proportion of enrolments of the senior secondary level are indeed high in quite a few countries of the region on which data are available. Such proportions are around 40 per cent in Indonesia, Thailand and Korea. Corresponding ratios, however, exceed 70 per cent in Czech Republic and Austria, 60 per cent in Belgium, Germanys, Italy, Netherlands, Switzerland, and 50 per cent in France, Denmark, Finland, (OECD, 2000, p. 146). Thus on the whole, vocational education in the Asian region is less developed than in Europe and other countries of the Organisation for Economic Co-operation and Development (OECD).

4. WHY UNEVEN PROGRESS?

While thus some countries in Asia have been successful, though not to the extent of the European and other OECD countries, in many Asian countries the performance record of these schools at secondary level "was burdened by disappointments and by shortfalls in earlier expectations" (Coombs, 1985, p. 115). Why have several countries made remarkable progress in vocational education and many others not? This depends upon social, economic and political factors, which also mutually interact with each other.

First are the social factors. Social attitudes to vocational education are not encouraging in many Asian countries. Negative attitudes to manual work severely dampen the demand for vocational education. Further, VET is conceived as a system of education for the poor, and for the educationally backward sections that are not eligible for admission into higher education. This is viewed as one that perpetuates inequalities in the system. For example, the experiment of providing a rural curriculum in *Tamil Nadu* in India, familiarly known as the Rajaji experiment, and the Handessa Rural Education Scheme in the 1930s in Sri Lanka, were abandoned not only because there was no demand for such education, but also because they came to be viewed respectively as a *Brahmincal* conspiracy and as "a ruse designed to keep the under-privileged away from the prestigious academic curriculum" (Wijemanne, 1978). In rural areas it is mostly considered as the second-class education against the expectations of pupils and parents. Low prestige attached to vocational education and its inherent inequities are somewhat a common phenomenon in many countries including, India, Indonesia, the Philippines and Sri Lanka and to some extent in Korea and Taiwan. This suspicion that vocational curricula provide "a second-class education and track [to] some individuals – lower class or lower caste, racial minorities and women – [to keep them] away from academic education and access to jobs of the highest pay and status" (Grubb, 1985, p. 529) became quite strong over the years and some public polices of ill-treatment of vocational education in educational planning and resource allocation contributed to strengthening this belief. As a result, vocational education in countries like India did not take off on a sound footing.

Second, enrolments in vocational education and level of economic development are related. Demand for vocational education seemed to exist in industrially developing societies, with growth and diversification of industrial structure. As Psacharopoulos and Loxley (1985, p. 228) observed, the lower the overall level of a country's development, the weaker is the case for introducing vocational curriculum and diversifying it. However, it is in these countries that the need for vocational education is felt most. Emphasis on diversified industrial production stresses the need for a labour force with vocational skills. Much growth in vocational education took place in countries like Korea during early industrialisation processes, when employment opportunities could increase. So vocational education becomes more popular in regions where jobs can be guaranteed. The other aspect can also be augured: unemployment rates may diminish, if people have vocational skills. For instance, Haq and Haq (1998, p. 96) observed that unemployment rates in the East Asian economies remained low essentially because the population possessed employable vocational and technical skills. However, the relationship between demand for vocational education and economic development may not be linear. When the economies move away from reliance on its agricultural and manufacturing sectors and in favour of the service sector, the demand for VET may indeed decline. A review of the experience of the East Asian countries led Mundle (1998, p. 664) to the same conclusion. Enrolments in vocational education in the region was substantial until a threshold level of gross national product (GNP) per capita (say about US $8000) was reached; thereafter the share of vocational education in senior secondary education seemed to have declined.

While the importance of VET in economic development was recognised, and detailed plans of providing VET were preceded by manpower analyses in some of the countries, in many developing countries in South Asia few planning exercises were preceded by manpower analysis, a necessary step to understanding the nature and quantum of demand for vocational skills, their employment potential, productivity and likely earnings, besides the existing mismatches between the skills of graduates and the requirements of the labour market. As a result, many programs were bound to fail.

Growth in VET in Asian countries is also influenced by the role of the state versus the role of the private sector. Governments have a dominant role in the provision of school-based VET in most Asian economies. Even in Korea, most enterprises rely on the government for trained manpower. The role of the state in provision of VET has been similar in Korea and Taiwan (Bennell & Segerstrom, 19998, p. 275). In Hong Kong too, the provision of public sector training has been strategic. In the South Asian countries, the government is the main provider of VET both at school level and also outside the school system. It is only in Japan that enterprise-based training is the dominant mode of training. In most other countries public education institutions have been the leaders. Though the private sector does play some role in VET in the East Asian countries and also to a meagre extent in South Asian countries, the quality of private institutions in providing VET has been found to be generally poor compared to public institutions in many countries, except in Japan. Taiwan and Korea also find that it is difficult to ensure reasonable standards and quality in private institutions.

An important aspect of vocational education refers to its financing. Vocational education is by definition costlier than general education. It was estimated that in South Korea secondary technical education costs more than ten times that of general secondary education per student (Middleton & Demsky, 1989, p. 65). In China the unit costs were 50 to 100 per cent higher in vocational and technical schools than in general secondary schools (Dougherty, 1990). Moreover, according to the estimates referring to 1980s and earlier periods, vocational education in South Asian countries was found to be 2–60 times higher than general education (Tilak, 1988c). However, mechanisms for the allocation of resources in education do not seem to favour vocational education in many countries. Public expenditure on vocational education – total as well as per student – has been remarkably low, compared to general secondary education.

Vocational education programs are costly and the meagre, dwindling educational budgets in several developing countries do not allow provision of sufficient resources for vocational education. Several developing countries, more particularly countries in South Asia have invested very little on vocational education. In the mid 1990s, Bangladesh invested 8.4 per cent of the total public expenditure on education in vocational and technical education, India and Nepal 4.4 per cent and Pakistan 2.6 per cent (Haq & Haq, 1998, p. 170). The current levels of public expenditures on vocational education are not particularly high even in East Asian countries. Only 5.7 per cent of the total education (current) budget goes to vocational education in Korea, 4.5 per cent in Singapore, and about three per cent in China and Hong Kong. In Taiwan, however, it is somewhat higher, 8.2 per cent in 1995 (Tilak, 2001). On the whole, these figures are very low compared to the figures in developed countries. Many OECD countries spend 11–18 per cent of their total educational expenditures on vocational education. After all, "poor and inadequate investments cannot produce higher returns" (Tilak, 1988a).

It appears that public expenditures on VET are not particularly high in East Asian countries, but private sector expenditures on training could be higher. Unfortunately no detailed and comprehensive data at macro level are readily available. For example, training is provided by enterprises in Singapore through the operation of the Skill Development Fund established in 1979 and financed through a levy on employers amounting to two per cent of salaries of all employees earning less than S$750 per month (Haq & Haq, 1998, p. 102). It is obligatory for the companies in Korea to finance public vocational and training programs (Lijima & Tachiki, 1994). Enterprise-based training is the most important form of VET in Japan.

Besides the scarcity of public resources, governments also face confusion on the efficacy of VET programs, which deter them from making required investments in VET. Available evidence on rates of return to education in countries does not indicate any advantage that vocational education will provide compared to general education. For example, Chung (1995, p. 177) reported 12 studies showing higher returns to vocational education than to general secondary education and ten studies otherwise; and five studies that yielded no clear results. Though there are certain well known problems with the estimates of rates of return to education, and a few other problems highlighted specifically in the context of returns to vocational education (e.g., Bennell, 1995; Bennell and Segerstrom, 1998), nevertheless, no conclusive evidence exists on the economic superiority of vocational education over general education (see also Tilak, 1988a,b).

Table 4 presents estimates of rates of return on this problem in five Asian countries. Though the estimates are somewhat dated, it can be noted that except in Taiwan where the difference is small, in general, vocational education does not pay as much as general secondary education. After all, costs of vocational education are extremely high, but the labor market benefits are not so high as to compensate for the huge costs. However, if productivity is measured not in earnings, but in physical terms, and not in relation to costs, some times it is found that workers with VET may be more productive than those with general academic education (e.g., Min & Tsang, 1990).

Another aspect of confusion for the governments in developing countries is changing policies of international organisations like the World Bank. World Bank supported VET in many countries in Asia for a long time. For example, in 1984–85 of the total World Bank lending for education, one-fourth was meant for VET projects. As stated earlier, World Bank and UNESCO have strongly argued in favour of investing in VET and its rapid expansion for economic growth. But by the late 1980s, the Bank policies took a ∩-turn on vocational

Table 4. Social rates of return to vocational versus general secondary education

Country	Year	General	Vocational/Technical
Taiwan	1970	26.0	27.4
South Korea	1981	9.0	8.1
Thailand	1970	10.0	8.0
	1990	11.4	6.7
Philippines	1960s	21.0	11.0
	1978	19.0	23.6
	1978	32.0	18.0
Indonesia	1982	23.0	19.0
	1986	19.0	6.0
	1986	12.0	14.0
	1986	11.0	9.0

Source: Psacharopoulos (1994); Tilak (1994, 2001); Bennell (1995, 1998).

education and strongly favoured investing away from VET (World Bank, 1995). World Bank's investment in VET came down to a meagre three per cent of the total education lending by 1996 (Bennell & Segerstrom, 1998, p. 271). The frequent ∩-turns of organisations like the World Bank in case of vocational education (and also manpower planning, rates of return to education and higher education) have caused considerable confusion among the governments of the developing countries on the wisdom of investing in VET. Countries that did not rely on World Bank assistance might not have suffered much.

5. WHERE DO WE GO FROM HERE?

From this review of Asian experience, a few important lessons can be drawn for the development of VET in developing countries.

- VET is important for economic growth. But the relationship is not linear. So each country has to decide the extent of VET that has to be developed, depending upon the level of development and demand for skills. As Foster (1965, p. 153) observed, "in the initial stages technical and vocational instruction is the cart rather than the horse in economic growth, and its development depends upon real and perceived opportunities in the economy. The provision of vocational education must be directly related to those points at which some development is already apparent and where demand for skills is beginning to be manifested." Plans for VET should be preceded by detailed manpower analyses and forecasts. Though the importance of manpower planning and forecasting *per se*, has declined, few doubt the importance of detailed manpower analysis.
- Since both general and specific human capital contribute to economic growth, a balance has to be struck between size of general education and vocational education. Further, vocational education need not necessarily be purely vocational and technical. It should also include, like in Japan and Korea, general skills and attributes that are useful across a wide variety of occupations. This is particularly important in the rapidly changing economic systems.
- As specific human capital development can take place both in formal schools and also in the firm-based institutions, it may be important to examine which vocational and technical skills are to be provided in schools and which in the training institutions and enterprise-based organisations. Comparative advantage of each system has to be taken into consideration.
- As vocational education is necessarily expensive, the government should make adequate allocation of resources for vocational education. Poor investments cannot yield attractive returns.
- Vocational education should not promote inequalities within the educational system. This requires provision of good quality vocational education and training, comparable, if not superior to, general secondary education that would avoid suspicions on the part of the people on the intentions of the

government in providing VET. It also requires effectively linking of vocational education with higher education, so that vocational education is not perceived as dead-end, with no opportunities to go on to higher education.
- Given the experience of many countries in Asia, except Japan, the government has to take a dominant role in promoting VET. The private sector may not be able to provide good quality VET.
- Lastly, issues relating to VET are not just curriculum questions, nor are they just economic. They are intricately linked with social, cultural, historical, economic, technical, and political parameters. Hence formulation of sound and effective policies and plans for VET require an inter-disciplinary development approach, treating VET as an integral part of overall educational planning.

REFERENCES

Anderson, C. A., & Bowman, M. J. (Eds.) (1965). *Education and Economic Development.* Chicago: Aldine.
Asian Development Bank (1991). *Technical and Vocational Education and Training.* Manila: ADB.
Balogh, T. (1969). Education and agrarian progress in developing countries. In K. Hufne & J. Naumann (Eds.), *Economics of Education in Transition* (pp. 259–268). Stuttgart: Ernst Klett.
Becker, G. S. (1964). *Human Capital.* New York: National Bureau of Economic Research.
Bennell, P. (1995). *General versus Vocational Secondary Education in Developing Countries: A Review of the Rates of Return Evidence.* IDS Working Paper 23. Brighton, UK.: Institute of Development Studies.
Bennell, P., & Sergerstrom, J. (1998). Vocational education and training in developing countries: Has the World Bank got it right? *International Journal of Educational Development, 18*(4), 271–287.
Blaug, M. (1973). *Education and the Employment Problem in Developing Countries.* Geneva: International Labor Office.
Boyd, T. F., & Lee, C. (1995). Educational Need and Economic Advancement: The Role of Vocational Education in the Republic of China, In Yee (Ed.), pp. 193–210.
Chung, Yue-Ping (1995). Returns to vocational education in developing nations. In M. Carnoy (Ed.), *International Encyclopedia of Economics of Education* (pp. 175–181). Oxford: Pergamon.
Coombs, P. H. (1985). *The World Crisis in Education.* New York: Oxford.
Crane, R. I. (1965). Technical education and economic development in India before World War I. In C. A. Anderson & M. J. Bowman (Eds.), *Education and Economic Development* (pp. 142–166). Chicago: Aldine.
Dougherty, C. (1990). Unit costs and economies of scale in vocational and technical education: Evidence from the People's Republic of China. *Economics of Education Review, 9*(4), 389–394.
Foster, P. J. (1965). The Vocational School Fallacy in Development Planning. In Anderson and Bowman (Eds.) (pp. 142–166).
Green, A. (1997). *Education, Globalization and the Nation State.* London: Macmillan.
Grubb, W. N. (1985). The convergence of educational system and the role of vocationalism. *Comparative Education Review, 29*(4), 526–548.
Haq, Mahbub ul & Khadija Haq (1998). *Human Development in South Asia 1998.* Karachi: Oxford University Press.
Lijima, K., & Tachiki, D. S. (1994). *Developing Human Resources for Sustainable Economic Growth: Public Policy Lessons from Japan, the Asian NIEs and DPEs.* Tokyo: Sakura Institute of Research.
Lillis, K., & Hogan, D. (1983). Dilemmas of diversification: Problems associated with vocational education in developing countries. *Comparative Education, 19*(1), 89–107.

Middleton, J., & Demsky, T. (1989). *Vocational Education and Training: A Review of World Bank Investment*. Discussion Paper 51. Washington DC: World Bank.

Min, Wei-fang & Tsang, M. C. (1990). Vocational education and productivity: A case study of the Beijing General Auto Industry Company. *Economics of Education Review, 9*(4), 351–364.

Mundle, S. (Ed.) (1998). Financing human resource development in the advanced Asian economies. *World Development, 26*(4), 657–742.

OECD (2000). *Education at a Glance: OECD Indicators*. Paris: Organisation for Economic Co-operation and Development.

Psacharopolous, G. (1987). To vocationalize or not to vocationalize: That is the curriculum question. *International Review of Education, 33*(2), 187–211.

Psacharopoulos, G., & Loxley, W. (1985). *Diversified Secondary Education and Development*. Baltimore: Johns Hopkins/World Bank.

Tilak, J. B. G. (1988a). Economics of vocationalization: A review of evidence. *Canadian and International Education, 17*(1), 45–62.

Tilak, J. B. G. (1988b). Vocational education and economic growth. *Journal of Educational Planning and Administration, 2*(1–2) (January – April), 157–184.

Tilak, J. B. G. (1988c). Vocational education in South Asia: Problems and prospects. *International Review of Education, 34*(2), 244–257.

Tilak, J. B. G. (1994). *Education for Development in Asia*. New Delhi: Sage.

Tilak, J. B. G. (2001). *Building Human Capital in East Asia*. Washington DC.: World Bank Institute.

UNESCO (1984). Technical and vocational education: Country studies. Bangkok: UNESCO Regional Office for Education in Asia and the Pacific.

UNESCO (1999). *Statistical Yearbook*. Paris.

Wijemanne, E. L. (1978). *Educational Reforms in Sri Lanka*. Report Studies C. 70. Paris: UNESCO.

World Bank (1974). *Education. Sector Paper*. Washington, DC.

World Bank (1995). *Priorities and Strategies for Education*. Washington DC.

Yamamoto, S. (1995). Traditionalism versus Research and Development at Japanese Universities. In Yee (Ed.) (pp. 25–35).

Yang, J. (1998). General or vocational? The tough choice in the Chinese Education Policy. *International Journal of Educational Development, 18*(4), 289–304.

Yee, A. H. (Ed.) (1995). *East Asian Higher Education: Traditions and Transformations*. Oxford: Pergamon.

47

Pacific Island Issues in Vocational Education and Training

PERIVE TANUVASA LENE
Samoa Polytechnic, Samoa

1. INTRODUCTION

This article is based on the developments of technical and vocational education and training (TVET) in the Cook Island, Fiji, Kiribati, Nauru, Niue, Samoa, Solomon, Tokelau, Tonga, Tuvalu, and Vanuatu. Details on the individual islands are given in Table 1. The first island nation in the Pacific to become independent was Samoa, on 1st January 1962, and since then, all the above mentioned island nations, have become self-governed. Much of the infrastructure put in place by colonial administrators and donors has been reviewed and renewed due to the changing needs and priorities of the island nations. In most island nations, the population growth is outstripping the capacities of the education system to provide adequate services resulting in a severe shortage of trained personnel to fill key positions in government and private sectors.

This article covers the challenges to Pacific Island nations, the current situation in TVET development on individual and regional levels and future strategies to improve the quality and standards of TVET to meet the countries' needs for better social and economic growth. Information for this article was provided by the main providers and planners of TVET in the 11 countries for accuracy and reality, as well as some regional reports and data compiled by donor organisations. The sources of information for the detailed statements presented in this article are for the Cook Islands (Ivaiti and Koteka, 2001), Fiji (Nabuka, 2001), Kiribati (Ereata, 2001), Samoa (Lene, 2001a), Tuvalu (Neemia, 2001), Samoa (Lene, 2001b) and UNESCO.

2. BACKGROUND

The development of technical and vocational education and training (TVET) in the island nations of the Pacific has undergone many changes in the past few years. This is due mainly to the increase in population and the need to have education as the main means of preparing people for employment. In most island nations, education is becoming more and more a priority in governmental economic strategies. Thus, TVET programs and their development and implementation are very important as they provide skills for young students as well as the working population wanting to attain higher skills and competency in their respective areas of profession. This is in support of lifelong learning and equity in education. As well, TVET development helps industries and communities to keep abreast of the fast changing technologies. This in turn has resulted in the trend of having industry more involved in education and training. This is done mainly through advisory panels or trade advisory committees consisting of stakeholders from industry and government departments that are directly involved in training, for example, Labour Departments. These panels identify industry training needs and make recommendations to incorporate them into the TVET provider's curriculum.

Every year there is an alarming increase in the number of student dropouts not completing secondary school education. The universities' entry level requirements for academic studies can accommodate only the top level students from the secondary schools. Similarly, the opportunities and vacancies available for TVET at a tertiary and college level are insufficient to meet the increasing demand. However, TVET providers have more flexible entry requirements and offer programs for students, people in the work force and communities. TVET therefore, can provide skills that most of the people can use for attaining jobs or can be applied in villages for community and domestic development. Nowadays, there is an increased demand for TVET providers to increase their enrolment capacities and consider other means of educational media to offer programs, for example, to introduce open distance learning to provide education for those islanders who lack the financial resources to go through the formal educational process or because of their isolated location from the main islands or capitals, find it difficult to attend programs on site. Because of the high costs of establishing and maintaining any technical and vocational institutions, most if not all of the island nations rely heavily on their governments, non-government organisations and donor assistance for their sustainable existence.

The introduction of new resources and equipment for national development in all the different sectors in the government and private sectors has increased the commitment by providers of education to educate people for employment and especially to prepare them for newer challenges as a result of fast changing technology. For the past 20 years, the island nations have recognised the need to increase investment and efforts in the development of TVET on a national level to ensure that skills education is available to as many students, existing workforce and people in communities, as possible.

3. KEY CHALLENGES FOR TVET IN ISLAND STATES

The Pacific Island nations exhibit an unparalleled diversity of culture and language as well as great variation in physical environment and political characteristics. The Pacific Island economies are small and remote from markets thus, they rely for revenue in economic and social developments on a narrow base of exports which include: fish, a few agricultural products, timber, tourism and labour to finance imports. In addition, island nations are very prone to natural disasters and other causes of environmental degradation and therefore rely mostly on foreign assistance from donor countries like Australia, New Zealand and Japan and multilateral organisations.

3.1. *Location and Sizes*

The geographical location of the different island nations plays a big role in their national development. Most of them are not in a situation where they can provide full control in transport, communication and other needed areas for a sustainable growth in economic and social developments. Thus, reliance on foreign influence plays a crucial role in how the future of TVET development is planned and implemented.

Daily airline flights or shipping services between the island nations and countries provide most of the basic and advanced resources for day to day and mid to long term existence of the islands. This is still very limited. In some islands, for example, Tokelau, the only way of commuting to the nearest island, Samoa is by the use of a small ferry on a monthly basis. In some islands, commuting by smaller planes is available on a weekly basis with only limited seats available. This geographic isolation, needs to be considered very seriously to enable students studying overseas to spend time with their families and maintain a good attendance record at the place of study.

Communication between the island nations is another factor which affects the development of education and especially TVET development because of its high demand for the use of modern methods of delivering education using information technology (IT). In most island groups, only the main islands would have access to power and telephone or satellite communication services. That leaves the outer islands to a limited choice of mail services only to communicate with the outside world.

The biggest challenge nowadays in support of what is referred to as 'equity in education' and 'education for all' is how can education reach, or be provided for, the rest of the population who do not have access to it, due to their isolated location.

3.2. *Political Situation*

The political stability level in some of the bigger island nations like Fiji, Solomon Islands, and Vanuatu is of concern in the development of education in the Pacific. Some of the Pacific Island nations are centres for regional academic and TVET tertiary institutions. As a result, the question of security for students and quality of programs offered arises and some students from the smaller island nations are now reluctant to attend some of these institutions.

On the other hand, how the governing political party in a country considers education as a national priority is of great importance. The trend nowadays in most island nations is to give education a priority due to several factors. This, includes education's role in national development and especially TVET for providing skills at different levels and for different target groups (see, for example, *Samoan Government Statement of Economic Strategies* for the last six years).

3.3. Population and Level of Mobility

The population of each island nation in the Pacific varies greatly from just under a million to just over a thousand depending on the land areas and island location (see Table 1). Within each country, those seeking TVET could come down to less than a 100 or just a handful on each island for a considerable area of the Pacific Ocean. The scattered population means that providing education for all

Table 1. Information on Pacific Island Nations

Country	Land area (square kilometers)	Exclusive economic zone (square kilometers)	Population (1998)	Main economic activity	No. of TVET providers
Cook Island	237	1,830,000	16,500	Tourism, remittances	None
Fiji	18,272	1,290,000	797,800	Sugar cane, tourism, gold mining, fishing, forestry, copra, manufacturing	na
Kiribati	811	3,550,000	85,100	Fishing, agriculture, remittances, copra	1
Nauru	21	320,000	11,500	Phosphate, mining, financial services, coconuts	1
Niue	259	390,000	2,100	Remittances	None
Samoa	2,935	120,000	174,800	Remittances, agriculture, tourism and light industry	9
Solomon Islands	28,330	1,340,000	417,800	Fishing, forest products, plantations	na
Tokelau	12	290,000	1,500	Coconut, copra, pigs, woodwork	None
Tonga	747	700,000	98,000	Remittance, coconut oil, manufacturing, tourism	8
Tuvalu	26	900,000	11,000	Fishing fees, remittances, copra	None
Vanuatu	12,190	680,000	182,500	Plantations, fishing, tourism	na

na not available.

is quite a challenging task. Islanders living on the remote islands will only have access to education if they move to the bigger or main islands. Providers for TVET education in the region or each island nation are limited in numbers due to the nature of the programs and the costly resources required to provide such education. It is not unusual to find only schools from primary to secondary level in several outer islands in a country with one institution for TVET located on one of the bigger islands. In some island nations, they are still in the process of gathering information to assess the feasibility of establishing an institute. Even if TVET is available, the level will be basic and the number of courses available will be very limited. Thus, students or people from these outer islands will still have to move to the central island if they need more advanced institutions or to travel to foreign countries for further studies. Students, who are qualified to undertake studies with institutions overseas, for example, mainly in New Zealand or Australia, will have to undergo a competitive screening process to win a national scholarship award as the fees will be unaffordable by their parents.

The constant high level of mobility by islanders between their own nation and foreign countries that provide more advanced training has created other challenges and problems.

4. CURRENT PROVISION OF TVET IN ISLAND STATES

Of the total number of students in the above countries that attend secondary school level, approximately 35 per cent make it to Year 12 and 13 to prepare for tertiary education. The other 65 per cent are either drop-outs after Year 10 or could not get places for further studies due to limited intake places. If they fail to get employment, they become dependant on their families and communities. This population is increasing at an alarming rate. The number of secondary schools offering TVET mainly in the form of industrial art subjects as part of their curriculum, varies from country to country depending on the national education system they use. The level of skills the above students gain after leaving secondary school level is either very limited or none.

The main providers of TVET at a college level in the region consists mainly of non-government or mission colleges. At the tertiary level, governments are usually the main providers. In smaller island nations like Cook Island, Niue, Tuvalu and Tokelau, they are still in the process of establishing formal national training centres or institutions in TVET. They are using as much information and feed-back from regional and international meetings on TVET development, to assess how and what would be the most feasible and cost effective process for them to undertake such a project. On the other hand they are also considering continually using the training opportunities already offered by TVET providers in other island nations like Samoa, Fiji and Tonga.

Even with the increased number of providers at regional and national levels, there is still an augmented demand to identify and develop other ways of providing TVET to cater for the increased number of students dropping out and graduating from secondary schools. The changing technology and its effect on industry through the need to upgrade continually the skills of employees is another justification of the need for more providers of TVET. As funding for such institutions is quite costly, government and non-government organisations are finding it difficult to cope financially with the demand from college and tertiary levels.

5. REGIONAL INITIATIVES IN TVET

The individual island nations in support of their economic and social developments, have identified the need to establish formal training centres or to continue to develop existing TVET education so that it can be offered to as many people as possible regardless of who they are and where they live. With the trend in improving the quality of the programs as a priority for a competent and skilled workforce, their qualifications will be recognised by other island nations in the region and especially countries like New Zealand and Australia to which most of the island people migrate. One of the issues raised during discussions and debates on investments and donor assistance in the development of TVET is whether all graduates will be able to get employment at the end of their studies considering the limited labour market in the island nations. The current notion by providers of TVET education is that if graduates cannot get formal employment, their skills can be applied in the development of their families, communities and better still, they can apply for jobs when they migrate overseas. One of the highest sources of revenue earned by island nations on an annual basis is in the form of remittances from relatives living overseas.

In support of future developments of TVET in the Pacific Island region, representatives for TVET providers and ministries or organisations that are directly related in the development of TVET from seven island nations in the Pacific met in Fiji, July 2001, to discuss the formation of a regional association of TVET providers.

It was unanimously agreed that an association be formed with the following goals:

- to get as many island nations as possible in the Pacific to become members;
- to develop a Vision Statement, Mission, Responsibilities, Activities Statement for the association;
- to share information and strategies to upgrade the level of TVET in each island nation;
- identify priority needs in TVET development on national and regional levels;
- to affiliate the association with regional and international donor countries and organisations for future assistance;
- for members to learn from each others' mistakes and develop realistic strategies to meet their specific needs based on past and current experiences and to prevent each nation from re-inventing the wheel of events and processes, which is both expensive and time consuming.

The trend for a successful future in TVET development in the Pacific region in the future, is for the island nations to work together by sharing ideas, resources and to explore together how to make the best of assistance offered by regional and international organisations.

5.1. Strategies for Future TVET Development

As part of the above resolutions and recommendations the following is a flow diagram showing how the regional association will function as well as its role at national and regional levels in the future.

It is seen in Figure 1, that the Pacific Regional Association of TVET Providers will be responsible in coordinating with their Governments the setting up of a Pacific TVET Council to govern, monitor and coordinate their activities. The Council being a representative body at a government level will include representatives from international organisations like UNESCO, Commonwealth of

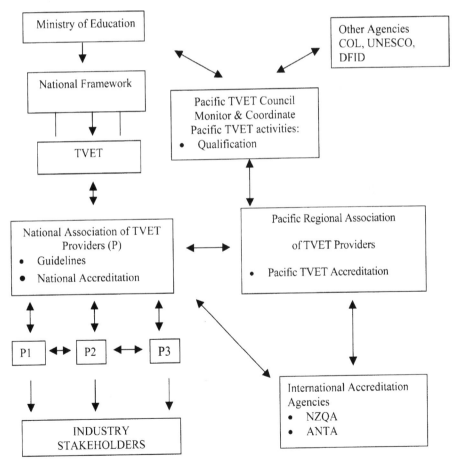

Figure 1. How the regional association will function.

Learning (COL), DFID, which can contribute or assist in getting funding from donors for the development of TVET in the Pacific. The Council will also play an important role in negotiating with foreign governments an accreditation process. This has been tried by some individual island nations for the past years but was unsuccessful and it was decided that perhaps it is time to try at a regional government level.

The Pacific Regional Association of TVET Providers will work directly with all the providers in the region through their National Association of TVET Providers.

This will include:

- developing of national standards and accreditation to be in line or similar with what is available and offered by the New Zealand Qualification Authority (NZQA) and the Australian National Training Authority (ANTA); and
- provide guidelines for designing and implementation of programs to meet local needs through sharing of experiences and ideas.

5.2. National Level

The bigger island nations like Samoa, Fiji, Solomon Islands, and Vanuatu, have several providers for TVET in place with more still developing to cater for the needs of outer communities. The level of programs and entry requirements are different pending on the target group the training is aimed at. In Samoa for example, there is one government-funded main national TVET provider at the tertiary level with 11 other non-government providers at the college level. At a tertiary level, students are required to complete and pass prescribed subjects in national and regional examinations. Some of the provider's intakes at a college level are aimed at students that have failed Years 10 to 12. Students from such providers who want to continue further studies at a tertiary level are always having difficulties because of their lower academic levels, though they are highly competent in their practical skills. A staircasing process will have to be developed and put in place by a national body, for example, the National Training or Qualification Authority, to set standards for students to achieve at different levels in order to acquire a formally recognised qualification and to be able to continue their studies at a higher level with less difficulties. Such national standards should be in line with other nations in the region, so that the qualifications can be transparent and accepted anywhere in the region.

Another important issue of vital importance is the need for providers in each island nation to work together in the area of program design and staff development. Government funded institutions benefit more on donor assistance because of its identity and as stated above, most of the providers around the region are non-government. Thus, one of the most important roles of the national association is to identify needs in such areas and request assistance from the government funded institutions or seek assistance from a donor through the national association. Current donor's requirements, show a preference to provide assistance to a national body or project rather than an individual or independent one.

5.3. Regional Level

The formation of a regional body to coordinate the developments of TVET on a national and regional level is an excellent step forward for education in the Pacific region. Such an initiative is well overdue because it was already indirectly indicated by donors through projects they have developed for the region. One such project that is currently being implemented for nine island nations is the Commonwealth of Learning (COL) project for developing of distance learning programs. The goal of the project is:

> Technical and Vocational Education and Training (TVET) which aims to increase the skill levels of the unemployed and under-employed is extended to those who have no access to conventional training.

The project was the result of a meeting by Ministers of Education for Fiji, Kiribati, Nauru, PNG, Solomon Islands, Samoa, Tuvalu, Tonga and Vanuatu in Kuala Lumpur, Malaysia in March 2000. With the development of the regional providers association, other island nations will benefit as well by sharing with the above nations. Indication from COL is already given on extending the assistance to other island nations. Similar projects can be negotiated with donors in future with a lot more weight behind them as a result of the regional providers association and especially with the Pacific TVET Council as the governing and monitoring regional body with direct input from local governments and donor agencies.

The issue of accreditation of qualifications is one of the most important developments on a regional level. Since the start of the independent era process in the 1960s among the island nations of the Pacific, education and training offered in the island nations especially in TVET are still being questioned and not accepted by the neighbouring developed nations although they have contributed a lot to their development through donor assistance. Again, the main reason perhaps is because the different island nations are trying their best to develop their programs and institutions on the limited funds available and subjected to the discretion of donors. The end result is that each country has its own system and standards that could be totally different from those of their neighbouring countries.

A highly successful example of providers working together at a regional level is in the maritime area. In the early 1990s, an association of maritime training providers was developed and established with its headquarters based in Suva, Fiji, under the umbrella of a regional organisation. Later, the national administrative bodies in maritime affairs were included and the body is now called Pacific Island Maritime Institutions and Maritime Authorities Association (PIMIMAA). The association was formed to coordinate and assist providers in maritime training in the region through its headquarters in Fiji, to develop and implement quality standards to meet international requirements set by the International Maritime Organisation (IMO), London. As of the end of 2000, most of the island nations in the association namely; Kiribati, Samoa, Solomon Islands, Tonga, Tuvalu and Vanuatu were included in the first ever White List of countries around the world that have met the required standards of maritime training. This is a positive result of all the providers of maritime training in the region working together as a regional body with the assistance from donors that establish and provide funding for the adviser and office to carry out the coordination and change implementation process. It would have been a very difficult task for each island nation to achieve due to the high cost involved.

6. FUTURE CHALLENGES FOR PACIFIC ISLAND NATIONS

With the current and future trends in globalisation and its effect on the small island nations, TVET plays an important role in keeping abreast of continual changes in economic and social developments overseas. Perhaps one of the main steps forward for all of the TVET providers through their national and the newly established regional association is to continue to convince their individual governments of how important their role is so that education would continue to be a priority in their economic strategies. This may be achieved through promotion in several areas, especially working closer with industry and community to meet their training needs.

The level of TVET development in the region varies substantially due to the factors stated in Section 2. Each island nation therefore, will have to identify clearly its needs and its level of capacity in comparison with other countries in the region. With the cooperation developed through the regional association of TVET providers, the main challenge now and in the future is how each island nation can learn from each other. Additionally, they must utilize information and strategies already developed and established by others to achieve successfully their individual goals from a single provider level to national and regional levels.

6.1. Communication

The development of a networking system, for example, e-mail and internet access, between providers on a national and regional level must be of high priority in order for any positive outcomes to be achieved in future. The introduction of IT and modern communications systems in the island nations should be adapted by providers as one of the common core programs that they teach and offer. This will help develop closer relationships with the industry and ensure future assistance from both industry and donor agencies especially for the provision of costly resources. At a global level, having access to international networking systems like UNEVOC would be of great value to all providers so that they could have access to the latest information from a research level to everyday classroom issues on TVET. The increased popular option and support by international organisations and donors of using open distance learning as a means of getting education to isolated islands is another valid reason for improving communication between islands.

With the increased demand of promoting open distance learning internationally as an option to provide and offer education to people living in remote islands, communication is an essential component in achieving such goals.

6.2. Quality Systems

In order to ensure future recognition and acceptance by non-island nation countries of the qualifications issued by island nation providers, one of the essential steps to be undertaken is to develop appropriate standards to meet regional and international requirements. This would be a challenging process especially in getting all of the regional association of TVET providers to agree on a common quality structure and framework. Such a process could be quite expensive so that island nations without such structures should make use of what had been done by other nations or providers already, and to develop guidelines for their own systems. Most of the providers would need to develop and establish documented charters with visions and goals, academic policies and procedures, and corporate plans, based on their national needs and economic strategies. At a national level, strategies should be developed to have in place a process to improve the standards at which providers at a college level would operate so that students from such institutions could continue with further studies at the tertiary level with limited problems. This would be a first step in developing an accepted quality system with more chance of getting financial support from local governments and especially foreign aid donors.

6.3. Staff Turn Over and other Developments

One of the most common challenges in all TVET providers is staff brain drain. It is often a critical issue when staff are sent overseas under scholarship awards to upgrade their qualifications and skills. If they come back, after a while they are often lost to the private sector or industry due to better salary packages offered to them. As this has been and will always be an on-going challenge, providers must work together at a national and regional level in sharing options and hopefully solutions on how to counter such a shortfall. In some island nations, for example, Samoa, structuring the salary packages to be in line with what the private sector offers is one option although it is not a solution as it depends solely to the availability of annual budgetary funding from a government.

A challenge in future for supporting quality systems and standards is to maintain qualified and competent staff. This is a serious issue in most island nations on top of the staff turnover issue and will have to be looked at seriously by all providers on national and regional levels. Again, the sharing of strategies and resolutions practised by other providers already within the region is essential, or to use as well as to share experiences with foreign providers.

6.4. Financial Support

This is the main fundamental and on-going challenge for any TVET provider because all of the developments and changes required to become a competent provider are costly and depend on the availability of budgetary funding. As stated before, most of the TVET providers in the island nations are non-government providers and therefore depend entirely on their own initiatives to get funding. Most of these institutions are owned and run by churches or religious organisations, so the local people are the ones that actually fund them with assistance from donors. In some island nations, governments are now providing non-government schools with annual financial grants but of limited amounts.

The experience of government institutions is similar although they can receive up to 90 per cent or more of annual funding requirements from government sources. The main reason being that they are involved mostly in developing programs to cater for a bigger and wider area of needs for students and industry. As well, they usually are and will always be the leaders in developing new or upgraded programs to meet the changes in modern technology, which are costly. Thus, the challenge will always be to convince local governments for increased annual funding or to get continuing assistance from foreign donors. For island nations that have not set up TVET institutions, the main challenge is to convince the local governments that such a development is not a cost but an investment in the future of their people and industries for a sustainable economic and social growth.

6.5. Employment Market

One of the most common questions raised by donors when negotiating assistance for a TVET provider is the level of employment for graduates. This is a vital issue because it could be a determining factor for donor assistance. The limited market for employment opportunities in the island nations does not allow much room for graduates and efforts will have to be directed now and in the future on how to resolve the issue. A good model that can be used is that of providers with maritime schools especially in smaller island nations like Kiribati and Tuvalu. They train their students for certification to international standards to be employed mainly on foreign owned ships. The main bulk of graduates from these institutions are therefore marketable overseas and are employed around the globe. Wages earned by seafarers from these island nations are the main form of foreign revenue for their individual countries. Similarly efforts through the national and regional providers association will be directed in getting the qualifications of graduates from other program areas to international standards so that they can get employment locally and overseas.

7. CONCLUSION

The situation in the Pacific region is unique because of its geographical background and how all of the island nations regardless of their size and remote location, are trying their best to keep up with the rest of the world. The issues in Technical and Vocational Education and Training (TVET) are very important as they play a major role for each island nation in providing sustainable economical growth. The development of TVET and the level of recognition by different governments in the region is of concern, especially those with political instability. Efforts by TVET providers to establish, develop and improve their institutions individually is and will always be a difficult task. The high costs for establishing and maintaining such institutes in the island nations is a big challenge considering such issues as population, quality of programs, marketability of graduates on local and overseas market, resources and equipment to meet changing technology, and the need to maintain qualified staff.

In light of the above issues, it is perhaps time for TVET providers in the region to start working together at a cross-national level to share information and resources and establish appropriate strategies to upgrade the standards of TVET from college level to tertiary level in close cooperation with industry. The use of open distance learning should be promoted and developed to offer programs to communities on the main islands and those on isolated islands. At the regional level, a body is now established to monitor and assist the TVET providers in the island nations with resolving issues that are common throughout the region through proper and consistent communication.

One of the strategies that should be considered by the regional association is to develop a research program in TVET development in the Pacific. At the moment there are very limited regional data available on the progress of TVET developments. Such research should concentrate on identifying the strengths and weaknesses of the current systems and how at national and regional levels could all island nations contribute and assist each other in supporting their strengths while reducing or finding ways to eliminate their weaknesses. Such research would also justify to donors the future trends of TVET development in the region in relation to international technology demands.

This, in the mid to long term would ensure assistance from regional and international donor countries and organisations as well as securing an accreditation process so that qualifications from any provider in the region would be recognised by overseas countries like New Zealand, Australia and the rest of the world.

REFERENCES

Ereata T. (2001). *Country Report, Kiribati*. Suva, Fiji: Pacific TVET Providers Association.

Ivaiti, H. & Koteka, F. (2001). *Country Report, Cook Island*. Suva, Fiji: Pacific TVET Providers Association.

Lene, P. T. (2001a). *Country Report, Samoa*. Suva, Fiji: Pacific TVET Providers Association.

Lene P. T. (2001b). *TVET Development in Small Countries, Samoa*. UNESCO TVET Conference Adelaide Treasury Department, Samoa. (2000). *Statement of Economic Strategy 2000–2001*.

Nabuka, J. (2001). *Country Report, Fiji*. Suva, Fiji: Pacific TVET Providers Association.

Neemia, N. S. (2001). *Country Report, Tuvalu*. Suva, Fiji: Pacific TVET Providers Association.

48

Transition from School to Work in East Asia

DAVID ATCHOARENA
International Institute for Educational Planning, Paris, France

EFISON MUJANGANJA
UNESCO (Bangkok Office), Thailand

1. INTRODUCTION

Transition from school to work in East Asia as in other regions forms an important part of the education policy agenda for the world of work. The issues involve preparation of learners for life in the workplace. They also pertain to pathways taken by students entering the labour market. In view of the importance of technical and vocational education (TVE) programs for acquiring workplace knowledge, skills and attitudes, this paper focuses on the vocational preparation of young people in East Asia.

The 1997–98 East Asian crisis, starting in July 1997 in Thailand, has had a massive impact on labour markets. Some observers expressed the fear that, having suffered a financial crisis, East Asian countries may now be facing a possible unemployment crisis (*The Economist*, 1998). This situation is particularly striking in a region that used to enjoy one of the world's lowest jobless rates. For school leavers, who are particularly exposed to deteriorating labour market conditions, the inability to find a job can lead to long lasting difficulties. Within this regional background, each country enjoys specific socio-economic conditions and faces particular development challenges as can be seen from the basic development indicators recorded in Table 1.

This article reviews the new conditions in which school to work transition takes place in five countries in East Asia, (Indonesia, Republic of Korea, Malaysia, Philippines, and Thailand) and in light of this, considers implications for technical and vocational education policies. The first section discusses the concept of 'youth in transition' and comments on the demographic changes affecting the supply of labour in the region. The next part of the article provides an overview of labour market changes and analyses their impact on youth employment. Following this overview, an analysis of educational developments

Table 1. Basic development indicators

Countries	Population (million) 2000	Annual population growth rate (%) 1995–2000	Human development index 1999	Per capita GNP (US$) 2000	Population in poverty (%) 1999
Indonesia	210.5	1.6	0.677	600	23.4
Korea	47.3	1.0	0.875	8490	7.4
Malaysia	23.3	2.4	0.774	3390	8.1
Philippines	78.4	2.2	0.749	1050	40.0 (2000)
Thailand	62.4	1.0	0.757	2010	12.9 (1998)

Source: Asian Development Bank, (2001) *Asia Key Indicators, 2001.*

completes the identification of the main factors affecting transition from education to working life. The last two sections outline the country responses in the field of technical and vocational education and present implications for policy.

2. THE ISSUE: JOBLESS YOUTH

Concerns about youth unemployment are the most common dimension of the transition from education to working life (OECD, 1999). Hence in many countries, unemployment rates among young people are much higher than total jobless rates. Although East Asia used to record one of the world's lowest unemployment rates, the deep financial crisis in 1997–98 gave rise to concerns about jobless youngsters. For most Asian governments, facilitating access to work has become a policy priority.

Yet, the transition issue is much broader than youth unemployment. Beyond immediate labour market prospects, successful transition involves preparing young people for learning throughout life in a context of increasing labour market instability and rapid technological change. Meeting this challenge is important in an attempt to restore and sustain the phenomenal growth rates of the early 1990s (Stiglitz & Shahid, 2001). Today, growth depends to a large extent, for the countries of the region, on raising productivity. That demands thorough reforms, including reforms in education and employment policies.

Finding appropriate solutions for those who did not stay long at school and who left the education system with low educational background and no qualification constitutes another aspect of the transition issue. In spite of the impressive educational progress accomplished by East Asian countries, a large number of young people, particularly among women, rural youth and ethnic minorities, are left behind with very limited literacy skills. This situation is due to the fact that in several countries of the region, while most children are now being admitted to school, too many do not stay the full course. Retention measures and the reduction of disparities now represent important challenges to reduce the number of young people who are at risk on the labour market. It is now widely accepted that improving the transition process also requires reducing the category of youth at risk and finding appropriate alternatives for them.

In East Asia, youth transition issues are taking place within a changing demographic fabric (OECD, 1996). The change in the structure of Asia's populations has been at least as profound as the economic transformation. As East Asian economies developed, they initiated their demographic transition in which improving living and health conditions and high birth rates resulted in rapid population growth. This trend was felt in most of Asia 30 years ago. Following this first phase of demographic change, birth rates eventually fell significantly, and population growth slowed down. This new demographic regime modified the age profile of the population with relatively few people in the youngest groups. For economies, this population profile means that a large share of the population is of working age, and the dependency ratio, given as "the proportion of people too old or too young to be employed", is relatively low. Among other effects, it is expected that people of working age will save a higher proportion of their incomes, contributing to favourable capital investment conditions, as experienced in Japan. For labour markets, this change is good news as it means that the pressure of new entrants is going down as is seen in Table 2 that records figures on the changing structure of the population by age. For youngsters, the demography of the region seems favourable for a smoother transition into the labour market. It is worth noting that in the West, the demographic transition took more than a century. In South-East Asia it took place within a single generation. For instance, in 1965, Thai women had an average of more than six children; now they have fewer than three. While the often overlooked demographic change has profound implications in order to understand the context of youth transition, a sound economy and favourable labour market conditions obviously constitute the key determinants for young people to enter into the world of work.

3. THE TRANSFORMATION OF THE TRANSITION CONTEXT

The Asian financial crisis has reversed decades of progress towards full employment in Indonesia, the Republic of Korea and Thailand, and has sharply reduced

Table 2. Structure of the population by age (%)

Countries	0–14 1980	0–14 2000	65+ 1980	65+ 2000
Indonesia	41.0	30.8	3.3	7.6
Korea	34.0	20.8	3.8	11.0
Malaysia	39.4	34.1	3.7	6.6
Philippines	41.9	37.5	2.8	5.5
Thailand	40.0	26.7	3.5	8.1

Source: Asian Development Bank, (2001), *Asia Key Indicators, 2001.*

job prospects for workers in countries throughout the Asia-Pacific region. The crisis has had massive effects on the labour markets (Betcherman & Islam, 2001). An increase in open employment and under-employment, changes in labour force participation, an increase in informal sector employment and degradation of youth transition patterns are some of the components of post-crisis adjustments.

The drop in demand for labour constituted an immediate adjustment. For some countries, this was felt both through decreasing employment and rising unemployment. Another significant impact was an increasing segmentation of the labour markets, the informal sector of the economy playing a growing role in labour surplus absorption. Of course the magnitude and the patterns of labour market adjustments differ across countries.

The immediate effect on open unemployment growth was the most severe in Korea and Thailand as can be seen in Table 3 that records change in growth and employment roles over the period 1996 to 2001. The increase in underemployment and the contraction of the labour market were also most pronounced in these two countries. The rise in the underutilisation of the workforce was the lowest in the Philippines and Indonesia experienced the lowest reduction in the number of jobs.

The vulnerability of young workers is often reflected in higher unemployment rates, indeed. In a context of severe labour market destabilisation, youth unemployment rates have reached very high levels. Korea experienced the sharpest increase in youth unemployment and reached the highest unemployment rate for males (20.8%). Table 4 records youth unemployment rates for before and after the 1998 crisis. The economies the most affected by the unemployment crisis, Korea and Thailand, also experienced a withdrawal of the workforce as reflected in falling participation rates. The trend was most pronounced in Malaysia.

Like the female workforce, juvenile labour is typically the most sensitive to the deterioration of labour market conditions. This greater exposure usually results in falling participation rates and possibly increasing school enrolment rates at the secondary and post-secondary levels. Not surprisingly, available

Table 3. Growth and employment rates (%)

Countries	Growth rates of GDP					Unemployment rates			
	1996	1997	1998	2000	1996	1997	1998	2000
Indonesia	7.8	4.7	13.1	4.8	4.9	4.7	5.5	6.1
Korea	6.7	5.0	6.7	8.8	2.0	2.6	6.8	4.1
Malaysia	10.0	7.3	7.4	8.3	2.5	2.4	3.2	3.1
Philippines	5.8	5.2	0.6	4.0	7.4	7.9	9.6	10.1
Thailand	5.9	1.4	10.8	4.4	1.1	0.9	3.4	2.4

Source: Asian, Development Bank, (2001), *Asia Key Indicators, 2001.*

Table 4. Youth (15-24) unemployment rates, by gender, before and after the crisis (%)

Countries	Male pre crisis	Male post crisis (1998)	Female pre crisis	Female post crisis (1998)
Indonesia	12.2 (1996)	15.7	15.0 (1996)	19.1
Korea	9.3 (1995)	20.8	6.0 (1995)	12.8
Philippines	25.9 (1995)	17.9	33.9 (1995)	22.1
Thailand	2.6 (1996)	11.2	2.3 (1996)	8.6

Source: Horton and Mazumdar. In Betcherman and Islam (2001).

data show a sharp decrease in labour market youth participation rates in Korea and Thailand. Table 5 records youth participation rates by gender before and after the 1998 crisis. This trend was not so significant in Indonesia, while the participation for young people increased in the Philippines.

In Korea, in 1998, the largest category of unemployed was the 20-29 year-old age group, representing 36 per cent of total unemployment. The youngest workers, while representing a smaller share of total unemployment, were the most exposed, displaying a 20.8 per cent unemployment rate in 1998, compared to 11.4 per cent for the 20-29 year-old age group. Traditionally the unemployment rate in Korea is higher for workers with a college-level education than for those with a high-school education or less. Recently, the gap between the two groups narrowed and the crisis reversed the trend. The transformation of the labour market reflected a substitution effect: more educated workers have taken low qualified jobs. Furthermore, the demand for high-school leavers tends to decrease while the labour market requests more college graduates. For the first quarter of 1999 the unemployment rates were 9.1 per cent for high-school level workers and 6.4 per cent for college-level workers.

Malaysia, during the high growth period, recorded a decline in the number of unemployed young workers, particularly in the 15-19 and 25-29 year-old age groups. However, in 1997, young people aged from, 20 to 24 years constituted the first group of unemployed workers, representing 44 per cent of the job-seekers.

In the Philippines, unemployment rates were already relatively high before

Table 5. Youth (15-24) participation rates, by gender, before and after the 1998 crisis (%)

Countries	Male pre crisis	Male post crisis (1998)	Female pre crisis	Female post crisis (1998)
Indonesia	61.4 (1996)	59.8	42.9 (1996)	41.1
Korea	31.0 (1994)	26.4	42.3 (1994)	35.8
Philippines	60.6 (1997)	61.9	35.9 (1997)	37.1
Thailand	64.4 (1996)	58.9	56.6 (1996)	50.1

Source: Horton and Mazumdar. In Betcherman and Islam (2001).

the crisis (7.8% in January 1997). To a large extent, this situation was due to the prevalence of jobseekers among youth. Therefore, the reduction of youth unemployment constitutes a major dimension of the employment policy. Already before the crisis, high school and college graduates displayed an unemployment rate higher than the overall rate. This pattern continued and the gap between college graduates' unemployment rate and overall unemployment worsened. According to some authors, this situation is not related to the structure of the demand for labour, but rather to the high level of graduates' expected wage (Esguerra et al., in Betcherman & Islam, 2001). As a consequence of high levels of migration, the importance of remittances in households' income could explain that youngsters, especially in well-off families, could afford long periods of unemployment, in other words, unemployment duration is likely to be longer for youngsters with higher reservation wages. It must be noted that in the Philippines decline in employment started in April 1998, several months after the beginning of the financial crisis in July 1997 and was largely due to the adverse effects of the so-called 'El Nino' phenomenon. While in 1999 unemployment had already decreased, the number of under-employed workers was still rising. In a context where college graduates are primarily affected by unemployment, rather than underemployment, this trend suggests that the situation of people with low levels of education continued to deteriorate.

The way Filipino households responded to the crisis created additional tension on children and adolescents who were often taken out of school. High school students were the most affected by this pattern. Survey data indicate that 6.4 per cent of households took children out of school (Esguerra et al., in Betcherman & Islam, 2001). Such a labour adjustment trend contributed to the rise of the labour force participation rate in the Philippines that is recorded in Table 5.

In Thailand, unemployment increased from 0.7 million people in 1997 to 1.7 million in 1999. In a situation of virtually full employment, this trend was reflected in a rapid increase in the open unemployment rate over the same period. In addition, underemployment reached 13.7 per cent of the labour force in 1998, as compared to 7.6 per cent in 1997.

While representing a central response to the labour market crisis, the expansion of the informal sector, including for young workers, is difficult to assess precisely due to limitations of data. However, available indicators, such as the number of workers registered in non-waged employment, suggested that informal sector work constituted a growing opportunity especially in Malaysia, Thailand and Indonesia (Betcherman & Islam, 2001). For the latter, the reported increase in total employment is due to significant growth of informal sector jobs.

In a region that had made impressive economic and social progress, rising unemployment and underemployment combined with the expansion of informal sector work contributed to fuelling an increase in poverty. Between 1997 and 1998 it is reported that the urban poverty rates more or less doubled in Korea (from 9% to 19%) and Indonesia (from 11% to 20%). It is expected that this rise in poverty indicators affected primarily vulnerable groups, including young people. Signs of declining labour force participation rates are already in evidence, and real wages are falling, by as much as 30 per cent in Indonesia, eight per cent in Thailand and five to ten per cent in Korea, depending upon the industry.

4. TRENDS IN EDUCATIONAL PARTICIPATION

The impressive growth record in educational participation experienced by East Asian countries generated a large debate on the factors explaining such success. Besides the macro-economic environment and the role of the state, a lot of attention was paid to skill formation (Tan, 1999). Relatively high levels of school enrolments contributed to increasing the stock of human capital. Hong Kong, Singapore, Korea and Taiwan (China) already enjoyed high levels of primary school enrolment in the early 1960s, at a time when their level of income was still relatively low. Malaysia displayed a similar pattern in the late 1970s. The growth in secondary enrolments followed the expansion of primary schooling (UNESCO PROAP, 1999). Investment in technical and vocational education has also been significant in most cases.

This human capital formation process is usually considered to have been instrumental in economic growth (Ashton et al., 1999). New growth theories emphasise the dynamic nature of human capital, since the level of human capital stock is considered to affect the rate of economic growth. Following the 1997 crisis, one of the important questions relates to the capacity of East Asian countries to rehabilitate their education and skill formation after the shock. Another issue is whether they will be able to continue to cope with the new conditions of the global economy (Lewin, 1998).

Besides economic trends, the demographic revolution experienced by East Asian countries has far-reaching implications for education systems and for transition issues. In the past decades, population growth has declined sharply. The annual demographic growth rate for East Asia dropped from 2.4 per cent between 1965 and 1970 to 1.3 per cent over the 1990–95 period.

The fertility transition, experienced in the sub-region, results in a changing age structure of the population that is already under way in all the countries of the sub-region (see Table 2). This process should both release the demands on education budgets and the pressure of school leavers on the labour market. However, the demographic prospects vary significantly in the different countries. The growth of the school age population aged 10–15 years over the 1990–2025 period is expected to range from −0.6 per cent in Korea to +1.0 per cent in Malaysia. While fewer children will need to be educated and inserted into the labour market in Korea, Thailand and Indonesia, school-age population growth will remain significant in Malaysia and the Philippines. Beyond these country differences, the overall trend of population ageing will raise new issues regarding the pattern of allocation of resources required by the presence of a larger and rapidly growing population of elderly people.

In a context of rapid economic expansion, some East Asian countries have already experienced a shortage of young workers (OECD, 1996). This imbalance fuels an international movement of labour from neighbouring countries experiencing a large surplus of labour. Such demographic patterns contribute to a shift in educational priorities, with increasing attention being paid to lifelong learning issues and policies. Allowing early school leavers to re-enter the system, facilitating the retraining of workers in updating their skills or preparing them for new occupations, and addressing the growing demand to learn for leisure will represent a growing challenge. This also implies that transition from school to work will no longer be a terminal process. At the end of compulsory schooling, combining or alternating work and learning will increasingly form a lifelong cycle.

In spite of high levels of enrolments, East Asian countries are still facing access and participation difficulties, often aggravated by the economic crisis (Ablett & Slengesol, 2000). Prior to 1997, Indonesia was suffering declining rates of primary school completion and transition to secondary education. A deterioration in quality was the explanation for most of this phenomenon. The crisis resulted in a drop in enrolment among low-income students, particularly at the secondary level. In Thailand, the financial crisis did not produce a significant impact on enrolments. In Korea, household and government responses managed, to a large extent, to protect education, and the overall gross enrolment rates continued to increase between 1997 and 1998. In the Philippines, the adjustment process between 1997 and 1998 was associated with a slower growth of primary school enrolments and a decrease, by eight per cent, in the number of secondary school students. The main effect observed in Malaysia was an increase in the demand for higher education due to the massive return of nationals unable to afford the cost of studying abroad anymore.

Levels of educational development remain contrasted across East Asia. Several countries are close to achieving universal primary and secondary education and Table 6 records gross enrolment ratios from 1980 to 1996. In Korea, the development of higher education increased the tertiary enrolment rate to one of the highest world levels (Varghese, 2001). Increasingly, educational pathways include technical and vocational education and higher education.

In spite of significant educational progress, quality and drop-outs remain

Table 6. Gross enrolment ratios (%)

Countries	Primary			Secondary			Tertiary		
	1980	1990	1996	1980	1990	1996	1980	1990	1996
Indonesia	107	115	113	29	44	56	4	9	11
Korea	110	105	94	78	90	102	15	30	60
Malaysia	93	94	103	48	56	61	4	7	12 (1995)
Philippines	112	111	116	64	73	77	24	28	29 (1995)
Thailand	99	99	87	29	30	56	15	19 (1985)	22

Source: UNESCO (1999), Statistical Yearbook, 1999.

concerns, notably in Indonesia and Thailand. Quality issues, drop-outs and increasing disparities in access and participation for low-income students and minorities will still constitute a challenge in the years to come for most East Asian countries. In countries where the informal sector represents a significant share of the labour market, the transition problem of young people who leave school early and with no qualifications or work skills is not likely to be reflected in unemployment or inactivity. Failure to take into account this dimension can result in overlooking the true magnitude of the transition issue, particularly for young people at risk. Besides strategies to prevent early drop-out, several countries have implemented nonformal education programs allowing children and adolescents who did not complete their basic education to re-enter the mainstream education system. In countries such as Thailand linkages exist between nonformal and formal vocational education programs.

One of the conclusions of the EFA 2000 review for East Asia underlined the need to strengthen educational information systems (UNESCO PROAP, 2000). Designing effective strategies requires an information base providing data and indicators on the transition from school to work. Today most of the information available concerns access and participation. While increasing attention is being paid to educational outcomes through learners' achievement measures, not much is being done at the moment to capture better and reflect the impact of various educational pathways on labour market outcomes.

5. EASING THE TRANSITION PROCESS: COUNTRY POLICY RESPONSES

Available information on ongoing strategies suggest that East Asian governments use two main instruments to improve youth transition namely technical and vocational education, and labour market programs (Betcherman & Islam, 2001). This pattern illustrates the increasing articulation between education policies and labour market policies. In this respect, the current trends in East Asia recall the patterns experienced by European countries where education responses and active labour market measures have been combined to improve youth transition processes and employment prospects (OECD, 1998).

Pathways from education to working life differ according to time and countries (Alto et al., 2001). While general education pathways remain an obvious option, many countries are giving increasing weight to vocational education pathways in an effort to facilitate the transition process and to increase labour productivity. Table 7 records the proportions of secondary school students in vocational education. In this context, the private sector can play an important role in increasing access to technical and vocational education.

Linkages between general education on the one hand, and technical and vocational education on the other, influence enrolments in technical and vocational education. Where technical and vocational education is stigmatised as a dead-end course, linkages have helped a lot in improving its attractiveness.

Table 7. Share of secondary school students in vocational education (%), 1996

Country	%
Indonesia	12
Korea	20
Malaysia*	3
Thailand (1997)	18

* Public sector.
Source: UNESCO (1999), Statistical Yearbook, 1999.

Increasingly, there is evidence of articulation between general education and technical and vocational education. As Haas (1999) observed "articulation pathways for technical and vocational education course graduates were evident in all countries ..., though such provision varied significantly from extensive linkages between TVE and higher education, through to quite limited opportunities for articulation" (Haas, 1999, p. 30).

6. TOWARDS IMPROVED TRANSITION PATHWAYS

While the existence of a growing level of youth unemployment is widely recognised, the nature of the problem is often a matter of debate. In many advanced economies, youth joblessness is described as 'super-cyclical', meaning that it is more sensitive to economic cycles than total unemployment (Ryan in OECD, 1999). However, the persistence of a hard core of unemployed youth often reflects a structural problem that cannot be solved by economic expansion alone. Among structural factors, educational failure is often cited as leading to labour market disability. In such cases, public policies tend to focus on the least employable young people in the United Kingdom and the United States. Understanding the exact nature of youth unemployment and the precise combination of structured causes and conjuncture-linked factors constitute a prerequisite for formulating effective policies. The variety of labour market conditions in East Asian countries suggests that the policy response has to be diversified to adjust to specific national features. Beyond this diversity, the financial crisis has revealed critical problems of productivity in some countries such as Thailand. In this context, strengthening training systems is seen as a priority to increase labour productivity and promote higher value-added forms of employment.

In order to respond to this challenge, East Asian countries have implemented comprehensive technical and vocational education reforms. Converging with international trends in training delivery, the focus of this policy agenda has been to establish closer links between supply and labour market demands and to shift responsibility from the public sector to the private provision. Eventually, public-private partnership will play a growing role to ease the transition from school to work.

The policy response articulated by most countries in the region can be grouped around six policy directions.

Improving co-ordination. In many countries of the region provision involves, besides the Ministry of Education, a number of other government bodies. In Indonesia for instance, 19 departments have been involved in over 800 training programs. Such fragmentation of public sector efforts leads to duplication and poor efficiency. The co-ordinating mechanisms or structures established in some countries have not yet produced their full impact

Increasing and improving private sector involvement in private provision. In some countries, like the Philippines and Indonesia, private institutions already enrol the vast majority of vocational education students. However, even in these countries, further steps are required to enhance the contribution of the private sector to the overall training system. Besides access to credit for private promoters, the development of quality control measures, including accreditation procedures and qualification frameworks are considered to be key elements to foster an enabling environment.

Several innovations are also being implemented for funding training programs. Notably, the introduction of voucher programs in Korea and to a larger extent in the Philippines, represents a significant change in view of introducing more competition among providers and more choice for individuals. The use of competitive tendering to access public resources is also increasingly considered to reduce costs while improving quality, 'institutional capability' being the first criteria considered for allocating funds in the Philippines.

Dual forms of training. Attempts to introduce dual forms of training also constitute significant reforms to bring delivery closer to the work place. Indonesia, the Philippines and Malaysia have introduced, around various modalities, apprenticeship programs. The outputs of these attempts on youth transition may lead to significant changes in the future balance of vocational pathways.

Lifelong learning policies. In the framework of lifelong learning, increasing consideration is given to policies that allow holders of TVE qualifications to move to tertiary and higher education programs.

Skilling. Although not always clearly expressed and materialised, the concern for upskilling, broad skilling and multi-skilling seems to inspire increasingly, the debate on technical and vocational reform. Primarily viewed as contributing to the productivity of the workforce and to the international competitiveness of the economy, these trends are also likely to improve the transition of youngsters into the working life and their participation in lifelong learning.

Nonformal education courses. Finally, a growing number of initiatives are implemented to provide nonformal education courses for skills-training for those who leave school without employable skills. Through such courses, learners may also be able to re-enter into mainstream technical and vocational education programs. Some countries, such as the Philippines, have initiated with some success specific training programs for the informal sector. Considering the important role that informal sector employment has played in absorbing a young low-qualified labour force, targeted training programs can constitute a strong instrument to protect disadvantaged young people from poverty. However, the Philippines' experience also shows that training in itself is not sufficient to improve productivity and security in the informal sector. Broader interventions, involving also NGOs and private institutions are required to forge effective integrated support packages.

The impact of these responses on youth transition patterns is not yet clear. In particular it is difficult to assess to what extent the measures recently taken have been contributed to absorb the effects of the crisis. Actually several countries had initiated the reform of vocational education before the crisis.

One of the problems in assessing the latest youth transition issues is the fact that many statistics, including educational data, are only available with a lag of several years. For this reason the analysis of the changes in the position of young people on the labour market for the various countries is difficult to conduct. In addition, the type of data required to review transition patterns is still rare. Looking at youth transition issues requires adopting a flow perspective. Yet, the availability of longitudinal data providing information on individual trajectories is limited. It is expected that the recent aggravation of youth unemployment may lead to expanding the collection of data and statistical analysis in order to fill this information gap.

7. CONCLUSION

In a context where youth transition is a relatively new domain of public policy, it is worth recalling some of the lessons drawn in other regions. The review conducted by the OECD on the transition from initial education to working life in the late 1990s identified key policy ingredients that determine successful transition (OECD, 1998). These include:

- the existence of open and coherent learning pathways and qualification frameworks designed in a lifelong learning perspective;
- he availability of opportunities for young people to participate in work-experience programs during their schooling;
- the provision of a broad range of vocational skills for young people not entering higher education;
- the existence of safety nets for young people at risk;
- the provision of information, guidance and follow-up services;
- the existence of an institutional environment allowing the involvement of all stakeholders and ensuring the co-ordination of programs; and

- the availability of relevant indicators and longitudinal data for monitoring and evaluation purposes.

Finally, it is worth stressing that the lack of training and skills is not the only factor explaining youth unemployment. Adequate responses need to include a policy mix in which training is one element among many. Besides technical and vocational education, work-experience programs and job counselling can also be effective measures to ensure that young people acquire the social skills and work habits required by the work place and for adulthood.

REFERENCES

Ablett, J., & Slengesol, I-A. (2000). *Education in Crisis: The Impact and Lessons of the East Asian Financial Shock 1997–99*. Paris: UNESCO.

Alto, R., Isaacs, I., Knight, B., & Polestico, R. (2000). *Training Systems in South-East Asia*. Leabrook, Australia: National Centre for Vocational Education Research.

Ashton, D., Green, F., James, D., & Sung, J. (1999). *Education and Training for Development in East Asia. The Political Economy of Skill Formation in East Asian Newly Industrialized Economies*. London and New York: Routledge.

Asian Development Bank (2001). *Asia Key Indicators, 2001*. Manila: Asian Development Bank.

Atchoarena, D. (Ed.) (2000). *Transition of Youth from School to Work: Issues and Policies*. Paris: UNESCO/International Institute for Educational Planning.

Betcherman, G., & Islam, R. (2001). *East Asian Labor Market and The Economic Crisis – Impacts, Responses and Lessons*. Washington, DC: The World Bank.

Haas, A. R. (1999). *Trends in Articulation Arrangements for Technical and Vocational Education in the South East Asian Region*. Melbourne: RMIT University.

Lewin, K. M. (1998). Education in emerging Asia: Patterns, policies, and futures into the 21st century. *Int. J. Educational Development*, 18(2), 81–118.

Organisation for Economic Cooperation and Development (1996). *Migration and the Labour Market in Asia: Prospects to the Year 2000*. Paris: Organisation for Economic Cooperation and Development.

Organisation for Economic Cooperation and Development (1998). *OECD Education Committee Thematic Review: The Transition from Initial Education to Working Life. Interim Comparative Report*. DEELSA/ED(98)11.

Organisation for Economic Cooperation and Development (1999). *Preparing Youth for the 21st Century, the Transition from Education to the Labour Market: Proceedings*. Paris: Organisation for Economic Cooperation and Development.

Stiglitz, J. E., & Shahid, Y. (2001). *Rethinking the East Asian Miracle*. Washington, DC: World Bank. New York: Oxford University.

Tan, J. L. H. (1999). *Human Capital Formation as an Engine of Growth: The East Asian Experience*. Singapore: Institute of Southeast Asian Studies.

The Economist (1998). Asia's new jobless. April 23rd.

UNESCO Principal Regional Office for Asia and the Pacific (1999). *Secondary Education and Youth at the Crossroads*. Bangkok: UNESCO Principal Regional Office for Asia and the Pacific.

UNESCO Principal Regional Office for Asia and the Pacific (2000). *A Synthesis Report of Education 2000 Assessment for the Asia-Pacific Region*. Bangkok: UNESCO Principal Regional Office for Asia and the Pacific.

United Nations Educational, Scientific and Cultural Organisation (1999). *Statistical Yearbook*. Paris: UNESCO.

Varghese, N. V. (2001). *Economic Crisis and Higher Education in East Asia.* Policy forum 29–31 January 2001, Selangor, Malaysia. Paris: UNESCO/ International Institute for Educational Planning.

49

Enterprise Education in Australia and New Zealand

MICHAEL LONG and CHRIS SELBY SMITH
Monash University – ACER Centre for the Economics of Education and Training, Australia

1. INTRODUCTION

Enterprise education and training (EET) refers to the development of knowledge and skills of workers within their enterprises. It includes activities undertaken as part of a course of study leading to a formally recognised qualification, formal (usually much shorter) courses of training that do not lead to a recognised qualification, informal on-the-job training by supervisors or co-workers and learning by doing. Because of the difficulty measuring informal training, much of the literature focuses on formal education, formal training and years of occupational or job experience.

EET often involves a combination of formal and informal learning situations. Indeed accrediting authorities can require that on-the-job experience forms part of a qualification or in some cases recognise informal learning or experience as the equivalent of educational courses. EET comes in a variety of forms. It can be undertaken on-the-job, off-the-job (either in the enterprise, a formal educational institution, or elsewhere) or both. It can build on previous education and training, as with increasing specialisation, or provide different skills, as with management training or retraining.

EET can either be initial education or continuing education and training. Both Australia and New Zealand have apprenticeship systems focused principally on school-leavers based on a mixture of work and off-the-job education. Much of the focus of this article, however, is on the continuing aspects of EET.

The boundaries of EET are not clearly defined. For instance, enterprises may provide paid or unpaid leave for workers to undertake further study that has little relevance to their current or any future job with the firm: a provision that might be more a fringe benefit than enterprise education. Workers may also pay for their own education or training in the hope of future promotion with either their current employer or a new employer. Although the enterprise does not pay for such education and training at the time, the worker may subsequently be reimbursed through a higher salary. Additionally students may undertake work experience in an enterprise as part of their course for no or only nominal pay. Such students are not employees and hence fall outside the scope of EET for the purposes of this article.

2. POLICY CONCERNS

The principal concern of government is that enterprises may provide less than socially optimal levels of education and training – that economic efficiency would be better served if enterprises provided more education and training. It is this belief that leads to policies that either mandate levels of expenditure on education and training by firms or that provide subsidies to enterprises for education and training courses.

Governments may be interested in the level of EET for many reasons.

- EET is a substantial economic activity. As with any part of the economy, governments wish to ensure that it functions efficiently.
- EET is considered a form of investment in human capital. As with some forms of initial education, the returns on that investment are thought to be high.
- Knowledge and skills are an increasingly important part of many economic activities.
- Economic, technological, organisational and demographic changes mean that greater emphasis needs to be placed on lifelong learning. Ongoing structural change in economies and increased occupational mobility imply a greater demand for retraining. Increased rates of technological, administrative and organisational change imply higher levels of training within occupations. The ageing of the workforce in Australia and New Zealand means that workers are exposed to change processes for longer and that their initial education and training is more likely to need to be supplemented before they leave the workforce.
- Given increased international competition, governments seek to improve the competitiveness of their economies. A more highly educated and trained workforce may provide a competitive advantage. EET delivers work-relevant knowledge and skills that match the needs of workers and enterprises.
- The level of EET differs among categories of firms and workers. Such differences may have implications for efficiency and equity.
- Access to education and training may be distributed differentially among countries in multi-national companies.
- The growth of casual and part-time employment may lower the tendency for enterprises to provide education and training their workers.
- Skills and training often feature in industrial and workplace relations agreements.
- The financing of EET leads governments (and some others) to suspect that enterprises may provide too little education and training for their employees. Enterprises pay for the training, but the worker receives the benefit. Other employers may poach trained workers by offering higher salaries.

- EET may provide reliable pathways from school to work that facilitate the continued skills development of young people.

3. THE EXTENT OF TRAINING

The amount of training, however defined, can also be measured in different ways – expenditure, participation, number of courses and hours (OECD, 1997). The emphasis in much survey work is usually on process rather than on outcomes, despite the latter's importance.

The amount of EET is not always obvious because it is often not captured as part of the statistics of an education system. It can, however, be surprisingly large. The 1996 *Survey of Training Expenditure* conducted by the Australian Bureau of Statistics (ABS) found that firms spent 2.5 per cent of their total wages and salary bill on the formal training and education of their employees, a total of $179m, which is a little over 0.8 per cent of GDP or equivalent to 15 per cent of the total expenditure on formal education in Australia (Long & Lamb, 2002).

The 1997 Survey of Education and Training found that 33.0 per cent of Australians aged 15 to 64 years who had been wage or salary earners in the preceding 12 months had participated in at least one in-house training course in the last 12 months, 20.0 per cent in external training (a component without any employer support) and 15.8 per cent in study for a qualification (ABS, 1998). On average employees receive 16.5 hours of employer-supported formal training in a year: this value translates into an additional year of schooling during an employee's working life, and much more for some workers. The hours of study for qualifications are not included in this estimate and given the generally longer duration of educational courses, might be expected to increase it substantially.

Results from the 1996 Education and Training Survey provide somewhat lower estimates for New Zealand. In the 12 months preceding interview for the survey, 23.2 per cent of wage and salary workers aged between 15 and 64 years had participated in an in-house training course, 14 per cent in external training, and 17 per cent in study towards a post-school qualification (Gobbi, 1998, p. 112). In all, 48.3 per cent of wage and salary earners participated in some type of formal education or training.

The International Adult Literacy Survey (IALS) shows slightly higher levels of training in New Zealand than in Australia. In the IALS, 45 per cent of employed Australians aged 25 to 54 years participated in training compared with 49 per cent for New Zealand and the mean hours of training were 61.3 for employed Australians compared with 69.0 for New Zealand. The IALS asked respondents about participation in one or more education and training course for 'career or job-related purposes' in the 12 months before the survey. The estimates from the IALS tend to be higher than for other surveys because the measures appear to capture some informal learning activities (OECD, 1999).

Using the IALS and other surveys of training, the OECD (1999) found that Australia and New Zealand were respectively eighth and sixth ranked out of 24 mainly OECD countries in terms of participation in training and third and second ranked respectively in terms of hours of training (see *Learning Across the Adult Lifespan*).

4. WHO GETS TRAINING?

Internationally, most studies show that the distribution of EET usually favours workers who are already advantaged in the labour market, namely, employees with higher educational qualifications, in professional or managerial occupations, in full-time permanent jobs, and from the majority ethnic grouping. EET therefore builds on initial education. Australia and New Zealand conform to this pattern except that in New Zealand workers in clerical and trades occupations have the highest incidence of in-house training (Gobbi, 1998). Early school leavers therefore risk entering a low-schooling-low-training trap that perpetuates their initial employment disadvantage.

Men and women are almost equally likely to participate in education and training, but male employees were more likely than female employees to receive employer support for study and external training and male workers receive more hours of training (Gobbi, 1998; Miller, 1994).

In both Australia and New Zealand, younger workers (15 to 24 years) are more likely to participate in education and training than older workers, but this is principally due to higher rates of participation in initial education. There is, however, a difference in the type of education and training undertaken. Older workers are more likely to participate in in-house and external training (Gobbi, 1998).

Participation rates in education and training in New Zealand vary with ethnicity. While 50 per cent of all European and other employees participated in education or training, only 41 per cent of Maori and 31 per cent of Pacific Islands peoples did so. In-house and external training, in particular, were less likely to have been undertaken by Maori (Gobbi, 1998). Similar differences exist between employees born in Australia and those not born in Australia and these differences cannot be entirely explained by other differences in education or employment (Baker & Wooden, 1991).

Public sector enterprises also provide more EET than private sector enterprises. From the perspective of the firm, the major structural driver of EET is the size of the enterprise: larger enterprises tend to train more. This is a concern in smaller economies such as Australia and (particularly) New Zealand in which a relatively higher percentage of employment is in smaller firms (Skill New Zealand, 2001b).

The 1996 Training Expenditure Survey showed that expenditure on training was 1.2 per cent of gross wages and salaries in firms with 1–19 employees, 1.9 per cent in firms with 20–99 employees, and 3.2 per cent in larger firms (ABS, 1997). Hayton et al. (1996) suggest on the basis of Australian case studies that small enterprises are less inclined to provide structured training because they:

- have fewer drivers of training, for example, small enterprises are less likely to have strategic plans or business plans with training clauses, and less likely to have high levels of workplace change;
- have fewer dedicated training resources, such as personnel and facilities;
- lack economies of scale that would assist class size and backfilling; and
- have organisational structures that provide little opportunity for upward mobility; and job roles are broad rather than specialised, with less opportunity for change horizontally to a new position within the enterprise.

The ABS 1997 Training Practices Survey, found that responding to new technology, enabling employees to move to other positions and developing a more flexible work force were much less important for smaller enterprises than for larger enterprises as reasons for providing structured training (Long & Burke, 1998). Small firms were also more likely to report that their current employees were adequately trained than were larger firms. The importance of structured training in improving the performance of personnel in their current jobs and in improving the quality of goods and services was similar regardless of firm size. It seems, when it comes to structured training, that the dominant concern of smaller enterprises is doing what is done already, but better.

Rogers (1999) found that small and medium-sized firms were much less likely to introduce an innovation in process or product and service than were larger firms. This is consistent with the lesser importance accorded to training to support technological change in small to medium sized businesses as compared with larger ones (Long & Burke, 1998). The apparent relationships between survival and growth, innovation, planning (Panizzolo, 1998) and human resource management (Ogunmokun et al., 1999) including training, suggest that promotion of training to the owners and managers of small to medium-sized enterprises may benefit from routinely highlighting the relationships (for further discussion see Selby Smith et al., 2001, pp. 39–52).

Variation in levels of training among enterprises and countries and over time can also reflect the economic and policy context within which enterprises and countries work. Unemployment levels may affect training provision, as may the extent of competition and the business, industrial relations and training policies and programs pursued by governments (Ridoutt et al., 2001).

Training and skills formation is encouraged to the extent that industrial and workplace agreements link remuneration to skills, include provisions for training and avoid narrow definitions of occupations. In the 1980s and 1990s both Australia and New Zealand implemented changes in their industrial relations systems that introduced greater flexibility in awards and workplace agreements.

In New Zealand, the *Employment Contracts Act 1991* introduced enterprise-based agreements that were designed to allow greater flexibility in the use of labour in individual workplaces. Workplace reform was stimulated by the establishment in 1991 of Workplace New Zealand, an organisation funded jointly by employers, unions and government. A small number of high-performance organisations were found to have increased their spending on training, with average payroll costs of between five and six per cent (Ryan, 1996).

The Australian industrial relations system has changed considerably since the mid-1980s. The Federal Government has legislated to encourage movement away from industry-based awards to workplace and individual agreements. The shift in employment towards individual contractual arrangements is estimated to account for up to one-third of the work force (ACIRRT, 1999). For the most part, awards can no longer regulate employer provision of training. While many employers have well-developed policies on skill formation, the changes require individual workers to take greater responsibility for their own training. For further discussion of possible effects on training levels, see Teicher and Grauze (1997) and Teicher and van Gramberg (2001).

Variation in the distribution of EET across categories is not necessarily evidence of an under provision of training or of barriers to training. Some occupations and some industries may simply not benefit from more EET as much as other occupations and industries. Similarly international differences in training levels may reflect the different industrial profiles of countries (OECD, 1998).

5. RETURNS

Studies of returns to EET have generally concluded that there are benefits to enterprises, the participating employees and society more generally. Definitive measurement of these benefits, however, can often prove elusive.

From the perspective of firms, EET contributes to workplace performance, competitiveness and profitability (OTFE, 1998; Billett and Cooper, 1998; Baker and Wooden, 1995; Blandy et al., 2000). Doucouliagos and Sgro (2001) estimated rates of return to the firm of between 30 per cent and 7,125 per cent for specific training programs in seven Australian companies from a cross-section of industries. Improved labour productivity from EET need not translate directly into improved profitability if competitors obtain similar benefits from training programs. Instead, the advantage might be survival.

Similarly, improved labour productivity that is totally absorbed in higher wages is not necessarily helpful for the firm. International studies indicate wage-benefits to workers from EET of between 7 and 9 per cent, although the estimates vary substantially (Long et al., 2000). Some of the variation is due to differences in the type and context of EET being measured. Some also reflects the difficulty in isolating any wage effect of EET from related work or worker characteristics. Apparently modest wage effects can translate into quite substantial returns on investment because expenditure is sometimes relatively small (Long, 2001).

Some benefits of training may be shared between the enterprise and trainees – higher morale and lower staff turnover, for instance (Orpen, 1997). Other employees of the firm may learn new skills by working with trained co-workers. Other firms are able to recruit trained workers. Prices for products may decline if productivity increases. Moreover, tax revenue may increase if profits or wages increase. The division of the total returns among these various stakeholders can vary widely among types of EET and are difficult to estimate.

6. WHO PAYS?

The principal theoretical perspective still derives from the original work by Becker (1964). Becker viewed EET as a form of 'human capital'. From this perspective, training is an investment and outlays on it are expected to yield a positive rate of return through increased productivity. It is an unusual form of 'capital', because unlike physical plant, it is likely to depreciate more quickly through lack of use.

In the context of EET, Becker made a distinction between the uses of the terms 'specific' and 'general' training. Specific training is useful only in the particular enterprise that provides it. Therefore enterprises are able to recover most of the productivity benefits and have an incentive to pay for specific training. General training, on the other hand, is useful to many other enterprises. Since workers are able to obtain the benefits of such training through higher wages, they have an incentive to pay for it and firms do not. The distinction allowed Becker to conclude that the market would ensure that appropriate levels of EET are provided.

Becker proposed that workers paid for general training principally by accepting lower wages. This is an appropriate model for initial education (especially apprenticeships and traineeships) where mainly young workers receive a relatively low wage while they are being trained and then higher wages later. For example, Blandy et al. (2000) found that Australian firms provide more extensive training for incoming employees than firms in the United States, but Australian workers paid more for their training (through accepting lower starting wages) and employers gained productivity increases from this training (not offset by wage increases for employees) of about two-thirds of those in the United States.

Becker's model, however, is not as useful for continuing training. Several studies suggest that firms do provide and pay for general training without any salary-sacrifice by their on-going workers (Osterman, 1995; Harhoff & Kane, 1994; Acemoglu & Pischke, 1998; Loewenstein & Splitzer, 1998; Barron et al., 1999; OECD, 1999). Although there are mechanisms that serve to insulate the training firm from poaching of trained workers (Long et al., 2000), these are unlikely to be totally successful. The lack of congruency between payment for training and benefit for training, together with benefits from training that may accrue to governments through higher taxation receipts, provides a possible basis for government intervention in the provision of EET.

7. POLICY AND PROGRAMS

In almost all countries, there is an implicit subsidy to EET. Most expenditure on physical capital is depreciated over several years, an approach that reflects both the gradual loss of resale value and the nature of the income stream against which the expenditure is offset. Expenditure on human capital, however, is treated as an accounting cost, which is equivalent to a (very advantageous) 100 per cent depreciation rate.

Because of concerns that enterprises do not provide socially optimal levels of education and training, governments in Australia and New Zealand, and many other countries, have introduced policies designed to increase the expenditure by enterprises, and workers on education and training.

7.1. Australia

Australia has a federal system of government, with six States and two Territories. The Federal Government has only limited constitutional authority in the area of education and training, but, prompted by an increasing recognition of the important economic role of education, has gradually increased its influence through its superior fiscal position. It now has primary responsibility for the university sector. The influence of the Federal Government in the vocational education and training (VET) sector is principally through the Australian National Training Authority (ANTA), which began operations in 1994.

ANTA is an agency overseen by an industry-based board, but accountable to a Council of Ministers of Federal, State and Territory Governments. ANTA's role is to provide strategic direction and advice to the States and Territories, to support innovation and to spread effective practice through the provision of Federally-provided growth funds, and generally to strengthen the quality, flexibility and responsiveness of the VET system to its clients and users. ANTA is supported by a network of Industry Training Boards (ITBs) that provide advice from enterprises and unions. Delivery of public vocational education and training, however, is still through State Government Institutes of Technical and Further Education (TAFEs).

Historically, cooperation in education and training policy and programs among the various State, Territory and Federal Governments has proved difficult to achieve. The disjuncture of responsibility, funding and accountability has contributed to the often slow progress in implementing change. Nevertheless, the Australian National Training Authority (ANTA) has overseen the introduction of a more uniform national training system, although considerable differences remain among the States.

The creation of ANTA was itself an expression of the reform of the vocational education and training sector that occurred from the mid-1980s, sponsored by governments, business and unions and underlain by concerns about international competitiveness. Much of the change is built on an acceptance of competency-based training. States and Territories agreed to link their awards to a national qualification framework, the Australian Qualification Framework, which was introduced in 1994. Training packages, introduced progressively by ANTA from the late 1990s, define the competency standards, assessment guidelines, and the qualification level for a given award. They also provide additional components such as learning strategies, professional development materials, and assessment materials. The training packages collectively define a defacto national training system.

The effect on EET has been considerable. Although substantial amounts of training remain outside the training system and are delivered in-house or externally, firms have been inevitably incorporated into the system. Attempts to create a more competitive and efficient training market encouraged the registration of private training providers. Many larger companies such as Bosch and Caterpillar registered as training providers to train their own apprentices and deliver a variety of other non-initial training courses through training packages. Other enterprises have then chosen to use industry providers rather than TAFEs. Registered public or private training providers may now deliver EET outside the training system. Competency-based training has also led to a focus on flexible delivery (self-paced study) and inevitably to greater work-place delivery.

Perhaps one of the most significant changes has been in the structure of apprenticeships which have long-formed an important part of the vocational education and training sector and an especially important educational pathway for young men. An apprenticeship was a contract of training between an employer and an apprentice. It was subject to government regulation. Employers received a government subsidy for each apprentice while apprentices were entitled to designated training and a training wage. An apprenticeship usually lasted three or four years.

There were several problems with the apprenticeship system. On the one hand, there was the impression that apprenticeships were often little more than timeserving. On the other, there was concern about the stability of the employer-apprentice relationship. The bankruptcy of an employer often posed severe difficulties for an apprentice. Large state-owned enterprises in utilities, transport and communication had traditionally employed many apprentices and served a valuable training function. Their corporatisation and privatisation during the 1980s and 1990s led to a reduction in apprenticeship places. Employment of apprentices now became more the province of smaller and medium-sized firms that were either less stable financially or less able to guarantee on-going work for an apprentice.

The creation of group training companies in the mid 1980s was a particularly successful innovation. These not-for-profit companies employed apprentices and then farmed them out to employers as required. These companies mobilised the goodwill of small employers towards the apprenticeship system by acting as a broker between the government and the employer. Small employers no longer had to deal with the paper work involved in employing an apprentice and did not have to worry about guaranteeing continuing employment of the apprentice. Group training companies now employ about 70 per cent of all apprentices.

Apprenticeships were based in the manufacturing and building trades. The growth in the economy was principally in the service sector in which there were few apprenticeships. Faced with the problem of increasing youth unemployment, the changing structure of the economy, and the perception of skill shortages, the

Federal Government moved to create a series of apprenticeship-like arrangements, which became known initially as 'traineeships' and later as 'new apprenticeships'. These were generally of shorter duration than 'old apprenticeships', perhaps by one or two years. As with apprenticeships, however, their defining feature was the contract of training between the employer and the trainee and government wage subsidies. The traineeships were located principally in the retail, hospitality and tourism industries, but also extended into real estate, information technology and office administration.

The take-up of traineeships and new apprenticeships was initially fairly low, but from the mid 1990s enrolments began to increase quite quickly and are now a significant element of the vocational education and training sector. Nearly 200,000 apprentices, trainees and new apprentices commenced courses in each of the years 1999 and 2000 – about two per cent of the labour force (NCVER, 2001). The combination of several elements has led to considerable concern about the quality of training delivered through traineeships. Firms could become registered training providers and deliver their own training to their own employers. Flexible delivery, workplace delivery, possibly low completion rates and the existence of government wage subsidies have raised questions about the quality of training. Several recent State Government reviews of the new apprenticeship system have confirmed this view and led to recommendations for far stronger government monitoring of the scheme (Schofield, 1999a, 1999b, 2000).

The Australian Government introduced a Training Guarantee in 1990, and suspended it in 1994. The legislation required firms with annual wages and salary expenditure above $200,000 to spend an amount equivalent to 1.5 per cent of their annual wages and salary expenditure on approved training. If the required amount was not spent on training, then the levy became a tax and any outstanding balance was paid to consolidated revenue.

A major review of the scheme found that for businesses with 20 to 99 employees, in the four years the scheme operated, it contributed to a growth of 60 per cent in average expenditure per employee and to a growth of 30 per cent in average hours of training per employee (Fraser, 1996; ABS, 1997). Robinson (1999) notes that such firms account for only 15 per cent of total training expenditure in Australia. The effect on expenditure, however, extended to both larger and smaller firms, although to a lesser extent. Surveys of employers are consistent with these estimates, and 40 per cent of eligible employers believed that the Training Guarantee had led to improvements in their methods of training and the way they planned their training. The review found that from the perspective of the government, the scheme was highly effective: between $20 and $100 of new training expenditure was generated for every government dollar spent.

It may be inefficient to treat all firms equally in the manner of the Training Guarantee. Some firms and industries may genuinely have a low requirement for training. Nevertheless, if some firms or industries are not aware of the benefits of training, mandated levels of expenditure may assist. The Training Guarantee did raise management's awareness of the need for training (Fraser, 1996).

7.2. New Zealand

In contrast to Australia, New Zealand has a centralised system of government. Authority for education and training lies with a single national government. Hence New Zealand has not faced the same set of jurisdictional issues as Australia. It has, however, faced similar economic issues, but has produced solutions of its own.

As with Australia, New Zealand began to reform its industrial training system in the late 1980s in response to concerns about rising unemployment, low productivity growth and the international competitiveness of its industries. Government, business and unions recognised that changes in initial education and training (especially the apprenticeship system) were inadequate to address the perceived skills deficit. Industry needed to provide for the continuing education and training of its workers. Further, the quality of training needed to be improved, with greater emphasis on demonstrated competence.

The major public infrastructure for the support of VET in New Zealand is the system of polytechnics that provides initial and post initial courses in industry training, often in conjunction with enterprises and other training authorities.

Two new bodies were created to oversee the changes. In 1991, the New Zealand Qualifications Authority (NZQA) was established to coordinate the implementation of a National Qualifications Framework (NQF). The framework was designed around units of competence (bundled to achieve qualifications established at the eight levels of the framework) with explicit learning objectives, performance criteria, and assessment. It facilitated assessment outside the formal training system, including recognition of prior learning (Hood, 1996). The credit received by learners is portable from one setting to another. Unit standards and qualifications are national standards that are developed largely by industry bodies and professional groups.

Skill New Zealand (originally known as the Education and Training Support Agency) was established in 1992 with Industry Training Organisations (ITOs). The ITOs are responsible for setting national skills standards, developing training packages for employers, arranging delivery of on- and off-job training, and assessing the competence of individual trainees. Skill New Zealand supports the ITOs and promotes the establishment and implementation of national standards at industry level.

The funding of industry training by Government is undertaken by Skill New Zealand through its administration of the Industry Training Fund (ITF), established in 1996. Funding is only available for training that is linked to the achievement of unit standards and qualifications registered on the NQF at Level 4 or below. Subsidies range from 82 per cent for the purchase of off-job training to 50 per cent for arranging on-job assessment of employees (Barker, 1998).

The intent of the policy is to encourage a greater extent and incidence of industry training by reducing the cost to enterprises. Since subsidised training is restricted to units of the NQF, employers are obliged to engage with externally moderated training. Frequently, however, qualified workplace assessors can undertake much of the assessment on-the-job. The system, however, is essentially voluntaristic: enterprises themselves decide whether to purchase training and, if so, the type of training.

A review of tertiary education initiated in 2000 prompted several changes to industry training in New Zealand (TEAC, 2000, 2001a, 2001b, 2001c). A Tertiary Education Commission, which has the role of overseeing and coordinating the various sectors of tertiary education, also has responsibility for the policy and operational responsibilities of Skill New Zealand. One purpose of the change is to incorporate better industry training within tertiary pathways.

The outcomes of the review largely strengthen the existing structures and programs for industrial training. The proposed legislation strengthens the role of the NZQA by allowing it to impose conditions on accreditations, course approvals and registrations. More funding will be made available to the ITF and previous restrictions on the level of training eligible for support through the fund will be lifted. More strategic planning about the supply of training will be expected from ITOs and more stringent quality controls will be imposed on their performance for registration and re-registration. Enterprises will have more freedom to choose among ITOs for the supply of training.

The major change in the funding of government-subsidised training is that an ITO may impose a training levy subject to a majority vote in a ballot of employers in the industry. The change recognises the potential externalities involved in the provision of EET and the benefits that may accrue to firms through training undertaken by other enterprises.

The Modern Apprenticeships program was introduced in 2000 and are a work-based education initiative designed to help more young people to access employment-based training and complete national qualifications. Apprentices are employed and have a registered training agreement with an ITO. The apprenticeship involves on-the-job and off-the-job training. Modern Apprenticeships extend the coverage of traditional apprenticeships into new industries such as retail, hospitality and business administration and provide for paid coordinators, who act as development officers for the scheme and case management for the apprentices. Pilot programs were begun in 2000 and by 2001 there were 1,212 persons enrolled in Modern Apprenticeships with the intention of greatly increasing this number (Skill New Zealand, 2001a).

In 2001, 66,390 industry trainees from 22,000 enterprises participated in at least one of about 2,500 ITF-funded courses. The courses were provided by 500 providers registered with 46 ITOs that covered about 76 per cent of the workforce. The courses resulted in 6,000 NQF awards and 1.5 million NQF credits. Skill NZ provided $NZ69.2 through the ITF (Skill New Zealand, 2001a).

Participants in the courses are only 3.6 per cent of the workforce. Hence substantial amounts of EET occur outside the system. The industry-based nature of the courses, and the time lags involved in developing courses to cover new skills, ensure that this will always be the case. But training through the fund has increased substantially during the last decade. Given the recent proposed changes to industry training, it is likely to increase in influence.

The value of such a subsidy scheme depends in part on how much additional training it generates. Some of the training funded under the ITF would occur in any case and be fully funded by employers. ITF-funding, however, seems to have been successful in providing training in industries and among categories of workers with previously low rates of training (especially Maori). As with Australia's Training Guarantee, an important contribution of the ITF, the ITOs and Skill New Zealand may be in raising awareness of the importance of EET. Additionally, however, the New Zealand arrangements provide an infrastructure through which training can be accessed and new training arrangements organised.

8. CONCLUSION

Enterprise education and training is a large and important economic activity. As with education in general, it contributes to the creation of a skilled workforce and, through that, to the competitiveness of enterprises. Broad economic and demographic changes have placed greater emphasis on the need for a skilled workforce. Governments worldwide have focused on providing a stronger infrastructure for vocational education and training. Governments in both Australia and New Zealand have introduced policies to improve the quality and efficiency of vocational education and training by creating national competency-based training packages linked to nationally recognised awards and delivered by registered providers in a training market characterised by increased competition. The shift to competency-based training, flexible delivery and workplace delivery in vocational education and training, and in enterprise education and training, requires new structures to ensure the quality of the training delivered (Schofield, 1999a, 1999b, 2000).

Without government support, the fact that workers ultimately own the outcomes of enterprise education and training is likely to lead enterprises to provide less than socially optimal amounts. To the extent that enterprise education and training is linked directly to the formal vocational education and training system, reforms of that system may lead to greater efficiency in the supply of education and training and greater demand for education and training from workers. Government policies and programs in Australia and New Zealand that reform the vocational education and training sector are therefore likely to have had a direct effect on enterprise education and training. Government contributions to the reform of this sector may therefore provide an indirect subsidy to enterprise education and training even if much of that education and training continues to be undertaken as in-house training.

The New Zealand Government provides substantial subsidies from its Industry Training Fund for industry-level enterprise education and training. The extent to which the subsidies have led to additional expenditure on enterprise education and training is unclear, although higher levels of training among categories of firms and workers with a traditionally low level of training might indicate some success. As with Australia's short-lived Training Guarantee, the contribution to the awareness of the value of training might well be as important as any direct effect on the amount of training.

The apprenticeship system in both Australia and New Zealand has been reformed and expanded. In existing apprenticeships, the focus has shifted to competency-based training and integration with the national qualification frameworks. New or Modern Apprenticeships have been introduced in part to address the need for initial industrial training in expanding industries that had been poorly represented in the existing apprenticeship system. In Australia in particular the new arrangements are not restricted to initial education. The existing and expanded apprenticeship systems in both Australia and New Zealand provide subsidies to employers and are usually associated with relatively low wages for the trainees. The apprenticeship system in Australia has benefited from the introduction of new structures to provide greater stability for the employment of apprentices.

REFERENCES

Acemoglu, D., & Pischke, J. (1998b). *The structure of wages and investment in general training*. NBER Working Paper 6357. Cambridge, MA: National Bureau of Economic Research.

Australian Bureau of Statistics (ABS) (1997). *Employer training expenditure, Australia July-September 1996*, Cat.no.6353.0, Canberra: ABS.

Australian Bureau of Statistics (ABS) (1998). *Education and training experience, Australia, 1997*. Cat. No. 6278.0. Canberra: ABS.

Australian Centre for Industrial Relations Research and Training (ACIRRT) (1999). *Australia at work: Just managing?*. Sydney: Prentice Hall.

Baker, M., & Wooden, M. (1991). *Immigration and training*. Canberra: AGPS.

Baker, M., & Wooden, M. (Eds.) (1995). Small and medium sized enterprises and vocational education and training, *Report to ANTARAC*. Adelaide: NCVER.

Barker, P. (1998). The New Zealand market approach. In C. Robinson & R. Kenyon (Eds.), *The Market for Vocational Education and Training*. Adelaide: NCVER.

Barron, J., Berger, M. C., & Black, M. (1999). Do workers pay for on-the-job training? *The Journal of Human Resources, 34*, 235–252.

Becker, G. S. (1964). *Human capital: A theoretical analysis with special reference to education*. New York: Columbia University Press.

Billett, S., & Cooper, M. (1998). *Returns to enterprises from the investment in VET*, Review of Research Series, Adelaide: NCVER.

Blandy, R., Dockery, M., Hawke, A., & Webster, E. (2000). *Does Training Pay? Evidence from Australian Enterprises*, Adelaide: NCVER.

Doucouliagos, C., & Sgro, P. (2000). *Enterprise return on a training investment*. Adelaide: NCVER.

Fraser, D. (1996). *The Training Guarantee: Its impact and legacy 1990–1994. Main report*. Canberra: Australian Government Publishing Service.

Gobbi, M. (1998). Participation in post-compulsory education and training, *Labour Market Bulletin, 1&2*, 108–126.

Harhoff, D., & Kane, T. (1994). *Financing apprenticeship training: Evidence from Germany*. NBER Working Paper 4557. Cambridge, MA: National Bureau of Economic Research.

Hayton, G., McIntyre, J., Sweet, R., McDonald, R., Noble, C., Smith, A., & Roberts, P. (1996). *Final report: Enterprise training in Australia*. Victoria: Office for Training and Further Education, pp. 65–66.

Hood, D. (1996). New Zealand: The development of a system of qualifications and certification based on skills. In OECD, *Assessing and certifying occupational skills and competences in vocational education and training*. Paris: OECD.

Loewenstein, M., & Spletzer, J. (1998). Dividing the costs and returns to general training. *Journal of Labor Economics, 16*, 142–171.

Long, M. (2001). Training and economic returns to workers. In A. Smith (Ed.), *Return on Investment in Training: Research Readings*. Adelaide: NCVER.

Long, M., & Burke, G. (1998). An analysis of the 1997 Training Practices Survey. *CEET working paper no. 20*. Monash University-ACER Centre for the Economics of Education and Training, Melbourne: Monash University.

Long, M., & Lamb, S. (2002). *Firm-based training for young Australians: Changes from the 1980s to the 1990s*. LSAY, Research Report No. 23. Melbourne: ACER.

Long, M., Ryan, R., Burke, G., & Hopkins, S. (2000). *Enterprise-based education and training: A literature review*, Wellington, NZ: Ministry of Education.

Maglen, L., Hopkins, S., & Burke, G. (2001). *Training for Productivity*. Adelaide: NCVER.

Miller, P. W. (1994). Gender discrimination in training: An Australian perspective. *British Journal of Industrial Relations, 32*(4), 539–564.

National Centre for Vocational Education and Training (NCVER) (2001). *Australian apprenticeships: Facts, fiction and future*. Adelaide: NCVER.

Office of Training and Further Education (OTFE) (1998). *Benefits to employers from an investment in training: Literature review*. Melbourne: OTFE.

Ogunmokun, G. O., Shaw, R. N., & Fitzroy, P. T. (1999). Determinants of strategic planning behaviour in small business: An exploratory investigation of small business organisations in Australia, *International Journal of Management, 16*(2), 190–202.

Orpen, C. (1997). The effects of formal mentoring on employee work motivation, organizational commitment and job performance, *The Learning Organization, 4*(2), 53–60.

Organisation for Economic Co-operation and Development (OECD) (1997). *Manual for better training statistics*. Paris: OECD.

Organisation for Economic Co-operation and Development (OECD) (1998). *Human capital: An international comparison*. Paris: OECD.

Organisation for Economic Co-operation and Development (OECD) (1999). Training of adult workers, *OECD Employment Outlook*. Paris: OECD.

Osterman, P. (1995). Skill, training, and work organisation in American establishments. *Industrial Relations, 34*, 125–146.

Panizzolo, R. (1998). Managing innovation in SMEs: A multiple case analysis of the adoption and implementation of product and process design technologies. *Small Business Economics, 11*(1), 25–42.

Ridoutt, L., Dutneall, R., Hummel, K., & Selby Smith, C. (2001). *Factors that influence the implementation of training and learning in the workplace*. Adelaide: NCVER.

Robinson, C. (1999). Promoting a training culture in Australia, In C. Robinson & K. Arthy (Eds.), *Lifelong Learning: Developing a Training Culture*. Adelaide: NCVER.

Rogers, M. (1999). The performance of small and medium enterprises: An overview using the growth and performance survey, *Melbourne Institute Working Paper no. 1/99*. The University of Melbourne: Melbourne Institute for Applied Economic and Social Research.

Ryan, R. (1996). *Workplace reform in New Zealand – the state of play*. Report prepared for Workplace New Zealand. Wellington: Workplace NZ.

Schofield, K. (1999a). *Independent Investigation of the Quality of Training in Queensland's Traineeship System*. Brisbane: Vocational Education, Training and Employment Commission.

Schofield, K. (1999b). *A Risky Business. Review of the Quality of Tasmania's Traineeship System* (2 vols.). Hobart: Office of Vocational Education and Training.

Schofield, K. (2000). *Delivering Quality. Report of the Independent Review of the Quality of Training in Victoria's Apprenticeship and Traineeship System* (2 vols.). Melbourne: Office of Post-Compulsory Education, Training and Employment.

Selby Smith, C., Ferrier, F., Burke, G. et al. (2001). *The Economics of Vocational Education and Training in Australia: CEET's Stocktake*. Adelaide: NCVER.

Skill New Zealand (2001a). *Annual report of Skill New Zealand for the year ended 30 June 2001.* Wellington: Skill NZ.

Skill New Zealand (2001b). *Knowledge at work: Workplace learning in New Zealand.* Wellington: Skill NZ.

Tertiary Education Advisory Committee (TEAC) (2000). *Shaping a shared vision.* Wellington: TEAC.

Tertiary Education Advisory Committee (TEAC) (2001a). *Shaping the system.* Wellington: TEAC.

Tertiary Education Advisory Committee (TEAC) (2001b). *Shaping the strategy.* Wellington: TEAC.

Tertiary Education Advisory Committee (TEAC) (*2001c). *Shaping a funding framework.* Wellington: TEAC.

Teicher, J., & Grauze, A. (1997). Enterprise bargaining, industrial relations and training. In C. Selby Smith & F. Ferrier (Eds.), *The Economic Impact of Training* (pp. 254–72). Canberra: Australian Government Publishing Service.

Teicher, J., & van Gramberg, B. (2001). 'The changing industrial relations environment'. In C. Selby Smith, et al. (Eds.), *The Economics of Vocational Education and Training in Australia: CEET's Stocktake.* Adelaide: NCVER.

Printed by Publishers' Graphics LLC

INTERNATIONAL HANDBOOK OF EDUCATIONAL
RESEARCH IN THE ASIA-PACIFIC REGION

A publication of the Asia-Pacific Educational Research Association

Kluwer International Handbooks of Education

VOLUME 11

A list of titles in this series can be found at the end of this volume.

International Handbook of Educational Research in the Asia-Pacific Region

Part Two

Editors:

John P. Keeves
Flinders University Institute of International Education, Australia

and

Ryo Watanabe
National Institute for Educational Policy Research of Japan, Tokyo, Japan

Section Editors:
John P. Keeves, *Flinders University Institute of International Education, Australia*
Rupert Maclean, *UNESCO-UNEVOC International Centre for Education, Bonn, Germany*
Peter D. Renshaw, *Griffith University, Southport, Australia*
Colin N. Power, *University of Queensland, St Lucia, Queensland, Australia*
Robyn Baker, *New Zealand Council for Educational Research, Wellington, New Zealand*
S. Gopinathan, *National Institute of Education, Nanyang Technological University, Singapore*
Ho Wah Kam, *National Institute of Education, Nanyang Technological University, Singapore*
Yin Cheong Cheng, *Hong Kong Institute of Education, Hong Kong*
Albert C. Tuijnman, *Institute of International Education, Stockholm University, Sweden*
Ryo Watanabe, *National Institute for Educational Policy Research of Japan, Japan*

APERA

KLUWER ACADEMIC PUBLISHERS
DORDRECHT / BOSTON / LONDON

Library of Congress Cataloging-in-Publication Data is available.

ISBN 1-4020-1007-9

Published by Kluwer Academic Publishers
PO Box 17, 3300 AA Dordrecht, The Netherlands

Sold and distributed in North, Central and South America
by Kluwer Academic Publishers,
101 Philip Drive, Norwell, MA 02061, U.S.A.

In all other countries, sold and distributed
by Kluwer Academic Publishers, Distribution Centre,
PO Box 322, 3300 AH Dordrecht, The Netherlands

A publication of the Asia-Pacific Educational Research Association

Printed on acid-free paper

All Rights Reserved
© 2003 Kluwer Academic Publishers
No part of this publication may be reproduced or utilized in any form or by any
means, electronic, mechanical, including photocopying, recording or by any
informations storage and retrieval system, without written permission from the
copyright owner.

Table of Contents

Overview and Introduction
John P. Keeves and Ryo Watanabe   xiii

PART ONE

SECTION 1: TRENDS AND ISSUES

Section Editor – John P. Keeves

1	Trends in Educational Reform in the Asia-Pacific Region *Yin Cheong Cheng*	3
2	Achieving Education for All in the Asia-Pacific Region *Rupert Maclean and Ken Vine*	17
3	Educational Expenditure and Participation in East Asia and Australia *Gerald Burke, Robert Lenehan, and Hing Tong Ma*	29
4	The Family and Schooling in Asian and Pacific Countries *Kevin Marjoribanks*	43
5	Cultural and Social Capital in Asian and Pacific Countries *Lawrence J. Saha*	59
6	Secondary Education Reform in the Asia-Pacific Region *Rupert Maclean*	73
7	Educational Research and Educational Policy-Making in Asian and Pacific Countries *T. Neville Postlethwaite*	93
8	Evaluation and Accountability in Asian and Pacific Countries *Ramon Mohandas, Meng Hong Wei, and John P. Keeves*	107
9	Educational Research in the Asia-Pacific Region *John P. Keeves, Ryo Watanabe, and Peter McGuckian*	123

SECTION 2: ACCESS AND EQUITY

Section Editor – Rupert Maclean

Education of Special Groups

10	Equality of Opportunity in Education *Rupert Maclean*	143
11	A Case Study of Learning Achievement in South Asia *Rupert Maclean and Ken Vine*	155
12	Education of Children in Remote Areas *Tiedao Zhang*	171
13	Education of Gifted and Talented Learners *Kenneth Kuen Fung Sin*	189
14	Inclusive Education for Students with Special Needs *David Mitchell and Ishwar Desai*	203
15	Issues for Urban Youth in Asia and the Pacific *Kerry J. Kennedy*	217
16	Drop-outs from School and How to Cope with this Problem *S. Srinivasan and S. Anandalakshmy*	231
17	Ethnicities, Minorities and Indigenous Groups in Central Asia *Joseph and Rea Zajda*	241
18	Sex and Gender Differences in Educational Outcomes *John P. Keeves and Malcolm Slade*	257
19	Gender-Sensitive Education for Bridging the Gender Gap *Namtip Aksornkool*	269
20	Gender Differences in Access to Education and Employment *Sharada Jain*	279

Lifelong Learning

21	Adult Literacy in the Asia-Pacific Region *Inayatullah*	293
22	Learning Across the Adult Lifespan *Erlinda C. Pefianco, David Curtis, and John P. Keeves*	305
23	Workforce Education *David N. Wilson*	321
24	Nonformal Education *Steve Wilson and Mona Shrestha*	335

SECTION 3: LEARNING AND HUMAN DEVELOPMENT

Section Editors – Peter Renshaw and Colin Power

25	The Process of Learning *Peter Renshaw and Colin Power*	351
26	Cognitive Development *Alison F. Garton*	365
27	Lifespan Human Development *Candida C. Peterson*	379
28	Values Education in a Changing World *Lourdes R. Quisumbing and Joy de Leo*	395
29	Measuring Attitudes by Unfolding a Likert-Style Questionnaire *David Andrich and Guanzhon Luo*	409
30	Bullying in Schools *Phillip T. Slee, Lang Ma, Hee-Og Sim, Keith Sullivan, and Mitsura Taki*	425
31	Student Learning: A Cross-Cultural Perspective *David N. Watkins*	441
32	Classroom Learning Environments *Barry J. Fraser and Swee Chiew Goh*	463
33	Metacognition *Christina E. van Kraayenoord and Merrilyn Goos*	477
34	Motivation and School Learning *Chi-Hung Ng and Peter Renshaw*	495
35	Problem Solving *Michael J. Lawson*	511
36	Technology and Learning *Kwok-Cheung Cheung*	525

SECTION 4: CURRICULUM AND TECHNICAL EDUCATION

Section Editor – Robyn Baker

Curricula of the Schools

37	Change in the School Curriculum: Looking to the Future *Robyn Baker and Andy Begg*	541
38	Civics and Citizenship *Thomas Kwan-Choi Tse*	555

viii Table of Contents

39	Environmental Education and Education for Sustainable Development *John Fien and Debbie Heck*	569
40	Literacy and Reading *Warwick B. Elley and Ho Wah Kam*	585
41	Mathematics Curricula *Andy Begg*	599
42	Science Curricula *Robyn Baker and Rosemary Hipkins*	615
43	Assessment Research in Second Language Curriculum Initiatives *Kathryn Hill and Tim McNamara*	629
44	Education for Peace and International Understanding *Yoshiyuki Nagata and G.R. (Bob) Teasdale*	641

Education and the World of Work

45	Planning Technical and Vocational Education and Training in Asia *David N. Wilson*	657
46	Vocational Education and Training in Asia *Jandhyala B.G. Tilak*	673
47	Pacific Island Issues in Vocational Education and Training *Perive Tanuvasa Lene*	687
48	Transition from School to Work in East Asia *David Atchoarena and Efison Mujanganja*	701
49	Enterprise Education in Australia and New Zealand *Michael Long and Chris Selby Smith*	715

PART TWO

SECTION 5: TEACHING, TEACHERS AND TEACHER EDUCATION

Section Editors – S. Gopianathan and Ho Wah Kam

Teaching

50	Issues and Concerns Regarding Teaching, Teachers and Higher Education *S. Gopinathan and Ho Wah Kam*	733

51	Class Size and Classroom Processes *Peter Blatchford and Gemma Catchpole*	741
52	Homework and Coaching *Ian David Smith*	755
53	Teacher Self-Evaluation *John MacBeath*	767
54	Time: Allocated, Institutional and Task Oriented *Maurice Galton*	781
55	Monitoring of Student Learning *Geoff N. Masters*	793

Higher Education and Teacher Education

56	Higher Education and Development *Jandhyala B.G. Tilak*	809
57	Financing Higher Education in the Asia-Pacific Region *N.V. Varghese*	827
58	Selection for Higher Education in the Asia-Pacific Region *V. Lynn Meek*	839
59	Adult Education in Universities in the Asia-Pacific Region *Darryl Dymock and Barrie Brennan*	853
60	Teaching as an Occupation and Learning Profession *Kerry J. Kennedy*	867
61	Research into Teacher Education *Sim Wong-Kooi*	883
62	The Recruitment and Reparation of Teachers *Chen Ai Yen, Lim Cher Ping, and S. Gopinathan*	899

SECTION 6: ORGANISATION AND MANAGEMENT OF EDUCATION

Section Editor – Yin Cheong Cheng

| 63 | Organisation and the Management of Education: Development, and Growth
Yin Cheong Cheng, Magdalena Mo Ching Mok, and King W. Chow | 915 |

64	Decentralization and the Self-Managing School *Brian J. Caldwell*	931
65	Quality Assurance and School Monitoring *Magdalena Mo Ching Mok, David Gurr, Eiko Izawa, Heidi Knipprath, Lee In-Hyo, Michael A. Mel, Terry Palmer, Wen-Jing Shan, and Zhang Yenming*	945
66	Staffing in School Education *Young-Hwa Kim*	959
67	School Leadership and Management *Allan Walker*	973
68	Effective Schooling in the Asia-Pacific Region *Clive Dimmock*	987
69	School Leadership Development *Philip Hallinger*	1001
70	Public and Private Education *Ramsey Ding-Yee Koo, Andy Man-Sing Yung, Kip Yuen Ip, and Wei-Chen Chuang*	1015
71	Policy-Making, Planning and Change in Tertiary Education *Alan Wagner and Philip Kwok-Fai Hui*	1031
72	Financing Education in Asian and Pacific Countries *Mark Bray*	1047
73	Family and Community Participation in Education *I-Wah Pang, Eiko Isawa, Anna Kim, Heidi Knipprath, Michael A. Mel, and Terry Palmer*	1063

SECTION 7: EDUCATIONAL RESEARCH AND NATIONAL DEVELOPMENT

Section Editor – Albert C. Tuijnman

74	Educational Research for National and Regional Development *Albert Tuijnman*	1081
75	Globalisation and Education in Asia *Francis O. Ramirez and J. Chan-Tiberghein*	1095
76	Comparative Educational Achievement Studies *Don Spearritt*	1107
77	Comparative Indicators in Education *Lawrence J. Saha and Albert Tuijnman*	1123

78	Dissemination of the Findings of Educational Research *Grant J. Harman and Kay Harman*	1137
79	Donor Support for Educational Research *William A. Loxley*	1151

SECTION 8: TOWARDS THE FUTURE

Section Editor – John P. Keeves

80	Educational Research for Educational Reform *John. P. Keeves and Rung Kaew Dang*	1167
81	The Impact of Educational Research on Decision Making and Practice *Victor Ordonez and Rupert Maclean*	1181
82	Research in Education: Nature, Impact, Needs and Priorities *Zhou Mansheng and John P. Keeves*	1193
83	University Education for National Development *Molly N.N. Lee and Suk Ying Wong*	1207
84	Culturally Inclusive Teacher Education in Oceania *Konai Helu Thaman*	1221
85	Reforming Secondary Education and the Education of Adolescents *Phillip W. Hughes*	1231
86	Reform in Science and Technology Curricula *Kok-Aun Toh and Ngoh-Khang Goh*	1243
87	Emerging Information and Communications Technology in Education *Sivakumar Alagumalai*	1257
88	Education Reform and the Labour Market in Pacific Island Countries *Gerald Burke*	1271
89	Training of Educational Research Workers *Barry J. Fraser and Angela F.L. Wong*	1285
90	Regional Cooperation in Educational Research *M.S. Kharparde and Ashok K. Srivastava*	1301
91	Challenges for Research into Educational Reform in the Asia-Pacific Region *Yin Cheong Cheng*	1315

92 Monitoring the Impact of Gobalisation on Education and Human Development
   John P. Keeves, Hungi Njora, and I. Gusti Ngurah Darmawan   1331

Index of Names   1347

Index of Subjects   1365

SECTION 5:

TEACHING, TEACHERS AND
TEACHER EDUCATION

Section Editors – S. Gopinathan and Ho Wah Kam

Teaching

50

Issues and Concerns Regarding Teaching, Teachers and Higher Education

S. GOPINATHAN and HO WAH KAM

National Institute of Education, Nanyang Technological University, Singapore

1. INTRODUCTION

There is now a general understanding that the cultural values of a country have a strong impact on instructional practices, classroom management and teachers in its education system. In other words, each culture has its own national teaching practices. From this perspective, it is often asked whether it is worthwhile for a country to try borrowing educational practices from another country. At the same time, given the internationalisation of information, there has been much borrowing of ideas by countries in the Asia-Pacific region from the centres of learning in the West. "Yet nothing is quite that simple", says MacBeath (see *Teacher Self-Evaluation*). He adds,

> There are common strands within Asia-Pacific countries which look to both East and West, factors not simply of recent history but of centuries of globalisation. The meeting ground of economics and religions in multiple manifestations has created common tensions but also unique challenges within each country and sub-region. The conflict between traditional values and emerging knowledge is a longstanding one.

This conflict is particularly evident in the case of English language teaching in East Asia.

At the same time, while policy-makers in both East and West have drawn heavily on school effectiveness research findings across countries, there are tensions when educational ideas from the East are introduced to schools in the West. In the United Kingdom, for example, the reactions to Reynold and Farrell's (1996) report *Worlds Apart?* were mixed and a little confused. The articles in this section on different issues of and concerns about schooling show the influences of the global and the national (or local) on teachers and instructional practices.

MacBeath (see *Teacher Self-Evaluation*) says that in Asia-Pacific countries, too, "policy-makers are no longer content to let teachers plough their own lone furrow". His topic, is particularly significant with the shift in paradigm in educational management, even in the Asia-Pacific region, from management by administrative decree to a greater degree of self-management. In his article, MacBeath argues that the best sources of information about the teachers' instructional practices are the teachers themselves. In such self-evaluation, teachers are expected to listen sensitively and attentively to the voices of the students as they have their own contributions to make. This means that the teachers should not only be better trained but should also have greater self-knowledge and self-confidence. The very qualities of teachers that have served well in the past may be detrimental to their success in the future. According to MacBeath, the schools of the future require a different cast of mind and a different repertoire of skills, among which is the ability to self-evaluate and the sensitivity to students' needs. The evaluation of teaching and learning becomes more rather than less important.

2. TEACHING, LEARNING AND TEACHERS

In his article, MacBeath (see *Teacher Self-Evaluation*) reviews a few studies carried out in the Asia-Pacific region in which researchers looked into the processes of learning – their thinking or engagement with learning – what he calls "the internal world of learning". He cites the work of Tay-Koay (1997) in Singapore, in which the researcher probed deeply the different levels of cognitive learning and emotive activities in an attempt to understand the learning behaviours of students that can affect teaching behaviour. In another case, mentioned in the chapter, a teacher in a small rural school in the Mekong Delta (in the Indochina region) built a database drawing on the views of pupils, parents and teachers about school climate, classroom teaching and pupil learning. In a sample of Hong Kong schools (as reported by MacBeath), teachers, while wary of evaluation of any kind, are not averse "to professional development that is grounded in their needs and priorities".

Getting closer into the world of teaching and learning, Smith (see *Homework and Coaching*) writes on homework and coaching, which are recognised in the Asia-Pacific region as important complements to classroom learning and teaching that are linked to higher achievement. Such coaching and the assignment of homework is often over-emphasized in some countries in the Asia-Pacific region. In China, for example, Prime Minister Zhu Rongyi, has commented on the negative effects of excessive homework, as Smith reported. Coaching, especially coaching (or what is called 'private tuition' in Hong Kong, Malaysia and Singapore) for high-stakes national examinations or for admission to university, is rampant in countries such as Japan, Republic of Korea and Taiwan. It is referred to as "hot-housing" and appears to be accepted in the high-achieving countries in the region.

While international comparisons of achievement have shown large differences in the amount of homework students have been receiving in different countries and while the consensus is that homework is worthwhile in motivating and reinforcing learning, there is little research evidence to show a positive relationship between homework and learning. In the East Asian context, there are contradictory conclusions from what little research there is about the effects of homework on coaching. On the one hand, Smith cites a study carried out in Japan (for example, attendance at the *juku* or cram schools) which showed time spent in coaching resulted in more opportunities to learn and higher scores in solving mathematical problems. On the other hand, in two Singapore research studies cited by Smith, it would appear that there was little statistically significant relationship between the amount of coaching or private tuition (represented by the number of hours spent) and achievement – in one case achievement in English language. In terms of research methods, researchers in the West have found it difficult to isolate the effects of homework and coaching from the many other variables that influence achievement, such as students' ability and prior knowledge. In the Asia-Pacific examples, Smith explains that attempting to explore the policy implications of homework and coaching can be problematic because there is a dearth of well-designed studies on the effects of homework and coaching on achievement.

Galton, in his article, writes on time and schooling (see *Time: Allocated, Institutional and Task Oriented*). The role of time in school learning has been a topic of great interest. The most well-known study carried out in the West, in which time was the key variable, was the Beginning Teacher Evaluation Study (BTES) (Fisher et al., 1978). In that study, time was classified under three categories: 'allocated time', 'engaged time' and 'academic learning time'. As most readers would realize, teachers in Asia-Pacific classrooms are certainly not tutors dealing with students on an individual basis. They are teachers of large classes, ranging from 40 to 70 students in a class, with very little time available, if there is any at all, to deal with individuals.

Galton has found time allocation in many Asia-Pacific countries a special problem because of the use of the double-shift system of schooling in which different pupils attend the same school in the morning and afternoon. In such a system, school facilities are fully used (i.e. Galton's institutional time, following his categorization, is very much extended) there are many implications for allocated and engaged time when double-session schools are compared with single session schools. In double-session schools, for example, in terms of engaged time, the chaos each day created by the transition from morning to the afternoon session can affect learning in the last hour of the morning session, while in hot climates, teachers and students become tired very easily and so teaching and learning in the afternoon session would inevitably suffer. As regards Galton's allocated time, in some areas or countries the school day is shortened to accommodate the double-shift system. However, the double-shift system is not necessarily a poor option. Bray (2000, p. 41) cites a 1972 study in Malaysia that shows that the achievement scores of English-medium students in secondary schools, which used English as the medium of instruction in those days, were as good as those obtained from single-session Malay-medium schools, in which Malay was the medium of instruction for most subjects.

Across both systems of schooling, double or single shift, time allocation to different activities in classrooms varies across some of the countries in the Asia-Pacific region. For example, on average revision occupies 13 per cent of lesson time in Singapore as against 12 per cent in Hong Kong and Taiwan, while it is 6 per cent in South Korea and Japan. Generally, time spent on lecturing and demonstrating is higher in Asian classrooms; the proportion ranges from 28 per cent in Singapore to 39 per cent in Taiwan. The greater use of the lecturing method in teaching is often attributed to the relatively large size of classes in the Asia-Pacific region.

In the last ten years in the United States and New Zealand, there has been a renewed interest in the question of class size for schools. To some extent, these different studies come to different conclusions about the relationship between class size and classroom processes as explained in Blatchford and Catchpole's article (see *Class Size and Classroom Processes*). Blatchford and Catchpole attempt to clarify classroom processes connected to differences in class size. Their conclusion is that while there has not been much research on the relationship between class size and classroom processes, the effects of class size on classroom processes are likely to be far from straightforward because other factors are involved and also the effects are likely to be multiple rather than singular. They have argued that class size is only a contextual factor that could influence teachers and students in a number of ways. It is not necessarily a case of merely reducing class sizes, if that were possible at all in the Asia-Pacific region because of the high costs, but there must be ways of making the most of opportunities afforded by relatively smaller classes.

The nature of assessment as a way of monitoring student learning is an increasingly important topic in education in the Asia-Pacific region when, according to Masters in his article (see *Monitoring of Student Learning*), most countries in the region recognize the need to monitor systematically levels of student learning. Masters' article outlines considerations in designing and implementing a program for monitoring student learning with reference to examples of initiatives already undertaken in several Asia-Pacific countries to collect relevant, reliable and timely information for good decision making in education.

3. HIGHER EDUCATION AND TEACHER EDUCATION

The second grouping of articles examines research in the Asia-Pacific region related to higher education and, in particular, the role of teacher preparation. It is issues of teacher preparation, the quality of teachers being produced in national education systems, how adequately their professionalism is recognised and rewarded that helps to link this section with the section on teachers and teaching.

Tilak, in his article, takes issue with policy analysts and planners who have argued that it is investment in elementary education rather than higher education that promotes economic growth and development. He notes that research on internal rates of return and the fact that, in many developing countries access to elementary education is still limited, as contributing to the argument that provision for higher education which necessarily is more demanding on limited resources is a misallocation of resources if economic growth is the policy goal; the phenomenon of graduate unemployment in South Asia in the 1960s and 1970s was also a contributing factor. Tilak points rightly to the fact that sectors for example, primary, secondary, tertiary are interrelated and that it is not possible to have good quality primary and secondary education without higher education. Economic development also requires a range of knowledge and skills in the workforce and neglecting higher education is thus poor policy with serious consequences (see *Higher Education and Development*).

Varghese looks at one aspect of the consequences arising from scepticism about the value of higher education, that of a progressive withdrawal of funding for higher education in developing countries (see *Financing Higher Education in the Asia-Pacific Region*). He notes that there is a progressive shift from single-source funding to reliance on diversified sources and the increasing role of the private sector in funding and managing universities. In some countries universities have been corporatized while in others there has been increased outsourcing of university operations, increases in student fees and a replacement of subsidies with loan schemes. Increasing globalisation trends and enhanced technological capability has led to higher education becoming even more international, thus creating strains on national regulatory mechanisms.

Meek's paper looks more closely at issues related to student selection into higher education institutions (see *Selection for Higher Education in the Asia-Pacific Region*). Meek's analysis centres on the socio-political context in which selection takes place with particular reference to access and equity. Given the general press politically and socially, for greater access, and the positive role that a better educated work force can play in fostering economic growth, the World Bank has nevertheless cautioned that flexibility at points of entry must be matched with measures to ensure quality at point of exit. Additionally, there has also occurred a greater diversification of institutional types in higher education thus making more complex issues of access and selection. Meek notes that in the more developed nations like Japan, Australia and New Zealand it is participation in tertiary education that will provide access to rewarding careers. In both developed and developing countries the pressure for greater access is leading to the emergence of private universities, in turn leading to charges of commercialisation of a public good and elitism.

In turn, Dymock and Brennan focus on one aspect of higher education, which is the provision of adult or continuing education in several universities in the Asia-Pacific region (see *Adult Education in Universities in the Asia-Pacific Region*). In particular, their article draws on four case studies based in New Zealand,

Japan, the South Pacific, and Australia. Although most of the courses or educational activities for adults started in these universities by being primarily not for credit, the authors find that increasingly accreditation towards a formal university qualification is possible. Under the rubric now of 'lifelong learning', the authors find that university continuing education programs, whether for credit or non-credit courses, for adults in the Asia-Pacific region are active, varied and expanding. However, in a concluding remark, Dymock and Brennan note that university continuing education in this region does not have a substantive research tradition.

Three articles, by Kennedy, Sim Wong Kooi and Chen Ai Yen and her colleagues look at research and issues related to teacher preparation, demand and supply for teachers and teaching as both occupation and profession. Sim's focus is on teacher education research not teacher education as training. Sim develops a typology for classifying and scrutinising teacher education research (see *Research into Teacher Education*). He cites research by Turney and Wright (1990) that concluded that teacher educators (in universities) are in a double bind, "criticised by their students as being too theoretical and out of touch with classroom realities and on the other hand held in low esteem by their university colleagues by having an inadequate disciplinary and theoretical base and a low commitment to pure knowledge". With regard to the potential of the new communications technology to overcome hinderances to quality, Sim cites Birch and Maclean's (1998) study that concluded that many developing countries still do not have ready access to basic information technologies such as radio and telephones and that within poor countries there is uneven access to technology with persistent gaps between the rich and the poor.

Ai Yen and her colleagues' article links issues of teacher recruitment to the concerns of governments to improve the quality and performance of schooling in their countries (see *The Recruitment and Preparation of Teachers*). The advent of the knowledge based economy has created a demand for school learners who are proficient in the new literacies, notably information and communication technology (ICT), who are creative, who show initiative and a capacity to learn and to solve problems. This in turn implies that teachers ought themselves to possess these qualities and to role model appropriate skills and behaviours to their pupils. They note the lack of quality recruits into the teaching force, a problem accentuated by the relative youthfulness of the population and the increasing demands placed on schooling. They note the wide diversity in the region, that while all Japanese teachers are trained in higher education institutions this is not the case with Indonesia. They cite innovative teacher preparation efforts in Australia and New Zealand to enable teachers to be more reflective and critical of their practice but note that lack of resources and expanding enrolments are limits to quality of preparation in South Asian countries.

Kennedy's article also alludes to the wide differences in conditions for teaching and in the treatment and regard of teachers in the Asia-Pacific countries (see *Teaching as an Occupation and Learning Profession*). There is wide variation in teacher salaries, incentives, and success, in persuading bright students to join teaching and in conditions of work. He cites a ILO/UNESCO (2000) report that points out that while expectations on teacher performance are high it is out of proportion to the rewards available. Despite progress made, countries like Sri Lanka, Maldives and Nepal have to rely on unqualified teachers. However, there are positive indicators as well. In the Philippines and Singapore teachers have received salary boosts and countries like Thailand and India are taking steps to develop quality assurance mechanisms to ensure that professional standards remain high.

4. CONCLUSION

In this overview we have drawn attention to the key issues and concerns identified by our contributors. The contributions themselves have ranged from higher education, teacher education research, student selection to higher education to instructional issues such as tutoring, class size and instructional time. The articles on teacher education, teacher self evaluation and teachers' work lives provide the link between the two subsections.

It is necessary to acknowledge that the intended wide coverage of the countries has not been realised as much as we would have wished. It has not been easy to access available research in some countries and in other countries the research, if it has been published, is available only in national languages. In other cases the quality of research has been suspect or dated.

Notwithstanding the above limitations some valuable findings are noted in the studies, some of which have significant policy implications. Smith notes, for instance, that there appears to be little statistically significant relationship between the amount of coaching and achievement. Given the burden that coaching imposes on many families in East Asia this issue is worth studying more intensively. A finding reported by Galton is that time allocation to different activities in classrooms varies considerably and that the greater use of lecturing or teacher dominated instruction is probably related to the relatively large class sizes in the Asia-Pacific region. It is necessary to ask how such differentiation is related to achievement and the relationship it bears to the status of some activities. Sim's paper contains the salutary reminder that, while some countries with enviable high standards of student achievement like Singapore are investing highly in ICT, too many countries in the Asia-Pacific region do not have even basic information technology infrastructure. Under these circumstances the learning gap is bound to grow wider.

It is to be hoped that these articles will provide a rich source of data for policy-makers and inspire younger researcher to probe deeper into the issues.

REFERENCES

Birch, I., & Maclean, R. (1998). Information and communication technologies for education and teacher development in the Asia-Pacific region: Issues and challenges. *Asia-Pacific Journal of Teacher Education and Development, 1*(2), 41752.

Bray, M. (2000). Education in Asia: Financing higher education – Patterns, trends and options. *Prospects, 30*, 331–347.

Fisher, C. et al. (1978). Teaching behaviors, academic learning time and student achievement. Beginning Teacher Evaluation Study (Phase IIIB, final report).

ILO/UNESCO (2000). *Report of the Committee of Experts on the Application of the Recommendation on the Status of Teachers*, CEART/17/2000/10.

Reynold, D., & Farrell, S. (1996). *Worlds Apart? A Review of International Studies of Educational Achievement Involving England*. A Review for the Office for Standards in Education (OFSTED). London: HMSO.

Tay-Koay, S. L. (1997). Students' reports of cognitive processes and levels of understanding. In J. Tan, S. Gopinathan, & W. K. Ho, *Education in Singapore*. Singapore: Prentice-Hall.

Turney, C., & Wright, R. (1990). *Where the Buck Stops*. Sydney: Southwood Press.

51

Class Size and Classroom Processes

PETER BLATCHFORD
Institute of Education, University of London, United Kingdom

GEMMA CATCHPOLE*
Institute of Education, University of London, United Kingdom

1. INTRODUCTION

In recent years there has been much debate about the size of classes in schools. The commonly held view of many teachers and parents, supported by some experimental research in the United States, is that children educated in small classes will academically outperform those taught in large classes. A contradictory picture is provided by results from international tests. These would seem to indicate that children from Asia-Pacific countries such as Taiwan, Japan, and Singapore which generally have larger classes, are better at science and mathematics than those from countries which have smaller class sizes such as the United States. Despite this, there have recently been moves by countries in the Asia-Pacific region to reduce class sizes. In this chapter we argue that further progress in this area rests largely on clarification of classroom processes connected to class size differences. The vast majority of research has been carried out in the United States and Europe but we also review research from other countries. We highlight cultural differences between countries, including those in the Asia-Pacific region, both in their teaching practices and views on education. We examine issues that remain unanswered and identify areas for educational research.

2. CLASS SIZE AND EDUCATIONAL ATTAINMENT

Many teachers and parents believe that small class sizes will allow a better quality of teaching and more individual attention to children, who will consequently achieve more. The STAR project in Tennessee in the United States has

---

* The authors would like to thank Judy Wright for information on research on class size in China.

been influential. Although findings are still contentious (see Goldstein & Blatchford, 1998; Grissmer, 1999; Hanushek, 1999; Prais, 1996), there is agreement that this is an impressive large scale study that provides evidence that smaller classes, at least below 20, have positive effects on pupil academic performance, and are most pronounced if introduced with the youngest children in school (e.g., Finn & Achilles, 1999; Nye, Hedges, & Konstantopoulos, 2000). In the United States, President Clinton pledged US$1.2 billion of the 1999 fiscal budget to reduce classes with a further US$1.3 billion awarded in the 2000 fiscal year. Class size reductions have been implemented by a number of states, for example, California, which has made class size reduction mandatory. This has been followed by much debate in other countries and also initiatives, for example, in the Netherlands, and Asia-Pacific countries as diverse as New Zealand and China. In China, the *Xinmin Evening News* (December 8, 1999) reported that there had been a reduction in class sizes following the Shanghai Education Commission call for a reduction in 1997. The Shanghai Education Commission was also reported to be planning to establish 100 small class experimental schools in 2000 (*Liberation Daily*, February 13, 2000). In Taiwan too, an organisation called the '410 Education Reform League' have called for smaller classes. Recently in the United Kingdom the Labour Government legislated for a maximum of 30 children per class at KS1 (5–7 years), and extra funding for teaching assistants in classrooms.

However, there is still considerable disagreement about the cost effectiveness of class size reductions, with some arguing class size reduction should be a main Government priority and others arguing that the academic gains are modest at best and funds would be better spent on other initiatives such as teacher training.

There are a number of reasons why results on connections between class size and educational achievement are difficult to interpret, and these difficulties mount when comparing results across countries with very different education systems. Factors such as the popularity of schools (which may result in larger classes but of more committed students and parents), special needs classes (where classes may be smaller but likely to have lower achievements), will affect the connection. In Singapore and China, elite classes tend to be larger than normal while in rural areas class sizes are smaller. Another factor that has contributed to difficulties in comparing studies concerns how class size is measured. As described in Blatchford, Goldstein and Mortimore (1998), defining class size may appear straightforward but there are actually difficulties, for example because the number of children in a class at a given time may be different to the number on a register. Pupil teacher ratios and class size are often used to be synonymous but they can be very different, for example because the number of teachers includes all teaching staff whether actually teaching in a classroom. Another complicating factor will be the physical size of classrooms. Physical limitations of the classroom such as not being able to move furniture or have pupils move around for group work, if this is desired, will be important, as well as physical problems encountered by the teacher, for example having to raise her voice, use of microphones, overhead projectors and sharing books. In

Thailand, many Thai English teachers are concerned by the physical constraints imposed by large numbers in their classrooms (Hayes, 1997, p. 77), not surprising given that the average size of classes in this study were between 45 and 55 people. Despite the fact that on paper some schools in China could reduce class sizes because of a low teacher-pupil ratio, the physical conditions in schools may not provide the extra room required (Jin & Martin, 1998, p. 127).

3. TEACHERS' VIEWS ABOUT CLASS SIZE

The effects of class size on student achievement will also be affected by the view that teachers have about the importance of class size. In the United Kingdom, Bennett's (1996) account of a survey of teachers' and head teachers' views shows that practitioners believe large class sizes affect teaching and learning, and they were particularly aware that larger classes could have an adverse effect on the amount of teacher attention. Research carried out in China (Din, 1998, p. 4; Din, 1998, p. 7; Din, 1999, p. 6) on teachers' attitudes towards class size indicated that both teachers from urban and rural areas preferred teaching small classes to large classes (defined as a class with more than 50 pupils). But in comparison to Western countries, classes in China are still large and it would seem unlikely that many of the teachers had experienced teaching small classes on a regular basis. Moreover, while it was found that teachers perceived small classes as beneficial, they did not believe they were necessary for academic achievement. Rather, the teachers felt that small classes facilitated more student-teacher interactions, better classroom management and reduced teacher workload. Many teachers do not see the point of trying to reduce class sizes. They believe that it is more important to present knowledge in a manner suitable for learning (Jin & Martin, 1998, p. 127).

Teachers in different countries may have a different view about what constitutes a large or small class. The STAR project compared class sizes quite out of the normal range for many countries, even by United Kingdom standards: it compared small with very small classes. In the United Kingdom classes over 30 are often considered large and those below 20 small (Blatchford & Mortimore, 1994). However, one study of English teachers in China found that most agreed a class of 50 to 60 pupils was large while the number of students in the larger classes ranged from 60 to 150 (Xu, 2001, p. 128).

4. CLASS SIZE AND CLASSROOM PROCESSES

There is some agreement among researchers in this field that the most important issue related to the effects of class size differences is not now whether they affect pupil achievement but what classroom processes are related to class size and therefore mediate effects of class size differences (Anderson, 2000; Grissmer, 1999). Another way to express this is to say that class size, that is, the number of children in a classroom, does not affect achievement directly; rather its influence is indirect and must be mediated through teachers' and pupils' behaviour. The focus of this chapter is to review what is known about these mediating processes.

At the outset it is necessary to say that knowledge about mediating classroom processes is relatively limited (Anderson, 2000; Grissmer, 1999). The STAR project, like many others, was predominantly interested in the relationships between class size and academic achievement, and has little to say about classroom processes that might explain effects found. Finn and Achilles, two of the STAR research team, acknowledge this when they argue: "Despite dozens of earlier studies, the classroom processes that distinguish small from large classes have proven elusive." (Finn & Achilles, 1999, p. 102). In a similar vein, Grissmer (1999) has concluded that there is a lack of coherent theories by which to guide and interpret empirical work on class size effects, and with which to make new predictions. The situation in countries other than the United States is much worse, in the sense that there has been little research on classroom processes connected to class size differences. Therefore, accounts of classroom processes that might explain why smaller classes differ from large classes are urgently needed.

5. CLASS SIZE AS A CLASSROOM CONTEXTUAL INFLUENCE

Main traditions of research on classroom processes including teaching effectiveness and pupil learning behaviour have in common a lack of interest in classroom contextual influences on teaching. There is an underlying assumption, in many studies, of a direct model, with teaching directly affecting pupils' achievements and learning. But teachers do not meet pupils out of context, and class size can be seen as one contextual influence on classroom life, which plays a part in the nature of the interactions between teachers and pupils. The conceptual roots of this view can be found in Bronfenbrenner (1979) and the ecological psychology approach of Barker (1968) and Kounin and Gump (1974). The basic idea is that the classroom context has distinctive forces or signals, different to other contexts, which pull events and participants along with them (Kounin & Gump, 1974). Here it is argued that different class sizes may well involve different forces or signals that influence both teachers and pupils.

6. CLASS SIZE AND WITHIN CLASS GROUPINGS

In line with this contextual approach there are also in some countries, and stages of education, learning contexts nested *within* classrooms. A main within-class context in countries like Britain, the United States and The Netherlands is the organisation of the class into separate groups of children within which they work. It is likely that the classroom environment, for example, class size, and within-class groups are connected, such as the number and size of groups. Blatchford et al. (2001) found that one consequence of larger classes is the likelihood of larger, less educationally effective groups. Lou, Abrami, Spence, Poulsen, Chambers and D'Apllonia (1996) also found, on the basis of their meta-analysis of within-class grouping studies, that smaller group sizes were optimal for students' learning; larger groups of six to ten members were less effective.

The effects of within class contexts will clearly depend on approaches to instruction and the curriculum in different countries. In the United Kingdom the issue of within class groups arises because teachers do not believe that teaching to larger groups or the whole class is appropriate with young children. They feel this may be possible in some curriculum areas, and for some activities, but will inevitably be of limited relevance to primary aged children, especially the youngest children. In Singapore the use of co-operative learning in the class has been promoted by educational departments since 1985. However, whole class teaching is the norm for most lessons followed by individual work after the class instruction. Ng, Chew, Lee and D'Rozario (1997) believe this is in response to large classes as well as tight curriculum time. The use of co-operative learning varies between subjects with the majority of group work being observed in science practical work and for certain English lessons, while pupils work individually in mathematics lessons. The authors have suggested that the prominence of individual learning in the core subjects such as Mathematics and English is a reflection of their concerns with monitoring and testing in these core examinable subjects. Indeed, the authors go so far as to suggest that due to parental demands for good examination results, teachers will be reluctant to abandon strategies that have served them well.

In China whole class teaching is the norm. This can be put into context when it is considered that teachers believe their pupils, apart from a few exceptions, are at the same level, and there is therefore no need for mixed ability groups in the classroom. Pairwork is used, although in a different manner to Western countries. It is nearly always prepared in advance and is performed to the teacher and class (Jin & Martin, 1998, p. 127). In Taiwan it has been proposed that whole-class teaching methods are possible because of the high levels of student motivation and attention. This is not always the case in other countries. Also, there is the expectation that all children in the class must reach the given standards and therefore there is no allowance for differentiation, unlike primary schools in other countries (Vulliamy, 1998, p. 134).

7. CLASS SIZE AND TEACHING

It might be expected that one set of classroom processes affected by class size would be aspects of teaching. The judgement and experience of many practising teachers is that, other things being equal, teaching is likely to be easier and more effective in smaller classes. Pate-Bain, Achilles, Boyd-Zaharias and McKenna (1992) report, on the basis of teacher interviews conducted at the end of each school year in the STAR research:

> A common benefit cited by teachers in small and regular plus aide classes

was that they were better able to individualize instruction. These teachers reported increased monitoring of student behaviour and learning, opportunities for more immediate and more individualized re-teaching, more enrichment, more frequent interactions with each child, a better match between each child's ability and the instructional opportunities provided, a more detailed knowledge of each child's needs as a learner, and more time to meet individual learners' needs using a variety of instructional approaches. (Pate-Bain et al., 1992, p. 254)

Teachers' reports are supported by the meta-analysis conducted by Glass, Cahen, Smith and Filby (1982) who found that smaller classes resulted in greater teacher knowledge of pupils, frequency of one-to-one contacts between teachers and pupils, variety of activities, adaptation of teaching to individual pupils, and opportunities to talk to parents (compare Cooper, 1989). Other studies report more individual teaching and attention (Harder, 1990; Pate-Bain et al., 1992; Turner, 1990), and more feedback (Pate-Bain et al., 1992; Cooper, 1989). However, in direct contrast to teacher views, Shapson et al. (1980), in a widely cited study, found no statistically significant differences between class sizes for most teacher activities. Worryingly, they found that these observation results were at odds with teachers' own views about the benefits of small classes.

There have been several more recent studies in the United States that have examined the effects of class size on teaching. Molnar et al. (1999) report results from the Wisconsin Student Achievement Guarantee in Education (SAGE) project; a five-year K-Grade 3 project begun in the 1996–7 school year. Though not a study of class size reduction as such, the program required participating schools to implement four interventions, one of which involved pupil teacher ratio reductions to 15 students per teacher. Teachers were asked to rank items in terms of the extent to which they were affected by reduced class size. The teacher behaviours that received the highest rankings were: (a) more individualised instruction; (b) more teaching time, (c) more discussion, sharing and answering, (d) more hands-on activities, and (e) more content coverage. The most important classroom processes, affected by reduced class size, according to Molnar et al. (1999) is therefore individualization. They put forward a tentative model of teaching in small classes which includes three elements: better knowledge of students, more instructional time, and teacher satisfaction, and these in turn lead to more individualized instruction.

In another recent study, Betts and Shkolnik (1999) present a sophisticated analysis, using an economic production function framework, to model relationships between class size and teacher time allocation. They conducted a secondary analysis of a national survey of students in middle and high schools in the United States. Results show some evidence that teachers substitute group instruction for individual instruction as class size increases, and devote less time to group instruction and more to individual instruction in smaller classes. There was a small effect on percentage overall instructional time. They argue that teachers would make better use of small classes if they did not reduce group instruction, though they agree that further research is needed to identify exactly what changes in teaching style might be most effective.

Rice (1999) also conducted a secondary analysis of teacher survey data. Data came from a national panel survey of students transferring to high school and appear to come from the 1990 follow up (again rather dated). Findings showed that in mathematics as class size increased less time was spent on small groups and individuals, innovative instructional practices, and whole group discussions, though increases in class sizes beyond 20 had little effect. There were no relationships between class size and instructional time allocation measures in science.

Both these last studies raise interesting questions about the effect of class size differences on teaching and non-teaching (e.g., procedural and managerial) time overall, and also on how it is shared between individuals, groups and the whole class. But the studies are limited in that they rely on a secondary analysis of rather general teacher retrospective estimates of time spent, and basic distinctions, for example, between individual, group and class contexts, which might be expected to be differently affected by class size, are not always clear. Another problem with the studies is the age of students involved. It has been found that greatest effects are reported with younger children and especially children immediately after entry to school, and so results involving much older children may underestimate effects of class size differences and involve different processes, than with younger children.

A quite different approach to teaching, with roots more in cognitive psychology, has drawn on Vygotskian thought, for example, on the Zone of Proximal Development (ZPD), and scaffolding to inform effective teaching and tutoring (see Tharp & Gallimore, 1991; Meadows, 1996; Wood & Wood, 1996; Wood, 1998). The underlying learning context in this tradition of thought is the one-to-one tutoring relationship. From this point of view the school classroom seems inherently disadvantaged as a site able to provide a contingent learning environment, and a classroom with a large number of young children is particularly problematic. Some studies have examined the reality of teacher scaffolding and contingent teaching in the context of everyday life in classrooms (Bliss, Askew, & Macrae, 1996), but connections with numbers of children in the class have not been worked through conceptually or empirically.

Blatchford et al. (2002) using a multi-method approach found consistent evidence that children in small classes were more likely to interact with their teachers, there was more teaching on a one-to-one basis, more times when children were the focus of a teacher's attention, more teaching overall, and more times when children were attending to the teacher and actively involved in interactions with them (i.e., responding or initiating rather than just attending). Complementary qualitative analyses of end of year teacher questionnaires and case studies, showed that class size affected (a) the amount of individual attention, (b) the immediacy and responsiveness of teacher response to children, (c) the sustained and purposeful nature of interaction between teachers and children, (d) the depth of a teacher's knowledge of children in her class, and (e) sensitivity to individual children's particular needs. Overall, Blatchford et al. (2002) conclude that in smaller classes there is more likelihood of what they call *'Teacher support for learning'*. One aspect of this is more likelihood of individualised teaching in small classes. In general, these results appear consistent with other studies reviewed earlier, although it is necessary to be clear about the nature of individualisation affected by small classes compared to large. Although there is more one-to-one teaching in small classes, the greater incidence of times when the child is the focus of attention indicates that children receive more attention in group and whole class situations as well. This needs to be born in mind when considering worries that smaller classes might encourage a reliance on individual teaching.

Again there are complications when comparing different countries. The relationship between class size and teaching will vary according to the way teachers are deployed in schools. In primary classrooms in the United States and the United Kingdom the class teacher takes the pupils for most, in not all, lessons. This is quite different to countries such as China, for example, where the primary school teacher may teach only one subject.

Blatchford et al. (2002) argue that although small classes allow teachers to be effective and large classes will present inevitable difficulties and hard choices, there is no immutable link between class size and teaching. Much will depend on how teachers adapt to class size differences. This in turn will be affected by views on curriculum coverage, and the demands of assessment arrangements. One study found that there were no differences in the teaching strategies employed by schools in rural and suburban areas of Queensland, Australia (Staunton, 1995, p. 131). This was somewhat surprising given that in the rural areas, class sizes rarely exceeded 10 students while classes in the suburban areas had, on average, between 25 to 28 students. The instructional approach employed was to the whole of the class, teacher centred and didactic. This persisted despite the teachers' stated preferences to be more accommodating in their instructional practices. It was reported that the teachers found it difficult to employ flexibility in their teaching methods due to the demands of the assessment program. In Singapore, the pressures of examination results mean that teachers appear reluctant to alter their teaching strategies. In Singapore, whole class teaching followed by individual work is perfectly suited to the requirements of the National Curriculum in Singapore (Ng et al., 1997, p. 126). In Taiwan, competition remains so intense that there is no time for diversion from the prescribed curriculum.

7.1. *Affective Considerations*

There is another effect of class size differences which illustrates the complexities involved. Effective teaching is possible in large classes, but this may be at some cost to teachers, for examples, in terms of eating away at spaces like breaks in the day, marking at weekends, but also in terms of the teacher's professional satisfaction and enthusiasm. Moriarty, Edmonds, Blatchford and Martin (2001) found that teachers' experiences of class sizes are connected to their emotional involvement in the job of teaching. It was very clear that some teachers with large classes considered that they could not provide the quality of education they felt was important for young children, and this upset them. This gap between a vision of what is appropriate for young children and the realities of teaching a large class may be particularly wide in the case of teachers of the youngest children in school.

8. CLASS SIZE AND PEER ATTENTIVENESS AND OFF-TASK BEHAVIOUR

Regardless of any connection with class size, studies of classroom processes related to achievement support the view that a key aspect of educational success is attentiveness, or active learning time, time on task or some equivalent term (e.g., Creemers, 1994). There is a good deal of evidence that pupil inattentiveness is a major variable having negative effects on pupils' achievement (Rowe, 1995).

Common sense and logic suggest that with more children in the class there will be more potential for distraction, and more possibility of being off task. Conversely in small classes there will be more opportunities to engage children and keep them on task. This might be expected to be particularly relevant in the case of the youngest children in school who are less likely to have developed the capacity for independent work.

Blatchford and Mortimore (1994) and Cooper (1989) in their reviews found several studies which indicated that pupils in smaller classes attend more and spend more time on task, participate more, and are more absorbed in what they are doing. These studies suggest that pupil attention is greater in smaller classes because pupils are not lost in the crowd and have more opportunities for participating, and that the effect of class size on attentiveness is most pronounced in the case of low attainers, because teachers can bring them out more.

Finn and Achilles (1999) have expressed the connection between small classes and pupil attention or engagement in class perhaps most clearly. They argue that:

> The evidence indicates that the key to the benefits of small classes is increased student engagement in learning. In a small class, every student is in the firing line. It is difficult or impossible to withdraw from teaching-learning interactions in a small-class setting. Social psychologists have long recognized the negative relationship between group size and participation of individuals – the principle underlying concepts such as 'social loafing' and 'diffusion of responsibility' ... When class sizes are reduced, the pressure is increased for each student to participate in learning, and every student becomes more salient to the teacher. As a result, there is more instructional contact, and student learning behaviors are improved. (Finn & Achilles, 1999, p. 103)

Blatchford (in press) found on the basis of systematic observations that children in large classes were less likely to attend to the teacher and to be off task in contacts with her, more likely to be actively off task with other children, and more likely to be off task when on their own, especially in the passive form of being disengaged from allocated work.

There does not appear to be much research from Asia-Pacific countries on connections between class size and attentiveness, though there is anecdotal evidence that children in large classes, especially those at the back of the classroom, lose attention. While behaviour and discipline does not really feature in the literature on the Asian countries, noise levels would appear to be a problem, and one of the main problems of large classes might be expected to be the noise produced. This is a particular problem for those countries which have open classrooms such as Singapore. This might in turn be expected to have an impact on student attention in class, though this will not necessarily follow.

9. CLASS SIZE AND PEER RELATIONS IN CLASS

There is a lot of evidence that children's early social behaviour toward peers is an important predictor of later social and personal adjustment (Parker & Asher, 1987). The effects of children's aggressive, withdrawn and pro-social behaviours toward peers have received most empirical support. There is also a large literature on the value of collaborative or cooperative group work in classrooms (see review in Galton, 1990), and naturalistic studies of children's interactions in classrooms, which will include those with peers (e.g., Galton, Simon, & Croll, 1980). However, as in the case of teaching and on pupil on task behaviour, there is little research on the effects of contextual classroom factors like class size on peer relations and behaviour. Research on children at nursery level indicates that less favourable staff pupil ratios can lead to more negative relations between children, including more aggression, annoying and teasing. This research has also found that increasing the numbers of adults can lead to more talking between adults rather than to pupils. But other research with older pupils seems less clear, and Shapson et al. (1980) found no difference in conflicts between pupils.

As with teaching, therefore, associations between peer relations and contextual factors like size of class are not clear. It might be expected that in large classes children will be more distracted and that this would include more off-task behaviour with their peers. It might also be expected that there would be more negative and aggressive behaviours between children in larger classes. Blatchford et al. (in press) found that class size differences affected the balance of interactions between pupils and teachers and pupils and other pupils. In large classes children spend more time with each other, working and socialising. Intriguingly, there were some signs that relationships between children, in terms of teacher ratings of asocial, aggressive and social exclusion behaviours were *worse* in smallest classes under 20 children. Smaller classes may be better academically but not necessarily socially.

There does not appear to be much research from Asia-Pacific countries relevant to the connection between class size and peer relations. In Singapore teachers do not believe in the benefits of children working with their peers; expressing the notion that learning is a passive process and a cognitive activity taking place in the head and not through talk (Ng et al., 1997, p. 126). One study of large English classes in China found that there were no significant differences in students' preference for learning English in large or small classes (Xu, 2001, p. 128). The author refers to cultural differences concluding that "Chinese students may not ... feel learning in large classes uncomfortable because large classes seem to suit their cultural characteristics more than small classes do". The same study also notes reports of the benefits of competition and the increased opportunities to make friends.

10. CONCLUSIONS

It seems clear that the effects of class size on classroom processes are far from straightforward because they will be affected by a number of factors, such as views on differentiation, the rigidity of the curriculum, deployment and views of teachers, and so on. It also seems clear that the effects will be multiple not singular, and it follows that multiple theoretical or conceptual frameworks are needed to account for these effects and to judge their implications, for example, connected to teaching, attentiveness and social relations. Further, the different effects may have conflicting outcomes, for example, in the sense that smaller classes can lead to positive academic outcomes but problematic social effects. There may be other complications, for example, a teacher compensation effect which may serve to cushion the expected effects of larger classes.

Perhaps the most sophisticated model to date of classroom processes affected by class size is by Anderson (2000). To this model should be added the separate level of within class learning contexts such as groupings and peer relations within classrooms.

We have argued that, though classroom processes have tended to be viewed in terms of a direct model, where teachers' actions toward pupils are seen directly in relation to pupils' learning or attainments, we suggest class size be considered as one environmental contextual factor that will influence teachers and pupils in a number of ways. It is not, as some argue, a case of either supporting teacher training to improve teacher quality, or reducing class sizes. We need to consider both together, and ways of making the most of the opportunities of smaller classes. An important next step is therefore to consider how teachers should best *deal* with this classroom contextual feature. A teacher can deal with it effectively, as shown in case studies from the London Class Size Study (Blatchford et al., in press). We have documented examples of teachers in small classes doing a marvellous job – with observers coming away inspired by the quality of teaching and children's educational experiences. In these classrooms teachers were taking full advantage of the extra opportunities for individual, focused and sustained attention provided by small classes. The benefits of having fewer children will not flow in any natural way – indeed, the benefits resulting from more contact with children can create problems, e.g. in terms of more interruptions. Teachers have to work just as hard to manage learning effectively.

This suggests that initial teacher training and professional development courses could do more to consider how to make the most of the opportunities provided by smaller classes, for example, in terms of opportunities for sustained and responsive contacts. In Britain, Galton et al. (1996) suggest that there is not likely to be much preparation in initial teacher training concerning ways of adapting teaching to class size. Student teachers on teaching practice tend to graduate through teaching individual children, then small groups and then the whole class. When they get their own class they are left to adapt to it on their own. Galton and his colleagues suggest allowing student teachers opportunities to teach with smaller classes. For example, with half the class, while the teacher takes the other half in another location. This would help the student teacher gain experience of teaching the whole class, and getting experience of the kind of sustained and focused teaching Galton and many others recommend.

REFERENCES

Anderson, L. W. (2000). Why should reduced class size lead to increased student achievement? In M. C. Wang & J. D. Finn (Eds.), *How Small Classes Help Teachers do Their Best* (pp. 3–24). Philadelphia, PA: Temple University Center for Research in Human Development and Education.

Barker, R. (1968). *Ecological Psychology.* Stanford, CA: Stanford University Press.

Bennett, N. (1996). Class size in primary schools: Perceptions of head teachers, chairs of governors, teachers and parents. *British Educational Research Journal, 22*(1), 33–55.

Betts, J. R., & Shkolnik, J. L. (1999). The behavioural effects of variations in class size: The case of math teachers. *Educational Evaluation and Policy Analysis, 21*, 193–213.

Blatchford, P. et al. (in press). A systematic observational study of teachers' and pupils' behaviour in large and small classes.

Blatchford, P., Baines, D., Kutnick, P., & Martin, C. (2001). Classroom contexts: Connections between class size and within class grouping. *British Journal of Educational Psychology, 71*, 283–302.

Blatchford, P., Goldstein, H., & Mortimore, P. (1998). Research on class size effects: A critique of methods and a way forward. *International Journal of Educational Research, 29*, 691–710.

Blatchford, P., Moriarty, V., Edmonds, S., & Martin, C. (2002). Relationships between class size and teaching: A multi-method analysis of English infant schools. *American Educational Research Journal, 39*(1), 101–132.

Blatchford, P., & Mortimore, P. (1994). The issue of class size for young children in school: What can we learn from research? *Oxford Review of Education, 20*, 411–428.

Bliss, J., Askew, M., & Macrae, S. (1996). Effective teaching and learning: Scaffolding revisited. *Oxford Review of Education, 22*(1), 37–61.

Bronfenbrenner, U. (1979). *The Ecology of Human Development.* Cambridge, MA: Harvard University Press.

Cooper, H. M. (1989). Does reducing student-to-teacher ratios affect achievement? *Educational Psychologist, 24*, 79–98.

Creemers, B. (1994). *The Effective Classroom.* London: Cassell.

Din, F. S. (1998). The benefits of teaching small classes perceived by Chinese urban school teachers. Annual Meeting of the Eastern Education Research Association, Hilton Head, SC.

Din, F. S. (1999). The benefits of teaching small classes – the Chinese perspectives. Annual Meeting of the Eastern Education Research Association, Hilton Head, SC.

Finn, J. D., & Achilles, C. M. (1999). Tennessee's class size study: Findings, implications, misconceptions. *Educational Evaluation and Policy Analysis, 21*, 97–109.

Galton, M. (1990). Grouping and group-work. In C. Rogers & P. Kutnick (Eds.), *Social Psychology of the Primary School*. London: Routledge.

Galton, M., Hargreaves, L., & Pell, A. (1996). *Class Size, Teaching and Pupil Achievement*. Report for National Union of Teachers, Leicester University.

Galton, M., Simon, P., & Croll, P. (1980). *Progress and Performance in the Primary Classroom*. London: Routledge and Kegan Paul.

Goldstein, H., & Blatchford, P. (1998). Class size and educational achievement: A review of methodology with particular reference to study design. *British Educational Research Journal, 24*, 255–268.

Glass, G., Cahen, L., Smith, M. L., & Filby, N. (1982). *School Class Size*. Beverley Hills, CA: Sage.

Grissmer, D. (1999). Class size effects: Assessing the evidence, its policy implications, and future research agendas. *Educational Evaluation and Policy Analysis, 21*, 231–248.

Hanushek, E. A. (1999). Some findings from an independent investigation of the Tennessee STAR experiment and from other investigations of class size effects. *Educational Evaluation and Policy Analysis, 21*(2), 143–163.

Harder, H. (1990). A critical look at reduced class size. *Contemporary Education, 62*(1), 28–30.

Hayes, D. (1997). Helping teachers to cope with large classes. *ELT Journal, 51*, 106–116.

Jin, L., & Martin, C. (1998). Dimensions of dialogue: Large classes in China. *International Journal of Education, 29*, 739–761.

Kounin, J. S., & Gump, P. V. (1974). Signal systems of lesson settings and the task-related behaviour of pre-school children. *Journal of Educational Psychology, 66*(4), 554–562.

Lou, Y., Abrami, P. C., Spence, J. C., Poulsen, C., Chambers, B., & D'Apllonia, S. (1996). Within-class grouping: A meta-analysis. *Review of Educational Research, 66*(4), 423–458.

Meadows, S. (1996). *Parenting Behaviour and Children's Cognitive Development*. Hove, East Sussex: Psychology Press.

Molnar, A., Cmith, P., Zahorik, J., Palmer, A., Halbach, A., & Ehrle, K. (1999). Evaluating the SAGE program: A pilot program in targeted pupil-teacher reduction in Wisconsin. *Educational Evaluation and Policy Analysis, 21*(2), 165–177.

Moriarty, V., Edmonds, S., Blatchford, P., & Martin, C. (2001). Teaching young children: Perceived satisfaction and stress. *Educational Research, 43*(1), 33–46.

Ng, M., Chew, J., Lee, C. K-E., & D'Rozario, V. (1997). *A Survey of Classroom Practices in Singapore – Preliminary Findings*. BERA Annual Conference, York, UK.

Nye, B., Hedges, L. V., & Konstantopoulos, S. (2000). The effects of small classes on academic achievement: The results of the Tennessee class size experiment. *American Educational Research Journal, 37*(1), 123–151.

Parker, J. G., & Asher, S. R. (1987). Peer relations and later personal adjustment: Are low-accepted children at risk? *Psychological Bulletin, 102*(3), 357–389.

Pate-Bain, H., Achilles, C. M., Boyd-Zaharias, J., & McKenna, B. (1992). Class size makes a difference. *Phi Delta Kappan, 74*, 253–256.

Prais, S. J. (1996). Class size and learning: The Tennessee experiment – what follows? *Oxford Review of Education, 22*, 399–414.

Rice, J. K. (1999). The impact of class size on instructional strategies and the use of time in high school mathematics and science courses. *Educational Evaluation and Policy Analysis, 21*, 215–229.

Rowe, K. J. (1995). Factors affecting students' progress in reading: Key findings from a longitudinal study. *Literacy, Teaching and Learning, 1*(2), 57–110.

Shapson, S. M., Wright, E. N., Eason, G., & Fitzgerald, J. (1980). An experimental study of the effects of class size. *American Educational Research Journal, 17*, 144–152.

Staunton, M. (1995). Instructional flexibility in rural and suburban secondary schools in north and north west Queensland: A comparative analysis. *Education in Rural Australia, 5*, 9–23.

Tharp, R., & Gallimore, R. (1991). A theory of teaching as assisted performance. In P. Light, S. Sheldon & M. Woodhead (Eds.), *Learning to Think*. London: Routledge.

Turner, C. M. (1990). Prime time: A reflection. *Contemporary Education, 62*(1), 24–27.
Vulliamy, G. (1998). Primary classroom practice: Some other lessons from Taiwan. *Education, 3–13*(26), 44–49.
Wood, D. (1998). *How Children Think and Learn* (2nd ed.). Oxford: Blackwell.
Wood, D., & Wood, H. (1996). Vygotsky, tutoring and learning. *Oxford Review of Education, 22*(1), 5–16.
Xu, Z. (2001). *Problems and Strategies of Teaching English in Large Classes in the People's Republic of China*. 10th Annual Teaching Learning Forum. Perth: Curtin University of Technology.

52

Homework and Coaching

IAN DAVID SMITH
The University of Sydney, Australia

1. INTRODUCTION

Homework and coaching are recognised by parents and students in the Asia-Pacific region as important complements to classroom learning and teaching. The explosion of knowledge in the past century has resulted in an increasingly crowded curriculum which teachers find difficult to cover during school hours. Moreover, the phenomenon of globalisation has placed a premium on formal educational qualifications to enable skilled workers to enter the workforce and to be mobile in an ever-changing job market. One consequence of these global forces is that examination performance is critical to a student's life chances. While teachers in some countries are ambivalent about the need for homework and coaching, many parents are willing to make considerable sacrifices of their time, effort and finances to support their children's education by helping them with their homework and paying for coaching. Indeed, coaching is a huge, growing, and largely unregulated industry in most Asian countries (Bray, 1998).

2. DEFINITIONS OF TERMS

'Homework' and 'coaching' (called 'private tuition' in some Asian countries) are widely used terms by teachers, parents and students. They are both designed to complement teaching and learning in the regular classroom. In most cases they both occur outside the normal school hours. In some Asian countries teachers supplement their income by coaching their students before or after school. The existence of low salaries in these countries increases the pressure on teachers to supplement their incomes by coaching students. This practice is generally frowned upon by educators (Bray, 1999a), because essential teaching content may be withheld from the regular school lessons in order for it to be taught by the same teacher before or after school for extra payment. This practice disadvantages those students whose parents cannot afford to pay for coaching. In other

Asian countries, such as Japan and Singapore, teachers are well-paid and seldom provide private tuition to their own students.

Homework is defined here as the practice exercises given by the teacher for the student to complete after a topic has been taught in class, the preparatory assignments for a future lesson, and extension tasks which apply the concepts or skills learned in class to new activities. These three types of homework – 'practice exercises', 'preparatory assignments', and 'extension tasks' – are all designed to reinforce or complement curricular material that has been taught during normal school hours and are meant to be completed outside those hours. They provide students with the opportunity to exercise self-discipline over *when*, *where*, and *how* to complete their homework (Hong & Lee, 2000). Some forms of homework, however, offer little scope for students to decide how the homework is to be completed. Forced-choice worksheets are an example of teacher-directed homework exercises. Open-ended book reviews, essays and science laboratory write-ups are homework examples that allow a considerable scope for student initiative.

The term 'coaching', sometimes called 'private tuition', is defined as teaching that complements the instruction given by a teacher at school. It is private because the cost of the tuition is paid, usually by parents, to a tutor who works for profit. The content of coaching is usually the curriculum of academic subjects, especially mathematics and foreign languages, which are important examinable subjects in the Asia-Pacific region. The form of the coaching may be individual tutoring, instructing small groups of students, or even large tuition centres, such as some *juku* or cram schools in Japan.

3. THEORETICAL PERSPECTIVE

The theoretical perspective that is used in this article to interpret the research findings on homework and coaching is the social-cognitive theory of Bandura (1997). Bandura believes that, as they mature, students rely less on teachers to control their learning. They increasingly use peer and adult models, whom they observe, imitate, and then they transfer their newly learned skill to other contexts. In her book, *The Japanese Educational Experience*, White (1987) relates the example of a Tokyo *juku* teacher who inspires his students by his caring attitude towards them, his skill in motivating them to learn, and his knowledge of the examination subjects. She recounts how his former students often return to his small *juku* to inspire and help current students. His skill in preparing his students for the university entrance examinations motivates them to take control of their studies and regulate their own learning in order to achieve their goals in gaining entrance to a prestigious university.

As students proceed through the school system, they are expected to become self-disciplined, no longer relying on the teacher for every direction, but taking control of their own learning and academic studying. Homework and coaching are mediators between the classroom instruction and students' independent learning, giving them a structure to learn more efficiently and effectively. Both have the potential to guide the student from teacher-dependence to self-regulated learning. They are like the scaffolding (Vygotsky, 1978) surrounding a new building as it is being constructed. The scaffolding provides the building with essential support while it is being constructed and is progressively removed as the building becomes capable of supporting itself.

A self-regulatory model of academic studying has been developed by Zimmerman (1998), who believes that self-regulated learning is cognitive, personal, and influenced by the social context, such as the value placed on homework and coaching by significant others like parents and teachers. In his model of self-regulated learning, Pintrich (2000) explains how students rely on three types of self-regulatory processes: cognitive, metacognitive and resource management skills. They learn to use cognitive skills such as 'remembering' key facts, concepts and principles in studying for an important examination. Secondly, they use metacognitive skills like planning, monitoring and evaluating, to review how successfully they are studying. They 'plan' their approach to studying the academic subject so that they systematically revise the key ideas in each subject. They 'monitor' their progress as they are studying to ensure that all the academic subjects are revised in sufficient depth. Next, they 'evaluate' whether they have achieved their study goals and re-revise certain subjects or topics until they are confident that their examination performance will meet the standards they increasingly set for themselves. Finally, they 'manage resources', such as time, homework and coaching. They may draw up a time management plan to revise the academic subjects efficiently. They will consult their homework completed during the school year to ensure that they understand the main concepts and skills taught in each subject. They may seek coaching during the year to supplement their teachers' instruction in order to optimise their examination performance.

Some learning activities like homework and coaching have social functions, as well as solitary self-regulatory functions (Alexander, 1996). The homework may be connected to social inputs from the teacher, who provides scaffolding to support the student's learning through homework. Coaching also has a strong social aspect, because the coach's role includes motivating the student to make best use of the extra tuition. In the Asian context, the student's motivation comes from external sources, such as the desire to please the teacher or tutor and parents, as well as from intrinsic sources, such as the desire to perform as well as possible in the examination. Thus, the social context of homework and coaching is just as important as the student's solitary use of self-regulatory strategies in Asian societies.

4. RESEARCH ON HOMEWORK

There is general agreement in the research literature that homework is associated with higher student achievement. The cross-national studies of the International

Association for the Evaluation of Educational Achievement (IEA) were influential in improving educational practice by revealing the significance of, among other things, time spent on homework as a predictor of school achievement (Keeves, 1995). The IEA's Third International Mathematics and Science Study (TIMSS) surveyed 9- and 13-year old students in approximately 50 countries on five continents. Japanese, Korean and Singaporean students performed particularly well, not only in the tests of mathematics and science facts and concepts, but also in their application of science laboratory skills to practical problems (Beaton, 1996). These findings demonstrated that their knowledge was based, not on rote-learning, but on their understanding of the underlying concepts and principles. It was also found that the amount of time spent on homework was associated with higher mathematics and science achievement.

A well-conducted study by Stevenson, Stigler and Lee (1986) tested first and fifth grade students in Japan and the United States in mathematics, reading, and cognitive abilities. They constructed their own mathematics achievement tests based on a careful analysis of the mathematics curricula at both grade levels in both countries. They also chose two ethnically homogeneous cities, Sendai and Minneapolis, and obtained representative samples of 240 first and fifth grade students in both countries. The researchers found that Japanese children scored significantly higher than American children at both grade levels. While there was some overlap in the average class performance in the two countries at the first grade level, in fifth grade the average score "of the American classroom with the *highest* average level of performance lies below that of the *worst* performing fifth-grade classroom of Japanese children" (Stevenson, Stigler, & Lee, 1986, p. 206). They concluded that these cross-national differences were not caused solely by differences in the quality of teacher instruction, because the mathematics achievement differences appeared as early as first grade. One of the variables they believed accounted for these achievement differences was the amount of homework done in Japanese homes as compared with American homes. Mothers were asked to estimate the time typically spent by her child each weekday and during each day of the weekend. The authors of this important study concluded that the combined effects of extra homework, parental involvement, and time spent on mathematics instruction were responsible for the growing achievement gap between students in the two countries from first to fifth grade.

It is generally agreed that homework improves students' study skills, helps students learn more factual information, involves parents in their children's education, and develops students' sense of self-direction and responsibility (Hong & Lee, 2000; Hong, Milgram, & Perkins, 1995). These findings, based on research conducted in the United States, Hong Kong and the Republic of Korea, have been replicated in recent research carried out in China.

Parental involvement in their children's education appears to be a critical factor in whether sound homework habits are formed early in their school experience. A recent review (Hoover-Dempsey & Sandler, 1997) found that the key factor in parents becoming involved in their children's education is that they have high self-efficacy beliefs in their ability and opportunity to assist their children's learning. Conversely, parents who have low self-efficacy beliefs, feeling that there is nothing they can do to help their children with their homework, are generally uninvolved in their children's education. There are policy implications for teachers in the need to empower parents to believe that their efforts can make a difference to their children's homework, study habits, and ultimately their educational achievement. Once parents believe that they can make a difference, specific strategies can be given to them by teachers in order to optimise the benefits of homework for the student. Even at the secondary school level, where parents' knowledge skills may be lacking, they can still be helpful in guiding their children's use of time and effort by helping them to locate relevant study resources at libraries, on the internet, and elsewhere.

Teachers' attitudes towards homework are also an important factor in the effective school homework policies to assist student learning. The Australian researchers, Bourke and Fairbairn (1995), found that five aspects of teachers' attitudes towards homework are important:

(a) homework is related to greater academic success;
(b) homework assignments need to be well-planned, clearly articulated, and meaningful to students;
(c) parents expect homework to be given to their children;
(d) feedback on the quality of the homework is essential; and
(e) parental involvement, especially with younger students, is necessary.

Teachers act as models for their students in reinforcing the important role that homework plays in practising skills learned in class, extending those skills and preparing for future lessons. Hong and Lee (2000) found that Hong Kong Grades 5 and 7 students' "self-perception of work accomplished at home was more positive in those students who were highly motivated by parents as well as teachers" (p. 125).

While it is generally agreed that homework is beneficial for student achievement, too much homework can be detrimental to student motivation and achievement. For example, it has been reported that primary school pupils in Hong Kong spend more time doing homework than any other Asian nation's children (Sharma, 1994). Excessive homework was cited as one of the reasons for a spate of suicides among children in Hong Kong in 1994. Care must be taken, however, not to oversimplify complex human behaviour. Newspaper reports, such as the one mentioned above, often attribute single causes to events which have multiple causes.

In conclusion, it is not known what is the optimal amount of homework. Asian students do more of it on average, than Western students. They begin earlier in their school lives and by the time they reach secondary school are expected to undertake several hours a day. In a study of over 1700 Hong Kong secondary students (Wong, 1992), it was found that more than a third of their considerable homework load was devoted to mathematics. The author also reported that mathematics achievement was most closely related to mathematics self-concept and positive student attitudes towards mathematics. The time spent on homework, however, was not related to mathematics achievement. It seems that it is not the quantity of homework that makes a difference to student achievement, but the quality of homework or how effective the homework exercises are in supplementing classroom instruction.

There is an ambivalent attitude towards homework by many Western educators (Hong & Lee, 2000; Stevenson, Stigler, & Lee, 1986; Whitton, 2000), with some arguing that it stifles the creative spirit in students who must spend hours over boring, rote-learning exercises in order to complete homework worksheets. This is a stereotype, which, like all stereotypes, is an exaggeration of the true state of affairs. Some homework may be boring and repetitive, especially if it requires many examples of the same mathematics algorithm to be solved. As stated earlier, there are at least three types of homework, each with different purposes. Imaginative homework exercises not only provide practice examples of concepts and principles already taught in class, but also allow students to prepare for future lessons and extend skills learned in class to new activities. Teachers who set such homework exercises motivate their students' learning. As discussed earlier, well-designed homework not only leads to higher student achievement, but it also helps students become self-regulating, independent learners. Homework may stimulate an intermediate phase of student learning between teacher-directed learning where the teacher is responsible for guiding the student's learning and independent learning where the student decides what and when to study.

5. RESEARCH ON COACHING

Research on coaching has found that it is widespread in the Asian region. In a recent review of the scale of coaching, Bray (1999a) found extensive use of private tutors to supplement regular classroom instruction. It appears that parents are prepared to pay for coaching of their children, even if they live in less developed countries. For instance, a majority of primary school pupils in Cambodia was reported to be receiving coaching (Bray, 1999b). Relatively fewer rural pupils were receiving coaching, presumably because their parents were less able to afford coaching than urban parents. Another reason for this urban-rural difference may be that rural parents perceive academic success as being less important in their children's lives than do urban parents. Nevertheless, almost one third of primary children in rural schools was receiving supplementary coaching. Furthermore, it has been found that a majority of students in Sri Lanka receives coaching, especially in the sciences (de Silva, 1994).

There is clear evidence that the scale of coaching is increasing. In Japan, for instance, attendance at primary school *juku* or cram schools has doubled from 1976 to 1993, with about 25 per cent of elementary school pupils attending *juku* in 1993 (Japan, 1995), while lower secondary level *juku* attendance has increased from almost 40 per cent to about 60 per cent over the same period. In Singapore, the proportion of primary and secondary students receiving private tuition almost doubled to approximately 50 per cent and 30 per cent respectively, in the decade from 1982 to 1992 (George, 1992). The fact that relatively more primary than secondary students were receiving private tuition is a reflection of the importance of national primary school examinations in the streaming of pupils into one of three streams, currently beginning in fifth grade.

The cost of coaching in the Asian region is immense. Bray (1999a, p. 27) states that the Japanese coaching industry in the mid-1990s had annual revenues of US$14 billion, with nine *juku* companies being listed on the Tokyo Stock Exchange. In Singapore, it has been estimated that the *per capita* expenditure on private tuition is approximately US$67 per annum, compared with US$112 in Japan. Bray (1999a) estimates that coaching consumes seven per cent of the total cost of schooling in Cambodia and 11 per cent of family incomes in Myanmar. Finally, the most extreme example of the burgeoning cost of coaching comes from Korea, where it is estimated that parents spend 150 per cent of the government's education budget. In other words, parents spend, on average, one and a half times what the Korean government spends on schools (*Asiaweek*, 1997, p. 20).

Why do Asian parents spend so much of their hard-earned income on education, especially coaching? First, it is well known that Asian parents value education highly. This is true, not only in Confucian heritage cultures, but also in most other Asian countries. For example, in multicultural Malaysia, it has been estimated that Indian parents spend more, on average, on their children's coaching than Chinese parents (Chew & Leong, 1995). The high value placed on education is not confined to cultures influenced by a Confucian tradition. Coaching is widespread in Hindu India, as well as in Buddhist Sri Lanka and Thailand.

The second answer to this question concerns the rewards for superior examination performance. In education systems which use national examinations to classify and select students for further educational opportunities, success on these examinations is crucial to students' career choices. In his influential book, *The Diploma Disease*, Dore (1976) argued that the later development begins in a country's push towards modernisation, the more important are the educational certificates for occupational selection. Students and their parents perceive this state of affairs and are willing to pay for coaching in examination subjects in order to optimise their children's chances of a rewarding career. In societies with a wider gap in salaries between professional or managerial jobs and semi-skilled or unskilled jobs, there is more pressure for students to perform well on examinations in order to qualify for the highly paid jobs. Also, if positions in prestigious universities are scarce, relative to the number of applicants, then there will be great demand for coaching in order to increase a student's chances of gaining a place in such institutions.

A third answer to this question of why coaching is so prevalent in Asian countries, is the phenomenon of large class sizes in the educational systems of the region. Classes of 40 or more students are common, with the result that individual attention from the teacher is less frequent than in the generally smaller classes in the West. Coaching in smaller classes or individual tutoring is a useful forum for students to be able to check their progress in a particular subject and to become motivated to perform to their potential.

In view of the widespread scope and cost of coaching in the Asia-Pacific region, its effects on student achievement is a critical issue. The data on this issue are scarce and inconclusive. There are several reasons for this lack of research. First, it is difficult to access students in private coaching schools, because they are outside the regular school system. The private coaching system is largely unregulated in most countries and so it is difficult to gain access to these students. While they may be asked questions when they are a captive audience at school, the precise impact on achievement of coaching undertaken outside school is difficult to measure. Second, it is difficult to isolate the effects of coaching from the effects of regular classroom instruction. A concept or skill, which was introduced in the classroom, may be consolidated in a coaching session. The student may have partially understood the concept at first, and then fully understood the concept as a result of this coaching session. Third, students who do and do not engage in coaching are different in other respects, such as their demographic background and past academic achievement. Socioeconomic and urban/rural differences need to be controlled. Bray (1999a) makes the important point that studies of the effects of coaching need to "allow for the fact that in many (but not all) cases the majority of pupils who receive supplementary tutoring are those whose academic performance is already good" (p. 49). Finally, the effects of coaching may be limited to a few subjects, such as languages and mathematics, which are assessed in public examinations. Any coaching effects in specific subjects cannot legitimately be generalised to other school subjects.

In his extensive review of the literature on coaching, Bray (1999a) could find only four studies which examined the impact of coaching on educational achievement, with only one of the four studies being carried out in the Asian region. That study was conducted by Sawada and Kobayashi (1986), who investigated the impact of *juku* attendance on mathematics achievement in upper elementary and lower secondary students. The sample consisted of 375 pupils in eight schools. Time spent in coaching was claimed to result in greater learning opportunities, with higher scores in mathematical problems involving arithmetic calculation and algebra. No differences were found in arithmetic application and geometry. Bray (1999a) interpreted the findings as reflecting the curricular emphasis of the *juku* classes. The lack of transfer of learning to application problems is a concern for educators who believe that education is more than examination success and involves preparing the student for practical application of skills learned in the classroom.

A recent Singaporean study of over 400 Secondary 2 students, matched for ability, examined the relationship between amount of private tuition and year-end examination performance (Cheo, 1998). He found that the students who spent more hours on coaching performed less well in their final examinations than those who spent fewer hours with private tutors. This surprising finding was explained in two ways. First, the students with more coaching may have over-studied for their examinations, resulting in lower motivation and lower achievement. Second, they may have received poorer quality tuition from tutors who emphasised quantity of revision, rather than the cognitive and metacognitive study strategies designed to prepare them for the examinations. A third possible explanation, that the more highly coached students were lower ability students in the first place, questions the efficacy of the matching process. These *post hoc* explanations require further experimental research. A second Singapore study investigated the relationship between hours of private tuition and English language achievement in Primary 3 children (Teo, 1987). It found a non-statistically significant relationship between the two variables.

Despite the lack of clear evidence as to the educational benefits of coaching, Asian parents continue to support the large and growing coaching industry. Involved parents often believe that their children will fall behind in their studies and not be competitive in examinations with other children who are receiving coaching. In a cross-cultural study of Grade 1 and Grade 5 pupils and their families in Japan, Taiwan and the United States, Stevenson and Lee (1990) found that Asian families placed greater emphasis on their child's academic achievement than did United States families. They were prepared to dedicate themselves to their child's academic success. According to Ng (2001, p. 110) parental dedication is demonstrated by the amount of space, funds and time allocated to the child. Parental dedication includes greater involvement in their children's homework and financial support for coaching.

6. POLICY IMPLICATIONS

Important implications for educational policy emerge from the research on homework and coaching. These implications are discussed separately in view of the fact that the research on the effects of homework and coaching draws different conclusions as to their relative effects on student achievement.

6.1. *Implications for Homework*

Most research has found that homework improves students' study skills, helps students learn more factual information, develops their sense of self-direction and responsibility, and involves parents in their children's education (Hong & Lee, 2000). In several Asian countries, however, there is growing concern that the amount of homework has become a heavy burden on students. There have been calls to regulate the amount and type of homework that is regularly given to children, often from their first year of schooling. In this way, children of all ages can enjoy a balanced life, with opportunities for leisure time to enable them to participate in recreational activities that are so essential for their growing bodies and minds. One such homework policy was announced recently by the

Minister for Education and Training in the State of New South Wales (NSW), Australia (Aquilina, 2000).

6.2. Implications for Coaching

The policy implications of the research on the effects of coaching are more problematic. Not only is there a dearth of research on the effects of coaching on student achievement in the Asia-Pacific region, but what little there is has reported conflicting results. Nevertheless, the scale of coaching across the region is immense and increasing. Recognising the different social contexts in which coaching takes place, Bray (1999a) proposed six possible policy approaches that could be adopted by different countries. These approaches ranged from a market-driven approach, to government monitoring of the scale of coaching, to more interventionist approaches, such as regulation, encouragement or even prohibition. The market-driven approach maintains that coaching is a choice parents make for their children and it provides an important source of income for students, mothers and others who want to work part-time. Prohibition has been adopted at times in Cambodia, Myanmar and Korea, with little impact on the private tuition system, because of a lack of enforcement of the bans (Bray, 1999a, p. 77).

Most educators advocate that, as a minimum, teachers should not be allowed to provide supplementary coaching to their own students. The omission of vital curriculum material from the school timetable in order to include it in the coaching lessons held outside school hours disadvantages those students whose parents cannot afford to pay for coaching. In addition, in countries where coaching is considered to be excessive, educational policymakers should search for the root causes, such as overcrowded curricula and public examinations that encourage rote learning. For example, the Singapore Ministry of Education has revised curricula in all subjects, reducing the content by up to 30 per cent. Teachers are being trained to engage students in critical and creative thinking, two vital skills in the knowledge economy of the twenty-first century. These skills are being applied in project work, where group and individual performance will contribute to student achievement scores in national examinations. Another example is Korea, where the government is reducing the reliance on rote learning in its public examinations by reducing the demand for facts and increasing the emphasis on critical thinking (Ng, 2001).

In defence of coaching, it has been argued that the Japanese *juku* is an important bridge between the school and the workplace (Kitamura, 1986; White, 1987). The egalitarian values of most teachers are at odds with the competitive nature of the job market. By preparing students for the entrance examinations of prestigious secondary schools and universities, *juku* serves an essential function which status-conscious parents are only too willing to support. Besides, it has been argued that *juku* also serves a social function by allowing students from different schools to meet and make friends. Finally, many private tuition centres teach their students the value of self-discipline, a value that is rewarded by most employers.

7. CONCLUSION

This literature review on homework and coaching in the Asia-Pacific region has found that both are occurring on a widespread and increasing scale. While it has been found that homework has definite academic and motivational benefits, increasing concern has been expressed by high officials in some Asian countries that excessive homework demands are having negative impacts on students and their families. There is an urgent need for educational policies which address these concerns. Otherwise, increasing numbers of students will suffer from anxiety, stress, school phobia and long-term dislike of learning. It is possible to design and implement a balanced homework policy, based on practice exercises, preparatory assignments and extension exercises.

The policy responses to the burgeoning growth of the coaching industry are complex. The educational benefits of coaching have not been demonstrated so far in the relatively few studies to be conducted. In some Asian countries, teachers' salaries are so low that they depend on coaching their own students after school to supplement their incomes. Most educators advocate that this practice should be discouraged or even prohibited. What is needed are policies designed to increase teachers' salaries by paying them for extra duties, such as marking public examination papers. Moreover, there needs to be more governmental regulation of coaching schools to ensure minimum standards of physical facilities, which already occurs in Singapore, and quality of service. Otherwise, parents will not be receiving value for money in an industry whose importance cannot be ignored. It is time that the coaching industry came out of the shadows and was recognised for the significant role it plays in most Asian societies.

REFERENCES

Alexander, P. A. (1996). The past, present, and future knowledge research: A reexamination of the role of knowledge in learning and instruction. *Educational Psychologist*, 31, 89–92.

Aquilina, J. (2000). *Homework Policy for NSW Government Schools*. Sydney: NSW Department of Education and Training.

Asiaweek (1997). Banning tutors, 23(17), 20.

Bandura, A. (1997). *Self-efficacy: The Exercise of Control*. New York: W. H. Freeman.

Beaton, A. (1996). *Mathematics Achievement in the Middle Years: IEA's Third International Mathematics and Science Study (TIMSS)*. Chestnut Hill, MA: Boston College.

Bourke, S., & Fairbairn, H. (1995). Reporting research for teachers: Teachers' attitudes to homework. *Unicorn*, 21, 95–102.

Bray, M. (1998). Financing education in developing Asian countries: Themes, tensions, and policies. *International Journal of Educational Research*, 29, 627–642.

Bray, M. (1999a). *The Shadow Education System: Private Tutoring and its Implications for Planners*. Paris: UNESCO.

Bray, M. (1999b). *The Private Costs of Public Schooling: Household and Community Financing of Primary Education in Cambodia*. Paris: UNESCO in collaboration with UNICEF.

Cheo, R. K. (1998). How home variables affect academic performance: A study of children in Singapore. *Unpublished M. A. thesis*. Singapore: National University of Singapore.

Chew, S. B., & Leong, Y. C. (Eds.) (1995). *Private Tuition in Malaysia: A Comparative Study*. Kuala Lumpur: University of Malaya.

de Silva, W. A. (1994). *Extra-school Tutoring in the Asian Context with Special Reference to Sri Lanka*. Maharagama: National Institute of Education.

Dore, R. (1976). *The Diploma Disease: Education, Qualification and Development*. London: George Allen & Unwin. (Reprinted 1997 by Institue of Education, University of London)

George, C. (1992). Time to come out of the shadows. *Straits Times* (Singapore), 4 April.

Hong, E., & Lee, K. (2000). Preferred homework style, and homework environment in high- versus low-achieving Chinese students. *Educational Psychology, 20*, 125–137.

Hong, E., Milgram, R. M., & Perkins, P. G. (1995). Homework style and homework behaviour of Korean and American children. *Journal of Research and Development in Education, 28*, 197–207.

Hoover-Dempsey, K. V., & Sandler, H. M. (1997). Why do parents become involved in their children's education? *Review of Educational Research, 67*, 3–42.

Japan, Ministry of Education, Science and Culture (1995). *Japanese Government Policies in Education, Science and Culture: New Directions in School Education – Fostering Strength for Life*. Tokyo: Ministry of Education, Science and Culture.

Keeves, J. P. (1995). The contribution of IEA research to Australian education. In W. Bos & R. H. Lehmann (Eds.), *Reflections on Educational Achievement*. Munster, Germany: Waxmann.

Kitamura, K. (1986). The decline and reform of education in Japan: A comparative perspective. In W. K. Cummings, E. R. Beauchamp, S. Ichikawa, V. N. Kobayashi & M. Ushiogi (Eds.), *Educational Policies in Crisis: Japanese and American Perspectives* (pp. 153–170). New York: Praeger.

Ng, A. K. (2001). *Why Asians are Less Creative than Westerners*. Singapore: Prentice Hall.

Pintrich, P. R. (2000). The role of goal orientation in self-regulated learning. In M. Boekaerts, P. R. Pintrich & M. Zeidner (Eds.), *Handbook of Self-Regulation* (pp. 451–502). San Diego, CA: Academic Press.

Sawada, T., & Kobayashi, S. (1986). *An Analysis of the Effect of Arithmetic and Mathematics Education at juku*. Translated by P. Horvath, compendium 12. Tokyo: National Institute for Educational Research.

Sharma, Y. (1994). Homework blamed for deaths. *Times Educational Supplement*, London, 1 July.

Stevenson, H. W., & Lee, S. (1990). Context of achievement. *Monographs of the Society for Research in Child Development*, serial no. 221, 55(1–2).

Stevenson, H. W., Stigler, J. W., & Lee, S. (1986). Achievement in mathematics. In H. Stevenson, H. Azuma & K. Hakuta (Eds.), *Child Development in Japan*. New York: W. H. Freeman.

Teo, E. K. (1987). Social correlates of English language proficiency of Primary 3 pupils in Singapore. Unpublished M.Ed. thesis. Singapore: National University of Singapore.

Vygotsky, L. (1978). *Mind and Society: The Development of Higher Psychological Processes*. Cambridge, MA: Harvard University Press.

White, M. (1987). *The Japanese Educational Challenge: A Commitment to Children*. New York: Free Press.

Whitton, D. (2000). Homework: Horror or heaven? *Classroom, 20*(2), 11–12.

Wong, N. (1992). The relationship among mathematics achievement, affective variables and home background. *Mathematics Education Research Journal, 4*, 32–42.

Zimmerman, B. J. (1998). Academic studying and the development of personal skill: A self-regulatory perspective. *Educational Psychologist, 33*, 73–86.

53

Teacher Self-Evaluation

JOHN MacBEATH
University of Cambridge, England

1. INTRODUCTION

Who knows best about what happens in classrooms? Who is best placed to judge the quality and effectiveness of teaching? While there may be many different answers to these questions this paper argues that the best source of information is the teacher himself or herself. Teacher self-evaluation is not, however, simply a matter of teachers making subjective judgements about their own teaching. It goes further, requiring a rigorous and systematic approach to evaluating learning and the context of learning. It requires teachers having a repertoire of self-evaluation tools as part of their professional armoury. It means listening sensitively and attentively to the voice of students – 'the treasure in our own backyard' – as they have their own expert contribution to make.

These issues must be put into a political context, a concern for international competitiveness, a drive for raised standards, and a push for external accountability and monitoring of school performance conjoined with a policy rhetoric of learning to learn and learning for life. So teacher self-evaluation serves the dual purpose – a formative and an accountability purpose. Evaluation tools are used not merely to defend reactively against external monitoring but proactively to inform, to educate and to demonstrate the complex inter-relationship of learning and teaching.

2. THE CHANGING POLICY CONTEXT

There was a time when it was assumed that teachers, having qualified, should be left alone to get on with the job. As autonomous professionals they could be trusted to put the interests of their children first, to be well versed in their subject and make informed choices as to the most appropriate methods. 'Qualified' was taken to mean qualified for life, certified as competent to go on teaching until a gracious and deserved retirement.

Few of these assumptions continue to hold good in the Third Millennium. In

Asia-Pacific countries, as in certain developed economies, policy-makers are no longer content to let teachers plough their own lone furrow. Research persistently identifies the impact of change and the importance of continuing professional development (Ho & Gopinathan, 1999).

It is no longer seen as acceptable for teachers to be qualified for life. The world has changed too much and too fast. Not only has knowledge proliferated out of control but access to knowledge has undergone an unforeseen and unimagined paradigm shift. The once widely accepted idea of transmission of information from teacher to pupil has been discredited by a more confident psychology of learning and a challenging neuroscience. Day by day doubt has been cast on cherished beliefs about the nature of 'intelligence', 'ability', and 'potential' (Perkins, 1995; Sternberg, 1996).

Paradoxically, while the nature of learning has been shown to be more determined by influences that lie outside of schools, teachers have become increasingly more accountable for the performance of their charges. More is known than ever before about the powerful formative influence of the early years, about the effects of deprivation and, most disturbingly, in recent times, about the shaping of children's intelligence, personality and behaviour in those critical inter-uterine years. Fetal alcohol syndrome, attention behavioural deficiencies, learning disabilities are attributable to the critical three months prior to birth (Caleekal, 2001) yet growing alongside this body of knowledge there is a political imperative to make schools more effective, more accountable and more transparent. And the burden falls squarely on teachers to demonstrate that indeed it is good teaching, not environment, not family, not socio-economic, not culture, not history, that makes the difference.

Policy-makers in both Western and Eastern countries have drawn heavily, and not always judiciously, on school effectiveness research. In countries with little tradition of research into whole school effects (Malaysia, for example) American studies have been referred to for guidance while countries with a significant repertoire of studies (Hong Kong, for example) have also tended to seek inspiration from North American, Australian, British and Dutch research. In these countries school effectiveness research has shifted focus progressively from school to department to classroom level and policy-makers have followed (MacBeath & Mortimore, 2001). So, in the minds of policy people, the onus of accountability moves from whole school to individual teachers. If it can be shown that teacher A is more effective than teacher B with the same students then teacher B may be called to account and performance rewarded or sanctioned accordingly.

Seen as the ultimate gatekeepers of standards it is the teacher who may be held responsible for lagging national performance or for maintaining high status. So comparisons among countries set the stage and provide the script for the players. Data from OECD, TIMMS and the European Commission have provoked a widespread urgency (some might say moral panic) among policy-makers. For relatively poorly performing countries the United States and the United Kingdom for example the pressure is on to push up measured performance. For the high performing countries – Singapore, Japan, Taiwan, Hong Kong, Korea, the challenge is, while remaining pre-eminent in measured attainment, to broaden the focus to deeper and more lifelong forms of learning. For countries still far short of comparable measurement – Pacific Island countries for example – the urgency takes a more basic form – recruitment and upskilling of teachers. Common to all, however, is the focus on the teacher, on his or her self-knowledge. Without this teachers will be prey to passing fads and ill-informed policy directives. Sacks' (1999) comments about the American scene is a salutary warning for countries of the Asia-Pacific region.

3. A PARADIGM SHIFT

Despite their relative high standings on international performance tables countries of the Asia-Pacific region have not been immune to the performativity agenda but at the same time there is an acknowledgement that high performance standards may have been bought at a high price. At the 1997 Seventh International Conference on Thinking, the Prime Minister of Singapore laid out a vision for a new, more learner-centred Millennium.

> What is critical is that we fire in our students a passion for learning, instead of studying for the sake of getting good grades in their examinations. Their knowledge will be fragile, no matter how many As they get ... It is the capacity to learn that will define excellence in the future not simply what young people achieve in school. (Goh Chok Tong, 1997)

This high rhetoric is paralleled in mainland China, Hong-Kong (Lo, 1999) and Japan where individuality, creativity and *ikuru-chikara* (ability to survive in a changing society) are rhetorically at a premium (Fujita & Suk-Yong, 1999).

Watkins (2001) has identified a categorical difference between a performativity and a learning agenda and his pattern of differences is presented in Table 1.

Watkins' two categories might be read as East and West. That is perhaps too

Table 1. Categorises differences between learning and performance

Learning	*Performance*
Belief that effort leads to success	Belief that ability leads to success
Belief in one's ability to improve and learn	Concern to be judged as able, concern to perform
Preference for challenging tasks	Satisfaction from doing better than others
Deriving satisfaction from personal success at difficult tasks	Emphasis on normative standards, competition and public evaluation
Using self-instruction when engaged in a task	Helplessness: evaluating self-negatively when task is difficult

(Watkins, 2001).

simplistic but many of the values of learning goals are more traditionally associated with the East – achievement through effort rather than ability, collaborative endeavour rather than individualistic gain. Lebra's (1976) study found that only one per cent of Japanese respondents attributed success to ability, a finding reflected with Korean students in 1998 (Kim & Park, 1998). Hampden-Turner and Trompenaars' (1993) comparative study of Japanese and American culture concurs with this essential contrast between conceptions of ability and effort.

Yet nothing is quite that simple. There are common strands within Asia-Pacific countries which look both to East and West, factors not simply of recent history but of centuries of globalisation. The meeting ground of economics and religions, in multiple manifestations have created common tensions but also unique challenges within each country and sub-region. The conflict between traditional values and emerging knowledge is a longstanding one. Confucianist beliefs promote collective good and harmony as an ultimate end but individual achievement is at a premium and too has to be harnessed, however uncomfortably, to the willingness to make sacrifices and put group interests before self. In Taiwan the tensions between collectivism and individualism are a recurring theme and how to integrate Western thought with Chinese philosophy remains in the forefront of debate and inquiry (Pan & Yu, 1999). In Malaysia the curriculum is intended to produce all-round development, emotional, spiritual and physical and intellectual, but overall academic performance remains the key discriminating factor (Ahmad et al., 1999). The Republic of Korea scores highly in international terms but also promotes shared effort, social harmony and social obligation (Kim & Park, 1998). In Hong Kong, the policy emphasis is on learning to learn but at the same time schools remain banded by ability of intake and fight hard to retain their academic reputation and selectivity.

Morris and Sweeting (1997) characterise student attitudes in the high achieving East-Asian countries as diligent, hard working and tolerant of boredom and their schools as inculcating social cohesion, national pride and competiveness. Referring to the Republic of Korea, Kim and Park (1998) argue that those very qualities which have served the system so well in the past will be detrimental to the future. The knowledge economy impatiently requires a different cast of mind and a different repertoire of skills. It is a task impossible to address without a change at the level of the classroom. The challenge for the future is expressed in these terms:

> the challenge for the school system in the immediate future is to combine the methodology and learning discipline that has produced high academic standards with new teaching-learning strategies and practices that will promote critical thinking, creativity and morality. (Ho & Gopinathan, 1991, p. 116)

Classroom teachers are aware that they should be more student-centred, more multi-disciplinary, multi-sensory and multiply intelligent but structures and conventions seem to push them back towards the comfort zone of what they know, what they can do and what they have done in the past. While deeply conservative by tradition they strive to think radically about the imperatives of change.

4. RAISING THE STAKES IN TEACHER EVALUATION

The class teacher is ultimately the gatekeeper of change, but currently is at the end of a long line of responsibility. This idea has resonance with teachers in Taiwan as reported by Pan and Yu.

> at present teachers seem to be in a passive position when facing the reform proposals. They feel that they are the subjects to be reformed rather than being the change agents. (Pan & Yu, 1999, p. 82)

All of this serves to make the evaluation of teaching and learning more, rather than less, important. Faced with superficial assessments of their performance, the authentic evaluation of teaching can become something of an educational crusade for the profession. In England it was the National Union of Teachers that commissioned research into school and teacher self-evaluation, published as *Schools Must Speak for Themselves* (MacBeath, 1999). It was taken up with enthusiasm by the Danish Union of Teachers and translated into Danish (MacBeath & Moos, 2001), used extensively with teachers in Hong Kong, translated in part into Thai where it was met with enthusiasm by teachers because its starting point was their concerns, their so-called 'careabouts'. One teacher in a small rural school on the Mekong Delta had, on her own initiative, put in place a sophisticated database drawing on the views of pupils, parents and teachers about school climate, classroom teaching and pupil learning.

Policy-makers tend to forget that teachers are natural evaluators. It is not something invented by governments and imposed on a recalcitrant profession. Evaluation is built into teaching. It is ongoing and implicit. An Exeter University study (Wragg, 2001) reported that teachers made, on average over a thousand decisions a day, each underpinned by an intuitive spontaneous evaluation – of behaviour, of attitude, of learning. More often than not these remained implicit and privatised rather than being formally articulated. Consistently from East to West, teachers welcome tools of evaluation which build on what they are already doing, which bring new insights and extend their pedagogic repertoire.

Teachers do not, by contrast, tend to welcome inspection and appraisal. They are suspicious of observation and monitoring of schools. Lee and his colleagues in Hong Kong (Lee et al., 2001), found teachers wary of appraisal and experiencing difficulty in keeping up with the pace of change. Teachers in their study were, like their counterparts elsewhere, wary of evaluation which fails to contextualise teachers' work, which misreads the delicate balance of relationships, or which lacks insights into the chemistry and physics of the classroom. Teachers are, however, willing to embrace strategies and tools designed to make them more effective, more reflective, more self-critical. They rarely object to professional development that is grounded in their needs and priorities.

Their understanding of teaching and learning is, by and large, more sophisticated than those who formulate policy and their understanding of their own classrooms is generally more deeply grounded than those who come to observe them. So, they tend to welcome measures which counter crude and simplistic assessments of teacher performance.

When teachers are equipped and confident in the use of self-evaluation tools they welcome the external critical eye. Rather than being embattled and defensive they are happy to open themselves to the challenge of the 'visitor's eye view' as Icelanders describe it. As professionals teachers are eager to learn and to improve and when they have a repertoire of self-evaluation tools it simply becomes part of their professional armoury. These tools are then used not merely to defend reactively against external attack, but proactively to inform, to educate and to demonstrate the complex inter-relationship of learning and teaching.

In 1990, writing about the relationship between teaching and learning Little (1990) advocated that teachers "pursue the connections with aggressive curiosity and healthy scepticism". This provocative statement describes the very essence of teacher self-evaluation. It describes what truly effective teachers do. Because the more informed they become about the frailty of the connection between teaching and learning the more they themselves becomes learners in their own classrooms. As a consequence the tools of self-evaluation are less concerned with the competencies of teaching than with the nature and process of learning.

When teachers set out to understand the individual child the more eager they become to find the appropriate modes of evaluation. The deeper the mystery of learning unfolds the greater the challenge to revisit and reframe conceptions of classroom learning. When seen from the standpoint of the individual student the same classroom may be both a comfortable place and a terrifying place. It may be both constructive and destructive, pro and anti-learning, depending on the perspective from which it is viewed.

The evaluation of teaching has taken its lead from school and teacher effectiveness literature, relying heavily on classroom observation and checklists of competency criteria. In contrast, learning-focused evaluation has looked to cognitive and social psychology, probing beneath superficial performance measures to grasp how the learner constructs his or her learning. In doing so its quest for understanding extends beyond the formal classroom to more informal contexts, of home, self-chosen learning, study, homework, tutorial centres, evening, weekend, Easter schools, Summer schools, *Mendaki* tutorial centres and *jukus*. It is these out-of-school contexts for learning that bedevil attempts to find accurate value-added measures at the school level (Fujita & Suk-Yong, 1999).

The quest for understanding starts not from the simple given of the classroom milieu but from the recognition that the multiple contexts of learning are powerful shapers of motivation, engagement, interest and attainment. Nor does evaluation start from the given of the teacher as instructor but explores the influence of others who may mediate learning – parents, peers, friends, mentors or private tutors.

As the main theatre in which teachers work, the classroom is an obvious and important focus for evaluation, but deeper insights come from setting that reflective inquiry in a wider frame of reference. So it allows learning to be more finely and sensitively apprehended.

5. EVALUATING CLASSROOM LEARNING

The twin principles of evaluation tools are, to draw on two Brunerian concepts (Bruner, 1970), economy and power. The economy, or parsimony, principle, requires that tools be simple, accessible, in-built rather than add on. The second principle requires they be power tools, capable of generating significant and transformative insights. So, starting with the simplest and least time-consuming approach, teachers may find a few moments in the ongoing life of the classroom to stand back from the lesson and reflect on three basic questions:

- What are the pupils doing?
- What are they learning?
- What am I doing?

This exercise is obviously best undertaken when pupils are engaged in some activity and the teacher is free to observe. It may serve as a formative prompt to a further question – 'What am I going to do next?'. The economy of this approach is obvious but its power may be more deeply hidden. The answer to the question 'what are the pupils doing?' may evoke a simple descriptive response such as 'writing', 'reading' or 'drawing', but a deeper probing is likely to tell a more complex and intriguing story. It may reveal something about the levels and quality of engagement from ritual performance through to creative understanding, from surface to deep learning (Entwistle, 1987), and from cognition to metacognition.

The following apparently simple set of questions, provided for Scottish schools (The Scottish Consultative Council on the Curriculum, 1997), has far-reaching implications when pursued with Little's combination of aggressive curiosity and healthy scepticism.

- How often do I encourage pupils to think for themselves and try out new ideas?
- What techniques do I use to help learners be more aware of how best to learn and why?
- What assumptions do I make about the individual learner when I teach?
- On what are these assumptions based?
- How would I describe the climate I am to establish in the classroom?
- What do I say and do to establish this climate? (SCCC, 1997)

Tay-Koay's (1997) study in Singapore throws interesting light on this. She asked students to report on their thinking during a series of lessons. These data were then disaggregated according to the ability level of the student, revealing the patterns shown in Tables 2 and 3.

Table 2. Engagement by ability

	Low ability		Average ability		High ability	
	n	%	n	%	n	%
not thinking actively	139	39.5	169	24.2	128	20.2
lesson-irrelevant thinking	88	22.4	196	28.0	262	41.3
lesson-relevant and irrelevant thinking	18	4.6	44	6.3	77	12.1
lesson-relevant thinking	147	37.5	290	41.5	167	26.3

Source: Tay-Koay (1997, p. 193).

Table 3. What pupils were doing – by ability group

	Low ability		Average ability		High ability	
	n	%	n	%	n	%
note-taking	7	1.8	9	1.3	98	15.5
paying attention	321	98.2	547	78.7	406	64.3
responding to questions	19	4.8	44	6.3	25	3.9
trying to understand	165	42.1	334	47.8	245	38.6
visualising	10	2.5	47	6.7	33	5.2
assimilating	21	5.4	27	3.9	27	4.3
applying	7	1.8	12	1.7	9	1.4
hypothesising	3	0.8	14	2.0	8	1.3
analysing	16	4.1	38	5.4	54	8.5
evaluating	11	2.8	16	2.3	125	3.9

Source: Tay-Koay, (1997, p. 195).

The Tables show that probing a little more deeply revealed not only different forms of behaviour but different levels of cognitive or emotive activity.

Without access to inner emotions and thoughts, only proxy measures can be used. Access can only be gained to the products of thinking, which may, in truth, be pale reflections of the inner life of children's minds. Such insights from research are of immense significance for the teacher while the strategies, which furnish them may easily be adapted as a self-evaluation instrument to potentially great effect.

Similarly, an approach known as 'subjective experience sampling' (Csikzentimaihalyi, 1997) can be put to the service of the individual teacher in his or her classroom. During one week researchers paged pupils at random intervals between 7.30 a.m. and 9.30 p.m., asking them to complete a simple rating scale to indicate their feeling, motivation, arousal at that particular moment. Over the course of the day and the week it told a graphic story of engagement, its peaks and troughs, apathy and boredom, curiosity and excitement, frustration and joy in learning.

An example of how this can be adapted as a self-evaluation tool comes from a study conducted in Japan along with seven other participating countries, namely the Learning School Project.

6. THE LEARNING SCHOOL

The Learning School Project (an ongoing international initiative) involves groups of students from schools in Japan, Korea, Hong Kong, Scotland, Sweden, the Czech Republic, Germany and South Africa. Students (two from each participating school) take a year out of their studies for their global journey, spending four weeks in each of the schools, evaluating the quality of learning and teaching and reporting back their findings to teachers and students. In its first year a week long conference was held in Japan to present findings to various audiences including academics and policy-makers.

Their use and adaptation of the Czikzentimahalyi (1997) instrument, shown in Figure 1, brought revealing insights to the research team, the teachers, the students and to leadership, for whom it presented a challenging set of findings.

Students take a minute, or less, to fill out the spot check before and after the lesson and at a given moment during the lesson at a signal from the teacher or the sound of an alarm clock. The Learning School students introduced a variation on the spot check – a 'triangulation' of three different viewpoints – student, teacher and student observer. At a given moment in the class lesson all three parties filled out the spot check sheet, the teacher and observer making a

Concentrating	1	2	3	Thinking about other things
Alert	1	2	3	Drowsy
Relaxed	1	2	3	Anxious
Wishing to be here	1	2	3	Wishing to be somewhere else
Happy	1	2	3	Sad
Active	1	2	3	Passive
Excited	1	2	3	Bored
Time passing quickly	1	2	3	Time passing slowly
Full of energy	1	2	3	Very little energy
Something at stake	1	2	3	Nothing at stake
Sociable	1	2	3	Lonely
Easy to concentrate	1	2	3	Difficult to concentrate
Cheerful	1	2	3	Irritable
Easy to be creative	1	2	3	Difficult to be creative

Figure 1. The spot check

judgement about the whole class, the student giving his or her own individual response. Aggregating all pupil responses with that of the teacher and observer gave an intriguing picture of quite different perceptions of what was happening in one classroom.

The value of these data was limited, however, without the further exploration. So the Learning School researchers sat down with an individual student in order to probe some of the inner feelings that provoked the completion of the spot check. As with the Csikzentimihalyi (1997) pager experiment, its greatest benefit comes from using this tool across a range of contexts and times of day. So, teachers can learn about different levels of motivation and thinking when a pupil is:

(a) listening to the teacher in a history lesson,
(b) working in pairs with a neighbour,
(c) engaged in role play in drama,
(d) reading a book in the library,
(e) looking for information on the net,
(f) doing mathematics homework,
(g) practising *Putonghua* as a second language,
(h) studying for a test while listening to music, and
(i) reading a novel in bed.

What does the teacher then do with this ambiguous information? He or she may dismiss it as worthless or may choose to engage with her class in a deeper exploration of what the data mean and where they may point in respect of future practice. The data, left to stand alone, are likely to be ambiguous and difficult to interpret. They require some qualitative information to help make sense of them. So, follow up dialogue is critical both to the benefit of the teacher and the class. In Tay-Koay's (1996) Singapore study interviews with students gave important clues to the meaning of the quantitative data.

"It was very detailed. The teacher used confusing terms. My friends asked deep questions beyond what the teacher taught ... I get very frustrated because everyone else seems to understand."

"I was distracted and could not concentrate".

"I was troubled with problems I had".

"I wasn't thinking of any stuff at that time because I was concentrating on writing the notes. I mean it is not easy to write and listen, for I can only do one thing at a time."

"The teacher's voice and expression can be very dull at times. I think tone and expression play a great part in helping students understand the lesson better." (Tay-Koay, 1997, p. 196)

These are thought provoking comments. As with the spot check, teachers are able to discover something about students' mental absenteeism. It is not surprising to find that they are worrying about problems located elsewhere but it is perhaps, more disturbing to find that they are taking notes, a task which seems to be divorced from thinking. Does it point to a certain kind of note-taking skill or, as the failure of higher order thinking suggests, a lack of training in the ability to abstract personal meaning from teacher talk?

7. THE INTERNAL WORLD OF LEARNING

This range of spot check instruments illustrate a way of ascertaining at any given moment what is happening in the internal world of thinking and feeling and the matching of this with what is observed by teachers or others in the external world of student behaviour. Wragg (2001) tells the story of the teacher who had asked the class to draw a head and shoulders. All but one dutifully produced a conventional portrait, face on or in profile. The one exception, however, was the student who had covered the sheet with bands of vivid colour, nothing like a head and shoulders, at least to the casual observer. The irate teacher might have interpreted this as an act of defiance or vandalism and required a more conventional illustration. A little patience allowed the student to explain that this was indeed a head but 'seen from the inside'. It is a telling metaphor for self-evaluation.

Damasio (1999) in his book entitled *The Feeling of What Happens* argues that to understand learning at work it is imperative to peel back layers of behaving and thinking from what happens – observable behaviour, through overt expression of emotions, to those things only accessible to the individual – the feeling of the emotions, the knowing of feeling, and the understanding of the feeling. It is these latter, higher, levels of apprehension which normally elude the teacher but can be probed through the use of relatively simple tools such as the spot check.

8. A LANGUAGE FOR LEARNING

All of this does, of course, presuppose students, and their teachers, are equipped with a language in which to discuss their thoughts and feelings. Our own ongoing research (MacBeath, Myers, & Demetriou, 2001) suggest that students tend not to have the language of metacognition and when presented with a question such as 'what did you learn in school today?' find it difficult to answer except in terms of content taught.

While probing of content is of itself important, teachers are sometimes shocked to find the misconceptions that students are working on and the erroneous assumptions they themselves have made. Watkins (2001) suggests there is a more probing question. The question 'What have you noticed about your learning?' gets more into the process and is a more challenging of a thought out response, demanding a more developed, conceptualised language. What this means is that for teacher self-evaluation to be maximally effective teachers need to work with their students over time to embed a language of self-evaluation integrally into the very process of learning and teaching. That in turn rests on a genuine desire to listen to students' and to believe that they are the most valuable source we have on their learning and our teaching.

A decade ago Fullan (1991) posed the question 'what would happen if we treated the student as someone whose opinion mattered?' thus alerting us not only to our failure to listen intelligently but also to the radical cultural change that this might provoke at the classroom level.

> Somehow educators have forgotten the important connection between teachers and students. We listen to outside experts to inform us, and, consequently overlook the treasure in our very own backyards, the students. (Soo Hoo, 1993, p. 389)

As an ardent advocate of students' role in informing learning and teaching Fielding (2001) suggests a taxonomy of the stages of student voice: (a) students as data source, (b) students as active respondents, (c) students as co-researchers, and (d) students as researchers.

While teachers who venture into this territory may find student data informative for their teaching, they can progress beyond this to involve students proactively as researchers into their own learning and as intelligent commentators on the quality of teaching. Embarking on the journey through the Fielding taxonomy is the challenge confronting schools. Much can be learned, even with very young children, although perhaps hampered by reading and writing abilities they are likely to be less inhibited than their older counterparts in their expression of feelings. Methods that work particularly well with young children are visual – drawing and painting, for example.

9. CONCLUSION

Synthesis is the key to effective evaluation, says House (2000). From all the information available, from multiple sources, diverse values, from various methods and inclusion of key stakeholders we arrive at 'an all-things-considered synthesis'. This does not imply a so-called 'definitive' conclusion rather the best, most honest, most considered judgement we can arrive at in the circumstances. All knowledge is conjectural, argued the philosopher Popper, and we know from our own experience that even the most definitive of scientific truths is likely to be questioned a few years down the line.

This has far-reaching implications for the classroom teacher, for school culture and for the nature of school leadership. It goes to the heart of educational purpose because it keeps to the forefront of practice the relationship between purpose and outcome. It brings teachers, students and school leaders back to the questions 'how good is our school?', 'how good is teaching and learning in our school?' and 'how do we know?' The implications are far-reaching because they require a cultural sea change at both classroom and school level. They imply an openness and receptivity to challenge, to learning from one's colleagues and from students. It means school leaders modelling learning and creating and sustaining a learning first culture.

Being open to new insights about schools and classrooms as places of professional knowledge creation has implications for continuing professional development at the individual school level as well as collaboratively and collegially among clusters of schools. But as research continues to show the autonomous teacher, the autonomous school will find difficulty in making real progress without the support and challenge of critical friends. We shall not cease from exploration, as the poet T.S. Eliot wrote many years ago, but the more we learn about learning the better we will know what the art and science of teaching really is.

REFERENCES

Ahmad, R., Zulkilfi, A. M., & Marzuki, S. (1999). School effectiveness and school improvement in Malaysia. In T. Townsend, P. Clarke & M. Ainscow, *Third Millennium Schools: A World of Difference in Effectiveness and Improvement* (pp. 265–283).

Bruner, J. (1970). *Towards a Theory of Instruction*. Boston, MA: Harvard University Press.

Caleekal, A. (2001). *Fetal Alcohol Syndrome*, retrieved from website digitalism.org/hst/fetal.html.

Csikszentmihalyi, M. (1997). *Talented Teenagers: The Roots of Success and Failure*. Cambridge: Cambridge University Press.

Damasio, A. (1999). *The Feeling of What Happens*. San Diego: Harcourt.

Entwistle, N. (1987). *Understanding Classroom Learning*. London: Hodder and Stoughton.

Fielding, M. (Ed.) (2001). *Taking Education Really Seriously: Four Years Hard Labour*. London: Routledge.

Fujita, H., & Suk-Yong, W. (1999). Postmodern restructuring of the knowledge base in Japanese mass education: Crisis of public culture and identity formation. *Education Journal, 27*(1).

Fullan, M. G. (1991). *The New Meaning of Educational Change*. New York: Teachers College Press.

Goh Chok Tong (1997). Opening speech at the Seventh International Conference on Thinking, Singapore, 1st–6th June.

Hampden-Turner, C., & Trompenaars, L. (1993). *The Seven Cultures of Capitalism*. New York: Doubleday.

Ho, W. K., & Gopinathan, S. (1999). Recent developments in education in Singapore. *School Effectiveness and School Improvement, 10*(1), 86–99.

House, E. (2000). *Schools for Sale*. New York: Teachers College Press.

Kim, H. W., & Park Y. S. (1998). The nature of achievement in Korean society. *Korean Journal of Educational Psychology, 12*(2), 51–58.

Lebra, T. S. (1976). *Japanese Patterns of Behavior*. Honolulu: University Press of Hawaii.

Lee, C. J., Chung, Y., Lo, N. L., & Wong, H. W. (2001). *Study of the Effectiveness of Hong Kong Secondary Schools*. Hong Kong: Hong Kong Education Department.

Little, J. W. (1990). Teachers as colleagues. In A. Liebermann (Ed.), *Schools as Collaborative Cultures: Creating the Future Now*. Basingstoke: Falmer Press.

MacBeath, J. (1999). *Schools Must Speak for Themselves*. London: Routledge.

MacBeath, J., & Mortimore, P. (2001). *Improving School Effectiveness*. Buckingham: Open University Press.

MacBeath, J., & Moos, L. (2001). *Skolan Kan Svaren for Sig Selv.* Copenhagen: CLUE.
MacBeath, J., Myers, K., & Demetriou, H. (2001). Supporting teachers in consulting pupils about aspects of teaching and learning, and evaluating impact. Paper delivered at the American Educational Research Association, Seattle, April.
Morris, P., & Sweeting, A. (1997). Human resource development in East Asia: A comparative analysis. *Asia Pacific Journal of Education, 17*(1), 7–27.
Pan, H. L., & Yu, C. (1999). Educational reforms with their impacts on school effectiveness and school improvement in Taiwan, R. O. C. *School Effectiveness and School Improvement, 10*(1), 86–99.
Perkins, D. (1995). *Smart Schools.* New York: The Free Press.
Scottish Consultative Council on the Curriculum (SCCC) (1997). *Teaching for Effective Learning.* Dundee: SCCC.
Soo Hoo, S. (1993). Students as partners in research and restructuring schools. *The Educational Forum, 57,* 386–393.
Sternberg, R. (1996). *Successful Intelligence.* New York: Simon and Schuster.
Tay-Koay, S. L. (1997). Students' reports of cognitive processes and levels of understanding. In L. Tan, S. Gopinathan & W. K. Ho, *Education in Singapore.* Singapore: Prentice-Hall.
Watkins, C. (2001). Learning about learning enhances performance. *Research Matters,* No. 13. London: Institute of Education.
Wragg, T. (2001). Breaking Through to Learning Conference, Unpublished conference Keynote address, Merchant's Hall, London, February 26th.

54

Time: Allocated, Institutional and Task Oriented

MAURICE GALTON
University of Cambridge, England

1. INTRODUCTION

For teachers, the degree of commitment exhibited by the pupils and the extent to which such pupils engage on their set tasks without distraction is usually accepted as the outward sign that the lesson is going well. The assumption behind this teacher maxim is that the more time a pupil spends working on the task, the more he or she will learn and the better he or she will do on tests designed to assess the knowledge, skills and ideas taught. However, matters are not as straightforward as they might at first appear. Pupil performance may be directly related to the time spent on the task but some of this time may be spent out of school doing homework or receiving additional tutoring. In class pupils may appear to be working but will do so at different rates so that one pupil may cover two pages with writing while another pupil has managed only half a side. The purpose of this article is to explore these different aspects of instructional time as they manifest themselves in different countries and in particular within the Asia-Pacific region.

2. THEORETICAL FRAMEWORK

As Simon (1981, p. 125) has pointed out, much of the debate about teaching has taken place at a somewhat superficial level because of the use of "crude, basically meaningless, generalised categories" and, in particular, the "wide acceptance of the unresolved dichotomies between traditional and progressive approaches, child centred and subject centred approaches or more generally between the formal and informal". In the United States and the United Kingdom this debate was a reaction against the reforms of the 1960s: reforms that grew out of a conviction that major problems to do with poverty and racial bigotry, were largely the result of ignorance so that with better education and fairer opportunities a more just and better society would emerge. There was widespread criticism of the practice of placing children in classes by ability (streaming) and following the work of Flanders (1964), a greater demand for greater student participation in the process of learning with less teacher direction. In the United Kingdom, for example, the 1967 Plowden Report specifically endorsed the maxim that 'finding out has proved to be better for children then being told'.

By the mid-1970s, however, much of the enthusiasm for reform had dissipated. The early results of the various American Headstart initiatives appeared to show that improving schooling made little difference to the existing social structures of the education system which tended to ensure that pupils from better-off home backgrounds achieved greater scholastic success. At the same time, the sharp decline in economic well-being following the oil crisis increasingly prompted governments in the developed countries to ask whether they were receiving sufficient value for the large sums of money they were investing in education. This, in turn, led them to question the use of what were often termed 'trendy teaching methods'. In the United Kingdom this debate was fuelled by the publication of Bennett's (1976) *Teaching Styles and Pupil Progress*, while in the United States Brophy and Good (1986) reviewed a large number of studies all of which tended to suggest that informal, more open forms of teaching were less successful where the outcomes used to measure success were standardised tests of numeracy and literacy. Central in this review was the study of beginning teachers, defined as teachers with less than five years' experience, in the State of California (Denham & Lieberman, 1986).

The problem for these and other researchers, who argued that when teaching so-called 'basic skills' teachers needed to take a more direct role than suggested by those in favour of indirect or informal teaching methods, was that this message was likely to be interpreted by politicians and the media as a call for a return to traditional teaching largely based upon rote learning. However, the philosophy behind the direct teaching approach was not inspired by a model of learning which conceived the pupil's mind as an empty vessel which needed to be filled with information provided by the teacher. Instead it developed out of the concept of 'mastery learning'. Theorists who sought to apply this concept to school learning, such as Carroll (1963) later followed by Bloom (1976), shared the optimistic notions of education current in the 1960s. For these theorists any pupil, in principle, could be taught anything if allowed sufficient time. Carroll expressed this proposition in the statement that the degree of learning was directly proportional to the ratio "of time actually spent by a pupil on a task divided by the time needed by the pupil to master the demands of that task."

This was a radical proposition, although not fully realised at the time, because it challenged the conventional view of ability. Psychometric approaches regarded a child's abilities, as measured by intelligence tests, to be fixed and largely predetermined so that only some children were capable of learning certain things. Hence it was sensible and more efficient to stream pupils according to their abilities so that the curriculum could be tailored to their specific needs, Carroll's self-evident proposition dispensed with this need to stream by ability in arguing that only time prevented a pupil from completing any task, irrespective of their initial ability and their aptitude.

Of course, this alternative model of school learning has practical limitations. Streaming, where retained, would be a function of pace (i.e. by putting children who were moving at the same speed together). There are also implications when planning the school curriculum since time spent on one subject in which the student had an interest and aptitude would need to be balanced against time spent on another which at that stage was not as central to the pupil's needs. For example, a pupil who showed the capacity to become a professional athlete might be timetabled for additional Physical Education lessons. This model contrasts with that used to construct the typical school curriculum (for example, the United Kingdom's National Curriculum) which is governed by notions of 'entitlement', that is all pupils are entitled to a statutory amount of time for every subject on the curriculum.

The purpose of providing this detailed explanation is not necessarily to support the validity of Carroll's ideas as applied to school learning. It is rather to underscore the point that the emphasis given by these researchers to time as a central feature in pupils' learning was, from the outset, part of an emancipatory and essentially democratic model of education designed to improve the circumstances of the disadvantaged in society. In the United States these ideas triggered a number of studies concerned with the allocation of time in schools. The findings showed that there was considerable variation in the amount of schooling that different pupils received. To begin with there were differences in the amount of **instructional time**, characterised by the start and end of the school day. There are also marked differences between the **allocated time**, that is time which was given over to the study of academic subjects as opposed to break and lunch times, periods for games, and classroom transitions when pupils move from one lesson to another. Most importantly in the model was the concept of **engaged time**, that is the time that pupils actually spent working during the course of the lesson on the set tasks. The difference between allocated time and engaged time has sometimes been referred to as **evaporated time** because it is the time that disappears through various interruptions during the class period when, for example, a pupil arrives bringing a message from the headteacher which has to be read out to the whole class, or the time spent in housekeeping duties such as tidying up the classroom at the end of the session.

Taking Carroll's ideas forward, Harnischfeger and Wiley (1978) produced a model of learning which mediated the influence of Carroll's key variable time, while maintaining that the allocated time was still the major determinant in predicting pupils' achievement. Among the teacher characteristics listed in the model, four major categories were identified: (a) the first concerned planning, which involved detailed specifications and guidelines of all classroom activities; (b) the second reflected a teacher's capacity to translate these plans into classroom plans and activities; (c) the third element refers to the teacher's ability to motivate pupils to increase their class involvement; and (d) the fourth, the teacher's communication skills to facilitate pupils' learning. In defining the curriculum Harnischfeger and Wiley were more concerned with what they term 'learning settings' to do with the grouping strategies, the kinds of teacher supervision and the teacher managerial activities rather than curriculum content.

A key question within this approach, therefore, is to identify those factors which maximise pupils' time on task and hence their achievement. Among the characteristics identified in the classrooms with highest levels of on-task behaviour were the following behaviours.

- Teachers were accurate in their diagnosis of pupil performance levels.
- Teachers were able to set appropriate tasks such that they matched the children's learning needs.
- High levels of pupil-teacher interaction took place concerning the presentation of information on academic content, monitoring work and giving feedback about performance. Such interactions usually took place in a group or class setting and were not characterised by individual work.
- Teachers spent more time discussing the structure of the lesson.
- Teachers gave satisfactory responses to students' requests.
- Teachers' value systems emphasised academic goals.
- Teachers encouraged students to take responsibility in helping each other and sharing materials.

When these characteristics are linked with concepts of mastery teaching (Block, 1971) then the process, first referred to as 'direct instruction' by Rosenshine (1979) emerges. The term, direct instruction, was deliberately chosen to distinguish the process from Anderson's (1939) and later Flanders' (1964) use of direct teaching. For Flanders direct teaching involved a teacher telling pupils things in an authoritarian manner. Rosenshine and others saw no reason why teachers could not instruct pupils within a warm friendly unthreatening classroom climate. The basic steps in direct instruction are that pupils are first presented with the new information, then allowed practice, then assessed either through testing or questioning, and then re-taught those parts which they have failed to master. Laslett and Smith (1984) offer a more detailed specification. The cycle is then repeated until the desired success rate is achieved. The success rate is readily determined by both the contexts in which the task is taking place and the nature of the task demand. For example, if problem solving of a particular kind generally takes place in groups it is not necessary that all pupils achieve high levels of success on the assumption that one of the group will find an acceptable solution on most occasions. However, if the task were to administer a dangerous drug to a patient such that the dose had to be accurate to a milli-litre then 100 per cent success rate would be required. One Singapore study found that in a comparison between mastery learning and non-mastery learning classes, the former group outscored the latter on a summative English test consisting of grammar, comprehension and spelling. The greatest gains occurred with comprehension where 80 per cent achieved mastery in the mastery learning group compared to 71 per cent in the control (Ho Wah Kam, 1983). Teachers, however, had to find additional time outside the existing timetable to implement the scheme in order to complete the teaching-testing-re-teaching cycle. They also spent up to two extra hours per week in lesson preparation, marking and recording individual pupil's progress.

Although, therefore 'time on task' is a central concept in the use of direct instruction its relevance may be of less importance with other teaching approaches which involve higher order cognitive activity. Rosenshine (1987, p. 258) has pointed out that:

> Findings on direct instruction are most relevant when the objective is to teach procedures, explicit concepts or a body of knowledge. Specifically, these results are most applicable when teaching mathematics concepts and procedures, English grammar, sight vocabulary, historical knowledge, reading maps and charts and science knowledge and procedures. These findings are less relevant when teaching implicit areas, that is where the skills to be taught cannot be broken down into explicit steps. Such areas include mathematics problem solving, analysis of literature, writing papers or discussion of social issues.

This issue will be taken up in the final section where the recent reforms now taking place in most Asia-Pacific countries are considered.

3. ALLOCATION OF TIME IN ENGLISH AND AMERICAN CLASSROOMS

Throughout the 1970s and 1980s a series of studies based upon systematic classroom observation was carried out into time allocation in British classrooms.

The first of these was Bennett's (1976) study, *Teaching Styles and Pupil Progress*. In this study teaching styles were identified through the use of a questionnaire, teachers were categorised as being either formal or informal. However, in attempts to explain differences between the relative success of the different styles pupils were observed and the amount of work related and social interaction between pupils noted. In the formal classrooms, the work rate was around 70 per cent at a maximum, where as in the informal classroom it never exceeded more than 60 per cent. A more detailed study (Galton et al., 1980) was then carried out between 1975 and 1980 at Leicester and was called the 'ORACLE Research' (Observational Research and Classroom Learning Evaluation). ORACLE is perhaps the most important study carried out in the primary classrooms in the United Kingdom and is still the most frequently cited piece of research concerning primary classrooms in the United Kingdom. The findings have been replicated in a number of other studies. During the 1980s, for example, two studies were carried out in London, one in upper primary schools (Mortimore et al., 1988), and the other in lower primary schools (Tizard et al., 1988). The Mortimore study used the same observation instrument as in ORACLE. During the late 1980s and early 1990s Alexander (1991), Pollard et al. (1994) and Croll (1996) carried out further studies. All these studies had figures for time on task in the same range as the earlier Bennett and ORACLE studies. More recently in a post National Curriculum survey Galton et al. (1999) produced averages of around 69 per cent. However, prior to the introduction of the National Curriculum there were wider variations in both instructional and allocated time. Bennett et al. (1980) found a variation of 17 per cent in the proportion of time allocated to mathematics and 30.7 per cent for work in English language.

In the United States similar findings emerged and are summarised in Brophy and Good (1986). Time on task averaged around 70 per cent although the proportions of allocated time to the main academic subjects was less at around 60 per cent. In the Beginning Teacher Education Study (BTES) in America more emphasis was placed on the time students spent engaging on tasks on which they made fewer errors and therefore needed less help from teachers. This led to the concept of '**academic learning time**' (ALT) defined as the amount of time students spent engaged in academic tasks that they could perform with high success. ALT varied considerably within a class and across grades. Fifth grade mathematics classes averaged only 35 per cent (see Brophy & Good, 1986, p. 352).

4. TIME ALLOCATION AND TIME ON TASKS IN ASIAN CLASSROOMS

Typically, Western writers tend to equate schooling in the East as mainly characterised by the predominance of whole class teaching and associated high levels of time on task (Reynolds & Farrell, 1996). In Western classrooms, on average, figures in the region of 20 per cent of lesson time can be spent on non-instructional matters (either disciplinary or routine administrative). The corresponding reported average figures for some Asian classrooms are much lower in the range 7 to 10 per cent (Anderson et al., 1989; Stigler & Stevenson, 1990). Unfortunately, there are few observation studies of the kind described in the previous section that can provide detailed comparative data. However, what is available suggests that across different countries there may be equally wide variations (World Bank, 1990). Alexander (2000, p. 416) in his study of five cultures noted that the highest levels of distraction occurred in Indian and American classrooms. The source of this behaviour differed in that while American children misbehaved, or engaged in casual conversations during the lesson, Indian pupils engaged in very few of these kinds of interactions. Instead they stopped working because they did not understand the task and were unable to proceed. Unlike their American counterparts they did not then distract other pupils who were still engaged but sat passively holding their pens and staring at the blackboard. Since the teacher monitored activity from the front of the class and the rooms were cramped and crowded, over time the divergence between those who understood and those who did not increased substantially (Alexander, 2000, p. 417). In contrast, data obtained during the evaluation of the Target Orientated Curriculum (TOC) in Hong Kong (Morris et al., 1999) showed that in Chinese language and mathematics lessons the average engagement of pupils when either listening to the teacher, attempting to ask or answer a teacher's question or engaging in some specific activity such as chanting responses in unison was over 77 per cent at its lowest and in some cases 86 per cent. In an earlier Singapore study Goh So Tian (1989) found that student teachers when teaching pupils to read spent 19 per cent of the time inducting pupils into the lesson by providing background information and stimulating pupils' thinking. Once the main part of the lesson was underway the bulk of the time (38 per cent involved the teacher asking questions or responding to the pupils' answers, leaving 28 per cent of the lesson for explaining and modelling and 14 per cent for feedback and evaluation. Pupils spent most of their time, in contrast to their peers in English classrooms either in reading (25 per cent) or in various forms of communicative activity (43 per cent). This involved making presentations, asking questions and various communicative activities.

Time allocation is complicated in many Asian countries by the use of the double shift system of schooling (Bray, 2000) in which different pupils attend the same school in the morning and afternoon. Bray's (2000, p. 44) data shows that the differences between single and double shift systems are not large. In single session primary schools in Hong Kong, for example, pupils receive 70 minutes additional teaching for a total of 23 hours and 20 minutes per week. In the Philippines the difference is 80 minutes per week while pupils in Singapore and Malaysia have exactly the same time in both types of schools (22 hours 30 minutes). However, as Bray points out such figures can be misleading in that where the amount of allocated time is reduced this is likely to be at the cost of the arts and physical education rather than core subjects such as languages, mathematics and science. Hence the general finding that overall, academic achievement in these subjects, is much the same in both types of school.

Recently, the repeat of the Third International Mathematics and Science Study (TIMSS-R) has collected information on the time allocation afforded to these subjects in the participating countries. Some caution needs to be exercised in interpreting these data because they are based on teacher estimates and not direct observation. Nevertheless, the proportions of time allocated to mathematics correspond closely to the ranking on the average attainment scores. For example, nine per cent of Singapore and Hong Kong pupils received over five hours of mathematics teaching per week and 37 per cent and 71 per cent respectively received between five and 3.5 hours teaching. The corresponding figures for the United Kingdom were two per cent and five per cent although the recent introduction of a daily numeracy hour in English primary schools will have improved these figures. In contrast there is a negative relationship between time allocation in science and attainment. In the United Kingdom, which scores well in science, 95 per cent of pupils receive between two and 3.5 hours instruction per week. In Singapore and Hong Kong, 46 per cent and 80 per cent of pupils received greater amounts of instruction respectively (Rudduck, 2000).

Teachers also reported on the time they spent on different classroom activities. Singapore and United States teachers spent most time on administration (6 per cent) with Japan the lowest (2 per cent). Homework revision occupies 13 per cent of the lesson time in Singapore, just below the highest level (15 per cent) in the United States. This contrasts with 12 per cent in Hong Kong and Taiwan but only 6 per cent in the United Kingdom, Korea and Japan. Generally, the time spent on lecturing and demonstrating is much higher in Asian classrooms according to these teacher reports. The proportions of time range from 39 per cent (Taiwan) to 28 per cent (Singapore). This contrasts with figures of 20 per cent and 18 per cent for the United States and the United Kingdom. Most countries spend about a third of the time on practice activities with the exception of the United Kingdom where the reported figure is 51 per cent. Just under half this latter figure (24 per cent) is taken up in independent practice or what Americans term 'seat work'. This is much higher than in Asian countries where the corresponding figure is around 10 per cent. Since the Western literature clearly establishes that time on task falls considerably when children work on their own on such activities, these reported figures help to explain the higher levels of pupil engagement in Asian classrooms.

5. TIME ALLOCATION OUTSIDE OF SCHOOL

The figures provided by Bray (2000) for the weekly amounts of allocated time in school are generally compatible with those recorded in Western classrooms (Galton et al., 1999; Alexander, 2000). Such comparative analysis, however, takes no account of the fact that some pupils remain on task for considerable periods after the school day ends or at weekends. These children spend time completing homework or receiving additional help through private tutoring. Postlethwaite and Wiley's (1992) survey showed that time spent on homework varied from 4.5 to nine hours per week with Hong Kong pupils spending just over six hours on such activity. A more recent survey of Singapore parents (Quah et al., 1997) reported that just over half (52 per cent) of high achieving pupils spent up to two hours per day on school work with nearly a quarter of pupils (24 per cent) doing between three and four hours. The corresponding figures for the low achieving pupils were 42 per cent and 16 per cent respectively which still represents an average estimate of some ten hours per week. In addition over 80 per cent spent at least one hour a day reading and in the case of girls this was more likely to be two hours.

In the same survey parents reported that a substantial proportion (44 per cent) provided extra tuition at home in mathematics and English language, figures supporting an earlier study (Kwan-Terry, 1991). A more comprehensive review of the use of private tutoring is provided by Bray (1999). In Hong Kong some 45 per cent of primary students received additional tutoring (Lee, 1996). In the Republic of Korea the figure for elementary students is nearly double (84 per cent) as reported in Bray (1999, p. 24). Most notably in Japan additional help outside school is supplied at formal establishments. Nine of these centres, known as *juku*, are sufficiently large to be listed on the Japanese stock exchange (Bray, 1999, p. 23) and nearly 70 per cent of all pupils have attended a *juku* at one point in their school career. Competition for places can be fierce. Bray (1999, p. 41) reports that one establishment accepted 1868 students from 11,000 Grade 4 applicants. Bray provides an interesting thesis, arguing that in countries that adopt egalitarian principles for public schooling, private tuition provides an important safety net. While helping the under-privileged to catch up it also allows affluent parents to accept the limitations within the school systems because they can afford to buy examination success for their children and provide opportunities for additional study of more neglected areas of the curriculum such as music and art.

How far additional tutoring leads to improved achievement is not totally clear. The evidence suggests that since students have greater opportunities to learn they should score higher on tests but results are mixed (Bray, 1999, p. 51). A recent Singapore study found that students who spent most hours a week having extra tuition the lower the grade scores obtained (*New Paper*, 1999). Benefits appear to be greater when the tests measure procedural knowledge rather than more complex abstract forms of problem solving.

6. TIME AND THE QUALITY OF INSTRUCTIONAL TASK

As Alexander (2000) notes in his international comparisons in primary education, 'time' is a problematic educational concept. He points to the experience of Berlack and Berlack (1981) who attempted to make sense of the dilemmas faced by teachers in the progressive schools of two English rural counties, Oxfordshire and Leicestershire. Teachers were constrained by the fact that the school day was finite and tasks had to be completed while at the same time seeking to "cede control of time to their pupils in order to foster autonomy and self-discipline" (Alexander, 2000, p. 411). Thus time as an educational concept implies more than the application of a managerial model designed to ensure maximum efficiency whereby most pupils spend most of their time successfully completing worthwhile tasks. It is also, as Alexander argues "a manifestation of conflicting versions of worthwhile education" (Alexander, 2000, p. 412), particularly in regard to the extent to which teachers are prepared to cede control of some part of the school day to their pupils. Allocating the amount of time required for pupils to complete activities such as a revision exercise in the mathematics textbook or a worksheet on the use of speech marks in English is a relatively straightforward task for the teacher. More difficult is the situation where pupils are expected to exercise some responsibility for their learning, as when planning and designing an experiment in science as a group or discussing ideas for a story or poem.

These are just the kind of dilemmas likely to face many Asian teachers in the light of recent attempts to reform the existing school systems to meet the challenge of globalisation. In Singapore, according to the Prime Minister, Lee Chok Tong "students need to develop their skills to cope with change to be independent learners and problem solvers, to acquire skills to seek out new information and knowledge to think critically and creatively ... to show initiative and to innovate" (Sharpe & Gopinathan, 1997, p. 377). Similar aims are set out in the recent Hong Kong Education Commission's Report, (2000, p. 4) *Learning for Life-Learning through Life,* to enable students to engage in "life long learning, critical and exploratory thinking" to be capable of "adapting to change and filled with self confidence and a team spirit". This implies a shift of emphasis away from formal compartmentalised academic studies to integrated learning, a shift from a focus on textbooks to greater use of diversified teaching materials, and above all, a shift from the transmission of knowledge model of pedagogy to one based on "learning to learn" (Hong Kong Education Commission, 2000, pp. 61–62).

The emphasis in these reforms is being placed on the acquisition of metacognitive knowledge (Alexander et al., 1991) and teaching for understanding rather than for transmission (Good & Brophy, 1994). This involves greater use of cooperative learning rather than direct instruction and thus challenges the utility of much of the time allocation models of schooling that for many years have underpinned the school effectiveness research movement. But the egalitarian principles first set out by the early reformers, which helped to define the key constructs of mastery learning, remain valid even if they must now be redefined within a different context.

REFERENCES

Alexander, P., Schallert, D., & Hare, V. (1991). Coming to terms: How researchers in learning and literacy talk about knowledge. *Review of Educational Research, 61*(3), 315–343.

Alexander, R. (1991). *Primary Education in Leeds.* Twelfth and Final Report from the Primary Needs Independent Evaluation Project. Leeds: University of Leeds.

Alexander, R. (2000). *Culture and Pedagogy: International Comparisons in Primary Education.* Oxford: Blackwell.

Anderson, H. (1939). The measurement of domination and of socially integrative behaviour in teachers' contacts with children. *Child Development, 10,* 73–89.

Anderson, L., Ryan, D., & Shapiro, B. (1989). *The IEA Classroom Environment Study.* Oxford: Pergamon Press.

Bennett, S. N. (1976). *Teaching Styles and Pupil Progress.* London: Open Books.

Bennett, S. N., Andreae, J., Hegarty, P., & Wade, B. (1980). *Open Plan Schools: Teaching, Curriculum, Design.* Slough: NFER.

Berlack, A., & Berlack, H. (1981). *Dilemmas of Schooling.* London: Methuen.

Block, J. (1971). *Mastery Learning: Theory and Practice.* New York: Holt, Rinehart and Winston.

Bloom, B. (1976). *Human Characteristics and School Learning.* New York: McGraw Hill.

Bray, M. (1999). *The Shadow Education System: Private Tutoring and its Implications for Planners.* Paris: International Institute for Educational Planning, UNESCO.

Bray, M. (2000). *Double-Shift Schooling: Design and Operation for Cost-Effectiveness.* Paris: International Institute for Educational Planning, UNESCO.

Brophy, J. E., & Good, T. L. (1986). Teacher behaviour and student achievement. In M. C. Wittrock (Ed.), *Handbook of Research on Teaching* (3rd ed.). New York: Macmillan.

Carroll, J. (1963). A model for school learning. *Teachers College Record, 64*, 723–733.

Croll, P. (Ed.) (1996). *Teachers, Pupils and Primary Schooling*. London: Cassell.

Denham, C., & Lieberman, A. (Eds.) (1986). *Time to Learn*. Report of the Beginning Teacher Education Studies. Washington, DC: National Institute of Education.

Flanders, N. A. (1964). Some relationships among teacher influence, pupil attitudes and achievement. In B. J. Biddle & W. J. Ellena (Eds.), *Contemporary Research on Teacher Effectiveness*. New York: Holt, Rinehart and Winston.

Galton, M., Hargreaves, L., Comber, C., & Wall, D. (1999). *Inside the Primary Classroom: 20 Years On*. London: Routledge.

Galton, M., Simon, B., & Croll, P. (1980). *Inside the Primary Classroom*. London: Routledge & Kegan Paul.

Goh Soo Tian (1989). Instruction research in reading comprehension: A preliminary observation study of reading comprehension classes taught by IE student teachers. *Singapore Journal of Education, 10*(2), 25–31.

Good, T., & Brophy, G. (1994). *Looking at Classrooms* (6th ed). New York: Harper Collins.

Harnischfeger, A., & Wiley, D. (1978). Conceptual issues in models of school learning. *Curriculum Studies, 10*(3), 215–231.

Ho Wah Kam (1983). *Mastery Learning Project: A Research Report*. Singapore: Institute of Education.

Hong Kong Education Commission (2000). *Learning for Life, Learning through Life: Reform Proposals for the Education System in Hong Kong*. Hong Kong: Hong Kong Special Administrative Region (SAR) of The People's Republic of China.

Kwan-Terry, A. (1991). The economics of language in Singapore: Students use of extra-curricular language lessons. *Journal of Asia-Pacific Communication, 2*(1), 69–89.

Laslett, R., & Smith, C. (1984). *Effective Classroom Management*. London: Croom Helm.

Lee, C. (1996). *Children and Private Tuition*. Hong Kong: Hong Kong Federation of Youth Groups.

Morris, P., Adamson, R., Au, M., Chan, K., Chee, M., Chik. P., Ko, P., Kwan, T., Lo, M., Mok, A., Ng, F., & Tong, A. (1999). *Target Orientated Curriculum: Feedback and Assessment in Hong Kong Primary Schools*, Final report. Hong Kong: Education Department.

Mortimore, P., Sammons, P., Stoll, L. D., & Ecob, R. (1988). *School Matters: The Junior Years*. Wells: Open Books.

New Paper (1999). Parents, listen: More tuition, lower grades. *The New Paper*, Singapore, 15 June.

Pollard, A., Broadfoot, P., Croll, P., Osborn, M., & Abbott, D. (1994). *Changing English Primary Schools*. London: Cassell.

Postlewaite, T. N., & Wiley, D. (Eds.) (1992). *The IEA Study of Science: Science Achievement in 23 Countries*. Oxford: Pergamon Press.

Quah, M. L., Sharpe, P., Eng, A., & Heng, M. (1997). Home and parental influence on the achievement of lower primary school children in Singapore. In J. Tan, S. Gopinathan & Ho Wah Kam (Eds.), *Education Singapore: A Book of Readings* (pp. 319–342). Singapore: Prentice Hall.

Reynolds, D., & Farrell, S. (1996). *Worlds Apart? A Review of International Studies of Educational Achievement Involving England*, A Review for the Office for Standards in Education (OFSTED). London: HMSO.

Rosenshine, B. (1979). Content, time and direct instruction. In P. Peterson & H. Walberg (Eds.), *Research on Teaching Concepts, Findings and Implications*. California, Berkeley: McCutchan.

Rosenshine, B. (1987). Direct instruction. In M. Dunkin (Ed.), *Teaching and Teacher Education*. Oxford: Pergamon.

Rudduck, G. (2000). *Third International Mathematics and Science Study Repeat (TIMSS-R): First National Report*, Research Report RR234. Slough: NFER.

Sharpe, L., & Gopinathan, S. (1997). Effective island, effective schools: Repair and restructuring in the Singapore school system. In L. Tan, S. Gopinathan & Ho Wah Kam (Eds.), *Education Singapore: A Book of Readings* (pp. 369–384). Singapore: Prentice Hall.

Simon, B. (1981). Why no pedagogy in England? In B. Simon & W. Taylor (Eds.), *Education in the Eighties, The Central Issues* (pp. 124–145). London: Batsford.

Stigler, J., & Stevenson, H. (1990). How Asian teachers polish each lesson to perfection. *American Educator, 15*(1), 12–20.
Tizard, B., Blatchford, D., Burke, J., Farquhar, C., & Plewis, I. (1988). *Young Children at School in the Inner City.* Hove: Lawrence Erlbaum.
World Bank (1990). *Primary Education.* Washington, DC: World Bank.

55

Monitoring Student Learning

GEOFF N. MASTERS

The Australian Council for Educational Research, Melbourne, Australia

1. INTRODUCTION

Most countries in the Asia-Pacific region recognise the importance of systematically collecting and monitoring levels of student learning. Under the Education For All initiative, many countries have turned their attention to developing reliable means of describing the knowledge and skills that comprise quality basic education and are developing the technical and organisational capacity to monitor student learning and to evaluate the effectiveness of educational policies and practices.

The reliable assessment of student achievement is required not only for improved teaching and learning, but also for the purposes of educational accountability and for the efficient allocation of human and financial resources. Substantial progress has been made in recent years in techniques for monitoring student achievement, and considerable attention has been paid to ways in which countries can use data from these programs to make the most effective and efficient use of limited resources.

The international Education For All Assessment drew attention to the important role of reliable and valid information about learning outcomes for monitoring and educational policy making. This exercise also revealed that achievement data were not always available in formats that could be used by policy-makers, and even when they were available, governments did not always take them into consideration in their educational decision-making.

This article outlines some considerations in designing and implementing a program for monitoring student learning. It includes examples of initiatives from several countries in the Asia-Pacific region.

2. DIMENSIONS OF LEARNING

The concept of individual progress – or growth, development, or improvement – is a fundamental idea in all teaching and learning. This concept is invoked whenever educators describe students as becoming better readers, using more sophisticated language, becoming more tolerant of others, developing deeper understandings, acquiring higher-order skills, solving more difficult problems, or mastering more advanced knowledge. Educators use words such as 'better', 'deeper', 'higher' and 'more' to describe the direction of student progress in particular areas of learning.

Educational programs and curricula in schools are designed to support and encourage student development on many different dimensions. School programs, at least in the compulsory years of schooling in the Asia-Pacific region, aim to develop students' skills and understandings in learning areas as diverse as languages, mathematics, physical education, music, and art. An academically well-rounded student makes progress on many fronts, including reading and writing in their first language, mathematical literacy, scientific literacy, health and physical education, studies of society and environment, technology, and the arts.

However, schools' concerns are not limited to the academic development of students. Schools in the Asia-Pacific region also seek to promote growth in personal and social skills such as leadership, the ability to work as a member of a team, self-confidence, empathy, self-motivation, and independence. Many aspects of student development are not specific to particular learning areas but are best thought of as general, cross-curricular skills or attributes.

Student development is thus multidimensional: students make progress on many dimensions simultaneously. However, when it comes to assessing and monitoring a student's development, it is usual, and probably necessary, to focus attention on one aspect of development at a time. For example, in monitoring levels of achievement nationally, a country may choose to focus on progress in mathematics, or perhaps more narrowly on students' levels of achievement in a particular aspect of mathematics, such as numerical reasoning, measurement, or chance and data. In monitoring developing competence in first language, countries sometimes make separate assessments in the areas of reading, speaking, listening, and writing.

Malaysia measures learning achievement at the national level through the Primary School Achievement Test (*Ujian Penilaian Sekolah Rendah*) administered in Year 6, the final year of primary school education. The PSAT assesses pupils' academic achievement in Bahasa Malaysia (the national language), English Language, Mathematics and Science. The objective of PSAT is to evaluate the achievement of primary students in reading, writing, scientific and numeracy skills in Malay and in the students' own language (Chinese or Tamil).

2.1. *Higher-Order Skills*

In today's world it is necessary, but not sufficient, for students to achieve minimal competence in areas such as reading, writing and numeracy. Most countries now recognise that, beyond the achievement of basic competence, students also need to develop critical literacy and numeracy skills of the kind required for effective functioning in everyday life. Skills of these kinds are now widely advocated by countries in the Asia-Pacific region and are being incorporated into some national assessment programs.

Basic reading proficiency involves an ability to decode text, to interpret word meanings and grammatical structures, and to understand meaning at least at a superficial level. But reading literacy for effective functioning in modern society requires much more than this: it also depends on an ability to read between the lines and to reflect on the purposes and intended audiences of texts, to recognise devices used by writers to convey messages and to influence readers, and the ability to interpret meaning from the structures and features of written materials. Reading literacy depends on an ability to understand and interpret a wide variety of text types, and to make sense of texts by relating them to the situations in which they appear.

In the context of the United States National Assessment of Educational Progress, Applebee et al. (1987) argue that, in today's world, literacy consists of much more than the ability to extract surface meaning from text and to express basic ideas in writing. They argue that there are two important components of literacy: (a) the ability to derive surface understanding from written materials and to express similar understanding in writing; and (b) the ability to reason effectively about what is read and written in order to extend understanding of the ideas expressed.

These authors go on to point out that in national assessments of reading and writing in the United States, most children and young adults can understand what they read and can express their thoughts in writing at a surface level. However, only a small percentage can reason effectively about what they read and write: in other words, function as literate consumers of text, including being able to recognise the techniques through which writers seek to influence and occasionally manipulate readers.

Numeracy similarly depends on a familiarity with a body of mathematical knowledge and skills. Basic number facts and operations, working with money, and fundamental ideas about space and shape, including working with measurements, form part of this essential body of knowledge and skills. But numeracy for effective functioning in modern society requires much more than this: it also depends on an ability to think and work mathematically, including modelling and problem solving. These competencies include knowing the extent and limits of mathematical concepts, following and evaluating mathematical arguments, posing mathematical problems, choosing ways of representing mathematical situations, and expressing ideas on matters with a mathematical content. Numeracy depends on an ability to apply these skills, knowledge and understandings in a variety of personal and social contexts.

When assessment programs include tasks that challenge students to think and to apply their learning, these programs set high rather than low expectations of performance. They also provide teachers and students with examples of the kinds of understanding and thinking to which all students should be aspiring. If the assessment programs being introduced across the Asia-Pacific region are to communicate high expectations of student achievement, then they must be designed to assess not only foundational knowledge and skills, but also higher-order skills, including students' abilities to apply their learning and to reason about the material they encounter.

Kazakhstan is an example of a country that has established procedures for the monitoring of educational achievement. The Kazakhstan assessment program, the Monitoring Learning Achievement project, has been supported by UNESCO-UNICEF assistance to countries in developing and strengthening national capacity to monitor the quality of basic educational programs.

The former Soviet education system in Kazakhstan placed considerable emphasis on the acquisition of factual, instrumental knowledge rather that on creative thinking and problem solving. Under that system, assessments of students' learning achievements and of the quality of education focused on what was referred to as 'memory control' and 'operational knowledge' to the exclusion of understanding, analysis, problem solving, and the identification of positive attitudes towards learning. Recent educational reform in Kazakhstan has had as an objective the development and assessment of higher-order competencies and the investigation of factors affecting the learning of these higher-order outcomes.

3. ASSESSMENT METHODS

Decisions about student achievement in an area of learning and about national progress over time can be based on observations and judgments of students' performances and work. Records of these observations and judgments provide the evidence required to draw conclusions about national levels of achievement and progress.

In planning the collection of evidence it is important that assessment methods are chosen carefully. Not all methods are capable of providing information about all learning outcomes. Some outcomes require particular methods. The assessment of students' abilities to find and select relevant information; to analyse collected material; and to write a report of their conclusions is probably best done through an assigned project, for example. The assessment of students' abilities to write for a range of purposes and audiences is probably best done through a collection or portfolio of their writing. And the assessment of oral language abilities is probably best done by observing spoken performances.

A complete picture of student achievement in an area of learning depends on useful information about a broad range of learning outcomes. A systemwide assessment program that addresses only a narrow range of outcomes provides a limited picture of achievement and so provides incomplete feedback to teaching and learning.

A second reason for choosing assessment methods carefully is that the choice of one method over another can send powerful messages to students about what is valued. If practical laboratory skills are said to be an important aspect of school science, for example, but course results are based entirely on paper and pencil tests, then students, and possibly teachers too, will focus their efforts on outcomes that can be assessed through paper and pencil tests. If the methods used to collect evidence address only a limited range of outcomes, then assessment procedures can distort teaching and learning.

3.1. *Considerations in Choosing Assessment Methods*

Ideally, the methods used to collect evidence about achievement in an area of learning would be designed to:

- reflect curriculum priorities;
- provide feedback that informs and guides instruction;
- be fair to all students;
- provide results that are reliable and comparable across schools and classes; and
- be administratively convenient and inexpensive.

In practice, methods of assessment usually are decided on pragmatic grounds and attach greater weight to some considerations than to others.

In a classroom, useful feedback to teaching and learning, practical convenience, and the availability of time and materials may be judged more important than considerations of reliability, fairness and comparability. In an admissions program, on the other hand, perceived objectivity and fairness may be judged more important than the accurate reflection of all curriculum priorities or the provision of instructionally useful feedback.

Curriculum relevance. In most educational assessment programs, the matching of assessment methods to curriculum content and goals is fundamental. Assessment methods are chosen to reflect faithfully, and provide evidence about, the range of knowledge, skills and understandings that make up an area of learning. Conclusions about student achievement are valid only when based on evidence about the intended range of outcomes.

The collection of evidence in an area of learning usually requires a variety of different assessment methods. Evidence about some outcomes may require observations and judgments of student behaviour in the classroom. Evidence about other outcomes may be collected through written work, including assignments, classroom quizzes and tests. Furthermore, evidence about still other outcomes may require the inspection and judgment of things that students have made.

In recent years many large-scale assessment programs have been reconstructed to provide evidence about a broader range of curriculum goals than have been traditionally addressed through written tests. These programs sometimes include portfolios of student work and assessments of oral communication skills, research skills, laboratory skills, and practical and manual skills.

However, considerations of reliability and comparability sometimes take precedence over curriculum coverage. In large-scale assessment programs, the requirements of fairness and objectivity often limit the range of assessment methods and hence the learning outcomes addressed. In the past, extensive use has been made of paper and pencil tests and examinations in these assessment contexts because of their perceived objectivity and reliability.

Practical convenience and cost also sometimes take precedence over curriculum fidelity. In large assessment programs in which tens or hundreds of thousands of students are assessed at a time, it may not be practicable to use particular methods of assessment, meaning that evidence may be collected on some kinds of learning outcomes but not on others.

Instructional utility. Ideally, methods for collecting evidence of student achievement are designed to provide information that is instructionally useful. Assessment methods are chosen and designed to yield insights into students' knowledge and conceptual understandings that can be used in future teaching and learning. In practice, of course, feedback to instruction is less important in some assessment contexts than in others.

One form of feedback likely to be useful in planning teaching and learning is a general estimate of where students are in their development: What levels of attainment have they reached? What kinds of skills, understandings and knowledge are typical of students at that level of attainment? What learning activities are likely to be most appropriate and useful next?

Fairness. Assessment methods also must be fair to students. This requirement is more important in some assessment contexts than others. It is especially important that assessments are made without prejudice in high stakes contexts where results can influence the allocation of resources or students' chances of employment or admission to other educational programs. But fairness is an important consideration in all assessment contexts.

Designers of assessment programs need to be aware of the ways in which the choice of an assessment method can influence the performances of students who do not speak the language of instruction as their first language, who come from particular cultural backgrounds, or who are physically disadvantaged. They also need to be aware of the ways in which the choice of assessment method can influence the relative performances of girls and boys.

Practical convenience. Another desirable feature of assessments is that they are convenient to implement. Practical convenience is especially important when there is a desire to collect evidence on a wide variety of learning outcomes for large numbers of students. When this is the intention, it is important that assessment procedures are manageable, easily incorporated into usual classroom activities, and capable of providing information that justifies the time and money required.

Practical feasibility takes on an even greater significance in assessment programs that attempt to provide both comprehensive curriculum coverage and high levels of reliability and comparability. It practice, these three intentions often prove difficult to satisfy simultaneously.

In Britain, for example, an attempt was made to collect evidence across the curriculum, for all students at particular Year levels, and in a way that would allow reliable comparisons across teachers and schools. Complex standard assessment tasks matched to curriculum goals were developed for administration by teachers. But these tasks took many hours of class time to administer, and tens of millions of pounds to develop. And, despite this effort, questions remained about the comparability of the resulting assessments because of differences in the conditions under which tasks were completed and the subjectivity of teachers' judgments.

Reliability and comparability. Assessment programs also must provide results that are reliable and comparable across schools and regions of a country. Reliability is particularly important when assessments are used to make comparisons of student groups. If the assessment of students' levels of attainment in an area of learning does not provide an accurate picture of their achievements, then any decision based on that assessment is likely to be unfair.

Reliable evidence is important in assessment programs designed to monitor standards across an education system over time. Because changes in average levels of student achievement over time tend to be small and difficult to detect, sensitive assessment methods and accurate data are essential.

4. ESTABLISHING AN ASSESSMENT PROGRAM

In establishing a system-wide assessment program, a number of fundamental decisions are required. These include decisions about:

- the subject areas to be tested;
- the grade levels at which testing is to occur;
- the assessment of a sample or all students in a grade;
- the nature of the tests to be used; and
- how performances are to be scored and results reported.

4.1. Subject Areas to be Tested

In many Asia-Pacific countries, assessment programs focus on literacy in the language of instruction, and sometimes on numeracy as well. Some large-scale assessment programs also assess student achievement in particular areas of the curriculum, such as science and health. Within literacy programs, the primary focus is inevitably on reading ability, with some programs also assessing writing.

4.2. Grade Levels to be Tested

It is common to test students at several key points in their schooling. Some assessment programs collect data on student progress early in their schooling with the intention of identifying students with learning difficulties. Many countries assess students in basic reading and perhaps writing at the completion of three or four years of schooling to identify students who have not yet mastered basic reading and writing skills and to take remedial steps to address reading difficulties. Education systems also sometimes conduct tests at other key points in the schooling process, such as the end of primary school (to assess readiness for secondary education) and at the completion of compulsory education.

4.3. Sample Versus Full-Cohort Testing

An important distinction in any discussion of the collection of outcome information on student learning is the distinction between full-cohort testing and a sample survey.

Full-cohort testing. Many education systems have put in place assessment programs to provide information to parents on student progress in some key learning areas at a few key times in the schooling process. In a number of Asia-Pacific countries, these assessment programs take the form of examinations at key stages in the schooling process (for example, the end of primary school).

The purpose of assessment programs of this kind is to collect and report reliable information on individual student progress in a few crucial areas of school learning. Data collected through these programs can be aggregated to provide summaries of group performances, either at the system level or at the school level.

Sample surveys. In contrast to full-cohort testing, a sample survey is designed to provide summary information at the system level only. Sample surveys allow trends in achievement levels to be studied over time and the performances of major subgroups of students to be compared and monitored. A survey can be used to compare student outcomes across systems and countries and to monitor the impact of educational initiatives on the achievements of identified student groups. But a sample survey usually does not provide reports on individual students.

A number of countries conduct surveys based on the performances of carefully drawn samples of students. Samples may be drawn to ensure adequate representation of particular categories of students so that the average performances of students in those categories can be compared and monitored. The United States National Assessment of Educational Progress is an example of a national survey of student achievement. But many other countries conduct similar surveys.

Although sample surveys obviously cannot fulfil the purposes of programs designed to provide parents with improved information on the progress of individual students, or to provide local school communities with information on school results, sample surveys have a number of important advantages over full-cohort testing.

One advantage of sample surveys is that they are capable of providing evidence about a rich and varied set of learning goals. Full-cohort testing programs inevitably address only those outcomes that can be assessed for many thousands of students at a time. Some full-cohort programs use machine-scored paper and pen questions. This constraint limits the range of learning outcomes that the program is able to address.

A second advantage is that, because sample surveys do not report on individual students, it is not necessary for all students to attempt the same set of assessment tasks. Different students can attempt different but overlapping sets of tasks (known as a 'multiple-matrix' design) to allow system reporting on a wide range of valued curriculum goals.

Finally, sample surveys have the advantage of being less expensive than full-cohort testing and tend to be less intrusive into classroom time. For these reasons, sample surveys are in general preferable to full-cohort testing for the purposes of collecting nationally comparable data on educational outcomes.

4.4. Nature of Tests

A decision also must be made about the format of the tests to be used in a system-wide assessment program. Will they be delivered orally with students writing their answers? Will students be given question booklets into which they write their answers? Is the use of machine-scored answer sheet feasible?

In addition to these questions, there is also a question about the types of test questions to be used. Will they require students to provide brief answers in their own words? Will they be multiple-choice? Will students be asked to write an extended written response? The choice of question format will depend in part on the outcomes to be assessed.

In most national assessment programs, students are provided with written question booklets to ensure a level of standardisation across classrooms and schools. When responses are not scored by machine, then scoring rules (rubrics) are required to ensure that students' answers are marked consistently and results are comparable from one school to the next and across different regions of the country.

4.5. Reporting and Evaluating Assessment Results

For most system-wide assessment programs there are multiple audiences for assessments of student achievement. Parents and students are audiences; other audiences include school communities, education systems, and the general public. These audiences usually are interested in different levels of detail about educational achievements.

Parents are likely to be most interested in knowing how students have performed in relation to teachers' expectations and in comparison with other children of the same age or grade. School communities may be most interested in knowing how children in a school are performing in relation to past levels of performance at that school or in relation to performances in other, similar schools. Education systems may be interested in monitoring the performances of particular groups of students, particularly if resources have been targeted at those groups. And the general public may be most interested in knowing that schools are teaching worthwhile knowledge and skills and that high educational standards are being achieved.

4.6. *Monitoring Progress*

It is important that reports of student achievement indicate overall levels of attainment and allow progress, including the progress of important subgroups of the student population, to be monitored over time. Ideally, reports of achievement:

- provide estimates of current levels of achievement;
- show progress or development;
- draw on a wide range of evidence about students' achievements;
- interpret levels of achievement descriptively in terms of the kinds of knowledge, skills and understandings typical of students at each level;
- display achievements graphically;
- interpret achievements by reference to the achievements of other students of the same age or grade.

For example, the national assessment in Thailand reports progress against a framework of achievement levels. The intention of the national assessment is to report students' levels of achievement, but also to provide information about what students typically are able to do at particular levels of achievement (Pravalpruk, 1996).

The survey of basic skills in Bangladesh also reports performance against four levels on a continuum of increasing proficiency. In reading, these levels are labelled 'non-reader', 'rudimentary', 'beginning' and 'minimally competent' and are illustrated with examples of the kinds of texts students at each level are able to read (Greaney et al., 1999).

Reporting against standards. When education systems report against standards, they make value judgements about the adequacy of student performance levels. Are students' performances at the desired levels? Are they good enough? In making judgements of this kind, reference can be made to either comparative or absolute benchmarks of achievement. Comparative benchmarks are set by reference to achievements in other places: for example, in other parts of the country or in other countries of the region. Comparative benchmarking looks to practices elsewhere as a guide to what can be achieved.

In education, the performances of students on past occasions, in other schools, other provinces, or other countries are sometimes used as comparative points of reference. In making judgements about current levels of achievement, education systems may seek answers to such questions as:

- how do science achievements in this country compare with achievements in other countries?

- how do levels of mathematics achievement in this province compare with the mathematics achievements of students in other provinces?
- how do students' literacy levels today compare with literacy levels ten years ago?

Absolute benchmarks, on the other hand, are set as desirable levels of performance for a particular purpose. In education, absolute standards are set by considering what it is that students should know and be able to do. For example,

- what kinds of mathematics knowledge and skill should be set as goals for all students by the end of the sixth grade?
- what minimum levels of knowledge and skill should be required for graduation from high school?

In the Cook Islands, Grade 4 assessments in English, Maori and mathematics were introduced in 1999. The Maori and English tests include tests of listening, reading, writing and dictation. The mathematics test contains tests in calculations, numbers, measurement, algebra, geometry and statistics. The Maori and mathematics tests are translated into seven island dialects. Students sit the Maori test in their local island dialect and elect to sit the mathematics test in either English or the local island dialect (Etches, 2000).

On each of English, Maori and mathematics, a test score corresponding to the minimum standard of basic competency in the subject is identified. Scores representing high standards of basic competency in each subject also are identified, and these performance standards are used in the reporting of student achievement. Results are reported for three geographical areas: northern, southern and Rarotonga.

The Cook Islands monitors trends over time by using the same Standardised Tests of Achievement in Grade 5 English, Grade 6 Maori and Grade 7 each year. Results on these tests showed a decline in Grade 5 English in the period 1994–99, although results from Rarotonga improved over this period and were significantly higher than in the outer islands. At the same time, achievement in Grade 6 Maori declined, mainly due to the lower achievement of students on Rarotonga. Achievement in Grade 7 mathematics increased slightly in line with improved performances on Rarotonga, despite a significant decline in the performance of students in the Southern Group (Etches, 2000).

Malaysia also has established minimum acceptable achievement levels on its Primary School Achievement Test (Year 6) and has monitored the percentage of students achieving these minimum performance standards over time. For example, in reading comprehension, the percentages of students achieving the minimum standard were: 1994 (95%), 1995 (93%), 1996 (96%), 1997 (96%); and in writing were: 1994 (78%), 1995 (79%), 1996 (80%), 1997 (81%), 1998 (79%).

4.7. An Example: Pakistan

In Pakistan it was recognised that neither the provincial assessment programs nor the government's traditional examination system had the professional or institutional capacity to undertake a rigorous assessment exercise that would yield valid and reliable national achievement data. It was decided to establish national achievement levels in the upper primary grades to monitor how the system was performing. A dialogue was commenced with the World Bank and donors to explore ways of establishing a credible assessment system in Pakistan in manageable stages (Hasan, 2000).

A first consideration was the number of grade levels at which assessments would be conducted. In order to collect data to satisfy Education For All requirements, it was decided to assess at only one grade level. Because most Provinicial and Area assessments were conducted at Grades 3 and 5, it was decided to conduct national assessments at Grade 4, the midpoint of the elementary structure. In addition, the low levels of achievement reported for Grade 3 and even Grade 5 suggested that Grade 4 would be the earliest that students were ready to take paper and pen tests. A further advantage of assessing at Grade 4 was that it would be technically possible to compare Grade 4 results with international studies of student achievement, such as the Third International Mathematics and Science Study.At a 1997 workshop in Lahore attended by representatives from all provinces or areas, it was estimated that 80 per cent of the curriculum content was common throughout the country and 20 per cent was province or area specific. However, since all provinces and areas followed the national curriculum, the competencies to be assessed would be the same. It was agreed that the national assessment should assess competencies only on the curriculum content common across all provinces and areas.

Sampling also posed a problem. It was recognised that, if provincial data were to be used for sample selection, then some cross-validation would be necessary. Reliable data on nonformal and private schools was unavailable, and consensus would be required at the national level in consultation with the provinces about what would be meaningful and practical sampling frames in terms of rural or urban, government or private, gender breakdowns, and the national-provincial curriculum mix in assessment instruments.

The planners of the national Grade 4 assessment recognised that care would be required in interpreting the findings of any national assessment. There were likely to be a number of socio-economic, cultural and regional variables affecting the levels of performance found through the national assessment. To allow more detailed study, it would be important to collect background information on schools (number of working days, student and teacher attendance, teacher-student ratio, participation of teachers and headteachers in training programs, annual examination results) and about communities (gross socio-economic level, involvement of Parent Teacher Associations or Village Education Committees in the schools, NGOs working for school improvement).

Finally, careful consideration would need to be given to the question of language. A decision would be required about the language in which tests of mathematics, science and other subjects were to be written. In the province of Sind, students studied both Urdu and Sindhi either as a first or second language, meaning that tests could be written in either language. But the situation in other provinces was more complex, with local languages sometimes being used, despite not being taught officially.

5. CONCLUSION

In education, good decision making is facilitated by access to relevant, reliable and timely information. Dependable information is required at all levels of educational decision making, from student, to parent, to classroom teacher, to school principal, to system manager, to identify areas of deficiency and special need, to monitor progress towards goals, and to evaluate the effectiveness of special interventions and initiatives.

Across the Asia-Pacific region, many indicators provide useful input to educational decision making. However, because almost all decisions and courses of action in education ultimately must be judged on the extent to which they result in improved student learning, measures of learning outcomes have a special significance as indicators of quality in education, as a basis for setting targets for improvement, and in monitoring progress towards educational goals.

Dependable information about student learning is required by policy makers and system managers if they are to exercise their responsibilities for the delivery of quality education to all students in a system. Effective management depends on an ability to monitor systemwide performances over time, to gauge the effectiveness of special programs and targeted resource allocations, to monitor the impact of systemwide policies, and to evaluate the success of initiatives aimed at traditionally disadvantaged and underachieving sections of the student population. Accurate, reliable data allow system managers to measure the progress of a system against past performances, to identify areas requiring special attention, and to set goals for future improvement.

Many countries in the Asia-Pacific region have established or are in the process of establishing national, sample surveys of student achievement in key areas of student learning. A number of these initiatives have been taken in response to the 1990 Jomtien World Declaration on Education For All and the 2000 Dakar Framework for Action.

In many countries, an important consideration in the introduction of new national surveys of student achievement is the need to build local technical capacity. Internationally, various agencies are working to support countries in the development of national capacity for monitoring educational achievement. These include the International Institute for Educational Planning(IIEP) (Kellaghan and Greaney, 2002) which has been involved in the Southern Africa Consortium for Monitoring Educational Quality (SACMEQ); the World Bank (Greaney and Kellaghan, 1996); Institute as part of its Strategic Choices for Education Reform program; and the UNESCO Institute for Statistics and the Australian Council for Educational Research as part of their Asia-Pacific regional conference on Indicators of Educational Performance (Forster, 2001a and b). Each of these initiatives is assisting developing countries in the region to plan programs for monitoring student learning and to establish the capacity to implement these programs.

REFERENCES

Applebee, A. N., Langer, J. A., & Mullis, I. V. S. (1987). *Learning to be Literate in America: Reading, Writing and Reasoning*. Princeton, NJ: Educational Testing Service.

Etches, P. (2000). *Report on Cook Islands Standardised Tests of Achievement 1999*. Cook Islands: Ministry of Education.

Forster, M. (2001a). *A Policy Maker's Guide to Systemwide Assessment Programs*. Melbourne: Australian Council for Educational Research.

Forster, M. (2001b). *A Policy Maker's Guide to International Achievement Studies*. Melbourne: Australian Council for Educational Research.

Greaney, V., & Kellaghan, T. (1996). *Monitoring the Learning Outcomes of Education Systems*. Washington, DC: World Bank.

Greaney, V., Khander, S. R., & Alam, M. (1999). *Bangladesh: Assessing Basic Learning Skills*. Dhaka: University Press.

Hasan, Parween (2000). EDI Workshop on Improving Learning in Primary Education in South Asia, February 7–10, 1999, Bhurban (Pakistan), Theme 3: Basic Skills Assessment – A Pakistan Case Study.

Kellaghan, T., & Greaney, V. (2002). *Using Assessment to Improve the Quality of Education*. Paris: International Institute for Educational Planning.

Pravalpruk, K. (1996). National assessment in Thailand. In P. Murphy et al. (Eds.), *National Assessments: Testing the System*. Washington, DC: World Bank.

Higher Education and Teacher Education

56

Higher Education and Development

JANDHYALA B.G. TILAK
National Institute of Educational Planning and Administration, New Delhi, India

1. INTRODUCTION

Higher education is an important form of investment in human capital. In fact, it can be regarded as a high level or a specialised form of human capital, the contribution of which to economic growth is very significant. It is rightly regarded as the "engine of development in the new world economy" (Castells, 1994, p. 14). The contribution of higher education to development can be varied: it helps in the rapid industrialization of the economy, by providing manpower with professional, technical and managerial skills. In the present context of transformation of societies into knowledge societies, higher education provides not just educated workers, but knowledge workers to the growth of the economy. It creates attitudes, and makes possible attitudinal changes necessary for the socialisation of the individuals and the modernisation and overall transformation of the societies. Fourthly, and most importantly, higher education helps, through teaching and research in the creation, absorption and dissemination of knowledge. Higher education also helps in the formation of a strong nation-state and at the same time helps in globalisation. Lastly, higher education allows people to enjoy an enhanced 'life of mind' offering the wider society both cultural and political benefits (TFHES, 2000, p. 37).

Developing as well as developed economies in the Asia-Pacific region, like most other economies of the world, have long recognised the importance of higher education in development. The human investment revolution in economic thought initiated by Schultz (1961) added a further boost to the efforts of the developing economies of the region during the post-War period. As Patel (1985) has noted, there was an educational miracle in the third world countries. Asia has its own major share in the miracle, and higher education has an important share in the education miracle. Compared to 1.1 million students enrolled in higher education institutions in 1950 in Asia, there are, according to the latest available figures, 35 million students in 1997. This means a phenomenal rate of growth of 65 per cent per year. Women constitute nearly 40 per cent of the total enrolments, representing a fair degree of gender equality in higher education. As a proportion of the relevant (17–23) age group, enrolments in higher education form more than 11 per cent, in contrast to about two per cent at the middle of the last century. The number of teachers in higher education institutions has increased from 0.1 million in 1950 to 2.3 million in 1997. All these figures are no mean achievements for countries of the region, which were economically backward, except Japan and a few oil-rich countries in West Asia.

All this does not meant that all countries in the region have developed their higher education systems uniformly well. There are indeed wide variations in the levels of development of higher education between several countries: some have very well developed higher education systems both in breadth and depth and in others it is highly restricted to a small minority of the populations. The five geographic regions in Asia – West Asia, Central Asia, South Asia, East Asia (including South-East Asia) and the Pacific (Oceania) – provide wide contrasts. There are wide regional disparities even between countries within the sub-regions and even within each country. Higher education has expanded well in some of the East Asian countries, apart from Japan, and in Australia and New Zealand in the Pacific region; but several countries in South Asia, Indochina and in West Asia lag far behind. The unequal levels of development in higher education also lead to unequal levels of economic development.

2. HIGHER EDUCATION AND ECONOMIC GROWTH

What is the effect of higher education on the economic growth of the countries? There is a general presumption that higher education is not necessary for economic growth and development, particularly in developing countries. On the other hand, it is literacy and primary education that is argued to be important. Estimates on internal rate of return also contributed to the strengthening of such a presumption. Conventionally, the contribution of education to economic development is analysed in terms of education-earnings relationships and more conveniently in the form of rates of return. Rates of return are a summary statistic of the relationship between lifetime earnings and the costs of education. Available estimates on rates of return, given in Table 1, clearly show that the social rates of return to investment in primary education are the highest, followed by secondary education. The returns to higher education are the least. This

Table 1. Rates of return to education in Asia (per cent)

	Primary	*Secondary*	*Higher*
Private	20.0	15.8	18.2
Social	16.2	11.1	11.0

Note: Asia includes non-OECD Asian countries.
Source: Psacharopoulos and Patrinos (2002).

pattern is more or less true in general with respect to private rates of return also, though in case of Asia, we note that higher education yields a higher rate of return than secondary education to the individuals.

Such evidence is extensively used to discourage public investment in higher education and to concentrate rather exclusively on primary education. Though the rate of return to higher education is less than that to primary education, it should nevertheless be noted that higher education does yield an attractive rate of return to the society (11 per cent) and to the individual as well (18 per cent).

The estimates in Table 1 are regional averages. There are wide variations in the rates of return in several countries. Table 2 presents the available estimates on rates of return to higher education in some of the Asian countries, for which data are available.

Despite some of the severe limitations that are held for estimates on rates of return, particularly social rates of return, these estimates are strongly believed to be a good indicator of the economic contribution of higher education. Some of the estimates are rather dated. Yet these estimates reveal (a) investment in higher education yields positive rates of return to the individual and also to the society at large; (b) in several countries social rates of return are high, above ten per cent, which can be considered as an alternative rate of return; and (c) rates of return seem to be increasing over the years. Generally, declining rates of return over time are often expected; but this is not the case in some of the Asian countries. This may be due to a rapid increase in the demand for higher educated manpower.

The contribution of higher education to economic development can also be measured better with the help of a production function or even a simple regression equation. The gross enrolment ratio, a flow variable, which is the most commonly used indicator of education development, reflecting the current level of efforts of the countries for the development of higher education, shows very unequal development of higher education between the several countries of the region. Table 3 presents estimates of the gross enrolment ratios for countries in the Asia-Pacific region for the latest year in the 1990s. The ratio ranges between one per cent and nearly 70 per cent. Higher education has expanded well in the East Asian tiger economies and a few Central and West Asian countries, the gross enrolment ratio being comparable to that in some of the developed countries. The gross enrolment ratios in the Republic of Korea, Singapore, Hong Kong, Thailand, Australia and New Zealand are above 20 per cent. Countries like Indonesia and Malaysia are rapidly expanding their systems, but still the enrolment ratios are only around ten per cent.

By contrast, all countries in South Asia and also those in Southeast Asia like Cambodia and Vietnam have very low enrolment ratios. Vietnam and Myanmar have had universal primary education for a long time. Even in the 1980s the gross enrolment ratios in primary education were above 100 per cent. They also have high literacy rates among adults (above 80 per cent). Yet they made little progress. Similarly, though Sri Lanka could attain a high level of performance in school education, economically it is still poor. This may be because Sri Lanka

Table 2. Rates of return to higher education in Asian countries

		Social	Private
China	1993	11.3	15.1
Hong Kong	1976	12.4	25.2
India	1965	10.3	16.2
	1978	10.8	13.2
	1995		18.2
Indonesia	1978	14.8	
	1986	22.0	
Iran	1972	11.5	
	1976	15.2	
Israel	1958	6.6	
	1969		8.0
Japan	1973	6.4	8.1
	1980	5.7	8.3
Malaysia	1983	7.6	12.2
Nepal	1999	9.1	12.0
Pakistan	1975	8.0	27.0
	1984–85	19.8	26.5
	1991		31.2
Philippines	1971	8.5	9.5
	1988	10.5	11.6
South Korea	1971	9.3	16.2
	1986	11.5	17.9
Singapore	1966	24.1	25.4
	1998	13.9	18.7
Sri Lanka	1981		16.1
Taiwan	1970	15.0	18.4
	1972	17.7	15.8
Thailand	1970	11.0	14.0
	1985	13.3	17.4
	1989		11.8
Asia (excl Japan)		11.0	18.2

Secondary Source: Tilak (1994), Psacharopoulos (1994) and Psacharopoulos and Patrinos (2002).

and these other countries have not paid adequate attention to higher education. For example, in Sri Lanka higher education is extremely restricted and secondary school graduates have to wait for 2 to 3 years in a queue for admission to higher education. Higher professional and technical education is much more restricted (see Tilak, 1996). All this suggests that primary education is not enough for economic development. It does not provide the wherewithal necessary for economic growth. On the other hand, it is clear that higher education is critically important for economic growth.

Table 3. Gross enrolment ratio in higher education in Asia and the Pacific – latest year in the 1990s

			Gross enrolment ratio (%)		
≤5	6–10	11–20	21–30	31–50	>50
Afghanistan	China	Armenia	Hong Kong	Japan	Korea
Bangladesh	India	Azerbaijan	Macao	Kazakhstan	Australia
Brunei		Bahrain	Philippines	Singapore	New Zealand
Cambodia		Indonesia	Thailand	Uzbekistan	
Lao		Iran	Turkmenistan		
Maldives		Kuwait			
Myanmar		Kyrgystan			
Nepal		Malaysia			
Pakistan		Mongolia			
Sri Lanka		Tajikistan			
Vietnam		UAE			
PNG		Fiji			
Samoa					

Source: Based on UNESCO (1999).

As earlier research (e.g., Tilak, 1989) has shown, gross enrolment ratios in education (GER) can be expected to have a positive effect on the level of economic development. In the production functions, time lag is also allowed, which yielded meaningful results. Here, using the data on 49 countries of the Asia-Pacific region, GDP per capita in 1999 (World Bank, 2000) is regressed on enrolment ratio around 1990 (UNESCO, 1999) and we note that the regression coefficient is positive and statistically significant at the one per cent level (see Equation 1 in Table 4), indicating a significant effect of higher education on economic growth of the nations.

The stock of adult population with higher levels of education is an important indicator of the level of development of higher education, that is referred to as the 'higher education attainment ratio' (HEA). This stock indicator represents the cumulative efforts of a country in the development of higher education over the years. Table 5 presents the higher education attainment ratios (HEA) for countries in the Asia-Pacific region where this information is available. In Nepal only 0.6 per cent of the adult (25+ age group) population have higher education; the corresponding ratio is 20 times higher in Japan, Korea and Philippines and 50 times higher in New Zealand. While Nepal and Cambodia figure at the bottom of the list of the countries in the region with respect to this indicator, in several developing countries of the region, the corresponding figure is less than five per cent; only in a few countries is it more than ten per cent. In contrast, in the United States nearly half the adult population has higher education. This attribute is also expected to have a stronger effect on development, as the group considered here forms a part of the labour force; it indeed forms

Table 4. Regression estimates of higher education on economic development in Asia

Dependent variable: ln GDP/pc

Eqn.	Higher education variable	Intercept	Coefficient	R-square	Adjusted R-square	F-value	Degrees of freedom
1	GER	3.3904	0.0162 (4.005)	0.2628	0.2464	16.038	46
2	HEA	3.3943	0.0195 (3.917)	0.3911	0.3469	15.343	28

Note: Figures in parentheses are *t*-values.
All coefficients are statistically significant at 99 per cent level of confidence.
Notation: GDP/pc: Gross Domestic Product per capita (PPP 1999).
GER: Gross Enrolment Ratio (per cent) around 1990.
HEA: Higher Education Attainment (proportion of population with higher education) (latest: 1990s).

Table 5. Higher education attainment in Asia-Pacific (% of adult (25+ age-group) population having post-secondary education (latest available data in 2001)

New Zealand	39.1	Turkey	10.8	Pakistan	2.5
Mongolia	23.4	Brunei Darussalam	9.4	Indonesia	2.3
Philippines	22.0	Singapore	7.6	Myanmar	2.0
Korea	21.1	India	7.3	Maldives	1.7
Japan	20.7	Malaysia	6.9	Afghanistan	1.6
Taiwan	17.8	Macao	5.9	Bangladesh	1.3
Hong Kong, China	14.5	Solomon Islands	5.6	Sri Lanka	1.1
Kazakhstan	12.4	Thailand	5.1	China	1.0
Tajikistan	11.7	Fiji	4.5	Cambodia	1.0
Israel	11.2	Vietnam	2.6	Nepal	0.6

Source: UNESCO (1999).

an important and even a large part of the skilled and educated labour force. The larger the stock of population with higher education, the higher the possibility for economic growth.

Equation 2 in Table 4 gives the regression estimates for the relationship between higher education attainment and GDP per capita. As expected, this gives a better result, with a higher coefficient of determination, and the variable has a higher effect, as the value of the coefficient suggests. Both the equations make it clear that higher education makes a significant and positive contribution to economic growth. Hence, it is clearly not appropriate to assume that its role is insignificant.

It may be argued that simple regression equations of economic development on education suggest only the correlations between the two, and not necessarily cause and effect relationships. Such an argument is partly pre-empted here, by allowing a time lag for higher education to cause economic development. Secondly, we also find very few countries with high levels of higher education being economically underdeveloped, while all the economically rich countries are not necessarily advanced in the development and spread of higher education.

In the rapidly technologically changing world, technology makes a significant difference to the economic growth of the nations. UNDP (2001) developed a technology achievement index (TAI), based on the degree of creation of technology in a given economy, the extent of diffusion of old and recent innovations, and human skills. The level of achievement in technology critically depends upon the level of higher education in a given economy. After all, it is higher education and research that help in developing new technology; it is higher education and research that contribute to innovations and their diffusion. Consequently, a very strong effect of higher education on the development of technology in any society can be expected. In fact, the level of achievement in technology may be a close indicator of economic growth itself. Most countries with high enrolment ratios in higher education have become leaders in technology, with high levels of achievement in technology, as shown in Table 6. The converse is also true: a large number of countries with low enrolment ratios (say less than ten per cent) are marginalised technologically. Those with the medium level of enrolment ratios, nearly 20 per cent, like Singapore and Hong Kong are indeed potential leaders in technology. A few countries like Philippines and Thailand with medium and high levels of enrolment ratios are classified by the UNDP (2001) as 'dynamic leaders'. The rest who did not expand their higher education systems well, are indeed marginalised. There is not even a single country with a low enrolment ratio (less than ten per cent) in higher education that has a high or medium level of the technology index.

Table 6. Higher education (GER) and technology (TAI)

Gross enrolment ratio	Technology achievement index		
	High (>0.5)	Medium (0.4–0.5)	Low (<0.4)
High (>20)	New Zealand, Korea Australia, Japan		Philippines
Medium (11–20)	Singapore	Hong Kong	Thailand
Low (<10)			Iran, Indonesia, Malaysia India, Sri Lanka, Nepal China, Pakistan

Source: Based on UNDP (2001) and UNESCO (1999).

Table 7. Regression estimates of higher education on achievement of technology in Asia

Dependent variable: In Technology Achievement Index (TAI)

Eqn.	Higher education variable	Intercept	Coefficient	R-square	Adjusted R-square	F-value	Degrees of freedom
1	GER	−0.7405	0.0143 (4.749)	0.570	0.545	22.552	17
2	HEA	−0.6535	0.0152 (3.055)	0.400	0.357	9.335	15

Note: Figures in parentheses are *t*-values.

The relationship between higher education and technology could be shown statistically. Table 7 records the regression estimates for the gross enrolment ratio (GER) and the higher education attainment ratio (HEA) as predictors of the technology achievement index (TAI). The simple correlation coefficient between gross enrolment ratio in higher education and technology achievement index is as high as 0.8 and that between technology and higher education attainment is 0.65. Though the number of observations is small, the simple regression equations estimated here (see Table 7) do show a very strong and statistically significant effect of higher education on the level of achievement of technology.

3. HIGHER EDUCATION AND SOCIAL DEVELOPMENT

The above rates of return and regression coefficients do not capture several non-economic benefits of higher education. Most studies of the relationship between education and development indicators, such as human development, health, life expectancy, mortality rate, and poverty, have concentrated on literacy and school education. Rarely has the role of higher education been examined in this context, probably on the presumption that higher education does not have any role in this. Such an assumption is widespread.

In order to present a brief idea of the relationship between higher education and a variety of aspects of well being, simple coefficients of correlation are estimated. Table 8 shows these correlations for gross enrolment ratios (GER) and higher education attainment (HEA) with seven social development indicators. All coefficients of correlation between higher education and development indicators have expected signs, whether it is in relation to the gross enrolment ratio or in relation to higher education attainment. Second, most coefficients are also statistically significant with high *t*-values. An exception is the coefficient between higher education attainment and poverty. All the other coefficients are significant at the 99 per cent level of confidence; except the coefficients relating to gender empowerment index and poverty, which are significant at the 95 per

Table 8. Coefficients of correlation between higher education and social development indicators

Between		GER (around 1990) [54]	HEA (latest year) [34]
And	n	r	r
Human Development Index (1999)	49	0.60	0.55
Gender Development Index	42	0.63	0.55
Gender Empowerment Index	11	0.61	0.65
Life Expectancy	54	0.53	0.54
Infant Mortality Rate	50	−0.46	−0.46
Total Fertility Rate	54	−0.57	−0.47
Poverty (International)	15	−0.57*	−0.30†

Note: Figures in [ ] refer to number of valid countries for which data are available; n: number of observations; r: coefficient of correlation.
Poverty (International): % of population below the line of income poverty of $1).
* Significant at 5% level; † not significant even at 10% level; all others are significant at 1% level.

cent level of significance, indicating that higher education is also positively related to several human development indicators, in addition to economic development.

Higher education is found to be very significantly related to the human development index and also to the gender development index. The higher the level of higher education in a society, whether in stock or flow forms, the higher is the level of human development, through its influence on two main components of human development index, namely, the life expectancy, and GDP per capita. It is not only life expectancy that is significantly related to higher education, but also infant mortality, another measure of health that is significantly related to higher education. Higher education helps a lot in reducing infant mortality rates, as people with higher education are more aware of the need for preventive health care measures and are also more aware of the availability of general healthcare facilities, leading to sound decision making within households regarding healthcare. Higher education can influence the health of the population in a different way as well, through the provision of skilled medical manpower to the society, thereby improving the quality and quantity of medical manpower in the society.

Similarly, the effects of higher education on fertility rates can also occur in two ways: on the one hand higher education may bring in attitudinal changes on the need to reduce fertility rates for development, and on the other hand, prolonged education, that is, enrolment in higher education may delay marriages, and lead to reduction in fertility rates. For example, Japan and Korea with the highest levels of higher education have the lowest levels of total fertility rates, 1.4 and 1.5 respectively. In contrast, the total fertility rates in Nepal and

Cambodia where hardly one per cent of the population have higher education, the fertility rates are 4.8 and 5.3 respectively.

Finally, the relationship between higher education and poverty. Data on poverty levels are very limited. Only 15 out of 49 countries in the Asia-Pacific region have data on poverty, that is, the percentage of the population living below the intentionally defined poverty line of US$ 1 per day. The estimated coefficients of correlation do suggest that poverty is inversely related to the level of higher education. The relationship between poverty and the gross enrolment ratio in higher education is negative and the coefficient is statistically significant; but the coefficient between poverty and higher education attainment is not significant, though negative as might be expected. In general, it can be argued that while basic education may take people out of poverty, this can be sustained well by secondary and higher education, which help in upward mobility and offer better economic opportunities.

Consequently, it is argued that higher education has a very significant role in the development of the societies in terms of economic development, human development, gender-based development, improvement in health, life expectancy, and reduction in fertility, infant mortality and poverty. Though, in general it is true that there exists a two-way relationship between higher education and development, the way and the facets of development analysed here, highlight the one-way relationship, namely, the contribution of higher education to development. For instance, it does not sound logical to argue that reduction in infant mortality rate or improvement in life expectancy leads significantly to development in higher education. Similarly, current national income may influence the growth of enrolment in the future, but enrolments a decade ago in higher education cannot be argued to be influenced by the current levels of national income, particularly in modern times, when rapid socioeconomic developments are taking place. In short, though the statistical analysis used is very simple, the group of countries is highly heterogeneous, and that there can be several factors influencing economic growth in addition to higher education; nevertheless, it indicates a strong and positive relationship, higher education clearly influencing development.

4. PUBLIC POLICY AND DEVELOPMENT OF HIGHER EDUCATION

Despite increasing awareness of the contribution of higher education to development, many developing countries in the Asian region have not expanded their higher education systems adequately, due to a variety of factors that are social, economic, political and cultural. However, one of the most important factors relates to public policies on the expansion of higher education. Several developing countries continue to pay inadequate attention to higher education. Two major areas of public policy are worth examining here. They are the financing of higher education, and privatisation.

4.1. Financing Higher Education

In most countries, higher education receives less than one per cent of GNP. It is only in the tiger economies of East Asia, oil-rich West Asia and Australia and New Zealand that the corresponding proportion is above one per cent. It is less than 0.2 per cent in quite a few developing counties such as Bangladesh, Myanmar, Lao and Tajikistan (Table 9). These statistics indicate the relative priority accorded to higher education in different countries.

Education, including higher education, is financed by the state in most societies, including the Asian economies. However, in recent years, there has been a steady decline in the public expenditures on higher education and several changes are taking place in the pattern of funding education all over the world in terms of the introduction of financial aid, student loans, and similar cost-recovery measures along with scholarships, vouchers and other protective measures (see Ziderman & Albrecht, 1995). An overall shift is taking place from financing the provision (or supply) of higher education to financing the demand for higher education all over. Methods of mobilizing non-governmental resources are being talked about essentially because of financial considerations, and, in particular, because of the increasing inability of governments to meet rapidly rising social demand for higher education. Universities, including public ones, are being required to generate resources on their own, and as a result many universities are making several innovations in the mobilization of non-governmental resources. For example, Hong Kong had a target of increasing the cost-recovery rate to 18 per cent through fees in higher education. China provided free higher education for a long time and also provided students with dormitory lodging and stipends for food and other allowances, but now marketization and quasi-marketization processes are occuring in post-Mao China. Fees have been introduced and student loan programs have been launched. Furthermore, China has

Table 9. Share of higher education in GNP (%)

Myanmar	1994	0.14	Nepal	1997	0.61
Lao	1997	0.16	Kazakhstan	1997	0.61
Tajikistan	1996	0.16	Philippines	1997	0.61
Bangladesh	1996	0.17	Kyrgystan	1996	0.75
India	1995	0.22	Thailand	1996	0.79
Azerbaijan	1996	0.25	Mongolia	1996	0.92
Armenia	1996	0.26	Iran	1995	0.92
Korea	1995	0.30	Uzbekistan	1993	0.92
Sri Lanka	1996	0.32	Singapore	1995	1.04
Vanuatu	1994	0.32	Hong Kong	1995	1.08
Indonesia	1996	0.34	Malaysia	1997	1.25
Pakistan	1997	0.35	Vietnam	1997	1.54
China	1996	0.36	Australia	1995	1.68
Japan	1994	0.44	New Zealand	1996	2.12
Solomon Islands	1991	0.52			

Source: Calculated by the author based on UNESCO (1999).

shifted its emphasis from traditional higher education to short-cycle programs, in which enrolment tends to increase rapidly. It has been shown that students are ready to pay for this kind of curriculum. Nonformal and on-the-job training are also preferred in China as these forms of training quickly fulfil the demand for skilled labor. Some of the predominant ways of generating money in Chinese universities include: (a) running factories, shops, stores, and so on; (b) selling research to industrial establishments; (c) procuring contracts and commissions for research and training; (d) offering consultancy services by the staff for a variety of activities including interpretation and translation; and (e) selling computer services. The system of financing higher education is gradually changing from one dominated by the state to one of multi-source funding, with the state taking care of the lion's, but gradually declining, share with the stipulation that it would be supplemented by multiple channels, including fund-raising campaigns and donations by individual citizens, enterprises, and other social bodies in addition to student fees. On the whole, more than ten per cent of higher education costs are recovered from students in several East Asian economies (see Tilak, 2001).

Many countries are experimenting with alternative forms of financing and cost recovery mechanisms. There are no recent detailed estimates on cost recovery in education. Table 10 records the share of fees in the costs of higher education in countries in the Asia-Pacific region compared with selected developed countries outside this region. Available evidence shows that the rates of cost recovery in higher education vary widely between zero per cent in Sri Lanka and 50 per cent in Korea. It is below 20 per cent in most of the public higher education systems in the Asian countries, except in Korea. It is quite interesting to note that rates of cost recovery in advanced countries are also not high: they are also less than 20 per cent, in fact less than 15 per cent. In this sense, the rates of cost recovery in Asian countries are somewhat comparable to those in the advanced countries and hence the general presumption that higher education in Asian countries is heavily subsidised by the state may not be true.

The rates of cost recovery in private higher education institutions in the Asian countries are alarmingly high. They are 50 per cent in Taiwan, 66 per cent in Japan, 82 per cent in Korea and 85 per cent in the Philippines. With such high rates of cost recovery, private higher education may be out of reach to a majority of the students belonging to weaker economic strata. This would indeed create serious problems of equity, if these countries have higher education systems that are predominantly private. The rate of cost recovery in private higher education in the United States is quite low: less than 40 per cent. Private institutions in the United States generate sizeable resources from non-governmental and non-student sources. But in Asian countries, education is funded either by the government or by the students in the form of fees. The non-governmental and non-student sources do not seem to exist. The levels of cost recovery in higher education are higher in developing countries in Asia than in many advanced countries. But again, it is in these countries that the arguments for higher and higher levels of cost recovery are being proposed. The dangers of high cost

Table 10. Share of student fees in costs of higher education in selected countries (per cent)

Name of the country		Share	Name of the country		Share
Public/predominantly public					
Asia-Pacific countries*			*Developed countries*		
Australia	1987	2.1	Norway	1987	0.0
	1999	18.6	France	1975	2.9
Japan	1970	2.0		1984	4.7
	1987	8.8	Italy	1989	7.3
Sri Lanka		..	Germany	1986	0.0
Pakistan		2.1	Canada	mid-1980s	12.0
Nepal	1986–87	4.4	Netherlands	1985	12.0
Malaysia		5.8	Spain	mid-1980s	20.0
	1991	20.0	United Kingdom		
Thailand		6.9	Universities	1970–71	12.6
Taiwan	1991	7.0		1988–89	6.4
Pakistan	1987–88		Polytechnics	1982–83	15.0
Colleges		7.4	United States	1969–70	15.1
Univs. (Gen)		1.9		1984–85	14.5
Univs. (Tec)		1.3			
China	1998	>10.0			
Philippines	1985	10.9			
Hong Kong	1988–89	6.5–12.1			
	1997	18.0			
Indonesia		13.0			
	1990	>20.0			
India	1984–85	15.0			
Vietnam	1993!	>20.0			
South Korea	1985	49.6			
Private					
Taiwan	Late '80s	50.0	United States	1969–70	38.6
Japan	1971	75.8		1984–85	38.7
	1985				
South Korea	1985				
Philippines	1977				

Note: .. Nil or Negligible; * around 1980, unless otherwise mentioned.
Source: Tilak (1997b, 2001a), Bray (2000), Catalano et al. (1992), Asonuma (2002); and Australia (2001), Woodhall (1991).

recovery are to be noted. Even if it is feasible to raise cost recovery rates to higher levels, it has to be seen whether it is desirable from the point of view of equity in higher education and the manpower needs of the developing economies. After all, the need for democratisation or massification of higher education is being increasingly felt everywhere.

On the whole, private higher education in Asia is financed mostly by the students in the form of fees, and public universities are mostly financed by the state, except in Korea. But all systems of higher education in the region are undergoing rapid changes, increasing their reliance on fees and other private finances. This so-called 'profit syndrome' is no longer uncommon in several Asian countries.

4.2. Private Higher Education

Another closely related and important issue of concern in the development of education in the last quarter century refers to private higher education. Private education is not a new phenomenon in the Asian region, though modern private education is of recent origin. Many of the private institutions in the region are privately managed, but are funded by the state to a substantial extent. So-called 'complete' or 'pure' private institutions may now be very few in number; but they are rapidly increasing in number. Unfortunately, data are not available to make such a distinction and to find out the exact share of the real private sector in education. State support to private institutions is quite common in the Asian countries.

Private higher education institutions in education have been growing rapidly in all countries of the region – not only in the transition economies of Central Asia, but also in South Asia, East Asia, including in China and the Pacific. The private sector meets a large part of the demand for higher education in Japan and Korea: its share in total enrolment in higher education is above 70 per cent in Japan, Korea, and Taiwan. As high as 73 per cent of all universities, and 84 per cent of all junior colleges in Japan are private, enrolling more than 70 per cent of the total student numbers in these institutions in 1992. Korea provides yet another example of extensive higher education operated by the private sector: 84 per cent of higher education institutions and nearly 80 per cent of higher education enrolment were in the private sector in 1993. Private higher education institutions in Taiwan outnumber public institutions by 2 to 1, capturing 70 per cent of the enrolment. The share of private enrolment in higher education in Japan, Korea, and Taiwan are among the highest in the world; and no country except the United States has enrolment in private institutions adding up to more than ten per cent of the total enrolment in higher education, and even there the figure is only ten per cent. In a sense, the Korean and Japanese experience seems to be in sharp contrast to the traditional welfare-state approach, not to mention the traditionally important role of the state in the provision of education that dominates the pattern of educational development in European economies such as the United Kingdom, Sweden, Switzerland and Italy, and in the United States and Canada as well. Many other economies of the region, Singapore, Taiwan, Hong Kong, and China, do not rely on private financing to the extent that Korea and Japan do.

Hong Kong was able to resist pressures to allow the establishment of private universities. However, the private or independent higher education sector is emerging slowly in China and a system of non-government-run higher education institutions is gradually taking shape, as non-state or private, or sponsored, institutions begin to take root. In Singapore, where there is only a very limited role for the private sector, the government takes the bulk of the responsibility for higher education. But the quality aspects of private higher education do not seem to be satisfactory. Despite flourishing growth and government support, private institutions in the region have failed to become top-quality institutions such as the ones founded in the United States. This shows what happens when quality controls are weak and profit motives dominate other considerations. The universities in Korea are said to be producing 'half baked graduates' necessitating huge investments by the government and the industry in R&D.

As private universities cater to the demands of the large population, neglect of public higher education goes unnoticed. More importantly, since higher education is allowed to be guided by market signals, most higher education institutions tend to concentrate on professional fields. As Clark (1995, p. 159) notes, humanities and social sciences are thrown aside; doctoral programs in not only social sciences but also in physical sciences are surprisingly weak; most advanced-level education is radically underdeveloped; and the research-teaching-study nexus has become highly problematic. This is believed to be mostly attributable to the dominant role of industry or private sector in higher education.

It is generally felt that rapid growth in public sector spending on education has resulted in rapid growth in public sector enrolment everywhere, including in East Asia, and that such a relationship between private sector investments and enrolment in private institutions (or total enrolments in all institutions) cannot be found. On the whole, the private sector is rapidly growing in size, and most public policies or the lack of the same are conducive for its growth.

5. CONCLUSIONS AND IMPLICATIONS

Higher education systems in many developing as well as developed countries including the Asia-Pacific region are also characterised by a crisis, rather a continuing crisis, with overcrowding, inadequate staffing, deteriorating standards and quality, poor physical facilities, insufficient equipment, and declining public budgets. More importantly, higher education is subject to neglect and even discrimination in public policy. As Verspoor (1994, p. 2) rightly observed, "the crisis is in part the reflection of the economic adversity that many developing countries have experienced in the 1980s, "but it is also **a crisis of policy or very often, lack of policies**" (emphasis added). Higher education systems are undergoing rapid changes in Asia. Some have followed the British mode of welfare stateism to some extent; others attach more value to individual economic gain (and thereby to the economic growth of the country) and expect the market to respond to economic incentives that higher education comes with; and a few others are indeed following *ad hoc* or no clear policies. Coherent long term policies for the development of higher education for development of nations are needed. Public policy has to recognise clearly the critical importance of higher education in development.

It is important to note that no nation that has not expanded reasonably well its higher education system can achieve a high level of economic development. International evidence shows that all advanced countries are those that have a gross enrolment ratio of above 20 per cent. Among the advanced countries there is no single country where higher education was not well expanded. In most developed countries higher education is fairly democratised, and is accessible to all. In fact, there are significant trends towards massification of the base of higher education. The gross enrolment ratio in higher education in advanced countries varies between 20 per cent and as high as 90 per cent. In contrast, in most of the developing countries, it is restricted to a small fraction of youth. No country could be found in the group of high-income countries with an enrolment ratio of less than 20 per cent. It is not only international evidence, but also the evidence from Asian countries supports this. The high-income countries in Asia, namely, Japan, Korea, Singapore, and Hong Kong, have an enrolment ratio between 20 per cent and 70 per cent. Many low income countries in the Asian region, except the Philippines, have an enrolment ratio much lower, below 20 per cent. Thus the 20 per cent enrolment ratio in higher education seems to be the critical threshold level for a country to become economically advanced.

The experience of the Asian countries with the policies of globalisation and structural adjustment is also rich (Tilak, 1997a). Comparing the experiences of several countries in the region, it may be concluded that these policies succeeded only in those countries that invested heavily in education, including specifically higher education. The converse is also true. These policies could not yield good results in those countries that have made low and inadequate levels of investment in higher education, reflected in low educational levels of the workforce, as in countries in South Asia, and also in Southeast Asia like Vietnam, Lao, and Cambodia, compared to the countries like Korea, and to some extent Thailand, Indonesia and the Philippines. After all, countries to be successful in international competition require highly skilled manpower, produced by higher education systems. Empirically, it has been found that globalisation has contributed to reduction in poverty and inequalities in East Asia, but 'globalisation has not allowed South Asia's progress towards poverty reduction to continue at its previous pace' (Khan, 1998). The reason could be found in the differences in investment in education, and higher education in particular.

Despite such an awareness, many countries in the Asian region are not able to accord due priority to higher education. South Asian countries lag far behind the other Asian countries in higher education. According to the predictions made by UNESCO (see Chapman & Adams, 1998), many of the developing countries in Asia, particularly in South Asia will continue to be lagging behind the developed countries in the development of higher education and will have low enrolment ratios, unless significant policies of expansion of higher education are adopted.

The case of Singapore and to some extent Hong Kong and Malaysia in the East Asian region, and of India in South Asia highlights the strengths of public higher education. The rapid growth in higher education in some of these countries is due largely to state funding. The role of the state is very important in providing and financing education everywhere. Excessive reliance of the governments on the private sector for the development of higher education may lead to strengthening of class inequalities and even produce new inequalities, besides adding to the problems of quality. On the whole, it seems that initial government investments on a large scale are important in higher education; but only after some time, and a certain level of educational and economic development is achieved, the private sector may complement the state efforts in higher education. This also depends upon the role of the private sector in economic development in general. The East Asian sequencing of funding – huge public funding first, and then only some private funding – is quite important (Thant, 1999).

REFERENCES

Asonuma, A. (2002). Finance reform in Japanese higher education. *Higher Education*, 43(1), 109–126.
Australia, Department of Education (2001). *Higher Education Report for the 2001 and 2003 Triennium*. Canberra: Commonwealth of Australia.
Bray, M. (2000). Education in Asia: Financing higher education – Patterns, trends and options. *Prospects*, 30, 331–347.
Castells, M. (1994). The university system: Engine of development in the new world economy. In J. Salmi & A. M. Verspoor, (Eds.), *Revitalising Higher Education* (pp. 14–40). Oxford: Pergamon.
Catalano, G., Silvestri, P., & Todeschini, M. (1992). Financing university education in Italy. *Higher Education Policy*, 5(2), 37–43.
Chapman, D. W., & Adams, D. (Eds.) (1998). Trends and issues in education across Asia. *International Journal of Educational Research*, 29(7), 581–685.
Clark, B. R. (1995). *Places of Inquiry: Research and Advanced Education in Modern Universities*. Berkeley: University of California Press.
Khan, A. R. (1998). The impact of globalization on South Asia [and] growth and poverty in East and South-East Asia in the era of globalization. In A. S. Bhalla, *Globalization, Growth and Marginalization* (pp. 103–124, 125–148). London: Macmillan.
Patel, S. J. (1985). Educational 'miracle' in the third world, 1950 to 1981. *Economic and Political Weekly*, 20(31), 1312–1317.
Psacharopoulos, G. (1994). Returns to investment in education: A global update. *World Development*, 22(9), 1325–1343.
Psacharopoulos, G., & Patrinos, H. (2002). *Returns to Investment in Education: A Further Update*. World Bank Policy Research Working Paper 2881. Washington, DC. [http//:econ.worldbank.org/files/18081-wps2881.pdf]
Salmi, J., & Vespoor, A. M. (Eds.) (year). *Revitalizing Higher Education*. Oxford: Pergamon.
Schultz, T. W. (1961). Investment in human capital. *American Economic Review*, 51(1), 1–15.
TFHES [Task Force on Higher Education and Society] (2000). *Higher Education in Developing Countries: Peril and Promise*. Washington, DC: World Bank.
Thant, M. (1999). Lessons from East Asia: Financing human development. In J. L. H. Tan (Ed.), *Human Capital Formation as an Engine of Growth: The East Asian Experience* (pp. 202–36). Singapore: Institute of Southeast Asian Studies.
Tilak, J. B. G. (1989). *Education and its Relation to Economic Growth, Poverty and Income Distribution: Past Evidence and Further Analysis*. Discussion Paper No. 46. Washington, DC: World Bank.

Tilak, J. B. G. (1994). *Education for Development in Asia*. New Delhi: Sage Publications.
Tilak, J. B. G. (1996). *Costs and Financing of Education in Sri Lanka*. Manila: Asian Development Bank/Brisbane: UniQuest.
Tilak, J. B. G. (1997a). Effects of adjustment on education: A review of Asian experience. *Prospects, 27*(1), 85–107.
Tilak, J. B. G. (1997b). Lessons from cost recovery in education. In C. Colclough (Ed.), *Marketising Education and Health in Developing Countries: Miracle or Mirage?* (pp. 63–89). Oxford: Clarendon Press.
Tilak, J. B. G. (2001). *Building Human Capital in East Asia*. Working Paper. Washington, DC: World Bank Institute.
Verspoor, A. M. (1994). Introduction: Improvement and innovation in higher education. In Salmi & Vespoor (Eds.), *Revitalising Higher Education* (pp. 1–11). Oxford: Pergamon.
UNESCO (1999). *Statistical Yearbook*. Paris: UNESCO.
UNDP (2001). *Human Development Report*. New York: Oxford University Press.
Woodhall, M. (1991). *Student Loans in Higher Education*. Paris: International Institute of Educational Planning.
World Bank (2000). *World Development Report 2000/01*. New York: Oxford University Press.
Yee, A. H. (Ed.) (1995). *East Asian Higher Education: Traditions and Transformations*. Oxford: Pergamon.
Ziderman, A., & Albrecht, D. (1995). *Financing Universities in Developing Countries*. Washington, DC: Falmer Press.

57

Financing Higher Education in the Asia-Pacific Region

N.V. VARGHESE
International Institute for Educational Planning, Paris, France

1. INTRODUCTION

Strategies for financing education vary according to the ideological orientation of the political process leading the country. There are those who argue that public funding of higher education, is regressive (Psachoropoulos, 1994). Others argue that although individual students benefit from higher education, the society also benefits and increased income leads to increased tax payable by individuals.

> Graduates are more likely to more than pay for their education over their working life via the tax system, so that the onerous fees that immediately recover the cost of providing higher education are not needed. (Heaton, 1999)

The debate essentially centres on the role of the state in development and the social cost of public subsidization. As the market ideology has become dominant, public subsidization of higher education is increasingly being questioned.

Higher education in the Asia-Pacific region has maintained three patterns of funding and managing. First, public funding and managing of the system were common in many countries. Countries in the South-Asian region, Australia, New Zealand and some countries of the South-East Asian region belong to this category. Second, private higher education traditions were common in many countries in the region. While private universities are predominant in the Philippines, they are also common in many of the East and South-East Asian countries. In countries, such as the Republic of Korea, Japan, Indonesia, and Thailand, the private sector in higher education is common. Third, foreign financing of education is mostly found in the Pacific Island states.

These traditional patterns have changed in the recent past. Most countries where public institutions and state funding dominated moved towards reforms to diversify funding sources, through a progressive shift from single-source state funding to cost sharing and income generating arrangements, whereas others have increasingly relied on the private sector for further growth and expansion of the sector. In other words, privatisation of public institutions and promotion of the private sector in higher education are two dominant trends in reforms to finance higher education in the Asia-Pacific region. These changes had considerable impact on the management of higher education, both at the system and at the institutional levels. The former implied granting more autonomy but less funding to the institutions of higher education, whereas the latter implied changing rules that govern the operation of the higher education sector and putting in place new regulatory mechanisms and quality control measures.

This article is organised as follows: the introductory section is followed by a section that discusses trends in the public financing of education and higher education in the region. Section 3 analyses patterns of privatisation in higher education. Section 4 describes the emergence and presence of private higher education in the countries of the region. Section 5 highlights some aspects of external funding, especially of the Pacific Island states. The concluding section revisits the issue of funding of higher education in the context of the East Asian economic crisis.

2. TRENDS IN PUBLIC FUNDING OF HIGHER EDUCATION

The level of public funding in higher education will generally correspond to the level of educational development of the country. Larger numbers of students usually imply a larger system and more public resources wherever the tertiary education system is predominantly public.

Countries in the region not only vary considerably in terms of the absolute size of the population but also in terms of the level of economic and educational development. Countries such as Japan, Australia, and Korea occupy one end of the spectrum indicating a significant leap in economic and educational development while Lao PDR, Bangladesh, and Nepal, are found at the other end, signifying low levels of development.

Australia, with 5401 tertiary students per 100,000 population occupies the highest position, closely followed by Korea (4974), whereas Lao PDR with 253 occupies the lowest position. Similarly, in terms of gross enrolment ratios the same trend is again revealed. Students in tertiary institutions account for 72 per cent of the age group population in Australia whereas the corresponding figure is only two per cent for Lao PDR, five per cent in Nepal and six per cent in Bangladesh (UNESCO, 1999). Needless to say, in some countries, the private sector is common and hence the level of public funding is low, even when tertiary education is fairly well developed.

In this article two indicators are considered to assess the changing pattern of public funding in higher education. They are the share of education to the total public expenditure and the share of higher education to the total education budget. The very commonly used indicator of share of education in GNP is not considered since the share of the private sector contribution to GNP is considerable in many countries of the region.

Table 1 shows several trends concerning the financing of education. First, from 1980 to the 1990s the share of education in public expenditure increased. This is the most general pattern in the region. Second, the share of educational budgets remained more or less the same in a few countries such as Australia, Jordan, and Israel. Third, the share of education in total budget declined. This is true of Nepal and some of the Central Asian republics.

As far as the financing of higher education is concerned, the trends are more interesting. First, there are quite a number of countries where an increase in the share of the education budget was accompanied by an increase in the share of higher education in total education budgets. These are mostly countries where higher education is expanding, especially through the public system. Singapore, Iran, Cyprus and New Zealand are examples of this category of countries.

Table 1. Public expenditure on higher education

Country	% Exp. education 1980	% Exp. education 1995 or latest	% HE in ed. budget 1985	% HE in ed. budget 1995	Aid % in investment 1995
Australia	14.8	14.8	30.5	29.8	–
Azerbaijan	23.5	17.5	–	7.8	14.8
Bangladesh	7.8	10.3	10.4	7.9	30.8
China	9.3	12.8	21.8	15.4	2.0
Cyprus	12.9	13.2	4.2	6.5	–
India	11.2	11.6	15.3	13.7	4.0
Iran	15.7	17.8	10.7	22.9	–
Israel	7.3	11.3	18.9	18.2	12.3
Jordan	14.4	17.1	34.1	34.9	23.9
Kazakhstan	17.6	17.6	–	12.5	–
Korea	23.7	17.5	10.9	9.5	–
Kuwait	8.1	8.9	16.7	29.9	–
Kyrgyz	22.2	22.5	8.8	8.3	62.9
Malaysia	14.7	18.3	14.6	16.8	–
Mongolia	19.1	17.6	17.3	17.9	130.6
Nepal	10.5	8.5	33.4	17.3	62.8
New Zealand	23.1	–	28.3	29.4	–
Oman	4.1	11.1	15.3	5.8	–
Pakistan	5.0	7.1	18.2	13.2	12.3
Philippines	9.1	10.1	22.5	–	–
Singapore	7.3	23.4	27.9	34.8	–
Sri Lanka	7.7	8.1	9.8	12.2	27.2
Syria	8.1	11.2	33.6	25.9	–
Tajikistan	29.2	16.1	7.7	10.3	–
Thailand	11.2	11.4	13.2	–	–
E. Asia & Pacific	9.7	10.7	21.4	15.4	–
South Asia	10.2	11.0	15.3	13.1	–

Source: UNESCO (1999).

Second, another set of countries experienced an increase in the share of the education budget accompanied by a declining share of higher education budgets. The most populous countries such as China, India, Pakistan, and Bangladesh belong to this category. Third, shares of both the education budgets and higher education budgets declined. In other words, the higher education sector received a declining share of a reduced public budget. Finally, in countries like Australia the share of educational budgets and that of higher education remained more or less the same.

The large-size countries certainly exert an influence on regional trends. Many countries of the East-Asian and Pacific region experienced no change to the share of higher education at the same level or an increase to it even when education budgets were declining. Other parts of the region, however, experienced a trend in the reverse order. Hence, it can be argued that the most common trend in public financing of higher education in the Asia-Pacific region is of an increasing share of public expenditure on education and a declining share on higher education in the 1990s. It seems that there is a correlation between the level of aid dependence of the countries and their expenditure on higher education. The share of education in total budgets increased in many countries due to the increase in aid flows, especially after the commitment of the donor community at the Jomtien conference of March 1990. However, external funding was directed to primary education.

Thus, it can be argued that external funding increased national educational budgets, but it could not increase higher education budgets. Under the structural adjustment programs, it was argued that investment in primary education brought more returns than that at the higher education level. The conditionalities, therefore, for structural adjustment loans included a reprioritisation of the sectoral allocations within education favouring primary education. Table 1 indicates patterns in aid flows in the 1990s; most of those countries that received aid to improve their investments increased their educational budgets. However, this trend did not translate itself into an increased share of higher education budgets

3. PRIVATISATION IN PUBLIC HIGHER EDUCATION INSTITUTIONS

The question of subsidising higher education was always a matter of controversy. In the 1960s public-subsidised education was in fashion and that generation enjoyed the highest level of subsidised higher education. By the 1980s the view had changed in that higher education, especially in developing countries, was benefiting students from the relatively richer socio-economic groups and hence subsidies to higher education were profiting in particular elite sections of society. This was joined by strong advocacy of the World Bank to reallocate priorities to primary education (World Bank, 1986). A reduction of subsidies to higher education meant transferring the incidence and burden to the households.

Privatisation took different forms. Cost recovery through student fees, student support through loan schemes, introduction of income generating activities are some of the forms in which public subsidy was reduced and higher education was privatized. However, the most common form in which incidence was transferred was by raising markedly fee rates in the universities.

3.1. *Cost Recovery through Student Fees*

In the late 1980s and early 1990s, student fees accounted for a low share of recurring expenditure on higher education in most of the South-Asian countries and were close to zero in the Central-Asian countries (World Bank, 1994). In the 1990s fees were enhanced in many Asian countries. For example, in the University of Hong Kong the authorities enhanced fees from 12 to 18 per cent of recurring expenditure by 1997. Even this 12 per cent was a substantial increased share when compared with the 1980s. The authorities are considering enhancing the fees further to 20 per cent (Bray, 2000; Mok, 1999).

Australia went back and forth on the issue of student fees. All institutions of higher education in Australia were government-funded and they charged a low level of fees up until the 1970s. In 1974, the government abolished fees to expand enrolment. A student fee was introduced for foreign students in the early 1980s when they were expected to pay 20 per cent of the cost. In 1988, the policy further changed and the fee rate for foreign students was increased to the equivalent of full fees and by 20 per cent for Australian students. In the 1990s, under the Higher Education Contribution Scheme (HECS) the students were paying up to 25 per cent of the cost of their higher education (NIER, 1998).

In India, the government appointed separate committees for technical and general higher education to explore possibilities and suggest measures for mobilizing non-governmental funds for the sector. The committee recommended that the fee should form at least 20 per cent of the cost. Many universities in India in the late 1990s enhanced student fees. In New Zealand, higher education institutions were administered through a buffer body called the University Grants Committee. The institutions are now under a newly created Ministry of Education. Tuition fees were low for a long time in New Zealand. The government is introducing a fee equivalent of 25 per cent of the cost of education. Institutions enjoy autonomy and actual fees are set by the council of each institution (NIER, 1998). In China there were no student fees prior to 1978. In the 1980s the student stipend system was changed and in the 1990s student fees were introduced. China introduced a differential fee structure whereby general students paid around Y 300–600 as annual tuition and Y 100–200 as boarding charges. However, self-financed students and those financed by enterprises had to pay around Y 2000–6000 annually (World Bank, 1996).

In all transitional economies of the Asian region, fees were introduced and many of student support systems were withdrawn. The examples of Mongolia, Kazakhstan, Uzbekistan, Tajikistan are cases in point for this trend.

3.2. Student Loan Schemes

Some of the countries in the region have had student loan schemes for a fairly long time (Woodhall, 1991). The government essentially provided these loan schemes at low or no interest rates to be paid back at a later stage in life when students found jobs. Nonetheless, from the late 1980s, and certainly from the 1990s student loans were introduced on a large scale in many countries as a mechanism to recover cost. In many cases higher education had become expensive due to the advent of the 'corporate managerialism and marketization process' (Mok & Lee, 2000) as a result of decline or withdrawal of the state from funding higher education. The student loan scheme was initiated on a larger scale to support students to pay high fees recently introduced and markedly raised. The loans mostly covered tuition and living expenses of students. Student loans could be either income contingent or mortgage type. Mortgage loans (see Ziderman, 1999, for different types of loans) have very often been a fixed monthly repayment amount, whereas as far as income contingent loans are concerned, the repayment is related to income earned by the individual. However, income contingent loans are more equity friendly and mortgage loans are more common because of ease of administration.

When student fees were increased in Australia, a loan scheme was introduced through the HECS (NIER, 1998). Mongolia introduced student loans in the 1990s as part of its transition from a socialist to a market economy. The loan schemes in India and Hong Kong are not related to the recent marketization process. Hong Kong introduced interest-free student loans in 1969; but in the 1980s an interest (low interest rate of 2.5 per cent) was added to the loan and in the 1990s the interest rates were further enhanced (Bray, 2000). In India (Tilak & Varghese, 1991) student loans were also in operation from the 1960s at a low rate of interest, more as a student support scheme. However, the 1990s reforms introduced student loan schemes in a big way, especially for students pursuing professional and technical education (Varghese, 2000). The country is introducing educational credit banks to provide loans to a larger number of students.

P.R. China introduced student loans as part of its transition from a centralized system to a socialist market economy (World Bank, 1996). Student stipends were converted into merit scholarships and loans from 1988 onwards. Thailand introduced student loan schemes on a large scale in the late 1990s (Ziderman, 1999). The loan scheme is for secondary and higher education. In fact, a majority of loan scholarships are distributed to secondary school students. This is one of the few examples where young students and minors are given loans and it did raise ethical issues on the desirability of children being made debtors.

A student loan scheme is available to meet the full cost of tuition, incidental expenses and living allowances in New Zealand (NIER, 1998). The repayment is through the income tax system, based on the earnings of the individuals. There is no repayment until the individual reaches the threshold income. Interest is charged on a compounded basis and is added to the loan every year. Malaysia has a student loan scheme for students in both public and private institutions. The loan amount is different for these two types of institutions. For example, in 1997–98, a total amount of RM 100 million was spent on 9091 approved student loans; the approved amount for 1998 is RM 203.5 million (NIER, 1998). Students in public institutions received a loan of RM 6500 and those in private institutions received a loan of RM 12,000 in 1997–98.

In Indonesia, a student loan scheme existed and it supported students from both private and public institutions of higher education (Purwadi & Muljoatmodjo, 2000). Similarly, the Government of Fiji introduced loan schemes in the 1990s (Crocombe & Crocombe, 1994).

All types of student loans have an element of subsidy. The low interest rate and easy instalments for repayment are indirect indications of extent of subsidy existing in loan schemes. Needless to say, recovery of student loans continues to be a severe problem in all countries, including the most advanced countries, that have introduced the scheme. Since the scheme is new in many countries of the region, it is too early to discuss the difficulties of repayment. New Zealand has already begun to experience the debt burden accumulated by students who received loans.

3.3. Income Generating Activities

Many universities in the region have adopted strategies for generating their own incomes. This is attained by different methods. Universities rent space and guest rooms, introduce consultancy services, establish linkages with other universities and industries, and introduce market friendly courses. The term, 'corporatisation' has become acceptable in China to signify the involvement of the university in business. One of the reports of SEAMEO PROAP (1996) indicates that universities are expected to mobilize around 50 per cent of their income through various activities in China. IIEP studies (Martin, 2000) have shown that university-industry linkages is an emerging area for income generation activities in many universities. The study on Papua New Guinea (PNG) (Satter & Pumwa, 2000) indicates that the main universities in the country have established commercial units to conduct business activities. These commercial units operate like private companies or corporations. The company at the Technical University of PNG has an annual turnover of 2.5 million Kina and employs around 57 full-time employees. There are many other innovative programs initiated by various universities (Sanyal, 1998) to generate their own income. The most widely cited cases are those in developed countries.

Australia attracts a large number of foreign students and they are a source of income for universities. In some universities the share of foreign students is substantial. Foreign students account for nearly 25 per cent of enrolment in Curtin University and 26 per cent in the Royal Melbourne Institute of Technology and an equal share may be found in the University of Southern Queensland, and the University of Woollongong (Kemp, 2000). Australian universities obtain funds from students abroad. New Zealand is another country that attracts many foreign students.

Malaysia is a classical example of the trend towards corporatising universities (Lee, 1998). Corporatized universities are able to borrow money, enter into business ventures, set up companies, and acquire and hold investment shares. The profits from these operations are expected to meet a good share of the operating costs of the universities. The government meets the capital expenditure part of the cost.

Capitation fee colleges in India (Tilak, 1992) are yet another mechanism to mobilize income. Under this arrangement, private colleges charge an initial amount and a high rate of fees not only to recover cost but also to enable profits to be made. The franchising and twinning arrangements made by many private and public universities provide a good source of income.

4. PRIVATE SECTOR IN HIGHER EDUCATION

The private sector in higher education was encouraged and promoted for various reasons. First, the social demand for higher education far exceeded the provisions that could be made by public authorities. Private sector operations were thus encouraged to expand access. Second, in many countries demand for courses and subjects of study had changed and public universities were unable to address this phenomenon. Third, in many centrally planned economies, transition from state planning to market forces was also associated with expansion of the private sector in higher education.

Many countries in the Asian region have a strong presence of the private sector in higher education. More than 80 per cent of enrolments in higher education in the Philippines, Korea, Japan, and Taiwan are accounted for by the private sector. In Japan and Korea private universities are under strict governmental regulations. Around three-fifths of the admissions in Indonesia and almost an equal share of enrolments in Malaysia are in private universities (Lee, 1999).

The number of private universities in Thailand is also increasing. The growth of the private sector was perhaps the fastest among transition economies. Within a short period of five to ten years, the growth rate of the private sector in transition economies was not only higher than that of state institutions, but also surpassed public institutions in number. In Mongolia, Kazakhstan and other Central Asian republics the private sector grew very fast. Consequently, the private sector has become an important, if not a dominant sector in these economies.

The growth of private universities in Bangladesh is a phenomenon of the 1990s after the amendment of the law in 1992 permitting private institutions to operate (Hopper, 1998). Most of these universities are located in the capital city of Dakka. In 1999, 13 out of 16 universities were located in the capital city. In India, private colleges were permitted to conduct technical and professional courses. Also, many provincial governments have now started self-financing colleges on a large scale in India.

Private institutions are established by religious organisations, private foundations and organisations and by for-profit private agencies. Some developing countries also experienced a very fast growth of private higher education institutions in the 1990s. The pattern was similar, although the reason was not political upheaval, but rather a more friendly approach to market forces.

While public universities receive a major share of their funding from the government, many private institutions established in the 1990s seldom obtain financial aid from public authorities. Many operate like an enterprise generating profit. Tuition fees form the financial backbone of many private institutions. They must meet their expenditure with what they collect from their students. The total income of private institutions is determined, therefore, by the number of students and the rate of tuition levied. For any given level of tuition fees, these institutions attempt to attract a larger number of students in order to maximize profitability. This is achieved through introducing courses that are popular on the employment market and not offered by traditional sectors. Courses on information technology, management and business studies, foreign languages (especially English), and tourism are very common among curricula proposed by institutions of private higher education in transition economies.

The profitability of these institutions depends on savings made by them on expenditure. Salaries, especially staff salaries, form a dominant part of expenditure of educational institutions in the public domain. Many private institutions make savings by employing teaching staff on a part-time basis. In some cases, staff members from the public sector teach in private institutions on this basis. In other words, high tuition fees, market friendly courses and part-time staff are common features of many private higher education institutions which appeared throughout the 1990s.

5. EXTERNAL FUNDING

External funding for higher education in the region is not very high. As mentioned in the introduction, many Pacific Island countries are too small and do not have universities. They traditionally send their students abroad for higher studies even after they have established universities. The unit costs are higher in smaller islands because they employ expatriates and they are unable to achieve economies of scale. A substantial share of external funding is to support study-abroad programs. The South Pacific region has the highest external funding support for higher education: "Nowhere else in the world is such a high proportion of post-secondary education carried out by international agencies" (Crocombe & Crocombe, 1994, p. 26). The post-secondary education of American Samoa and Micronesian territories of the North Pacific is supported by the United States. The migration of students for studies to Japan, China and Taiwan has now increased. However, the main destination continues to be the United Kingdom.

The trend in overseas education has changed from church-based education to education in public universities. The major contribution once came from the

United Kingdom, Australia and New Zealand. However, their contributions declined in the 1990s and Japan and other East Asian countries have increased their contribution. Irrespective of the changes in the source of external funding "the Pacific Island states receive more aid per capita than any other part of the world. That which is allocated to education is almost all to post-secondary" (Crocombe & Crocomnbe, 1994, p. 141).

There are few other countries that traditionally send a large share of their students abroad for higher studies. For example, Cyprus continues to send more than 50 per cent of their university students abroad for pursuing studies, even though a university was established within the country in 1992 (Menon, 1998). Nearly one-fifth (19.7%) of the tertiary education students of Singapore go abroad for studies. Malaysia sends 21.6 per cent of its university students abroad for studies (UNESCO, 1999). However, these students receive national scholarships rather than external funding and hence their situation is different from the Pacific Islands cases.

6. CONCLUDING OBSERVATIONS

Central to the issue of financing of higher education is the role of the state. When the public sector was growing, the state needed higher educated persons to manage the economy and it subsidised provisions for higher education. Now the public sector is shrinking and the state is no more the major consumer of educated manpower. An application of the same principles may demand that the state should withdraw its subsidies and allow and facilitate the private sector to finance higher education. However, setting priorities in higher education cannot be left to the market forces alone. The state has a responsibility to direct and regulate the changes in higher education, even when it cannot fully fund the sector.

The recent trends in cost recovery and income generating activities of entrepreneurial universities indicate the capacity of institutions to mobilize resources on the one hand and to set limits to such efforts on the other (Varghese, 2002). The efforts in the future need not be to substitute funds from one source by another but to increase total resources available to higher education. Redefining the resource sharing responsibilities between the state and the non-governmental sectors can accomplish this. A partnership based more on this shared view should shape future funding arrangements for higher education. A brighter future for higher education lies in the development of a mutually beneficial and socially responsible relationship between market forces and state interventions.

Unfortunately the role of the state is not confined to funding alone. There are instances when the move towards the private sector was encouraged when the public sector did not respond to the felt needs of the community, either in terms of expanding access or delivering market friendly courses. But the recent experience of the East Asian economic crisis indicates that markets are unable to function properly in the absence of state support in terms of policy and regulation. More importantly, the state came forward to support private universities from insolvency in Korea by investing 990 billion won in 1998. Again, the state introduced student support systems to retain students in private universities in Korea, Thailand and Indonesia (Varghese, 2001). In other words, the extreme case of aid of state-only or market-only is not a pragmatic approach to find a sustainable solution for paucity of funds in higher education. The public universities need to be more entrepreneurial and private institutions more sensitive to play a socially responsible role in their operations.

REFERENCES

Bray, M. (2000). Financing higher education: Patterns, trends and options. *Prospects, 30*(3), 332–348.
Crocombe, R., & Crocombe, M. T. (1994). *Post-secondary Education in the South Pacific.* London: Commonwealth Secretariat.
Heaton, C. (1999). The equity implications of public subsidization of higher education: A study of the Fijian case. *Education Economics, 7*(2), 153–166.
Hopper, R. (1998). Emerging private universities in Bangladesh: Public enemy or ally? *International Higher Education, 10,* 5–6.
Kemp, D. (2000). *Higher Education Report for the 2000–2002 Triennium.* Canberra: Commonwealth Secretariat.
Lee, M. N. N. (1998). Corporatisation and privatisation of Malaysian higher education. *International Higher Education, 10,* 7–8.
Lee, M. N. N. (1999). *Private Higher Education in Malaysia.* Penang: University Sains Malaysia.
Martin, M. (2000). *Managing University-Industry Relations: A Study of Institutional Practices from 12 Different Countries.* Paris: International Institute for Educational Planning.
Menon, M. E. (1998). Factors influencing demand for higher education: The case of Cyprus. *Higher Education, 35*(5), 251–266.
Mok, K. H. (1999). The cost of managerialism, the implications for 'McDonaldization' of higher education. *Journal of Higher Education Policy and Management, 21*(1), 117–127.
Mok, K. H., & Lee, H. H. (2000). Globalization and re-colonization: Higher education reform in Hong Kong. *Higher Education Policy, 13*(14), 361–378.
National Institute for Educational Research (NIER) (1998). *Recent Reforms and Perspectives in Higher Education.* Tokyo: NIER.
Psacharopoulos, G. (1994). Returns to education: A global update. *World Development, 22,* 1325–1343.
Purwadi, A., & Muljoatmodjo, S. (2000). Education in Indonesia: Coping with challenges in the third millenium. *Journal of South East Asian Education, 1*(1), 79–112.
Sanyal, B. (1998). *Strategies for Higher Education in Asia and the Pacific in the Post-Cold War Era,* IIEP contributions No. 29. Paris: International Institute for Educational Planning.
Satter, M. A., & Pumwa, J. (2000). The management of university-industry relations in Papua New Guinea. In M. Martin (Ed.), *Management of University-Industry Relations: Five Institutional Case Studies from Africa, Europe, Latin America and the Pacific Region* (pp. 75–144). Paris: International Institute for Educational Planning.
SEAMEO-PROAP (1996). *Re-engineering Higher Education for the Twenty-first Century.* Bangkok: PROAP (UNESCO).
Tilak, J. B. G. (1992). Capitation fee colleges. *Journal of Higher Education, 16*(1).
Tilak, J. B. G., & Varghese, N. V. (1991). Financing higher education in India. *Higher Education, 21*(1), 83–101.
UNESCO: United Nations Educational Scientific and Cultural Organisation (1999). *Statistical Year Book.* Paris: UNESCO.
Varghese, N. V. (2000). Reforms in financing higher education, *Seminar,* no. 494, 20–25.
Varghese, N. V. (2001). Impact of the economic crisis on higher education in East Asia: An overview.

In N. V. Varghese (Ed.), *Impact of the Economic Crisis on Higher Education in East Asia: Country Experiences* (pp. 23–60). Paris: IIEP.

Varghese, N. V. (2002). *Limits to Diversification of Sources of Funding in Higher Education.* Paris: IIEP.

Woodhall, M. (1991). *Student Loans in Higher Education: Asia.* Paris: International Institute for Educational Planning.

World Bank (1986). *Financing Education in Developing Countries: An Exploration in Policy Options.* Washington, DC: World Bank.

World Bank (1994). *Higher Education: The Lessons of Experience.* Washington, DC: World Bank.

World Bank (1996). *China Higher Education Reform.* Washington, DC: World Bank.

World Bank (1996). *Philippines Education Financing and Social Sector Reform Agenda.* Washington, DC: World Bank.

Ziderman, A. (1999). *Student Loan Schemes in Thailand: A Review and Recommendation for Efficiency and Equitable Functioning of the Scheme.* Bangkok: PROAP (UNESCO).

58

Selection for Higher Education in the Asia-Pacific Region

V. LYNN MEEK
Centre for Higher Education Management and Policy, University of New England, Australia

1. INTRODUCTION

This article reviews the selection and admission policies of various higher education institutions and systems in the Asia-Pacific region. It is not so much concerned with the mechanics of selection (e.g., public examination, moderation and setting of entry scores for particular courses; see Keeves, 1998) as with the socio-political context in which selection takes place, particularly with respect to access and equity. The article begins with an overview of current issues of concern to selection for higher education. The next section presents a brief summary of what appear to be two important issues for a number of countries in the region: privatisation of higher education and differentiation of institutional type coupled with the rise of distance education and the open university. The article then looks at the case of India as an example of a huge system of higher education attempting to cope with the complex issues of equity and access. The conclusion speculates on what might be the most important issues with respect to selection over the next decade.

2. OVERVIEW: SELECTION AND THE MASSIFICATION OF TERTIARY EDUCATION

With respect to selection policies and procedures *per se*, the focus of this article is mainly on higher or university-level education with the discussion limited to selection and admission at the undergraduate level. However, no categorical distinction is made between the terms higher and tertiary education for they are often used interchangeably in the literature. Also, space does not allow for rigorous and detailed delineation between a number of related concepts: selection, admission, access, entrance, and participation. For a more fine-grained consideration of these conceptual issues see Harman's (1994) extensive review of selection in the Asian region.

Generally, there are three types of admission for higher education:

> competitive or selective admissions, in which a limited supply of places is awarded to selected applicants in order of their merit on entry or pre-entry tests; qualifying admissions, in which all those who reach a set minimum mark are entitled to a higher education place, subject only to administrative, not competitive requirements ... ; and open admissions, in which anyone may enrol regardless of previous educational achievement. (Fulton, 1998, p. 8)

Selection becomes a contentious issue when the number of applicants greatly exceeds the number of student places available (Harman, 1994, p. 314). If all potential students could gain access to the institution and course of their choosing, selection would be a topic hardly worth discussing. But with the massification of higher education following the Second World War, access to higher education has become an issue for most countries, whether they are classified as industrialised, newly industrialised or developing. According to a World Bank report:

> To educate their students effectively, institutions should be able to enrol only as many applicants as they can responsibly teach, and to accept only students who possess the knowledge and ability to fully benefit from their studies. Selectivity should help ensure that enrolment growth is related to instructional capacity and, if selection criteria have good predictive validity, that opportunities for further study will be allocated to those who are most likely to benefit academically. (*Higher Education: Issues and Options for Reform*, 1993, p. 32)

A more recent World Bank report recognises the importance of value-added higher education in the light of ever increasing enrolments. "As higher education systems expand, they must become more tolerant at points of entry, while ensuring the quality at the point of exit is maintained" (*Higher Education in Developing Countries: Peril and Promise*, 2000, p. 87). However, while arguing the benefits of a more general or liberal higher education curriculum over early narrow disciplinary specialisation, the report also recognises the tradeoffs necessitated by the tension between available financial resources and the proportion of the population that can be allowed to participate in higher education at the highest level: "the more extensive general education programs are not meant for all, or even the majority, of students. They should be aimed at the brightest and most highly motivated in any cohort, with a broader cross-section of students offered less intensive forms of general education" (p. 88). But in many developing and developed countries alike, both the proportion of the population who can effectively participate in higher education and the political importance attached to such participation has in recent decades been continually re-defined upwards. This makes policies and procedures concerning selection all the more important and complex, and directly ties questions of selection to the way in which higher education systems are differentiated into diverse types of institutions, representing different points of access.

In the period covering the 1960s up to the late 1980s, many higher education systems in developing countries, including those in the Asia-Pacific region (notably India, Pakistan and Bangladesh) were heavily criticised for producing too many graduates with qualifications and knowledge of little relevance to the employment and development needs of the nation. But as Teichler (2001, p. 3) notes, "the widespread concern prevailing in the past about 'over-education' or 'over-qualification' gave way in the 1990s to views that further expansion might be inevitable, might be an appropriate foundation of a 'knowledge society'". This view is strongly reinforced by the OECD publication *Redefining Tertiary Education* (1998).

Redefining Tertiary Education concentrates on the first years of tertiary education participation, and is based on country-specific reports from a number of nations, including Australia, Japan and New Zealand. Whereas in the past, universal participation was taken to mean about 50 per cent of the age cohort, now 80 per cent or more is becoming the average. Hence, it appears even another "new paradigm is emerging whereby participation in some form of tertiary education may be expected to become the norm in our societies" (p. 9). The elements of this new paradigm include:

- the continually rising aspirations and expectations among individuals and societies;
- the universalisation of full secondary education, a phenomenon in most countries of only the past three or four decades;
- the directions of public policy in many countries which project eligibility for tertiary education of 60, 80, or 100 per cent of those completing secondary education ... ;
- the realisation by adults of the need to continue or restart formal learning and of the opportunities to do so;
- the constantly reiterated social demand and human capital theses which are a stimulus to individual and social investment in ever higher levels of skills and competences;
- the equity-based attention to previously under-represented groups; and
- the relative ease of access to highly flexible and accommodating forms of study whether home-, workplace- or institution-based. (*Redefining Tertiary Education*, 1998, p. 37)

In the more advanced nations of the Asia-Pacific region, such as Australia, Japan and New Zealand, "tertiary education is replacing secondary education as the focal point of access, selection and entry to rewarding careers for the majority of young people". Moreover, "there is an increased risk to social structure and cohesion and a threat to equity and social justice if a significant proportion of the population is excluded or discouraged from participation in a stage of education which clearly confers benefits" (*Redefining Tertiary Education*, 1998, p. 20).

Once commenced, the student flow towards mass and universal tertiary education cannot be easily slowed, much less stopped, providing it with about the same political and financial importance to government as secondary education. Clearly, both private and public resources must be mobilised if tertiary education institutions are going to accommodate effectively increasing participation. The crucial question for all countries is how to provide an affordable but high quality education in the face of soaring demand.

Universal tertiary education coupled with the notion of life-long learning places selection in quite a different context compared to the situation in some of the less advanced nations of the Asia-Pacific region that have yet to achieve universal primary education (e.g., Bangladesh, India, Indonesia, Pakistan and Thailand). For example, the majority of the higher education systems in the region use some form of public examination to select aspiring applicants straight from school. But in countries like Australia, this group of applicants has become increasingly less significant, as have the examinations themselves, given the fact that about 50 per cent of new undergraduate students are selected on the basis of other criteria: mature age, experiential learning, prior learning, and other higher education studies.

What appears to be universal to the higher education systems of the region is the challenge of providing a high quality tertiary or higher education for all who are capable of benefiting from it at an affordable price. Two important strategies commonly employed to achieve this end have been the privatisation of higher education and the differentiation of institutional type, including the proliferation of the open university model and distance education.

3. HIGHER EDUCATION: PRIVATISATION AND DIFFERENTIATION

Obtaining accurate information on levels of access and participation in the various higher education systems across the Asia-Pacific region is virtually impossible. But one thing can be said with conviction – participation in higher education is increasing everywhere, though not at a uniform rate. Barro and Lee (2000) provide some interesting comparative figures with respect to level of educational attainment of the population over 25 years in East Asia-Pacific and South Asia that are recorded in Table 1.

In both regions, the proportion of the population participating in higher education has risen substantially over the last four decades, although the rates of participation have stayed well below that of developed countries. Grouping countries in this manner masks substantial differences in nations' educational attainment levels, particularly with respect to countries constituting the East Asia-Pacific region, where for the year 2000, 20 per cent or more of the population over 25 years in Korea, the Philippines and Taiwan have participated in higher education, while the corresponding proportion for a number of the other countries is 10 per cent or less (the range being 1.4% in Papua New Guinea to 25.8%

Table 1. Trends of educational attainment of the total population aged 25 and over by region

Region (no. of countries)	Year	Pop. over 25 (mil.)	No School (%)	Primary education (%)	Secondary education (%)	Higher education (%)	Average years of school
East Asia-Pacific	1960	79	61.3	31.4	5.7	1.6	2.26
(10 countries[a])	1970	100	43.7	43.8	9.7	2.8	3.29
	1980	131	30.1	49.4	15.6	4.8	4.39
	1990	178	33.1	35.1	24.1	7.6	5.35
	1995	205	27.1	36.6	26.2	10.1	6.03
	2000	233	22.8	37.7	27.4	12.1	6.50
South Asia	1960	248	77.3	19.3	3.3	0.1	1.31
(7 countries[b])	1970	304	74.2	19.8	4.6	1.2	1.75
	1980	382	72.4	12.2	13.1	2.3	2.48
	1990	499	60.3	21.8	14.2	3.7	3.34
	1995	574	54.7	26.2	15.2	4.0	3.73
	2000	660	48.4	30.6	16.7	4.3	4.19
Advanced countries	1960	362	6.5	53.6	32.2	7.5	6.97
(23 countries[c])	1970	404	5.1	50.6	34.4	9.9	7.50
	1980	467	5.3	35.1	43.2	16.4	8.67
	1990	535	4.2	31.2	40.5	24.0	9.25
	1995	582	4.0	28.7	41.4	25.9	9.57
	2000	612	4.1	27.4	39.4	29.1	9.80

Adapted from Barro and Lee (2000). Regional averages are computed by weighting each country's observation by its share of the regional population aged 25 years and over.
[a] Fiji, Hong Kong, Indonesia, Korea, Malaysia, Papua New Guinea, Philippines, Singapore, Taiwan, and Thailand.
[b] Afghanistan, Bangladesh, India, Myanmar, Nepal, Pakistan, Sri Lanka.
[c] Australia, Austria, Belgium, Canada, Denmark, Finland, France, Germany, Greece, Iceland, Ireland, Italy, Japan, Netherlands, New Zealand, Norway, Portugal, Spain, Sweden, Switzerland, Turkey, United Kingdom, United States.

in Korea). The disparities in the proportion of the population for whom higher education is the highest level attained are much less for the seven countries constituting South Asia, ranging from 2.2 per cent in Afghanistan to 4.8 per cent in India for the year 2000.

3.1. *Selection and Privatisation*

Questions of who participates in higher education are never far removed from those concerning who pays for it. A general trend in this respect has been the privatisation of higher education and a change in attitude from higher education being a public to a private good. Australia, for example, has moved from a situation where the government was the primary funder of higher education to the present where the government considers itself a subsidiser, contributing less than 50 per cent to the overall funding of the sector. While the establishment of fully private higher education institutions has made little impact on Australian higher education, the privatisation of the public sector has been extensive, brought about mainly through the introduction of student tuition fees. At the undergraduate level, Australian students pay fees through the Higher Education Contribution Scheme, collected through the tax system only when the graduate is employed and reaches a prescribed income level. But prospective students who miss out in the normal selection process, can gain a place at university by paying up front fees if their score in the public examination is no more than five per cent below the selection cut-off score for the courses in which they are interested. While this has sparked some concern of a two-tier system where the rich can buy their way into a course, so far, relatively few students have chosen this option.

Up to the mid-1980s in Australia, the education of overseas students was seen mainly as a form of foreign aid. Students were subsidised by government aid programs and fees were not paid directly to institutions. But, in the late 1980s, government foreshadowed a more market oriented approach to foreign students – from 'aid' to 'trade' – by indicating that full-fee paying overseas students provided another important source of potential revenue growth. In 2000 there were 153,372 international students enrolled in Australia with a further 34,905 enrolled with Australian providers operating overseas. A relatively new phenomenon in this area is for Australian universities to enrol overseas students through distance education or at an offshore campus established by a university in collaboration with a foreign partner. The great majority of students are from the South East Asia region and Australia has a higher proportion of international students in its higher education sector than any other major exporter within the OECD.

Each Australian university sets it own entry standards and prospective overseas students must meet the same selection criteria as that prescribed for domestic students. They must also have the financial support to pay the substantial tuition fees (on average about $12,000 per annum) plus living costs. In recent years there have been allegations that at least some universities are lowering their entry standards in order to attract more international students and engaging in soft marking to ensure that they continue once enrolled. While such allegations have not been substantiated, they highlight potential problems created by the continued commercialisation of higher education.

With the globalisation and liberalisation of its centrally planned economy, China has made substantial reforms to its higher education system, including the recent establishment of some 1,800 private colleges and universities enrolling about one million students. However, it appears quality is a substantial problem: "only 37 of these colleges and universities have approval to issue standard credentials. Of these 37, only 4 issue a standard undergraduate degree" (Postiglione, 2001, p. 11).

In response to both the soaring demand for higher education and the considerable degree of student violence on the campuses of the country's 13 public universities, privatisation has also been a response pursued by Bangladesh. In contrast to Australia, in Bangladesh, privatisation of higher education has occurred through the country's 19 private universities, all created since 1992 as a result of changes in the laws governing higher education that year. Up to 1992, Bangladesh had a purely public higher education system, but one that could accommodate only about 25 per cent of the some 80,000 annual eligible aspirants (Hopper, 1998, p. 5).

In Bangladesh, admission to higher education is based on a nation-wide selection and placement examination, though students attending the private universities must pay substantial tuition fees (public higher education is virtually "free"). In a country where the per capita income is less than $300 per annum, the annual tuition fee of about US$5,000 at such private universities as the Independent University of Bangladesh is entirely out of the reach of the vast majority of the population.

The emergence of private universities in Bangladesh has both its critics and supporters. Critics argue that private universities are elitist and entirely inappropriate for such a poor country, and maintain that higher education is a public good and a "powerful instrument for building a more equitable society. By providing equal access for good students from the lower social and economic backgrounds, the public university can become a great social and economic equaliser" (Quddus, 1999, p. 15). Proponents see that the benefits of higher education accrue mainly to the individual rather than society, and also maintain that increasing numbers in private universities frees up places in public institutions. "Fears that the emergence of private higher education will result in commercialisation through 'purchasing' of degrees and development of a profit motive behind higher education have been somewhat tempered by ... provisions in the Non-Government Universities Act" (Hopper, 1998, p. 6). The Act also demands that five per cent of all student places in private universities be reserved for "poor but meritorious students". Nonetheless, Hopper argues that "with the shift of university costs to the individual through the creation of private universities, the rise in elitism is unavoidable" (p. 6).

But the problem of elitism is not peculiar to Bangladesh. Of particular concern to many if not most nations has been the continuing imbalances in the social composition of the student population. In Australia, for example, the participation rate of a number of equity groups has improved substantially in recent years. Women, for instance, made up 57 per cent of all 2001 non-overseas commencing students, a considerable improvement on their participation a decade earlier. Indigenous Australians and persons from non-English speaking backgrounds with respect to overall participation have become over represented. However, little or no progress has been made on the relative access by rural and isolated students, or by persons of low socio-economic status. Despite a dramatic increase in student numbers since the mid-1980s, participation in higher education by persons of low socio-economic status has not improved; in fact, evidence suggests that it has worsened (Meek & Wood, 1998).

The Philippines has one of the largest, well established private higher education systems in the region. The nation's 1147 private and 210 public higher education institutions cater for close to two million students, representing about 35 per cent of the relevant age cohort. This impressive rate of participation in higher education would be impossible without the extensive system of private institutions. However, many of these institutions are of low quality, with weak admission standards, charging minimal tuition fees and having few resources to maintain educational infrastructure and hire appropriately qualified academic staff. Moreover, many students come to higher education in both the public and private sector ill prepared for study at this level. One problem is that in the Philippines the average student enters higher education with only ten years of prior schooling, compared to 12 years in many countries. In April 2000, the Philippine Commission on Educational Reform recommended a pre-baccalaureate year after high school for students intending to attend university. "This pre-baccalaureate year will be implemented for all students, with the provision that universities may allow some students to enter directly after high school, either because they have already had more than 10 years of schooling or because of proven aptitude" (Nebres, 2001, p. 16). It is interesting to note that in the past the University of Papua New Guinea used the successful completion of a post-school, pre-university preliminary year as its main selection device for undergraduate entry, while the University of the South Pacific continues to do so.

3.2. Selection and Alternative Institutional Types

With the rising cost of higher education, particularly university education, coupled with soaring demand, many nations have attempted to channel a proportion of their aspiring students into less costly alternatives. New Zealand, for example, has retained a binary system of higher education that differentiates between universities and polytechnics, with entry into the polytechnics slightly less competitive. Another model that has proved popular is that of the community college adapted from North America. For example, in Thailand a new initiative to help the nation cope with the rising number of students expecting to participate in post secondary education is the introduction of community colleges in the outlying provinces and districts. This initiative is designed not only to cope with increasing numbers of tertiary education applications, but to further principles of equity and access in the provinces (Burian & Komolkiti, 2001).

Throughout the region there has been a dramatic rise in the open university model based on distance education and flexible entry. Initially, the open university model was regarded as a panacea for the exploding demand for higher education in developing countries. But by the late 1980s and early 1990s, there was growing criticism that the introduction of the open university and the use of distance education in developing countries had not met its promises of widening access and increasing participation. Ali et al. (1997) in reviewing the related literature summarise a number of the issues: poor quality teaching materials, high drop-out, infrastructure deficiencies, student-teacher isolation, and failure to reach the rural masses and the most disadvantaged groups.

But over the last decade rapid developments in the area of new information and communication technologies (ICTs) have greatly increased expectations of what can be achieved by distance education. One of the more extreme views is that the so-called 'virtual university' will replace the traditional university in developed and developing countries alike. While this appears to be unlikely, there is no doubt about the rapid growth in distance education and the establishment of open universities throughout the region. The Asian Association of Open Universities (AAOU) established in 1987 to widen the educational opportunities available to all the people of the region had by the end of 2000, 28 full members drawn from Bangladesh, China, Chinese Taipei, Hong Kong SAR, India, Indonesia, Iran, Japan, Korea, Pakistan, Palestine, The Philippines, Sri Lanka, Thailand and Vietnam. In 2000, AAOU member institutions enrolled over four million students with some ten member institutions classified as 'mega-universities'.

Clearly, online delivery, computer simulation, television and satellite delivery, the expanding internet and other ICTs have allowed open universities to overcome the tyranny of distance, while simultaneously increasing rates of participation. Though generally, open universities select from a wider pool of applicants than those who aspire to enter a traditional university, there is still some doubt about their ability to reach the most disadvantaged groups in particular societies. Dhanarajan (1998, p. 3) complains that "institutions that proclaim to be 'open' still continue to select their enrollees", and advocates that "institutions genuinely committed to open access must attempt to identify the learners' academic needs first before designing courses rather than starting with courses and looking for students to fit them". In reality, there is probably no such thing as pure "open access" in higher education. Rather, higher education systems everywhere must balance competing demands for participation against available resources necessary to preserve an acceptable standard of quality. Nowhere is the complexity of these demands more apparent than in India.

4. INDIA: A CASE STUDY

With nearly one billion citizens, 16 per cent of the world's population lives in India in an area that constitutes 2.4 per cent of the world's land mass. India spends 3.8 per cent of its GNP on education, but still has yet to achieve universal elementary education and is home to about one third of the world's non literate population aged 15 years and above (Ministry of Education, 2001).

Since India's independence, there has been a huge growth in the number of institutions and the number of students has increased twenty-nine fold. There are 244 universities, Deemed Universities, Institutions of National Importance (of which 16 are central universities funded by the Union Government, 47 Deemed to be Universities, five joint state/central government institutions) and 11,381 colleges. The university level institutions include 34 agricultural universities, 25 technical, 18 medical and 10 open universities.

With increased demand for higher education places, an escalating problem has been the growing number of fake universities functioning without authority in different parts of the country. The India University Grants Commission (UGC) has established a Special taskforce (the Malpractices Cell) to deal with matters relating to fake universities.

Admission to undergraduate courses requires candidates to complete 12 years of schooling and to achieve passes at the 60 to 70 per cent level in five subjects in the Senior Secondary or equivalent examination. Admission to technical courses requires candidates to pass at the 75–80 per cent level and include the subjects physics, chemistry, biology, mathematics and English. While generally admission to an undergraduate pass course is not rigid, admission to places in central universities and institutes of technology is far more competitive. Professional courses in most states also demand special entrance examinations.

In 2000–2001, of a total of 7,734,000 student enrolments, 1,277,000 were studying in university departments and 6,457,000 in affiliated colleges. The bulk of enrolments (81%) were in Arts (40%), Science (19%) and Commerce (22%). About 68 per cent of the enrolments were studying at the undergraduate level. Women accounted for 35.5 per cent of the total 2000–2001 enrolments, a proportion that varies greatly from province to province: 54 per cent in Kerala and 20 per cent in Bihar.

Indian higher education continues to face problems with respect to the standards and quality of education, as well as social disparities and regional imbalances in higher educational access and facilities. While in many developed nations, female participation in higher education is now substantially above 50 per cent, in India, as indicated above, women students constitute just a little over one-third of all students. The overall literacy rate in India is 62 per cent, but just 50 per cent for women. The districts of Barmer and Jalor of Rajasthan have female literacy of 7.68 per cent and 7.76 per cent respectively, the lowest in the country (Ministry of Education, 2001, p. 12). The *Annual Report 2000–2001* (2001, p. 41) states that "though there have been some significant results ... gender disparities continue to persist with uncompromising tenacity, more so in rural areas and among disadvantaged communities". Several Indian States have made education free for girls up to university level.

In order to address these problems the UGC has initiated a number of programs for enhancing access and equity. With respect to increasing the participation of women students in higher education, the Commission is assisting universities in the construction of hostels for women that provide a safe environment and encourage mobility of women students. Such assistance has been provided to 23 universities and 438 colleges. The UGC also provides assistance for the establishment of study centres to undertake research and develop curricula in the area of women studies. In order to enhance equity in the areas of engineering and technology, the UGC has introduced a scheme to assist the introduction of undergraduate courses in these areas in selected women's universities. The All India Council for Technical Education (AICTE) has created a Board on Women Participation in Technical Education, and special incentives, including scholarships and stipends, are provided. Another new scheme supported by the UGC is the introduction of day care centres in universities and colleges through a one-off grant. Other planned initiatives include infrastructure for women students, scholarships for women in professional courses, databases for women, and gender sensitivity programs.

The educational development of children belonging to the Scheduled Castes (SCs), Scheduled Tribes (STs), other Backward Castes and educationally backward minorities is a government priority. The National Policy on Education makes a number of special provisions for SCs and STs.

- There is the reservation of seats for SCs and STs in Central Government Institutions of Higher Education, Regional Engineering Colleges, Central Universities, etc. In universities, colleges and technical institutions, apart from reservation, there is also relaxation in the minimum qualifying cut-off percentages for admission. The UGC has established SC/ST Cells in 103 universities, including Central Universities to ensure proper implementation of the reservation policy.
- In order to improve academic skills and linguistic proficiency of students in various subjects and raise their level of comprehension, remedial and special coaching is provided for SC/ST students. The Indian Institutes of Technology have a scheme under which SC/ST students who fail marginally in the entrance examination are provided one year's preparatory course.
- Out of 43,000 scholarships at the secondary stage for talented children from rural areas, 13,000 are reserved exclusively for SC and ST students, while 70 scholarships are reserved exclusively for SC and ST students under the National Talent Search Scheme (*Annual Report 2000–2001*, 2001, p. 45).

There are coaching classes for students belonging to educationally backward minority communities to compete in various competitive examinations for securing admission to professional courses. By 2000 there were 77 coaching centres, including 10 coaching centres for women, in 22 universities and 55 colleges. The program is monitored by the Standing Committee on Minorities.

The prescribed reservation quota for SCs and STs in teaching is not filled and, in order to remedy this situation, the UGC has established a Central Pool Database of eligible SC and ST candidates that universities and colleges can access.

Another major initiative in India intended to broaden access and equity in higher education participation is the open university system. In addition to the nine state controlled open universities and 52 distance education units in the traditional universities, there is the Indira Gandhi National Open University (IGNOU) established expressly by an Act of National Parliament in 1985 to democratise higher education. The major objectives of the University include widening of access to higher education by providing opportunities to larger segments of the population, particularly to the disadvantaged groups, organising programs of continuing education and initiating special programs of higher education for specific target groups. IGNOU has both a flexible entry and delivery program, with courses offered through a network of 34 regional centres and 557 study centres. In 2000, more than 231,000 students were registered in some 56 programs consisting of 604 courses offered by IGNOU. The Indian government expects that by the end of its ninth Five Year Plan, 20 per cent of total enrolments in higher education will be in the open university system. The open university network has created a common set of programs consisting of contributions from the different open universities which can be accessed by any individual open university (Joshi, 1998).

Despite all the efforts to improve equity and access to higher education, a number of problems persist. First, India has a massive system of higher education and a feature since independence has been rapid expansion. But despite phenomenal growth, total enrolment represents only about six per cent of the relevant age-group population (17–23 years). This compares quite unfavourably to some of India's Asian neighbours: the Philippines (27.8%), Thailand (19.0%) and Malaysia (10.1%) (Joshi, 1998, p. 14). Access to Indian higher education remains an issue. Second, as the nation heads towards universal primary education and increased participation at the secondary level, it is likely that the access problem will merge with those created by the continued massification of the higher education system in general where the adequacy of the preparation of the candidates for higher education becomes even more diverse. "Increasing access and decrease in quality have been major issues confronting higher education with a very large young population and increasing strain in government resources" (Joshi, 1998, p. 15). Third, despite relatively cheap tuition fees, the higher education student population is dominated by those from the upper social and economic sections of society. As Joshi (1998, p. 15) notes, there is a continued need "to place greater emphasis on enrolment of students from underprivileged backgrounds such as the rural areas, the scheduled castes and tribes and other backward groups, minorities, the disabled and others who have suffered from discrimination which has existed for centuries". Fourth, as a by-product of inadequate selection methods, high student waste rates and low academic standards continue to be problems for many higher education institutions.

5. CONCLUSION

Nearly a decade ago, Harman (1994, p. 314) summarised a number of issues relevant to student selection for the higher education systems of the Asia-Pacific region:

- inefficiencies in selection and admission methods, with many inadequately

prepared students gaining entry to higher education and with institutions being forced to enrol more students than they can handle;
- lack of effective coordination in selection and admission policies and practices between government agencies and higher education institutions;
- a strong belief that the quality of teaching and learning in higher education has suffered because of too rapid expansion in enrolments;
- continuing imbalances in the social composition of student populations;
- unfair and biased selection criteria;
- limited progress with equity programs aimed to broaden access;
- mismatches between the outputs of higher education and labour market needs; and
- concern about the poor quality of secondary schooling, and in particular the inadequate backgrounds of many students in science, mathematics and languages.

None of these issues has been entirely resolved, and problems associated with imbalances in the social composition of student populations and equity in the participation of minority groups have proved to be particularly intransient. There is some indication that access and participation is improving through the application of ICTs by open universities and other distance education providers. But these strategies have their own in-built equity constraints for if students are going to participate they must have access to the new technology. The so-called 'digital divide' between developed and developing countries and between the rich and poor in all nations is one of the biggest problems facing higher education systems everywhere.

Most of the countries in the region, in attempting to balance the pressures of soaring demand for higher education against those of maintaining quality, have transferred some of the cost from government to the individual. But there is a limit to how much the individual can and should pay for higher education. Higher education is inexorably linked to the development of the knowledge economy, and both countries and individuals prevented by whatever means from effectively participating in the knowledge economy face a dim future. Selection for higher education remains one of the most important social and political issues faced by all nations of the Asia-Pacific region.

REFERENCES

Ali, M., Shamsher, A. K., Haque, E., & Rumble, G. (1997). The Bangladesh Open University: Mission and promise. *Open Learning, 12*(2), 12–17.

Government of India (Department of Elementary Education and Literacy, Department of Secondary Education and Higher Education, Ministry of Human Resource Development). (2001). *Annual Report 2000–2001*. New Delhi.

Barro, R. J., & Lee, J. W. (2000). International Data on Educational Attainment: Updates and Implications. CID Working Paper No. 42. Boston: Center for International Development, Harvard University.

Burian, C. N., & Komolkiti, S. (2001). *Community Colleges in Thailand: A New Option*. Institute of International Education. http://asia.iienetwork.org.

Dhanarajan, G. (1998). Access to Learning and the Asian Open Universities: In Context. Paper delivered at the 12th Annual Conference of the Asian Association of Open Universities, *The Asian Distance Learner*, The Open University of Hong Kong, 4-6 November.

Fulton, O. (1998). Equality and higher education. *Education: The Complete Encyclopaedia*. Oxford: Elsevier Science, CD-ROM.

Harman, G. (1994). Student selection and admission to higher education: Policies and practices in the Asian region. *Higher Education, 27*, 313-339.

Hopper, R. (1998). Emerging private universities in Bangladesh: Public enemy or ally? *International Higher Education, 10*, 5-7.

Joshi, M. M. (1998). Higher Education in India: Vision and Action. Country Paper. UNESCO World Conference on Higher Education in the Twenty-First Century. Paris, 5-9 October.

Keeves, J. P. (1998). Examinations: Public. In *Education: The Complete Encyclopedia*. Oxford: Elsevier Science, CD-ROM.

Meek, V. L., & Wood, F. (1998). *Managing Higher Education Diversity in a Climate of Public Sector Reform*. Canberra: AGPS.

Ministry of Education (2001). *Education Statistics*. Government of India. www.education.nic.in/htmlweb/edusta.htm#intro.

Nebres, B. F. (2001). The Philippines: Current trends. *International Higher Education, 24*, 15-17.

Organisation for Economic Cooperation and Development (OECD) (1998). *Redefining Tertiary Education* (1998). Paris: OECD.

Postiglione, G. (2001). China's expansion, consolidation, and globalisation. *International Higher Education, 24*, 10-12.

Quddus, M. (1999). Access to higher education in Bangladesh: The case of Dhaka University. *International Higher Education, 17*, 15-16.

Teichler, U. (2001). Mass higher education and the need for new responses. *Tertiary Education and Management, 7*, 3-7.

World Bank (1993). *Higher Education: Issues and Options for Reform*. Washington, DC: The World Bank.

World Bank (2000). *Higher Education in Developing Countries: Peril and Promise*. Washington, DC: The World Bank.

59

Adult Education in Universities in the Asia-Pacific Region

DARRYL DYMOCK
Centre for Lifelong Learning and Development, Flinders University, Australia

BARRIE BRENNAN
University of New England, Armidale, Australia

In many countries the education of adults has taken second place to the education of children, because school education is usually compulsory until a specified age, and governments have tended to focus their efforts and resources on that period. Adult education has generally been left to non-governmental agencies, except sometimes in specific areas, such as literacy, where national campaigns to educate adults have been government-initiated.

Because the term 'adult education' encompasses such a diverse range of educational programs and sometimes specific target audiences, it has been covered in this *Handbook* in several different sections and in a number of articles, (see *Lifelong Learning, Adult Literacy, Learning Across the Adult Lifespan, Workforce Education*, and *Nonformal Education*). This article is specifically about adult education in universities in the Asia-Pacific region, where it is generally termed 'continuing education'. The authors take as their starting point a definition of university continuing education as courses and other educational activities offered by universities which are primarily not for credit, although accreditation towards a formal university qualification may be possible. The article draws in particular on four case studies from across the Asia-Pacific region: New Zealand, Japan, the countries of the South Pacific, and Australia, with reference to university continuing education in Hong Kong and India.

1. UNIVERSITY CONTINUING EDUCATION

As the twentieth century progressed, adult education outside of formal degree offerings became relatively commonplace in the major British universities and subsequently in universities in other parts of the then British Empire, including Australia, New Zealand, Hong Kong, Fiji and India. It became known also variously as 'university extension', 'extra-mural education' and, more latterly, 'continuing education'. In its early years it was strongly liberal, and intended for individual development and the pursuit of knowledge rather than for vocational purposes, but since about the early 1980s there has been a decided swing to fee-paying professional development courses. In countries not from the British tradition, such as Japan, other imperatives have driven university continuing education, as will be seen.

Research has not been a strong point of university continuing education, despite the latter's location in institutions for which research is one of the major objectives. In relation to Centres for Continuing Education (CCEs) at New Zealand universities, it can be said that while the traditional functions of universities are to engage in teaching, research and community service, CCEs do not undertake much direct teaching, do little research (this fact is related to the absence of academic staff) but fulfil a major community service role as a primary public face of the university to the public.[1]

Similarly, at the University of the South Pacific (USP), although the USP has a mechanism to monitor and direct its various continuing education providers and their focus areas, there appears to be an absence of research in this field.[2] A similar view is held in Japan.[3]

A major reason for the lack of research is that continuing education personnel tend to be employed for their practical skills, rather than for their research abilities, even when they have academic status. They are administrators, program planners, coordinators, facilitators and sometimes financial experts, but the data they are required to produce tend to be statistical information about the number and nature of enrolled students and, increasingly, the strength of the financial return to the university in which the courses are given.

Publications from continuing education units tend to be in the form of annual reports that justify their existence within the institutional framework, rather than an analysis of the program profile or philosophy, or an explanation of program changes over a period of time. Even when continuing education is closely related to the main objectives of the university, there appears to be little research into its processes, purposes or outcomes apart from the statistics already alluded to. As a result, what emerges are issues that require research, rather than findings from research already undertaken. The main purpose of this article, therefore, is to provide a framework for future research rather than present a substantive report of it.

2. CONTINUING EDUCATION IN NEW ZEALAND UNIVERSITIES[1]

While some of the early-established universities such as Auckland and Canterbury set up university extension programs based on the British extra-mural model (Dakin, 1992), the more recent trend for the newer universities (e.g., Waikato) has been to develop Centres for Continuing Education (CCEs). The differences between the two types is more than semantic – the original extension departments employed academic staff to teach non-credit courses popular within the university's credit program, usually in a modified format; CCEs are predominantly administrative centres where professional continuing education staff (program planners) endeavour to link the university's resources to various publics' learning needs (Findsen, 1996). In New Zealand today, only CCEs continue to exist.

The plight of continuing education in New Zealand universities cannot be divorced from the wider political economy of the country nor the development of adult and higher education in this setting. In the last decade there have been massive economic, political and educational changes, initiated by the fourth Labour Government (1984–1990) and since carried on by successive governments, irrespective of political persuasion. The changes have been characterised by neo-liberal reforms in line with a New Right ideology – the streamlining of government-owned enterprises, deregulation, competition and restructuring in accord with a free market. These principles, according to Dale and Robertson (1997), have been translated into (a) cuts in public spending, (b) the minimisation of state obligations (in particular, the redirection of state funding from program provision towards increased program regulation), (c) the depoliticising of education away from the state, and (d) drives for increased efficiency and accountability. In higher education (including universities and their sub-units such as CCEs) practices which embody the following features are highly valued: greater entrepreneurialism, more user-pays, streamlining of decision-making, increased commercialisation, control of quality and firm strategic planning. In all but one case, CCEs managers have been appointed as leaders rather than academics, most of whom have not been replaced or have been moved into academic departments.

In 1994, the then director of continuing education at the University of Auckland stated the mission of that unit as:

> The University of Auckland Centre for Continuing Education contributes to the cultural, social and intellectual life of Auckland city and region. It exists to provide opportunities for all adults to have access to the distinctive educational expertise and resources of the University of Auckland. The centre aims to provide a range of quality courses and programs to the community, basing its own standards on the scholarship, research, skills and values of the wider University, and in acknowledgment of the Treaty of Waitangi. (Peddie, 1994, p. 1)

This mission statement would not vary much across the centres for continuing education at the five universities which currently have CCEs. The broad aspiration of serving communities would be present in all units though the quality of that provision is likely to vary considerably because most have become very oriented towards user pays and business models. The commitment to upholding the principles of the Treaty of Waitangi (a founding document between the early

European settlers and the indigenous Maori people) would be omnipresent as this is a major social equity goal of New Zealand society. Hence, there is always an active tension between profit-generating activity and wider social education goals.

Other factors affecting the direction of continuing education at respective locations have been the relative importance of adult and continuing education as a function of each university, physical and infrastructural positions of the Centre, the leadership of various directors and the extent of embeddedness of the unit within local and national communities (Findsen & Harre-Hindmarsh, 1996). In general terms, CCEs are expected to make their own way financially or cost the university as little as possible. Programs vary, with recent strengthening in vocational provision at the expense of liberal adult education. Duke, a former director of continuing education at the Australian National University and more recently at the University of Auckland, once commented that continuing education reflected a pluralism – "the seamless web or robe" (Duke, 1991, p. 61) – prevalent in British forms of provision. In New Zealand, there appears to be little philosophical coherence. A complicating factor in most universities has been the *laissez-faire* attitude of the parent institution as to who can undertake continuing education within the institution, producing *de facto* competitive internal markets.

In a recent case study of the Auckland CCE, Findsen (2001) discussed a number of issues requiring closer scrutiny in university-based continuing education in New Zealand. A fundamental concern is for the clarification of the role of continuing education in universities, yet this is seldom discussed with proper rigour. Unless the vision for continuing education is made known and explicit, CCEs remain vulnerable to managerial whim and cost-cutting exercises. Strong links need to be made between the mission of the unit with the parent institution to maximise the continuity of the service.

The marginalisation of continuing education in New Zealand universities will continue unless the field is reconfigured as a mainstream activity. The renewed interest at a societal level in lifelong learning and the learning society gives the field a chance to rebuild in universities.

3. CONTINUING EDUCATION IN JAPANESE UNIVERSITIES[3]

In recent years, Japan has shifted toward a lifelong learning society. A lifelong learning society implies that people can learn at any stage of life, can choose and participate in learning opportunities and that the results of their learning can be adequately evaluated and utilised. It is this philosophy rather than the British extra-mural tradition which underpins current university continuing education developments in Japan.

Although the notion of lifelong learning itself was established as early as the mid 1960s, it was around 1990 that Japanese society started to transform into a lifelong learning society. Recent surveys with regard to lifelong learning consistently showed that almost 80 per cent of Japanese were inclined toward study throughout their lives for personal fulfilment.

The Japanese higher education system has also shifted toward a lifelong learning society. During the 1990s, Japanese universities experienced major transformations such as shifting from the traditional structure which consisted of younger students, to more lifelong learning institutions with non-traditional students. Conventional Japanese universities focused only on the traditional age group of students in terms of program content, admission and so on. There are no national statistics which show the student population over the age of 25 years in Japanese higher education institutions. However, social, economic and demographic circumstances have rapidly changed in Japanese society from the 1990s. For instance, globalisation and technological innovation have developed rapidly, and Japan must deal with global market competition; therefore people are forced to catch up with the speed of technological changes and new knowledge. Many people are demanding opportunities to acquire specialised knowledge and skills. Secondly, the 18 years-of-age population peaked in 1992 and since then it has decreased year by year. These environmental changes have made Japanese higher education institutions shift to become more institutions of lifelong learning. As a result, the number of adult entrants has been increasing steadily.

The programs targeting adults and working professionals can be defined as continuing higher education programs. Usually, continuing higher education programs in Japanese universities can be divided into non-degree based extension courses as well as open classes and degree programs in regular courses of both undergraduate and graduate programs.

Although some universities have focused on establishing full-fledged extension or continuing education programs, they still account for a small percentage of all university courses. On the other hand, almost all national as well as private universities have recently developed degree programs for working professionals. It is expected that these programs will cover the decreased 18-year-old population and play an important role for training working professionals for enterprises. Although these degree programs are in the category of regular university courses, universities have established special recruiting systems for adults and special night-time classes for working professionals. Of course, many universities accept adult students and there is a demand for undergraduate programs among adult students. However, there is a greater demand for graduate programs for adult students or working professionals from the view point of development of highly skilled labour in the global competition era. By 2002, out of a total of 600 universities, 362 undergraduate programs and 276 graduate schools accepted adult students.

Those social, economic and demographic factors as well as governmental policy toward transforming Japanese higher education institutions to more lifelong learning institutions became the incentive for higher education institutions to establish graduate programs for working professionals. Most of these new programs are business-related or policy-related programs. These new programs for working professionals put more emphasis on practical knowledge and obtaining skills required for professionals. Business-related graduate programs have introduced case study analysis or other clinical teaching methods, in order for working professionals to develop more practical knowledge and strategic problem solving skills.

For higher education institutions which expect more adults to enter their graduate programs, there are at least two problems to be solved. One is to develop curricula and instruction methods appropriate for working professionals, since most Japanese graduate programs are mainly research oriented and those curricula are less attractive for working professionals who aim at acquiring professional knowledge and skills in order to prepare for global competition in economy and technology. The other problem is that it will take years for Japanese higher education institutions to introduce prior learning assessment of adults and working professionals. Nevertheless, the development of a lifelong learning system is almost inevitable and, although continuing higher education programs have only recently been introduced in Japanese universities, they are now no longer marginal nor cost consuming centres, but seem likely to play an important role in the university reform movement in the twenty-first century.

4. CONTINUING EDUCATION IN THE SOUTH PACIFIC[2]

Providers of continuing education in the South Pacific region are challenged by the socio-cultural diversity of learners, and their geographical spread over vast oceanic distances coupled with their varying economic status. The University of the South Pacific (USP) as the principal indigenous provider of university education in the region, had to design and develop its continuing education program in the face of the diversity and disparity of its community of learners. The USP is a regional institution providing various forms of education to its 12 member countries namely Cook Islands, Fiji, Kiribati, Marshall Islands, Nauru, Niue, Samoa, Solomon Islands, Tokelau, Tonga, Tuvalu and Vanuatu.

The learners' languages are diverse and the population ranges from 2000 as in Niue to 750,000 in Fiji. Two countries are one-island states (Nauru and Niue) and the rest are made up of groups of islands spread over miles of ocean. With the exception of Nauru and Niue and Tuvalu, more than 70 per cent of the population are rural dwellers. Another issue is the high rate of unemployed youth school-leavers coupled with underemployed adults, along with a lack of skilled workers for the small manufacturing and service sectors.

Continuing education is seen as a social and legitimate function of the university. Based on the University's mission to provide education to the community where they are and the level they are at, the USP has over the last 33 years become a multi-modal and flexible provider of learning. USP defines continuing education as the "non-credit offerings of the University, flexible in its mode of delivery, open and flexible in its entry qualification". The purpose of continuing education is to improve practice, up-skilling, and re-skilling for public education and for personal development and leisure. The learners take continuing education to meet their professional and personal needs and more, the collective needs of their community. Each year some 10,000 learners directly participate in continuing education activities (USP, 2001) and many thousands more indirectly benefit.

The USP reaches out to the member communities outside the University's proverbial 'wall', through University Extension. A national USP Centre is based in the main urban centre of each of the 12 member countries. Larger countries like Fiji, Solomon Islands, Vanuatu and Tonga have USP Sub-Centres in the other major centres. University Extension headquarters is based in the USP Laucala campus in Fiji from where it delivers and coordinates with the national university centres. Modern telecommunication technology supports the networking and administration of University Extension. USP Centres identify and organize continuing education activities to meet the learning needs of their local constituent community.

University Extension is a unique provider in the USP. First, it delivers continuing education at a distance to regional learners in the 12 countries. Second, telecommunication facilities, including satellite access, which are available to the delivery of distance credit courses and program, are also available for its continuing education activities. University Extension also organizes national continuing education programs through the national USP Centres. Third, its continuing education activities are mainly targeted at improving the practice of Non-Government Organisations (NGOs), civil society groups and other non-state actors. Unlike the other organisations that provide continuing education to the formal sector, University Extension provides for other sectors in the community. Many students after completing these study programs become confident enough to enrol in credit courses in related fields offered by the USP.

The value of continuing education is little understood by those in the credit faculties, with the result that it gets the so-called 'cinderella' treatment in the allocation of resources. Various departments of the USP provide continuing education but do not necessarily label their activity under the practice. University Extension is the only provider that labels its activity under continuing education and has a constituted Continuing Education section. The principal providers of USP are the seven Institutes, a number of Centres and Sections and University Extension. A role of these providers is to deliver continuing education related to their focus issue; however, their clientele are from the formal sector, that is, either the private sector or the government.

Distance is a barrier to education both at national and regional levels in the South Pacific. Except for one-island states in the region, the quality and quantity of national transport and communication facilities affect any educational program delivered at distance by a regional provider like the USP.

5. CONTINUING EDUCATION IN AUSTRALIAN UNIVERSITIES

From the late nineteenth to the late twentieth centuries, there appears to have been a disparity between what Australian universities have espoused about adult (or continuing) education as a distinct form of educational provision and what adult education these same institutions provided. Using Johnson and Hinton's (1986) main title of their report on adult and continuing education in Australia, *It's human nature*, Brennan (1988) argued that, as far as universities had been concerned, adult education had never been an easily accepted and valued, part of their educational provision.

In the early 1980s, Smith (1985), the director of an adult education unit at the University of Newcastle, visited each of Australia's then 19 universities and recorded what he perceived was their adult education provision. All institutions offered adult education. Many had a specially designated Department or Centre but the adult education provision extended beyond that of these units. This range of diversified activity was not always encapsulated in institutional policy documents or administrative procedures.

Smith's view of adult education in universities perhaps represents fairly accurately the situation in the mid-1980s on the eve of a major re-restructuring of Australian universities at the beginning of the 1990s under the reforms of the then Federal Education Minister (Dawkins, 1988). As the ongoing reform and restructuring continued in the 1990s, adult education in universities was not a major focus. One feature has been the closing of the central departments in some universities, for example, the University of New England that in 1996 closed its Department of Continuing Education, which had been set up when the university gained independence from the University of Sydney after the Second World War (Lucardie, 1996).

A 2002 Internet survey of selected universities by Brennan indicated that a replication of the Smith survey would reveal a great deal of adult education and continuing education activity but perhaps under different titles and organised in a variety of ways. For example, Sydney University (2002) (www.usyd.edu.au/cce) still retains its Centre for Continuing Education that offers courses from business and information technology to languages and fine arts. At the University of Queensland (www.uq.edu.au) there is now the Institute of Continuing and TESOL Education (ICTE) offering community and professional programs. At the University of Adelaide (www.adelaide.edu.au), radio 5UV that was noted by Smith (1985, p. 25) remains and offers a wide range of programs on radio seven days a week. One of the newer universities, the University of Southern Queensland (www.usq.edu.au) has a special continuing education centre that offers professional development, tertiary preparation, foundation studies and more general interest programs particularly by distance education and the residential McGregor Schools.

These activities, in the older tradition of the centralised department, indicate some continuity but do not cover the full range of continuing education activities in Australian universities. Outside the group of central providers, and often competing with them, are many Continuing Professional Education programs aimed at the graduates of the professional faculties, with the common expectation that graduates from other universities will also participate. Some faculties and special agencies with their own specialist continuing education staff also offer these activities. In the last 20 years or so, most Australian universities have established commercial education arms or technology transfer centres of some sort, which are expected to bring revenue to the university. Newly established Cooperative Research Centres (CRCs), offer activities that may be focused on the dissemination of their research findings but they are also concerned with generating new research and retaining the support of their industry partners. A quite different range of programs emanate from the universities' many galleries and museums.

Brennan (1999, pp. 18–19) used the work of Schroeder (1970) and Kowalski (1988) to develop a typology of providers of adult education programs according to the centrality of adult education to the organisation's purposes. The first type of organisation is one set up primarily to provide adult education programs; the second is an organisation set up to provide other types of education but has included adult education as an additional mode; a third type distinguishes organisations that use adult education to assist the organisation to achieve other, frequently non-educational, purposes.

Universities in Australia were never of the first type, according to Brennan. Universities may have been considered as illustrating the second type, but wrongly. Australian universities' adult education provision, as illustrated by the Smith survey and in the more contemporary examples noted above, demonstrates that their provision is more closely associated with the third type. Australian universities have not viewed adult education as part of their core business but have used adult education, and appear to be continuing to do so, to achieve a number of their other objectives with varying client groups. They may have a public relations goal; many of them, but not necessarily all, probably also have the goal of creating a profit or at least a cost recovery goal. In research terms a major task is for the adult education provision of Australian universities to be surveyed according to the role described for a Type 3 provider.

6. OTHER EXAMPLES OF UNIVERSITY CONTINUING EDUCATION

6.1. *Hong Kong*

One of the few significant research publications in the last decade on continuing education in universities in the Asia-Pacific region came from Hong Kong. *Professional and Continuing Education in Hong Kong: Issues and Perspectives* (Ngok and Lam, 1994) attempted to link the provision of continuing education to human resource planning in Hong Kong. It included consideration of the role of government, tertiary expansion, the contribution of local and overseas educational providers, the characteristics of adult learners in Hong Kong, staff training by companies, and support for mature age students returning to school. One of the authors' specific recommendations was for more comprehensive planning: "If universities round the world are juggling with funding constraints and finding part-time degree structures more economical, perhaps the Hong

Kong government can be more pro-active in planning, guiding and funding such options" (Ngok & Lam, 1994, p. 124).

Government policy has had a significant influence on the direction that continuing education at University of Hong Kong has taken. For example, in 2000 the School of Professional and Continuing Education (SPACE) established a Community College in response to the Education Commission's recognition of the need for a more versatile and flexible educational structure to support a strategy to raise the level of tertiary education participation from 30 per cent to 60 per cent for the relevant age group within ten years (Young, 2001). A year later the SPACE Director wrote: "We are fully in support of the government's vision and are now more than ever convinced that the Community College curriculum provides an excellent alternative to the conventional patterns of post-secondary education." (Young, 2001).

Another SPACE initiative which linked pragmatism with government policy was the launching of collaborative business programs with several Chinese mainland universities, anticipating China's entry to the World Trade Organisation (SPACE, 2001). In 1953, the Extra-Mural Department at Hong Kong University, had two staff members and 330 students studying 12 courses (Ngok & Lam, 1994). At the turn of the century the renamed SPACE had over 1300 courses and 650 full-time and 1700 part-time staff (SPACE, 2001). There were 95,000 enrolments, the equivalent of 15,000 full-time students (SPACE, 2001).

There are of course other universities in Hong Kong with substantial continuing education programs, but SPACE demonstrates how continuing education can become both a substantial contributor to university finances and a major flag bearer of the university's programs, with a mix of credit and non-credit courses.

6.2. India

There has been a long tradition of university involvement in education beyond formal courses in India, where higher education is seen as one instrument of social transformation (Menon, 1998). The country's University Grants Commission recognised the significance of this element of university activity in 1977 when it added 'extension' to teaching and research as the major responsibilities of Indian universities:

> If the university system has to discharge adequately its responsibility to the entire education system and to the society as a whole, it must assume extension as the third important responsibility and give it the same status as research and teaching. (University Grants Commission, 1977, quoted in Menon, 1998, p. 7)

An example from that time is the involvement from 1978 to the early 1980s of many Indian universities in the National Adult Education Program which aimed particularly to increase the level of literacy across the nation (Ministry of Education and Social Welfare, 1978). Twenty years later, more than 100 universities in India had extension departments or centres funded by the University Grants Commission to offer programs such as literacy and post literacy, science for people, environmental education, and technology transfer (Menon, 1998, p. 3). Ahluwalia (1998) pointed out that continuing education has different functions in creating a learning society from the point of view of countries in less advanced stages of development, such as India, than in the model envisioned by Faure (1972).

7. RESEARCH ISSUES

There are two main research issues arising from the case studies and other data above, which are interlinked:

- the extent to which external factors influence the nature of continuing education programs; and
- the purpose and place of university continuing education, as perceived by the institution and by the continuing education centre.

In three of the four cases described above, the broader social context plays a significant part in the sorts of continuing education programs offered by universities. In New Zealand, for example, changing government policy on higher education has found expression in the increasing entrepreneurialism of universities which is partly manifested in the latter's continuing education activities. Changes in continuing education in Japanese universities have been triggered by government policy as well as market forces as the demographics change and mature age students form an increasing proportion of the higher education population. In Australia, however, the lack of clear government policy (and funding) has seen the significance of adult or continuing education in universities diminish considerably as a distinct entity in the last decade or so, to re-emerge in different forms.

In some countries, universities have a much more overt link with the development of their immediate and wider communities. For example, the University of the South Pacific sees itself as having a responsibility for regional development, delivering education for the residents of 12 countries, and continuing education is part of this strategy through University Extension. India provides a prime example of university extension consciously operating within a broader social context, and appears to be one of the few countries in the Asia-Pacific region where university extension or continuing education is still substantially government funded. At Hong Kong University (HKU), the School of Professional and Continuing Education (SPACE), provides a different model of response to external influences. The SPACE approach seems to overcome the tension between the need for financial viability and the need to meet community and government expectations. Financial viability appears to be one of the criteria for continuing education in Australian and New Zealand universities. However, in this regard the contrast between the USP and the HKU experiences, highlights the significance of population size and institutional accessibility.

In aiming for financial viability, there are implications of course for the nature of the programs offered, both in terms of the curricula and the accreditation of courses. The HKU programs and, for example, the Agriculture, Resources, Infrastructure and Management Program (formerly Continuing Education Center) at the Asian Institute of Technology, Bangkok (http://www.cec.ait.ac.th), are designed primarily for sub-professional and professional, fee-paying students. The liberal education programs referred to in the New Zealand case study above are a casualty of such policies. On the other hand, vocationally-oriented courses can be more readily credited towards a formal university qualification and thus encourage learning pathways.

At this stage continuing education makes up only a very small proportion of university courses in Japan, as reported in the case study above, but under the influence of government policy, programs for working professionals are becoming increasingly important. However, while the changing continuing education policy has seen a mix of non-degree and both undergraduate and postgraduate programs emerge for adults, recognition of prior learning (RPL) in Japan is still not well advanced. RPL has become much more common in recent years in Australia with the development of pathways through the Australian Qualifications Framework, and in New Zealand through similar competency-based programs, particularly in the vocational education and training sector, although most Australian universities now have procedures for recognising prior learning for credit purposes.

In recent years the emergence of the concept of lifelong learning within the context of globalisation and widespread technological and organisational change has helped to bring a new significance to the need for adult education, as exemplified by developments in many Japanese universities. As globalisation increases, so universities are seeking to position themselves to serve the needs of wider educational markets. In Australia, for example, many universities are utilising online technologies for continuing education, and at Hong Kong University, SPACE had developed what is referred to as an 'Online Universal Learning' platform for teaching and learning purposes. The University of the South Pacific has of course been using distance methods for its regional continuing education program since its establishment. In Singapore and Hong Kong in particular, but also elsewhere in the region, continuing education collaboration with universities in other countries is increasingly common.

What the discussion above highlights is the variety of perceptions of continuing education within institutions. In the case study of Australian universities adult education *per se* is much less of a focus than it has been but it is much in evidence under other guises: adult education is not their core business, but they use it to achieve other goals. In universities in countries where it has a more defined role, such as in New Zealand and at the University of the South Pacific, specialised continuing education centres often struggle for professional recognition and compete with other parts of the institution, particularly for ongoing professional education. In such cases there seems to be an ambivalence in the attitude of the parent institution to the continuing education function. The examples from the Asia-Pacific region cited above suggest that continuing education achieves its highest recognition when it is linked to the mainstream purposes of universities, particularly when the institutions themselves are overtly seeking to meet community and government objectives.

8. CONCLUSION

The definition of university continuing education initially adopted by the authors turned out to be too limited to encompass the range of continuing education in universities across the Asia-Pacific region. The available data indicate that the practice of continuing education in universities across the region is active, varied and in many cases expanding, and includes both credit and non-credit programs. If there is serious acceptance of the concept of lifelong learning by governments and universities, then continuing education may continue to be offered in a variety of ways in the region's universities. Under the banner of lifelong learning, distinctions between credit and non-credit and vocational and non-vocational continuing education, as well as the focus on the young, may assume less importance. In these ways continuing education may help countries in the region to become learning societies whatever their stages of development.

What this review has also shown is that university continuing education is a field of professional practice without a tradition of substantive research. The issues discussed in this article are intended to point the way for further research into adult education in universities across the Asia-Pacific region.

ENDNOTES

[1] Case study contributed by Brian Findsen, School of Education and Social Sciences, Auckland.
[2] Case study contributed by Cema Bolabola, The University of the South Pacific, Laucala Campus, Fiji.
[3] Case study contributed by Reiko Yamada, Department of Literature, Doshisha University, Kyoto, Japan.

REFERENCES

Ahluwalia, M. (1998). Role and status of continuing education in creating [a] learning society. *Papers from the 2nd Asia Regional Literacy Forum*, www.literacyonline.org/products/ili/webdocs/manjeet.

Australian National University, Centre for Continuing Education. http://www.anu.edu.au/cce/, accessed May 2002.

Brennan, B. (1988). It is not necessarily natural: University adult and continuing education in Australia. *International Journal of University Adult Education*, 28(1), 1–22.

Brennan, B. (1999). *Unit Notes AET470: Introduction to adult education and training 2000*. Armidale: University of New England.

Dakin, J. (1992). Derivative and innovative modes in New Zealand adult education. *The New Zealand Journal of Adult Learning*, 20(2), 29–49.
Dale, R., & Robertson, S. (1997). 'Resiting' the nation, 'reshaping' the state: Globalisation effects on education policy in New Zealand. In M. Olssen & K. Morris Matthews (Eds.), *Education Policy in New Zealand: The 1990s and Beyond*. Palmerston North: Dunmore Press.
Dawkins, J. S. (1988). *Higher Education: A Policy Statement*. Canberra: Australian Government Publishing Service.
Deeks, J., Crosthwaite, J., & Nicoll, W. (1998). *Report of the committee for the internal operational review of continuing education and the Centre for Continuing Education*. Auckland: The University of Auckland.
Duke, C. (1991). Restructuring for better service? Continuity and change in university adult education. *New Education*, 13(1), 57–67.
Faure, E. (Chair) (1972). *Learning to Be*. Paris: UNESCO.
Findsen, B., & Harre-Hindmarsh, J. (1996). Adult and community education in the universities. In J. Benseman, B. Findsen & M. Scott (Eds.), *The Fourth Sector: Adult and Community Education in Aotearoa New Zealand*. Palmerston North: Dunmore Press.
Findsen, B. (1996). University-based adult and continuing education in New Zealand: Trends and issues. *Access – Critical Perspectives on Cultural and Policy Studies in Education*, 15(2), 21–37.
Findsen, B. (2001). A road travelled too far?: A case study of the restructuring of university adult and continuing education. *Studies in Continuing Education*, 23(1), 71–94.
Johnson, R., & Hinton, F. (1986). *It's Human Nature: Non-award Adult and Continuing Education in Australia*. Canberra: Commonwealth Tertiary Education Commission.
Kowalski, T. J. (1988). *The Organising and Planning of Adult Education*. New York: State University of New York.
Lucardie, D. (1996). University continuing education – dollars or sense? *Adult Learning Australia*, September, 12–13.
Menon, P. (1998). Promoting women's literacy through universities: Challenges for higher education. *Papers from the 2nd Asia Regional Literacy Forum*, www.literacyonline.org/products/ili/webdocs/menon, accessed February 2002.
Ministry of Education and Social Welfare, Directorate of Adult Education (1978). *National adult education program: Training of adult education functionaries*. New Delhi: Directorate of Adult Education, Government of India.
Ngok, L., & Lam, A. (1994). *Professional and Continuing Education in Hong Kong: Issues and Perspectives*. Hong Kong University Press.
Peddie, R. (1994). *Centre for Continuing Education, Strategic Plan, 1994–97*. Auckland: The University of Auckland.
School of Professional and Continuing Education (SPACE). (2001). Hong Kong: Hong Kong University, www.hku.hk/space, accessed February 2002.
Schroeder, W. L. (1970). Adult education defined and described. In R. M. Smith, G. F. Aker & J. R. Kidd (Eds.), *Handbook of Adult Education*. New York: Macmillan.
Smith, B. (1985). *A review of continuing education provision by the Australian universities*. Newcastle: Department of Community Programs, University of Newcastle.
University of Sydney (2002). Centre for Continuing Education, http://www.usyd.edu.au/cce, accessed March 2002.
University of the South Pacific (2000). *University Extension Annual Report 1999*. Suva: USP.
University of the South Pacific (2001). *The University of the South Pacific Calendar 2000*. Suva: USP.
Young, E. (2001). Message from the Director, School of Professional and Continuing Education, Hong Kong University. www.hku.hk/space/about_space, accessed February 2002.

60

Teaching as an Occupation and Learning Profession

KERRY J. KENNEDY

Hong Kong Institute of Education, Hong Kong

1. INTRODUCTION

The teaching profession is currently the subject of many high level international discussions involving organisations such as the United Nations Scientific and Cultural Organisation (UNESCO), the International Labour Organisation (ILO), the Organisation for Economic Cooperation and Development (OECD), the Asian Development Bank and the World Bank. There is agreement across these agencies that teachers and the quality of the teaching workforce are central to the future development of all nations, irrespective of their global location. This point was made most trenchantly by OECD's *Schooling for Tomorrow* project. It posed a 'meltdown scenario' for the future in which it flagged the possibility of there not being enough teachers to meet the needs of systems and governments for the educational imperatives of the twenty-first century (OECD, 2001). Such a scenario, if realised, would pose a serious threat to meeting national goals and objectives as well as to the aspirations that students and parents have for the future.

The centrality of teachers to modern nation states can be gauged by the extent to which teachers are being asked to do more and more in relation to priorities such as lifelong learning, new information and communications technologies (ICT) and new ways of preparing students for the information society. Yet there remain significant issues, both within and across national jurisdictions, relating to remuneration, professionalism, teaching conditions and status that call into question the commitment of governments to ensuring a high quality teaching workforce. A report issued jointly by UNESCO and the ILO summed up these tensions well.

> What is currently expected of teachers may well be out of proportion to the rewards countries are prepared to reward them for their efforts, the means typically put at their disposal, the difficult conditions under which many of them work, and the present knowledge base which defines effective

teaching and learning. Moreover there is still much to be done to address continuing problems of equal opportunity for women in the teaching workforce ... (ILO/UNESCO, 2000, p. 17)

Nowhere are these issues more vital, and in a sense more obvious, than in the Asia-Pacific region. Many countries have enjoyed sustained economic growth, despite the economic crisis, while others are still developing, so that the disparities in the region are very marked. The contexts in which teachers work, as varied as they are, have in common a general set of problems.

- Even where there has been economic growth it does not seem that teachers have always benefited. Where there has not, teaching conditions continue to be inadequate.
- The digital divide exists within the region providing access to ICT for some but not for others.
- Status as a profession seems to elude teachers irrespective of where they are located. The sheer size of the teaching workforce within national jurisdictions seems to militate against status as much as it does against adequate remuneration.

Teaching and teachers may well be necessary to the future of the region, but this has not meant that their employment conditions, remuneration or benefits have been improved to match the new roles they are expected to play.

The purpose of this article, therefore, is to canvass significant policy issues relating to the teaching workforce in the Asia-Pacific region. This will involve the use of key statistical indicators that will demonstrate the size and relative costs of the teaching profession as well as its relative efficiency and effectiveness. This statistical representation will be complemented with an analysis of the new challenges that face the teaching profession and how these challenges might be met in different national jurisdictions. Finally, options will be canvassed as to how the teaching profession might transform itself into a learning profession in order to meet the challenges that lie ahead.

2. TEACHING PROFESSION: DEMOGRAPHICS, CONDITIONS, COSTS AND STATUS

Teachers in the Asia-Pacific region make up a sizable proportion of the world population of teachers. UNESCO (2000, p. 117) reported a world population of 58,973,000 teachers in 1997 (including tertiary teachers). Of these, 2,214,000 were in the more developed regions of Asia and Oceania while 17,532,000 were in the less developed regions of Eastern Asia and Oceania (of whom 11,659,000 were in China) and 7,417,000 were in Southern Asia (of whom 5,019,000 were in India). Based on these figures some 46.06 per cent of the world population of teachers can be found in the Asia-Pacific region, although it is of interest to note that some 61 per cent of the region's teachers are in two countries: China and India, with some 70 per cent of these being in China. Despite the concentration of teachers in the two main population centres of the region, teachers play an important role in every country. Table 1 shows the dispersion of teachers across the region and the school populations for which they are responsible.

Table 1 indicates that education represents a key activity across the region, that it is enacted in a diverse range of contexts and it has significant support from national authorities. This latter point can be made more cogently by considering the range of economic indicators set out in Table 2.

A key point to note from Table 2 is that the main input costs of educational development as a component of national development is the compensation paid to teachers in terms of salaries and benefits. Thus attempts to improve rumuneration and benefits for teachers will always represent a significant cost for governments. Even when the cost is seen as an investment on the part of governments it nevertheless has to be justified against other spending priorities of governments. It is for this reason that this human capital formation function of teachers has received more attention in recent times with increased scrutiny and monitoring of teacher performance (UNESCO, 1998, pp. 31–32).

What does this teaching work force look like in terms of both personal characteristics and professional contexts? Females do not dominate the teaching profession in the Asia-Pacific region but their numbers are steadily increasing. In 1995, there were 7.8 million female teachers and the same number of males in Eastern Asia and Oceania compared with 4.7 and 7.4 million respectively in 1980. In South Asia there were 2.3 million females and 4.3 million males compared with 1.2 and 3.0 million respectively in 1980 (UNESCO, 1998, p. 43). These figures contrast with those of industrialised countries where it was reported that some 80 per cent of primary school teachers are female. Female representation in the teaching workforce is important since female teachers have an important role to play as role models for girls. For example, research has indicated that the presence of female primary school teachers encourages girls to stay on at school (Higginson, 1996, p. 12).

Using traditional indicators of teacher quality, the quality of the primary teacher education work force in the Asia-Pacific region is generally high, and 94 per cent of teachers in East Asia and the Pacific and 87 per cent in South Asia have the required academic qualifications (World Bank, 2001, p. 84). In countries like Vietnam, for example, the numbers of primary teachers with adequate teaching qualifications increased by about 20 per cent over the decade from 1990 (Vietnam Ministry of Education, 2000, p. 23). Yet a neighboring country like Cambodia has not seen such progress. Despite significant aid efforts and with a focus on the in-service training of teachers, it seems that little progress has been made since. On other fronts such as curriculum development there has been little change (Duggan, 1996). This raises the issue of whether a quality indicator like qualifications is directly related to student outcomes (Hanushek, 1995). The question of quality is a difficult one when output rather than input factors are considered. There is little doubt that a qualified teaching workforce

Table 1. Numbers of teachers, schools and students in selected Asia-Pacific countries

Country	Data	Teachers Primary	Teachers Secondary	Schools Primary	Schools Secondary	Students Primary	Students Secondary
Australia	1999	65,000 →		9,600 →		1,985,400	1,341,300
Bangladesh	95/96	—	2,636	75,594	12,858	17,580,000	5,788,000
Brunei	1998	3,858[a]	17,720	184	38	58,548	30,956
Cambodia	92/93	43,205	3,912,000[c]	4,899	na	1,918,985	331,951
China	1998	5,819,000	23,304	609,626	81,822[e]	139,530,000	67,070,000[e]
Hong Kong	1998	20,606	1,577	832	507	476,682	467,487
Macau	97/98	1,744	98,857	81	47	47,235	28,280
Taiwan	1997	95,029	10,757	2,557	1,158	1,910,000	1,814,202
East Timor	94/95	42,135	—	4,001	na	1,462,722	240,441
Fiji	1996	16,228	2,081,223[b]	450	232	185,000	38,300
India	97/98	1,871,542	781,755[d]	610,763	261,836[b]	108,781,792	57,433,776[b]
Indonesia	97/98	1,158,616	540,036[b]	151,064	34,404[d]	25,689,693	12,683,199[d]
Japan	1998	415,680	215	24,295	16,729[b]	7,633,533	8,638,689[b]
Kiribati	1997	727	110,000	86	9	17,594	4,403
Korea (DPR)	87/88	59,000	198,548[b]	4,810(97)	4,840(97)	54,300	2,408,000
Korea (Rep)	1999	137,577	10,717	5,544	4,684[b]	3,935,537	2,440,835[b]
Laos	96/97	25,831	97,401	7,896	na	786,335	180,160
Malaysia	1997	150,681	—	7,084	1,561	2,870,667	1,804,519
Maldives	1999	—	314(84)	230	287[b]	47,479	41,559[b]
Micronesia, F.S.	1995	1,051(84)	10,400	174	24	27,281	6,896
Mongolia	98/99	7,700	71,904[b]	96	534[b]	195,000	252,100[b]
Myanmar	94/95	169,748	16,336	35,856	2,916[b]	5,711,202	1,390,000
New Zealand	1998	75,032[c]		2,282	343	448,058	234,174

(Continued)

Table 1 (Continued)

Pakistan	98/99	374,500[a]	262,800[b]	163,746	27,526[b]	17,298,000	3,984,000
PNG	1995	13,457	3,293(92)	–	–	516,797	78,759
Philippines		341,183	154,705	37,645	5,880(93/94)	11,902,501	4,888,246
Samoa	1996	1,479	665	155(95)	–	35,649(97)	21,315[b]
Singapore	1998	11,406	9,141	193	147	288,311	178,795
Solomons	1993	2,514(94)	618(95)	523	23	60,493(94)	7,981(95)
Sri Lanka	1995	70,537	103,572	9,657	5,771	1,962,498	2,314,054

Source: The data in this table is drawn from the country profiles in *The Europa World Book, 2000 and 2001*, Volumes 1 & 2. London: Europa Publications.

Annotations
[a] Includes Pre-primary schools
[b] Includes Middle and High schools.
[c] Includes General and Vocational Secondary.
[d] Includes General Secondary (Junior and Senior) and Vocational Secondary.
[e] Not including composite schools or special schools.

Table 2. Economic indicators relating to education in the Asia-Pacific region

% of Gross National Product spent on education[a]	4–5.6%
% of Total Government Outlays spent on education[b]	10–17%
% of Educational Expenditure spent on teacher compensation[c]	62.3%

[a] In the more developed countries of Oceania the figure in 1995 was 4% and in the less developed countries of East and South Asia the figure ranged from 4–5.6% (Bray, 1998, p. 629).
[b] These figures are for Asian Development Bank countries and they exclude extremes (Bray, 1998, p. 628).
[c] World Bank (2001, p. 84).

is better than an unqualified one, but exactly how it makes a difference is little understood at this stage and is at best contested.

Some countries have no choice but to draw on unqualified teachers. For countries like Nepal, Sri Lanka and the Maldives lack of qualified teachers represents a real problem. Even in India, for example, while 87 per cent of primary teachers are qualified, there has been a need in some states to draw on the local community to combat the issue of teacher absenteeism. The Shiksa Karmi Project has been operating in Rajasthan since 1987. Here local community educators, known as 'barefoot teachers', often substitute for qualified teachers (UNESCO-PROAP, 2000, pp. 32–33).

While the productivist function of teachers highlights their important role in relation to national development, and teacher qualifications are one indicator of teacher quality, the actual conditions under which teaching is conducted does not always reflect the importance attached to teachers. Teacher pupil ratios in the primary schools of the region are usually higher than in high-income European countries. For 1997, in East Asia and Oceania the ratio is 1:25, for South Asia it is 1:59 compared with European countries where it is 1:16 (World Bank, 2001, p. 84). Corresponding pupil teacher ratios in secondary schools tend to be lower than in primary schools and somewhat closer to the European equivalent (UNESCO, 1998, p. 56). Yet these figures mask significant national differences across a range of professional contexts in which teachers work. In Bangladesh, for example, while the teacher pupil ratio in primary schools was 1:59 in 1998 it was expected to rise to 1:82 at the turn of the century (UNESCO-PROAP, 2000, p. 33). Data of a more qualitative kind in this area is neither strong nor extensive. A survey conducted by UNESCO revealed, for example, that in a sample of schools in Nepal, 84 per cent of students in the top grade did not have textbooks in their mother tongue, and 58 per cent did not have a mathematics text. In a sample of schools in Bangladesh, 44 per cent did not have a teacher's table and 31 per cent did not have a teacher's chair (UNESCO, 1998, pp. 55–56). Such data can only be regarded as anecdotal, but it is illustrative of the diverse contexts in which teachers have to carry out their professional work, the heavy demands that are placed on them and the kinds of problems that they face on a day-to-day basis.

Teacher salaries also demonstrate the somewhat ambivalent position of teachers in the countries of the Asia-Pacific region. Chapman and Adams (1998a, p. 649) have reported that while some countries in the region (Republic of Korea, Bangladesh and Thailand) increased teacher salaries between 1985 and 1995, that this was not the case throughout the region. Data reported from Mehrotra and Buckland (1997, and cited in Chapman & Adams, 1998b) indicate that teachers' salaries as a multiple of per capita GDP are lower in Asia (1.84) than they are in West and Central Africa (7.28) and South and Eastern Africa (5.90) and only slightly better than in Latin America (1.79).

Table 3 indicates the relative salary levels of senior secondary teachers in selected low income, developing and developed countries. It demonstrates the diversity of salary levels within the region and how these compare with OECD countries.

Despite the obvious discrepancies displayed in Table 3, within some national jurisdictions there has been considerable commitment displayed to enhance the benefits that teachers receive. In the Philippines, for example, between 1985 and 1995 there was a 400 per cent increase in teacher compensation resulting in a five per cent increase in real income (Department of Education, Culture and Sport, 2000, p. 126).

All of the above have implications for the status of the teaching profession across the region. The weight of opinion very strongly suggests that the status of teaching as a profession is not high (Ramanthan, 1995; Chapman & Adams, 1998b; UNESCO, 1998). Where there are countries like Japan in which actual salaries are high, the conditions of teaching are often so stressful, that community pressures sometimes lead teachers to suicide (Shimahara, 1991). There has been the recent case in Hong Kong of an outstanding teacher committing suicide (*South China Morning Post*, 22 September, 2001) with considerable follow up action by trade unions emphasizing the stressful conditions under which teachers now work.

In countries like Thailand, there is considerable concern about the status of the profession (UNESCO, 1998, p. 37). Salaries are still perceived to be low

Table 3. A comparison of senior secondary teachers' salaries, 1997

Type of salary	United States[a]	South Korea[a]	OECD mean[a]	Malaysia	Indonesia	Chile
Starting salary (US$)	23,815	23,960	20,527	12,535	3,659	12,711
Salary after 15 years	33,953	42,597	29,114	19,819	5,150	15,915

Source: Office of Research and Development, Indonesian Ministry of Education (2000), Table 10.8.
[a] 1996 data.

compared with other professions, the workload is high and the morale is low. There is very often the need for teachers to take a second job. These characteristics of the profession are by no means confined to Thailand. Malaysian authorities report similar problems despite strong support from the Ministry of Education to regard teachers as professionals (UNESCO, 1998, p. 52). Enhancing the status of the teaching profession across the region remains a priority.

2. NEW CHALLENGES FOR THE TEACHING PROFESSION

There is no dearth of literature pointing to the new roles required of teachers. There is the productivist literature linking teachers to national development goals, the conceptual literature that notes the shift from industrial to information societies or the teaching effectiveness literature that highlights increasingly the powerful role that individual teachers play in relation to student learning. In a very real sense, this literature is at odds with the actual status of teachers. Much more is now expected but little is given in the way of incentives or motivation to contribute to a more complex and demanding environment. Yet the pressures for change are great.

A number of writers have pointed to the significant changes required of the teaching profession in the future (Stanley, 2000; Carneiro, 2000; Ralph, 2000). Cheng, for example, has pointed to the "paradigm shift in teaching as well as teacher education for the new century" as summarised in Table 4.

Cheng's vision is contextualised by the needs of a new economic paradigm, the creation of a knowledge society and the increased demands that will inevitably be placed on schools. For teachers, the demands of change are quite severe and the expectations are significant. The teaching profession of the future needs to be better educated, better prepared, more adaptable, more flexible and better able to meet the needs of an ever-changing society. Key questions, therefore, are related to the capacity of present educational resourcing to deliver these outcomes and the capacity of the profession to respond to such widespread changes.

This theme of the challenges facing the teaching profession was taken up by the OECD's project, Schooling for Tomorrow. That project took the view that it was not possible to predict a single policy scenario for the future of schools and so it generated six possible scenarios:

- bureaucratic schools systems continue,
- extending the market mode,
- schools as core social centre,
- schools as focussed learning organization,
- learning networks and networked schools, and
- the melt down scenario. (Istance, 2001, pp. 15–19)

The important point about these scenarios is not so much their substance as

Table 4. Cheng's paradigm shift in teaching

New tripilization paradigm	Traditional site bounded paradigm
Individualized teacher and teaching	*Reproduced teacher and teaching*
• Teacher is the facilitator to support students' learning • Multiple intelligence of teacher • Individualized teaching style • Teaching is to arouse curiosity • Teaching is a process to initiate, facilitate, and sustain students' self-learning and self-actualisation • Sharing joy with students • Teaching is a lifelong learning process	• Teacher is the centre of education • Partially competent teacher • Standard teaching style • Teaching is to transfer knowledge • Teaching is a disciplinary, delivering, training and socialising process • Achieving standards in examinations • Teaching is a transfer and application process
Localized and globalized teacher and teaching	*School-bounded teacher and teaching*
• Multiple local and global sources of teaching knowledge • Networked teaching • World-class teaching • Unlimited opportunities for teaching • Teacher with local and international outlook • As a world-class and networked teacher	• Teacher as the sole source of teaching and knowledge • Separated teaching • Site-bounded teaching • Limited opportunities for teaching • Teacher with only school experiences • As a school bounded and separated teachers

Source: Cheng (2001, p. 52).

the extent to which they indicate the social, economic and political constructions of the teaching profession. Policymakers can make distinctive choices about the policy settings they wish to put in place and schools and teachers will be affected by those settings.

Teaching and learning will also be affected so that under one scenario referred to as 'learning networks and networked schools', teachers become almost superfluous to the kind of learning it is envisaged will dominate schools, or whatever replaces schools in this futuristic scenario. Teachers might also disappear under the meltdown scenario where it is suggested that there simply may not be enough incentives to attract people to the teaching profession in the future or that the replacement rate for an aging profession will be so great that it will not be possible to keep up with demand. These scenarios contrast with others (for example, schools as social core centres) where the social role of the school is enhanced in contexts where other aspects of economic and social development downplay the need for cohesion and common values. In this scenario, the social role of teachers comes to the fore as schools provide even more than they do now the so-called 'social glue' that holds diverse and often fragmented societies together. All of these scenarios, however, predict a complex and demanding role for teachers and one that might well change in changing social, political and economic conditions.

Cheng (2000) has pointed to the particular challenge that the creation of an information society poses for the teaching profession. The mere transmission of information, a traditional way for conceiving of teaching in many Asian countries, will no longer be a valued function, for access to information will come in many different ways without the assistance of a teacher. So where does this leave teachers? Cheng outlines a new role for teachers in the information society:

> Teachers would then restore their dignified role of being a leader in learning and a sage in the learning community (school). Raw information is not yet useful knowledge. Teachers have the undeniable role of helping students in selecting, analysing and synthesising available information, and facilitating students in the application and creation of knowledge – developing students' capacity to generate wisdom. (Cheng, 2000, p. 3)

This transition will by no means be easy either for teachers or students. Facilitating learning is not the same as providing information: it requires new skills, new ways of planning and new ways of organising classrooms and classroom management. Students who may be used to a more passive learning style will need to be taught how to be active learners. The recent work of Watkins and Biggs (2000) on the characteristics of Chinese learners and their learning styles is important here since they have shown that apparently passive forms of learning do result in the acquisition of significant knowledge and skills. It will not be a simple case of changing teaching strategies since student learning characteristics will need to be understood and provided for in new contexts that will demand independent learning, critical thinking, cooperative work and the development of a thirst for learning. These are the challenges that will face teachers in this new century.

These views, or similar ones, have now found their way into policy in major education systems in the region so that they do not just represent the views of visionaries. *Learning to Learn – Lifelong Learning and Whole-person Development* (Curriculum Development Council, 2001) has set out a plan for the next decade that seeks to transform curriculum, teaching and learning in Hong Kong schools. The emphasis of the reforms is on learner centred approaches to teaching, catering for the needs of all students, school based curriculum development and a greater emphasis on critical thinking, creativity and communication skills (Curriculum Development Council, p. v). In Malaysia teachers have been charged with a mission to create knowledge workers who will become a critical national resource with the capacity not only to absorb and master the new and emerging, but also to innovate and manage change" (*Agenda on Education*, nd). Singapore's Minister for Education recently highlighted the role of teachers in producing a culture of innovation so necessary to national development.

As teachers, you hold the important responsibility of encouraging your pupils to be more innovative. The pupils see you as role-models in the way you approach idea-generation and problem solving in the classroom. For example, if you accept only one fixed answer to problems and do not encourage pupils to "think out of the box" and generate new ideas or new perspectives to a problem, your pupils are unlikely to develop a creative and innovative mindset. (Teo, 2001)

In another part of the region, the government of Taiwan released a *White Paper* in 1998 entitled *Towards a Learning Society*. The *White Paper* set out a program of reform designed to remove structural barriers to participation in education and to create a lifelong learning culture. In its 1999 *Progress Report*, the Ministry of Education outlined the full extent of the reforms which made it clear that teachers would be required to cope with a more flexible education system that catered for all students and not just an elite group. At the same time there was a commitment to reduce class sizes in primary schools and junior colleges and experiment with small class teaching (Ministry of Education, 1999). In this sense the reform program has recognised the need for much needed structural reforms to be put in place if teaching is to be effective in this new age of mass education.

UNESCO (1998) has noted that one way in which this new emphasis on the importance of education has been manifested has been through increased monitoring and evaluation of teaching performance. The application of this business model to teaching has come about because, as governments increase their investment, there is greater concern about the outcomes of schooling. Teachers play a fundamental role in securing these outcomes. The issue is often put in the context of ensuring the quality of education in which the quality of the teaching workforce becomes a significant and measurable variable in contributing to this overall quality. Another side of this process is the emphasis on measuring student outcomes as well so that student progress can be monitored. Outcomes rather than inputs are seen as the key ingredients in this productivist model of education and schooling.

4. TEACHING AS A LEARNING PROFESSION

The new roles required of teachers undoubtedly demand that greater attention be paid to lifelong learning for the teaching profession. It is constant professional renewal that will ensure that teachers are able to meet the challenges of the future. There are many different ways in which this is being and can be achieved. The ILO has placed a great deal of emphasis on what it calls 'workplace learning', especially as it relates to the role of employers, employer associations and unions (ILO, 2000). While employer and employee relationships are often seen as confrontational, the ILO has argued that employees and employers have much in common in seeking to meet the challenges of globalisation, new skill requirements and new strategic objectives. The reasons for this are not difficult to understand

Enterprises perform effectively when their employees are learning faster than – or keeping up with– the pace of external change. This presupposes that learning has to focus on the enterprise's current and future outputs – what people have to know and do to produce the outputs. (ILO, 2000, Part 3)

Attempts have been made in the United States to promote this kind of learning through direct negotiations between employers and teacher unions (Bredeson, 2001). Yet there appears to be a long way to go before this so-called 'new unionism' is able to deliver the kind of culture and professional development outcomes that are needed. Nevertheless, it is an important avenue to explore since it provides teachers with greater control over their own learning and has a greater likelihood to produce a teaching workforce based on self-directed lifelong learning.

From another perspective, the Taiwan Ministry of Education has recognized the need for a new learning culture amongst teachers. As part of *Towards a Learning Society*, the following initiatives have been proposed:

... the improvement of teachers' professional abilities in elementary and junior high schools, as well as the establishment of a lifelong learning system for teachers, in order to improve the quality of education. Strategies include:
a. regulating a lifelong learning system for teachers,
b. integrating lifelong learning organisations for teachers,
c. increasing lifelong learning paths for teachers, and
d. designing lifelong learning curricula for teachers.
(Ministry of Education, 1999).

This teacher learning initiative goes hand in hand with attempts to undertake a significant program of reform as mentioned earlier. It is a recognition by the government that both resources and support are needed if teachers are to take on new roles and responsibilities in the light of social and economic restructuring.

In India, the National Council for Teacher Education (NCTE) was established in 1993 under its own legislation. It has a very broad remit to oversee all stages of teacher education and to guarantee its quality. A very clear intention of NCTE is to ensure that the initial stage of teacher education, pre-service training, is carried out to a level and standard that will meet the new social and economic requirements. This had led to the development of standards for all levels of provision from undergraduate to postgraduate. This standard setting process has characterised a number of countries' approaches to the quality issue as the NCTE's constitution makes clear.

It shall be the duty of the Council to take all such steps as it may think fit for ensuring planned and co-ordinated development of teacher education and for the determination and maintenance of standards for teacher education. (The National Council for Teacher Education Act, 1993, Chapter 111)

A similar approach has been adopted in Thailand. The Teachers Council of Thailand (*Khurusapha*) has adopted 11 standards for the teaching profession. These standards highlight the professional role of teachers both within school communities and in the broader society. Alongside this is the Thai Government's commitment to reform "... welfare and social benefits for teachers and educational personnel at all levels ... so as to boost their morale, thereby creating a pride in their profession, while also strengthening their job security" (The Cabinet's Statement on Educational and Social Matters, 1997). As mentioned earlier, higher expectations and the monitoring of effectiveness accompany greater investment.

Developing teaching as a learning profession is given high priority in those countries which see themselves on the cusp of new economic and social realities and where the need for transformation is clear. At the same time there needs to be funding available to make this transformation a reality. While progress is being made in low-income countries such a Vietnam and Cambodia there is little evidence of the kind of advanced strategies for teacher renewal that can be seen in countries seeking to prepare for the development of the information economy. Low income countries continue to cope with basic issues of teacher supply and quality. It is the human resource needs of the information economy that is a driving force in those countries that can afford to develop their teaching workforces. This creates a kind of 'learning divide' in the region where some teachers are able to benefit from local policies of support while other teachers are not so fortunate. It seems clear, though, that as new economic realities make themselves felt in low-income jurisdictions that teacher development will need to be given a higher priority.

5. CONCLUSION

It is clear that across the region, teaching as an occupation plays an important social and economic role. Different jurisdictions handle this role in different ways so that it is diversity rather than commonality that characterises the profession on a regional basis. The issue of the status of the profession remains problematic across the region even where governments are able to provide adequate funding and support. The key to the future in all countries is the extent to which teaching can become a self-directed learning profession capable of meeting the high expectations that are now demanded. In the future, the skill level of the teaching profession may well be a deciding factor in a country's ability to advance and develop as a member of an increasingly globalised and competitive community. This is a challenge that needs to be confronted by individual teachers, their employers and governments.

REFERENCES

Agenda on Education (nd). http://www.moe.gov.my/teacher.htm
Bredeson, P. (2001). Negotiated learning. Union contracts and teacher professional development. *Educational Policy Archives*, 9(26), http://epaa.asu.edu/epaa/v9n26.html

Bray, M. (1998). Financing education in developing Asia: Themes, tensions and policies. *International Journal of Educational Research, 29*, 672–642.

The Cabinet's Statement on Educational and Social Matters (1997). http://www.moe.go.th/main2/part2.htm

Carneiro, R. (2000). The quest for a new learning paradigm. http://www.austcolled.com.au/resources.html

Chapman, D. W., & Adams, D. (1998a). The quality of education in Asia: The perennial priority. *International Journal of Educational Research, 29*, 643–665.

Chapman, D. W., & Adams, D. (Eds.) (1998b). Trends and issues in education across Asia. *International Journal of Educational Research*.

Cheng, K. (2000). Personal capacity, social competence and learning together. http://www.austcolled.com.au/resources.html

Cheng, Y. (2001). New education and new teacher education: A paradigm shift for the future. In Y. Cheng, K. Chow & K. Tsui (Eds.), *New Teacher Education for the Future – International Perspectives*. Hong Kong: The Hong Kong Institute of Education and Kluwer Academic Publishers.

Curriculum Development Council (2001). *Learning to Learn – Lifelong Learning and Whole Person Development*. Hong Kong: Curriculum Development Council.

Department of Education, Culture and Sport (2000). *Report of the Philippines Country EFA Assessment*. http://www2.unesco.org/wef/countryreports/philippines/rappport_1.html

Duggan, S. (1996). Education, teacher training and the prospects for economic recovery in Cambodia. *Comparative Education, 32*(3), 361–375.

Hanushek, E. (1995). Interpreting recent research on schooling in developing countries. *The World Bank Research Observer, 10*(2), 227–237.

Higginson, F. (1996). Teacher Roles and Global Change – An Issues Paper. Prepared for the 45th Session of the International Conference on Education.

ILO/UNESCO (2000). *Report of the Committee of Experts on the Application of the Reccomendation on the Status of Teachers*, CEART/17/2000/10.

Istance, D. (2001). Teachers, quality and schools in the future. In K. Kennedy (Ed.), *Beyond the Rhetoric – Building a Teaching Profession to Support Quality Teaching*. Australian College of Education Yearbook, 2001 (pp. 12–20). Canberra: Australian College of Education.

Ministry of Education (1999). The Ministry of Education 1999 Progress Report. http://www.edu.tw/english/index.htm

The National Council for Teacher Education Act (1993). http://www.ncte-in.org/noti/act.htm

OECD (2001). *What Schools for the Future?* Paris: OECD.

Office of Research and Development (ORD) Indonesian Ministry of Education (2000). *Indonesian Education Statistics 1999/2000*. Jakarta: ORD.

Ralph, D. (2000). Learning cities for the new millennium. http://www.austcolled.com.au/resources.html

Ramanathan, R. (1995). Teacher Organisations' Perspective on the Status of Teachers. In *Partnerships in Teacher Development for a New Asia*. Report of an International Conference (pp. 213–217). Bangkok: UNESCO Principal Office for Asia and the Pacific.

Shimahara, N. (1991). Teacher education in Japan. In E. Beauchamp (Ed.), *Windows on Japanese Education*. New York: Greenwood Press.

Stanley, G. (2000). Teacher as knowledge engineer. http://www.austcolled.com.au/resources.html

Teo, C. (2001). Speech at Ministry of Education's *Excel Day*. Townsville Primary School, September 29.

UNESCO (1998). *World Education Report, 1998: Teachers and Teaching in a Changing World*. Paris: UNESCO.

UNESCO-PROAP (2000). *Sub-Regional EFA 2000 Assessment Synthesis: South and West Asia*. Bangkok: UNESCO PROAP.

UNESCO (2000). *World Education Report, 2000 – The Right to Education*. Paris: UNESCO.

Vietnam Ministry of Education (2000). *Education for All 2000 Assessment – Country Report – Viet Nam*. Bangkok: UNESCO PROAP.

Watkins, D., & Biggs, J. (2001). *Teaching the Chinese Learner: Psychological and Pedagogical Perspectives*. Hong Kong and Melbourne: Comparative Education Research Centre, University of Hong Kong and the Australian Council for Educational Research.

World Bank (2001). *World Bank Development Indicators, 2001*. New York: World Bank.

61

Research into Teacher Education

SIM, WONG-KOOI
University of Brunei Darussalam, Brunei, Darussalam

1. INTRODUCTION

It may be considered disputable as to what countries should constitute the Asia-Pacific region. The UNESCO Principal Regional Office for Asia and the Pacific, which has teacher education as one of its priority areas (e.g., APEID, 1990) includes most of the countries in the region, but excludes Brunei Darussalam, Hawaiian Islands, New Caledonia, Singapore, Taiwan and Timor. This article makes no such exclusions and it is necessary to refer occasionally to some research that has been conducted in the United States, a country that borders on the region.

In terms of publications in English, Australia is probably the most prolific country in the region. For example, as its *Inaugural Yearbook*, the South Pacific Association for Teacher Education published a very impressive collection of reviews on Australian teacher education, which illustrate extensive and intensive research activities (Eltis, 1987). However, only a few Australian examples were used, so as not to exclude illustrations from other countries. This article is also confined to teacher education research, rather than teacher education *per se*, for which the reader should refer to the comparative study by Morris and Williamson (2000) (see *The Need for and Recruitment of Teachers*).

2. A TYPOLOGY: SEEKING A PANORAMIC VIEW

As part of the state-of-the-art reviews of the Southeast Asian Research Review Advisory Group (SEARAG), reviews of research on teacher education were conducted in five countries, a little more than a decade ago, namely Indonesia, Malaysia, Philippines, Singapore and Thailand. In attempting to synthesise these reviews, Sim (1991) employed a common framework for classifying the 281 research studies according to the two dimensions of 'focus' and 'scope.' In terms of 'focus', each study was classified into one of four categories, which are associated with different phases of pre-service and in-service teacher education, namely: (a) inputs, (b) initial training, (c) induction and (d) in-service, as well as several sub-categories for each category, such as (e) selection criteria and needs survey, (f) school teaching practice and program evaluation, (g) quality of beginning teachers and problems of beginning teachers, and (h) effectiveness of in-service training and teacher supervision.

With respect to 'scope', which referred to 'how intensive or extensive the study is, in terms of coverage and analysis', four main categories were used.

(1) *Micro-mirrors* refer to studies which focus on a limited set of concerns in an attempt to reflect and understand the nature of the concerns.
(2) *Mini-mousetraps* refer to studies which are usually small-scale and attempt to explore an innovative approach which is likely to improve practice.
(3) *Mega-mixes* refer to multi-faceted studies which involve multiple sources of data and more elaborate, often multivariate, forms of analysis.
(4) *Macro-maps* refer to studies which attempt to develop a more comprehensive perspective in establishing important linkages, such as between research and training, theory and practice or pre-service and in-service teacher education.

The resultant distribution of studies for the five countries, namely, Indonesia (I), Malaysia (M), Philippines (P), Singapore (S) and Thailand (T) are as shown in Table 1.

In their review of the reports on research in teacher education in 12 countries, including Australia, China, India, Japan and Singapore, Tisher and Wideen (1990) identified nine neglected areas, which could be included in a classification scheme for teacher education research. The nine research lacunae were concerned with: selection, the curriculum of pre-service, development of teaching skills, practice teaching and its supervision, the participants, in-service education, institutional contexts, entry to teaching, and the future of teacher education.

In studying the main features of, and the issues and tensions affecting teacher education, in a geographically diverse range of 21 countries, Leavitt (1992) identified eight key areas affecting teacher education systems: recruitment, curriculum content, control, research, professionalism, teacher educators, in-service education and indigenisation. Three of those countries, Australia, Japan, and the People's Republic of China, are included in this volume. There were earlier surveys of teacher education in the Asia-Pacific region, which include the APEID report (APEID, 1990), that provided a fairly comprehensive review of innovations in the field of teacher education. A more recent study, undertaken for the Asia Pacific Economic Co-operation (APEC) by Darling-Hammond and Cobb (1995), has provided a rich source of descriptive data, primarily from the perspective of governmental agencies, on the characteristics of the teaching force, how teachers are selected, the duration of teaching practice and the nature of the curriculum of teacher education programs.

It is apparent that, besides the two dimensions of 'focus' and 'scope', or stages in teacher education and research methods, respectively, in classifying teacher

Table 1. Distribution of research studies on teacher education according to focus and scope (Sim, 1991)

Focus of study	Scope of study				Total
	Micro-mirrors	Mini-mousetraps	Mega-mixes	Macro-maps	
Inputs	5I, 3M, 15P, 11S, 9T	3I, 1M, 2S,	1I, 2M, 4P, 6S, 10T	3P, 3S, 1T	9I, 6M, 22P, 22S, 20T
Initial training	10I, 17M, 13P, 20S, 26T	15I, 5M, 1P, 6S, 9T	4I, 2M, 1P, 2S, 4T	1S, 1T	29I, 24M, 15P, 29S, 40T
Induction	4I, 1M, 5P, 6S, 1T		1I, 2T		5I, 1M, 5P, 6S, 3T
In-service	2M, 15P, 7T	2I, 6P	2M, 11T		2I, 4M, 21P, 18T
Total	19I, 23M, 48P, 37S, 43T	20I, 6M, 7P, 8S, 9T	6I, 6M, 5P, 8S, 27T	3P, 4S, 2T	45I, 35M, 63P, 57S, 81T

Legend: I = Indonesia, M = Malaysia, P = Philippines, S = Singapore, T = Thailand.

education research (Sim, 1991), another important dimension refers to the various 'areas of concern' in teacher education, such as the main players, the curriculum, the processes and the context. For the purpose of this article, it is suggested that, instead of using a three-dimensional model, only two dimensions on aspects of teacher education should be employed, as is shown in Table 2. For each dimension, a minimum number of categories are used. For example, only

Table 2. Suggested typology for classifying and scrutinising teacher education research

	Main areas of concern in teacher education			
Main stages in teacher education	A Who & Whom? [Main Players: Educators & Teachers]	B What & Why? [Curriculum: Content & Rationale]	C How & How Well? [Processes: Teaching & Evaluation]	D When & Where? [Context: Place & Time]
1 Pre-service	1a	1b	1c	1d
2 In-service	2a	2b	2c	2d

two stages of the teacher education continuum are identified. Even so, they are not necessarily mutually exclusive.

The scope or types of research methods employed are, however, not specifically discussed. The purpose of using such a typology is to try and characterise the main areas of concern for the main stages in teacher education, within which suitable research may be conducted. For each of the eight combinations, some pertinent questions or issues are raised, even though the state-of-the-art in teacher education research has not adequately nor appropriately addressed many of them. A few examples of research are, however, mentioned in this article. These are merely to provide glimpses of the kinds of research that are being undertaken, and they are, by no means, representative of the numerous studies that have been conducted in the Asia-Pacific region.

3.1. *Who and Whom in Pre-Service Teacher Education (1a)*

'Who' refers to teacher educators. Among the pertinent issues that could be raised are the following questions.

- Who are the people who serve as teacher educators and what are their profiles in terms of age, gender, qualifications, experience and country of origin (if foreign)? Are more of them inclined to be generalists or specialists, to prefer qualitative or quantitative research, what are their teaching styles and do they practise what they preach regarding teaching and learning?
- Who should become teacher educators and what is the desirable mix of characteristics in terms of age, gender, teaching qualifications, teaching experience, sociability and country of origin? What dispositions, in terms of cognitive styles and approaches to research, teaching and evaluation are preferable for what situations?

'Whom' refers to student teachers, for whom the pre-service program is intended. Important issues to raise could include the following questions.

- What are the characteristics of student teachers – before, during and after pre-service education – in terms of possible misconceptions, prior teaching experience and practical theories, attitudes, beliefs and concerns, as well as self-esteem, self-efficacy and self-regulation?
- What are the desired characteristics of future teachers in terms of professional attitudes, pedagogical skills and knowledge base, especially pedagogical content knowledge?

For those countries, where teacher education institutions are part of a university, the findings of Turney and Wright (1990) in Australia are probably applicable. In their survey of Australian teacher educators, they found that:

> A majority of teacher educators believe that there is insufficient time for

research and preparation, that there is too much of class contact time, and that there is a lack of student interest. ... Teacher educators find themselves in a double bind. They are, on the one hand, criticised by their students and teachers as being too theoretical and out of touch with classroom realities and on the other hand they are held in low esteem by their university colleagues by having an inadequate disciplinary and theoretical base and a low commitment to pure knowledge.

In an Australian study, Yarrow et al. (1996) found various discrepancies between the perceived actual and ideal characteristics of university practicum supervisors. While the lowest discrepancies were in terms of friendliness, being well-qualified and treating other participants as fellow professionals, the greatest discrepancies were in terms of consistency, awareness of student teachers' individual development and stating expectations explicitly.

Although most teacher education institutions in the region have difficulty in attracting the best candidates for pre-service teacher education, the use of alternative selection criteria to purely academic grades has been explored in Singapore. In reviewing several studies on the use of alternative selection criteria, Soh and Ho (1990) raised a number of technical issues in conducting such research, including possible interaction effects among the cognitive and affective predictors used.

There has been increasing interest in studying student teachers' beliefs. Chan and Elliott (2000) maintained that "Of all the beliefs held by teachers, the beliefs about the nature of knowledge and learning (known as epistemological beliefs) appear to influence teachers' choice and decisions in classroom teaching, including what methods to use, how to manage the class, what to focus in learning and so on." Recently, there has been some interest in pre-service teachers' practical theories. In Australia, the case for embarking on such studies was made by Marland (1998).

3.2. *Who and Whom in In-Service Teacher Education (2a)*

While 'who' refers to teacher educators, 'whom' refers to practising teachers who participate in in-service education. Although most of the questions in the preceding section are probably applicable, there are additional questions which may be raised.

- Are teacher educators role models in pursuing lifelong continuing education and applying up-to-date knowledge and methods of teaching, such as the use of information and communication technology and andragogical techniques?
- How motivated and job-satisfied are teachers and what are the beliefs and perceptions of in-service teachers?

The motivation of practising teachers to teach is of particular importance to in-service teacher education. Thus, there have been a number of studies on teachers' motivations and concerns and job satisfaction in some countries. For example, several studies in Brunei Darussalam have been directed at teachers' motivation to teach. One study by Wong et al. (1998) focused on teachers' main concerns. A key finding was that "Most teachers, irrespective of their demographic characteristics, tend to have high levels of concern about pupils' lack of basic skills, poor motivation and attitudes, not completing homework and discipline behaviours."

As part of a cross-national study on job satisfaction, a Singapore study by Sim (1989) found two well-defined factors: 'overall satisfaction' and 'work orientation'. It is interesting that the 'experience of stress' variable loaded negatively on the former and positively on the latter, suggesting that stress has an ambivalent role, functioning as 'distress' and 'eustress', respectively. Thus, in the Singapore context, stress can function negatively as well as positively. From focus group interviews with some of the secondary school teachers, Lee (1989) found that students were sources of encouragement as well as of discouragement, teaching their own subject and continuing professional learning were sources of encouragement, while non-teaching duties and the work environment were sources of discouragement.

More recently, another study in Singapore by Stott and Tan (1999) investigated job satisfaction. Their sample of teachers seemed to view job satisfaction in three different ways, namely, in terms of the satisfaction gained from being a professional, empowerment and recognition, and the importance of rewards and conditions.

3.3. *What and Why in Pre-Service Teacher Education (1b)*

'What' refers to the content of the curriculum, while 'why' refers to its rationale. The following questions may be asked.

- What goals and objectives, short-term and long-term, are being pursued and to what extent are the teacher education institutions autonomous in determining them? What attitudes, skills and knowledge are being emphasised, and to what extent, in pre-service teacher education?
- Should the ultimate objective of teacher education be to develop competence and confidence in improving the performance of all children in all schools, while recognizing that every child and every classroom is unique? Should student teachers be prepared for immediate realities of classroom instruction and management or future possibilities as reflective professionals, including anticipated educational reforms?

In an APEC document for the meeting of Education Ministers in Washington, it was observed that

> in systems with centrally established standards, pre-service teacher education often focuses on curriculum and standards. In more decentralised systems,

however, where teacher-training institutions sometimes are located far from the new teacher's place of employment, pre-service programs cannot focus on the specifics of any given curriculum, and thus may emphasize pedagogy over curriculum content. (APEC, 1992)

According to Cobb et al. (1995), many APEC countries identified so-called 'quality teachers' as the goal and focus of their teacher education programs. Quality teachers are described as having some combination of the following attributes: pedagogical knowledge, subject area content knowledge, skills and attitudes necessary for effective teaching, strong understanding of human growth and child development, effective communication skills, strong sense of ethics, and capacity for renewal and ongoing learning.

It would therefore be useful to compare teachers' and teacher educators' perceptions of practising and ideal teachers in order to design the pre-service curriculum. Cortes et al. (1986) conducted a survey of teachers, mainly in the Philippines, and sought to characterise not only the 'teacher-in-practice' but also the perceived 'ideal teacher'. They concluded that

All in all, the most highly rated attributes are predominantly moral and social, and the skills to which great importance is attached are predominantly pedagogical. It is along these skills and personality traits, that objectives of teacher education programs should be addressed. (Cortes et al., 1986)

The practicum or field experiences or teaching practice has often been viewed as the central core of the pre-service curriculum, as exemplified by developments in Australia (Turney et al., 1982), Singapore (Sim & Ho, 1990) and Brunei Darussalam (Sim, 1999). Lovat (1999), has pointed out:

Field experiences must be more than practice without reflection, rules without understanding. They need to provide opportunities for students to inquire, to experiment, and to reflect on the subtleties and complexities of the classroom, including the moral as well as technical dimensions of teaching. The learning, both formal and informal, which occurs in schools and other settings will be a central concern in all field experience.

Student teachers are, understandably, anxious when it comes to having to perform in the classroom, especially when they are being observed and supervised during the practicum. In one study of a sample of student teachers in Singapore, Mau (1997) found that maintaining class control and meeting the needs of different students were the major concerns. In another study, D'Rozario and Wong (1998) found that practicum-related stresses were associated with such factors as their own and others' expectations of their teaching performance, the need to manage and discipline their classes effectively, establishing rapport and communicating with principals and parents.

3.4. *What and Why in In-Service Teacher Education (2b)*

Again, 'what' and 'why' refer to the content and rationale of in-service teacher education. The questions for pre-service teacher education would also be relevant. However, there are additional questions that could be raised.

- Have needs surveys been carried out periodically to ascertain the needs – and not just the wants – of teachers in terms of 'uplifting', 'updating' and 'upgrading' in-service programs or courses?
- What kinds of induction programs, if any, are available for beginning teachers to induct them not only to the school but also to their profession?

There have been numerous studies on in-service education and induction of beginning teachers in Australia, as reported by Tisher (1990). In many other countries, in-service education tends to be *ad hoc* and sporadic rather than systemic and systematic, and teacher induction programs are quite rare.

Eleven APEC countries contributed to a major study on teacher induction (Moskowitz & Stephens, 1997). Of particular interest are the lessons learned, which arose mainly from comparing the situation in the United States with the situations in Japan, New Zealand and the Northern Territory in Australia, which apparently have the following common characteristics.

- New teachers are viewed as professionals on a continuum, with increasing levels of experience and responsibility; novice teachers are not expected to do the same job as experienced teachers without significant support.
- New teachers are nurtured and not left to flounder on their own; interaction with other teachers is maximized.
- Teacher induction is a purposive and valued activity.
- Schools possess a culture of shared responsibility and support; all or most of the school's staff contribute to the development and nurturing of the new teachers.
- Finally, the study found that in all three countries, assessment of new teachers is down-played.
- Policy makers everywhere want to improve teacher induction.

3.5. *How and How Well in Pre-Service Teacher Education (1c)*

'How' and 'how well' refer to the processes of teaching and evaluation, respectively, with regard to pre-service programs. There are some pertinent questions that could be raised.

- How are pre-service programs preparing student teachers to meet the existing and emergent needs of schools and what strategies are being used to facilitate the development of relevant attitudes, skills and knowledge?
- How are student teachers being assessed and how are the outcomes of pre-service programs being evaluated in terms of the criteria of effectiveness, efficiency and equity?

The major outcome of pre-service education is often regarded as the development of competence and confidence in teaching. Hence, as indicated earlier, teaching practice or the practicum is generally regarded as the core component in the pre-service curriculum. Brady et al. (1998) highlight the importance of "establishing theory-practice nexus". The crucial role of supervision has therefore been much researched (Dunkin, 1996). Hope (1999) talks of the need for "reshaping primary teacher education in New Zealand" in order to strengthen the partnership between teacher education institutions and schools. The practicum has been particularly useful in enhancing student teachers' reflectivity (e.g., Dunkin, 1996; Mills & Satterthwait, 2000). Potentially, microteaching has also been used to develop reflectivity and there seems to be a revival of interest in using microteaching, or adapted forms of it, in pre-service teacher education (e.g., Cornford, 1996; Francis, 1997).

During the 1980s, when the presage-process-product paradigm for research on teaching and teacher education was declining in popularity in the West, there was a plethora of such studies in ASEAN countries. In Indonesia, for example, there were as many as 30 such studies, as reported by Djalil (1990). Interestingly, there has recently been a resurgence of interest in the so-called 'outcomes' question in the West (e.g., Cochran-Smith, 2001), accompanied by interest in providing evidence that teacher education programs and procedures are accountable, effective, or value-added. It is also noteworthy that both qualitative, which is currently more in vogue, and quantitative, approaches are being employed in evaluating the outcomes of teacher education. For example, in reporting a major synthesis of studies of excellence in teachers, Darling-Hammond (2000) concluded that:

> The findings of both the qualitative and quantitative analyses suggest that policy investments in the quality of teachers may be related to improvements in student performance. This analysis suggests that policies adopted by states regarding teacher education, licensing, hiring, and professional development may make an important difference in the qualifications and capacities that teachers bring to their work.

The evaluation of pre-service programs and courses is often carried out routinely through end-of-program or course evaluation and feedback. Different approaches to the assessment of student teachers have been employed. In reviewing various studies on the use of a variety of modes of assessment in pre-service teacher education in Singapore, Soh and Ho (1990) concluded that, in terms of assignments, the open-ended form was more efficacious, while in terms of examinations, the written form tended to assess recall rather than higher order thinking.

3.6. *How and How Well in In-Service Teacher Education (2c)*

Again, in examining 'how' in-service teachers are being developed and 'how well' they have succeeded in attaining the desired outcomes, similar questions to those in Section 3.5 could be raised. In addition, the following questions might be asked.

- How are practising teachers being motivated to invest their time and energy in continuing professional development and how do in-service providers capitalise on the potentials of information and communication technology?
- How are quality assessment and quality assurance being conducted and to what extent has the feedback from evaluation been used to improve the conduct of in-service programs and courses?

The potential of information and communication technology (ICT) is increasingly being tapped in providing in-service training for practising teachers, who, for reasons of distance and time have difficulty in attending centralised courses, as illustrated, for instance, by studies conducted in India (Maheshwari & Raina, 1998) and Australia (Watson et al., 1996). Birch and Maclean (1998) have provided a useful analysis of the development of ICT in relation to teacher education in the Asia-Pacific region. In their conclusion, they pointed to the disturbing phenomenon of a 'digital divide' between the rich and the poor in the region.

How to sustain in-service teacher education has also been a concern, as shown by Yuen-kwan's (1998) study in Hong Kong. Chareonwongsak (2001) referred to Thailand's efforts to devolve in-service teacher education from a government-controlled to a market-driven situation. Corrie (2000) reported an attempt to involve newly qualified teachers in Australia as collaborative practitioners, but found that they tended to use cooperative rather than collaborative strategies.

In some countries, in-service training is regularly conducted and it is customary for evaluation to be in-built, as shown by the nine studies in Thailand conducted during the 1980s, and reported by Chantavit (1990). When new curricula are introduced, it is also quite common for in-service courses or workshops to be conducted for teachers. Likewise, end-of-course evaluation is usually incorporated, but, less frequently, a major evaluation exercise is undertaken to evaluate the impact of such courses as well as the underlying factors influencing the implementation of the new curricula. An example of such in-service evaluation is the study by Noor Azmi (1991) on the New Primary Curriculum in Malaysia. A major finding was that the courses had only a "surface effect but not the impact that could bring deep assimilation of all the (New Primary Curriculum) features." Among the possible causes he suggested were: (a) the informative rather than experiential nature of the courses, (b) credibility of some key personnel, (c) teachers' restricted professionality, and (d) limited time allotted and poor facilities.

3.7. *When and Where in Pre-Service Teacher Education (1d)*

'When' and 'where' refer to the time and place, respectively, of the pre-service program or course. Some pertinent questions could be raised.

- When is it most appropriate for certain pre-service activities, such as the practicum, to take place and for what duration? What are the progressive changes, if any, in student teachers' attitudes and beliefs?

- Where and when would it be appropriate or inappropriate to adopt or adapt certain innovative practices from other systems?

Williamson and Morris (2000) have highlighted the importance of taking cognizance of cultural context in comparing teacher education across countries. For example, they pointed out the difference between countries with a Confucian culture, which may be represented by countries like Japan and the People's Republic of China, and an Anglo-celtic culture, which may be represented by Australia and New Zealand. While the former tend to be oriented towards academic content knowledge, the latter are more practice oriented.

Drawing on the findings of various research studies with subjects from Australia, New Zealand, Papua New Guinea, and other island nations in the South Pacific, as well as from Indonesia, Vietnam and Thailand, Teasdale (1997) has cautioned against the tendency for less developed countries to ape the more developed countries.

3.8. When and Where in In-Service Teacher Education (2d)

Contextual questions pertaining to pre-service teacher education are highly relevant to in-service teacher education.

- What in-service programs or courses are needed to cater for the changing needs of teachers at different stages of their careers?
- What adaptations are needed to cater for the differing needs of teachers in different geographical or other contexts?

For a vast country like the People's Republic of China, teachers who are posted to remote rural areas would have to make use of limited opportunities for continuing their professional development. Wu and Chang (1990) reported a case study of a very dedicated teacher of English, who achieved remarkable successes with her students, despite the fact that most people in the community considered the subject as useless. As she had studied English for only two years at Beijing's Teachers' College, she seized every available opportunity to improve herself, by observing demonstration classes, attending refresher courses and applying new principles and methods to her teaching.

Another relatively vast country is India, where, according to Govinda and Buch (1990), the in-service education of teachers is the weakest link in the whole system of teacher education. From their review of research on in-service education, they concluded that the situation was quite discouraging in terms of quantity as well as quality. They maintained that research studies should have provided an empirical base for assessing overall in-service requirements at different levels. Studies should also be conducted to work out alternative models for organising in-service programs.

5. FUTURE DIRECTIONS: VISUALISING A PLAUSIBLE FUTURE LANDSCAPE

While all the countries in the Asia-Pacific region, as well as their teacher education institutions, are probably unique in terms of their desirable, feasible and actual practice of teacher education and research, it may be helpful to use a generic typology, such as the one in Table 2, to provide a holistic snapshot of the current situation.

In particular, each country needs to decide whether each of the main concerns – pertaining to teacher educators and student teachers, teacher education curricula and their rationales, teaching and evaluation approaches employed, as well as the cultural contexts in various spatial and temporal locations – have been addressed appropriately and adequately. If not, how urgent is it to secure research-based answers that would help improve teacher education?

Besides teacher education institutions, there are a number of national and regional organizations that conduct courses for teachers and are therefore very much involved in in-service teacher education. These organisations should be persuaded to become engaged in conducting research and evaluation studies on the impact of their programs and activities. An example of such a study is the evaluation of the programs and activities of two SEAMEO (South-East Asian Ministers of Education Organisation) Centres (SEAMEO-INNOTECH and SEAMEO-RECSAM) by a SEARRAG team.

Finally, especially with the increasing opportunities for electronic networking, there are many advantages in cross-national collaborative research. However, for a symbiotic meta-strategy to work, it may not be advisable for countries that are vastly different to undertake fully collaborative research. Within countries, and even within institutions, many trade offs could arise from a team approach in researching important problems in teacher education, which are generally complex in nature. Teacher educators could also employ the strategy of training teachers as researchers, who could subsequently become partners in collaborative research, especially when it is school-based or school-focused.

A unique approach in stimulating teachers to collaborate in conducting action research and sharing their findings has been the setting up of the Teachers' Network in Singapore. Judging from its highly frequented website, its regular newsletters, and the many workshops and conferences, its mission "to serve as a catalyst and support for teacher-initiated development, thought sharing, collaboration and reflection, leading to self-mastery, excellent practice and fulfilment" is certainly not mere rhetoric. Such activities augur very well for the kind of symbiosis that ought to develop between teacher education institutions and schools through research.

Needless to say, the foregoing suggestions are not meaningful for some countries in the Asia-Pacific region, while some other countries are probably further along in attaining some of the ideals envisaged in the suggestions. Hopefully, they might serve as reference points for some to compare with what they have, or have not, thus far been able to achieve by way of using research for improving teacher pre-service and in-service education. At the same time, it is doubtful that any country can afford to ignore having to confront the realities of globalisation and the need to develop technoliteracy (Lankshear & Snyder, 2000), that increasingly impinge on education, in general, and pre-service and in-service teacher education, in particular. It is by no means coincidental that the second volume of the *Journal of Southeast Asian Education* is devoted to the theme, "New literacies in the 21st century: Thinking and information technology." The articles by researchers from Brunei, Hong Kong, Malaysia and Singapore invariably underscore the need for teacher education and research to address the new literacies.

REFERENCES

APEC (1992). *Education Standards in the Asia-Pacific Region: Preface and Summary of Survey Findings*. Document No. 2. for the APEC Education Forum, 7–8 August, Washington, DC.

APEID (1990). *Innovations and Initiatives in Teacher Education in Asia and the Pacific Region*. Bangkok: UNESCO Regional Office for Education in Asia.

Birch, I., & Maclean, R. (1998). Information and communication technologies for education and teacher development in the Asia-Pacific region: Issues and challenges. *Asia-Pacific Journal of Teacher Education and Development*, 1(2), 41–52.

Brady, L., Segal, G., Bamford, A., & Deer, C. E. (1998). *Student perceptions of the theory/practice nexus in teacher education*. Paper Presented at the Annual Conference of the Australian Association for Research in Education, 29 November to 3rd December, Adelaide.

Chan, K.-W., & Elliott, R. G. (2000). Exploratory study of epistemological beliefs of Hong Kong teacher education students: Resolving conceptual and empirical issues. *Asia – Pacific Journal of Teacher Education*, 28(3), 225–234.

Chantavit, S. (1990). *A Review of Teacher Education Research in Thailand*. Bangkok: SEARRAG.

Chareonwongsak, K. (2001). From government-controlled to market-driven: The case of Thailand's in-service teacher development. In Y. C. Cheng, K. W. Chow & K. T. Tsui (Eds.), *New Teacher Education for the Future: International Perspectives* (pp. 187–218). Dordrecht: Kluwer Academic Publishers.

Cobb, V. L., Darling-Hammond, L., & Murangi, K. (1995). Teacher preparation and professional development in APEC members: An overview of policy and practice. In L. Darling-Hammond & V. L. Cobb (Eds.), *Teacher Preparation and Professional Development in APEC Members: A Comparative Study* (pp. 1–16). Washington, DC: U.S. Department of Education.

Cochran-Smith, M. (2001). The outcomes question in teacher education. *Teaching and Teacher Education*, 17, 527–546.

Cornford, I. R. (1996). Is there a role for microteaching in the 1990s? *Asia-Pacific Journal of Teacher Education*, 24(1), 83–94.

Corrie, L. (2000). Facilitating newly qualified teachers' growth as collaborative practitioners. *Asia-Pacific Journal of Teacher Education*, 28(2), 111–121.

Cortes, J. R., Anunciacion, R. M., & Santos, L. O. (Eds.) (1986). *Perceptions of the 'Ideal Teacher' and the Teacher-in-Practice in the ASEAN*. Philippines: National Development Education Centre (NADEC).

Darling-Hammond, L. (2000). Teacher quality and student achievement: A review of state policy evidence. *Education Policy Analysis Archives*, 8(1).

Darling-Hammond, L., & Cobb, V. L. (Eds.) (1995). *Teacher Preparation and Professional Development in APEC Members: A Comparative Study*. Washington, DC: US Department of Education.

Djalil, A. et al. (1990). *A Review of Teacher Education Research in Indonesia*. Jakarta: SEARRAG.

D'Rozario, V., & Wong, F. L. A. (1998). A study of practicum-related stresses in a sample of first-year

student teachers in Singapore. *Asia-Pacific Journal of Teacher Education and Development*, 1(1), 39-35.
Dunkin, M. J. (1998). *Current Trends in Teaching Practice*. Paper presented at the National Colloquium on: 'Towards developing and strengthening partnership in teacher education,' Brunei Darussalam, 16-18 September.
Eltis, K. (1987). *Australian Teacher Education in Review*. Adelaide: South Pacific Association for Teacher Education.
Francis, D. (1997). Reconceptualising microteaching as critical inquiry. *Asia-Pacific Journal of Teacher Education*, 25(3), 207-224.
Govinda, R., & Buch, M. B. (1990). Indian research in teacher education: A review. In R. P. Tisher., & M. F. Wideen (Eds.), *Research in Teacher Education: International Perspectives* (pp. 141-162). London: Falmer Press.
Hope, J. (1999). Reshaping primary teacher education in New Zealand: Compressed courses and school partnership. *Asia-Pacific Journal of Teacher Education*, 27(4), 183-192.
Lankshear, C., & Snyder, I. (2000). *Teachers and Technoliteracy: Managing Literacy, Technology and Learning in Schools*. St Leonards, NSW: Allen & Unwin.
Leavitt, H. B. (1992). *Issues and Problems in Teacher Education: An International Handbook*. New York: Greenwood Press.
Lee, F. M. F. (1989). Sources of enthusiasm and discouragement: Another aspect of teacher professional satisfaction and its link with quality of teaching and learning. *Singapore Journal of Education* (Special Issue), 69-87.
Lovat, T. J. (1999). Searching for best practice in initial teacher education: Responding to the challenges. *Asia-Pacific Journal of Teacher Education*, 27(2), 119-126.
Mau, R. Y. (1997). Concerns of student teachers: Implications for improving the practicum. *Asia-Pacific Journal of Teacher Education*, 25(1), 53-66.
Maheshwari, A. N., & Raina, V. K. (1998). Inservice training of primary teachers through interactive video technology: An Indian experience. *International Review of Education*, 44(1), 87-101.
Marland, P. (1998). Teachers' practical theories: Implications for preservice teacher education. *Asia-Pacific Journal of Teacher Education and Development*, 1(2), 15-23.
Mills, M., & Satterthwait, D. (2000). The disciplining of pre-service teachers: Reflections on the teaching of reflective teaching. *Asia-Pacific Journal of Teacher Education*, 28(1), 29-38.
Morris, P., & Williamson, J. (Eds.) (2000). *Teacher Education in the Asia-Pacific Region: A Comparative Study*. New York: Falmer Press.
Moskowitz, J., & Stephens, M. (1997). *From Students of Teaching to Teachers of Student Teachers: Teacher Induction around the Pacific Rim*. Washington, DC: U.S. Department of Education.
Noor Azmi, I. (1991). Inservice training in Malaysia for the new primary nurriculum. In K. M. Lewin & J. S. Stuart (Eds.), *Educational Innovation in Developing Countries: Case Studies of Changemakers* (pp. 95-126). London: Macmillan Press.
Sim, W. K. (1989). The job satisfaction of teachers in Singapore. *Singapore Journal of Education* (Special Issue), 48-68.
Sim, W. K. (1991). *A Review of Teacher Education Research in Five ASEAN Countries: A Synthesis*. Singapore: SEARRAG.
Sim, W. K. (1999). *Towards a paradigm shift in teacher education in Brunei Darussalam*. Paper presented at the Australian Council of Deans of Education (ACDE) Conference, Canberra, 20-22 September.
Sim, W. K., & Ho, W. K. (1990). 25 years of teacher education. In J. S. K. Yip & W. K. Sim (Eds.), *Evolution of Educational Excellence: 25 Years of Education in the Republic of Singapore* (pp. 157-186). Singapore: Longman.
Soh, K. C., & Ho, W. K. (1990). Teacher selection research: The Singapore experience. *Singapore Journal of Education*, 11(1), 29-37.
Stott, K., & Tan, A. L. (1999). Exploring teacher job satisfaction in a Singapore secondary school. *Asia-Pacific Journal of Teacher Education & Education*, 2(1), 41-49.
Teasdale, G. R. (1997). *Globalisation; Localisation: Impacts and Implications for Teacher Education in*

the Asia-Pacific Region. Paper presented at the 27th Annual Conference of the Australian Teacher Education Association, Rockhampton, 5–8 July.

Tisher, R. P. (1990). One and a half decade of research on teacher education. In R. P. Tisher & M. F. Wideen (Eds.), *Research in Teacher Education: International Perspectives* (pp. 67–87). London: Falmer Press.

Tisher, R. P., & Wideen, M. F. (Eds.) (1990). *Research in Teacher Education: International Perspectives.* London: Falmer Press.

Turney, C. et al. (1982). *The Practicum in Teacher Education: Research, Practice and Supervision.* Sydney: Sydney University Press.

Turney, C., & Wright, R. (1990). *Where the Buck Stops.* Sydney: Southwood Press.

Watson, J. M., Baxter, J. P., Olssen, K. H., & Lovitt, C. (1996). Professional development at distance as an information-technology enterprise. *Asia-Pacific Journal of Teacher Education, 24*(2), 139–146.

Williamson, J., & Morris, P. (2000). Teacher education in the Asia-Pacific region: A comparative analysis. In P. Morris & J. Williamson (Eds.), *Teacher Education in the Asia-Pacific Region: A Comparative Study* (pp. 265–284). New York: Falmer Press.

Wong, K. Y., Nannestad, C., Lourdusamy, A., & Veloo, P. (1998). What are secondary school teachers in Brunei Darussalam concerned about? *CARE Review,* 50–56.

Wu, Z., & Chang, J. (1990). Education reforms and research on teacher education in China. In R. P. Tisher & M. F. Wideen (Eds.), *Research in Teacher Education: International Perspectives* (pp. 227–239). London: Falmer Press.

Yarrow, A., Millwater, J., & Foster, B. (1996). University practicum supervisors: Marching to a different drummer. *Asia-Pacific Journal of Teacher Education, 24*(2), 197–210.

Yuen-kwan, W. L. (1998). How sustainable are in-service teacher-training courses? *Asia-Pacific Journal of Teacher Education, 26*(1), 65–74.

62

The Recruitment and Preparation of Teachers

CHEN AI YEN, LIM CHER PING and S. GOPINATHAN
National Institute of Education, Nanyang Technological University, Singapore

1. INTRODUCTION

This article focuses on the challenges and demands for quality education in the Asia-Pacific region and the responses of different countries as expressed in their efforts to bridge the gap between the supply of and demand for quality teachers in the last two decades. In the face of rapid technological and economic developments globally, education institutions in the region have been under increasing pressure to prepare learners who are adaptable to change, who are creative and innovative, who can apply knowledge and solve problems with confidence. There is consensus that teachers are no longer the exclusive source of expertise and authority in education. While other resources, human as well as material, are being made available by various agencies and institutions, the major problem in meeting these new educational challenges is that of teacher shortage. The crux of the problem is the challenge to ensure the sustained supply of well prepared and motivated teachers for the education of citizens in a much more complex new world and new global economy (World Bank, 2000b).

The teacher in reformed education systems has to take on the more demanding role of a mediator and a knowledge broker: to provide guidance, strategic support, and assistance to help students, even adult learners, to assume responsibilities for their own learning. In order to take up this role, teachers have to be equipped with lifelong learning skills in addition to timeless qualities such as love and care of their students, as well as teaching by example as flexible learners working collaboratively and utilising a range of resources. There is a pressing need for each teacher to be open to new ideas, new methods and technologies, to learn how to learn, unlearn and relearn, and to understand and accept the need for change (Muller, 1998).

In this article an analysis of the need for the supply and recruitment of teachers of quality among a purposive sample of Asia-Pacific countries is framed by the following three dimensions:

(a) planning for the supply of quality teachers (policies and reforms);
(b) preparation for the supply of quality teachers (training systems, agencies, institutions and alternative resources); and,
(c) teacher recruitment strategies and outcomes.

2. PLANNING FOR THE SUPPLY OF TEACHERS OF QUALITY

Different Asia-Pacific countries have responded to the global challenges and demands for quality education in their own ways, according to their goals of education – nationalistic, economic, and professional. In the 1970s and 1980s most of the countries in the region initiated timely educational reforms to keep pace with globalisation and technological developments. These reforms were inevitably linked to an increasing emphasis on the strategic role of teachers, and thus teacher education as a means of upgrading the workforce and through them developing the economy and building the nation. As a result, different approaches have been employed to recruit and develop quality teachers to meet the increasing demand for quality education. Countries that have been responsive to globalisation and have enjoyed relative political stability, as well as investing heavily in human capital in terms of the training of skilled and adaptable workers have done better in nurturing an adequate supply of quality teachers. This in turn has brought about the transformation of these countries through rapid economic growth and technological development in the last two decades. Outstanding examples are Japan, Republic of Korea, Taiwan, Malaysia, Singapore, Australia and New Zealand. In the last decade, the People's Republic of China has also made great progress in providing improved multi-level and multi-media conventional and distance teacher training.

The demand for and the supply of quality teachers has been a major concern in the national development plans of every one of the Asia-Pacific countries in the past three decades. Stated in different terms and languages, different agencies and institutions directly or indirectly responsible for formulating educational policies, reforms and strategies have published their needs and plans nationally (e.g., Green Paper on Education in China, 2000; Reports of the Japanese National Council on Educational Reforms, 1985–2000; Sri Lanka's Staff Appraisal Report, 1996; the Malaysian 5 year Plans, 1981–2000; and Singapore's IT Masterplan in Education, 1997), and internationally (e.g., World Bank Reports on Education, 1990–2000; UNESCO Report on Innovations and Initiatives on Teacher Education, 1990). By and large, the demand for and supply of teachers at different levels: elementary or primary, secondary, tertiary, and for different programs: in-service, pre-service, and specialisations vary from country to country, from one geographical region to another and from year to year. One element, however, appears to be constant, that is the perennial problem of teacher shortage and diverse national strategies for the supply of qualified teachers by institutional training or by less formal methods of teacher development. Only Japan in the region seems to have overcome the problem of teacher shortage by according higher socio-economic status, working conditions and salaries to teachers.

Generally speaking, most Asia-Pacific countries define the quality of a professional teacher by a qualification based on either the number of years of education a teacher receives or by the level of teacher education undertaken. UNESCO (2000) statistics indicate a wide range in the number of years of education required of teachers. At the primary level, the average is about 13 years and at the secondary level, the average is about 16 years. In China, Japan, the Republic of Korea, and Singapore, all secondary teachers and school administrators have university level education. Many Asia-Pacific countries have also developed in-service and further teacher education programs for educational administrators, higher level professional teachers, and different curricular specialists in addition to the basic two or four year teacher training for primary or secondary level teaching.

In Australia, China, Japan, New Zealand, Singapore, and Korea, additional theoretical knowledge inputs through seminars, workshops and conferences, even televised courses as well as skill training programs for in-service teachers in conventional classroom situations and in e-learning courses have resulted in the teachers becoming more adaptable and able to perform at higher levels. In most instances, the wise and appropriate integration of information and communication technologies (ICT) has complemented the pace of teacher development in tandem with the provision of general staff development programs, salary increases and improving teachers' working conditions. Since quality teachers are nurtured and not born, enlightened educational policies and sound infrastructures for the recruitment and nurture of teachers must be in place to ensure quality supply.

This article looks more closely at the specific agencies and recruitment strategies for building a supply of quality teachers in five clusters of countries in the Asia-Pacific region. The five clusters are (a) Australia and New Zealand; (b) Japan and Korea; (c) P.R. China; (d) India, Pakistan, Bangladesh and Sri Lanka; and (e) Malaysia and Singapore.

3. THE PREPARATION AND RECRUITMENT OF TEACHERS

The demand for quality teachers is a pressing issue in the Asia-Pacific region. This is because about a third of its population is under 15 years of age and all need to be educated so that they can become employable workers and useful citizens. Illiteracy rates among the young in the four developed countries of the region (Australia, Japan, New Zealand, and Singapore) are negligible. However, to remain economically competitive, even these countries continue to need quality teachers. Therefore, all the countries in the region need quality teacher education for the untrained, beginning, specialist and expert teachers and administrators to manage and teach both the young and the adult learners to cope with the demands and challenges of a global economy.

3.1. *Australia and New Zealand*

Australia and New Zealand have been clustered together because of their similar historical, geographical and political backgrounds as well as their economic status. Located along the southern rim of the Asia-Pacific region, the two countries, played two alternating roles: first as fore-runners of innovative non-formal technology-enhanced teacher education, and, second as preservers of the high standards required for formal professional teacher education.

In Australia, both the Australian Commonwealth and State Governments have been addressing the quality of teaching in schools since 1978. In reports in 1990, the Schools Council indicated both a decline in the number of applicants for teaching, the changed nature of teacher's work and the need to improve working conditions and conditions of employment. Changes have been made in the selection for training, pre-service and in-service preparation of teachers, and the development of a national teaching profession with clear criteria for improving the process of accreditation and recognition of the profession. A requirement that entrants to teaching should be drawn from the top academic quartile was implemented. Every potential teacher trainee has a university degree while staff development is organised mainly at the school level, and special and higher degree programs are taught in the universities. State authorities determine the entry qualifications of teachers into their systems even though the Federal Government provides most of the funding for higher education (Preston, 2000). With regards to teacher professional quality, their image and conditions of service, there is overall upgrading in all the states as evident in the creation of a more defined career path and professional program (UNESCO, 1990; Lake & Williamson, 2000).

Despite the diversity of teacher education courses in Australian universities, educational reforms during the 1990s have recast professional teachers as learners and researchers actively engaging in improving teaching practices and student learning outcomes. This is evident in two recent initiatives aiming at revitalizing teacher professionalism within Australia. They are the National Schools Network (NSN) and the Innovative Links Between Schools and Universities Project that have sought to broaden the base of school restructuring beyond organizational change to reconceptualise teacher professionalism. Teachers working on the projects have developed skills and competencies to undertake classroom based action research, they have looked into dilemmas of teaching and problem aspects of the curriculum, difficult student behaviour and other demanding aspects of school life. These two projects have provided the opportunities for 14 universities representing all Australian states and one territory to strengthen further the building of a quality teaching service in Australia (Sachs, 1997).

New Zealand is a developed country whose wealth has largely been dependent on the use of new technology, particularly in agriculture. These have created new demands for educational planners to provide appropriate training opportunities, particularly at technical levels and for post-secondary education. In contrast to Australia where university-based teacher education is dominant, New Zealand authorities have adopted a more diversified, privatised structure. As early as the 1970s, so-called 'teacher outposts' were established to train students in school-based practices. Research seems to support the view that this provides effective initial teacher training, particularly in the one-year postgraduate course for secondary teaching. Additionally, 20 per cent of teachers' college positions in New Zealand are short-term contracts to attract teachers and other specialists from and into the teaching field. The positions of these personnel are protected while they are in college (APEID-UNESCO, 1990). In more recent years, the emphasis on teachers as self-regulating learners, improving their own practice and their students' independent learning, has been considered in contemporary curriculum reforms (Muller, 1998). The ten state-funded teacher education institutions and nearly 30 other agencies have different recruitment criteria but all act as agents of change in training and curriculum reforms as well as in their market approach to education (Ramsey, 2000). Colleges of education provide professional training for future teachers mainly at the primary education level, while the seven universities provide training for secondary teachers as well as postgraduate training for in-service teachers. Better quality and qualified teachers as well as teacher educators of diverse backgrounds are being trained and employed to meet the challenges of a new world economy.

3.2. *Japan and Republic of Korea*

Japan and Korea have been clustered together because of their geographical proximity and high standard of economic and educational development. In Japan, educational policies for the last three decades have been characterized by an emphasis on sustaining national competitiveness for an economy already dominant in Asia. The Japanese National Council on Educational Reforms was created in 1984 to install a comprehensive series of reforms as part of the government's modernisation efforts. The improvement in the quality of teachers has been perceived as important for improving the quality of elementary and secondary education. All Japanese teachers are trained in universities or colleges approved by the Ministry of Education (MOE). Secondary teachers are trained in four-year courses in national universities, while others are trained in two or four year courses at a small number of local and private institutions of Higher Education (UNESCO, 1997).

Japanese schools reached their peak of modernisation in the mid-1970s, when school attendance reached 95 per cent in senior high school and nearly 40 per cent in universities. Quality teachers were needed to man these institutions and expansion of teacher education took place in the 1970s until the supply reached saturation point in the 1980s with a rapid decline in the birth rate. A situation of oversupply of teachers emerged with teacher education colleges switching to catering for more in-service education in specialized areas such as early childhood education, counselling and ICT (Sato & Asanuma, 2000). Despite the oversupply of teachers in Japan, all Japanese teachers continue to be recruited by the appropriate authorities from among those who hold relevant teacher certification. In order to secure the best personnel for teaching, the salaries of teachers are pitched higher than those of regular public employees.

All teachers are required to participate in in-service education immediately after their employment, and many are granted study leave with pay to study for higher degrees. The reforms also focus on improving the educational environment including reduction in class size, the teaching process, research and technological development and teacher education. There are special programs for the training of school principals and senior teachers, Science and English language teachers; a number have been received overseas training soon after pre-service training (APEID-UNESCO, 1990). Efforts for the professional development of teachers in schools through various modes of delivery including the use of ICT continue unabated.

Across the Sea of Japan in North-Eastern Asia, the Republic of Korea focuses its attention on teacher education to upgrade the quality of teachers and the quality of education as a whole. The needs of in-service teacher education, strongly proposed at the beginning of the 1980s, and the needs of in-service education for educational administrators and professionals were raised simultaneously and resulted in the establishment of the National Institute for Educational Research and Training and 11 national teachers' colleges for elementary school teachers (UNESCO, 1997).

In connection with policies to raise teacher quality, different methods are employed. These include recruitment and selection methods, improvement of the training curriculum, certification, employment and internship systems as well as in-service teacher education. According to the APEID-UNESCO (1990) Report, Korean education has witnessed an intermittent fluctuation of surplus and shortage in teacher demand and supply because of the drastic curtailment of the total number of students, classes and teachers in the education system. One outcome is quality assurance of the teachers trained and their positive contribution to the development of the nation. The other is the use of ICT in teacher education. The concept of adapting education to the information age or 'educational informatisation' was popularised after the launching of the Education Reform Measures and then the Comprehensive Education Information Plan in May 1995. This Three-year Plan aims to provide an environment in which the customers of education including teachers and students have access to various educational resources and teacher training programs so that they have the skills for using educational software and information network management (Looi, 2001).

3.3. China

The People's Republic of China has made the most progress since its modernisation efforts at the end of the Cultural Revolution in 1976. Education, particularly teacher education, has played a strategic role in China's restoration, development and innovation in four areas, namely, agriculture, industry, science and technology since the 1980s. As a result of the various educational reforms, the number of normal universities and colleges (at least 95% are government aided), and the pre-service and in-service enrolment into these institutions increased exponentially, sometimes a nearly 200 per cent increase for pre-service admission and an almost 300 per cent increase for in-service training enrolment (APEID-UNESCO Report, 1990). There was an increase of 11 per cent in the enrolment in higher education in 2000. This is expected to reach 15 per cent in 2010 (Chinese Educational Development and Research Center, 2000). More specifically, the training of pre-service and in-service physical education, music, arts, physiology and hygiene specialists has been stepped up. Following the reorganization of secondary education with a strong emphasis on vocational education, the training of vocational teachers in various fields has also been stepped up, particularly in border areas and minority regions. Concurrently, there is also great expansion in the establishment of multi-level, multi-pattern network for in-service teacher education in universities, colleges and through broadcasting and online courses.

Great efforts have also been made to upgrade teacher educators' qualification, salary and working conditions since 1985. As a result, a number of the teacher educators have been sent overseas for upgrading purposes. Although the United Kingdom, the United States and Australia have been the main postgraduate teacher education training grounds, Singapore has been playing an important role in this connection, particularly in the training of teacher educators involved in the teaching of English. At least 700 Chinese teacher educators have been formally trained in postgraduate programs in Singapore, not to mention the hundreds of Singapore teachers and teacher educators who have been officially or unofficially assisting China in short-term in-service training programs.

From a comparative perspective, the problems of training and recruiting teachers faced by China is similar to those faced by other countries. Like most countries in the world, China has difficulty in recruiting the most promising teaching talent because of competition from more prestigious and lucrative professions. The rigid regulation of teacher education by the state and the central government may have hampered the recruitment and development of quality teachers in a rapidly expanding market economy. In order to meet the huge demand for teachers at all levels of schooling, the Chinese State Commission is resolving the policy dilemma of maintaining strict control over teacher education or encouraging self-sufficiency and diversification of teacher education institutions, in addition to taking more drastic measures to boost the morale and social status of teachers in order to attract the young and keep the older people in the teaching profession (Leung & Hui, 2000).

3.4. *India, Pakistan, Bangladash and Sri Lanka*

All the three countries in the Indian sub-continent and Sri Lanka have made some progress in educational reforms since their independence and more significantly in the past two decades. This is particularly noticeable in the field of basic education in the rural areas and for women. India has increased its public expenditure on education to 3.8 per cent of its GNP on education, yet 46 per cent of its 930 million people in 1995 were illiterates (MOE, India, 2001). Sri Lanka has a well-developed education system that is closely related to its economic development. It has a literacy rate of over 90 per cent and the highest basic and secondary education participation in South Asia. However, like the other three countries on the Indian sub-continent, the shortage of trained teachers is an acute problem that demands attention. This is because only some 18 per cent of new recruits to teaching are trained before entering the service (World Bank, 1996).

Since the formulation of the National Policy on Education in 1986, Indian education has witnessed a quantitative expansion at all levels and recent efforts have been directed towards qualitative improvement. As early as 1976, the administration of education has been transferred from the 31 state departments of education to the National Council for Educational Research and Training (NCERT). All the educational reforms including policies regarding the recruitment and training of teachers now come under the NCERT. Despite a sizable annual education budget, the country continues to face a shortage of teachers, particularly quality teachers, and more acutely in rural areas. This is due to its two per cent population increase in both the rural and urban areas in the 1990s (MOE, India, 2001).

In Pakistan, the establishment of different types of teacher training institutions including those for specialized training has narrowed the gap between supply and demand of teachers and upgrade the quality of teacher education to some extent. To achieve its national and economic objectives, the curriculum from primary to higher education was revised in 1971, and the teacher training centres were upgraded into teacher education colleges and new training institutes were established. Some universities started new in-service teacher education programs through distance delivery systems for example, the Allama Iqbal Open University.

Since its independence nearly 30 years ago, Bangladesh has tried to provide basic education for its children under 12 years of age by both formal and nonformal education means. According to the Bangladesh Education Sector Review published by the World Bank, enrolments cover 90 per cent of primary school age group, 44 per cent at lower secondary and 27 per cent at upper secondary. Almost as many girls are enrolled as boys in the primary and lower secondary schools. To overcome its acute qualified teacher shortage problem, a number of nonformal programs conducted for non-professional teachers have been successful in reducing the number of illiterates. National plans for mass secondary education are being implemented with the support of well-designed textbooks and teaching materials. Non-government institutions have also organised vocational skill training programs for pre-service and in-service teachers (World Bank, 2000a).

Sri Lanka has nearly 190,000 teachers in public sector primary, secondary and collegiate schools. Since the 1990s, it has faced the problem of a decline in the quality and efficiency of education, particularly in schools in the slums and rural areas. In spite of immense efforts in stepping up training programs in colleges and distance learning programs in nonformal institutions, the supply of teachers cannot keep pace with the demand and need, and the quality of education in general has declined. This is particularly apparent in Tamil-speaking schools where the shortage of teachers is more acute than Sinhala-speaking schools. The main reason for the decline is the fragmentation of the teacher education system in terms of policies, support and funding. Sri Lanka spends relatively little on education (3% of GNP and 10% of total public expenditure) by international (20% of total public expenditure) and even Asian standards (about 11–18% of public expenditure). Four different types of rather autonomous teacher training institutions with little regard to national needs and priorities manage the funds. The result is an oversupply of qualified Sinhalese teachers and a very short supply of trained Tamil teachers, Mathematics, Science and English teachers, and an inflexibility in teacher deployment particularly to so-called 'difficult' schools.

In order to improve the quality, equity and cost effectiveness of teacher education and to ensure a supply of quality teachers, the Sri Lanka Government has proposed certain initiatives which include: (a) consolidating smaller primary and secondary schools and eliminating the position of principal in schools with five teachers or less; (b) training all primary teachers to teach all subjects including English; (c) undertaking special recruitment of Tamil medium teachers on a contract basis; and (d) introducing a post-graduate Diploma in Education as an initial training course for an identified number of graduates annually prior to their employment as teachers (World Bank, 1996).

3.5. Singapore and Malaysia

Singapore and Malaysia are discussed as a cluster for two main reasons, namely, (a) their goals and policies of education are economic-driven, (b) their common sociocultural-historical background of the supporting infrastructure, especially the training agencies and institutions. Although the teacher recruitment and career development strategies have been quite different since Singapore left the Malaysian Federation in 1965, the two main reasons and the countries' close physical proximity and economic interdependence justifies the clustering.

The education systems in both Singapore and Malaysia are seen principally as engines for producing manpower, and where the policies and plans for the supply of teachers in both countries are economically motivated. As both economies move towards more value-added industries in the face of intense competition from other emerging Asian economies, there is increasing pressure for teachers to have a strong mastery of the disciplines that they teach, an ability to model higher-order thinking processes and work in multi-disciplinary teams, and leadership and communication skills needed in knowledge-based economies.

In order to ensure the quality of the teachers who will meet these challenges, academic qualification is still the main consideration. In both countries, their Ministries of Education (MOE) have always targeted to recruit the top one-third of each cohort from the university and 'A' level/SMTP graduate pool, and the academically stronger Polytechnic graduates in the case of Singapore. Usually, it is the university graduates who are trained to teach in and posted to secondary schools and the junior colleges. However, both ministries offer university graduates the option of being trained to teach in primary schools. On top of academic credentials, the teachers-to-be are also assessed in the following areas: aptitude and interest for teaching, communication skills and values. The selection process for teachers is stringent to ensure that quality is not compromised. In 1998, for example, the MOE of Singapore only selected 1,572 university graduates out of the 4,026 who applied. To augment the local graduate teacher pool, about 400 foreign teachers including Chinese language teachers, were recruited in 2000. As a result, the quality of teachers has been improving as the MOE (Singapore) is recruiting one out of every eight university graduates (Minister of Education's Speech in Parliament, 15 March 2001).

In the last decade, the supporting infrastructure in place for the professional development and networking of teachers in both Singapore and Malaysia has shifted away from a fragmented vision of discrete 'pre' and 'in' service training to one of professional development and networking as a continuum of 'initial education', 'induction' and 'in-service continuous professional development and networking'. Such a shift of paradigm in the infrastructure is characterised by "iterations between theory, practice and research; interaction between inductees and experienced mentors; feedback from in-service to initial education programs" (Delannoy, 2000, p. 11).

The initial education in the training institute provides the teachers with a basic toolkit that consists of a repertoire of skills and a conceptual framework to understand and organise these skills. As the basic training in the institutes cannot be expected to prepare the teachers fully to the basic level of competency to operate effectively in schools, an induction program is absolutely crucial. Moreover, the entry into the teaching profession may prove to be a traumatic experience for the young teacher, triggering many to dropout or become discouraged or cynical. In Singapore, the MOE has a centralised induction program conducted by the Teachers' Network for new teachers that is dedicated to providing vital information, survival tips, platforms for discussion and sharing among beginning teachers, and between beginning teachers and more experienced ones in face-to-face and electronic environments. In both Singapore and Malaysia, individual schools also have their own school-based induction training to enculturate the new teachers to their particular school culture and ethos.

Through much fine-tuning by the MOE and teachers' training agencies, the transition from initial teacher education to induction is moving towards being seamless. And this transition is also becoming seamless from induction to in-service continuous professional development and networking. The teachers in both countries have various opportunities to refresh constantly their skills and knowledge to keep up with the latest developments in education, both pedagogies and technologies. The MOE and the teachers' training institutions usually provide these opportunities. In Singapore, teachers are entitled to 100 hours of in-service training each year. Teachers are also fully sponsored or highly subsidised for courses, conducted by private training agencies that enhance their professional competence (Gopinathan & Sharpe, 2002).

In Singapore, the National Institute of Education (NIE), the sole teachers' training institute in the country, has established a set of Advanced Diploma and

Advanced Postgraduate Diploma programs to enable teachers to upgrade and keep up-to-date in their content knowledge of school subjects or state-of-the-art educational methods or technologies, guidance and counselling methods. These advanced diplomas then provide an alternative route for admission into the institute's bachelor's and master's degree programs. The teachers, however, can opt to sign up for individual modules in the program, and hence, having a wider choice of in-service continuing professional development. The advanced diplomas and their accreditation framework also ensure better articulated linkages between in-service and career paths of teachers by providing greater opportunities for serving teachers to upgrade to degree and postgraduate qualifications, even to doctoral level (Gopinathan, Ho, & Tan, 2001).

The teachers' training institutes in both countries have also focused on milestone training that allows teachers to acquire new skills, knowledge and networks to perform their new tasks as they move up the professional ladder. These highly intensive and executive-type programs are run to develop school leaders to operate with confidence and competence in the highly demanding school environment. Besides professional development programs, there are also teachers' networks in both countries that serve as a catalyst and support for teacher-initiated development through sharing, collaboration and reflection leading to self-mastery, excellent practice and fulfilment. The internet and intranet are mediating many of the teachers' network activities due to the sound technological infrastructure in both countries.

In Singapore, the Masterplan for IT in Education was launched in 1997 as a blueprint for the integration of IT in education as a strategy to meet the challenges of the twenty-first century. By 2001, all teachers in school have received at least 40 hours of basic ICT training and a large number of the teachers have learned to integrate IT into the curriculum and school administrators are all using ICT for administration, management and communication system-wide. In Malaysia, the Smart School Project was launched by the MOE in 1997 to prepare all schools to be electronically networked by 2010. The smart schools will continue to use the existing school curriculum but multimedia technology will be used to enhance the quality of teaching and learning. The MOE has since taken steps to develop courseware for Science, Mathematics, Bahasa Malaysia and English. 1,780 master teachers are trained in ICT, who in turn, will train 30,000 other teachers (Lee, 2002).

The instruments (teacher professional development and networking) to improve the supply of quality teachers have been quite similar in both Malaysia and Singapore. However, the recruitment strategies and outcomes are quite different. Singapore has been doing extremely well in its recruitment of teachers due to its recruitment efforts and the introduction of new career paths for teachers. Over the last five years, the MOE has recruited an average of about 2000 trainee teachers per year and it intends to maintain that over the next decade to compensate for retirement and attrition. The recruitment efforts involve intensive media publicity campaigns to increase public awareness of teaching as a challenging and rewarding career, and targeting mid-career candidates (both graduates and non-graduates).

Moreover, the MOE in Singapore has recently introduced more rewarding career paths for teachers under the Education Service Professional Development and Career Plan (Edu-Pac). This plan allows teachers opportunities to develop and climb the professional ladder according to their interests, abilities and aspirations. The Edu-Pac has three main components: a new career structure, recognition structure and enhancements to the performance management system. It offers three career paths that the teachers can choose: the teaching track, leadership track or senior specialist track. It also strengthens the link between pay and performance through its career and recognition structures. Consequently, the recruitment outcome of quality teachers has been much more encouraging in Singapore than Malaysia.

4. TRENDS, ISSUES, AND THE FUTURE

In comparing the supply and demand of quality teachers for the education of a rapidly increasing population in the vast Asia-Pacific region, several trends and issues have emerged. The increasing emphasis on the strategic role of teacher education as a means of upgrading the workforce and indirectly developing the economy and building the nation has been recognized by some Asia-Pacific countries. Deliberate and systematic planning and formulation of sound educational policies by the federal governments, as well as the wise and appropriate application of technology in terms of systems and methods, software and hardware have hastened the pace of the preparation and supply of quality teachers as in Japan, Malaysia and Singapore. Extending the length of training and upgrading the quality of teacher education might also have improved the quality of teacher supply. Other recruitment measures including raising teachers' salaries and improving teachers' working conditions have played an important part in Australia, Japan, Korea, New Zealand and Singapore.

However, the rigid regulation of teacher education by the state and the central government within the context of a rapidly expanding market economy as is the case in China has hampered the recruitment and development of quality teachers. To meet the huge demand for teachers at all levels of schooling, the Chinese State Commission has to resolve the policy dilemma of maintaining strict control over teacher education and encouraging self-sufficiency and diversification of teacher education institutions, in addition to taking more drastic measures to boost the morale and social status of teachers in order to attract the young and keep the older people in the teaching profession.

Increasing the use of ICT for learning and teacher development seems to be one of the emerging trends in sustaining the supply of quality teachers to meet with the needs and challenges of an information age and knowledge economy. Another trend is the increasing partnership between the training institutions and the government in the recruitment and development of quality teachers as in

Singapore, Hong Kong and Taiwan which deploy education and ICT more and more for both training and nation building purposes.

REFERENCES

APEID-UNESCO (1990). *Innovations and Initiatives in Teacher Education in Asia and the Pacific region, Volume 1: Overview and Volume 2: Case Studies*. Bangkok: UNESCO.
Chinese Educational Development and Research Center. (2000). *Green Paper on Education in China*. Beijing: Educational Scientific Publishing Co.
Delannoy, F. (2000). *Teacher Training or Lifelong Professional Development: Worldwide Trends and Challenges*. TechKnowLogia, Nov/Dec, pp. 10–13.
Gopinathan, S., & Sharpe, L. (2002). The teacher is the key: Professionalism and the strategic state. In Elwyn Thomas (Ed.), *Teacher Education: Dilemmas and Prospects*. World Yearbook of Education 2002. London: Kogan Page.
Gopinathan, S., Ho, W. K., & Tan, J. (2001). Teacher education and teaching in Singapore: Recent trends. *Asia-Pacific Journal of Teacher Education and Development*, June 1999, 2(1), 3–14.
Lake, J., & Williamson, J. (2000). Australia. In P. Morris & J. Williamson (Eds.), *Teacher Education in the Asia-Pacific Region – A Comparative Study*. New York and London: Falmer Press.
Lee, M. N. N. (2002). Teacher education in Malaysia: Current issues and future prospects. In E. Thomas (Ed.), *Teacher Education: Dilemmas and Prospects*. World Yearbook of Education 2002. London: Kogan Page.
Leung, J. Y. M., & Hui, X. (2000). People's Republic of China. In P. Morris & J. Williamson (Eds.), *Teacher Education in the Asia-Pacific Region – A Comparative Study*. New York and London: Falmer Press.
Looi, C. K. (2001). Regional Editorial: IT programs and policies in the Asia-Pacific region. *Journal of Computer Assisted Learning, 17*, 1–3.
Malaysia 5 Year Plans 1981–2000.
Ministry of Education, China. www.education, cn, 2000.
Ministry of Education, India. www.education, nic.In, 2001.
Morris, P., & Williamson, J. (2000). *Teacher Education in the Asia-Pacific Region – A Comparative Study*. New York and London: Falmer Press.
Muller, J. (1998). The well-tempered learner: Self-regulation, pedagogical models and teacher education policy. *Comparative Education, 34*(2), 177–193.
Preston, B. (2000). *Teacher Supply and Demand to 2005 – Projections and Contexts*. Canberra: Australian Council of Deans of Education.
Ramsey, P. D. K. (2000). New Zealand. In P. Morris & J. Williamson (Eds.), *Teacher Education in the Asia-Pacific Region – A Comparative Study*. New York and London: Falmer Press.
School Council (1990). *Australia's Teachers: An Agenda for the Next Decade*. Paper prepare by the School Council for the National Board of Employment Education and Training.
Sachs, J. (1997). Reclaiming the agenda of teacher professionalism: An Australian experience. *Journal of Education for Teaching, 23*(3).
Sato, M., & Asanuma, S. (2000). Japan. In P. Morris & J. Williamson. (Eds.), *Teacher Education in the Asia-Pacific Region – A Comparative Study*. New York and London: Falmer Press.
UNESCO (1997). *World Guide to Higher Education: A Comparative Survey of Systems, Degrees and Qualifications*. Paris: UNESCO.
UNESCO (2000). *Statistics 2000*. Paris: UNESCO.
World Bank (1996). *Staff Appraisal Report: Democratic Socialist Republic of Sri Lanka for A Teacher Education and Teacher Deployment Project*. Washington, DC: World Bank.
World Bank (2000a). *Bangladesh: Education Sector Review Volume 1*. Dhaka: The University Press.
World Bank (2000b). *Reports on Education, 1990–2000*. Washington, DC: World Bank.

SECTION 6:

ORGANISATION AND MANAGEMENT OF EDUCATION

Section Editor – Yin Cheong Cheng

63

Organisation and Management of Education: Development and Growth

YIN CHEONG CHENG, MAGDALENA MO CHING MOK and KING W. CHOW

Centre for Research and International Collaboration, Hong Kong Institute of Education, Hong Kong

1. INTRODUCTION

In the last few decades in the Asia-Pacific region and other parts of the world, education was clearly assumed to be the key for economic, social and political developments, and was thus expanded quickly (Fullan, 1998; Lieberman, 1998). Given the limited resources and various kinds of contextual constraints, inevitably there are dilemmas and tensions in the efforts of expanding education systems, financing the increasing educational provision, ensuring the accountability of educational services to the public and improving the effectiveness of learning and teaching during the growth of educational services in the Asia-Pacific countries. Particularly in response to the challenges of globalisation, information technology, international competitions, knowledge-based economy and fast societal developments in the new millennium, more and more issues in educational management, organisation and provision have been raised for discussion, debate and research (Chapman, Sackney, & Aspin, 1999). Since the 1990s, there has been numerous educational reforms launched in nearly all countries in the Asia-Pacific region (Cheng & Townsend, 2000). The various waves of education reforms (Cheng, 2001a) have induced a lot of changes in different aspects of organisation and management of education.

Based on the findings and observations from numerous country reports and policy documents of Australia, Japan, Hong Kong, Republic of Korea, Malaysia, mainland China, New Zealand, the Philippines, Thailand, Vietnam, Lao, Taiwan, India and Indonesia in the past five years, some main trends of educational reforms in the Asia-Pacific region have been identified by Cheng (2001b) and Cheng and Townsend (2000), as shown in Table 1. At the macro-level, the main trends include 'towards re-establishing new national vision and education aims'; 'towards restructuring education system at different levels'; and 'towards market-driving, privatising and diversifying education'. At the meso-level, 'towards parental and community involvement in education and management' is an important

Table 1. Trends of educational reform and key issues of administration and organisation of education in the Asia-Pacific region

Levels	Trends of education reform in the region	Key issues in organisation and management of education in the region	Chapters and contributors in this section
Operational level	• Towards paradigm shift in learning, teaching and assessment • Towards using information technology in learning and teaching and applying new technologies (such as development planning and strategic management) in management	• How can management and organisation of education provide sufficient and appropriate support to facilitate teaching and learning and enhance their relevance to the future?	• To be explored and addressed by the articles
Site-level	• Towards ensuring education quality, standards and accountability • Towards decentralisation and school-based management • Towards enhancement of teacher quality and continuous lifelong professional development of teachers and principals	• How to ensure quality, effectiveness and accountability of educational services to the diverse aims, expectations and demands at the individual and society levels • How to decentralise authority and maximise the flexibility and efficiency in using resources to solve problems and meet the diverse needs at the site-level • How to develop leadership and strengthen human resources for better educational services in such a fast changing and challenging environment	• Quality assurance and school monitoring: by M. Mok et al. • Effective schooling in cultural contexts: by C. Dimmock • Decentralisation and self managing school: by B. Caldwell • School leadership and management: by A. Walker • Leadership development and training: by P. Hallinger • Staffing in school education: by Y.H. Kim

(Continued)

Table 1 (Continued)

Meso-level	• Towards parental and community involvement in education and management	• How to manage and facilitate various kinds of participation and partnership to support educational services and practices	• Family and community participation: by I.W. Pang et al.
Macro-level	• Towards re-establishing new national vision and education aims • Towards restructuring education systems at different levels • Towards market-driving, privatising and diversifying education	• How to re-develop or re-structure education systems to face up with the challenges in the new century • How to plan, expand and manage education systems and provision to meet the changing and increasing demands • How to finance and resource various educational provision and services in a more fair and efficient way	• Development of public and private education: by R. Koo et al. • Policy-making, planning, and change: by A. Wagner and P. Hui • Financing education: by M. Bray

trend. At the site-level, there are also some salient trends, such as 'towards ensuring educational quality, standards and accountability'; 'towards decentralisation and school-based management'; and 'towards enhancement of teacher quality and continuous lifelong professional development of teachers and principals'. At the operational level, the main trends include 'towards using information technology in learning and teaching and applying new technologies in management'; and 'towards paradigm shift in learning, teaching and assessment'.

How the growth of educational services echoes these trends of educational reforms and provides sufficient and appropriate support to facilitate teaching and learning and enhance their relevance to the future becomes a core concern in the field of organisation and management of education. Parallel to each trend of educational reform at the site-, meso- and macro-levels, there may be different implications and issues for organising and managing of educational services, as shown in Table 1.

At the site-level, the key issues for educational management may include the following:

- how to ensure quality, effectiveness and accountability of educational services to the diverse aims, expectations and demands at the individual and society levels (Adams & Kirst, 1999; Goddard & Leask, 1992);
- how to decentralise authority and maximise the flexibility and efficiency in using resources to solve problems and meet the diverse needs at the site-level (Caldwell & Spinks, 1998; Murphy & Beck, 1995); and
- how to develop leadership and strengthen human resources for better educational services in such a fast changing and challenging environment (Bush & Coleman, 2000).

At the meso-level of educational institutions or schools, how to manage and facilitate various kinds of participation and partnership to support educational services and practices is a key concern (Wang, 2000). And at the macro-level, people are concerned with the issues, such as how to re-develop or re-structure education systems to face up with the challenges in the new century; how to expand and manage education systems and provision to meet the changing and increasing demands; and how to finance and resource various educational provision and services in a more fair and efficient way (Cheng, Ng, & Mok, 2002).

Given the large scope of trends in educational reform and the complexity of the aforementioned issues in the field of organisation and management of education, there is an urgent need to pursue a wide range of educational research for supporting the ongoing policy debate and practice in the Asia-Pacific region (Cheng & Townsend, 2000). The articles included in this section of the *Handbook* are part of collective efforts to start the analysis and review of the various complex issues in the growth of educational services with a focus on organisation and management of education in the region.

At the site-level, there are six articles reviewing the various issues in quality assurance and school monitoring, effective schooling in cultural contexts, decentralisation and the self-managing school, school leadership and management, leadership development and training and staffing in school education in some countries of the region. At the meso-level, one article addresses the issues and perspectives in family and community participation in school education in the region. At the macro-level, there are three chapters focusing on the issues of the development of public and private education, the concerns in policy-making and planning when expanding education and the efforts and dilemmas in financing educational services.

In facing the complexity, multiplicity and huge coverage of issues in development, reform and growth of educational services in the Asia-Pacific region, this *Handbook* of eight sections is just a start to providing an overview of key observations on some important aspects of organisation and management of education at different levels in the Asia-Pacific region. With the collective efforts in this *Handbook*, we believe, more research and review will be encouraged and promoted to broaden and deepen the understanding of crucial issues in this region such that policy development, educational management and reform in the region or individual countries will be advanced.

2. ISSUES OF ORGANISATION AND MANAGEMENT AT SITE-LEVEL

As discussed above, the development, reform and growth of educational services should be aimed at supporting and facilitating the processes of learning and teaching at the operational level and ensuring their relevance to the future needs of individuals and the society. Clearly, how to organise and manage education at the site-level to support learning and teaching in the classroom inevitably becomes a direct and important concern. As shown in Table 1, there are six chapters reviewing the issues of educational management and organisation at the site-level.

2.1. *Quality Assurance and School Monitoring*

To ensure quality, effectiveness and accountability of educational services and practices at the site-level in order to meet the planned educational aims, the diverse expectations and needs of multiple stakeholders at both the individual and society levels are now core functions of educational management in many countries in the Asia-Pacific region. The article (see *Quality Assurance and School Monitoring*), prepared by Mok, Gurr, Lee, Izawa, Mel, Palmer, Shan, Knipprath and Zhang, examines the quality assurance (QA) processes and mechanisms in Australia, Hong Kong, Japan, Korea, New Zealand, Papua New Guinea, Singapore and Taiwan.

The authors report the emergence of a clear trend in the eight education systems: there is now an increasing emphasis on process monitoring, with this emphasis reflecting a move away from either the input model or the input-output model toward an input-process-output model. Other trends that have emerged in the region and are identified by the authors include decentralisation of QA mechanisms; internationalisation of QA systems; increasing emphasis on teacher quality and reform in teacher education; more reform in the public examination systems; attaining enhanced openness and transparency; the increasing use of multidimensional indicators for QA on process and output of educational institutions; and the establishing of designated offices for QA and funding for research and development in education quality.

According to the authors, the efforts expended to ensure educational quality in these eight national systems have been impressive. Nevertheless, a number of issues and barriers still exist, with remedial policy actions awaiting, which include the needs for having better alignment between education aims and QA focus; for neutralising oppositions from the government and key parties; for gaining obvious effect of initiatives on student learning; and for satisfying an urgent need for capacity building for effective, efficient, valid and reliable QA processes.

To draw implications, the authors highlight the challenges ahead: better alignment between educational aims and QA focus must be made; what is expected to be measured and what is actually being measured must be made to coincide; external and internal reviews have to be aligned; government expectations and stages of school development must be made compatible; the methods for monitoring and expertise support given to schools must come hand-in-hand; and the effort spent on the review exercise and expected outcomes must be aligned.

2.2. Effective Schooling in Cultural Contexts

Since the 1990s, there has been a strong worldwide movement of pursuing school effectiveness through various initiatives at the site-level. The International Association for the Evaluation of Educational Achievement (IEA) studies have also stimulated a lot of concerns and debates about how to improve the practice of school processes for enhancing students' achievements and about the impacts of cultural factors on the effectiveness of school practices. In order to give a more comprehensive discussion of school processes within the Asia-Pacific context, Dimmock focuses on effective schooling in his article (see *Effective Schooling in the Asia-Pacific Region*). Specifically, the article explores the meanings attached to effective schooling in four systems of education within the Asia-Pacific region: mainland China, Hong Kong, Japan and Taiwan, which are generally dominated by the Confucian heritage culture, with effective schooling seen as a culturally-sensitive and contextually-based phenomenon. Dimmock points out that the relationship between effective schooling and cultural context can be framed in terms of four propositions: a close harmony and alignment with family and home values; an inordinate emphasis on homework and examination success; systems of teaching, learning and school organisation that are reflective of, and are adapted to, deep-seated societal values and cultural environments; and teaching conditions and teacher professional development that is highly conducive to effective teaching.

Dimmock's discussion also sheds lights on the issues of research. He notes that empirical studies on effective schooling in the Asia-Pacific region are relatively few, and there are the needs to chart a future research agenda. For example, rigorous and systematic comparative studies are needed in order to take full account of cultural contexts and influences. Related to this is also the need to conduct in-depth, small-scale case studies that compare schools operating in different cultural contexts. Further, as Dimmock pointed out, there is also a need for comparative studies that adopt a holistic approach which would encompass cultural values transmitted by parenting, socialisation and the home, the curriculum, teaching and learning, and school organisation and leadership. To Dimmock, the deployment of this approach is important as schooling is influenced by the aforementioned factors, and thus omitting any of them in the studies would make acquiring a complete picture difficult.

2.3. Decentralisation and the Self-Managing School

School-based management (SBM) has become an important international trend of school management reform since late 1980s, with emphasis on decentralisation to the site-level and maximising flexibility and efficiency in using resources to solve problems and satisfy the diverse needs at the site-level (Cheng, 1996). In the article (see *Decentralisation and the Self-Managing School*) on decentralisation and the self-managing school, Caldwell reviews the scale of change in the patterns of centralisation and decentralisation around the world, and then gives an account of the developments of self-managing schools in Australia, Hong Kong, Indonesia, Thailand and New Zealand.

With particular reference to an international comparative study conducted in association with the Third International Mathematics and Science Study (TIMSS), Caldwell finds the current developments as follows. First, there is now a robust body of theory on learning in self-managing schools. Second, many governments have stopped conducting experiments on 'self-governing schools' while the notion of 'self-managing schools' has been maintained and extended. Third, the trend of decentralisation in the form of self-managing schools is irreversible. Fourth, the expectations for schools to establish the link between the school reform program and learning outcomes for students are becoming more explicit in policy-makers' preference. Finally, researchers are utilising an increasingly sophisticated array of techniques for the analysis of data to generate meaningful findings for documenting program effectiveness, with effectiveness measured particularly in terms of student learning outcomes.

The major implications identified by Caldwell are that, first, further change may be more by nature professional than structural, with the creation of organisations on a national or sub-national scale to set standards and provide accreditation and certification for educators whose roles have already been profoundly changed by decentralisation: for example, for teachers, teaching as a profession is becoming research-based, outcomes-oriented, service-driven and team-focused, and teachers are now expected to focus on student learning outcomes; for school leaders, self-management is in essence mainly about the management of learning, and they are now accountable for students' learning outcomes. Second, what is needed is further research that focuses on the nature of decentralisation as manifested in the form of the operation of self-managing schools; on factors that hinder or facilitate the implementation of change; and on impact on learning outcomes of students and on the professional lives of teachers and school leaders.

2.4. School Leadership and Management

In such a fast changing educational environment, educational institutions have to face a lot of internal and external challenges and uncertainties. Whether in the Asia-Pacific region or in other parts of the world, educational leaders are often perceived as the key actors mobilising their institutions and members at the site-level to face up with those challenges and make educational services and provision more quality effective and accountable (Cheng, 2002). Walker focuses on school leadership and management in his article (see *School Leadership and Management*). He outlines the common threads that run through the general reform environment in the Asia-Pacific region, revealing that all school principals in different countries must operate within multiple contexts that influence the role that school principals are expected to play. Then, Walker reports that the current policies on decentralisation and school-based management place tremendous demands on school principals to change. He highlights some of the ways in which the principalship is changing within the context of decentralisation and how a reshaping of the role of the principal is becoming inevitable.

Finally, Walker discusses three major challenges that need to be faced if principals are to reshape meaningfully their role in line with current reforms: the first challenge is the degree of fit between reform components and the societal culture and context within which they are implemented; the second challenge to the meaningful reshaping of the principalship is the lack of preparedness and professional support provided to principals; and the third challenge is about how decentralisation and other reforms have or have not been implemented to encourage a meaningful reshaping of the principalship.

Walker highlights that the processes, relationships and functions related to the principalship have been neglected by the educational research enterprise. It is therefore important that researchers help to develop a better understanding of the work of principals and of the ways principals promote and cope with change. To Walker, the job awaiting is thus the development of mid-range theories about various aspects of the principalship, with the theory-building studies conducted to explore fully the different cultures and contexts that exert a powerful influence on principals.

2.5. School Leadership Development

Parallel to the challenges to principalship in a changing environment is the development and training of educational leaders in the Asia-Pacific region. In the article (see *School Leadership Development*) on leadership development, Hallinger reviews the recent trends in the development of school leadership in Malaysia, Thailand, Singapore and Hong Kong. Three questions guide the analysis of his article: 'What do we know about principal effectiveness and how does this knowledge base transfer to the Asian context of schooling?' 'What trends have emerged in school leadership development in East and South-East Asia over the past decade?' 'What are emerging issues and directions for practice and research in school leadership development in this area of the Asian region?'

Hallinger's review of the trends in school leader preparation in East and South-East Asia furnish a basis for generating several recommendations for practice in school leader preparation and development. The first recommendation is that new globally-derived, research-based findings, as well as indigenous craft knowledge about teaching and learning and leading schools, should be considered legitimate subjects for learning among prospective and practising school leaders. Second, the changing knowledge base and context for school leadership have turned lifelong learning into a fundamental facet of the professional role of school leaders and thus continuous professional development must be considered normal and inevitable. Third, one of the foci in the process of leadership development should be on the problems that school leaders face in their work. Fourth, the use of new knowledge and skills by school leaders requires a flexible combination of on-site coaching and networks of support in schools. Finally, professional development of school leaders must be contextualised so that the development is compatible with and relevant to the educational change at the macro-level.

2.6. Staffing in School Education

As reflected in the trends of educational reforms, enhancement of teacher quality and continuous professional development of teachers are crucial concerns to be attended to if educational practices and services at the site-level are to be effectively carried out. The article (see *Staffing in School Education*) prepared by Kim examines the issues of teacher supply and demand, recruitment, career ladder and promotion, performance standards and appraisal of teaching personnel in Japan, Korea, New Zealand and Singapore.

The author has identified the following trends. First, the imbalance between teacher supply and demand is a common problem in many Asia-Pacific countries, with the problem caused by non-rational teacher policy or the changing demographic structure in the four countries. Second, the countries have tried to diversify the employment status of teachers and to encourage people at different ages with diverse experience to become teachers through diverse paths. Third, under the assumption that teachers could excel when a rational system is established to assess teacher competence and evaluate their performance, efforts have been expended in the four countries to develop and refine teachers' performance standards for implementing the merit-based compensation system. Fourth, efforts have been expended to institutionalise more career ladders in the classroom teaching job category so as to encourage competent teachers to devote themselves to teaching. And fifth, the staffing system in school education has to be restructured on the basis of merits and to enhance openness and flexibility.

On the research side, Kim finds that various policy studies which tackle staffing issues in school education have been conducted in the four countries. All of those studies, which tend to employ simultaneously various research methods, are in essence policy-oriented research. Further, those studies tend to employ a comparative perspective to examine four or five foreign country cases in order to draw implications for reform or improvement in the respective country. Based on the findings, it is possible to draw an important implication that, while various countries are already making efforts to rationalise their policy on staffing in school education, particularly by making their policy research more comparative and more methodologically rigorous, there is still the need to take a proactive perspective such that staffing policy formulation and reformulation could be made more relevant to future development of the countries within a context of globalisation and information technology.

3. ISSUES OF ORGANISATION AND MANAGEMENT

All the site-level, management and operation of education are within a larger social context; at work within the context are the factors at the meso- and macro-levels. In other words, how the organisation and management at these two higher levels can facilitate and support the development of educational practices at the site-level is also important and necessary in the review of the growth of educational services in the Asia-Pacific region.

3.1. *Family and Community Participation*

At the interface between educational institutions and the society, family and community participation in education has received growing attention in the last decade in the Asia-Pacific region. How to manage and facilitate various kinds of participation and partnership to support educational services is often one of the key concerns in educational management. The article by Pang and others (see *Family and Community Participation in Education*) focuses on family and community involvement in school education, which is important for inducing positive learning outcomes in children. The authors provide an overview and then examine the unique features of the family and community participation in Australia, Hong Kong, Japan, Korea and Papua New Guinea. In order to guide the analysis, the authors employ a refined Epstein's typology of school-family-community partnership, including such components as parenting and learning at home, communicating, volunteering and collaborating with the community and decision-making.

The authors have noted that observable in the various countries examined in the article are unique trends since each country has its own socio-economic and cultural properties influencing the values and practices of family and community involvement. For example, the role of parents in supporting children' education at home remains a prominent feature in such Confucian influenced regions as

Hong Kong, Japan and Korea while, in contrast, family efforts are supported by professionals in Australia. The authors have nonetheless identified some general trends. First, in these Asia-Pacific region countries, there has been an increased concern over family and community participation. Second, there is now an expectation that parents should play a greater role in the schooling of their children. And third, there is an increased comprehensiveness of the school-to-home communications.

In view of the diversity and variety of the approaches to and patterns of family and community involvement in the Asia-Pacific region, the authors draw some key research implications. First, in most of the countries examined, there is the need to have surveys conducted to provide an overview of the perceptions and practices of various actors in family and community involvement in school education. And second, there should be more focused studies on the specific mechanisms that contribute to the enhancement of meaningful family and community participation in relation to educational reform.

3.2. Public and Private Education

At the macro-level, the development of education systems including public and private education to meet the growth needs of educational services is necessary. The article (see *Public and Private Education*) prepared by Koo, Yung, Ip and Chuang is on the development of public and private school education in some areas of the Asia-Pacific region. The article has four parts in which the authors examine various aspects of public and private education in mainland China, Taiwan, Hong Kong and Macao. In the analysis, the authors pay particular attention to some fundamental questions about the provision, scope and orientation of public and private education within the socio-economic and political contexts of these societies.

In order to provide a conceptual framework for guiding the analysis, the authors give a description of the main features of educational provision in the public and private sectors. The authors then examine some of the forces that have shaped public and private school education in the four societies that are deeply rooted in the Confucian ethical values, before turning to the comparisons of these particular systems. The authors report that there are some remarkable similarities and differences in the provision of public and private education in the four systems. For example, there is: (a) common concern for equality, effectiveness, diversification and autonomy; (b) public education has been a successful endeavour for the four societies, while the proportion of youngsters successively completing their education in the private sector has increased rapidly during the past two decades; and (c) the increase of private schools generates the issues of inequality and elitism.

In view of the similarities and differences in the provision of public and private education in the four systems, the authors underscore that ongoing and further research through a comparative perspective is much needed to ascertain the dynamics of the current changes and to give an account of how and why parents and their children would reap the benefits of private or public education. The authors also note that another relevant area of future research is the possibility of using vouchers as a means to, on the one hand, facilitate parents and their children in their making of their educational choice and, on the other hand, meet the costs of attending private or public schools.

3.3. *Educational Policy-Making, Planning and Change*

Given the rapidly changing environment of education and various challenges from local and global contexts, educational policy-making and planning are inevitably necessary to ensure the provision of educational services at different levels, appropriately and promptly responding to the emerging demands at both the individual and society levels. Wagner and Hui examine in this article (see *Policy-Making, Planning and Change in Tertiary Education*) the perspectives, trends and research on policy-making, planning and changes in education. The authors explore in greater detail the planning and policy approaches accompanying the development of tertiary education policy in Japan, Korea and Australia in order to identify and document emerging and newly reinforced directions for policies arising out of the current challenge for growth.

The authors identify some current trends. First, with the emergence of what is referred to as a 'new managerialism', the trend to decentralise or to devolve some elements of planning, decision-making and administration has been reinforced. Thus, planning activities at all levels of decision-making in education and in various agencies outside or within ministries of education can be observed. Second, popularly employed is the market-based approach, reflecting the advancement of a neo-liberal view that tertiary education generates returns to individual students and thus reliance on the market mechanism is justifiable. And third, the current policy approaches pay more attention to the clear specification of the desired educational results and, as a result, policies now tend to place a premium on the skills and competences to be acquired by individual students as evidenced in the adoption of standards, detailed curriculum guidelines and assessments.

In view of the three trends of devolution of planning and policy, demand-driven planning and policy and outcome-based policies and monitoring, the authors use the Australian, Japanese, and Korean cases to highlight three key policy considerations: (a) the shift from a supply-led (government) to a demand-driven (market) mechanism shapes policy responses and effects; (b) a dilemma present in the context of expansion of tertiary-level education is formulating and implementing policies that not only support and drive development but are flexible and responsive to the program diversity in order to accommodate demands from society and individual students; and (c) in the continuous development of capacities at the institutional level to set standards and to enhance quality assurance. These three key policy considerations together demand further in-depth comparative research on the linkages among appropriate policy actions and the realisation (or not) of clearly identified policy goals.

3.4. Financing Education

The provision of educational services and practices consumes various types of resources. But within the constraints of resources, how to finance a wide range of educational services and initiatives at different levels is often perceived as the core issue of organisation and management of education in the Asia-Pacific region. The article (see *Financing Education in Asian and Pacific Countries*) prepared by Bray focuses on the sources of financing for education in the Asia-Pacific region. Bray examines issues relating to financing formal education at all levels. Bray begins the discussion by pointing out that governments are the dominant sources of finance for education, in addition to other important sources, including households, communities and private entrepreneurs. Bray then elaborates on the forms of cost-sharing in education, particularly noting the roles of fees and community financing. To Bray, the features of educational financing in Asia and the Pacific show both diversity and commonality: while a quick look may give the impression that diversity is an obvious feature, a more thorough review would point to the fact that commonalities can be found throughout the region.

Bray's analysis reveals a number of common themes. First, throughout the region, the role of the state in financing education is now under review while non-government actors are expected to play a more prominent role. The advance of the market economy, even in such countries as China, Laos and Vietnam, which are officially socialist states, has brought some convergence within the region. Second, students' paying fees for the education they received has become a generally accepted feature, especially at the tertiary level. In some countries, the fee-charging policy is extended to the level of primary schooling; and effective schemes for grants and loans may not be in place to help alleviate the hardship created by the policy. This development leads to the raising of major questions of equity, as well as questions about the scale of taxation, and in turn the government resources available for education and other activities. Third, external aid is also significant in many countries in the region, where a major source of finance for education is estimated. And fourth, to be handled in the educational finance domain are not only educational issues but political issues as well, with the coping of the latter requiring more than professional education and financial knowledge and experience.

4. CONCLUSION

Organisation and management of education in the Asia-Pacific region as a field of practice and research to support the development and growth of educational services is changing very rapidly in response to the challenges from numerous educational reforms in an era of globalisation, knowledge-based economy and international competition. From the trends in the region as discussed in the preceding pages, we can find that some important issues and implications emerge for appreciating how management and organisation of education should change and for supporting the development, reform and growth of educational services and practices in the Asia-Pacific region (see Table 1).

The ten articles in this section of the *Handbook* provide a review of the developments in different aspects of organisation and management of education in the region and furnish a basis for drawing implications for research and further development. At the site-level, quality assurance and school monitoring, effective schooling, decentralisation and the self-managing school, school leadership and management, leadership development and training, as well as staffing in school education are the key areas of concern for supporting and developing effective educational practices, such as teaching and learning at the individual or group level. There are six articles covering the various issues in these areas.

At the meso- and macro-level, there are four articles reviewing the various issues in the management of family and community participation, development of public and private education, and policy-making and planning as well as financing education. Clearly how the initiatives and practices at these two levels can contribute to the development and growth of educational services at the site-level or operational-level is inevitably a key concern for organising and managing education.

From the observations of these ten chapters, it is clear that the macro- and meso-environment of education will shape the nature, scope and quality of educational provision and practices at the site-level that will consequently influence in significant ways the effectiveness, quality and relevance of educational output at the operational level. Of course, it is not surprising that the nature and quality of outputs from the educational practices at the operational and site levels may finally produce feedback to or impact on the development of policy factors and initiatives at the meso- and macro-level. In other words, there is a need to examine how the various developments at different levels are interrelated, and how their interrelatedness would affect the development, growth and effectiveness of educational provision and services to meet the increasing but diverse demands of individuals and the societies. Future research with this orientation is likely to generate findings that can give a more comprehensive picture of the causes and consequences of the various issues in organisation and management of education in a context of numerous ongoing education reforms in the Asia-Pacific region.

Given the diversity and variety of the socio-economic and political values of the many countries in the region, there are inevitably differences in how educational issues are to be coped with and how research is to be pursued in the field of organisation and management of education. The articles in this section represent an important intellectual endeavour to review the complex issues in the development, reform and growth of educational provision and services in the Asia-Pacific region. This collective effort will be a significant first step to start a long journey for understanding and preparing effective organisation and management of education to meet the challenges in the new century in the Asia-Pacific region.

REFERENCES

Adams, J. E., & Kirst, M. W. (1999). New demands and concepts for educational accountability: Striving for results in an era of excellence. In J. Murphy & K. S. Louis (Eds.), *Handbook of Research on Educational Administration* (2nd ed.) (pp. 463–490). San Francisco: Jossey-Bass.

Bush, T., & Coleman, M. (2000). *Leadership and Strategic Management in Education.* London: Chapman.

Caldwell, B. J., & Spinks, J. M. (1998). *Beyond the Self-Managing School.* London: Falmer Press.

Chapman, J. D., Sackney, L. E., & Aspin, D. N. (1999). Internationalization in educational administration: Policy and practice, theory and research. In J. Murphy & K. S. Louis (Eds.), *Handbook of Research on Educational Administration* (2nd ed.) (pp. 73–97). San Francisco: Jossey-Bass.

Cheng, Y. C. (1996). *School Effectiveness and School-Based Management: A Mechanism for Development.* London: Falmer Press.

Cheng, Y. C. (2001a). *Education Reforms in Hong Kong: Challenges, Strategies, & International Implications.* Plenary speech presented at the International Forum on Education Reform: Experiences in Selected Countries, Bangkok, Thailand.

Cheng, Y. C. (2001b). *Educational Reforms in the Asia-Pacific Region: Trends, Challenges and Research.* Paper presented at the Second IAPED International Conference on Education Research, Seoul National University, Seoul, Korea.

Cheng, Y. C. (in press). The Changing context of school leadership: Implications for paradigm shift. In K. Leithwood, J. Chapman, D. Corson, P. Hallinger & A. Hart (Eds.), *International Handbook of Research in Educational Leadership and Administration.* Dordrecht: Kluwer Academic Publishers.

Cheng, Y. C., Ng, K. H., & Mok, M. M. C. (2002). Economic considerations in educational policy making: A simplified framework. *International Journal of Educational Management, 16*(1), 18–39.

Cheng, Y. C., & Townsend, T. (2000). Educational change and development in the Asia-Pacific region: Trends and issues. In T. Townsend & Y. C. Cheng (Eds.), *Educational Change and Development in the Asia-Pacific Region: Challenges for the Future* (pp. 317–344). Lisse: Swets and Zeitlinger Publisher.

Fullan, M. (1998). The meaning of educational change: A quarter of a century of learning. In A. Hargreaves, A. Lierberman, M. Fullan & D. Hopkins (Eds.), *International Handbook of Educational Change* (pp. 214–228). Dordrecht: Kluwer Academic Publishers.

Goddard, D., & Leask, M. (1992). *The Search for Quality: Planning for Improving and Managing Change.* London: Chapman.

Lieberman, A. (1998). The growth of educational change as a field study: Understanding its roots and branches. In A. Hargreaves, A. Lierberman, M. Fullan & D. Hopkins (Eds.), *International Handbook of Educational Change* (pp. 13–22). Dordrecht: Kluwer Academic Publishers.

Murphy, J., & Beck, L. G. (1995). *School-Based Management as School Reform: Taking Stock.* Thousand Oaks, CA: Corwin Press.

Wang, Y. (Ed.) (2000). *Public-Private Partnership in the Social Sector.* Tokyo: Asian Development Bank Institute.

64

Decentralisation and the Self-Managing School

BRIAN J. CALDWELL
University of Melbourne, Australia

1. INTRODUCTION

In this article, decentralisation refers to the systematic and consistent delegation to the school level of authority and responsibility to make decisions. Decentralisation to the school level is often referred to as school-based management or local management or self-management. Self-management is used here. The creation of regional units of administration within national or sub-national jurisdictions may involve decentralisation of authority and responsibility to such units but, in most instances, it is referred to as a 'de-concentration' or 'dispersion' of authority and responsibility from a central location rather than a transfer of authority and responsibility from one level of government to another.

The starting point is a description of the scale of change in patterns of centralisation and decentralisation around the world. Then follows a definition of self-management and an account of developments in the Asia-Pacific region, commencing with nations that have made significant progress, namely, Australia, Hong Kong and New Zealand, followed by short accounts of interest and intentions in other places, illustrated by Indonesia and Thailand. The evidence of impact on learning is assessed, with particular reference to an international comparative study conducted in association with the Third International Mathematics and Science Study (TIMSS) and case study research that maps the link to learning in Victoria, Australia. While the critics of decentralisation are acknowledged, the long-term prognosis is that decentralisation in the form of self-managing schools is likely to be irreversible. The article concludes that further change may be more professional than structural, with the creation of organisations on a national or sub-national scale that set standards and provide accreditation and certification for educators whose roles have been changed profoundly by decentralisation.

2. SCALE OF CHANGE

Decentralisation and the building of systems of self-managing schools have been major components in educational reform in nations in the Asia-Pacific region for several decades. At the same time, almost paradoxically, a higher level of centralisation has been sought for some functions, and national and international frameworks have emerged. Together, these two developments were included in a list of so-called 'megatrends' that were evident on a broader international scale in the early 1990s. Writing in the future tense to indicate that momentum was building in each instance, Caldwell and Spinks (1992) included the following in a list of ten megatrends in school education.

1. There will be a powerful but sharply focused role for central authorities, especially in respect to formulating goals, setting priorities, and building frameworks for accountability.
2. National and global considerations will become increasingly important, especially in respect to curriculum and an education system that is responsive to national needs within a global economy.
3. Within centrally determined frameworks, government [public] schools will become largely self-managing, and distinctions between government and non-government [private] schools will narrow.

Three other megatrends highlighted concern about quality, the dispersion of education, and the nature of learning. These shaped the nature of work in systems of education that were, at the same time, more centralised and more decentralised.

4. There will be unparalleled concern for the provision of a quality education for each individual.
5. There will be a dispersion of the educative function, with telecommunications and computer technology ensuring that much learning that currently occurs in schools or in institutions of higher education will occur at home and in the workplace.
6. The basics of education will be expanded to include problem solving, creativity and a capacity for lifelong learning and re-learning.

Four further megatrends of a societal nature have been identified.

7. There will be an expanded role for the arts and spirituality, defined broadly in each instance; there will be a high level of 'connectedness' in the curriculum.
8. Women will claim their place among the ranks of leaders in education, including those at the most senior levels.
9. The parent and community role in education will be claimed or reclaimed.
10. There will be unparalleled concern for service by those who are required or

have the opportunity to support the work of schools. (Caldwell & Spinks, 1992, pp. 7-8)

By the late 1990s, these megatrends were more sharply focused, and it became difficult to identify any nation that was not moving along tracks of educational reform. Caldwell and Spinks (1998) identified three tracks.

Track 1: The building of systems of self-managing schools;
Track 2: An unrelenting focus on learning outcomes; and
Track 3: Creating schools for the knowledge society.

The notion of 'tracks' conveyed the image of all nations moving in each of these directions, but differing in the distance each has moved.

Particular attention is given in this article to movement on the first track ('building systems of self-managing schools'), with a self-managing school defined by Caldwell and Spinks (1988, pp. 4-5) in the following terms:

A self-managing school is a school in a system of education to which there has been decentralised a significant amount of authority and responsibility to make decisions related to the allocation of resources within a centrally determined framework of goals, policies, standards and accountabilities. Resources are defined broadly to include knowledge, technology, power, material, people, time, assessment, information and finance.

3. REVIEW OF DEVELOPMENTS IN SELECTED SYSTEMS

Attention is given in this section to developments in five education systems, namely, Australia, New Zealand, Hong Kong, Indonesia and Thailand.

3.1. *Australia*

Australia is a federation of six states and two territories. The constitution of the nation assigns to the states and territories the responsibility to make laws on education, but the national government has considerable power because of its capacity to raise funds and make grants. All states have created regional units of administration. As far as decentralisation is concerned, there has been a steady shift to self-management in Australia since the early 1970s, with South Australia and then the Australian Capital Territory making the first moves, followed by Tasmania and Victoria. A major thrust was made in Victoria in the 1980s but momentum was lost toward the end of the decade, when New South Wales took up the running until the early 1990s when resistance to further change was evident. Victoria then achieved dramatic change from 1993 with its landmark Schools of the Future program, first under the reforming Kennett Liberal National Government and then referred to as 'enhanced self-management' when the Bracks Labor Government was elected in 1999. Queensland stepped forward in 1998 with its Leading Schools program, continuing without a label with a change in government at the end of the decade. South Australia recaptured its early leadership in the field from 1999 with its Partnerships 21 program that has many similarities to what has been achieved in Victoria. There has been steady but incremental change through this period in Tasmania and the Northern Territory. Western Australia has a relatively modest program in local management.

What has been achieved in Victoria is noteworthy in many respects, accounting for international interest in reform since the early 1990s. By 2001, about 94 per cent of the state's school education budget was decentralised to the school level in what are known as 'school global budgets'. A curriculum and standards framework covers all years of primary and secondary schooling. Schools have the capacity to select their own staff members who are employed by the state government. An accountability framework provides for annual and triennial reporting. A mechanism that gives a high degree of coherence to arrangements is the school charter, a document of about 20 pages that sets out the distinctive nature of the school and the manner in which it addresses system and local priorities. The charter has a life of three years, and the triennial review is intended to guide the writing of the next charter. A similar reform is under way in South Australia under the title of Partnerships 21 (Spring, 2001).

3.2. New Zealand

After Victoria, and to a lesser extent, South Australia, the most comprehensive reform in the region with a decentralisation theme may be found in New Zealand, a nation with a unitary system of government. There are no states or territories. Regional units of administration have been weak or non-existent. Decentralisation or self-management followed a review of the administration of the public school systems in 1988, the same year as the Education Reform Act in Britain called for the introduction of local management of schools. These reforms on opposite sides of the globe are often bracketed together in a critical sense as illustrations of a market approach to the reform of school education. In New Zealand, a high level of self-management followed the scaling down of the Education Department and the creation of a national curriculum and standards framework. The so-called 'bulk funding' of schools to cover staff, as achieved in the 'school global budget' in Victoria, did not achieve a critical mass and was abandoned with the election of the Clark Labour Government in 2000. It is noteworthy that, as in Victoria, little momentum was lost with change of government in New Zealand, with the initial reform set in train by the Lange Labour Government, with extension by the Bolger National Government, and a minimal scale back by the Clark Labour Government.

3.3. Hong Kong

There have been important developments in Hong Kong, a former British colony before 1997 and a Special Administrative Region (SAR) of China afterwards, with the concept of the self-managing school helping to shape the School Management Initiative (SMI) that got under way in the early 1990s following a review of the public sector. The education system has a form of district administration. Only about eight per cent of Hong Kong's approximately 1,200 schools are government schools, with the rest in the aided sector, owned by a range of foundations, trusts, churches and private organisations. All receive substantial funding from the government. There are very few truly private schools. Under the SMI, a larger proportion of government grants was decentralised to schools for local decision-making. By 1998, barely 200 schools had volunteered to join the scheme, with most of these being government schools. The Education Commission, established in 1984 to make recommendations on educational policy, called for full implementation of school-based management by 2000 but, significantly, proposed that it be integrated with a range of practices in pursuit of quality schooling for all (Education Commission, 1996). By 2001, Hong Kong was characterised by literally hundreds of school-based schemes for enhancing the quality of schooling, resourced by the substantial Quality Education Fund established after Hong Kong became an SAR.

3.4. Indonesia

United Nations Educational, Scientific and Cultural Organization (UNESCO) and United Nations International Children's Emergency Fund (UNICEF) (UNESCO-UNICEF, 2001) are supporting an interesting approach to decentralisation in Indonesia under the title 'Creating Learning Communities for Children'. Four initiatives were combined in a pilot project conducted in 79 schools in three provinces (Central Java, East Java and South Sulawesi), including the introduction of a limited form of self-management, with a small budget for each school; professional development for teachers; encouragement of parents and other members of the community to support their schools; and most important, changes to learning and teaching under the theme 'active joyful effective learning'.

3.5. Thailand

An ambitious reform in decentralisation is under way in Thailand following the passing of the National Education Act in 1999 (Office of the National Education Commission [ONEC], 1999). Section 39 states that:

> The Minister shall decentralise powers in educational administration and management regarding academic matters, budget, personnel and general affairs administration directly to the Committees and Offices for Education, Religion and Culture of the educational service areas and the educational institutions in the areas.

Section 40 provides that:

In each institution providing basic education and [also] at lower-than-degree level, there shall be a board supervising and supporting the management of the institution. The board shall be comprised of representatives of parents; those of teachers, community and local administration organisations, alumni of the institution, and scholars. A pilot project in 2001 involved 250 schools.

4. THE IMPACT OF DECENTRALISATION ON LEARNING OUTCOMES

An important issue in every nation where decentralisation has been a feature of educational reform is the extent to which there has been an impact on learning. On an international scale, it is sobering to note the consistent finding in early research that there appeared to be few if any direct links between local management, self-management or school-based management and learning outcomes (Malen, Ogawa, & Krans, 1990; Summers & Johnson, 1996). Some researchers have noted that such gains are unlikely to be achieved in the absence of purposeful links between capacities associated with school reform, in this instance, self-management, and what occurs in the classroom, in learning and teaching and the support of learning and teaching (see Cheng, 1996; Hanushek, 1997; Smith, Scoll, & Link, 1996; Organisation for Economic Co-operation and Development [OECD], 1994).

Research of the kind cited above can now be seen as constituting the first generation of studies of self-management, and that second and third generations of studies are now discernible. It is in the third generation that the nature of the linkage between self-management and learning outcomes can be mapped in a manner that can be trustworthy in policy and practice.

4.1. *The Inconclusive Nature of the Linkage in First and Second Generation Studies*

Findings in the first two generations were largely inconclusive in respect to impact on learning. Summers and Johnson (1996) provided a meta-analysis of the first generation of research. They located 70 studies that purported to be evaluations of school-based management, but only 20 of these employed a systematic approach and just seven included a measure of student outcomes. They concluded that

> there is little evidence to support the notion that school-based management is effective in increasing student performance. There are very few quantitative studies, the studies are not statistically rigorous, and the evidence of positive results is either weak or non-existent. (Summers & Johnson, 1996, p. 80)

Apart from the "overwhelming obstacles" in the way of assessing impact, Summers and Johnson drew attention to the fact that few initiatives identify student achievement as a major objective. The focus is on organisational processes, with virtually no attention to how process changes may affect student performance. (Summers & Johnson, 1996, pp. 92–93)

In a report on the effects of school resources on student achievement, Hanushek (1997) drew attention to the finding "that simply decentralising decision-making is unlikely to work effectively unless there exist clear objectives and unless there is direct accountability" (p. 156). It is the absence of this framework that characterises the context for what are described here as first generation studies.

The second generation of studies accompanied the more far-reaching reforms in self-management, with most of the available budget in a school system decentralised to the local level within a comprehensive and centrally determined curriculum, standards and accountability framework. In general, the findings were as inconclusive as those from the first generation.

4.2. *Specifying the Links in the Third Generation of Studies*

A third generation of studies emerged in the late 1990s. The policy context was the same as for the second generation, with three important differences marking this generation of study. First, by the late 1990s, a substantial set of data on student achievement had been established as a result of system-wide tests that enabled change at the local level to be tracked over several years. Schools were also able to draw on an increasingly deep pool of other indicators. Second, the policy framework had become more explicit with respect to expectations for schools to make the link between elements in the school reform program and learning outcomes for students. This reflected change on Track 2 ("an unrelenting focus on learning outcomes") in the classification of Caldwell and Spinks (1998). Third, researchers were utilising an increasingly sophisticated array of techniques for analysis of data, including structural equation modelling, along with more focused approaches to case study

Third International Mathematics and Science Study. The most comprehensive study of learning outcomes that explored the impact of decentralisation is the Third International Mathematics and Science Study (TIMSS). Several nations in the Asia-Pacific region participated, including Australia, Hong Kong, Japan, Republic of Korea, New Zealand and Singapore. Information was gathered on a range of factors, including: (a) student and family characteristics, (b) resources and teacher characteristics, (c) institutional settings including the extent of centralisation in examinations, (d) distribution of responsibilities between centre and schools, (e) teachers' and parents' influence in decision-making, and (f) extent of competition with independent private schools and incentives for students. Analysis of the performance of more than 260,000 students from 39 countries was undertaken at Kiel University in Germany and reported by Woessmann (2001). Regression analysis yielded interesting findings:

They show that institutions strongly matter for cross-country differences in students' educational performance, while increased resource inputs do not contribute to increased performance. Controlling for indicators of parents' education levels and resource inputs, three indicators of institutional features of the education system have strong and statistically significant effects on country-level student performance. Increased school autonomy in supply choice and increased scrutiny of performance assessment lead to superior performance levels, and a larger influence of teacher unions in the education process leads to inferior performance levels. Together, the variables explain three quarters of the cross-country variation in mathematics test scores and 60 per cent of the variation in science test scores, whereas previous studies which focused on family and resource effects explained only up to one quarter of the cross-country variation in student performance tests. (Woessmann, 2001, p. 6)

Woessmann (2001) suggested that nine features are favourable to student performance:

- central examinations,
- centralised control mechanisms in curricular and budgetary affairs,
- school autonomy in process and personnel decisions,
- an intermediate level of administration performing administrative tasks and educational funding,
- competition from private educational institutions,
- individual teachers having both incentives and powers to select appropriate teaching methods,
- limited influence of teacher unions,
- scrutiny of students' educational performance, and
- encouragement of parents to take an interest in teaching matters.

There are some important observations to make about the list. First, "centralised control mechanisms in curricular and budgetary affairs" refers to centrally determined frameworks, not to the manner of implementation at the school level. In the case of the budget, this refers to the existence of a funding mechanism that specifies how funds shall be allocated to schools; schools then determine how these funds are deployed at the local level. Second, Woessmann (2001) is cautious about the findings on the influence of teacher unions. It is important to record his caution, because the matter is contentious (see Steelman, Powell, & Carini, 2000) for findings that suggest unions have a positive impact on educational performance). He notes that the indicator of influence in the study might serve as a "proxy for the effect of a standard salary scale as opposed to merit differentials in teacher pay" (p. 81).

This international study provides evidence on an international comparative scale of the efficacy of approaches such as school-based management, local management or self-management that are set in a centrally determined framework.

Schools of the Future in Victoria. The nature of the linkages between a capacity for self-management and the achievement of improved learning outcomes for students became clearer in studies conducted in Victoria, Australia, in the late 1990s. Research was carried out in the Schools of the Future program from 1992 to 1999. The objectives and purposes of the reforms in Victoria in the 1990s in the Schools of the Future (SOF) program range over educational ("to enhance student learning outcomes", "actively foster the attributes of good schools"); professional ("recognise teachers as true professionals", "allow principals to be true leaders"); community ("to determine the destiny of the school, its character and ethos"); and accountability ("for the progress of the school and the achievement of its students").

Successive surveys in the Cooperative Research Project (1994, 1995a, 1995b, 1996, 1997, 1998) consistently found that principals believed there had been moderate to high level of realisation of the expected benefit in respect to improved learning outcomes for students. In the final survey in 1997, 84 per cent gave a rating of 3 or more on the 5-point scale (1 is "low" and 5 is "high"). As in the second generation of studies, such findings do not illuminate the issue of the extent to which the capacities fostered by the reform impact on learning outcomes. Structural equation modelling using LISREL 8 (Jöreskog & Sörbom, 1993) was employed in the analysis of data in the 1995, 1996 and 1997 survey. The effects reported here derive from the 1997 survey (Cooperative Research Project, 1998).

The first step was to create seven variables derived from 45 survey items. These were concerned with attitude to the reform (Confidence in the Attainment of Schools of the Future Objectives), support (Curriculum and Standards Framework Curriculum Support) and outcomes (Curriculum and Learning Benefits, Curriculum Improvement due to the Curriculum and Standards Framework, Planning and Resource Allocation Benefits, School and Community Benefits, and Personnel and Professional Benefits). Three variables have a direct effect on Curriculum and Learning Benefits, which includes improved learning outcomes for students. These are Personnel and Professional Benefits (which reflects ratings for realisation of the expected benefits of better personnel management, enhanced professional development, shared decision-making, improved staff performance, more effective organisation following restructure, increased staff satisfaction and an enhanced capacity to attract staff); Curriculum Improvement due to CSF (which reflects ratings for improvement of capacity for planning the curriculum, establishing levels and standards for students, moving to a curriculum based on learning outcomes and meeting the needs of students); and Confidence in Attainment of SOF Objectives.

Noteworthy are the pathways of indirect effects, which may be illustrated by the effect of Planning and Resource Allocation Benefits, that is mediated in respect to its effect on Curriculum and Learning Benefits through Personnel and Professional Benefits and Confidence in Attainment of SOF Objectives. Expressed in another way, realising the expected benefits of better resource management, clearer sense of direction, increased accountability and responsibility, greater financial and administrative flexibility and improved long-term planning will have no direct effect on Curriculum and Learning Benefits, but will have an indirect effect to the extent they impact on Personnel and Professional Benefits, which in turn have a direct effect on Curriculum and Learning Benefits. Also noteworthy are the variables that have direct effects on Confidence in Attainment of SOF Objectives. High ratings of confidence were associated with high ratings for the achievement of Planning and Resource Allocation Benefits, School and Community Benefits and CSF Curriculum Support. The likely explanation is that unless principals experience benefits in these last three domains, they are unlikely to have confidence in the reform.

The findings in these surveys are limited to the extent that they are based on the perceptions of principals rather than measures of student achievement. This has been a concern in most efforts to determine the impact of reform in recent years. In the case of the Cooperative Research Project (1998), there was no system-wide base-line data on student achievement when the reform was implemented. Case studies in Victoria (Wee, 1999) helped illuminate the links under conditions where principals' report improved learning outcomes. Were the linkages evident in the model confirmed in deep on-site investigations in particular schools where improvement is claimed? The research design in both studies thus started with schools where principals made such a claim. The first task was to test the validity of these claims, drawing on evidence in the particular schools selected for study. The second task was to seek explanations for how such improvement occurred and then to match it against the linkages or pathways described above.

The study was conducted in four schools in late 1997, when the pool of indicators was well developed and a substantial body of evidence was available to test claims of improved learning outcomes. Findings revealed that schools could cite evidence that their efforts had led to improved outcomes for students. They drew on many sources of data in recognising improved student learning in their schools. This illustrated the capacity being developed in the system to gather information about the performance of schools. Maps of direct and indirect links were prepared for each school using the rigorous approach to data collection, data display and data reduction for qualitative research proposed by Miles and Huberman (1994). These maps show how school capacity associated with being a School of the Future had led to improved outcomes for students. Actions at the school level that had a direct impact on student learning are in the domains of professional development, implementation of the curriculum and standards framework and monitoring. The impact of resource allocation is indirect, mediated through curriculum, professional development, monitoring and staffing.

4.3. *Self-Managing Schools in Developing Nations*

The world-wide trend to self-management is further illustrated by initiatives in developing nations, supported by international aid agencies, including the World

Bank, UNESCO and UNICEF. UNESCO hosted a forum in Paris in February 2001 that provided an opportunity for the sharing of experiences in recent years. It is likely that some of the best evidence of the impact of self-management on learning outcomes may come from these settings. An explanation lies in the manner in which self-management has been linked to learning. This is illustrated in the UNESCO-UNICEF project in Indonesia described earlier. This involved the introduction of a limited form of self-management, with a small budget for each school; professional development for teachers; encouragement of parents and other members of the community to support their schools; and most important, changes to learning and teaching under the theme 'active joyful effective learning'. Improvement on key indicators such as student attendance and learning outcomes was documented (UNESCO-UINCEF, 2001) for most of the 79 schools within 12 months of commencement.

5. THE CRITICS OF DECENTRALISATION

Several critiques of decentralisation, as defined in this article, were mounted in the early years of reform, especially when local management or self-management was part of a package of reforms introduced by conservative, market-oriented governments in Australia (the Kennett Liberal-National Government and Schools of the Future in Victoria from 1993), Britain (the Thatcher Conservative Government and the 1988 Education Reform Act), and New Zealand (the Bolger National Government in the 1990s but also its predecessor Labour Government). Among the critics were Smyth (1993), Blackmore, Bigum, Hodgens and Laskey (1996), and Whitty, Power and Halpin (1998). Evidence was generally drawn from very small numbers of schools relatively early in the respective reforms, with the main thrust of the argument based on a perceived connection between the introduction of self-management and the creation of a market in school education (for a counter argument, see Caldwell and Spinks (1998) and Caldwell (1999)).

The criticisms of self-management have been muted in recent years, especially as successors to the governments listed above extended the reform, notably in the case of the Bracks Labor Government in Victoria (with 94 per cent of the State's school education budget now decentralised for local decision-making) and the Clark Government in New Zealand. Like the Blair Government in Britain in 1997, these governments abandoned experiments in what was referred to as 'self-governing schools' but maintained and extended the notion of 'self-managing schools'. Powerful criticisms of continuing efforts at reform are still mounted, but these tend to focus on other issues, including levels of resourcing, curriculum and standards frameworks and matters related to public and private schooling.

6. PROGNOSIS

Attention in the early years of the twenty-first century is turning to what may initially be seen as a consequence of decentralisation, but is in fact a concomitant of reform on the three tracks described at the outset ('building systems of self-managing schools', 'an unrelenting focus on learning outcomes' and 'creating schools for the knowledge society'). Effort on the three tracks is now integrated in efforts to create a stronger connection between the different dimensions of the education reform agenda and learning outcomes at the level of the individual student. This has meant that large-scale professional development programs for principals, other school leaders and teachers in general have concentrated on state-of-the-art approaches to learning and teaching. A noteworthy example in several educational systems, particularly Australia and New Zealand, is in the area of literacy in the early years of schooling, often leading to dramatic improvements in student achievement. System-wide professional development programs have attracted thousands of teachers. With self-management, schools have substantial control of the budget and many design their own programs to supplement those at the system level. The major implication of these developments is that teachers need to learn about learning. For school leaders, self-management is mainly about management of learning. They are accountable for the outcomes.

Teaching is becoming research-based, outcomes-oriented, service-driven and team-focused in much the same way as medical practice. It is a development that parallels decentralisation in the form of the self-managing school, with the most powerful driver being the 'unrelenting focus on learning outcomes'. There is interest in several education systems in the establishment of professional bodies that will set standards, accredit preparation and professional development programs and certify membership in an educational parallel to what already exists in the medical profession. There are likely to be counterparts in these nations to the establishment in Britain of the General Teaching Council and the National College for School Leadership. In Victoria, Australia, for example, there is an Institute of Teaching that incorporates a College of Principals.

The prognosis for reform is that further change may be more professional than structural, with the creation of organisations on a national or sub-national scale that set standards and provide accreditation and certification for educators whose roles have been changed profoundly by decentralisation. Further research is needed on the nature of decentralisation as it is manifested in self-managing schools; factors associated with successful and unsuccessful implementation of change; and impact on learning outcomes and the professional lives of teachers and their leaders.

REFERENCES

Blackmore, J., Bigum, C., Hodgens, J., & Laskey, L. (1996). Managed change and self-management in schools of the future. *Leading and Managing, 2*(3), 193–204.

Caldwell, B. J. (1999). Market, choice and public good in school education. *Australian Journal of Education, 43*(3), 257–272.

Caldwell, B. J., & Spinks, J. M. (1988). *The Self-Managing School.* London: Falmer Press.

Caldwell, B. J., & Spinks, J. M. (1992). *Leading the Self-Managing School.* London: Falmer Press.

Caldwell, B. J., & Spinks, J. M. (1998). *Beyond the Self-Managing School.* London: Falmer Press.

Cheng, Y. C. (1996). *School Effectiveness and School-Based Management: A Mechanism for Development*. London: Falmer Press.
Cooperative Research Project (1994). *Base-Line Survey*. Report of the Cooperative Research Project on Leading Victoria's Schools of the Future, Directorate of School Education, Victorian Association of State Secondary Principals, Victorian Primary Principals Association, The University of Melbourne (Fay Thomas, Chair) [available from Department of Education, Employment and Training].
Cooperative Research Project (1995a). *One Year Later*. Report of the Cooperative Research Project on Leading Victoria's Schools of the Future, Directorate of School Education, Victorian Association of State Secondary Principals, Victorian Primary Principals Association, The University of Melbourne (Fay Thomas, Chair) [available from Department of Education, Employment and Training].
Cooperative Research Project (1995b). *Taking Stock*. Report of the Cooperative Research Project on Leading Victoria's Schools of the Future, Directorate of School Education, Victorian Association of State Secondary Principals, Victorian Primary Principals Association, The University of Melbourne (Fay Thomas, Chair) [available from Department of Education, Employment and Training].
Cooperative Research Project (1996). *Three Year Report Card*. Report of the Cooperative Research Project on Leading Victoria's Schools of the Future, Directorate of School Education, Victorian Association of State Secondary Principals, Victorian Primary Principals Association, The University of Melbourne (Fay Thomas, Chair) [available from Department of Education, Employment and Training].
Cooperative Research Project (1997). *Still More Work to be Done But ... No Turning Back*. Report of the Cooperative Research Project on Leading Victoria's Schools of the Future, Department of School Education, Victorian Association of State Secondary Principals, Victorian Primary Principals Association, The University of Melbourne (Fay Thomas, Chair) [available from Department of Education, Employment and Training].
Cooperative Research Project (1998). *Assessing the Outcomes*. Report of the Cooperative Research Project on Leading Victoria's Schools of the Future, Department of Education, Victorian Association of State Secondary Principals, Victorian Primary Principals Association, The University of Melbourne (Fay Thomas, Chair) [available from Department of Education, Employment and Training].
Education Commission (1996b, March). *The Education Commission Report No. 6* [Online]. Available: Http://www.info.gov.hk/ed/english/resource/education_documents/download/ecr6_e_2.PDF [2000, October 26].
Hanushek, E. A. (1997). Assessing the effects of school resources on student performance: An update. *Educational Evaluation and Policy Analysis, 19*(2), 141–164.
Jöreskog, K. G., & Sörbom, D. (1993). *LISREL 8: User's Reference Guide*. Chicago: Scientific Software, Inc.
Malen, B., Ogawa, R. T., & Krans, J. (1990). What do we know about site-based management: A case study of the literature – A call for research. In W. Clune & J. Witte (Eds.), *Choice and Control in American Education Volume 2: The Practice of Choice, Decentralisation and School Restructuring* (pp. 289–342). London: Falmer Press.
Miles, M. B., & Huberman, A. M. (1994). *Qualitative Data Analysis: An Expanded Sourcebook* (2nd edn). Thousand Oaks, CA: Sage Publications.
OECD, Directorate of Education, Employment, Labour and Social Affairs, Education Committee (1994). *Effectiveness of Schooling and of Educational Resource Management: Synthesis of Country Studies*. Points 22–23, Paris: OECD.
ONEC (1999). *National Education Act of B. E. 2542 (1999)*. Bangkok: ONEC.
Smith, M. S., Scoll, B. W., & Link, J. (1996). Research-based school reform: The Clinton administration's agenda. In E. A. Hanushek & D. D. Jorgenson (Eds.), *Improving America's Schools: The Role of Incentives* (Paper 2, pp. 9–27). Washington, DC: National Academy Press.
Smyth, J. (1993). *A Socially-Critical View of the Self-Managing School* (pp. 417–466). London: Falmer Press.

Spring, G. (2001). *Frontline Services and the New Economy: Schools as the Units of Innovation.* Presented at the Policy Network Education Workshop on the theme 'Frontline Services: Unleashing the Energy', British Council, London, September 2001, published as No. 109 of the Seminar Series, IARTV (Incorporated Association of Registered Teachers of Victoria), December. (This paper is available from IARTV, 82 Jolimont Street, Jolimont, Victoria 3002).

Steelman, L. C., Powell, B., & Carini, R. M. (2000). Do teacher unions hinder educational performance: Lessons learned from state SAT and ACT scores. *Harvard Educational Review,* 70, 4.

Summers, A. A., & Johnson, A. W. (1996). The effects of school-based management plans. In E. A. Hanushek & D. W. Jorgenson (Eds.), *Improving America's Schools: The Role of Incentives* (Paper 5, pp. 75–96). Washington, DC: National Academy Press.

UNESCO-UNICEF (2001). *Creating Learning Communities for Children.* Report of an evaluation of a pilot project in decentralisation conducted by UNESCO, UNICEF and the Government of Indonesia (B. J. Caldwell, Chair). Djakarta: UNESCO.

Wee, J. (1999). *Improved Student Learning and Leadership in Self-Managed Schools.* Unpublished thesis for the degree of Doctor of Education, University of Melbourne.

Whitty, G., Power, S., & Halpin, D. (1998). *Devolution and Choice in Education: The School, the State, and the Market.* Buckingham: Open University Press.

Woessmann, L. (2001). *School Resources, Educational Institutions, and Student Performance: The International Evidence,* Kiel Institute of World Economics, University of Kiel (available at http://www.uni-kiel.de/ifw/pub/kap/2000/kap983.htm). This paper was presented at the annual conference of the Royal Economic Society, Durham, April 9–11, 2001.

65

Quality Assurance and School Monitoring

MAGDALENA MO CHING MOK[1], DAVID GURR[2], EIKO IZAWA[3], HEIDI KNIPPRATH[4], LEE IN-HYO[5], MICHAEL A. MEL[6], TERRY PALMER[7], WEN-JING SHAN[8], ZHANG YENMING[9]

1. INTRODUCTION

Responding to the rapid development of new knowledge, new technology and globalisation, education quality, quality assurance and school monitoring are key policy issues in many countries around the world, particularly those in the Asia-Pacific region (Cheng & Townsend, 2000). Quality in education can be defined in a number of ways, including the fitness of educational outputs for use (Juran & Gryna, 1988); the achievement of the mission and goals (Crosby, 1979; Mukhopadhyay, 2001); adding values to students or institutes (Saunders, 1999); continuous improvement (Deming, 1986); excellence, exceptional or high standard (Gaither, 1998); lack of defects (Crosby, 1979); and satisfying the needs and expectations of strategic constituencies (Cheng & Cheung, 2001; Crosby, 1979). Quality in education is multifaceted and multidimensional (Cheng & Cheung, 2001) and is described by some as a dynamic positive concept (Mukhopadhyay, 2001). One of the consistent features of concern with quality has been the establishment of quality assurance and school monitoring systems.

Quality assurance (QA) can take on many approaches. Stanley and Patrick (1998) classified QA systems into 'self-regulating', ' externally regulated' and a 'mixture of the two' according to whether the process is regulated by the institutes, imposed by an external agency or is a combination of both. The orientation of the QA systems can be disposed towards surveillance by identifying

---

[1] *The Hong Kong Institute of Education, Hong Kong*
[2] *University of Melbourne, Australia*
[3] *Asian Development Bank, Manila, The Philippines*
[4] *University of Twente, The Netherlands*
[5] *Korean Education and Development Institute, Seoul, Korea*
[6] *University of Goroka, Papua and New Guinea*
[7] *National Taiwan Normal University, Taipai, Taiwan*
[8] *National Taiwan Normal University, Taipai, Taiwan*
[9] *National University of Singapore, Singapore.*

areas of weaknesses or alternatively, towards improvement through cooperative strategies between the government and schools. Many countries follow the 'loose-tight coupling' approach (Tse, 2000) whereby schools are given autonomy on school-based decisions, while at the same time the government closely monitors school quality. Whichever approach has been taken, there are pitfalls in the QA processes. A number of researchers (e.g., Fuller, 1989) have highlighted the importance of finding a balance between accountability (i.e., the pressure for change) and improvement (i.e., the support of change).

This article presents the QA processes of eight education systems in the Asia-Pacific region, based on national reports compiled by the authors from analysis of available documents and research reports. The systems included are Australia, Hong Kong, Japan, Republic of Korea, New Zealand, Papua New Guinea (PNG), Singapore and Taiwan. Three questions have guided discussions in this chapter: What are the QA models practised in the Asia-Pacific educational systems? What are QA trends that have emerged in these systems? What are the issues and barriers faced by these systems in QA of school education? For each country the QA processes of the dominant educational system have been reviewed. It is hoped that through analysing these eight cases, learning can be shared about the conceptions, processes and mechanisms of QA of school education, ultimately contributing to further the development of quality education in the region and elsewhere.

2. QUALITY ASSURANCE FRAMEWORK

Visscher (1999) identified three meanings of control, namely, describing what should be done (input control), monitoring whether it has been done (process control) and checking the results (output control). According to this conception, QA frameworks can be broadly classified into the 'Input Model', 'Input-Output Model' and 'Input-Process-Output Model' according to whether the inclination is towards prior control (both prior and output control) or control over input, process and output.

Understandably, such classification can only be approximations as there are many variants of these models. For instance, before its recent education reforms in 1993, Japan followed an Input QA model (Nakadome, 1999). Japan used to exercise stringent prior control over the education budget, teacher quality, curriculum and textbook, making sure that everything was uniform and highly satisfactory before the system began to function.

1.1. Input-Process-Output Model

The Input-Process-Output model is characterized by a set of QA mechanisms, usually in the form of QA cycles at each of the input, process and output stages of the education process. It is a common model either currently practised or moving towards being practised by several systems in the Asia-Pacific region, including Australia, Hong Kong, Japan, Korea, New Zealand and Singapore.

Input QA generally includes the central quality control of teachers, centralized resources allocation and centralised curriculum. Process QA is typically in form of school self-review complemented by external review. Output QA commonly takes the form of system-wide testing of student learning in literacy, numeracy and other curriculum subject areas at key stages.

Perhaps one of the most elaborate Input-Process-Output QA systems is the Singapore School Excellence Model (SEM), practised by Singapore schools since 2000. The SEM framework comprises the 'Enablers', which are critical processes impacting on educational outcomes, and the 'Results', which are what the school has achieved or is achieving. SEM emphasises both processes and outcomes, and it looks at outcomes beyond students' academic performance (Ministry of Education, Singapore, 2001).

3. NEW DEVELOPMENTS

As revealed in the previous analysis, a major development on QA of school education in the region is moving towards the adoption of various nuances of the Input-Process-Output model with process and output monitoring taking prominence. Several other trends have emerged in the region including:

- decentralisation of QA mechanisms,
- internationalisation of QA systems,
- emphasis on teacher quality and reform in teacher education,
- reform in the public examination systems,
- enhanced openness and transparency,
- the use of multidimensional indicators for process and output QA,
- designated offices for QA and funding for research and development, particularly that pertaining to education processes.

3.1. *Decentralization*

QA in the region can be classified into 'centralised', 'decentralised' (or 'partnership') and 'autonomous' systems. In a centralised system, exemplified by Papua New Guinea, Japan and Korea, the government undertakes school reviews which are often inspectorial (school audit for Korea) in nature, with aims to ensure compliance so that schools implement the curriculum and assessment according to government policy directives. The Inspections and Guidance Division of National Department of Education (NDOE) in Papua New Guinea is responsible for the appraisal of teachers and school administrators on matters relating to promotions and continuity of service. School inspections are compulsory and inspectors may visit a school three to four times in one year. In Korea, school audits by the central government has replaced school inspections since 1995 using models developed by the Korean Educational Development Institute (KEDI). Evaluation results are linked with administrative and financial support to encourage greater accountability in accordance with recommendations by the Education Reform Committee. In Japan, external monitoring of schools comprises: (a) school review aiming at providing advice in the form of regular school visits by an ex-teacher who works for the education board (*shidou shuji*); and (b) external monitoring (*gaibu hyouka*) performed by higher education institutions. External monitoring is referred to as evaluation by people of the community (including parents) at lower education levels.

The decentralised or partnership system, comprising a double-loop with both external review (usually in a 3 to 5-year cycle) by the government and internal review (usually annually) according to strong directives from the government, is a significant trend to have emerged in the region. It has many variants in Asia-Pacific systems (e.g., Australia, Hong Kong, New Zealand and Singapore) but they share in common the characteristics of: (a) greater autonomy of local authority and schools; (b) more reflection of local needs; (c) stronger partnership between the government and schools; (d) increased accountability of schools; (e) more transparency of decision making processes; (f) a shift from emphasis on input to process and output; and (g) the use of reviewers or auditors instead of inspectors. In the region, decentralisation manifests in the form of school-based management and the use of both external review and internal school-based review in the QA process.

Australia and New Zealand are the frontiers of implementing school-based management in the region (Caldwell & Spinks, 1988, 1998). The most decentralised example is that of the State of Victoria (Gurr, 1999) where a school self-review and external verification process is used. Schools are required to have a school charter (a three-year planning document in which schools indicate their own educational plans and priorities within government guidelines) and report on school progress annually. Every three years schools are required to prepare a school self-assessment, summarising the school performance over the past three years. The school self-assessment is monitored through an independent external verification process.

The New Zealand Education Act of 1989 requires all schools to have a Board of Trustees for developing a school charter, comprising a set of goals for the school that drives its operation and translates the Government's guidelines and initiatives into reality, in consultation with the school community. The charter is the basis of the Government funding through which school education can take into account priorities of the local community. The school Board of Trustees must report annually to the stakeholders and this involves both the community and the Ministry of Education.

School-based management was fully implemented in Hong Kong in 1997, drawing upon experiences from the earlier School Management Initiative implemented in 1991 (Cheng, 2000). In Singapore, the SEM framework (Ministry of Education, Singapore, 2001) is a full-fledged school-based management model for school self-evaluation and improvement. Although currently Japanese schools do not have much autonomy for individual development plans, several education boards and their allied research centres have written evaluation criteria recently for schools to experiment with self-evaluation (Kenkyuujo, 2000a, 2000b; Yaosaka, 2001).

Examples of autonomous QA systems are found in the private school system of Australia, Hong Kong, New Zealand and Taiwan whereby government inspection is generally only to ensure that they are *bona fide* schools (e.g., curriculum plans, qualified staff, adequate buildings, satisfaction of fire regulations etc.).

3.2. Internationalisation of QA Systems

To face up to challenges of globalisation and advancements in information and communication technology, QA in Asia-Pacific education systems has taken on stronger international features in recent years. It is now common practice for governments to encourage collaboration with overseas educational institutes; engage international consultants in policymaking; host international conferences to facilitate input from overseas experts; make use of quality standards developed overseas; maintain Ministry of Education (MOE) web-sites to facilitate international exchange and participate in system-wide international assessment and evaluation exercises.

In Australia, internationally recognised QA systems are evident in some states. The two most common systems are the International Schools Council and ISO 9000. Both provide detailed and prescriptive self-assessment tools and the opportunity for external monitoring of progress. In some states, schools can substitute these programs (e.g., South Australia) or use them in addition to (e.g., Victoria) the locally derived monitoring and QA programs. Taiwan is another country that has been proactive in internationalisation. In Taiwan, the Ministry of Education has promulgated rules for assisting academic cooperation between domestic and foreign higher education institutions.

Countries in the region have been active in participating in The Organisation for Economic Cooperation and Development (OECD) projects in developing cross-national educational indicators. For instance, Australia, Hong Kong, Japan, Korea, New Zealand, and Singapore participated in the OECD Programme for International Student Assessment (PISA) project. Many of these countries also participated at international studies on student achievement conducted by the International Association for the Evaluation of Educational Achievement (IEA) including the Second International Mathematics Study in 1981, the Second IEA Science Study in 1983–84, the Reading Literacy Study in 1990–91 and TIMSS in 1994–95 and 1999.

3.3. Emphasis on Teacher Quality and Reform in Teacher Training

Acknowledging the importance of teacher quality on education quality, Asia-Pacific governments show strong commitments to ensuring teacher standards. Initiatives in the region include (a) regulation on teacher registration, recruitment and promotion; (b) monitoring and reporting of teacher performance; and (c) reforms on teacher education with emphasis on teacher professionalism and professional status.

In Australia, Japan, Korea and Taiwan, teachers are monitored through annual reviews at the school level. Teacher appraisal in Papua New Guinea is by inspectors who furnish a report on the teaching. In Hong Kong, the Education Ordinance mandates that all teachers are registered with the Director of Education. In Korea, teacher quality is assured by certification according to national standards and government regulations on recruitment and promotion. Japan controls teacher quality by (a) vigorous selection through competitive examinations; (b) a 12-month induction training of teachers with appointment conditional on favourable evaluation at the end of training; and (c) annual review of teachers by the principal and of the principal by the education board.

Major teacher education reforms in the region can be illustrated by those undertaken in Hong Kong and Taiwan. The Hong Kong Institute of Education was established in 1994 as a major provider of teacher education and came under the aegis of the University Grants Committee in 1997. In addition, the Advisory Committee on Teacher Education and Qualification (ACTEQ) was established in 1993 to monitor teacher quality standard, advise on teacher education policy development and enhance teacher professionalism and their professional status. A HK$20 million (approximately US$2.6 million) one-off grant is earmarked to establish the core generic competencies for teachers and subject-specific teacher competencies, as well as for the setting up of a General Teacher Council. Further, the government pledges to have all graduates of pre-service school teachers as degree holders from the 2004–2005 school year (Education and Manpower Bureau, 2001, p. 14). Statistics shows that the percentage of degree-holding teachers has risen from 65 per cent in 1990 to 85 per cent in 1999 at the secondary level, and from five per cent in 1990 to 38 per cent in 1999 at the primary level (Lai, Ko, & Li, 2001, p. 6).

The Taiwan teacher education reform emphasises diversification and excellence. Under the auspices of a diversified teacher education system, coupled with the constant effort of the teacher education review committee to introduce reform initiatives in:

- policy and related measures,
- the materialisation of the internship and counselling system,
- the implementation of teacher qualification through testing,
- the promotion of in-service training and lifelong education, and not least,
- the guidance of a comprehensive teachers' law.

The professional status of elementary and secondary school teachers in Taiwan has remained high, and thus the quality of the teachers and the quality of the education provided is likely to be high.

3.4. *Reform in the Public Examination Systems*

Performance at system-wide examination is often used as an important quality indicator. Recent educational reforms in Hong Kong, Taiwan and Papua New

Guinea included changes to system-wide examination as a central feature of the reforms. In Hong Kong, the high-stake public examination at P6 is to be replaced by a low-stake formative Basic Competency Assessment by 2005, emphasising assessment for learning (Education Commission, 2000).

Assessment reform in Taiwan concerns, among other issues, the promotion of internal and external assessment mechanisms in order to enhance the quality of school education. With respect to internal assessment mechanism, all Taiwan schools have to assess their students on moral values, intellectual development, physical health, social skills and aesthetic appreciation with regard to the cognitive, affective and skill dimensions. There is also emphasis in the education reform on using a variety of approaches in the assessment of students.

Assessment reform plays a central role in the recent education reform in Papua New Guinea. The NDOE implements a national system of examinations at the completion of each cycle of education. A careful record of examination data over the years is kept to monitor standards in the country. Summary reports of the examination results, which enable comparison across schools, cohorts and subject areas, are published each year (e.g., *Standards and Monitoring Project 12, 1987–1997*). In addition, the NDOE publishes a range of documents (e.g., *Dealing with Assessment Marks*) to ensure that schools follow the guidelines closely and accurately.

3.5. Enhanced Openness and Transparency

Information gathered through QA processes may be sensitive and potentially damaging to the system, unit, government, school or individual. The extent to which such information is put in the public domain usually causes high anxiety among those concerned, and it demands certain courage of the political and educational leaders to exercise an open system. In a review of issues associated with school performance indicators, Rowe (1996) utilised a set of principles articulated by Goldstein and Myers (1996); the principle of unwarranted harm and the principle of right to information. The right to information needs to be balanced with a concern for the unwarranted harm that this information may cause. Achieving this balance is difficult although there are ways of minimising potential harm (Rowe, 1996).

Partly in relation to decentralization of the QA of school systems in the region, there has been more transparency in the QA processes. The Ministry of Education in many countries now maintain a comprehensive website with education policies, the school system and accountability information for wide access and scrutiny by parents and the general public. There are at least two levels of transparency in education QA, that at policymaking levels through open consultation, and that at process and output level through the publication of school performances. Transparency at the policymaking level is illustrated by the Hong Kong political system, described as a 'consultative autocracy' (Cheng, K. M., 1997), which involves wide consultation efforts whereby policy-advisory bodies (e.g., ACTEQ), academics, principals, the general public and overseas consultants are engaged extensively in major policy formulation.

Transparency at the reporting level is best illustrated by Singapore where school excellence is publicly acknowledged through the Masterplan of Awards for schools. These awards are linked to SEM, and used to show that students have met the required standards and give recognition to schools' efforts on excellence. Similarly, some states in Australia give public reporting of individual school performance in system-wide testing of student learning in literacy and numeracy (in a quasi-league table format). In Japan, although some schools are well-known to be 'closed schools' (*heisateki*), the Ministry and its advisory councils admit now the need for so called 'open schools' (*hirakareta gakkou*), schools that are open towards the community, consequently making information more publicly accessible.

3.6. *The Use of Multidimensional Indicators for Process and Output QA*

The use of performance indicators for the monitoring of educational progress and performance at the systemic level has become a common international practice (Husén & Tuijnman, 1994; Mong, Wang, & Yang, 1997). In line with the recent revision in the educational aims of many Asia-Pacific systems with renewed emphasis on whole person development, the welcoming trend is the inclusion of both academic and non-academic performance indicators. Japan, Taiwan, Singapore and Hong Kong are good examples to illustrate this development. Since 1993, Japanese schools not only assess the academic performance of students, but also include in their assessment such other aspects as motivation to learn, willingness to participate, creativity and zest for living as major school outcomes.

In Hong Kong, schools are measured on four performance domains – namely, 'management and organisation', 'teaching and learning', 'support for pupils' and 'school ethos', and 'attainment and achievement' in the academic as well as social and affective dimensions and with indicators in each (Education Department, 2001).

Indicators in the SEM framework in Singapore involve the levels of school management, teacher, curriculum and student. Nine criteria are used, namely, leadership, strategic planning, staff management, resources, student-focused processes, administrative and operational results, staff results, partnership and society results and key performance results (Ministry of Education, Singapore, 2001).

3.7. *Office Designated for QA and R&D Funding for Quality Education*

Another trend observed in Asia-Pacific systems involves the establishment of offices akin to the Office for Standards in Education in the United Kingdom, designated for QA of school education and the generous allocation of research funding earmarked for quality education.

In Hong Kong, the QA Inspectorate was established in 1997 to develop the QA framework and undertake school review. In addition, a HK$5 billion (approximately US$0.65 billion) Quality Education Fund was established in

1998 to finance projects promoting quality education, covering such domains as effective learning, all-round education and school-based management across all school sectors (http://www.info.gov.hk/qef/stat/index.htm, 2001).

In Japan, a new committee with members comprising government officials and academics was established in 2001 to monitor government department performance and to evaluate the policy of the Ministry of Education, Culture, Sports, Science and Technology (MECSST). The MECSST provides generous research funding (*Kagaku kenkyuu hojokin*), amounting to yen 131.4bn in 1999, to support academic research in all scientific fields (Akao et al., 2000).

KEDI, established in 1972 by the Korean government, has been recently commissioned to undertake the Comprehensive School Evaluation Project, which aims to establish quality control systems for school education. In New Zealand, the Education Review Office was established in 1989 for conducting formal accountability school reviews and submission of reports to the government on the health of the education system.

4. ISSUES AND BARRIERS TO QUALITY ASSURANCE

QA by its very nature requires careful negotiation among key stakeholders in its aims, meanings and interpretations. Different parties have different expectations of the QA process and its outcomes. Further, since different levels (system, local government, school, principal, teacher, students, advisory bodies, pressure groups and parents), domains (policy, resource, curriculum, management, teacher professionalism, academic outcomes and non-academic outcomes) and purposes (accountability, development, improvement, reward, remediation, promotion and comparison) are involved, the process is necessarily complicated. In addition, sophisticated methods and technical skills are necessary on top of developing mutual trust and rapport among key players. Opening up more channels for discourse among key stakeholders may solve some but not all of the problems. It is pleasing to note that the regional trend is towards increasing transparency through such processes as consultation, internet dissemination, public reports and both international and national forums. Nevertheless, a number of issues and barriers still exit. These include the mismatch between education aims and QA focus; opposition from the government and key parties; no obvious effect of initiatives on student learning; and capacity building for effective, efficient, valid and reliable QA processes.

4.1. *Lack of Alignment Between Educational Aims and QA Focus*

As Cheng and Townsend (2000) have highlighted, countries in the region that have heavily revised their educational aims in recent educational reforms. The commonality in these educational aims is the emphasis on whole person development, creativity, problem solving, learning skills and lifelong learning. Nevertheless, there is yet to be developed explicit QA mechanisms to gauge system performance in these domains. It is encouraging to note that (a) countries like Australia, Singapore and Hong Kong have each made serious attempts to include social and affective schooling outcomes in their QA systems; (b) Japan and Korea are committed to lifelong learning, with Korea setting up the National Centre for Lifelong Education within KEDI; (c) Singapore and Japan include creativity and thinking skills as their national education priorities; and (d) PNG and Taiwan have each made good progress in their assessment and teacher education reforms. Despite these efforts, there needs to be stronger alignment between the educational aims and the QA systems. Questions need to be addressed are: Are these traits observable and, if so, are they measurable? How can they be measured? What indicators would reflect the status of system, school and student performance on the educational aims (Cheng, Y. C., 1997)? And above all, research needs to be undertaken to develop parallel packages for change and improvement if performances are found to be unsatisfactory.

Two research areas particularly needing urgent attention are the integration of information and communication technology (ICT into teaching and learning, and the individualisation of learning. While the expenditure remains high, the importance and potential of ICT in education is widely acknowledged and many systems have been proactive in its development. There needs to be developed systematic monitoring and evaluation of the effectiveness of ICT.

Regulations and monitoring very often bring about uniformity and standardisation. However, over-standardisation can result in rigidity and stagnation. It discourages innovation, as well as stamps out zest for excellence beyond minimum standards. Standardisation is also in opposition to the spirit of individualisation of learning to cater for differences in local contexts and the diverse ability and needs of individual learners. Research is needed to identify the best balance between individualisation and standardisation within each local context, as well as for the development of QA mechanism that could reflect whether or not the balance has been achieved (Cheng, Y. C., 1997).

4.2. Opposition from the Government, Unions, Schools, Teachers, Students and the Public

For the same reason that QA is multilevel and multidimensional, the outcomes of QA processes have policy and resources implications for players in different layers of the hierarchy; are expected to impact on student learning; and may affect the job opportunities or promotion prospects of individuals. Naturally, many parties who all claim to have ownership of student learning have strong views and different opinions on what is the best QA approach.

4.3. Sources of Opposition to Reform

Asia-Pacific systems are not unfamiliar with strong opposition from the government, pressure and political groups, schools, teachers, students and the public to the methods, emphasis, components or expected outcomes of QA. Some of this opposition may be violent, others constructive but all point to the fact that quality education is a treacherous enterprise. In South Australia, for instance, despite positive reports about the Education Review Unit, it was closed by an incoming government and replaced by a QA unit that had only a quarter of its original staff (Cuttance et al., 1998). The school review program initiated by the New South Wales (NSW) Government in 1994 was banned by the Teachers' Federation, which subsequently contributed to the demise of the NSW QA Unit. The Tasmanian Education Council report, which strongly recommended school-based management, was rejected by the Minister (Cuttance et al., 1998). In Hong Kong, government request for benchmarking of English language teachers through examination also met with apprehension in 2000 (Downson, Bodycott, Walker, & Coniam, 2000). In Japan, national achievement assessments on all second and third grade lower secondary students held in the 1960s were subsequently abolished because of harsh protest by the teachers' unions and schools (Sakamoto & Kouzou, 1992).

Cheng (1997) (see also Cheng & Townsend, 2000) has highlighted several sources of tension in the monitoring of school effectiveness, namely, (a) that between the purposes of school improvement and public accountability; (b) between school self-evaluation and external evaluation; (c) between system level and school-site level effectiveness; (d) among the choices of combinations of indicators; and (e) between choosing effective indicators and performance standards. Such tensions contribute to the conflicts between the government and schools. Systematic research is urgently needed to identify ways of managing differences between school-site level and system level quality concerns (Cheng, Y. C., 1997).

The success of QA requires the cooperation of many parties. Very often such cooperation relies on goodwill and confidence in ultimate positive impact on student learning. Unfortunately, it is not always easy to demonstrate direct relationships between QA implementations and increase in student achievement (see, e.g., Wong, 1997). One of the areas that QA systems promote is the construction of better data and better management information systems to manage the data. This leads to better school improvement plans as they are data-driven. Unfortunately, evidence on student learning improvement remains difficult to connect with QA, as QA is normally constructed as part of a larger reform effort. A school review team, in most cases, stays for a couple of days in the school whereas developing an effective school is a long-term process. School review team members may find it difficult to provide explicit advice and guidance and school review may thus be criticized as being a mere formality. In fact, for most national systems, school effect on student achievement variables tends to be small and around ten per cent of the total variance. Although the result is not surprising given the complexity in school operations and the differential degree of variation between macro- and micro-level variables, as QA tends to be a demanding process on time and resources, its lack of thrust seriously undercuts willingness for further cooperation. An important research area concerns the refinement of technology for the measurement of effectiveness of school-based management (Cheng & Townsend, 2000).

4.4. The Need for Capacity Building for School Self-Review

School review is a complex process requiring training. Schools have to be supported in addressing such question as how to choose an appropriate combination of indicators? How to collect and collate classroom observation data? How to interpret, make use of and respond to external review reports? If the cognitive or procedural demand exceeded what could be met by the schools, the data collected would be invalid, unreliable, irrelevant or not useful.

5. CONCLUSION

This article reports on the quality assurance and school monitoring of eight systems, namely, Australia, Hong Kong, Japan, Korea, New Zealand, Papua New Guinea, Singapore, and Taiwan in the Asia-Pacific region along three themes: 'What are the models used?' 'What trends have emerged?' 'And what are the issues and barriers?' A number of similarities and differences are identified among these countries in their QA systems. Notably, these countries share the commonality in their commitment for quality education, which is manifested in a myriad of QA mechanisms. Although the countries are at different stages of development, the trends are from assuring minimal standards to continuous quality improvement; from the centralized system demanding conformity to decentralization enabling individualism and openness; from monolithic focus on academic cognitive outcomes to multilevel, multidimensional review of performance of the system, schools, teachers and students; and from within-system reporting to international comparisons and sharing.

There are still many challenges ahead, not the least the better alignment between education aims and QA focus; between what is expected to be measured and what is being measured; between external and internal review; between government expectations and stages of school development; between the methods for monitoring and expertise support given to schools; and between the effort spent on the review exercise and expected outcomes.

REFERENCES

Akao, K., Arai, A., Ito, M., Sato, H., Shimizu, K., Fujita, T., & Yaosaka, O. (Eds.) (2000). *Kyouiku deeta bukku 2000–2001* [A databook of educational statistics]. Tokyo: Jiji tsuushinsha.

Caldwell, B. J., & Spinks, J. M. (1988). *The Self Managing School*. London: Falmer Press.

Caldwell, B. J., & Spinks, J. M. (1998). *Beyond the Self Managing School*. London: Falmer Press.

Cheng, K. M. (1997). The policymaking process. In G. A. Postiglione & W. O. Lee (Eds.), *Schooling in Hong Kong: Organization, Teaching and Social Context* (pp. 65–78). Hong Kong: Hong Kong University Press.

Cheng, Y. C. (1997). Monitoring school effectiveness: Conceptual and practical dilemmas in developing a framework. In H. Meng, Y. Zhou & Y. Fang (Eds.), *School Based Indicators of Effectiveness: Experiences and Practices in APEC Members* (pp. 197–206). Guangxi, China: Guangxi Normal University Press.

Cheng, Y. C. (2000). Educational change and development in Hong Kong: Effectiveness, quality, and relevance. In T. Townsend & Y. C. Cheng (Eds.), *Educational Change and Development in the Asia-Pacific Region: Challenges for the Future* (pp. 17–56). Lisse, The Netherlands: Swets and Zeitlinger.

Cheng, Y. C., & Cheung, W. M. (2001, September 5–8). *A Typology of School Environment: Multilevel Self Management and Education Quality*. Paper presented at the Annual Conference of the European Educational Research Association, Lille, France.

Cheng, Y. C., & Townsend, T. (2000). Educational change and development in the Asia-Pacific region: Trends and issues. In T. Townsend & Y. C. Cheng (Eds.), *Educational Change and Development in the Asia-Pacific Region: Challenges for the Future* (pp. 317–344). Lisse, The Netherlands: Swets and Zeitlinger.

Crosby, P. B. (1979). *Quality is Free: The Art of Making Quality Certain*. New York: McGraw Hill.

Cuttance, P., Harman, G., Macpherson, R. J. S., Pritchard, A., & Smart, D. (1998). The politics of accountability in Australian education. In R. J. S. Macpherson (Ed.), *The Politics of Accountability*. Thousand Oaks, CA: Corwin Press, Inc.

Deming, W. (1986). *Out of the Crisis*. Cambridge, Mass.: MIT Press.

Dowson, C., Bodycott, P., Walker, A., & Coniam, D. (2000). Education reform in Hong Kong: Issues of consistency, connectedness and culture. *Education Policy Analysis Archives* [On-line serial], 8(24). Available: Http://olam.ed.asu.edu/epaa

Education and Manpower Bureau (2001). *2001 Policy Address: Quality Education: Policy Objective for Education and Manpower Bureau*. Hong Kong: Printing Department Hong Kong Special Administrative Region (HKSAR) Government.

Education Commission (2000). *Reform Proposals for the Education System in Hong Kong*. Hong Kong: Printing Department, HKSAR Government.

Education Department (2001). *School Education Quality Assurance: Performance Indictors (Primary schools) Domain of Teaching and Learning (2nd ed)*.. Hong Kong: Advisory Inspectorate Division, Education Department.

Fuller, B. (1989). Defining school quality. In J. Hannaway & M. E. Lockheed (Eds.), *The Contribution of the Social Science to Educational Policy and Practice: 1965–1985* (pp. 33–69). San Francisco, CA: McCutchan Publishing Corporation.

Gaither, G. H. (Ed.) (1998). *Quality Assurance in Higher Education: An International Perspective*. San Francisco: Jossey-Bass Publishers.

Goldstein, H., & Myers, K. (1996). Freedom of information: Towards a code of ethics for performance indicators. *Research Intelligence*, 67.

Gurr, D. (1999). *From Supervision to Quality Assurance: The Case of the State of Victoria (Australia)*. Paris: UNESCO, International Institute for Educational Planning.

Husén, T., & Tuijnman, A. C. (1994). Monitoring standards in education: Why and how it came about. In A. C. Tuijnman & T. Husén (Eds.), *Monitoring the Standards of Education: Papers in honor of John P Keeves* (pp. 1–22). Oxford: Elsevier Science.

Juran, J. M., & Gryna, F. M., Jr. (Eds.) (1988). *Juran's Quality Control Handbook* (4th ed.). New York: McGraw Hill.

Kenkyuujo, K. K. (Ed.) (2000a). Gakkou hyougiin no secchi to unei [The establishment and running of the school council] [Special issue]. *Kyoushoku kenshuu tokushuu* [Journal for Training in the Teaching Profession], 28(9).

Kenkyuujo, K. K. (Ed.) (2000b). Gakkou no jiko tenken hyouka no suishin [The propulsion of self-evaluation by schools] [Special issue]. *Kyoushoku kenshuu tokushuu* [Journal for Training in the Teaching Profession], 28(11).

Lai, K. C., Ko, K. W., & Li, C. (2001). *Teacher Education Planning Digest. Profile of the Teaching Profession in Hong Kong in the 1990s, Issue 5*, January 2001. Hong Kong: Office of Planning and Academic Implementation, The Hong Kong Institute of Education.

Ministry of Education, Singapore (2001). Information sheet on best practice award (BPA). [On-line], Available: Http://www1.moe.edu.sg/press/2001/pr15082001.htm

Mong, H. W., Wang, X., & Yang, N. (1997). School based indictors of effectiveness in APEC members: Experiences and practices. In *APEC Education Forum: School Based Indicators of Effectiveness: Experiences and Practices in APEC Members*. The People's Republic of China: Guangxi Normal University Press published for APEC.

Mukhopadhyay, M. (2001). *Total Quality Management in Education*. Sri Aurobindo Marg, New Delhi: National Institute of Education Planning and Administration.
Nakadome, T. (1999). *Gakkou keiei no kaikaku senryaku (Strategies to reform school management)*. Tokyo: Tamagawa Daigaku Shuppanbu.
Rowe, K. (1996). Assessment, performance indicators, league tables, value added measures and school effectiveness: Issues and implications. *IARTV Seminar Series, 58*.
Sakamoto, H., & Kouzou, Y. (Eds.) (1992). *Monbushou no kenkyuu* [Research on the Ministry of Education]. Tokyo: Sanichi shobou.
Saunders, L. (1999). *'Value Added' Measurement of School Effectiveness: A Critical Review*. Slough, England: National Foundation for Educational Research.
Stanley, E. C., & Patrick, W. J. (1998). Quality assurance in American and British higher education: A comparison. In G. H. Gaither (Ed.), *Quality Assurance in Higher Education: An International Perspective* (pp. 39–56). San Francisco: Jossey-Bass Publishers.
Tse, K. C. (2000). *Jiao Gai He Jia? Xiang Gang Zhi Jing Yan* [What is the value of education reform? The experience of Hong Kong]. In China Comparative Education Society (Ed.), *The New Era Education: Challenges and Responses* (pp. 95–124). Taipei: Yang-Chih Book.
Visscher, A. J. (Ed.) (1999). *Managing Schools Towards High Performance: Linking School Management Theory to the School Effectiveness Knowledge Base*. Lisse, The Netherlands; Exton, PA.: Swets & Zeitlinger.
Wong, K. C. (1997). Organizing and managing schools. In G. A. Postiglione & W. O. Lee (Eds.), *Schooling in Hong Kong: Organization, Teaching and Social Context* (pp. 81–94). Hong Kong: Hong Kong University Press.
Yaosaka, O. (2001). *Gendai no kyouiku daikaku to gakkou no jiko hyouka* [Recent education reforms and self-evaluation by schools]. Tokyo: Gyousei.

66

Staffing in School Education

YOUNG-HWA KIM
Hongik University, Seoul, Republic of Korea

1. INTRODUCTION

The concept of staffing includes different elements depending on the context in which it is used. According to the Oxford American Dictionary that defines staffing in the narrowest terms, staffing means providing a staff of employees or assistants. In general, however, it is used with a broader meaning. Internal staffing includes policies, practices and procedures relating to promotion, transfer, demotion, resignation, disability, retirement, severance and death (Castetter & Young, 2000). McPartland and Fessler (1992) suggest three overlapping dimensions of staffing patterns at primary and secondary schools: the extent of hierarchy of differentiated staff roles and responsibilities; the way that individual staff responsibilities are associated with curricular specialisation; and the degree to which the roles of instructional staff are interdependent or interactive.

Staffing is strongly associated with the areas that current teacher policy and further school reform policy give high priority. They are connected with the issues, such as how to attract and hold highly qualified teachers and how to provide teachers with an improved professional working environment (McPartland & Fessler, 1992). Choosing common elements of various definitions and rather a broader concept of staffing, this article examines the issues of teacher supply and demand, recruitment, career ladder and promotion, performance standards and appraisal and placement in the Asia-Pacific region, focusing on Korea and referring to Japan, New Zealand and Singapore.

2. PROBLEMS AND ISSUES

2.1. *Teacher Supply and Demand*

Many Asia-Pacific education systems are experiencing the imbalance between teacher supply and demand.

Korea. In Korea, due to continuous increase in university enrolment and lapses in long-term planning for teacher training and recruitment policy, there has been chronic over-supply of teacher certificate holders over the last two decades. As the economy slows, more college students have chosen to become teachers, and the turnover rate for teachers has decreased. Further, both a decrease in school enrolment and the subsequent integration of small rural schools have resulted in a decrease in employment opportunities for graduates from teacher training institutions.

The problem is particularly serious at the secondary school level. The number of teacher certificate holders for secondary education conferred by teachers' colleges, teacher training courses at universities and graduate schools of education is nearly five times as large as that of those successful job applicants. Thus, applicants for secondary school teacher positions have piled up greatly with little opportunity to get hired. For instance, among the applicants who graduated from teacher training institutions in 1994, only 20 per cent (4,968) out of the 25,340 entire pool of new certificate-holders were employed in 1995; only 14 per cent (3,428) out of 24,461 and 27 per cent (4,227) out of 15,665 entered the teaching profession in 1996 and 1997, respectively (Kwak, 1999).

With respect to the primary school sector, the extent of over-supply of teacher certificate holders has not been as large as that at the secondary school level. In 1996, 74 per cent of certificate holders from national institutions were actually employed. The situation, however, drastically changed into a serious teacher shortage due to the abrupt lowering of the retirement age from 65 to 62 in 1998. In 1999, a total of 15,890 primary school teachers (12%) retired, including those who did because they reached the set retirement age (5,135) and those who chose early honorary retirement (10,755). Considering that the total figure was 4,873 in 1998, we can figure out the seriousness of the shortage of teachers (Korean Ministry of Education and Human Resource Development [MOEHRD], 1999).

In order to fill the vacancies, teacher selection examinations were conducted five times in 1999. This was extraordinary, when compared with the one to two examinations per year practice in the past. Despite the increased number of teacher selection examinations, 8,073 primary school vacancies that should have been filled could not be filled. Only 5,621 teacher candidates participated in the examination, and 5,346 candidates passed the examination.

With respect to secondary school teachers, meeting new demands does not seem so difficult because of the large pool of trained teachers, but the supply of primary school teachers is problematic since the pool itself is not large enough to meet the demand due to the closed training system. This imbalance between teacher supply and demand is likely to continue for at least several years (Kim, H. S., 2000).

The government has attempted to cope with the situation by allowing schools to hire secondary school teacher certificate-holders as contract teachers exclusively responsible for specialised subjects and those who already retired as contract teachers on request. However, this measure is being exposed to criticism in that it is a try to patch the problem up and not to find a more permanent solution. Students and professors in primary school teacher training institutions, such as national universities of education strongly protested against the measure, highlighting differences in the professionalism required as a primary school teacher and a secondary school teacher. Parents are also complaining about hiring teachers again who once retired (Kim, Y. H., 2000).

Japan. Japan has also faced a situation of teacher surplus over the past ten years. As a rapid decrease of the young population continues for many years, the number of students is falling year by year. Besides, the number of smaller schools below 11 classrooms with less than 300 students is increasing in primary schools particularly. Accordingly, the graduates who want to be teachers find it extremely difficult to enter the teaching profession. The proportion of graduates from teacher training institutions who were hired within three months of graduation was merely 14 per cent in 1998 (Accanokazya, 2000). The situation of teacher surplus is anticipated to remain unchanged in the years to come. In the 1980s, teaching had been named a 'greying' and 'ageing' profession because the average ages of teachers were over 40 years already, and it was almost impossible to find school principals under 50 years of age (Masami, 1999).

2.2. Recruitment

Recruitment refers to those activities designed to make available the number of applicants, the diversity of applicants and the quality of staff needed to perform the work of the school system. Recruitment is an essential part of a comprehensive plan to secure excellent personnel who will accomplish the purposes of school education. Both short- and long-range planning activities are involved in recruitment. The short-range activities aim at meeting present demands for personnel that exist in an organisation; the long-term activities are those needed to ensure a future supply of qualified personnel (Castetter & Young, 2000).

Korea. Several countries in the Asia-Pacific region, such as Korea, have changed their teacher recruitment policies, promoting a shift in the recruitment system from a closed to an open system and a shift in the recruitment methods from a uniform method to diverse methods. For the pre-service training of primary school teachers, Korea has a so-called 'closed objective-oriented training' system, which limits the opportunity for a teaching job only to those who major in teacher education at the national universities of education. The government tightly controls the enrolment quota of the national universities of education according to the projected demand for the teaching force, and those graduates of the universities are automatically awarded the teacher certificate when they complete their undergraduate studies in teacher education.

The pre-service training system of secondary school teachers is a relatively open system where teacher-applicants are trained through such diverse educational channels as colleges of education, teacher certification programs in universities, departments of education in universities and graduate schools of education. However, the system normally only allows teacher-applicants to enter teaching jobs at the beginning of their career and prevents people of diverse ages with diverse experience from becoming teachers through diverse paths.

Consequently, the teaching force in Korea is characterised by a lack of diversity in its employment status. Non-regular teaching staff such as part-time teachers, represent only four per cent of the Korean teaching force, compared with 16 per cent in the United States and 21 per cent in Japan. This low percentage indicates that most teachers are tenured full-time teachers in Korea (Kim, G. J., 1999). The personnel policies that are full-time faculty oriented for both primary and middle schools inhibit the encouraging of the flexibility in the recruitment of teachers in response to rapid changes in the Korean society.

In order to provide opportunities for capable professionals with extensive work experience to enter the field of teaching and to prepare for the sound operation of the seventh curriculum in Korea, a teacher qualification examination that is open to everyone is being considered. Those applicants who pass this examination are to be provided with necessary training programs for teaching and student guidance. The Korean MOEHRD has made a decision to implement this new system for securing teachers in such special fields as technical education, but teacher unions and associations are opposing such a decision.

Japan. In 1998, the Central Educational Council in Japan suggested that the requirements for appointment to the position of principal or vice-principal should be changed to allow persons who did not have a teaching certificate and teaching experience, but had experience and skill in a job related to education or in the management of organisations to be appointed. Accordingly, the regulations of the School Education Act were revised to include an article which would allow those who had worked in a job related to education for ten years or more to be appointed to the position of a principal or vice-principal from the year 2000. Thus, a person who had experience of ten years or more in the job related to education was able to be appointed to a principal's or vice-principal's position even without a teacher certificate (Central Educational Council, 1998).

2.3. *Performance Standards and Appraisal for Teaching Personnel*

The performance appraisal of teachers aims at achieving reasonable personnel management, quality improvement, and conscious and substantial guidance for students. As many Asia-Pacific countries are attempting to change the promotion and reward system from a seniority-based to a merit-based system, they are developing and refining job performance standards for teachers.

In Korea, it has been pointed out that the promotion and pay system based on the seniority rule was a fundamental factor causing teachers to neglect their self-development. Teachers think that the compensation for their work is not rationally determined. The decisions for promotion are based mainly on seniority rather than on the results of a performance-oriented and fair evaluation method. A teacher hardly expects promotion to administrative positions unless he or she has attained 25 years of experience. The seniority-based promotion system and salary structure have weakened the competitive nature of the teaching job, losing the opportunity to reward younger competent teachers. The desirability of establishing a merit-based personnel system was documented and the need to set standards for the critical jobs of teaching and educational administration underscored. Effective lessons, student guidance, development and implementation of a creative plan for school management, and the ability to carry out effective supervision of instruction were made valid criteria for selection and appointment (Kim, Y. C., 1994).

Evaluation of job performance in Korea was to be carried out for all education officials according to the regulations for promotion. After the evaluation, those with excellent results would go through a special assessment of their job performance. The personnel division, after the assessment, would select the top 20 per cent and rank the recommended candidates. The list of candidates would then be handed over to the judging committee that would be comprised of three to seven members who would be superiors of the objects of evaluation. Based on the list and the ranking of the candidates, the committee would choose the persons for appointment and set the percentage of the bonus awarded. The heads of departments or superintendents determined the factors and the methods for the special assessment. In the case that the assessment was carried out in a school, teachers could also participate in the decision-making in setting up procedures and in identifying factors to be assessed during selection (Yang, 2000).

As a consequence of the nation's economic crisis of 1998, the merit-pay system was discontinued. Nevertheless, the major causes of discontinuation were not limited to financial constraint. The results of a nationwide survey conducted in March 1999 by MOEHRD, involving 1,554 teachers, showed that 59 per cent opposed the merit-pay system. A similar survey conducted by a teachers' union showed that 77 per cent negatively considered it. It was found that without sufficient discussion on teachers' professional advancement, the system could not succeed. Furthermore, teachers had shown antipathy as the nominees were in fact selected according to the seniority rule rather than merit, and many had considered that the merit payment was largely used up for the purpose of entertaining colleagues (Yang, 2000).

MOEHRD intends to establish job performance criteria for each of the positions advertised (teacher, teacher-administrator, vice-principal and principal), certificates awarded (nurse and teacher, librarian and teacher, professional counselling teacher and art teacher), employment status granted (full-time teacher and contract teacher), and teaching grades (K-12) allocated. There would also be a review of points and various criteria used in the evaluation of a teacher's performance so that teachers who were outstanding in teaching and student guidance would receive higher points. Under the observation of principals, a Teacher Evaluation Committee would be set up for each school with the participation of teachers to secure objective and fair evaluation. When necessary, parents might participate in this process. Each individual Teacher Evaluation Committee would have the authority to request retraining of those teachers who were found to need further professional development in academic competence or student guidance (MOEHRD, 2000).

Japan. Japanese teachers in public schools as public employees are appraised for their achievement of duties and fulfilment of responsibilities, as well as their character, capacities and aptitude as observed in relation to their performance of duties according to the Local Public Service Personnel Law. Teachers in private schools are free from the legal requirements, but the administrators of these schools are expected to appraise their teachers in compliance with the practices of the public sector. The school principal evaluates the teachers and the superintendent of the education board makes any necessary revisions. Evaluation results are to be used in individual teacher placement and promotion and so on, in general, on a yearly basis. For each individual evaluation item, observation points are awarded as are specified in the scales prepared by the board of education concerned, as follows: (a) class management, academic guidance, student guidance, student performance and achievement, in-service training and self-improvement, dealing with school affairs as achievement of duties and (b) capacities, zeal for teaching, leadership, sincerity, sense of responsibility, fairness, generosity, cooperation and dignity, special characteristics and capabilities (Masami, 1999).

The result of the job performance evaluation, however, may not be fully used in practice, for example, in awarding payment and promotion, since in Japan personnel management in schools is also characterised, like Korea, by a seniority-based reward and promotion system. The average age for being promoted to a vice-principal is consequently very high: it is in the late 40s for the primary and lower secondary school level and the early 50s for the upper secondary school level; as for a principal, it is the early 50s and the late 50s respectively (Department of Region of Japanese Ministry of Education, 1999).

However, in parallel with changes in employment practices in private enterprises from the lifelong employment practices to the merit-based ones on the one hand and with the weakening of the power of the teacher union on the other, the necessity to appraise teacher performance more actively and expand the pay difference among teachers according to the results of the performance appraisal has been strongly emphasised in recent years. Since 2000, the Tokyo Province is attempting to abolish the egalitarian seniority-based personnel management system and to introduce a new appraisal system based on capability and job performance. The results of the teacher appraisal are expected to be reflected in salaries and allowances and in promotion to administrative positions (Department of Personnel Management of the Tokyo Office of Education, 2000). In addition to the Tokyo Province, several other boards of education are considering the introduction of a new personnel management system, and other provinces are expected to reform their personnel management system (Kim, Yang, & Kim, 2000).

New Zealand. In New Zealand, prior to and following the Tomorrow's Schools reforms starting in 1987, there had been concern about the performance of some teachers. The community had been very dissatisfied with the lack of accountability with respect to teacher performance (Picot, 1988). The School Trustees Association and a number of politicians also expressed this dissatisfaction (Awatere-Huata, 1998). As a way of increasing educational accountability, two sets of performance standards for teachers were developed during the 1990s: the so-called 'satisfactory teacher' standards developed by the Teacher Registration Board (TRB) and the professional standards developed by the Ministry of Education (Langley, 1999).

From its inception in 1989, the TRB had been charged with developing the standards for the entry of teachers into the profession and the standards by which teachers could remain in the profession. The TRB developed the dimensions of the satisfactory teacher after reviewing literature about teacher effectiveness and after consulting about effective professional practice with many educational and community groups (Langley, 1999).

The definition of a 'satisfactory teacher' holds that any teacher must show that acceptable learning occurs for all students in their charge, within an environment that affirms the bi-cultural and multi-cultural nature of New Zealand (TRB, 1994). The conditions under which the above prescription can most likely be met are identified as the four key dimensions of the satisfactory teachers: (a) professional knowledge; (b) professional practice; (c) professional relationships; and (d) professional leadership. Each of these dimensions has a number of more specific behavioural descriptors which expand on the meaning of that dimension (Langley, 1999).

After 1990, a teacher can become registered and therefore be employed in a school or kindergarten only when that teacher meets all of the dimensions of the 'satisfactory teacher' in addition to being of good character and being fit to be a teacher. Every three years and before a teacher can renew their practicing certificate, their principal or professional leader has to confirm that they are still classed as 'satisfactory' and meeting those dimensions. In general, teachers tend to be favourable to these new standards. There has been consultation in the process of developing the standards, and teachers regarded the standards as a clear means of setting better expectations for entry into the profession (Langley, 1999).

In the mid-1990s, the New Zealand Ministry of Education promulgated a further set of performance standards. The professional standards were in 11 areas: professional knowledge, professional development, teaching techniques, student management, motivation of students, Maori language and culture, communication, cooperation with colleagues, contribution to school activities, resource management, staff and student management, and professional leadership. Each of these categories contained a number of descriptors defining the category (Langley, 1999).

Besides the development of the professional standards, a performance management system (PMS) was established in each school. The PMS required each teacher to be appraised annually against the professional standards and to be meeting those standards before any salary increase would be granted (Langley, 1999).

As the result of the development of professional standards and the introduction of PMS, employment and industrial relationships have come to dominate professional relationships. Performance is now tied to professional standards which were introduced as part of an industrial negotiation rather than as a result of professional consultation and commitment (Langley, 1999). The result in many cases has been that teachers feel they ought to comply, not for reasons of delivering a better service for children, but because it is required to get a salary increase. In a case study which sought to analyse the influence of the standards and PMS in a large New Zealand school, McNay (1999) discovered that no more than half of the teaching staff perceived the system as improving their performance. The current system tends to focus solely on a series of teaching behaviours which are appraised, sometimes isolated from each other rather than to depend on a framework that integrates elements of teacher effectiveness, elements of high performance and human resource functions (McNay, 1999).

2.4. Career Ladders and Promotion in Teaching

Instituting hierarchical career ladders in teaching is expected to (a) help attract and retain top talent in teaching, and (b) provide quality control mechanisms through the use of stringent criteria for selection to upper levels and through periodic renewals of advanced certificates or regular evaluations of teachers (McPartland & Fessler, 1992).

In many Asia-Pacific education systems, the potential for teachers to advance through career paths is extremely restricted as the availability of positions to which teachers can be promoted is limited. The development of career ladders for classroom teachers is often centred on preparing for administrative positions, rather than improving teaching performance or the educational program. The competition for administrative positions, with their higher compensation, has resulted in a loss of outstanding classroom teachers. Extensive encouragement of classroom teachers to prepare for an administrative position tends to preclude maintenance of superior staff with teaching skills.

The career ladder of teachers in Korea and Japan is very short and simple. Teachers are classified, according to their educational background and experiences, into assistant teachers, second level teachers, first level teachers, vice-principals and principals. In practice, promotion from the second to first level teachers is made automatically after a certain period of experience. The nature and difficulty of duty, the authority and responsibility and role expectation of the two levels are rather similar. Since assistant teachers are very few, regular teachers develop to have a sense of promotion only when they move to an administrative position and, therefore, teachers are not likely to invest their effort in developing their professional skills in teaching.

Because of this career structure, competent teachers favour being promoted to vice-principal, principal or other educational administrators or professional grades, instead of remaining as classroom teachers. Teachers who are devoted to teaching and produce excellent educational achievement among their students are not treated as favourably as those who are performing administrative jobs. In fact most teachers give excessive importance to status upgrading to the positions of vice-principal or principal. Excessive competition for promotion to administrative positions has led to many teachers neglecting their intrinsic task (Seo, 1994).

In order to nurture a social climate that respects teachers who are committed to teaching, the Korean Government is attempting to restructure the current personnel system of teachers, vice-principal and principal to adopt a head teacher position that is the highest position for classroom teachers being separated from the administrative track. It is suggested that the candidate for a head teacher position should have a certain level of teaching experience and professional expertise in subject education or other specialised field of education. It is also suggested that the certificate for the head teacher position should be given following the completion of a qualification training program, and an appropriate compensation level should also be determined (MOEHRD, 2000).

Singapore. In contrast, Singapore's teaching profession has a multi-stage (13 ranks) career ladder and teachers can get promoted every two to three years. Teachers are classified into college graduates and non-graduates. Each group of the teachers is supposed to go through three stages of general education officer, two stages of senior education officer and eight stages of super senior officer. The two groups of teachers, namely, college graduates and non-graduates, have a different salary structure at each stage (Kim, Yang, & Kim, 2000). The promotion of teachers is recommended by the principal and decided by the board of teacher promotion. The most important agents in the recommendation and decision of promotion are principals and chief teachers. In the appraisal of job performance, leadership, teaching skill and capability, it is difficult to guarantee complete objectivity. In particular, the appraisal of teacher's capability depends completely on the subjective judgment of the principal and chief teachers. Therefore, those teachers who do not maintain a good relationship with the principal and chief teachers tend to complain about the promotion results (Kim, Yang, & Kim, 2000).

2.5. Placement

The setting up of reasonable standards for the placement and duty performance of teachers is a very important agenda in teacher policy. In Korea, the government is attempting to improve the standards for the placement and duty performance of teachers in primary and secondary schools. It has been pointed out that according to the current *Regulation of Education Act*, differences in various factors between school levels and regions are not considered in the allocation of teachers to each school since the allotment of the teacher placement quota is determined in a uniform way. Consequently, a serious teacher shortage occurs in a certain level of schools in certain regions. Furthermore, many teachers complain about the inequity of teaching hours per week (Park, Lee, & Hong, 2000).

Moreover, with the recent introduction of the Seventh National Curriculum, which drastically expands the student choice of subjects in a situation of teacher strategies, the revision of teacher placement standards has become inevitable (Kim, Y. H., 2000). The problem of supply with the additional demand for teachers is one of the most important factors limiting the efficient operation of the Seventh National Curriculum. As the demand for contract teachers for the subjects (for which the securing of regular teachers is difficult) is increasing, it becomes necessary to set up the standards for securing contract teachers and those for duty performance very clearly. It is emphasised that the teacher placement standards should be improved in such a way as to support the rational management of the new curriculum. It is also emphasised that the duty which teachers should perform including teaching hours have to be clarified through setting up standard teaching hours (Park, Lee, & Hong, 2000).

The Korean MOEHRD is attempting to determine standard teaching hours for each grade of each school level. It plans to consider the number of students and standard teaching hours when calculating the legally established standard for the allocation of teachers in addition to the current number of classes. In the long run, the city and province would be allowed to determine the maximum number of teachers based upon the standard teacher-student ratio.

The Korean MOEHRD is also reviewing a new way to calculate the maximum number of teachers in cases of contract teachers, part-time teachers with jobs in the private sector, and part-time lecturers. Further, MOEHRD is examining the ways to hire these teachers as long as the funding is available, even though the maximum number of the legal teacher placement quota has been filled. Each of the municipal and provincial offices of education will independently need to establish reasonable and effective teacher placement criteria.

3. RESEARCH

A number of research studies have been undertaken to tackle the problems and issues examined above in the Asia-Pacific education systems. In this section, the research studies are examined, with particular reference made to the studies conducted in Korea in recent years. As Korea was approaching the twenty-first century, MOEHRD (1999) established and announced "A tentative comprehensive plan for the development of the teaching profession" and sought to prepare a final version of the policy plans (MOEHRD, 2000). In the plans, MOEHRD placed an emphasis on the systematic and comprehensive restructuring of the basic framework for teacher policy. While establishing and implementing the plans, MOEHRD has launched 31 research projects among which there are a couple of research studies related to staffing in schools, including the following: "A study on the development of competency-based duty of teachers" (Park &

Chung, 1999a); "A study on job performance standards by school level, teacher rank, and certificate" (Park & Chung, 1999b); "A study on the improvement of appraisal system for the promotion of teaching personnel and the rational evaluation" (Park et al., 2000); "A study on reasonable teaching hours per week and teacher placement standards by school level" (Chung & Park, 1999); "A study on the establishment of standards for the reasonable placement and job performance of regular and contract teaching personnel for the operation of the Seventh National Curriculum" (Park, Lee, & Hong, 2000); "A study on the restructuring teacher career ladder and certification system in Korea" (Kim, Yang, & Kim, 2000).

All of these research studies are basically policy-oriented studies rather than foundation studies. Most of them have a similar structure: (a) identifying the main problems of current status; (b) reviewing theoretical background and previous studies; (c) examining four to five foreign country cases and drawing implications for pursuing the direction and measures for reform or improvement; (d) collecting empirical data using in-depth interviews or questionnaire surveys and analysing the result; and (e) searching for the direction and measures for reform or improvement.

In order to tackle these research questions, these research workers have employed various research methods: (a) reviewing the existing studies and proposals; (b) examining cases of developed countries; (c) carrying out a survey using questionnaires to teachers, school administrators, school inspectors, educational experts or parents; (d) conducting in-depth interviews with those groups of people related to education; and (e) collecting opinions and advice of educational experts through discussions and an open forum. Some research studies have employed all of these methods.

These research studies provide the data about public opinion on the major policy issues concerned. They also provide the information about the experience of foreign countries. They suggest policy directions and concrete measures to be taken. The findings of these studies have been carefully examined in the development and implementation of public policy.

4. FUTURE DIRECTIONS

Imbalance between teacher supply and demand is a common problem in many Asia-Pacific education systems due to either an unreasonable teacher policy or the age structure of population. It is likely to remain a problem in the near future. The shift of teacher policy promoting changes from a closed to an open system of teacher training and recruitment, and from uniform to diverse ways of teacher training and recruitment may be one of the more efficient ways of maintaining the elasticity of teacher supply and demand and solving the problem of imbalance between teacher supply and demand. Such Asia-Pacific systems as Korea and Japan are attempting to create opportunities to provide a teacher qualification examination for everyone and the opportunities to become teachers or school administrators to those experts without teacher certificates but who have job experience related to education. These countries are also attempting to diversify the employment status of teachers. These attempts are expected to encourage people of diverse ages with diverse experience to become teachers through diverse paths.

Many Asia-Pacific education systems are developing and refining teacher's job performance standards to implement the merit-based compensation system under the assumption that the teachers would cultivate and make use of their abilities to the best when an acceptable system is established to evaluate their professional competence. The lesson from the experience of the Asia-Pacific countries is that the appraisal system should incorporate into it all elements of teacher effectiveness, high performance and human resource functions, rather than focusing merely on a series of teaching behaviours which are sometimes isolated from each other.

There has been an attempt to establish better career ladders for classroom teaching jobs in some of Asia-Pacific systems in order to avoid the drain of competent classroom teachers to administrative positions and to encourage teachers to remain devoted to teaching. Despite teachers' resistance to the development of teacher career ladders with differentiating compensation according to job ranks or levels, the efforts to develop policies to stretch the career ladder of the teaching job is expected to continue.

A variety of policy studies to tackle these issues in staffing have been conducted in the Asia-Pacific education systems reviewed here. These studies and the experience of those systems suggest that the staffing structure in school education should be restructured to respect the ability and achievements of teachers and to introduce greater openness and flexibility. Furthermore, from the findings presented in this article, an important implication can be drawn that, while various countries are already making efforts to rationalise their policy on staffing in school education, particularly by making their policy research more comparative and more methodologically rigorous, there is still the need to take a proactive perspective such that staffing policy formulation and reformulation could be made more relevant to the future development of the education systems within a globalised and information technology-intensive context.

REFERENCES

Accanokazya (2000). *Educational Data Book 2000–2001*. Tokyo: *Sisatongshinsa* (Japanese).
Awatere-Huata, D. (1998). *Zero Tolerance*. Wellington: Parliament Buildings and Government Press.
Castetter, W. B., & Young, I. P. (2000). *The Human Resource Function in Educational Administration* (7th edn). Upper Saddle River, New Jersey: Merrill.
Central Educational Council (1998). On the way of the existence of local educational administration [On-line]. Available: Http://www.monbu.go.jp/singi/cyukyo/00000253 (Japanese).
Chung, K. H., & Park, Y. S. (1999). *A Study on Reasonable Teaching Hours per Week and Teacher Placement Standards by School Level*. Seoul: MOEHRD & KEDI (Korean).

Department of Personnel Management of the Tokyo Office of Education (2000). *About the Introduction of the Educational Personnel Evaluation System in Tokyo Province.* Quarterly Educational Law No. 124. Tokyo: Office of Education.

Department of Region of Japanese Ministry of Education (1999). On the current status of the appointment of principals and chief teachers in public schools in 1999. *The Monthly Magazine of the Board of Education Dec. 1999* (Japanese).

Kim, G. J. (1999). Issues and tasks for development of Korea's teacher policy. In *Korea-OECD Seminar on Teacher Policy: Cases of Selected OECD Member Countries* (pp. 99–112). Seoul: MOEHRD & KEDI.

Kim, H. S. (2000). Towards achieving high quality pre-service teacher training in Korea. *Asia-Pacific Journal of Teacher Education & Development, 3*(1), 55–77.

Kim, H. S., Yang, S. S., & Kim, A. N. (2000). *A Study on the Restructuring Teacher Career Ladder and Certification System in Korea.* Seoul: KEDI (Korean).

Kim, Y. C. (1994). Development direction for teacher personnel policy. In *Academic Seminar of Korean Public Policy Conference.* Seoul: KEDI.

Kim, Y. H. (2000). The 21st century vision of the Korean teaching profession: Issues and policy plans. *Asia-Pacific Journal of Teacher Education & Development, 3*(1), 35–54.

Kwak, B. S. (1999). Call for a reform in Korea's primary and secondary education and improvement of teacher policy. In *Korea-OECD Seminar on Teacher Policy: Cases of Selected OECD Member Countries* (pp. 79–96). Seoul: Korean MOEHRD & KEDI.

Langley, J. (1999). A professional renaissance in teaching: The case for a genuine partnership between teachers and the state. In *Korea-OECD, Seminar on Teacher Policy: Cases of Selected OECD Member Countries* (pp. 175–202). Seoul: MOEHRD & KEDI.

Masami, M. (1999). Teacher policies in Japan. In *Korea-OECD Seminar on Teacher Policy: Cases of Selected OECD Member Countries* (pp. 233–255). Seoul: Korean MOEHRD & KEDI.

McNay, M. (1999). *Performance Management in Primary Schools: A Case Study.* Unpublished MSc thesis. University of Canterbury.

McPartland, J. M., & Fessler, R. (1992). Staffing patterns. In M. C. Alkin et al. (Eds.), *Encyclopedia of Educational Research* (6th edition) Vol 4 (pp. 1252–1259), New York: Macmillan.

MOEHRD (1999). The current status of teacher training institutions (Internal data) Seoul: MOEHRD (Korean).

MOEHRD (2000). *Comprehensive Plans for the Development of Teaching Profession.* Seoul: MOEHRD (Korean).

Park, D. K. et al. (2000). *A Study on the Improvement of Appraisal System for the Promotion of Teaching Personnel and the Rational Evaluation.* Seoul: MOEHRD & KEDI (Korean).

Park, Y. S., & Chung, K. H. (1999a). *A Study on the Development of Competency-Based Duty of Teachers.* Seoul: KEDI (Korean).

Park, Y. S., & Chung, K. H. (1999b). *A Study on Job Performance Standards by School Level, Teacher Rank, and Certificate.* Seoul: MOEHRD & KEDI (Korean).

Park, Y. S., Lee, M. H., & Hong, H. J. (2000). *A study on the establishment of standards for the reasonable placement and job performance of regular and contract teaching personnel for the operation of the 7th national curriculum.* Seoul: MOEHRD & KEDI (Korean).

Picot, B. (1988). *Administering for Excellence: Effective Administration in Education.* Wellington: The Task Force.

Seo, J. H. (1994). *The Educational Personnel Management.* Seoul: Seyoungsa (Korean).

Teacher Registration Board (TRB) (1994). *The Registration of Teachers in Aotearoa New Zealand.* Wellington: The Board.

Yang, S. S. (2000). Improving Korean teachers' professionalism: Issues of recent personnel management reform. *Asia-Pacific Journal of Teacher Education & Development, 3*(1), 99–116.

67

School Leadership and Management

ALLAN WALKER

Chinese University of Hong Kong, Hong Kong

1. INTRODUCTION

Any attempt to cast a net across a large and diverse area, such as the Asia-Pacific region, is fraught with pitfalls. The societies which comprise the region differ tremendously both within and between national boundaries. They differ in terms of long-standing cultural values and beliefs, social expectations, educational structures, political governance and ideologies and stages of economic development, to name but some. Any attempt to outline and comment comprehensively on the state of, in this case, school leadership and management in the region, risks painting a sketchy and generalised picture at best.

Given the difficulties of accounting for the multifarious contexts and cultures present in the region in such a short piece, this article sets out to outline some common elements of the current educational reform context in the region and to explore how this is remaking the role of the principal across a number of Asia-Pacific education systems. In outlining common reforms, it is suggested that policies pursuing decentralisation and school based management (SBM) are especially influential in shifting the role of the principal in the region. Such an approach is defensible given that throughout the last decade the Asia-Pacific region has witnessed unprecedented and broad-based movement toward decentralisation. Although these reforms have touched all levels of education, the dominant target has been the school and hence, unavoidably, the principal.

While starting from a reform perspective, it should be noted that educational policy, particularly at the school implementation level, constantly interacts with shifting local conditions and societal cultures that filter its shape and efficacy. Although the article touches on some such areas, it is impossible to do their intricacies justice. The article is also bounded by its concentration on the principalship. This is not to deny the importance of other forms and sources of leadership that operate throughout school communities in the region. However, a focus on the principalship is justified in terms of its key role in school operation, school change and policy implementation. Rightly or wrongly, the principal often stands at the centre of school level reform – often alone and often confused – as perhaps the key figure.

This article has four main sections. The first section briefly outlines common threads running through the general reform environment in the region. This is important as it recognises that principals must operate within multiple contexts and that these influence the role they are expected to play. The second section suggests that policies that can be grouped under decentralisation, and SBM strike closest to the everyday role of the principal and place tremendous demands on them to change. The third section summarises some of the ways in which the principalship is changing in reaction to decentralisation and how this calls for a reshaping of the role of the principal. The final section discusses three major challenges that need to be faced if principals are to reshape meaningfully, their role in line with current reforms.

2. THE REFORM CONTEXT

Given the vast social, cultural and political diversity of the Asia-Pacific region, it would appear a daunting task to sift general school reform trends. However, there appear to be a cluster of reforms which seem remarkably similar, at least in espoused intent, across the region, and which hold increasing sway over the lives of school leaders. As Hallinger (1998) notes: "... one is (also) struck by the overlapping nature of the reforms within the Asia-Pacific region. There remain wide differences in national cultures and institutional systems of education within the region. Yet, the nature of the reforms selected by policy makers for implementation is uncanny in its similarity" (p. 423). The reforms also have remarkably similar roots and mirror global, often neo-liberalist, trends which explicitly link economic productivity and education. As Gopinathan and Ho (2000) show clearly in Singapore, politicians and policy makers "... believe in a positive relationship between education and (economic) development" (p. 166). Likewise, schools in Hong Kong, Thailand and China have been clearly identified as the vehicles for preparing young people capable of meeting the needs of rapidly changing societies.

Following a comprehensive review, Cheng and Townsend (2000) have identified a number of reform trends common across the region. These include new visions for education, the expansion and restructuring of education and, importantly, the quest for quality education. This quest for quality has been manifest in policies targeting, for example, individual student needs, thinking and problem solving skills, improving teacher qualifications and skills and a growing emphasis on improving the curriculum. The quality movement is exemplified in a Hong Kong report, *Quality School Education* (Education Commission, 1996), which concentrates, among other themes, on "ways to improve school management and performance towards the provision of quality school education to better meet the needs of students" (p. x).

Other reforms focus on increased accountability and quality assurance, the privatisation of education, requirements for strategic planning, the development of new curricula and improvement in teaching and learning and the use of information technology. Reformers have also begun examining rigid and all-consuming examination and evaluation practices. Recent reform in China has seen much attention focused on how to move from "test-oriented education" towards "quality-focused education", which includes ways to improve curriculum and instructional content, teacher education and educational evaluation (Tang, 2001). Reform also targets the professional development of principals and teachers and, importantly, a marked and quite radical shift to decentralisation and SBM, including community involvement in school decision-making. As governments struggle to legitimise the communities' voice, school principals find themselves forced into sharing power with parents, community members and teachers alike. While each of the above trends is present to varying degrees in many countries across the region their scope, pattern, progress and impact differ, depending upon the contextual conditions within which they were introduced.

3. DECENTRALISATION

The reform environment within which principals in the region work has shifted spectacularly over the last decade – and will almost certainly continue to do so (Hallinger, 1998). Perhaps the reform that has had the most telling impact on the role of the principal is the shift toward decentralisation and SBM. Decentralisation reforms have impacted on almost all areas of school operation throughout the region and aim to alter substantially the role of school leaders. As with other reforms, those targeting decentralisation follow different motivations and forms but generally include school restructuring; school-based curriculum development; school development planning; increased teacher and parent involvement and the formation of school councils, delegated budgeting and human resource management; centralised curriculum planning using a learning outcomes framework; increased accountability to the central bureaucracy; increased parental choice; and greater competition between schools.

As mentioned above, not all such initiatives have been implemented in all systems, but it is difficult to find a country in the region that has not been touched in some way by decentralisation. This is illustrated in Singapore where decentralisation in one form or another has persisted unabated since 1988 (Gopinathan & Ho, 2000). This has contributed immensely to the evolution of the principal's role. Chew, Stott and Boon (2000) claim that by the early 1990s principals' roles had changed drastically: "Principals were no longer to function as passive managers but as 'Chief Executive Officers' responsible for designing the future of their schools" (p. 4). Similar influences linked clearly to decentralisation policies are apparent in the lives of principals across the region, including those in Thailand, mainland China, Republic of Korea, Malaysia, Hong Kong and Taiwan.

The situation in Taiwan and Hong Kong exemplify the influence of decentralisation across the region. In Taiwan, decentralisation and school restructuring are a central pillar of current reform and, as such, have a substantial impact on principals as they strive to exercise their leadership. Yang (2001) claims that the role of principals has become "diverse and paradoxical" as they are charged with control and responsibility for curriculum, personnel and budget, but are also expected to share decision-making power with parents, teachers and other community members. Cheung echoes similar concerns for Hong Kong principals.

> Hong Kong principals face an uncertain, constantly changing and rather stressful future ... they face wave upon wave of reform initiatives. Additional responsibilities without adequate resources have made the role changes much more painful than necessary. How to find more room and time for principals to metamorphose into a new breed needs pondering and concern by both authorities and the principals themselves. (Cheung 2000a, p. 62)

4. RESHAPING THE PRINCIPALSHIP

Although decentralising reforms come in an assortment of shapes and sizes and follow diverse rationales, all basically aim at one level, namely, to transfer greater responsibility from central authorities to the principal and, often simultaneously, teachers and the wider school community. In Japan, the 1998 report *Policies on the Educational Administration of Local Governments* recommended the extensive decentralisation of educational administration and, "the enhancement of autonomy and initiative by schools and the strengthening of community participation in educational activities" (Muta, 2000, p. 461). A key foundation underpinning decentralisation is the need to provide schools with increased flexibility and responsibility, so they can better cater to the unique needs of their communities. This motive is apparent in the Thai Basic and Occupational Training Project (BOET), which reinforced the importance of "decentralising decision making and enhancing local capacities for problem solving and change implementation" (Hallinger, Chantarapanya, Sriboonma, & Kantamara, 2000, p. 207). Likewise, Taiwan schools and principals are expected to respond to their constituents' voices and work closely with them to reach consensus on school-level decisions (Shen, 2001).

Increased autonomy and flexibility brings with it increased accountability for principals and an expectation that they relinquish some of their traditional power and authority. In Taiwan, Zhang (1999; cited in Fwu & Wang, 2001) claims that: "The top-down school decision making system in which the principal plays the dominant role is criticised for its inertia to enhance professional collaboration among teachers and actively respond to public needs" (p. 4). This means that principals confront not only the complexities accompanying the devolution of power to them at a school level, but also its redistribution within the school community itself. In Taiwan, for example, communities now have legislated power to make real decisions relating to the staffing and functioning of the school.

The sharing of decision-making power with teachers and parents threatens the traditional role of the principals in many regional societies. One notable example of this can be seen in Taiwan's *1994 Teachers Act*. The *Act* transferred the principal's power to hire teachers to a school-based search committee comprising administrators, teachers and parents and granted teachers the right to form union-like associations with the power to negotiate their rights and obligations with administrators. The *Education Act of 1999* further diluted the traditional in-school power of the principal by legislating more parental involvement in the internal decision-making processes of the school and radically changing the principal selection and tenure mechanisms. Since 1999, principals are selected and contracted for four years by district-level search committees composed of other administrators, parents, teachers and other educational experts. These changes have forced Taiwan's principals to "feel stressful, insecure and powerless" (Fwu & Wang, 2001, p. 18).

Involving parents and teachers in change and policy decisions is problematic for many principals, given their history of often-unquestioned authority. Rightly or wrongly, an influential 1991 report in Hong Kong claimed that principals were insufficiently accountable for their actions and "see their post as an opportunity to become 'little emperors' with dictatorial powers in the school" (Education and Manpower Branch and Education Department, 1991, p. 14). Cheng's (2000) research found that Hong Kong principals were weakest in providing incentives for teachers and encouraging participation in decision-making. Also in Hong Kong, Pang (1997) found that schools were generally highly centralised and that teachers seldom participated in decision-making or leadership. Principals in Taiwan are now expected to adopt a power-sharing mechanism which forces them to change their approach to decision-making from one based on traditional bureaucratic authority to one based on professional authority. This does not sit well with some principals who complain about the imbalance between their responsibility and authority due to constant reforming, and feel that they actually have less formal control over budgeting, planning and personnel. Taiwanese principals suggest that although teachers have more power, they are not subject to the same accountability criteria as principals (Fwu & Wang, 2001). As in many Asia-Pacific societies, relationships between principals and their school communities have been based on status and seniority where principals expected to be obeyed. A breaking down of such values can be an unsettling affair for principals.

The other side of the coin is that teachers can be equally reluctant to engage in shared decision-making. Hallinger and Kantamara (2000) cite an example in Thailand, which they describe as a vertically aligned culture system, which "exerts great influence upon social relations in the workplace. Persons of lower status (i.e. age, position, and seniority) naturally defer to those of higher status, accepting differences in power as a normal feature of social relations" (p. 49). Similarly, parents in Hong Kong are often reluctant to participate actively in school-level decision-making because this is seen as the responsibility of the professionals. Likewise, schools themselves may be seen as somewhat inept if they rely on parents to make decisions. In high power distance societies like Thailand and Hong Kong, it can be difficult for principals to encourage teachers to become openly and honestly involved in decision-making. So while principals are expected to involve actively, school community members in decision-making, they are hindered not only by their own traditional values and authority, but also by the reluctance of teachers and parents to become involved. In some cases, principals are seen as neglecting their leadership role if they do not take a strong, personal stand.

Gopinathan and Ho (2000), however, paint a different picture in Singapore. They suggest that new curricular demands have provided more opportunities for teachers to work together and that this has promoted a shift from enforced collegiality to more spontaneous collegiality. This, in turn, has resulted in a change in the working style of principals. Gopinathan and Ho (2000) thus conclude: "In the past, enforced collegiality was administratively regulated, while now collegiality among teachers is increasingly seen as a way of fostering staff development in the school and this has in fact changed the very way school principals manage their schools" (p. 180).

Principals are also being driven to shift from their traditional management role to that of educational, curriculum or instructional leader. Concerns for quality have prompted policy focusing on curriculum, teaching and learning. In Taiwan, for example, the implementation of curriculum reforms has been accompanied by an expectation that principals change from a traditional administrator into a curriculum leader. Fwu and Wang (2001) claim that this is a difficult transition for principals who are more accustomed to playing an administrative rather than an instruction or curriculum role. Cheng (2000) found that principals in Hong Kong displayed low levels of direct involvement in curriculum leadership and higher levels of indirect involvement.

Although the discussion has only touched upon a small number of factors reshaping the role of the principal, these show that the last decade in the Asia-Pacific region has seen a dramatic shift in the conception and expectations of principals. Throughout the region principals are being called upon to change the way they work and lead in at least five ways. First, principals are asked to become more proactive – to direct actively meaningful change and not just sit back and watch the world go by. In Singapore, "They (principals) were expected to respond to the growing dynamism and unpredictability of the external school environment and to steer their school forward as innovative leaders" (Chew, Stott, & Boon, 2000, p. 4). Second, principals are told to be consultative, open and democratic, to promote staff ownership and to create a school culture which nurtures shared leadership. Third, principals as educative leaders are increasingly charged with promoting a more integrative, coherent school.

Fourth, the move to SBM is based on the premise that there is no all-encompassing remedy to school level needs and problems. Leaders must help develop within their own community a capacity to identify and fashion solutions to local concerns. Such demands are only likely to intensify. This is shown clearly among the Chinese Ministry of Education's main tasks for 2002, namely, to: "Emphasize innovation in educational management, deepen the reform of educational administration, employ laws and regulations for school management" (Tang, 2001, p. 18). Fifth, in addition to expectations targeting internal school operation, principals in the region are more and more involved in the environment beyond the school. School leaders are held more accountable for the success or otherwise of their organisations, and the success of local initiatives depends on the principals' abilities to adapt their roles to new realities.

When put together, such pressures on principals produce an environment of excitement, uncertainty, confusion and paradox. As they face often-contradictory demands, many struggle to find their place and make sense of their new roles. On the one hand, they are expected to retain their traditional role as 'stabiliser' in the school and uphold tradition. On the other hand, they are being increasingly called upon to change, reform and redefine their schools. In the midst of such demands, principals are also pushed to reshape their own place and power in relation to parents and teachers. On a more positive note, at the same time as reforms such as decentralisation threaten the traditional role and comfort of principals, they also expose unheralded opportunities to change schools and improve the range of student outcomes.

Given the increasingly complex role expected of school principals in the region, it is not surprising that doubts have been expressed about the principal's capacity to deal with the changes associated with decentralisation reforms and make them work. For example, Muta (2000) questions whether Japanese principals are able to carry out what he calls "non-traditional tasks". Similarly, Yang's (2001) research found that although educational reforms expected Taiwan's principals to be change agents rather than managers, principals tended to reject change in favour of maintaining the *status quo*.

5. CHALLENGES TO RESHAPING THE PRINCIPAL'S ROLE

Thus far, it has been argued that the educational reforms currently in train in the region, and particularly those aimed at decentralisation and SBM, call for radical changes in the role of the principal. Principals are being driven to reshape their values, ways of working and positioning in the school. It is unclear, however, whether the reshaping that is called for will in fact be successful: that is, whether principals will be able to reshape positively their role to make the raft of reforms work. The transformation of the principalship faces a number of challenges to education systems, school communities and principals themselves. Although there are obviously many factors that impede the reshaping of the principalship, only three are dealt with here.

As touched upon in the previous section, the first challenge is that the nature of the reforms themselves may not take enough account of the cultures within which they are implemented. A corollary of this is that deeply rooted cultural values and norms may not be congruent with many of the reforms demanded and that this may inhibit acceptance of certain elements, such as shared leadership. The second challenge is the inadequate provision of professional development in many countries to help principals understand, believe in and implement, changes in their work and relationship with others. The third challenge is that reforms in different settings often lack linkage to each other and either go too far or not far enough in bringing about a change in the principalship.

The first challenge to the extent to which the principal's role will actually change is the degree of fit between reform components and the societal culture and context within which they are implemented. With increasing globalisation, societies in the region are exposed to values, knowledge and skills that, even under colonisation, were heretofore unavailable. As the social and cultural influence of globalisation continues across the region, its influence on educational policy and the principalship is indisputable. However, theories, policies and practices implemented in specific social settings may not be valid and applicable in other social-political-cultural contexts. This is because societal cultures, along with local economic, political and religious conditions, act as mediators and filters to policies and practices imported from overseas. In this mediating role, three reactions or responses are possible: adoption or complete acceptance, adaptation, and rejection (Dimmock & Walker, 2000).

It is customary to recognise three stages in the policy process: formulation, adoption, and implementation. The role of the principal is pre-eminent at the implementation stage. It is relatively easy to formulate and adopt policies from elsewhere but the real test of their suitability and efficacy comes at the implementation level. If the policy formulation and adoption stages fail to act as effective filters and mediators, the policy may meet its first real opposition at the school and principalship level. When reform policies aimed at reshaping the role of the principal fail to account adequately for cultural and contextual conditions, it becomes unlikely that the role will be genuinely transformed. One example of this, as touched upon earlier, is the attempted widespread implementation of collaborative leadership in schools.

Reforms across the region strongly advocate a change in principals' leadership style, from an authoritarian to a more participative style. There is an obvious attempt to disperse some of the present power and authority exercised by principals and for them to develop collaborative leadership styles, a trend in vogue in many Western societies. Broad involvement or shared leadership in schools is a new concept to both principals and teachers in many societies throughout the region and, in some cases, may be incongruent with existing cultural values and norms. Hui (1990), for example, while arguing that participative leadership is counterproductive in Chinese societies, states, "a participative superior is seen as indecisive and, therefore, not worthy of respect" (pp. 203–204). Cheung (2000b) supports this assertion in schools: "the large power distance traditionally renders the principal the most powerful figure in the school ... Administrative decisions are final and to be obeyed without question. The staff is kept in line through veiled threats or open sanctions and also through the promotion system which often rewards the obedient" (p. 241). Lin (2000) reveals a similar picture in mainland China, where despite mandated decentralisation to the school level, teachers have little motivation to engage in meaningful collaborative decision-making. Lin cites research that showed that over 50 per cent and 75 per cent of teachers respectively described their relationship as 'obedience' and 'unequal'. Because of the structure of many Chinese schools, Lin suggests that teachers tend to feel dependent on the principal.

Since leadership styles are intertwined with power, authority and responsibility, more participative approaches, at least as in some of the forms proposed in the region, may be ill-suited to the cultural conditions within which they are to be implemented. It may be that the cultural and contextual preferences of principals will reshape the form of specific reforms and, accordingly, the transformation of their own role. For example, while participation increases across the region, its practice may remain bounded by hierarchy and other status differences (Cheng and Wong, 1996). In other words, broader participation may well be implanted in schools, but look very different from that adopted by policy-makers and practised outside the region.

In summary, the exercise of leadership in the region is influenced by the values principals bring with them to school (Walker & Dimmock, 2002). These values are partly influenced by societal culture. For example, Walker and Dimmock (2000) found that the ways in which a number of Hong Kong principals perceived, managed and solved dilemmas were profoundly influenced by entrenched values that highlighted the importance of relational and organisational harmony, and respect for hierarchy and those in authority. If decentralising reforms overtly clash with such values, or are implemented too quickly, it becomes more difficult for principals to adopt meaningfully, new ways of working. Many reforms targeting the principalship demand deep and rapid participation, this may well contradict the high power distance prevalent in societies such as Hong Kong, China and Thailand and so minimise the chances of real change in the role of the principal.

A second challenge to the meaningful reshaping of the principalship is the lack of preparedness and professional support provided to principals. As Lin (2000) states forcefully, in Taiwan, "reinventing schools requires exceptional school leaders" – such leaders require a commensurate level of support and professional development to make the required role shift and, in many cases, this has not been forthcoming. This casts some doubt on whether they can adopt the new roles. As Muta (2000) explains in Japan, "The leadership and management skills of school principals are indispensable, but the current requirements for those positions are very strict making it very difficult to find qualified persons" (p. 464). While discussing whether principals will be able to cope with new responsibilities associated with decentralisation, Muta continues: "... some questions exist as to whether the principals can carry out such non-traditional tasks" (p. 464).

With the exception of a small number of countries, such as Singapore, most regional societies have only recently acknowledged the need for meaningful principal professional development to help principals reshape their roles. Lin (2001) states: "In Taiwan, with regard to principalship, most efforts had been focused on the issues of selection, before-job training, and transference. There were no specific preparation programs for principals ... Most of the opportunities for professional development for principals in Taiwan are sparse, unplanned, incoherent, spontaneous and without sequence" (p. 305). In January 1999, the Hong Kong Education Department released a consultative framework for principal development, which was designed "to equip and develop school principals with the necessary knowledge, skills and attitudes to become competent to lead schools into the new millennium" (Cheng, 2000, p. 68). Although some work has been done toward operationalising such a lofty goal (e.g., Walker, Begley, & Dimmock, 2000) its efficacy remains in question.

For principals to reshape successfully their role, they must have access to meaningful professional development. For such development to become relevant and offer any chance of real change, it should be developed in concert with principals themselves and be adequately resourced and rewarded by departments and ministries of education. It should also be linked closely to the reforms principals are expected to implement and shaped to form a coherent program, rather than the piecemeal, fragmented attempts that comprise the norm. Much of the responsibility for making professional development meaningful, of course, lies with principals themselves and their willingness to take some control of their own destinies.

In addition to re-examining the professional development provided to principals, some countries, such as Hong Kong and Japan, need to examine carefully their principal selection procedures. Other countries, such as Singapore, have carefully conceptualised and standardised selection criteria and processes in place (Chew, Stott, & Boon, 2000). Careful selection and principal-needs driven, contextually sensitive, professional development is paramount if principals are to remake their role effectively.

A third challenge to reshaping the principalship in the Asia-Pacific region is related to the degree to which decentralisation and other reforms have or have not been implemented, and to whether the depth of the reforms is either too extensive or too narrow to encourage a meaningful change. An example of reforms, perhaps not going far enough, may be found in mainland China (Tang, 2001). Recent SBM reform in China has implemented a "principal responsibility system" that gives increased responsibility to the principal within three organic elements that seek to increase teacher and community involvement. While acknowledging the positive impact of the reform on school efficiency and operation, Tang (2001) suggests that it has fallen down at the implementation stage, because it failed to include key functions such as teacher recruitment and school-based curriculum development. For principals to reshape their role in line with the demands of decentralisation reforms, it may not be enough to implement piecemeal reforms which, for example, force principals to share power with teachers but give them no say over the teachers hired.

On the other hand, some commentators might claim that reforming the role of the principal has gone too far too quickly in other countries. The *1994 Teachers Act* and *1999 Education Reform Act* in Taiwan may be examples of this. As mentioned above, in the course of the introduction of these *Acts*, principals have lost tenure, lost much of their power to hire teachers, had their own selection placed in the hands of teachers and community members and been forced to institute shared decision-making. At the same time the reforms have demanded that they be proactive, change and instructional leaders. The Curriculum Reform Program instituted in 2001 will apply further pressure as it deregulates curriculum to the school level and expects principals, "... to assume a major responsibility and lead staff to develop school based curriculum" (Fwu & Wang, 2001). A similar range of reforms also face principals in Hong Kong and Japan.

The effect of too many reforms, and reforms that appear to run in assorted directions, is that they further confuse principals by presenting them with more contradiction, incoherence and conflict. Reforms that appear to lack connection are unlikely to encourage a meaningful reshaping of the principalship. Overly crowded and unclear reform environments can result in rejection of reforms and a yearning for what "used to be". Following a small-study in Taiwan, Yang (2001) claims that as the role of the principal becomes more complex and contradictory, "most (principals) tend to support the *status quo* rather than change" (p. 9). An overly demanding and incoherent reform environment can also lead to a situation where potential leaders simply do not want to be school principals. Multiple reforms, especially if they lack coherence, may retard the reshaping of the role of the principal: after all, it is not easy to reshape your role if you are unsure what the role is meant to be.

6. CONCLUSION

As noted at the outset, painting a comprehensive picture of the state of school leadership and management in a region as vast as the Asia-Pacific region is all but impossible given the diversity of the region. However, a number of general themes can be discerned. The most obvious of these is that under the weight of multiple reforms, the role of the school leader has undergone substantial broadening, deepening and externalising. In focusing its attention, this article has sought to outline the reform policies calling for the transformation of the principalship and then suggested that policies focusing on decentralisation and SBM place special demands on principals in the region.

There is little doubt that regional principals continue to work in the midst of substantial change. At the same time as their roles undergo multiple shifts, their importance to school improvement, school change and student outcomes has increased rather than diminished. In order to understand fully the changing roles of the principal in the Asia-Pacific region, there is a real need for more empirical studies, particularly at the school level. To date, very little is known about what transpires in schools: the processes, relationships and functions related to the principalship have been sorely neglected. It is important that researchers supplement large scale policy commentaries with deeper examination of the work lives of principals and how they promote and cope with change. In other words, there is a need to build mid-range theories into various aspects of the principalship.

It is also important that these studies fully explore the different cultures and contexts that exert such a powerful influence on principals. For example, while current educational reform provides an important part of the context to school leadership, especially that part concerned with its changing nature and form, societal culture also provides an important backdrop to, and influence on, leadership.

Within multiple contexts, research is also needed into the skills, knowledge, values and attributes future school leaders throughout the region may require. As well as knowledge building such research can also inform ongoing personal and professional development opportunities: something traditionally missing in many regional systems. Investigations in this area may target, among other areas, leading autonomous organisations, leading learning, and how to involve usefully, others in school decisions.

While research in settings outside the region can certainly be informative to understanding the dynamics of the principalship in times of change, it would be a mistake to accept unquestioningly the outcomes of such research and apply them blindly to the Asia-Pacific region. Both the region as a whole and each individual society require a more realistic and contextually grounded understanding of school leadership and management and its place in educational reform and school change.

REFERENCES

Cheng, K. M., & Wong, K. C. (1996). School effectiveness in East Asia: Concepts, origins and implications. *Journal of Educational Administration, 34*(5), 32–49.

Cheng, Y. C. (2000). The characteristics of Hong Kong school principals' leadership: The influence of societal culture. *Asia Pacific Journal of Education, 20*(2), 68–86.

Cheng, Y. C., & Townsend, T. (2000). Educational change and development in the Asia-Pacific region: Trends and issues. In Y. C. Cheng & T. Townsend (Eds.), *Educational Change and Development in the Asia-Pacific Region: Challenges for the Future* (pp. 317–343). Lisse, The Netherlands: Swets & Zeitinger.

Cheung, M. B. (2000a). The changing roles and needs of school principals in Hong Kong. In A. Walker, P. Begley & C. Dimmock (Eds.), *School Leadership in Hong Kong: A Profile for a New Century* (pp. 61–62). Hong Kong: Hong Kong Centre for the Development of Educational Leadership.

Cheung, M. B. (2000b). Securing a better future: A Hong Kong school principal's perception of leadership in times of change. In C. Dimmock & A. Walker (Eds.), *Future School Administration: Western and Asian Perspectives* (pp. 225–248). Hong Kong: Chinese University Hong Kong Press.

Chew, J., Stott, K., & Boon, Z. (2000, September). *The Making of Secondary School Principals: Some Perspectives from Singapore*. Paper presented at the Australian Council for Educational Administration Conference Community Building in a Global Context, Tasmania, Australia.

Dimmock, C., & Walker, A. (2000). Globalization and societal culture: Redefining schooling and school leadership in the 21st century. *COMPARE, 30*(3), 303–312.

Education & Manpower Branch & Education Department (1991). *The School Management Initiative: Setting the Framework for Quality in Hong Kong Schools*. Hong Kong: Government Printer.

Education Commission (1996). *Quality School Education*. Report No. 7. Hong Kong: The Government Printer.

Fwu, B. J., & Wang, H. H. (2001, March). *Principals at the Crossroads: Profiles, Preparation and Role*

Perceptions of Secondary School Principals in Taiwan. Paper presented at the International Conference on School Leaders Preparation, Licensure, Certification, Selection, Evaluation and Professional Development, Taipei, Taiwan.

Gopinathan, S., & Ho, W. K. (2000). Educational change and development in Singapore. In Y. C. Cheng & T. Townsend (Eds.), *Educational Change and Development in the Asia-Pacific Region: Challenges for the Future* (pp. 163–184). Lisse, The Netherlands: Swets & Zeitinger.

Hallinger, P. (1998). Educational change in Southeast Asia: The challenge of creating learning systems. *Journal of Educational Administration, 36*(5), 492–512.

Hallinger, P., & Kantamara, P. (2000). Leading at the confluence of tradition and globalisation. *Asia Pacific Journal of Education, 20*(2), 46–57.

Hallinger, P., Chantarapanya, P., Sriboonma, U., & Kantamara, P. (2000). The challenge of educational reform in Thailand: Jing jai, jing jung, and nae norn. In Y. C. Cheng & T. Townsend (Eds.), *Educational Change and Development in the Asia-Pacific Region: Challenges for the Future* (pp. 208–226). Lisse, The Netherlands: Swets & Zeitinger.

Hui, H. (1990). Work attitudes, leadership styles and managerial behaviours in different cultures. In R. Brislin (Ed.), *Applied Cross-Cultural Psychology*. Beverly Hills, CA: Sage.

Lin, J. (2000). Reform in primary and secondary administration in China. In C. Dimmock & A. Walker (Eds.), *Future School Administration: Western and Asian Perspectives* (pp. 291–310). Hong Kong: Chinese University Hong Kong Press.

Lin, M. D. (2001, March). *Professional Development for Principals in Taiwan: The Status Quo and Future Needs Trends*. Paper presented at the International Conference on School Leaders Preparation, Licensure, Certification, Selection, Evaluation and Professional Development, Taipei, Taiwan.

Muta, H. (2000). Deregulation and decentralisation of education in Japan. *Journal of Educational Administration, 38*(5), 455–467.

Pang, S. K. (1997). The binding forces that hold school organisations together. *Journal of Educational Administration, 36*(4), 314–333.

Shen, W. J. (2001, February). *Centralisation or Decentralisation: International Experiences and the Implications for Taiwan*. Paper presented at the International Forum on Education Reforms in the Asia-Pacific Region, Hong Kong.

Tang, X. (2001). *Education Reform and Development in the People's Republic of China: Issues and Trends*. Paper presented at the International Forum on Education Reforms in the Asia-Pacific Region, Hong Kong.

Walker, A., & Dimmock, C. (2000). Leadership dilemmas of Hong Kong principals: Sources, perceptions and outcomes. *Australian Journal of Education, 44*(1), 5–25.

Walker, A., & Dimmock, C. (2002). Moving school leadership beyond its narrow boundaries: Developing a cross-cultural approach. In K. Leithwood & P. Hallinger (Eds.), *Second International Handbook of Educational Leadership and Administration* (pp. 167–204). Dorchecht, The Netherlands: Kluwer.

Walker, A., Begley, P., & Dimmock, C. (2000). *School Leadership in Hong Kong: A Profile for a New Century*. Hong Kong: Hong Kong Centre for the Development of Educational Leadership.

Yang, C. L. (2001). *The Changing Principalship and its Implication for Preparing Selecting and Evaluating Principals*. Paper presented at the International Conference on School Leaders Preparation, Licensure, Certification, Selection, Evaluation and Professional Development, Taipei, Taiwan.

68

Effective Schooling in the Asia-Pacific Region

CLIVE DIMMOCK

Centre for Educational Leadership and Management, University of Leicester, United Kingdom

1. INTRODUCTION

This article focuses on the idea of 'effective schooling' rather than on 'school effectiveness', and does so within the context of the Asia-Pacific region. Adopting such a focus is significant in three ways. First, it promotes a conceptualisation of schooling as located within a broader context involving the family, home, parenting and socialisation. Second, it is conducive to a more comprehensive discussion of school processes – especially curriculum, teaching and learning – than would otherwise be the case. Third, by contextualising the discussion within the Asia-Pacific region, attention is diverted away from a narrow ethnocentric concentration on Anglo-American research that has tended, hitherto, to dominate the field.

The article explores the meanings attached to effective schooling in four systems of education within the Asia-Pacific region, namely, mainland China, Hong Kong, Japan and Taiwan. All are described as Confucian heritage cultures. A number of propositions underpin the argument, some of which are developed in this chapter. First, the concept of 'effective schooling' is culturally, and contextually sensitive. Second, societies may view the concept differently, and such differences may be as wide within the Asia-Pacific region as between it and the rest of the world. Third, the key stakeholders in each of the school systems – teachers, parents, government and employers – have their own perceptions of the concept and its meaning. Fourth, these separate perceptions may or may not align. Fifth, the concept of effective schooling is transient and changing. Hence, the model of effective schooling advocated at any given moment in time by parents, employers or government may not be the model espoused at a subsequent or future point in time. Sixth, a mix of forces – some enhancing, others hindering and threatening, effective schooling – tends to exist simultaneously within every system and school.

An understanding of effective schooling in Asia, as elsewhere, needs to be grounded in the cultural context (Dimmock, 2000; Dimmock & Walker, 2000).

Perceptions of effective schooling are dependent on the extent to which schools reflect the wider society's cultural values, including its socio-political environment. Thus, a school in mainland China that overtly fails to support the political system would not be thought as providing so-called 'effective schooling', particularly by the government. The same is true in Taiwan. Similarly, given the emphasis on harmonious ethnic relations by the government and society of Singapore, a school that failed to promote such relationships between the three main ethnic groups that comprise the population, Chinese, Malay and Indian, would likely be discounted from that society's definition of 'effective schooling'. Consequently, definitions and perceptions of effective schooling are subject to local or national, rather than international or global, interpretation (Dimmock & Walker, 2000). While the approach adopted is based on a cultural exposition, it is wise to heed Cheng's (2000) advice, that cultural approaches are fraught with complexity and difficulty.

The aim of this article is to focus on particular features of effective schooling in the four systems, not to provide a comprehensive assessment of their strengths and weaknesses.

If 'effective schooling' is seen as a culturally-sensitive and contextually-based phenomenon, then within the cultural contexts of East Asia, it can be framed in terms of four propositions:

- a close harmony and alignment with family and home values;
- an inordinate emphasis on homework and examination success;
- systems of teaching, learning and school organisation that are reflective of, and are adapted to, deep-seated societal values and cultural environments; and
- teaching conditions and teacher professional development that is highly conducive to effective teaching.

2. CLOSE HARMONY BETWEEN SCHOOL, HOME AND FAMILY VALUES

Where parental and school values align, and where parents actively support the aims of the school, student achievement and behaviour are improved and effective schooling is more likely to result (Biggs, 1994; Hess & Azuma, 1991). In the Asia-Pacific region, it can justly be claimed that the values underlying societal culture and those underpinning school missions and aims seem to be more aligned than is the case in Western countries (Biggs, 1994). As Stevenson and Stigler (1992) point out, however, there are variations in parental practices and roles within the region, just as there are differences in schooling.

Children in these four Asian societies spend more days in school and more time each day in school than do their Western counterparts. For example, Stevenson and Stigler (1992) report that students in Beijing (China), Sendai (Japan) and Taipei (Taiwan) spend more hours at school, namely, eight hours during the week and four hours on Saturdays, than their American counterparts.

In addition, they spend more days each year at school. In Japan, for example, the legal minimum school year is 210 days, but most local school officials insist on 240 days. In Taiwan, 220 days is a typical school year.

However, the main point is not that this considerable time spent in school translates into more time devoted to academic learning. Rather, a good part of it is taken for extra-curricular activities. This means that the school occupies a central place in the social as well as academic life of the student. Even during holiday periods, Chinese and Japanese children rarely lose contact with their teachers and school friends (Hess & Azuma, 1991). School and home activities tend to merge, since the structure of the school year is punctuated by relatively more but short breaks between terms, than is the case in America (Watkins & Biggs, 1996).

Parents in the four Asian societies demonstrate strong support for their children's learning at school by sparing little expense in providing conditions conducive for learning in the home (Hess & Azuma, 1991). This is despite home conditions that are, at least physically, anything but favourable. Even among first year elementary school students, very high proportions of Japanese and Taiwanese parents invest in desks and make space available at home for children to focus on their homework (Stevenson & Stigler, 1992). The average living space for the Japanese family is only 900 square feet. In China and Hong Kong, family living space is even less, typically 500 square feet, yet even here, the present author has noticed that parents are keen to make the dinner table available after the family meal if there is insufficient space for a separate desk.

Parents are especially keen to encourage their children to read outside of school. For example, Asian children spend more time reading books and comics than their American counterparts, but help less, than their American counterparts, with domestic chores. Japanese mothers, in particular, claim that they would rather their children get on with their homework, and that in any case, living in small homes makes chores less onerous. Stevenson and Stigler (1992) found that Taiwanese, Japanese, and Chinese children in that order spend more time reading at home than do their American counterparts. Parents endorse children spending extra hours on homework, reading and filling in workbooks since they believe these activities are likely to enhance their children's progress at school.

The critical relationship between the home and school is well summarised by Stevenson and Stigler (1992):

> Japanese and Chinese appear to maintain a relatively sharp differentiation between the functions of home and school. Schools are primarily held responsible for developing academic skills, and the social skills required for integration into group life; the home is responsible for supporting the school's role and for providing a healthy emotional environment for the child. Parents and teachers work together, but do not duplicate each other's efforts. (p. 83)

Close communication between teachers and parents in China and Japan is often maintained through the use of notebooks that pass between them and which monitor the students' progress.

Moreover, children in mainland China, Taiwan and Japan are socialised in ways that endorse and support school success (Holloway, 1988; Salili, 1996). For example, role models that represent virtuous individuals, and selfless contributions to the welfare of the group or state, are extolled. In mainland China, Lei Feng, Chairman Mao's good soldier, is immortalised. In Taiwan, Sun Yat-sen and Chiang Kai-shek are highly honoured. In Japan, Kinjiro's efforts to learn two centuries ago are held up to today's youth (Stevenson & Stigler, 1992). Second, pre-schools and kindergartens in Japan and China place great emphasis on building socially interactive skills and strengthening group identification. Pressure on young children to conform is strong, coming from teachers, who are usually held in high esteem, and peers, through strong group identification (Salili, 1996). This same group identity means that Japanese and Chinese children are likely to feel that they are letting their parents down if they do not perform at school (Watkins, 2000). Third, Japanese and Chinese teachers explicitly teach skills and routines that help children learn, adjust and contribute to the smooth organisation and running of the classroom. This caring relationship (Gao, 1998; Jin & Cortazzi, 1998) includes imparting skills such as personal management, keeping tidy desks, use of the bathroom, taking notes and performing classroom duties.

Parental expectations are influential in student achievement and effective schooling. Cross-cultural comparisons of parental levels of satisfaction with schooling have been made by Stevenson and Stigler (1992), who asked parents in Chicago, Minneapolis, Beijing, Taipei (Taiwan) and Sendai (Japan) how satisfied they were with their children's performance at school. Only five per cent of the Chinese and Japanese mothers reported being 'very satisfied' with their child's school compared with 40 per cent of American mothers. While Japanese and Chinese children perform well on international academic achievement tests, compared with their American counterparts, their parents think less positively about their performance and their schools.

This attitude of non-complacency among parents, children and teachers establishes conditions conducive to effective schooling in the four Asian societies. Asian parents are generally more demanding and more stringent in their evaluations. Japanese and Chinese parents apply higher standards than do their American counterparts when judging their children's academic performance. Asian children, in turn, accept these standards and are motivated to work hard to meet them. In accounting for these differences in parenting, Stevenson and Stigler (1992) point out that by comparison with Japan, America lacks a common national curriculum and standard public examination system; it has relatively poor contact between home and school; and it generally accords lower priority to academic achievement.

Above all, Asian children are motivated to work hard and to succeed as a mark of respect for their parents. Success at school reflects well on the parents and family. Children are highly conscious of parental pressure and expectation on them to do their best at school. In summary, Japanese and Chinese children spend considerable time at home working on activities related to school, much more than their American counterparts. Such activities are strongly supported and nurtured by their families, whose values place education at the forefront of their priorities. Effective schooling therefore spreads well beyond the gates of the school into the home.

3. EMPHASIS ON HOMEWORK AND EXAMINATION SUCCESS

Research evidence shows that homework, providing it has certain characteristics, is a key factor in promoting student academic achievement (see Fraser, Walberg, Welch, & Hattie, 1987). In respect of the four Asian school systems, the importance attached to homework is so great that it is often excessive (Turay, 1994). Strong pressure to set homework comes from both parents and teachers (Stevenson & Lee, 1996).

Despite the cramped and overcrowded conditions in Asian homes, teachers assign more homework and children spend more time doing it, than their American counterparts. Interviews the author conducted with a group of primary school teachers in Hong Kong revealed that it is not atypical for elementary school children aged eight and nine years to spend four and five hours a night on homework. Such is the homework pressure on young children in mainland China, that the central government has instituted a decree forbidding all homework during the first year of elementary school. By contrast, in the year 2000, the Chicago Board of Education imposed a requirement of 30 minutes of homework per day for the first three years of elementary school. Taiwanese teachers tend to set more homework than even Japanese teachers, elementary school children being assigned homework during most of the year, including holidays.

Contradictory evidence exists on whether the effects of excessive homework on students in the four Asian societies are harmful. Stevenson and Stigler (1992) found little or no evidence that the stronger work ethic of Asian children translated into greater psychological problems, although their studies were confined to primary aged children. On the other hand, the pressure of homework combined with university entrance examinations at the upper secondary stage often manifest in severe stress and occasional personal and family tragedy.

In Japan, it is generally the mother who assumes the main role in assisting her children to complete homework, while in Chinese families, this role is shared with the father. In contrast, American parents place less importance on helping their children with homework. Chinese and Japanese parents are likely to be disciplined over their children completing homework, insisting on its completion before they are allowed to watch television (Stevenson & Stigler, 1992).

At the upper secondary stage, there is an equal pressure placed on examination success (Gow, Balla, Kember, & Hau, 1996). This is partly explained by the limited number of university places available. In Taiwan and China, for example, only one place per one hundred applicants may be available. Pressure on Japanese high school students' results in about 90 per cent attending *juku* or cram schools in evenings, weekends and holidays, in addition to their normal school (McAdams, 1993).

The double effect of excessive amounts of homework and overly competitive examination systems may have negative effects on schooling. For example, the main preoccupation becomes passing the examination rather than learning *per se*. Even in Hong Kong, where the number of university places has increased six-fold during the 1990s, there is still considerable pressure on prospective university entrants. Educational policy makers in Hong Kong have recently advocated a reduction in examination pressure at both primary and secondary school, arguing that children are over-examined throughout their school lives, which in turn has a negative effect on quality schooling.

4. LEARNING, TEACHING AND SCHOOL ORGANISATION

Successful learning on the part of students, quality teaching, and school organisation conducive to successful learning and teaching – are all intrinsic elements of effective schooling. This section argues that, in general, all three conditions exist in the four Asian systems being reviewed. It further claims that a key aspect contributing towards their effectiveness, in all four societies, is the extent to which they reflect particular cultural characteristics, which in turn distinguish them from practices elsewhere in the world. They are reflective of and adapted to deep-seated societal values and cultural environments.

4.1. *Cultural Assumptions Underpinning Learning: Effort and Ability*

A key feature of effective schooling in Asia is the cultural basis on which children's learning takes place. Japanese and Chinese societies uphold a different view of the relationship between effort, ability and achievement from Westerners (Biggs, 1994; Stevenson & Lee, 1996). Asian societies believe that effort and hard work are the keys to learning and that they can compensate for lack of ability. By contrast, Americans tend to attribute academic success more to innate ability. These different social philosophies about what accounts for success, in the case of the Chinese, tracing back to the teachings of Confucius, have ramifications for parental expectations, behaviour at home and teaching at school (Biggs, 1994; Hess & Azuma, 1991; Holloway, 1988).

The Chinese and Japanese belief, particularly espoused by parents, that effort will lead to achievement tends to act as a motivation to work long hours. In contrast, American belief in ability and a preoccupation with measuring it through intelligence tests, means that children are soon labelled as either high or low achievers and no amount of hard work can compensate for lack of ability. Parental attitudes and expectations adjust accordingly (Stevenson & Lee, 1996). For example, a much lower percentage of Chinese and Japanese mothers believe that their children's final school performance is predictable from an early age than is the case with American mothers (Stevenson & Stigler, 1992). The Asian view, referred to as the 'effort model' offers a more optimistic scenario for learning outcomes than the American 'ability model', and explains why Asian students are willing to work hard and long to achieve.

4.2. Learning: A Culturally-Related Process

Learning styles and how learning takes place are influenced by culture. Chinese students in Hong Kong, and it is claimed Japanese and Chinese generally, learn differently from Western students (Watkins & Biggs, 1996). Asian students have a well acknowledged tendency to rote learn, a characteristic assumed by Westerners to mean that only surface learning, rather than deep understanding, takes place. However, Watkins and Biggs (1996) argue that for Chinese students, memorisation leads to understanding, although whether it deepens understanding or is a precondition for it is not clear. For Hong Kong students, their studies show that rote learning is a necessary part of memorisation, which in turn is linked to deeper understanding (Kember & Gow, 1990; Watkins & Biggs, 1996). While memorisation is used to deepen understanding, it can also be used for passing examinations. Asian students may thus be sophisticated enough to vary the process to suit the objective. Westerners generally fail to see the advantages of rote learning, instead regarding it as a lower-order form of learning and contrasting it with higher-order learning skills associated with deep learning and learning for understanding. Rote learning leading to memorisation, deep understanding and examination-passing is a central characteristic of effective schooling in the four Asian systems.

4.3. Teaching: A Culturally-Related Process

In understanding the major differences between teaching in mainland China, Taiwan, Japan (and America), it is helpful once more to refer to the Stevenson and Stigler (1992) research in scores of classrooms in these countries from 1980 onwards. They found major differences within and between Asian (and Western) countries. Their conclusions are summarised below.

(1) Asian teachers have relatively few class contact hours (Cheng & Wong, 1996; Reynolds & Farrell, 1996). In Japan and Taiwan, teachers teach about 60 per cent of the lesson time. In China, teachers might only teach three or four hours each day (Cheng & Wong, 1996; Stevenson & Lee, 1996). This allows them to plan lessons more carefully, spend more time seeing students who need help and discuss teaching techniques with their colleagues. This is not the practice, however, throughout Asia. For example, the author having supervised teachers in Hong Kong is aware that they have class contact hours similar to American teachers, namely, 90 per cent of the total weekly lesson time.
(2) Japanese, mainland Chinese and Taiwanese teachers generally spend more

time working together and helping each other design lessons. Their collaboration is facilitated by, first, the existence of a national curriculum, which means that they are often teaching the same material at about the same time; second, more non-contact time; and third, close proximity in the same workroom. Hong Kong teachers, by contrast, often lack the time and incentive to engage in such collaboration since they lack the preparation time.

(3) Teachers in Japan, mainland China and Taiwan come close to practising the principles of 'informed teaching' (Dimmock, 2000). In general, they are well informed and well prepared, guiding their students through the material. Lessons are clearly structured: each lesson starts with aims and purposes and finishes with a summary. During the lesson, there is interaction and discussion and students are active participants in problem solving.

(4) Teachers display technical proficiency in basic teaching techniques, which helps explain why students concentrate in class more than their Western counterparts.

(5) Lessons are characterised by seatwork interspersed with teacher input in brief but frequent periods throughout the lesson, rather than the lesson being divided into two halves, with teaching first, followed by seatwork, as in the America classroom. Asian children thus have more opportunity to interact with their teachers than do American students.

(6) Teachers give a lot of corrective feedback and this serves to motivate the students. Corrective feedback is given in various ways. For example, a Japanese lesson might be based on a poor piece of work completed by a particular student, with the teacher exposing all the weaknesses to the whole class so that all can learn from the individual's mistakes. The individual student whose work is exhibited withstands attention and personal embarrassment for the benefit of the whole group. Such a practice in a Chinese classroom would lead to loss of face (Biggs, 1994; Gow et al., 1996).

(7) Asian teachers try to make subjects more relevant and interesting by relating material to be learned to the children's everyday lives. For example, word problems in mathematics often serve this function, turning the lesson into an active problem solving exercise.

(8) When Beijing teachers were asked to rank the most important attributes of good teaching, they ranked 'clarity' first, whereas Chicago teachers ranked 'sensitivity to the needs of individuals'. Beijing teachers ranked 'enthusiasm' second, while Chicago teachers chose 'patience'. While American teachers see their main role as catering to the needs of individual children, possibly at the expense of whole class teaching, Asian teachers devote their attention to the principles and processes of whole-class teaching, while still acknowledging the needs of individual children. Despite class sizes of 60 or more, teachers still manage high levels of individual interaction with students (Jin & Cortazzi, 1998).

(9) Asian teachers tend to stick to the basic principles of teaching, and have more time and energy to apply them (Biggs, 1994; Hess & Azuma, 1991).

They incorporate a variety of teaching techniques into a lesson, rely frequently on discussions rather than lectures, achieve smooth transitions from one activity to another and spend more time on task (Reynolds & Farrell, 1996).

While Stevenson and Stigler (1992) and Biggs (1994) conclude that certain teaching stereotypes in regard to Confucian heritage societies are valid, for example, large class sizes, some authoritarianism and high examination pressures, in other respects, the stereotypes fail to capture reality because they ignore cultural factors. The teacher in Confucian heritage societies has developed culturally-adaptive ways of teaching to circumvent what is regarded in the West as unfavourable conditions, especially in terms of large class sizes, for effective teaching. Teachers in such hierarchical societies enjoy considerable respect; yet, they exercise warmth and care in their relationships with students. They typically blend whole-class teaching in classes of 40 to 60 students with student-centred approaches and group work (Watkins, 2000). They develop with the student a functional joint responsibility for learning and teach in ways that push for high cognitive level outcomes. Above all, they place great store in planning and cooperating with their colleagues as part of a professional community.

Other favourable factors are supportive of teachers and teaching in Confucian heritage societies in relation to their Western counterparts. Generally, they enjoy higher social and professional status (Hofstede, 1991). They are accorded more respect by students and parents, and they are more supported by the home and family in their efforts to encourage children to learn. Students are more self-disciplined in the classroom and more willing to be attentive, collaborative and more adept at so-called 'cue-seeking', especially in regard to assessment, and are more task-oriented in their class work and homework.

The moral is that cultures are systems (Biggs, 1994). It is, therefore, misleading to look at specific practices or features on their own, and then to identify their presence or effectiveness in another culture. If certain Western features do not seem to be present in Asian settings, it might be that they exist in a disguised or different form, or that they are compensated for by other sets of factors. The dynamic interplay between all of the parts, not the presence of any one part, is what makes it all work. In short, culture provides the context within which the parts of effective schooling interact.

In summary, Taiwanese, Japanese and Chinese schools have achieved high levels of harmony between their core values and those of parents and society at large. Although class sizes tend to be large, schools and teachers, through adaptation, have circumvented these otherwise negative features. For example, they have devised low teaching loads allowing for better quality preparation; informed teaching practices, such as more wait time and more individual attention within whole-class teaching; more peer interaction and a belief in greater effort when faced with failure (Watkins, 2000). None of these alone makes a significant difference. Rather, it is the harmony achieved between teaching and learning and between the school and society, which matters. There is much about the methods of teaching and learning in Japanese and Chinese schools that would be unworkable in Western schools. In Japan, for example, the student, not the school, is seen as the 'twig to be bent'. Western cultures, receptive to the notion that the school accommodates the child, continue to grapple with the problem of putting this ideal into practice.

4.4. *School and Class Organisation Reflect Cultural Values*

Children's experiences at school in the four systems are highly structured. For example, the school day, as well as the content and sequence of lessons, are tightly planned (Jin & Cortazzi, 1998; Reynolds & Farrell, 1996). Yet, despite tight structure, schools promote high levels of social interaction (Watkins, 2000). Teachers give thought to the grouping of students, such that they can learn from one another. Children tend to do a lot more group work rather than individual work. In Japan, this group emphasis is known as the '*han*'. Membership of each *han* is carefully planned by the teacher to ensure that each student plays a team role and performs to achieve an expected outcome. Moreover, students in these four Asian societies display a liking for school more than do their American counterparts (Stevenson & Stigler, 1992). Asian elementary school classrooms not only manage to promote children's learning, but do so while instilling structure, order and discipline and at the same time, a liking, for school.

5. TEACHING CONDITIONS SUPPORT EFFECTIVE TEACHING

Good quality teaching lies at the heart of effective schooling (Cheng, 1994). The quality of teaching relies on the calibre of entrants attracted to the profession, the pre-service and in-service training provided, and the working conditions under which teachers perform. These leading conditions and teacher professional development support effective schooling in the four systems being reviewed.

Teacher training methods in the four Asian systems vary considerably. In Japan, teacher training is like an apprenticeship. There is a systematic effort to pass on the accumulated wisdom of past generations of teachers to new entrants and to keep perfecting that practice by providing for continued professional interaction. Beginning teachers, by law, must receive a minimum of 20 days of in-service training, supervised by master teachers, during their first year on the job. Many teachers in mainland China have only rudimentary training. However, conditions vary widely between the more prosperous cities and the poor rural areas. In Hong Kong, teachers receive a preponderance of up-front training in college, supplemented by brief spells of teaching practice in schools, before starting teaching. Thereafter, they receive limited opportunities for in-service training by comparison with Japanese and mainland Chinese teachers, and they certainly lack the school-based professional development practices engaged in by Japanese teachers. It is worth describing these practices in more detail.

Japanese teachers, both beginners and experienced, are expected to hone their skills through interaction with other teachers. Meetings are organised to discuss specific teaching techniques and skills and to devise lesson plans and handouts. '*Kouaikenshuu*' is the term used for the continuous process of school-based professional development engaged in by groups of Japanese teachers throughout their careers. According to Stigler and Hiebert (1999), "These groups play a dual role: not only do they provide a context in which teachers are mentored and trained; they also provide a laboratory for the development and testing of new teaching techniques" (p. 110).

Run by teachers who work together in grade-level, subject, or special purpose groups, such as the school technology committee, a range of diverse activities is undertaken all within the auspices of the school improvement plan that sets the goals and focus for each year's efforts. At the heart of the '*kouaikenshuu*' is the lesson study, or '*jugyou kenkyuu*', the principle behind which is that the classroom is the best place to improve teaching. Grounding pedagogic research and experiment in classroom practice mitigates the problems encountered later when transferring ideas developed out of the classroom. Groups of teachers meet regularly over long periods of time (up to a year) to work on the design, implementation, testing and improvement of one or several research based lessons. Practices similar to these also occur among mainland Chinese teachers whose teaching conditions and patterns of school organisation are conducive to collaborative peer professional development based on effective pedagogy.

How teachers approach their work is partly dependent on their social status and the degree to which, as stated earlier, home and school values align (Stigler & Hiebert, 1999). Japanese teachers, for example, enjoy relatively high salaries and social status when compared with other public sector workers. The supply of applicants generally exceeds demand for teachers, resulting in a higher calibre of entrant to the profession. In contrast, teachers in mainland China are poorly paid, but like teachers in the other three systems, generally exhibit strong levels of commitment. High expectations are placed on them by principals and others, exemplified by many teachers spending long hours at school.

In summary, differences in the organisational and structural arrangements for teaching mean that teachers' work roles differ markedly between cultures. The fact that teachers in Hong Kong typically teach 90 per cent or more of total lessons each week, while their mainland Chinese counterparts teach about one half of the total lessons, makes a significant difference to their pattern of work and their involvement in professional development. Mainland teachers have more time to plan and prepare high quality lessons and more opportunity to collaborate with peers and to engage in professional development. Time for collaboration and preparation is directly linked with teaching quality and effective schooling.

6. ISSUES AND IMPLICATIONS FOR FUTURE RESEARCH

Empirical studies on effective schooling in the Asia-Pacific region are relatively few. With globalisation and the growing reciprocal interest between Asian and

Western societies in the effectiveness of schooling, there is need to chart a future research agenda.

In regard to methodology, rigorous and systematic comparative studies are needed that take full account of cultural contexts and influences. In this regard, authentic and well validated frameworks and dimensions need developing by which to compare, first, societal cultures and social practices, and second, school structures and practices (see Dimmock & Walker, 1998a, 1998b). Country-by-country descriptions will not do. Authentic comparison and explanation needs to be underpinned by generic frameworks and dimensions. In turn, there is need for reliable and valid instruments, of both a qualitative and quantitative kind, for data collection in the field. Stevenson and Stigler (1992) have shown how large-scale studies involving schools in a number of cities in America and Asia can yield exciting benefits to knowledge and cultural-comparative insights hitherto unrecognised. Equally, there is need for in-depth, small-scale case studies comparing schools in different cultures. Cross-cultural collaboration between researchers would be a good start.

In regard to content, relatively few studies of effective schooling in Asia have been published in English. More studies of the primary sector to complement Stevenson and Stigler's work are needed. The dearth of cross-cultural comparative studies is even greater in the secondary sector. There is also a need for comparative studies to adopt a holistic approach that encompasses values and culture transmitted by parenting, socialisation and the home, the curriculum, teaching and learning, and school organisation and leadership. Schooling is influenced by all of these: to omit any of them is to obtain a partial picture. Finally, the appeal of a holistic socio-cultural approach to effective schooling, one that emphasises context by linking school, home and values, is that it presents an alternative to, and complements, the positivistic, measurement-oriented, student achievement focus of traditional school effectiveness studies.

7. CONCLUSION

While the chapter has focused on many of the positive aspects of effective schooling in the Asia Pacific region, important challenges and problems are evident. These stem from important changes, driven by globalisation, taking place within each society, concerning economy, politics and culture within the global economy. Governments, employers and parents are forced to re-define their expectations of effective schooling.

The first concerns the growing influence of Western cultural values that are seen as threats to traditional Asian values underpinning schooling. A second issue centres on the extent to which schooling maintains a collective (Asian), rather than an individual (Western) focus. The key question here is the extent to which diversity in, and individualised approaches to, curriculum, should be promoted.

A third concern is the emphasis placed on passive learning at the expense of problem solving and creativity, and in association, the need for greater integration of computer technology in learning and teaching (Dimmock, 2000). As the long-term competitiveness of economies such as Hong Kong, Taiwan and Japan are challenged in the global market place, so will the ways in which these societies define 'effective schooling'. Hong Kong, for example, with few natural resources other than its geographical position, will need to invest heavily in skilled human resources and high value-added products and services, for its continued economic prosperity. Taiwan and Japan will need to diversify if they are to recover from the present economic downturn. China has a tremendous challenge in meeting the labour demands needed to fuel its continued growth and to bring even a basic education to scores of millions of its citizens, especially in the rural areas. Each of the four societies has its emerging place in the global economy. How each responds to these challenges, through effective schooling, will undoubtedly reflect its cultural disposition.

REFERENCES

Biggs, J. (1994). What are effective schools? Lessons from East and West. *Australian Education Researcher, 21*(1), 19–39.

Cheng, K. M., & Wong, K. C. (1996). School effectiveness in East Asia: Concepts, origins, and implications. *Journal of Educational Administration, 34*(5), 32–49.

Cheng, Y. C. (1994). Teacher leadership style: A classroom-level study. *Journal of Educational Administration, 32*(3), 54–71.

Cheng, Y. C. (2000). Cultural factors in educational effectiveness: A framework for comparative research. *School Leadership and Management, 20*(2), 207–226.

Dimmock, C. (2000). *Designing the Learning-Centred School: A Cross-Cultural Perspective*. London & New York: Falmer Press.

Dimmock, C., & Walker, A. (1998a). Towards comparative educational administration: Building the case for a cross-cultural, school-based approach. *Journal of Educational Administration, 36*(4), 379–401.

Dimmock, C., & Walker, A. (1998b). Comparative educational administration: Developing a cross-cultural comparative framework. *Educational Administration Quarterly, 34*(4), 558–595.

Dimmock, C., & Walker, A. (2000). *Future School Administration: Western and Asian Perspectives*. Hong Kong: Chinese University Press.

Fraser, B. J., Walberg, H. J., Welch, W. W., & Hattie, J. (1987). Syntheses of educational productivity research. *International Journal of Educational Research, 11*(2), 145–252.

Gao, L. B. (1998). *Conceptions of teaching held by school physics teachers in Guangdong, China, and their relations to student learning*. Unpublished PhD thesis, University of Hong Kong, Hong Kong.

Gow, L., Balla, J., Kember, D., & Hau, K. T. (1996). The learning approaches of Chinese people: A function of socialization processes and the context of learning? In M. H. Bond (Ed.), *The Handbook of Chinese Psychology* (pp. 109–123). Hong Kong: Oxford University Press.

Hess, R. D., & Azuma, M. (1991). Cultural support for schooling: Contrasts between Japan and the United States. *Educational Researcher, 20*(9), 2–8.

Hofstede, G. H. (1991). *Cultures and Organisations: Software of the Mind*. London: McGraw Hill.

Holloway, S. D. (1988). Concepts of ability and effort in Japan and the US. *Educational Research, 58*, 327–345.

Jin, L., & Cortazzi, M. (1998). Dimensions of dialogue, large classes in China. *International Journal of Educational Research, 29*, 739–761.

Kember, D., & Gow, L. (1990). Cultural specificity of approaches to study. *British Journal of Educational Psychology, 60*, 356–363.

McAdams, R. P. (1993). *Lessons from Abroad: How Other Countries Educate their Children.* Lancaster, Pennsylvania: Technomic Publishing Co.

Reynolds, D., & Farrell, S. (1996). *World's Apart? A Review of International Surveys of Educational Achievement Involving England.* London: Her Majesty's Stationery Office.

Salili, F. (1996). Accepting personal responsibility for learning. In D. Watkins & J. Biggs (Eds.), *The Chinese Learner: Cultural, Psychological, and Contextual Influences* (pp. 85–106). Hong Kong: Comparative Education Research Centre, University of Hong Kong.

Stevenson, H. W., & Lee, S. Y. (1996). The academic achievement of Chinese students. In M. H. Bond (Ed.), *The Handbook of Chinese Psychology* (pp. 124–142). Hong Kong: Oxford University Press.

Stevenson, H. W., & Stigler, J. W. (1992). *The Learning Gap: Why our Schools are Failing and What we can Learn from Japanese and Chinese Education.* New York: Simon & Schuster.

Stigler, J. W., & Hiebert, J. (1999). *The Teaching Gap: Best Ideas from the World's Teachers for Improving Education in the Classroom.* New York, NY: The Free Press.

Turay, A. (1994). All homework and no play for HK schoolkids. *South China Morning Post*, April 3, p. 3.

Watkins, D. (2000). Learning and teaching: A cross-cultural perspective. *School Leadership and Management, 20*(2), 161–174.

Watkins, D. A., & Biggs, J. B. (1996). *The Chinese Learner: Cultural, Psychological and Contextual Influences.* Hong Kong: Comparative Education Research Centre, University of Hong Kong.

69

School Leadership Development

PHILIP HALLINGER
Mahidol University, Chiang Mai, Thailand

1. INTRODUCTION

Since the early 1990s, the status of education in the Asia-Pacific region has changed dramatically. Once an afterthought of government policy-makers, education has assumed centre-stage in recent years. The result has been the passage of significant legislation aimed at aligning educational policies and practices with evolving social, political and economic aims (Caldwell, 1998; Cheng & Townsend, 2000; Hallinger, 1998; Rahimah, 1998). This global love affair with educational reform has not, however, been without disappointments. With the ever-increasing rate and scope of global changes, governments are finding it ever more difficult to put their new policies into practice (Cheng & Townsend, 2000; Dimmock & Walker, 1998; Hallinger, 1998; Lam, in press). The implementation of change in educational practice that is directed by policy decisions demands effective leadership of schools and educational institutions. This article considers trends and directions for future research and development in the field of school leadership in the Asia-Pacific region.

The need to increase effectiveness of reform implementation has refocused policymakers' attention on school principals. This rediscovered interest in the principal's role in policy implementation has coincided with research findings that consistently point to the key leadership role of the principal in school improvement (Hallinger & Heck, 1996, 1997). The confluence of these trends has led to a new focus on the preparation, training and development of school leaders internationally (Caldwell, in press; Hallinger, in press; Huber, in press).

While this trend is apparent throughout the world (e.g., Caldwell, in press; Hallinger, in press; Huber, in press; Murphy & Shipman, in press) it is especially evident in East and Southeast Asia. Since 1990, a wave of interest in school leadership development has swept the Asia-Pacific region including the United States (Hallinger, 1992; Hallinger & McCary, 1990; Murphy & Shipman, in press), Malaysia (Abdullah, 1999; Bajunid, 1995, 1996), Australia (Caldwell, in press), Hong Kong (Lam, in press; Walker, Bridges, & Chan, 1996), People's

Republic of China (Li, 1999), Singapore (Chong, Stott, & Low, in press; Gopinathan & Kam, 2000; Low, 1999), Thailand (Hallinger, 2000; Hallinger & Kantamara, 2000a, 2000b; Ministry of Education-Thailand, 1997a, 1997b), and the People's Republic of China (Fwu & Wang, 2001; Ministry of Education-ROC, 1998; Yang, 2001). This focus on school leader preparation and development reflects an optimistic belief in both the impact of leadership on school improvement as well as in the capacity of school systems to develop more effective school leaders.

This article focuses on a subset of Asia-Pacific education systems: Malaysia, Thailand, Singapore and Hong Kong. All four represent traditionally centralised education systems. Yet, each is moving towards the implementation of educational reforms that would change many features of management, teaching and learning. All four assert the desire to transform their education systems into so-called 'learning organisations' and their nations into 'knowledge-based societies' (e.g., Chong et al., in press; Ministry of Education-R.O.C., 1998). This evolving vision would require a changing role of the school principal. Thus, school leader preparation is now high on national agendas for educational reform.

Three questions frame this chapter: What do we know about principal effectiveness and how does this knowledge base transfer to the Asian context of schooling? What trends have emerged in school leadership development in East and Southeast Asia over the past decade? What are emerging issues and directions for practice and research in school leadership development in Southeast and East Asia?

2. THE STATE OF THE ART ON PRINCIPAL EFFECTIVENESS

The issue of principal effectiveness has been addressed at length elsewhere (Hallinger & Heck, 1996, 1997). In brief, research conducted over the past 20 years finds that school leaders influence the capacity of schools to change and improve. More specifically, the research base also finds that principals exercise a positive, measurable and indirect effect on student learning outcomes.

While it may be comforting to know that empirical research supports conventional wisdom, this finding is of limited utility without elaboration of how leadership contributes to school effectiveness. Though far from complete, researchers have begun to describe the avenues through which principals and other school-level leaders enhance school effectiveness. Principals achieve these positive effects through their efforts to create a shared vision and mission for the school; restructure the formal organisation of the school (e.g., class schedules, teacher's time, grade/unit organisation) in order to support instructional effectiveness and enhance staff collaboration, decision-making and communication around teaching and learning; provide stimulation and individualised support for development of the teaching, and learning capacities of staff; and reshape the school culture in order to emphasise norms of continuous learning and collaborative work (Hallinger & Heck, 1997).

These conclusions imply that professional preparation for school leaders should address both 'management' and 'leadership' competencies. Management competency involves making the school run efficiently. This has been the traditional focus of training for school leaders, especially in Asia. However, in this era of rapid change, management competency alone is insufficient (Hallinger, 1998). If schools are to keep pace with changing societal demands, it will also require leadership. Leadership represents the capacity building, creative, and innovative roles of the school principal (Caldwell, in press; Hallinger, 1998).

3. APPLICATION OF THIS KNOWLEDGE BASE TO EAST ASIA

The knowledge base that underlies the practice of school management and leadership globally is incomplete and ever changing. Yet, the breadth and depth of empirical research on school leadership in East Asia appears to lag behind that of Western nations. How well does the trend of Western findings on school leadership transfer to the Asian region? A quick scan of the literature reveals that the trend of empirical research in East Asia supports the general pattern of international research findings.

For example, empirical studies conducted in Hong Kong have examined the role of the principal in school effectiveness (Cheng, Y. C., 1991, 1994, 2001; Cheng, K. M., 1994, 1995; Cheng, K. M., & Wong, 1996; Dimmock & Walker, 1998; Pang, 1998). In general terms, these results confirm the general direction of findings concerning the impact of school leadership.

Research on principal leadership in East Asian system's reports is also beginning to generate interesting findings concerning the avenues through which school leaders achieve desired results. Such research has been conducted in Thailand (e.g., Hallinger & Kantamara, 2000a, 2000b), Hong Kong (Dimmock & Walker, 1998), Malaysia (Bajunid, 1995, 1996) and Singapore (Gopinathan & Kam, 2000). Although it is too early to generalise, this emerging body of work does suggest several propositions worthy of further exploration.

(1) Principals in East Asian education systems have an impact on the effectiveness of their schools and that effect is mediated by internal school factors as well as contextual factors.
(2) Principal leadership in East Asian systems is strongly shaped by the cultural and institutional context of their schools. There is a tradition of strong hierarchical authority complemented by cultural norms that support the centralisation of power and authority. On the one hand, these forces limit the systemic authority of principals. On the other hand, the same contextual factors increase the day-to-day influence East Asian principals' exercise over their schools.
(3) East Asian principals achieve results through similar avenues (i.e., goals, school structure, people and culture) as principals in the West. However, the day-to-day practices by which principals enact leadership through these variables differ in response to the cultural and institutional context.

East Asian principals operate within a traditional system role as bureaucratic administrators rather than as school leaders. Their institutional norms and policies shape their behaviour as administrators whose role is to implement orders rather more than as leaders of programs or change at the school level. This change in role conception may prove to be the most important target for efforts at training and development in East Asian school systems.

4. EMERGING TRENDS IN SCHOOL LEADERSHIP DEVELOPMENT IN EAST ASIA

In this section I will discuss general trends in school leader preparation and development as they have emerged over the past decade in East and Southeast Asia. I will accomplish this through a quick tour of several countries that have been active in this domain.

4.1. *Malaysia*

Malaysia's foray into school leader preparation began during the 1980s with funding from the World Bank. The *Institute Ahminuddin Baki* (IAB) was established as a central training centre for school administrators from throughout Malaysia. It boasts a central campus with dormitories and a large staff comprised of managers, trainers, curriculum developers and evaluators.

Over time the IAB has developed an extensive curriculum that incorporates both international and local topics (Bajunid, 1996). This curriculum is delivered cyclically in both pre-service and in-service formats to the administrators of Malaysia's schools. As an arm of the Ministry of Education, the IAB has the authority to implement mandatory training programs.

During the 1990s Malaysia further developed its capacity as an institution of higher learning. In this period the IAB was granted the authority to offer Master-level training. Subsequently, the IAB has awarded hundreds of Master degrees in educational administration. This was a significant development in that it began to raise the standard expected of educational administrators in this country.

In 2000, Malaysia further expanded its provision of leadership preparation and development through the opening of a National Principals' Centre at the University of Malaya. This centre is taking primary responsibility for Masters degree training of educational administrators. The location of this centre in a university also signals the recognition of a need for more research and development to underlie the training of educational managers in Malaysia.

Malaysia, which has perhaps the longest formal experience in school leadership development in the region, offers an instructive perspective on the development of its school leaders. Bajunid, Director of the IAB for over a decade, has made among the most cogent cases internationally for using indigenous (i.e., locally generated craft knowledge or wisdom of practice) as well as global (i.e., generally empirically derived knowledge from the West) sources of knowledge for school leadership development. His assertions echo the views of Barth, founder of the Principals' Centre Movement in the United States, who has long asserted that craft knowledge represents a key foundation of the knowledge base of school leaders. However, Bajunid goes further as he makes the case that craft knowledge must be derived from within the local context

> With the forces of globalization and internationalization and competition, there is a trend to achieve world standards. This aspiration for world class standards is casting new meaning towards the indigenization efforts. It is likely that such world standards criteria will be tempered and coloured by unique national and cultural local nuances. (Bajunid, 1996, p. 272)

This is significant and represents the most salient contribution made by the leadership development experience in Malaysia. Under Bajunid's intellectual leadership, the IAB initiated a research and development effort designed to generate useful cases and perspectives on indigenous and global leadership practices and perspectives. This knowledge base was intended to shape leadership development as well as the role of school administrators in Malaysia. This is an agenda that needs to be extended further.

4.2. Thailand

Thailand initiated its preparation for school administrators during the early 1980s under similar funding as in Malaysia. The Institute for the Development of Educational Administrators (IDEA) was initially comprised of a central campus outside of Bangkok with dormitories and instructional facilities. Following the same model as the IAB in Malaysia, IDEA has an instructional and curriculum development staff responsible for delivery of pre-service and in-service training school administrators throughout Thailand. Over time, regional training centres have been set up nationwide under the overall supervision of IDEA. These centres as well as the home campus are responsible for providing a wide range of administrative preparation and development programs. These include programs designed to prepare staff for the assumption of new roles as well as programs designed for general development purposes.

Similar to the IAB, IDEA is viewed primarily as a policy implementation arm of the Ministry of Education. Both nations share a similar tradition of centralised bureaucracy in education. The IDEA's role has explicitly revolved around the goal of transferring to school administrators the knowledge needed to implement national educational polices. The underlying conception of administrative preparation has been explicitly managerial in nature with school leaders viewed very much as order-takers and system maintainers.

This vision of the role of Thai school administrators is beginning to change, at least in the national rhetoric of reformers. Educational reforms such as school-based management, student-centred learning, learning technologies and parental and community involvement are quickly becoming part of the Thai language of school reform (Hallinger, 2000). To the extent that these reforms actually move forward towards implementation, the role and capacities of school leaders will need to undergo dramatic changes.

One recent research and development effort was undertaken to explore school improvement in Thailand and has generated some data that complements findings on indigenous knowledge from Malaysia. Hallinger and Kantamara (2000a, 2000b, 2001) studied the relationship of school leadership and school improvement in a series of case studies. Their findings suggest the following conclusion.

> In closing we are cognizant of the fact that we have only begun to scratch the surface of the most intriguing aspect of this topic: the interaction between the traditional cultural norms that shape behaviour in Thai schools and external change forces. We assert that future leaders in all nations will need to be adept at negotiating the norms of the traditional culture *and* the global culture. The extent to which the norms of the local culture differ from the global norms will determine the types of adaptation. Our experience in Thailand suggests that this dual set of skills is in short supply. This suggests an important challenge for the future for those engaged in school improvement research and practice. (Hallinger & Kantamara, 2000b, p. 45)

4.3 Singapore

Singapore's efforts in school leadership development reflect the city-state's long-standing commitment to human resource development (Low, 1999). During the 1980s this effort was encompassed in a university-delivered diploma program in educational administration. Chong, Stott and Low (in press) note:

> For over fifteen years, the Diploma in Educational Administration (DEA) was known for its excellence in training school leaders. Indeed, many of Singapore's senior educators, including superintendents and directors have passed through this prestigious programme. It was a programme characterised by executive skills training and learning from excellent principals through a mentoring process. (in press)

With the advent of 1990s, however, Singapore's educational policymakers recognised the need for a broader and deeper program aimed at raising the knowledge and skills of its school administrators. At that time, Singapore was undertaking a new set of educational reforms organised around the framework of learning organisations. As a country, Singapore had conceived of a new goal encapsulated in the phrase, 'Thinking Schools, a Learning Nation'.

This conveyed a new conception of the role of schools in society. It also implied new forms of school organisation and delivery of educational services. Together these new conceptions led to a new role for school leaders. As Chong, Stott and Low (in press) have articulated:

> Indeed, the new educational agenda demanded a new type of school leader,

one who could cope proactively with a dynamic, complex and sometimes uncertain context. The old leadership thrived on conformity. The new leadership had to be ambitious and independent, innovative, and able to succeed in conditions that were less clearly defined .... It was also clear as we talked to educators both in Singapore and abroad that the new principal would have an expanded and more intellectually demanding role. We needed to train principals who could 'think' their way through complex, sometimes unique, and often persistent issues in schools. Such individuals would need – as we said earlier – to guarantee high degrees of quality in teaching and learning, orchestrate the strategic agenda and direct operations at the school-community interface. (in press)

This recognition demanded an expanded approach to the development of Singapore's school leaders. This led to the opening of the Singapore Principals' Executive Centre (PEC) in 1996. The PEC is operated through the joint efforts of the National Institute of Education (NIE) at Nanyang Technological University and the Ministry of Education. Since its opening, the PEC has built on the earlier efforts to reshape the landscape of school leadership development in Singapore. Today a full range of preparation and development programs is offered for Singapore's school leaders from pre-induction through all phases of career development.

The PEC and other programs offered at NIE represent the core delivery mechanism. These programs combine the advantages of university's intellectual assets with the focus and support of the Ministry of Education. The PEC's programs are strongly linked to the delivery structure of Singapore's schools. For example, the PEC's programs support clusters of Singapore schools, a feature of recent educational reforms. Yet, it does this within the context of a strongly held, shared vision of the role of school education.

This represents perhaps the strongest feature of Singapore's efforts in this domain. They have integrated school leadership preparation and development into a broader systemic model of educational reform rather than as a separate entity. School leadership development is linked to the system's vision of lifelong learning and productive personal, professional development. If successfully implemented, Singapore's model of school leadership development addresses the core tension in system-led attempts at school leader preparation. This concerns how to meet system needs while honouring the aspirations and needs of individual school leaders. While the results of this approach remain anecdotal, the approach itself is worthy of both emulation and further study.

4.4. *Hong Kong*

Up until the year 2000, the Hong Kong Education Department held no system-wide expectations for the training of school leaders. Lam summarises the situation:

> Rising through the teaching rank and file, most did not receive formal

training in administration or leadership. Most will have attended a few workshops provided by the Department of Education. These ad hoc sessions would have focused primarily on clarifying education policies, curricular matters and foreign educational concepts. What we think of as true professional development opportunities for them are few and far between. Further studies beyond the basic degree are not required; therefore, only a handful have pursued graduate studies on their own. (Lam, in press)

Although the Education Department is responsible for the overall standard and curriculum of education in Hong Kong, it supervises an unusual mix of government-controlled and independent schools. Its power over the independent schools, which serve a significant percentage of the population, is more limited than in Thailand, Singapore or Malaysia. This was reflected in their *ad hoc* approach to the preparation and development of school leaders.

Several Hong Kong universities have offered preparation programs in educational administration for many years. As suggested by Lam (in press), however, participation in these programs was entirely voluntary. Moreover, in contrast to Singapore for example, there have never been links between training and promotion, certification or system goals in Hong Kong.

In 1999, under the leadership of a new Director, the Education Department placed school leader preparation and development in the spotlight. The Director of Education asserted that the city's aspirations for educational reform would be for naught unless the system's school principals were able to operate at a higher level of effectiveness. Indeed she made an explicit assertion that the limited leadership capacity of the current cohort of school principals represented an impediment to system-wide reform.

This led to a series of initiatives aimed at upgrading the professional preparation, training, selection and certification of principals. In response several universities have since established centres called 'educational leadership centres'. The mission of these centres is still unclear and will probably remain so until greater clarity emerges from the Education Department itself. Lam (in press) notes that

> The government has attempted to rectify the situation by making professional training mandatory for principals at different stages of their careers. In the blueprint, which is being developed and refined, three categories of individuals are recognised: 'aspiring' principals, 'newly appointed' principals, and 'experienced' principals' (Lam, in press). Unfortunately, as is too often the case, system priorities have shifted as the Director who was providing the impetus for this reform has been promoted and some momentum has been lost. It is too soon to tell whether Hong Kong will be able to meet the challenge of implementing its ambitious goals for school leader preparation and development.

5. RECOMMENDATIONS FOR PRACTICE IN SCHOOL LEADERSHIP DEVELOPMENT

This brief review of trends in school leader preparation in East and Southeast Asia suggest several recommendations for the organisation and practice of school leader preparation and development. These derive from the past decade of emerging efforts among practitioners and researchers in this field in the Asian region.

> 5.1 *New globally-derived, research-based findings as well as indigenous craft knowledge about teaching and learning and leading schools represent legitimate subjects for learning among prospective and practising school leaders.*

As noted above, a knowledge base drawn from the fields of leadership (inside and outside of education) as well as from teaching and learning provides the basis for forthcoming leadership development efforts. There is knowledge and there are skills worthy of mastery by school leaders and that knowledge base is not static. The lessons learned from each of the education systems mentioned in this chapter emphasise the need to localise the curriculum. This is true even as global issues (e.g., student-centred learning, use of IT in management and in teaching and learning) also increase in salience.

> 5.2 *The changing knowledge base and context for school leadership makes lifelong learning a fundamental facet of the professional role.*

Annual attendance at a convention no longer suffices as a leader's efforts at professional development. Lifelong learning has become a necessary and fundamental facet of the school leader's role. Encouragement of a norm of lifelong learning stands as one of the hallmark achievements of the principal's centre movement started at Harvard University in the early 1980s. It would be a serious mistake for Asian systems to stop their efforts at leadership development at the end of the preparation and induction stages.

> 5.3 *The process of leadership development should actively engage learners and be organised, at least in part, around the problems that school leaders face in their work.*

One innovation of the 1990s in professional education generally, as well as in school leadership was problem-based learning (PBL). PBL places the academic disciplines and formal knowledge base at the service of the profession and provides an active means of instruction that respects and builds upon the prior knowledge of learners (Bridges & Hallinger, 1995). Moreover, PBL seems highly adaptable as a means of responding to the need to integrate indigenous craft knowledge into the training for school leaders (e.g., Hallinger & Kantamara, 2001; Walker et al., 1996).

Moreover, other non-traditional approaches to professional learning have found their way into practice in recent years. For example, apprenticeships and mentorships also have the potential to develop dimensions of leadership that are seemingly immune to traditional lecture and discussion on leadership topics (Chong, Stott, & Low, in press; Low, 1999). Simulations and the use of information technology likewise have the potential to reenergize learning and develop the thinking of school leaders (Hallinger & McCary, 1990).

5.4 *Implementation of new knowledge and skills requires a flexible combination of on-site coaching and networks of support in the schools that function as and within learning organisations.*

Evaluations of leadership development efforts find that exposure to new knowledge through training bears only a small relationship to change in practice at the school (Hallinger, 1992). Leadership development intended for behavioural change must include a support component that all too often is absent. The operative principle is that school leaders need the same support for behavioural change as teachers: motivation to learn, time to learn, resources for learning, a model, a coach and opportunities for practice.

To the extent that twenty-first century schools can foster the norms and practices of learning organisations, they can mitigate some of the obstacles to professional learning. Again Singapore's attempt to develop "thinking schools and a learning society" exemplifies this approach (Chong, Stott, & Low, in press).

5.5 *Professional development of school leaders must take place in a broader context of professionalisation of education.*

The past two decades have seen demonstrable progress in the attitude of school leaders towards the notion of lifelong learning. This must, however, be strengthened further through government policy as well as through the active engagement of the profession in charting the course of professional learning. Local school authorities need to examine the implicit expectations conveyed by the system, as well as formal policies with respect to professional development: Does the system expect school leaders to engage in ongoing development? Do governmental units provide resources to support both learning and implementation? Do policies provide a framework of support for prospective and current leaders?

The time has come for school leaders to engage with parties inside the profession (e.g., universities, research institutions and professional associations) as well as outside the profession (e.g., governments, corporations and community institutions) to define the agenda for professional learning and development in the coming years (Caldwell, 1998, in press; Davis, 1999).

6. EMERGING DIRECTIONS FOR RESEARCH

As suggested in the body of this article, there is much to be learned from empirical research into school leadership development in the Asia-Pacific region.

A framework for thinking about important areas and questions for research in this domains is required.

Who participates? Although descriptive research on the nature of participants is not an obvious topic, this would prove to be useful information. There is little information available across the region about who is participating in pre-service and in-service preparation and development. Gender, years of experience and other personal variables, when combined with patterns of participation and career advancement through the system, would represent interesting data.

Curriculum, delivery, organisation and governance. As suggested above, dual goals for system change and personal, professional development create tension for providers and school leaders. Better information is needed on curricula, instructional methods in use, delivery methods and forms of governance. A data bank of such information would be invaluable to local providers in the region who often find themselves reinventing the wheel.

Research on the impact of training and development. A weakness internationally in studies of leadership development is the tendency to stop at descriptive studies. There is a clear need for empirical studies that examine the impact of training on knowledge, skills and attitudes of learners. This is unfamiliar territory for many students of educational administration. Heck (in press) offers useful examples. In particular, longitudinal studies that also explore transfer of learning seem appropriate here.

Impact on the system. Research that examines system changes that result from leadership development efforts is also needed. One clear lesson from learning organisations is that training alone does not bring about substantial changes. It is only when implemented in concert with other reforms that the impact can be adequately assessed. This is especially true when reference is made to the education system.

Next generation studies of the impact of leadership development, therefore, ought to be both micro-studies and macro-studies. Micro-studies would examine the impact on individuals. Macro-studies would explore effects of training along with other variables that would combine to create effects on the education system. Outcomes variables of interest would include professionalism, change capacity and impact on teachers.

This article has sought to provide an overview of trends in school leadership development in the Asia-Pacific region. More specifically, the article has focused on the challenges of preparing school leaders to assume the tasks of educational reform and improvement in East and Southeast Asian education systems. This is an exciting time full of challenges and opportunities in this domain of educational development. It is hoped that the profession will take advantage of these opportunities for the benefit of the region's youth.

REFERENCES

Abdullah, A. S. (1999). *The school management and leadership directions in Malaysia for the 21st century*. Paper presented at the 3rd Annual Asian Symposium on Educational Management and Leadership, Penang, Malaysia.

Bajunid, I. (1995). The educational administrator as a cultural leader. *Journal of the Malaysian Educational Manager*, 1(1), 16–29.

Bajunid, I. A. (1996). Preliminary explorations of indigenous perspectives of educational management: The evolving Malaysian experience. *Journal of Education Administration*, 34(5), 50–73.

Bridges, E., & Hallinger, P. (1995). *Implementing problem-based leadership development*. Eugene, OR: ERIC Clearinghouse for Educational Management.

Caldwell, B. (1998). Strategic leadership, resource management and effective school reform. *Journal of Educational Administration*, 36(5), 445–461.

Caldwell, B. (in press). A blueprint for successful leadership in an era of globalisation in learning. In P. Hallinger (Ed.), *Reshaping the Landscape of School Leadership Development: A Global Perspective*. Lisse, The Netherlands: Swets & Zeitlinger.

Cheng, K. M. (1994). Quality of education as perceived in Chinese culture. In T. Tanaka (Ed.), *Quality of Education in the Context of Culture in Developing Countries* (pp. 67–84). Tampere: Tampere University Press.

Cheng, K. M. (1995). The neglected dimension: Cultural comparison in educational administration. In K. C. Wong & K. M. Cheng (Eds.), *Educational Leadership and Change: An International Perspective* (pp. 87–104). Hong Kong: Hong Kong University Press.

Cheng, K. M., & Wong, K. C. (1996). School effectiveness in East Asia: Concepts, origins and implications. *Journal of Educational Administration*, 34(5), 32–49.

Cheng, Y. C. (1991). Leadership style of principals and organisational process in secondary schools. *Journal of Educational Administration*, 29(2), 25–37.

Cheng, Y. C. (1994). Principal's leadership as a critical factor for school performance: Evidence from multi-levels of primary schools. *School effectiveness and school improvement*, 5(3), 299–317.

Cheng, Y. C. (2001). Multi-models of education quality and principal leadership. In K. H. Mok & D. Chan (Eds.), *The Quest for Quality Education in Hong Kong: Theory and Practice*. Hong Kong: Hong Kong University Press.

Cheng, Y. C., & Townsend, T. (2000). Educational change and development in the Asia Pacific region: Trends and issues. In T. Townsend & Y. C. Cheng (Eds.), *Educational Change and Development in the Asia Pacific: Challenges for the Future* (pp. 317–344). Lisse, The Netherlands: Swets & Zeitlinger.

Chong K. C., Stott, K., & Low, G. T. (in press). Developing Singapore school leaders for a learning nation. In P. Hallinger (Ed.), *Reshaping the Landscape of School Leadership Development: A Global Perspective*. Lisse, The Netherlands: Swets & Zeitlinger.

Davis, B. (1999, June). *Credit where credit is due: The professional accreditation and continuing education of school principals in Victoria*. Paper presented at the Conference on Professional Development of School Leaders, Centre for Educational Leadership, University of Hong Kong, Hong Kong.

Dimmock, C., & Walker, A. (1998). Transforming Hong Kong's schools: Trends and emerging issues. *Journal of Educational Administration*, 36(5), 476–491.

Fwu, B. J., & Wang, H. H. (2001). *Principals at the crossroads: Profiles, preparation and role perception of secondary school principals in Taiwan*. Paper presented at the International Conference on School Leader Preparation, Licensure, Certification, Selection, Evaluation and Professional Development, Taipei, ROC.

Gopinathan, S., & Kam, H. W. (2000). Educational change and development in Singapore. In T. Townsend & Y. C. Cheng (Eds.), *Educational Change and Development in the Asia Pacific: Challenges for the Future* (pp. 163–184), Lisse, The Netherlands: Swets & Zeitlinger.

Hallinger, P. (1992). School leadership development: Evaluating a decade of reform. *Education and Urban Society*, 24(3), 300–316.

Hallinger, P. (1998). Educational change in the Asia-Pacific region: The challenge of creating learning systems. *Journal of Educational Administration, 36*(5), 492–509.

Hallinger, P. (2000). The changing context of Thai education: New challenges for school leaders. *Chulalongkorn Educational Review, 7*(1), 1–13.

Hallinger, P. (in press). School leadership development: Global challenges and opportunities. In P. Hallinger (Ed.), *Reshaping the Landscape of School Leadership Development: A Global Perspective*. Lisse, The Netherlands: Swets & Zeitlinger.

Hallinger, P., & Heck, R. (1996). Reassessing the principal's role in school effectiveness: A review of empirical research, 1980–1995. *Educational Administration Quarterly, 32*(1), 5–44.

Hallinger, P., & Heck, R. (1997). Exploring the principal's contribution to school effectiveness. *School Effectiveness and School Improvement, 8*(4), 1–35.

Hallinger, P., & Kantamara, P. (2000a). Educational change in Thailand: Opening a window onto leadership as a cultural process. *School Leadership and Management, 20*(1), 189–206.

Hallinger, P., & Kantamara, P. (2000b). Leading at the confluence of tradition and globalization: The challenge of change in Thai schools. *Asia Pacific Journal of Education, 20*(2), 45–57.

Hallinger, P., & Kantamara, P. (2001). Learning to lead global changes across cultures: Designing a computer-based simulation for Thai school leaders. *Journal of Educational Administration, 39*(3), 197–220.

Hallinger, P., & McCary, M. (1990). Developing the strategic thinking of instructional leaders. *Elementary School Journal, 91*(2), 90–108.

Heck, R. (in press). Examining the impact of professional preparation on beginning school administrators. In P. Hallinger (Ed.), *Reshaping the Landscape of School Leadership Development: A Global Perspective*. Lisse, The Netherlands: Swets & Zeitlinger.

Huber, S. (in press). School leader development: Current trends from a global perspective. In P. Hallinger (Ed.), *Reshaping the Landscape of School Leadership Development: A Global Perspective*. Lisse, The Netherlands: Swets & Zeitlinger.

Lam, J. (in press). Balancing stability and change: Implications for professional preparation and development of principals in Hong Kong. In P. Hallinger (Ed.), *Reshaping the Landscape of School Leadership Development: A Global Perspective*. Lisse, The Netherlands: Swets & Zeitlinger.

Li, W. C. (1999, June). *Organizing Principal Training in China: Models, Problems and Prospects*. Paper presented at the Conference on Professional Development of School Leaders, Centre for Educational Leadership, Hong Kong University, Hong Kong.

Low, G. T. (1999, June). *Preparation of aspiring principals in Singapore: A Partnership Model*. Paper presented at the Conference on Professional Development of School Leaders, Centre for Educational Leadership, University of Hong Kong, Hong Kong.

Ministry of Education-R. O. C. (1998). *Towards a Learning Society*. Republic of China: Ministry of Education, Taipei.

Ministry of Education-Thailand. (1997a). *Introducing the Office of the National Primary Education Commission*. Bangkok, Thailand: Ministry of Education.

Ministry of Education-Thailand. (1997b). *The Experience from the Basic and Occupational Education and Training Programme*. Bangkok, Thailand: Ministry of Education.

Murphy, J., & Shipman, N. (in press). Developing standards for school leadership development: A process and rationale. In P. Hallinger (Ed.), *Reshaping the Landscape of School Leadership Development: A Global Perspective*. Lisse, The Netherlands: Swets & Zeitlinger.

Pang, N. S. K. (1998, April). *Organisational Cultures of Excellent Schools in Hong Kong*. Paper presented at the annual meeting of the American Educational Research Association. San Diego, CA.

Rahimah, H. A. (1998). Educational development and reformation in Malaysia: Past, present and future. *Journal of Educational Administration, 36*(5), 462–475.

Walker, A., Bridges, E., & Chan, B. (1996). Wisdom gained, wisdom given: Instituting PBL in a Chinese culture. *Journal of Educational Administration, 34*(5), 98–119.

Yang, C. L. (2001). *The changing principalship and its implications for preparing, selecting and evaluating principals*. Paper presented at the International Conference on School Leader Preparation, Licensure, Certification, Selection, Evaluation and Professional Development, Taipei, ROC.

70

Public and Private Education

RAMSEY DING-YEE KOO, ANDY MAN-SING YUNG, KIN YUEN IP
The Hong Kong Institute of Education, Hong Kong

WEI-CHEN CHUANG
Da-Yeh University, Taiwan

1. INTRODUCTION

This article contains four parts in which various aspects of public and private education in mainland China, Taiwan, Hong Kong and Macau, are examined with particular attention to some fundamental questions concerning the provision, scope and orientation of public and private education within the contexts of these societies. To provide a conceptual framework, the chapter begins with a description of the main features of educational provision in the public and private sectors; it then examines some of the forces that have shaped public and private education, before turning to the comparison of similarities and differences in these particular systems. It should be pointed out that one important reason for the selection of the four societies is that, apart from geographic location, they all share many important common features such as language, culture and social customs. Predominately, people in these East Asia territories are of Chinese origins and have a common heritage which is deeply rooted in the Confucian ethical values.

2. CHINA

2.1. *The Contexts of the Minban (Private) Schools*

In socialist China, the terminology of 'public' and 'private' education can be problematic. For several decades after the 1960s, independent institutions outside the state establishment were simply non-existent. Terms such as 'schools run by social forces' (*shehui liliang banxue*) or 'people-run schools' (*minban* schools) have been used to describe schools not directly run by a government bureau. However, many of them are in fact using public money through partnership with government organisations; and some of the state enterprises are actually running *minban* schools too (Cheng, Cheung, & Ip, 2000). Conceptually, *minban* is not totally equivalent to 'private', although they are often used interchangeably in some studies.

2.2. Historical Development of Private and Public Education

Modern schools in China appeared at the beginning of the twentieth century. Both public and private schooling grew steadily until the socialist take-over in 1949. In the 1950s, private schools were totally wiped out from China. Education was considered to be apparatus for the revolutionary party in its pursuit of socialist idealism. The government's objective was to provide public schooling under the leadership of the Communist Party for all children and free of charge, from elementary education up to university, within the framework of a highly-centralised planned economy (Miao, 1994, pp. 8–13). Public schools became the predominant form of schooling. However, many poor rural areas could not depend on government revenue for providing basic education. *Minban* schools or so-called 'teaching points' in very primitive form were supported by local communities often without government financial support (Gao, 1985, p. 330).

After the Cultural Revolution (1966–77), private schools re-emerged and their development has been closely related to the socio-economic and political changes. In the first phase (1978–1991), the government gradually relaxed its control over the economy and abandoned the orthodox planned economy model, and some forms of non-government schools were allowed to operate under the new constitution (Wang & Xu, 1996, 21, p. 7). In the second phase (1992–1998), the development of private schools was triggered by the Deng Xiaoping's famous visits to the south in 1992. Deng called for more market economy reform and ended the temporary setback in economic reform due to the 1989 Tiananmen Square crackdown. In response, the number of new *minban* schools significantly expanded (Lu, 2001).

Since 1999, the latest policy of the Chinese government is to encourage further the expansion of private education. The new rich and growing middle class seek alternative ways to educational success for their children, thus creating a huge demand for private schooling. Private schooling being seen as a kind of business generating handsome profits also facilitates the increase in the supply side. Comprehensive legislation has become one of the recent foci in the agenda (Hu & Ding, 2001; Shao, 2001). Development of private education over the past two decades has been significant. However, it comprises only 0.7 per cent of all schools in China (Lu, 2001).

2.3. Public Schools

Most schools in China are public schools, normally fully funded by government money. All personnel are government employees, directly administered by the government, which also determines the school curriculum and operational system. The mission of public schools in the country is to preserve the dominant ideology of socialism and to contribute to the national development, as prescribed in laws. Government control has been comparatively tight.

Public schools in China are directly administered by the government, without a school board or similar body. Since the 1980s, decentralisation of educational administration has been taking place. More autonomy is now delegated to the local administration especially at the county or district level (Cheng, 1992). The Chinese Communist Party (CCP) also extends its influence to the school and university. Principals are responsible for the day-to-day operation of the schools while the chapter secretaries of the CCP assumes the role of ideological leadership, which is critical in understanding education in China (Yiu, 1984).

Public school finance has long been a major problem for China due to the huge population and the poor economy. Many public schools attempt to obtain extra funding through various means. They include collecting miscellaneous fees from students directly, setting up factories or companies to do business and renting out part of the campus to shop-owners. Many popular schools also levy large fees on students (who fail to meet the admission standard) applying to enter the school (Ng, 2001). This has led to certain issues relating to the problem of inequality. Another factor that adds to the inequality in available resources for Chinese schools is the increasing regional disparity. As a result of decentralisation in both administration and financing of schools, the difference between the better-off coastal regions and less developed inland regions has been gradually growing during the past two decades (Cheng, 1992, p. 78–80).

One more factor leading to inequality in public education has been the setting up of key-point schools in the 1980s. The selected schools are provided with a better campus, better equipment, greater financial support and teachers with better qualification and performance, and are also allowed to select the best students in the areas in which the schools are located. The policy of a key-point school is to aim at guaranteeing an output of well above average graduates. This is done by concentrating limited resources in the selected key-point schools. This policy has been attacked by some academics for contradicting the principle of equal opportunity and causing excessive competition among students.

2.4. Private Schools

The private school system in China has been developing rapidly since the 1980s. The existence of private schools within a socialist system is always justified on financial grounds. Given that China is "a poor country running a huge education system", as is frequently cited in official documents, the private school is considered to be an important means of supplementing the inadequacy of public provision (Lu, 2001). On the other hand, it is also seen as a sign of loosening ideological control and expanding the private market sector. In 1999, a small but significant number of *minban* tertiary institutions do not have a CCP chapter (Chen & Li, 2001), which was unimaginable in the past. One distinct feature of private education in China, as Kwong (1997) observes, is the drive behind its rapid growth. Moreover, there are no missionary run private schools in China today. Very few private schools are operated solely as non-profit making schools. This leads to a fierce debate about profit-making in a socialist regime.

People run *minban* schools for various purposes. Government officials admit that most people running *minban* schools want to achieve both public purpose and private return at the same time (Lu, 2001, p. 42), although the "purpose to make profit" through providing private education is forbidden by the law. Nonetheless, observers like Kwong (1997) and Miao (1994) believe most of them are in fact for-profit schools.

Great variety can be found in *minban* schools in China, representing different levels of government control. On the one hand, public schools that are converted to state-owned *minban* schools and are contracted to people to run, represent the highest level of government control in *minban* schools. They are aimed at self-financing through the collection of tuition fees, thus easing the overall financial burden on the government. On the other hand, a small number of private schools were set up through an Education Reserve Fund (*Jiaoyu chubeijin*) in 1993. This required each student to make a deposit of US$ 30,000 to 40,000 into the school fund. This money would be returned in full but without interest to students upon graduation. As these schools acquired a high level of financial autonomy in this way, government control became extremely difficult. Crises eventually emerged after the outbreak of the 1997 economic crisis when some schools were unable to return *Jiaoyu chubeijin* deposits to parents. Consequently, this practice was prohibited in at least one province in 1999 (Lu, 2001, p. 44). The converted schools and *Jiaoyu chubeijin* schools represent the two extremes of the range of private schools while one continues to be state-owned the others chasing after huge profits in the financial market.

All in all, different people see private schools in China in different ways. Lin (1999, p. 184) sees the re-emergence of the private school as the result of a social transformation that is causing the breaking down of the government monopoly on education. Kwong (1997), however, argues that private schools mostly being driven by profit-making, do not question the prevailing educational philosophy and thus have not caused any fundamental change to the Chinese education system. Private schools help to complement the inadequacy of educational provision (Deng, 1997, p. 137), but the issue of inequality has become a major concern.

3. TAIWAN

In Taiwan, the government provides most of the education at the compulsory education level (Ministry of Education, 2001). Privatisation of education increases significantly beyond primary schooling, particularly in the vocational track. Of the total 468 high schools, 47 per cent are private (Ministry of Education, 1997). Since more than half of the vocational institutions are privately run, the academic track is primarily provided for by the public sector. Since education is highly controlled by the central government in most respects, there are not many different types of schools for parental choice. However, privatisation of high school education has taken place in such a way that it would seem to have resulted in creating barriers blocking access to an equal and quality education for all citizens.

3.1. School Governance and Decentralisation of the Curriculum

Despite the fact that the government is vested with the responsibility and power to enact laws for education, it has been criticised for the lack of commitment to providing a diversification of school types to meet the needs of people from many different backgrounds (Humanistic Education Foundation, 1998; see http://hef.yam.org.tw/index.html). However, with the impact of globalisation and the influence of educational reform elsewhere, curriculum development and implementation strategies in Taiwan have recently been shifted from the extreme of being highly centralised to the opposite extreme of decentralisation. A few private experimental schools as well as public-sponsored educational programs with approaches based on non-traditional educational philosophies have also been founded. Schools at the compulsory education level are encouraged to develop their own curricula (Ministry of Education, 2001). However, the change in educational philosophy revealed in the recent trends in educational reform has given rise to some problems and issues (Mao, 2001).

3.2. Privatisation of Vocational High Schools

In Taiwan traditional education in the academic track is dominated by the public sector, while over half of the education in the vocational track is offered by private institutions. Except for a few (academic) high schools in the private sector, public high schools are the most prestigious and are favoured by the elites. Students with lower academic standing in junior high schools will usually end up in private vocational high school programs, which is also the last resort for most students seeking to complete their high school education. Statistics reveal that slightly over half of the total 204 vocational high schools are in the private sector, representing 64 per cent of students in vocational education. In contrast, of the total 217 high schools, half of them are in public sector having 71 per cent of the student enrolment (Ministry of Education, 1997).

Privatisation is not a panacea. The study by Young (1995) indicates that students enrolled in the vocational track differ significantly from those in the academic track. That is, students enrolled in the academic track of the public schools have higher socio-economic status than those in junior colleges and vocational high schools. However, increasing privatisation in vocational education could be detrimental to those students from a disadvantaged socio-economic environment. A recent study examining the feasibility of maintaining a high ratio of private schools in the vocational track provides further evidence to support the view that a high percentage of private schools in the vocational track tends to reduce the chance for females and economically disadvantaged students to move up the social scales through participation in education. Hence, these private vocational schools are reproducing the existing social class structure. The findings of an empirical study in Taiwan focusing on the influence of background factors on attendance in public or private schools and on years of completed education in Taiwan are also in agreement with this speculation (Chang & Chen, 2000). More research should be undertaken to provide evidence on the efficacy of public and private education. The lack of empirical studies into this issue also shows that the problem is attracting less attention than it should.

3.3. Governance of Private Vocational High Schools

Apart from equity and privatisation, school governance is another important issue. The government seems to lack effective policies to regulate private schools as profit-making institutions, particularly those in the vocational track. In Taiwan, private schools are mostly governed by their respective trustee boards, and many such bodies have a questionable reputation for their conduct and accountability, because many entrepreneurs investing in the private schools want to make substantial profits from education. Thus, the emergent challenge for the government in private school governance is to strengthen its review of the existing regulations and laws regarding the rights and duties and operations of the boards of trustees (Hu, 1995; Tseng, 1997). Furthermore, a report of the Educational Reform Committee in 1996 urges that government auditing practices should also be applied at all levels of the private school sector (Huang, Chou, & Chen, 1996). Although the report has been released for five years, the recommendations made by the Educational Reform Committee have not yet been put into practice.

All in all, in Taiwan, private education serves the function in reducing the financial burden of the government as well as in providing greater choice for the public. Given that public schools dominate all levels of compulsory education and because of the long history of centralisation in education, privatisation could only find a place in the vocational track of the high schools. The expected diversity and flexibility in the process of privatisation is still far from satisfactory. Expanding vocational education in the private sector alone does not operate as a desirable educational alternative for most parents and children, and in the long run it may reproduce the existing social class structure. How to restructure both the financing and governance of the existing public and private school systems and offer citizens better educational choices while ensuring the quality of education provided as well as ensuring autonomy and accountability in the private sector remains a fundamental issue and challenge for future educational reform.

4. HONG KONG

Hong Kong's formal education features three-years of early childhood education, universal elementary education, with six years of primary and three years of junior secondary education, an increasingly competitive intermediate level education with two years of senior secondary and two years of sixth form education, and highly competitive higher education, in most cases, a three-year first degree program. Public funding plays a dominant role in the supply of formal education at different levels except for early childhood education. The Hong Kong public education sector includes government schools and subsidised schools, both at the primary and secondary levels, as well as eight University Grants Committee (UGC) funded degree granting institutions (UGC, 1996). The private education sector is relatively small. It mainly includes the great majority of the early childhood or pre-primary educational institutions, about ten per cent of the primary and 17 per cent of the secondary schools, the Open University and two smaller private higher education institutions, namely, Hong Kong Shue Yan College and Chu Hoi College. This section of the article focuses mainly on the different ways and issues in the governance and financing of education in the Hong Kong public and private education sectors from early childhood to the intermediate level.

4.1. *The Governance and Financing of Public Education*

In the public education sector, the major difference between government schools and subsidised schools is financial autonomy, which in many ways also affects decision making and outcomes produced by individual schools. Government schools, which are directly funded by the Education Department, and teachers, who are employees of the public service, have a relatively smaller degree of freedom in how the money is spent. The Education Department and the general public regard government schools as so-called 'defacto pioneers' or 'pilots' in trying out or testing government educational policies at the school level. In contrast, subsidised schools, mainly operated by independent school sponsoring bodies, though also receive funding from the government, enjoy more financial freedom and flexibility. This is especially so for those schools which have joined the School Based Management Scheme in recent years, a decentralisation policy for improving administrative efficiencies. Also, subsidised schools are allowed to appoint their own staff such as principals and teachers and administrators according to the sponsoring body's own preference, that involves for example, academic and religious orientation and community needs including admission of new immigrant children or other disadvantaged groups, as long as it is consistent with the requirements of the government regulations. Obviously, the wealthier the school sponsoring body, the greater the degree of independence the school experiences.

4.2. *The Governance and Financing of Private Education*

Private education plays a dominant role in early childhood education in Hong Kong. Kindergartens are operated in two different categories: kindergartens regulated by the government's Education Department, and child-care centres monitored by the Social Welfare Department. Most kindergartens offer bi-sessional classes of three hours each, while most child-care centres offer whole-day programs. Most kindergartens follow a common curriculum, *Guide to the Pre-Primary Curriculum* endorsed by the Curriculum Development Council since 1996 (Wong, 1999) and are self-financed and exist on fees paid by parents. In recent years, kindergartens may receive extra funding from the government through the Quality Education Fund. Yet, despite the introduction of an agreed upon pay scale, kindergarten teachers are mostly underpaid (Cheng, 1997). As such, they are considered to be the Cinderella of the entire education sector.

Private schools at the elementary and intermediate levels in Hong Kong are funded and operated in two main ways. First, there are private schools which are financed by their individual providers or investors or are education trust foundations, but at the same time they are subsidised or assisted by the government, in the form of capita grants and bought places, for example, the Bought Place Scheme (BPS) before 2000 or the Direct Subsidy Scheme (DSS) since 1991. However, the government decided to phase out the BPS scheme by 2000 and to replace it with Direct Subsidy Scheme (Bray, 1995).

4.3. *Educational Choices and Autonomy through Subsidy Scheme and Trust Fund*

The DSS is a means of maintaining a strong, independent private education sector for Hong Kong's pluralistic society, while allowing schools maximum freedom with regard to curricula, fees and entrance requirements that is consistent with maintaining a basic educational standard (Education Commission, 1988, p. 55). It is indeed an educational practice that uses marketisation and privatisation to provide an emphasis on diversity and choice in education (Whitty, 1997, pp. 299–302; Bray, 1998). The Direct Subsidy Scheme is targeted at four groups of schools: BPS private schools, non-BPS private schools, international schools and aided schools. The scheme was launched in 1991 by the government with the intention of giving public grants to schools according to a sliding scale while allowing them autonomy in making curricular choices, changing tuition fees and employing entrance requirements. The grant to a given school should equal the difference between the school's income from fees and the notional cost to the government of an aided school with a similar number of pupils. Other sources of income through gifts and donations would be excluded from these calculations. Schools with low fees would receive the full grant for each pupil, while schools with the highest income would receive a minimum proportion of the full grant.

Current development of the DSS accelerates the adoption of market practice and privatisation policies in the provision of basic education by the Hong Kong Special Administrative Region government. Inevitably, it has important implications for basic education in Hong Kong. First, the government encourages school sponsoring bodies to join DSS when they apply to set up new schools; priority for a new school allocation depends greatly on compliance. Second, the government seeks to transform the mode of operation of a government school by allowing it to join the DSS. This tests the viability of a full-scale transformation of all government schools into the DSS scheme in the future. Third, it attracts many well established subsidised or grant schools, those so-called 'elite schools', to join the DSS scheme as a means of strengthening their autonomy in school management, rather than adhering to the government's centralised policies on fees, school finance, students' allocation, entrance requirement, and curriculum design. As such, this gives rise to new issues and challenges with respect to equality of educational opportunity, a segmented student market, and management practices.

Another type of private primary and secondary schools is solely financed by the individual providers and investors or education trust foundations, without receiving any subsidy from the government. Distinctive examples are international schools, which depend largely on parent and student contribution in the form of tuition fees and debentures, for example, English Schools Foundation. These schools are mainly private schools catering the needs of children of the expatriate families and a growing number of local children whose parents have either a preference for the educational system of a particular country and curricula or a dislike for the local education system. They enjoy independent school decision making over matters such as the curriculum, student admission policy, and language policy, based on the pattern of the host countries (Education Department, 2000). Thus, Hong Kong maintains a diversified basic education catering for the needs of a pluralistic society.

All in all, the effects of marketisation and privatisation on diversity in basic education require and deserve further analyses and exploration, since marketisation and privatisation have just started. While the public education sector in Hong Kong plays the role of the mainstream education provider, the private sector helps maintain diversity, open educational opportunities and provides greater choice. The aim is to ensure that the private sector also provides quality education as in the public sector, which it is envisaged will facilitate the long-term social and economic development of Hong Kong. The private sector therefore should not be regarded as a competitor of the mainstream public sector, but its essential supplement (Bray, 1998). Together, the public and private education sectors contribute to each individual participant's enhancement of his or her quality and ability and, in aggregate, to society's progress and prosperity. Notwithstanding the situation, both the public and private education sectors share one thing in common. That is, they must ensure that the quality of their service is maintained and delivered at a level that would justify the continuing supply of their respective funding. This explains the vigour shown in the proposals for educational reform in both education sectors at the turn of the millennium.

5. MACAU

Macau emerged as part of the Portuguese empire in the sixteenth century, and recently became, after Hong Kong, another special administrative region within China on 20 December 1999. The *entrepôt* has its economic, political and social systems, which resemble Hong Kong but are significantly different from those in China and Taiwan (Bray & Koo, 1999). The Basic Law of Macau guarantees a high degree of autonomy for its people to maintain their own social, economic and political systems for 50 years, including operating its own educational system independently from the rest of China. The two official languages in Macau remain Chinese and Portuguese after the handover.

5.1. The Diversified Systems of Education

Macau has an uncoordinated and diversified education system, in which the operation of schools is based on models in Portugal $(4+2+3+2+1)$, People's Republic of China $(6+3+3$ or $6+5)$, Hong Kong $(6+5+1$ and $6+5+2)$ and Taiwan $(6+3+3)$. Among these four basic types of systems, other combinations have been adopted by schools at various levels. Official schools follow the Portuguese model and private schools generally adopt models from Hong Kong, China or Taiwan (Almeida & Bray, 2001).

There is no uniform curriculum in Macau. The *laissez-faire* policy of the colonial government has resulted in the absence of a coherent and coordinated system of education. The curriculum of the private schools differs from that in the public or official schools. While the curriculum in government schools is centrally controlled, the lack of standard syllabi and a common curriculum in the private sector has posed severe problems of curriculum relevance for many years (Tang, 1999; Tang & Morrison, 1998). The over-dependence on imported textbooks and teaching and learning materials (usually from Hong Kong, Taiwan and China) which are of limited specific relevance for schools in both public and private sectors could result in students' learning much more about these external places than about Macau (Bray & Hui, 1999). Since the handover, the government has embarked on a series of reform initiatives in improving education, including the provision of funds to localise textbook contents and teaching supplements in various subjects.

5.2. Private and Official Schools

Private schools play a dominant role in education since public or official schools account for only 12 per cent of the total. Most private institutions are owned or managed by religious bodies (mainly the Roman Catholic Church and the Protestants Churches) and social service organisations. Within the public sector, two types of schools exist with respect to the medium of instruction, namely, the Portuguese official school and Luso-Chinese official school. The Portuguese official schools follow a common curriculum and use textbooks imported from Portugal. Bray and Koo's (1999) account of Macau education in political transition observes that as many Portuguese-speaking people and their children left the enclave, the government found new ways to reduce responsibility for its major Portuguese secondary school by handing it over to a private Portuguese-medium secondary school, the *Escola Portuguesa de Macau* (Bray & Koo, 1999, p. 1). The Luso-Chinese schools use Cantonese as the medium of instruction and teach Portuguese and *Putonhua* and use textbooks imported from Hong

Kong. English is not taught until the fourth grade. In contrast, most private schools teach either in English or in Chinese, but Portuguese is seldom included in the curriculum (Choi & Koo, 2001).

All official schools are under the control of the Education and Youth Affairs Department. The laws and regulations used to control the operation of the private schools are relatively relaxed as the government does not want to interfere with the autonomy and internal politics of the private sector. Private schools are free to devise their own curricula, recruit their own staff, determine their own conditions of service, and decide on the size of classes (Bray & Hui, 1991). Teachers in private schools have heavy workloads and, in addition to Saturday sessions, may well be teaching four or five core subjects as well as performing class teacher and other duties and extracurricular activities (Choi & Koo, 2001).

Macau derives its revenue mainly from its tourism and gambling enterprises. Traditionally, the government has invested only a small proportion of its budget in education. Private schools only share about one-third of the financial resources. Nevertheless, public spending on education in recent years has increased to about 10 per cent of government's total recurrent expenditure (or round 1.7% of GDP), the figure is still considered small when compared to China, Taiwan and Hong Kong. Allocation of resources to public and private education has been under great debate (Lau, 2000; Wu, 1994) since the average educational expenditure per student head in public schools is six times more than that in private schools (*Macau Daily*, 11 November 2000). In 1998, the government has expanded the network subsidy scheme in order to provide subsidies to private schools from kindergarten up to nine years of basic education. Doubts exists for the government to impose controls on private schools since schools joining the scheme must first reduce their class sizes to 45 or below and follow prescribed guidelines advanced by the government.

As Macau has no compulsory educational policy, severe academic competition coupled with shortage of school places has caused many children to drop out of school before completing their middle school education. Repetition is common in both private and official schools. Research indicates that repetition rates in Luso-Chinese primary schools are much greater than those of their private counterparts (Chan, 2001; Lau, 2001). The problems of dropout and repetition have caused great concern to educators and the government.

In summary, Macau has a diversified and uncoordinated system of education. Government investment in education is small, it relies heavily on the private sector in its provision of education for its citizens. There is a strong need for Macau to improve the existing conditions and structures in its public and private education. Apart from the challenging tasks of unifying the curricula and narrowing the disparity in resource allocation and governance of public and private education, the government should assume a greater role in (a) facilitating and enhancing the development, (b) cooperation and innovation among institutions in the public and private sectors, and (c) in the enactment of nine years of compulsory education in the future.

6. DISCUSSION

A review of the four societies in this article points to some remarkable similarities and differences in their provision of public and private education. Comparison reflects a concern for equality, effectiveness, diversification and autonomy. On the whole, public education has been successful in the four societies, while the fractions of peoples successively completing their education in the private sector have increased rapidly during the past two decades. However, the increase in the strength of the private schools is giving rise to inequality and elitism. There is also a deliberate effort to decentralise through the governments (except in Macau) by delegating more powers and autonomy to schools with respect to curriculum development, school management and staff recruitment in the public sector.

Several differences have been observed in individual societies. Perhaps, the most highly centralised of the four systems is China where, mainly for political commitment and ideological leadership, the central government has largely determined the nature and content of public and private systems of education. China has to strike a balance in retaining a certain degree of state control when opening up to the market forces. In late 2001, the country has become a member of the World Trade Organisation, foreign operators will in the future be allowed to operate schools in some forms not yet known. State control over the school administration, curriculum and textbooks, religious affiliation and endowment, student enrolment, will be open to future challenges. It is important to investigate the tensions, that have created conflict between the state and the church and private schools through further research in this area.

By contrast, in the more economically developed Taiwan, the role of private education is not merely to reduce the burden on the government, rather it has an important function to offer more school choice and to provide a safety valve. Nevertheless. a large private sector exists at the high school level, with most students in the vocational track. Increasing privatisation in the vocational sector has a marked impact on the provision of equality of educational opportunity at the high school level and gives rise to issues of equity. Indeed, the government policy towards centralisation of school governance and decentralisation of curriculum development and implementations has posed some important issues and challenges to private and public education which may well be summarised in terms of the following questions. What is the role of privatisation in the context of moving toward a diversified systems of education in Taiwan? Is it feasible to create an environment for the development of different types of schools with everything being centralised except the development of curriculum and implementation? Will the situation become similar to that in the United States in which only the families that have the luxury of educational choice are those from higher socio-economic backgrounds? Ongoing inquiry and further research in comparative perspectives in this direction is needed in order to understand the nature and complexities of the problems and issues (Chang & Chen, 2000; Mao, 2001) before researchers and educators could provide answers.

Hong Kong has a rather distinctive system of education, in which private schools at elementary and intermediate levels are funded and operated through financing by individual providers or by subsidies from the government in the form of the Bought Place Scheme (BPS) and the Direct Subsidy Scheme (DSS). After the 1997 handover, one major issue is that the DSS may offer protection to the international schools (Bray, 1995). It is recommended that further studies should be conducted to ascertain the effect of the DDS on school performance as well as related issues of equality of educational opportunity through decentralisation and privatisation.

Macau is unique in terms of its *laissez-faire* system of education. The Macau Government relies heavily on the private sector in its provision of education. The diversity and complexity have emerged as a result of colonial neglect of education. Since the return of sovereignty in 1999, the increase of state control with more government subsidies towards a more regulated education system to improve the standard of public and private education has become the central issue in education (Lau, 2001). Another equally important issue and challenge confronting the Macau Government is whether effective partnership could be accomplished between private and public schools given that both sectors have ignored each other since the time of colonisation and not until the recent political handover has dialogue begun to take place.

Finally, with the impact of economic crisis and rapid technological advancement and global competition (Cheng, 2000), China, Taiwan, Hong Kong and Macau must continue to commit themselves to both public and private education and to provide an efficient channel of resources for lifelong learning and innovation for its citizens. On the other hand, while Hong Kong and Macau have already returned to China and both are subject to the "One Country, Two Systems" policy, social, economic and political concerns have caused educators and stakeholders in both territories to become interested in forms of privatisation of schooling across the border (or vice versa), in some cases leading to changes in what has been a supply and demand imbalance between the public and private sectors. Such phenomena and movement will certainly have important implications for the process and outcomes of education in these societies. Ongoing and further research in comparative perspectives is much needed to ascertain the dynamics of this change as well as why parents and their children would take advantage of private or public education across the border. Another relevant area of future research is the possibility of vouchers as a means of helping parents and their children make their educational choice and meet the costs of attending private or public schools.

REFERENCES

Almeida, C., & Bray, M. (2001). Macau: System of education. In T. Husér et al. (Eds.), *The Complete Encyclopaedia*. Oxford: Elsevier Science.
Bray, M. (1995). The quality of education in private schools: Historical patterns and the impact of

recent policies. In Siu Ping-kee & Tam Tim-kui, Peter (Eds.), *Quality in Education: Insights from Different Perspectives*. Hong Kong: Hong Kong Educational Research Association.

Bray, M. (1998). *Privatization of secondary education: Issues and policy implications. Education for the 21st Century*. Paris: UNESCO.

Bray, M., & Hui, P. (1991). Curriculum development in Macau. In C. Marsh & P. Morris (Eds.), *Curriculum Development in East Asia*. New York: Falmer Press.

Bray, M., & Koo, R. (Eds.) (1999). *Education and society in Hong Kong and Macau*. Hong Kong: Comparative Education Research Centre, University of Hong Kong.

Chan, K. (2001). *A preliminary report on student retention in Luso-Chinese schools: Perspectives on family background and learning difficulties*. Macau: DSEJ.

Chang, J. N., & Chen, Y. G. (2000). The influence of background factors on attending public or private schools and on years of education in Taiwan area. *Journal of the Research on Compulsory Education*, 6, 103–140.

Chen, B. Y., & Li, G. Q. (2001). *Varieties in higher education institutions in China: A survey of 115 institutions*. In B. Y. Chen (Ed.), *Rich Harvest in Minban Higher Education*. Beijing: Guoji Wenhua Publishing Company.

Cheng, K. M. (1992). *Education Reform in China*. Hong Kong: Commercial Press.

Cheng, K. M. (1997). The education system. In G. A. Postiglione & Wing On Lee (Eds.), *Schooling in Hong Kong: Organization, Teaching and Social Context*. Hong Kong: Hong Kong University Press.

Cheng, K. M., Cheung, K. W., & Ip, K. Y. (2000). *Marking Minban education from public education*. A paper presented to the expert discussion on the legislation of Minban Education in China, hosted by Centre of Research on Education in China, University of Hong Kong (February).

Cheng, Y. C. (2000). Strategic leadership for educational transformation in the new millennium. *Chulalongkorn Educational Review*, 6(2), 15–32.

Choi, C., & Koo, D. Y. (2001). Characteristics of public and private primary schools in Macau in the early nineties. In B. C. Choi & R. D. Y. Koo (Eds.), *Education and Social Development in Macau*. Hong Kong: The Hong Kong Institute of Education.

Deng, P. (1997). *Private Education in Modern China*. Connecticut: Praeger.

Education Commission. (1988). *Education Commission Report No. 3: The structure of tertiary education and the future of private schools*. Hong Kong: Government Printer.

Education Department. (2000). *Education Facilities for Non-Chinese Speaking Children*. Hong Kong: Government Printer.

Gao, Q. (Ed.) (1985). *A History of Modern Education in China*. Beijing: Beijing Normal University Press.

Hu, R. P. (1995). An investigation on the role and function of the boards of trustees of the private schools in Taiwan. *Journal of Jurisprudence and Politics*, 4, 113–123.

Hu, W., & Ding, X. J. (Eds.) (2001). *A focus on the Legislation for Minban Education*. Beijing: Educational Science Press.

Huang, C. T., Chou, Y. H., & Chen, T. H. (1996). *The allocation of the educational resource and tuition of higher education: The forming of the auditing committee of education at all levels of education*. Taiwan: Auditing Committee of Educational Reform.

Kwong, J. (1997). The re-emergence of private schools in socialist China. *Comparative Education Review*, 41(3), 244–259.

Lau, S. P. (2000). The basic law: Blueprint for our future education. In *A collection of conference papers on education development in Macau after the change of sovereignty*. Macau: Macau Return to China Committee Press.

Lau, S. P. (2001). An analysis of diversity in Macau education. *Macau Education*, 11(2), 10–19. Macau: Macau Education Committee Publisher.

Lin, J. (1999). *Social Transformation and Private Education in China*. New York: Praeger.

Lu, G. Q. (2001). The present situation of *minban* education in China. In National People's Congress, Education Office and Centre for Research of Education in China, University of Hong Kong (Eds.), *Study on Minban Education and Exploration in Related Legislation*. Guangzhou: Guangdong Higher Education Press.

Mao, L. R. (2001). An analysis of curriculum reforms in Taiwan from the perspective of political sociology. *Taiwan Journal of Sociology of Education, 1*(1), 80–101.

Miao, S. F. (1994). *From free education to education that collects fees*. Sichuan: Sichuan Education Press.

Ministry of Education (1997). *Educational Statistics of ROC*. Taipei: The Ministry.

Ministry of Education (2001). *Summary of Statistics*. Taipei: The Ministry.

Ng, H. M. (2001). Creation of income by schools in China. *Educational Management and Administration, 29*(4), 387–403.

Shao, J. R. (2001). *Study on Legislation for Minban Education in China*. Beijing: People's Education Press (in Chinese).

Tang, F. H., & Morrison, K. (1998). When marketisation does not improve schooling. The case of Macau. *Compare, 28*(3), 245–262.

Tang, K. C. (1999). Secondary school mathematics curricula. In M. Bray & R. Koo (Eds.), *Education and Society in Hong Kong and Macau*. Hong Kong: Comparative Education Research Centre, University of Hong Kong.

Tseng, A. S. (1997). A study on the organization of the foundation in the private school law. *The Hwa-Kung Quintessence of Jurisprudence, 25*, 11–35.

University Grants Committee (1996). *Higher Education in Hong Kong: A Report by the University Grant Committee*. Hong Kong: Government Printer.

Wang, Z. M., & Xu, G. Y. (1996). *Study on Minban Schools in China*. Tianjin: Tianjin Science and Technology Press.

Whitty, G. (1997). Marketisation, the state, and the re-formation of the teaching profession. In A. H. Halsey et al. (Eds.), *Education: Culture, Economy, Society*. Oxford: Oxford University Press.

Wong, N. C. M. (1999). Pre-school education. In M. Bray & R. Koo (Eds.), *Education and Society in Hong Kong and Macau: Comparative Perspectives on Continuity and Change*. Hong Kong: University of Hong Kong.

Wu, K. L. (1994). A critique on the financial resources and educational policies. In D. Y. Koo & H. T. Ma (Eds.), *Macau Education: Continuity and Change*. Macau: Macau Foundation.

Yiu, Y. B. (1984). *Chinese Education, 1949–1982*. Hong Kong: Hua Fung Bookstore.

Young, Y. (1995). *The Equality of Educational Opportunity – An Investigation of Sociology of Education*. Taipei: NTNU Press.

71

Policy-Making, Planning and Change in Tertiary Education

ALAN WAGNER
University at Albany, State University of New York, United States

PHILIP KWOK-FAI HUI
Hong Kong Institute of Education, Hong Kong

1. INTRODUCTION

Almost all countries undertake educational planning in some form. Educational planning is said to be "the application of rational systemic analysis to the process of educational development with the aim of making education more effective and efficient in responding to the needs of its students and society" (Forojalla, 1993, p. 39). Planning is thus closely linked to policy development and implementation, for the aims of planning are to inform decisions on appropriate goals and the approaches used to realise them. Given that growth has been a feature of world-wide development in education and a key challenge for education planning and policy, this article examines the developments and perspectives that are shaping educational planning and policy making with regard to educational expansion, particularly in relation to the experiences with tertiary education in three countries in the Asia-Pacific region: Japan, Republic of Korea and Australia.

While perspectives and considerations of planning, policy making and change cover all levels and sectors of education, there are good reasons for focusing in greater detail on planning and policy for tertiary education. First, tertiary education enrolments as well as participation rates are growing throughout the region, even in countries that had experienced substantial growth at this level prior to the 1990s. Second, high levels of participation in tertiary education mean that the directions followed and decisions taken at this level have influence on policy and practice at lower levels and affect provision and policy measures for adults as well. Indeed, the boundaries in programs and teaching are blurring across stages of learning, and thus make less appropriate and less meaningful strong distinctions in policy and planning across stages of learning. So, with expansion, the leading edge of reflection and action on education planning and policy making is shifting to the level of tertiary education. Through its focus on tertiary education planning and policy, then, this article aims not so much to provide a comprehensive overview of education planning and policy as a whole; rather, it seeks to identify and document emerging and newly reinforced directions for policy arising out of the current, identified challenge of growth.

2. PERSPECTIVES ON EDUCATION PLANNING AND POLICY

2.1. *The mergence of Educational Planning*

Perspectives and influences on planning practices have evolved over time and vary among countries. As Prakash (1999) observes, "the meanings and connotation of the concept of 'planning' have [changed] over time, over space, and between disciplines and socio-economic systems to which the concept is applied" (p. 93). In the last half of the twentieth century, there has been a steady growth of continuous systematic planning in all social policy portfolios. This development reflected a growth in public expenditure for social services, the growing importance of the contribution of such services to economic, civic and social life, and an increasing capacity within ministries and agencies to guide and administer social service provision.

The so-called 'rational paradigm' (Wildavsky, 2001) for centralised planning was favoured until the 1970s, when evidence of weak implementation and weak results encouraged a shift away **from** detailed direction and administration from the centre **to** regional, local and institution-level planning and decision making within a broad framework of guidelines and incentives (Tuijnman, 1996, Chapter 6). Education planning, policy development and change mirrored these trends. From the 1960s, one or more planning units were established in ministries but, by the mid-1990s, planning activities could be found at all levels of decision-making in education and in various agencies outside as well as within ministries of education (Caillods & Hallak, 1995). Planning processes now increasingly embrace a range of disciplinary perspectives and so serve to inform or guide different policy development needs. Economic analyses, for example, focus on allocative efficiency and resource use. In contrast, systems analysis, operations research and studies of administrative behaviour seek "consistency rather than optimality, and also ... use non-price strategies and rules of co-ordination rather than purely pricing considerations" (Fox, 1972, p. 37).

Throughout this period, intergovernmental organisations and development banks were also promoting educational planning throughout the region. These agencies not only sought to assist countries develop the expertise to undertake planning, they provided specific advice on both the volume and types of education to be accorded priority in planning and, in the case of the development banks, provided access to financing in support of those priorities.

2.2. *Planning and Policy Making for Growth*

Educational expansion continues as a feature of worldwide development in education. Toward the end of the 1990s, growth in enrolments was manifested in higher and still rising rates of participation in tertiary-level education (OECD, 1998, 2001). The observed trends and patterns accorded with positions advocated by the intergovernmental organisations as well as national authorities. Through the early 1990s, the World Bank and the United Nations Educational, Scientific and Cultural Organization (UNESCO) advocated rapid development of primary education in developing countries and less emphasis on tertiary, technical and professional education. The Asian Development Bank (ADB) provided substantial support especially for primary and nonformal education to assist its developing member countries in the Asia-Pacific region (ADB, 1995). OECD, (2000) giving emphasis to economic performance and overall well-being in its advanced, democratic market economy. Member countries, identified the important role played by professional and technical education. However, at the turn of the millennium, a higher priority for tertiary education was being signalled by the three global intergovernmental organisations as well as the ADB. The World Bank and UNESCO released *Higher Education in Developing Countries: Peril or Promise?* (Task Force, 2000), and OECD published its first major report in over ten years on higher and tertiary education, *Redefining Tertiary Education* (OECD, 1998). The Asia-Pacific Regional Follow-up Committee for the UNESCO's World Conference on Higher Education confirmed the newly reinforced tertiary education policy emphasis for the region (UNESCO, 2001).

The volume and patterns of educational participation have been seen to follow from two perspectives. The functionalist view regards educational expansion as linked to economic productivity and growth (see, e.g., Postiglione, 1997; Mauch, 2000). Growing interdependency among economies, partly driven by rapid development and use of information technologies, has encouraged economic restructuring that exploits advanced and widely developed capacities for knowledge, creativity and skills. On this view, differences in competence and skill levels account for differences in economic performance. Indeed, the most recent OECD analyses show that such skill and competence levels, measured by educational attainment, account for more of the inter-country variation in economic performance than previously estimated (Bassanini & Scarpetta, 2000). The findings apply particularly to the most advanced countries where rates of participation in education through secondary education are very high, and so partly explain the interest in expansion of tertiary education as an emphasis in policy making and planning in those countries as well as developing countries (Blöndal, Field, & Girourard, 2001).

In contrast, the conflict perspective regards educational expansion through the lens of social class differences, and particularly for participation patterns to reflect the reproduction of those differences. This view has special weight in tertiary education, and in such societies as colonial Hong Kong. Policy making and planning, then reflect or seek to overcome the social, political and economic influences giving rise to the observed patterns of difference.

Both perspectives are relevant when approaches and tendencies of planning, policy and change in education are examined at each educational level and sector. They play out in different measure in each country, but our view is that neither the functionalist perspective nor the conflict perspective is sufficient to explain educational growth in the Asia-Pacific region. Fuller consideration needs to be given to the role of the state, both in the ways it undertakes to plan for educational development and in the extent to which it seeks through various policy measures to reinforce or overcome the new or continuing tendencies identified by these two perspectives. It is to an examination of the features and tendencies in educational planning, policy development and change in three selected countries that we now turn.

3. TERTIARY EDUCATION PLANNING, POLICY DEVELOPMENT AND CHANGE

As just described, wider economic and social developments are according greater weight to the skills, competencies and dispositions embodied in individuals and to growing diversity in the backgrounds and interests within the larger pool of current and potential learners. Such breadth encompasses in some measure the perspective of lifelong learning for all. As used by OECD Education Ministers, lifelong learning emphasises a lifelong, also called 'cradle to grave' perspective, and stresses continuity and transition, learning and learners of all ages, not sectors or boundaries, whether with respect to contents, methods and contexts of teaching and learning. Lifelong learning is broader than recurrent adult and nonformal education, because it embraces all learning from that of young people in pre-primary schooling through to adults of *troisième âge* (Tuijnman, 1996; Wagner, 1999).

Paradoxically, much greater competition on seemingly constrained public and private budgets introduces another dynamic: societies expect more from education, yet find it difficult to agree through political processes to invest more. So, while there are good reasons for increasing the investment in education, both private and public, competing demands for available resources require more, and more hard-headed bases for the levels and deployments of resources in education. Education planning and policy development are being shaped in the Asia-Pacific region, and specifically in the systems under review, by such considerations. Three directions may be identified.

First, new policy approaches rely to a greater extent than previously on demand, individual and social. This partly reflects recognition of the inability of policy makers to anticipate or to provide for rapidly changing skills and competences profiles required to cope in complex modern societies, let alone in dynamic economies. Demand-oriented policies are more welcoming to wider diversity in provision, within and across the state and private sectors.

Second, new policy approaches feature a new organisation of planning and policy-making responsibilities, in which some decisions are moved closer to the level of the educational institution. A devolution or decentralisation of responsibilities, particularly in the ways resources are deployed to take into account the diversity in backgrounds and interests of learners at institution-level and across the system, may be seen as a part of the shift from supply-led to demand-driven provision.

Third, new policy approaches give greater attention to the clear specification of the results desired. Often expressed in terms of pass, retention or graduation rates, policies now focus more on the skills and competences to be acquired by individuals as reflected in standards, detailed curriculum guidelines and assessments. Specific approaches range from extensive monitoring and accountability efforts to the widespread dissemination of improved information for institutional administrators, learners and third parties, among which are employers as well as policy makers.

The general tendencies may be seen in other policy fields and, as is often the case in other fields, the reach and influence of demand requires policy approaches that extend beyond the education portfolio (see, e.g., Osborne & Gaebler, 1993). The trends point to a key dilemma in planning and policy making for education, particularly at the tertiary level. The flexibility and diversity introduced along with educational growth, for example, means that policies aimed at one type of program or pattern of participation may have different, adverse consequences for other programs or participation patterns. Put more positively, policies need to be mindful of the diversity of provision and the variety of settings, pathways and linkages through which learners acquire skills and competences. In particular, quality assurance arrangements and criteria established for first formal discipline-based degrees at state universities may be less appropriate for private or more professionally-oriented first tertiary-level qualifications. At a minimum, such quality assurance arrangements should use criteria that reflect the breadth and flexibility as well as the depth of learning at this level. Cheng (1995) signals the emergence of such flexibility and dynamism in education planning in the Asia-Pacific region when he concludes from his analysis of practices that planning has become forward looking and is evolving in terms of the goals identified as it reflects in different measure in different countries social demand, quality improvement and labour market needs among others.

3.1. *Japan*

Participation in tertiary education in Japan continues to grow from already high levels. Growth dates from the beginning of the post-war period, based at least partly on the evolution of the population of 18-year olds in the years to the mid-1980s (Shiozawa, 2000). That age group was expected to reach its post-war peak in 1991, so there was less provision for further expansion in the national universities. Enrolments in programs in private, local and non-university institutions were left to absorb fluctuations in demand around the long-term trend. These trends are shown in Tables 1–3. Enrolments in tertiary-level courses at the mostly full-fee, private special training colleges accounted for a large part of enrolment growth from the late 1970s to the early 1990s, as the measured rate of entry of 18-year olds into these programs more than doubled to about 20 per cent. In the course of the 1990s, both entry rates and enrolments in these

Table 1. Trends and projections in participation rates in Japanese universities and junior colleges, 1955 to 2009

Tertiary education providers	1955	1960	1970	1980	1990	1995	1998	2004	2009
University	7.9	8.2	17.1	26.1	24.6	32.1	36.4	–	–
Junior colleges	2.2	2.1	6.5	11.3	11.7	13.1	11.8	–	–
Total	10.1	10.3	23.6	37.4	36.3	45.2	48.2	54.9	62.9

Source: Reiko (2001, p. 281 Table 1 & P.287 Table 3). Participation rate is defined as enrolment as a percent of the eligible age group.

Table 2. Average annual growth rates of enrolments in Japanese university and non-university-type higher education

Period	1975–80	1980–85	1985–90	1990–96
University	1.2	0.1	3.1	3.6
Non-university+	25.4	2.6	8.0	0.0

+ = Includes junior college and special training college enrolments.
Source: Estimated from Ministry of Education, Science, Sports and Culture, Statistical Abstract of Education, Science, Sports and Culture (1997, p. 19).

Table 3. Numbers and percentage of public and private tertiary education institutions and students in Japan, 1970 to 1998

Year	Number of institutions			Number of Students (in 000s)		
	Total (N)	Public (%)	Private (%)	Total (N)	Public (%)	Private (%)
1970(1)	930	25.3	74.7	1714	24.7	75.3
1980(1)	1025	26.3	73.7	2253	23.8	76.2
1998(2)	1254	24.3	75.7	3141	25.4	74.6

Data refer to technical colleges, junior colleges and universities.
Sources: 1. James and Benjamin (1988, p. 20, Table 1.3); 2. MESSC (2000, p. 22).

programs have declined (Ministry of Education, Science, Sports and Culture [MESSC], 1997). The enrolment trends have been shadowed by weak economic performance in the last half of the 1990s, leading to calls for economic restructuring and a leaner, more responsive public administration. With respect to the latter, pressures for greater efficiency have led to efforts to consolidate ministerial portfolios and to reduce public sector spending. Education, and particularly tertiary-level education, has been affected by these developments.

Demand-driven planning and policy making. Tertiary education provision in Japan has long followed demand, at least insofar as students pay a substantial share of the costs of their education (40 per cent and 80 per cent, respectively, in public and private institutions) and private education in universities, two-year colleges and colleges of technology and special training colleges account for more than three-fourths of overall enrolments as just described. Further, some 30-branch campuses of United States universities were established or expanded around 1990 and enrolled at that time nearly 100,000 Japanese students. Public expenditure on tertiary education was 0.6 per cent of GDP, compared with 1.2 per cent in Australia (OECD, 2001). Together, these features describe a tertiary education market that is highly commercialised and privatised (Shiozawa, 2000), and strongly driven by demand.

Decentralisation and devolution of planning and policy making. The planning for the reforms of the 1990s called for the voluntary engagement of tertiary education institutions, to a greater extent than in the past (Reiko, 2001). At the turn of the millennium, planning and new policies aim for a harder edge to reforms in the form of even greater reliance on market mechanisms and a more targeted role for government funding for research and for financial support for those with low incomes.

One of the key reforms is a change in the legal status of national universities, from administrative extensions of the Ministry to entities as independent foundations. This reform has been embraced by the University Council, an advisory body to the Ministry, as one of a much more extensive set of reforms envisaged for higher education. Under the reform, each national university is responsible for its own management and have even greater flexibility to adapt study programs, secure and deploy resources, and enter into partnerships. Employees in national universities will no longer carry formal status as public civil servants, although national funding for and job responsibilities and security of post holders are expected to be retained in a different form (MESSC, 1998).

In addition, the Ministry formally withdrew from immediate oversight of study programs and curricula. Universities and colleges have been encouraged to modify the organisation of their degree programs in ways that better integrate general and more specialised contents. Institutions and programs were left to decide what changes they wanted to make. In fact, some opted for greater specialisation in study programs while others made no changes. Some institutions lacked the administrative capacity and vision to make changes without guidance from the Ministry, but, under the reform, the Ministry no longer provided such detailed advice.

Output- and outcome-based policies and monitoring. At the same time, the Ministry sought to strengthen quality monitoring through a new initiative located at the National Institution for Academic Degrees, an independent body tasked to work with all higher education institutions in establishing an approach for quality assurance. The approach being adopted follows a model of institutional self-evaluation to be carried out with the participation of an external team. This is new to Japanese higher education.

Taken together, the intent of the implied changes is far-reaching. It is not clear whether arrangements and capacities for policy development and management within the Ministry or within individual higher education institutions have been strengthened in those areas most likely to support the desired results. Arrangements for the allocation of public funds remain apart from the more strategic and flexible institution-based framework now being put into place. However, institutions now will have greater scope to seek out funding from other sources and partnerships that enhance institutional goals. On balance, the changes open the potential for the Ministry, designated agencies, and representative bodies to take a more strategic role in advancing the development and responsiveness of the breadth of tertiary education provision by treating private and municipal universities and colleges as well as the very wide variety of mostly private special training colleges as elements of provision to meet learning needs at this level. Further movement in this direction is essential, not least because private universities and two-year colleges as well as special training colleges as just mentioned account for more than three-fourths of tertiary-level enrolment.

3.2. *Republic of Korea*

Tertiary education enrolment has increased strongly in the four decades to 2000. The fastest growth occurred in the 1980s, first with the expansion of junior vocational colleges and then through enrolment growth in colleges and universities. The unification of all high-level vocational schools in vocational colleges partly fuelled that growth, as did policies that increased admission quotas and led to the establishment of new colleges and universities to meet social and economic needs. However, a large share of the growth has taken place in private tertiary education institutions; this growth is particularly marked in the last half of the 1990s. Provision is differentiated, with four-year colleges and universities (national, public and private), teachers colleges (national), junior colleges (national, public and private), the Air and Correspondence University and other open universities (national and private) and a range of other types (private). Tables 4 and 5 present the trends of expansion, by type of institution, in Korea.

Overall expansion has strongly followed economic development. Indeed, according to early and more recent research, the contribution of tertiary education graduates to economic performance has increased over time and remains high (Park, 2000). However, growth has also been influenced by the society's Confucian heritage culture. Great value is placed on education, and policies and reforms thus reflect society-wide views as well as economic imperatives. The prominence of education is reflected in the attention given by newly-elected presidents to policies and reforms in this sector (Park, 2000; Weidman & Park, 2000).

Demand-driven planning and policy. The high degree of private funding of education, particularly tertiary-level education, means that provision is strongly linked to payments of students and their families. Overall, families account for about

Table 4. The trend of tertiary education expansion in Republic of Korea from 1970 to 1998

Year	No. of vocational colleges	Total no. of students in vocational colleges	Per cent increase in student enrolment (%)	No. of 4-year colleges and universities	Total no. of students in 4-year colleges and universities	Percent increase in student enrolment (%)
1970	65	33,483	–	71	146,414	–
1975	101	62,866	88	72	208,986	43
1980	128	165,051	163	85	402,979	93
1985	120	242,117	47	100	931,884	130
1990	117	323,825	34	107	1,040,166	12
1995	145	569,820	76	134	1,187,735	14
1998	158	801,681	41	181	–	–

Source: Data adapted from Park (2000, pp. 130–131); and Weidman and Park (2000, p. 239); and UNESCO (1998).

Table 5. Number of tertiary education students per 10,000 population in Korea

	1965	1970	1975	1980	1985	1990	1996
Population A (in 1000s)	28,794	31,466	34,707	37,436	40,448	43,411	45,545
H.E Studs. B (in 1000s)	141.6	201.4	318.7	647.5	1,455.8	1,691.4	2,541.7
B/A × 10,000	49.5	63.9	91.9	173.0	360.0	389.6	558.1
Per cent increase (%)	–	129	144	188	208	108	143

Source: Weidman & Park (2000, p. 240).

three-fourths of the resources available to education at all levels: government expenditure amounts to 3.7 per cent of GDP, privately-paid tuition fees amount to 2.1 per cent of GDP, and spending on private tuition amounts to another 6 per cent of GDP (Ashton, Green, James, & Sung, 1999). The patterns may be seen in tertiary education, where tuition and fees paid by students and their families account for 50 per cent of revenues at public institutions; the comparable share for private institutions is 80 per cent. Table 6 shows that government expenditure on tertiary education as a share of total public expenditure has remained about the same since 1980. The share of the Ministry of Education's budget devoted to higher education has declined somewhat from its 1980 peak. Such high levels of private spending and provision mean that access to tertiary education is relatively open and responsive. Private tertiary education institutions have served this function, by accommodating growth in earlier years and

Table 6. Trends in Government expenditure for tertiary education in Republic of Korea (unit: billion Won)

Year	GNP (A)	Govt' Budget (B)	Budget of MOE (C)	MOE Budget for higher education (D)	D/B (%)	D/C (%)
1970	2,776	446	78	4	0.9	5.1
1975	10,064	1,586	227	12	0.8	5.3
1980	36,672	5,804	1,099	99	1.7	9.0
1985	78,088	12,532	2,492	179	1.4	7.2
1990	168,437	22,689	5,062	362	1.6	7.2
1994	299,436	47,593	10,879	734	1.5	6.8

Source: Weidman and Park (2000, p. 170).

attracting new clienteles of women, returning students and adults over the 1990s as the size of the traditional young adult cohort has declined.

Decentralisation and devolution of planning and policy making. Over much of this period, the government has managed development largely through regulation and controls. For example, the July 30 Education Reform of the early 1980s introduced changes in admission policies to boost enrolment, confirmed the move to a national entrance examination and upgraded teachers college and National Open University study programs from two to four years.

The Presidential Commission on Education Reform (the May 31 Educational Reform Initiative), under President Kim Young Sam, called for more substantial changes in the organisation of education. There is enlarged scope to establish universities under specific and transparent criteria, and greater autonomy afforded to individual institutions in admissions and program development. On one assessment,

> the university's influence on moral standards, visions and strategies, and autonomous effectiveness does not seem to be higher than the government's influence through administrative control, policy initiatives and financial support programs. Therefore, the university's institutional autonomy is still guided by governmental policy guidelines and indirectly controlled by government. (Lee, 2000, p. 12)

The constraints in both regulation and decision-making expertise appear to be recognised at least in part. In response, the Ministry plans to introduce a new fiscal system for the national universities that will bring general funding and special funding together in an integrated account. The national universities would have full autonomy in the use of resources, and scope to establish the level of tuition fees as well. The proposals are seen to go either too far, by setting out an open-ended commitment for government, or not far enough, by stopping short of establishing universities as corporate entities, responsible for fully managing their financial affairs (Lee, 2000).

Output- and outcome-based policies and monitoring. As economic performance has weakened, there are heightened concerns about the quality of tertiary education. Existing evaluation procedures, handled through the Korean Council for University Education, provides for an independent accreditation and assessment of institutions – the Korean Council for College Education performs evaluations for junior colleges. The Ministry uses the assessments of its own higher education evaluation committees in making funding decisions. Moreover, targeted funding provided through contracts with the Ministry are being used to promote qualitative improvements in research and international competitiveness, both of which are new directions in the Brain Korea 21 project.

In general, planning and policy development for change in tertiary education thus are in a dynamic phase in South Korea. The transition from military to civilian government has ushered in an opening up of tertiary education to a wider set of society-wide expectations and movement toward a new balance in how decisions are made about the volume and type of provision. Regulation and controls, particularly for the national universities, mean that centralised planning and decision-making still holds influence. But, both the President's Commission on Education Reform and the Brain Korea 21 project signal a qualitative change in orientation. These planning exercises involved wide participation and envisage both more autonomy and less insulation from demand and the market for institutional providers. If the directions are clear, progress in policy development and implementation is uneven.

3.3. *Australia*

The Commonwealth Government aimed for enrolment expansion from the late 1980s, partly in view of individual demand and partly in response to a perception of needs emerging from the economy. As part of restructuring efforts intended to shift the economy from reliance on exports of unprocessed products to high performance, high value-added and internationally competitive activities, government planning and policies sought to boost and expand higher and tertiary education. In this regard, policy has emphasised the supply of knowledge workers. Finance and Treasury authorities have recently examined the economic role of education, while for its part the Department for Education, Employment, Training and Youth Affairs has stressed links between the economic sector and the education sector to enhance quality in tertiary education (Marginson, 1997).

Under the Unified National System, the majority of tertiary institutions are classed and funded as universities. Harman (2001) highlights the diversity that remains, noting that the universities can be placed into four major groups: the leading so-called 'Group of Eight', with 30 per cent of student enrolment and

50 per cent of Ph.D. candidates; small-scale institutions established in demographics-based expansion of the 1960s and 1970s, with 25 per cent of first degree enrolment; technical universities, with 21 per cent of overall enrolment; and eight newer universities together with the University of the Sunshine Coast (Harman, 2001). In addition, there are four specialist colleges, a university college, 285 colleges of technical and further education and several open learning institutions. Patterns and trends in enrolments by type of program and institution are presented in Tables 7 and 8.

Demand-driven planning and policy making. Linked in part to the vigorous micro-economic reforms underway, the Dawkins government in the late 1980s re-introduced private student payments in the form of an innovative Higher Education Contribution Scheme (HECS) (DeAngelis, 1998). HECS is now differentiated into three bands, according to the relative costs of the study program (cost-based) or the attractiveness of the study program (demand-based, partly in relation to employment prospects for program graduates). Thus, program demand is both guided by the private contribution expected and by the allocation of resources (expenditures) for each program. The demand-based approach has been strengthened under a new policy allowing institutions to

Table 7. Students in Australian higher education, by level of course, 1987 to 1995

	Number of all students in higher education, enrolled in						
	Research higher degrees	Coursework higher degrees	Post-graduate diplomas	Bachelor degrees	Other courses	Total	Growth
1987	14,567	13,401	35,745	264,177	65,844	393,734	–
1990	16,535	19,782	42,445	340,598	65,715	485,075	23%
1993	28,345	33,584	51,714	430,204	31,770	575,617	18%
1995	32,646	41,373	50,106	454,846	25,206	604,177	5%
1987 = 100	224.1	308.7	140.2	172.2	38.3	153.4	

Source: Marginson (1997, p. 188).

Table 8. Growth in education, population and labour force, Australia 1955, 1965, 1975 (1955 = 100)

Year	Primary schools	Secondary schools	Higher education	Technical education	All education	Population (all ages)	Labour force
1955	100.0	100.0	100.0	100.0	100.0	100.0	100.0
1965	130.8	220.2	270.6	203.7	157.3	123.3	123.7
1975	142.8	314.2	887.0	294.4	202.7	151.0	161.6

Sources: Marginson (1997, p. 21).

enrol a limited number of so-called 'full-cost/full-fee' students, beyond the government-determined number of state-funded places. Although most tertiary education institutions are funded by the Commonwealth Government, planning and policy also allow for the establishment and recognition of privately-funded institutions. Some established universities have developed separate, full-fee certificate programs.

Decentralisation and devolution in planning and policy making. The reforms also aimed to encourage institutions to take decisions on profile, scale and resource allocation. In the early stages, public financing for funded places was withdrawn from institutions that fell below a minimum size or adequate profile. This led to consolidation and mergers within the sector and realised economies of scale and scope (DeAngelis, 1998). Universities are expected to manage their own affairs, including recruitment and site-based negotiation of pay.

Output- or outcome-based policies and monitoring. The government has developed institution-level indicators of profile and performance to enable comparisons by students and the wider public. Monitoring has been strengthened with the establishment of a new quality assurance effort through which each institution will be evaluated. Further, the Minister of Education, proposed in a 1998 policy statement to administer a common test to all those graduating from tertiary education, the results to be used to demonstrate the quality of Australian tertiary education to multi-national enterprises and employers. The proposal has not advanced very far but instruments have been piloted. Quality judgments have been left to the market, although the Commonwealth Department has also provided incentive funding for institutions capable of demonstrating quality initiatives or proposing innovative teaching and learning approaches.

So, with the movement toward a free market economy, tertiary education has come to be regarded in planning and policy terms as the source of high skill workers. The tertiary education sector underwent its own micro-economic reform, steered partly through the market and partly through market-based funding incentives, monitoring and information efforts organised by the Commonwealth Department with the engagement of system-wide advisory bodies and boards such as the National Board of Employment Education and Training (Vidovich & Porter, 1997). Under such a policy menu, analysts have noted the emergence of a "bifurcation between educational haves and educational have-nots" and a weakening of overall investment in the knowledge sector (Marginson, 2001). Notwithstanding these concerns, the policy directions developed thus far look set to be continued. The West Committee, in its report, *Learning for Life* (Committee to Review Higher Education Financing and Policy, 1998), called for further expansion and a student-centred orientation which would be advanced by bridging the divide between technical and further education institutes and university sectors, a gradual movement toward a voucher-type funding mechanism to implement what was referred to as a 'lifelong learning entitlement', and eased entry and recognition of private tertiary education establishments.

4. CONCLUSION

This article has examined perspectives, trends and research on policy making, planning and changes in education and explored in greater detail planning and policy approaches accompanying growth in tertiary education in Japan, Korea and Australia. As enrolments and diversity increased in these countries, market-based approaches and a trend to decentralise and devolve at least some elements of planning, decision-making and administration have been reinforced. These directions for policy and planning reflect the emergence of what is referred to as a 'new managerialism', and the advance of a neo-liberal view that participation in tertiary education yields returns to the individual student and thus justifies reliance on the market. The alternative development view, that investment in tertiary education requires largely state investment, has lost favour (Marshall & Peters, 1999). However, as Olssen (1999) points out, "neo-liberalism has come to represent a positive conception of the state's role in creating the appropriate market by providing the conditions, laws and institutions necessary for its operation" (p. 341). So, the state does not withdraw from tertiary education policy, but rather adopts a different policy approach that seeks to harness the market mechanism in the pursuit of excellence, increased competitiveness and efficiency. Education planning plays an important role, both in the analysis of private and public incentives for students, institutions and those who work in them, and third parties and in the dissemination of information on the performance within the system including variations in quality.

The evolution of education planning and policy development reflects such features, and dilemmas arise as countries seek to adopt this new perspective. The review of experiences with tertiary education planning, policy and change in Japan, Korea and Australia highlight three key considerations for policy making. First, the shift from supply-led (government) to demand-driven (market) is shaping policy responses and their effects. Second, a dilemma, in the context of expansion of tertiary-level education, is to have in place policies that support and drive development yet that are also flexible and responsive to the program diversity needed to accommodate the range of society-wide and economic demands as well as student profiles and interests. Third, while the giving over to demand and to autonomy are evident, there is still some room to go in developing capacities at the institution level, to standard setting (appropriate to diversity in provision and learning) and to quality assurance and information. That is, development is uneven.

All in all, the effects of the policy approaches already adopted are not yet fully understood, and further in-depth comparative research on the links between concrete policy actions and the realisation (or not) of identified policy goals will yield benefit to policy makers, planners and researchers.

REFERENCES

Ashton, D., Green, F., James, D., & Sung, J. (1999). *Education and Training for Development in East Asia: The Political Economy of Skill Formation in East Asian Newly Industrialized Economies.* New York: Routledge.

Asian Development Bank (ADB) (1995). *Case Studies in Education Research and Policy.* Manila: ADB.

Bassanini, S., & Scarpetta, S. (2001). Does human capital matter for growth in OECD countries? Evidence from pooled mean-group estimates. *OECD Economics Department Working Papers*, No. 282, Paris: OECD.

Blöndal, S., Field, S., & Girouard, N. (2001). Investment in human capital through post-compulsory education and training. *OECD Economics Department Working Papers* (forthcoming). Paris: OECD.

Caillods, F., & Hallak, J. (1995). Introduction: A new scope for educational planning. In J. Hallak & F. Caillods (Eds.), *Educational Planning: The International Dimension.* New York: Garland.

Cheng, K. M. (1995). Commonality among diversity: A review of planning and administration of education in Asia. In J. Hallak & F. Caillods (Eds.), *Educational Planning: The International Dimension.* New York: Garland.

Committee for the Review of Higher Education Financing and Policy (1998). *Learning for Life.* Commonwealth of Australia, Canberra: AGPS.

DeAngelis, R. (1998). The last decade of higher education reform in Australia and France: Different constraints, differing choices, in higher education politics and policies. In J. Currie & J. Newson (Eds.), *Universities and Globalization: Critical Perspective* (pp. 123–139). Thousand Oaks CA: Sage.

Forojalla, S. B. (1993). *Educational Planning for Development.* London: St. Martin's Press.

Fox, K. A. (1972). *Economic Analysis for Educational Planning.* Baltimore: The Johns Hopkins University Press.

Harman, G. (2001). Academics and institutional differentiation in Australian higher education. *Higher Education Policy*, 14(4), 325–342.

Lee, C. J. (2000). Emerging patterns of relations between government and university: Riding a horse with carrots and whip. Country case study prepared for international workshop on *University and Government: Changing Patterns of Relation.* Center for National University Finance and Center for Research and Development of Higher Education, University of Tokyo.

Marginson, S. (1997). *Education Australia: Government, Economy and Citizen since 1960.* Cambridge: Cambridge University Press.

Marginson, S. (2001). Australia: Higher education moves up the political agenda. *International Higher Education, Fall 2001.* Retrieved from website: Http://bc.edu/bc_org/avp/soe/cihe/newsletter/News25/text012.htm on 24 December 2001.

Mauch, J. E. (2000). The impact of higher education on emerging markets. In M. S. McMullen, J. E. Mauch & B. Donnorummo (Eds.). *The Emerging Markets and Higher Education* (pp. 25–44). New York: Routledge.

Marshall, J., & Peters, M. (1999). Studies in educational policy at the end of the millennium. In J. Marshall & M. Peters (Eds.), *Education Policy.* Cheltenham: An Elgar Reference Collection.

MESSC. (1997). *Statistical Abstract of Education, Science, Sports and Culture. 1997 Edition.* Tokyo: Research and Statistics Planning Division, MESSC.

MESSC (1998). *A Vision for Universities in the 21st Century and Reform Measures – To Be Distinctive Universities in a Competitive Environment: University Council Report.* Tokyo: University Council, MESSC.

MESSC. (2000). *Education in Japan, 2000: A Graphic Presentation.* Tokyo: Research and Statistics Planning Division, MESSC.

OECD (1998). *Redefining Tertiary Education.* Paris: OECD.

OECD (2000). *Investing in Education. Analysis of the 1999 World Education Indicators.* Paris: OECD.

OECD (2001). *Education at a Glance: OECD Indicators.* Paris: OECD.

Olssen, M. (1999). In defense of the welfare state and publicly provided education: A New Zealand perspective. In J. Marshall & M. Peters (Eds.), *Education Policy*. Cheltenham: An Elgar Reference Collection.

Osborne, R. J., & Gaebler, T. (1993). *Reinventing Government: How the Entrepreneurial Spirit is Transforming the Public Sector*. New York: Plume.

Park, N. (2000). Higher education in a rapidly developing country: The case of the Republic of Korea. In M. S. McMullen, J. E. Mauch & B. Donnorummo (Eds.), *The Emerging Markets and Higher Education* (pp. 125–146). New York: Routledge.

Postiglione, G. A. (1997). Asian higher education: Growth, diversity, and change. In M. F. Green. (Ed.), *Transforming Higher Education: Views from Leaders Around the World* (pp. 57–72). Phoenix, AZ: The American Council on Education and The Oryx Press.

Prakash, S. (1999). *Education Planning*. New Delhi: Gyan.

Reiko, Y. (2001). University reform in the post-massification era in Japan: Analysis of government education policy for the 21st century. *Higher Education Policy, 14*, 277–291.

Shiozawa, K. (2000). *Globalization of higher education in Japan*. Doctoral dissertation. University of Hawaii.

Task Force on Higher Education and Society (2000). *Higher Education in Developing Countries: Peril and Promise*. The World Bank, Washington, DC: The World Bank.

Tuijnman, A. C. (1996). *Lifelong Learning for All*. Paris: OECD.

UNESCO (1998). *Handbook on Diplomas, Degrees and other Certificates in Higher Education in Asia and the Pacific*. Asia-Pacific Centre of Educational Innovation for Development, UNESCO, retrieved from the website: Http://www.unescobkk.org/education/aceid/higher-edu/Handbook/Handbook.htm on November 29, 2001.

UNESCO (2001). *Asia-Pacific Regional Follow-up Committee for the World Conference on Higher Education. Higher Education in Asia and the Pacific: A Collection of Seven Publications and One Handbook*. CD-ROM. Bangkok: UNESCO.

Vidovich, L., & Porter, P. (1997). The Recontextualisation of 'quality' in Australian Higher Education. *Education Policy, 12*, 4.

Wagner, A. (1999). Tertiary education and lifelong learning: Perspectives, findings and issues from OECD work, *Higher Education Management, 11*(1), 46–58.

Weidman, J. C., & Park, N. (2000). *Higher Education in Korea: Tradition and Adaptation*. New York: Falmer Press.

Wildavsky, A. B. (2001). *The New Politics of the Budgetary Process* (4th Edn.). Boston: Longman.

72

Financing Education in Asian and Pacific Countries

MARK BRAY

Comparative Education Research Centre, University of Hong Kong. Hong Kong

1. INTRODUCTION

As in other domains, the features of educational financing in Asia and the Pacific show both diversity and commonality. At first sight, diversity is perhaps the more obvious feature. However, commonalities may also be found throughout the region. This article discusses issues relating to financing at all levels of formal education. The article begins by noting that governments are the dominant sources of finance for education, but that other important sources include households, communities and private entrepreneurs. The article then elaborates on forms of cost-sharing in education, noting in particular the roles of fees and community financing.

Some observers disapprove of cost-sharing, arguing that governments should provide fee-free education for all in order to ensure that nobody is discriminated against by inability to pay. In most settings, fee-free education can only be achieved if taxation is high enough to provide adequate resources. However, the article notes that data on taxation show wide variations in levels. The next two sections focus on institutional revenue-earning schemes and on external aid for education. Both involve complex issues of control as well as support for education. The following section has the rather different focus of supplementary private tutoring. This is a major activity in some countries, but has been given little attention in policy statements and research literature. The final section presents the conclusions.

2. THE VOLUME OF EXPENDITURES

2.1. *Public Expenditures*

Table 1 shows information on the volume of public expenditures on education in 27 countries. The first two columns show expenditures as proportions of Gross National Product (GNP) and of total government budgets. The diversity

Table 1. Public Expenditures on Education in Asia and the Pacific (per cent)

Country	Public expenditures on education as % of GNP	Public expenditures on education as % of total govt. budget	% Distribution of recurrent expenditure Pre-primary and primary	Secondary	Tertiary
Bangladesh	2.2	8.7	44.2	43.3	7.9
Bhutan	4.1	7.0	41.5	18.4	22.3
Cambodia	1.0	10.0	–	–	–
China	2.3	12.2	36.9	31.5	16.5
Fiji	5.4	18.6	50.5	37.0	9.0
Hong Kong	2.9	17.0	21.9	35.0	37.1
India	3.3	11.6	38.4	26.1	13.6
Indonesia	2.2	–	–	–	–
Kazakhstan	4.7	17.6	–	–	12.5
Kiribati	6.3	17.6	–	–	–
Kyrgyz Republic	5.3	23.5	–	–	–
Laos	2.5	10.3	42.2	43.5	3.9
Malaysia	5.2	15.5	35.4	41.2	16.8
Maldives	6.4	13.6	67.0	32.0	5.0
Mongolia	6.0	15.1	24.4	–	–
Nepal	3.1	13.2	44.5	17.7	28.1
Pakistan	3.0	7.9	48.0	24.0	14.0
Philippines	3.2	17.9	63.9	10.1	22.5
Samoa	4.2	–	52.6	25.2	–
Solomon Islands	4.2	–	56.5	29.8	13.7
South Korea	3.7	17.4	45.5	34.4	7.9
Sri Lanka	3.4	8.1	–	–	12.2
Taiwan	6.2	17.9	–	–	–
Thailand	4.8	20.1	52.8	21.5	16.5
Tonga	4.7	17.3	38.8	24.2	7.3
Vanuatu	4.8	18.8	57.9	33.0	6.4
Vietnam	2.9	7.4	40.0	20.0	16.0

– Data not available.
Note: Most data refer to the period around 1996.
Sources: Haq and Haq (1998); UNESCO (1998, 2000); various national sources.

around the region is evident in the ranges. Whereas expenditures by the Cambodian government represented only 1.0 per cent of GNP, the figure for Kyrgyz Republic was 6.8 per cent; and public expenditures on education as a proportion of the total budget ranged from 7.4 per cent in Vietnam to 23.1 per cent in Kyrgyz Republic. In general, education was always among the largest items in government budgets.

Table 1 also shows statistics on the distribution of recurrent government budgets at different levels of education. Again the statistics show major variations. Whereas the government of Laos spent only 3.9 per cent of its education budget on higher education, the Hong Kong figure was 30.0 per cent. The Laos figure reflected the fact that the tertiary sector was very small, though scheduled for major expansion. The Hong Kong figure reflected a tertiary sector which had already been expanded to cover 25 per cent of the age group and which was basically publicly-funded. Tertiary enrolment rates in the Republic of Korea were higher than in Hong Kong; but since the bulk of provision in Korea was private, only 7.9 per cent of the government's recurrent budget for education was allocated to the sector.

Table 2 shows regional aggregates over time. In Eastern Asia, public expenditures on education as a proportion of GNP rose slightly between 1980 and 1995, but in Southern Asia they fluctuated. In general, the less developed countries of Asia devoted a smaller proportion of GNP to education than did their counterparts in Africa. This particularly reflected the low level of teachers' salaries in Asia as a proportion of per capita GNP. The proportion was also below that in the more developed countries of North America, Asia and Oceania and Europe. The proportion was particularly low in China.

2.2. Private Expenditures

The nature of educational expenditures in Korea deserves elaboration, because it underlines the danger of citing government expenditures as if they were the only ones. Such a tendency is evident in many documents, but may lead to a very biased picture. In Korea, non-government expenditures on education in 1994 formed 71.1 per cent of total expenditures. During the period since 1977, private expenditures had grown much more rapidly than public ones (Paik, 1995, p. 15).

Although detailed data are regularly collected on private expenditures in

Table 2. Public expenditures on education as a percentage of GNP, by World Regions, 1980–95

Region	1980	1985	1990	1995
More developed regions	5.2	5.0	5.0	5.1
North America	5.2	5.1	5.4	5.5
Asia and Oceania	5.0	4.5	4.0	4.0
Europe	5.2	5.2	5.1	5.4
Less developed regions	3.8	3.9	3.9	4.1
Africa (excluding Arab States)	5.1	4.8	5.1	5.6
Eastern Asia	2.8	3.1	3.0	3.0
China	2.5	2.5	2.3	2.3
Latin America and the Caribbean	3.8	3.9	4.1	4.5
Southern Asia	4.1	3.3	3.9	4.3
Arab States	4.1	5.8	5.2	5.2

Source: UNESCO (1998), p. 110.

Korea, the same cannot be said of most other countries. As a result, cross-national statistics cannot be systematically displayed in the same way as can be done for public expenditures. Table 3 presents information on private enrolments in a number of countries. In particular, Table 3 shows the high percentages of private enrolments at the pre-primary level. However, Table 3 should be viewed with caution, especially because definitions of private schools varied in different countries. Thus, many students in Fiji and Tonga were in schools which were legally private but which were heavily subsidised by the government and were generally considered part of the public sector of education.

A further weakness of Table 3 is that although it shows the percentages of private enrolments in various countries, the proportion of financing coming from private sources might be very different. Figure 1 shows estimates of the proportions of household and government expenditures in public primary schools of eight countries of East Asia during the mid-1990s. Particularly dramatic was the picture in Cambodia, where government inputs were small and where gaps were bridged by parents and communities. The non-government figure included fees, transport, supplementary tutoring, and other items. Household cost were also high in Vietnam, though formed much smaller percentages in Mongolia and the Philippines. The high household expenditures in Cambodia and Vietnam were not the result of deliberate government policies. Rather they arose because the

Table 3. Private enrolments as a percentage of total enrolments, Asia and the Pacific, 1995

Country	Pre-primary	Primary	Secondary
Cambodia	–	1	1
Fiji	100	96	87
Hong Kong	100	10	12
Indonesia	100	18	42
Kazakhstan	–	0	0
Kiribati	–	0	77
Laos	11	2	0
Malaysia	42	–	5
Maldives	93	–	31
Nepal	–	6	–
Papua New Guinea	41	2	3
Philippines	53	7	35
Samoa	–	13	43
Solomon Islands	9	11	17
South Korea	78	2	37
Sri Lanka	–	2	2
Thailand	26	12	6
Tonga	–	7	80

– Data not available.
Source: UNESCO (1998), pp. 158–159.

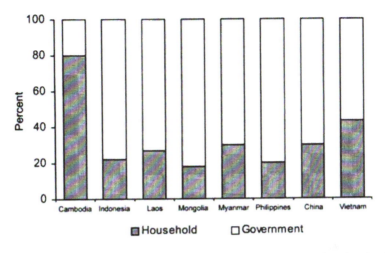

Figure 1. Government and household financing of public primary education in eight countries of East Asia, mid-1990s.

Note: The chart shows only household (including community) and government financing. It ignores inputs from external donors and other sources. The figures apply only to schools officially classified as public, and thus exclude private schools. Items included in calculations are not standardised by country. For example, some include transport to and from school, whereas others do not. See the individual sources for details.

Sources: Asian Development Bank (2000); Bray (1996a, 1999a); Bray and Thomas (1998); Evans and Rorris (1994); Hossein (1996); Jiang (1996); Maglen and Manasan (1999); World Bank (1997a).

governments were unable by themselves to meet needs, and households found that if they wanted to have schooling of even minimum quality, they had to provide resources by themselves.

Figure 1 refers only to the primary level, and would show even greater proportions of household financing at the secondary level. In Vietnam, for example, households were estimated in 1994 to be meeting 44.4 per cent of the costs of public primary education, but 48.7 per cent of the costs of public lower secondary education and 51.5 per cent of the costs of public upper secondary education (The World Bank, 1997a, p. 68). Similarly, in Indonesia households were estimated in 1995/96 to be meeting 22.2 per cent of the costs of public primary education, but 37.2 per cent of the costs of public lower secondary education and 41.2 per cent of the costs of public upper secondary education (Bray & Thomas, 1998, pp. 42, 47).

At the tertiary level, countries with high proportions of enrolments in private institutions include Bangladesh, India, Indonesia, the Philippines, Korea and Thailand. The scale of private higher education in the Philippines deserves particular comment because it is at the extreme. In 1998, 1,118 out of 1,383 institutions (80.8 per cent) were operated by private bodies (Johanson, 1999,

p. 1). Of these, 281 institutions were run by sectarian organisations, particularly the Roman Catholic Church. Some private universities were operated by churches and other not-for-profit agencies, but others were operated as companies with shares quoted on the stock exchange.

3. COST-SHARING IN EDUCATION

3.1. *Forms of Cost-sharing*

The most obvious form of cost-sharing is in fees paid by the consumers of educational services. Fees may be determined at the school level by institutions and communities, or they may be determined at the government level. The latter is particularly common in higher education.

In 1994, the World Bank presented statistics on the proportions of recurrent expenditures in higher education met from tuition fees in different countries. The Bank indicated that at the time that the document was written, in only 20 countries of the world did tuition fees account for over 10 per cent of recurrent expenditures (The World Bank, 1994, p. 41). The scale of fees was not related to the incomes of countries, but there was variation across regions. Sub-Saharan Africa, North Africa, the Middle East and Eastern Europe had little or no tradition of cost recovery in public higher education. However, public-institution fees exceeded 10 per cent of recurrent expenditures in one out of five Latin American countries and in half of the Asian countries in the sample.

As the 1990s progressed, in some parts of Asia fees increased further. In Hong Kong, where the government imposed uniform fees across all public institutions, the authorities decided in 1991 to raise fees from 12 per cent of recurrent costs (which was already a substantial increase from the situation in the mid-1980s) to 18 per cent in 1997. Fees also greatly increased in mainland China. Many institutions admitted self-sponsored students for high fees, and in the late 1990s the average fee in many institutions was between 25 and 30 per cent of recurrent costs. In Singapore, fees were increased from 10 per cent of the recurrent cost in 1986/87 to 21 per cent in 1996/97 (Zhang, 2000).

Another form of cost-sharing may involve communities. Such communities may be of many kinds, including ones based on geographic proximity, religion, ethnicity and race. In several countries of the region, community financing reaches significant levels.

- In Bhutan, in 1998, 115 community primary schools operated in parallel with 128 fully-government primary schools and 42 government junior high schools with primary sections (Royal Government of Bhutan, 1999, p. 25).
- In China, in 1994, 32.4 per cent of primary teachers and 7.4 per cent of lower secondary teachers were '*minban*' personnel, most of whom were employed by collectives and village communities (People Republic of China, 2000, p. 55).
- In Bangladesh, government primary schools comprised only 48.7 per cent of all formal primary schools in 1993. Non-government schools, of which the

majority were operated by villages and other communities formed 22.2 per cent; and the remainder were Islamic *madrasahs* (The World Bank, 1996, p. 29).

When it works well, community financing can spread the burden of resourcing education so that it does not rest solely with either governments or parents; and community financing can also promote local interest in schools. However, community financing can exacerbate regional and social inequalities, and does not always operate efficiently (Bray, 1996b; Bray, 2002). Partly for these reasons, the Chinese government aims to phase out community employment of teachers. Between 1994 and 1998 the number of community-employed teachers was reduced significantly, though the reduction was offset in some parts of the country by an increased number of substitute teachers employed on comparable terms (People Republic of China, 2000, p. 56). Moreover, in other systems communities have been given greater rein than before. In Cambodia, for example, communities used to be prohibited from employing their own teachers, but this is now permitted.

3.2. Alternatives to Cost-sharing

Many observers, including some United Nations bodies, disapprove of fee-charging, especially in public institutions. They do so particularly on the grounds that fees are likely to exclude individuals from the poorest segments of society. The question arising concerns the alternatives to cost-sharing.

The chief alternative is a system of taxation which generates sufficient revenue for the government to pay for services. Of course even in such a system the costs are still ultimately borne by society, which includes the consumers of services; but the payment is indirect rather than direct.

Table 4 provides some statistics on the scale of central government tax and non-tax revenues in 13 countries. In this sample of countries, the average of both tax and non-tax revenue formed a larger share of GDP in 1995 than in 1980. However, the capacity and willingness to generate income from taxation was lower in some countries than in others. China, for example, had moved to a market economy, and did not have the type of taxation infrastructure of more established capitalist economies. Similar comments applied to Laos, Mongolia and Vietnam (Rana, 1993, p. 12), though the figure for Mongolia in Table 4 suggests that in that country the capacity of the taxation system had been considerably increased by 1995.

Burgess (1997, p. 309) has argued that taxation is the only sustainable way to finance basic education in less developed countries. Aid, debt and inflation finance, he pointed out, are not sustainable and may ultimately reduce financing capacity. Contributory social security schemes are not a promising source of additional funding for most developing countries, and Burgess argued that the bulk of additional finance should come from broad-based domestic indirect taxes such as value added taxes. Direct taxes, he suggested, are less suitable, both because of difficulties in collection and because of their limited scope for achieving redistribution.

Table 4. Central Government Revenues as Percentages of GNP, Asia and the Pacific

Country	Tax revenue 1980	Tax revenue 1995	Non-tax revenue 1980	Non-tax revenue 1995	Total revenue 1980	Total revenue 1995
Bangladesh	7.7	–	2.9	–	10.6	–
China	–	5.7	–	4.6	–	10.3
Indonesia	20.2	16.4	1.8	6.2	22.0	*22.6*
Malaysia	23.4	20.6	4.4	6.6	27.8	27.2
Mongolia	–	20.3	–	5.0	–	25.3
Nepal	6.6	9.1	2.9	4.3	9.5	13.4
Pakistan	13.3	15.3	5.5	7.2	18.8	22.5
Papua New Guinea	20.5	18.9	2.8	*2.3*	23.3	*21.2*
Philippines	12.5	16.0	5.9	4.9	18.4	*20.9*
Singapore	17.5	17.2	4.0	4.6	21.5	*21.8*
South Korea	15.3	17.7	8.0	6.5	23.3	24.2
Sri Lanka	19.1	18.0	5.4	10.8	24.5	28.8
Thailand	13.2	17.1	6.6	7.4	19.8	24.5
Average	15.4	16.0	4.6	5.9	20.0	21.9

– Data not available.
Note: Figures in italics are for years other than those specified.
Source: World Bank (1997b), pp. 240–241.

4. INSTITUTIONAL REVENUE-EARNING SCHEMES

In some countries, institutions have been increasingly required to secure additional funds from other sources. Some institutions gain income from factories, businesses and other enterprises. This was especially common in communist societies during the period of central planning, when factories were seen as part of the social fabric of their localities. The advent of market economies has required enterprises to pay more attention to profits, and in many instances has reduced their willingness to contribute to schools. However, even in longstanding capitalist societies examples of enterprises contributing to schools are common. Martin (1996) gave examples of corporations in the Philippines which have become part of adopt-a-school programs. In Manila, three elementary and two secondary schools have benefited, receiving inputs from an oil refinery, a match manufacturer, a detergent company and a large multinational hamburger outlet. In Singapore, banks, supermarkets and other companies have donated cash and goods to schools, and have been able to claim taxation relief on these donations from the government. In Mongolia, some schools manage their own flocks of sheep; and in Nepal and China, schools commonly rent out buildings and use land for other non-educational purposes. Tertiary institutions in many countries have also been required to generate their own revenues through consultancies, publishing and endowments.

The scale of revenue obtainable from such sources depends strongly on the general wealth of the societies in which the institutions operate, on the specialisms offered by the institutions, and on the frameworks set by governments. Prosperous societies are obviously better able to support such initiatives than impoverished ones, though institutions in prosperous societies have in general faced less need to secure independent revenues, because their governments have been more easily able to provide substantial budget allocations. In the marketing of skills, institutions and individuals specialising in applied science and commerce have more opportunities than their counterparts specialising in history or philosophy. Governments can facilitate moves by offering tax exemptions for donations to public institutions.

Vietnam is among the countries in which higher education institutions have been forced by the escalating cost of living and the inadequacy of revenues from the government to earn independent revenues. Pham and Sloper (1995, p. 174) indicated that in 1991 Vietnam's College of Construction was able to add 28.3 per cent to its budget by taking on external contracts. Comparable figures were 22.0 per cent for the Foreign Languages University, and 11.0 per cent for the College of Mining and Geology. Pham and Sloper (1995) commented that the scale of such income generation chiefly depends on the product or service that can be provided (which does not always relate to the primary mission of the institutions), the entrepreneurial capability and culture within the institution, and the state of institutional infrastructure (personnel, organisational and technical) which creates the basis for delivering a desired product or service. Urban institutions generally have greater opportunities than rural ones. However, in Vietnam, rural institutions have been able to generate revenues by raising poultry, producing vegetables, managing restaurants and tailoring clothes. Critics observe that such activities deflect the staff from their primary missions as specialised providers of higher education. Advocates usually agree, but point out that the activities at least permit the institutions to survive in harsh economic climates.

An example of a very different sort may be taken from Singapore. Although the country has a buoyant economy and a history of government budget surpluses, even in Singapore the 1990s brought a philosophy that higher education institutions should develop their own sources of revenue and reduce dependence on the government. In 1991, appeals were launched by Singapore's two universities for newly-created Endowment Funds with a target of S$1 billion (Selvaratnam, 1994, p. 81). To boost the funds, the government contributed S$500 million, and committed itself to match up to S$250 million during the following five years if the universities could secure that amount from non-government sources.

5. EXTERNAL AID

External aid is a significant source of finance for education in many countries of the region. Table 5 presents data on the scale of Official Development Assistance flows to the developing member countries of the Asian Development Bank (ADB) between 1982 and 1997. The volume of flows reflected not only the sizes of the countries concerned but also various political factors. For some

Table 5. Official development assistance[a] flows to ADB developing member countries (US$ million)

Country	1982	1987	1992	1997
Afghanistan	9.3	45.0	204.3	278.9
Bangladesh	1,341.2	1,790.3	1,820.7	1,144.0[b]
Bhutan	11.3	42.1	56.2	67.5[b]
Cambodia	43.9	14.2	206.8	370.0[b]
China	524.0	1,381.6	3,049.6	5,042.2[b]
Cook Islands	10.4	11.0	17.2	10.0
Fiji	35.4	35.9	63.4	38.8[b]
Hong Kong	7.9	19.4	−39.0	–
India	1,643.9	1,702.9	2,423.0	591.6[b]
Indonesia	906.3	1,245.9	2,078.9	1,106.6
Kazakhstan	–	–	9.5	519.6
Kiribati	15.1	18.4	26.8	15.8
Kyrgyz Republic	–	–	3.5	214.7[b]
Laos	38.3	55.0	164.9	327.7[b]
Malaysia	135.3	363.4	205.5	−70.2[b]
Maldives	5.4	18.6	38.1	15.0[b]
Marshall Islands	–	–	7.7	63.0
Micronesia, Federated States of	–	–	13.9	96.0
Mongolia	–	3.0	122.9	322.1[b]
Myanmar	318.9	352.6	115.1	102.5[b]
Nauru, Republic of	–	–	0.2	2.6
Nepal	200.9	353.0	433.2	454.8[b]
Pakistan	915.6	820.2	1,009.3	1,103.9[b]
Papua New Guinea	310.7	317.7	442.1	296.5[b]
Philippines	333.4	732.2	1,718.0	549.3[b]
Samoa	22.8	34.6	53.4	28.2[b]
Singapore	20.5	23.3	19.9	–
Solomon Islands	28.4	57.1	44.7	36.3[b]
South Korea	34.0	11.2	−3.0	4,502.0[b]
Sri Lanka	415.5	477.0	638.0	510.0[b]
Taiwan	−6.4	−8.5	5.9	–
Tajikistan	–	–	9.7[b]	92.5[b]
Thailand	388.9	469.9	772.5	6,231.7[b]
Tonga	17.4	21.3	23.6	25.4[b]
Tuvalu	6.2	25.7	8.4	10.1
Uzbekistan	–	–	1.4	74.7[b]
Vanuatu	26.0	51.0	40.6	27.5[b]
Vietnam	135.5	111.0	575.1	849.6[b]

– Data not available.
[a] Official Development Assistance is defined as concessional flows to developing countries and multi-lateral institutions provided by official agencies, including state and local governments, or by their executive agencies, administered with the objective of promotion of economic development and welfare of the developing countries and containing a grant element of at least 25 per cent.
[b] Refers to net flows of long-term public and publicly-guaranteed debt from official creditors and grants, including technical cooperation grants. This category is wider than that of Official Development Assistance.
Sources: Asian Development Bank (1996, p. 49); (1999, p. 49).

countries in some years a negative sign is recorded, meaning that resources flowed out rather than in. For the years 1982 and 1987, no figures are recorded for Kazakhstan, Kyrgyz Republic or Uzbekistan since, while presumably resources flowed within the Soviet Union, they were part of a different framework.

Indonesia is among the countries in which external aid for education has played an increasingly prominent role. Figure 2 shows the percentages of contributions of three major donors, namely the United Nations Development Programme (UNDP), the World Bank and the Asian Development Bank (ADB), to the total education budget during the periods of five five-year plans (*Repelitas*). The picture is of significant growth, from 0.6 per cent in the first plan (1968–73) to 12.1 per cent in the fifth (1988–93).

In Nepal, external assistance has played an even more major role. Table 6 indicates the trend between 1981–85 and 1997/98. External financing was already substantial, forming 19.7 per cent of the total public budget for education in 1981–85; but by 1997/98 it had expanded to 52.8 per cent. Statistics such as these raise questions (both in Nepal and in other countries where aid levels have been comparable) about the extent to which policies and priorities are dominated by external agents rather than by the governments and peoples of the countries concerned. In Nepal, much of the early assistance was for technical higher education, but the bulk of assistance in 1997/98, reflecting the priorities of

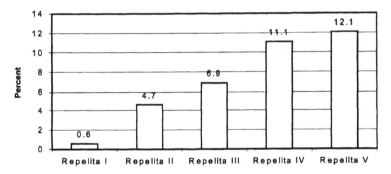

Figure 2. Contributions of major aid agencies as a proportion of the total national education budget, Indonesia.

Table 6. Trends in external and internal mobilization of resources for education, Nepal (per cent)

	1981–85	1986–90	1991–92	1993–95	1997/98
Internal	80.3	83.6	92.0	68.7	47.2
External	19.7	16.4	8.0	31.3	52.8
Grants	68.2	31.4	27.2	44.0	22.5
Loans	31.8	68.6	72.8	56.0	77.5

Source: Bajracharya et al. (1997, p. 76).

external agencies, was for basic and primary education. Whereas in 1981–85, 68.2 per cent of assistance was in the form of grants, in 1997/98 the proportion was only 22.5 per cent. From the viewpoint of the external agencies, the importance of loans rather than grants lay not only in the fact that the resources of the agencies would be repaid and thus would be self-sustaining, but also that, at least in theory, the recipient governments would scrutinise projects more carefully and would be more committed to their success. However, at the national level short-term political considerations have often taken precedence over long-term economic ones, and one effect of the expanded proportion of loan assistance has been greatly increased national debt.

In the socialist and former socialist states, patterns of external assistance changed markedly during the 1990s. Up to the end of the 1980s, resources flowed within and from the Soviet Union, but few resources for education came into the Soviet Union from outside. Mongolia was among the countries receiving substantial resources from the Soviet Union. Indeed in some years inflows of Soviet resources amounted to over 30 per cent of Gross Domestic Product. In 1988, about 50,000 Soviet civilians and large numbers of military personnel worked in Mongolia, contributing to all aspects of the economy and government. By 1993, however, this had collapsed. Since that time, external aid has been received from many bilateral and multilateral agencies in the Western bloc, but this has not completely replaced the scale of resources that had been received from the Soviet Union.

Among the issues which confront both donors and recipients are absorptive capacity, coordination with and between external agencies, and the conditionalities imposed by some donors. In Cambodia, nearly half the government's 1994 budget for education was financed by bilateral and multilateral agencies. Some projects were in competition with each other for scarce counterpart personnel, and major inefficiencies were caused by limitations in national infrastructure. Some of the conditionalities imposed by the external agencies concerned technical matters such as the availability of management structures, but others had broader political implications. For example, in 1997 the government of the United States suspended most of its aid, including in the education sector, in protest against what it perceived to be anti-democratic actions and a quasi *coup d'état*. These political factors underline the fact that external aid is rarely a stable source of finance for national governments.

6. SUPPLEMENTARY PRIVATE TUTORING

The scale, modes of operation, and implications of supplementary private tutoring have been neglected in both policy debates and the academic literature (Bray, 1999b). In some countries such tutoring is a massive enterprise. For example, a Sri Lankan survey found that in Colombo, 60 per cent of Ordinary Level students and 84 per cent of Advanced Level students received private tutoring (De Silva, 1994, p. 4); in Korea, private tutoring consumed 37.4 per cent of out-of-school educational expenditures in 1994 (Paik, 1995, p. 24), far exceeding the proportions devoted to books (19.3 per cent), stationery (7.4 per cent), transportation (6.4 per cent) or uniforms, boarding and other expenses (29.5 per cent); in India, a 1997 survey of 7,879 primary school pupils in Delhi found that 39.2 per cent received tutoring (Aggarwal, 1998, p. 65); and a 1992 survey of urban Bangladesh found that 65 per cent of pupils in government primary schools received private tutoring, which consumed 43 per cent of the direct private costs of education for the total number of parents in the sample (The World Bank, 1996, p. 53). Private tutoring has also been shown to be a substantial activity in parts of Cambodia (Bray, 1999a), Japan (Russell, 1997), Malaysia (Marimuthu et al., 1991), Taiwan (Zeng, 1999) and Singapore (George, 1992).

While more research is needed on the topic, some points are clear.

- Private tutoring is a major sphere of activity, not only in prosperous countries but also in impoverished ones.
- Private tutoring is growing. In societies such as Singapore and Hong Kong where it has long roots, it is expanding; and in countries where it was not previously evident, such as China and Vietnam, it has emerged.
- Private tutoring is found at all levels, but is especially common in the years in which students take public examinations, both primary (where relevant) and secondary.
- The organisational structures for private tutoring are varied. Some tutoring is individualised and takes place in either the clients' or the tutors' homes. At the other end of the scale are institutions which operate from many campuses. Some enterprises even operate on an international basis. Kumon, which is a company specialising in mathematics tutoring and is headquartered in Japan, is an example.
- The quality of private tutoring is also very varied. In few societies do governments set (let alone enforce) regulations on teacher qualifications, class size and so forth.
- Private tutoring may be found in both urban and rural areas, though is more common in the former than in the latter.

It is far from certain that the unfettered growth of private tutoring is desirable. Governments should at least monitor the scale and nature of private tutoring, so that they are aware not only of its impact on household budgets but also of its implications for the quality and effectiveness of mainstream schooling. Private tutoring maintains or increases social and geographic inequalities. While it presumably gives good private rates of return to the individual clients, it is not self-evidently an activity deserving encouragement.

7. CONCLUSION

This article commenced by noting aspects of diversity around the Asia-Pacific region. The region displays wide variations in the scale of resources available for education, and in the respective roles of governments, the private sector, households and communities.

However, the article also shows a number of common themes. Throughout the region, the role of the state has been brought into question, and non-government actors are expected to play a larger part than was generally the case between the 1960s and the 1980s. The advance of the market economy, even in China, Laos and Vietnam which officially remain socialist, has brought some convergence within the region. Fees for education have become a generally-accepted feature, especially at the tertiary level. In some countries, fee-charging extends down to the primary level; and it is not always supported by effective schemes for grants and loans. This raises major questions of equity. It also raises questions about the scale of taxation, and thus the government resources available for education and other activities. Also significant in many countries, particularly the poorest ones, is external aid. In addition to the educational issues are many political ones. This illustrates the links between matters of financing and other domains. The politics of aid are, arguably, of even greater importance than the technical issues. Finally, the chapter has highlighted the scale of private tutoring, which is commonly overlooked in analyses of the financing of education. In many societies of the region, supplementary private tutoring demands substantial financial inputs from households. It has major implications for social stratification, and also for the nature of teaching and learning in mainstream classes. This is among the domains needing further research in the future.

REFERENCES

Aggarwal, Y. (1998). *Primary Education in Delhi: How Much do the Children Learn?* New Delhi: National Institute of Educational Planning and Administration.
Asian Development Bank (1996). *Key Indicators of Developing Asian and Pacific Countries.* Manila: Asian Development Bank.
Asian Development Bank (1999). *Key Indicators of Developing Asian and Pacific Countries.* Manila: Asian Development Bank.
Asian Development Bank (2000). *Lao People's Democratic Republic: Education Sector Development Plan Report.* Manila: Asian Development Bank.
Bajracharya, H. R., Thapa, B. K., & Chitrakar, R. (1997). *Nepal Case Study. Study of Trends, Issues and Policies in Education.* Manila: Asian Development Bank.
Bray, M. (1996a). *Counting the Full Cost: Parental and Community Financing of Education in East Asia.* Washington DC: The World Bank in collaboration with UNICEF.
Bray, M. (1996b). *Decentralization of Education: Community Financing.* Washington DC: The World Bank.
Bray, M. (1999a). *The Private Costs of Public Schooling: Household and Community Financing of Primary Education in Cambodia.* Paris: UNESCO, International Institute for Educational Planning in collaboration with UNICEF.
Bray, M. (1999b). *The Shadow Education System: Private Tutoring and its Implications for Planners.* Fundamentals of Educational Planning No. 61. Paris: UNESCO International Institute for Educational Planning.
Bray, M. (2002). *The Costs and Financing of Education: Trends and Policy Implications.* Series,

Education in Developing Asia. Manila: Asian Development Bank, Hong Kong: Comparative Education Research Centre, University of Hong Kong.

Bray, M., & Thomas, R. M. (Eds.) (1998). *Financing of Education in Indonesia.* Manila: Asian Development Bank, Hong Kong: Comparative Education Research Centre, University of Hong Kong.

Burgess, Robin S. L. (1997). Fiscal reform and the extension of basic health and education coverage. In C. Colclough (Ed.), *Marketizing Education and Health in Developing Countries: Miracle or Mirage?* (pp. 307–346). Oxford: Clarendon Press.

De Silva, A. (1994). *Extra-school Tutoring in the Asian Context with Special Reference to Sri Lanka.* Maharagama, Sri Lanka: Department of Educational Research, National Institute of Education.

Evans, K., & Rorris, A. (1994). *Cost-effectiveness of Primary Education in Myanmar.* Yangon: UNICEF.

George, C. (1992). About $260 million a year spent on tutors' fees. *Straits Times,* 4 April.

Haq, M., & Haq, K. (1998). *Human Development in South Asia 1998.* Karachi: Oxford University Press.

Hossein, S. (1996). Unpublished data on costs and financing of education in Mongolia. Washington DC: The World Bank.

Jiang, M. (1996). *Education Sector in Transitional Economies: China Case Study Report.* Document for TA project: Social Sectors in Asian Transition Economies. Manila: Asian Development Bank.

Johanson, R. K. (1999). Higher education in the Philippines. Technical background Paper No. 3 for Asian Development Bank and World Bank *Philippine Education for the 21st Century: The 1998 Philippines Education Sector Study.* Manila: Asian Development Bank.

Maglen, L., & Manasan, R. G. (1999). *Education Costs and Financing in the Philippines.* Technical background Paper No. 2 for Asian Development Bank and World Bank. *Philippine Education for the 21st Century: The 1998 Philippines Education Sector Study.* Manila: Asian Development Bank.

Marimuthu, T., Singh, J. S., Ahmad, K., Lim, H. K., Mukherjee, H., Oman, S., Chelliah, T., Sharma, J. R., Salleh, N. M., Yong, L., Leong, L. T., Sukarman, S., Thong, L. K., & Jamaluddin, W. (1991). *Extra-school Instruction, Social Equity and Educational Quality.* Report prepared for the International Development Research Centre, Singapore.

Martin, A. H. (1996). *A Case Study of School-Parent-Community Partnerships via the Parent Teacher Associations (PTA).* Bangkok: East Asia and Pacific Regional Office, UNICEF.

Paik, S. J. (1995). *Educational Finance in Korea: Its Development, Current Issues and Policy Directions.* Paper for the workshop on Financing Human Resource Development in Asia. Manila: Asian Development Bank.

People's Republic of China (2000). *National Report for EFA 2000 Assessment.* Beijing: National Commission for UNESCO, Ministry of Education.

Pham, Q. S., & Sloper, D. (1995). Funding and financial issues. In D. Sloper & Le Thac Can (Eds.), *Higher Education in Vietnam: Change and Response* (pp. 161–181). Singapore: Institute of Southeast Asian Studies.

Rana, P. B. (1993). *Reforms in the Transitional Economies of Asia.* Occasional Paper No. 5. Manila: Economics and Development Resource Centre, Asian Development Bank.

Royal Government of Bhutan (1999). *Education for All: An Assessment of the Progress.* Thimphu: Education Division, Ministry of Health and Education.

Russell, N. U. (1997). Lessons from Japanese Cram Schools. In W. K. Cummings & P. Altbach (Eds.), *The Challenge of Eastern Asian Education: Lessons for America* (pp. 153–170). Albany: State University of New York Press.

Selvaratnam, V. (1994). *Innovations in Higher Education: Singapore at the Competitive Edge.* Technical Paper No. 222. Washington DC: The World Bank.

The World Bank (1994). *Higher Education: The Lessons of Experience.* Washington DC: The World Bank.

The World Bank (1996). *Bangladesh: Education Expenditure Review.* Washington DC: The World Bank.

The World Bank (1997a). *Vietnam: Education Financing.* Washington DC: The World Bank.

The World Bank (1997b). *World Development Report 1997.* Washington DC: The World Bank.

UNESCO (1998). *World Education Report 1998: Teachers and Teaching in a Changing World*. Paris: UNESCO.
UNESCO (2000). *World Education Report 2000: The Right to Education*. Paris: UNESCO.
Wirjomartono, S. H., Jiyono, S. A., Indriyanto, B., Purwadi, A., Cahyana, A., & Chamidi, S. (1997). *Indonesia Case Study*. Study of trends, issues and policies in education. Manila: Asian Development Bank.
Zeng, K. (1999). *Dragon Gate: Competitive Examinations and their Consequences*. London: Cassell.
Zhang, M. (2000). *Differential or flat? A comparative study of tuition policies in the world*. Study prepared for the Hong Kong University Grants Committee. Hong Kong: Comparative Education Research Centre, University of Hong Kong.

73

Family and Community Participation in Education

I-WAH PANG[1], EIKO ISAWA[2], ANNA KIM[3], HEIDI KNIPPRATH[4], MICHAEL A. MEL[5], TERRY PALMER[6]

1. INTRODUCTION

The study of family and community participation in children's school education is complex, given the different actors and institutions involved, the different levels of operation, the range of activities, the cultural dimensions and the differing perspectives and ideologies. Research studies on family and community participation in the Asia-Pacific region are very few as compared to those in the United States. The National Institute for Educational Research (NIER) Report (1996) documented the family and community involvement in some of the regions, including Australia, Hong Kong, Japan and the Republic of Korea; yet, no comparison has been made between them. The Organisation for Economic Co-operation and Development Report (OECD) (1997) and Kelley-Laine (1998) examined the parent as partners in schooling of nine countries; yet, only Japan came from the region. A thematic study of the United Nations Educational, Scientific and Cultural Organization (UNESCO) (Bray, 2000) highlighted the practices of community participation in a few Asian and African countries, including Papua New Guinea (PNG).

This article provides an overview and examines the unique features of the family and community participation in five education systems in the Asia-Pacific region, including Australia, Hong Kong, Japan, Korea and Papua New Guinea. The above list of countries is a convenient selection.

---

[1] *Hong Kong Institute of Education, Hong Kong*
[2] *Asian Development Bank, Manila, the Philippines*
[3] *Korean Educational Development Institute, Seoul, Republic of Korea*
[4] *University of Twente, the Netherlands*
[5] *University of Garoka, Papua New Guinea*
[6] *National Taiwan Normal University, Taipai, Taiwan*

2. PRACTICES AND ISSUES

In this study, the typology proposed by Epstein (1995) is adopted as the analytical framework. There are six suggested types of school-family-community partnership: namely, 'parenting', 'communicating', 'volunteering', 'learning at home', 'decision-making', and 'collaborating with the community'. Owing to the close relationships between types 'Parenting' and 'Learning at home', and between 'Volunteering' and 'Collaborating with Community', these types are grouped together, respectively, in the discussion in this article.

2.1. *Parenting and Learning at Home*

Parenting is referred to as assisting families with parenting skills and setting home conditions that support children, and assisting schools in understanding parents. 'Learning at home' is defined as involving families with their children's learning at home including homework and curriculum-linked activities (Epstein, 1995).

The term 'parent education' has not been found in the literature on Papua New Guinea (PNG). In this country, the focus has largely been on improving and enhancing the education system to overcome the high illiteracy rate, the low student enrolment rate, curriculum development and teacher education programs.

In Australia, in states like New South Wales and Northern Territory, a project called 'Parents as Teachers' has been organised for parents prior to and after a child's birth. Parent literacy and numeracy programs are also offered by most Australian states in junior schools (Townsend & Walker, 1998) and in community centres to help parents assist their children in pre-schools and primary schools, including those with special needs (NIER, 1996). Examples of numeracy programs include the Family Mathematics Project Australia, which has been used extensively in schools.

Parent education in Hong Kong has been offered in the past mainly by non-government organisations (NGOs) in community centres. In the last few years, schools have taken initiatives in organising parent education with the professional support from NGOs and the financial support from the Government through the Quality Education Fund (http://www.info.gov.hk/qef) and the Committee on Home-school Cooperation (http://edhsc.hkcampus.net). In 2000, the Government further allocated US$8 millions for promoting parent education (http://www.info.gov.hk/emb). A steering committee was set up and headed by the Director of Education. Hong Kong schools have become more aware of their role in parent education and see educating parents as a way to improve children's behaviour and school performance. Drawing examples from Mainland China, a systematic training of parents called Parent School has also been initiated in some schools.

In Japan, the Ministry of Education has established children's centres in local communities to provide parents with information on various parent-child activities, and the *Home Education Handbook and Notebook* to support home education has been distributed. In 1992, the Ministry started to lessen school hours by introducing gradually a five-day school week in order to encourage children to spend more time with the family as a part of the policy to reduce the share of school in education (*Monbushou hen*, 1999, pp. 1–37).

Korean mothers assume responsibility for their children's education and view unselfish devotion to their children as a critical feature of their personhood and motherhood. They visit the school four or five times a year and are well acquainted with their children's teachers (Ellinger & Beckham, 1997). The relationship between teachers and students is seen as an extension of the mother-child relationship (Kim & Choi, 1994). Parent education programs are offered by schools, parent associations and adult education organisations. Reports have also suggested that there should be more opportunities for parents to acquire parenting knowledge (Korean Educational Development Institute [KEDI], 2000).

Despite the societal change, the role of parents in supporting children's education at home remains a prominent feature in the Confucian heritage cultures: Hong Kong, Japan and Korea. In particular, the phenomenon of the 'education mother' is often quoted in the literature on Japanese and Korean education (OECD, 1997; Park & Kim, 1999). Stevenson and Stigler (1992) argued that

> In contrast to the common stereotype ... the Japanese mother does not adopt the rule of a pushy, demanding home-bound tutor. It is more accurate to describe the Japanese mother as a provider of a nurturant and protected atmosphere for learning. (p. 82)

The popularity of tutorial schools or private tutoring in these regions has shown the importance that parents attach to school education, and parents perceive that they are incapable of or unavailable to assist their children's learning at home. In recent educational reforms, parents in these regions have been called upon by the government to attend to the all-round development of their children. In contrast, some state governments in Australia have given increasing attention to children's homework. In Australia, there are alternative forms of learning at home, including home schooling (Klicka, 1999) and the education of those children with special needs living in remote areas. In these cases, family efforts are supported by the professionals at central delivery points.

2.2. Communicating

Communicating refers to the school-to-home and home-to-school communication about school programs and student progress. Communication appears to be the most common type of partnership between school and family in these regions. The teacher-parent contacts in Hong Kong, Japan and Korea are often described as 'problem oriented', focusing on children's academic and behavioural problems. It was reported, however, in Australia, that parents feel schools avoid telling the hard truths about student progress. In Australia, efforts are made to ensure that the community and parents know what is happening in schools (Cuttance & Stokes, 2000). Findings indicate that parents place a higher priority on receiving information about their child's progress than any other type of information they receive from schools (ACSSO & APC, 1996).

A trend in these regions is the increased comprehensiveness of the school-to-home communications. Examples include the publication by schools in Australia on how schools perform against various benchmarks and the release of school information and plans in Hong Kong as a requirement of school-based management (Education Department, 1999).

It is noteworthy to find out how similar are the activities linking homes and schools in various places, including school reports, notices to parents, newsletters and teacher-parent meetings on students' progress. In Australia and Hong Kong, school-home communication also makes use of new technologies, including e-mail, mobile phones and websites. In Japan and Hong Kong, the *Daily Communication Notebook* and *Student Handbook* are used for school announcements to parents and students' recordings of daily homework. However, similar to that in the United States, the school-home communication in these systems tends to decrease as the child grows up (NIER, 1996; OECD, 1997; Osakafu Kyouiku Iinkai, 1999; Shen et al., 1994).

Among the home-school links, Home Visit and Classroom Observation Day are practised in Japan and Korea. In Japan, teachers of Grades 1 to 7 visit all the families of the children in their classes when a new academic year begins. These visits are to find out the home learning environment of the children, parenting measures and family expectations. Schools also offer demonstration classes for parents for one to five times a year to allow parents to see their children learning. Usually observations are followed by a discussion of the class and individual children's performance (OECD, 1997). The above structured parent involvement is consistent with comments about the tight school control of communication processes and the passive role of parents. In fact, in places where there are strong parent bodies, like Australia, the parent-initiated communication is more apparent. In recent years, a number of Hong Kong schools have established parent resource rooms. This move implies that the parents could play a more active role in home-school communication.

2.3. *Volunteering and Collaborating with Community*

Volunteering is defined as the recruitment, training, activities and schedules involving families as volunteers and audiences at the school, or in other locations to support school programs. Collaborating with the community is defined as coordinating resources and services for families, students and the school with businesses, agencies and other groups, and providing services to the community by students, families and schools (Epstein, 1995).

In Australia, which has a relatively long history of family and community involvement, the Parents and Citizens Associations and Infants' Mothers Clubs are the source of volunteer support for schools. They provide assistance in classroom instruction, canteen and library services, after-hours maintenance, fundraising and special interest activities, depending on the school settings. To a much lesser extent they are involved in high-level school governance. Each of these groups is usually affiliated with a state parent body that is, in turn, affiliated with the Australian Council of State School Organisations (ACSSO) (http://www.acsso.org.au). Government departments acknowledge the importance of the state parent bodies and often provide support for their activities. These state and national bodies see themselves as strong lobby groups to support schools.

In Hong Kong, parent volunteering has increased as a result of setting up of the parent-teacher associations (PTA). However, parental assistance mainly occurs outside the classroom and is not connected with the core school activities, that is, teaching and administration (Pang, 1997). PTA has been used to enhance school-family communication. In recent years, it has become the vehicle for parental assistance in school operations, such as conducting extra-curricular activities, supporting school functions, helping with children's lunch, staffing the library and providing clerical support to class teachers. Traditionally, school students participate in various types of community services, such as selling flags for Non Government Organisations (NGO). Recently, there has been increasing involvement of the community in school instruction. Schools, which have been provided with additional grants by the Government, bought services from NGOs to provide parent education, students' activities and assistance to low-performers. Community participation has become more extensive and commercialised.

In Japan, PTA was established after the World War II, and at first along with the elective education board was considered as an opportunity for parents and the community to participate actively in school education. Now PTA seems to be troubled by a lack of interest of the members in the activities, as well as a huge difference in the amount of administrative burden between the members and control by the school (Hiroki, 1996, p. 88; Sumida, 2001). PTA is very often no more than a voluntary group of a limited number of parents helping staff with school events or sharing the financial burden of the schools. Since the advent of the five-day week, PTA has been more involved in extra-curricular activities and forming links between the school and the community. The kinds of activities range from facilitating sport and recreation for children, teaching greetings, encouraging safe traffic, patrolling the neighbourhood, publishing the PTA newspaper and cleaning the school grounds (Sumida, 2001). Most local PTAs do not have any significant relationship with their communities and there is usually no channel for interaction between communities and schools. Except for parents under strictly limited conditions, many Japanese schools were closed off to community members (OECD, 1997). However, in the introduction of a new subject called 'Integrated Study', the Ministry of Education encouraged schools and local education authorities to solicit support from community members (*Monbushou hen*, 1999). Furthermore, less-selective schools often encourage students to participate in internship programs in local companies and volunteer activities organised by the chambers of commerce.

In Korea, one of the roles of the School Council is to manage after-school programs to develop students' talent, aptitude, hobby and specialties. In 1999, about 97.5 per cent of schools were operating various after-school programs (Korea Institute for Youth Development [KIYD], 1999). To enrich the programs, various resources in the community have been used. For example, more field trip centres to increase experiential learning are being set up in local neighbourhoods, and persons with various work experiences are frequently invited to speak to classes. Schools often set aside one day per week for the purpose of so-called 'learning by experiencing', and students are also encouraged to visit their parents' workplaces to broaden their life experiences (KIYD, 2000). Youth activities, welfare, and exchange form the scheme called the 'Basic Plan for Youth of Korea' (Ministry of Culture and Tourism, 2000). In vocational education, the so-called '2+1 system', that is, two-years of general school education and one year of on-site training, has been in operation since 1994. Schemes involving secondary schools being attached to industrial companies have also been expanded (Ministry of Education, 2000).

In the past, children in Papua New Guinea (PNG) were taken from homes and kept at the school and were taught and trained in the ways of the colonisers. Time away from home inevitably meant that children did not learn about their own community activities and ways of life. In recent years, the participation of the family and the community has been made possible by bringing schools physically closer to the community and using the local vernacular in elementary education. Elders and other members of the community are brought into the school to provide additional knowledge and to support teachers. Parents assist teachers with field trips and voluntarily work as classroom aids from time to time. They can contribute to their children's education because language is no longer a barrier. Community members help develop the materials for the curriculum (Josephs, 2000). They take part in programs called 'Cultural Days', when they help dress up children in traditional costumes and finery and take part in traditional singing and dancing. In many rural schools, the community members also build houses for teachers, and students' toilets and classrooms.

2.4. Decision Making

There is a range of decision making structures in education systems within Australia. These encompass all the known models with school councils or school boards mandated in some places (Victoria, Australian Capital Territory and South Australia), optional in other places (Queensland, Tasmania, Northern Territory) and encouraged in others when the context is appropriate (New South Wales, Western Australia). Many Australian schools use the expertise of parents and community through a range of committee structures. Some have budgetary committees that advise the principal on all expenditures. Others have school uniform, canteen, fundraising, curriculum, and welfare committees that comprise representatives of staff and parents. In some cases, Parents and Citizens Associations are empowered by the principal to be involved in key decision-making. They are not, however, involved in the monitoring or evaluation of staff performance and in decisions about the nature and scope of reporting to parents on student progress (Cuttance & Stokes, 2000). Parents are encouraged throughout Australia to have a say in the appointment of key staff to their schools. Most notably this occurs at the level of the principal. In special cases, other staff members are selected by a panel involving parents.

In a review of Australian parent organisations (Wang, 1996, pp. 134–135), the organisations were commended for their success in securing large amounts of resources for education, solving educational problems and raising the Government's concern in educational matters. Yet, the national and state parent organisations were said to be limited in influencing government and state policies in education partly because individual members might base their decisions on the interest of their political parties rather than on educational grounds. The difficulties of involving parents in school decision making can be illustrated in the case study by Hatton and Eddy (1997) on involving parents in developing a school development plan. Parents were found to be unprepared for such involvement, and the school sent the parents on the curriculum committee to attend in-service courses. The dual parent organisations of the Parents and Citizens Committee and the Aboriginal Education Consultative Group within the school were said to add more burden to the teachers.

In Hong Kong, community involvement in school education is characterised by the school sponsorship of NGOs. The sponsoring agencies are responsible for a portion of the school setting up fund. Llewellyn (1982) Report drew attention to the fact that school sponsoring bodies "are not federated on a neighbourhood basis makes it impractical to contemplate local control". These bodies, traditionally, have been resistant towards opening up their school boards to incorporate a wider representation of stakeholders. This situation is somewhat changed owing to the fact that most schools have already established a parent-teacher association at the Government's request, which makes possible the election of the parent representative. However, in early 2002, the Government is considering a proposal to increase wider representation on school board. In recent years, a number of District Parent-Teacher Associations have been set up (see http://edhsc.hkcampus.net). Some parent leaders also have been invited to serve on various advisory committees of the Education Department.

Although most of the Japanese public schools have a PTA, they have had no influence on school management and policy making (Hiroki, 1996). A typical example is that the Parent-Teacher Association will support schools in disciplining students but is prone to keep quiet about issues that would bring shame to the community (Wray, 1999, p. 101). PTA members are often nominated and appointed by school principals, not selected by democratic election as the representatives of parents. Most PTAs cannot manage their financial affairs without permission or at least prior consultation with principals even though their monetary resources mainly come from family donations (Japan National Association of Parent-Teacher Associations, 1995). In 1998, the Central Council on Education (CCE) emphasised anew the need for improvement of the educational functions of the community and that schools should strengthen bounds with the community and parents (*Chuuou Kyouiku Shingikai*, 1998). Based on this report, the Ministry of Education promulgated an ordinance to encourage schools to install a School Council. This School Council, consisting of people of the community and parents, are informed by the principals of the school's policies. Yet, a Council can express its own opinions only when the principal asks for advice. Some schools have already started to implement a School Council and to encourage a more active partnership with the community and parents, while others prefer to be closed off.

Until recently the role of parent organisations in Korea has been limited to financial support for schools that their children attend. The idea of a School Council was proposed in 1995. The ratio of composition is set at 40–50 per cent of parents, 30–40 per cent of teachers, and 10–30 per cent of community figures. The Council is to deliberate on school budgets, settle financial accounts, propose elective courses and other after-school programs and consider the school charter and regulations (Ministry of Education, 2000). By 2001, School Councils have been implemented in most public schools. However, there are many concerns about the lack of parents' knowledge about school management, the ambiguous relationship between the principal and other members, and the extent of the representativeness of the council (Kim, 2000). There are two parent bodies, which are influential in education at the national level: the National Parents Association for True Education organised in 1989, and the Parents Joint for Realization of Human Education established in 1990 (KEDI, 1998). These bodies, supported by the government, suggest improvement to educational environments, fostering educational autonomy and democracy, and the expansion of parents' right and participation (Ministry of Education, 2000).

In Papua New Guinea, it is mandatory that primary schools have a Board of Management (BOM) and that secondary schools have a Board of Governors (BOG). Both the BOMs and the BOGs are important bodies in the overall co-ordination and management of each school. These bodies have representatives from churches, local community groups, the professionals, businesses, and also female representation. There are important links between the community and the schools particularly in exchanging information and bringing to light areas of concern that may need attention by those charged with the responsibility for action. School budgets, discipline of teachers, development plans, staff appointments and other areas of interest are coordinated between the BOMs or BOGs and the school administration. Chairs of the BOM or BOGs are elected by members of the Boards and are members of the local community. Such organisations allow parents and guardians access in school decisions and to make important contributions to school policies and practices. Among various functions listed by the Law, the construction and maintenance of buildings were taken most seriously by the majority of Boards (Bray, 2000).

3. AN OVERVIEW OF RESEARCH

The research in this area in the Asia-Pacific region seems to be more related to the family and community environment and parental role, than school programs.

The studies in different systems have, to some extent, addressed their own concerns about schooling.

In Australia, there is significant concern over parental involvement in children's literacy in terms of practices, influences and models (Spreadbury, 1995; Townsend & Walker, 1998). Marjoribanks (1999) demonstrated the significant relationship between the family social and ethnic background and the educational outcomes of Australian students. There are some studies that are concerned with parents' rights in their children's schooling. The Australian Council of State School Organisations Inc. (ACSSO) and the Australian Parent Council Inc. (APC) (1996) have developed 12 key principles in relation to parent consensus on assessment and reporting practices, which reflect the parents' perceptions of their rights and children's rights as consumers in education. Groundwater-Smith and White (1997) discussed the implications of this parental consensus and expressed concern over the availability of quality information both from schools and families about children's progress and learning. With regard to the marketisation of schools, Kenway and Fitzclarence (2000) examined how parents and children had become educational commodities of the schools, that is, they were seen as value added or negatively value based on their behaviour and the support given to the schools.

Hong Kong researchers have given increasing attention to parent involvement during the past decade. Shen et al. (1994), depicted an overall picture of the attitudes and behaviour of the various actors in the school system. Tam, Cheng and Cheung (1997) argued for a conceptual model of total home-school cooperation. Ho, (1995), who argues that parent involvement is a multi-dimensional construct, examined the effects of family background and school policies on parental involvement (Ho, 2000). Pang (1997) developed a matrix model for the functions of Parent-Teacher Associations (1997). He also examined the school-family relations from theories of social psychology (Pang, 2000a), and developed and evaluated a psychological model for teacher-parent communication (Pang, 2000b). Ng (2000) examined the impact of social class on home-school relations and found that parents of the working class are in a less favourable situation in participating in school activities.

Research studies in Japan are focused on issues relating to school reform and parental roles in school education. Examples include: (a) the development of the child in the community (Sumida, 2001), (b) change in the perceptions of parents towards the education of the child and towards the school-family-community relationship after the introduction of a five-day school week (Hayashi, 1998), (c) school organisation (Teruhisa & Toyokazu, 1996), (d) family effects on academic performance (Lummis, 1988), and (e) mothers' efforts (Stevenson & Stigler, 1992).

Research studies in Korea place a premium on issues in relation to parental roles in child development and school education (Kim & Choi, 1994) and family effects on educational attainment and success (Rodd, 1996; Sorensen, 1994). Park and Kim (1999) linked Korean's parental practices to Confucianism and highlighted the congruence between the values emphasised in the home environment and those learned in the school. In the OECD (1998) study on Korea, the school-industry partnership in vocational and technical education was examined.

Research in Papua New Guinea is limited. Demerath (1999) described how social and economic conditions in 1995 led to an emerging ambivalence toward education among villagers. He concluded that the support by the local community and parents and community and parental participation in program development were elements crucial to contextualising primary school instruction about agriculture. In an extensive discussion of community teacher education, McLaughlin and O'Donoghue (1996) emphasised that it should include an understanding of how traditional village life provides purpose as well as the means for the survival and identity of Papua New Guinea people. In the *Education For All Assessment 2000* of UNESCO, the country report of Papua New Guinea recognised the role of the village and community in the provision of further education, training, non-formal education and literacy programs (Josephs, 2000).

4. CONCLUSION AND RESEARCH IMPLICATIONS

4.1. *Driving Forces*

In the Asia-Pacific region, there has been an increased concern about family and community participation. The various governments have recognised the importance of enhancing school-family-community partnerships and taken the lead in promoting these partnerships using different approaches. In the case of Hong Kong, Japan and Korea, the increased involvement is associated with the education reforms in these school systems initiated in the 1990s. The School Councils in Japan and Korea were introduced as a part of the educational reform. The Korean model has been extensively implemented, and the School Council is meant to promote changes in both the structure of school management as well as in the nature of school programs. In Hong Kong, the government initiated to involve parents in school management much earlier than the comprehensive education reform (Education Commission, 2000). The target of school accountability has shifted gradually from the government bureaucracy towards the school parents as users. This shift may be triggered by the democratic concern of the then colonial government in view of the change of sovereignty of Hong Kong in 1997. The Australian model of partnership is characterised by the strong parent bodies. The family and community participation in Australia seems to derive from democratic as well as educational concerns. In Papua New Guinea, the parent and community involvement is tied with the access to education as well as the improvement of schools as a whole. The educational reform system that began with the Matane Report (1986) was precisely about expansion, access and the organisation and relevance of curriculum. The driving forces for family and community participation in various regions are summarised in Table 1.

Table 1. Driving forces for family and community participation

	Accountability to users	Learning support	Access to education
Australia	+	+	
Hong Kong	+	+	
Japan		+	
Korea	+	+	
Papua New Guinea	+	+	+

+ applicable.

4.2. Roles of Family and Community

The school systems in the Asia-Pacific region increasingly expect parents to play a greater role in the school education of their children. Evidence for this claim is seen in the variety of programs and activities that schools have provided for parents and the increased involvement of parents in school operation and management in recent years. Apparently schools, families and the community increasingly share experience with each other, and interact in various ways, including informing, discussing, consulting and participating in decision making in relation to their children's education; and in some systems, these activities are also extended to school management. The involvement of parents and community members as decision makers are apparent in Korea, Australia and Papua New Guinea, but was seldom reported in Japan. Hong Kong schools have just begun to include parents on school boards.

Parents in these Asia-Pacific school systems were found to be strong supporters of their children's school education either at home (Learning at Home) or in school (Volunteering) or both. In the Confucian influenced cultures, Hong Kong, Japan and Korea, parents play an important role in supporting their children's school education at home, and for some parents, at school as well. Parents also act as learners in attending education program organised by schools. Table 2 summarises the role of parents in school education in the various systems. The agent for participation refers to the typical organisation through which families' and communities' influence acts.

Concerning the role of the community, it appears that there are three types: represented by communities' supporting the school (for example, in Australia, Korea and Papua New Guinea), schools' supporting the community (for example, in Hong Kong) and cooperation between the two, like the school-industry attachment in Korea and the internship program in Japan.

4.3. Limitations of this Study

Community participation in school education is especially complex, as it includes all the links to the external community established by the school, in various settings (formal and informal; voluntary and commercial) and in relation to

Table 2. Agent for Family and Community Participation and Parent Role

	Agent for family and community participation	Parent role in school education			
		L	Sh	Ss	D
Australia	Parents and Citizens Association		*	*	*
Hong Kong	PTA	*	*	*	
Japan	PTA	*	*	*	
Korea	School Council	*	*	*	*
Papua New Guinea	BOG & BOM			*	*

L = learner: Sh = supporter at home; Ss = supporter at school; D = decision maker.
* Applicable.

various aspects of school programs. Family participation is more limited in scope. Yet, to provide an updated and comprehensive overview of family participation is still difficult, owing to the lack of naturally representative surveys in individual regions, except for Hong Kong. Another barrier concerns the language in which research is published. The publications are to a large extent in their own languages, posing considerable difficulties in terms of accessibility and systematic review of the materials of various systems.

4.4. Suggestions for Further Research

The strength of doing research in the Asia-Pacific context has to do with the diverse cultural background. The East-West links have provided the Asia-Pacific region with diverse cultural characteristics and different perspectives in order to examine the issues involved. The existence of countries at various stages of economic and educational development also presents many educational issues for meaningful comparison, and can provide insights into the fundamentals of school education.

What is lacking in most of these regions are basic surveys, that provide an overview of the perceptions and practices of the various actors involved. Critical to more successful schooling, more focused studies are needed into the specific mechanisms or vehicles that contribute to meaningful family and community participation in relation to educational reform. For example, research may examine the impact of parent and community involvement in school management and children's learning, and also the perceptions of the parent and community members concerned. Another type of studies may be related to the strong tradition of parents' involvement in their children's education at home. It is important to examine, for example, the changing roles of 'education mothers' in the Confucian heritage cultures in light of various educational reforms. It would be equally interesting to know how a Western-influenced country, like Australia, caters for the family practices of Asian immigrants and other Asian values. In order to inform and deepen understanding of the perceptions and practices of various actors involved in different systems, studies may apply sociological and psychological theories, such as symbolic interactionism and exchange theory, and examine the relevance of these theories (Pang, 2000a). These analyses should be able to lead to further improvement of theory and at the same time contribute to the global understanding of school-family-community partnership in children's education.

REFERENCES

Australian Council of State School Organizations Inc. (ACSSO), & Australian Parents Council Inc. (APC) (1996). *Assessing and Reporting Student Achievement: A Report of the National Parent Consensus.* Canberra: ACSSO & APC.

Bray, M. (2000). *Community Partnership in Education: Dimensions, Variations, and Implications.* Paris: UNESCO.

Chuuou Kyouiku Shingikai (1998). *Kongo no chihou kyouiku gyousei no arikata ni tsuite* (How local administration on education should be). Tokyo: Central Council on Education.

Cuttance, P., & Stokes, S. (2000). *Reporting on Student and School Achievement.* Canberra: Department of Education, Employment and Youth Affairs.

Demerath, P. (1999). The cultural production of education utility in Pere Village, Papua New Guinea. *Comparative Education Review, 43*(2), 162–192.

Education Commission (2000). *Learning for Life Learning through Life – Reform Proposals for the Education System in Hong Kong.* Hong Kong SAR Government: Printing Department.

Education Department, Hong Kong (1999). *Implementation of school-based management in all public schools.* Administration Circular No. 3/99.

Ellinger, T. R., & Beckham, G. M. (1997). South Korea: Placing education on top of the family agenda. *Phi Delta Kappan, 78*(8), 624–625.

Epstein, J. L. (1995). School/family/community partnerships. *Phi Delta Kappan,* 701–712.

Groundwater-Smith, S., & White, V. (1997). What is being learned here: Trends in assessment and reporting. In L. Logan & J. Sachs (Eds.), *Meeting the Challenges of Primary Schooling* (pp. 161–173). London: Routledge.

Hatton, E., & Eddy, B. (1997). Managing school development: A case study. In L. Logan & J. Sachs (Eds.), *Meeting the Challenges of Primary Schooling* (pp. 53–64). London: Routledge.

Hayashi, T. (1998). *Katei, gakkou, chiiki shakai no kyouiku renkei* (The educational partnership between family, school and community). Tokyo: Taga Shuppan.

Hiroki, K. (1996). *Kyouiku ni okeru kodomo, oya, kyoushi, kouchou no kenri, gimukankei* (Rights and duties of principals, teachers, parents and children in education). In Horio Teruhisa & Urano, Toyokazu (Eds.), *Soshiki toshite no gakkou* (School as an organization) (p. 88). Tokyo: Kashiwa Shobou.

Ho, S. C. (1995). Parent involvement: A comparison of different definitions and explanations. *Chinese University Education Journal, 23*(1), 39–68.

Ho, S. C. (2000). The relationships between family factors, institutional policies and parental involvement in children's education. *Educational Research Journal, 15*(2), 275–298.

Japan National Association of PTA (1995). *Report of Survey of the Reality of PTA and the Parents' Consciousness of Education.* Tokyo: National Association of PTA.

Josephs, J. (2000). *Education for All: Assessment 2000 – Papua New Guinea Country Report.* Document presented in the Asia-Pacific Conference on Education for All, Bangkok, 17–20 January.

KEDI. (1998). *Educational Partnership Buildup Schemes for a New Educational Community Formation.* Seoul: KEDI.

KEDI. (2000). *Parent as Partners in Schooling,* Seoul: KEDI.

Kelley-Laine, K. (1998). Parents as partners in schooling: The current state of affairs. *Children Education, 74*(6), 342–345.

Kenway, J., & Fitzclarence, L. (2000). *Institutions with Designs: Consuming School Children.* Camberwell, Victoria: The Australian Council for Educational Research.

Kim, H. S. (2000). *A study on the school council in secondary schools*. Unpublished Master's Thesis, The Dankuk University.

Kim, U., & Choi, S. C. (1994). Individualism, collectivism, and children development: A Korean perspective. In P. M. Greenfield & R. Cocking (Eds.), *Cognitive Socialization of Minority Children: Continuities and Discontinuities*. Hillsdale, NJ: Lawrence Erlbaum.

KIYD. (1999). *A Study on the Connection Extra-curricula Activity in School with Community Training Activity*. Seoul: KIYD.

KIYD. (2000). *Community Networking for Youth Career Development*. Seoul: KIYD.

Klicka, C. J. (1999). *Australia: Home Schooling in the Land Down Under*. Virginia, USA: National Centre for Home Education.

Llewellyn, G. E. J. (1982). *A Perspective on Education in Hong Kong*. Hong Kong: Government Printer.

Lummis, J. M. (1988). *The effects of families and schools on academic performance in Japan, Taiwan, the People's Republic of China, and the United States*. Ph.D. Thesis, University of Michigan.

Marjoribanks, K. (1999). Social context of education. In J. Keeves & K. Marjoribanks (Eds.), *Australian Education: Review of Research 1965–1998* (pp. 3–30). Melbourne, Victoria: The Australian Council for Educational Research.

Matane, P. (1986). *A Philosophy of Education for Papua New Guinea*. Port Moresby: Papua New Guinea National Department of Education.

McLaughlin, D., & O'Donoghue, T. (1996). *Community Teacher Education in Papua New Guinea*. [On-line] Available: Http://www.pngbuai.com/300socialsciences/education/training/teacher-ed-mclaughlin1of6.htm.

Ministry of Culture and Tourism (2000). *Young people in Korea*. Seoul: MOCT.

Ministry of Education. Korea (2000). *Education in Korea: 1999–2000*. Seoul: MOE.

Monbushou hen (1999). *Heisei 11 nendo, wagakuni no bunkyoushisaku: Susumu kaikaku* (Japanese government policies in education, science, sports and culture 1999: Educational reform in progress). Tokyo: Author.

National Institute for Educational Research (NIER) (1996). *Partnership in Education: Home, School and Community Links in the Asia-Pacific Region*. Tokyo: NIER.

Ng, S. W. (2000). The impact of social class difference on parent involvement in school education in Hong Kong. *Chinese University Education Journal*, 28(2), 35–62.

Organization for Economic Cooperation and Development (OECD) (1997). *Parents as Partners in Schooling*. Paris: OECD.

Organization for Economic Cooperation and Development (OECD) (1998). *Reviews of National Policies for Education: Korea*. Paris: OECD.

Osakafu Kyouiku Iinkai (Osaka Prefecture Education Board) (1999). *Gakkou kyouiku jiko shindan shikou no matome* (Report on the self-evaluation trial by schools). Osaka: Osaka Prefecture Education Board.

Pang, I. W. (1997). Functions of PTA and PTA networking: A Hong Kong perspective. *Chinese University Education Journal*, 25(1), 81–106.

Pang, I. W. (2000a). Home-school relations: An exploration from the perspective of social psychology. *Chinese University Education Journal*, 28(2), 157–172.

Pang, I. W. (2000b). *Teacher-parent communication: The developing and evaluating of a model of intention and behavior in Hong Kong primary schools*. Unpublished Ph.D. Thesis, University of Hong Kong.

Park, Y. S., & Kim, U. (1999). The educational challenge of Korea in the global era: The role of family, school and government. *Chinese University Educational Journal*, 27(1), 91–120.

Rodd, J. (1996). Socialization attitudes and practices of Korean mothers of young children: The influence of context. In E. Hujala (Ed.), *Childhood Education: International Perspectives* (pp. 63–73). Finland: Oulu University Early Education Centre.

Shen, S. M., Pang, I. W., Tsoi, Y. S., Yung, K. K., & Yip, S. F. (1994). *Home-school Co-operation Research Report*. Hong Kong: Government Printer.

Sorensen, C. W. (1994). Success and education in South Korea. *Comparative Education Review*, 38(1), 10–35.

Spreadbury, J. (1995). Why parents read to children. *Australian Journal of Early Childhood, 20*(1), 1-6.
Stevenson, H. W., & Stigler, J. W. (1992). *The Learning Gap.* New York: Simon & Schuster.
Sumida, M. (2001). *Chiiki shakai to kyouiku* (The community and education). Fukuoka: Kyuushuu Daigaku Shuppankai.
Tam, W. M., Cheng, Y. C., & Cheung, W. M. (1997). A re-engineering framework for total home-school partnership. *International Journal of Educational Management, 11*(6), 274-285.
Teruhisa, H., & Toyokazu, U. (Eds.) (1996). *Soshiki toshite no gakkou* (School as an organization). Tokyo: Kashiwa Shobou.
Townsend, T., & Walker, I. (1998). Different families: New issues for schools. In T. Townsend (Ed.), *The Primary School in Changing Times* (pp. 80-100). London: Routledge.
Wang, B. H. (1996). *Australian Education.* Shanghai: East China Normal University.
Wray, H. (1999). *Japanese and American Education: Attitudes and Practices.* London: Bergin & Garvey.

SECTION 7:

EDUCATIONAL RESEARCH AND NATIONAL DEVELOPMENT

Section Editor – Albert C. Tuijnman

74

Educational Research for Regional and National Development

ALBERT TUIJNMAN
Institute of International Education, Stockholm University, Sweden

1. INTRODUCTION

Since the 1960s scholars have spent much time exploring the relationship between education and educational research, on the one hand, and several aspects of national development, whether economic, social, cultural or political, on the other. Studies have pointed out that there exists a significant relationship between the two, even if it is thought to be non-linear and indirectly mediated by other variables (Fägerlind & Saha, 1983; Schofer et al., 2000). The entries in this section all contribute to the still on-going discussion about the importance and role of research in improving educational outcomes and promoting wider social and economic goals. The entries also take a regional perspective, centred on the contribution of educational research in the Asia-Pacific region. What emerges clearly from the entries is the fact that there is an international dimension to all educational research. Even if much fruitful research is undertaken at a micro level, with a focus on locally defined problems and engaging teachers in specific schools or classrooms, such studies still form part of a larger and multi-layered tapestry, and they all, in one way or another, draw on and also contribute to the international body of knowledge of education.

In this article a definition of educational research is presented first. In subsequent sections some broad historical developments are traced in the relationship between educational research and policy, and educational research and practice. Further sections address issues of research capacity and training in the Asia-Pacific region, and discuss some possible ways of strengthening the potential benefits of educational research for policy and practice. A brief conclusion is also offered.

2. A DEFINITION OF EDUCATIONAL RESEARCH

In examining the educational research and policy systems of different countries it should be borne in mind that there is no agreement at the international level about the precise meaning of the term, 'educational research and development'. The basic issues concerning the definition of research and development, and the conventions associated with its use, are provided in Chapter 2 of the fifth edition of the *Frascati Manual: Proposed Standard Practice for Surveys of Research and Experimental Development* (OECD, 1993). This manual, which is named after the town in Italy where it was first adopted in 1963, was written by and for the experts who collect, publish and use national research and development data. The latest edition of the manual defines the terms as follows:

> Research and experimental development (R&D) comprise creative work undertaken on a systematic basis in order to increase the stock of knowledge, including knowledge of man, culture and society, and the use of this stock of knowledge to devise new applications. (OECD, 1993, p. 29)

The key distinguishing characteristics of research and development, as defined by the manual, are originality and investigation as a primary objective. The manual also lists a large number of activities that should be excluded from the definition of research and development. Several of these exclusions pose problems, however, because the field of education is of relatively recent origin and draws on a variety of disciplines. Educational research is also conducted in different settings, including universities, schools, work places and special research centres. Multi-discipinarity is an essential and defining feature of educational research, but this inevitably also poses some challenges, not least in terms of academic allegiances and identities.

A crucial problem concerns the balance between research initiated by the public authorities and field-initiated research. The latter can be divided into research initiated by practitioners and studies initiated by the researchers themselves. Field-initiated research can play a major role in promoting partnerships among researchers, teachers and other practitioners. On the one hand there is a need for so-called 'quick-and-dirty', problem-oriented studies in the applied sector, which may be small-scale, short-term and rather disconnected from the mainstream of academic research. On the other hand, research also needs to be co-ordinated and sustained over a long time period. The scale and duration of support provided for educational research is often less than that needed to make substantial progress on the complex and difficult problems faced by decision makers and by teachers in the classroom.

The following definition of educational research and development is offered by Kogan and Tuijnman in a report commissioned by the OECD (1995, p. 37):

> Educational R&D is systematic, original investigation or inquiry and associated development activities concerning the social, cultural, economic and political contexts within which educational systems operate and learning takes place; the purposes of education; the processes of teaching, learning and personal development of children, youth and adults; the work of educators; the resources and organisational arrangements to support educational

work; the policies and strategies to achieve educational objectives; and the social, cultural, political and economic outcomes of education.

The breadth of the potential topics encompassed by these two definitions, and the range of academic disciplines that may be involved, suggest that education is best viewed as a multidisciplinary research field.

OECD (2001) makes further distinctions between basic, strategic and applied research. Basic research is mainly curiosity driven is not tied to any immediate practical goal. Strategic research operates between basic and applied research and has a longer time horizon and broader goals than the latter. Applied research is defined as original investigation directed primarily towards a specific practical objective.

3. FROM SYSTEM RESEARCH TO PRACTITIONER KNOWLEDGE

In the early days, educational research in the Asia-Pacific region developed in accordance with models emanating from the fields of psychology and related behavioural sciences in mainly Western European nations. Austrian and German scholars set many examples of empirical, even experimental research with a basis in educational psychology during the 1920s and 1930s. After World War II academics in Great Britain also played an important role in encouraging the development of the field, especially within the context of the British Commonwealth. However, educational research in the countries of the Asia-Pacific region has been most significantly influenced by developments occurring in the United States since the end of World War II. Compared with Western Europe, educational research as a field of study had in that country moved early on and without much controversy beyond psychology and had adopted a broader organising framework based in the social sciences. It was this broader framework that set the stage for the development of educational research in the Asia-Pacific region.

During the 1950s and 1960s, there was a firm belief in certain scholarly circles in the United States in what social science research, including educational research could do in providing the scientific and rational basis for the solving of concrete problems – knowledge that could be applied directly in the framing of better public and educational policies (Atkinson & Jackson, 1992). This belief in the fact-finding mission of research was present also in academic circles in other nations in both Asia and Europe, for example Australia and Sweden, but there the critical mass to produce large-scale studies was often lacking. This functionalist or linear model of the role of social and educational research in producing facts and applying knowledge in problem solving offered a rallying point around which policy-oriented and quantitative research gradually gained legitimacy during the 1960s (Kogan & Tuijnman, 1995). Much of this early educational research was anchored strongly in the social sciences.

Discussions on the role of research in elucidating the policy implications of changes in the relationships between education, the labour market and the economy continued. By the mid-1960s it had become clear that the industrialised countries faced similar problems in developing and expanding their education systems, for example, problems concerning the satisfaction of individual and social demand, the planning of resource allocation and particularly the development of the scientific and technical manpower needed in order to sustain development in modernizing economies (Husén & Tuijnman, 1990). Because many of the questions were identical, the result was a degree of similarity even in the orientation of the research programs that were being developed at that time. Recognition of this commonality led to a demand for the international dissemination of research findings. In turn this led to the creation of common research programs and the establishment of international platforms for research collaboration, for example, under the auspices of regional UNESCO agencies, the International Institute for Educational Planning, and the Centre for Educational Research and Innovation (CERI) established at the OECD in Paris in the late 1960s.

In a study conducted for the latter centre, Eide (1971) examined the role of research in the planning of social policy. A central consideration then was whether educational research should provide technological prescriptions or whether it should concentrate on the restatement of problems and the formulation of policy options. The conclusion offered was that researchers could not seek to realise their contributions though prescribing solutions but rather through "constructing, challenging, and changing cognition", as Shavelson (1990) put the message much later. Other studies assessing the relationship between educational research and policy were conducted as well (OECD, 1974, 1987). The main themes addressed were the goals of educational research and the problematic relationship with decision making. The study noted that considerable difficulties were encountered in preparing the survey because the institutional status of educational research had remained uncertain in the majority of the countries. The survey also identified three basic issues in the development of an effective relationship between educational research and policy systems. The first was that an unambiguous relationship between research and development was as a rule lacking. The second issue was the absence of a linear relationship between educational research and policy-making. A third was the lack of confidence and trust between the two communities, with policy makers often dismissive of the usefulness of research findings.

The general inability to address these issues led to a gap between high expectations and promises, on the one hand, and frustration with actual performance on the other. Thus disappointment and scepticism replaced some of the previous enthusiasm. This sparked a heated discussion about the proper role of social and educational research. The ensuing *Methodenstreit* or paradigm controversy – an often heated argument within the academic community about the validity and value of competing theoretical and methodological frameworks in the social sciences – did little to restore faith in the applicability of the knowledge produced by research workers in education (Husén & Tuijnman, 1990). By the end of the 1970s, a sense of resignation concerning the possibility of realizing major educational reforms through empirical research focused on the pursuit of generalized knowledge had become widespread not only among decision makers and teachers but, significantly, also among many researchers.

The apparent so-called 'crisis of confidence' in educational research, as documented by numerous reports of Congressional Committees and study groups in the United States and elsewhere in Asia and Europe led to dramatic cut backs in funding for educational research. This situation prompted academics in the field to undertake critical studies of the relationships between research, policy and school improvement (Weiss, 1982; Whyte, 1986; Gage, 1991; Kaestle, 1993). Husén and Kogan (1984), for example, noted on the basis of a review of the functions of research that the crisis besetting the research system was partly due to the overselling of the findings produced by research. This attitude was seen as reflecting an almost naive belief in the linearity of the relationship between quantitative social science research and decision making. Planners and administrators, in their search for empirical facts in support of rational decision making, as well as educators seeking to improve the teaching and learning process, were supposed to be the passive consumers of the products created by social and educational researchers.

Once it was acknowledged that a functionalist interpretation of the relationship between educational research and policy-making – the dominant model until the early 1980s – was no longer tenable, the debate gradually shifted to the ways in which the potential contribution of research could be realized. The main questions were still the same, but in addition to highlighting the expectations and needs of government officials in charge of the system as a whole, those of a new consumer group were increasingly brought to the fore. The central issue emerging during the 1980s became less how educational research could inform policy formation and more how it could contribute to improving educational practice: How can research findings benefit teachers, school leaders and local administrators? With this orientation came a new set of questions, answering them required a different methodological toolbox and a wholly different approach to engaging in research (see Biddle & Saha, 2002).

Thus during the 1990s there developed a strong emphasis on practice-oriented research that would, it was hoped, immediately benefit teachers and school leaders and assist them in solving practical problems of teaching and learning in the classroom. A report prepared by the New Zealand Ministry of Education (2001) shows how this so-called 'practice-utility' perspective became an important criterion applied in research funding in the country. A recent and related development that also impacts on research priorities and research funding regimes are the development and refinement of knowledge management tools and their applications to schools and universities (Gibbons et al., 1994; OECD, 2000). In this perspective, every person involved in the educational process, whether as teacher, administrator or student, is through the act of their engagement in learning and its organisation automatically also engaged in a personal research project. As Anderson and Herr (1999) point out in their essay on the

'New Paradigm Wars' that have emerged over the knowledge base of educational practice in America, Europe and increasingly also in Asian nations, whether rigorous practice-derived knowledge can classify as research is a matter of definition and perspective.

What is very clear, though, at this early stage in the twenty-first century, is that a new phase has begun in the politics of research in education in America and Europe (see Randall, Cooper, & Hite, 1999), one that emphasises pedagogy and didactics, the empowerment of practitioners and the legitimacy of their knowledge base, and one that down the road may well impact on funding regimes for educational research. Whether and how this tendency will play out across the countries of the Asia-Pacific region is less clear at present. There are important differences between the countries, and not only in cultural respects. But as the next section seeks to show briefly, international trends in educational research, planning and training have exerted strong influences on the development of research in the region. If the past is anything to go by, then the current trend that seeks to empower practitioners by including them as full members of the knowledge production system may well gain strong footholds also across the Asian region (see also *Research in Education: Nature, Impact, Needs and Priorities*).

4. INTERNATIONAL CO-OPERATION IN RESEARCH AND TRAINING

International agencies and national donor agencies have played important roles in the development of educational research in many Asian countries. Moigiadi (1991), for example, recounts how the Office of Educational Research was established in Indonesia within the Ministry of Education and Culture in 1969 with major funding from the Ford Foundation and the United Nations Development Programme. A five-year program of work involving large-scale data collection from schools, teachers and students at all levels of education and focusing on a wide array of variables ensued. Moigaidi also describes how most of the research staff, both senior and junior, took part in training programs abroad, ranging from three to nine months non-degree studies to full Masters. and doctoral programs in different institutions in the United States, Australia, Europe (United Kingdom and the Netherlands) and Asian States.

A large number of government officials from many Asian nations have taken part in the annual training program and intensive courses and workshops organised by the International Institute for Educational Planning (IIEP) at UNESCO in Paris since the early 1970s. The speciality of the IIEP program has always been to combine training and planning with educational research and the effective dissemination of new concepts, methods and techniques in educational planning and research. Thus the IIEP has acted as a major channel for the dissemination of examples of best practice to different Asian nations. UNESCO, through its Principal Regional Office for Asia and the Pacific, has also initiated and supported many innovative programs with the participation of many countries in the region. Some of the most important programs were those that supported the countries in the drawing up and also the monitoring of their five-year development plans for the education sector, plans that did assist some of the countries in achieving universal primary education at an early stage.

The World Bank and the Asian Development Bank have also played major roles in supporting and developing research in the Asia-Pacific region (see *Donor Support for Educational Research*). Lockheed (1991, p. 185), for example, notes that of 146 education projects initiated by the World Bank between 1982 and 1989, 116 included research components with a total of 436 identifiable, planned studies. The policy to embed specific research studies and surveys into larger education funding projects has continued and even intensified during the 1990s. The World Bank currently views itself as a knowledge bank and knowledge broker, and it accordingly emphasizes modern knowledge management practices, according to which all participants in a given development project are learners and researchers, and all have to contribute insights to a common data base. Many researchers in Asian nations ranging from Laos, Cambodia and Vietnam to the Philippines and Myanmar have participated and contributed to such development and research programs, that have provided not only new findings but also offered advanced training in research methods and opportunities to work in international, cross-disciplinary teams.

Despite all the effort and time and money spent, however, there still is a great need for research capacity building in many countries in the Asia-Pacific region. Hamid Latif and Fazlul Majid (1994) list a large number of critical issues that need to be addressed. All of these issues would still seem important and urgent today.

5. SCHOOLING AND GROWTH OF NATIONS

The critical issue confronting all who are involved in educational programs is whether or not participation in schooling is related to the growth of nations through raising the quality of the labour force within countries. The challenge for educational research has been to show this relationship, because the presence of such relationships is politically necessary to support financially the maintenance and increase of educational programs at all levels. With the increasing costs of educational provision, particularly in the fields of mathematics and science, it is necessary to consider whether mathematical and scientific knowledge and skills are a primary component of the human capital that is relevant to the quality of the labour force of a country. The key problem associated with this issue is one of how human capital should be measured. It is commonly argued that national growth rates are influenced by ideas and invention, through either research and development or through adoption, and that these are dependent on the stock of human capital which is reflected in the quality of the labour force of the country. Previous studies of this issue have used primary and secondary school enrolment rates and levels of attainment, as assessed by the number of years of schooling completed for a measure of human capital. However, Hanushek and Kimko (2000) have employed new and alternative measures of student performance on international achievement tests of mathematics and science to assess differences in labour force quality, that they consider are valid indicators of both human capital and the outcomes of educational programs.

Data were assembled for 39 countries that participated in international studies of student achievement on at least one occasion with 31 of these countries having the measures of economic performance that were needed for the estimation of rates of economic growth. There were six testing programs that provided the data, covered the years from 1964 to 1993, and included countries where estimates of economic growth could be calculated. The countries drawn from the Asia-Pacific region were: Australia, China, Hong Kong, India, Japan, Republic of Korea, New Zealand, the Philippines, Singapore, Taiwan, Thailand, and Russia that bridged into the region. Labour force quality differences measured in this way were shown to have extremely strong relationships with growth rates. These effects were particularly strong for the countries of the Asia-Pacific region. While the effects were stronger when the East Asian countries considered as three groups: (a) the four Tigers (Hong Kong, Korea, Singapore and Taiwan), (b) the four Tigers and Japan, and (c) the five High Performers with the newly industrialised countries of Indonesia, Malaysia and Thailand, were included, they were sustained even when these sets of countries were excluded. However, Ramirez and Chan-Tiberghein (see *Globalisation and Education in Asia*) contend that these relationships were reduced when additional statistical controls were employed, and when the Asian economic crisis period of the late 1990s was included in the economic growth calculations. Nevertheless, it is clear that the measures of educational achievement employed are related to economic growth. This finding not only endorses the emphasis on mathematics and science in the curriculum of the schools in the Asia-Pacific region, but also the importance of both educational research efforts that have been carried out over the past 40 years to collect these data, and the efforts to raise the quality of education in the Asia-Pacific region. Moreover, under these circumstances, a case can be argued for the strengthening of work in the field of educational research in the Asia-Pacific region in order to maintain the collection of data to monitor student achievement in mathematics and science in the countries of the region.

6. STRENGTHENING THE CONTRIBUTION OF EDUCATIONAL RESEARCH

The studies already referred to above have identified a number of perceived weaknesses and issues that could be addressed if educational research is to realise better its potential for informing and improving educational policy and practice. Among these are the following issues (Kogan & Tuijnman, 1995, pp. 22–23).

- *Fragmentation.* Political agents, policy makers, practitioners and educational researchers often operate at a long distance from each other. Moreover, educational researchers are as a rule divided in their views on all important issues.
- *Irrelevance.* The work educational researchers do and the outcomes of their work are often perceived as irrelevant by other constituencies, including the higher education sector.
- *Low quality.* It is often claimed, and with some justice, that much of what is presented as educational research is of poor quality and cannot stand up to rigorous scholarly scrutiny or the conventional criteria of validity and reliability.
- *Low efficiency.* Crude outcome indicators suggest that educational research, as a field, is less efficient and less productive than other disciplines in the natural as well as social sciences.
- *Low utility.* There is a persistent perception among the user communities that the findings of educational research have limited practical applicability.

In order to improve the potential of educational research and innovation as a means for monitoring progress and identifying areas where improvement may be needed, strong support is obviously needed. However, an increase in the input and output of the research system does not necessarily produce the desired outcomes, since this to a large extent depends on the methods and channels for research utilization that are in place. Careful thought must therefore be given to the ways in which an increase in the funds available for educational research may be optimally beneficial to all parties, both the consumers and the producers in both the short and the long term.

Political agents and the educational research community often operate at a long distance from each other, and mutual appreciation is often lacking. A dearth of systematic communication also besets the relationships between school practitioners and researchers in education and related disciplines. The policy and research system can therefore be made more effective in some respects if the interaction among policy makers, researchers and practitioners is improved. This naturally depends on which perspective is taken regarding the role of the research community with respect to the policy community and practitioners. Improving communication and co-operation are central elements in strategies to strengthen the research system.

Some strategies for overcoming the general concerns and structural problems identified above have been suggested by different authors (e.g., Kogan & Tuijnman, 1995; Ginsburg & Gorostiaga, 2001; Adams, Hwa Kee, & Lin, 2001). A key suggestion is that it would be important for researchers to involve practitioners in the design and actual conduct of school innovation projects, and to advertise and disseminate their findings more effectively. Connecting theory to practice is more than examining instructional effectiveness or devising new forms of professional development. It also means placing research in the service of teaching and school improvement. The same principle applies to effective policy analysis in education.

In 1999, the New Zealand Ministry of Education (2001) adopted a strategic research initiative (SRI) designed to ensure that policy work is underpinned by sound educational research and development. The national R&D plan identified the following priority themes:

- the effects of family and community resources on education outcomes,
- early childhood education,
- the effects of curriculum and assessment on education outcomes,
- the effects of school governance, ownership, and management on educational outcomes,
- the effects of school resourcing on educational outcomes,
- post-compulsory education,
- human capital development in organisations,
- influence of peer effects on learning outcomes, and
- enterprise based education and training.

New Zealand's R&D plan suggests a return to the belief that policy makers can identify research priorities and that commissioned research projects can be directly relevant to policy and practice. Whether this position will hold up in reality remains to be seen in the years to come.

In 2000, the Centre for Educational Research and Innovation of the OECD launched a new series of thematic reviews of educational R&D policy in its Member Countries. New Zealand was the first country to undergo such a review. The purpose was to examine the extent to which the national educational R&D system is functioning as an effective means for creating, collating and distributing the knowledge on which practitioners and policy makers can draw. In their report (OECD, 2001, p. 21) the examiners draw a number of conclusions. Among them the following are thought to have more general relevance for educational R&D in smaller countries across the Asia-Pacific region.

(1) Strengthening educational R&D will require additional resources, but this should not be seen as expanding the system in its current form. Expansion may best be seen as part of an overall increase of funding for social sciences. Resources also need to come from more diverse sources, as there is at present over-reliance on government, and especially the New Zealand Ministry of Education.
(2) Some concentration of research capacity is necessary. This does not necessarily mean physical concentration but the explicit development of critical research masses around certain fields and themes.
(3) There is a need to pay special attention to develop the capacity to use and analyse large data sets. Large data bases with relevance for the field of

education are built up but not effectively utilized, partly because of a lack of expertise and partly due to low interest on the part of researchers.

7. THE ISSUES RAISED IN THIS SECTION

The articles in this section of the *Handbook* address aspects of educational development that are directly related to the strengthening of educational research in the Asia-Pacific region in ways that lead on to regional and national development. Ramirez and Chan-Tiberghein examine the relationships between globalisation and education in Asia (see *Globalisation and Education in Asia*). They focus on the expansion of mass primary and secondary schooling and examine the influence of national characteristics and of economic, political and cultural globalisation on enrolments, curricula, the training of teachers, governance and finance. They next examine a similar set of issues for tertiary and higher education. In the following article (*Comparative Educational Achievement Studies*), Spearritt addresses the issues related to the cross-national studies of educational achievement that have been conducted across the world and have included countries in the Asia-Pacific region. The demand for such studies is growing rapidly within the region, not only for the information on comparative performance provided, but also for the training that participation in such studies gives to the educational research workers within the countries involved. Saha and Tuijnman (see *Comparative Indicators in Education*), provide an account of the development of educational indicators and the use of such indicators in educational research for the purposes of national evaluation and policy making.

Not only is the advancement of the conduct of educational research within the Asia-Pacific region of critical importance for the development of the region and also the countries within the region, but the dissemination and sharing of the findings of educational research studies across the region is of great benefit to all the countries taking part. The Harmans address the questions associated with the dissemination of the findings of educational research undertaken within the region, between and within the countries involved. There is much to be gained from cooperation and the sharing of both efforts and findings between countries, (see *Dissemination of the Findings of Educational Research*).

The states within the Asia-Pacific region range from countries that are very small to ones that are very large; from underdeveloped countries, to highly developed and industrialised countries; and from countries in which large numbers never learn to read and write, to countries where around 60 per cent of an age cohort might expect to participate in higher education with a further 20 per cent participating in technical education at some time in their lives. The organisations that sponsor and facilitate the sharing of educational services between the privileged countries in the region and the under privileged countries, are the aid agencies. Loxley discusses in his article, the support provided in the fields of education and educational research by the aid agencies in order to raise the levels of economic and human development within the region. (see *Donor Support for Educational Research*). The importance of economic development can not be denied, but it is in the end, the lives of the individual people throughout the region that is of greatest concern, and education plays a key role in all aspects of human development.

8. CONCLUSION

The Asia-Pacific region has changed markedly as a result of a series of remarkable accomplishments, economically, politically and culturally, particularly since the 1970s. In parallel with these changes the education systems of countries have also seen rapid growth. Universal primary schooling has been achieved in most countries, and many are well on the path towards achieving universal secondary education. Tertiary enrolments have also exploded across the region. Simplifying, the relationship between education and national development can be seen as dialectic, with education serving as an engine of economic growth, which in turn yields benefits and the resources needed for new investment in the education sector (Fägerlind & Saha, 1983). In this sense the education systems of the nations in the Asia-Pacific region have contributed importantly to both national and regional development. Their education systems have not merely expanded linearly, however, as there have been numerous reforms as well, with major implications for funding, institutional arrangements, curricula, methods of teaching and learning, quality assurance and school effectiveness. Many of these more qualitative changes have built, in one way or the other, on the findings of educational research and the fruits of more applied development programs.

In this instrumentalist perspective (see Schofer et al., 2001), it can safely be assumed that educational research has made a contribution, albeit mostly indirectly, to the series of remarkable successes recorded in national and regional development in East Asia and the Pacific countries. Describing more precisely the nature of this contribution and calculating the return on investment in educational R&D is a large and difficult undertaking (Shavelson, 1990). Given that educational R&D, as a field and discipline of study, is of a relatively recent origin, the returns to educational R&D are best examined over a long time period. The publication of the current *Handbook* is itself good testimony to the progress that has been made in many aspects of the field over the years. In order to sustain this trend educational R&D deserves to be given strong support in the years to come. Preserving a good balance between basic research and more applied development work will be one key to achieving this.

For national governments and international agencies the rationale for investment in educational research and research training is not the development of the field *per se*, but lies in achieving certain ends. Educational research is expected to contribute new knowledge and insights that can be used to improve education and create learning environments where the aptitudes and capacities of all individuals can be developed and applied. In order to achieve this, educational research must draw on the full range of available methods, both quantitative and qualitative, and would cover a large variety of topics and themes. The challenge is a substantial one, but the benefits are potentially also huge. Even a small improvement in the quality of schooling, for example, can have a major impact on gross educational yield. In this context it is necessary to remember that education is among the largest of all human enterprises: nearly one in five inhabitants of the earth currently attend classes in an educational establishment, the teaching profession is among the largest, and educational expenditure generally accounts for between 10 and 25 per cent of total public expenditure. Even if educational research is funded on a relatively modest basis, and even if the research does not generally or directly lead to large improvements, the incremental benefits that accrue to educational research over time must be highly significant (see also *Educational Research for Educational Reform*).

REFERENCES

Adams, D., Hwa Kee, G., & Lin, L. (2001). Linking research, policy, and strategic planning to education development in Lao People's Democratic Republic. *Comparative Education Review*, 45(2), 220–241.

Anderson, G., & Herr, K. (1999). The new paradigm wars: Is there room for rigorous practitioner knowledge in schools and universities? *Educational Researcher*, 28(5), 12–21.

Atkinson, R. C., & Jackson, G. B. (Eds.) (1992). *Research and Education Reform: Roles for the Office of Educational Research and Improvement*. Washington, DC: National Academy Press.

Biddle, B., & Saha, L. J. (2002). *The Untested Accusation: Principals, Research Knowledge, and Policy Making in Schools*. Westport, CN: Ablex Publishing (Greenwood).

Eide, K. (1971). *Educational Research Policy*. Paris: Centre for Educational Research and Innovation, OECD.

Fägerlind, I., & Saha, L. (1983). *Education and National Development*. Oxford: Pergamon Press.

Gage, N. L. (1991). The obviousness of social and educational research results. *Educational Researcher*, 20, 10–16.

Gibbons, M. B., Limoges, C., Nowotny, H., Schwartzman, S., Scott, P., & Trow, M. (1994). *The New Production of Knowledge*. London: Sage Publications.

Ginsburg, M., & Gorostiaga, J. M. (2001). Relationships between theorists/researchers and policy makers/practitioners: Rethinking the two-cultures thesis and the possibility of dialogue. *Comparative Education Review*, 45(2), 173–196.

Hamid Latif, A., & Fazlul Majid, A. F. (1994). *Educational Research Environment in South Asia*. Dhaka: Bangladesh Forum for Educational Development.

Hanushek, E. A., & Kimko, D. D. (2000). Schooling, labor-force quality and the growth of nations. *American Economic Review*, 90(3), 1184–2008.

Husén, T., & Kogan, M. (Eds.) (1984). *Educational Research and Policy: How do they Relate?* Oxford: Pergamon Press.

Husén, T., & Tuijnman, A. C. (1990). *The Uses of Educational Research: Epistemological, Ideological and Comparative perspectives*. Stockholm: Swedish Social Sciences and Humanities Research Council.

Kaestle, C. F. (1993). The awful reputation of education research. *Educational Researcher*, 23, 23–31.

Kogan, M., & Tuijnman, A. C. (1995). *Educational Research and Development: Trends, Issues and Challenges*. Paris: Centre for Educational Research and Innovation, OECD.

Lockheed, M. (1991). World Bank Initiative: Building Educational Research and Assessment Capacity. In W. Gmelin & K. King (Eds.), *Strengthening Analytical and Research Capacities in Education: Lessons from National and Donor Experiences*. Report on a Meeting in Bonn, July 1–5, 1991. Bonn: German Foundation for International Development.

Moigiadi (1991). Strengthening analytical and research capacities in education: The case of *'Balitbang Dikbud'* in Indonesia. In W. Gmelin & K. King (Eds.), *Strengthening Analytical and Research Capacities in Education: Lessons from National and Donor Experiences.* Report on a Meeting in Bonn, July 1–5, 1991. Bonn: German Foundation for International Development.

New Zealand Ministry of Education (2001). New Zealand's Educational Research and Development Systems: Background Report. *Document CERI/CD/RD(2001)2.* Paris: CERI, OECD.

OECD (1974). *Research and Development in Education: A Survey.* Paris: OECD.

OECD (1987). *Evaluation of Research: A Selection of Current Practices.* Paris: OECD.

OECD (1993). *Frascati Manual 1992. Proposed Standard Practice for Surveys of Research and Experimental Development.* Paris: OECD.

OECD (2000). *Knowledge Management in the Learning Society.* Paris: OECD.

OECD (2001). Educational Research and Development Policy in New Zealand: Examiners' Report. *Document CERI/CD(2001)4.* Paris: CERI, OECD.

Randall, E. V., Cooper, B., & Hite, S. (1999). Understanding the politics of research in education. *Educational Policy, 13*(1), 7–22.

Schofer, E., Ramirez, F. O., & Meyer, J. W. (2000). The effects of science on national economic development, 1970 to 1990. *American Sociological Review, 65*(4), 866–887.

Shavelson, R. J. (1990). Contributions of educational research to policy and practice: Constructing, challenging, changing cognition. *Educational Researcher, 17,* 4–11.

Weiss, C. (1982). Policy research in the context of diffuse decision making. In G. Kosse (Ed.), *Social Science Research and Public Policy-making.* London: NFER-Nelson.

Whyte, W. F. (1986). On the uses of social science research. *American Sociological Review, 51,* 555–563.

75

Globalisation and Education in Asia

FRANCISCO O. RAMIREZ
Stanford University, Palo Alto, CA, United States

JENNIFER CHAN-TIBERGHEIN
University of British Columbia, Vancouver, Canada

1. INTRODUCTION

Economic, political, and cultural globalisation processes have characterised the world for centuries; different theories have highlighted the rise and dynamics of the world capitalist economy (Wallerstein, 1974), the world system of nation-states (Anderson, 1991) and worldwide cultural rationalisation (Meyer, Boli, Thomas, & Ramirez, 1997). Theories vary in the weight they assign to different sources of influence, from global organisation of production and exchange to hegemonic powers to transnational organisations, professionals and experts. Theories also vary in the emphasis given to mechanisms of diffusion, from market adaptation to coercion to imitation to enactment of policy models and prescriptions. However, a common theme is the premise that an understanding of national phenomena requires an understanding of the broader world within which the national phenomena are embedded (Therborn, 2000). As globalisation processes intensified after World War II, this premise gained greater currency in the social sciences (Guillen, 2001) and its educational implications have become the focus of more comparative research. Much work centers on economic globalisation and its impact on nation-states and national educational policies (see for instance the papers in Burbules & Torres, 2000 and in Stromquist & Monkman, 2000). Alternatively, worldwide political and cultural dynamics are emphasised in other lines of inquiry that examine the development of scientific and educational knowledge structures and their societal effects (see, for example Drori, Meyer, Ramirez, & Schofer, 2003).

Throughout the globalisation and education literature an important distinction can be made between those who assume a more or less bounded nation-state and a national character and those who, on the contrary, assume stronger world dynamics and transnational influences. Scholars of the national character group emphasise the distinctiveness of national educational patterns and structures and their capacity to resist external pressures or to adapt to them in unique ways. World dynamics scholars are more likely to emphasise the strength of exogenous factors and their isomorphic or common educational outcomes. These differences in perspective are especially evident with respect to education in Asia, both as regards mass schooling and higher education. Both perspectives are considered in this review of the literature on globalisation and education in Asia. The first section of this review focuses on mass primary and secondary schooling and considers the influence of national character and of economic, political, and cultural globalisation on enrolments, curricula, teacher training, governance, and finance. Next, a similar set of issues for higher education, bearing in mind both general perspectives is considered.

2. MASS SCHOOLING

2.1. Enrolments

Enrolment growth has characterised Asia as well as other regions for several decades. Education as human capital and education as a human right are highly institutionalised beliefs throughout the world. Much of the phenomenal growth of education is due to the internal and external political legitimacy nation-states acquired as a result of national mass schooling policies. Mass schooling as a nation-state project has been globally institutionalised throughout the twentieth century and the Asian countries are no exception to this rule. There is little evidence of recent primary or secondary enrolment expansion or contraction in Asian countries that can be attributed to the recent wave of economic globalisation. Some scholars, though, argue that a distinctive Asian resource development perspective accounts for an Asian educational advantage (Cummings, 1995) However, while enrolment development in Asian countries compares favourably with patterns in Sub-Saharan Africa, the average Asian country is not more developed with respect to secondary enrolments than a number of Latin American and Middle Eastern countries (Baker & Holsinger, 1996). There is also intra-regional variability, with some countries, Malaysia, for example, expanding secondary education more so than others, Thailand, for instance (Baker & Holsinger, 1997).

2.2. Curriculum

The quality of schooling though has increasingly commanded greater attention and this has led to a proliferation of cross-national educational assessments. While earlier studies emphasised the importance of expanded access to schooling more recent research focuses on upgraded learning and achievement. The literature has shifted from a focus on having more schools and more students to issues of educational quality. as indicated by achievement levels. Given the worldwide emphasis on science and technology for development, cross-national science and mathematics assessments have attracted both more scholarly and popular attention. In study after study Singaporean, Taiwanese, Korean, and Japanese primary and secondary students have outperformed their counterparts elsewhere. This pattern is quite clear in the Third International Mathematics and Science Study (Beaton et al., 1996). The Asian economic miracle of the 1980s has often been attributed to the character of the Asian schools that produced the technically skilled and productive workers.

But what is it about Asian schools that made them appear to be distinctive and successful laboratories of human capital? Scholars such as Cummings (1997) have highlighted several features of what they view as a Japanese educational model influential through much of Eastern Asia. These include a Confucian tradition that emphasises a disciplined orientation toward the collective good, strong central educational bureaucracies that can create and impose high quality national curricular and teacher training standards, and a more focused emphasis on specific learning outcomes that prominently include science and mathematics. The Confucian tradition is also reflected in a greater emphasis on moral education with a focus on values inculcation rather than the values clarification aim more likely to be found within a Western civics education perspective (Cha et al., 1988) The more direct and extensive role of national educational bureaucracies may result in more tight coupling between policies and practices and thus less variability in what is taught and what is learned. Greater collaboration among teachers may be due to both the cultural emphasis on the group versus the individual as well as the greater clarity and cohesiveness of educational goals. These more transparent and better integrated goals are in turn due to the pervasive influence of national educational authorities over more limited subject matter terrain.

However, other scholars have raised questions regarding the distinctiveness of Asian curricular systems and teaching practices. Meyer and his colleagues (1992) make a strong case for increasing cross-national curricular isomorphism with respect to the distribution of time across curricular subjects; the official intended curriculum of primary schools appears to be more trans-nationally standardised than nationally unique. This is consistent with the earlier finding that classroom environments were surprisingly similar across countries (Anderson et al., 1989). Working with TIMSS survey data, LeTendre et al. (2001) show that Japanese teachers do not much vary from their American and German counterparts with respect to their beliefs about how mathematics is learned or how much their teaching is affected by variation in student abilities (see Stigler & Heibert, 1999, for an opposing view). Most researchers, however, do find some differences; Japanese teachers, for instance report more time spent on administrative tasks and counselling students than do Western teachers. This and related findings suggests that teacher-student ties in some Asian countries may be diffuse in their scope, affecting students in school as well as at home (LeTendre, 1994). Researchers often conclude that teachers are affected by both global expectations regarding curriculum and teaching as well as by national laws and customs regarding teaching and classroom management (LeTendre, et al., 2001; see also Anderson-Levitt, 1987), for a discussion of national legacies and school cultures).

Much of the interest in issues regarding mathematics and science achievement in Asian countries presupposes a link between achievement in these subjects and economic growth. One cross-national study finds evidence supporting this link; the authors conclude that net of other factors, higher quality schooling results in a higher quality labor force, and thus, in higher levels of economic growth (Hanushek & Kimko, 2001). However, using similar cross-national achievement data other scholars show that this finding is somewhat diminished if the models include additional statistical controls, for example, domestic capital formation, or if the so-called 'Asian Tigers' are excluded from the analyses, or if the period of study is extended to include the recent Asian economic crisis (Ramirez, Luo, Meyer, & Schofer, under review). If and how academic achievement contributes to human capital formation and economic growth continues to be a contested issue. (see *Educational Research for Regional and National Development*).

Asian education for development success stories, ironically, have globalised and influenced many educational reform discussions in the West (Stevenson & Stigler, 1992; Smith & O'Day, 1990). These discussions often assume a competitive global economic context within which those countries that fail to make the needed curricular reforms will "face the consequences" (Schmidt et al., 1999). The Asian economic decline in the late 1990s undercuts the more exaggerated claims made on behalf of Asian curriculum and invites further comparative research on this important topic.

3. TEACHER TRAINING

Much recent educational reform centres on teacher training. Here again Asian success is touted (Stigler & Stevenson, 1991). Asian teachers, it is argued, are expected to master subject matter content to a higher degree than their American counterparts. Furthermore, the former receive better on the job training and support from master teachers. While comparative research sheds little light on what school teachers actually know about their subject matter, there is evidence that out of field teaching is much more prevalent in the United States than in Japan (LaTendre et al., 2001). Furthermore, there is evidence of the negative effect of out of field teaching (Ingersoll, 1999). Lastly, there is evidence that teachers are more likely to interact with other teachers on subject matter issues in Japan than in the United States.

Recent developments with regard to teacher training reforms are also ironic. Calls for teaching and curricula that will promote broad competencies and the ability to engage in independent thought and learning are on the rise in Asia. The 1998 reforms in Japan explicitly emphasise problem creation and problem solving skills that transcend academic subject boundaries and downplay factual knowledge (Parameter, 2000 in Stromquist & Monkman, 2000). These reforms take into account international competition and assume that a more independent minded, flexible, and creative Japanese graduate is needed for the good of the nation. What makes this ironic is that the good of the nation was also invoked in the American 'nation at risk' reform proposals but the product of the reforms was supposed to be an American graduate more grounded in factual knowledge and subject matter mastery.

A global competitive economic order is often invoked in fostering educational reforms throughout the world. This in and of itself is evidence of globalisation at work. It is, however, unclear how much the reforms are attuned to new objective national requirements as distinguished from triumphant belief systems or models and their educational implications. The latter emphasise the importance of mathematics and science literacy for individual productivity and economic growth. However, the latter also highlight a broader vision of citizenship and human rights and the importance of individual choice and initiative. This vision propels education systems away from curricula solely rationalised around economic demands and includes the rise of subject matter that may constrain unbridled economic growth but may be attuned to the broader sustainable development idea, for example, environment education in China (Lee & Tilbury, 1998). The less than consistent implications of a less than cohesive belief system may account for the different directions educational reforms take in different parts of the world. However, it is difficult to discern educational reforms that only reflect local circumstances or proceed from assumptions that cannot be understood save in local currency.

In order to illustrate this point, consider the 1997 educational reforms in Singapore. Its three components were: (a) Thinking Schools, Learning Nations (TSLN), (b) Masterplan for Information Technology (IT, 2000), and (c) National Education (NE). The TSLN reforms sought to reduce current curricular content by 30 per cent so as to add new curricular emphases that would encourage independent learning, creativity, and critical thinking. The National Education component called for young Singapore students to be better instructed in the recent history of Singapore so that they would better internalize those attitudes that constitute part of the 'cultural DNA' of Singapore. This call was framed as an extension of moral education in Singapore and this framing may be seen as distinctively Confucianist and Asian. But the independent minded and critically thinking learner hardly fits the more hierarchical and collective good Confucianist and Asian emphasis. These apparently inconsistent elements are reconciled in the overall goal of promoting and harnessing individual creativity for national development. So, while the moral education framing element may be nationally distinctive in tone, the overall goal is clearly a transnationally validated one in the contemporary world (Ko, 1999). Exogenous and endogenous factors appear to characterise these reforms. This point is further illustrated as we turn to issues of governance and finance.

4. GOVERNANCE AND FINANCE

Asian education systems are generally characterised by national bureaucracies that exercise authority and control over important governance and finance issues, in addition to curricular and teacher training matters. These systems have been praised for their cohesion and integration, but they have also been criticized for their rigidity (Schoppa, 1991). Some critics have called for more local autonomy and educational decentralisation to meet better local and community needs. These calls sometimes include proposals for privatisation (Roesgaard, 1998). Other scholars, though, contend that both decentralisation and privatisation are policy initiatives shaped by triumphant neoliberal beliefs, rather than by national needs created by economic globalisation (Carnoy, 1999; Horio, 1998). In the Asian context calls for flexibility have not given rise to strong voucher movements. As regards mass schooling there is little evidence of growth of private schools, as such, or of more localized financial arrangements, although the growth of cram schools and shadow education in Korea and Japan is well-documented (Baker et al., 2001) But, as indicated earlier, some curricular reforms are guided by ideas regarding the need for producing more creative persons with greater problem solving capacities. These ideas are sensitive to transnational currents, even as mass schooling governance and financing structures continue to reflect national historical legacies.

5. HIGHER EDUCATION

5.1. Enrolments

The global increase in mass schooling is not a phenomenon that characterises only lower (and in most cases, compulsory) levels of schooling. The worldwide expansion of higher education is a striking trend after World War II and this trend can be observed among Asian countries as well. Economic globalisation arguments emphasise the demands for more technically sophisticated workplaces that are capable of producing high value added consumer goods (Carnoy, 1999). To be sure the growing policy emphasis on science and technology for development reflects economic globalisation; countries with higher levels of science and engineering enrollees do in fact undergo greater economic growth between 1965 and 1995 (Schofer, Ramirez, & Meyer, 2000). However, for most countries the growth in science and engineering enrolments is exceeded by the increase in the non-science and non-engineering enrolments. Increased demand for entry into higher education is broad based with respect to field of study. An analysis of this trend for nine Asian countries shows that between 1972 and 1992 the average science and engineering share of total enrolments slightly decreased, from 22.3 per cent to 20.6 per cent (Wotipka, 2001) The countries that decreased the most include Korea, Malaysia, and Sri Lanka; the countries that increased the most were India, Pakistan, and the Philippines. Japan, Nepal, and Thailand remained stable.

The Asian trend is also similar to the world trend with respect to women's expanded entry into higher education (Bradley & Ramirez, 1999) and into the science and engineering sectors of higher education (Ramirez & Wotipka, 2001). Consistent with feminist critiques of the status of women in some Asian countries, the Asian levels are below those of the Western countries. In 1972 for example, while women's share of science and engineering higher education was 17 per cent in the West, it was only 9.1% in Asia. These differences persist up to 1992, but by that period the women's share in Asia was up to 16 per cent in comparison with 24 per cent in the West. Historical legacies and national culture may account for the persistent differences, but the common upward trends may reflect the global impact of the institutionalisation of women's rights in international agendas (Chan-Tiberghein, 2001).

Not only has higher education expanded dramatically but its credentials have become the most legitimated path to occupational mobility worldwide (Blossfeld & Shavit, 1993). Even in countries earlier characterised by a command economy and mobility through party membership, China, for example, recent studies show that the recruitment of young party members often involves party sponsorship of their attainment of higher education, often through their participation in adult education programs (Li & Walder, 2001). Thus, the new Chinese elite are as likely to be characterised by higher educational credentials as their counterparts in Asia, and indeed, throughout the world. Alternative mobility routes lack credibility and tend to diminish.

5.2. Curriculum

Much of the literature emphasises the extent to which business and technology related subjects have become more fashionable academic courses in the last two decades. There is indeed evidence of the rise of new post secondary educational institutions emphasising business and technology curricula in Asia (Lee, 2000). There is also evidence of calls for and attempts to create more internationally relevant higher education curricula (Lee, 2000). These developments seem to be closely attuned to economic globalisation dynamics. But curricular changes are broader in scope and multiple globalisation dynamics appear to be at work. Internationalisation, for example, is not simply about highlighting international trade and the need for skills and know how to be internationally competitive. Comparative analyses of university history curricula show a sharp rise in the proportion of these courses with a world history focus and a concomitant decline in the percentage of courses with a Western core powers emphasis (Frank, Wong, Meyer, & Ramirez, 2000). So, while the importance of Western competitors influences some curricular developments in Asia, other changes are shaped by world pressures to celebrate the equality of nation states. These pressures give rise to more national and more regional history courses. These pressures also legitimate social movements and these in turn give rise to curricular innovations such as women's studies in Japan (Chan-Tiberghein, 2001).

These curricular changes are mirrored by shifts in the faculty composition of universities across Asia and throughout the world. What is found as a worldwide trend is a relative increase in faculty numbers in technology and business but also in the social sciences and a relative decrease in the humanities. Change in university curricula reflect changes in how nature and society are envisioned, analysed, and discussed and these changes are triggered by exogenous economic, political, and cultural influences. To be sure, these influences stress international economic competitiveness but they also emphasise human rights and sustainable development (Chabbott & Ramirez, 2000).

5.3. Governance and Finance

Some commentaries on globalisation and higher education contend that a worldwide rise of private colleges has been triggered by an increased demand for skilled labor in business, tourism, and information technology (Cohen, 2001). This increased demand in turn is due to economic globalisation dynamics which compel nation-states to become more tolerant of private higher education or even actively to encourage its development. In some Asian countries the private sector of higher education has long been established, for example, Indonesia, Japan, Korea, the Philippines, and Thailand. But interest in and growth of private higher education is a relatively recent development in other countries, for example, in China, India, Malaysia, Vietnam (Wongsthorn & Yibing, 1995). In Malaysia, for example, the rapid expansion of private higher education in the 1990s reflects increased social demand, budgetary constraints, and the high costs of overseas education due in part to currency devaluation (Lee, 1999). Unlike the elite private universities in Japan (e.g., Waseda or International Christian University) or the Philippines (e.g., the Ateneo or De La Salle University) the new Malaysian colleges often cater for students not able to attain admission into the public universities. These colleges often develop ties with foreign universities, ties that give their students increased access to a variety of degree programs and credit transfers. Moreover, the restructuring of higher education in Malaysia also leads to public universities engaging in market-related activities with goals such as the improvement of efficiency, productivity, and accountability. These goals and the innovations designed to attain them are much discussed in the Western context as well (Clark, 1998).

The softer role of the Asian states with respect to the governance of higher education has gone hand in hand with diminished central funding. This is especially evident after the financial crisis that hit Asia in 1997. In Singapore the share of government's current expenditures in education dropped from an all time high of 30.7 per cent in 1992 to 23.3 per cent in 1998. In Korea public educational expenditures as a percent of gross national product fell from 4.0 per cent in 1997 to 3.6 per cent a mere two years later. In Thailand, Malaysia, and Indonesia, support for public higher education declined (UNESCO, 2001). In Taiwan the decline in government expenditures has gone hand in hand with calls for increased tuition, user fees, and other initiatives to raise funds. In this and in other Asian countries a common globalisation discourse has been utilized to justify educational reforms in the direction of privatisation and marketisation (Mok, 2000). In the Taiwanese case the discourse of world economic competition is linked to a socio-political liberalization discourse, a development overlooked in theories solely focused on economic globalisation. These developments further propelled students in the direction of the private sector.

While many of the above developments illustrate the influence of exogenous factors on national institutions of higher education, there are also some cross-national differences. Private higher education is more extensive in some countries than others. The level of state regulation over private higher education cross-nationally varies, as does the extent to which private higher education aspires to international ties with foreign universities. These differences have led some scholars to conclude that while educational paradigms and policies may be global in character, national legacies affect implementation and practice (Gopinathan, 1996). Others see this as evidence of widespread loose coupling between principles, policies, and practices in the domain of educational transfers and implementation (Weick, 1976).

6. SOME CONCLUDING THOUGHTS

This review suggests that changes in schools and universities in Asia are due in part to economic, political, and cultural globalisation processes. These changes partially reflect adaptations to an international economic order and to widespread beliefs about what is to be done to become or to remain competitive. Such beliefs are often stored in international organisations such as the World Bank and articulated with authority by experts such as professional economists. Education as human capital is a widespread belief that is consequential in promoting the growth of schooling and even university enrolments, especially in fields such as a science and engineering. These educational changes, however, reflect broader political and cultural changes. The educational product is imagined not just as a value adding labourer or producer but also as an engaged citizen and creative person. Education as a human right is also a widespread belief that further accelerates educational growth and accounts for why some educational changes cannot be explained on economic grounds alone. These changes include enrolment increases in the social sciences, curricular developments such as women's studies and environmental education, and reforms that highlight the importance of civic education.

These changes are propped up by the professional expertise of social scientists and educators. Lastly, some changes can count on justifications from both education as human capital and education as human rights perspectives, the greater inclusion of women at all educational levels, for example, may be simultaneously celebrated as national investment in human capital and as national commitment to human rights. This expansion symbolises a rational and humane nation-state, a symbolization that garners much internal and external legitimacy for the nation-state. These changes may turn out to be more stable than changes driven by narrower criteria emphasising only efficiency or equity, changes such as decentralisation in educational governance structures or curricular innovations resulting in greater flexibility and individual choice. The impact of globalisation on education in Asia is more likely when different dimensions of globalisation create different but compatible rationales favoring the same educational outcomes.

This review also recognises intra-regional variability with respect to some educational structures, the likelihood and extent of private higher education, for instance. The role of historical legacies in shaping national responses to globalisation pressures is also recognised. It is assumed that more isolated nation-states are likely to have better buffered and thus more distinctive education systems. But it is also assumed that isolation was a more viable option in prior eras. Much of the economic globalisation literature emphasises the extent to which national borders cannot effectively shield a country from modern communication technologies. A broader understanding emphasises the political and cultural dimensions of globalisation and the pressures these create on all peoples to assemble themselves as nation-states committed to mass schooling as a nation-state project and increasingly to the massification of higher education. National character and historical legacies are more evident in the internal organisational characteristics of schools and universities, but even these increasingly reveal exogenous influences. Broad educational principles, purposes, and policies tend to employ a worldwide idiom and are likely to continue to do so in the foreseeable future.

REFERENCES

Anderson, B, (1991). *Imagined Communities: Reflections on the Spread and Origin of Nationalism*. New York: Verso.

Anderson, L., Ryan, D., & Shapiro, B. (1989). *The IEA Classroom Environment Study*. New York: Pergamon.

Anderson-Levitt, K. (1987). National culture and teaching culture. *Anthropology and Education Quarterly, 18*, 33–37.

Baker, D., & Holsinger, D. (1996). Human capital formation and school expansion in Asia: Does a unique regional model exist? *International Journal of Comparative Sociology, 37*, 159–173.

Baker, D., & Holsinger, D. (1997). Human capital formation and school expansion in Asia: Does a Unique regional model exist?. In W. Cummings & P. Altbach (Eds.), *The Challenge of Eastern Asian Education* (pp. 115–134). New York: SUNY Press.

Baker, D., et al. (2001). Worldwide shadow education: Outside-school learning, institutional quality of schooling, and cross-national mathematics achievement. *Educational Evaluation and Policy Analysis, 23*(1), 1–18.

Blossfeld, H-P., & Shavit. Y. (1993). *Persistent Inequality*. Westview Press.

Bradley, K., & Ramirez, F. O. (1996). World polity and gender parity: Women's share of higher education, 1965–1985. *Research in Sociology of Education and Socialization, 11*, 63–91.

Burbeles, N., & Torres. C. (1999). *Globalisation and Education: Critical Perspectives*. New York: Routledge.

Carnoy, M. (1999). *Globalisation and Educational Reform: What Planners Need to Know*. Paris: International Institute for Educational Planning.

Cha, Yun-Kyung, Suk-Ying Wong, & Meyer. J. W. (1988). Values education in the curriculum: Some comparative empirical data, In W. Cummings, S. Gopinathan & Y. Tomoda (Eds.), *The Revival of Values Education in Asia and the West* (pp. 11–30). Oxford: Pergamon.

Chabbott, C., & Ramirez, F. O. (2000). Development and education. In M. Hallinan (Ed.), *Handbook of Sociology of Education* (pp. 163–187). New York: Plenum.

Chan-Tiberghein, J. (2001). The Rise of a Women's Human Rights Epistemic Network: Global Norms and Local Education. Unpublished doctoral dissertation. School of Education, Stanford University.

Clark, B. (1998). *Creating Entrepreneurial Universities: Organisational Pathways of Transformation.* Surrey, UK: Pergamon.

Cohen, D. (2001). The worldwide rise of private colleges. *The Chronicle of Higher Education,* March, 47–50.

Cummings, W. (1995). The Asian human resource approach in global perspective, *Oxford Review of Education, 21,* 67–81.

Cummings, W. (1997). Human resource development: The J-model. In W. Cummings & P. Altbach (Eds.), *The Challenge of Eastern Asian Education* (pp. 275–292). New York: SUNY Press.

Drori, G., Meyer, J. Ramirez, F. O., & Schofer. E. (2003). *Science and the Modern World Polity: Institutionalisation and Globalisation.* Stanford CA: Stanford University Press.

Frank, J. D., Wong, S-Y. Meyer, J. W., & Ramirez, F. O (2000). What Counts as History: A Cross-National and Longitudinal Study of University Curricula, *44,* 29–53.

Gopinathan, S. (1996). Globalisation, the state, and educational policy in Singapore. In W. O. Lee & M. Bray (Eds.), *Education and Political Transition: Perspective and Dimension in East Asia.* Hong Kong: Comparative Education Research Center, University of Hong Kong.

Guillen, M. F. (2001). Is globalisation civilizing, destructive, or feeble? A critique of five key debates in the social science literature. *Annual Review of Sociology, 27,* 235–276.

Hanushek, E., & Kimbo, D. D. (2000). Schooling, labor-force quality and the growth of nations. *American Economic Review, 90*(3), 1184–2008.

Horio, T. (1988). *Educational Thought and Ideology in Modern Japan.* Tokyo: University of Tokyo Press.

Hanushek, E., & Kimko. D. (2000). Schooling, labor force quality, and the growth of nations. *American Economic Review,* December, 1184–1208.

Ingersoll, R. (1999). The problem of underqualified teachers in American secondary schools. *Educational Researcher, 28*(2), 26–37.

Ko, C. T. (1999). Shaping Instincts and Attitudes: Moral Education in a Singaporean Secondary School. Unpublished Masters Monograph. School of Education, Stanford University.

Lee, J. C. K., & Tilbury, D. (1998). Changing environments: The challenge for environmental education in China. *Geography, 83,* 227–36.

Lee, Mm. (2000). The impact of globalisation on education in Malaysia. In N. Stromquist & K. Monkman (Eds.), *Globalisation and Education: Integration and Contestation Across Cultures* (pp. 315–332). New York: Rowman and Littlefield Publishers.

Lee, M. (1999). *Private Higher Education in Malaysia.* Penang, Malaysia: Universiti Sains Malaysia.

LeTendre, G. (1994). Guiding them on: Teaching, hierarchy, and social organisation in Japanese middle schools. *Journal of Japanese Studies, 20*(1), 37–59.

LeTendre, G, Baker, D., Akiba, M., Goesling, B., & Wiseman, A. (2001). Teachers' work: Institutional isomorphism and cultural variation in the U.S., Germany, and Japan. *Educational Researcher, 30,* 3–16.

Li, B., & Walder, A. (2001). Career advancement as party patronage: Sponsored mobility into the Chinese administrative elite, 1949–1996. *American Journal of Sociology, 106,* 1371–1408.

Meyer, J., Kamens, J., & Benavot, A. (1992). *School Knowledge For the Masses: World Models and National Primary Curricular Categories in the Twentieth Century.* Washington, DC: Falmer Press.

Meyer, J., Boli, J. Thomas, G., & Ramirez, F. O. (1997). World society and the nation-state. *American Journal of Sociology.*

Mok, K-H. (2000). Reflecting globalisation effects on local policy: Higher education reform in Taiwan. *Educational Policy, 15,* 637–660.

Parameter, L. (2000). Internationalisation in Japanese education: Current issues and future prospects. In N. Stromquist & K. Monkman (Eds.), *Globalisation and Education: Integration and Contestation Across Cultures* (pp. 237–254). New York: Rowman and Littlefield.

Ramirez, F. O., Luo, X., Schofer, E., & Meyer, J. W. (under review). Does Academic Achievement in Mathematics and Science Promote Economic Growth?

Ramirz, F. O., & Wotipka, C. M. (2001). Slowly but surely? The global expansion of women's participation in science and engineering fields of study. *Sociology of Education, 74,* 231–251.

Roesgaard, M. (1998). *Moving Mountains.* Aarhus, Denmark, Aarhus University Press.

Schmidt, W, McKnight, C. C., Cogan, L. S., Jakwerth, P., & Houang, R. T. (1999). *Facing the Consequences: Using TIMSS for a Closer Look at U.S. Mathematics and Science Education*. The Netherlands: Kluwer Academic Press.

Schofer, E., Ramirez, F. O., & Meyer, J. W. (2000). The effects of science on national economic development, 1970–1990. *American Sociological Review*, 65, 877–898.

Schoppa, L. (1991). *Education Reform in Japan: A Case of Immobilist Policies*. New York: Routledge.

Smith, M. S., & O'Day, J. (1991). Systemic school reform. In S. Fuhrman & B. Malen (Eds.), *The Politics of Curriculum and Testing* (pp. 233–67). Bristol, Penn: Falmer Press.

Stevenson, H., & Stigler, J. (1992). *The Learning Gap*. New York: Summit Books.

Stigler, J., & Stevenson, H. (1991). How Asian teachers polish each lesson to perfection. *American Educator*, 15(1), 12–20.

Stromquist, N., & Monkman, K. (Eds.) (2000). *Globalisation and Education: Integration and Contestation Across Cultures*. New York: Rowman and Littlefield.

Therborn, G. (2000). Globalisations, dimensions, historical waves, regional effects, normative governance. *International Sociology*, 15, 151–179.

UNESCO (2001). *Proceedings of Policy Forum on Economic Crisis and Higher Education in East Asia*. Selangor, Malaysia: UNESCO.

Wallerstein, I. (1974). *The Modern World System I: Capitalist Agriculture and the Origins of the European World Economy in the 16th Century*. New York: Academic Press.

Weick, K. (1976). Educational organisations as loosely coupled systems. *Administrative Science Quarterly*.

Wongsothorn, T., & Yibing, W. (Eds.) (1995). *Private Higher Education in Asia and the Pacific*. Bangkok: UNESCO PROAP and SEAMEO RIHED.

Wotipka, C. M. (2001). Beyond Access to Transformations: A Cross-National Analysis of Women's Participation in Science and Engineering Education, 1970–200. Unpublished doctoral dissertation. School of Education, Stanford University.

76

Comparative Educational Achievement Studies

DONALD SPEARRITT
University of Sydney, Australia

1. INTRODUCTION

Comparative studies of educational achievement have constituted one of the major growth areas of educational research in the last 50 years. This article traces the development of cross-national comparative studies of educational achievement, with particular emphasis on those undertaken by the International Association for the Evaluation of Educational Achievement (IEA). Critical issues involved in conducting international comparative studies are discussed. The participation of Asia-Pacific countries in these studies is outlined, and the educational achievement levels attained by these countries in mathematics, science, reading and written composition are presented. A brief account is given of background factors shown to be associated with educational achievement, and likely future developments in cross-national studies of achievement in Asia-Pacific countries are indicated.

2. ORIGIN AND AIMS OF INTERNATIONAL STUDIES OF EDUCATIONAL ACHIEVEMENT

Prior to the 1960s, comparative studies of education systems in different countries had been largely descriptive in form, addressing such aspects as their organization and administrative arrangements, the sources and extent of their economic support, curriculum patterns, student enrolments, teacher qualifications and teaching methods. Little data were available to assess an important outcome of the different systems, namely, the achievement of the students in those countries.

The origin of the current large-scale international studies of comparative educational achievement came with the establishment in 1959 of a body which became known as the International Association for the Evaluation of Educational Achievement, or IEA. This body addressed the problem of developing tests and survey instruments which would be suitable for use in different countries with their different languages and differing curricula. These tests and instruments formed the basis for large-scale IEA cross-national surveys of educational achievement in a range of school subjects. Commencing with a survey of mathematics achievement in 12 countries in 1964, the IEA studies have covered science achievement, reading comprehension, reading literacy, written composition, literature, civic education, English as a Foreign Language, and French as a Foreign Language. Approximately 40 countries were involved in IEA's Third International Mathematics and Science Study (TIMSS) in 1995 and in a repeat survey in 1999; in future studies the acronym stands for Trends in Math and Science Study. Information from these studies has provided a much more comprehensive and solid foundation for comparative studies of education systems than was previously available.

The report on the first international study of educational achievement (Husén, 1967) emphasizes that the overall aim of these studies was not only to compare outcomes in different educational systems, but to relate these outcomes to relevant input variables, such as the structure of the school system, level of teacher training, social background of students, level of parent education, money spent on education and so on. In effect, the studies aim to explore two questions: (a) To what extent do countries differ in levels of student educational achievement? (b) Why do they differ? By identifying factors exerting a positive influence on educational achievement, countries would be in a position to formulate policy which might be expected to improve their education system.

3. CRITICAL ISSUES IN COMPARATIVE EDUCATIONAL ACHIEVEMENT STUDIES

Educational achievement can be compared across countries or within countries. Comparisons within countries may be made with respect to political divisions (states, provinces), type of schooling (government versus non-government), gender, urban versus rural location and so on. Given that the problems of difference in language and culture are of much less importance in national than in international surveys, this article has been restricted to the issues raised and the results obtained in comparing educational achievement across countries.

For cross-national comparison of educational achievement, the same task has to be applied to students in the different countries. The construction of a test question measuring the attainment of a particular skill or understanding or item of knowledge may be relatively straightforward in a linguistically homogeneous country, but poses considerable problems when the question has to be presented in several different languages. In this situation it is of critical importance that the question or test or other instrument to be used to compare cross-national educational achievement be fair or equally valid for all of the participating countries.

Curricula vary for a given age or grade level in different countries. Test development for cross-national studies therefore calls for a detailed analysis of the objectives and content of the curriculum for a given subject in each of the participating countries and a rating of the importance of the topic by the responsible national committee. International coordinating committees use this information to establish, in effect, a common curriculum in the subject area, which includes most of the content areas specified by the participating countries. Test questions are written to reflect this common curriculum. Although the common curriculum may not be identical with the actual curriculum followed in any of the participating countries, it provides the basis for developing a balanced test representing the major curriculum emphases in all countries (Beaton, Postlethwaite, Ross, Spearritt, & Wolf, 1999).

In IEA studies, test items have generally been prepared in English and then translated into other languages. A critical question is whether the items continue to measure the same skills or understanding after this translation. To help ensure this, tests are usually translated independently by two translators, and their translations compared. Back translation into English is also employed (Postlethwaite, 1999). Empirical tools and their associated fit indices can now be used to identify items affected by the process of adaptation.

Cross-national comparisons of educational achievement may also be affected by differences in student motivation, such as attitudes towards test-taking. In making cross-national comparisons, it is assumed that there are no substantial differences in the level of student motivation across countries.

The validity of cross-national comparisons of educational achievement also depends on the comparability of the target populations at each age or grade level in participating countries. Age level provides a better basis than grade level for defining equivalent target populations across countries, as grade level is affected by country variations in age of entry to school and in progression policies from grade to grade. Because of the practical difficulties of drawing age samples in schools, populations are often defined in terms of both age and grade. The lower secondary TIMSS 1995 population, for instance, was defined as "students enrolled in the two adjacent grades that contained the largest proportion of 13-year-old students at the time of testing" (Beaton et al., 1996, p. A-2). In most countries these were seventh- and eighth-grade students. Agreement also has to be reached on which small segments of the population might be excluded, for example, schools for students with special needs.

Tests are generally applied to samples of students at a given age or grade level in a participating country as it is usually impracticable to test all students. These national samples need to be comparable if achievement is to be compared across countries. To achieve this comparability, each country has to follow rigorous procedures in drawing two- or three-stage probability samples of students, involving random selection of schools within strata and of students or classes within schools. The sample design is taken into account as well as the sample size and standard deviation of test scores in calculating the standard error of the mean for each country. This standard error is used in determining the 95 per cent confidence interval within which the population mean for that country would fall.

4. PARTICIPATION OF ASIA-PACIFIC COUNTRIES IN INTERNATIONAL STUDIES

Since the early 1960s, many countries in the Asia-Pacific region have undertaken a substantial amount of research into comparative educational achievement as a result of their involvement in IEA studies. The extent of participation in Asia-Pacific countries in these surveys at one or more of the age or grade levels of 9 and 10 years, 13 and 14 years and the final year of secondary school is set out in Table 1.

Asia-Pacific participation in the IEA surveys has been strongest at the 13 and 14 year level. In mathematics or science some countries (e.g., China, Taiwan, Indonesia, Malaysia, and Papua New Guinea) have participated only at this level. The Republic of Korea, Taiwan, some provinces and cities from China, and 14 republics from the Soviet Union, participated in surveys of the achievement of 13 year-old students in mathematics and science, undertaken by the Educational Testing Service for the International Assessment of Educational Progress (IAEP) in 1987 (Lapointe, Mead, & Phillips, 1989) and 1991. Australia, China, Japan, Korea, New Zealand and the Russian Federation are participating in the PISA (Programme for International Student Assessment) project of the

Table 1. Participation of countries in the Asia-Pacific region in educational achievement surveys conducted by IEA

Year 19	Mathematics				Science				Reading	
	64	80	95	99	70	83	95	99	70	90
Australia	×		×	×	×	×	×	×		
China						×				
Hong Kong		×	×	×		×	×	×		×
India					×				×	
Indonesia				×				×		×
Japan	×	×	×	×	×	×	×	×		
Korea, Rep of			×	×		×	×	×		
Malaysia				×				×		
New Zealand		×	×	×	×		×	×	×	×
Papua New Guinea						×				
Philippines				×		×		×		×
Russian Federation			×	×			×	×		
Singapore			×	×		×	×	×		×
Taiwan				×				×		
Thailand		×	×	×	×	×	×	×		×

Asia-Pacific countries participating in other IEA surveys of achievement. Indonesia: Written composition (1980). New Zealand: Literature, Civic Education, French For. Lang. (1970), Written Composition. China tested in three provinces only.

OECD, which is assessing the reading literacy, mathematical literacy and scientific literacy of 15 year-old students in 32 countries in three-year cycles, commencing in 2000.

Although these international surveys of educational achievement have been organized by international bodies, a substantial amount of the work involved in analysis of curricula, test item preparation and analysis, sample selection, test administration and collection of results for a particular country has been undertaken within that country under the supervision of its National Research Coordinator for the study. As a result, educational research organizations within several Asia-Pacific countries have been heavily involved in the processes required to carry out large-scale comparative studies of achievement in school subjects. Organizations also involved at the level of international coordination have included the Australian Council for Educational Research for the PISA and Second IEA Science Study and the New Zealand Department of Education for the Second International Mathematics Study. While the international reports on IEA surveys are generally written by the international coordinating centre for the study, participating countries often prepare reports outlining the results for their own student body in more detail. A considerable amount of expertise in areas of curriculum analysis, test item preparation and statistical analysis of test results and associated factors has now been built up in many countries in the Asia-Pacific region.

Levels of student achievement attained in Asia-Pacific countries in major school subject areas in the various IEA studies are presented in subsequent sections. The form of presentation has been designed to show where Asia-Pacific countries stand in relation to all participating countries as well as showing how they compare among themselves. Detailed information is provided for the more recent TIMSS surveys, and condensed information for the earlier surveys.

5. EDUCATIONAL ACHIEVEMENT IN ASIA-PACIFIC COUNTRIES

Information provided by comparative educational achievement studies in Asia-Pacific countries is outlined in this section for the subject areas of mathematics, science, reading and written composition. As countries choose both the age and grade levels and the subject areas in which they participate, a complete comparative picture of educational achievement is not available. Interpretation of the data is subject to qualifications indicated in the text.

5.1. Achievement in Mathematics

In the 1964 IEA survey of mathematics achievement (Husén, 1967), Japan had the highest mean score (31.2) of all ten countries participating at the 13-year-old level, and Australia (20.2) was a little above the international average of 19.8. Japan ranked sixth among the 12 countries at the final secondary year level and Australia eleventh, but only eight per cent of the student age group stayed to final secondary year and took mathematics in Japan as against fourteen per cent in Australia.

At the 13 and 14 year level in the IEA's Second International Mathematics Study (1980–82), Japan's mean score was the highest of 18 countries in arithmetic, algebra, geometry and descriptive statistics and the second highest in measurement (Garden & Robitaille, 1989). Hong Kong's results were close to the international average, while those for New Zealand were below the international average, except in geometry and statistics. Thailand's performance was at the lower end of the distribution of national averages in most mathematical areas. Hong Kong ranked first, and Japan second in the achievement levels of students taking mathematics as a substantial part of their program in the final year of secondary school. On average, New Zealand ranked sixth among the 15 education systems and Thailand ranked fourteenth. The proportion of school students taking a substantial program in mathematics at this level, however, was only six per cent in Hong Kong as against twelve per cent in Japan, and eleven per cent in New Zealand.

More recent results of comparative educational studies of mathematics achievement in the Asia-Pacific region come from the IEA's Third International Mathematics and Science Study (TIMSS) in 1994–95 in up to 41 countries (Beaton et al., 1996), A TIMSS-Repeat survey of eighth-grade students was carried out in 1998–99 in 38 countries, 25 of which had participated in the 1994–95 study (Mullis et al., 2000). Thirteen of the 38 countries were Asia-Pacific countries.

Item response theory was used to establish scales with a mean of 500 and a standard deviation of 100 for reporting the performance of students. As the scales were based on different groups of students, scale scores and international averages shown in Table 2 are not comparable for Grade 4 and Grade 8 students. Nor are the Grade 8 scores comparable for TIMSS95 and TIMSS99 as in the latter case they were based on the performance of students in countries taking the mathematics achievement test in both 1995 and 1999 (Mullis et al., 2000).

Table 2 presents the order of the countries in terms of their average scale score at the Grade 4 level in 1995 and at the Grade 8 level in 1995 and 1999. Grade 4 and Grade 8 results are presented as the students tested were in Grade 4 rather than Grade 3, and in Grade 8 rather than Grade 7 in most countries. Bold-type is used to highlight the position of Asia-Pacific countries in mathematics achievement in relation to other countries. Since the average or mean scale scores are almost always based on samples of the relevant population, cross-national comparisons of performance have to take account of the standard error of the mean and the number of cases for each country, as well as the number of countries being compared. Such comparisons are available in the relevant reports for each subject. For the present, it is sufficient to note that countries in the lists without fairly large differences in their mean scores are unlikely to have differed significantly in their performance. A further qualification to be taken into account in considering Table 2 is that countries listed in italics were unable to implement

Table 2. Average scores of countries on mathematics achievement – Third International Mathematics and Science Study

Grade 4–10 years		Grade 8–14 years			
TIMSS95		TIMSS95		TIMSS99	
	Average		Average		Average
Singapore	625	**Singapore**	643	**Singapore**	604
Korea	611	**Korea**	607	**Korea**	587
Japan	597	**Japan**	605	**Taiwan**	585
Hong Kong	587	**Hong Kong**	588	**Hong Kong**	582
Netherlands	577	Belgium (Fl)	565	**Japan**	579
Czech Rep	567	Czech Rep	564	Belgium (Fl)	558
Austria	559	Slovak Rep	547	Netherlands	540
Slovenia	552	Switzerland	545	Slovak Rep	534
Ireland	550	*Netherlands*	541	Hungary	532
Hungary	548	*Slovenia*	541	Canada	531
Australia	546	Bulgaria	540	Slovenia	530
United States	545	Austria	539	**Russian Fed**	526
Canada	532	France	538	**Australia**	525
Israel	531	Hungary	537	Finland	520
INTERNAT'L AV	529	**Russian Fed**	535	Czech Rep	520
Latvia (LSS)	525	***Australia***	530	**Malaysia**	519
Scotland	520	Ireland	527	Bulgaria	511
England	513	Canada	527	Lativia (LSS)	505
Cyprus	502	*Belgium (Fr)*	526	United States	502
Norway	502	***Thailand***	522	England	496
New Zealand	499	Israel	522	New Zealand	491
Greece	492	Sweden	519	INTERNAT'L AV	487
Thailand	490	INTERNAT'L AV	513	Lithuania	482
Portugal	475	*Germany*	509	Italy	479
Iceland	474	**New Zealand**	508	Cyprus	476
Iran, Islamic Rep	429	England	506	Romania	472
Kuwait	400	Norway	503	Moldova	469
		Denmark	502	**Thailand**	467
		United States	500	Israel	466
		Scotland	498	Tunisia	448
		Latvia (LSS)	493	Macedonia Rep	447
		Spain	487	Turkey	429
		Iceland	487	Jordan	428
		Greece	484	**Iran, Islamic Rep**	422
		Romania	482	**Indonesia**	403
		Lithuania	477	Chile	392
		Cyprus	474	**Philippines**	345
		Portugal	454	Morocco	337
		Iran, Islamic Rep	428	South Africa	275
		Kuwait	392		
		South Africa	354		

Note: Asian countries are shown in **bold type**.
Countries shown in *italics* did not comply fully with the sampling procedures required.

fully the required sampling procedures or to attain the specified participation rates of at least eighty-five per cent of the relevant population.

The superior achievement in mathematics of Grade 4 and Grade 8 students in a group of Asian countries (Singapore, Korea, Japan, Hong Kong and Taiwan) in comparison with all other participating countries is a striking feature of Table 2. This continues a pattern for Japan which was evident in the earlier IEA surveys of mathematics in 1964 and 1980–82. From average levels of performance in mathematics at the 13 and 14 year level in 1980–82, Hong Kong had clearly improved its position by 1995. In the 1988 IAEP study, 13-year-old students in Korea also attained the highest overall mathematics achievement score, well above the mean of other participating countries (Lapointe, Mead, & Phillips, 1989).

The mathematics performance of Grade 4 students in Australia and Grade 8 students in Australia, Malaysia and the Russian Federation was considerably lower than that of the above mentioned Asian countries but significantly higher than the international average. New Zealand and Thailand were below the international average at Grade 4 but closer to the international average at Grade 8 8. Lower-performing countries in mathematics at the Grade 8 levels include Indonesia and the Philippines.

In the TIMSS 1995 survey, all students in the final year secondary sample took a test of mathematics literacy, comprising questions likely to occur in real-life situations, covering fractions, percentages, proportionality, measurement, estimation, data analysis and so on. On the scale described earlier (mean 500, SD 100), Australia and New Zealand with a cohort representation of about seventy per cent obtained the same mean score of 522, but ranked eighth among the 21 countries. The Russian Federation with a cohort representation of only forty-eight per cent attained a mean score of 471.

An advanced mathematics test was applied to final year secondary students who had taken advanced mathematics courses. Mean scale scores for the 16 countries ranged from 436 to 557 with an average of 501, the Russian Federation ranking second and Australia fourth, with mean scores of 542 and 525 respectively. This difference was not significant. The cohort representation for the Russian Federation was only two per cent as against Australia's 16 per cent. In both countries performance in each of the three main content areas reflected their overall performance (Mullis et al., 1998).

Evidence from all of the IEA surveys suggests that Asia-Pacific countries fall into four broad groupings in mathematics achievement at the Grade 4 or Grade 8 levels: (a) Singapore, Korea, Japan. Hong Kong and Taiwan achieve at the highest international levels; (b) Australia, the Russian Federation and Malaysia fall well above the international average; (c) New Zealand and Thailand approximate the international average; and (d) Indonesia and the Philippines perform well below the international average.

5.2. *Achievement in Science*

In the first IEA comparative study of achievement in science in 1970/71 (Comber & Keeves, 1973), Japan's mean score was the highest of all countries at the

10-year and 14-year levels, and New Zealand's the highest of all countries at the final secondary level. Australia and New Zealand were above the international mean for developed countries at both the 14-year and final secondary levels. In less developed countries, which included India, and Thailand, mean scores were much lower than the international mean for developed countries, the lowest-scoring country at the upper level being India. The opportunity to learn the material covered in the test was much lower for India than for developed countries.

Mean percentage scores of countries participating in the Second International Science Study in 1983-84 (Postlethwaite & Wiley, 1992) were computed on core items common to all students at ages 10 and 14 years and on biology, chemistry and physics items for students studying science at the final secondary level. Japan was again the highest-scoring country at the 10-year level, closely followed by Korea. Japan also scored well at the 14-year level. For students studying specialist sciences at the final secondary level, Hong Kong (Form 7 students) was the highest-scoring country in chemistry and physics and was second to Singapore in biology. Japan was above the international average in chemistry and physics but not in biology. Korea was below the international average in all three subjects. Singapore and Hong Kong scored below the international median at the 10-year and 14-year levels, but improved their position substantially in the specialist science subjects at the final secondary level. Australia scored at about the international median at all age levels, with Thailand and Papua New Guinea falling below the median and the Philippines much lower. Although China's mean score fell at about the international median at age 14 years, it was based on only three metropolitan areas, Beijing and two other cities, and their surroundings.

Mean scale scores of 10-year-olds and 14-year-olds on the science tests in the TIMSS 1995 and 1999 surveys are presented in Table 3. The scores have been based on an international achievement scale in science with a mean of 500 and a standard deviation of 100. International averages for the 1995 survey are considerably higher than 500, as results are presented only for the higher grade at each grade level, namely Grade 4 and Grade 8. Scale scores and international averages are not comparable across the three data columns in Table 3 because of the different groups on which the scales were established. Bold-type is again used in Table 3 to highlight the position of Asia-Pacific countries in science achievement as compared with other countries.

Table 3 indicates that a small group of Asia-Pacific countries, namely Singapore, Taiwan, Japan and Korea, were generally the highest-scoring or close to the highest-scoring of all participating countries in science achievement at the 10- and 14-year levels (Martin et al., 1997; Beaton et al., 1996a). Although the average scores of Australian students were slightly lower, in general they did not differ significantly from those of the above-mentioned countries. The performance of students from the Russian Federation, New Zealand, Hong Kong and Malaysia was above the international average. Thailand was below the international average at the 10-year level but close to the average at the 14-year level. Mean scores of Indonesia and the Philippines were well below the average.

Table 3. Average scores of countries on science achievement – Third International Mathematics and Science Study

Grade 4–10 years		Grade 8–14 years			
TIMSS95		TIMSS95		TIMSS99	
	Average		Average		Average
Korea	597	**Singapore**	607	**Taiwan**	569
Japan	574	Czech Republic	574	**Singapore**	568
United States	565	**Japan**	571	Hungary	552
Austria	565	**Korea**	565	**Japan**	550
Australia	562	Bulgaria	565	**Korea Rep of**	549
Czech Rep	557	*Slovenia*	560	Netherlands	545
Netherlands	557	*Netherlands*	560	**Australia**	540
England	551	*Austria*	558	Czech Rep	539
Canada	549	Hungary	554	England	538
Singapore	547	England	552	Finland	535
Slovenia	546	Belgium (Fl)	550	Slovak Rep	535
Ireland	539	**Australia**	545	Belgium (Fl)	535
Scotland	536	Slovak Rep	544	Slovenia	533
Hong Kong	533	**Russian Fed**	538	Canada	533
Hungary	532	Ireland	538	**Hong Kong**	530
New Zealand	531	Sweden	535	**Russian Fed**	529
Norway	530	United States	534	Bulgaria	518
INTERNAT'L AV	524	Canada	531	United States	515
Latvia (LSS)	512	*Germany*	531	**New Zealand**	510
Iceland	505	Norway	527	Latvia (LSS)	503
Israel	505	**New Zealand**	525	Italy	493
Greece	497	***Thailand***	525	**Malaysia**	492
Portugal	480	*Israel*	524	Lithuania	488
Cyprus	475	**Hong Kong**	522	INTERNAT'L AV	488
Thailand	473	Switzerland	522	**Thailand**	482
Iran, Islamic Rep	416	Spain	517	Romania	472
Kuwait	401	*Scotland*	517	Israel	468
		INTERNAT'L AV	516	Cyprus	460
		France	498	Moldova	459
		Greece	497	Macedonia Rep	458
		Iceland	494	Jordan	450
		Romania	486	Iran, Islamic Rep	448
		Latvia (LSS)	485	**Indonesia**	435
		Portugal	480	Turkey	433
		Denmark	478	Tunisia	430
		Lithuania	476	Chile	420
		Belgium (Fr)	471	**Philippines**	345
		Iran, Islamic Rep	470	Morocco	323
		Cyprus	463	South Africa	243
		Kuwait	430		
		Colombia	411		
		South Africa	326		

Note: Asian countries are shown in **bold type**.
Countries shown in *italics* did not comply fully with the sampling procedures required.

In countries participating in the TIMSS 1995 survey, a science literacy test was taken by a sample of all students in the final secondary year, whether they were studying science or not. The test was designed to ascertain how well students could use their scientific knowledge in real-world problems. Sweden's mean score of 559 was the highest of 21 countries. Means were 529 for New Zealand and 527 for Australia, with cohort coverage of 70 per cent and 68 per cent respectively. With a smaller cohort coverage of 48 per cent, the mean score of 481 for the Russian Federation was below the international mean of 500.

Achievement levels for students specialising in science in their final secondary year were assessed only for those studying physics. The Russian Federation ranked third and Australia seventh among 16 countries. Mean scores of 545 for the Russian Federation and 518 for Australia did not differ significantly, both being above the international mean of 501. Only 1.5 per cent of the age cohort took physics in the Russian Federation as against 13 per cent in Australia (Mullis et al., 1998).

On the evidence from the three IEA science surveys, Asia-Pacific countries can be classified into five broad groupings in science achievement at the 10-year-old and 14-year-old levels: (a) Singapore, Japan, Korea and Taiwan achieve at the highest international levels; (b) Australia and the Russian Federation fall in the next highest grouping; (c) Hong Kong and New Zealand perform above the international average, with Hong Kong moving into the next higher group in 1999; (d) Malaysia, Thailand, China and Papua New Guinea achieve close to the international average; and (e) India, Indonesia, and the Philippines perform well below the international average.

5.3. Achievement in Reading

In an IEA study in 1970–71, tests of reading comprehension, reading speed and word knowledge were applied in up to 15 countries to samples of 10-year-olds, 14-year-olds and students in the final year of secondary school (Thorndike, 1973). Reading comprehension scores for each country were derived from multiple-choice reading comprehension tests, extensively pre-tested to confirm that items discriminated appropriately between good and poor readers in each of the languages used. Cross-national comparisons are discussed only for reading comprehension as this aspect of reading is of most relevance for comparative studies of achievement.

For 10-year-old students, country mean scores ranged from 3.7 to 21.5, one of the lowest-scoring countries being an Asia-Pacific country, India (8.5). At the 14-year-level, the country with the lowest mean scores was India (5.2), while New Zealand had the highest mean score (29.3) of all countries. This pattern was repeated for students at the final secondary year level, mean scores ranging from 3.5 for India to 35.4 for New Zealand.

New Zealand's superior performance in reading was maintained in an IEA study involving 32 countries in 1991–92 (Elley, 1994). Multiple choice tests of reading literacy covered a wider range of reading activities than in the earlier survey, and included the interpretation of graphs, maps, timetables and the like. Scores were computed for narrative, expository and document reading, but comparative performance of countries has been restricted here to overall scores. New Zealand was among the high-achieving countries, ranking sixth at the 9 and 10 year level and fourth at the 14 and 15 year level. Hong Kong and Singapore were a little below New Zealand at the 9 and 10 year level but above the international median; at the 14 and 15 year level, they were well above the international median and not significantly lower than New Zealand. Their internationally superior performance in mathematics and science did not extend to reading literacy. Thailand and the Philippines were below the international median at age 14 and 15 years, and Indonesia had the second lowest mean of all countries at the 9 and 10 year level.

5.4. *Written Composition*

Cross-national studies of achievement in written composition pose many more problems than in mathematics and science, and even in reading. Curricula in the area of writing are not only less structured, but there is less agreement among countries in the types of writing that are valued. In IEA's study of written composition in 14 countries in the early 1980s, compositions were written in 11 different languages. Indonesia and New Zealand participated at the 10 to 12-year level, New Zealand at the 15 to 17-year level, and Thailand, at the final secondary year level. Each student wrote three compositions, including a common task and two rotated tasks. Functional, narrative and argument compositions were assigned at all age levels, supplemented by reflective writing tasks at the two higher age levels.

In an extensive pilot study, compositions written in each country were scored by native speakers and teachers of the language in that country, with the aid of international scoring criteria and international scales of benchmark compositions for each task and for the four main aspects rated, namely, overall impression, content, organization, and style and tone (de Glopper, 1988). These scales and scoring criteria were developed by international juries of raters drawn from the participating countries. Although the pilot study indicated that compositions from different cultures could be put on the same scale by an international jury, equivalent location of the scale points across countries could not be assured, thereby precluding direct comparisons of country means.

Countries can be compared, however, in terms of their relative performance on the different types of writing task undertaken by students at a given age or grade level. At the 10 to 12 year level, Indonesia showed very little variation in performance on functional, narrative and argument tasks, whereas New Zealand students performed much better in functional than in argument writing tasks. At the 15 to 17-year-old level, New Zealand was relatively high on functional writing, and relatively poor on reflective writing; the survey revealed that reflective composition was not taught to students at this age level in many countries.

Thailand performed much better in argument and reflective writing than in functional writing at the final secondary year level (Purves, Lehmann, & Degenhart, 1992).

The IEA study of written composition highlighted the difficulties involved in conducting comparative educational achievement studies in subjects which are highly culture dependent, and in which performance is affected not only by language differences but by the way in which performance is rated.

6. FACTORS ASSOCIATED WITH EDUCATIONAL ACHIEVEMENT

The IEA comparative studies have provided a large amount of data for each of the Asian-Pacific countries, as well as for other countries, on variables likely to be related to student achievement, for example, home background and educational resources, attitudes towards school subjects, instructional time devoted to particular subjects, class size, amount of homework, curriculum emphases, teaching approaches and so on. Tables summarizing such information can be found in the relevant reports.

Relationships between levels of achievement in a school subject and other variables of interest, taken one at a time, provide useful preliminary information about the likely importance of factors, which may influence achievement. These relationships, however, are susceptible to selective and simplistic interpretation, as background factors are themselves interrelated. For a proper identification of factors associated with educational achievement, multivariate analyses are required.

In all of the IEA studies in which the relevant analyses have been completed, home background factors have shown a strong relationship to educational achievement, after the influence of other factors has been taken into account. This relationship holds in both developed and less developed countries. These factors comprise such variables as the educational levels and occupations of parents, and educational resources within the home, for example, number of books, availability of newspapers and access to computers. Again, after other factors have been accounted for, educational achievement has been found in many countries to be positively related to:

(a) school characteristics, for example, school size, library and science facilities;
(b) teacher characteristics, for example, level of teachers' education and training;
(c) teaching and learning practices, for example, number of in-class instructional hours per subject, amount of homework, opportunity to learn the material tested, and
(d) student motivation, e.g. liking for school, interest in subject.

Sophisticated forms of multivariate analysis, such as hierarchical linear modelling, are now available for identifying factors associated with achievement which are unique to particular countries that is, country-specific factors. With countries as a level of analysis in this type of modelling, Leitz (1996) has shown that the relationship between reading achievement and the average level of reading resources in the homes served by schools was considerably greater in New Zealand and the United States than in the other countries surveyed.

In seeking to establish why countries differ in achievement, a number of small-scale intensive studies of student achievement and its correlates have compared the performance and background of Chinese and Japanese students with that of American students, especially in school subjects with lower mean scores in the United States. In addition to demonstrating differences in such variables as instructional time and amount of homework, Stevenson and Stigler (1992) argued that Japanese mothers placed more emphasis on effort and less on ability than American mothers in accounting for academic achievement, but others argue that these concepts cannot be assumed to have the same meaning across cultures (Bempechat & Drago-Severson, 1999). Sociologists have pointed to the contrasts between child socialisation practices adopted at home and in school in Japan and the United States (Fuller, Holloway, Azuma, Hess, & Kashiwagi, 1986). Videotape studies of mathematics classes have contrasted an emphasis on teaching methods of problem solving in the United States with an emphasis on helping students understand mathematical concepts in Japan (Stigler, Gonzales, Kawanaka, Knoll, & Serrano, 1999).

Asia-Pacific countries cover a wide span of levels of development. On a Composite Development Index incorporating measures of wealth, health and adult literacy, Thailand, the Philippines and Indonesia had very low index rankings (Elley & Schleicher, 1994). In his review of the six-subject survey of 1970/71, Walker (1976, p. 238) concluded that "the most dramatic differences in achievement" were those between the developed and less developed countries. The data presented in Tables 2 and 3 from the TIMSS survey suggest that this state of affairs still applies among Asia-Pacific countries, as elsewhere.

7. FUTURE DEVELOPMENTS

The effects of comparative educational achievement studies on educational policy and practice in Asia-Pacific countries are difficult to quantify. Much of the benefit to educational systems in these countries comes from their engagement in the process of carrying out the studies. This requires them to undertake regular reviews of their subject curricula in the light of what is being taught in other countries. It also keeps their researchers abreast of latest developments in methods of curriculum analysis, test and scale construction and analysis, sampling and data processing procedures and statistical methodology. Although the PISA project will monitor more generalised achievement in reading, mathematical and scientific literacy in OECD and some other countries, this will not diminish the need for regular international monitoring of curricula and achievement in school subjects such as mathematics and science and at age levels not covered by PISA. Cross-national comparisons of educational achievement in relation to curriculum sequencing and content and to teaching approaches provide information of crucial importance to educational systems in reviewing their school curricula and teaching and learning practices.

In order to maintain the value of the information from cross-national studies, Asia-Pacific countries will need to ensure that criteria set out for sampling guidelines, response rates and procedures for the coding and entry of data are fully achieved. Advances in research and statistical methodology, such as hierarchical linear modelling, will allow them to identify achievement-related factors operating in their own education systems, and to institute policy reforms where necessary in factors amenable to change such as curriculum content, teaching conditions and educational resources. Continued studies of classrooms with the aid of videotapes and other *in situ* studies of socialisation and pedagogical practices would illuminate cross-national differences in teaching and learning procedures.

Educational achievement in a country may well be related to the socialisation processes and values accepted by the society, but changes in values are not readily transferable or even acceptable to other societies. Probably the most significant step that could be taken to improve the overall levels of achievement in Asia-Pacific countries would be to increase the educational resources, including number of years of schooling and levels of teacher education, available to the low-performing countries.

REFERENCES

Beaton, A. E., Mullis, I. V. S., Martin, M. O., Gonzales, E. J., Kelly, D. L., & Smith, T. A. (1996). *Mathematics Achievement in the Middle School Years: IEA's Third International Mathematics and Science Study*. Chestnut Hill: IEA-TIMSS.

Beaton, A. E., Martin, M. O., Mullis, I. V. S., Gonzales, E. J., Smith, T. A., & Kelly, D. L. (1996a). *Science Achievement in the Middle School Years: IEA's Third International Mathematics and Science Study*. Chestnut Hill: IEA-TIMSS.

Beaton, A. E. Postlethwaite, T. N., Ross, K. N., Spearritt, D., & Wolf, R. M. (1999). *The Benefits and Limitations of International Educational Achievement Studies*. Paris: International Institute for Educational Planning/International Academy of Education.

Bempechat, J., & Drago-Severson, E. (1999). Cross-national differences in academic achievement: Beyond etic conceptions of children's understanding. *Review of Educational Research, 69*, 287–314.

Comber, L. C., & Keeves, J. P. (1973). *Science Education in Nineteen Countries: An Empirical Study*. New York: Wiley.

de Glopper, J. (1988). The results of the international scoring sessions. In T. P. Gorman, A. C. Purves & R. E. Degenhart (Eds.), *The IEA Study of Written Composition I: The International Writing Tasks and Scoring Scales*. Oxford: Pergamon.

Elley, W. B. (Ed.) (1994). *The IEA Study of Reading Literacy: Achievement and Instruction in Thirty-two School Systems*. Oxford: Pergamon.

Elley, W. B., & Schleicher, A. (1994). International differences in achievement levels. In W. B. Elley (Ed.), *The IEA Study of Reading Literacy: Achievement and Instruction in Thirty-two School Systems* (pp. 35–63). Oxford: Pergamon.

Fuller, B., Holloway, S. D., Azuma, H., Hess, R. D., & Kashiwagi, K. (1986). Contrasting achievement rules: Socialisation of Japanese children at home and in school. *Research in Sociology of Education and Socialisation, 6*, 165–201.

Garden, R., & Robitaille, D. F. (1989). *The IEA Study of Mathematics II: Contexts and Outcomes of School Mathematics*. Oxford: Pergamon.

Husén, T. (Ed.) (1967). *International Study of Achievement in Mathematics: A Comparison of Twelve Countries*, Vols. 1–2. Stockholm: Almqvist and Wiksell.

Lapointe, A. E., Mead, N. A., & Phillips, G. W. (1989). *A World of Differences: An International Assessment of Mathematics and Science*. Princeton, NJ: Educational Testing Service.

Leitz, P. (1996). International comparisons through simultaneous and conjunct analysis: A search for general relationships. *International Journal of Educational Research, 25*, 669–792.

Martin, M. O., Mullis, I. V., Beaton, A. E., Gonzales, E. J., Smith, T. A., & Kelly, D. L. (1997). *Science Achievement in the Primary School Years: The IEA's Third International Mathematics and Science Study*. Chestnut Hill: IEA-TIMSS.

Mullis, I. V., Martin, M. O., Beaton, A. E., Gonzales, E. J., Kelly, D. L., & Smith, T. A. (1998). *Mathematics and Science Achievement in the Final Year of Secondary School: IEA's Third International Mathematics and Science Study*. Chestnut Hill: IEA-TIMSS.

Mullis, I. V., Martin, M. O., Gonzales, E. J., Gregory, K. D., Garden, R. A., O'Connor, K. M., Chrostowski, S. J., & Smith, T. A. (2000). *TIMSS 1999: International Mathematics Report*. Boston: International Study Center, Boston College.

Postlethwaite, T. N. (1999). *International Studies of Educational Achievement: Methodological Issues*. Hong Kong: Comparative Education Research Centre. The University of Hong Kong.

Postlethwaite, T. N., & Wiley, D. E. (1992). *The IEA Study of Science II: Science Achievement in Twenty-three Countries*. Oxford: Pergamon.

Purves, A. C., Lehmann, R., & Degenhart, R. E. (1992). *The IEA Study of Written Composition II: Education and Performance in Fourteen Countries*. Oxford: Pergamon.

Stevenson, H. W., & Stigler, J. W. (1992). *The Learning Gap: Why Our Schools are Failing and What Can We Learn from Japanese and Chinese Education?* New York: Summit Books.

Stigler, J. W., Gonzales, P., Kawanaka, T., Knoll, S., & Serrano, A. (with Derghazarian, E., Huber, G., Ichioka, F., & Kerstin, N.). (1999). *The TIMSS Videotape Classroom Study: Methods and Findings from an Exploratory Research Project on Eighth-grade Mathematics Instruction in Germany, Japan, and the United States, NCES 1999–074*. Washington, DC: US Department of Education, National Center for Education Statistics.

Thorndike, R. L. (1973). *Reading Comprehension Education in Fifteen Countries: An Empirical Study*. New York: Wiley.

Walker, D. A. (1976). *The IEA Six Subject Survey: An Empirical Study of Education in Twenty-one Countries*. New York: Wiley.

77

Comparative Indicators in Education

LAWRENCE J. SAHA
Australian National University, Canberra, Australia

ALBERT TUIJNMAN
Institute of International Education, Stockholm University, Sweden

1. INTRODUCTION

This article first provides a definition of educational indicators and describes some of the main reasons why countries have supported international work on them since the late 1980s. The following section traces the development of educational indicators both in the context of comparative educational research and of national evaluation and policy-making regarding education systems. This section also includes a description of the relatively recent OECD-INES project and some of its accomplishments, including the revision of the International Standard Classification of Education. The development of educational indicators in Asia-Pacific countries is presented in a third section. An organising framework for the selection of indicators is also given. Finally, some of the main challenges confronting continued work on educational indicators are listed, particularly in so far as these relate to indicators of educational outcomes in the Asia-Pacific region.

2. DEFINITIONS OF EDUCATIONAL INDICATORS AND THEIR USE

2.1. *Definitions*

An indicator is a single or complex statistic that conveys essential information about the condition of a major aspect of a social or economic system, such as the economy, health or education. The information that is conveyed by indicators can be used for a variety of purposes, and these include both academic understanding and policy-making. However, the term 'indicator' is usually reserved for the latter, and is usually linked with the performance evaluation and condition of a goal-oriented action or system.

An indicator usually presents information on some sort of scale, often a continuous one. Yet it is normally impossible to set an unambiguous cut score or benchmark on such scales. Hence it cannot be known precisely whether an indicator value signifies an adequate or an inadequate condition. An indicator can therefore never be a very precise instrument for policy evaluation. Interpretations of indicator values that signify adequate or inadequate performance and that suggest a need for policy intervention will differ depending on the perspective of the beholders. It follows that an indicator can point to a problem area but cannot offer a diagnosis of this problem or prescribe what should be done to remedy it.

Educational indicators are best described as derived statistics with an added evaluative character to the informative nature of statistics in general. "An indicator is an individual or a composite statistic that relates to a basic construct in education and is useful in a policy context" (Shavelson et al., 1987). At the same time, however, an indicator

> ... is not simply a numerical expression or a composite statistic. It is intended to tell something about the performance or behaviour of an education system, and can be used to inform the stakeholders – decision-makers, teachers, students, parents and the general public. Most importantly, indicators also provide a basis for creating new visions and expectations. (Bottani & Tuijnman 1994, p. 26)

The above definitions suggest a number of criteria to which indicators should comply (Bottani and Tuijnman 1994; Wyatt 1994).

- They are quantitative and include an aggregation of qualitative, value- and policy-oriented attributes.
- They are intended to convey summary information about an important aspect of the performance of an education system.
- They need to communicate different types of information to satisfy different user needs, from the students and their parents, teachers and school principals, school inspectors, local administrators, employers, and policy makers in government agencies.
- They are intended as a basis for evaluation and are therefore inherently related to questions of policy.
- Indicators are mutually interdependent; they cannot stand on their own. To be useful, indicators are part of a set of multiple indicators with an understanding of how they are interrelated.
- Indicators most often operate at a macro or aggregate level of analysis and should contain information on outcomes at different levels, for example, students, institutions, systems and labour markets.
- In order to be functional an indicator system must be selective of the data it seeks to communicate.
- Indicators must be embedded in time series so that developments in education policy can be understood.

- Comparative indicators are intended to increase the understanding of similarities and differences, strengths and weaknesses, between the education systems of different countries.

As a result of the above criteria, there are limitations to the utility of social and educational indicators for policy-making. First, they imply that it is difficult to reach valid conclusions that are based only on one indicator. It is necessary to take into account the broader context of how the indicator relates to others. Second, these criteria highlight the necessity of applying a logically consistent theoretical framework that makes the relationships among multiple indicators explicit. Third, the criteria suggest the need for a careful and comprehensive approach in collecting and aggregating statistical data as a prerequisite for indicator construction.

When applied to education, these criteria make it possible to evaluate the extent to which an education system has the capacity to meet the social, political and economic goals of a country. Therefore, like social indicators of any kind, educational indicators cannot be used in isolation from other social indicators. Hence the selection of any type of social indicator, including education, should be guided by the following additional criteria.

- Social indicators should be a part of a wider politically motivated process of selection, based on political consensus and support.
- A balance between the diagnostic and suggestive nature of the social indicators should be maintained.
- An explicit conceptual and theoretical model should guide the selection of indicators.
- Any collection of social indicators should be in a form that allows a variety of analytic procedures to be used in the study of their interrelationships.

The definition of educational indicators and the criteria for their selection make clear that their uses are closely linked to both political and research agendas. In general, their use is either related to the reporting of the current condition of a system or an aspect of that system, or geared towards the analysis of present or future trends affecting the education system. In both scenarios, however, the indicators must offer a basis for making judgements with respect to system performance. A second implication in this view of education is increasing the potential for accountability in the system. Because the construction of educational indicators is related to goals and targets, the failure to attain them can be more closely analysed and the cause of failure more easily identified and remedied.

2.2. Early Development of Educational Indicators

Porras-Zuniga (1994) notes that already in 1926 there were efforts to develop standardised educational statistics. By the late 1950s and early 1960s, particularly with the rapid expansion of national education systems and the need for educational policy and planning, work on standardised statistics rapidly developed. Already by 1975 there were two instruments to meet this need: *Recommendation Concerning the International Standardization of Educational Statistics*, which was first approved by UNESCO in 1958, and the *International Standard Classification of Education* (ISCED) approved in 1975 by the International Conference of Education. The two classification systems were made compatible in 1978 so that comparisons between systems of education might be possible (Porras-Zuniga, 1994).

At the same time, researchers in the new field of comparative education advocated the identification and measurement of relevant factors or variables that would make the comparative study of education systems possible. Holmes, one of the pioneers of comparative education, argued that comparative education was related to educational policy and planning. He advocated the identification and measurement of the contextual determinants of education systems, the selection of the relevant variables with respect to an educational problem, and finally some assessment of the relationship between the factors must be made (Holmes, 1967).

The interest in and development of standard educational indicators occurred in an environment of rapid change in the education systems in most countries of the world. During the 1960s and 1970s many countries were preoccupied with the design and implementation of strategies for dealing with the pressures of numbers in their education systems. The emphasis was mainly on growth in education and relatively less attention was paid to aspects of educational quality and cost-effectiveness.

This orientation changed, and quite radically so, during the early 1980s. The impact of continued financial austerity on public finance led politicians in many industrialised countries to consider the implementation of cost saving programs. The shift from policies concerned with educational expansion, to strategies aimed at increasing cost-effectiveness, was striking when education ministers met at the OECD in 1984. Concepts of 'quality assurance' and 'accountability' were introduced and advocated. Thus a new stage was set for the development of educational policy, with an emphasis on issues of quality and outcomes rather than quantity and inputs.

During this period of educational change, many countries had specified broad goals for school education, but it was less common for them to have formulated specific goals. If goals were stated at all, then they often included general statements about the purposes of education, written in the context of the nation state, and they were phrased in ways that did not require benchmarking against a national or international standard. In contrast, the trend emerging in the late 1980s was not only to write down explicit goals but also to formulate them in terms of targets to be achieved. This development reflected the thinking that if high-quality education for all is to be achieved, then goals combined with high standards must be agreed upon, and performance must be measured and assessed against those standards. These ideas clearly provided support for the effort to develop educational indicators at the international or comparative level (Husén & Tuijnman, 1994). An outcome of these developments was the largest international project on educational indicators.

2.3. The OECD-INES Project

The Centre for Educational Research and Innovation (CERI) of the OECD launched its project on Indicators of Education Systems (INES) in 1987. The overriding goal for the project was to develop a limited set of comparable and international indicators of education systems. This was to be achieved in phases and through a collaborative framework comprising several technical groups and networks dealing with specific indicator areas, such as educational finance and enrolment, educational outputs and outcomes, education and labour market destinations, and attitudes and expectations of students, parents and other stakeholders.

Two international conferences laid the foundation for the INES project. The United States Department of Education hosted the first of these conferences in Washington, DC in November 1987. The second was sponsored by the Ministry of National Education of France and convened in Poitiers in March 1988. It is interesting to note that the CERI Governing Board had not been unanimous in launching the INES project. Several nations had expressed reservations but strong political pressure and also financial support supplied by the United States National Center of Education Statistics had carried the decision. The first phase of the work was exploratory and designed to demonstrate country interest as well as the feasibility of developing comparable educational indicators. Once the CERI Governing Board was satisfied that these two conditions were met, the second phase was launched following the ministerial meeting convened in November 1990. The objective was to develop a limited, still preliminary set of educational indicators. This work was accomplished and led to a stocktaking exercise hosted by Swiss federal authorities in Lugano in September 1991.

The preliminary set of indicators that was presented in Lugano was far from ideal. There were problems of inconsistency in applied definitions, important indicators were missing, relationships among indicators were not specified, and the data underlying the indicators were not strictly comparable, either because of national differences in the fiscal and school reference years or because of differences in the way information was collected by the countries. Nevertheless, it was decided that the OECD should seek to publish the first results, because this would provide a strong incentive to press on and improve both the reliability and coverage of the indicators. The first version of *Education at a Glance* was published in September 1992. This was an achievement in both a political and a scientific sense, and it signified a distinct political will in member countries to build up an improved framework of comparative educational indicators.

With the publication of *Education at a Glance* (OECD 1992a) the project found itself at the beginning of a third phase. Then the four main aims were: (a) to improve still further the reliability, comparability and political relevance of the indicator set; (b) to develop new indicators in areas such as equity, quality, schooling processes, external efficiency, research systems, and post-initial education and training; (c) to collaborate with UNESCO and the statistical office of the European Union in developing new questionnaires and adapting the ISCED classification system to new and emerging needs; and (d) to improve the mechanisms for the routine collection of data and their transfer to the OECD and UNESCO secretariats.

The OECD published its second educational indicators report in December 1993. This included 38 indicators, two more than had been included in the first edition. The target for the second edition had not been to enlarge the set but to update the indicators and reduce the time lag between data collection and reporting. This goal was met, as was that of improving the reliability and comparability of the data on educational finance. The repetition of the data collection exercise also made it possible to improve somewhat the adequacy of the data transfer mechanisms and the co-operative procedures involving the secretariat and the Member Countries.

The *Education at a Glance* reports have been published on a regular basis since 1995. Subsequent editions have included new indicators as well as their underlying basic statistics. Consequently the publication has tended to grow in size over time. An important comparative database has thus been built up, one that has also become available electronically on cd-rom as well as on-line. Further developments have seen the launch of the World Education Indicators initiative, a joint effort by OECD, UNESCO and the World Bank. Several countries in the Asia-Pacific region joined the international work on educational indicators through this initiative. Since 1996, the OECD has also regularly published a companion volume to *Education at a Glance*, entitled *Education Policy Analysis*. The purpose of the latter is to promote and refine the application of indicators in policy analytical work.

2.4. *Frameworks for Organising Indicators*

Given that multiple factors should be considered within an indicator framework it is useful to apply a systems approach, defining indicators within the framework of their possible associations. Thus a relational structure is required with an interface to select and examine indicators within their hierarchical organisation. Two limitations suggest themselves. The first concerns the availability of the underlying statistics needed to build more synthetic indicators. The second results from a lack of consensus on clear organisational principles guided by social theory.

The theoretical framework for the organisation of indicators adopted by the OECD as a basis for its 1992 indicator report comprises four clusters of indicators, as shown in Figure 1, Panel 1 (OECD, 1992b). Four levels of outcomes are seen as covering the totality of possible results, ranging from the individual to the society.

Productivity, efficiency and equity are treated for the purposes of the adopted

The system dimension	Contexts	Inputs	Processes	Outcomes
Level				
Individual level	×	×	×	×
Institutional level	×	×	×	×
Labour market level	×	×	×	×
Societal level	×	×	×	×
Criteria				
Productivity	×	×	×	×
Efficiency	×	×	×	×
Equity	×	×	×	×

Figure 1. A framework for organising educational indicators.

model as three cross-cutting dimensions, as is shown in Figure 1, Panel 2. Combined together, they can be treated as overall quality measures, assessing the suitability of the national education systems to accomplish the tasks they are entrusted with by society. The emphasis is on quality.

> The quality of education and training is considered in all Member States to be a concern of the highest political priority. High levels of knowledge, competencies and skills are considered to be the very basic conditions for active citizenship, employment and social cohesion. (EU, 2000, p. 3)

The resulting general framework is summarised in the matrix in Figure 1, Panel 2. The purpose of the framework is not only to describe the indicator domains that ideally should be covered as part of a systematic and comprehensive system but also to suggest how these indicator domains might be presented in a logical or sequential order. The cross-cutting policy dimensions, in turn, are used to ensure that the measures that are actually used to cover the indicator domains are explicitly related to issues deemed important by policy makers. The framework is therefore a matrix suggesting a graphical layout of the web of indicators that should be encompassed. It is defined both in terms of a theoretically motivated sequential order and according to politically motivated issues for evaluation.

2.5. The International Standard Classification of Education

The International Standard Classification of Education (ISCED) is a classification of educational programs designed to serve as an instrument for assembling, compiling and presenting comparable statistics and indicators of education both within individual countries and internationally. It presents standard concepts, definitions and clarifications for statistics on many different aspects of education, such as statistics on student enrolment, on the human or financial resources invested in education, or on the educational attainment of the general population.

Within the ISCED framework, the term 'education' is taken to comprise deliberate, systematically organised and sustained communication designed to bring about learning. The underlying notion in this definition is that while all education involves learning, not all learning can be regarded as education. The application of the framework is believed to facilitate the transformation of detailed national-level educational statistics defined in accordance with the specific customs and system characteristics of a country into consistent aggregate categories of levels and fields of education that are deemed to be internationally comparable and that can be meaningfully interpreted. However, the following qualifications to the above apply:

> It must be recognised that ISCED has natural limitations for the direct classification and assessment of competencies and qualifications of the participants in educational activities. This is because there is no close and universal relationship between the programs a participant is enrolled in and actual educational achievement. The educational programs an individual has participated in or even successfully completed are, at best, a first approximation to the skills and competencies he or she has actually obtained. (UNESCO, 1997, p. 5)

The ISCED framework was originally adopted in 1976 and implemented during the following years. Because of the considerable leeway allowed in interpretation by the definitions and the lack of an adequate co-ordinating mechanism for data producers, the quality of the data and especially their international comparability have not always been of the standard deemed desirable. In order to improve data quality, consistency and international comparability, a decision to revise and update the ISCED framework was passed in 1992 and work began in earnest in 1994.

By early 1997 a draft of a revised classification had been prepared by a task force appointed to carry out the work. The revised framework was reviewed by stakeholders in individual countries and by international organisations and was subsequently approved at the twenty-ninth session of the UNESCO General Conference in October 1997 (UNESCO, 1997). During 1998 a new technical manual containing detailed definitions, specifications and numerous guidelines for implementation was prepared, and provisions were put into place gradually to phase in the new classification during 1998 and 1999. As the new classification was to be applied globally, and in both developed and developing countries, there obviously were numerous challenges that had to be overcome. UNESCO and its specialised agencies such as the International Institute for Educational Planning and the UNESCO Institute for Statistics organised a number of meetings and training sessions for educational planners and statisticians also in the Asia-Pacific region.

Because individual or micro-level data are not normally used for international comparisons of educational attainment, the indicators available at the international level rely on broad taxonomies in which aggregates of the educational programs that exist at the national level provide the basis for the comparisons. The term 'levels of education' thus broadly relates to the degree of complexity of the content of an educational program. The levels refer to graduations of learning experiences and the skills and competencies that educational programs require of the participants. Accordingly, the educational levels represent an ordered series of categories roughly corresponding to the overall complexity of the knowledge, skills and competencies that are thought to be required for the successful completion of an educational program.

The new ISCED framework has six main levels. But most of these are in turn sub-divided into several separate but related dimensions that make it possible to undertake more detailed comparisons. The six main levels of education according to ISCED-97 are the following:

- ISCED 0   Pre-primary education
- ISCED 1   Primary education; first stage of basic education
- ISCED 2   Lower secondary education; second stage of basic education
- ISCED 3   Upper secondary education
- ISCED 4   Post-secondary education, non-tertiary
- ISCED 5   Tertiary education, first stage
- ISCED 6   Tertiary education, second stage
- ISCED 9   Education not definable by level

Main criteria, subsidiary criteria and complementary dimensions are used by country data producers to map empirically their national educational programs and assign them to the agreed international levels as defined by the ISCED framework. Main criteria include the following: (a) the educational properties of the program; (b) whether school- or centre-based provision; (c) the minimum age of the children catered for; and (d) the upper age limit of the children attending the program. Subsidiary criteria refer mainly to the qualifications of the staff, age of entry into the nationally designated institutions or programs, or the end of compulsory schooling. Complementary dimensions refer to the type of subsequent education or cumulative duration.

3. EDUCATIONAL INDICATORS IN ASIA AND PACIFIC COUNTRIES

There are at least three reasons why a discussion of educational indicators in Asian and Pacific countries might be different from European or North American countries. First, the structure and organisation of their education systems differ in certain respects. Second, there are cultural specificities, and hence the public aspirations and expectations for education may differ. Third, many Asia-Pacific countries began their rapid educational expansion later than did other Western countries.

The development of educational indicators in OECD and UNESCO was not entirely a Western activity. Japan, which became a member of OECD in 1964, participated throughout the educational indicator project. The Republic of Korea, which became a member in 1996, has participated only in recent years. Japan has been publishing its own educational statistics since 1955 (Japan, Ministry of Education, 2000), but has also been included in the OECD project from the beginning (see OECD, 1992a). In addition to these countries, other initiatives for the development of educational indicators have been more specific to the Asia-Pacific region.

3.1. *APEC: Comparative Educational Statistics in the Asia-Pacific Region*

In January 1989 a group of 18 Pacific Rim countries formed an organisation called Asia-Pacific Economic Cooperation (APEC) which had as its objective "... to sustain the growth and development of the region; to enhance the positive gains resulting from increasing economic interdependence; to develop and strengthen multilateral trade; and to reduce trade barriers" (APEC, 1998, p. v). The Members included the following Asia-Pacific territories: Brunei Darussalam, People's Republic of China, Hong Kong, Indonesia, Japan, Republic of Korea, Malaysia, Papua New Guinea, the Philippines, Singapore, Chinese Taipei and Thailand. Other Pacific Rim countries are Australia, Canada, Chile, Mexico, New Zealand and the United States.

In 1992, the APEC Human Resources Development Working Group (HRDWG) met in Washington, DC and endorsed a theme of 'Towards Education Standards for the 21st Century'. In 1993, HRDWG met in Tokyo and decided to collaborate in the preparation of common educational statistics to guide policy-making and evaluate educational programs. Although HRDWG did not call these statistics 'indicators', the data, which have been subsequently collected and reported, meet the definition of educational indicators provided in Section 2.1 above.

In 1994 the first report, *School Education Statistics in the Asia-Pacific Region*, was published which contained preliminary educational statistics from 11 countries. A second report with revised and expanded statistics was published in 1998. The report included 24 tables that included time-series data, starting with 1990, and the most recent year. The report also included statements of school education priorities and organisational diagrams from each of the APEC countries. These statements provided the background against which the statistics could be interpreted. Separate chapters described in detail information on pre-primary education, completion and transition rates from primary to secondary school, and finally on student attainment. The latter presentation also included educational statistics derived from UNESCO sources and comparative data on student achievement in mathematics and science derived from the Third International Mathematics and Science Study (TIMSS) conducted under the auspices of the International Association for the Evaluation of Educational Achievement (IEA), an association in which a number of Asia-Pacific education systems had been active since the 1960s (see *Evaluation and Accountability in Asian and Pacific Countries. Comparative Educational Achievement Studies*).

3.2. WEI: Asia-Pacific Countries and World Education Indicators

In 1997, building on the OECD indicators program (see Section 2.3 above), and with the assistance of UNESCO and the World Bank, the World Educational Indicators (WEI) initiative was launched. Eleven countries were included in the project, six of which were Asian, namely China, India, Indonesia, Malaysia, the Philippines, and Thailand. Sri Lanka joined the project in its second year. The purpose of this project was to develop further the OECD indicators methodology and to improve the application of this methodology to policy. A further goal was to test the possibility of reaching an agreement among the countries on a small but critical set of indicators which could measure educational performance in an international, comparative manner (UNESCO/OECD, 2000).

As a result of participation in this project, the seven Asian countries have been able to improve their educational indicators and to measure the performance of their education system in a comparative context. In the initial report, an overview of the advantages of the development of international indicators was reviewed. The WEI countries were compared on resource allocation to education, the lengthening of educational attainment, equity in educational provision, and the improvement of the quality of education. Each country's education system was profiled in a way that made comparisons possible.

By its own admission, WEI is still in its early stages. The collection of data from each country remains incomplete. In addition the interpretation of the indicators at an international level often overlooks the differences between them, which are only in part due to national idiosyncratic structures of education (UNESCO/OECD, 2000, p. 18). Nevertheless, the seven Asian countries that participate in the project have benefited from the development and maintenance of their own educational statistics and indicators.

3.3. Specific Indicators for National Educational Reform: Hong Kong

Many countries of the world from time-to-time embark upon reforms of their education systems. Because of the cultural and structural characteristics of countries, the indicators that are used to guide and monitor reform projects are specific to the countries, and as a result depart from, or are added to, the international indicators pursued by OECD, APEC or WEI projects. This is the case of the current education reform in Hong Kong.

In order to prepare for the needs of the twenty-first century, the Education Commission in Hong Kong, after considerable consultation, has embarked on a comprehensive educational reform at all educational levels, from early childhood education to higher education and adult continuing education. The reform is to focus on seven key areas: curriculum, language education, support for schools, professional development of teachers and educational leaders and administrators, admission systems, assessment mechanisms, and increase in post-secondary education opportunities (Hong Kong, 2002a). As a background to the reform, a comprehensive set of trend statistics showing the changes in Hong

Kong education during the 1990s into 2000/2001 was developed and published (Hong Kong, 2002b).

In order to guide and monitor the reform, the Education Commission set out to develop specific educational indicators. In the first instance the performance indicators for early childhood education were developed. While these were closely modelled on the OECD-INES indicators, it was also recognized that some aspects of the Hong Kong education system were unique and therefore required indicators that were specific to the system. One of these unique areas is moral education, which clearly relates to the cultural fabric of Hong Kong society.

The use of educational indicators to guide and monitor educational reform in Hong Kong represents a good example of their application in the Asia-Pacific region. Not only is Hong Kong's educational reform based on international standard indicators, but it also requires the development of unique indicators specific to Hong Kong culture. The experience of Hong Kong reflects similar circumstances in other Asia-Pacific countries. The use of OECD international indicators is valuable for the comparative assessment of an education system, but indicators specific to the cultural setting of an education system are also necessary if the use of the indicators for the assessment of performance and policy-making is to be effective.

4. ISSUES AND CHALLENGES

Despite the progress made since the late 1980s many gaps still remain in the development and use of educational indicators, in the Asia-Pacific countries and elsewhere. Basically, the challenges are of an instrumental, a technical-statistical and a logistical nature.

In the initial phases of the work, much of the discussion focused on what then was labelled 'the uncertain connection' between indicators and educational improvement. The INES project carried a utilitarian, instrumental perspective. This leads to wondering whether and how the indicators have been used, and whether this use has led to improvement. This is a difficult question to answer. There is some evidence that ministries of education and other government agencies in the Asia-Pacific region are carefully examining the OECD indicator data, and that this reflection leads to policy action. An encouraging signal is that quite a few education systems, such as Hong Kong, are developing their own indicator reports, in which they follow the OECD model and complement it with additional data that are seen as particularly relevant in the national context.

The OECD indicators reports were envisaged as a means of providing snapshots of the education systems of the Member Countries. This they did, but they have also grown in size and become more statistically oriented. As technical complexity has increased the readership, which originally was intended to be very broad and non-specialist, has become more restricted. This makes it imperative not to lose sight of the main goal of the activity, which is to produce synthetic or summary information useful for accountability and policy making. Strengthening the policy relevance of the indicators will require an analysis of the relationships between the context, input, process and outcome variables. It will also require that the indicator data are combined with other sources of information, both nationally and internationally.

This leads to an extension of the type of research studies that the International Association for the Evaluation of Educational Achievement (IEA) initiated over 40 years ago. In these studies it has been found that comparative analysis was seriously handicapped by the lack of sound educational indicators that applied both across countries and over time. Only from such comparative studies is it likely that a better understanding can be gained of the forces at work in the provision of educational services across the countries of the world, and the Asia-Pacific region in particular.

In instances where indicators are used out of context and in highly selective ways, there is a risk of bias in interpretation. Indicators can be useful tools for benchmarking and assessment, but all too often their potential is not realized. This is true of all countries, including the Asia-Pacific countries. A challenge of a logistical nature is thus posed, because further development and innovation in the area of educational statistics and indicators depends on a range of activities being undertaken both within countries as well as at the international level. Improved co-ordination between and within nations and co-operation among international agencies, as well as strong political support and continued investment, are important considerations.

REFERENCES

APEC (1998). *School Education Statistics in the Asia-Pacific Region.* Canberra: Department of Employment, Education, Training and Youth Affairs.

Bottani, N., & Tuijnman, A. C. (1994). International education indicators: Framework, development and interpretation. In A. C. Tuijnman & N. Bottani (Eds.), *Making Education Count: Developing and Using International Indicators* (pp. 21–35). Paris: Centre for Educational Research and Innovation, OECD.

EU (2000). *European Report on the Quality of School Education: Sixteen Quality Indicators.* Brussels: Commission of the European Communities, Directorate-General for Education and Culture.

Holmes, B. (1967). *Problems in Education: A Comparative Approach.* London: Routledge & Kegan Paul.

Hong Kong, Education and Manpower Bureau (2002a). *Education Statistics.* Hong Kong: Education and Manpower Bureau, Hong Kong Special Administrative Region of The People's Republic of China.

Hong Kong, Education Commission (2002b). *Progress Report on the Education Reform (1): Learning for Life – Learning Through Life.* Hong Kong: Education Commission: Hong Kong Special Administrative Region, The People's Republic of China.

Husén, T., & Tuijnman, A. C. (1994). Monitoring standards in education: Why and how it came about. In A. C. Tuijnman & T. N. Postlethwaite (Eds.), *Monitoring the Standards of Education: Papers in Honor of John P. Keeves* (pp. 1–21). Oxford: Pergamon.

Japan: Ministry of Education, Sports and Culture (2000). *Education in Japan.* Tokyo: Ministry of Education, Sports and Culture.

OECD (1992a). *Education at a Glance: OECD Indicators.* Paris: Centre for Educational Research and Innovation, OECD.
OECD (1992b). *The OECD International Educational Indicators: A Framework for Analysis.* Paris: Centre for Educational Research and Innovation, OECD.
Porras-Zuniga, J. (1994). Comparative statistics in education. In T. Husén & T. N. Postlethwaite (Eds.), *The International Encyclopedia of Education* (pp. 2: 958–964). Oxford: Pergamon Press.
Shavelson, R. J., McDonnell, L., Oakes, J., Carey, N., with Picus, L. (1987). *Indicator Systems for Monitoring Mathematics and Science Education.* Santa Monica, CA: The Rand Corporation.
UNESCO (1997). *International Standard Classification of Education.* Paris: UNESCO.
UNESCO/OECD (2000). *Investing in Education: Analysis of the 1999 World Education Indicators,* Paris: UNESCO/OECD World Education Indicators Programme.
Wyatt, T. (1994). Education indicators: A review of the literature. In A. C. Tuijnman & N. Bottani (Eds.), *Making Education Count: Developing and Using International Indicators* (pp. 99–121). Paris: Centre for Educational Research and Innovation, OECD.

78

Dissemination of the Findings of Educational Research

GRANT J. HARMAN and KAY HARMAN
Centre for Higher Education Management and Policy, University of New England, Armidale, Australia

1. INTRODUCTION

This article describes the organisation and recent expansion of educational research in the Asia-Pacific region and how findings are disseminated, particularly to educational practitioners and policy-makers as well as to other researchers. It also discusses the use and impact of research findings, and possible means to improve utilisation of the findings of educational research.

The Asia-Pacific region is a vast area stretching from the Middle East in the west to various Pacific Island nations in the east, and including the Indian subcontinent, China and other North Asian countries, South East Asia, and Australia and New Zealand. Together this region with well over three billion people and approximately 60 per cent of the world's population presents a picture of impressive diversity and variety, and rapid change. The region includes two countries each with populations of over one billion as well as very small nations. It is home to major economies such as Japan, as well as to some of the world's poorest nations. Similarly, education systems and educational research capacities vary greatly. In a small number of countries, particularly OECD member countries and China and India, educational research is well supported and well developed, with strong regional and international links. In contrast, in small and far less wealthy nations, educational research efforts are limited and often consist of little more than the collection and analysis of basic student enrolment statistics.

While educational researchers in the region have made important contributions to the better understanding of educational processes and issues, they are often criticised for not producing sufficient relevant knowledge valued by educational bureaucracies and key personnel in educational institutions. Researchers, however, tend to be more optimistic, hoping that more effective mechanisms can be developed for the dissemination of findings so that new partnerships can be forged between researchers, policy makers and professionals.

2. ORGANISATION OF EDUCATIONAL RESEARCH

Educational research can be defined as systematic and original investigation into: (a) the processes of learning and development of children, youth and adults; (b) the contexts in which learning and teaching takes place; (c) the work of educators; (d) resources and organisational arrangements to support educational work; (e) the purposes and outcomes of education; and (f) education policy issues. This definition is derived mainly from more comprehensive OECD definitions of educational research and development (Centre for Educational Research and Innovation, 1995, pp. 36–37) (see *Educational Research for Regional and National Development*).

Admittedly, across the Asia-Pacific region there is by no means any clear consensus about the precise meaning of the term educational research, or about its purposes. Some researchers define educational research narrowly, seeing its focus solely on formal schooling and drawing almost exclusively from the discipline of psychology. At the other end of the spectrum, others take a much broader view, conceiving the purposes of educational research in broader terms, and believing that research should focus not only on formal education for all age groups but also on the social, economic and political contexts in which such education takes place, the administrative and financial support for education and educational policy issues. They also recognise that valuable contributions can be made by scholars from a wide range of disciplinary backgrounds outside of educational studies.

Over recent years two main paradigms about the nature of research in education and the knowledge it yields have dominated a great deal of discussion across the countries of the region. Many senior officials in education ministries and researchers working closely with them have looked to the social and behavioural sciences to produce knowledge that is seen to be independent of context, that may be generalised to many learning situations, and that is neutral with respect to social values. In contrast, school principals and teachers have often adhered to the view that sophisticated, theoretical educational research has very little to contribute in terms of decision making in the classroom and school, and the improvement of professional practice and policy. Relevant knowledge, according to this latter view, is a product of reflective practice; it is dependent on context, is particularistic, and is related to specific social and personal values. These two paradigms have often been seen to be in conflict with one another, one being positivist, using measurable and objective criteria, seeking to explain and build a science of education, while the other being humanistic and critical, deriving from the humanities and social sciences and emphasising qualitative information and interpretative approaches. For many years, these two perspectives coexisted uneasily. The positivist view where measurement was a key focus dominated for a long time in many countries. In India, for example, during the initial years of independence, educational phenomena were "studied by reducing them to more specific aspects and examining relationships amongst variables" with the aim of making educational research "an academic exercise of great methodological rigour and objective scrutiny of variables" (Yadav & Lakshmi, 1998, p. 2). But in the late 1960s and 1970s, a crisis of confidence in the positivist approach led to major expansion of the interpretative approach and qualitative work. More recently, open conflict has been replaced by recognition that the two paradigms are best seen as complementary. Thus pluralism in approaches gained increasing favour, with many researchers supporting the idea expressed by Lakomski (1991) as moving 'beyond paradigms'. With this more holistic view, choice of methodology and approach is dependent upon the research questions being asked and not upon the belief that one paradigm is necessarily superior to the other.

Since the 1950s, there has been an impressive expansion in educational research throughout the Asia-Pacific region. Even the smallest nations have made efforts to establish and enhance their educational research capacity, whereas in countries such as Japan, China, India, Australia and New Zealand educational research is well developed, addressing a wide range of topics that use sophisticated methods. According to two Indian scholars,

> over the past five decades [in India] educational research has evolved into a significant component of the educational scene. That this has developed from an almost nonexistent component makes it impressive. (Yadav & Lakshmi, 1998)

In China, there are now more than 10,000 full-time researchers working in national and provincial or municipal educational research institutions and universities and colleges, with many more engaged in action research at grass roots level (Nanzhao et al., 1999, p. 80).

Despite some measure of skepticism about the value of educational research from particular policy makers and practitioners, the expansion of educational research has been driven by reform movements to improve education and schooling, by new emphases on public accountability and by strong beliefs, especially among educational professionals, that educational research can make important contributions to improving practice and policy. According to the Asian Development Bank, educational research 'is the tool which enables policy makers to determine national educational needs, to assess new approaches to resolving issues, and to evaluate the effectiveness of policies and strategies (Asian Development Bank, 1996, p. i). Behind many reform efforts has been a belief that education is an important factor in national innovation, economic growth and international competitiveness while an increased emphasis on public sector accountability has produced enhanced interest in measuring the effectiveness of investment in education. Associated with this new emphasis on accountability in some countries is increased use of market driven models for the provision of government services, leading to greater use of evaluation and performance indicators.

Educational research is conducted from a variety of institutional settings. In many countries, ministries of education and other government agencies are of key importance, but other providers include universities and colleges of education, specialist educational research organisations and more recently consulting firms and individual consultants. Arrangements differ considerably, from country to country, reflecting different organisation of their public sectors, different intellectual and educational traditions, and differing financial support and national priorities.

Ministries and departments have had substantial involvement in educational research for many years. Many education ministries have major research divisions that undertake a range of different research programs, such as the Educational Research and Planning Division of the Malaysian Ministry of Education. In New Zealand, while the Ministry of Education has its own research division, recently it has moved increasingly to sponsor research activities in universities and buy research services from both private and overseas providers, rather than actually carrying out research projects (Burgon, Philips, & Nana, 2000; New Zealand Council for Educational Research, 2000). Outside of ministries, other government agencies sometimes play important roles in both conducting and sponsoring research, particularly in specialised areas such as curriculum, examinations, and early childhood education and adult education.

Universities and colleges are major producers of educational research in many countries, largely because of the research expertise of their academic staff and their commitment to the notion that advanced level teaching needs to be supported by research (Harman, 2000). In Australia and New Zealand, not only are faculties and schools of education major research producers but also important are special research centres, teaching and learning centres (Hayden & Parry, 1997) and staff in disciplines such as psychology and sociology. In other cases such as in Iran, educational research is conducted as part of internal university evaluations (Bazargan, 2000). In New Zealand in the financial year 1999–2000, the Ministry of Education funded some 40 projects in New Zealand universities and colleges of education (Burgon, Philips, & Nana, 2000) while in Australia educational research is undertaken in all 37 public universities, with external funding coming from a large variety of sources. These include the Australian Research Council; the Commonwealth (Australian) Department of Education, Science and Training; the Commonwealth University Teaching and Staff Development Committee; the Australian National Training Authority; and state and territory ministries and educational agencies. An Australian Research Council sponsored review of education research (McGaw et al., 1992) reported that 80 per cent of the educational research effort in Australia is the product of higher education institutions, with the remainder being from government funded institutions.

In a number of countries important roles are played by specialist educational research organisations, irrespective of whether they are government agencies or independent. An example of such a major government agency is the National Institute for Educational Policy Research (NIER) in Japan, which was established in 1949 as one of a number of government research institutes under the general supervision of the Ministry of Education. Its main objectives are to collect and disseminate relevant information on education and educational research, provide assistance and advice to educational institutions and educators, cooperate with international organisations, organise workshops and seminars for educators from Asian and Pacific countries, and exchange educational information with educational institutions outside Japan. In 1997, it had a total staff of 89 which included 68 researchers (National Institute for Educational Policy Research, 2001). Other major government educational research agencies are the Korean Educational Development Institute, the Chinese National Institute for Educational Research, the Indonesian Office of Educational and Cultural Research and Development, and Bahrain's Educational Research and Development Centre.

In a small number of countries, independent educational research organisations play important roles. Examples are the Australian Council for Educational Research (ACER) in Melbourne and the New Zealand Council for Educational Research (NZCER) in Wellington. Both are comprehensive in their focus and both were established in the 1930s with grants from the Carnegie Foundation of New York. Both are organised as not-for-profit companies. While they receive considerable government support in the form of grants, contracts and sale of materials, they have been successful is distancing themselves from day to day operations of government. ACER has a total staff of over 170 including some 85 professional and research staff (Australian Council for Educational Research, 2001).

Consulting firms and individual consultants are playing an increasingly important role in a number of countries. Generally they win competitive contracts from government departments and agencies, and from universities, and tend to concentrate in specialised areas relating to management restructuring, evaluation, and information technology.

The scale and focus of educational research activity in any country are directly affected by the total volume of resources devoted to educational research, and where those resources are located. Unfortunately, published data for the Asia-Pacific region are limited and relate mainly to Australia and New Zealand, although it could be assumed that the broad trends identified by OECD would apply to the various OECD countries of the region. Not surprisingly, OECD data indicate that educational research and development (R&D) is only a minor activity in education sectors as a whole. For the early 1990s across six OECD countries including Australia and New Zealand, only between 0.37 per cent and 0.18 per cent of total educational expenditure was allocated to educational R&D while on average educational R&D accounted for only a small proportion of total R&D (Centre for Educational Research and Innovation, 1995, pp. 44–45). Governments typically are the principal source of funding for educational R&D across the Asia-Pacific region, although in a small number of cases private foundations play important supplementary roles. Educational research generally is a highly labour intensive activity, with labour costs often accounting for about 75 per cent of total expenditure. Person years devoted to R&D on education and training in Australia increased from 1117 in 1986–87 to 2933 in 1996–97.

In 1996–97, 92 per cent of this effort was located in higher education institutions (Holbrook et al., 2000, pp. 63–64).

3. DISSEMINATION MECHANISMS

Dissemination of research findings is handled by a variety of mechanisms, including reports and monographs, professional and scholarly journals, conferences, seminars, workshops and short courses. Increasing use is be made of web-based and on-line provision. Other important mechanisms are initial teacher education courses and postgraduate courses in education. The main institutional bases for dissemination are the key providers of educational research, especially education ministries, university faculties of education, and specialist research organisations, but also important are scholarly and professional associations and commercial publishers (of journals, monographs, education textbooks, and educational tests and teaching materials). Frequently, organisations that fund research also provide funds to facilitate dissemination, while in other cases government ministries often publish and distribute project reports from work they undertake.

Apart from this, studies demonstrate that research findings are often disseminated by various informal means, including advice from principals to teachers and from one teacher to another teacher, while in some school systems teachers and principals are being increasingly involved in research from its design to its implementation. One recent Australian study of the links between educational research and the teaching profession reported as follows:

> Indeed, the practitioners in the current study cited high levels of involvement in research-based professional development sessions, involvement in formal research projects, and significant collaboration with research-oriented colleagues, including 'lighthouse' local researchers. (McMeniman et al., 2000, p. 494)

Many educational research providers and funders of research projects now have well developed dissemination mechanisms. This is particularly true of specialist research organisations. ACER, for example, operates ACER Press, which publishes a wide range of research reports, tests and educational materials as well as two scholarly journals and a bibliography of educational research theses, while in China the National Institute of Educational Research publishes a large number of books and monographs and seven professional periodicals, including *Educational Research* and *Educational Abstracts Weekly*. Many education ministries have extensive lists of publications on various educational research topics while more recently some have provided free access to the public to download reports from their web-sites. Some individual university education faculties and government agencies publish their own journals or use other methods of dissemination; for example, in Papua New Guinea, the University of Goroka publishes the *Papua New Guinea Journal of Teacher Education* while in Hong Kong the Chinese University has established an electronic Chinese-oriented educational information publication called Chinese ERIC to serve Chinese communities. In other cases, considerable administrative support is provided to journals from within university faculties and specialist educational research organisations. The Indian *Journal of Educational Planning and Administration*, for example, is edited by a senior member of the National Institute of Educational Planning and Administration in New Delhi.

Professional and scholarly associations now play an increasingly active role in supporting educational research and disseminating findings. Almost all countries of the region have at least one scholarly or academic educational research journal, while those countries where educational research is well developed have a multiplicity of specialist journals. Some of the leading national research journals have been published for many years. The *Indian Educational Review*, for instance, was founded in 1966 and is currently published by the National Council of Educational Research and Training. According to a recent report for the OECD, Australia has 33 professional education associations that publish research-based journals, with 23 of them having been established in the past three decades (Centre for Educational Research and Innovation, 1995, p. 109). Generally, professional and scholarly associations run their own programs of conferences, seminars and workshops which often bring together both researchers and practitioners as well as publishing journals and newsletters. Thus, in Hong Kong, since the mid-1980s the Hong Kong Education Research Association has run annual conferences as well as publishing the *Education Research Journal* and sponsoring other activities. Recent annual conference topics have included beyond compulsory education, equal opportunities for students with disabilities, and educational reform.

Even in single specialist fields, there is an increasing number of separate associations and journals. This is well illustrated by the field of tertiary education studies in Australia. Not only do many researchers belong to broader national bodies such as the Australian Association for Research in Education and the Australian College of Educators, but there are a number of more specialist associations including the Higher Education Research and Development Association of Australasia, the Association of Tertiary Education Managers, the Australian Association for Institutional Research, and the Australian Vocational Education and Training Association. Each has its own journal and newsletters, and runs its own conferences and workshops. While this multiplicity of associations caters well for specialist interests, it tends to lead to increased fragmentation of the educational research community.

A recent trend has been transfer of ownership of many leading educational research journals of the region to leading international publishers. Thus, the Australian founded *Journal of Educational Administration* is now published by MCB University Press, while the *Journal of Higher Education Policy and Management*, *Higher Education Research and Development*, the *Asia Pacific Journal of Teacher Education*, and the *International Journal of Disability*,

Development and Education have all gone to Carfax Publishing in England. Editorial leadership, however, in each case still comes from researchers in Australian universities.

While educational researchers from each country contribute articles to their local journals, many leading researchers contribute significantly to international journals and international conferences, and to cross-country collaborative research projects. Various efforts have sought to assess the contributions of Australian and New Zealand scholars to leading American and international journals. In the late 1980s, White (1988, p. 9) reported on an analysis of author affiliation for all articles published in 1967–69, 1976–78 and 1985–87 in two leading American educational research journals, the *American Educational Research Journal* and the *Journal of Educational Psychology*. He found that Australian contributions started from no articles in 1967–69 for both journals and rose to two and then eight for the *American Educational Research Journal* and to 13 and then 11 for the *Journal of Educational Psychology*. More recently Phelan, Anderson and Bourke (2000) carried out a bibliometric analysis counting publications and citations attributed to Australian researchers in journals listed in the ISI database. Of the 169 educational research journals identified on the ISI database, Australian researchers had published in most of these. Using a composite productivity measure of educational research output taking into account publications, citations, population size, and economic factors, Australia came fifth in rank order internationally after the United States, Israel, New Zealand and Canada (Phelan et al., 2000).

4. UTILISATION AND IMPACT

While educational researchers take considerable pride in their achievements, both practitioners and senior bureaucrats are often highly critical of the contributions of research, especially more academic research conducted in universities. Particular problems mentioned by critics include lack of relevance, low quality, poor or inappropriate dissemination of findings, alienating technical language and concepts, and "problems associated with different 'cultures' including the receptiveness and knowledge of potential users" (Holbrook et al., 2000, p. 42). On the other hand, in some countries of the region with more highly centralised education control, "the relationship between educational research and decision making is close, since a committee under the State education commission is responsible for planning and management of educational research" (Ordonez & Maclean, 1997, p. 651). In such situations, political leaders are often more positive about the value of educational research in guiding policy directions.

This phenomenon of substantial criticism of educational research is by no means unique to the Asia-Pacific region but rather is international in character. Indeed, at their meeting in Paris in November 1990 in addressing the importance of strengthening the knowledge base for educational practice and policy, OECD Ministers of Education commented as follows:

In general, the level of investment in research and development in education and training is far lower than in any other sector of comparable size. The potential of educational research as an integral element of improvement remains largely under-developed, whether at the national, regional or local level. Traditional academic research has its own special part to play. More important still, much research and development needs to be grounded in practice, involving staff and institutions, whether individually or collectively, in a constant process of diagnosis, comparison and analysis. (Quoted in Centre for Educational Research and Innovation, 1995, p. 9)

Researchers have responded to such criticisms in various ways. Some have put greater efforts into school-based action research projects, working directly with teachers and principals, while others have attempted to involve teachers more in educational research conferences and workshops. In other cases, educational research organisations have invested more of their resources in dissemination activities including press releases, summary digests of findings for distribution in schools, and other efforts to build new and ongoing channels of communication between producers and consumers of educational research. Still others have responded by changes in research topics, priorities and methodologies in an attempt to produce work more likely to be regarded as relevant and useful. These efforts have produced useful achievements, particularly leading to better understanding of the processes by which teachers acquire new information and the links between educational research findings and policy making. While both researchers and policy makers in the past often believed in a linear relationship between quantitative research, educational reform planning, and improved practice, recent work has shown that the linear model of research utilisation is fundamentally flawed, and that educational research findings can very seldom be applied directly in practice.

Criticisms of the utility of educational research have led other researchers to increased reflection on their work. Some have urged that educational research should recognise its limitations, particularly its inability to play decisive roles in setting national policy goals. Others have warned that researchers should be more careful in making prescriptions or playing the role of social reformers, pointing out that practitioners, policy makers and researchers frequently work from different conceptual bases (e.g., Anderson & Biddle, 1991).

In the Asia-Pacific region considerable effort over the last decade has gone into various efforts to overcome problems in utilisation identified by policy makers and practitioners. Education ministries and international agencies such as the Asian Development Bank, UNESCO and the OECD have played constructive roles in funding studies and in contributing to the debate on research dissemination and utilisation. Significantly, a number of studies have produced a more positive view of the role of educational research in the region.

One study conducted by senior staff of the UNESCO regional office in Bangkok reported on opinions of high-ranking educational administrators from 19 countries in the Asia Pacific region (Ordonez & Maclean, 1997). This group expressed concern that many educational decisions are made without sufficient attention to research and about the absence of a culture amongst politicians valuing the possible contributions of research to major policy decisions. They saw the potential for research not only to address particular issues but also to identify priorities for government action and felt that the impact of educational research was often greater than commonly recognised. On the other hand, this group recognised that in some Asian countries 'critical enquiry and challenges to basic assumptions are likely to be regarded as generally unacceptable and offensive by senior policy makers' (Ordonez & Maclean, 1997, p. 653) (see *The Impact of Educational Research on Decision Making*).

Another study conducted by the China National Institute for Educational Research for the State Education Commission looked at the use of student grading methods in pilot schools in certain areas. The results of this research were highly positive and the wide dissemination of the results of this research led to the adoption of the reforms in other cities (Nanzhao et al., 1999, pp. 102–103).

However, by far the most substantial studies to evaluate the role of educational research and understand better the problems of research dissemination and utilisation have been conducted in Australia over the past decade. These began with a review in the early 1990s which concluded that, while Australian educational research had many strengths, the enterprise was a fragile resource that needed reorientation and increased support if it was to contribute more effectively to improving Australian education (McGaw et al., 1992). Various recommendations were made for improving dissemination and the application of findings, included closer links between researchers, funding agencies and research users in the process of identifying priorities. The review also pointed to the need for better understanding of the concept of research impact: that is, whether the research is used, what kinds of research are influential, and what forms of interaction are most useful.

In 1997, a major study reported on the influence of research on decision making in policy formulation in the Australian vocational education and training sector. It pointed out that decision makers could use research without the research leading to changes in policy directions and that research findings can have an impact on many different levels in large education systems. On the other hand, it warned that researchers should have modest expectations since policy direction is influenced by a range of other factors, including pragmatic and political considerations (Selby Smith, 1997).

More recently in Australia, the Commonwealth Department of Education, Training and Youth Affairs commissioned four major studies of research impact and utilisation and the findings were published in a single major report entitled, *The Impact of Educational Research* (2000). The first study which examined how teachers make decisions on classroom practice found that teachers generally seek out the sources they believe will build upon their existing knowledge and that this is a very individual process. Teachers rely to different degrees on a variety of sources, including direct research involvement, professional development courses, formal postgraduate studies and professional reading. The aspects of teaching most affected by these sources are strategies to engage students with learning generally as well as with specific content, and ways of meeting the needs of individual learners (McMeniman et al., 2000).

The second study (Figgis et al., 2000) used the work context of educators to map backwards the effects of research on policy and practice. The study involved extensive interviewing, observation and document analysis related to four program and policy areas – improving literacy, gender equity, students at education risk, and the introduction of new information and communications technologies. Educators interviewed attributed their commitment to a specific policy or program to a wide range of motivations. While for teachers the search for information was limited to readily available sources, policy makers and school administrators turned more readily to researchers, talking to them and commissioning research. The gap between researchers and research users is linked by a complex connecting web, with research users being able to access research information through one of the nodes. But for communication to take place, research users must be interested in accessing information, thus pointing to the need for greater efforts in marketing research results.

The third study provided a comprehensive charting of educational research in Australia (Holbrook et al., 2000), with the main focus being university-based research, which accounts for some 90 per cent of educational research in Australia. While the study found a relatively stable pattern of output, at the same time there was evidence of flexibility to take up new issues and respond to new situations. Evidence of links between researchers and schools were clearly evident, with school principals, professional associations and school system administrators all of the view that educational research benefited Australian education. The study highlighted the role of postgraduate students who constitute the largest single group involved in research, with most of them being teachers or educational professionals. Postgraduate students reported that their research had a personal impact on their work, although a smaller proportion considered that it had an impact in a more general way on schools. Even more encouraging were the views of policy makers, who reported growth in the use of research, pointing out that much of the work that had an impact had been commissioned by them. But in comparison, the influence of university research on schools was largely indirect, unstructured and often mediated through individuals.

The fourth study was the bibliometric analysis already referred to (Phelan et al., 2000). One important conclusion was that, of the 104 most cited articles with Australian authors in the periods 1981–87 and 1988–95, a high proportion of articles were about matters of direct interest to practitioners. Some 14 per cent of articles were directly relevant to teaching practice, almost 20 per cent to educational policy making, about 25 per cent to administration and about 15 per cent to methodological or highly theoretical inquiries that would be less easily accessed by practitioners.

Taken together, these four studies produce a more positive and optimistic interpretation than much of the previous work. They point to the inadequacy of conceiving the relationship between researchers and practice as being linear, with the impact being clearly identifiable, direct and measurable. Rather, the picture emerges of a multi-layered interacting process of engagement between researchers and educators, resulting in communication of both instrumental and conceptual knowledge. While much research output is applied in nature and has responded to new challenges driven by funding priorities, possibly even more could be done for research to address educators' problems. The studies document an expectation that policy shifts will be supported by research but in schools the contact with research is likely to be more diffuse and *ad hoc*. Despite this, extensive evidence points out that by both direct and indirect means research has an influence on individual educators, whether their work involves teaching or policy development. Further, teachers need to disseminate more the results of their class-based research efforts.

5. CONCLUSIONS

Since the 1950s there has been an impressive expansion and development of educational research in the countries of the region, but at the same time today educational research capacity and achievement vary greatly. The main providers in rank order are universities and colleges, education ministries and government agencies, and specialist educational research organisations. Governments typically provide the main source of funding with the main mechanisms of dissemination being research reports and monographs, professional and scholarly journals, conferences, seminars and workshops, and informal means. Many educational research providers and funders now have well developed dissemination mechanisms. While educational researchers have made important contributions, they are often criticised for not producing sufficient relevant knowledge valued by educational bureaucracies and key personnel in educational institutions. Particular criticisms relate to lack of relevance of much research, low quality, poor or inappropriate dissemination of findings, alienating technical language and concepts, and different cultural settings of research and policy making and practice.

Recent studies of the use and impact of educational research within the Asia-Pacific region, however, have produced more positive results about the value and utility of educational research, while at the same time pointing to the inadequacy of traditional linear models of research utilisation and consequently the desirability of conceptualising the relationship between key stakeholders in terms of multi-layered interaction processes. Researchers possibly need to be more modest in their expectations concerning possible impact, but at the same time clearly there is value in strategies which build closer links between researchers, policy makers and practitioners, and for research topics to be guided more closely by educators' concerns. The considerable variations in research capacity and expertise across the region point to the value of increased international and regional cooperation in future developments. Hopefully, researchers in each country will be encouraged to reflect increasingly on their research focus and methods, and ways how they might best interact with other educational professionals and policy makers. In this way, further progress might be made towards achieving the potential of educational research to contribute more effectively to policy and practice.

REFERENCES

Asian Development Bank (1996). *Case Studies in Educational Research and Policy*. Manila: Asian Development Bank.

Anderson, D. S., & Biddle, B. J. (Eds.) (1991). *Knowledge for Policy: Improving Education through Research*. London: Falmer Press.

Australian Council for Educational Research (2001). *70th Annual Report 1999–2000*. Melbourne: Australian Council for Educational Research.

Bazargan, A. (2000). Internal evaluation as an approach to revitalise university systems: The case of the Islamic Republic of Iran. *Higher Education Policy*, 13, 173–180.

Burgon, J., Philips, A., & Nana, P. (2000). *Annual Research Report 1999–2000*. Wellington: Research Division, New Zealand Ministry of Education.

Centre for Educational Research and Innovation (1995). *Educational Research and Development: Trends, Issues and Challenges*. Paris: Organisation for Economic Co-operation and Development.

Figgis, J., Zubrich, A., & Alderson, A. (2000). Backtracking practice and policies in tesearch. In *The Impact of Educational Research* (pp. 279–374). Canberra: Higher Education Division, Department of Education, Training and Youth Affairs.

Harman, G. (2000). Research on tertiary education in Australia. In S. Schwarz., & U. Teichler (Eds.), *The Institutional Basis of Higher Education Research: Experiences and Perspectives*. Dordrecht: Kluwer Academic Publishers.

Hayden, M., & Parry, S. (1997). Research on higher education in Australia and New Zealand. In J. Sadak & P. G. Altbach (eds), *Higher Education Research at the Turn of the New Century: Structures, Issues and Trends* (pp. 163–188). Paris: UNESCO Publishing.

Holbrook, A. Ainley, J., Bourke, S., Owen, J., McKenzie, P., Misson, S., & Johnson, T. (2000). Mapping educational research and its impact on Australian schools. In *The Impact of Educational Research* (pp. 15–279). Canberra: Higher Education Division, Department of Education, Training and Youth Affairs.

Lakomski, G. (Ed.) (1991). Beyond paradigms: Coherence and holism in educational research. *International Journal of Educational Research*, 15(6), 501–597.

McGaw, B., Boud, D., Poole, M., Warry, R., & McKenzie, P. (1992). *Educational Research in Australia: Report of a Review Panel*. Canberra: Australian Government Publishing Service.

McMeniman, M., Cumming, J., Wilson, J., Stevenson, J., & Sim, C. (2000). Teacher Knowledge in Action. In *The Impact of Educational Research*. Canberra: Higher Education Division, Department of Education, Training and Youth Affairs.

Nanzhao, Z., Mujue, Z., Jiguang, B., & Tienjun, Z. (1999). The relationship among educational research, information and policy-making: A case study of China. In W. Rokicka (Ed.), *Educational Documentation, Research and Decision-Making: National Case Studies*. Paris: UNESCO International Bureau of Educational Research.

National Institute for Educational Policy Research (2001). website: Http://www.nier.go.jp/homepage/kyoutsuu/index.htm

Ordonez, V., & Maclean, R. (1997). Asia: The impact of educational research on decision making. *Prospects*, 27(4), 645–654.

New Zealand Council for Educational Research (2000). *Annual Report 1998–99*. Wellington: New Zealand Council for Educational Research.

Phelan, T., Anderson, D. S., & Bourke, P. (2000). Educational research in Australia: A bibliometric analysis. In *The Impact of Educational Research* (pp. 573–671). Canberra: Higher Education Division, Department of Education, Training and Youth Affairs.

Selby Smith, C. (1997). *The Relationship Between Research and Decision-Making in Education: An Empirical Investigation.* In *The Impact of Educational Research.* Clayton: Monash University, CEET Working Paper.

The Impact of Educational Research (2000). Canberra: Higher Education Division, Department of Education, Training and Youth Affairs.

Yadav, M. S., & Lakshmi, T. K. S. (1998). Educational research: The Indian scene. *Indian Educational Review, 33*(1), 1–15.

White, R. T. (1988). Indigenes and Exotics: Balance of Trade in Research between Australia and the United States. Melbourne: Paper presented to the annual conference of the Australian Association for Research in Education.

79

Donor Support for Educational Research

WILLIAM A LOXLEY

Asian Development Bank, Manila, The Philippines

1. INTRODUCTION

Education is a major determinant of development everywhere as neither economic nor social change is likely to occur without a literate and healthy population. This is especially true in Asia where educational diversity is widespread. With over three billion people, Asia contains both the world's most populous countries and some of its smallest. Partly because the two most populous nations, China and India, are found in Asia, the region dominates education systems worldwide in terms of number of children and classroom teachers. Table 1 shows the enrolments in the five major regions of the world. When individual nations are aggregated by region and contrasted, it can be seen in Table 1, for example, that 42 per cent of all teachers (25 million) and 50 per cent of all students (655 million) are found in Asia. Each of these students represents a valid reason why it is important for schooling to become an effective and productive means to a good education in Asia (Loxley, 2002).

In a way, the variety of education systems in Asia serve as a natural laboratory for researchers to conduct research in order to discover ways to improve educational efficiency through policy making. Furthermore, the level of economic resources among nations in Asia ranges from some of the highest in the world (Japan, Republic of Korea, Hong Kong and Singapore) to the lowest (Bangladesh, Nepal, Vietnam). Resources spent on salaries for 25 million teachers and non-salary budgets in education amount to many billions of dollars each year. Therefore, research to support policies is needed to ensure efficiencies within the many systems of education in Asia. Without reliable policies, those countries with high populations and low economic resources find it difficult to raise productivity if their people have not invested enough in themselves to take advantage of future opportunities. Likewise, the more advanced countries will find it difficult for the next generation to compete in the global economy if educational policy is ignored. Consequently, the Asian educational landscape suggests that hundreds of millions of students will suffer if good education

Table 1. Worldwide school enrolment, 1997 (in millions)

Region	World population Number	%	Preschool students Number	%	Primary students Number	%	Secondary students Number	%	Tertiary students Number	%	Teachers (all grades) Number	%
East Asia/Pacific	1,800.0	30	33.0	35	214.0	32	113.0	29	17.0	19	17.6	30
South Asia	1,200.0	20	7.0	7	158.0	23	95.0	24	9.5	11	7.4	13
Latin America	700.0	11	15.0	16	85.0	13	29.0	7	9.5	11	6.8	11
Africa/Arab	1,200.0	20	6.0	6	118.0	18	40.0	10	6.0	7	6.2	10
Developed Countries	1,100.0	19	35.0	36	93.0	14	121.0	30	46.0	52	21.0	36
World Total	6,000.0	100	96.0	100	668.0	100	398.0	100	88.0	100	59.0	100

Source: UNESCO (1997).

policies are not provided. In order to ensure good policies, educational research is needed to improve schools, teaching and learning.

An examination of how research is organised in Asia is useful for understanding the role of research in educational decision making. How does the public sector with government-run educational ministries, universities and national institutes interact with private sector institutions such as foundations, corporate businesses and associations? And how do public and private associations in the form of bilateral and multilateral arrangements provide for the flow of support for educational research in Asia? Upon closer inspection the reader will learn that donor funds from outside the region support educational research and development to improve schooling. These funds have in the past and will continue to be a significant and effective means to support educational development budgets throughout Asia. What follows is a typology and detailed description of donor support for educational research in Asia.

2. TYPOLOGY OF DONOR SUPPORT FOR EDUCATIONAL RESEARCH IN ASIA

Historically, the colonial powers from Europe forged educational links with many nations in Asia and from these associations between universities, and among various philosophies of education, local policy and research evolved over time. For example, colonial history invited connections between the Dutch and Indonesia, the French and Vietnam, the British and India, the Spanish and the Philippines. A subsystem of influence also evolved between Malaysia, Brunei, the Middle East and North Africa, on the one hand and Bangladesh, Pakistan and Indonesia on the other hand. These links included ministry to ministry and university to university contacts but relatively little effort was given to research. Research played no critical role in influencing educational policy in the region because resource levels in most countries were too low to sustain a quality research base and because the connection between educational research and development was not fully appreciated. This situation changed, beginning in the 1960s and 1970s, as the Ford and Rockefeller Foundations provided funds to new universities. In Southeast Asia, the Canadian International Development Agency (CIDA) developed a network of institutes that laid the foundations for indigenous efforts to build research networks in the region (Gopinathan and Nielsen, 1988). Through the decades, several tens of thousands of Asian students studied abroad and returned to Asia to provide a critical mass of teachers, researchers and planners in government and universities. In more recent times a wider proliferation of efforts has emerged from outside the public sector both within and outside Asia.

If policy prescription is a key ingredient of educational research, governments either must develop their own capacity or else purchase expertise from the market. For this reason, universities and institutes funded by Asian Governments are commonplace with the public sector schools predominating over private schools. In order to protect academic freedom, the public universities are usually semi-autonomous. Several examples of world class institutions include the University of the Philippines and Chulalongkorn University in Thailand. Gadja Mada University in Yogyakarta, Indonesia and the National Institutes of Education in Hong Kong and Singapore that provide high quality policy research. Often public institutions band together in the form of associations within and across nations in the region. For example, the Asian Network of Training and Research Institutions in Educational Planning (ANTRIEP) that was created in 1995 to provide a forum for collaborative research and training includes 17 member institutions from Bangladesh, China, India, Indonesia, Korea, Malaysia, Nepal, Pakistan, Philippines and Sri Lanka. This institutional network organises annual seminars on educational topics in the region. As such, the Asia region currently has a rich tradition of public sector involvement in education.

In addition, philanthropic associations, foundations, corporations and institutes fund private universities and centres to redirect educational policy making. Selected examples include the International Association for the Evaluation of Educational Achievement (IEA) that includes a dozen Asian member institutes, Bill Gates, Ford, Rockefeller, Van Leer Foundations as well as transnational companies such as IBM and Siemens Corporations that provide funds for education in the region. Finally, governments often band together starting with simple bilateral arrangements to multilateral associations designed to address real needs such as pro-poor growth and cooperation. In Asia, the multilateral arrangements serve to focus attention on ways to address longer-term solutions to perennial problems. The multilateral arrangements can be within the region such as the South East Asian Ministers of Education Office (SEAMEO) or the South Asian Association for Regional Co-operation (SAARC) located in Kathmandu. Other organisations that span countries inside and outside Asia include the Asian Development Bank (ADB), the Islamic Development Bank (IDA), the World Bank and various United Nations (UN) agencies. This general typology of the various bilateral and multilateral public and private institutions is presented in Figure 1 where each type is explained in detail.

2.1. Individual Government Networks

Asian governments have a strong interest in public education with most ministries actively involved in data collection, monitoring and evaluation. They are also the primary recipients of aid to education even though together governments spend billions of dollars on recurrent education budgets each year. Because education is costly given the large teacher payrolls, these ministries are responsible for extremely large budgets used to cover both recurrent and non-salary expenditures. Consequently, government ministries provide the bulk of funds for recurrent budgets but may not be able to meet the development needs of the system. Education ministries may include research and evaluation units but sometimes, separate national education institutes and centres are set up to

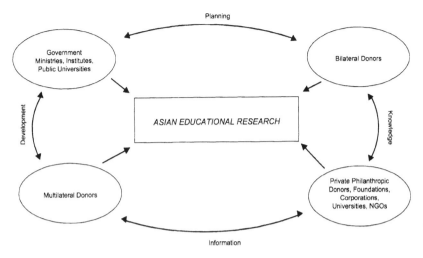

Figure 1. Sources of support for educational research in Asia.

conduct educational research most often associated with policy and planning. Examples of government research institutes include the Office of National Education Commission (ONEC) in Bangkok, the National Institute of Education in Colombo, the China National Institute for Educational Research (CNIER), The Office of Educational and Cultural Research and Development in Indonesia, the Bangladesh Institute of Development Studies (BIDS) and the National Institute of Educational Policy Research in Tokyo. These institutes represent some of the major monitoring and evaluation research agencies in Asia today. In addition, public universities and teachers colleges are commonplace in Asia and most conduct educational research for theses and on contract for Governments. Some national university systems are almost entirely public such as in Sri Lanka, India and Bangladesh, while in other countries, private universities predominate, such as in the Philippines and, to some extent, in Thailand.

Occasionally government ministries and research centres in the region join together to increase capacity through economies of scale. Examples of these associations within the region include South East Asia Ministers of Education Officer (SEAMEO) and the Association of South East Asian Nations (ASEAN). In South Asia, the South Asian Association of Regional Cooperation (SARAC) includes Afghanistan, Bangladesh, Bhutan, India, Maldives, Nepal, Pakistan and Sri Lanka. Each of these countries provides support for a forum to debate and conduct research in education. In all cases, the major role of research support from government agencies is to collect data to monitor policy that addresses very specific issues, which arise from time to time, such as information technology and technical education, mathematics and science, and language learning.

2.2. Bilateral Government Networks

Bilateral arrangements include government to government support for educational research that often conducts regional studies to find solutions to common problems such as measuring quality assurance, teacher education, preschool and special education. Bilateral arrangements within the region are less frequent than those from outside the region as regional governments often lack funds for cooperation with other countries. However, Japan, Australia and New Zealand are three major exceptions because the Ministry of Education in Japan is provided with a budget line item to fund educational programs for ministries of education on other Asian countries. Australia and Japan also provide funds to support Asian education systems through direct foreign assistance. The Japanese International Cooperation Agency (JICA) and the Australian Aid for International Development (AusAID) provide funds for large programs in many countries throughout Asia. To a lesser extent, New Zealand provides extensive support to the many smaller Pacific Island nations. Foreign assistance from individual nations within the Organization of Economic Cooperation and Development (OECD) outside Asia is considerable, with funds earmarked for specific projects often through ministries of foreign affairs disbursed through embassies. There are many examples of bilateral ties often based on commercial and educational interests to attract university students to study abroad or to allow companies to procure equipment abroad.

2.3. Private Sector Philanthropic Networks

The private sector has the most varied arrangements influencing educational research in Asia. This is because the category includes universities, research institutes, corporate sponsored foundations, consortia, non-governmental organisations (NGO) and joint public-private sector enterprises as well. For example, foundations including Van Leer, Ford and Rockefeller have long been involved in Asian education. Private universities in the region that have influenced education include the Agha Khan University in Pakistan, Tata Institute of Social Sciences in Bombay, Bangkok University in Thailand, the new Multi-Media University outside Kuala Lumpur and Tamagawa University in Tokyo. Universities outside the region that have sponsored arrangements with universities in Asia are too numerous to mention. Corporate foundations recently formed such as the Bill Gates, Soros, and MacArthur Foundations have also taken interest in educational research by sponsoring programs in Asia. Usually the research is targeted at specific topics germane to each foundation's mandate and this may include a large component of fellowships and training abroad. Non-governmental organisations serving as consortia include the IEA that promotes educational assessment, the Commonwealth of Learning (COL) as well as the Australian Council for Educational Research (ACER) and the Asia Foundation.

2.4. Multilateral Networks

The multilateral networks revolve around formal international arrangements among governments based on agendas to promote development. In Asia, the Asian Development Bank (ADB), the regional development bank, is perhaps the largest lender for education in the region followed by the World Bank. To a lesser extent, the Islamic Development Bank (IDB) lends for education to the region but this goes mostly to Muslim countries such as Bangladesh, Indonesia and Pakistan. Malaysia and Brunei also provide resources for education in the region. In addition to the development banks, other multilateral networks include the United Nations networks such as UNDP, UNICEF, UNESCO and IIEP. Often, the UN family of service providers to education operated from Bangkok, Thailand and provides funds for conferences, studies, and training. While the sums are small compared to the development banks, nevertheless, the research is valuable because it is often innovative and conducted on a pilot basis to provide knowledge.

In Asia, education ministries are highly centralised and tasked with carrying out policy and planning for primary and secondary education. Only recently have they developed links between policy making and research by undertaking research through national institutes and public universities. While the research priorities have varied from decade to decade, educational research remains committed to classroom learning, teacher training, aspects of curriculum development, school management including decentralisation and improving learning materials. More recently, the donors have given priority to crosscutting issues of equity especially for females, minorities and the rural poor.

3. ANALYSIS OF BILATERAL LENDING TO EDUCATION

Perhaps OECD or the European Commission (EC) has prepared statistics on member contributions to education in Asian Countries on a bilateral basis, but the money, while little reported, is considerable and amounts to tens of millions of dollars annually. These funds are distributed through embassies or development aid offices within embassies under foreign assistance programs found in major capitals of the region. OECD countries that represent the 26 wealthiest nations, are a main source of outside financial assistance to Asian nations among bilateral nations including many European Union (EU) members. Within Asia, Japan, New Zealand and Australia (three OECD countries) are major bilateral donors. Each bilateral donor prepares a lending profile jointly with its Government to fund projects each year. In education, funds typically go for overseas training, equipment and small-scale development projects aimed at a particular issue. These portfolios can shift dramatically over a short time. Examples of topics to support education include Information and Communications Technology (ICT) for learning, provision of curriculum, management and administration, extensive training programs in all areas of instruction.

Typically, bilateral agencies are eager to support educational programs including cross-national training, conferences and studies, surveys and policy dialogue. The motivation is to support crosscutting issues such as children's rights, gender equity and poverty reduction. While general support for international growth and development come through trade and treaties, the bilateral donors are eager to assist nations fill gaps in research and training support to raise global standards and seek common ground for discussions and action. Bilateral donors are helpful in funding overseas fellowships, local training, conferences and collaboration in conducting national surveys and research studies. Funding amounts to tens of millions of dollars spent by each donor in the region with greater amounts spent on large and poor countries. The monies are channelled through embassies and the amounts fluctuate from year to year depending on foreign assistance priorities and specific institutions sponsored. Some governments have banded together to form the Nordic Development Fund (NDF) and the European Commission (EC) to provide development funds to Asia in addition to the bilateral funding from the individual member country.

In order to understand how the bilateral donors provide aid to education in Asia, it is necessary to consider how the typical bilateral lending operates. In the home capital, the government apportions funds for overall grants in aid. Larger amounts are provided under favourable loan agreements. Typically, the donor country prioritises the countries in the region and the sector support based on past support and ongoing programs. This is often formulated in league with other donor agencies to avoid overlap and give the strongest position to the donor with the most experience and expertise in the area concerned. In the case of education, funds are often supported directly to the recipient ministry, university or non-governmental organisation. In some cases, the aid is tied and the provider selects the consultants and procurement under the project. Most countries operate in this manner given historical precedent and convenience of administration. The larger bilateral donors listed below generally follow the practices sketched above.

The Japanese Bank for International Cooperation (JBIC) along with the Japan International Cooperation Agency (JICA) provide low cost loans and grants to education departments throughout Asia. These are in addition to bilateral programs, sponsored by the Japanese National Ministry of Education through JICA and through the National Institute of Educational Policy Research (NIER) in Tokyo.

The Australian Aid for International Development (AusAID) is active in the region in education. AusAID draws extensively from its own staff and Australian universities to serve most education systems in Asian countries.

The British Department for International Development (DFID) along with the British Council are very active in the Asia region providing study grants and conducting studies of education.

The French Government provides educational support to the region through the *Agence Francaise de Development* (AFD) and for education and cultural activities through the *Alliance Francais* especially in India, Pakistan, the Philippines, Malaysia, Indo-China and the South Pacific.

The German Government provides support through the *Kreditanstalt fur Wiederaufbau (FfW)* and the German Technical Cooperation (GTZ) as well as through the education and culture activities of the Goethe Institute. Special emphasis is given to vocational and technical education in the Asia region.

The Canadian International Development Agency (CIDA) has provided assistance to educational institutions in the region for 40 years and is especially known for promoting research cooperation in Southeast Asia in the 1980s. In the early 2000s, CIDA re-examined its global strategy that continued to stress involvement in Asia.

The United States Aid for International Development (USAID) has provided bilateral funding for education to numerous countries in Asia including innovative programs in interactive radio instruction in Pakistan and Papua New Guinea. In Indonesia alone, USAID has sent a minimum of 15,000 Indonesians abroad to the United States for training. Each of these graduates can contribute to national development after returning home.

4. ANALYSIS OF MULTILATERAL LENDING TO EDUCATION

The multilateral donors are the major international agencies consisting of numerous governments organised to address specific problems. The major donors discussed below include the multilateral donor banks such as the Asian Development Bank (ADB), Islamic Development Bank (IDB) and the World Bank that provide low cost loans to assist countries to support education. In addition, there exists the family of United Nations Agencies mandated to support various aspects of education. The regional office for the UN is located in Bangkok, Thailand. Some of these UN agencies, including the United Nations Education and Scientific Cooperation Organization (UNESCO), provide research and training support throughout Asia. The United Nations International Children's Emergency Fund (UNICEF) is committed to supporting children's rights. The International Institute of Education Planning (IIEP) in Paris is a major training and research centre for conducting studies around the world and in the Asia region. The United Nations Development Fund (UNDP) and the International Labor Organization (ILO) are to some extent oriented to higher levels of education and on-the-job training. Each of the above institutions is making a major contribution to educational research in Asia. Their contribution and impact are discussed below.

Established in 1965, the ADB is the premier development bank in Asia (ADB, 2001). It is located in Manila, Philippines and serves the Pacific Island nations, Southeast Asia, North Asia, South Asia and the newly emerging Central Asian republics of the former Soviet Union. Through a wide network of national offices, the ADB provides about US$6.0 billion in loans annually for all sectors in most countries through the approval of about 80 distinct projects each year. About six per cent of these funds go for education and of that perhaps about five per cent or US$18 million goes for educational research and evaluation mostly through mandated analyses required to assess project impact. The ADB's overriding commitment is to poverty alleviation in the region but this can be accomplished by targeting cross-cutting issues such as gender, environment, human resource development and many other highly focused social issues such as child labour, street children, nutrition and teen pregnancy. In addition to the education loans enacted annually which include surveys and research studies mandated as a condition of the loan, the ADB provides grant funds distributed to firms, institutions, NGOs and individuals on a competitive basis to undertake national and regional studies.

The technical assistance concept is not new to ADB. Since its inception more than 35 years ago, over 4,500 technical assistance studies in all development sectors have been implemented at a cost of US$1.8 billion. The education share was about seven per cent totalling US$125 million. This technical assistance went for conferences, survey studies, research and training. The research portion directed at studies and surveys was about ten per cent of the education total, or US$12 million. Recent examples of technical assistance provided under project loans or separately include monitoring and evaluating the social protection sector development program, research studies of the scholarship programs and planning and evaluating street children programs in Indonesia. In China, technical assistance strengthened the Department of Ethnic Minority Education and provided a series of research studies on ethnic minority education and training. Technical assistance studies and conferences focus on evaluating policy and outcomes of key crosscutting issues affecting education such as governance, poverty alleviation and gender equity (ADB, 1999). When technical assistance is included under loans, the funds belong to governments and they contract consultants, studies and conferences. When technical assistance is provided by the ADB, each assistance is opened to firms or individuals to compete. Winning proposals are rated on content but also heavily on the consultants proposed.

In addition to technical assistance provided to individual countries either through loans or separate grants, research studies are also conducted on a regional basis. Regional technical assistance in the past has been provided on many issues facing Asia. About 900 regional technical assistance studies have been carried out for a total of US$340 million of which education represented about six per cent or US$20 million.

For example, distance education for primary teacher training was examined in a number of countries and publications provided. Typical regional studies and workshops cover financial support for regional institutions to undertake education policy. Major studies included primary school dropout prevention in South Asia (ADB, 1997). In that study conducted in 1995, longitudinal data were collected on primary school students in Bangladesh, Bhutan, Nepal and Pakistan and analyses carried out to understand better the process of school retention in primary schools throughout South Asia. The study findings provided support for designing educational investment loans in the region. The ADB also funds international conferences like the Education For All Conferences especially the regional meeting in Bangkok, Thailand leading up to the international meeting held in Dakar, Senegal in April 2000. Recent initiatives to support education in the Mekong River basin has allowed regional governments in China, Cambodia, Laos, Myanmar, Thailand and Vietnam to explore issues common to the subregion. In general, ADB sponsored educational research is aimed at addressing issues of poverty, gender disparity, labour market problems and rural development. Major support for monitoring and evaluation is designed to strengthen educational management information systems that track trends in the region (ADB, 2000).

A semiautonomous unit of the ADB is the Asian Development Bank Institute located in Tokyo. The ADBI undertakes research studies to investigate specific issues pertinent to the Asia region. In education, the ADBI has previously investigated ways to improve school learning and public-private partnerships. The ADBI conducts workshops and conferences whose participants are selected from public and private educational institutes in Asia.

The Islamic Development Bank (IsDB) commenced operations in 1975 with the stated purpose of fostering economic development and social progress of member countries and Muslim communities in non-member countries. Programs generally extend to health and education for Muslim communities in non-member countries. Interestingly, when IsDB purchases assets under a project, it sells them to the beneficiaries at a higher premium on delivery. In education, IsDB is most often concerned with civil works and procurement of equipment, but consultants are often contracted to conduct studies.

The World Bank is the premier development bank in the world established after the World War II and serving the entire globe (World Bank, 2001). Over the past ten years, World Bank lending has averaged about US$2.0 billion each year of which 40 per cent went to East and South Asia and half of that for basic education. It lends on average, about US$800 million for education in Asia, but when educational lending in the form of soft loans for China and India are subtracted then education lending is comparable to the US$360 million annual lending of ADB for education in the region. However, China and India do not borrow from ADB for social sectors because they do not qualify for soft loans from ADB. The World Bank functions in a similar way to ADB as in fact all development banks lend to governments and to a lesser degree to private entities with the government acting as a guarantor. Consequently, the World Bank similarly lends for projects in education designed to improve equity, access, quality and efficiency. Most projects contain training and research grants targeted at beneficiaries.

The World Bank also has the in-house capacity to conduct its own research in education especially through evaluation of projects designed to address implementation problems as well as theoretical underpinnings of development theory. The World Bank carries out extensive policy research in its Policy Research Departments and makes these high quality reports available to the public for a small cost. The cross-national studies are extremely useful because often the World Bank is in a position to collect materials and undertake survey studies that would otherwise be difficult to obtain through other agencies. These studies benefit Asia especially when they pertain to Asian countries. In addition, the Educational Development Institute (EDI) in Washington supports the regional offices around the world to train staff and expand the human resource development in particular countries where gaps arise in the academic or human resource base needed at any given time. The EDI has slowly evolved into the premier research and training institute for development world wide where most Bank research is conducted in-house in a number of departments. The World Bank provides global information generally free of cost and this is very effective for the world community. The World Bank provides professional development and advisory services through global information in thematic areas of education including early childhood, teacher education, adult education outreach, educational technologies and educational management reform.

The World Bank also undertakes major research endeavours when preparing its international reports. For example, the World Development Report for 2000 was devoted to poverty alleviation. As part of this activity, the Voices of the Poor Project was launched to improve the understanding of poverty seen through the eyes of the poor. The World Bank has also embarked on innovative educational programs through its World Links for Development Program of the World Bank Institute designed to link schools of the world to an on-line internet system so students can learn about students and schools in other lands. This program has proved to be extremely innovative and relevant for transferring knowledge across borders including those in Asia (World Bank, 2001).

The European Union (EU) was established in the late 1940s but only in the 1990s has it expanded greatly funding for international development under the European Commission (EC). In Asia, the EC combines the funds of its member countries and together they provide budgetary support for educational interventions. These funds can be tapped for consultants, conferences, procurement and a number of educational research studies in all countries in the Asia region (European Commission, 2001).

The United Nations system of institutions that serve the Asia region provides ongoing departmental programs annually to member countries and sometimes these endeavours involve co-financing with the multilateral banks and other bilateral organisations. The UN agencies charged with various aspects of education not only collect information but also provide small grants and innovative programs targeted specifically at particular issues facing member states. Some of these agencies and their programs are now described.

The United Nations Educational, Scientific and Cultural Organization (UNESCO) has offices in Bangkok, Thailand. The organisation is committed to providing training, conferences and conducting research with regional centres on educational matters especially those related to science and culture.

The International Institute of Educational Planning (IEEP) with offices in Paris serves UNESCO as a training, conference and planning agency. IIEP has recently carried out school surveys in the Asia region and helps to train staff from various educational institutes in areas of planning and analysis.

The United Nations Children's Fund (UNICEF) has regional offices in Bangkok and heavily leverages its programs with other bilateral agencies through joint activities and through joint consultations. The agency is well known for its emphasis on children's rights and works closely with NGOs and with governments, for example, to improve education through feeding programs and policies to reduce child labour.

The United Nations Development Program in Asia aims to support all sectors and countries in their development efforts. Its budget provides the largest UN agency funding in the region. With respect to education, UNDP supports human resource development programs, training conferences and consultations.

5. CONCLUSION AND SUMMARY

Education is an enormous enterprise in Asia with roughly half of all students in the world attending schools in the region and 43 per cent of all teachers worldwide are in Asian classrooms. Governments and private organisations in the region clearly recognise the need for good policy decisions backed by solid educational research. As such, educational research is rapidly advancing in Asia creating sufficient critical mass to sustain future growth in education. Local donor funding within the region such as from Japan and Australia is slowly supplanting donor funding for education from outside the region. Several tens of thousands of university graduates have been trained abroad over the past 30 years under various donor grant and scholarship programs but today there are many Asian universities producing graduates in educational research. While aggregate data are hard to come by, trends have been noted among donors showing that these programs have declined slightly to be replaced by more private sector done linkages between multinationals, corporations and foundations. The remaining donor programs tend to be more targeted at poorer segments of the population. It is also true that local multilateral donor funding within the region continues to support education through targeting specifically aimed at the disadvantaged.

Donor support for educational research in the region has culminated in a unique mix of public and private, bilateral and multilateral assistance in the form of grants and loans both local and foreign. While traditional multilateral efforts by ADB, IDB, World Bank and the UN agencies continue to support education, important new sources of funding have arisen from associations of government agencies as well as private corporations and foundations. Areas of expansion also are found in local associations of universities such as ATRIEP as well as collaboration with IEA in school assessment within and across countries (Plomp & Loxley, 1991).

Areas of support have changed over the decades from human development to capacity building in management and evaluation for policy making and monitoring. The fine-tuning of donor support for education will continue to reallocate scarce funding to special topics such as information technology, privatization and participation by NGOs and community organisations as well as decentralised approaches to educational administration and management. In each case, educational research will continue to play an important role, and donor funding will be central to these efforts.

REFERENCES

Asian Development Bank (1997). *Combating Primary School Dropout in South Asia.* Manila: ADB.
Asian Development Bank (1999). *The Quality of Life in Rural Asia.* Manila: ADB.
Asian Development Bank (2000). *Education Policy in Asia.* Manila: ADB.
Asian Development Bank (2001). http://www.adb.org
European Commission (2001). http://www.europa.eu.int
Gopinathan, S., & Nielsen, H. D. (Eds.) (1988). *Educational Research Environments in Southeast Asia.* Singapore: Chopmen Publishers.
Loxley, W. (in press). The role of education in the Asia region. In C. de M Castro & A. Verdisco (Eds.), *Making Education Work: Latin American Ideas and Asian Results.* Tokyo: Inter-American Development Bank.
Plomp, T. J., & Loxley, W. (1991). IEA and the quality of education in developing countries. In P. Vedder (Ed.), *Measuring the Quality of Education.* Amsterdam: Swets and Zeitlinger.
UNESCO (1997). *Statistical Yearbook.* Paris: UNESCO.
World Bank (2001). *The World Program.* Washington, DC: Economic Development Institute. http://www.worldbank.org/worldlinks
World Bank. http://www.worldbank.org/world

SECTION 8:

TOWARDS THE FUTURE

Section Editor – John P. Keeves

80

Educational Research for Educational Reform

JOHN P. KEEVES
Flinders University Institute of International Education, Australia

RUNG KAEW DANG
National Education Commission, Bangkok, Thailand

1. INTRODUCTION

The fields of policy-oriented research in education (Nisbet, 1997), policy analysis (Trow, 1997), and educational research and policy making (Husén, 1997) have been reviewed by many scholars. Moreover, it is not uncommon for educational research institutes to have sections of their organisations given over to policy research studies (for example, The Australian Council for Educational Research). While not all policy-oriented research in education is directed towards reform, since some studies serve a legitimatory function (Keeves, 1997) seeking to maintain and consolidate existing policy, much research in education is oriented towards change and the making of new policy. Consequently, Postlethwaite (see *Educational Research and Educational Policy-Making in Asian and Pacific Countries*) argues strongly for the involvement of policy makers, commonly ministers of education in participating countries, in the planning and review of major cross-national educational research studies, in order to facilitate the use of the findings from such studies in the making of policy. Nevertheless, Husén has drawn attention to the pressing need for investigation into how new policy is made in the field of education and how that policy is implemented in practice. In conversation, Tjeldvoll asked Husén the question: "What would be your dream research project?" To which Husén replied:

> It would be a comparative study of education reforms, on the extent to which what I call the 'strategic principles' have been followed. I have recently spelled out these principles in various contexts, trying to answer the question to what extent they apply to education change occurring within the framework of change in socioeconomic context. How much time does it take to prepare, draw up the blueprint, get it through the political process, and

implement it in the classrooms. Further, it is of great interest to get more insights about the role of participation of those who are affected, parents, local politicians, and so forth. Then there is the cost connected with these processes. The historical aspect of the changes over time is also of interest. This, I think, would be a big, important, and challenging project. (Tjeldvoll, 2000, p. 170)

Husén (1994) had previously considered the problems facing schools and educational institutions and had referred to the "rigidity of the system in the midst of a changing society" (p. 3) that had increased because of the increase in power of the different interest groups that were operating within education systems. Although this made it more difficult than before to introduce reforms, there were certain rules associated with reform, involving "time, participation, resources, political stability, and consensus" (Husén, 1994, p. 3).

Clearly, too little research and theorising has been undertaken into the processes by which policy-making and change occurs, and too little is known about how the theorising that has been done relates to policy-making and reform in education. As a consequence, the policy-oriented research that is undertaken is commonly under-valued and remains unused or not taken into consideration when reform is being planned, when change is being introduced, and when new policies are being made. This article seeks to consider theoretical perspectives for the study of change and reform in education and to examine briefly examples of reform in countries within the Asia-Pacific region that have been derived from research, and have been or are being introduced into the education systems of those countries.

2. TOWARDS A THEORY OF SOCIAL ACTION

The operation of societal processes is highly complex and as a consequence there has, in the past, been a tendency to construct a simple dualism between, for example, the individual and the society, or the subject (people) and the object (social structure), where a more complex duality is involved. This use of a dualism has led to an over-emphasis on an analysis of function and to ignore the processes by which human beings are active as human agents operating within society. These human agents are motivated and driven by ideas to implement reform or to restrict and prevent change.

There are many theoretical approaches to the study of the processes operating in societies, but one approach advanced by Giddens (1984), a British sociologist, provides an excellent framework from which to examine social forces. This approach is integrative in nature, in so far as it links together many earlier theoretical perspectives. In *The Constitution of Society* (Gidden's, 1984) introduces two extremely important social processes, namely, the 'double hermeneutic process' and 'structuration theory'.

2.1. The Double Hermeneutic Process

The hermeneutic process is well known. It involves the influence of the context within which new ideas and discoveries are advanced to provide greater understanding of the world in which human beings live, work and play. The process is named after Hermes, the messenger of the Gods in classical Western mythology, who brought new ideas and knowledge to humankind. Giddens (1984) argues that the new ideas and relationships, which are advanced by social and natural scientists change the ways in which people think about their world. These new concepts and generalisations subsequently change the understanding of social processes, and thus alter the operation of these processes in ways that are guided by the knowledge and explanations that human agents hold concerning those situations in which they are living. This return of new ideas and generalisations to change the nature and conditions in a society is referred to by Giddens as a 'double hermeneutic' process.

Education has a key role in the operation of both the hermeneutic and double hermeneutic processes. Not only does education provide the skills and procedures within which new knowledge and generalisations are advanced, but it also provides the mechanisms by which those new ideas and understandings are spread throughout society, and thus changes the ways in which people think about the world in which they live (see *Educational Research: Nature, Impact, Needs and Priorities*). These ideas of Giddens are not completely new in the field of education since they are incorporated in some of Weiss' (1979) models of research utilisation. However, in a democratic society, the dissemination of new ideas and understandings must spread beyond the policy makers to a wider based group of people who think about education and act through democratic processes to introduce change and reform.

2.2. Structuration Theory

Giddens (1984) has also advanced a set of concepts that are used to explain how human agents reproduce or transform the processes that operate within a society. Education is one of the key social processes that is acquiring increasing prominence in societies in the Asia-Pacific region as schooling expands to include greater proportions of an age-cohort engaged in education at the primary, secondary and tertiary levels and continues on in the form of lifelong and recurrent education and training. Giddens rejects the exclusive use of such approaches as (a) functionalism, in which social phenomena are analysed in terms of the needs that social structures encounter; and (b) evolutionism, in which there is a specified series of stages through which societies pass as they move towards modernity. These approaches have their place, as do many other approaches in the examination of social processes. However, Giddens (1984) provides a unifying framework within which many of the different understandings of social processes advanced during the twentieth century can be incorporated. This integrative view is a great strength of Giddens' work. Space does not permit the further elaboration of Giddens' theory of structuration. However, Turner

(1986, pp. 456–478) provides a relatively concise and clear account of Giddens' ideas. Within this account of social processes, there are places for research that could be conducted under different disciplinary perspectives and different research traditions to provide input to clarify the particular processes that are operating in an educational situation. In addition, such research could also provide evidence that would inform the development of new policy or would recommend the adoption of one practice rather than another in the process of reform.

2.3. Structuration and Policy Research

A recent study in Australia by Kenny (2000) has examined the relevance of Giddens' ideas to a problem situation in which initially integration and subsequently inclusion, had become accepted as the appropriate approaches for the education of young children with disabilities in contrast to the approach of segregation that had been exclusively practised 20 years earlier. The changes that had occurred in the making of policy and the proposals for practice had their origins in two different research and disciplinary traditions. As a consequence, very considerable tension had developed both in the administration and implementation of the successive changes that were introduced. The conflicts and contradictions that emerged could not be readily resolved because they were derived from two different research and scholarly perspectives. One perspective stemmed from the child study movement that had its origins in the 1880s in the work in the United States of Hall and in England of Sully, who was concerned with children's language and imagination (De Landsheere, 1997, p. 8). The second perspective derived from medical research and the study of disabilities that emerged more recently, also in the United States and England. The first tradition expected children to be left free to play and grow in a garden-like environment. The other perspective expected children to be supported in a clinical or semi-clinical fashion with planned developmental exercises. With limited resources, it was perhaps not surprising that such tensions and conflicts would develop, since there were large gaps in the provision of services.

Kenny's (2000) study described the complexities of the social processes that operated, and from interviews with key agents in the introduction of change showed how the different traditions led to different expectations and the advancement of conflicting policies and practices. There was no simple solution to the problems that emerged. The origins of the problems were deeply ingrained in teacher education programs, both in-service and pre-service, in the limited financial resources available, and in the lack of stability and leadership in the school system at the times when successive changes to policy and practice were proposed. There would appear to have been a failure to recognise the complexity of the reform processes and a failure to allow sufficient time in the planning of successive changes, as different influential administrators and policy makers took charge at different stages over the time when the change processes were operating. The principles of functionalism and evolution are too simplistic to explain the complex net of processes that operated in these situations. Giddens' theory of structuration, as portrayed in this work by Kenny serves to provide an understanding of the forces involved in introducing change and reform.

3. EXAMPLES OF EDUCATIONAL REFORM

In the sections that follow, examples of educational reform are drawn from different systems in the Asia-Pacific region. These examples seek to consider (a) the extent of dependence of the reform on research; (b) the recognition of the complexity of the reform process in laying down foundations for change; (c) the occurrence of tensions that arose in the introduction of reform; (d) the success of the reform; and (e) the long term maintenance of the processes of reform. It is clearly necessary to recognise that because of the complexity of the social processes involved in education, a long-term perspective is required. Consequently, some examples that are discussed below, may not have been in operation for a long enough period for the success of the reform to be viewed in an appropriate perspective.

3.1. *Indonesia: National Assessment of Education Project*

In the late 1960s the Indonesian Government foresaw that within five years it would have considerably more money to spend on the provision of education within the country. The then Minister of Education sought an evaluation of the existing educational services across Indonesia and how the nation might effectively spend its new-found wealth to improve the provision of education in the future. During the previous two decades, since the establishment of the Indonesian nation, there had been an extraordinarily rapid growth of schools and universities. Under these circumstances, there had also probably been a decline in the standard of education provided. The Minister of Education did not seek a detailed plan, or highly specific recommendations for the future, but rather a broad strategy that would guide development over the coming decades. This required an investigation into the existing education system, conducted with a view towards the future rather than the past. While the study was referred to as an 'assessment project,' it would seem to be better described as a 'prospective evaluation' or 'prospective accountability study' that was conducted by Beeby (1979) from New Zealand and was formulated at three levels. The level 1 report was formed from a series of case studies and small investigations, with no attempt being made at an integration of the findings from other parts of the study. At level 2, each team or task force reporting at level 1 completed the writing of a report in which it integrated the findings of other teams and task forces. These level 2 reports were checked in workshops against the judgments of men and women who through long experience in the school system in different branches, were very familiar with the system and its strengths and weaknesses. The level 3 report brought together the findings from the level 2 reports and was presented in two stages, one concerned with primary education and the other with secondary education.

In preparing a report for wider distribution seven years after the completion of the study, Beeby (1979) structured his book in three parts. Part 1 consisted of an introductory chapter describing the country of Indonesia and its schools. Part 2 was a more detailed description of the school system in 1970–72, and took a retrospective view. Part 3 took a more prospective view setting the problems of the system in a wider political and social context and advanced strategies for the resolution of these problems. This study has clearly guided developments in education in Indonesia for much of the past three decades. The report considered the broad areas of (a) buildings, equipment, books, (b) teaching and teachers, (c) leadership and supervision, (d) examinations, (e) teacher training, (f) the curriculum, (g) student flow, (h) structure of the school system, and (i) administrative structures.

This study by Beeby (1979) examined all aspects of the Indonesian education system including the administrative structure, leadership and supervision at the system and subsystem levels, and the provision of buildings, equipment and books. These were necessary for a complete investigation that would help to reshape education in Indonesia.

3.2. India: The Indian Education Commission (1964–1966)

The Indian Education Commission was set up in 1964 and reported in 1966. In contrast to the Indonesian study conducted by Beeby (1979) it prepared a report (India, Ministry of Education and Social Welfare, 1966) that was required to make specific recommendations for the conduct of education in India. After consultations with the State Governments and with the approval of the parliament, the Indian Government announced a national policy for education in 1968. Included in the reforms were (a) a nationally accepted structure of education, of $10+2+3$ years; (b) a response to policies advanced by Mahatma Gandhi for a curriculum that differentiated between the needs of different groups in Indian society in which learning was organised around productive manual work with an increased emphasis on work experience, that was closely related to the lives of the people; (c) a continued effort to expand educational opportunity; and (d) the cultivation of moral and social values.

Approximately 20 years later, in 1985, the Indian Government reviewed the existing educational situation and decided to introduce new educational policies. The 1986 policy envisaged subsequent reviews taking place every five years. A country with a rapidly growing population and as large as India, faces many challenges and a regular and planned program of reform is clearly required to meet the problems raised by social change and globalisation.

3.3. The Australian Schools Commission

In the decades following the World War II, Australia undertook an extended and planned program of immigration that at its peaks exceeded in proportional terms the peaks of the immigration programs in the United States of the late nineteenth and early twentieth centuries. This was coupled with a high fertility rate that arose, in part, from curtailment during the great depression of the 1930s and the years of war during the early 1940s. It also arose from the high level of affluence in Australia during the 1950s. However, it was not until the mid-1960s when the first wave of students was completing school that the strains imposed on the school systems of the Australian States became apparent. Research required for an international study showed that information was not available to make accurate estimates of the retention rates and participation rates at successive grade levels of schooling across Australia that were changing rapidly due to "staying longer at school" (Radford, 1966). This research study led subsequently to the collection of the necessary data, and drew attention to the need for a strong office of education for the national planning of educational services. In 1968, under the auspices of the Australian National Advisory Committee for UNESCO, a highly significant National Seminar on Educational Planning was held. This seminar was planned and reported by the leading educational researchers in Australia and provided a review of existing research that was relevant to educational planning (Bassett, 1970). Moreover, a summary statement of this report was published under the title *National Survey of Educational Needs* (Australian Education Council, 1970) that had wide distribution. In 1972, an Interim Committee of the Australian Schools Commission was established that reviewed the state of affairs in the schools across Australia, with respect to the limited and equitable distribution of resources for education (Karmel, 1973).

The Committee proposed a range of programs in seven areas: (a) General Recurrant Resources, (b) General Buildings, (c) Primary and Secondary School Libraries, (d) Disadvantaged Schools, (e) Special Education, (f) Teacher Development, and (g) Innovation. The proposals of the Interim Committee were accepted by the Australian Government and a very large sum of money was allocated in the first instance to establish a permanent Schools Commission in order to implement the programs that covered the major recognised areas of need. However, the Commission encounted several problems in the implementation of its programs. First, it rode over the domains of the Australian States, that had statutory responsibility for education, running counter to the planned development of educational services in each of the Australian States. Second, it sought to influence and control the curriculum of the schools and failed in its attempts, with an independent statutory authority, the Curriculum Development Centre being set by the Australian Government in collaboration with the States. Third, its Innovations Program ignored the emerging concern for the achievement outcomes of education, while its Disadvantaged Schools Program argued for the attainment of equality of achievement outcomes between different social groups, largely ignoring the growing body of research into both innovation and factors influencing educational outcomes. Its programs also, at least initially, largely ignored the needs of students with specific learning difficulties and a further inquiry was set up to examine these problems (Cadman, 1976). Moreover, its Teacher Development program set out to replace existing activities providing for the inservice education of teachers.

There is little doubt that the Australian Schools Commission which was formed had a major impact on the renewal of Australian education with the large amounts of money injected through its General Recurrant Resources and General Buildings Programs. Unfortunately, however, it largely ignored the need for continuity in planning for the provision of educational services, as well as the need for research and the monitoring of change in the social and economic context of education. By the time the Commissison was initially established, the birth and fertility rates in Australia had started to fall dramatically. Furthermore, through the politicisation of education, expectations had been set up that could not be fulfilled, and the Commission clashed with the Teachers Unions, which sought indirectly to control its deliberations and progams. After seven years of operation, both the Schools Commission's and the Curriculum Development Centre's activities were scaled down, and the Commission was formally closed seven years later, while the Curriculum Development Corporation has been retained with largely a service and commercial role. It is clear, from this experience that not only is research required before reforms are considered, but also ongoing research, monitoring and independent evaluation, with open debate of the findings are necessary if the reforms are to be sustained and long term planning is to be maintained. The short term introduction of reform is not enough. Problems arise from the limited terms of office of ministers of education and political parties and the failure of senior educational administrators to be adequately trained in the review of evidence collected from research, monitoring and evaluation studies.

3.4. Lao PDR

Lao PDR ranks as one of the smallest and poorest countries in Asia. It has a population of approximately five million people with 44 per cent of the population under the age of 15 years. The people of Lao PDR are very diverse in ethnicity and language and 85 per cent live in rural and mountainous areas. Life expectancy in Lao of 57 years is one of the lowest in the world, and while the fertility rate is 6.7, the annual population growth rate has been reduced to 2.4 per cent. The country currently has estimated adult literacy rates of 75 per cent for men and below 50 per cent for women, and clearly has immense problems in building a strong education system. The challenge for its government is to fight poverty through education, and through the participation of the people in national development with financial support being obtained through foreign investment (Lao PDR, 2000b).

The Ministry of Education, at the end of the twentieth century sought to construct a strategic vision for education in Lao PDR for the 20 year period to the year 2020. The report that was prepared (Lao PDR, Ministry of Education, 2000b) provided a brief overview of socio-economic development as well as the regional economic situation that was based on national statistics and estimates made by The World Bank. From this evidence, the main issues for education were identified that included the need to raise the quality and relevance of education, together with the need to improve the planning and management of educational services. In addition, policy recommendations were advanced that focused on equitable access, quality, relevance and management, as well as strategies to achieve these goals with specific targets set for the year 2005 and with the required activities and outcomes clearly stated. Nevertheless, the major question for the development of educational services in Lao PDR involved the financing of education. The budget allocation for education in 1997-98 of 1.0 per cent of Gross Domestic Product (GDP) would appear very low, since this constituted only 10.1 per cent of the national budget. Nevertheless, the education budgets grew rapidly during the 1990s, but declined as proportions of GDP, of government spending, and domestic recurrent spending. It was noteworthy that the expenditure over the period on the international component would appear to have increased markedly. However, it was clear that the development of education within Lao PDR required strong financial support from the international banks and donor agencies.

This strategic vision for education up to the year 2020 became a key document for the Government Report to the Seventh Round Table Meeting in Geneva (Lao PDR, 2000a) where financial assistance was sought from overseas sources. Education is central to the alleviation of poverty, and the decentralisation of administration to the provinces, districts and villages. The roles and functions of research in this context involve the collection and analysis of statistical information on all aspects of educational participation and expenditure as well as the monitoring and examination of change over time. In addition, since the outcomes of the program of development are expressed in specific terms, evaluation of the program during the period under review requires the examination of both the attainment of the specified outcomes and the appropriateness of the activities undertaken to achieve those outcomes.

3.5. *Thailand: The National Education Commission*

A major review of education has, in recent years, been conducted in Thailand by the National Education Commission that led to the *National Education Act* (BE 2542 (1999)). The activities of the Commission involved: (a) the conduct of 42 detailed research studies on major issues in education; (b) the thorough scrutiny of the reports of the Commission and the drafts of the Parliamentary Bill by scholars and two special committees of the House of Representatives and of the Senate; (c) widespread consultations with the many stakeholders; and (d) public polls involving over 100,000 persons. The thoroughness of the consultations in the preparation of the report and the Act was an important aspect of the work of this Commission that led to widespread agreement with the recommendations that have been enacted by law (Thailand, NEC, 2000).

General objectives and principles. The act was developed around four major objectives each involving several key principles.

(1) Education in Thailand should aim for the full development of the Thai people and should involve all aspects: physical health, mental health, intellect, knowledge, morality, integrity, and the ability to live in harmony with other people.
(2) The learning processes should aim at developing a sound awareness of a democratic system of government under a constitutional monarchy.
(3) The provision of educational services should be based on (a) lifelong education for all, (b) participation by all segments of society, and (c) continuous development of the bodies of knowledge and learning processes.
(4) The system, structure and processes of educational provision should be based on the following principles: (a) unity in policy and diversity in implementation, (b) decentralisation of authority to institutions and organisations, (c) the setting of educational standards at all levels and for all types of education, with a system of quality assurance, (d) lifting the professional standards of teachers, (e) raising of financial support from different sources for the provision of education, and (f) forming partnerships with individuals, families, committees, organisations and institutions.

Essential features of the Act. There are four key features of the Act.

(1) All individuals have equal rights and opportunities to obtain a basic education of quality and free of charge for at least 12 years.
(2) Special educational services will be provided for the disabled and disadvantaged free of charge.
(3) Education for gifted persons will be provided in appropriate forms.
(4) Education will be compulsory for nine years from Grades 1 to 9.

Education system, curriculum reform and the learning process. There will be three types of educational provision: formal, non formal and informal. Credits obtained and accumulated by learners will be transferable within the same type or between different types of education, including vocational training, work experience and nonformal and informal education. Educational institutions are authorised to provide any one or all of the three types of education. The features of provision of these types of education are listed as follows.

(1) Formal education is provided at two levels: basic education and higher education.
(2) Early childhood education and basic education are provided in early childhood institutions, schools and learning centres organised by nonformal educational agencies.
(3) Higher education is provided in universities, institutes and colleges.
(4) The teaching-learning process aims to enable learners to develop themselves at their own pace and to the best of their potential.
(5) Core curricula for basic education are prepared by the Basic Education Commission.

(6) Curricula at all levels of education are diversified, aiming at human development with a balance between knowledge, critical thinking, virtue and social responsibility.
(7) The State will promote the establishment and running of many different types of lifelong learning resources, including public libraries, museums, art galleries, zoological gardens, botanical gardens, science and technology parks, sport and recreation centres, data bases and other sources of informal educational provision.

Encouraging participation and partnership. Great flexibility will be provided in the provision of educational services.

(1) In addition to the State, private persons, local administration organisations, individuals, families, community organisations, private organisations, professional bodies, religious institutions, enterprises and other social institutions have the right to provide basic education. They will be given government support and grants, tax rebates or exemptions for bringing up children and providing basic education.
(2) Educational institutions, in cooperation with all sectors of society will contribute to strengthening communities by encouraging learning within the communities.

This program of reform is very flexible and diversified and requires the restructuring of existing educational administrative structures as well as enthusing all members of Thai society to participate fully in the opportunities provided for education. The mobilisation of resources for education in such a diffuse and diverse education system presents considerable challenges. However, the use of information and communications technology is likely to be greatly facilitated by the flexibility of the proposed system. The proposals for the implementation of the reform and the specification of actions to be taken within one year, within three years, and within five years indicate that the proposed reforms have been carefully planned with a view towards quality assurance. While strategies and plans for the introduction of reform have been laid down, the reorganisation of the educational administrative structure and the management of the education system involves major change at a time when Southeast Asia is still recovering from the financial set backs of the late 1990s.

The changes associated with the reform also envisage a new approach to learning built around research and development institutes for learning reform as well as a National Institute for Learning Reform. These institutes will inform a network of teachers and educational institutions that will develop their own approaches to learning reform, together with regular and systematic use of daily television and radio programs for communication with the wider public. Annual national and regional symposia on learning reform will also be held.

4. CONCLUSION

The conduct of research that leads to the planning and implementation of educational reform in the Asia-Pacific region would seem to be best undertaken through cooperative research studies. In countries where there are separate education systems for state or regional units, and where each state or region has research units of sufficient strength to conduct worthwhile research studies into policy issues, it would seem possible for the collaborative research studies to be carried out within a single country. However, such situations are the exception rather than the common place. Consequently, cooperative research studies are more likely to be carried out between countries in the region rather than within countries. Cooperation has many advantages, particularly at the design stage, where expertise can be shared in the design and planning of a study. However, cooperation and the undertaking of similar studies in several different countries, provides the opportunity for replication, that is a necessary condition for claiming generality for the findings. Moreover, if sufficient countries are involved in a common study it is possible to examine the data collected in the search for cross-country relationships. The earlier studies conducted by the International Association for the Evaluation of Educational Achievement (IEA) sought relationships of this kind between and within countries (see Keeves, 1995). Purves (1989) and his colleagues have also written on *International Comparisons and Educational Reform* drawing on evidence from IEA studies.

In the absence of large studies in the Asia-Pacific region that permit cross-system comparisons, a valuable alternative is the holding of cross-national seminars to discuss and debate the findings of research studies conducted within a single country. A first seminar of this kind was held in Tokyo in 1979 under the auspices of UNESCO at the suggestion of Raja Roy Singh, the then Director of the Unesco Regional Office in Bangkok. The report of this seminar was published by NIER (UNESCO/APIED-NIER, 1979) with comment on research conducted within 15 countries of the Asia-Pacific region. In a renewal of interest in cooperative research, a second seminar was held in Bangkok in collaboration with the Hong Kong Institute of Education, in September 2002. This second seminar focused on several issues of importance: (a) learning reform, (b) school reform, (c) institutional reform, (d) decentralisation, (e) education standards and quality assurance, (f) implementation of reform, and (g) system reform. These are clearly issues that are shared by countries across the region, and countries have much to learn form each other.

Relatively little is known about how the processes of reform in education operate and about the roles of ideas, policy, human agency, leadership, both for and against change, as well as the financial conditions in the society. Consequently, it would seem important that, as reform is introduced, studies should be set up to investigate thorougly the reform processes. Giddens' ideas, discussed briefly above in Section 2 of this article, provide a largely untested theoretical framework for inquiry into the processes of reform. The study of the reform process and educational change is clearly a major field of research in education awaiting investigation.

REFERENCES

Australian Education Council (1970). *Nation-wide Survey of Educational Needs.* Sydney: Australian Educational Council.

Bassett, G. W. (1970). *Planning in Australian Education.* Melbourne: ACER.

Beeby, C. E. (1979). *Assessment of Indonesian Education: A Guide in Planning.* Wellington: NZCER and Oxford Press.

Cadman A. G. (Chair) (1976). *Learning Difficulties in Children and Adults: Report* (House of Representative Select Committee on Specific Learning Difficulties). Canberra: AGPS.

De Landsheere, G. (1997). History of educational research. In J. P. Keeves (Ed.), *Educational Research, Methodology and Measurement: An International Handbook* (pp. 8–16). Oxford: Pergamon.

Giddens, A (1984). *The Constitution of Society.* Oxford: Blackwell.

Husén, T. (1994). Problems of educational reforms in a changing society. *International Perspectives on Education and Society, 4,* 3–22.

Husén, T. (1997). Educational research and policy-making. In J. P. Keeves (Ed.), *Educational Research, Methodology and Measurement: An International Handbook* (pp. 251–257). Oxford: Pergamon.

India, Ministry of Education and Social Welfare (1996). *Education and National Development, Report of the Education Commission (1964–66).* New Delhi: Ministry of Education.

Karmel, P. H. (Chair) (1973). *Schools in Australia: Report* (Report of the Interim Committee for the Australian Schools Commission). Canberra: AGPS.

Keeves, J. P. (1995). *The World of School Learning: Selected Key Findings from 35 Years of IEA Research.* The Hague: IEA.

Keeves, J. P. (1997). Legitimatory research. In J. P. Keeves (Ed.), *Educational Research, Methodology and Measurement: An International Handbook* (pp. 193–198). Oxford: Pergamon.

Kenny, K. S. (2000). Inclusion in early childhood education in South Australia. An Hermeneutic Study of the Role of Gaps and Tensions between Theory, Policy and Practice in the Standardisation of Educational Transformation. Unpublished PhD. Thesis, Flinders University.

Lao, PDR (2000a). *Fighting Poverty through Human Resources Development, Rural Development and People's Participation* (Government Report to the Seventh Round Table Meeting, Geneva, November, 2000). Vientiane: Ministry of Finance.

Lao, PDR. Ministry of Education (2000b). *The Education Strategic Vision up to the Year 2020.* Vientiane: Ministry of Education.

Nisbet, J. (1997). Policy-oriented research, In J. P. Keeves (Ed.), *Educational Research, Methodology and Measurement: An International Handbook* (pp. 211–217). Oxford: Pergamon.

Purves, A. C. (Ed.) (1989). *International Comparisons and Educational Reform.* Alexandria VA: Association for Supervision and Curriculum Development.

Radford, W. C. (1966). *Staying at School Longer.* Melbourne: ACER.

Thailand, Office the National Education Commission (2000). *Education in Thailand 1999.* Bangkok: National Education Commission.

Tjeldvoll, A. (2000). *Torsten Husén: Conversations in Comparative Education* (edited by H. G. Lingens). Bloomington, Indiana: Phi Delta Kappa.

Trow, M. (1977). Policy analysis. In J. P. Keeves (Ed.), *Educational Research, Methodology and Measurement: An International Handbook* (pp. 205–211). Oxford: Pergamon.

Turner, J. H. (1986). *Structure of Sociological Theory* (4th edn.). Chicago: Dorsey Press.

UNESCO/APEID-NIER (1979). *Educational Research in Relation to Educational Reform in Asia and Oceania.* Tokyo: NIER.

Weiss, C. (1979). The many meanings of research utilisation. *Public Admin. Review, 39,* 426–31.

81

The Impact of Educational Research on Decision Making and Practice*

VICTOR ORDONEZ
East-West Centre, Honolulu, Hawaii

RUPERT MACLEAN
UNESCO-UNEVOC International Centre for Education, Bonn, Germany

1. INTRODUCTION

In both developed and developing countries in the Asia-Pacific region governments and administrators involved with educational decision making are exploring innovative solutions, including the re-engineering of their educational systems, to address various key concerns. These include:

- the most cost effective ways to expand access to education;
- ways of improving equity, especially for women;
- increasing the relevance of education;
- upgrading the quality of education while at the same time maintaining the quantitative expansion of education systems to cope with an increasing demand for their services; and,
- ways to enhance both the internal efficiency of education systems to ensure that limited resources are put to best use and external efficiencies to ensure that the products generated by the content and processes of an education system best satisfy economic and social requirements.

In addressing these key concerns, it is widely held that educational research has the potential to play an important role in policy formulation and decision making aimed at improving education and schooling, since it "is the tool which enables policy makers to determine national educational needs, to assess new approaches to resolving issues, and to evaluate the effectiveness of policies and

---

* This article is derived from an article published by the same authors in *Prospects, 30*(3), September 2000 – Education in Asia.

strategies" (ADB, 1996, p. 1). Yet decision makers do not use research as much as they could and do not actively seek it out, thereby largely neglecting or overlooking the opportunity for better policy or decisions that research findings provide.

Despite the potential of educational research to making an important, some would say essential, contribution to decision making in education, many researchers complain that education decision makers pay insufficient attention to research findings. Policy makers and implementers, on the other hand, argue that much of the available educational research is unintelligible and lacking in relevance for educational decision making purposes. Examples where educational research could usefully inform decision makers include monitoring the health of education systems, investigating options for reform and change, evaluating intended and unintended outcomes of interventions and the provision of assessment strategies which focus on student learning rather than on rank ordering which ignores the quality of learning.

Much has been written (e.g., Husen and Kogan, 1984; Brown, 1994; Hallinan, 1996; McGaw, 1996) which analyses the relationship between education decision making, research and educational information. Some of this writing presents the views of researchers and others who express a concern about the marginal attention given to research in policy formulation and educational decision making. Many (e.g., Shavelson, 1988; Harlen, 1996, Biddle & Saha, 2002) provide suggestions as to what needs to be done to increase the impact of research in this area.

Agencies such as the Asian Development Bank (e.g., 1996), OECD (e.g., 1994; 1995; 1996) and UNESCO (e.g., ACER/ACEID, 1995; IBE/NIER, 1996) have also contributed to the debate on this topic, vigorously seeking pathways to improve the flow of information between the producers and consumers of educational research, and providing case studies to illustrate where this communication has been successful.

It is also clear from the literature that due to radical and widespread changes occurring in the use of information technologies, much more information is now more readily available for policy makers to use as an input to the decision making process. In some ways this makes the decision making process more difficult than it was when information inputs were more restricted.

The debate and discussions on this topic have been largely confined within the halls and journals of the academic community. This article presents the perspective of decision makers, who are the consumers of research, regarding the impact of educational research on the decision making process, to add balance to the debate. This article presents, in the form of a case study, the views of a small group of senior educational decision makers from countries in the Asia-Pacific region on the possible link between educational research and improved educational practice, and on what they believe can realistically be done to improve the usefulness and influence of educational research on decision making in education. The extent to which the views expressed here are generalisable more widely to other decision makers in the Asia-Pacific region remains to be tested.

As governments are the main providers of school education in the region, in this article the emphasis is on decision makers working in or for government, rather than those in private enterprise.

2. DIFFERENT TYPES OF RESEARCH: DIFFERENT LEVELS OF DECISION MAKING

When considering the relationship between research and decision making in education, it is important to recognise that there is not one, but many different types, of educational research. These range from reviews of the research literature which present an overview of the research done by others on a particular matter (such as on the influence of socio-economic status or gender on educational outcomes) to sophisticated and detailed research studies which examine a particular question in great depth (such as the impact of particular teaching methods on the development of convergent contrasted with divergent thinking in a group of students).

Sometimes a particular body of research (such as that linking socio-economic background to education outcomes) has had a profound and far-reaching influence on public opinion and decision makers alike, so that the findings become part of the taken for granted reality as to how education and schooling systems function. In such a case it is not generally possible to say that a particular research study influences a particular policy, but the influence of research on policy and practice in a more general sense is there for all to see.

Educational research may serve many different functions, besides informing those who make educational decisions. Some academic research in universities, for example, may be undertaken for no other reason than that it reflects the particular interests and inquisitiveness of the researcher or researchers involved. In our view, there is perhaps too much of this type of research being generated in universities, and not enough of the type of research which policy makers need.

In addition, educational researchers work in very different types of work settings, such as universities, research units in government departments and in independent or semi-independent research units. With the growing popularity of action research, and the notion of the teacher as researcher, educational practitioners in schools and teacher training institutions are also undertaking research, as an input to help improve their educational practice. When this occurs the producers and consumers of research may in fact be one and the same entity.

The motivations of these different groups of researchers can vary considerably. For instance, independent researchers in universities tend to be much more critical in their approach to their research than are those working as part of government research units.

Just as there are many different types of research and researchers, so there are many different types, and levels of decision makers. Decision makers include both Ministers of Education and other politicians who make policy decisions that may influence a whole education system, as well as high ranking civil servants who themselves assert a great deal of decision making influence when implementing the policy decisions of their political masters. In addition, moves towards a greater decentralisation of education, the forging of home-school links and the development of genuine partnerships in education has had important implications for the decision making process, with an increasing proportion of decisions now being made at the level of the community, school and classroom where, for example, the decisions of classroom teachers on matters such as teaching methods can have a profound influence on the educational outcomes of a particular group of children in a particular setting.

3. OPINIONS OF DECISION MAKERS ON EDUCATIONAL RESEARCH

The data presented below was drawn from two main sources: first, the opinions of high ranking education decision makers and administrators from 19 countries in the Asia-Pacific region whose views were recently surveyed, through open ended questions, by the authors, when these officials attended meetings in Bangkok organised by UNESCO PROAP and, second, the views of the authors of this article, both of whom have had experience to varying degrees as education decision makers and researchers.

The decision makers were surveyed as a group, and also interviewed individually, respondents being invited to present their views on a range of matters. These are discussed under five main headings: (a) the influence of educational research on establishing priorities for the education sector in their country; (b) expectations regarding research and decision making in education; (c) evidence regarding the overall impact of educational research on the decision making process in their country; (d) views on who should determine the research questions to be answered and who should do the research; and, (e) specific suggestions on how the relationship between researchers and decision makers can be improved.

Despite the diverse nature of the countries surveyed with regard to such matters as their level of economic development, the features of their education systems, socio-cultural characteristics and the like, there was a surprisingly high level of agreement among them regarding the views expressed. Respondents were assured that their responses would be treated anonymously, with no individual respondent or their country being identified in the write up of the material collected without their prior approval.

3.1. *Research and Education Priorities*

The chasm between academic research and the need by administrators for information upon which to base policy and priority setting has been discussed in many places. However, partly because the academic community seems satisfied with the discovery of its own knowledge, and is more comfortable talking with their peers than with the rough and tumble world of government and politics, they have never developed the skills and aggressiveness needed to capture the attention of the bureaucrats and meaningfully channel their attention and priorities. As a result, the combination of media blasts and politicians' inquiries and outbursts channel the administrators' attention to issues that are most spoken about, whether they are in fact the most fundamental or not.

Decision makers expressed their concern that many education decisions are made without enough attention being given to research. This occurs because politicians often make decisions on the basis of prior experience and hunches, not on the basis of research. One of the big weaknesses in the system is that there is no culture among politicians of basing decision making on research, which is a big weakness in most education systems. Research is important to help achieve some continuity over time between successive governments, but this often does not happen, one difficulty being that many political parties and ministers want to push their pet theories and ideas, generally based on political ideology rather than hard data, unless the data accord with the ideology.

There are other reasons why researchers and academic institutions often do not play that significant a role in influencing policy changes and day to day decisions in the Ministry. When looking at how priorities are set and how energy is focused, there are many other players on the scene, competing more effectively than research, for their share of attention. These include: the legislators, the national and local government leaders, the media, the parents and teachers' associations, and the decision makers at lower levels within the bureaucracy itself.

In order to explain the context of this reality, it must be remembered that senior administrators are more than merely armchair thinkers analysing situations and evolving policy. More often than not, especially in developing countries, the time for policy analysis and reformulation is the last luxury to be enjoyed, as the time and energy of administrators is more than taken up by a perpetual series of crises and urgent problems to be solved, for example, teacher or student strikes, budget deficiencies, requests from politicians, or conflicts within the bureaucracy. When not tackling crises, administrators spend the rest of the available time seeing to it that the system does not break down but keeps running reasonably well. This means endless meetings with curriculum developers, with superintendents, with textbook publishers, and with public works officials.

If researchers are to be influential in changing this situation they need to identify and address those matters which would help in or facilitate the use of their research by decision makers. Only in this way are they likely to become more influential in the education decision making process. In those areas where the views of decision makers are justified, researchers will need to change their approaches, while in other areas it may be a matter of researchers better communicating with the decision makers to convince them that it is in their own interests to take greater account of research in the decision making process. However, the core of the matter is that researchers need to produce research findings on relevant and useful topics.

3.2. Expectations of Research

The role of research as a tool for administrators is twofold. More commonly it is used to investigate a particular issue, for example, school dropouts, to analyse the seriousness of the problem, and possibly its underlying causes, and then second, to test the validity of alternative policy measures to address the issue. Most of the project related research is of this type.

However, in a more fundamental sense, there is a priority role for research that the administrators more desperately need. It is the role of scanning the entire sector and providing a calibrated topography of the range of issues and suggesting means according to which they can be prioritised. This type of research does not point to better ways of doing things already being done, but better things that ought to be done in the first place. In working with several Ministries of Education in the Asia-Pacific region, UNESCO has found this to be true. All too often a Minister or senior official is fired by a single cause or major idea, often an opportunity to make a visible impact, and then devotes most of his or her effort to this. Often it is the right priority, but other priorities, often vital, are overlooked, and if it is not the right priority in the first place, then the entire system suffers.

While administrators must therefore make special efforts to ensure that these two types of research are available and utilizable by them, there is an equivalent responsibility on the part of the research community to base its agenda more closely on the expressed concerns of the policy makers, which are in turn reflective of media, legislators, and society at large. To the extent that its research is at least implicitly mandated by the decision makers, it will be guaranteed a fair hearing and used for actual policy making.

Making decisions often requires speed, and research often takes too long to give an adequate answer. In addition, the decision maker is in a more complex situation regarding the wide range of variables to consider and accommodate, while the researcher is generally more autonomous. These are but two of many differences between the culture of the researcher and that of the decision maker.

It was widely felt by those surveyed that if education research is to be taken more seriously by decision makers it is necessary for them to be convinced that available research will make their job easier and that it will provide guidance of a type that makes the decision making easier and more reliable. In other words, the yardstick by which research will be judged is highly practical in nature.

Some respondents felt it not unreasonable that academic researchers accept some academic, political and practical constraints when engaged in policy orientated projects. They must also be able to adopt a policy minded mode of thought over the customary research minded approach. In accepting policy orientated research projects, researchers can shape policy rather than merely comment on it after the fact.

The view was expressed by the interviewees that researchers need to present their findings in a form that is most likely to be used by decision makers. It was felt that the most important dictate in this regard is to present decision makers with the bare minimum of information necessary for the task: the material should be simple, short and succinct. The key is to provide findings that can be understood by someone who is very busy. At the same time, more detailed information should also be available in order that the assistants to the decision maker can check the accuracy of what is being presented, whether it is a proposal or an evaluation.

3.3. Impact of Research

Respondents felt that there is, in fact, a greater impact of research on decision making than is commonly recognised because this impact is often not identifiable in a cause-effect sense. An example was given of the work on the impact of restricted and elaborated language codes in classrooms, and on the definition and distribution of success and failure in schools in ways that favour middle to upper socio-economic groups in society. Such research has had a profound impact on public opinion and on the views of decision makers regarding education and schooling but in ways that are not readily apparent or easily identifiable.

There was a consensus that the extent to which research is used depends on the level of decision making involved, since research is used differently at various levels of decision making. Many decisions are made on a political basis, so research is not used. However, with regard to specific policies in areas such as assessment research this is more likely to be used as an input to the decision making process. So whether or not research is used by decision makers depends in part on the type of decision to be made.

However, although decision makers driven by political considerations will look for research to support their ideologies or pet projects, this interdependence can also work the other way. If compelling and persuasive research is properly presented, the research agenda could generate a politically powerful agenda or cause that the decision makers could adopt, use and capitalize upon.

Although research has little direct impact on policy decisions taken at the political level, it was felt that it does have an important impact with decision makers at the lower levels, such as with regard to evaluation at the school level. As education systems become more decentralised, educational research becomes increasingly important in many countries since there was general agreement that the lower the level in the decision making hierarchy, the greater appears to be the likely impact of educational research on the decision making process.

A respondent noted that although decision makers in the civil service generally realise the importance of research to the decision making process, a problem occurs when their political masters want action to be taken which flies in the face of available evidence. Although this puts the civil service decision maker in an uncomfortable position, the bottom line is that they must do what the politician wants, regardless of what the research evidence may say. Another difficulty is that educational reforms are often introduced but not given time to take root and be evaluated, further change from politicians occurring before adequate evaluation and research on the outcomes has taken place. There is thus a need to convince politicians, decision makers and the general public that education decisions should be based on research, not just political ideology or intuition, and, indeed, that it is in their interests to do this, since if this approach is adopted, decisions are more likely to meet with success. However, even when policies are developed according to political ideology, the researcher can still be of assistance in finding those decision making pathways that are likely to succeed and be effective.

It was noted that in some countries with centralised bureaucracies the relationship between educational research and decision making is close. Decision makers themselves help to determine and identify the research questions examined, and so have a clear stake in the process and outcomes. In addition, educational researchers provide advice to decision makers on how to gain information on various topics examined. It was also felt that all countries could benefit by encouraging such a dialogue.

3.4. Determining Research Questions

The fact that many Ministries of Education establish their own research branches to undertake policy-oriented research and to monitor education outcomes was quoted as indicating that government decision makers recognize the value of research, but that they find most of the research generated by outside bodies does not meet their needs in terms of policy orientation and is not generally presented in a form that is readily usable. One way in which Ministries of Education seek to determine the research agenda is by funding particular studies in areas of special interest.

It was also noted that members of the research community and decision makers respond to different pressures in their educational endeavours, which results in a serious communications gap. It was argued that one of the big differences in perspective between researchers and decision makers is that while researchers value neutrality in their research, many decision makers have a clear orientation which they want to have justified or reinforced by researchers. Thus there are quite different expectations between the two groups. The challenge is to find an effective solution to this problem.

In practice, many decision makers find that the only times when they are pushed into a more systematic analysis is when they have to initiate or evaluate a sector study or sub-sector study as a prerequisite to a major capital investment, often connected to a loan or a grant from an external source. Because the funding sources in their turn have to justify the projects to their principals in a coherent and defensible fashion, they feel the need to urge the national decision makers to generate the needed research information and analysis to justify major interventions. In reality, therefore, the only research that some top level decision makers consistently look at are those mandated by and associated with externally supported, large-scale projects. It seems ironic that this occurs in countries where there are many colleges, universities and centres of research.

Reference was also made to scanning or watchtower type research for innovations or to identify so-called 'research tragedies'. Most research has a predetermined focus, such as to examine dropout rates, the extent of textbook distribution or factors affecting learning achievement. This type of research, which is sometimes undertaken by Ministries of Education or teacher training institutions, scans the sector but not for the purpose of a sector study or analysis but to identify innovations from the field that might flower or can be institutionalized and so become widespread.

There was much discussion about the merits and demerits of an in-house research arm within the bureaucracy of an Education Ministry itself, whether the planning office of the Minister houses it, or whether it is a quasi-autonomous Educational Research Institute with its own governance mechanism. In either case, such a body becomes effective to the extent that it co-opts other academic institutions to participate in its task, rather than to try to do everything in-house and thus be suspected of producing findings that legitimate decisions that have already been made at higher levels.

It was also felt that too much research is being conducted by too many institutions, with there being a need for more focus and concentration. Governments in many countries are becoming more actively involved in the allocation of funds for research and so, through controlling the purse strings, they have an important impact on setting the research agenda and priorities.

3.5. *Improving the Research and Decision Making Relationship*

The decision makers spoken to felt that too few researchers in academic institutions are concerned with the linkage between their research and the real world. One of the ways in which governments try to overcome this difficulty is to provide funding for research projects, which they regard as being particularly important or relevant. Another, perhaps cheaper way of improving this linkage is for decision and policy makers to give some thought to producing and then disseminating a list of priority research topics that can guide university and other researchers looking for relevant areas and issues to focus upon.

The view was expressed that a lack of resources makes it difficult to conduct research on all issues that are deemed to be important. In addition, outside research is often not in a form that is readily accessible and usable by the decision maker, and too much research is not sufficiently focused. There needs to be a closer dialogue between decision makers and researchers to try and ensure they are thinking along the same lines.

There is also a need to develop closer partnerships between both decision makers and researchers, involving such groups as the teaching profession, and the local community.

It was also felt that in order to inform policy the research conducted must be useful, accessible, of high quality, relevant and timely. The decision makers complained that researchers do not give them the answers they need, when they need them. Political agendas have their own time frame and the need for advice may not be able to wait for properly collected evidence.

Respondents agreed with the views of some (e.g., Shaeffer & Nkinyangi, 1983; Bray in ADB, 1996), who argue that since research is at least in part a cultural phenomenon tied to ideology and communication patterns, there are some important ways in which the environments for research and policy making are different in Asia from those in other parts of the world. They agreed that, in Asia, critical enquiry and challenges to basic assumptions are likely to be regarded as generally unacceptable and offensive by senior policy makers, particularly if such research leads to social disharmony and a loss of face by the decision maker involved.

This is generally very different to the situation in the West, where criticism is generally encouraged and officials are not expected to take such views personally. In addition, respondents noted that male decision makers in Asia find it particularly difficult to be challenged by researchers, who are female, and by those who are younger or of lower rank than themselves. To the extent this applies, there is a need to address this question, if research is to contribute to decision making. It would appear that the debates on research and policy point to a need to locate more explicitly, the proper niche of researcher and policy maker dialogues in the context of the larger picture of managing a large bureaucracy in the Asia-Pacific region.

4. SUMMARY AND CONCLUSIONS

There is no doubt that educational research has the potential to make an important contribution to policy formulation and analysis. However, there appears to be at the current time a strong feeling amongst many educational decision makers and administrators in the Asia-Pacific region that educational research has a long way to go before it reaches its potential in the region. In order to improve the current situation, there is a need for all parties concerned to examine critically the current relationship between research and policy-making with a view to identifying constructive and realistic ways in which policy makers and education researchers can work together most effectively in this regard.

Participants at the UNESCO meetings referred to above were in agreement as to what can best be done by researchers to improve their relationship with policy makers, and to increase the likelihood that their research findings would be taken into account by educational authorities. In their view it is essential that researchers do more to ensure that:

- their research is conducted on topics that are of interest to decision makers;
- researchers clearly specify the policy implications of their findings;
- research is of high quality, with rigorous methods of inquiry;
- claims made in the research are realistic, in terms of data collected and methods adopted;
- research findings are expressed precisely, concisely and in concrete form; and
- decision makers take the trouble to articulate more explicitly their research needs to researchers.

They also felt that decision makers should be more open-minded with regard to the contribution of research to improving educational practice, rather than being quick to dismiss it as largely irrelevant, which currently and frequently happens. Although it is not easy to resolve the current long standing differences that exist between researchers and decision makers in the areas referred to in this article, there was a common agreement among those surveyed that all parties needed to work together more constructively to ensure that available research and decision making resources were harnessed most effectively to help improve the quality and relevance of education in the Asia-Pacific region.

REFERENCES

Asian Development Bank (ADB) (1996). *Case Studies in Education Research and Policy.* Manila: ADB.

Australian Council for Educational Research (ACER) and the Asia-Pacific Centre of Educational Innovation for Development (ACEID) (1996). *Educational Research in the Asia-Pacific Region, Report on the UNESCO-ACEID/ACER Asia-Pacific Regional Seminar, 1–5 May 1995.* Melbourne.

Biddle, B. J., & Saha, L. J. (Eds.) (2002). *The Untested Accusation: Principles, Research Knowledge and Policy Making in Schools.* New York: Ablex Publishing (Greenwood).

Brown, S. (1994). Research in education. What influence on policy and practice? *Knowledge and Policy, The International Journal of Knowledge Transfer and Utilisation,* 7, 94–107.

Hallinan, M. T. (1996). Bridging the gap between research and practice. *Sociology of Education,* 69, 131–134.

Harlen, W. (1996). *Educational Research and Educational Reform.* Paper presented at an International Conference to Celebrate the 50th Anniversary of the National Foundation for Educational Research (NFER), UK. December.

Husen, T., & Kogan, M. (1984). *Educational Research and Policy: How do they Relate?* Oxford: Pergamon Press.

International Bureau of Education (IBE) and National Institute for Educational Research of Japan (NIER) (1996). *Educational Reform and Educational Research: New Challenges in Linking Research, Information and Decision making.* Report on an International Meeting in Tokyo, Japan, 4–14 September, 1995.

McGaw, B. (1996). Linking educational research with policy and practice. *ACER Newsletter,* 85.

Organisation for Economic Co-operation and Development (OECD) (1994). *Education Research and Reform: An International Perspective.* Paris: OECD, CERI.

Organisation for Economic Co-operation and Development (OECD) (1995). *Educational Research and Development: Trends, Issues and Challenges.* Paris: OECD, CERI.

Organisation for Economic Co-operation and Development (OECD) (1996). *Knowledge Bases for Education Policies.* Paris: OECD, CERI.

Shaeffer, S., & Nkinyangi, J. (Eds.) (1983). *Educational Research Environments in the Developing World.* Ottawa: International Development Research Centre.

Shavelson, R. J. (1988). Contributions of educational research to policy and practice: Constructing, challenging, changing cognition. *Educational Researcher,* 17, 4–22.

82

Research in Education: Nature, Impact, Needs and Priorities

ZHOU MANSHENG
National Center for Education Development Research, Beijing, P.R. China

JOHN P. KEEVES
Flinders University Institute of International Education, Australia

1. INTRODUCTION

The provision of educational services and the conduct of education in the Asia-Pacific region faces many problems. These problems differ between the large nations in the region (China, India and Indonesia) with huge populations and the smaller Pacific Island nations. Nevertheless, the tasks for educational research are the provision of soundly based information and evidence, as well as guidance and recommendations, that would help in the development of policies and practices contributing to the resolution of these problems. The simple categorisations of research activity into 'quantitative or qualitative', 'pure or applied', 'conclusion oriented or decision oriented', 'analytic or systemic' and 'discipline research or policy research' do not provide adequately for the range of approaches and the variety of activities that are undertaken in educational research. The use of these simple dualisms only serves to divide the teams of educational research workers undertaking research studies within the countries of the region. These categories create tensions between researchers as they approach the conduct of their investigations and inquiries in different ways, within different disciplinary research traditions, with different types of procedures for the collection of evidence and data, and with different approaches to the examination of the information collected. The problems faced in educational research are so many and so large, that it would seem necessary to develop a view of the research endeavours into educational problems that emphasises the essential unity of this field of inquiry. Educational research activity has a unity of purpose and a unified epistemological basis that demands the rejection both of alternative paradigms of inquiry and of simplistic dichotomies. The choice of the procedures to be employed in each research investigation in the field of education must ultimately depend on the nature of the problem involved. It is the purpose of this article to emphasise the essential unity of research activity in education, so that research programs in the Asia-Pacific region are not diverted from valued purposes by dissent based upon simple categorisations.

The success of educational research activity in the Asia-Pacific region since the late 1960s, has led to the need to prepare this *Handbook* because little of this research is visible outside the countries of the region. The body of knowledge assembled over this period is rather more than the accumulated wisdom held by the leaders in the field of education who have lived and worked in the region, and the names of former leaders, Dr. C. E. Beeby and Dr. M. Hiratsuka from New Zealand and Japan respectively, come quickly to mind. The findings of educational research in the Asia-Pacific region are now forming a coherent body of knowledge that warrants presentation to the research workers, scholars, administrators and policy makers of the region, and indeed, the wider world.

2. CONCERNING THE NATURE OF KNOWLEDGE

Before considering the impact, needs and priorities of educational research, it is necessary to examine the nature of educational processes and educational research activity in its many forms. Popper and Eccles (1977) have drawn attention to three conceptually different worlds that exist in the setting in which the quest for knowledge and scholarly inquiry is conducted. World 1 is the world of material objects, to which must be added the various structures created by human societies. Thus World 1 includes the natural physical world as well as schools, universities, homes and the mass media. World 2 is the world of subjective and personal experience involving the human mind. World 3 is a new and objective world that includes the body of knowledge developed by humans and stored in various forms in libraries, and more recently on network systems. It contains the corpus of knowledge about educational processes that has emerged during the past century. It also includes the knowledge developed in the many disciplinary and interdisciplinary fields related to education that is growing at a rapid pace. This body of knowledge, that has been subjected to both logical and empirical testing and that is growing rapidly, may be regarded as having an existence of its own.

World 3 has also recently given rise to a new sub-world of Information and Communications Technology, World 3T. It is convenient in this article to separate the sub-world of Information Technology from World 3, The Body of Knowledge, because the development of information technology is an important new frontier in education in the Asia-Pacific region. There is also a sub-world that has formed from World 2, The Human Mind. This sub-world, World 2B, involves the Collective Views of Cultural and Social Groups. It is comprised of the religious and other views and ideas that are accepted by groups, with the consent and consensus of the individuals within each group. These views and ideas may not be amenable to logical or empirical examination, in the ways that knowledge can be tested. World 2B has nevertheless, a role in education, particularly in the Asia-Pacific region, where there is growing concern for moral and social values and beliefs. In so far as some beliefs and values have not been tested either empirically or logically they do not belong to World 3, The Body of Knowledge.

Figure 1 shows in diagrammatic form these three worlds and the two sub-worlds, as well as the interrelations between them that are concerned with the processes of education, together with educational research and scholarly inquiry. The arrows drawn between the worlds in Figure 1 indicate the different processes involved in the many different facets of education. It is of interest to examine each of the components in turn, considering first the teaching and learning processes and second, the processes of research and inquiry.

2.1. Educational Processes

The body of knowledge held in World 3 is systematically compartmentalized into disciplinary and interdisciplinary fields. This body of knowledge is constantly changing, and has grown very rapidly during the twentieth century and continues to expand at a remarkable rate. It is constantly being checked in a variety of ways against World 1, The Real World.

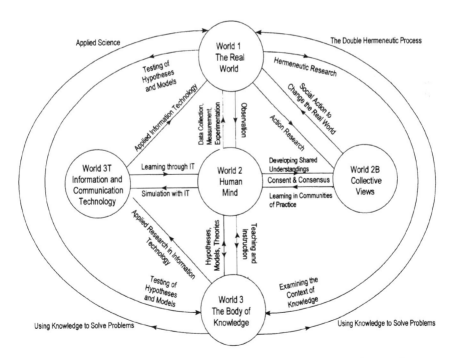

Figure 1. The nature and processes of education and educational research.

Teaching and instruction. Teaching and instruction involves the passing on of selected aspects of the body of knowledge that forms World 3 to the minds of individual students, who build their own World 2. Today there is so much knowledge stored in World 3 that selections must be made regarding the knowledge from World 3 that is passed to individuals. Nevertheless, the knowledge that is taught, while initially accepted, may later be shown to be incomplete and inadequate and is liable to be fallible.

Metacognition. World 2 (The Learner's Mind) is centrally located in the reciprocal processes that operate between World 1 (The Real World) and World 3 (The Body of Knowledge). The processes of education involve the students being concerned with how information and ideas are structured in their own minds. This process is referred to as metacognition, and an awareness of and attention to metacognitive processes are argued to be of considerable benefit to the learners.

Learning through information technology. Advancements in the power of computers and the consequent developments in information technology have not only changed how students can now obtain access to information, but are also changing the ways in which students learn, in so far as they are potentially becoming less dependent on traditional methods of teaching and instruction. The link between World 3T and World 2 is emerging as a radically new and very important educational process. It is important to note that all information that is today stored in World 3T has not been rigorously tested.

Consent and consensus. The interactive processes between World 2 (Human Mind) and World 2B (Collective Views) are the processes of consent and consensus that are developed through both formal and informal education in order to prepare individuals to live in social groups.

Social action to change the real world. Those educational processes that are associated with debate and discussion between individuals and groups of individuals with respect to how best knowledge should be used to change The Real World and its institutions are represented by the arrow from World 2B (Collective Views) to World 1 (The Real World). Social action has long been of concern to many educators and issues such as poverty and educational disadvantage are given prominence in the Delors Report: *Learning: The Treasure Within* (Delors, 1996). Consequently, consideration must be given in educational programs at all levels to appropriate ways in which such issues should be addressed and how change might be brought about.

2.2. *Educational Inquiry and Research*

There are many different processes that together constitute educational inquiry and research. It is necessary to examine how these processes are interrelated and linked to the three worlds shown in Figure 1 in order to see the essential unity of educational inquiry and research. The initial and major processes of educational inquiry involve the building up of the body of knowledge in World 3. This process of educational inquiry has several component parts.

Observation. Observation is a part of the process of inquiry in which an individual in World 2 is involved in perception of World 1, The Real World, using the five senses. However, what an individual perceives is influenced by what the individual is predisposed to perceive.

Data collection, measurement and experimentation. A further step in inquiry is the collection of evidence, the measurement of qualities referred to as quantification, and where possible the conduct of surveys, experiments, and controlled investigations (Kish, 1987). What is observed, collected or measured is greatly influenced by the knowledge, the views and the understandings of the individuals conducting the inquiries. Consequently, this process involves the link between World 1 and World 2, in which data and information obtained from World 1 are assembled and held in World 2 (The Human Mind).

Testing of hypotheses, models and theories. The individual research worker has almost certainly formulated hypotheses and models, derived from theory and previous research, prior to the collection of data and information. In the process linking World 2 and World 3, the learner or research worker formulates propositions, hypotheses, models and theories, and designs studies to examine these for their adequacy as representations of the real world or for logical consistency. The process of testing hypotheses, models and theories is best seen as a reciprocal link from World 3 back to World 1, where the hypotheses and the structure of the models as well as the components of theories stored in World 3 are tested against data and evidence collected from World 1.

Hermeneutic and Historical Research. Two areas of research in education, commonly referred to as historical and hermeneutic research, investigate the context of educational change and ideas in order to provide an understanding of the development of new ideas and processes.

Action research. An area of research associated with social action is the investigation of the conditions and the development of plans for making changes in World 1 (The Real World). This area of research requires that social groups in World 2B act as human agents both individually and collectively to gather evidence, prepare for change and introduce change in World 1.

Applied research with information and communications technology. An emerging field of research into educational processes involves the application of Information and Communications Technology both to change the thinking of individuals in World 2 and to change the operation of institutions in The Real

World (World 1). This field of investigation is concerned both with the development of information and communications technology and the examination of the conditions under which it operates most effectively to introduce change. It seems likely that information technology is capable of influencing the ways in which people think and learn, through the provision of virtual or simulated experience.

The hermeneutic processes. The conduct of educational research involves rather more than the investigation of the conditions provided for teaching and learning in schools. This is only one of the many facets of the processes of education. Educational processes also involve investigating how research is conducted in other fields, how change is currently introduced, was introduced in the past, and will be introduced in the future. Thus, educational research is concerned with the conditions and the context within which change occurs, commonly referred to as hermeneutic research. Furthermore, educational research involves the introduction, development and use of knowledge through the process of education referred to as the double hermeneutic process (Giddens, 1984). In the double hermeneutic process ideas and knowledge are brought into operation from World 3 through the minds of individuals in World 2, and acting collectively in World 2B to produce change in World 1. These many areas form a very rich and varied field for educational inquiry in the future (see *Educational Research for Educational Reform*).

3. THE NATURE OF EDUCATIONAL RESEARCH

Much has been written about the nature of educational research. There is a stereotyped view, that is still held by many educational research workers, in which initial training in the discipline of psychology provides a theoretical basis from which the 'dos' and the 'don'ts' for pedagogical practice may be derived. The audience for the advice and guidance of the educational research worker is seen to be the practising classroom teacher in the schools, who seeks to improve the effectiveness and efficiency of her or his daily work (Jackson & Kiesler, 1977). It is evident (McGaw, 1992) that at least in Australia the primary discipline apart from education itself, from which the largest proportion of research workers in education is drawn, is that of psychology. However, this perspective of placing psychology in the key role, involves a failure to understand the complexity of educational research and the ways in which educational research influences not only policy and practice in education, but also the development of bodies of knowledge that in turn lead to the implementation of social change through the double hermeneutic process.

3.1. *The Multidisciplinary Nature of Educational Research*

Educational research workers may be drawn from a very wide range of disciplinary areas, including psychology, sociology, history, anthropology, linguistics, economics, the natural sciences, political science, demography, law, and more recently information and communications technology. Each different field provides perspectives, theories and knowledge as well as methods of inquiry that are relevant to the examination of educational problems. Moreover, the educational problems that warrant investigation, and for which a solution must be sought, are not simply those that occur in the classroom, however important such problems might be seen to be. Education takes place within the home, and within the peer group, through religious institutions and through the mass media, in libraries and museums as well as at work and at play. Furthermore, the findings of educational research are of concern not only to teachers, but also to politicians and legislators, school administrators and school board members, parents and caregivers, as well as employers and youth workers.

3.2. The Multvariate Nature of Educational Research

A second key characteristic of educational research is that it must deal with very complex relationships, that involve many variables. It is rare for an educational problem to be reduced to the study of the relationship that exists between only two variables. In general, there is a plethora of factors that may be relevant to a problem situation, which is under investigation, and consequently the research study must be conducted in a multivariate context. However, the experimental strategies that are employed by the agricultural scientist and the psychologist for removing the effects of many unknown variables by randomisation and control are, in the main, denied to research workers in education and the social sciences, because they are not permitted to and do not wish to influence unduly the lives of people by allocating them at random to treatment or control groups.

3.3. The Multilevel Nature of Educational Research

A third key characteristic of educational research is that it is multilevel in nature, since individuals are taught in classroom and school groups, and schools are set within districts and regions. Most problem situations in education are multilevel. However, the analytical procedures that have been employed in the past have been designed to analyse data at one level only.

In the latter decades of the twentieth century statistical techniques have been developed that are not only multivariate in nature, but also make allowance for the multilevel structure of the data collected. Furthermore, the greatly increased power of desktop computers now permits the analysis of such data to be carried out very rapidly. Under these circumstances the types of research studies that can be designed, the amounts of data that can be collected, and the wealth of detail extracted by statistical analysis have been markedly changed. As a consequence, the field of educational research itself has also been changed.

4. THE IMPACT OF EDUCATIONAL RESEARCH

A recent Australian report (Holbrook et al., 2000) has identified four main ways through which systematic inquiry in education has an impact on educational policy and practice: (a) the production and dissemination of ideas and knowledge; (b) investigator controlled applied research; (c) investigator-user linkages; and (d) user-oriented action research. These four modes of impact may be seen in Figure 1, as knowledge and ideas from World 3 are brought back to change World 1 (The Real World).

4.1. Production and Dissemination of Knowledge and Ideas

The link from World 3 back to World 2 involves both formal instruction and the less formal dissemination of knowledge and ideas back into the minds of individual persons, to change the ways in which they (in World 2) and social groups (in World 2B) think about World 1 (The Real World) that confronts them. The distinctions between basic, strategic and applied research do not apply as readily in the social and behavioural sciences as they do in the natural sciences.

4.2. Investigator Controlled Applied Research

The impact of research by means of which the investigator operates through technology to change the real world has not been prominent, although not completely absent in the field of education, during the twentieth century. However, today it assumes greater prominence, due to the emergence of World 3T, (the world of Information and Communications Technology). There are ways in which the investigator can apply information and communications technology both to change the processes of learning and to change the manner in which World 1 (The Real World) is operating.

4.3. Investigator – User Linkages

In the impact of educational research through investigator-user linkages, the knowledge and ideas stored in World 3 not only changes the way in which the user in World 2 views the real world, but also, since that world is in part, created by the user, changes can be made directly to World 1 itself, through changes in both policies and practices. Thus, there is a link back from World 3 to World 1, operating necessarily through individuals in World 2 and groups of individuals in World 2B, in which the findings of research are used to change World 1 (The Real World) within which the human agents of change live, work and learn.

4.4. User-oriented Action Research

This form of impact involves the link between World 2B and World 1. Within this link the user undertakes action research to examine the real world, to investigate the conditions and need for change, and through controlled investigation examines the conditions required to optimize the desired changes. Subsequently social action takes place to change World 1 (The Real World) employing knowledge and ideas drawn from World 3 through the minds of the group of individuals in World 2B who have conducted action research prior to the introduction of change.

The commonly held scientific and technological view of the application of research is seriously inadequate in the field of education since it is primarily concerned with only investigator controlled applied research. Moreover, it grossly underestimates the practical impact of social science research (Giddens, 1984) and, in particular, educational research. In the study of social and educational processes people do not remain the passive subjects of inquiry. They are responsible for their own ideas and actions. They understand the debate about ideas arising from research and they not only assimilate these ideas, but they also accommodate to them and are changed. The real world is not only unknowable without the views and perceptions of the people in it, but also, the ideas generated in research in education have a very significant impact on the world, as they know it. As a consequence they change World 1 (The Real World) through the double hermeneutic process.

4.5. *The Power of New Ideas*

There are important reasons why it is not possible to point specifically to a substantial number of universal generalizations or very significant applications and discoveries that have been generated by research in education. When, from the study of human action, new ideas and concepts emerge that explain educational processes in a clearer way than the members of the educational world are able to provide, these ideas are appropriated by those members and are built back into their thinking and their working lives. These ideas also have the effect of changing educational processes. It is not that the views and relationships previously associated with educational processes are necessarily wrong, but rather that the new ideas are so powerful that they change not only the perceptions of the educational processes, but also the operation of the processes themselves. Ideas about the roles of women in society, educational disadvantage, ethnic and racial relations, and lifelong learning are obvious examples of such important changes that have occurred in education during recent decades.

5. FACTORS INFLUENCING EDUCATIONAL RESEARCH

An awareness of some of the factors that influence developments in the field of educational research has emerged from the studies reported and examined by Conant (1947) and Suppes (1978). Three factors can be identified, namely: (a) a response to critical issues and problems, (b) the impact of technology, and (c) new ideas and new perspectives that are derived from other disciplinary areas.

5.1. *Response to Critical Issues and Problems*

Emerging issues and problems in the field of education have the capacity to change the direction of educational research while these issues and problems are being investigated. The public concern for such issues commonly releases funds for this type of research, and public debate about the issues helps to generate ideas about the underlying nature of the problems involved, as well as to identify the aspects of the problems that are amenable to research. Unfortunately, public awareness of the issues and the demands for research and investigation arise only when the problems have become obvious. Good research takes time to conduct. Consequently, persons responsible for the identification of research priorities must attempt to anticipate such issues and have research studies in progress before the problems become critical. Educational research workers must become aware of the long-term needs of society and seek to investigate research issues related to those needs, well in advance of the emergence of problems that demand resolution.

5.2. *The Impact of Technology*

The development of computers and their rapid advancement in both power and ease of use changed the ways in which research in education could be conducted. This led to marked changes in the nature and support for educational research in the mid-1960s and is likely to lead to further change through the investigation of the uses of information and communications technology. Much more is involved than arises from changes in the storage and analysis of data. However, the emphasis on data has divided the field very superficially into qualitative and quantitative studies and into interpretative and explanatory research.

The rapid growth in the amount of research being conducted over recent decades, not only into educational processes, but in all fields has given rise to the knowledge explosion, to the expansion of higher education and to the availability and widespread use of computers. Furthermore, the storage and dissemination of this new knowledge is greatly facilitated by the use of computers through the emerging field of information and communications technology. Consequently, it is not appropriate to view education as involving only the training and induction of young people into the adult world. Education is a process that operates throughout life, and all people need to become self-directed learners who are able to access new knowledge through the new information and communications technology, and who wish to do so at all stages in their lives.

5.3. *New Ideas from Other Disciplines*

A further consequence of the expansion of knowledge in other disciplinary areas is the impact of key new ideas in other fields that have a relevance and potential influence on the field of education. Recent and ongoing research into the operation of the brain and the field of neuroscience is a highly significant area for research into educational processes. Likewise, advances in the field of medicine have changed markedly life expectancy and the health of people, as well as leading to a population explosion in certain regions of the world. These changes have very significant implications for research in the field of education. Furthermore, changes in the fields of economics, and international finance, coupled with expansion in the provision of educational services, place immense strains on the operation of educational institutions. These strains demand research and investigation.

The determination of priorities in educational research solely through consideration of the existing magnitude and consequences of current issues would seem unwise. It is also necessary to consider the researchability of the problem and whether new technology, new methods of inquiry from other disciplines and new conceptual frameworks from other fields would make a particular problem more amenable to investigation than it was previously.

5.4. *Criteria for the Setting of Priorities in Educational Research*

An Australian Panel for a Strategic Review of Research in Education (McGaw et al., 1992, pp. 72–75) identified six criteria for the setting of priorities in a national research agenda that would seem to apply to all levels of inquiry in education.

Social and economic needs. Research into issues and problems in education is undertaken within a changing social, political and economic context and this context must be taken into consideration in identifying priorities for research. Studies that anticipate changes in society are of particular importance although they may be very difficult to sell to administrators and politicians who have perspectives that are restricted to the short-term and the resolution of currently critical problems.

Equity, social and racial justice. Because educational research is conducted in the realm of ideas, and has the capacity to change the ways in which people think, as has been discussed in previous sections of this article, it would seem essential that in establishing priorities for educational research, consideration is given to questions of equity and the tensions identified in the Delors Report (Delors, 1996). The tensions involving equity and justice, the identification of strategies to overcome barriers and the use of these tensions productively are major factors in advancing priorities for research.

Needs for professional development. All who are involved in a teaching role in education have a need to keep abreast of the remarkable expansion of knowledge. Thus educational research has a particular obligation to assist all workers in the field of education to accept a problem-based or research-based approach to learning in their own lives, and to convey this perspective to their students in their teaching.

Existing research strengths. Each individual, team, research organisation, university department and national research tradition has existing strengths that need to be consolidated and developed. No single person or national body can seek to cover all aspects of the field of educational research. Consequently, choices must be made in setting priorities that build on existing strengths.

Advances in the research field. In the setting of priorities, consideration must be given not only to recent advances in the field, but also to the identification of areas where advance is possible within the constraints of expertise of research workers, availability of finance and the time required to achieve substantial findings and conclusions.

Important gaps. One of the functions of identifying priorities is to fill significant gaps in existing research programs. By focusing attention on the deficiencies that exist in research programs more complete views of problem situations are obtained that provide guidance for contributing to the resolution of the problems.

6. STATEMENT OF PRIORITIES

Each individual, team, organisation and national educational body must implicitly or explicitly identify its priorities for the conduct of research into educational problems in its sphere of influence. In the section that follows, statements on the research priorities from several different countries are presented.

6.1. *Australia*

Nearly a decade ago The Review Panel for the Strategic Review of Research in Education in Australia in 1992 proposed nine priority areas that it considered should stand for a minimum period of several years before being reviewed (McGaw et al., 1992, pp. 78–81). These may be considered as three groups of priority areas. The first group comprises research in areas of continuing importance to education and the improvement of professional practice, in particular: (a) the teaching of thinking skills, (b) learning in the preschool and adult years, and (c) assessment of student learning. The second group concerns research into the organisation and management of educational structures, in particular: (a) leadership and management in devolved educational systems, (b) education, training and work, and (c) teachers' work. The third group involves research directed towards the revision and improvement in specific areas of the curriculum, in particular: (a) mathematics education, (b) science education, and (c) language and literacy education.

6.2. *The Peoples Republic of China*

During the past five years (1996–2001) educational research in China has experienced marked growth and educational research workers have become much more active than ever before. Research programs have been introduced that are based on: (a) the ongoing development of basic educational theory; (b) the investigation of problems and application of research findings that focus on current educational issues; (c) the advancement of learning and teaching; and (d) the undertaking of cooperative research activities in new and diversified fields of inquiry.

Ongoing development of basic educational theory. This type of research has been traditional in the field of education in China. Current programs emphasise (a) the integration of different fields of knowledge (the social sciences, the natural sciences and the human sciences); (b) links between education and industry, between education and technology and between education and the making of policy; and (c) studies of the tensions between traditional culture and modern culture as well as between the East and the West.

Application of findings that focus on current issues. The major issues facing education in China are: (a) the development of private education, (b) the funding of educational expansion, (c) curriculum reform, (d) the education of teachers, and (e) the conduct of examinations and student assessment.

Advancement of learning and teaching. One of the important areas for studies involves the use of computer technology, particularly with regard to the development of software, as well as multimedia teaching, and the use of information and communications technology. In addition, problems associated with learning how to study and activity teaching are considered to be very important.

Undertaking of cooperative research activities. There is recognition that the fields of educational inquiry are becoming more extensive, and links with research workers in other parts of the world can be more readily established. Consequently, there is need to diversify research programs and become more involved with scholars working in other lands.

Priorities for future studies. The range of research studies that might be undertaken in the coming five year period is wide and a listing of priorities for research is essential. The following 12 issues are seen to have high priority:

- adjusting educational structures to meet the needs of modernisation,
- developing the system of compulsory education,
- reform in rural education and development in rural areas and the western regions,
- use of educational information technology,
- sustainable development of higher education,
- lifelong education and learning,
- strengthening moral education,
- reform and modernising the curriculum and teaching methods,
- reform of the examination system and standards of assessment,
- investigating the development of the brain and the implications for educational practice,
- the development of students with a healthy personality and an innovatory spirit, and
- research into the making of educational policy and the educational legal system.

7. CONCLUSION

In recent decades, a conflict has developed in educational research concerned with both the methods of inquiry and the purposes of research and scholarly work. This article argues for the unity of the field of educational research, that lies in the investigation and resolution of the many complex problems involved in educational processes, as well as in the testing of knowledge within the framework of coherentism. Quine and Ullian (1978) have advanced five criteria for the unifying and systematising of knowledge, namely, fruitfulness, testability, generality, coherence and simplicity. In addition, there is the recognition that the quest for knowledge is never fully achieved and theory is never complete or fully developed. However, in the field of education remarkable progress has been made in the years from the mid-1960s. This was the time when educational research started to become firmly established in the Asia-Pacific region. Now nearly 40 years on, educational research in the region is clearly entering a highly productive phase and is being strengthened by a unity of purpose and scholarly efforts.

REFERENCES

Conant, J. B. (1947). *On Understanding Science: An Historical Approach*. New Haven, Connecticut: Yale University Press.

Delors, J. (1996). *Learning: The Treasure Within* (Report to UNESCO of the International Commission on Education for the Twenty-first Century). Paris: UNESCO.

Giddens, A. (1984). *The Constitution of Society*. Cambridge: Polity Press, and Oxford: Blackwell.

Holbrook, A. et al. (2000). Mapping educational research and its impact on Australian schools. In Department of Education, Training and Youth Affairs. *The Impact of Educational Research* (pp. 15–278). Canberra: DETYA.

Jackson, P. W., & Kiesler, S. B. (1997). Fundamental research and education. *Educational Research*, 6(8), 13–18,

Kish, L. (1987). *Statistical Design for Research*. New York: Wiley.

McGaw, B. (Chair) (1992). *Educational Research in Australia* (Report of the Review Panel Strategic Review of Research in Education). Canberra: AGPS.

Popper, K. R., & Eccles, J. C. (1997). *The Self and Its Brain*. London: Routledge and Kegan Paul.

Quine, W. V., & Ullian, J. S. (1978). *The Web of Belief*. London: Random House.

Suppes, P. C. (Ed.) (1978). *Impact of Research on Education: Some Case Studies: Summaries*. Washington, DC: National Academy of Education.

83

University Education for National Development

MOLLY N.N. LEE
Universiti Sains Malaysia, Malaysia

SUK YING WONG
Chinese University of Hong Kong, Hong Kong

1. INTRODUCTION

University education is the apex of any education system and it is also the most costly when compared to the other levels of education. Throughout the world, national governments invest heavily in tertiary education with a strong belief that universities play an important role in national development. It is no different in the Asia-Pacific region. Despite theoretical scepticism and ambiguous research findings, the connection between higher education and development continues to be featured in many national development plans. Discourses and research on university education for national development usually seek to address a multidimensional concept of development. The key question that is commonly asked is, how do universities contribute to the economic, the political and socio-cultural development of a nation? Others have asked more critical questions such as: What kind of development? For whom? For What purpose? How? (Saha, 1991).

The relationship between universities and national development may not be a one-way relationship but could possibly be dialectical. On the one hand, higher education may be a vehicle for national development, and national development can also affect the development of the higher education system in general, and universities in particular. As pointed out by Wang (1992) in his essay on universities in transition in Asia, when societies change, universities are expected to respond accordingly. It is possible for societies to be changing faster than universities as well as universities to be changing faster than their societies. A review of the literature shows that policy makers and educational administrators are generally more interested in how higher education can contribute to national development, whereas scholars and academicians tend to be more interested in how higher education systems are affected by the contextual change of the societies concerned.

The aim of this article is two-fold, one, to review research studies on the role of university education in national development in the Asia-Pacific region, focusing on the theoretical underpinnings of these studies and on some of the empirical findings. The article also examines how national development has resulted in many educational reforms as illustrated by the development of universities in selected countries. Although the Asia-Pacific region is a vast and diverse one, many of the countries do share a variety of common characteristics in terms of their educational performance and development paths. Because of the constraints of the length of the article and the availability of relevant literature, it is not possible to cover every single country or all the research studies that have been done on this region. However, every effort has been made to provide cross-national coverage and references are made to specific countries in this region to illustrate certain developments in this area of educational research.

2. THEORETICAL PERSPECTIVES

Since the end of World War II much has been written on the relationship between education and development, starting with the so-called 'age of innocence' and leading onto the 'age of scepticism'. This section reviews critically the various theoretical underpinnings of the discourse and research on this important topic with specific reference to university education. The structural functionalist perspective views education as an instrument of development by directly socialising individuals into those skills, attitudes, and values deemed crucial to the development of modern institutions (socialisation theory), and by improving the quality of human capital required for economic growth (human capital theory). University education is often viewed as an avenue for social mobility, and a vehicle to promote national identity and national unity. Much of the research literature on national development, especially those publications that were produced by international agencies and bodies focused on the utilitarian functions of universities in contributing towards economic growth, social equality, cultural transmission and good citizens. For examples, the Association of Commonwealth Universities organised a congress on *The Contribution of Universities to National Development* in Perth, Australia in 1988. In the same year, the Asian Development Bank came out with a publication entitled *Education and Development in Asia and the Pacific*, and in 1990, the Association of Southeast Asia Institutions of Higher Learning (ASAIHL) organised a conference and report on *The Role of ASAIHL Universities in Promoting Economic Development Through Regional Cooperation* in Manila, Philippines.

The structural functionalist perspective of education and development has been heavily criticised for overlooking the element of conflict as a major dimension in social change. Critical theorists have argued that education is a system of allocation, conferring success on some and failure on others (allocation theory), and instead of promoting social equality, it reproduces the class structures that exist in society (reproduction theory). The critical perspective views education as a contested terrain where different social groups struggle to protect and advance their interests. This perspective sees access to university education as part of a mechanism of domination and social class reproduction. The universities also play an indirect role in maintaining social order by promoting the legitimacy of the state and the credentials it confers. It is argued that the state represents the interests of the ruling power bloc, and it is not as independent as it often likes to project itself, but rather it is a contested terrain where the conflicts and contradictions of different social groups or classes in a nation-state are played out. In the contested state theory, the university is referred to as a potential 'site of struggle' between state hegemonic and counter-hegemonic activities, to use Gramsci's terms.

Institutional theorists have espoused the notion of the link between the modern university and the nation-state as part and parcel of the modernity project. According to Readings (1996), the university as a modern institution plays a central role in the formation of citizens for the nation-state by producing the ideology for national culture and social cohesion. The alliance of power and knowledge, following Foucault (1980), and the use of the modern university to provide the legitimisation to power by building national identity has been exploited by nation-states. As pointed out by Meyer (1977), university education functions in society as a legitimating theory of knowledge defining certain types of knowledge as extant and as authoritative, and at the same time functions as a theory of personnel defining categories of professional elites who possess these bodies of knowledge and forms of authority. He also maintains that university education becomes institutionalised in nearly every country throughout the world because of both the symbolic and utilitarian functions it plays in the process of nation building.

More recent discourse on the relationship between university and the nation-state alludes to the possibility that there is a decoupling of the university and the nation-state. Kwiek (2001) argues that, in the age of globalisation, the university seems no longer to be able to maintain its modern role as a cultural institution closely linked to the nation-state because national identity ceases to be the most important social glue in a globalising society. Furthermore, the university in its traditional modern form is incompatible with the perspective of global consumerism. Therefore, the university needs to re-formulate its role and re-institutionalise itself in a context characterised by the decline of the nation-state. As observed by Readings (1996), "the contemporary university is busily transforming itself from an ideological arm of the state into a bureaucratic organized and relatively autonomous consumer-oriented corporation" (p. 11).

The modern university is a product of Western traditional culture and the impact of Western academic models, practices and orientations on Asian universities has been studied by a number of scholars. Altbach and Selvaratnam (1989) edited a volume entitled *From Dependence to Autonomy* which is comprised of research on the development of universities in ten countries in various parts of Asia. The central argument running through this volume is that Asian universities have a great deal of autonomy to set policies and priorities but the power of Western research and publication system as well as the English language remain key influences. Other studies indicate that the pace of change in Asian higher education is as much a function of economic development as it is of sociopolitical change experienced in each of the countries (Yee, 1995; Postiglione & Mak, 1997). Besides these edited volumes, there are other studies on the development of higher education in Asia-Pacific countries initiated by international bodies like ASAIHL (1989), Institute of Southeast Asian Studies (Ahmat & Siddique, 1987) and SEAMEO RIHED (1996).

3. UNIVERSITY EDUCATION AND ECONOMIC DEVELOPMENT

The contribution of universities to economic development has been identified along three dimensions: (a) producing and accumulating human capital, (b) generating, disseminating, and applying knowledge, and (c) innovating and inventing new information and technology. Many countries in the Asia-Pacific region, especially countries that lack natural resources like Japan, Singapore, and Taiwan, have continued to place faith in human resource development with the expectation of high economic growth. The discourse on investment in human capital may have reached its high-water mark in the 1960s, but it continues to attract much attention among researchers and policy-makers in countries that strive to develop a globalised knowledge economy.

The evidence for linkages between investment in human capital and economic growth is represented by an extensive literature with many nuances. Empirical studies on this topic include individual countries, cross-country surveys, growth accounting exercises and rates of return analysis. On the last point, rates of return to investment in education have generally been found to be high, especially at the private level (see *Higher Education and Development*). In general, private rates of return exceeded the social rates and in both cases returns are highest in the primary sector and that the rate of return is higher in developing countries than the developed countries. Furthermore, in the developing countries the social rates of return to higher education are lower than the returns to primary and secondary education (Psacharopoulos & Woodhall, 1985). However, this does not seem to be the case in some of the newly industrialised Asian countries. Rates of return studies on Singapore in 1980 show that the social rates of return for tertiary, secondary, and primary education are 18.9, 16.9, and 9.0 per cent, respectively; and the private returns are 29.1, 22.9, and 18.1 per cent, respectively (Ng, 1987). A similar study in Malaysia shows that the private rate of return is higher for tertiary education (34.5 per cent) than for secondary education (32.6 per cent) (Lee, 1980).

The high private rates of return for higher education have led to a vast expansion of higher education in the Asia-Pacific region. The growth of enrolment ratios in higher education during the period 1960–1992 is as high as 29 per cent in Japan, 34 per cent in Korea, 14 per cent in Taiwan and Singapore

(Mingat, 1995). When the private rates of return for higher education are greater than the returns to society, the financing of higher education becomes problematic. It is not surprising that many countries have reverted to user-pays or cost-recovery policies. For example, in 1989 Australia implemented fee charges in what had become 16 years earlier, a free university system, and the public universities increased their market-related activities when public funding was reduced by 12 to 15 per cent over the 1997–1999 period (Marginson, 1997). In other countries, the private sector plays a significant role in providing higher education to meet the ever-increasing social demand. Private enrolments as a percentage of all enrolments at the tertiary level are as high as 85 per cent in Philippines, 79 per cent in the Republic of Korea, 70 per cent in Taiwan, 65 per cent in Indonesia, and 57 per cent in India (Lewin, 1998). In the recent years, even socialist countries like China and Vietnam have allowed the involvement of the private sector in higher education.

In the 1990s, there was a lot of interest in the rapid economic growth of a cluster of countries in East Asia and a debate ensued on the role played by educational investment in bringing about this so-called 'economic miracle'. The economic success of the Asian Tigers has generated a range of studies which have attempted to identify the sources of that growth. The 1993 World Bank study of eight high growth Asian economies (Japan, Singapore, Republic of Korea, Hong Kong, Taiwan, Indonesia, Malaysia and Thailand) suggested that educational investment in these countries was both more strategically focused, on basic education first, and in most cases a subsequent emphasis on vocational and technical training at higher levels, and more efficiently managed and that this produced improvements in access and quality which were translated into economic benefits (World Bank, 1993). Other cross-country studies adopted the statist approach and argued that the state had played an active and critical role in promoting the process of economic growth and at the same time in engendering a high-quality, well-controlled labour force (Castells, 1992; Aston et al., 1999).

In essence, the economies in Korea, Taiwan, Hong Kong, and Singapore have been restructured to slow down agricultural production and to expand the industrial, manufacturing and service sectors. In order to sustain the planned industrialisation, among other things, there should be a right mix of skills in the labour force. In this respect, the universities clearly play a prominent role in the training of technologically skilled human resources. The universities also help to develop the specialised personnel and infrastructure for the scientific and research enterprise in each of these countries (Altbach et al., 1989). Through funding managed by national research councils, the governments concerned are able to orient the research agendas to problems of national priority.

However, there is an element of oversimplification in the human capital explanation of the economic success of these four countries because not only are there other factors at work, there are also variations in education's effects on economic growth among these countries. Morris (1996) found a substantial degree of variation across societies in terms of funding for education, the role of the state in providing tertiary education, and the relative emphasis on general and technical education. His study showed that Taiwan and Korea had focused on vocational and technical education whereas Singapore and Hong Kong had relied on more academic curricula. A single case study on Taiwan indicates that senior high school and tertiary education had no significant positive effects on economic growth using time-series data for 1976 and 1986. However, this study shows that primary and junior high school education had strong and positive effects on economic growth in Taiwan. The explanation for these findings lies in the characteristics of the economic structure of Taiwan (Liu & Armer, 1993).

4. UNIVERSITY EDUCATION AND POLITICAL DEVELOPMENT

Within the structural-functional perspective, the notion of political development involves concepts like national integration and political participation. University education can contribute to political development by playing three main functions: (a) political socialisation, (b) selecting and training political elites, and (c) promoting national identity and unity. Universities have a great variety of roles to play. Many multicultural societies like Malaysia, Indonesia, Singapore, look to their universities to promote social and political harmony. The university is the single most important institution which provides future political leaders as well as leaders in bureaucracy, the armed forces and the economy. The most spectacular example is when academics become political leaders and share in the ruling of the country as found in Singapore, Korea, Thailand, Taiwan and Malaysia. On the other hand, universities are often called upon to establish a particular political ideology for the ruling power. Ideological education aimed at socialising the young is observed in China where "education must serve socialist construction"; in North Korea where the officially stated purpose of education is to produce a socialist mind and body through the principle of *Juche*; and in post-revolutionary Iran where Islamic education is heavily stressed in the universities (Postiglione & Mak, 1997).

As mentioned before, the modern university has been linked to the nation-state project. A historical study on higher education in Indonesia shows that Indonesian universities had emerged as an integral component of the revolutionary effort to throw off Dutch and Japanese oppression (Cummings & Kasenda, 1989). Even today, most of the academics in Indonesia look to their national leaders for indication and direction of the preferable course of their work and their institutions. In the case of Japan, the modern university was established during the Meji Period to help to transform the country "from a feudal to modern, unified nation-state composed of a citizenry obedient and loyal to the new nation" (Fujimura-Fanselow, 1997, p. 138). Even the small nation states in the Pacific Ocean grouped together to establish a regional university, namely, University of the South Pacific to promote national unity and regional identity.

Within the critical perspective, the university is a state ideological apparatus and a site of struggle among the ruling groups to serve their political and ideological purposes. An analysis by Mehran (1997) shows how the universities in Iran have been used by different ruling groups for "elite formation, status perpetuation, nation building, creating a new class of technocrats, and bringing about a cultural revolution" (p. 115). She traces the conflict between the *ulama* and the secular elite and shows how their competition for power had been played out in the universities. She observes that the universities have been used both as an element of Westernisation, modernisation, and secularisation and as a tool for Islamisation and political socialisation, depending on who was in power in pre- and post-revolutionary Iran. Another case in point is China. It is interesting to note that China's four modernisations do not include political modernization. Universities in China are to serve the needs of economic, social development but not political development. In fact, during the Cultural Revolution the universities were attacked by the communist state as places disseminating bourgeois ideologies and were not allowed to enrol students for more than four years (Min, 1997). Similarly, between 1975 and 1979 the Khmer Rouge under Pol Pot destroyed all the institutions of higher learning in Cambodia.

The political role of the university is to assume a critical stance to the sociopolitical *status quo* so as to bring about political development and social transformation. Academics and students are public intellectuals and social critics and they are supposed to be agents of change. However, they are more successful in some countries than others. For example, the student revolution of October 1973 had resulted in the downfall of the then military regime in Thailand, and later in October 1976 another student revolt had led to a return of military influence and joint civil-military rule (Watson, 1989). More recently, student political activism contributed to bringing down the Suharto regime in Indonesia. However, the political dissent initiated by students in China during the *Tien An Men* incident in 1989 was squashed by the state. In Burma, Bangladesh, and Sri Lanka universities were frequently closed down by their respective governments when political security was threatened. In Malaysia and Singapore, the governments used legislation and interventionist strategies to suppress academic freedom and curb student activism.

5. UNIVERSITY EDUCATION AND SOCIO-CULTURAL TRANSFORMATION

Following the three dimensions outlined above, this section discusses the extent to which universities are related to the social and cultural development of a society, and thus to national development and national building. This discussion includes an examination of the issue of widening access to higher education, the problem of educated unemployment, the question of financing higher education, and the dilemma of cultural transmission.

One of the most popular topics of research is access to higher education in general and universities in particular. Access to tertiary education has grown at very different rates in the Asia-Pacific countries. The emerging trends in Asia between 1980 and 1992 are well documented in Lewin (1998). The enrolment ratios at the tertiary level in 1991 are the highest in countries where private financing is most significant such as Korea (41%), Philippines (26%), and Thailand (16%). Both Singapore and Hong Kong also have high enrolment ratios, 22 per cent and 19 per cent respectively even though most of the higher education places are publicly funded, partly because of their small populations and resources. During this period, the growth in enrolments as a ratio is found to be high in Fiji (3.9), Lao PDR (2.6), Indonesia (2.9), and Korea (2.5). The high rate of growth in Fiji and Lao PDR is partly due to their low base lines as reflected by the small number of higher education students per 100,000 which, in 1980, was 44 and 275 in Lao PDR and Fiji, respectively, and these jumped to 1112 and 1076 in 1992. On the other hand, tertiary enrolments seem to have been declining in newly independent central Asian countries such as Uzbekistan, Kazakhstan and Azerbaijan.

Higher education has become more diversified with more and more enrolments in institutions outside the traditional universities. Many countries have established junior colleges, community colleges, technical institutes, and polytechnics to accommodate the increasing numbers and diverse backgrounds of the student populations. In China, there are adult higher education institutions such as Workers' Colleges, Management Training Colleges and Educational Colleges (Min, 1997). All kinds of certificate, diploma, and other short-cycle post-secondary courses have become available. In some countries distance and open learning systems have developed to meet the ever-increasing social demand for higher education. For example, Thailand had over 500,000 students enrolled in distance learning at tertiary level in the early 1990s which is more than two and a half times the number in conventional universities (Lewin, 1998). Pakistan, Sri Lanka and Korea also had significant enrolments in distance education.

The widening of access to higher education to non-traditional students and marginalized groups, brought about by demographic changes or political struggle, has also been observed in many countries. Traditionally, universities in Japan are extremely youth-centred and closed to adult learners. But with an aging population and the anticipated decline in the traditional college population, universities are increasingly being forced to attract non-traditional and part-time students like working adults and women including housewives (Fujimura-Fanselow, 1997). The aging of the population is also occurring in Korea, Singapore, China, Sri Lanka, and Thailand and there will be more demand for adult continuing education, either for mid-life career changes, or learning for leisure, in the coming years.

Research findings in this region have shown educational inequalities in higher education along class, gender, ethnic, and regional lines. Differences in educational opportunities among different social strata are most marked at the tertiary level. It is a well-established fact that educational attainment is closely related to the socio-economic status of the student. Competition for admission to universities, especially to top universities, is very stiff in some Asian countries like Japan, Korea, and Thailand, for access to these universities also provides access to desirable and prestigious employment. The high cost of private higher education also disadvantages students from lower income groups.

Regional disparities, urban-rural differences, ethnic and gender differences in access to university education are prevalent in all countries throughout the Asia-Pacific region like India, Sri Lanka, Malaysia, Myanmar, and China. In the functionalist view, the university is a social institution that, as one of its functions, allocates personnel to positions according to educational credentials. The desire for higher status leads people to compete for better jobs by striving for university credentials. But critical theorists argue that it is in the interests of the political elites to marginalize the masses from obtaining university education. However, political contestation among different ethnic groups has resulted in various forms of affirmative actions being taken to widen access to university education in some of these countries (Wang, 1983). Malaysia has, since 1970, implemented an ethnic quota policy whereby student admission to public universities is based on the racial composition of the population. A quota policy based on districts has been implemented in Sri Lanka since 1972 (Jayaweera, 1997). In the case of China, ethnic minorities have been given enrolment priority in the universities (Min, 1997), and in India places in the universities are reserved for the scheduled castes and tribes as well as the so-called 'natives' of certain states (Wang, 1983). All these positive discrimination policies are attempts to redress some of the social inequities that are found in these societies because if there is no widening access of higher education to the economically and educationally disadvantaged groups, then universities tend to work to increase social divisions. Gender inequities in higher education are common in most countries with few exceptions like Philippines and Malaysia. In Malaysia, female students in public universities exceed male students in the ratio of 58:42.

In order to increase educational opportunities, several countries have established new types of institutions like regional universities and colleges so that those who are located in provinces and regions away from the metropolitan centres can also have easy access to higher education. Myanmar has broken new ground in the decentralisation of higher education by establishing 20 regional colleges in 1976–1977. Junior colleges were set up in Vietnam to provide education to the community by helping it to tap the local resources with the use of science and technology (Goel, 1983). Regional universities in Thailand were established to meet the increasing demand for higher education among the youth in rural areas, to prevent rural-urban drift, and to stimulate growth in economic, social and cultural development in each region (Watson, 1989). However, the existence of a regional university does not necessarily mean that it will automatically become an agent for rural development and there are real dangers that its graduates may not be able to find employment which can lead to further social and political problems.

One of the consequences of increasing access to universities is the problem of graduate unemployment which is widespread in some countries like India, Bangladesh, Pakistan, Philippines and Indonesia. The relationship between education and employment is well researched and documented. In countries where the expansion of higher education has not been accompanied by corresponding economic expansion, the problem of oversupply of graduates emerged. Studies on the employment prospects of the graduates in these countries have shown that there is a mismatch between education and employment. More than 50 per cent of the job seekers in India are found to be educated, including many with a university degree (Jayaram, 1997). In the Philippines, the unemployment rate was about 8.8 per cent and the underemployment rate was almost 18.6 per cent in 1997. Many of the graduates do get employed but often with jobs that are either not in their field of study or at the lower end of the social scale (Gonzalez, 1997). The educated underemployed have resulted from the escalation of educational qualification for jobs that occurs when the supply of people with educational credentials exceed the demands of the labour market. The downgrading of university graduates can be observed in the hiring of teachers from the Philippines as domestics abroad in Asia, the Middle East, and Western Europe.

Asian universities have often been criticised for "producing long queues of poorly trained graduates seeking unavailable jobs" (Wang, 1992, p. 21) because many of these universities are poor imitations of the Western model which may not suit the socio-economic conditions and development requirements of the societies concerned. There is a tendency for the university to overplay its credentialing function leading to a so-called 'paper chase' for those who view higher education as the only means for upward mobility. Where the problem arises, it is counterproductive for the government to restrain access to higher education for it may lead to social unrest. As pointed out by Gonzalez (1997), most of the 1,090 colleges and universities would have to continue to play a necessary custodial role for Philippine society. In Sri Lanka, graduate unemployment had to be contained in a politically volatile context by special state interventions to absorb unemployed graduates into the service sectors (Jayaweera, 1997). For example, thousands of arts graduates were appointed by the government as teachers on the eve of a general election in 1976. In China, the problem of graduate employment takes a slightly different form, for during the communist regime jobs were assigned to graduates but since the 1980s, a job market had emerged and today graduates have to seek their own jobs and a policy of 'employment by merit' is practised throughout the country (Cheng, 1994).

The issue of the social relevance of universities becomes more complicated when universities are required to play the dual role of preserving a cultural heritage on the one hand and to promote cultural change on the other. The dilemma of cultural transmission is reflected in the tension between the new and the old. Bray's study (1997) of the Pacific Islands shows that all these societies face considerable tension between the traditional and the newly imported Western ways of life, and the modern universities transmit values that often conflict with those held in indigenous cultures. Universities in Indonesia and Malaysia have made conscious efforts to promote the indigenous cultures by adopting the national language as the medium of instruction after gaining political independence.

The issue of cultural transmission gets even more complex when the question of 'whose culture?' is raised. This question is particularly pertinent in multicultural societies. In India, Philippines, and Indonesia, religious bodies have set up their own universities to promote their religious beliefs and values. The notion of cultural dominance is detected in a collection of articles on the contribution of universities to development in Muslim societies in Southeast Asia (Ahmat & Siddique, 1987). In Muslim dominant societies like Indonesia and Malaysia, writers note the importance of higher education based on Islamic philosophy and cultural traditions to train political elites, and the role of the universities to supply Malay managerial, professional and scientific personnel for the modern economy. On the other hand, in societies with Muslim minorities like Singapore, Thailand and Philippines, contributors note the failure of the universities to transmit and sustain the Muslim culture. Mehran (1997) analysed the role of the universities in transforming Iran from a traditional and religious society to a modern and secular one and then back to a religious society. According to her, "the post-revolutionary Islamic universities were to be fundamentally transformed to provide Islamic education and spiritual/moral training as well as teach sciences to bring about self-reliance for the nation" (Mehran, 1997, p. 126). Her study shows that universities reflect the existing socio-political realities of the place and period.

A key role of the modern university is to generate new knowledge, to disseminate knowledge, and to apply and utilize knowledge. Research efforts have focused on questions like what kinds of knowledge and for what purpose? Whose knowledge? and Who get access to what knowledge? In the era of globalisation, it is possible to observe the internationalisation of higher education with the continuous flow of knowledge, academic staff, students and educational programs which tend to lead to cultural convergence in terms of academic knowledge, information and ideas that get transmitted to the students all over the world. This trend has led to the influence of external international standards on educational programs offered in the local universities (Lewin, 1998). In trying to emulate and compete with universities of international standing, some local universities often become out of step with their own culture and insensitive to their own society's needs. Studies on the relationship between university education and national development have raised questions of how to adapt foreign knowledge to serve national needs (Zhong & Hayhoe, 1993), and how local universities in this region attempted to shift from knowledge seeking to knowledge creation (Cummings, 1994).

A study by Altbach et al. (1989) on the universities and scientific development in Malaysia, Singapore, Taiwan and Korea shows that a sufficiently indigenous scientific base has developed so that science and technology as taught and researched in local universities have made important contributions to the national development of these four countries. The search for complementarity of local and global knowledge in the Asia-Pacific region is a topic of research done by Teasdale and his team in Flinders University in Australia (Teasdale, 1998). This research project used a variety of research methods to investigate the interplay of local and global culture and knowledge in schools and universities. Some studies have described and documented local cultures of knowledge in indigenous Australian settings, in Aotearoa New Zealand, and the South Pacific Region, and others are case-studies of schools and higher education institutes that have attempted to seek ways to blend local and global processes of knowledge to create new ways of teaching, learning and knowing. These studies indicate that universities are often called upon to reconstitute and reformulate their roles and functions in the era of globalisation. There are calls for the universities to provide a counterweight against the 'de-culturing' and 'de-nationalizing' forces of globalisation and at the same time to "avoid the socially and politically crippling extremes of nationalism, parochialism, and social fragmentation" (Johnstone, 2001, p. 6).

6. CONCLUSION

The university can shape society and in turn it is shaped by society. This article has reviewed the discourse and research done on the dialectical relationship between university education and national development in the Asia-Pacific region. National development can be interpreted in various ways to mean economic growth, equitable distribution of wealth, full employment, promotion of social welfare, and enhancement of cultural satisfactions, all which would lead to a better quality of life. The review shows that university education alone cannot bring about the desired social change or improve the material conditions of the people. Educational development must be accompanied by political and economic strategies of national development. The contribution of universities to national development is complex and multidimensional and may take different forms in different countries depending on the historical context of the countries concerned. On the other hand, universities seldom rise above the socio-economic and political context in which they are embedded. Universities are both international and national institutions with commitments to their own countries as well as commitment to the international academic community. Therefore, the development of universities is shaped and influenced by global challenges and national responses.

REFERENCES

Ahmat, S., & Siddique, S. (Eds.) (1987). *Muslim Society, Higher Education and Development in Southeast Asia.* Singapore: Institute of Southeast Asia.

Altbach, P. G., & Selvaratnam, V. (Eds.) (1989). *From Dependence to Autonomy: The Development of Asian Universities.* Dordrecht: Kluwer Academic Publishers.

Altbach, P. G., Davis, C. H., Eisemon, T. O., Gopinathan, S., Hsieh, H. S., Lee, S., Pang, E. F., & Singh, J. S. (1989). *Scientific Development and Higher Education: The Case of Newly Industrializing Nations.* New York: Praeger.

Association of Southeast Asia Institutions of Higher Learning (ASAIHL) (1989). *University Education in the 1990s.* Proceedings of a seminar in Bangi, Malaysia, 4–7 December 1989.

Aston, D., Green, F., James, D., & Sung, J. (1999). *Education and Training for Development in East Asia*. London: Routledge.

Bray, M. (1997). Papua New Guinea and the Pacific Islands. In G. A. Postiglione & G. C. L. Mak (Eds.), *Asian Higher Education* (pp. 245–264). Westport, Connecticut: Greenwood Press.

Castells, M. (1992). Four Asian tigers with a dragon head: A comparative analysis of the state, economy, and society in the Asian Pacific Rim. In R. P. Appelbaum & J. Henderson (Eds.), *States and Development in the Asian Pacific Rim* (pp. 33–70). Newsbury Park: Sage Pub.

Cheng, K. M. (1994). Young adults in a changing socialist society: Post-compulsory education in China. *Comparative Education*, 30(1), 63–73.

Cummings, W. K., & Kasenda, S. (1989). The origin of modern Indonesia higher education. In P. G. Altbach & V. Selvaratnam (Eds.), *From Dependence to Autonomy: The Development of Asian Universities* (pp. 143–166). Dordrecht: Kluwer Academic Publishers.

Cummings, W. K. (1994). From knowledge seeking to knowledge creation: The Japanese university's challenge. *Higher Education*, 27, 399–415.

Foucault, M. (1980). *Power and Knowledge: Selected Interviews and Other Writings, 1972–1977*. Brighton: Harvester Press.

Fujimura-Fanselow, K. (1997). Japan. In G. A. Postiglione & G. C. L. Mak (Eds.), *Asian Higher Education* (pp. 137–164). Westport, Connecticut: Greenwood Press.

Goel, S. C. (1983). *Higher Education in Asia and the Pacific: A Perspective Study*. Paris: Unesco.

Gonzalez, A. (1997). Philippines. In G. A. Postiglione & G. C. L. Mak (Eds.), *Asian Higher Education* (pp. 265–284). Westport, Connecticut: Greenwood Press.

Jayaram, N. (1997). India. In G. A. Postiglione & G. C. L. Mak (Eds.), *Asian Higher Education* (pp. 75–91). Westport, Connecticut: Greenwood Press.

Jayaweera, S. (1997). Sri Lanka. In G. A. Postiglione & G. C. L. Mak (Eds.), *Asian Higher Education* (pp. 325–343). Westport, Connecticut: Greenwood Press.

Johnstone, B. D. (2001). Globalisation and the Role of Universities, http://www.gse.buffalo.edu/FAS/Johnston/RoleofUniversities.htm/.

Kwiek, M. (2001). Globalisation and higher education. *Higher Education in Europe*, 26(1), 27–38.

Lee, K. H. (1980). Education, Earnings and Occupational Status in Malaysia, 1978, unpublished Ph.D. thesis, London School of Economics.

Lewin, K. M. (1998). Education in emerging Asia: Patterns, policies, and futures into the 21st century. *International Journal of Educational Development*, 18(2), 81–118.

Liu, C., & Armer, M. J. (1993). Education's effect on economic growth in Taiwan. *Comparative Education Review*, 37(3), 304–321.

Marginson, S. (1997). Imagining Ivy: Pitfalls in the privatization of higher education in Australia. *Comparative Education Review*, 41(4), 460–480.

Mehran, G. (1997). Iran. In G. A. Postiglione & G. C. L. Mak (Eds.), *Asian Higher Education* (pp. 115–136). Westport, Connecticut: Greenwood Press.

Meyer, J. W. (1977). The effects of education as an institution. *American Journal of Sociology*, 83(1), 55–77.

Min, W. (1997). China. In G. A. Postiglione & G. C. L. Mak (Eds.), *Asian Higher Education* (pp. 37–56). Westport, Connecticut: Greenwood Press.

Mingat, A. (1995). Towards Improving Our Understanding of the Strategy of High Performing Asian Economies in the Education Sector. International Conference on Financing Human Resource Development in Advanced Asian Economies. Manila: Asia Development Bank.

Morris, P. (1996). Asia's four little tigers: A comparison of the role of education in their development. *Comparative Education Review*, 32(1), 95–109.

Ng, S. F. (1987). Returns to Investment in Education in Singapore, unpublished Master thesis, National University of Singapore.

Postiglione, G. A., & Mak, G. C. L. (Eds.) (1997). *Asian Higher Education*. Westport, Connecticut: Greenwood Press.

Psacharopoulous, G., & Woodhall, M. (1985). *Education for Development: An Analysis of Investment Choices*. New York: Oxford University Press.

Readings, B. (1996). *The University in Ruins*. Cambridge, Massachusetts: Harvard University Press.

Saha, L. J. (1991). Universities and national development: Issues and problems in developing countries. *Prospects, 21*(2), 248–257.

SEAMEO, RIHED and UNESCO, PROAP (1996). *Reengineering of Higher Education for the 21st Century.* First SEAMEO-UNESCO PROAP Regional Conference on Higher Education in Penang, Malaysia.

Teasdale, G. R. (1998). Local and global knowledge in higher education: A search for complementarity in the Asia-Pacific region. *International Journal of Educational Development, 18*(6), 501–511.

Wang, B. L. C. (1983). Positive discrimination in education: A comparative investigation of its bases, forms, and outcomes. *Comparative Education Review, 27*(2), 191–203.

Wang G. W. (1992). Universities in transition in Asia. *Oxford Review of Education, 18*(1), 17–27.

Watson, K. (1989). Looking west and east: Thailand's academic development, In P. G. Altbach & V. Selvaratnam (Eds.), *From Dependence to Autonomy: The Development of Asian Universities* (pp. 63–95). Dordrecht: Kluwer Academic Publishers.

World Bank (1993). *The East Asian Miracle: Economic Growth and Public Policy.* Washington, DC: World Bank.

Yee, A. H. (Ed.) (1995). *East Asian Higher Education: Traditions and Transformations.* Great Britain: International Association of University Press and Pergamon.

Zhong, W., & Hayhoe, R. (1993). Higher education in China: Challenges of making foreign knowledge serve China. In Smart, J. C. (Ed.), *Higher Education: Handbook of Theory and Research* (Vol. 9, pp. 389–427). New York: Agathan Press.

84

Culturally Inclusive Teacher Education in Oceania*

KONAI HELU THAMAN
University of the South Pacific, Suva, Fiji

1. SCHOOLING AS CULTURALLY ALIENATING

European and United States colonial activities in the islands of the Pacific Ocean resulted, among other things, in the introduction of schools and the teaching of European and Anglo-American based knowledge, skills and values. This led to the transformation not only of the structures and processes of our cultures but also our worldviews.

Today, the degree to which such processes influence the way we think and learn largely depends on our ability to clarify for ourselves the differences between our received wisdom, from our formal, mainly Western education, and the wisdom of the home cultures in which we grew up and were socialised, and from which we continue to learn important knowledge, skills and values. In the context of formal education, the difference between these two sources is the cultural gap, which is small for those students whose home cultures are attuned to the culture of formal education but wide for those whose home culture is different.

2. EDUCATION AND CULTURE

For my purposes I define education as an introduction to worthwhile learning, and culture as a way of life of a people which includes their store of important knowledge, skills and values expressed through a language and transmitted to the young for the sake of cultural continuity and survival. In this context, education and culture are inextricably interwoven since the content of all education has value underpinnings that are always associated with a particular cultural agenda, given that no education can be culture-free. In most Oceanic societies today, traditional cultural values underpin much of what people emphasise and

---

* This article is reprinted from the *International Education Journal*, 2(5), 1–8 with the permission of the editors of the journal.

think about, and continue to be the framework that people use to justify their behaviour and to explain the behaviour of others (Thaman, 1988).

In most Oceanic communities, people still share a worldview in which life is a web of interrelationships that provide meaning to and a framework for their existence in a particular society. This framework, often manifested in different types of kinship relationships, defines particular ways of being and behaving as well as knowledge and wisdom, and how these are passed on from one generation to another. In this context, worthwhile learning ought to be about cultural survival and continuity, with a curriculum that is similar to that described by Lawton (1974) as a collection of the best of a culture, the transmission of which is so important that it must not be left to chance but to specially prepared people – teachers. Sadly, though, most of our schools and institutions of higher learning, such as teachers' colleges, are actually sites of struggle as most of our teachers and learners continue to teach and learn about knowledge, skills and values that are almost exclusively associated with cultures other than their own, and often very alien to their lived realities, making schooling irrelevant and meaningless for many learners as well as teachers.

3. THE SCHOOLING AGENDA

In so-called 'developed countries' the school is normally expected to serve three functions, namely to promote economic progress, to transmit culture and to cultivate children's intellectual and moral development (Serpell, 1993). We know, however, that in practice schools fall far short of the ideal synthesis of all of these functions. In Oceania, as in most developing, post-colonial contexts, the economic and cultural agendas of schooling continue to come into conflict, mainly because of different perceptions about children's upbringing and its relationship to their moral and intellectual development. The cultural agenda is embedded within Pacific Island indigenous cultural traditions, while the economic agenda is European-based, informing what teachers and students are supposed to do in school.

In such a situation, many teachers occupy a culturally ambiguous position. On the one hand their professional training commits them to the rationale, processes and practice of a culturally alien school curriculum, while on the other their personal identities are usually rooted in their Pacific Island cultural traditions and norms. Their training makes them part of a group whose knowledge and skills help set them apart from the rest of the community, yet their early upbringing was mainly in the medium of an indigenous or local language that is similar to if not directly continuous with that in which most of their pupils are growing up. Furthermore, the relationships between pupils and teachers as well as those between pupils and their parents are negotiated within the terms of reference of local and indigenous cultures which have their own ideas about moral and cognitive development, interpersonal and social responsibility, as well as the development of wisdom.

In Oceania the extent to which the school represents the cultures of teachers and students is minimal. The officially sanctioned values are those of the school bureaucracy, the introduced curriculum and the teaching profession, not those of the majority of teachers and learners. Moreover, as alluded to earlier, school culture relies on universalism and impersonality while the cultures of most teachers and students rely on specific contexts and interpersonal relationships (Thaman, 1988). Schooling promotes individual merit while Oceanic cultures are still generally based on the primacy of the group. At best schooling offers the fortunate few access to the modern, monetised sector; at worst, it is a recipe for cultural destruction and systematised selfishness. Today, as we grapple with increasing student underachievement, high push-out rates and general ineffectiveness, many people are asking the question: "What and whose knowledge is considered worthwhile to teach and to learn in school?"

4. CURRICULUM RELEVANCE

The concern with curriculum relevance in our region dates back to the early 1970s when the school curriculum was seen by Pacific Island leaders as an important instrument in preparing people for independence from various colonial masters. A major regional curriculum project funded by UNDP and managed by UNESCO was based at the University of the South Pacific from 1970 to 1975. Charged with the development of curriculum materials for junior high schools (in Mathematics, English, Science, Social Science, Home Economics and Industrial Arts), the project involved foreign experts and local teachers; some of the curriculum materials produced are still used in our schools today.

An important lesson learnt from this project was the realisation by some curriculum personnel that the products as well as the process of curriculum development needed to be more culturally sensitive and inclusive (Thaman, 1985). The designation by the United Nations of a World Decade for Cultural Development (1987–97) served to strengthen this concern and a UNESCO regional seminar in Rarotonga, Cook Islands in 1992 provided an opportunity for Pacific Island educators to reaffirm the need for them to have ownership of their formal education, for the betterment of their various societies. The establishment of a UNESCO Chair in Teacher Education and Culture at the regional University of the South Pacific five years later was evidence of the international community's commitment to teacher education as a vehicle for ensuring cultural inclusiveness in formal education in our region.

5. THE IMPORTANCE OF TEACHERS

Teachers have not always been at the centre of the international community's attention. In 1995, for example, the World Bank Education Sector Review of six key options for reforming education systems did not even mention teachers, their selection or training. Such evident neglect of teachers reinforced a belief in many of our countries, including for example, in the regional curriculum reform project I mentioned earlier, that education systems could be changed without having to deal with teachers. By the mid-1990s teachers throughout the world, including Oceania, had been relegated to an inferior role both in relation to their working conditions and from the viewpoint of teaching itself.

Teachers, however, have finally attracted attention. In 1996 for example, the Report to UNESCO of its Commission on Education for the Twenty-first Century (the Delors Report), devoted a whole chapter to teachers, and warned that countries that wish to improve the quality of education must first improve the recruitment, training, social status and working conditions of their teachers. In 1998, a sub-regional seminar, held in Fiji, agreed that teachers in Oceania had low levels of remuneration and status, and in their joint message to commemorate World Teachers Day in October, 2000 the chief executives of UNESCO and ILO appealed to the world community to renew their commitment of support to teachers. They also asked governments to find ways of honouring the pledge made at the World Education Forum held in Dakar in 2000, and to endorse the Dakar Framework for Action in order to enhance the status, morale and professionalism of teachers and to reaffirm the claim that teachers will remain the core of education systems.

The general neglect of teachers in the educational reforms of the last 30 years in Oceania reflects the global picture. However, there were also other factors. The first relates to a general belief that teachers did not need formal training, a view that is particularly unfortunate when held by key people such as Ministers of Education. Another reason might have been the emphasis, placed by overseas curriculum development consultants, on learners rather than teachers and their attempts to produce so-called 'teacher-proof' curricula, based on the assumption that pupils would learn in spite of their teachers. Finally, teachers were generally left out because of our various countries' heavy dependence on overseas aid donors and their foreign consultants, most of whom brought with them their own educational philosophies and ideologies which, together with the absence of clear national education visions, resulted in the uncritical acceptance of educational theories and ideas by their Pacific counterparts.

6. TARGETING TEACHERS

The remainder of this article outlines how some of us in Oceania are attempting to help teachers ensure that more pupils benefit from their school education by creating culturally inclusive learning environments. I shall explain a joint effort among regional teacher education institutions and the University of the South Pacific (USP), through its UNESCO Chair and its Institute of Education, to assist teacher educators to contextualise better their work in the hope that their students, who would be teachers, would do the same.

In 1992, principals of teachers colleges in the Oceania region met in Suva, Fiji, to form the Pacific Association of Teacher Educators (PATE) and to discuss issues of mutual concern. Among these was the appropriateness of the teacher education curriculum for preparing teachers who understood and appreciated students' needs and backgrounds. It was felt that even though a lot of new curriculum materials had been developed, few teachers understood what curriculum reform was about and fewer still were able to implement satisfactorily new curricula. Participants at the PATE consultation also agreed on the need for cultural relevance not only in the content of the school curriculum but also in its philosophy. A paper presented at that first meeting introduced the idea of a culturally inclusive metaphor '*kakala*' as a framework for both curriculum development and teacher education (Thaman, 1992).

Three years later, at another meeting of PATE, I was asked to present another paper on how Pacific cultural knowledge, skills and values might be incorporated into the curriculum, not only of schools but also of post-secondary institutions. At this meeting, participants agreed to review their respective teacher education curricula in order to make them more culturally democratic. The mechanism for this review was a UNESCO-funded research project that was undertaken jointly by the UNESCO Chair, the USP Institute of Education and regional teachers' colleges. The aim of the project was to find out the extent to which teacher education curricula incorporated aspects of Pacific Island cultures. The results showed a need for improved contextualisation of teacher education courses and a decision was made in 1998 to develop and produce materials in the form of modules which teacher educators in the region might use to help them understand and incorporate indigenous and local Pacific Island knowledge and processes in their work.

The authors of the modules are Pacific Island researchers and educators who recognise the important role of teachers in any attempt to change what goes on in schools. The modules are intended for use by staff of teachers' colleges to help them to contextualise better their teaching as well as to stimulate debate on the relationship between culture and formal education in the Pacific Island region. So far, six modules have been published. The first was entitled *Towards Culturally Democratic Teacher Education*. It introduces the project as well as making brief suggestions about how elements of Pacific Island cultures might be incorporated into different subject areas such as language and communication studies, expressive arts, science, mathematics, human development and education.

The second module, *Vernacular Languages and Classroom Interaction in the Pacific*, by Dr. Ana Taufe'ulungaki from Tonga, examines the use of the mother tongue in basic education as a medium of teaching and learning, and the implications for teacher education. Module 3, *Incorporating Local Knowledge in Teaching about Education and Society* is authored by Ms Una Nabobo and describes a very successful course which she and an Australian colleague, Ms Jennie Teasdale, designed and taught at the Fiji College of Advanced Education. Module 4 was written by New Zealand born Samoan researcher Anne-Marie Tupuola. Entitled *Making Sense of Human Development: Beyond Western Concepts and Universal Assumptions*, she interrogates western psychological theories of human development and examines, in particular, the stage of adolescence as well as notions of individuality and independence. She concludes that it is culturally inappropriate to interpret human development in Pacific Island societies using only Western psychological terms and concepts.

Module 5, *Ways of Mathematising in Fijian Society*, by Dr. Sala Bakalevu, suggests that the problems Fijian students face in learning mathematics is largely due to a mismatch between the students' cultural background and the expectations of schooling. She also says that the Fiji school mathematics curriculum does not recognise Fijian ways of mathematising, such as how Fijians count, measure and practice traditional economy and exchange although Fijian notions have the same mathematical purposes as those described in school mathematics. She suggests that an understanding of ethnomathematics would help teachers encourage students to use strategies derived from their own ways of mathematising, and proceed to formal operations only when pupils are ready. Module 6 is authored by Dr. Kabini Saga of Solomon Islands. Entitled *Learning from Indigenous Leadership*, Saga raises the issue of schools not reflecting the important values of their communities, leading to a denial of ownership of schooling. He urges teachers to help develop ownership and representation and suggests that the study of indigenous leadership processes and structures be included in the teacher education curriculum. Through such studies, he argues, teachers would not only become more sensitive to the cultures of the communities they serve but become better cultural bridges for their students. Four more modules are being prepared for publication.

7. COMPARATIVE STUDIES

As well as materials production, research into indigenous educational ideas is also being encouraged as a major activity. During the past five years, staff and students at our University have been gathering information on various indigenous communities' notions of learning, knowledge and wisdom as part of a course that is taught on *Educational Theories and Ideas*. A summary of this course appears in Teasdale and Ma Rhea (2000). An important part of the course is students' exploration of their own cultural values and educational ideas, and comparison with those of other students. The exercise has proved to be both interesting and instructive as students become aware of the similarities and differences between their own cultural values and those of other Pacific Island cultures as well as between Pacific Island and Western values (Thaman, 2000). A collection of essays about vernacular educational ideas from Oceania is currently under preparation; when completed it will be the main text for the course.

8. A WAY FORWARD

This article concludes with a summary of a Pacific Island education symposium held at the University of the South Pacific early in 2001. A group of about 15 concerned educators from the region met to discuss educational issues currently facing the various Pacific Island nations with a view to future collaboration especially in the areas of educational research and development. A summary of the main recommendations was presented to a meeting of Ministers of Education from the region that was held in Auckland in May 2001.

The symposium was made possible by a grant from the New Zealand Overseas Development Agency. Participants came from Fiji, New Zealand, Tokelau, Samoa, Solomon Islands, Vanuatu, Tonga, Papua New Guinea, Marshall Islands and the University of the South Pacific in Fiji. The meeting was jointly hosted by the USP Institute of Education and Victoria University of Wellington, New Zealand. Participants were chosen because of their reputation in the areas of innovative teaching, consultancy and research as well as their commitment to seeking alternative ways of addressing long established educational issues. Although participants identified many issues, the two overriding ones were: (a) lack of ownership by Pacific Island peoples of the formal education process, and (b) lack of a clearly articulated vision that could inform both development and education in the region, assuming of course that education is accepted as an instrument in achieving national visions and developmental goals. Symposium participants agreed that the main challenge facing the Pacific Island region today had to be the reconceptualisation of education in a way that would allow Pacific peoples to reclaim the education process and at the same time allow for the articulation of a Pacific Island vision for education. Interestingly enough the issue of ownership had already been identified at the Rarotonga meeting of 1992. A new metaphor, *The Tree of Opportunity*, was endorsed by participants as an appropriate framework for re-thinking Pacific Island education.

The *Tree of Opportunity* is firmly rooted in Oceanic cultures. The strengths and advantages that the tree gains from its root source will facilitate growth and strength, and allow for the incorporation of foreign or external elements that could be grafted on to the tree without altering its identity. In educational terms, this would mean ensuring that Pacific Island cultural values are appropriately embedded within the processes and structures of formal education in order to provide a strong foundation for worthwhile learning.

The symposium also considered the various implications of their accepted metaphor. Politically it means defining a new vision for education that recognises the contributions and roles of Oceanic cultures in modern development in general and educational reforms in particular. Such a vision needs to be supported by political commitment and resource provisions, and formalised by various appropriate policies and legislations. Economically, it means focusing on the most disadvantaged groups and ensuring that adequate financial and human resources are allocated in order to facilitate desired results. It would also mean enhancing and strengthening village economies in order to ensure sustainability and security, important bases for developing modern cash economies. Socially it means strengthening relationships and partnerships at all levels, especially links between schools and their communities in order to ensure that all stakeholders are participating in the formulation of national visions and processes of education and development. It will also require the development of appropriate school language policies and the active involvement of custodians of Pacific Island cultures in the process of schooling in order to identify skills and behaviours as well as values, beliefs and knowledge systems that are considered critical for the survival and sustainability of Pacific Island cultures and societies.

Finally, it would mean broadening the outcomes of education in order to ensure that Pacific Island heritages are enhanced and maintained while at the same time provide a foundation for building other types of worthwhile learning that are a synthesis of indigenous and global knowledges. This may be achieved through:

(a) better contextualising the curriculum;
(b) developing a new pedagogy based on Pacific Island values, beliefs and knowledge systems that incorporate Pacific Island styles of learning and ways of knowing;
(c) reorienting teacher education and training in order to ensure that all teachers are competent in, and have a deep understanding of, as many Pacific Island languages and cultures as possible;
(d) developing new forms of student assessment that take account of the anticipated changes in curriculum and pedagogy;
(e) incorporating indigenous Pacific Island processes, ways of management and administrative structures; and
(f) strengthening research capabilities in Pacific Island post-secondary institutions as well as in the various Pacific Island communities.

The symposium also made a number of recommendations both short and long-term in nature, focussing on national as well as regional contexts. These recommendations were grouped under headings such as: Educational Policy Formulation and Development; Curriculum Reform; Teacher Education; and Financing of Education, including the role of foreign aid. However, the recommendations did not seem to sit comfortably with the widely-held view that promotes education almost entirely for economic reasons, concerned largely with the issue of human resource development and widening paid employment opportunities. Although the importance of the economic agenda of schooling cannot be over emphasised, it is felt that the other agendas of the school needed to be taken seriously if student achievement is going to be an important criterion for assessing the success of national investment in formal education.

If, however, we wish to use an economic lens to view schooling in Oceania, we would have to ensure that there is a strong link between a community's economically productive activities and the content of basic education, or primary schooling. Unfortunately the primary school curriculum has been neglected for many years with school examination results, for entry into secondary schools, being used as the main indicator of what a student knows, based on a prescribed program, rather than what a student may know as a result of the quality of teaching experienced. It is therefore important for the schools to place more emphasis on the other agendas of schooling, especially its moral and pedagogical agendas, even though the scope for religious and political manipulation may seem great to some people. Given the contrast mentioned earlier between the practices of children's home cultures and that of the school it would seem desirable for school authorities to consult with adult members of different communities as part of the process of curriculum development. Another factor which was seen as significantly contributing towards students' underachievement in school has to do with the Pacific Island region's heavy reliance on English or French as the mediums of instruction, languages that are the second, third or even fourth languages of many school children. This is a major educational issue that merits deeper analysis.

9. CONCLUSION

The contrast between the culture of modern schooling and most Oceanic cultures as these are lived today and its implications for formal education cannot be over-emphasised. It is, however, not an unbridgeable gap. The main bridge, in the view of many Pacific Island educators, must be the teacher, and it is essential to focus attention on those who prepare teachers in our colleges and higher education institutions. We understand that this is not the only solution, however. We continue to encourage research on Pacific Island indigenous knowledge systems as well as pupils' learning styles, in the knowledge that these would help inform our work. Much remains to be done as we continue to interrogate our different ways of seeing the world in general, and our education in particular. We hope that collectively we will be able to find better and more culturally inclusive ways of ensuring that the majority of our children will benefit from their school education and to have the opportunity to learn about the best their cultures have to offer so that they can create for themselves a synthesis for the purposes of cultural continuity and sustainability.

REFERENCES

Bakalevu, S. (2000). *Ways of mathematising in Fijian society.* Module Five, Pacific Cultures in the Teacher Education Curriculum Series. Suva: UNESCO Chair/Institute of Education, USP.

Lawton, D. (1974). *Class, culture and the curriculum.* London: Routledge and Kegan Paul.

Little, A. (1995). In conclusion: Questions of culture and education. *Prospects: UNESCO Quarterly Review of Comparative Education,* 25(4), 777–782.

Nabobo, U. (2000). *Incorporating local knowledge in teaching about education and society: A Fiji case study.* Module Three, Pacific Cultures in the Teacher Education Curriculum Series, Suva: UNESCO Chair/Institute of Education, USP.

Saga, K. (2000). *Learning from indigenous leadership.* Module Six, Pacific Cultures in the Teacher Education Curriculum Series, Suva: UNESCO Chair/Institute of Education, USP.

Serpell, R. (1993). *The significance of schooling.* Cambridge: Cambridge University Press.

Taufe'ulungaki, A. M. (2000). *Vernacular languages and classroom interaction in the Pacific.* Module

Two, Pacific Cultures in the Teacher Education Curriculum Series. Suva: UNESCO Chair/Institute of Education, USP.

Taufe'ulungaki, A. M. (2001). *The Tree of Opportunity: Re-thinking Pacific Education*. Suva: Symposium Summary, USP.

Teasdale, G. R., & Teasdale, J. I. (Eds.) (1992). *Voices in a seashell: Education, culture and identity*. Suva: IPS/UNESCO.

Teasdale, G. R., & Ma Rhea, Z. (2000). *Local knowledge and wisdom in higher education*. Oxford: Pergamon.

Thaman, K. H. (1988). Ako and Faiako: Cultural values, educational ideas and teachers' role perceptions in Tonga. Unpublished PhD thesis, University of the South Pacific, Suva.

Thaman, K. H. (1992a). Towards a culture-sensitive model of curriculum development for Pacific Island countries. *Directions*, *13*(1), 1–11.

Thaman, K. H. (1992b). Looking towards the source: A consideration of (cultural) context in teacher education. In C. Benson & N. Taylor (Eds.), *Pacific Teacher Education Forward Planning Meeting: Proceedings*. Suva: Institute of Education, USP.

Thaman, K. H. (1995). Concepts of learning, knowledge and wisdom in Tonga, and their relevance to modern education. *Prospects*, *25*(4), 723–735.

Thaman, K. H. (2000a). Towards a new pedagogy: Pacific cultures in higher education. In G. P. Teasdale & Z. Ma Rhea (Eds.), *Local Knowledge and Wisdom in Higher Education* (pp. 43–50). London: Pergamon.

Thaman, K. H. (2000b). *Towards cultural democracy in teacher education*. Introductory Module, Suva: UNESCO Chair/Institute of Education, USP.

Thaman, K. H. (2001). Towards a Pacific philosophy of education: The role of teachers. Keynote address, Fijian Teachers Association AGM, Suva.

Tupuola, A. (2000). *Making sense of human development: Beyond western concepts and universal assumptions*. Module Four, Pacific Cultures in the Teacher Education Curriculum, UNESCO Chair/Institute of Education, USP, Suva.

85

Reforming Secondary Education and the Education of Adolescents

PHILLIP W. HUGHES

Centre for UNESCO, Australian National University, Canberra, Australia

1. INTRODUCTION

Education has felt the impact of dramatic change, particularly over the past 50 years. Its responses have often been ineffective largely because they react to immediate rather than long-term issues. Secondary education has a crucial part in achieving more successful responses since it prepares the young people who will be the managers of future change. Without a major reform secondary education will not be effective in this preparation since it fails to engage a substantial proportion of its students. As this sector is the connecting link for the education system this makes it difficult to improve the effectiveness of the whole. The means for reform are available. The will to apply them is the necessary ingredient.

2. SECONDARY EDUCATION AS A GATEWAY TO THE FUTURE

Education must take account of the breadth and variety of change.

2.1. *Significant Factors of the Period, 1959 to 2000*

- There has been no global war since 1939–45 but it has been a period of continuing violence in which as many people were killed as in that war.
- The world population grew from 2 billion to 6 billion and still grows.
- Life expectancy increased from 47 to 65 years but is unevenly distributed.
- Student numbers rose from 252 million to over 1200 million.
- More that half of the nations existing now became independent in this period.
- City-dwellers increased from 30 to 51 per cent of the world population, an increase of almost 2.5 billion.
- New technology revolutionised communication, transport, work, science and medicine.

- All countries have become part of a global economy, affected by forces which they cannot control individually.
- The world environment is threatened by irreversible deterioration of its forests, its water supply, its top-soil and its atmosphere.
- Social institutions like religion, government and the family have had major changes.
- Young people more than other groups, feel the impacts of change in employment, issues of crime, drug abuse, family break-up, violence and war.

2.2. Education as an International Response

International bodies now see education as so crucial to the future that they are not only making it a key priority but are working together to achieve common goals. The United Nations Declaration of Human Rights specified the right to education: "all people had the right to education, free and compulsory in the elementary stages and generally available for technical and professional education" (United Nations, 1950). For the United Nations (UN) and its member bodies, notably UNESCO, the achievement of that declaration has been a continuing and a cooperative quest. In 1990, in a major effort to assess progress towards universal elementary education, 155 countries, 20 intergovernmental bodies and 150 non-governmental organisations, met at Jomtien in Thailand. The meeting issued the *World Declaration on Education for All*, agreeing unanimously to restate the current significance of the 1948 declaration that "everyone has a right to education" in terms of 'basic education', as an enabling process, providing access to social participation, productive employment and individual fulfilment (UNICEF, Jomtien, 1990). This commitment has enormous implications, given that none of the participating countries were then, or are now, fully meeting two demanding requirements of the declaration: first, access to education for all people; second, a basic education of great breadth and power.

The *World Education Report* noted that this effort was having limited success in achieving universal schooling (UNESCO, World Education Report 2000a). This assessment was confirmed when the international agencies and member countries met again, at Dakar, seeking to assess the extent of achievement and to move beyond declarations to real achievement. The assessment showed a bleak picture with none of the six aims from Jomtien being fully realised including the key aim of basic education for all by 2000. The assessment noted that real progress had been made but that great steps still remained to be taken.

- Between 1990 and 1998 the numbers in primary school rose from 509 to 591 million, a significant advance, but in the age group 6 to 11 years in 1995 there were still 85 million girls and 60 million boys receiving no schooling. For 2010, the estimates were 86 million girls and 68 million boys out-of-school.
- While the number of literate adults had increased to more than 3 billion, still there were more than 880 million adults who were illiterate.
- In addition, gender discrimination, racial and ethnic discrimination, continued

to reduce life chances for many, and the quality of learning and the acquisition of human values and life skills fell far short of the aspirations and needs of individuals and societies.
- Great differences existed in attendance rates at primary school, in rates of survival to Year 5, in hours of instruction, in pupil-teacher ratios and there was a high proportion of students repeating grades with little progress (UNESCO, Dakar, 2000b).

Many events have contributed to diminish the hope of basic education for all. In Asia, the economic resurgence has proved difficult to maintain. In Africa, war and violence, and the AIDS epidemic have cut short many of the efforts to achieve basic learning for all. In Eastern Europe, ten years after the change to democracy, young people are in most ways more disadvantaged than before (UNICEF, 1998). In the industrialised countries, even the most advanced, the high level of unemployment for young people is one of the many indicators that this age group is experiencing such severe disadvantages that there is a danger of creating a deep social gulf.

The United Nations General Assembly in 1995 noted the importance of young people at the present time to the well-being of future generations and recognised the aspirations of this group to participate fully in the life of society. The Assembly adopted a World Programme of Action for Youth to the Year 2000, identifying ten priority areas: education, employment, hunger and poverty, health, environment, drug abuse, juvenile delinquency, leisure-time activities, girls and young women, and the full and effective participation of young people in the life of society and in decision-making. Three concerns were noted.

> The first is the inability of many parents in developing countries to send their children to schools because of local economic and social conditions. The second concerns the paucity of educational opportunities for girls and young women, migrants, refugees, displaced persons, street children, indigenous youth minorities, young people in rural areas and young people with disabilities. The third concerns the quality of education, its relevance to employment and its usefulness for assisting young people in the transition to full adulthood, active citizenship and productive and gainful employment. (UN General Assembly, 1995)

In an effort to meet this situation UNESCO established the International Commission on Education for the Twenty-First Century. The Commission supported strongly the Jomtien commitment but stressed the need to broaden that effort.

> The Commission considers, however, that a similar commitment, to secondary education in this case, should be written into the agenda ... for the next century. Secondary education must be seen as a crucial point in the life of individuals: it is at this stage that young people should be able to decide

their own futures, in the light of their own tastes and aptitudes, and that they can acquire the abilities that will make for a fully successful adult life. Education, at that level should thus be adapted to take account both of the different processes whereby adolescents attain maturity ... and of economic and social needs. (Delors, 1996)

In addition to the need to assign a high priority to the reform of secondary education the report stressed the parallel importance of the special place of adolescents in reform.

2.3. *The Key Place of Adolescents*

Adolescents are crucial to reform because they, more than any other group, are radically affected by the changes in society. Communication, work patterns, transport, social customs, relationships and values: all are part of the process of change. The majority live in developing countries where the numbers are still increasing. The difficulties of providing opportunities are illustrated by figures for Asia. In Southern Asia, the out-of-school numbers for secondary ages were given as 42 million males and 55 million females. Those figures were found to be 39 and 58 million respectively by 2000 and were estimated to be 39 and 55 million by 2010 (UNESCO, Dakar, 2000b).

3. ISSUES FOR RESOLUTION: ADOLESCENTS AND EDUCATION

3.1. *Marginalisation: A General Issue*

Particular aspects of change bring to young people a marginalisation, a sense of exclusion, precisely at the time when the need for their full participation is so evident. As industrialisation, in its current form, spreads, there is a greatly increased period of dependence for young people. In the past, there was immediate access from school to work. For many people that access was early, at age 14 years when the first job was taken. With that job came many of the responsibilities of adult life. With the transformation of the nature of work, the large number of jobs for manual and unskilled labour has reduced dramatically with opportunities for employment for young people now depending more heavily on further education and training. This often means that young people are dependent on help from their family until well into their twenties. Given the degree of family dislocation in many societies, this dependence imposes further strains. For many young people, achieving the necessary levels of education required for employment is proving very difficult. For others, even when they do proceed further in education, structural change in the workplace has severely limited their options for employment. To act effectively in this area demands a much more coherent social policy than currently exists. That policy must recognise the need for close links between those organisations that are working in areas related to the concerns of young people. Just as providing full opportunity for young people requires a coherent social policy so too it demands a coherent education pattern. The divisions and barriers that have developed between and even within the various sectors and areas of education only add to the problems of those who already feel marginalised by society. Education, nonformal, informal and formal, must be part of a cohesive whole if the stringent challenges of the future are to be met.

3.2. Violent Circumstances

Wars or other involvement in violence may not only prevent young people from attending school, but actively enlist them in military or other violent activity. The child soldier with an automatic weapon has become a feature of many conflicts. In such cases it is not only the loss of time and opportunity to learn but the development of anti-social skills which may make such young people difficult, even dangerous, members of a civil society. Their self-esteem is built upon their destructive skills and they may actively resist any circumstances which seem to devalue those skills or emphasise other values such as learning. Even those not active in violence find themselves in situations where the circumstances are dominated by a violent past from which it is difficult to escape. In many countries such as Cambodia and Vietnam, those who have been severely affected by violence find themselves side by side with those whom they see as causes of that violence.

3.3. Poverty

Currently 1.3 billion people live on less than $US1 per day, with this number growing daily as newly impoverished groups are being created by violence, loss of employment and the restructuring of society. Two-thirds of these people are women and a high proportion are young people and children. In many parts of Asia, youth employment under harsh conditions is a problem both because of the effects on health but also because it limits opportunities for education and self-improvement. Yet, the opportunity to earn may be an important contribution to family income. In other countries, young people suffer disproportionately high rates of unemployment. In both instances employment status is closely linked with poverty. Disadvantages tend to be compounded. People who are poor, tend to be illiterate, and to have: poor health, fewer employment opportunities, inadequate nutrition, sanitation and housing. They will tend to lack political influence and to suffer social or racial discrimination. Thus, they are often unable to change the circumstances which keep them poor. Young people growing up in such an environment become conditioned to poverty, developing the values and characteristics which perpetuate it.

3.4. Unemployment Among Youth

Employment is a major means through which young people achieve independence and are able to contribute to society. Traditionally, the route for young people to adult working life has been through a full-time job. This has taken place at different stages of the education system, depending on the skill level or formal preparation required. With changes in work patterns this simple relationship no longer applies and the former route through full-time employment is now less accessible. Alternative routes to employment are also difficult. In the industrialised countries, OECD surveys show that entry to a low-paid or part-time job can be part of a carousel effect, a cycle of insecure, casual, temporary and part-time work from which it is difficult to escape (OECD, 1997, 1998). Since the number of full-time jobs available to teenagers has radically diminished in these countries, there is a large proportion of young people who find it increasingly difficult to gain a secure footing in the workforce. This creates more barriers for young people who seek adult status. The completion of initial education, finding a secure job, leaving home, making new living arrangements and new personal relationships: all these are difficult but the gaining of productive work is crucial in this sequence (Sweet, 1998).

3.5. *Family and Other Circumstances*

The contribution of changes in work patterns has been identified above as a major practical and emotional contributor to marginalisation. Compounding this structural factor in societies, other basic social institutions have tended to lose their capacity to support and provide guidance. Religious institutions frequently have lost contact and authority in relation to young people. Similarly, the family, another fundamental social institution, is working under difficult conditions and suffers more instability and a greater sense of uncertainty than ever before. Dysfunctional families are the reality for many young people, either through family break-up or the loss of parents from violence and other factors. Not only the lack of financial support but the reduction in guidance and caring is more often a feature. Homelessness is an increasing feature, not just in developing countries but also in the large cities of industrialised nations. The lack of resources and of family support also often leads to criminal activity, drug abuse or prostitution. Young people in many countries have the highest suicide rates of any age group within the population. The central task is to assist them in building hope for the future, a sense of meaning and purpose.

4. REFORM AND RESEARCH: TWIN NEEDS

4.1. *Need for Combined Action*

The International Conference on Population and Development stressed the unique opportunities, which now exist to find solutions to long-entrenched problems. The meeting identified a growing consensus on the need for increased international co-operation in regard to population growth in the context of sustainable development. That consensus is a hopeful sign for the future but must be fostered and developed, not just in conferences but in planning, in priorities and in programs.

UNESCO has built upon this need for international bodies and donor communities to co-operate with each other. That need has been further emphasised for all the major agencies by the increased number of approaches from their member countries which are aware of the magnitude and complexity of the need and increasingly keen to work together. This need applies equally to the international agencies themselves, which have a great number and considerable range of programs. Cooperation between these bodies clearly is a considerable advance where priorities are consistent. Where they are not consistent it is equally useful to seek some common agreement to ensure worthwhile results rather than conflict or confusion. To this end UNESCO initiated a meeting in 1998 of a substantial group of such agencies. Their agreed task was to consider individual priorities and to consider the possibilities and modes for cooperative effort. The meeting agreed on the key importance of secondary education and the clear need for substantial reform in that area noting the findings of inquiries such as by the Principal Regional Office for Asia and the Pacific.

A variety of problems plague secondary education in the countries of the region: wastage, low teacher morale, under-trained, poorly motivated teachers, sub-standard teaching of literacy and numeracy, deficient teaching materials and school environments, student health and nutrition problems, low parental support for education, unenforced legislation on child labour and compulsory schooling, inaccurate baseline data including achievement levels and so forth. All these factors, when combined, result in reduced efficiency, quality and equity at the secondary level ... secondary education is currently the weakest link in the education chain. (UNESCO, PROAP, 1997)

The meeting defined areas of cooperation: cooperating in a major review of secondary education; establishing a web-site for information exchange, focusing on issues of values education such as citizenship education; strengthening the support for teachers; and, seeking new approaches to access and to financing secondary education.

UNESCO has also been active in developing cooperative approaches at the regional level through its Asia-Pacific Programme of Educational Innovation for Development, APEID. This organisation was initiated at a regional meeting in 1971 and adopted by UNESCO in 1972. It was conceived as a cooperative endeavour of member countries and institutions in those countries, working from the countries own national goals (Singh, 1986). APEID has pursued a successful course for almost 30 years, using the resources of the region to solve the problems of the region (Churchill, 1988; Hughes, 1995). APEID now comprises 199 centres in 29 member countries and in its endeavours has placed secondary education as one of its major priorities. This type of cooperative action may not guarantee more effective patterns of reform but it greatly increases the probability of success. A very successful project has been the Joint Innovative Project (JIP), with China. This has augmented the major national effort involved in the move to nine years of compulsory education in China. This makes very heavy demands on resources and personnel. The JIP has augmented this program, directing effort and attention to the qualitative aspects, especially in diversifying teaching and learning approaches (UNESCO, PROAP, 1997).

4.2. *New Strategies for the Use of Research*

Research in areas such as medicine and engineering has revolutionised not only the techniques of those professions but their organisational forms, their means of communication and their concepts of the profession. Yet in education, research still plays a marginal role. The great benefits which a fundamental research-practice link could show, remain to be implemented. A number of major research organisations have looked at the needs in this area and one of UNESCO's regional offices, PROAP Bangkok, has studied the situation and reported (see *The Impact of Research on Decision-Making in Education*). Their findings emphasise the gulf that exists between researchers, policy-makers and practitioners and make useful suggestions. The changes must involve both teachers and researchers. Researchers need to include in their work issues, which are felt to be important to teachers and to write in more accessible language. Teachers need to interact much more with research, suggesting issues for investigation and seeking ways to use research results in their daily tasks.

4.3. *Using Principles Involved in Current Successful Reform*

A considerable improvement in performance for international bodies, school systems and individual schools is possible given more careful use of past experience and a willingness to share experiences and studies together. As has been noted, almost all the necessary improvements have been successfully achieved, somewhere, at some time (Barber, 1996). Using such successful experience, it is possible to identify some of the principles which guide worthwhile and effective programs for young people.

An evaluation orientation. Care is now taken in planning, documenting and assessing projects to ensure that they make the best use of resources, benefit from past experience and use evaluation techniques both to monitor progress during a project, in formative evaluation, and to assess the final results, through summative evaluation. This implies that evaluation must be a part of the planning from the beginning and not an afterthought.

Inclusiveness. Every effort is made to be inclusive in projects, that is to ensure that equity applies in gender, race, economic circumstances and disabilities.. This is done not only for the benefit of the disadvantaged students, who will gain from working in the regular curriculum wherever possible. It will be of value to all students who will learn how to relate to a full span of people, rather than to an excluding group.

Participatory approaches. A vital aspect of work with young people is to ensure full involvement in all aspects of projects, from planning through to implementation, assessment and follow-up. A major benefit to young people from inclusion in a project is to gain a sense of responsibility and ownership. Again, this is a principle that will apply increasingly to schools, which now include in many countries the full range of the adolescent population. In past years, this group would have been at work, undertaking adult responsibilities. That responsibility needs now to be exercised at school, if it is to develop at this important stage. Schools have a much wider role to play than merely preparing for the next educational stage. In the secondary years, and particularly the latter years, the students are about to exercise the responsibilities of citizenship, hopefully democratic citizenship. The attitudes and capacities for that vital role must also be developed at school. Peer tutoring is not a new concept but offers much more in these days when individual students have access to so much information and can gain significantly from the opportunity to order and communicate that information. The Creativity-Action-Service Program of the International Baccalaureate Organisation is an example of what can be done in schools to involve young people in constructive service activities which are useful in themselves but which change young peoples' attitudes to their own responsibilities in their own society and, often, in world society. This program involves students in providing help to individuals or groups through activities, which may take many forms. The value lies not only in the usefulness and variety of the activities themselves but also in the attitude changes for the participating students, realising in practical terms the humanity and vulnerability of other people. For example, the students at Li Po Chun World College, Hong Kong were concerned to develop their understanding of minority groups in China. They formed a link with the *Yao* minority, a small ethnic group living in isolated conditions in the Canton Province. Now, each year a group of the students go to live in the area, visiting and working with the *Yao* people in their fields, building houses, improving roads and, in particular, forming relationships with the young people.

A recognition of urgency. Reform can be a process, which becomes an end in itself, neglecting its original purpose. That purpose is always to help those in need, as immediately and as effectively as possible. In many countries this means that action cannot wait until system reform has been completed. Where education infrastructure does not exist or is inadequate, the process of nonformal education can help immediately and its help is a spur to further success. The strength of many initiatives in nonformal education is that they begin with purposes, which derive from the needs of those who are involved. These purposes may include improved crops, safer child-birth procedures, better hygiene, clean water supplies and can progress to effective marketing, use of finance and capacity to use the legal system. Each of these purposes can be powerful in providing motivation to proceed with further aspects of basic education. As part of the global UN campaign against poverty and marginalisation, UNESCO has launched a six-year Learning and Working Programme for practical training of youth at risk, linked with their basic education. Given nearly one billion illiterate people in the world, and over 130 million out-of-school, their needs cannot be supplied by the formal system. The program works with specific groups in difficulty: ethnic minorities, migrants, refugees and those in slum areas. All countries involve certain common features: linking immediate needs with a training program that teaches relevant skills and knowledge while at the same time strengthening literacy, helping towards economic independence through assisting with marketing and showing the relevance of numeracy, involving the learners in the running of their own communities, seeing social integration as a necessary adjunct to economic independence.

4.4. *New Approaches to Organisation and Process for Schools*

The situation faced by young people is so different from anything in the past that if we were to develop our organisations *ab initio* we would do so very differently from the present patterns. These, with their strong boundaries and their structures from the past, do not meet current needs. We cannot start from the beginning as we have real structures in place but radical thinking is necessary if we are to begin to meet perceived and emerging needs. Some areas for action are listed.

Values education. One of the areas emphasised by the Delors (1996) Report was the vital importance to all people of "learning to live together". This type of initiative and the parallel emphasis by so many countries on citizenship make values education a central priority. Values education raises quite distinct emphases since it concerns not only studies in school but also all processes at the school and in cooperation with the community. Schools must not only talk of democracy but practise it in appropriate ways, providing real responsibility to students at school, with increasing emphasis on the later years.

Effective early intervention. The radical differences in student performance at the secondary levels are a matter of deep concern and require early identification and remedial action. Research by Hill (1998) indicates that the gap between the top ten per cent and the bottom ten per cent of readers at Grade 3 level is already five years of schooling. By Grade 10 this gap is much wider, with the lower ten per cent reading at Grade 3 level or below. The research results indicate that a determined and individual effort at the early stage can bring the weaker performers up to satisfactory levels

The school as a learning community. Research studies have demonstrated effectively the need for schools to set learning as their central priority. This may sound obvious but it is not, as schools frequently set other priorities in their practice, whatever the rhetoric may say. A determined effort to put learning as the central purpose requires that the rituals and myths, the celebrations and heroes, are chosen for that predominant purpose. It means, too, that all those associated with the school are learners, not just the students. School leaders, teachers and parents need to become part of this process (McMullen, 1996).

Peer teaching. A valuable corollary to the idea that teaching and learning are inter-related is in the use of students as teachers. Peer teaching or other forms of teaching by students of other students has been shown to be of considerable value to both student-teacher and student-learner. At a time when the pressures on regular teaching staff are heavy, such a system, carefully organised by the school, can be of benefit but not only in adding to the teaching strength of the school, valuable as that is. The main beneficiaries are the students involved and their gain in learning from the process. The Perach Project in Israel, whose purpose is to assist and to culturally enrich Jewish and Arab children from disadvantaged families, involves over 45,000 children and has proved very successful.

Learning entitlement. The Delors (1996) Report suggested that each person should have a 'learning entitlement'. This concept involves a specified number of years to be taken up by the student at times of choice, depending only on the capacity to use the opportunity effectively. In terms of the urgency of the situation for young people and the benefits now appearing in many societies experimenting with the idea of 'second-chance education'. This concept deserves careful attention, and the Republic of Korea has already moved in this direction.

Development of a learning society. Earlier it was pointed out that the school cannot successfully take on the total responsibility for students' learning. Natural helpers are the parents of students. Their agreed and organised involvement in their children's learning can be of benefit to both student and parent. Other people in the community can help, given encouragement and support: grandparents, older citizens, specialists in various fields. Increasingly, the school can become a learning centre for the community, with a great increase in its use and its value. The school can profitably reduce the barriers between themselves and their communities, not only in the increased physical contacts and greater time usage but in a more fundamental sense, becoming the educational arm for the whole community. Schools have made little use in the past of other groups in the community which may be potential sources of teaching and learning, such as scouts and guides, churches, temples and mosques, sporting clubs, museums, art galleries. The community has a great range of institutions which can become part of a learning network (Raizen, 1994). The Asian tradition of respect for teachers and education will greatly strengthen such approaches.

5. CONCLUSION

The central concept of the Delors Report, 'the hidden treasure' is the richness and diversity of talent possessed by every human being. Just as there is concern to retain the wealth of plant and animal life as a key resource, so, too, there is a need to develop the richness of talent that all people possess as individuals. Recent research on multiple intelligences (Gardner, 1993), stresses the distinctness of a number of human abilities, verbal, logical, spatial, musical, physical, understanding others, understanding ourselves. Education in the future must recognise and encourage this diversity. Music, the arts, sports and physical education are areas that are important to young people in terms of their interests and also important if there is to be balanced development. There is a danger that emphasis could be too exclusively on those issues of relevance to employment and the economy. Central as these are for the future of young people and to society generally, the full development of personality and capacities is equally so.

REFERENCES

Barber, M. (1997). *The Learning Game*. London: Victor Gollancz,.
Churchill, S. (1988). *Impact Evaluation Report on the Regional Network of Educational Innovation for Development*. Bangkok:. UNESCO.
Delors, J. (Chair) (1996). *Learning Evaluation Report on the Regional Network of Educational Innovation for Development*. Bangkok: UNESCO.
Gardner, H. (1993). *Frames of Mind: The Theory of Multiple Intelligences*. London: Fontana.
Hill, P. W. (1998). The literacy challenge. *Education Review*, 2(4).
Hughes, P. W. (1995). *UNESCO Innovative Network Synergy or Chaos?* Bangkok: UNESCO.
Jomtien, (1990). *World Conference on Education for All*. New York: UNICEF.
McMullan, P. (1996). *A Survey of School Reform*. New York: AERA Convention.
Organization for Economic Cooperation and Development (OECD) (1997). The OECD employment outlook: Low-wage jobs: Stepping stones or traps? *The OECD Observer*, No. 208,
Organization for Economic Cooperation and Development (OECD) (1998). *Thematic Review: The Transition from Initial Education to Working Life.*, Paris: OECD.
Raizen, S. (1994). *Learning and Work: The Research Base in Vocational Education and Training for Youth*. Paris: OECD,.
Singh, R. R. (1986). *Education in Asia and the Pacific*. Bangkok: UNESCO.
Sweet, R. (1998). Youth: The rhetoric and the reality of the 1990s. In *Australia's Youth: Reality and Risk*. Sydney: Dusseldorp Skills Forum.
United Nations General Assembly (1995). *World Programme of Action for Youth towards the Year 2000*. New York: United Nations.
United Nations (1950). *Universal Declaration of Human Rights*. New York: United Nations.
UNESCO. Proap (1997). *Work Plan for ACEID for the Sixth Programming Cycle. 1997–2001*. Bangkok: UNESCO, PROAP.
UNESCO, (2000a). *World Education Report: The Right to Education: Towards Education For All Throughout Life*. Paris: UNESCO.
UNESCO (2000b). *World Education Forum Report* (Dakar) *The Right to Education: Towards Education For All Throughout Life*. Paris: UNESCO.
UNICEF (1990). *World Conference on Education for All* (Jomtein). New York: UNICEF.
UNICEF (1998). *Children at Risk in Families and the Community. The MONEE Project*, Florence: UNICEF.

86

Reform in Science and Technology Curricula*

KOK-AUN TOH and NGOH-KHANG GOH

National Institute of Education, Nanyang Technological University, Singapore

1. INTRODUCTION

The marked growth of scientific knowledge over the past 30 years, and the realisation that science and technology could be harnessed for economic and technological development, have in no small way led science to assume an increasingly important role in education. This is reflected in a growing and coherent body of scientific ideas and principles that have gained acceptance across the world as being appropriate content for inclusion in school science curricula.

Expectations on what science curricula content should deliver are quite ambitious. They usually include scientific literacy for all citizens, helping them to be interested in and understand the world around them, to engage in the discourse of and about science, to be sceptical and questioning of claims made by others about scientific matters, to be able to identify questions and draw evidence-based conclusions, and to make informed decisions about the environment and their own health and well-being (Goodrum, Hackling, & Rennie, 2001).

In view of the above, there is therefore concern within the education community in the West, particularly the United States, over the low rate of ten per cent of United States secondary school students electing to study science beyond the compulsory courses. Fewer still decide to major in the sciences in universities, and an even smaller number elect to pursue advanced degrees (Feldman & Atkin, 1993). This trend has also been reported for Australia, with researchers at Monash University expressing concern over the fact that there are fewer students as well as fewer of the more able students opting to pursue courses and careers involving science (Dobson & Calderon, 1999). However, the decline in enrolments in the physical sciences may be masked by high growths seen in the

---

* The authors gratefully acknowledge with thanks the valuable inputs provided by Sivakumar Alagumalai and T. H. Wee in the preparation of this article.

broader life sciences and information technology areas and changes in the size of the age and grade cohorts.

This narrowing science-education funnel, a limiting pipeline that leads people to careers in science, does not seem to hold true for countries in the Asia-Pacific region. Recognition of the argument that claims a causal relationship between a strong program in science education and economic success seems to be the engine for growth in Asia, particularly the newly industrialised economies of the Republic of Korea and Singapore. The commitment to science and engineering fields in these countries is reflected in their relatively high rankings in the Third International Mathematics and Science Study (TIMSS). Singapore and Korea came out first and second, respectively, in the seventh grade scores in the international science rankings to lend support to this (Beaton et al., 1996, p. 26).

This article examines the key issues associated with science curricula in three domains: at the grassroots level, at the level of policy makers, and at the level of the science education community (Feldman & Atkin, 1993). A so-called 'key issues' approach is adopted because it provides an in-depth look into what happens in a particular country, thus giving solid information about the educational issues involved.

2. KEY ISSUES AT THE GRASSROOTS LEVEL

2.1. Interest in the School Curricula at the Grassroots Level

All parents want their children to succeed in school, and Asian parents in particular have traditionally placed a strong emphasis on the academic achievement of their children. Success in school seems to be equated with scoring high marks and doing well in examinations. This link has sparked off intense competition to do well in schools, and many parents in the Asia-Pacific region feel compelled to send their children to private tuition centres or enrichment classes to give them the needed support to excel in their studies. A manifestation of this obsession is noted across a number of different countries, albeit with different degrees of emphasis. Several examples are of interest and concern:

(a) the practice of Japanese students spending their time in special out-of-school education called *juku* or more popularly known outside of Japan as 'cram schools', in preparation for their examinations;
(b) the reports of pressure on students in Hong Kong to perform well and the medical problems arising from their over-exertion and lack of sleep in the process (*The Straits Times*, 9 May 2001);
(c) the camping overnight to enrol kids in particular schools in Malaysia (*The Sunday Times*, 27 May 2001); and
(d) the perceived need in Singapore for private tuition even though the students are doing well for these subjects in school, because their peers are having private tuition.

This interest by parents for their children to do well in school is commendable, and stems from Asian societies having a special reverence for education. Many of them do not have a good education themselves and therefore it is understandable for them to ensure that their children do not miss out on opportunities that education can offer. Education opens doors, which were closed to them because they did not have the requisite education. For those parents with good educational background, their belief in a strong education being able to provide for a better future for their children is even stronger (see, *Homework and Coaching*).

2.2. Science Curricula Development in Thailand

Most countries have a central body taking charge of curriculum development. In Thailand, for example, the Department of Curriculum and Instruction Development defines the curricula structure and scope, while the Institute for the Promotion of Teaching Science and Technology (IPST) is responsible for the development of curricula and instructional materials including teaching-learning activities corresponding to the prescribed structure and scope. The Thai science curricula are unique for their appropriateness to the local context and responsiveness to the needs of the country (Soydhurum, 2001). In the main, Thailand followed the English traditions of science teaching, but more recently has been influenced by American approaches.

The primary science content is in general agreement with what is being offered in other countries. It aims at enabling children to learn about problem solving processes through their environment, in conformity with the four characteristics identified by Harlen (1985), namely:

(a) science curricula are manifested as one unified subject and not as separate subjects (physics, chemistry, biology);
(b) children are involved in direct experience with living and non-living things;
(c) the science curriculum is expected to cater to the twin aims of developing both cognitive skills and attitudes; and
(d) it is important to make use of the children's immediate environment for studying scientific subject matter.

At the secondary level the science curricula aim at ensuring an understanding of the basic principles and theories as well as the nature, scope and limitations of science. Students should also learn to be rational while being receptive to opinions and comments of others. In Thailand, science and science education are valued by the community, have high priority in the school curriculum, and are perceived as contributing significantly to the economic and social well-being of the nation.

Like most countries, the Thai science curricula have undergone changes in response to local needs and environment. The curricula are the outcomes of work by experts at the grassroots level, namely scientists, science teachers, science education faculty, curriculum development specialists, and particularly those specialising in science content, teaching methods and evaluation,. The design and development process took into consideration the needs and suggestions of science teachers throughout the country. Pertinent documents, articles and research reports were used by the working groups developing the curriculum. The working groups ensured that there is consistency and continuity of science curricula from one level to another, and provided for the necessary foundation for tertiary education in science and technology. The manner of curriculum development is an example reflecting grassroots level involvement in the developmental process.

More recently, however, the government has given an added boost by stepping in with a whole slew of changes being instituted in an attempt to replace rote learning and boring classes with stimulating lessons where children can ask questions. Teachers, who are "used to ruling their classrooms like kings and having pupils soak up information like sponges" (*The Straits Times*, 6 June 2001), are required to move towards a child-centred approach where children are encouraged to ask questions, to learn by doing and analysing, and where pupils are taught to think for themselves. Some teachers are upset. Thai culture traditionally holds the teacher in high regard; teachers should not be challenged and to be questioned smacks of rudeness. The Thai Prime Minister Thaksin Shinawatra himself encouraged all Thais to "think out of the box" because the old Thailand tended to inhibit new thinking and entrepreneurship. This is a great step forward and represents a significant paradigm shift in how students are taught.

2.3. Science Curricula Implementation in Japan

Many readers remember vividly the headlong plunge into ambitious new science curricula in the United States in the post-Sputnik years. The success or failure of the different programs provided valuable lessons on curricula implementation. The limited success of the majority of these efforts points to the importance of teachers in the equation. Teachers are not easily moved away from their day-to-day practices despite the avalanche of changes emanating from different sectors, and this can be likened to ducks floating serenely on the water surface, when underneath there is frantic paddling. A classic example is the need to encourage teachers in their implementation of science curricula to shift from a 'teaching by telling' approach to 'teaching for understanding.' The pressure of getting students to perform well during examinations has, in no small way, detracted teachers away from the role of teaching for understanding. It is therefore useful to take a leaf from the Japanese education scene by looking at the way in which the undercurrent at the grassroots level in Japan is succeeding in this basic change in the implementation of science curricula. The undercurrent being referred to here is the impact being created in Japanese classrooms by what are called 'research lessons' (*kenkyuu jugyou*).

While the cultural upbringing of most teachers in Asian countries tends to make them somewhat reserved, particularly in regard to having an audience observe them while they are teaching an actual lesson, the Japanese culture seems to have got around this problem by convincing both novice and experienced teachers of the benefits of using research lessons to improve the implementation of new curricula. The use of observers to provide feedback is very much in line with the videotaping of micro-teaching lessons for later review as is typically done in initial teacher certification programs. They observe a teacher teaching a class, take copious notes, record class activities with their cameras, or videotape the lesson. After the lesson the teacher and observers move to another room to discuss the lesson. The teacher explains the intent of the lesson, justifies why a particular approach is taken and not another, and the observers give their candid feedback, with both parties discussing how the lesson can be improved. The comments from the observers help the teacher to see things that might otherwise have escaped attention.

A typical research lesson can be given before an audience made up of other teachers in the same school (*kounai kenkyuu jugyou*). The research lesson system is valued very highly by Japanese teachers, and can even be found in very remote mountain schools where there are fewer than 20 students. It is pervasive in all schools, and this accounts for the uniformity in the standard of education in Japan (Lewis & Tsuchida, 1998). There are no rules being laid down requiring research lessons to be carried out. They are embedded in the practice of ordinary teachers in ordinary classrooms. The teachers themselves feel that it is of such basic importance and that it is the way to go to improve upon what they are doing. Collaborations are routine for Japanese teachers. The spirit of camaraderie is apparent when teachers plan the research lessons in collaboration with several other colleagues in the same school, working as a team and deciding on the theme and frequency of research lessons.

The research lesson can also be open to teachers from outside the school, with invitations sent to educators in the district, or even the entire country. University faculty are often invited as commentators in such situations. Public research lessons (*koukai kenkyuu jugyou*) like these help prepare teachers for changes in Japan's national curriculum, with teachers flocking to those schools that are piloting the change. This provides a shining exemplar for the implementation of new curricula and, in particular, how stakeholders at the grassroots level can make a success or failure of the curricula. While a new curriculum may attempt to influence what happens in the classroom, the influence from within oftentimes provides a better chance of success. This interest generated at the grassroots level is an extension of the Western ideas of self-reflection and acceptance of peer critique. The keen desire to improve oneself seems to overshadow any apprehension arising from the scrutiny of one's practices by others.

3. KEY ISSUES AT THE LEVEL OF POLICY MAKERS

3.1. *Bold Initiatives Undertaken in Singapore*

At the level of policy makers, it is important to have a mission and vision to set the direction. Also important is the political will to put resources into the enterprise. It is this forward planning that has put many Asian countries in the international league alluded to at the beginning of this article. Singapore, in particular, has demonstrated astonishing transformation in its economy within a short span of 35 years. The transformation from a struggling post-colonial society plagued with problems of survival to a politically and economically stable country, rated amongst the world's best, is a success story to which few countries can lay claim. A study of the ingredients which made for this success shows the pivotal role of education in the task of nation-building, and in particular, the fashioning of a vibrant economy with a competitive edge in the world market (Yip & Sim, 1990).

If there is anything certain, it is that the economic and educational success did not materialise overnight. In retrospect, the major changes in the education system of the last three-and-a-half decades fall into a number of reasonably well-marked phases:

- the survival-driven years (1965–1978),
- the efficiency-driven years (1979–1998),
- the ability-driven years (1999–present).

The survival-driven years were characterised by heavy investments in education by sheer political will. The massive school building program, at an average rate of one new school per month for a number of years to provide every child of school-going age with a place in school, was seen as a necessary base to support the economic growth of the country. Besides science, which was already well-entrenched as an important subject in the school curriculum for economic growth, technical education was introduced as a compulsory subject for boys and as many as 50 per cent of girls took the subject as well at the lower secondary level. The Industrial Training Board, the forerunner of the Institute of Technical Education today, and later, a second university, the Nanyang Technological University, were established to spearhead the drive for engineers and technicians in the work-force.

As a small country, Singapore cannot afford educational wastage, and the efficiency-driven years saw the introduction of ability-based streaming against a backdrop of much heated public debate. Notable curricula changes included the decision to focus on literacy and numeracy in the first two grades of formal schooling and the relegation of science as a subject to begin at the third grade. These reforms were arguably controversial but were calculated as the best way of achieving the fullest potential with optimal use of resources available.

While the efficiency-driven years saw the goal as obtaining a pre-determined output with as little resources as possible, the ability-driven years are likely to see a continuation of this efficiency-driven system with special attention given to developing the full spectrum of talents and abilities in every child. This entails putting in place general ability testing, aptitude testing, career counselling, project work, as well as out-of-school activities to identify and help every child maximise his or her talents.

Going forward, a number of initiatives are also being put together to prepare the school-going students to meet the challenges for the next stage of Singapore's economic growth. Towards this end there is a very strong commitment towards:

(a) the importance of the study of life sciences,
(b) information technology and e-learning in the school science curricula,
(c) ensuring that thinking skills are being built into the science curricula.

Study of the life sciences. The completion of the draft sequence of the human genome in 2000 caught the interest and fired the imagination of the world. Research in the life sciences has opened up many possibilities for a better quality of life through the promise of more effective medicines and food with higher yield and better nutritional value. Jobs in the life sciences industry are expected to have a high growth potential and create new economic opportunities for countries that have equipped their people well for developments in this field. It is with this view in mind that the learning of the life sciences in schools is being given a tremendous push across all grade levels. The ultimate goal is to make it the fourth pillar of the industrial sector, alongside electronics, chemicals and engineering. Massive revisions to the science curricula at all levels were undertaken to ensure that the life science component is adequately represented and relevant. External inputs were sought to fire up the imagination of those involved in the delivery of this program to give it a fresh impetus.

Incorporation of IT and web-based learning into the school science curricula. Investment in the IT industry has accelerated worldwide, and the pervasive availability of personal computers in each country has resulted in a steady expansion of e-learning. Singapore is one of the most extensively wired countries, with nearly every household owning a computer. These computers are used in a vast array of applications, from sending email and surfing websites, to doing research and web-based learning using the internet. Web-based education removes all barriers of time and distance, and is therefore expected to have an explosive effect on school learning as well as lifelong learning. The use of IT and web-based learning is fairly well entrenched across all disciplines in the school curriculum. With the IT Masterplan (Teo, 1997) covering investments in IT hardware, software and training, many science teachers are now familiar with the use of Java applets and Blackboard as part of their e-teaching tools. The more progressive schools are going ahead by having courses online, and web-based assessment and assignment management. The challenge is to produce students who are technologically skilled and flexible in the face of changing job demands.

Commitment to thinking and problem solving skills. There seems to be unanimous agreement by different countries of the importance of promoting thinking skills across the school curriculum. The use of investigative work, with its inherent hypothesis testing, observing skills, experimentation, and making inferences, has become a natural vehicle for the promotion of thinking and problem solving as core skills. The commitment to have the science curricula include these aspects is fairly well entrenched as evidenced from the:

(a) use of an inquiry approach as the framework for all science teaching from the elementary grades;
(b) incorporation of a project work initiative into the formal science curricula, and as a means to nurture creativity, and develop self-directed inquiry and lifelong learning skills;
(c) inclusion of Scholastic Achievement Test (SAT) as one of the criteria for university admissions with a science and mathematics component;
(d) empowerment to teachers for the assessment of practical skills (such as planning investigations, implementing, handling data, evaluating evidence, and drawing conclusions).

These initiatives in the life sciences, technology and the promotion of thinking skills are intended to keep pace with a changing world and opportunities provided as a result of advancement in science and technology.

3.2. Integrated Curriculum Initiative in Hong Kong

There is much emphasis on integrating the three science curriculum areas (biology, chemistry and physics) using unifying themes like energy, diversity, cycles, systems and interactions, and admittedly some of the curricular materials drawn up have worked quite well at the elementary grade levels. Attempts to couple science with other subject areas, creating an inter-disciplinary subject, have also been argued for at different times.

It is therefore of particular interest to the science education community that policy makers and curriculum designers in Hong Kong have recently started to implement a new integrated curriculum called General Studies (an integration of three elementary grade level subjects, namely, Science, Social Studies and Health Education). This integration is a move to reduce the time needed to cover similar overlapping topics, and allow children to look at issues from various perspectives.

However, there is little integration among the four content areas, namely healthy living, living environment, natural world, and science (Cheng, So, & Tsang, 1998). The shadow of the three former conventional syllabuses is heavily cast upon these content areas and it is felt that the General Studies syllabus is merely an amalgamation rather than an integration of subjects. Consequently, science-related content areas can easily be identified from the syllabus. The constraints and impediments of the structure of the General Studies syllabus create three concerns for the teachers teaching the subject:

(a) the subject concepts and ideas presented in the integrated approach are not very systematic;

(b) a large number of the primary school teachers do not understand and see the need and rationale for integration;
(c) there are difficulties in teaching the science-related subjects, in particular, those teachers who were only teaching social studies and health education *a priori*.

Despite these concerns, more and more teachers are involved in teaching General Studies as the new curriculum takes up a significant amount of lessons in the primary school weekly time allocation.

One interesting emergent trend occurring in some schools is that more than one teacher is teaching the same class, thus thwarting the intent of the new curriculum. General Studies is intended to be an integrated curriculum and teachers should aim at linking up all the subjects (Science, Social Studies and Health Education) into one entity in their teaching. It is undesirable to carve it up into its three former constituent subjects and allocate the same class to different teachers. This reflects the belief among some schools that General Studies is better served and implemented by different teachers, each specialising in a particular area. This arrangement actually reduces the anxiety among some teachers who do not possess the background to teach unfamiliar subject matter.

It is necessary to recognise, however, that this goes against the intent of General Studies as an integrated subject. The original purpose to reduce the time needed to cover overlapping topics might not be best served under the circumstances. Much prior preparation to acquaint teachers in topics with which they are unfamiliar could perhaps avert the problems encountered.

3.3. *Educational Reform in China*

Science curricula in the People's Republic of China, a country of 1.3 billion people, are influenced in many ways by centuries of traditions. Additionally the traditions in one part of the country vary from those of another part. What happens in one part of the country is in support of the traditional continuity of the environment in that region. Indeed it is this deeper level of tradition that must influence the direction of science education and thus affect the Chinese science and technology achievements.

China suffered setbacks during the two decades of the Great Leap Forward and the Cultural Revolution. In 1985, by drawing from the science and technology experience of other nations, China began a major review of educational policy, including science education. This educational policy emphasised the aims of improving the quality of the nation and producing as many scientific and technological skilled people as possible through re-structuring the educational provisions (Keith, 1987). They therefore advocated the idea that "science and technology are the chief productive forces" of social and economic development. Yet such an idea has not been fully put into practice because of old thinking and old systems which block the linking of science and technology with the economy. With the firm conviction that advancement in science, technology and education is necessary to enable China to boost its productivity and consequently improve the lives of its people, the Chinese government backed educational reform efforts, promoted quality-oriented education and implemented the strategy of "invigorating China through science, technology and education" (U.S. Embassy in Beijing, 1996).

In 1998, the Chinese authorities announced the working guidelines for further promoting science and technology education at primary and secondary school levels. The guidelines covered the rationale, the framework, how to proceed, and other supporting actions. There are two main features under this new development, namely,

(a) an integrated type of science and technology education, and
(b) the infusion of science and technology education into the subject-based curricula.

Science and technology are actually closely related to each other. Technological application of modern science and scientific-based research of modern technology are the linkages for science and technology. It is their belief that a curriculum that favours pure science over technology appears to miss the vital link that provides the essential component of relevance for the students. As a result, differences in objectives in different schools in different parts of the country have now given way to a more unified trend of an integrated type of science and technology education. The framework of such science and technology education, as quoted by Qi Dian Qiang is as follows:

> It is an educational activity which is based on the fundamental education, through rational integration of science education and technology education. Through such activity, the objectives of nurturing and training students to possess scientific attitude, scientific spirit, scientific value, scientific methods and experimental skills of science and technology can be achieved. Consequently, the students' quality in science and technology can be promoted. (Qi Dian Qiang, 1999, p. 4)

In terms of strategy for implementation of an integrated type of science and technology education, it is suggested that science and technology education, at the primary and secondary levels, should be infused into each of the subject-based curricula, including language, mathematics, moral education, music and physical education. There are three obvious advantages of doing so, namely, in terms of (a) position, (b) quantity, and (c) time. Since all the curriculum subjects are those which are in place in the school time-table, the infusion of science and technology education into all these subjects implies that width and depth of its application in education and sufficient time for a complete infusion can be guaranteed (Zhu, 2000).

In terms of curriculum design, the Science, Technology and Society (STS) education model (Ratcliffe, 2001) is more popular and well accepted. The guidelines also suggest that teacher-based research for finding out appropriate content and teaching methods should be carried out.

Making changes to a system the size of China is not easy. In addition, China is also facing the challenge of closing the gap between rhetoric and reality in providing quality and equal science education for all students.

4. KEY ISSUES AT THE LEVEL OF THE SCIENCE EDUCATION COMMUNITY

Changes implemented in most countries arise as a result of the need to keep the curricula up to date, or to make a shift in emphasis of societal goals. How then is the science education community involved in curriculum research, particularly the systematic study and analysis of curricula? Are they providing the basis for curriculum reform or curriculum implementation?

Unfortunately the authors of this article detect very little link between science education researchers' efforts and the work undertaken by those who are involved in curriculum changes in schools. This conclusion is arrived at from an overview of recent issues of journals that report on science education research, albeit some are in the general educational research domain, namely:

- *Journal of Research in Science Teaching & Science Education* (United States),
- *International Journal of Science Education & Research in Science and Technological Education* (Europe),
- *Research in Science Education* (Australia),
- *Asia-Pacific Journal of Education* (Singapore),
- *New Horizons in Education* (Hong Kong),
- *Journal of Science and Mathematics Education in S.E. Asia* (Malaysia).

Most of the time the reasons for curriculum changes are other than scholarly analysis. It is not the authors' intent to suggest that curriculum changes should necessarily be rooted in research. Most research reports found in journals are the outcomes of some individual doctoral study, and the connection to curriculum issues is, at best, marginal.

This is not to say that science educators are not involved entirely. Most of them are sited in faculties of education and are actively involved in interpreting curriculum changes or giving meaning to the changes as part of the initial teacher education programs. They are the intermediary between curriculum and the teacher trainees. Their pre-occupation is with enhancing the teachers' role, passing on the excitement they have for the subject, and assisting the trainees in distinguishing between knowledge of the subject matter for teaching from knowledge of subject matter *per se*. Shulman (1986) has referred to the former as "pedagogical content knowledge" or knowledge of the ways of representing and formulating the subject to make it comprehensible to others.

The reform of science curricula will definitely demand certain reforms in pedagogical content knowledge, for example, specific teaching skills and knowledge in using information technologies that are required to enact curricula intended to result in better performance for all. As a result, science educators also have to provide continual education training programs for teachers to upgrade themselves in terms of science content and pedagogical skill in order to meet the new challenges. Therefore science educators play a key role in the implementation of new curricula.

5. EDUCATIONAL RESPONSE AND CONCLUSION

Policy makers recognise the importance of adjusting to the changing world and shifts taking place in the science education scene in other countries. A number of international studies have also taken place in the last few decades to provide policy makers with information on the relative standing and effectiveness of their education systems. Science educators from around the world are also continuing to make efforts to improve the quality of science education by learning from different countries.

Improving the scientific literacy of students is the main purpose of school science education. Scientifically-literate persons will contribute to both the social and economic well-being of the country. Modern and progressive science curricula that will make a difference in the lives of all students are important at the beginning of the third millennium.

The importance of examinations and schools and the dictates of science and technology in the lives of the school-going population seem to be a common feature across many Asia-Pacific nations. A recognition by governments of the importance of the school science curricula as a determinant of future economic and technological welfare seems to be fairly well accepted.

Most nations are taking the cue concerning the importance of IT and e-learning, and how it will feature as the education of choice of the future. No country or individual can afford to choose to be isolated from the internet and the vast potential that can be opened up as a result of web-based learning.

Owing to the immense size of the Asia-Pacific region and the vast number of different systems in place, this article must necessarily be limited to only a selection of systems with specific key issues for illustration. The two scenarios of curriculum implementation exhibited by Japan and Hong Kong reflect contrasting styles being adopted. While teachers in Japan are involved in the change process, those in Hong Kong might not have been so well prepared for the change. The winning ways exhibited in the classrooms of the former seems to point to the way to go. The integration of science and technology education as well as the infusion of science and technology education into the subject-based curricula in China may have advantages in promoting science and technology.

From the point of view of improving the quality of teaching and learning science-related topics, the notion of specialisation seems to make sense and should not be brushed off too lightly. Teachers with insufficient background in science lack the pedagogical competence to guide children to look at issues from different perspectives to create a holistic learning experience. Their lack of sufficient science background might be an important factor why schools in Hong Kong are keeping the various areas distinct and insulated in the extended block of time allocated to General Studies. This will seriously hamper their effectiveness and confidence to assist someone else to learn the science-related topics. Having said this, it is imperative to emphasise that teaching of all the science-related components in each class at the elementary grade level by one teacher is the norm rather than the exception in most countries. Team teaching or cooperative teaching might be a way to solve this problem.

Under the current international reform of science curricula, the nature of teaching cannot be reduced to the performance of a prescribed set of behaviours. Teachers are required to make numerous and instant decisions in response to students' questions, level of understanding and behaviours. Teachers are professional with specific pedagogical training, carrying with them expert knowledge of multi-faceted roles, which include that of a surrogate parent, entrepreneur, counsellor, IT expert, mentor, facilitator and administrator. They have to take on increasingly, roles emphasising ethics, moral education and promoting the integration of community values. The respect for such a figure has been left fairly intact for centuries in Asia. While some Asian countries may have shifted from this stance, such a position is still largely in place for countries such as Taiwan and China, despite the test of time. For these cultures critical comments about teaching performance of another teacher have not been encouraged. This may have some adverse effects on alternative approaches, and consequently success in science education reform. Countries which have the resources and the will to move ahead in the science education reform movement can be expected to reap rich rewards in the years ahead.

REFERENCES

Beaton, A. E., Martin, M. O., Mullis, I. V. S., Gonzalez, E. J., Smith, T. A., & Kelly, D. L. (1996). *Science Achievement in the Middle School Years: IEA's Third International Mathematics and Science Study*. Boston: Boston College, (IEA).

Cheng, M. H. M, So, W. M. W., & Tsang, C. L. J. (1998). Teachers' concern about the implementation of an integrated curriculum: A Hong Kong study. *Journal of Science and Mathematics Education in S.E. Asia*, 21(1), 22–32.

Dobson, I. R., & Calderon, A. J. (1999). *Trends in Science Education: Learning, Teaching and Outcomes 1989–1997*. Australia: Australian Council of Deans of Science. Available at: Http://www.acds.edu.au/members/issues.htm [2001, 8 June].

Feldman, A., & Atkin, J. M. (1993). Research in science education in the USA. *Journal of Curriculum Studies*, 25(3), 281–289.

Goodrum, D., Hackling, M., & Rennie, L. (2001). *The Status and Quality of Teaching and Learning of Science in Australian Schools*. Australia: Department of Education, Training and Youth Affairs. Available at: Http://www.detya.gov.au/schools/publications/2001/science/index.htm [2001, 31 May].

Harlen, W. (1985). Science education: Primary-school programmes. In T. Husen & T. N. Postlewaite (Eds.), *The International Encyclopedia of Education*. Oxford: Pergamon Press.

Keith, M. L. (1987). Science education in China: Transformation and change in the 1980s. *Comparative Education Review, 31*, 419–441.

Lewis, C. C., & Tsuchida, I. (1998). A lesson is like a swiftly flowing river: How research lessons improve Japanese education. *American Educator*, Winter, 2–17 & 50–52.

Qi, D. Q. (Ed.) (1999). *Zhong Xiao Xue Xian Dai Ke Ji Jiao Yu Dao Lun*. China: Qing Dao Ocean University Publisher.

Ratcliffe, M. (2001). Science, technology and society in school science education. *School Science Review, 82*(300), 83–92.

Shulman, L. S. (1986). Those who understand: Knowledge growth in teaching. *Educational Researcher, 15*(2), 4–14.

Soydhurum, P. (2001). *Science Education in Thailand*. Thailand: Institute for the Promotion of Teaching Science and Technology.

Teo, C. H. (1997). Opening new frontiers in education with Information Technology (IT). Opening address delivered at the launch of the Masterplan for IT in Education on 28 April 1997 at Suntec City. Available: Http://www.gov.sg/mita/speech/speeches/v21n2014.htm [2001, 24 May].

The Straits Times (2001). One dies as HK's exam fever takes its toll. Report on happenings in Asia. Straits Times, 9 May 2001, pp. A4.

The Straits Times (2001). Thailand's teachers left behind in reforms. Straits Times, 6 June 2001, pp. A6.

The Sunday Times (2001). Queuing Parents: Chinese camp overnight to enrol kids in schools. Sunday Times, 27 May 2001, pp. 28.

U.S. Embassy, Beijing (1996). *A Report of the U.S. Embassy in Beijing*. China: U.S. Embassy.
  – Science and education for a prosperous China: Lessons from abroad.
      Available at: Http://www.fas.org/nuke/guide/china/doctrine/stabrd4.htm
  – Science and education for a prosperous China – A brutal and frank assessment.
      Available at: Http://www.fas.org/nuke/guide/china/doctrine/stsum3.htm
  – PRC State Council: Decision on accelerating S&T Development
      Available at: Http://www.fas.org/nuke/guide/china/doctrine/stdec2.htm.

Yip, S. K. J., & Sim, W. K. (Eds.) (1990). *Evolution of Educational Excellence: 25 Years of Education in the Republic of Singapore*. Singapore: Longman.

Zhu, J. H. (Ed.) (2000). *Xian Dai Xiao Xue Ke Ji Jiao Yu*. China: China Construction Material Industry Publisher.

87

Emerging Information and Communications Technology

SIVAKUMAR ALAGUMALAI*
EDICT Research Group, Flinders University, Adelaide, Australia

1. INTRODUCTION

Information literacy includes the ability to search, locate, evaluate, manage, use, present and communicate information and to engage in problem solving, self-directed learning, autonomous-targeted learning, and research skills and all are fundamental to education. Information and communications technology (ICT) is a means of searching, storing, archiving, processing and presenting information electronically through a number of media and technologies. The convergence of information systems and global communication infrastructures, for example the internet and wireless systems, have initiated this fusion of information and communication technologies. ICT is the use of computers in instruction and communication for the purposes of learning and teaching that takes place mainly through information networks with the help of communication technology.

ICT is also a pertinent aspect of work that expands significantly into education through workplace and informal learning. An internet search of 'ICT and education' would present numerous hits including websites that reflect the importance of ICT,

> ICT will be the medium of education in the foreseeable future, and will change many aspects of the education system as we have known in the twentieth century, ICT should be introduced into the education system within a framework of a national computerisation plan that is based on a holistic and systemic understanding of the role of ICT in education. Aviram (2000)

---

* The author acknowledges the support provided by Prof. John P. Keeves (Flinders University), Prof. Jonathan Anderson (Flinders University), Prof. Toh Kok Aun (Nanyang Technological University), Prof. S. Gopinathan (Nanyang Technological University) and Prof. Cedric Hall (Victoria University of Wellington).

ICT is not a static entity, but involves a dynamic system of software, hardware, mindware and conceptions that is constantly evolving. This article examines the evolution and emerging trends in ICT and its implications for education and educators.

2. OPERATIONALISING ICT

During the past two decades software and hardware have undergone constant development and updating. However, little or no work has been done to reflect on how education systems have adopted and adapted to these changes in ICT. Part of the problem may be attributed to the different terminology associated with ICT and the perceptions of implementers and researcher workers in the area of education. Although there are widely accepted definitions of ICT, Bruce (1998, p. 41) indicates that "there are different ways in which educators experience information literacy". She argues that the use of different terminology in ICT reflects personal experiences and is "not a linear process, nor is it technologically driven and not readily definable in terms of skills or attributes" (Bruce, 1998, p. 42). Various terms have been used interchangeably to describe technology that facilitates and enhances education. Learning technologies focus on learning and refer to devices and systems that promote it. Instructional technologies refer to devices and systems that facilitate the delivery of instruction. Content management systems like WebCT, TopClass and Blackboard, to name a few, fall under the domain of instructional technology (Curtin, 2002; Rogers, 2001). Educational technologies include both the learning technologies and instructional technologies. Although educational technologies cover a breadth of systems and devices, it is not clear that the different types of software and hardware are included in its definition. To present information technology (IT) with the broadest perspective, EdNA (1996), defines IT to include the "processes applications and equipment by which we access, create, organise, analyse, present and communicate information in a range of formats including text, images and sound."

A number of educational organisations recognise the importance of both information and communications technology to account for the diverse functions of education, which include instruction, learning, assessment, evaluation, and learning-tracking and reporting systems. The significance of both information and communication is recognised and operationalised in a number of strategic plans and actions:

> Information technology (IT) is the term used to describe the items of equipment (hardware) and applications (software) that allows us to access, retrieve, store, organise, manipulate, and present information by electronic means. Personal computers, scanners, and digital cameras fit into the hardware category. Database storage programs and multimedia programs fit into the software category. NZ-MOE (2002, p. 4)

> Communications technology (CT) is the term used to describe telecommunications equipment through which information can be sought and accessed,

for example, phones, faxes, modems, wireless ports, and computers. NZ-MOE (2002, p. 4)

ICT use in schools focuses on multimedia-enabled systems. The communication aspect of ICT involves communication between and within systems and institutions. Information and data are transmitted to enable meaningful knowledge construction and presentation.

Thus, the term ICT brings together the optimal capacities of systems and devices to enhance lifelong learning, and allow for learners to solve innovative problems (DETYA, 2000). However, ICT is an evolving entity. What then is this 'emerging ICT'? Roberts (2000) indicates that the newer technologies are highly interactive and provide greater motivation. She highlights the view that "the motivational, empowering, engaging capabilities of these technologies are particularly important for students who are under-challenged and under-motivated" (Roberts, 2000, p. 2). Anderson (1985, 2002a) argues that it is inevitable that ICT will play a major role in the way we instruct, learn, assess and manage courses in the future.

3. CURRENT USE AND IMPLICATIONS OF ICT IN EDUCATION

Traditional technology and traditional practices do not adequately prepare our students for the workplace or further education. Lee (2001, 2002) and Tan (2001) report that today's learning environments must equip students with appropriate tools and strategies to operate effectively to solve problems, collaborate and cooperate, and interact with others. The availability of ICT has initiated a shift in both pedagogy and instructional practices. Table 1 summarises the emerging trends in education and the eminent shift in learning environments.

ICT impacts greatly on student's lives. Schools (K-12) and institutions of higher education use ICT to enhance learning, teaching, assessment and administration. ICT also facilitates communication between individuals and organisations. Researchers in Australia have highlighted the importance of ICT in supporting cooperative learning (Larkin, 2002; McLoughlin, 2002) They further argue that ICT benefits the students through:

- greater motivation,
- increased self-esteem and confidence,
- enhanced questioning skills,
- promoting independent and cooperative learning,
- improving presentation,
- developing self-directed learning capabilities,
- promoting critical information handling skills,
- optimising time on task,
- improving social and communication skills, and
- supporting a global network of learners.

Table 1. Pedagogical and methodological shifts (adapted ISTE, 1998)

Traditional Learning Environment	→	New Learning Environment
Teacher-centred instruction	→	Student-centred instruction
Course design	→	Instructional design
ICT-based design	→	Adaptive systems
Single-sense stimulation	→	Multisensory stimulation
Single path progression	→	Multipath progression
Single media	→	Multimedia
Isolated work	→	Collaborative work
Information delivery (instructivist)	→	Information exchange (constructionist)
Passive learning	→	Active/inquiry-based learning
Factual, knowledge-based	→	Critical and informed decision-making
External motivation	→	Autonomous-targeted learning
Reactive response	→	Proactive/planned action
No interaction between system and individual	→	Importance of Human-computer interactions
Isolated, artificial context	→	Authentic, real-world context
Single-media/form assessment	→	Multimedia/form assessment
Written text feedback	→	Multimedia/form feedback

Although numerous research studies indicate the positive effects of ICT use in education, Fumihiko (1990) and Lee (2002) warn that introducing ICT into higher education is more complex, and implementers need to consider the value it brings to the learning process and the ways and means of creating knowledge. They argue that pedagogy, content, cooperation and risks have to be examined prior to embarking on implementing an ICT solution in an organisation. This warning is further compounded by the *World Education Report* (UNESCO, 1998) which notes that "education worldwide is facing a significant challenge in preparing students and teachers for the future during a time when most teachers are not prepared to use ICT and education systems are not equipped to integrate the new ICT." A recent report by Anderson (2002a) highlights some of the problems educators would face and outlines useful strategies that they could adopt.

Research and developments in ICT are growing at a relatively faster rate than educator's pace of acceptance of these technologies. The relative distance between the developments and ICT acceptance is further compounded by those educators who focus on the technology alone. They have moved from using horse-driven carts to solar-energy driven vehicles. However, they have failed to take notice of both the drivers of these machines and that gravel-paths have been upgraded to slip-proof roads. Current users of ICT have different needs and expectations. Students at both schools and universities are exposed to stereophonic sounds, DVD movies, and multimedia interactive games and simulation at home and their leisure environment. However, are their teachers ready for these students?

Information technology jobs in industry demand specialised training in

Computer Science or Information Science. Unfortunately, the growing demands of teachers with necessary ICT skills and knowledge has spawned a new generation referred to as "self-taught ICT users" (Browne, 2002).

Taylor (1983) reports major problems with self-taught teachers who were certified in certain subject areas and authorised to be information technology or computer science teachers, regardless of how much computer-related training they may have had. Kiper et al. (cited in Duncan, 1992) caution that those with "some ICT experience continue to lack the skills required for using computers effectively." ICT includes related disciplines of computer science, information science, information systems, data processing, computer information systems, management information systems, business information systems and computer literacy (Duncan, 1992, p. 2). Some basic understanding of word-processing, presentation software or web-page development does not constitute an expertise in ICT and many of these self-taught teachers are misinformed about the broader implications of ICT. Self-taught computer ICT specialists could distort both instruction and learning through and with ICT (Gupta & Houtz, 2000). Moreover, Wenglinsky (1998) emphasises that "students whose teachers received professional development on computers showed gains in mathematics scores of up to 13 weeks above grade level" He concludes that teachers' professional development in ICT is positively related to students' academic achievement in mathematics.

Apart from placing demands on teacher's ICT proficiency, emerging ICT has made the roles of educational technologists even more important in facilitating instruction and learning. Wasser, McGillivary and McNamara (1998) highlight that educational technologist will continue to support the instructors in enhancing learning and the delivery of meaningful instruction. Educational technologist's roles require expertise in teaching, curriculum and pedagogy. Institutions of higher education in the Republic of Korea, Japan, Singapore and Taiwan offer specialist programs in educational and instructional technology. However, the increased use of ICT in education has led technicians, who have been self-taught, to become educational technologists. A few, with some knowledge of ICT and some experience of tutoring, have assumed the so-called 'credentials' of educational technologists. McGillivary (2000) and Ely (2000) highlight the need for appropriate qualifications and training through recognised accredited institutions. Further to the need of having an appropriate training in educational technology, Dowling, Foord-May and Mathera (2001) have proposed the 'National Standards for Educational Technologists'. Thus, as highlighted by Hirumi and Isidro (1996), it is imperative that teachers acquire the necessary training in ICT to support better their students in the tasks of learning. (see also *Technology and Learning*).

4. IMPLICATIONS FOR PROFESSIONAL DEVELOPMENT

There has been a keen interest in autonomous targeted learning, self-directed learning and self-regulated learning that focuses on the individual learner

(Alagumalai, Keeves, & Njora, 2002). It is timely and useful to examine and investigate the effectiveness of adaptive learning environments and intelligent tutoring systems, that provide students with individualised ability-appropriate instruction and supported practice through an interactive environment that enhances active learning. Use of metadata generation techniques and associated wait-time monitoring processes (Alagumalai & Larkin, 2001) would allow both learners and teachers to monitor and track latent cognitive processes. Emerging ICT has initiated a shift in both educational and pedagogical paradigms. The use of adaptive and intelligent education systems would emphasise the importance of learning how to learn rather than ICT being a repository and transmitter of domain facts and rules of application.

Moreover, emerging online learning systems support collaboration between users. Developments in computer-supported collaborative learning (CSCL) tools seek to provide simulated learning companions who cater for the learner's needs and demands adaptively. In the real classroom situation the difficulty of matching learners to mutual support is overcome through a CSCL system.

A number of research organisations and institutes have started employing the frontiers of emerging technology to facilitate group work. Traditional individual-based research endeavours are being replaced with group initiatives. Collaboration between teams of experts has become the prime mover of ICT related research and development. The multimedia technology group in the Universiti Technologi Malaysia, the Science and Technology Group at the Nanyang Technological University in Singapore and the EDICT Research Group at Flinders University, as part of their initiatives seek to examine the use of ICT to enhance instruction, learning, and school management.

A number of ICT innovators, namely the Universiti Technologi Malaysia (Aris et al., 1999) and SEAMEO-INNOTECH (Pefianco, 1999) seek to examine how they can address individual learning styles, cultural and linguistic diversity, needs of children with disabilities, geographic or temporal barriers, and the provision of values education. Similarly, EDICT has committed itself to exploring the use of adaptive, intelligent and virtual-simulation systems to enhance instruction, learning, assessment and evaluation, education management and administration. Innovative use of emerging ICT has already started.

The roles of learning-facilitators and learners are evolving with emerging ICT. Anderson (2002a) indicates that the educator's role is not to provide information but to guide and encourage students through the information flood. The move away from a content laden curriculum to that of processes and metacognition by the Japanese (Machida, 2000; Tanaka & Suzuki, 2000), Korean (Sung, 2000), Singaporean (Singapore MOE Press Release, 1999, 2000), and Taiwanese (Chin and Lin, 2001) education systems is fortuitous and is a positive step towards using ICT effectively. Hence, the emerging ICT necessitates the construction of a newer and richer context for instruction and learning more necessary.

Wright (1998) highlights the adoption of new philosophies in integrating ICT into the curricula. She argues that ICT empowers the learners to guide the development of curriculum and to pace knowledge construction (Wright, 1998).

Authentic field experiences can be captured and shared through dynamic web pages and media. Learning from vicarious experiences presents a new dimension. Portable digital assistants (PDA) and wireless slates would help validate experiences and experiential diaries.

Learning is not about how much information can be stored and recalled, but how appropriate information can be retrieved quickly and utilised optimally and efficiently. Emerging ICT enables educators to monitor effectively the cognitive and metacognitive processes of their learners and prepare students for their role in society. Feedback can be reviewed synchronously or asynchronously during learnable moments.

ICT has been deployed and integrated into instruction and learning for a long time. In the past technologies have examined performance on lower order tasks and basic skills (Kubasek, 2000; Nair, 2000). They highlight that there has been little research that reports on the gains associated with ICT in higher order skills.

Fischer and Scharff (1998) highlight that "new technologies alone will not provide answers to the challenges that self-directed learning presents." They propose that technology needs to be "applied to best solve the fundamental problem that people encounter in actual learning situations" (Fischer & Scharff, 1998, p. 28). Roberts (2000, p. 2) argues that "getting the technology into the school in itself won't improve education ... the effective use of technology goes hand-in-hand with a high-powered, demanding curriculum, with highly-trained, dedicated talented teachers."

A rethinking of emerging ICT is not to view education as the platform into which ICT is integrated or embedded, but ICT involves the infusion of education within the ICT. Each generation of educators aspires to lift their learners to higher order thinking. Newer ICT may mean faster processing speeds or larger storage space for data. However, faster hardware or optimised software does not automatically transform learners into higher order thinkers nor does it make teachers into effective instructors. Although we may be witnessing the transition from e-learning (online) to m-learning (mobile, Wireless Application Protocol-based learning) the quality of teaching does not become better with newer technology. However, the way in which instructions are optimised through the available technology may be the key to better learning and reflection. For example, spell checkers, simulations and applets or learning objects have an educational effect. Education is infused or embedded within these technologies.

In infusing education into the constantly evolving ICT, specific disciplines and essential learning areas and pedagogy attain prime importance. Infusing education into ICT, forces the need to review the way learners model their thinking and a reflection of educational practices. Integrating or embedding ICT, into say mathematics or science, would fixate particular practices and ways of knowing with a particular technology. Infusing education into emerging ICT allows for constant review of the focus on practices and thus shifts the levels of thinking and knowing. ICT is merely a means to achieve an improvement in student learning performance. Thus, the best use of any current or emerging technology should be determined by the curriculum and an instructor who has a sound knowledge of content, pedagogy, instructional design and ICT.

Alagumalai (1999, 2002a, 2002b) and Hammond (2001) indicate that recent developments in Artificial Intelligence, Adaptive Learning and Testing Systems and an understanding of Human Computer Interactions allows educators to understand better cognitive and metacognitive processes involved during learning. ICT provides a lens and probe with which to track learning development and thus allow educators to offer effective extension and remedial individualised solutions to their learners. Emerging ICT is not about en-mass education, but is about adaptive individualised support to learning and discovery. LOTS (Alagumalai, 1998), MCATS (Alagumalai, 1999), MTDFS (1998–2000), IOCADS (Alagumalai, 1999–2002) and metadata-associated learning objects present learners with the virtual facilitator by the side, negotiating and sustaining learning over time. Static tacit knowledge, encapsulated through texts and figures in print media, is being replaced with dynamic simulations that allow high levels of interaction and reactivity. Reactivity here refers to the proactive strategising and the activation of cognition, metacognition, and affects and attitudes.

Authentic representations of learning situations through virtual environments allow students to move more rapidly to hypothetical-deductive reasoning and symbolic modelling stages. Virtual dissections (for example, www.froguts.com) and simulations like SimCity allow the learners to transfer contrived knowledge to more authentic problem-solving tasks. The initiatives of the Learning Federation, Australia (socci.edna.edu.au/), move in the direction of promoting authentic learning. Emerging ICT with the supported bandwidth and fidelity will encourage and permit students to engage actively in meaningful learning.

In the traditional schooling model, teachers dictated content and provided resources for their students. The new learner is presented with all the tools and techniques for engineering their own learning. Teachers may have to catch-up with the ICT skills and knowledge of their students. These concerns are being echoed across all education departments around the world (DEST, 2002; Lourdusamy, Hun, & Wong, 2001; NZ-MOE, 2002; Segumpan, 2001; Singapore-MOE, 2000). Emerging ICT forces a rethinking of how not to overload students with content, but how to optimise learning through the best available systems and solutions. It is a major move away from attaching learning preference to the students and to consider the many-to-one interactions the learner could have through their individual learning space. Emerging ICT addresses the need to extend student's learning space through communication, knowledge recognition and construction, and modelling.

5. FUTURE DIRECTIONS – FROM PORTABLE TO WEARABLE SYSTEMS

There have been numerous research studies undertaken to examine differences between males and females in cognitive and metacognitive processes. The debate, whether males and females operate differently from a psychological perspective, is still continuing. Emerging technologies, especially the use of radiological tracking, is starting to provide insights into brain activity. Various imaging techniques, namely Positron Emission Tomography (PET), Single-Photon Emission Computed Tomography (SPECT), Magnetic Resonance Imaging (MRI) [also referred to as Nuclear Magnetic Resonance Imaging (NMR)], and Functional Magnetic Resonance Imaging (FMRI) allow the identification of functionally active regions in the brain. Techniques like Electroencephalography (EEG) (Willoughby, 2002) and Magnetoencephalography (MEG) record the minute electrical and associated magnetic fields generated at the neuron or cellular level. The PET, SPECT, fMRI, EEG and MEG are functional imaging techniques that provide information on the physiological state of cerebral tissues (Fantini et al., 2001).

Studies of brain activity have triggered a re-examination of how learning occurs (Bradford, 1990; Lazimy, 2000, Willoughby, 2002). However, most of the functional imaging techniques require special rooms and centres and are restricted to one or a few patients at any one time. With the miniaturisation of technology and equipment, emerging technology would be able to provide useful tools and techniques for studying brain activity more flexibly. We are not too far away from using wearable ICT, with tiny monitoring probes and wireless transmitting devices that could provide data for a number of students solving a problem or even undertaking practical laboratory tasks. Students could use optimised software involving portable digital assistants (PDAs) and wireless slates that track and report progress and diagnostic information. Positive and corrective information could be fed back to users instantaneously to extend and remediate learning. The learner could be provided with the opportunity both to regulate and direct learning.

Emerging ICT in the hands of the qualified and capable teacher will become an invaluable tool. ICT development will not slow down for teachers to catch up, but it is imperative to accelerate professional development to keep abreast of current practices. Education departments and systems, and teacher education providers play a vital role in professional development. Learning and reflection about practice is not an individual challenge, but could be shaped and refined by colleagues and through collaboration. As ICT evolves, there is a need to move towards a Community of Practice (CoP), where professional development is a shared process with colleagues playing dynamic mentor-mentee roles. The internet (for example, through CoPweb.org) allows educators to raise questions and seek information about practice. We are at the beginning of the use of the emerging ICT, and it will be useful to start reflecting on our current practices, and use ICT to optimise related processes.

This would mean a rethinking of research directions. Research and development in ICT should not happen just in the close confines of certain faculties and schools, but should have cross-disciplinary foci. Research in education should be extended to developing systems that support and enhance instruction, learning, assessment, evaluation, administration and management. We have moved from the era when programmers designed applications for educators to implement in the classroom with little or no consideration for methodology and pedagogy. Educators should become designers and engineers of learning and instructional systems.

Traditionally, teachers reviewed and selected print materials for their students. Print information was scrutinised for misconceptions, appropriateness of layout, font size, and accuracy of graphics, figures, content and information. McKenzie (1995) highlighted the problems of bias associated with software evaluation. Similar rigour in evaluation in the selection of digital material, as had been exercised in textbook reviews, has to be exercised by educators. This would imply a thorough understanding of instructional design and human-computer interactions. Hypermedia and learning objects have their inherent problems, and client-centred (learner focused) evaluation of any digital media prior to its use in instruction would be fortuitous.

However, the emerging technologies present ethical problems (Ward & Morgan, 2001) and the possibility of plagiarism (Le Heron, 2001), and have implications for privacy and confidentiality (Cady & McGregor, 2002). These new technologies have activated a rethinking of teacher education, and professional development to address these issues.

Emerging ICT should allow teachers, students, parents and community members to help shape automated learning. The 'C' in ICT has to make communications the core of any form of learning and enhance better thinking. ICT should allow all new knowledge to be translated to community practice, and not allowed to idle in elite libraries and on degenerating hard-disks. This parallels the so-called 'jump-shifts' in e-knowledge advanced by Norris, Mason and Lefrere (2002), where learning and knowledge will be used in both theory and practice to transform social and economic systems based on knowledge sharing. We need to "harness new technologies to carve out niches in the newly emergent global economy" (Gopinathan, 1997, p. 45).

Emerging ICT presents educators with an opportunity to shape and direct learning through the community. New knowledge, unlike in the past which sat at elite libraries and on degenerating hard-disks, can be made accessible and useable by community access through emerging ICT. We have to act immediately to be able to hold the reins to where we want to education to go, and not allow the emerging ICT to dictate our directions. However, to be effective in driving learning and empowering learners through the superhighway ahead, educators need sound grounding in both educational principles and practices, and ICT (see also *Challenges for Research into Educational Reform in the Asia-Pacific Region*).

REFERENCES

Alagumalai, S. (1998). *Software/Application: Linear Online Testing System (LOTS)*. Singapore: Trident Groups Pty Ltd.

Alagumalai, S. (1999). *Software/Application: Multimedia Computer Adaptive Testing System (MCAT)*. Singapore: Trident Groups Pte Ltd.

Alagumalai, S. (1998–2000). *Software/Application: Multi-test Diagnostic Feedback System (MTDFS)*. Singapore: Trident Groups Pte Ltd.

Alagumalai, S. (1999–2002). *Software/Application: Intelligent Online Computer Adaptive Diagnostic Systems (IOCADS)*. Patent Pending – Flinders Technologies. Adelaide.

Alagumalai, S. (2002a). Infusing Higher-Order Thinking Skills through Information and Communications Technology. Paper presented at the Singapore Educational Research Association Conference 2002. Singapore. 20–22 Nov.

Alagumalai, S. (2002b). 19th Century Tools, Techniques and Technology for 21st Century Students! Paper presented at the Singapore Educational Research Association Conference 2002. Singapore. 20–22 Nov.

Alagumalai, S., Keeves, J. P., & Njora, H. (2002). Meaningful Assessment: A Case for Intelligent Adaptive Testing Systems. Paper presented at the Inaugural International Test Users' Conference – Testing: Now and the Future. Sydney, Australia. 3–5 Jul.

Alagumalai, S., & Larkin, A. (2001). Beyond learning objects: Implications of metadata. Paper presented at the Educational Research Conference 2001. Flinders University, Adelaide, 27 Nov.

Anderson, J. (1985). *A rationale for the educational use of computers in South Australia*. A discussion paper prepared for the Education and Technology Task Force. South Australia.

Anderson, J. (2002a). *Information and Communication Technology in Secondary Education*. A Curriculum for Schools and Programme of Teacher Development. Paris: UNESCO.

Anderson, J. (2002b). *CDROM: Teaching Ideas for Teacher Educators – Database of Good Practice in Use of ICT*. Paris: UNESCO.

Aris, B. B., Abu, M. S. B., Ellington, H. I., & Dhamotharan, M. (1999). Integrating multimedia technology in the curriculum: Universiti Teknologi Malaysia's experiences. *The INNOTECH Journal*. Jul-Dec Issue.

Aviram, A. (2000). Integrating ICT and Education in Israel for the Third Millennium. Keynote address at The International Conference on Education in the Age of the Information Revolution. June 2000. Available at: Http://www.21learn.org/acti/aharonict.html. Accessed: 22 Dec 2001.

Bradford, J. H. (1990). The semiotic organ: Language and the brain, cited in D. N. Osherson & H. Lasnik, *Language: An Invitation to Cognitive Science*. Cambridge, MA: MIT Press.

Browne, E. (2002). Beyond our wildest dreams, an evaluation of conversational learning using Information and Communication Technology. Paper presented at the Networked Learning Conference, 26–28 March. Lancaster University, UK.

Bruce, C. S. (1998). The Phenomenon of Information Literacy. *Higher Education Research and Development*, 17(1), 25–42.

Cady, G. H., & McGregor, P. (2002). *Protect your Digital Privacy: Survival Skills for the Information Age*. USA: Que.

Chin, C., & Lin, F. L. (2001). Value-loaded activities in mathematics curriculum. Values & Mathematics Project: A joint mathematics educational research project conducted by Monash University and Australia Catholic University and funded by the Australian Research Council. Available online at: Http://www.education.monash.edu.au/projects/vamp/chin_&_lin2001.pdf

Curtin, J. (2002). WebCT and online tutorials: New possibilities for student interaction. *Australian Journal of Educational Technology*, 18(1), 110–126.

DEST (2001). *Department of Education, Science and Training – Making Better Connections: The Models of Teacher Professional Development for the Integration of ICT into Classroom Practice*. Canberra: DEST.

DEST (2002). *Department of Education, Science and Training – Raising the Standards: A Proposal for the Development of an ICT Competency Framework for Teachers*. Canberra: DEST.

DETYA (2000). *Department of Education, Training and Youth Affairs – Learning for the Knowledge Society*. Canberra: DETYA.

Duncan, D. (1992). Qualifications of information technology teachers: The role of education and certification. *Journal of IS Education*, 4(1), 1–5.

Dowling, L. J., Foord-May, M., & Mathena, C. (2001). *Proposing National Standards for Educational Technologists.* Walden University. Available online at: Http://www.dowlingcentral.com/gradschool/EDUC6400/nationalstandards_2.html

EdNA (1996). *Gateways – Information Technology in the Learning Process.* Available at: Http://www.edna.edu.au/sibling/learnit/itdef.html. Accessed: 6 Aug 2001.

Ely, D. P. (2000). The Field of Educational Technology. *Update 2000.* ERIC Clearinghouse on Information Technology. Syracuse, NY. Document No. EDO-1R-2000-01.

Fantini, S., Aggrawal, P., Chen, K., & Franceschini, M. A. (2001). Monitoring brain activity using near-infrared light. *American Laboratory.* Oct 2001, 15–17.

Fischer, G., & Scharff, E. (1998). Learning technologies in support of self-directed learning. *Journal of Interactive Media in Education, 98*(4), 1–32.

Fumihiko, S. (1990). Basic position concerning the revision of the junior high school course of study in science education. *Journal of Science and Mathematics Education in South East Asia.* Penang, Malaysia: SEAMEO-RECSAM, *14*(3), 18–29.

Gopinathan, S. (1997). Education and development in Singapore. In J. Tan, S. Gopinathan & H. W. Kam (Eds.) (1997). *Education in Singapore: A Book of Readings.* Singapore: Prentice Hall.

Gupta, U. G., & Houtz, L. E. (2000). High school students' perceptions of information technology skills and careers. *Journal of Industrial Technology, 16*(4), 1–8.

Hammond, J. (2001). Guest editorial: Human computer interactions. *Journal of Research and Practice in Information Technology, 33*(1), 1–2.

Heinich, R., Molenda, M., Russell, J., & Smaldino, S. (2002). *Instructional media and technologies for learning* (7th ed.). Columbus, OH: Prentice Hall.

Hirumi, Atsusi & Isidro, Grau IV (1996). A review of computer-related state standards, textbooks, and journal articles: Implications for preservice education and professional development. *Journal of Computing in Teacher Education, 12*(4), 6–17.

ISTE (1998). *International Society for Technology in Education – National Educational Technology, Standards for Students.* Eugene, OR.

Kiper, J., Rouse, B., & Troy, D. (1989). Inservice education of high school computer science teachers. *SIGCSE Bulletin, 21*, 193–203.

Kubasek, N. K. (2000). I Found it on the Internet: Critical Thinking and Your Computer. Paper presented at the 6th SEAMEO INNOTECH International Conference: The Learning Society of the Future – Reconciling Education, Values and Technology for Social Transformation. Manila, Philippines. Dec 2000.

Lazimy, Y. (2000). *A Study of Recent Advances in Electroencephalography.* University of Wisconsin-Madison. Available online at: Http://www.cae.wisc.edu/~meditate/EEGpaper.doc

Larkin, A. T. (2002). Globalisation in Tertiary Education. Paper presented at the Hong Kong Educational Research Association Conference. Hong Kong. 10–12 Dec.

Le Heron, J. (2001). Plagiarism, learning dishonesty or just plain cheating: The context and countermeasures in information systems teaching. *Australian Journal of Educational Technology, 17*(3), 244–264.

Lee, K. T. (2001). Information technology integration in teacher education: Supporting the paradigm shift in Hong Kong. *Asia-Pacific Journal of Teacher Education, 4*(1), 157–178.

Lee, K. T. (2002). Effective teaching in the information era: Fostering an ICT-based integrated learning environment in schools. *Asia-Pacific Journal of Teacher Education, 5*(1), 21–45.

Lourdusamy, A., Hun, C., & Wong, S. K. (2001). Impact of hand-held wireless electronic device (Edupad) on science and mathematics teaching-learning environment. *Journal of Science and Mathematics Education in South East Asia, 24*(2), 51–66.

Machida, S. (2000). Development of hypermedia-based mathematics sub-textbooks by a conceptual and procedural mapping method. Paper presented at the ICME-9 Conference. Tokyo, Makuhari.

McGillivray, K. (2000). Educational technologists as curriculum specialist: Part 1. Help outside the classroom. *Learning and Leading with Technology, 28*(1), 36–41.

McKenzie, J. (1995). Did anybody learn anything? Assessing technology programs and the learning accomplished from now on. *A Monthly Electronic Commentary on Educational Technology Issues, 5*(4), December.

McLoughlin, C. (2002). Computer supported teamwork: An integrative approach to evaluating cooperative learning in an online environment. *Australian Journal of Educational Technology*, 18(2), 227–254.

Nair, V. K. K. (2000). Interactive Multimedia Courseware in Education: Issues and Challenges. Paper presented at the 6th SEAMEO INNOTECH International Conference: The Learning Society of the Future – Reconciling Education, Values and Technology for Social Transformation. Manila, Philippines, Dec 2000.

Norris, D. M., Mason, J., & Lefrere, P. (2002). *A Global Initiative – Transforming the e-knowledge Industry: A Revolution in the Sharing of Knowledge*. A Manifesto for a New Industry: A TKI Initiative. Australia: MIS.

NZ-MOE (2002). *Information and Communication Technologies (ICT) Strategy for Schools, 2002–2004*. Ministry of Education, Wellington, New Zealand.

Pefianco, E. C. (1999). The third millennium's challenges to the knowledge builders of the Asia-Pacific region. *The INNOTECH Journal*, Jul-Dec Issue, 2–4.

Roberts, L. (2000). *Nobody believes it's the quick-fix for America's K-12 ills: Linda Roberts on the role of technology in the classroom*. Washington, DC: US Government Report.

Rogers, G. (2001). Information and communication technology in practicum: A Charles Sturt university experience. *Asia-Pacific Journal of Teacher Education and Development*, 4(1).

Segumpan, R. G. (2001). Bruneian education – student's science process skills: Implications to curriculum and management. *Journal of Science and Mathematics Education in South East Asia*, 24(2), 21–34.

Singapore MOE Press Release (1999). Available online at: Http://www1.moe.edu.sg/press/1999/pr990712.htm

Singapore MOE Press Release (2000). Available online at http://www1.moe.edu.sg/press/2000/pr23102000adm.htm

Sung, I. (2000). Korea's experiment with virtual education. *Education and Technology Technical Notes Series*. A publication of the World Bank Human Development Network. Bangkok: UNESCO.

Tan, K. S. (2001). Addressing the lifelong learning needs of teachers: A continuing teacher education framework. *Asia-Pacific Journal of Teacher Education*, 4(2), 173–188.

Tanaka, N., & Suzuki, N. (2000). Japanese Experiences in the Promotion of Computer Use in Education. Paper presented at the 6th SEAMEO INNOTECH International Conference: The Learning Society of the Future – Reconciling Education, Values and Technology for Social Transformation. Manila, Philippines. Dec 2000.

Taylor, H. (1983). Computer science – the illegitimate child of secondary education. *SIGCSE Bulletin*, 15, 200–203.

UNESCO (1998). *World Education Report 1998: Teachers and teaching in a changing world* (Summary). Available at: Http://www.unesco.org/education/educprog/lwf/doc/IA1.html Accessed: 18 Jul 2001.

Ward, D., & Morgan, J. (2001). *Ethics in Emerging Technologies in Education. Emerging Technologies – TKT 8703 Section 1*. Available online at: Http://www2.Msstate.edu/~lsa1/et/ethics.html

Wasser, J. D., McGillivray, K., & McNamara, E. T. (1998). Diary of an Educational Technologist. *Hands On*, 21(2), 1–6. Available online at: Http://www.terc.edu/handsonIssues/f98/diaries.html

Wenglinsky, H. (1998). *Does it Compute? The relationship between educational technology and student achievement in mathematics*. Princeton. NJ: Educational Testing Service Policy Information Centre.

Willoughby, J. O. (2002). Observing how the Brain Works. Paper presented at the EDICT Seminar. School of Education, Flinders University. Adelaide. 4 Oct. Details available at: Http://som.flinders.edu.au/FUSA/NEROSCIENCE/EPILEPSY/EpilepsyLab.html

Wright, J. L. (1998). Computers and young children: A new look at integrating technology into the curriculum. *Early Childhood Education Journal*, 26(2), 107–109.

88

Education Reform and the Labour Market in Pacific Island Countries

GERALD BURKE*

*Monash University – ACER Centre for the Economics of Education and Training,
Melbourne, Australia*

1. INTRODUCTION

The article is concerned with the changes in the world economy, how these impinge on the international labour markets and of Pacific Island countries' labour markets in particular, and the implications for education. The article reviews briefly what is happening in the global economy and labour market, dominated by the rich and large countries of the world. The key features are technological change and accompanying new forms of work organization including the globalisation of production. Production is tending to be relocated to where productivity is high relative to costs. The consequences of these changes for the labour markets of both rich and poor countries are considerable. Some of the common features are an increase in overall unemployment, casualisation of work and a shift in manufacturing employment from the rich countries. Increasing income among some sectors of the world population is leading to a growth in employment in some service sectors such as tourism. While there appears to be a growth in some areas of low skilled work on balance it appears that the changes are increasing the rewards for those with high level skills suited to the emerging new industries.

The impact of these changes on the economies and labour markets of Pacific Island countries is not always positive though there are opportunities as well as disadvantages. One thing seems clear: in any country exposed to international competition those persons with low levels of education and skills are likely to experience low rates of employment and low rates of income. It is also clear that education and training for persons of all ages needs to expand in quantity and quality. The expansion of education and training has to be financed. This

---

* The author is grateful to Don Brewster for his comments.

raises the issues of how to tap new sources of finance for education and training. And how can the efficiency of the provision of education and training be increased so that more can be achieved with the finances. This article takes as given that education is crucial to the improvements in the economic well being of nations. A number of aspects of this relationship are considered in the article. However, it is important to state that economic outcomes are not the only focus of the education system. Education is concerned with personal development, citizenship, social equity and cohesion. It may not be assumed that policies concerned with the economy necessarily will achieve the social goals.

2. THE WORLD ECONOMY AND LABOUR MARKET

The expansion of world trade, new technologies and production organised across nations has led to a changing pattern of employment and remuneration within high-income countries. There has been a reduction in routine production jobs in rich countries in manufacturing. Higher productivity and the shift of production to lower wage countries are the main reasons for these changes. Accompanying the higher productivity in manufacturing is the greater economy in the use of materials. A result quite surprisingly different from the predictions of the 1960s is that the value of commodities has tended to decline relative to manufactures, particularly highly technical products, and services.

Productivity growth has been particularly high in areas such as communications where production has grown at a remarkable rate but where total employment has not grown much. There has been strong growth in employment in areas where it is difficult to measure productivity, such as property and business services, associated with the outsourcing of both public sector and private sector work and the growing internationalisation of business. These jobs are often in areas of high skill professional employment. There has also been strong growth in retail trade, restaurants and accommodation that are on average relatively low skill areas.

The changes in industrial structure have tended to reduce employment and earnings of both skilled and unskilled men and low skilled women and to expand employment in areas in which females had above average employment. The areas of job expansion are not readily accessible to many of the older workers displaced by the decline in manufacturing. The education and skills that older workers had acquired may not be relevant to the changed work environment. Employment has not expanded sufficiently to employ those wanting to work. This is indicated by the high levels of measured unemployment in many high-income countries. The average unemployment rate for the OECD has risen from 5.3 per cent in 1990 to 6.3 per cent in 2000. Underemployment, indicated by persons working part-time but seeking full-time work, indicates a still larger problem. There are also a large number, about equal to the official number of unemployed, who would like work but are not actively looking for work. Most of these are older adults whose plight has not attracted the same attention as that of unemployed youth.

Overall, the changes involve increasing the earnings of highly skilled persons relative to unskilled, and increasing the private benefits of high levels of education and training. It is less clear what the effects are on middle level jobs. There has been a widening in the distribution of earnings in many high-income countries. The workforce participation rate of adult males has fallen whereas the participation rate of adult females has tended to rise. In the majority of high-income countries there has been a relative growth in part-time employment (OECD, 1999, p. 240).

In some countries there has been an increase in casual or temporary employment. While overall employment protection has been maintained, there are examples of substantial changes in employment protection in a few countries especially in the regulations governing temporary employment (OECD, 1999, p. 87). There is an increase in the proportion of persons perceiving a rise in job insecurity (OECD, 1997, p. 129). While job turnover does not appear to have increased, the consequences of job loss for some and especially for older workers in a period of high unemployment and varying degrees of unemployment compensation, is greater than in the past. There is also evidence that for workers with low levels of education, who already have relatively low rates of job tenure, that tenure is decreasing relative to persons with higher levels of education (OECD, 1997, p. 143).

3. POLICIES COMMON ACROSS LARGE ECONOMIES

These changes in the world economy have been aided and accompanied by a common adoption of policies aimed at containing the size of government and increasing the role of the private sector and the market. The stagnation of some of the wealthy economies in the 1970s and 1980s and the collapse of the communist regimes a decade ago were factors in the surge in belief in the virtues of the private profit motive and free markets. Governments in many countries have divested themselves of activities in gas, electricity, transport and communications. In some areas they have moved towards freer international trade, though the rhetoric of some of the larger players is not always matched by their policies. The reduction in protection of manufacturers allows the development of global production practices of many corporations.

A common development is the move to deregulate labour markets. The rich economies differed in the extent to which workers had won particular job conditions and wages. The strongly held belief by some governments has whittled back the restrictions and regulations in many rich countries. Those countries retaining regulatory and protective practices for workers have felt the pressure of competition from more deregulated economies.

High levels of taxation are seen as reducing the attractiveness of investment and hence limiting the growth of the private sector, the engine of development. Hence a range of practices has been adopted to restrict public expenditure and the level of taxation. These include improved management in the public sector, often involving devolution of management but increased assessment of performance against specified objectives. It also includes reduction in the range of government services and in some cases income support. The effects include a decline in public employment.

4. EDUCATION AND TRAINING

The policy response for education and training to the changes in the global economy varies, but virtually all the high-income countries are seeking an increase in education and training. However, they are attempting to provide it at lower unit cost or to finance it through the private sector. The reasons for the policy of expansion are that at least a substantial proportion of new jobs requires new knowledge, and higher skill levels. The rapid introduction of new technology in some areas means a faster obsolescence of old skills and the need to acquire new ones throughout working life. This is most obvious in the information technology areas.

The other main reason for expansion is related to equity and the ageing of the populations of many of the high-income economies. As already mentioned older and low skilled males have been displaced in the recent economic change. Education and training is seen as assisting in their reemployment or even in supporting life choices for those not in the paid workforce.

For these reasons many countries have endorsed the concept of lifelong learning in place of policies focused on formal education for children and young adults. This involves improved basic education for children and a much-increased participation in learning by adults throughout their life. The learning for adults is seen to take place in a range of settings: formal education, training in the workplace, community education and self-education. Such policies, when implemented, mean that a much greater proportion of the population is involved in education and training. If unit costs remain unchanged then this means a substantial increase in expenditures.

There is a wide range of measures either adopted or under consideration either to reduce unit cost or to shift costs from the public sector to employers or to students and their families. Measures include improved management of education resources, introduction or increase in fees charged, mandated or encouraged additional training by employers, and increased competitive pressures in the provision of education and training.

5. EFFECT OF THE GLOBAL CHANGES ON PACIFIC ISLAND COUNTRIES

Globalisation has been associated with rapid economic growth in several previously low-income economies especially in Asia, though this was temporarily slowed by the economic crisis of 1997 to 1999. This has not been the experience of the Pacific Island countries. Table 1 shows that in general the level of production per head remains very low and the growth rates not high compared with the high performing economies of the 1990s. Income per head is higher than GDP per head in most of these countries due to remittances from former emigrants now living abroad and from overseas aid.

The small population of most Pacific Island economies is a major disadvantage for the potential scale of production. Table 1 provides some summary statistics on the selected Pacific Island countries (PICs). With the exception of Papua New Guinea (PNG) with nearly five million people, all have populations under one million and six of the 11 have populations between 10,000 and 100,000. Only Fiji has developed a substantial manufacturing industry, in garments, and that is under threat from changes in access to markets in Australia, the main destination for its exports. The very small countries with many islands suffer from small internal markets and high costs of transport and other infrastructure, and from remoteness from external markets.

The dependence on agriculture of most Pacific Island nations is made more precarious by the tendency noted earlier for commodity prices to fall relative to the general level of prices in the world economy. Table 1 shows that a majority of the population is engaged in agriculture or fishing in most countries for which data are available. Though agriculture engages such a large proportion of the population, in general the output per head is low and hence agriculture's share of GDP is much lower than its share of the workforce. In contrast, in high-income countries the proportion engaged in agriculture is often less than five per cent.

The growth in income of persons in the large and high-income economies and relatively low cost international travel has led to the subsequent increase in world tourism. Fiji has benefited from this.

6. IMPLICATIONS FOR EDUCATION AND TRAINING

The changes in the world economy and their impact on the Pacific Island economies do have implications for education and training. The implications need to be set against the current levels of provision and the particular circumstances of each country. As already indicated the impacts vary considerably across the Pacific Island economies, which have varied populations and resources. They have particular histories of economic, political and educational development, in part indicated by the data in Tables 2 and 3.

Table 2 indicates that universal primary education has not been achieved. The World Bank's recent analysis concluded that educational outcomes, except in Tonga, have been poor. There are insufficient qualified teachers and:

> By the time students graduate from primary school, they are several years behind same-age students in industrial countries. In Fiji, FSM, Marshall Islands and Samoa, only about half of the students who finish primary

Table 1. Economic and demographic indicators, Pacific Island Countries

	Population '000 estimate 1999[†]	Population % 0–14[†]	Life expectancy*	Labour force % agriculture[*]	Agriculture % share of GDP 1996	GDP growth rate 1987–91 %**	GDP growth rate 1992–97 %**	GNP per capita US$ 1995**	GDP per capita PPP 1996[†]
Fiji	813	33	73	67 (1987)	19	2.4	2.5	2,440	6,700
Micronesia, F.S.	132	na	67	na	na	4.4	1.2	2,010	1,760
Kiribati	86	na	58	na	na	2.9	1.6	920	800
Marshall Islands	66	50	61	na	na	4.4	−0.3	1,670	1,450
Palau[†]	18	27	68	na	na	na	na	na	8,800
Papua New Guinea	4,705	39	58	64	26	na	na	na	2,400
Samoa	230	39	69	65	40	−1.8	2.6	1,120	2,100
Solomon Islands	455	45	63	41	48	3.2	4.4	910	2,600
Tonga	109	na	69	67	30	1.2	1.7	1,630	2,100
Tuvalu*	11	35	64	na	na	2.8	na	na	800
Vanuatu	189	39	65	65	23	na	2.6	1,200	1,300

Sources:
* World Bank (1999). [Online] Countries 'At a Glance', Economist Intelligence Unit Country Reports.
** World Bank (1998). Pacific Islands: Regional Economic Report.
[†] CIA World Factbook 1999 [online].
na. not available.

Table 2. Selected measures of educational provision

	% of age cohort reaching grade 5 in 1994*	Progression to secondary school	Adult illiteracy rates age 15+ % 1995	Student teacher ratio Prim.†	Student teacher ratio Second.†
Fiji	87	na	8	34	20
Micronesia Federated States	na	na	na	na	na
Kiribati	90	23	10	24	17
Marshall Islands	na	na	9	na	na
Palau	na	na	na	na	na
Papua New Guinea	59	38	28	38	27
Samoa	85	na	98	24	19
Solomon Islands	81	na	62	24	18
Tonga	92	76	na	22	18
Tuvalu	96	na	na	na	na
Vanuatu	61	25	30	31	19

UNESCO *Indicators [online]*, † World Bank (1998). *Pacific Islands: Regional Economic Report Chapter 3, UNDP (1998)*.

Table 3. Government expenditure on education in Pacific Island Countries

	Per cent of current government expenditure 1990–95	1996	Per cent of GDP early 1990s*	1990–95	1996
Fiji	19	14	5	6	4
Micronesia Federated States	na	na	na	na	na
Kiribati	20	21	6	11	13
Marshall Islands	15	17	na	11	10
Palau	na	na	na	na	na
Papua New Guinea	na	na	na	na	na
Samoa	18	18	4	5	5
Solomon Islands	17	15	4	5	4
Tonga	19	18	5	10	10
Tuvalu	na	na	na	na	na
Vanuatu	22	23	5	5	5

World Bank (1998). *Pacific Islands: Regional Economic Report Chapter 3*, *UNESCO Indicators [online]*.

school go on to secondary education and in the rest of the PICs, the numbers are much lower, ranging from 17 percent in Vanuatu to 7 percent in Kiribati. (World Bank, 1998 p. 29)

Public expenditure in the high-income OECD countries averages about five per cent of GDP. Table 3 shows that public expenditure on education in Pacific Island countries (PICs) is generally quite high in comparison. The fact that this level is associated with low levels of school completion by comparison with high-income countries reflects the low level of GDP and the difficulties of providing well-qualified teachers and education and training for dispersed and usually small populations. The PICs also have the additional costs associated with relatively high rates of population growth, a young population and high rates of adult emigration. Table 1 shows for the countries listed that 27 to 50 per cent of the populations were aged 0 to 14 years. The average for high-income countries is about 20 per cent aged 0 to 14 years.

7. ESTIMATING THE EDUCATION AND TRAINING NEEDS

It is no easy task to forecast the future development and labour force needs of any economy let alone for Pacific Island economies. For a number of the smaller countries the training needs of the workforce are complicated by internal migration and by external migration to countries such as New Zealand and Australia. Even in high-income countries with sophisticated collections of economic and demographic data there is not a great degree of reliance on manpower forecasts in forming government policy on education and training. There are too many uncertainties in regard to the likely growth in the economy, the industrial distribution of the growth, the particular skill needs of industry and the rate of labour turnover. However, forecasts can provide part of the data for policy formation. Other data needs to be considered too, such as current rates of employment and unemployment, graduate destinations and salaries and known policy changes, for example, the restriction on government employment implemented in some countries. Such data can be used to sketch scenarios of future employment.

If education and training were to be set to meet the labour force needs of a depressed economy there would often be little indication of a need for expansion. However, it is also clear from the review of the experience of the global changes, that a high education path is a necessary condition for achieving a high-income economy. There is also the case for improved education and training for social as well as labour force reasons.

The problem is how this is to be achieved given that education already absorbs a considerable proportion of public outlays and most governments, often with the advice of international agencies or donor countries, are trying to contain the levels of public expenditure. Table 4 shows the level of public revenue, external grants and expenditure relative to GDP. Fiji, Vanuatu and Tonga are the only countries where expenditure is less than 50 per cent of GDP. In some cases, assisted by external grants, expenditure is about the same size as the GDP. The average for OECD countries is about 40 per cent though some European countries exceed 50 per cent.

Though not the whole answer, it is clear that attention needs to be given to

Table 4. Government revenue, external grants and expenditure as per cent of GDP, average 1990-95

	Revenue	External grants	Total revenue	Expenditure
Fiji	27	0	27	28
Micronesia Federated States	30	60	89	90
Kiribati	79	39	119	101
Marshall Islands	32	55	87	98
Palau	na	na	na	na
Papua New Guinea	na	na	na	na
Samoa	42	13	55	70
Solomon Islands	29	15	44	53
Tonga	26	15	41	43
Tuvalu	na	na	na	Na
Vanuatu	24	15	38	39

Source: World Bank (1998), p. 12.
na. not available.

- improving the efficiency of the delivery of education and training and
- examining new forms of finance.

8. EFFICIENCY

Given the need to improve quality and quantity of education and training and the scarcity of financial resources, increased efficiency in the delivery of education is essential. The usefulness of any particular measure will vary among Pacific Island nations, depending on the structure of government and the skills of the administrators in the education system. The major cost is for teaching personnel. This accounts for over 70 per cent of current expenditures in primary and secondary education. Teacher quality is vital and is unlikely to be enhanced by a low salary rate. However, attention might be given to the range of salaries paid with incentives in career earnings to retain good teachers.

Activities by governments to economise on resources include the development of funding models whereby schools with the same needs in terms of student numbers and student learning difficulties are funded at the same level. Governments also need additional data on the performance of the education system, particularly to identify what works. This includes measures of attainment in key learning areas as well as measures of participation, retention and post school destination. Such data should inform policy development. Where there is a large degree of devolution of control of schools it may help in identifying what forms of school organisation are most effective.

One of the ways of promoting the efficiency of schooling is the provision of better learning materials to schools and provision of teacher development. These are aspects of efficiency that involve increased expenditure, not less. For Pacific

Island countries providing materials in their own languages is a particularly expensive problem.

The main approach to economising on capital costs is through mergers of institutions, but there is very little prospect of this across a country of many islands. Usually the annual costs of the use of capital facilities are not a matter for the budget of a public educational institution so it has no reason to try to economise on them. The increasing use of accrual accounting which identifies annual capital costs will draw more attention to the costs of facilities.

New technology is seen as the means of cost reduction in the formal education and in the workplace. The usual high initial costs of course development in using the new technology must be noted though there are examples of low cost provision. There is also a very strong need for expenditure on staff development if the new technologies are to be used to provide quality education and training. It appears that mixed-mode teaching which could combine on- and off-campus activities and the use of new technologies may offer the most prospects for lower costs and better learning (Rumble, 1997). The use of technology in the collaborative delivery of post secondary education across several Pacific Island countries is a matter for consideration: its effectiveness may be limited by the quality of telecommunications.

Organisational changes are seen as a means of promoting cost savings in personnel, capital or other costs. One change that is certainly needed is the better coordination of policies across the various ministries of education, training and employment. One major change occurring in most high income countries is the devolution of decision making to as close to the delivery of services as possible (OECD, 1996, Chapter 5). The role of central government is in the provision of the infrastructure of the curriculum and qualifications framework. It monitors the outcomes rather than engaging in bureaucratic determination of resource allocation. In some cases this involves a system of funding at least partly related to outcomes, and the compilation of indicators of those outcomes. It is clear however that devolution of financial decision making requires a high level of staff development for school administrators.

A more radical approach is the promotion of competition among providers. Competition encourages meeting the needs of the clients – students, trainees or employers. In some high-income countries governments have put to tender the provision of publicly funded training. However, competition promotes efficiency when there are large numbers of buyers and sellers and the small dispersed nature of the PICs suggests that most are too small for this more radical approach.

9. FINANCE AND WHERE DIRECTED

When government finance is insufficient to meet the demands for improving the quantity and quality of education then consideration has to be given as to where the public finance will be directed and at providing means of increasing the private levels of finance. Mingat (1995) in an analysis of high performing Asian economies, Japan, Republic of Korea, Singapore and Taiwan, found that an early commitment to primary and basic education, relative to other levels of education was common among those economies. The World Bank (1998) endorses the need for the concentration on achieving quality primary education.

For high-income countries where there is near universal secondary education there is still debate about the size of the post secondary sector and also about the extent to which secondary education should be explicitly vocational. There are considerable variations across successful economies in these aspects. Middleton et al. (1993, p. 16) find that employers want the competencies that general or academic education can provide, but with the attitudes that practical education is thought to supply.

In general, studies in individual economies have not shown school level vocational education to be a good investment compared with general education, but there are exceptions. When vocational education is leading effectively to job entry Middleton et al. (1993) find it can also be useful in pursuing social objectives such as providing for the less able or helping less advantaged groups. But it is of little value for the less advantaged in periods of high unemployment and when there is little direct connection to employers. Ziderman (1997, p. 362) concludes that vocational schools in the ongoing period of rapid economic change will need to concentrate on broader training, emphasising the capacity for subsequent worker training and with links to the workplace.

The prevailing view (Bray, 1998, p. 12) is that vocational education is considerably more expensive than general education because of smaller practical classes and expensive equipment. Training in the workplace has not been considered in this article but is important in any assessment of the success of education and training strategies. There may be substantial differences in the extent of workplace training and in government regulation or funding of it. France and Malaysia are examples of countries that require employer expenditure or contributions to training as a means of increasing the level of training and having it financed by the private sector.

Private finance is one means of funding the expansion of enrolments in education and training in a period of tightened government budgets. Across the world there has been a tendency to reduce public funds per student in higher education. Ziderman and Albrecht (1995, p. 23) document that the decline has occurred across economies at all income levels, though the experience has been worst in the poorest economies.

Private finance is advocated in post-basic and non-universal education as a means of lessening the spending of government funds on those in the community already well off. It is advocated along with private provision as a means of promoting competition and efficiency in education, though there are counter arguments concerning lack of information, externalities and thin markets. The force of these counter-arguments is strongest at the lowest levels of education.

Private finance is particularly important in Korea, Japan and Taiwan where tertiary participation rates are high. Among low-income economies, Vietnam has made the expansion of its education system dependent on fees, despite being a socialist economy.

The World Bank (1998, p. 30) raises the issue of whether students in Pacific Island countries in tertiary education should bear more of the costs. Many high-income countries have student loan schemes, which involve some degree of government subsidy. Ziderman and Albrecht (1995) review them. The Higher Education Contribution Scheme in Australia is worth attention. Students may defer payment of fees until they enter the paid workforce. At that point they begin to repay their debt if their income exceeds a specified minimum level. The scheme's effectiveness does depend on a high level of efficiency in the tax system and may be difficult to enforce in countries with high levels of emigration.

10. CONCLUSION

This article takes as given that education is crucial to the improvements in the economic and social well being of nations, as well as in the degree of its social cohesion and participation.

The article outlines some of the key features of the changes occurring internationally in employment and earnings. In the globalised economy there is a tendency for earnings to increase for the more highly educated and to decline for the least skilled, who also suffer the highest levels of unemployment. New technology implies that new skills will have to be acquired throughout working life. Production is tending to be relocated to where productivity is high relative to costs.

While some previously low-income countries have benefited from this, on the whole PICs have not. Manufacturing industry has not gone to the PICs except for the garment industry in Fiji and its future is threatened by changing trading arrangements. The PICs have also suffered from the economizing on commodities that is occurring with the introduction of new technologies in the global economy. Tourism is an area benefiting from growth in the world economy but many of the PICs (again excepting Fiji) are remote and transport remains more expensive.

Analysis of the data on the changing economies, government and private employment and new industrial opportunities can help in sketching scenarios of the areas for development of education and training in PICs. However the development of any economy and its educational needs are subject to considerable uncertainties. At present most of the PICs lag well behind modern industrial economies in participation rates and in the quality of their education and training. Raising the levels of provision and the quality of provision will be difficult given the already high levels of public expenditures and the pressures to reduce them being exerted by donor agencies. Given the scarcity of financial resources increased efficiency in the delivery of education is essential. The new multi-media technologies need attention. While still expensive they are becoming less costly and offer great potential for dispersed populations.

Efficiencies will not be achieved unless some incentives are provided and some mechanisms for monitoring efficiency are implemented. These include mechanisms to promote efficiency and equity in funding. Methods for consideration include the use of funding models, performance measures, accounting for capital on an annual basis as with accrual accounting, devolution of management, and increased competition among providers. As well as increased efficiency there is a need to tap increased private sources of finance for education and training. Employers can be required by legislation to provide training or to fund education for their employees.

Instead of compulsion, governments can consider a range of methods of providing incentives to individuals and employers to invest. These forms of incentives include grants or subsidies to cover part of the costs of education. Loans for education and training can also provide access to education and training, eventually at a lower cost to the government than grants. Loans for which the repayment is contingent on the individual achieving a certain level of earnings reduce the risks of investment in education. Collection of such loans through the taxation system as in Australia appears to be efficient and effective. One problem of an income contingent loan scheme in Pacific Island countries is the tracking of persons who migrate to other countries. Increased information on education and employment opportunities can increase incentives to invest in education. This implies a good information and guidance system across countries.

REFERENCES

Bray, M. (1998). Financing Education in Developing Asia: Oatterns, trends and policy implications, Asian Development Bank, Working paper for the Study of Trends, Issues and Policies in Education, University of Hong Kong

Middleton, J., Ziderman, A., & Van Adams, A. (1993). *Skills for Productivity, Vocational Education and Training for Developing Countries.* New York: World Bank, Oxford University Press.

Mingat, A. (1995). *Towards Improving our Understanding of the Strategy of High Performing Asian Economies in the Education Sector.* France: IREDU CNRS, University of Dijon.

OECD (1996). *Lifelong Learning for All.* Paris: OECD.

OECD (1997). *Employment Outlook June 1997.* Paris: OECD.

OECD (1998). *Employment Outlook June 1998.* Paris: OECD.

OECD (1999). *Employment Outlook June 1999.* Paris: OECD.

Rumble, G. (1997). *The Costs and Economics of Open and Distance Learning.* London: Kogan Page,

World Bank (1998). *Pacific Islands: Regional Economic Report* [online].

Ziderman, A. (1997). National programmes in technical and vocational education: Economic and education relationships. *Journal of Vocational Education and Training, 49,* 3.

Ziderman, A., & Albrecht, D. (1995). *Financing Universities in Developing Countries.* Washington DC: Falmer Press.

89

Training of Educational Research Workers

BARRY J. FRASER
Curtin University of Technology, Perth, Australia

ANGELA F.L. WONG
National Institute of Education, Nanyang Technological University, Singapore

1. INTRODUCTION

The future of educational research in the Asia-Pacific region depends critically on the adequacy of training for the next generation of educational researchers in these countries. The purpose of this article is to overview some of the existing provisions for formal and informal training of educational research workers in the region. The historical reliance on sending a small elite overseas for higher degrees is too expensive to implement on the scale needed, and provisions for educational research training in universities in the Asia-Pacific region are too few and too inflexible. Therefore, to cater for the needed supply of educational researchers for the region, there is an urgent need for more flexible higher degree programs that allow people to work and live in their own area while undertaking world-class programs at selected universities in the Asia-Pacific region. This article is structured using the following sections: types of research training; coursework and support materials for research degrees; research training programs in the Asia-Pacific region; flexible provisions for part-time distant research students; and concluding and forward-looking remarks.

2. TYPES OF RESEARCH TRAINING

Although people often first think of formal university courses when asked about educational research training, there also are many important informal approaches to research training (e.g., conference attendance and publishing). Below, formal university courses are considered prior to discussing some of these important informal sources of research training.

2.1. Formal University Courses

Preservice teacher education courses in education seldom provide substantial training in research, which usually has to wait until after graduation with a Bachelor's degree. For example, perusal of the undergraduate education programs at the National Institute of Education in Singapore, Universiti Brunei Darussalam and University of Malaya indicates an absence of research methods courses. However, some preservice courses in these universities do offer a certain amount of research training through an introduction to action research or other research approaches as a minor part of courses on other topics.

In Australian universities, research training in the field of education typically has the following structure.

- *Level 1:* Bachelor of Education (Honours) is for people with a first degree in education. This program typically consists of both coursework and a thesis.
- *Level 2:* Master of Education/Arts consists either of a major research thesis or a combination of coursework and a minor project/thesis.
- *Level 3:* Either a Doctor of Philosophy by major thesis or a professional doctorate (e.g., Doctor of Education) involving professional coursework training plus a smaller thesis.

In contrast to typical Australian universities, however, Asian universities often have a focus on research in a content area (e.g., science) rather than research in education at the Bachelor's Honours level, prior to undertaking professional coursework and research training in education.

At the three Asian universities mentioned above (National Institute of Education in Singapore, Universiti Brunei Darussalam and University of Malaya), there are Doctor of Philosophy degrees by research only, while Masters degrees consist of coursework and a minor research dissertation or project. Courses on research methods and statistics are common in these Masters programs, but are not covered in bachelor or doctoral programs.

2.2. Informal Sources of Research Training

Although formal university courses provide an important approach to research training, much professional development in educational research also is gained from informal sources. For example, engaging in action research on one's own teaching can yield important insights, as can attending and presenting papers at educational research conferences (e.g., Educational Research Association in Singapore, American Educational Research Association and Australian Association for Research in Education).

Acting as an author or reviewer of journal articles provides excellent training, as does membership and active participation in national and international research associations. Some people also get worthwhile opportunities for internships in research centres, or at least the chance to participate in workshops or seminars.

The new Centre for Research in Pedagogy and Practice at the National Institute of Education at Nanyang Technological University in Singapore is about to provide some unique opportunities in educational research training (www.nie.edu.sg/html/crpp.htm). This Centre's major objective is to generate research-based information that can be used to inform educational decision making. In order to meet this goal, the Centre will appoint about 30 full-time staff to undertake research with the support of research assistants and other personnel. Therefore, this Centre will provide an exciting framework for research and the implementation of the research findings in the schools, as well as the opportunity for researchers, teachers and administrators to work together to develop and implement new ideas in the schools to educate better, students for the challenges in the decades ahead. These activities will provide training in educational research for a large group of people associated with the new Centre.

3. COURSEWORK AND SUPPORT MATERIALS FOR RESEARCH DEGREES

Many universities offer coursework on research methods as part of professional doctorates or Master's degrees in the field of education. However, few universities provide the breadth of coursework in research methods that is offered by the Flinders University of South Australia, whose courses include:

- Introduction to research
- Qualitative research methods
- Introduction to statistics
- Advanced educational measurement
- Advanced multivariate and multilevel analysis
- Use of information and communications technology
- Recent advances in research in learning and development.

At other Australian universities various materials have been designed to help students who are undertaking research degrees. For example, to assist further the teaching of postgraduate research students at Curtin University of Technology, a team of academic staff co-authored materials on writing research proposals for approval by a graduate studies committee. The 74-page *A Guide to Preparing your Application for Candidacy* (Rennie et al., 1999) is available (http://www.smec.curtin.edu.au/candid/). Thus, given the diverse backgrounds of the students (e.g., international, interstate, different disciplines, levels of education), the monograph attempts to meet very specific needs. Various sections provide ideas to help students to conceptualise their research program, a bibliography of useful references, and some examples of other students' summaries of their proposed research programs.

Numerous books have been published to help supervisors and graduate students come to grips with the nebulous task of either supervising or undertaking higher degrees by research. These include *Supervising the PhD: A Guide to Success* (Delamont, Atkinson, & Parry, 1997), *Working for a Doctorate: A Guide for the Humanities and Social Sciences* (Graves & Varma, 1997), *Supervision of Postgraduate Research in Education* (Holbrook & Johnston, 1999), *Establishing Effective PhD Supervision* (Cullen, Pearson, Saha, & Spear, 1994), *Writing Your Doctoral Dissertation: Invisible Rules for Success* (Brause, 2000), *Successful Dissertations and Theses: A Guide to Graduate Student Research from Proposal to Completion* (Madsen, 1992).

4. RESEARCH TRAINING PROGRAM IN ASIA-PACIFIC REGION

This section of the article provides an overview of the training of educational researchers in each of the following countries: Brunei Darussalam, Indonesia, Malaysia, the Philippines, Singapore and Thailand. For each country, we document the historical beginnings and development of educational research training, and try to answer questions about what kinds of institutions are involved in the training, who the trainers are, who the participants are, what kinds of courses the participants undertake, and where the graduates of these courses are employed after completing their training.

We found it difficult to find published information about research training in the field of education in the Asia-Pacific region. In some cases, this may be because relatively little work is being undertaken in the training of education researchers. In cases where interesting work is going on, there would appear to be few written records. There is clearly the need for programs to be developed for the training of educational research workers.

4.1. Brunei Darussalam

In Brunei Darussalam, there have been several initiatives which attempt to encourage educational practitioners and policy-makers to be more research-oriented. Most of these initiatives over the previous decade originated from the Sultan Hassanal Bolkiah Institute of Education (SHBIE), which is the sole teacher education institution in the country. However, there are no programs which set out specifically to train educational researchers.

A Master of Educational Management program was introduced in 1989 when SHBIE became a part of Universiti Brunei Darussalam. A course entitled 'Introduction to Educational Research' was included during the last semester of the program when the course projects were being conducted concurrently. The participants were either officers from the Ministry of Education or senior school personnel. Because of the nature of their jobs, they could not be regarded as trained educational researchers as such, except perhaps for the very few who were enrolled in the dissertation strand and learned to conduct more rigorous research from their supervisors.

Later, in 1995, the Master of Education program was introduced. It placed greater emphasis on the development of research competence through two core courses on educational research. Introduction to Educational Research provided a basic introduction to both quantitative and qualitative methods of inquiry, while Research Methodology allowed the students to go deeper into either quantitative or qualitative approaches. The MEd program also allowed for areas of specialization, namely, Educational Management, Science and Mathematics Education, and Language Education. In 2001, some further changes were introduced. The first course became more philosophical and qualitative in nature, while the second became either solely quantitative, qualitative or action-research oriented.

A doctoral program has also been included at the SHBIE. However, the few candidates who are enrolled are all from overseas because local candidates, who are mostly tutors at SHBIE, prefer to wait to be sponsored by the government for overseas studies. So far, many of those who were sponsored for overseas studies have returned with doctorates, while a few have not. Unfortunately, because nearly all of these trained research workers are appointed to senior administrative positions, a neglect of research activities results.

4.1. *The CARE Program*

Besides formal training through the MEd and doctoral courses in Brunei, several other initiatives have also brought about a greater awareness of the need to conduct educational research. In 1994, the systematic and systemic CARE Program with five components was introduced. It began with two workshops involving representatives from SHBIE and the Ministry of Education and schools, and it aimed at developing a Collaborative Agenda for Research in Education. This was referred to as CARE3, which was one of the five CARE activities introduced to boost educational research in Brunei Darussalam.

CARE1: Committee for Applied Research in Education,
CARE2: Centre for Applied Research in Education,
CARE3: Collaborative Agenda for Research in Education,
CARE4: Criteria for Applied Research in Education,
CARE5: Confederation of Associations for Research in Education.

CARE3 originally identified four priority areas for research, namely, motivation to learn, motivation to teach, improving language competence, and improving professional competence. However, with the request from the Ministry of Education that SHBIE adopts six primary schools for investigating the application of research in education, there was a shift in emphasis for CARE3 towards developing Strategies for Optimising Learning and Development (SOLD) and Thoughtful Schools. The enthusiasm for collaborative research even extended towards the development of the Inter-institute Dialogue on Educational Advances (IDEA), for which representatives from SHBIE and the National Institute of Education in Singapore (NIE) would meet each year, in alternating venues, to plan and share the outcomes of collaborative research. In December

2001, a symposium on IDEA was presented at the annual conference of the Australian Association for Research in Education (Sim et al., 2001).

Brunei Darussalam provides a good example of how its research training has been enhanced through cooperation with an overseas institution. This cooperation has led the Brunei government to sponsor five DOSME staff for full-time doctoral study at Curtin University (e.g., Cheong, 2001).

A more significant outcome of the cooperation is the provision of arrangements whereby people residing and working in Brunei can work part-time towards a Curtin University doctorate or Masters degree. The centrepiece of this arrangement is an annual week-long short course held at UBD and co-taught by Curtin and UBD staff. Attendance at this course, followed by reading, email communication, and the completion of various assignments, enables participants to gain credit towards a coursework unit in Curtin University's professional doctorate (Doctor of Science Education or Doctor of Mathematics Education) or Master of Science (Science Education or Mathematics Education). A number of secondary and tertiary teachers in Brunei already have successfully completed Curtin doctorates under this model (e.g., Khine, 2001; Scott, 2001).

In addition to catering for people who want to enrol in a Curtin degree, these short courses are open to all science and mathematics teachers in Brunei. To date, nine of these short courses, on topics such as conceptual change, learning environments, curriculum, student assessment and curriculum evaluation, and leadership and professional development, have been attended by over 1000 science and mathematics teachers in Brunei.

4.2. *Indonesia*

Educational research in post-independence Indonesia has spanned a period of close to 30 years. During that time, there has been a large expansion of institutional capacity and research productivity. In 1976, research capacity was further strengthened when the government decided to launch a nationwide PhD program in which nine state universities were involved. Three of the nine specialized in educational studies. In addition, another university outside the nine was assigned the task of setting up a special graduate-level program in educational research, as well as the provision of short courses on research for Ministry officials.

Educational research in Indonesia serves three main purposes: (a) to fulfil general and postgraduate academic degree requirements; (b) to further research interests of university-based scholars; and (c) to examine a practical policy or issue. Thus, educational research workers comprise undergraduate and postgraduate students, staff from the Institutes and Faculties of Education, and officials from government organisations such as the Office of Educational and Cultural Research and Development, as well as non-government organisations like the Institute of Economics and Social Research, Education and Training and private universities (Setijadi et al., 1988). In order to improve the quality of research, undergraduate and postgraduate students and the researchers from the Office of Educational and Cultural Research and Development were given more opportunities to attend short courses, workshops, seminars, or even studies on research methods, both at home and abroad.

Despite these training opportunities, there are still many obstacles which impede research productivity, such as the lack of professional status and non-material rewards, and the scarcity of research workers. In universities and government offices, conducting research does not command high social value, thus non-material rewards are almost non-existent. For example, in tertiary institutions, staff gain only 20 per cent of their credit points for promotion from research activities (Setijadi et al., 1988). With regards to the number of so-called 'real' researchers in Indonesia, experts claim that it is very small relative to the need for researchers. To make matters worse, many good research workers have been offered more lucrative administrative jobs in the public or private sector, resulting in a further reduction in the number of researchers.

4.3. Malaysia

The training of educational researchers in Malaysia began with the establishment of the Faculty of Education at the University of Malaya in 1965. Its first Dean, the late Professor Ruth Wong, concentrated her early years there recruiting high-quality staff, particularly those with postgraduate degrees. As a long-term plan, promising local staff were sponsored to undertake doctoral studies in prestigious universities overseas (e.g., Harvard and Stanford), while well-qualified expatriate staff were employed in several areas of specialization. Upon their return from their postgraduate studies, the local staff would then supervise the research of newer staff members as well as that of their MEd and PhD students (Ho, 1995).

Professor Sim Wong Kooi, who was at Universiti Brunei Darussalam at the time of writing this article, was among the first four local staff whom Professor Wong recruited. He recalled that she strongly encouraged her staff to conduct research, which would hopefully enlighten policy and practice in education, including teacher education.

Since the early 1970s, various national and international organisations have invited the more experienced staff from the Faculty of Education, University of Malaya, to undertake research and evaluation projects. Typically, a research team comprising these staff, as well as some younger members, would be formed. Later, postgraduate students from the Master of Education program, which was introduced in 1971, were included. These projects then served as authentic training grounds for many an aspiring educational researcher.

An example of such a project is the South-East Asian Science and Mathematics Experiment (or SEASAME), under the auspices of the South-East Asian Ministers of Education Organisation's Regional Education Centre for Science and Mathematics (or SEAMEO RECSAM). Since 1973, a team of researchers from the University of Malaya has helped to conduct a variety of courses in primary science and mathematics curriculum development, resource materials development, curriculum evaluation, and teacher inservice education. The participants have come from the SEAMEO countries. They have been involved in developing prototype curriculum modules, including resource materials, and the trying out of the modules, as well as developing materials for inservice education of teachers. Participants in each course therefore contributed towards specific components of a major curriculum research and development project.

In addition to the Faculty of Education of the University of Malaya, the School of Educational Studies at the Universiti Sains Malaysia, established in 1967, also emphasised the importance of educational research. Since the 1980s, some members of staff were involved in some of the projects at SEAMEO RECSAM. The late Professor Zainal Ghani played a key role, for he served as Secretary to the Southeast Asian Research Review and Advisory Group (SEARRAG) and as one of Malaysia's representatives since its inception in 1980. Besides being instrumental in the development of a Southeast Asian Bibliographic and Abstracting Service (SEABAS), he also co-ordinated a number of the state-of-the-art and state-of-the-practice reviews in which each of the six member countries (Brunei Darussalam, Indonesia, Malaysia, Philippines, Singapore and Thailand) participated (Ghani, 1988). These reviews provided excellent opportunities for researchers to be involved in reviewing and undertaking research in their respective countries.

Besides his involvement with SEARRAG, Professor Zainal also played an important role in obtaining funds for Project InSPIRE (Integrated System of Programmed Instruction for Rural Environments) in 1990. This project provided useful opportunities for young researchers to obtain on-the-job training. He was also responsible for the formation of the Malaysian Educational Research Association (MERA). However, it was most unfortunate that he passed away before its inaugural conference in 1998.

With the subsequent increase in the variety of universities in Malaysia, there can be little doubt that educational researchers, including teacher researchers, are being trained by the respective faculties of education in a number of ways. One such example of the informal process of developing science teachers as researchers has been the annual awards for innovative science teaching by the Malaysia-Toray Science Foundation, which began in 1993. Each year, science teachers from various parts of Malaysia submitted reports of school-based research projects which were scrutinised by a panel of professors from various universities. The shortlist candidates were invited to present and demonstrate their project to the panel. Between 15–20 winners were selected for cash awards at a prize-giving ceremony.

4.4. Singapore

The beginnings of educational research training in Singapore can be said to have started in the 1973 when the Institute of Education (IE) was formed to be the sole teacher-training institution, taking over the functions of the Teachers Training College, the School of Education (University of Singapore) and the

Research Unit (Ministry of Education). Professor Ruth Wong, who was concurrently holding the positions of Director of Research at the Research Unit, MOE, and the Principal of the Teachers Training College, was appointed the first Director of IE. Besides revamping the academic structure, Professor Wong was given the responsibility for enlarging the role of teacher training to include research and postgraduate work.

In her previous appointment as the Dean, Faculty of Education, University of Malaya, Professor Wong devoted much of her time and energy to staff training and development. She used the same staff development scheme at IE involving "... building a core of indigenous manpower with postgraduate qualifications from prestigious universities overseas was with her a top priority in terms of staff development" (Ho, 1995). Even though Professor Wong had left IE by then, by 1980, this objective was achieved to a large extent.

The period when the profile of educational research at IE really reached new heights was during the leadership of Professor Sim Wong Kooi, who was its Director from 1981 to 1990 and "a teacher educator in the Ruth Wong mould" (Gopinathan, 2002). It was during his tenure when IE built up a critical mass of educational researchers, and when the first budding of research culture appeared. The launch of the Master of Education coursework-cum-research program in 1984 marked a significant milestone for educational research in Singapore. For the first time, a systematic program for the training of educational research workers was in place. With respect to PhD training, it wasn't until the late 1980s that IE had the staff capacity to supervise a significant number of doctoral students.

Besides providing formal training for educational researchers, IE also provided other mechanisms to sensitise and encourage teacher trainers and school teachers to be more research-oriented. In 1986, the Educational Research Association (ERA) was established. One of the objectives of the association was "to seek to improve the training and facilities for educational research personnel in order that their expertise could be used for educational improvement" (Gopinathan & Gremli, 1988). Local avenues for sharing research findings have also been provided. NIE publishes three journals for this purpose – *REACT* (Review of Educational Research and Advances for Classroom Teaching), *Teaching and Learning*, and the *Asia Pacific Journal of Education* (formerly known as the *Singapore Journal of Education*).

In 1991, IE became part of the Nanyang Technological University. It was renamed the National Institute of Education (NIE). With this upgrade in status, the importance of educational research was further enhanced and emphasised. Academic staff without a doctoral degree were encouraged to pursue doctoral studies. Recruitment of new staff became more stringent, preferring to take in those with no less than a doctorate. To date, almost 70 per cent of the academic staff at NIE have doctorates. This has resulted in the launching of several more Master's programs – the Master's of Arts in Applied Linguistics, Applied Psychology, Educational Management, Instructional Design and Technology, Education (Mathematics Education), Science (Exercise and Sport Studies).

In January 2002, when the NIE officially opened its new $400 million purpose-built campus, the Minister for Education announced that the Ministry of Education (MOE) would be investing $48 million over the next five years to help NIE to develop its educational research capability in the areas of Mathematics and Science Literacy, Language Literacy, and ICT (Teo, 2002). The money would also be used to help set up a new Centre for Research on Pedagogy and Practice. These initiatives strongly indicate that MOE is interested in using educational research findings to provide the basis for policy making. The education system has become much more complex in recent years, and so school principals cannot just be administrators and give stock answers to the stakeholders of education anymore. What they propose and implement in their schools for their students must be substantiated by what research says. At the same time, the MOE has also been encouraging teachers to upgrade and update. Non-graduate teachers are encouraged to work for a degree, while graduates are expected to pursue postgraduate degrees. Hence, NIE is the obvious choice to provide the necessary leadership and training in the conduct and interpretation of educational research in the South-East Asian region. The future for educational research in Singapore is bright. The training of educational researchers will have to keep up with it to maintain the momentum. More avenues for doctoral studies for education officers are being explored. For example, the MOE is actively encouraging NIE to cooperate with overseas institutions to co-award degrees. In this way, teachers can do most of their doctoral work locally, and need only to do a short period of residency at the overseas university. It is hoped that such a flexible arrangement will attract more education officers, especially married women, to pursue graduate degrees.

4.5. *The Philippines*

The development of educational research in the Philippines began during the time of rapid expansion of education in the late 1940s. The country was busy rebuilding schools ravaged during the Second World War and to meet the increasing demand for education. At the same time, the number of teacher education institutions increased rapidly in response to the demand for better trained teachers. Incentives for upgrading teachers' educational qualifications also led to the establishment of more graduate schools of education.

Sutaria and Elequin (1988) reported that the demand for educational research continued to be on the rise. The number of researchers was also growing and their skills were being improved to meet the requirements for more sophisticated research. These Filipino researchers were generally drawn from colleges and universities, government institutions, the Ministry of Education, Culture and Sports (MECS), non-government institutions, and professional associations.

Like in all tertiary institutions, postgraduate students and staff provide the main research workers in the country. Relevant courses on the conduct of educational research are offered as part of coursework for the students. The Institute for Science and Mathematics Education Development's main business is curriculum development and training, while its research activities are linked with the MECS. However, in MECS, most of the personnel have been in either supervisory or curriculum coordination positions. Training programs to strengthen the educational research staff of the Ministry thus have been launched.

Non-government organisations like INNOTECH (Regional Centre for Educational Innovation and Technology), which is one of the centres of SEAMEO (Southeast Asian Ministers of Education Organisation), conduct training courses, workshops and seminars for selected educational staff from the member countries. Topics include how to carry out research, develop new approaches, and devise solutions for the problems that are identified. All research is conducted in-house by staff recruited from member countries. Some professional associations also conduct educational research that is mainly commissioned.

4.6. Thailand

Educational research in Thailand is mainly conducted at the universities or government agencies. According to Sapianchai and associates (1988), the bulk of educational research has been done as graduate theses in the university departments of education, while some has been done by individuals in the teaching profession or by institutions (mostly work units in the Ministry of Education and National Education Commission, and a few teaching departments in universities and teacher training colleges). From a survey, it was found that most of these researchers had a BA in education, with three-quarters of them having an MA in education studies too. There were also some who possessed doctoral degrees (Sapianchai et al., 1988).

In order to promote research, a range of activities is organised. Conferences and symposia allow for the presentation of research projects to large audiences. Meetings and seminars provide opportunities for researchers to define research problems, develop research designs and discuss research results and their implementation. Training is another avenue for encouraging research. It comes in the form of staff development and aims to furnish personnel with knowledge of research methods and statistics. Staff development for potential researchers is conducted either overseas or in Thailand. Overseas postgraduate training is often funded by Aid Organisations. Many people have been trained in this way. Another form of training allows external researchers to be invited to provide the training. Hence, institutions would either send their staff on training courses or they would organise inservice training for them in-house. Sometimes, the research personnel could also be sent to other institutions as resource persons to encourage an exchange of expertise.

The training courses deal mainly with research and statistics, so that trainees are provided with information about various methods of statistical analysis. However, they do not seem to be able to go beyond conducting surveys. For instance, participants often are not able to define a realistic research problem, or to make research findings match with reality, or to interpret statistics meaningfully. It was noted that a better method of training seemed to be the apprenticeship of novice researchers with experienced researchers.

In order to improve graduate research training, it was also noted that university professors might need to link theory and practice better. They themselves need to be more exposed to the real and urgent problems of educational development, and collaborate actively with practitioners to seek practical solutions. It is considered that such a practice would help to bring about useful changes in the training of future researchers.

5. FLEXIBLE PROVISIONS FOR PART-TIME RESEARCH STUDENTS

As the above case studies from six countries show, the scope of provision for formal graduate programs in education is limited in universities in the Asia-Pacific region, especially at the doctoral level. The traditional practice of sending a small elite to prestigious overseas universities for a doctorate is even more limited as high costs preclude this approach from being tenable for anything but a relatively small number of the people who can obtain funding from governments or aid agencies. Therefore, this final section illustrates the valuable contribution that overseas universities can play by providing the sort of flexible arrangements that permit people to obtain their doctorates while working and residing in their own countries.

In the previous section on Brunei Darussalam, a description was given of a partnership between Universiti Brunei Darussalam and Curtin University of Technology which enabled people to undertake postgraduate programs with Curtin while residing in Brunei. A hallmark of these postgraduate programs in science and mathematics education at Curtin University of Technology in Western Australia is that they have the flexibility to allow a person anywhere in the world to study part-time while residing at home and continuing in full-time employment. Not only is sophisticated information technology used to deliver coursework through distance education and to maintain regular contact, but postgraduate programs are taken to students by establishing nodes and offering institutes in numerous locations to address the specific needs of the students.

Because postgraduate students in groups need support and a significant degree of face-to-face contact, especially when distant and isolated from campus, Curtin staff have established an increasing number of so-called 'nodes' of students interstate and around the world. Students in these nodes undertake the same doctoral coursework as internal students by attending concentrated institutes taught by Curtin staff in remote locations at times convenient to students (e.g., in school holidays). Assessment tasks are undertaken after the institutes while maintaining email contact. In these nodes, students who have reached the research stage also meet regularly face-to-face to gain support from each other, from their visiting Curtin thesis supervisors, and from local adjunct staff who have been appointed to assist. Currently, approximately 150 Curtin doctoral students meet together in groups on a regular basis in places including Miami (USA), Thailand, New Zealand, South Africa and Brunei. Students in these nodes receive support, motivation guidance and care from Curtin staff from the beginning of their research studies, and therefore their specific needs are identified through early contact with staff.

The postgraduate program in Thailand illustrates the operation of nodes and institutes. The 19 doctoral students in this location are employed by Rajhabat Institute Udon Thani as tertiary lecturers in science. Curtin staff travel to Thailand to teach professional doctoral coursework units (each running for five weekdays) and to meet with a thesis class. The topics and timing of institutes, and the range of research topics offered for supervision, are decided only after extensive consultation with doctoral students and the employer.

Students' deep appreciation of the flexibility of these postgraduate programs is illustrated in many testimonial letters. For example, doctoral students describe how they were able to undertake a doctorate without giving up their academic position, moving away from home, and leaving their families.

6. CONCLUDING REMARKS: LOOKING AHEAD

Although finding reliable and accessible sources of information has proved difficult, generally it can be surmised that the training of educational researchers in the Asia-Pacific region is achieved through a variety of mechanisms. Some of these are formal (e.g., university graduate programs), while others are informal (conference attendance, publishing, membership of professional associations). But graduate education abroad has been and continues today as a major strategy for research training. Although there is local capacity to train researchers up to Masters and doctoral levels, indigenous capacity is still considered inadequate on the scale needed to satisfy current needs. Overseas training continues to be in demand, especially because some financial aid from local agencies, foreign agencies and universities is available for graduate programs.

However, given the extremely high costs of sending people overseas for postgraduate research degrees, this effort must be considered far too limited to satisfy the need for so many leaders with educational research expertise in teacher training, ministries of education and elsewhere throughout the Asia-Pacific region. Moreover, it might not always be in a country's best long-term interests to take people out of key employment positions to send them overseas for several years to undertake doctorate or Masters degrees.

The provisions for higher degrees by research throughout the Asia-Pacific region not only are too few, but they also tend to be too inflexible. For example, at the doctoral level, there is an emphasis on thesis-only degrees and full-time on-campus study. Given the diversity of the backgrounds of potential doctoral students, there is a need for some professional doctorates that provide some coursework, in addition to a major study or two or three minor studies to broaden students' knowledge and skill bases before commencing sustained research activity. Because most graduate students in education are likely to be mature-aged, to be in important employment positions already, and to have family responsibilities, there is a need for flexible graduate programs that permit them to study part-time and through distance education while residing at home and continuing in their jobs.

This article has provided one case study, that of doctoral programs in science and mathematics education at Curtin University of Technology in Australia, which provides a model of the flexibility needed for the Asia-Pacific region. This doctoral program not only provides coursework options that are available through distance education and online methods, but also Curtin staff travel to nodes around the world for face-to-face contact, to run coursework units as short courses, and to run thesis classes for students in the research study phase of their programs.

It would be unrealistic to imagine that a large number of well-established universities in the Asia-Pacific region would be able to mount a major graduate program that offers a high level of flexibility. Rather, it would make sense for a small number of universities, in locations such as Singapore, Hong Kong and Delhi, to act as central providers of these flexible graduate programs for the region. Not only would these universities need to provide coursework for distance education study, but also would need to build in an all-important face-to-face component by having students visit these universities at times convenient to students and, more importantly, having staff from these universities take their graduate programs to their students by setting up study nodes outside their own countries.

In providing such centres of flexible graduate studies in several countries, partnerships with other universities will be important. Such partnerships could involve universities in Australia and New Zealand, with highly-developed graduate programs.

In addition, it has been noted that the academic staff at the education faculties of universities and the teacher training institutes within the Asia-Pacific region have been the main recipients of research training in recent years. However, there has been a move to encourage teachers to pursue postgraduate degrees, especially in Singapore; whether the notion of 'teachers-as-researchers' really catches on is left to be seen. Moreover, there is a pressing need for the staff of administrative centres to receive training in research, in order to inform the making of policy that would advance national development.

REFERENCES

Brause, R. S. (2000). *Writing your doctoral dissertation: Invisible rules for success.* London: Falmer Press.
Cheong, I. P.-A. (2001). *Evaluation of environmental education and environmental attributes in Brunei.* Unpublished PhD thesis, Curtin University of Technology, Perth, Australia.

Cullen, D. J., Pearson, M., Saha, L. J., & Spear, R. H. (1994). *Establishing effective PhD supervision.* Canberra, Australia: Australian Government Publishing Service.

Delamont, S., Atkinson, P., & Parry, O. (1997). *Supervising the PhD: A guide to success.* Buckingham, UK: The Society for Research into Higher Education & Open University Press.

Ghani, Z. D. (1988). The educational research environment in Malaysia. In S. Gopinathan & H. D. Nielsen (Eds.), *Educational Research Environments in Southeast Asia* (pp. 51–82). Singapore: Chopmen Publishers for Southeast Asia Research Review and Advisory Group (SEARRAG).

Gopinathan, S. (2002). Speech given at the symposium on 'Valuing the Teaching Profession: Purpose, Passion and Hope', National Institute of Education, Singapore.

Gopinathan, S., & Gremli, M. S. (1988). The educational research environment in Singapore. In S. Gopinathan & H. D. Nielsen (Eds.), *Educational Research Environments in Southeast Asia* (pp. 135–184). Singapore: Chopmen Publishers for Southeast Asia Research Review and Advisory Group (SEARRAG).

Graves, N., & Varma, V. (1997). *Working for a doctorate: A guide for the humanities and social sciences.* London: Routledge.

Ho, W. K. (1995). *The educational legacy of Dr Ruth Wong Hie King.* Singapore: National Institute of Education.

Holbrook, A., & Johnston, S. (Eds.) (1999). *Supervision of postgraduate research in education* (Review of Australian Research in Education No. 5). Coldstream, Australia: Australian Association for Research in Education.

Khine, M. S. (2001). *Associations between teacher interpersonal behaviour and aspects of classroom environment in an Asian context.* Unpublished Doctor of Science Education thesis, Curtin University of Technology, Perth, Australia.

Madsen, D. (1992). *Successful dissertations and theses: A guide to graduate student research from proposal to completion* (2nd ed.). San Francisco: Jossey-Bass Publishers.

Rennie, L., & Gribble, J. with Downie, J., Fisher, D., Rapley, P., Taylor. P. (1999). *A guide to preparing your application for candidacy.* Available: Http://www.smec.curtin.edu.au/candid/

Sapianchai, P., Jitjang, A., Phopruksawong, S., Saihioo, P., Chantavanich, S., & Thongutai, U. (1988). The educational research environment in Thailand. In S. Gopinathan & H. D. Nielsen (Eds.), *Educational Research Environments in Southeast Asia* (pp. 185–234). Singapore: Chopmen Publishers for Southeast Asia Research Review and Advisory Group (SEARRAG).

Scott, R. H. (2001). *Students' perceptions of science teachers' behaviour in Brunei Darussalam.* Unpublished PhD thesis, Curtin University of Technology, Perth, Australia.

Setijadi, Moegiadi, Hardjono, Idris, N., Soekamto, T., Djalil, A., Indrijathno, B., Suksmo, A., & Nielsen, H. D. (1988). The educational research environment in Indonesia. In S. Gopinathan & H. D. Nielsen (Eds.), *Educational Research Environments in Southeast Asia* (pp. 27–50). Singapore: Chopmen Publishers for Southeast Asia Research Review and Advisory Group (SEARRAG).

Sim, W. K. et al. (2001, December). *Bilateral research in education: Putting IDEA into practice in Singapore and Brunei Darussalam.* Symposium presented at the annual conference of the Australian Association for Research in Education, Fremantle, Australia.

Sutaria, M., & Elequin, E. (1988). The educational research environment in the Philippines. In S. Gopinathan & H. D. Nielsen (Eds.), *Educational Research Environments in Southeast Asia* (pp. 83–134). Singapore: Chopmen Publishers for Southeast Asia Research Review and Advisory Group (SEARRAG).

Teo, C. H. (2002). *Making NIE an international leader in professional teacher training and educational research by 2010.* Speech by the Minister for Education at the official opening of the National Institute of Education (NIE) complex, Singapore, 26 January 2002.

90
Regional Cooperation in Educational Research

M.S. KHAPARDE and ASHOK K. SRIVASTAVA
National Council of Educational Research and Training, New Delhi, India

1. INTRODUCTION

A research study generally refers to an investigation that is taken up to uncover novel facts and arrive at new conclusions by methodical inquiry of a subject or by engaging in a course of scientific pursuit. It subsumes the study of materials and sources in order to establish facts and compile information. Since the countries in a region face problems in their educational development that are altogether distinct from those of the countries in other regions, it is fundamental that a system of cooperation exists among the educational researchers of a particular region for undertaking collaborative research, collating information, and establishing facts. It is, however, observed that educational researchers in the Asia-Pacific region frequently work alone or in small teams without being aware of similar or related efforts taking place in other countries of the region. Often these researchers look to Europe and the United States for inspiration without showing regard for the local and regional problems. There are rapid educational changes occurring in the Asia-Pacific region, which are not based on dependable research evidence. Further, isolated research efforts carry little meaning for policy initiatives and practice. Greater collaboration among the researchers in the region is likely to reinforce them to situate their research in the local and regional context and will also greatly enhance the implementation of research findings in policy and practice. The twin goals of this paper are (a) to examine various policy initiatives undertaken to improve cooperation in educational research in the Asia-Pacific region, and (b) to analyse the existing arrangement of collaboration among educational researchers in the region.

2. POLICY INITIATIVES FOR REGIONAL COOPERATION

2.1. *Regional Diversity*

The Asia and the Pacific region which accounts for approximately 60 per cent of the world's population, consists of a wider range of diverse societies encompassing all aspects of life than any other region in the world. The region includes some of the largest and smallest countries in terms of population size and area, some of the richest and poorest countries, technologically advanced countries, as well as countries with a large aboriginal population, many diverse political systems and linguistically diverse countries. (Singh, 1986). About 75 per cent of the world's illiterates are found in this region. Though there has been overall improvement in enrolment and participation rates at all levels of formal education, the education of girls and other hard-to-reach people continues to be a major challenge in the development of some of the countries. For example, surveys conducted by the World Bank (Filmer & Pritchett, 1999) report great variations in the patterns of educational achievement across countries and across population groups within the countries of the region. For instance, in India 70 per cent of the children in the age group of 15 to 19 years have completed Grade 1, and 56 per cent have completed Grade 6. By contrast, in Indonesia virtually all have completed Grade 1, 85 per cent have completed Grade 6, but only 53 per cent have completed grade 7. In many countries, for example Pakistan, India, and Nepal, almost all children from rich households have completed at least one year of schooling, and in many countries they have completed the entire primary cycle. The shortfalls from universal primary education are, for the most part, due to children from the poorest households. Girls are at a great educational disadvantage in many of the Asia-Pacific countries and socio-cultural sections of the society and there are major differences between the educational attainment of males and females. While this gap does not exist in Indonesia, males reach six grades higher than females in Pakistan. There are wide variations in the ratios of pupils to teachers among countries, ranging from 14 to 63 pupils to each teacher in primary schools. The proportions of graduates of higher education vary from one in every four inhabitants to one in every 200 inhabitants. Many countries in the region continue to devote three per cent or less of GNP to education. Only a few developed countries in the region spend the equivalent of five per cent or more of GNP on education. Teachers' emoluments in general account for between 58 to 86 per cent of all public current expenditure on education. With very few exceptions, less than ten per cent of expenditure is devoted to teaching materials, scholarships, and welfare services in education taken together.

In the contemporary Asia-Pacific region, the economic benefits, health care, and educational facilities are distributed very unevenly between and within countries. Also, the processes of modernisation and globalisation are threatening the sustenance of cherished values and goals of the countries of this region. Many countries have begun the process of examining ways in which education, through both formal and informal means, can be used to help grapple with such problems (Maclean, 1992). It is in this context that cooperation and collaboration in educational research assumes greater significance in the Asia-Pacific region so that countries could benefit from each other's experiences.

2.2. *Regional Cooperation: Education Ministers' Policy Conferences*

The concept of regional cooperation in the Asian region came into existence during the period 1960–62. The representatives of the governments of various countries met in Karachi in 1961 to draw up a regional plan for compulsory primary education in their countries. The Karachi Plan was adopted at the first meeting of Ministers of Education of Asian Member states. In the second Ministers' Conference held at Bangkok in 1965 an Asian Model for Educational Development was considered. It was at this conference that the incipient stage of education in developing regions was highlighted. This led to the development of a regional program of educational research centred on the National Institute of Educational Research (NIER) of Japan, with the support of UNESCO. The Singapore Conference in 1971 highlighted the critical importance of educational innovation in the educational development in the region. It recommended educational innovations as a priority area in inter-country and regional cooperation. These recommendations led UNESCO to promote inter-country networking of national centres and programs as the principal medium of regional cooperation in the sharing of experiences and expertise. A new program, called the Asian Program of Educational Innovation for Development (APEID), was initiated. (The name was later changed to Asia and the Pacific Program of Educational Innovation for Development, but with the same acronym, APEID.) Also, programs for cooperative studies and innovative projects of research-based experimentation related to educational development, particularly in the areas of moral education, aesthetic education, and cultural identity, were proposed. The later conferences, namely the Colombo Conference (1978), the Bangkok Conference (1985) and the Kuala Lumpur Conference (1993), reinforced the policies and programs related to cooperation in educational research in the region. The International Meeting on Educational Reform and Educational Research in 1995 at NIER in Japan identified international and regional cooperation as one of the research needs and included it in the priority areas of research.

3. REGIONAL COOPERATION IN EDUCATIONAL RESEARCH

The need for regional cooperation in the field of education in the Asia-Pacific region has been consistently emphasised in all the regional ministerial conferences since the meeting in Tokyo in 1962. The word 'cooperation' literally means the action of working together for the same purpose or on the same task. The essential characteristic of cooperation is a union of capital and labour. Viewed in this context, the term 'regional cooperation in educational research' stands for the joining the countries of the Asia-Pacific region together to find the solutions to the problems in the educational development of each country and to profit from each other's experiences.

Regional cooperation in the development of education is an expression of international cooperation, which is linked with the fundamental principle of UNESCO. It is enshrined in UNESCO's Constitution, Article 1, which states:

> The purpose of the organisation is to contribute to peace and security by

promoting collaboration among the nations through education, science and culture in order to further universal respect for justice, for the rule of law and for the human rights and fundamental freedoms which are affirmed for the people of the world, without distinction of race, sex, language or religion, by the charter of the United Nations.

It further states that UNESCO will help to maintain, increase and diffuse knowledge

> ... by encouraging cooperation among the nations in all branches of intellectual activity, including the international exchange of persons active in the fields of education, science and culture and the exchange of publications, objects of artistic and scientific interest and other materials of information.

The establishment of cooperation between the countries fosters understanding among them by promoting the free flow of ideas and exchange in the sphere of intellectual and cultural activities. It must be noted that the relationship of cooperation is not one of a donor on the one hand, and a receiving beneficiary on the other. Rather, each participating country has something to give and something to receive. The capacities of ideas, skills and experience have evolved in all the countries and their mobilization for common sharing should be the substance of inter-country and regional cooperation. Cooperation is based on the notion that there is no single model of development, which can be transferred or otherwise imposed. There are diverse and alternative paths to development and the choice is to be defined by the country concerned in the context of its own social, economic and cultural conditions. Regional cooperation provides a focus for cooperative problem solving, complimentarity in development efforts and pooling of experiences and resources. Participation is the cornerstone of regional cooperation. In the field of education or educational research, it is essential that countries participate in the designing, developing, implementing, supervising and evaluating the research. Networking of the countries, educational workers and researchers is another predominant mode of regional cooperation.

4. THE ROLE OF LEADING INSTITUTIONS

UNESCO has assumed a significant role in fostering cooperation and collaboration in educational research in the Asia-Pacific region. In particular, the contribution of some of its programs and associated institutes, namely Asia and the Pacific Program of Educational Innovation for Development (APEID) in Bangkok, The Asian Centre of Educational Innovation for Development (ACEID) in Bangkok, the UNESCO Principal Regional Office for Asia and the Pacific (PROAP) in Bangkok, as well as other organisations including the Southeast Asian Ministers of Education Organisation (SEAMEO) in Bangkok, SEAMEO Regional Centre for Educational Innovations and Technology in

Quezon (Philippines), and the South East Asia Research Review and Advisory Group (SEARRAG), the United Nations Children's Emergency Fund (UNICEF), the Swedish International Development Agency (SIDA), and Overseas Development Administration (ODA) are noteworthy. The National Institute for Educational Policy Research of Japan, The Australian Council for Educational Research in Melbourne, the National Council of Educational Research and Training in New Delhi, and the Centre for Research and International Collaboration at the Hong Kong Institute of Education, are all playing significant roles in this direction.

As a cooperative endeavour of the member states, APEID was launched in 1973. It nurtures technical cooperation among developing countries in partnership with developed countries of the region and international bodies having similar objectives. Its goals are: (a) to promote awareness of the need for innovation and of possibilities for change; (b) to promote understanding of the processes and practices of innovation; (c) to identify and stimulate innovative activities and cooperative action among the Member States; (d) to assist the Member States in strengthening ongoing national programs which are developing innovations dealing with one or more aspects of development-oriented education; and (e) to promote the inter-country transfer of experiences and technical cooperation, particularly through exchange activities, advisory services and the flow of information. APEID is not an institution; rather it is a mode of inter-country cooperation for mutual help. Its institutional framework consists of Associated Centres, National Development Groups, Regional Consultation Process, and the ACEID. APEID has a network of 199 Associated Centres in 29 countries throughout the Asia-Pacific region to assist in implementation of the program activities. APEID's program areas are determined in consultation with UNESCO Member States and Research and Innovation is one of the major program areas for APEID's Sixth Programming Cycle (1997–2001).

As an integral part of the UNESCO Regional Office for Education in Asia and the Pacific, ACEID functions as a facilitator of programs especially by: (a) promoting inter-country cooperative action, (b) serving as a catalytic agent for stimulating innovations in the countries, (c) identifying gaps and growth points in national efforts, (d) developing information materials, and (e) promoting the exchange of educational media resources. One of the notable activities of ACEID is the development and dissemination of information and materials on educational development and innovation.

The UNESCO Principal Regional Office for Asia and the Pacific (PROAP) is the main coordinating agency for the organisation of international conferences on educational research in the Asia and the Pacific region. It also promotes the conduct of collaborative educational research in the Member States.

SEAMEO is a chartered intergovernmental organisation, consisting of ten Member States: Brunei Darussalam, Cambodia, Indonesia, Lao PDR, Malaysia, Philippines, Singapore, Thailand, Myanmar, and Vietnam. The Southeast Asian Ministers of Education Council (SEAMEO) is the policy making body of the organisation, and is comprised of the Ministers of Education of all member countries. The organisation promotes the development of educational innovation and technology, and the conduct of research in nonformal education, education in science and mathematics, language education, higher education, and vocational and technical education. The SEAMEO Regional Center for Educational Innovation and Technology promotes the conduct of research related to different aspects of education and also organises training programs, seminar workshops, and conferences for educational research workers in the Member Countries. Many countries are Members of the South-East Asia Research Review and Advisory Group (SEARRAG), that is a regional network on educational research and information.

UNICEF aims to help children throughout the world, with a focus on the neediest children, particularly their survival, development, and protection. Its programs seek to ensure that children have the greatest possible care from birth and develop to their full potential. UNICEF conducts research, policy analysis and the evaluation of program performance to help fine-tune its work in many countries of the Asia-Pacific region. In India, UNICEF provides financial and technical support to several important and innovative projects including the Minimum Levels of Learning (MLL), the Project for evaluating Total Literacy Campaigns, the Project Radio Education in Adult Literacy, and the Area Intensive Education Project. The Swedish International Development Agency and the Overseas Development Administration are also associated with the promotion of educational research in the region.

There are a few national institutes located in the Asia-Pacific region, which on their own or in collaboration with international agencies are engaged in the development of educational research. The National Institute for Educational Research in Tokyo is one such institute whose main functions are: (a) to conduct basic and applied research in education; (b) to disseminate research results; (c) to give assistance and advice to educational organisations and educators; (d) to organise regional workshops and seminars for educators from other Asian and Pacific countries; and (e) to exchange educational information with educators and educational institutions in other countries. The National Institute of Special Education at Yokosuka in Japan conducts special education seminars for researchers and teachers of special education in 14 Asian and Pacific countries. The mission of the Australian Council of Educational Research (ACER) in Melbourne is to create and disseminate knowledge and tools that can be used to improve learning. It is engaged in carrying out large-scale survey research, longitudinal studies of student progress, and studies related to classroom teaching and learning.

The National Council of Educational Research and Training in New Delhi conducts research related to all aspects of school education. It is also engaged in the dissemination of the educational research findings through the publication of reports of surveys of educational research (so far five surveys have appeared and the sixth is in preparation), and journals like *Indian Educational Review* and *Indian Educational Abstracts*. It supports research activities by providing training in research methodology to teacher educators and researchers and making finance available for educational research in the country. The Centre for Research and International Collaboration in Hong Kong aims to become a centre of excellence in research, development and global networking and collaboration in education. It supports research that promotes educational innovation and change, enhances educational quality in schools, and contributes to the development of educational policy. The contributions of various other national institutes, such as the Korea Educational Development Institute, the New Zealand Council for Educational Research, the Academy of Sciences in China and the Indian Council of Social Science Research towards the promotion of educational research in the region are noteworthy.

5. COLLABORATION IN EDUCATIONAL RESEARCH

It is clear that the issue of regional cooperation and collaboration in the Asia-Pacific region is about four decades old. It may, therefore, be appropriate to examine in some detail the extent to which regional cooperation actually operates in the field of educational research in this region. To this end, this section examines the attempts made towards (a) the organisation of seminars, conferences and training of educational researchers, (b) the conduct of collaborative research, and (c) the sharing of research findings in educational research.

5.1. *Organisation of Seminars, Conferences and Training Programs*

One of the major initiatives to augment the educational research programs in the Asia-Pacific region was the holding of a training workshop under the direction of Professor Lee Cronbach in the late 1960s. This was followed for a decade or more by the activities of SEARRAG, which established collaborative links between educational research workers in the region.

At the request of UNESCO Regional Office in Bangkok, the first Regional Seminar on Educational Research in Relation to Educational Reform was organised in 1979 by the National Institute for Educational Research in Tokyo. Since then NIER has been organising regional seminars on an annual basis, and in some years more frequently. As Maclean (1997) notes, "NIER has been a 'light house' institution over the past 30 years which has made a very significant contribution to educational research and development world-wide, but particularly in the Asia-Pacific region" (p. 34). APEID, under the umbrella of UNESCO, has organised more than 100 regional seminars, workshops, meetings of experts, editorial and consultative committees related to educational research. Countries, including Australia, Bangladesh, People's Republic of China, India, Indonesia, Japan, Malaysia, Nepal, New Zealand, Pakistan, Philippines, Republic of Korea, Sri Lanka and Thailand have participated in these activities in a substantial way. Some of the major workshops and seminars have been:

(a) Educational Research Workshop on Problems Related to School Curriculum in Asia (1969);

(b) Regional Workshop on Problems faced by Asian Teachers and Their Attitudes Towards Innovation in Classroom Teaching (1975);
(c) High Level Seminar on Moral Education in Asia (1978);
(d) Regional Seminar on the Contribution of Inter-disciplinary Research to the Development of Education in Asia and the Pacific (1984);
(e) Regional Training Workshop on School Mathematics and Microcomputers in Asia and the Pacific (1987);
(f) International Meeting on Educational Reform and Educational Research: New Challenges in linking Research, Information and Decision-making (1995);
(g) Regional Seminar on Learning for a Sustainable Environment: Teacher Education and Environmental Education in Asia and the Pacific (1996); and
(h) Regional Seminar on Educational Research for Policy and Practice with Particular Reference to Secondary Education Reform and the Education of Youth (2000).

Table 1 lists some of the seminars, conferences and training programs being organised for educational researchers in the Asia-Pacific region. The institutes and organisations like NIER, AusAID, the National Institute of Special Education in Japan, the Korean Educational Development Institute, the National Centre for Vocational Education Research in Australia, the National Council of Educational Research and Training in India, the Islamic Center for Technical and Vocational Training and Research in Bangladesh, and the Higher Education Research and Development Society of Australasia have been actively involved in conducting seminars, workshops and conferences for educational researchers in other countries of the region.

5.2. *Collaborative Research Programs*

Collaborative educational research in the Asia-Pacific region has primarily been conducted on the initiatives of UNESCO. The collaboration between individual researchers of different countries in the region is relatively low. This section contains examples of some of the collaborative research carried out in this region. The regional cooperative program in Asia and the Pacific in the fields of educational research and development was initiated in 1967 by NIER in collaboration with the UNESCO Bangkok Office. The program implemented a cooperative study of curriculum and educational content in the schools of Asian countries. The NIER, in cooperation with APEID, carried out a cooperative study on moral education, with the participation of the Member States in the region. The project started with a regional workshop in 1978 and was completed in 1980. The outcome of the project has been published and widely disseminated. The NIER also carried out the following studies in which different countries of the region participated: The Problems of Asian Teachers and Their Attitudes Towards Innovation in Classroom Teaching (1975), A Study of Elementary Education Curriculum in Asia and the Pacific (1986), and Study of Secondary Education in Asia and the Pacific (1988).

Table 1. Regional Seminars/Conferences/Training Programs for Educational Researchers

Institution	Country	Course
AusAID	Australia	Scholarship for suitably qualified students from African and Asia-Pacific regions for Ph.D. work.
Islamic Centre for Technical and Vocational Training and Research	Bangladesh	Vocational training courses for Islamic countries
Korean Educational Institute Development	Republic of Korea	International study visits, seminar and symposia. Short-term training program for foreign educators.
National Centre for Vocational Educational Research	Australia	International conferences in vocational education
National Council of Educational Research and Training	India	International seminars on research in primary education. Training in research methods for SAARC countries.
National Institute for Educational Policy Research	Japan	Regional research workshops and seminars
National Institute of Special Education	Japan	APEID special education seminars in 14 Asia-Pacific countries
SEAMEO Regional Centre for Educational Innovation and Technology	Philippines	Training programs, seminars, workshops, conferences for 10 Member Countries.
The Higher Education Research and Development Society of Australia	Australia	Annual international conference, workshops and seminars
The Flinders University Institute of International Education	Australia	Scholarships to overseas students for pursuing Ph.D.

In a study conducted by UNESCO (1997), efforts were made to analyse the importance being given to adult, nonformal education in the Asia-Pacific region. Four countries, namely India, Nepal, Philippines, and Thailand participated in the study. The UNESCO Regional Office in Bangkok provided the broad framework for the research design. The finer details of the study were left to the participating countries.

A number of collaborative research studies in the area of higher education have occurred in the Asia-Pacific region. UNESCO (1991) investigated trends and issues facing higher education in Thailand, Indonesia, India, Bangladesh,

Philippines and Australia. In another study (UNESCO, 1990), women's participation in higher education was the focus of research in which China, Nepal, and Philippines participated. Govinda (1997) examined the decentralisation of educational management in which educational researchers from Bangladesh, India, Nepal, Pakistan, and Sri Lanka were associated. The educational research environments in Southeast Asia, particularly in Indonesia, Malaysia, Philippines, Singapore, and Thailand have been the focus of the research reported by Gopinathan and Nielsen (1988).

The Australian Council for Educational Research in Melbourne is leading a consortium appointed by the Organisation for Economic Cooperation and Development (OECD) to develop the Programme for International Student Assessment (PISA) in which several countries of the Asia-Pacific region are currently participating. PISA is concerned with conducting surveys of literacy and achievement in mathematics and science (i.e. the knowledge and skills to cope with changes in society, etc.) of 15-year old students. The literacy survey was conducted in 2000, while surveys in mathematics and science will be undertaken in 2003 and 2006. The results of these surveys are expected to set and achieve a standard for quality in international comparisons that has never been attained before.

The International Association for Evaluation of Educational Achievement (IEA) has maintained its program of cross-national studies that have involved many of the countries within the region, with 13 educational systems within the Asia-Pacific region currently being members of IEA. The current study is an extension of the Third International Mathematics and Science Studies conducted in 1995 and 1999, referred to as Trends in Mathematics and Science Study (TIMSS). In addition to providing an international measure of educational achievement of 13-year-olds in science and mathematics, the study also examines the correlation between achievement levels and factors such as pedagogical methods and the learning environment (see *Comparative Educational Achievement Studies*).

The Asia Pacific Centre for Educational Leadership and School Quality at the Hong Kong Institute of Education has conducted an international school effectiveness research project involving several countries in the region including Hong Kong and Australia. The findings made a substantial contribution to ongoing policy efforts in these countries.

5.3. *Sharing of Research Findings*

Each university and educational research institute of a country in the region is engaged in pursuing some research programs. The knowledge of the results of these studies to other researchers in the region may provide them with valuable insights in order to solve educational problems in their countries. The research results are generally published in local, regional or international journals, as these are the universally accepted outlets for empirical research. Table 2 contains the list of journals published in countries in the Asia-Pacific region. Countries

Table 2. Journal in Educational Research in the Asia-Pacific Region

	Journals	Periodicity	Language	Country of origin
1	APEID/UNESCO Bulletin	Annually	English	Japan
2	Australia and New Zealand Journal of Vocational Education	Semi-annually	English	Australia
3	Comparative Education Review	—	—	China
4	Educational Development	Bimonthly	Korean	Korea
5	Education Review	Annually	—	Korea
6	Foreign Education in Primary and Secondary Schools	—	Chinese	China
7	Higher Education Academic Journal	Quarterly	Chinese	China
8	Indian Educational Review	Semi-annually	English	India
9	Indian Journal of Psychometry and Education	Semi-annually	English	India
10	INNOTECH Journal	Semi-annually	English	Philippines
11	International Journal of Disability, Development and Education	Quarterly	English	Australia
12	Journal of the Centre for Educational Research and Practices	—	English	Japan
13	Journal of Foreign Education Studies	—	—	China
14	Journal of Royal Institute	Quarterly	Thai	Thailand
15	Journal of Value Education	Semi-annually	English	India
16	Korean Education	Annually	Korean	Korea
17	New Explorer in Psychology	Bimonthly	Chinese	China
18	New Zealand Journal of Educational Studies	Semi-annually	English	New Zealand
19	NIER Newsletter	Quarterly	English	Japan
20	Perspectives in Education	Quarterly	English	India
21	Research and Exploration in Higher Education	Quarterly	Chinese	China
22	The Journal of Science	—	Korean / English / French / German	Korea
23	Teacher's World	Annually	English	Bangladesh
24	The Australian Journal of Education	Three per year	English	Australia

such as China, Japan, Korea, Australia, and India are the major publishers of research journals. The journals published in China and Korea are in their national languages (i.e. Chinese and Korean). Thus the information available to the researchers is severely restricted to a few journals published in selected countries. In a region containing 52 educational systems, the effective research results presents a major challenge towards the realisation of cooperation and collaboration among the researchers.

The preceding discussion clearly indicates the paucity of collaborative efforts in educational research in the Asia-Pacific region. Reviewing the research environment in developing countries including India and Bangladesh, Adair (1995) identified three factors responsible for a poor research environment in these countries: (a) political intervention, (b) the lack of accountability and consensus on research standards, and (c) the lack of meaning of the research. Intense collaborative efforts are required to bring about an improvement in the research environment of the countries in the region.

6. FUTURE CONCERNS

It is important to emphasise that in view of the educational development required in the countries of the Asian-Pacific region, there will always be a need for maintaining stronger regional cooperation in educational research. Moreover, it is evident from the earlier discussion, that despite the policy initiatives and also the activities of the UNESCO Regional Office at Bangkok, cooperation in educational research in this region remains at a low level. In addition to the work of UNESCO, the national institutions located in this region need to play a more proactive role towards this end.

The opportunities for collaboration lie in diverse fields. Listed below are some areas, which need to be strengthened in the Asia-Pacific region.

(1) Strong cooperation among regional organisations for the conduct and use of findings of educational research is required. Regional designs for undertaking collaborative research studies into important educational problems could be developed and implemented in countries facing similar problems. A certain amount of flexibility could, of course, be built into the designs to allow the participating countries to accommodate the demands of their socio-cultural milieu.
(2) There is need to adopt a regional perspective on educational developments, qualifications, education systems, and interdependent relationships among the countries. The variation between countries in these structures and practices would provide a base for the investigation of the causes of this variation in a way that is not possible within a single system.
(3) Regional cooperation in planning the training of researchers and users of research needs to be developed. The training should focus on: (a) synthesis or meta-analysis of research in different countries, (b) use of comparative

indicators, and (c) the use of advanced research methods of inquiry.
(4) There should be a regular forum of regional researchers, practitioners and policy makers to take stock of major changes and trends in practices in different countries. There is a need to improve communication and interaction among professionals through conferences, seminars and research workshops. Some programs that would bridge national boundaries would stimulate professional interaction strategies, would improve communication, and would also promote a consensus on research standards.
(5) A regional database on comparative studies needs to be established which is accessible both to users and suppliers of information.
(6) The networking of educational researchers, and research institutions in the region of Asia-Pacific is essential. This would prove helpful to satisfy the needs of those who are less able to develop their own skills to work with the diversified body of information.

In summary, considering the diversities in the educational development of the countries in the Asia-Pacific region, cooperation and collaboration among countries in the region assumes greater significance. Efforts in this direction have been initiated in the Education Ministers' Conferences of the Asia-Pacific region, and also by leading institutions in the region including APEID, ACEID, PROAP of UNESCO, SEAMEO, NIER, NCERT, ACER and others. However, the impact of these initiatives, as is evident from the analysis of various collaborative efforts, does not seem to be widespread. There remains a need for establishing stronger cooperation in educational research among countries of this region.

REFERENCES

Adair, J. G. (1995). The research environment in developing countries: Contributions to the national development of the discipline. *International Journal of Psychology, 30*, 643–662.
Filmer, D., & Pritchett, L. (1999). The effect of household wealth on educational attainment: Evidence from 35 countries. *Population and Development Review*, 25(i).
Gopinathan, S., & Nielsen, H. D. (1988). *Educational Research Environments in Southeast Asia*. Singapore: Chopmen Publishers.
Govinda, R. (1977). *Decentralization of Educational Management: Experience from South Asia*. Paris: International Institute for Educational Planning.
Maclean, R. (1992). Innovations and reforms in schooling in Asia's developing countries. *Prospects, 22*, 366–378.
Maclean, R. (1997). APEID and NIER: Meeting the challenges and opportunities of the past and the present. In *Educational Cooperation in Asia and the Pacific: 30 years of NIER's activities*. Tokyo: National Institute of Educational Research.
Phelan, T. J. (2000). Is Australian educational research worthwhile? *Australian Journal of Education, 44*, 175–194.
Singh, R. R. (1986). *Education in Asia and the Pacific*. UNESCO, Bangkok.
UNESCO (1990). *Women's Participation in Higher Education*. Bangkok: UNESCO Principal Regional Office for Asia and the Pacific.
UNESCO (1991). *Trends and Issues Facing Higher Education in Asia and the Pacific*. Bangkok: UNESCO Principal Regional Office for Asia and the Pacific.
UNESCO (1997). *Impact of nonformal adult education in the Asia-Pacific region: A four country synthesized study*. Bangkok: UNESCO Principal Regional Office for Asia and the Pacific.

91

Challenges for Research into Educational Reform in the Asia-Pacific Region*

YIN CHEONG CHENG
Hong Kong Institute of Education, Hong Kong

1. INTRODUCTION

Witnessed since the 1990s are numerous educational reforms in nearly all countries in the Asia-Pacific region, in response to the challenges and impacts of globalisation, information technology, international competitiveness, the knowledge-based economy and fast societal developments in the new millennium (Cheng & Townsend, 2000). A huge amount of resources and effort have been put into various types of educational changes and initiatives implemented in such different areas of the region as Australia, PR China, Hong Kong, India, Indonesia, Japan, Republic of Korea, Lao PDR, Malaysia, New Zealand, the Philippines, Taiwan, Thailand and Vietnam. Based on findings and observations from numerous country reports and policy documents of these areas released in the past five years, an article in Section 1 of this Handbook (see *Trends in Educational Reform in the Asia-Pacific Region*) has identified some major trends in educational reform in the region. It provides an overall picture of the region for understanding the direction, nature and progress of the various national initiatives and efforts for the development of education in facing the challenges in the new millennium.

These trends represent the major educational reforms addressing issues of development at four different levels. At the macro-level, the main trends include: (a) towards re-establishing a new national vision and educational aims; (b) towards restructuring an education system at different levels; and (c) towards market-driving, privatising and diversifying education. To a great extent, these trends address the important issues at the societal level, particularly the following issues.

---

* Note: Part of the materials in this chapter are adapted from Cheng (1999, 2001b) and Cheng and Townsend (2000).

- How can the national vision and aims in education be redefined and correspondingly the education systems be restructured to cope effectively with the challenges in an era of globalisation, information technology and a knowledge-based economy?
- How can the consumption of limited resources be maximised in planning and managing educational provision for meeting new educational aims and satisfying the diverse and increasing demands from the society, the community and individuals?
- How can the various educational services be financed to achieve national aims in a more equitable, efficient and effective way?

At the meso-level, increasing parental and community involvement in education and management is a salient trend. The educational reforms in this trend often encourage and promote wide participation and partnership in education in order to broaden the support from the community and family for the provision of quality educational services and to ensure the accountability of educational institutions to the public, particularly when the educational services provided are funded with public money.

At the site-level, the major trends are: (a) ensuring education quality, standards and accountability; (b) increasing decentralisation and school-based management; and (c) enhancing teacher quality and the continuous lifelong professional development of teachers and principals. In general, these trends address the issues at the institutional level, which include the following questions.

- How can the quality, effectiveness and accountability of education be provided to meet diverse expectations and demands?
- How can authority be decentralised to maximise the flexibility and efficiency in consuming resources to solve problems and meet diverse needs at the site-level?
- How can teacher quality and educational leadership be enhanced to provide better educational services in such a fast changing and challenging environment?

At the operational level, the main trends include (a) using information technology in learning and teaching and applying new technologies in management, and (b) making a paradigm shift in learning, teaching and assessment. The reforms aim to facilitate change and development of educational practices, particularly at the classroom or operational level, in order to meet the future development needs of individuals and society.

Even though during the last decade many countries have poured in huge amounts of money to reinforce their educational reforms, unfortunately, most of the reformers are still disappointed with the performance of their education systems, and they doubt whether their graduates have been well prepared to face the challenges of the new century. Inevitably, policy-makers, educators and researchers have to be concerned with the following two questions related to these trends in educational reform.

- What are the major challenges in current trends in educational reform in the Asia-Pacific region particularly in such a new era of globalisation, information technology, competition and the knowledge-based economy?
- What implications can be drawn from these challenges of education reform for research?

This article aims to explore these two questions so as to provide a common ground for sharing the issues and concerns of educational reform among countries in the region as well as drawing implications for building up a knowledge base that can fill the gaps between research and policy making and inform the formulation and implementation of educational reform in the region.

2. CHALLENGES AND IMPLICATIONS AT THE MACRO AND MESO LEVELS

2.1. *Challenges and Implications in Re-establishing New National Visions and Educational Aims*

Numerous examples of reviewing educational aims and establishing new goals that reflect new national and global visions can be found in Australia, Cambodia, China, Hong Kong, India, Japan, Korea, Malaysia, New Zealand, the Philippines, Singapore, Taiwan and Thailand. Nonetheless, the changing role of education in national development has created serious challenges for educators, leaders and practitioners at the system and site levels. They have to echo these new national visions and goals and consider changes in the aims, content, process and practice of education. They are facing important challenges, such as the following ones.

- How should they plan and conduct these necessary changes at different levels effectively?
- How should they lead their teachers, students and other stakeholders to face up to the changes and pursue a new education that is relevant to the future?
- How can they ensure that educational change and reform are relevant to national growth and development in a competitive global environment?
- How can the knowledge base of educational aims and school functions be broadened to support more relevant policy-making and educational planning?
- Given that there are many new functions for educational institutions at individual, institutional, community, societal and international levels in the new century, including the technical, economic, human, social, political, cultural and educational functions (Cheng, 1996), it is necessary to ask 'to what extent do the current educational reforms take all these many functions at different levels into consideration?'

- How can the initiatives and reforms ensure a balance in achieving these functions and aims on the one hand and also reflect national priorities within the many constraints on the other hand?

All these are important issues and challenges for educational reform in the region. Unfortunately, there seems to be a lack of a comprehensive knowledge framework for policy makers and country leaders of these countries and areas to provide a broad perspective for review, assessment and development of educational aims. There is an urgent need to pursue educational research in this area to help tackle these issues and challenges in the process of redefining and re-establishing educational aims in the light of new national visions in the new century.

2.2. Challenges and Implications in Restructuring the Education System at Different Levels

Whether in response to the fast increasing developmental needs of the society or to the challenges of globalisation and international competitiveness, many countries have begun to review and restructure their education systems from early childhood education to tertiary and lifelong education. Their purposes are to echo the changes towards new educational aims, improve the selection and allocation of students, enhance educational equality and practice and redress serious drawbacks of an examination-oriented culture, particularly in some Asian countries.

In the process of reviewing and restructuring their education systems, policy makers, educators and researchers in the region have to face some important challenges in such a fundamental structural change. Examples of the challenges are given below.

Relevant to the future. Given changes in educational aims and national vision, how can the expansion of education and the restructuring of the academic system reflect or serve the needs of these changes? How is it shown that the structural changes to the system are relevant to the future?

Appropriate alternatives. There may be a number of alternatives for education systems that can serve new educational aims and national visions. How can policy makers identify those alternatives and understand which one is most appropriate for their country within the existing cultural, political and economic constraints? (Cheng, Ng, & Mok, 2002)

Balance between quality and quantity. In Korea, Taiwan and Hong Kong, for example, many people are concerned that the rapid expansion of higher education may be at the cost of the quality of graduates (Lee, 2001). How can the changes maintain a balance between expansion and the quality of education? To what extent should the traditional elite system be retained?

Difficulties in fundamental structural change. Review and reform of an education system is in fact a fundamental structural change, involving complicated and extensive political interests and concerns of nearly all key parties and actors in education and the larger community. As such, how can policy makers and stakeholders overcome all existing structural and political difficulties and conflicts involved in review and reform, and then reach a rational, feasible and commonly acceptable plan for action? (Cheng & Cheung, 1995)

Lack of knowledge base. Since the review and reform of an education system is a very complex and large-scale social endeavour affecting the future of so many students and teachers and the society, it should be based on a very comprehensive knowledge base for review, planning and implementation at different levels of the education system. But then, how can policy makers, educators and other key actors be provided with such a knowledge base for their actions?

The above are just some of many challenges of review and reform. Clearly, all these challenges and issues would inevitably become a core agenda for policy debate that needs to be examined and investigated extensively by research. Unfortunately, there would seem to be a gap between the ongoing reform and the research being undertaken in many countries. In other words, there is an urgent need for a very wide spectrum of research to address the policy concerns of system change in education in different countries in the region during the years ahead.

2.3 Challenges and Implications in Market-Driving, Privatising and Diversifying Education

The trend of educational reforms towards privatisation, marketisation and diversification has become more and more important in the Asia-Pacific region, particularly when most countries are suffering from a limitation of resources to expand their educational services to meet the diverse and increasing demands of education. Some critical issues are emerging that challenge policy-makers, social leaders and educators. Salient examples are listed below.

Equity and quality. How can equity and quality in education be ensured for students in disadvantaged circumstances? This is often a crucial issue in policy debate in many developing countries in the region (Cheng, Ng, & Mok, 2002).

Diverse and conflicting expectations. There are diverse and conflicting expectations of stakeholders about education in the region. For example, teachers or educators emphasise the citizenship quality of their graduates. Parents are more concerned with whether their children can pass the examinations and get the necessary qualifications for employment. Employers often doubt whether the graduates have the necessary knowledge and skills to perform in the workplace. In view of the above, how should the expectations of these key stakeholders be identified and given priority if schools have to survive in a competitive market environment? How should schools deal with the diverse and even conflicting expectations of different stakeholders on the aims, content, practice and outcomes of school education?

Market forces and national aims. The market forces may or may not aim at achieving and realising the national aims and visions through education. As such, how can policy makers and educators ensure that the market forces at the local or community level are in operation in the direction of development at the national or international level?

Parental choice and national visions. Specifically, how consistent are the parental or individual choices with the national visions and goals? How should these choices be supported by the state?

National framework and privatisation. To what extent should a national framework be set in terms of the market system and privatization without hindering initiatives from the marketplace but maintaining the national direction and forces within global competitiveness?

All these are just some of the dilemmas and issues that policy makers and educators face in formulating educational changes towards marketisation and privatisation. Unfortunately, the knowledge for understanding and handling these challenges in the region is slight. Research in this important area to address and inform the management of the above challenges is inevitably necessary in the coming years if the trend towards marketisation and privatisation in education is to be maintained.

2.4. *Challenges and Implications for Parental and Community Involvement in Education*

Parental and community involvement in education has not been traditional in many Asian areas, such as Hong Kong, Japan, Korea, Malaysia, Taiwan, and Thailand. Recently, people in these countries have become more aware of the importance and necessity for a wider partnership and involvement in education. There is a growing trend for educational reform to promote this kind of involvement and participation. The major concerns and implications in this trend may include the following issues.

Culture for parental and community involvement. Even though parental and community involvement has many advantages, how to promote and implement it effectively is still a core issue in the current educational reforms in the region. Most Asian countries lack a culture of accepting and supporting the practice of parental and community involvement. Teachers are traditionally highly respected in the community. It is often believed that school education should be the sole

Challenges for Research into Educational Reform in the Asia-Pacific Region 1321

responsibility of teachers and principals. Parents have tended to view them as the experts in education. Parental and community involvement is often perceived as the act of distrust of teachers and principals; to involve parents can be perceived as a loss of face among professionals. How can the policy makers and educators change this culture to encourage more parental and community involvement?

Inducing more political problems. Parental and community involvement in school management and leadership will inevitably increase the complexity, ambiguities and uncertainties in the political domain of educational institutions. How can educational leaders be prepared to lead parents and the community, build up alliances, balance diverse interests between parties and resolve different conflicts of interest in order to bring in benefits while avoiding or reducing negative effects of parental and community involvement? Would the induced political problems and difficulties from external involvement in fact dilute the scarce time and energy of teachers and leaders from educational work with students? How can they handle these dilemmas in managing parental and community participation in education?

In order to understand and manage all these questions and issues urgently needs support and advice from research if the reforms involving policy initiatives are to be successful. Unfortunately, research in this area is still underdeveloped, particularly in the context of the Asian tradition.

3. CHALLENGES AND IMPLICATIONS AT THE SITE LEVEL

3.1. *Challenges and Implications in Ensuring Educational Quality, Standards and Accountability*

In the region, many countries have introduced different types of quality assurance initiatives to monitor and promote educational quality and accountability. In planning and implementing these initiatives and efforts, there are some important issues challenging policy makers, educators and researchers (Cheng, 1997a). Examples are given below.

- How is it known that the existing stakeholders' satisfaction and expectations are relevant to the future of new generations and the society in the new millennium? If the satisfaction and expectations are not relevant, how can the gap be handled?
- How can they ensure a balance between a school's internal development and accountability to the public? A very strong emphasis on accountability to the public is often accompanied by close supervision and control that restrict initiatives for internal development and create stronger defensive mechanisms that limit effective learning by organisations.
- How can different stakeholders with diverse and even conflicting interests

handle the potential contradictory purposes between school self evaluation and external evaluation for quality assurance?
- Educational processes are complicated, involving many factors; how can it be known what indicators are valid and reliable to reflect quality and effectiveness in education and what combinations of indicators of input, performance and outcomes are appropriate to the educational institutions in specific contexts or a specific time-frame?
- On what basis should the quality standards and benchmarks be set? What are the measures to be taken to ensure that they are acceptable and fair to all involved parties and feasible in management and implementation?
- Monitoring education quality at the school-site level should be different from that at the system level. How could this difference be managed in a more efficient and effective way such that educational institutions or schools are not overburdened?
- Given the importance of leadership in pursuing educational quality, how can educators and leaders implement and develop quality assurance and quality inspection effectively? (Cheng, 1997b)

The existence of these issues and challenges makes it necessary to conduct research which informs leaders, educators and policy makers who are responsible to the public for ensuring educational quality and accountability at different levels.

3.2. Challenges and Implications in Decentralization and School Based Management

The trend of educational reforms towards decentralisation and school based management (SBM) becomes more and more important in the many countries of the region. According to Cheng and Townsend (2000), the change from traditional external control management to SBM in the countries of the region confronts a number of issues that have to be tackled in the process of educational transformation.

Decentralisation and accountability. After decentralising authority and power to the school-site level, there is a need to keep the self managing schools and teachers accountable with respect to the quality of education provided and the use of public money. Even though a concept of 'tight-loose coupling' (Cheng, 1996) has been proposed to tackle this issue, it is still a long way from being put into practice and the issue remains a key area in ongoing policy discussion about decentralization in education (Cheng & Ng, 1994).

SBM and educational equality. People often believe that with greater autonomy better schools may take advantage of this situation to recruit better students and teachers and procure more resources such that educational inequality will not only be maintained but enlarged, particularly for the students from disadvantaged backgrounds. For example, Townsend's previous analysis and his work on the Australian case have raised concerns about this problem (Townsend, 1996, 1997).

SBM as technological change and cultural change. The shift to SBM represents a type of change in management technology. Yet, whether or not it can be effectively implemented at both the system and school site levels depends heavily on the cultural change among those concerned (Levy, 1986; Ng & Cheng, 1995). Numerous studies have reported that there are various barriers and conflicts in implementing SBM because both educational officers at the system level and school practitioners at the school level still have the mind-set of external control management when implementing the management change towards the SBM model (Cheng & Chan, 2000).

SBM and educational outcomes. Many contemporary SBM studies address self management only at the school level and often assume that increased autonomy and responsibility given to schools will result in increased school effectiveness in producing quality. Yet, this assumption is questionable and past empirical studies do not yield a consistent view (Sackney & Dibski, 1994). From the perspective of Cheung and Cheng (1996), the linkage of SBM to educational outcomes should be strengthened through multi-level self management at the individual, group and school levels. Even though multi-level self management may be one of the theoretical efforts to bridge the gap between management change and student performance, the debate on this issue is still strong and ongoing until there is sufficient empirical evidence to show a clear linkage.

Downsizing the central education departments. Following the decentralisation of authority from the central office to the schools, the major roles and responsibilities of the central education department largely disappears, and the structure of the existing central bureaucracy in education has to be downsized and reformed. For example, the Education Department of the State of Victoria in Australia was largely cut to pieces in the process of implementing SBM. Downsizing a central education department is one of the hardest parts of educational change in most countries of the region. Most educational changes are often initiated and planned by the central office and the downsizing of an education department inevitably is in conflict with the interests of the bureaucracy.

The above issues together present a wide spectrum of research areas that need a great deal of intellectual effort in order to understand the complexity of school transformation and to inform policy making and implementation of school-based management.

3.3. Challenges and Implications for the Enhancement of Teacher Quality

In current educational reform, the trend towards enhancement of teacher quality and the promotion of continuing lifelong professional development of teachers and principals is important for ensuring educational effectiveness and quality in a rapidly changing environment. In such a trend, educators, leaders and researchers are facing some new challenges (Cheng, in press).

- How can school leaders build up a new culture of continuous lifelong staff development among their colleagues and related school stakeholders? (Cheng, 2000c). In other words, how can they develop their schools as learning organizations that can support all types of learning and development? (Senge et al., 2000)
- How can the relevance of professional development or formal teacher education ensure ongoing educational reforms and major shifts in education? (Elliot & Morris, 2001)
- How can a knowledge management system be built in schools to encourage active learning, accumulate experiences and knowledge from daily practices, and inform further development of staff?
- How can the diverse needs of ongoing school and staff development be identified and satisfied within a limited resource framework?
- How can internal and external networks be built to provide the necessary support and resources for ongoing school development, professional development and teacher education? (Mok & Cheng, 2001)
- With the aim of pursuing new approaches to education for the future, there is a strong local and international demand for a major shift in approach to educational leadership. What kind of new approach to leadership should be developed in such a context? How should the necessary shift be conceptualised, organised and implemented successfully among educational leaders?

When compared with the magnificent scale of ongoing educational reforms, the existing advances in understanding the nature of staff development, teacher education and leadership development are still insufficient. Clearly, a broad spectrum of research efforts is needed in these areas in coming years.

4. CHALLENGES AND IMPLICATIONS AT THE OPERATIONAL LEVEL

4.1. *Challenges and Implications in Using ICT in Education*

Many countries in the region take information and communications technology (ICT) in education as one of the most strategic initiatives in ongoing educational reform (Birch & Maclean, 2001; Gopinathan & Ho, 2000). As pointed out by Cheng and Townsend (2000), the initiatives for promoting ICT in education proposed in the past few years are confronting some basic issues.

Gaps between ICT and new education aims. While ICT is very powerful for creating opportunities for learning and facilitating learning and teaching in a very efficient way, its functions should not be over-emphasised, because ICT is a means rather than the end of education. Therefore, both policy makers and educators have to consider its relevance for the achievement of educational aims when formulating strategies for ICT in education. Some basic issues have to be tackled. How and what types of ICT are related to existing or new aims? To what extent and in what aspects can the use of ICT help to achieve educational aims? What are the potential limitations for ICT within education?

Gap between hardware, software and training. From experiences in some countries, it seems to be easier to purchase hardware, such as computers and other ICT facilities for schools, than it is to provide appropriate software and training for teachers and students. Many school practitioners spend a lot of their energy and time developing so-called 'home-made' software due to a lack of a more comprehensive and sophisticated software system to support teaching and learning in ICT. Unfortunately, the quality of the home-made software is often questionable while the development is time-consuming. How to provide a comprehensive package including the necessary hardware, software and training, as well as an ICT platform to support and maintain the effective and efficient use of ICT in teaching and learning, is an important issue, particularly in some developing sub-regions and countries where resources for development are limited.

Gap between ICT and curriculum development. Stakeholders wonder whether the existing curriculum should be changed in terms of aims, subject content, instructional process or assessment to adapt to the new ICT learning environment. Moreover, teachers do not know how to do it. There is often a lack of new frameworks for integrating the strengths and benefits of ICT into curriculum development. The advances in ICT happen too fast. There is a clear gap between the rapidly changing ICT environment and curriculum development in most countries in the Asia-Pacific region.

Gap between technological change and cultural change. In the past few years, the efforts to implement ICT in schools expended by many policy makers in the region met with strong resistance from school practitioners. There have been not only technological difficulties but also cultural problems. Implementation of ICT in education is an extensive technological transformation and inevitably involves cultural change among teachers, principals, education officers, other change agents and even students, if successful change is expected (Levy, 1986; Cheng, 1996). Therefore, how to change the existing attitudes and beliefs into a new ICT culture is clearly a serious challenge for the reform program, whether in developing countries or developed sub-regions.

How to lead effectively the implementation of ICT and other new technology in education is a completely new issue for most policy makers, educators and leaders in the region. The effective responses and strategies for handling the issues and challenges raised above depend heavily on a deep understanding of them and a knowledge base of implementation of cultural and technological changes in different contexts. All these are in need of support from educational research.

4.2. *Challenges and Implications in the Shift in Learning, Teaching and Assessment*

There is a growing trend for educational reform which emphasises major shifts in learning, teaching and assessment. Many countries are making efforts in this direction through various types of curriculum reform and initiatives in globalisation, localisation and individualisation in education. These shifts in education inevitably induce a completely different set of concerns and challenges for educational reform. The following are just some of them.

Cultural change and major shift. A major paradigm shift is not only a kind of technological and theoretical change but also a kind of deep cultural change including changes in all concerned stakeholders' and key actors' attitudes and their whole line of thinking about the future of the global world, the vision, aims, contents, methods, processes, practices, management and funding of education. How can such a comprehensive paradigm shift be achieved at different levels in ongoing educational reforms?

Teachers prepared as key actors for paradigm shifts. Clearly, teachers will play a very crucial role in the whole process of globalisation, localisation and individualization in education and development of students' contextualised multiple intelligences (CMI) (see Cheng, 2001c). Without them, such a major shift in learning and teaching is impossible. How then can teachers be prepared to develop themselves as globalised, localised and individualised CMI teachers, transform their educational institutions into CMI institutions and facilitate their students' becoming CMI leaders and citizens? Also, how can they help transform curriculum and pedagogy into those that live up to the world class standard to meet the challenges and needs of the new millennium? These are really important questions to be addressed.

New quality assurance for paradigm shift. As explained by Cheng (2001a), there should be a new conception of quality assurance responding to the paradigm shift in learning, teaching and assessment. In other words, the reform efforts and quality initiatives should be driven by the new paradigm of education. The following issues therefore become important challenges for policy makers, educators and researchers.

- How well can learning and teaching be organised in the ongoing educational reforms? In other words, how can students' learning and teachers' teaching be well placed in a globalised, localised, and individualised context?
- How well can students' learning opportunities be maximised through ICT application and networking of teachers in educational reforms? How can the

policy makers and educators ensure the linkage of ICT and the environment in order to maximise the opportunities for students' learning and development?
- How well can students' self-learning be facilitated and sustained as potentially lifelong in all the initiatives proposed for the educational reforms? In other words, how can the opportunities created in the educational reforms be maximised and ensured to be clearly converging in order to make students' self-learning sustainable over time?
- How well can students' CMI and their ability to organise their self learning be developed with respect to the new initiatives for learning and teaching? Basically, how can the policy makers and educators ensure the relevance and outcome of students' learning in terms of multiple intelligences, multiple values and ability to organise self learning?

Clearly, the implications from these issues and challenges for research are very substantial. It needs a great deal of inter-disciplinary and long-term research effort to study major shifts in learning, teaching and assessment, to investigate and understand the above issues in policy making, management and practice, and to propose appropriate strategies and methods in order to implement major shifts and reforms at different levels.

5. CONCLUSION

There are some crucial challenges arising from the ongoing trends in educational reform in different parts of the Asia-Pacific region. The challenges are impacting on the success of policy formulation and reform implementation in education in many countries. It is therefore of great concern to consider how those challenges and issues can become prioritised items on the urgent agenda of educational research if reforms are to be fully informed and finally successful in formulation and implementation. The implications derived from these issues for educational research and policy analysis are important.

All in all, given the complexity of research on such comprehensive educational reforms in many countries in the region, there is an urgent need to develop a critical mass of research intelligence through different types of networking in the region, which is a necessity not only for individual countries but also for the whole Asia-Pacific region to meet the numerous challenges in education reforms in the new millennium. It is hoped that this article will open a wide range of issues and implications for policy debate as well as educational research on educational reforms in the region and other parts of the world.

REFERENCES

Birch, I., & Maclean, R. (2001). Information and communication technologies for education and teacher development in the Asia-Pacific region: Issues and challenges. In Y. C. Cheng, M. M. C. Mok & K. T. Tsui, (2001) (Eds.), *Teaching Effectiveness and Teacher Development: Towards a New Knowledge Base* (pp. 347–370). Dordrecht, The Netherlands: Kluwer Academic Publishers.

Cheng, Y. C. (1996). *School Effectiveness and School-based Management: A Mechanism for Development.* London: Falmer Press.

Cheng, Y. C. (1997a). Monitoring school effectiveness: Conceptual and practical dilemmas in developing a framework. In H. Meng, Y. Zhou & Y. Fang (Eds.), *School Based Indicators of Effectiveness: Experiences and Practices in APEC Members* (pp. 197–206). China: Guangxi Normal University Press.

Cheng, Y. C. (1997b). A framework of indicators of education quality in Hong Kong primary schools: Development and application. In H. Meng, Y. Zhou & Y. Fang (Eds.), *School Based Indicators of Effectiveness: Experiences and Practices in APEC Members* (pp. 207–250). China: Guangxi Normal University Press.

Cheng, Y. C. (1999). Recent education developments in South East Asia: An introduction. *School Effectiveness and School Improvement, 10*(1), 3–9.

Cheng, Y. C. (2001a). *Paradigm Shifts in Quality Improvement in Education: Three Waves for the Future.* Paper presented at the Second International Forum on Quality Education: Policy, Research and Innovative Practices in Improving Quality of Education, Beijing, China, 12–15 June 2001.

Cheng, Y. C. (2001b, October). *Educational Reforms in the Asia-Pacific Region: Trends, Challenges and Research.* Paper presented at the Second iAPED International Conference on Education Research, Seoul National University, Seoul, Korea.

Cheng, Y. C. (2001c). New education and new teacher education: A paradigm shift for the future. In Y. C. Cheng, K. W. Chow & K. T. Tsui (Eds.), *New Teacher Education for the Future: International Perspective* (pp. 33–67). Dordrecht, The Netherlands: Kluwer Academic Publishers.

Cheng, Y. C. (in press). The changing context of school leadership: Implications for paradigm shift. In K. Leithwood, J. Chapman, D. Corson, P. Hallinger & A. Hart (Eds.), *International Handbook of Research in Educational Leadership and Administration.* Dordrecht: Kluwer Academic Publishers.

Cheng, Y. C., & Chan, M. T. (2000). Implementation of school-based management: A multi-perspective analysis of Hong Kong Case. *International Review of Education, 46*(3–4), 205–232.

Cheng, Y. C., & Cheung, W. M. (1995). A framework for the analysis of educational policies. *International Journal of Educational Management, 9*(6), 10–21.

Cheng, Y. C., & Ng, K. H. (1994). School management initiative and strategic management. *Journal of Primary Education, 4*(2), 1–16.

Cheng, Y. C., & Townsend, T. (2000). Educational change and development in the Asia-Pacific region: Trends and issues. In T. Townsend & Y. C. Cheng (Eds.), *Educational Change and Development in the Asia-Pacific Region: Challenges for the Future* (pp. 317–344). The Netherlands: Swets & Zeitlinger.

Cheng, Y. C., Ng, K. H., & Mok, M. M. C. (2002, in press). Economic considerations in educational policy making: An simplified framework. *International Journal of Educational Management, 15*(4).

Cheung, W. M., & Cheng, Y. C. (1996). A multi-level framework for self-management in school, *International Journal of Educational Management, 10*(1), 17–29.

Elliott, J., & Morris, P. (2001). Educational reforms, schooling, and teacher education in Hong Kong. In Y. C. Cheng, K. W. Chow & K. T. Tsui (Eds.) (2001). *New Teacher Education for the Future: International Perspectives* (pp. 147–166). Dordrecht, The Netherlands: Kluwer Academic Press.

Gopinathan, S., & Ho, W. K. (2000). Educational change and development in Singapore. In T. Townsend & Y. C. Cheng, (2000) (Eds.), *Educational Change and Development in the Asia-Pacific Region: Challenges for the Future* (pp. 163–184). Lisse, The Netherlands: Swets & Zeilinger.

Lee, M. H. (2001, February 14–16). Restructuring of higher educational institutions in Korea. Paper presented at the International Forum on Education Reforms in the Asia-Pacific Region 'Globalisation, Localization, and Individualization for the Future', HKSAR, China.

Levy, A. (1986). Second-order planned change: Definition and conceptualization. *Organizational Dynamics, 38*(7), 583–586.

Mok, M. M. C & Cheng, Y. C. (2001). Teacher self learning in a networked environment. In Y. C. Cheng, K. W. Chow & K. T. Tsui (Eds.) (2001). *New Teacher Education for the Future: International Perspectives* (pp. 109–144). Dordrecht, The Netherlands: Kluwer Academic Press.

Ng, K. H. & Cheng, Y. C. (1995). Research on school organizational changes: Approaches and strategies. *Educational Research Journal*, 10(1), 73–93.
Sackney, L. E., & Dibski, D. J. (1994). School-based management: A critical perspective. *Educational Management and Administration*, 22(2), 104–112.
Senge, P., Cambron-McCabe, N., Lucas, T., Smith, B., Dutton, J., & Kleiner, A. (2000). *Schools that Learn*. New York: Doubleday/Currency.
Townsend, T. (1996). The self managing school: Miracle or myth. *Leading and Managing*, 2(3), 171–194.
Townsend, T. (Ed.) (1997). *Restructuring and Quality: Issues for Tomorrow's Schools*. London: Routledge.

92

Monitoring the Impact of Globalisation on Education and Human Development

JOHN P. KEEVES
Flinders University Institute of International Education, Adelaide, Australia

HUNGI NJORA
Flinders University Institute of International Education, Adelaide, Australia

I GUSTI NGURAH DARMAWAN
Pendidikan Nasional University, Bali, Indonesia

1. INTRODUCTION

During the twentieth century marked advances occurred in science and technology that spread across the world and greatly changed the way in which we live. While the term 'globalisation' that refers to these changes, has its origins in the twentieth century, the processes that involve global development had their beginnings in Europe in the seventeenth and eighteenth centuries. The growth of modern science and technology accelerated this development during the latter half of the twentieth century to such and extent that Giddens (1999), in speaking and writing about the effects of globalisation refers to the *"Runaway World"* in his Reith Lectures, two of which were given in the Asia-Pacific region in Hong Kong and Delhi as part of what he referred to as a "global electronic conversation". It has been the very rapid developments in the process of global change that have drawn attention both to the benefits and the problems that accompany globalisation. However, instead of being more and more under our control, the world seems to be running out of control.

> ... some of the influences that were supposed to make life more certain and predictable for us, including the progress of science and technology, often have quite the opposite effect. (Giddens, 1999, pp. 2–3)

These developments had their origins in the writings of scholars who challenged the influence of dogma and religion in Europe, and particularly in France in the eighteenth century, in a movement referred to as the 'Enlightenment'. These thinkers argued in a rational way and for a reasoned approach to practical life and social change. The scholars of the Enlightenment included two Frenchmen, (a) Fontenelli, who argued for the modern theory of development; and (b) Descartes, who established the supremacy of rational knowledge; and two Germans, (c) Kant, who held to the belief in the unlimited progress of all mankind; and (d) Leibniz who contended that progress took place in a continuous and cumulative way. These ideas have helped to change the way in which scholars in Europe and North America have argued and written about the world in which we live.

Four great books of modern times have supported this movement that has led to global change. These books are *The Principia* by Isaac Newton, *The Origin of Species* by Charles Darwin, both from Great Britain, *Das Kapital* by Karl Marx from Russia, and *Democracy and Education* by John Dewey from the United States. These works helped form the five general perspectives from which globalisation can now be viewed: (a) Newton laid the foundations for the development of science and technology; (b) Darwin showed the importance of the environment; and (c) gave support for the ideas of social and cultural evolution; (d) Marx emphasised the consequences of an economic view and approach; and (e) Dewey established the significance of the modern political perspectives of democracy and their relationship to education. Much of the debate about globalisation has been limited in discussion to only one of these five perspectives at a time. They are not five separate views of the world inhabited by human beings, but are necessarily inter-related perspectives. They have all informed advances in educational theory and practice, and have all drawn extensively from developments in the field of education during the latter half of the nineteenth century and the twentieth century. Moreover, they have fed the rapid growth in globalisation that has occurred, and they are all dependent on education for establishing controls on what Giddens (1999) has termed the "runaway world". However, it is the development of the six billion individual people living in all the countries and states of our world and, in particular, in the Asia-Pacific region, that is of interest and concern in the discussions about education in the articles of this *Handbook*. Consequently, it is to the consideration of human development that we turn in this concluding article.

This article examines briefly, each of these five perspectives of globalisation, namely, (a) developments in science and technology, (b) changes in the world environment, (c) social and cultural evolution, (d) economic growth and (e) democracy and political processes. It considers both the impact of education on globalisation as well as the impact of globalisation on education in the past, the present and the future. In addition, this article argues that research workers in education and other fields have an obligation to monitor change and the effects of globalisation, not only on the provision of education, whether formal, nonformal or informal, but also of human development in each of the countries and states within the Asia-Pacific region.

2. LEARNING – THE TREASURE WITHIN

The strongest response to the global problems of poverty, ignorance, exclusion, oppression and war has come from the International Commission on Education for the Twenty-first Century that reported to UNESCO in a volume titled *Learning: The Treasure Within* (Delors, 1996). As its title implies, this report emphasises the importance of education in the resolution of the problems confronting all people living in our world. However, it recognises seven tensions that must, if possible, be overcome, namely, the tensions between:

- the global and the local as people become citizens of the world, without ignoring their roots both within their homeland and their local community;
- the universal and the individual, as people support the groups to which they belong without forgetting the unique character of each individual human being;
- tradition and modernity, as people accommodate to and assimilate the new without rejecting what is of value in the past;
- long-term and short term considerations, as people react to the immediate and new instantaneous reporting of events that involve long-term problems and considerations;
- the need for competition and concern for equality of opportunity, as people seek to live, work and play in a world where its resources are not readily accessible to all people;
- the extraordinary growth of knowledge and human beings' capacity to assimilate it, as people recognise that learning can not be limited to the early years but must continue throughout life; and
- the spiritual and the material, as people recognise the importance of values and moral precepts in a world where advertising emphasises material possessions (Delors, 1996, pp. 16–18).

The structure of education advanced by the Delors Commission is built upon four pillars that provide the foundations from which the problems faced by people around the world might be tackled in a cooperative way, both within and between social and cultural groups. These four pillars are:

- learning to live together, through the possession of an understanding of other cultures and their history, traditions, and spiritual values;
- learning to know, through the possession of a sufficiently broad general education together with a willingness to continue learning in both formal and informal ways throughout life;
- learning to do, through not only the competence and skill to act in a variety of situations as an individual, but also as a member of a team; and
- learning to be, through the need of everyone to exercise greater independence and judgment as well as a greater sense of responsibility to work with others to attain common goals.

These four pillars of learning reflect traditional Western culture that has its origins in classical Greek philosophy. This is perhaps not surprising since the pressures for globalisation and for change, that have formed through recent centuries, have been developed and have grown, as has been argued in the earlier section of this article, from the Enlightenment and have been fostered in Europe and North America. However, conviction with respect to the desirability and inevitability of social and cultural change supported by scientific and material developments, while flowing from Darwinian ideas of evolution, is not inconsistent with the perspectives of Confucian teaching and of earlier Chinese civilisations that have held to an intellectual tradition which recognises the continually changing nature of society through the establishment of harmony. Likewise, Islamic thought advanced by Ibn Khaldun, views change and development in terms of dialectic and cyclical processes that are ordered and not random processes (Fagerlind & Saha, 1989).

The many different social and cultural groups within the Asia-Pacific region recognise the material benefits that flow from modern science and technology and the consequences of these benefits for a national economy and the well being of the individuals within those groups. As a consequence, these people seek to learn about modern science and technology, as well as the framework of thinking that underpins this knowledge. Nevertheless, it is not immediately clear as to whether the material benefits of science and technology can be made available to all such groups without fundamental changes to the ways of thinking of some individuals and some groups. The challenges to some societies and cultures in the Asia-Pacific region, as well as to some groups in Western countries, that would seem to be holding to a self-centred and isolationist perspective at a time when globalisation is permeating all parts of the world in which we live together, can only be tackled through sustained programs of education. These programs of education must focus not only on the five perspectives that lie beneath the movement towards globalisation but also on the human development of all people, irrespective of race, creed, sex or class, living in the different social and cultural groups within the Asia-Pacific region. However, change has already occurred and is continuing to occur through both dialogue and educational programs in all countries and states with respect to these five perspectives, as well as that of human development. The documenting of the change that has occurred as well as the monitoring of the change that is occurring are initial first steps in the future provision of educational programs that will support future human development within the Asia-Pacific region.

3. MONITORING CHANGE THAT RELATES TO GLOBALISATION

The five perspectives that relate to globalisation have been identified above to be the political, the scientific and technological, the economic, the socio-cultural, and the environmental perspectives. There are more than 50 national entities in the Asia-Pacific region that hold approximately 60 per cent of the world's population. Some nations are very large, both with respect to the physical space they occupy and with respect to the number of people they contain. Others are small island nations with relatively few people. Some are among the most industrially developed nations, and others are among the least developed nations. Some have strong data recording systems, and some are even uncertain about the number of people they contain. Nevertheless, it is necessary to obtain and record data of interest from all countries within the Asia-Pacific region, if development across the Asia-Pacific region under the influences of globalisation is to be monitored effectively.

The monitoring of change in a form that can be readily comprehended by those who undertake the policy-making and planning for the many different social and cultural groups within the region requires the use of indicators (see *Comparative Indicators in Education*). The work on the development of such indicators is being carried out under the United Nations Development Programme, and the *Human Development Report 2001: Making New Technologies Work for Human Development* provides information produced by a team of people engaged in a program which considers the estimation and use of indicators to assess and monitor human development (UNDP, 2001). This article draws heavily on the work of the team responsible for the *Human Development Reports 2001* and *2002*. The indicators that this team have developed would seem to satisfy the requirements advanced by Gilomen (2002), drawing together information from some of the five perspectives discussed above into a composite indicator concerned with human development. Other scholars and teams have sought to present and use such indicators on previous occasions, for example the International Association for the Evaluation of Educational Achievement (IEA) in the reports of its cross-national studies (for example, Husén, 1967; Passow et al., 1975) have employed similar indicators and related them to educational outcomes.

Likewise, the Organization for Economic Cooperation and Development (OECD) has used indicators in its publications titled *Education at a Glance* (1995, et seq.) and has presented detailed information on many different aspects of education. Furthermore, the Asia-Pacific Economic Cooperation Human Resources Development Working Group Education Forum has published two reports on *School Education Statistics in the Asia-Pacific Region* (APEC HRDWG, 1994, 1998). However, while education is central to planning and policy making for human development, the effects of globalisation and educational programs worldwide involve the five perspectives referred to above as well as the provision of education. Moreover, educational programs would seem to be generally restricted to the provision of formal education while both nonformal and informal education must be considered in the future alongside formal education (Desjardins and Tuijnman, in press) in any comparative analyses of learning outcomes. In the sections that follow in this article the indicators that have been advanced by UNDP (2001) with respect to the five perspectives referred to above and human development in general, are examined.

4. DEMOCRACY AND POLITICAL CHANGE

Giddens (1999, p. 68) has argued that the most powerful idea associated with political and social change and the process of globalisation during the twentieth century has been the idea of 'democracy'. The concept of 'democracy' has a long history, but was seen to encompass the related ideas of 'liberty' and 'equality' during the Enlightenment, that led to the French Revolution. However, it was in the United States that these ideas led to a major civil war for the abolition of slavery, and the establishment in the United Kingdom as elsewhere, of procedures and policies for the emancipation of women, and the provision of universal suffrage, as well as the eradication of constitutional discrimination based in wealth, race and religion. The idea of 'democracy' also involves the establishment of equality of educational opportunity, commonly implying a liberal education in order for all people to be able to exercise meaningfully their right to vote, as well as providing for all adult people to fulfil their right to work and to have adequately paid employment. Giddens (1999, p. 70) draws attention to the fact that under the forces of globalisation the number of democratic governments in the world has more than doubled since the mid-1970s. Pintor and Gratschew (2002), in a study of voter turnout since 1945 across the world, have identified countries that can be classified as democracies, and report an increase from 27 per cent in 1974 of the countries of the world endorsing democracy to 62 per cent in 2000. Nevertheless, there has also at times, in some countries, been opposition to democratic processes, with Myanmar and Pakistan in the Asia-Pacific region reverting to authoritarian rule during recent decades.

In addition, the employment of democratic processes has been extended to larger units through the formation of the United Nations Organisations, the British Commonwealth, and the European Union, as well as the economic trading blocks, such as the OECD group of wealthier countries, the military blocks that seek to establish and maintain world peace and the courts that support international law and justice. The employment of democratic processes has been made possible through developments in education and can only be sustained and developed further, particularly in the Asia-Pacific region, through advances in education throughout the region. UNDP (2001) records both the status of major international human rights instruments, and the acceptance of fundamental labour rights conventions in the countries of the world.

5. THE SCIENTIFIC AND TECHNOLOGICAL EXPLOSION

It has been the scientific and technological advances that flowed during the twentieth century from the discovery of the atom and the electron that have transformed very rapidly not only global travel but also more recently the transfer of information around the world through new information and communication technologies. Modern societies face major challenges that may be seen from the different perspectives of the 'New Economy' or the 'Information

Society' or some other label. However, the range and scope of these challenges are not as yet clear and demand systematic monitoring as the advance of new scientific knowledge increases at an ever growing rate.

UNDP (2001) presents information on:

- a technology achievement index,
- investment in technology creation,
- diffusion of technology in agriculture and manufacturing, and
- diffusion of technology in information and communications.

Societies clearly face the challenges of managing the risks of technological change, particularly with respect to genetically modified crops and the use of pollutants, alongside the use of nuclear and biochemical weapons. Educational programs within which such issues are debated in an informed way are necessary for sound policy decisions to be made and adhered to by the peoples of the Asia-Pacific region.

6. ECONOMIC GROWTH

For both highly developed and relatively undeveloped countries, levels of employment and economic participation are linked to the levels of educational achievement and attainment that have been reached at school, college and university through a wide range of formal programs, as well as through nonformal and informal learning experiences. Moreover, the well being of the people in a country or a state would appear to be closely related in a period of globalisation to the level of economic activity and the rate at which it is developing. While this perspective is strongly challenged by many, it is clearly difficult for a country to turn its back on economic growth. UNDP (2001) records information on indicators of:

- economic performance,
- the structure of trade,
- flows of aid, from and to countries, and
- priorities of public spending.

These indicators are concerned with the provision of access to the resources needed for all people within a country to obtain an improving standard of living. However, access to these resources is greatly influenced by levels of unemployment for different social groups within a country. Only through well developed educational programs can a country lift its level of economic performance. However, many wealthier countries seek to import teachers, skilled workers, medical practitioners and technologists, in order to raise their level of economic growth at the expense of less developed countries, instead of planning in advance to meet their national needs.

7. ENERGY AND THE ENVIRONMENT

The material resources available to provide the energy needed to support scientific and technological development and an expanding economy must be regarded as limited within the world in which we are presently living. Moreover, the consumption of many material resources has effects on the global environment to the extent that there is serious doubt whether the environment in which we live will be preserved for future generations over a long period of time.

UNDP (2001) provides information on indicators concerned with:

- energy consumption,
- carbon dioxide emissions, and
- ratification of environmental treaties.

The reluctance of many countries to address these issues involving energy usage and the environment in circumstances where it is seen to be prejudicial to scientific and technological development and economic growth, particularly where such countries are heavy consumers of the limited energy resources and heavy contributors to carbon dioxide emissions across the world, is of concern. It has been through ecologically oriented courses in biology at schools and universities, that the people of many countries have become acutely aware of these problems, and it will only be through sustained programs of formal, nonformal and informal education that societies will be led to take the necessary steps to conserve both local and global environments.

8. SOCIAL AND CULTURAL CHANGE

The perspective that is perhaps the most difficult to examine through the use of indicators, that record the effects of globalisation, involves social and cultural change.

UNDP (2001) provide indicators concerned with:

- refugees and armaments that relate to protecting personal security,
- gender related development,
- gender empowerment,
- gender inequality in education,
- gender inequality in economic activity, and
- woman's political participation.

While gender related issues have been found to be relatively easy to examine through the use of indicators, issues relating to indigenous peoples, minority social and ethnic sub-groups, religious groups, and child and slave labour would appear to some degree to be intractable. Nevertheless, it is only through educational programs that build on the guidelines laid down within the Delors report, referred to above, that resolution of these problems will be possible.

9. MONITORING OF EDUCATIONAL CHANGE

Work has already commenced on a collaborative program between some of the countries of the Asia-Pacific region to monitor change in the provision of education within the region. The Asia-Pacific Economic Cooperation Human Resources Development Working Group Education Forum (APECHRDWDEF) has been set up by the Ministers representing the 18 member economies that form APEC (Asia-Pacific Economic Cooperation). In establishing the APEC Education Forum the Ministers have identified education as the key to developing and extending the skills required to sustain economic development in the region during the coming decades. The Education Forum identified three priority areas for its work:

- providing instruction of a high quality in key areas,
- monitoring the performance of education systems, and
- facilitating information exchange and the movement of people to support human resource development.

An initial report was prepared and presented (APECHRDWGEF, 1994) that provided data on 11 of the APEC members' education systems. In 1998, a second and more extensive report was prepared (APECHEDWGEF, 1998) with 18 APEC members making contributions that described their education systems and provided policy-relevant statistics relating to schools. It is nevertheless, important to recognise that the provision of education in a country extends not only beyond the school system to pre-school centres and technical institutes and colleges and centres for lifelong learning, but also to the many different types of nonformal and informal educational services. Moreover, the countries in South Asia that have been shown in this *Handbook* to have major problems in the provision of educational services are not active members of the Asia Pacific Economic Cooperation Education Forum. There is clearly a need for improved recording of educational statistics in some countries of the Asia-Pacific region. There is also scope for organisations like APEC to pay greater attention to the education systems of the member countries in order to obtain, not only economic benefits, but also to realise the many social and cultural benefits that flow from higher levels of educational attainment.

10. HUMAN DEVELOPMENT INDEX

The combining of the several perspectives considered in the previous sections, to form a single index that provides a way to enable changes which arise from the effects of globalisation to be monitored, is of practical significance for the purposes of planning and policy making particularly in the field of educational provision. An appropriate index for these purposes should focus on aspects of human development and the essential components of a human development index are taken by the UNDP (2001) Team to be:

- life expectancy at birth,
- adult literacy rate,
- primary, secondary and tertiary gross enrolment ratio, and
- gross domestic product per capita.

Figure 1 shows in diagrammatic form how the UNDP (2001) Team has calculated the human development index that has been constructed from the four component parts listed above.

The index calculated by UNDP (2001) would appear analogous to the resource conversion process developed by Coleman (1971) that combines financial resources (GDP per capita) with social resources (life expectancy at birth) and human resources (adult literacy rate and gross enrolment rates). In addition these ideas are consistent with the views of the Indian scholar, Amatyr Sen (1999) winner of the 1998 Nobel Prize, for his contributions to welfare economics. Whether other resources should be taken into consideration and whether alternative indicators might be employed in the calculation of the index is an issue for debate.

Table 1 records the trend in the values of the human development index (HDI) for five-year intervals from 1975 to 2000 for countries in the Asia-Pacific region for which data are available. The data used In the calculation of this index are recorded in Table 1 and are taken from UNDP (2001, pp. 141–144) and the values of HDI that are given in Table 1 are taken from UNDP (2001, pp. 145–148), and UNDP (2002). The countries in the Asia-Pacific region are grouped into three categories, 'high human development', 'medium human development' and 'low human development' and the World HDI rank as well as the Asia-Pacific HDI rank ordering are also given in Table 1.

Furthermore, it should be noted that some UN Member Countries are not included in Table 1, in the main, because GDP per capita data are not available for these countries, namely: Afghanistan, Kiribati, Democratic Republic of Korea,

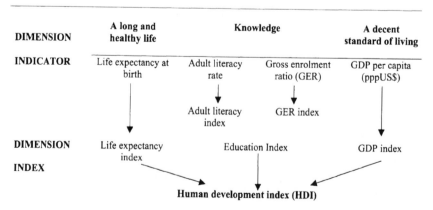

Figure 1. Calculation in the human development index (UNDP, 2001, p. 239).

Marshall Islands, Federated States of Micronesia, Nauru, Palau, Tonga, and Tuvalu. In addition, there are some entities, namely: Macao, Taiwan, and East Timor that are not considered in the UNDP (2001) report.

11. CONCLUSION

The major issues raised repeatedly in the articles throughout this *Handbook* are concerned with the effects of globalisation and their relationships with human development and education. Since it is difficult to predict with certainty the long-term influences of globalisation on the diverse groups of people in the Asia-Pacific region, the one course of action that must be undertaken involves the systematic monitoring of change. From the evidence presented in Table 1 it is clear that over the 25 year period from 1975 to 2000 during which globalisation has been operating in a way that Giddens (1999) refers to as the "runaway world" there has been a clear trend across the countries of the Asia-Pacific region for which there is strong evidence available, of an increase in the development of human resources in most countries of the region. This is seen in longer life expectancy, increased participation in formal education and a general rise in gross domestic product per capita with the increase in quality of life that these might be expected to bring. Whether this trend will be maintained over time as globalisation continues its driving influence is not clear. However, it is obviously necessary to monitor change with respect to human resource development as well as with respect to the other five perspectives of political processes, science and technology, economic growth, energy consumption and the environment, and society and culture. Moreover, it is a task for educational researchers to monitor and interpret the evidence on the changes that occur in the decades ahead.

Educational research also faces the challenge of advancing the provision of education, whether the services provided are formal, nonformal or informal services in order to advance human well-being. The specific tasks of inquiry confronting educational research workers are sometimes difficult to foresee. Nevertheless, it is necessary to ensure that optimal use is made of new information and communication technology in the variety of settings that exist in the region. The developments that have occurred during the decade from 1990 to 2000 were difficult to foresee a decade earlier in 1980, and yet the potential for change was clear. Moreover, it is difficult to envisage the challenges and changes that will occur for more than a decade ahead. Perhaps the greatest danger ahead lies in the bifurcation that may arise both within and between countries of those people who can reap the benefits of the new information and communication technology and those who can not. The tackling of this particular problem is only one of the many challenges that lie ahead.

There is also concern in many countries of the Asia-Pacific region for the changes in moral values that are said to be occurring, particularly among young people in the Asia-Pacific region. This concern is leading to a growing emphasis

Table 1. Human Development Indicators (source UNDP, 2001)

Country for 1999	Life expectancy at birth[b]	Adult literacy rate[c]	Gross enrolment ratio[d]	GDP per capita[e]	\multicolumn{6}{c	}{Human development index trends (HDI)}	HDI (2000) World rank	HDI (2000) A-P rank	Democracy[a]
					1975	1980	1985	1990	1995	2000			
High human development													
Australia	78.8	—[x]	116[y]	24,574	0.842	0.859	0.871	0.886	0.926	0.939	5	1	*
Japan	80.8	—[x]	82	24,898	0.851	0.876	0.891	0.907	0.920	0.933	9	2	*
New Zealand	77.4	—[x]	99	19,104	0.846	0.853	0.865	0.873	0.900	0.917	19	3	*
Hong Kong, SAR	79.4	93.3	63	22,090	0.754	0.793	0.820	0.857	0.875	0.888	23	4	
Singapore	77.4	92.1	75	20,767	0.719	0.753	0.779	0.816	0.853	0.885	25	5	
Korea Rep of	74.7	97.6	90	15,712	0.687	0.729	0.771	0.814	0.851	0.882	27	6	*
Brunei Darussalam	75.7	91.0	76	17,868	—	—	—	—	—	0.856	32	7	
Medium human development													
Malaysia	72.2	87.0	66	8,209	0.614	0.657	0.691	0.720	0.758	0.782	59	8	*
Russian Federation	66.1	99.5	78	7,473	—	0.809	0.826	0.823	0.778	0.781	60	9	
Thailand	69.9	95.3	60	6,132	0.603	0.645	0.675	0.713	0.749	0.762	70	10	*
Fiji	68.8	92.6	84	4,799	0.656	0.679	0.693	0.719	0.740	0.758	72	11	*
Armenia	72.7	98.3	80	2,215	—	—	—	—	—	0.754	76	12	
Philippines	69.0	95.1	82	3,805	0.649	0.683	0.687	0.716	0.733	0.754	77	13	*
Kazakhstan	64.4	99.0	77	4,951	—	—	—	—	—	0.750	79	14	
Maldives	66.1	96.2	77	4,423	—	—	—	—	—	0.743	84	15	
Turkmenistan	65.9	98.0	81	3,347	—	—	—	—	—	0.741	87	16	
Azerbaijan	71.3	97.0	71	2,850	—	—	—	—	—	0.741	88	17	
Sri Lanka	71.9	91.4	70	3,279	0.614	0.648	0.674	0.695	0.717	0.741	89	18	*
Uzbekistan	68.7	88.5	76	2,251	—	—	—	—	—	0.727	95	19	
China, People's. R.	70.2	83.5	73	3,617	0.522	0.553	0.590	0.624	0.679	0.726	96	20	

(Continued)

Table 1 (Continued)

Iran, Islamic Rep of	68.5	75.7	73	5,531	0.556	0.563	0.607	0.643	0.688	0.721	98	21	*
Samoa (Western)	68.9	80.2	65	4,047	—	0.555	0.646	0.661	0.685	0.715	101	22	*
Kyrgyzstan	67.4	97.0	68	2,573	—	—	—	—	—	0.712	102	23	
Vietnam	67.8	93.1	67	1,860	—	—	0.581	0.604	0.647	0.688	109	24	
Indonesia	65.8	86.3	65	2,857	0.467	0.529	0.581	0.622	0.662	0.684	110	25	*
Tajikistan	67.4	99.1	67	1,031	—	—	—	—	—	0.667	112	26	
Mongolia	62.5	62.3	58	1,711	—	—	0.535	0.554	0.545	0.655	113	27	*
India	62.9	56.3	56	2,248	0.406	0.433	0.472	0.510	0.544	0.577	124	28	*
Myanmar	56.0	84.4	55	1,027	—	—	—	—	—	0.552	127	29	**
Cambodia	56.4	68.2	62	1,361	—	—	—	—	—	0.543	130	30	*
Papua New Guinea	56.2	63.9	39	2,367	0.420	0.442	0.463	0.481	0.521	0.535	133	31	*
Low human development													
Pakistan	59.6	45.0	40	1,834	0.343	0.370	0.403	0.441	0.476	0.499	138	32	*
Bhutan	61.5	42.0	33	1,341	—	—	—	—	—	0.494	140	33	
Nepal	58.1	40.4	60	1,237	0.292	0.329	0.370	0.415	0.451	0.490	142	34	*
Lao Peoples Dem R	53.1	47.3	58	1,471	—	—	0.372	0.402	0.443	0.485	143	35	
Bangladesh	58.9	40.8	37	1,483	0.332	0.350	0.383	0.414	0.443	0.478	145	36	*

Source: Voter Turnout; Since 1945; [b] in years for 1999; [c] % aged 15 and above, 1999; [d] Combined primary, secondary and tertiary gross enrolment as a % for 199; [e] ppp US$ for 1999.

[x] For purposes of calculating HDI – 99.0% was used; [y] For purposes of calculating HDI – 100% was used; [z] UNDP (2001) records values of the HDI and world ranking for Solomon Islands (0.622 and 120) and Vanuatu (0.542 and 131).

** Returned to authoritarian rule: Myanmar (1990) (UNDP, 2002, p. E-1-3).

on moral education and values education (see *Values Education in a Changing World*, and *Education for Peace and International Understanding*) in the education systems of East Asia and the Pacific Islands. While it is extremely difficult to monitor such human characteristics as attitudes and values, the wave of democracy-building that occurred in the 1980s and 1990s is an indicator of a growing dimension of human values and development in the Asia-Pacific region. There is clearly a need for maintaining the wave of democracy building and extending it to a deepening of democracy by giving ordinary people a greater say in the making of local, national and global policies. Nevertheless, we are moving towards a world society that is marked by new uncertainties with increasing individualism and fundamental changes to important social and religious institutions (Beck, 1992). Different scholars take opposing and contradictory views about globalisation and its effects on different parts of our world and on our lives. A final word in this consideration of globalisation must go to Giddens (1992, pp. 81–82), who, in speaking about the "runaway world", said:

> One might be forgiven for thinking that some problems are simply intractable, without hope or resolution. ... Nothing comes without struggle. But the furthering of democracy at all levels is worth fighting for and it can be achieved.

The effective operation of democratic processes resides in the highest possible levels of educational attainment within our social institutions. In the countries and states of the Asia-Pacific region like the countries and states that occupy the world in which over six billion people are now living, educators and educational research workers must collaborate in their endeavours to share their knowledge and expertise. This *Handbook* presents evidence of the very considerable body of knowledge and expertise that exists within the Asia-Pacific region. It is the sharing of these products of previous research studies and the undertaking of cooperative investigations and inquiries in the future across countries and states within the region that presents a major challenge to all educators in the region. However, it is only through cooperation and collaboration in the provision of education, and in the use of new information and communication technology by educators working within the region that the many problems facing the countries of the region will begin to be resolved.

REFERENCES

Asia-Pacific Economic Cooperation Human Resources Development Working Group Education Forum (APECHRDWG) (1994). *School Education Statistics in the Asia-Pacific Region*. Canberra: DEETYA for APEC.
Asia-Pacific Economic Cooperation Human Resources Development working Group Education Forum (APECHRDWG) (1998). *School Education Statistics in the Asia-Pacific Region*. Canberra: DEETYA for APEC.
Beck, V. (1992). *Risk Society: Towards a New Modernity*. London: Sage.

Coleman, J. S. (1971). *Resources for Social Change: Race in the United States.* New York: Wiley.

Delors, J. (Chair) (1996). *Learning: The Treasure Within.* Paris: UNESCO.

Desjardins, R., & Tuijnman, A. (in press). A General Approach for Using Data in the Comparative Analyses of Learning Outcomes.

Fagerlind, I., & Saha, L. J. (1989). *Education and National Development: A Comparative Perspective* (2nd edn.). Oxford: Pergamon.

Giddens, A (1999). *Runaway World: How Globalisation is Reshaping our Lives.* London: Profile Books.

Gilomen, H. (2002). Education in the New Economy: A statistical framework for strategic monitoring and management. Paper presented to the IAOS Conference London 2002, Part II, Section 2. Neuchâlat, Switzerland: Swiss Federal Statistical Office.

Husén, T. (Ed.) (1967). *International Study of Achievement in Mathematics.* Stockholm: Almqvist and Wiksell, and New York: Wiley.

Organisation for Economic Cooperation and Development (OECD) (1995). *Education at a Glance,* Paris: OECD.

Passow, A. H., Noah, H. J., Eckstein, M. A., & Mallea, J. R. (1976). *The National Case Study: An Empirical Comparative Study of Twenty-One Educational Systems.* Stockholm: Almqvist and Wiksell.

Pintor, R. L., & Gratschew, M. et al. (2002). *Voter Turnout since 1945: A global report.* Stockholm: International Institute for Democracy and Electoral Assistance.

Sen, A. (1999). *Development as Freedom.* Oxford: Oxford University Press.

United Nations Development Programme (UNDP) (2001). *Human Development Report 2001: Making New Technologies Work for Human Development.* New York: Oxford University Press.

United Nations Development Programme (UNDP) (2002). *Human Development Report 2002:* /www.undp.org/, 24 July 2002.

Index of Names

(**bold** type indicates a chapter by that author)

Abbey, J. 342, 343, 347
Abbott, D. 791
Abdullah, A. S. 1001, 1012
Abdullah, H. M. 10, 13
Abe, Y. 209-10, 213
Abel, M. 644, 652
Ablett, J. 708, 713
Abrami, P. C. 745, 753
Abu Bakar Nordin 118, 120
Abu, M. S. B. 1267
Accanokazya 961, 970
Acemoglu, D. 721, 728
Achilles, C. M. 742, 744, 745-6, 749, 753
Acker, S. 268
Adair, J. G. 1312, 1313
Adair, V. A. 436, 437, 438
Adams, D. 260, 267, 824, 825, 873, 880, 1089, 1093
Adams, J. E. 8, 13, 918, 929
Adamson, R. 791
Adey, P. 309, 320
Adibnia, A. 481, 490
Adorio, P. 211, 213
Advani, L. 207, 215
Aggarwal, S. 229
Aggarwal, Y. 1059, 1060
Aggrawal, P. 1268
Ahlstrand, B. 671
Ahluwalia, M. 863, 865
Ahmad, K. 289, 290, 1061
Ahmad, R. 770, 779
Ahmat, S. 1210, 1217, 1218
Ahmed, A. 603, 612, 613
Ahmed, H. 336, 347
Aikenhead, G. 623, 626
Aikin, W. M. 120
Ainley, J. 352, 362, 1149
Ainscow, M. 189, 200, 779
Ainsworth, S. 551, 553
Akaev, Askar 248, 252
Akane, A. 509
Akao, N. 953, 956
Aker, G. F. 866
Akiba, M. 1105
Aksornkool, Namtip **269-78**

Alagumalai, Sivakumar **1257-69**, 1262, 1264, 1266, 1267
Alam, M. 806
Albrecht, D. 39, 42, 819, 826, 1281, 1282, 1283
Alderson, A. 1149
Alderson, J. C. 640
Aldridge, J. M. 464, 465, 469, 470, 472, 473, 474
Alexander, P. A. 757, 765, 790
Alexander, R. 785-6, 788, 789, 790
Ali, M. 847, 851
Alkin, M. C. 971
Allen, K. 325, 331, 332, 587, 596
Almeida, C. 1024, 1027
Altbach, P. 441, 453, 557, 566, 1062, 1104, 1105, 1149, 1211, 1217, 1218, 1219, 1220
Alto, R. 709, 713
Alur, – 208, 213
Amadeo, J.-A. 567
Amara Sawadisevee 118, 120
Ames, C. 500, 505
Anandalakshmy, S. **231-40**
Anas, A. P. 382, 392
Andersen, E. B. 412, 422
Anderson, B. 1095, 1104
Anderson, C. A. 685
Anderson, D. S. 140, 1144, 1145, 1149, 1150
Anderson, G. 1085-6, 1093
Anderson, G. J. 464, 475
Anderson, H. 784, 790
Anderson, J. 1259, 1260, 1262, 1267
Anderson, L. 786, 790, 1097, 1104
Anderson, L. W. 743, 744, 751, 752
Anderson, M. 493
Anderson, R. C. 358, 362, 596
Anderson-Levitt, K. 1097, 1104

Andreae, J. 790
Andrich, David 352, **409-24**, 412, 414, 417, 418, 422, 423
Ang, R. P. 497, 505
Anunciacion, R. M. 895
Aoki, T. 599, 612
Appelbaum, R. P. 1219
Applebee, A. N. 551-2, 554, 795, 806
Aquilina, J. 764, 765
Arabsolghar, F. 487, 490
Arai, A. 956
Arcelo, A. 667
Archer, J. 500, 504, 505
Aris, B. B. 1262, 1267
Armer, M. J. 1212, 1219
Asam, C. 590, 594
Asanuma, S. 903, 911
Asghar, M. 464, 473
Asher, S. R. 750, 753
Ashley, L. 486, 491
Ashman, A. 214
Ashoka, Emperor of India 651
Ashton, D. 707, 713, 1039, 1045
Ashton-Warner, S. 587, 589, 594
Askew, M. 747, 752
Asonuma, A. 825
Aspin, D. N. 915, 929
Astilla, E. 456, 497, 498, 508
Aston, D. 1211, 1219
Atchoarena, David 669, **701-14**, 713
Atkin, J. M. 1243, 1244, 1255
Atkinson, J. W. 496, 505
Atkinson, P. 1288, 1299
Atkinson, R. C. 1083, 1093
Atran, S. 376
Atweh, B. 544, 554
Au, K. 590, 594
Au, M. 791
Austin, G. 373, 376
Aviram, A. 1257, 1267
Awatere-Huata, D. 965, 970
Awkerman, G. 657, 671

1347

1348 Index of Names

Ayres, D. M. 68, 71
Azizian, R. 242, 246, 255, 256
Azuma, H. 355, 356, 357, 362, 766, 988, 989, 992, 994, 999, 1120, 1121

Bacon-Shone, J. 201
Baden, S. 271, 277
Baha'i, – 338, 340, 347
Bailey, J. 205, 213
Baine, D. 215
Baines, D. 752
Baird, J. 485, 490
Bajracharya, H. R. 1058, 1061
Bajunid, I. 1001, 1003, 1004–5, 1012
Bakalevu, Sala 1226, 1229
Baker, D. 1096, 1100, 1104, 1105
Baker, D. P. 258, 267
Baker, M. 718, 720, 728
Baker, R. 7, 13, 626
Baker, Robyn **541–54, 615–27**
Balderston, J. B. 667–8, 671
Ball, K. 331, 332
Balla, J. 991, 999
Balogh, T. 674, 685
Baltes, P. B. 379, 380, 381, 384, 385, 386, 387, 388, 389, 390, 391, 392
Bamford, A. 895
Bandura, A. 513, 523, 756, 765
Baquer, A. 207, 213
Barber, M. 1238, 1242
Barfett, S. 489, 491
Barker, M. 626
Barker, P. 725, 728
Barker, R. 744, 752
Barnett, J. 595
Barr, R. 597
Barratt-Pugh, C. 594
Barro, R. J. 842, 843, 851
Barron, J. 721, 728
Bassanini, S. 1033, 1045
Bassett, G. W. 1173, 1179
Basu, C. K. 668, 671
Batten, M. 362
Baxter, J. P. 897
Bazargan, A. 1140, 1149
Beaton, A. 605, 612, 613, 758, 765, 1097, 1109, 1112, 1115, 1121, 1244, 1255
Beaty, E. 443, 455
Beauchamp, E. R. 766
Beaver, B. 499, 505
Beck, L. G. 918, 929
Beck, V. 1344
Becker, G. S. 673, 685, 721, 728
Becker, J. P. 547, 554, 603, 612
Beckham, G. M. 1065, 1075
Beckwith, J. 454
Bednarz, N. 493
Beeby, C. E. 101, 105, 130, 140, 174, 188, 1171, 1172, 1179, 1194

Begg, Andy **541–54**, 548, 554, **599–614**, 612
Begley, P. 982, 984, 985
Behrendt, H. 626
Belfiore, P. J. 207, 208, 214
Bell, B. 626
Bempechat, J. 1120, 1121
Benavot, A. 120, 557, 558, 567, 1105
Benjamin, – 1036
Bennell, P. 681, 683, 684, 685
Bennett, N. 743, 752
Bennett, S. N. 782, 785, 786, 790
Benseman, J. 866
Benson, C. 1230
Berger, M. C. 728
Berlack, A. 789, 790
Berlack, H.. 789, 790
Bernard, D. 314, 319
Bernardo, A. B. I. 517, 523
Berry, J. 444, 454, 455
Bertrand, O. 657, 658–9, 663, 671
Berwick-Emms, P. 586, 594
Bessant, B. 134, 135, 140
Betcherman, G. 704, 705, 706, 709, 713
Betts, J. R. 746–7, 752
Bhalla, A. S. 825
Bhanthumnavin, D. L. 496, 507
Bhardwaj, M. 157, 169
Biddle, B. J. 443, 454, 791, 1085, 1093, 1145, 1149, 1182, 1191
Biggs, J. B. 308, 319, 320, 354, 355, 359–60, 362, 363, 442, 443, 444, 446, 447, 450, 452, 453, 454, 456, 490, 506, 508, 514–15, 523, 524, 876, 881, 988, 989, 992, 993, 994, 995, 999, 1000
Bigum, C. 941, 942
Billett, S. 720, 728
Birch, I. 11, 13–14, 738, 739, 892, 895, 1324, 1327
Birren, B. A. 380–1, 385, 392
Birren, J. E. 380–1, 385, 392
Bisaria, S. 271, 277
Bishop, A. J. 554, 609, 611, 613
Black, M. 728
Blackledge, D. 6, 14
Blacklock, D. 425, 437
Blackmore, J. 941, 942
Blanc, C. 226, 228
Blandy, R. 720, 721, 728
Blatchford, D. 792
Blatchford, Peter 736, **741–54**, 742, 743, 744–5, 747–8, 749–50, 751, 752, 753
Blaug, M. 664, 671, 675, 685
Bliss, J. 747, 752
Block, A. 608, 613
Block, J. 784, 790
Blöndal, S. 1033, 1045

Bloom, B. S. 111, 112, 120, 782, 790
Blossfeld, H.-P. 1101, 1104
Bodycott, P. 955, 957
Boekaerts, M. 766
Boli, J. 1095, 1105
Bolstad, R. 626
Bond, M. H. 507, 509, 999, 1000
Bond, N. 455
Bonstead-Bruns, M. 54, 56
Boo, H. 621, 624, 627
Boon, Z. 975, 978, 982, 984
Booth, T. 189, 200
Bordia, A. 338, 339, 341, 343, 344, 345, 346, 347
Borkowski, J. 478, 490
Bose, A. 645, 652
Bottani, N. 1124, 1135, 1136
Boud, D. 1149
Boulton-Lewis, G. M. 451, 454
Bourdieu, Pierre 44, 45, 50, 53, 55, 59, 61, 71
Bourke, P. 140, 759, 1144, 1150
Bourke, S. 204, 214, 765, 1149
Bowden, J. 442, 454
Bowey, J. A. 486, 490, 588, 594
Bowman, M. J. 685
Boyd, T. 677, 685
Boyd-Zaharias, J. 745–6, 753
Boyer, E. L. 549, 554
Bradford, J. H. 1265, 1267
Bradley, K. 1100, 1104
Bradnock, R. 217, 218, 226, 228
Brady, L. 891, 895
Bramald, R. 548, 554
Bransford, J. D. 309, 320, 351, 358, 360, 362, 477, 490, 513, 523
Brause, R. S. 1288, 1298
Bray, Mark 35, 39, 41, 325, 332, 333, 559, 567, 735, 740, 755, 760, 761, 762, 764, 765, 787, 788, 789, 790, 825, 831, 832, 837, 880, 917, 927, 1022, 1023, 1024, 1025, 1027–8, 1029, **1047–62**, 1051, 1053, 1059, 1061, 1063, 1070, 1075, 1105, 1190, 1216, 1219, 1281, 1283
Bredeson, P. 878, 879
Breen, M. 586, 594
Brekelmans, – 464
Bremmer, I. 243, 255, 256
Brennan, Barrie 737–8, **853–66**, 860, 861, 865
Brenner, M. E. 519, 523
Breuss, T. 383, 392
Bridges, E. 1001, 1009, 1012, 1013
Brim, O. G. 392
Brinton, M. C. 46, 56
Broaded, C. M. 47, 55

Broadfoot, P. 551, 554, 791
Brock, C. 215
Brockeroff, M. 218, 219, 221, 228
Bronfenbrenner, U. 44, 55, 744, 752
Brophy, J. E. 782, 786, 790, 791
Brouilette, R. 214
Brown, A. 633, 637, 639, 640
Brown, A. L. 309, 320, 351, 358, 360, 362, 477, 478, 479, 490-1, 493
Brown, R. 215, 479, 493
Brown, R. K. 551, 554
Brown, S. 1182, 1191
Brown, T. 6, 14
Browne, E. 1261, 1267
Bruce, C. S. 1258, 1267
Bruce, M. 489, 491
Bruner, J. S. 373, 376, 773, 779
Bryk, A. S. 466, 473
Buch, M. B. 893, 896
Budge, D. 551, 554
Bunruangrod, D. 648, 652
Burapharat, Chitrlada 329, 332
Burbeles, N. 1095, 1104
Burden, R. L. 472, 474
Burgess, Robin S. L. 1053, 1061
Burgon, J. 1140, 1149
Burian, C. N. 846, 851
Burke, G. 719, 729, 730
Burke, Gerald 29, **29-42, 1271-83**
Burke, J. 792
Bush, T. 12, 14, 918, 929
Byrd, M. 383, 392
Byrne, B. 486, 491, 588, 595

Cadman, A. G. 1173, 1179
Cady, G. H. 1266, 1267
Cahen, L. 746, 753
Cahyana, A. 1062
Cai, D. 393
Cai, J. 519, 520, 523
Caillods, F. 78, 91, 1032, 1045
Calderon, A. J. 1243, 1255
Caldwell, Brian J. 7, 14, 916, 918, 921, 929, **931-44**, 932, 933, 937, 941, 942, 948, 956, 1001, 1003, 1010, 1012
Caleekal, A. 768, 779
Calkins, M. A. 671
Cambourne, B. 588, 595
Cambron-McCabe, N. 1329
Campbell, A. 336, 337, 347
Campbell, J. R. 586, 595
Campbell, W. J. 495, 505
Campion, M. 591, 595
Campione, J. 477, 490
Carey, N. 1136
Carini, R. M. 938, 944
Carlson, R. V. 657, 671
Carneiro, R. 874, 880
Carnoy, M. 557, 567, 1100, 1104

Carr, M. 478, 490
Carr, T. 594
Carroll, J. B. 308, 320, 782, 783, 791
Carroll-Lind, J. 437, 438
Carss, M. 613
Carswell, S. 436, 438
Cashmore, J. A. 498, 505
Caspi, S. J. 49, 55
Cassidy, M. F. 60, 71
Castells, M. 809, 825, 1211, 1219
Castetter, W. B. 959, 961, 970
Castillo, E. S. 7, 14
Castro, C. de M. 1164
Catalano, G. 825
Catalano, R. F. 439
Catchpole, Gemma 736, **741-54**
Cavallo, D. 341, 347
Cazden, C. 356, 362
Ceci, S. J. 44, 55
Center, Y. 205, 214, 592, 595
Cha, Yun-Kyung 108, 120, 558, 563, 567, 1097, 1104
Chabbott, C. 7, 14, 1102, 1104
Chadha, A. 207, 214
Chambers, B. 745, 753
Chamidi, S. 1062
Chan, B. 1001, 1013
Chan, C. 483, 484, 491
Chan, D. W. 189, 196, 198, 200, 496, 497, 498, 505, 507, 1012
Chan, H. K. 201
Chan, I. 454
Chan, K. 791, 1025, 1028
Chan, K.-W. 887, 895
Chan, L. K. S. 486, 488, 489, 491, 493, 497, 499, 505
Chan, M. T. 1323, 1328
Chan-Tiberghein, Jennifer 1088, 1091, **1095-1106**, 1101, 1104
Chang, A. S. C. 455
Chang, C. C. 7, 15
Chang, C. K. 517, 523
Chang, C. M. 498, 506
Chang, C. Y. 522, 523
Chang, H. G. 196, 200
Chang, J. 893, 897
Chang, J. N. 1020, 1028
Chang, K. S. 528, 536
Chang, S. 482, 491
Chang, S. C. A. 487, 494
Chang, W. C. 497, 498, 500, 502, 505
Chantarapanya, P. 976, 985
Chantavanich, S. 1299
Chantavit, S. 892, 895
Chapman, D. W. 260, 267, 824, 825, 873, 880, 1328
Chapman, E. S. 500, 501, 508
Chapman, G. 217, 218, 226, 228
Chapman, J. D. 915, 929

Chapman, J. W. 486, 492, 493, 589, 592, 595, 597
Chareonwongsak, K. 892, 895
Chase, W. G. 358, 362
Cheah Yin Mee 596, 597
Chee, M. 791
Chelliah, T. 1061
Chen Ai Yen 531, 536, 738, **899-911**
Chen, B. Y. 1017, 1028
Chen, C. C. 469, 473, 505
Chen, J. H. 176, 188, 500, 502
Chen, K. 1268
Chen, L. 428, 438
Chen, M. F. 198, 200
Chen, S. 428, 438
Chen, T. H. 1020, 1028
Chen, Y. G. 1020, 1028
Chen, Y. Y. 205, 206, 214, 215
Cheng, B. S. 497, 505
Cheng, K. 876, 880
Cheng, K. M. 453, 455, 951, 956, 981, 984, 993, 999, 1003, 1012, 1016, 1017, 1022, 1027, 1028, 1035, 1045, 1216, 1219
Cheng, M. H. M. 1250, 1255
Cheng, S. K. 211, 214
Cheng, Y. 454, 874, 875, 880
Cheng, Yin Cheong 3, **3-16**, 4, 5, 7, 9, 12, 13, 14, 16, 119, 120, 895, 915, **915-29**, 921, 922, 929, 936, 943, 945, 948, 953, 954, 955, 956-7, 974, 977, 978, 982, 984, 985, 988, 996, 999, 1001, 1003, 1012, 1028, 1071, 1077, 1315, **1315-29**, 1317, 1318, 1319, 1321, 1322, 1323, 1324, 1325, 1326, 1327, 1328, 1329
Cheo, R. K. 762-3, 765
Cheong, I. P. A. 1290, 1298
Cheung, C. H. 498, 506
Cheung, D. 615, 618, 626
Cheung, K. M. 1016, 1028
Cheung, Kwok-Cheung 361, **525-37**, 527, 536
Cheung, M. B. 976, 980, 984
Cheung, W. M. 13, 14, 957, 1071, 1077, 1319, 1323, 1328
Chew, J. 745, 753, 975, 978, 982, 984
Chew, S. B. 761, 765
Chia, L. S. 521, 522
Chia, R. C. 497, 505
Chiba A. 646
Chieh, J. J. 196, 200
Chien, M. F. 191, 200, 201
Chik, P. 791
Chikarmane, P. 341, 345, 347
Chin, C. 521, 522, 524, 1262, 1267
Chinapah, M. 271, 277
Chinnappan, M. 518, 524
Chionh, Y. H. 465, 473

1350 Index of Names

Chitraker, R.   1061
Chiu, C. Y.   500, 506, 508
Chiu, K. H.   527, 536
Chiu, S. Y.   515, 523
Cho, S.   190, 192, 194, 200, 201
Choi, C.   1025, 1028
Choi, S. C.   1065, 1071, 1076
Chong, K. C.   1002, 1006–7, 1010, 1012
Chong, Y.   483, 491
Choo, O. A.   502, 505
Chou, C.   616, 627
Chou, W.   194, 198, 200
Chou, Y. H.   1020, 1028
Chow, King W.   880, 895, **915–29**, 1328
Chrostowski, S.   626, 1122
Chu, C. P.   496, 505
Chuang, C. J.   496, 497, 505, 506
Chuang, Wei-Chen   925, **1015–29**
Chudowsky, N.   359, 363, 514, 524
Chui, H.   484, 491
Chung, K. H.   968–9, 970, 971
Chung, Y.   779
Chung Yue-Ping   683, 685
Churchill, S.   1237, 1242
Chuuou Kyouiku Shingikai   1070, 1075
Chyn, M. C.   497, 505
Ciolek, M.   254, 255
Clark, B.   1102, 1105
Clark, B. R.   823, 825
Clark, D. A.   327, 332
Clark, R. J.   554
Clarke, P.   779
Clarkson, P.   544, 554, 611, 613
Clay, M. M.   586, 588, 592, 594, 595
Clayton, J.   587, 595
Clayton, V. P.   385, 392
Cleary, M.   437, 438
Clements, M. A.   554
Clinton, Bill   742
Clune, W.   943
Cmith, P.   753
Cobb, P.   603, 608, 613, 614
Cobb, V. L.   884, 889, 895
Cochran-Smith, M.   891, 895
Cocking, R. R.   309, 320, 351, 358, 360, 362, 1076
Cogan, J.   558, 566, 567
Cogan, L. S.   617, 626, 1106
Cohen, D.   1102, 1105
Colclough, C.   826
Cole, P. G.   489, 491
Coleman, J. S.   43, 45, 48, 53, 55, 60, 62, 71, 1340, 1345
Coleman, M.   12, 14, 918, 929
Coll, R.   626
Colletta, N. J.   307, 320
Collins, –   264, 265
Collins, C.   362
Collins, J.   61, 71

Collins, K.   386, 391, 392
Collins, S.   627
Collins, W. A.   383, 392
Collis, K. F.   308, 319, 320
Comber, B.   596
Comber, C.   791
Comber, L. C.   468, 473, 1114, 1121
Conant, J. B.   1201, 1206
Conaty, J. C.   215
Coniam, D.   955, 957
Connell, W. F.   135
Cook, K. S.   57
Cooke, S.   370, 376
Coombs, C. H.   410, 423
Coombs, P. H.   336, 347, 680, 685
Cooper, B.   626, 1086, 1094
Cooper, H. M.   746, 749, 752
Cooper, M.   720, 728
Cornford, I. R.   891, 895
Corrie, L.   892, 895
Corson, D.   929, 1328
Cortazzi, M.   450, 454, 990, 994, 996, 999
Cortes, J. R.   889, 895
Costa, F.   229
Covington, M. V.   497, 505
Cowie, C. R.   593, 595
Crane, R. I.   676, 685
Crawford, J.   382, 393
Crawford, N.   206, 214
Creemers, B.   749, 752
Crocombe, M. T.   833, 835, 836, 837
Crocombe, R.   833, 835, 836, 837
Croft, A.   591, 595
Croll, P.   750, 753, 786, 791
Cronbach, L. J.   126, 423
Crosby, P. B.   945, 957
Crosthwaite, J.   866
Crunkilton, J. R.   657, 658, 661, 664, 671
Cruz, T. M.   647–8, 652–3
Csikzentimihalyi, M.   774, 776, 779
Cubberley, E. P.   110, 120
Cullen, D. J.   1288, 1299
Cullen, J. L.   489, 491
Cumming, J.   1149
Cummings, W. K.   567, 766, 1062, 1096, 1097, 1104, 1105, 1212, 1217, 1219
Currie, J.   1045
Curtain, R.   225, 226, 228
Curtin, J.   1258, 1267
Curtin, P.   336, 337, 347
Curtis, David   **305–20**, 308, 320
Cuttance, P.   955, 957, 1066, 1069, 1075
Czikzentimahalyi, M.   774, 775, 776, 779

Dahlin, B.   359, 362, 445, 454
Dahnke, H.   626
Dai, C. Y.   333
Dakin, R.   854, 866

Dale, R.   855, 866
Dall'Alba, G.   443, 455
Damasio, A.   777, 779
D'Ambrosio, U.   609, 613
Damon, W.   377
Daniels, H.   215
D'Apllonia, S.   745, 753
Dar, A.   325, 327–8, 332
Darling-Hammond, L.   884, 891, 895
Darmawan, I Gusti Ngurah   **1331–45**
Darwin, Charles   1332
Das, A.   207, 209, 214
Dasen, P. R.   366, 376
Davidson, G. R.   373, 376
Davidson, J. E.   201
Davies, A.   632, 639
Davis, B.   548, 554, 609, 611–12, 613, 1010, 1012
Davis, C.   596
Davis, C. H.   1218
Davis, P.   604, 613
Dawkins, J.   588, 595, 860, 866
de Bruyn, E.   44, 55
De Carvalho-Filho, M. K.   488, 491
De Ford, D. E.   596
de Glopper, J.   1118, 1121
De Groot, E.   478, 493
de Lacey, P. R.   376
De Landsheere, G.   96, 105, 124, 140, 1170, 1179
de Lemos, M.   370, 376
de Leo, Joy   353, **395–407**, 653
De Silva, A.   1059, 1061
de Silva, W. A.   760, 766
de Soete, G.   424
De Vos, G. A.   496, 505
DeAngelis, R.   1042, 1043, 1045
De'Ath, P.   55, 590, 595
Deeks, J.   866
Deer, C. E.   895
Degenhart, R. E.   1119, 1121, 1122
Delamont, S.   1288, 1299
Delannoy, F.   908, 911
Delors, J.   77, 259, 267, 396, 401, 407, 653, 1196, 1203, 1206, 1234, 1240, 1241, 1333, 1345
Demerath, P.   62, 71, 1072, 1075
Demetriou, H.   777, 780
Deming, W.   945, 957
Dempsey, I.   204, 214
Demsky, T.   682, 686
Deng, M.   205, 206, 214
Deng, P.   1018, 1028
Deng Xiao-ping   563, 1016
Deng Zongyi   105
Denham, C.   782, 791
Derghazarian, E.   1122
Derricott, R.   558, 567
Desai, I. P.   **203–15**, 205, 214
DeSarbo, W. A.   423
Descartes, René   1332

Index of Names 1351

Desjardins, R. 307, 320, 1335, 1345
Dev, P. C. 207, 208, 214
Dewey, John 124, 608, 1332
DFID 17, 27
Dhamotharan, M. 1267
Dhanarajan, G. 847, 852
Dhillon, A. S. 522, 523
Dibski, D. J. 1323, 1329
Dickson, W. 492
Dienstbier, R. 506
Diken, I. H. 212, 214
Dimmock, Clive 916, 920–1, 980, 981, 984, 985, 987, **987–1000**, 988, 994, 998, 999, 1001, 1003, 1012
Din, F. S. 743, 752, 753
Ding, X. J. 1016, 1028
Dixon, R. S. 437
Djalil, A. 891, 895, 1299
Dobson, I. R. 1243, 1255
Dockery, M. 728
Donnorummo, B. 1045, 1046
Donoghue, J. R. 414, 423
Dore, R. 761, 766
Doucouliagos, C. 720, 728
Dougherty, C. 682, 685
Douglas, G. 449, 455
Dowling, L. J. 1261, 1268
Downie, J. 1299
Dowson, C. 955, 957
Dowson, M. 500, 501, 505
Drago-Severson, E. 1120, 1121
Drew, P.-Y. 454
Drori, G. 1095, 1105
D'Rozario, V. 745, 753, 889, 895–6
Du Plessis, D. 205, 213
Dudgeon, P. 369, 373, 375, 376
Duggan, S. 869, 880
Duit, R. 621, 627
Duke, B. 588, 595
Duke, C. 856, 866
Duncan, D. 1261, 1267
Dung, P. 522, 523
Dunkin, M. J. 443, 454, 791, 891, 896
Duschl, R. 627
Dutneall, R. 729
Dutt, A. 217, 218, 226, 228, 229
Dutt, S. 338, 340, 341, 343, 348
Dutton, J. 1329
Dweck, C. S. 478, 491, 498, 506
Dymock, Darryl 737–8, **853–66**

Eason, G. 753
Eccles, J. C. 1194, 1206
Eckstein, M. A. 1345
Ecob, R. 791
Eddy, B. 1069, 1075
Edgar, A. 247, 255
Edmonds, S. 748, 752, 753

Ee, J. 211, 214
Ehrle, K. 753
Eide, K. 1084, 1093
Eisemon, T. O. 1218
Ekanayaka, S. B. 335, 347
Ekblad, S. 429, 438
Elder, C. 634, 640
Elequin, E. 1294, 1299
Eley, M. 454
Eliot, T. S. 779
Elkins, J. 214, 487, 490, 588, 596, 597
Ellena, J. 791
Eller, W. 596, 597
Elley, W. B. 101, 267, **585–97**, 586, 587, 589, 590, 591, 593, 594, 595, 597, 1117, 1120, 1121
Ellinger, T. R. 1065, 1075
Ellington, H. I. 1267
Elliot, J. 1324, 1328
Elliott, R. G. 887, 895
Ellis, P. 336, 341, 347
Elson, D. 285, 290
Eltis, K. 883, 896
Ely, D. P. 1261, 1268
Eng, A. 791
Engelbrecht, J. 601–2, 613
English, L. D. 520, 523
Entner Wright, B. R. 49, 55
Entwistle, N. J. 442, 443, 454, 455, 773, 779
Epstein, J. L. 1064, 1066, 1075
Ereata, T. 687, 699
Erikson, E. H. 380, 386, 392
Eripek, S. 212, 214
Esguerra, – 706
Eshanova, Z. 249, 255
Etches, P. 803, 806
Evans, K. 1051, 1061
Evensen, D. 513, 521, 523
Evers, B. 285, 290

Fägerlind, I. 254, 255, 563, 565, 567, 1081, 1092, 1093, 1334, 1345
Fairbairn, H. 759, 765
Fang, Y. 119, 120, 956, 1328
Fantini, S. 1265, 1268
Farnsworth, E. B. 205, 214
Farquhar, C. 792
Farrell, S. 733, 740, 786, 791, 993, 995, 996, 1000
Faure, E. 400, 401, 407, 863, 866
Fazlul Majid, A. F. 1087, 1093
Feldman, A. 1243, 1244, 1255
Fensham, P. 621, 626
Ferger, H. 424
Ferguson, L. W. 412, 423
Ferguson, P. D. 472, 473
Ferrara, R. 477, 490
Ferreira, J. 582, 583
Ferrier, F. 333, 730
Fessler, R. 959, 966, 971
Field, S. 1033, 1045
Fielding, M. 778, 779

Fielding-Barnsley, R. 486, 491, 588, 595
Fien, John **569–84**, 576, 582, 583, 584
Figgis, J. 1147, 1149
Filby, N. 746, 753
Filmer, D. 1302, 1313
Finch, C. R. 657, 658, 661, 664, 671
Findsen, B. 855, 856, 866
Finn, B. 320
Finn, J. D. 742, 744, 749, 752, 753
Firsov, V. 610–11, 613
Fischer, G. 1263, 1268
Fisher, C. 735, 740
Fisher, D. 1299
Fisher, D. L. 465, 466, 468, 470, 471, 473, 474
Fitz-Gibbon, C. T. 10, 15
Fitzclarence, L. 554, 1071, 1075
Fitzgerald, J. 753
Fitzroy, P. T. 729
Flanders, N. A. 782, 784, 791
Flavell, J. 477, 480, 491, 492
Fleming, N. 54, 56
Flood, J. 594
Fluitman, F. 332
Fogarty, G. J. 454
Fontenelli, – 1332
Foong, P. 480, 492
Foord-May, M. 1261, 1268
Foorman, B. R. 596
Foreman, P. 204, 214
Forest, J. F. 455
Forlin, C. 204, 214
Forlin, P. 204, 214
Forojalla, S. B. 1031
Forret, M. 626
Forster, M. 352, 353, 362, 594, 806
Fortson, J. L. 201
Foster, B. 897
Foster, M. 596
Foster, P. J. 675, 684, 685
Foucault, M. 1209, 1219
Fowler, – 370
Fox, K. A. 1032, 1045
France, B. 626
Franceschini, M. A. 1268
Francis, D. 891, 896
Frank, J. D. 1101, 1105
Franken, R. E. 495, 506
Fraser, Barry J. 51, 56, 57, 354, 355, 446, 454, 463, **463–75**, 464, 465, 466, 467, 468, 469, 470, 471, 472, 473, 474–5, 991, 999, **1285–99**
Fraser, D. 724, 728
Freebody, P. 486, 491, 586, 595, 597
Freeman, L. 595
Freire, P. 335, 340
Freudenthal, H. 604, 613
Freyberg, P. 603, 613, 621, 627
Frost, R. 204, 214

1352 Index of Names

Fu, X.   516, 523
Fuhrman, S.   1106
Fujimura, N.   516, 523
Fujimura-Fanselow, K.   1212, 1214, 1219
Fujita, H.   769, 772, 779
Fujita, T.   956
Fullan, M. G.   778, 779, 915, 929
Fuller, B.   946, 957, 1120, 1121
Fulton, O.   840, 851
Fumihiko, S.   1260, 1268
Funder, D. C.   392
Fung, K. C.   498, 506
Fwu, B. J.   976, 977, 978, 983, 984–5, 1002, 1012

Gabel, D.   473
Gadamer, H.-G.   599, 613
Gaebler, T.   1035, 1046
Gaffney, J. S.   589, 595
Gage, N. L.   1085, 1093
Gaither, G. H.   945, 957, 958
Galbraith, P.   480, 481, 492
Gallimore, R.   747, 753
Gallois, C.   393
Galton, Maurice   735, 739, 750, 752, 753, **781–92**, 785, 786, 788, 791
Gandhi, Mahatma   644–5, 674, 1172
Gao, L. B.   454, 990, 999
Gao, Q.   1016, 1028
Garden, R.   626, 1112, 1122
Gardner, H.   191, 195, 201, 357, 362, 527, 1242
Garmezy, N.   388, 392
Garner, P.   215
Garofalo, J.   481, 492
Garton, Alison F.   358, **365–77**, 367, 376
Garvey, D.   369, 370, 373, 375, 376
Gates, A.   486, 491
Gault, U.   382, 393
Gaur, G.   157, 169
Gelman, S. A.   372, 377
George, C.   761, 766, 1059, 1061
Ghafari, E.   596
Ghani, Zainal   138, 1292, 1299
Gibbon, M.   338, 344, 347
Gibbons, J.   586, 595
Gibbons, M. B.   1085, 1093
Gicain, M. S.   648, 652
Giddens, Anthony xxiii, 1168, 1169–70, 1171, 1178, 1179, 1198, 1201, 1206, 1331, 1332, 1336, 1341, 1344, 1345
Giles, H.   393
Giles, L.   388, 392
Gill, I.   325, 327–8, 332
Gilomen, H.   1335, 1345
Gilroy, A.   590, 595
Ginsburg, M.   1089, 1093
Girourard, N.   1033, 1045
Giroux, H.   566, 567

Gizewski, P.   217, 218, 226, 229
Glaser, R.   359, 363, 514, 524
Glass, G.   746, 753
Gleason, G.   242, 245, 255
Glenn, J.   243, 245, 255, 513, 523
Glynn, T.   592, 593, 596, 597
Gmelin, W.   1093, 1094
Gobbi, M.   717, 718, 728
Goddard, D.   918, 929
Goel, S. C.   1215, 1219
Goesling, B.   1105
Goh, C.   488, 492
Goh Chok Tong   769, 779
Goh, Ngoh-Khang   521, 522, 524, **1243–56**
Goh So Tian   787, 791
Goh, Swee Chiew   51, 56, 354, 355, **463–75**, 464, 465, 466, 467, 468, 473
Goldin, G.   608, 614
Goldring, E. B.   9, 15
Goldstein, H.   742, 752, 753, 951, 957
Gonzales, E.   353, 362, 605, 612, 613, 626, 1120, 1121, 1122, 1255
Gonzales, P.   1120, 1122
Gonzalez, A.   1216, 1219
Good, T. L.   782, 786, 790, 791
Goodnow, J.   368, 372, 373, 374, 375, 376, 377, 382, 383, 392, 498, 505
Goodrum, D.   618, 622, 625, 626, 1243, 1255
Goodson, I.   543, 554
Goos, Merrilyn   **477–94**, 480, 481, 482, 492, 493–4
Gopinathan, S.   7, 10, 11, 15, 105, 567, **733–40**, 740, 768, 770, 779, 790, 791, **899–911**, 908, 909, 911, 974, 975, 978, 985, 1002, 1003, 1012, 1103, 1105, 1153, 1164, 1218, 1266, 1268, 1293, 1299, 1310, 1313, 1324, 1328
Gordon, C.   454
Gorham, A.   334
Gorman, T. P.   1121
Gorostiaga, J. M.   1089, 1093
Goswami, U.   365, 376
Goulet, L.   381, 391, 392
Govinda, R.   158, 169, 896, 1310, 1313
Gow, L.   444, 455, 991, 993, 999
Goyette, K.   54, 56
Graham, S.   425, 438
Gramsci, A.   1209
Graney, K.   253, 255
Grant, H.   498, 506
Grant, N.   250, 255
Gratschew, M.   1336, 1345
Grauze, A.   720, 730
Graves, N.   1288, 1299

Gray, K. C.   321–2, 333, 660, 661–2, 671
Greaney, K. T.   486, 492
Greaney, V.   802, 805, 806
Green, A.   677, 685
Green, C.   271, 277
Green, F.   713, 1039, 1045, 1219
Green, M. F.   1046
Greenfield, P.   357, 362, 1076
Greeno, J.   359, 362, 514, 523
Greer, B.   608, 614
Greer, J.   537
Gregario, L.   570, 583
Gregory, K.   626, 1122
Gremli, M. S.   1293, 1299
Gribble, J.   1299
Griffin, R.   215
Grigorenko, E. L.   50, 55, 56
Grissmer, D.   742, 743, 744, 753
Groome, H.   53, 56
Groundwater-Smith, S.   1071, 1075
Grouws, D. A.   493, 605, 613
Groves, S.   604, 613
Grubb, W. N.   674, 675, 680, 685
Gryna, F. M.   945, 957
Gu, C.   429, 439
Gubhaju, B.   220, 221, 229
Guest, P.   226, 229
Guilford, J. p. 191, 201
Guillen, M. F.   1095, 1105
Gulliksen, H.   411, 423
Gump, P. V.   744, 753
Gunstone, R.   603, 614, 624, 627
Gupta, U. G.   1261, 1268
Gurr, David   919, **945–58**, 948, 957
Gustafsson, J. E.   308, 320
Guttman, C.   335, 347

Haas, A.   328, 333, 710, 713
Habisch, A.   228, 229
Hackling, M.   618, 626, 1243, 1255
Haertel, G. D.   48, 49, 57
Hagan, J.   57
Haigh, M.   626
Hakuta, K.   766
Halbach, A.   753
Halford, G. S.   365, 372, 374, 375, 376
Hall, –   1170
Hallak, J.   174, 188, 1032, 1045
Halliday, M.   591, 595
Hallinan, M. T.   47, 56, 72, 1104, 1182, 1191
Hallinger, Philip   916, 922–3, 929, 974, 975, 976, 977, 985, 1001, **1001–1013**, 1002, 1003, 1006, 1009, 1010, 1012, 1013, 1328
Halpin, D.   941, 944
Halsey, A. H.   1029
Hamid Latif, A.   1087, 1093

Hamid, P. N. 496, 506
Hamilton, A. 53, 56
Hammond, J. 1264, 1268
Hampden-Turner, C. 770, 779
Han, Y. H. 496, 506
Hanushek, E. A. 742, 753, 869, 880, 936, 937, 943, 944, 1088, 1093, 1098, 1105
Hao, L. 54, 56
Haq, F. S. 210, 214
Haq, K. 281, 284, 290, 681, 682, 685, 1048, 1061
Haq, M. 281, 284, 290, 681, 682, 685, 1048, 1061
Haque, E. 851
Haque, M. 335, 347
Harbison, F. 659, 660, 661, 663, 671
Harder, H. 746, 753
Harding, A. 601–2, 613
Hardjono 1299
Hare, V. 790
Hargreaves, A. 929
Hargreaves, L. 753, 791
Harhoff, D. 721, 728
Harlen, W. 1182, 1191, 1245, 1256
Harlow, A. 626
Harman, G. 839, 840, 850, 852, 957, 1041, 1042, 1045, 1091, **1137–50**, 1140, 1149
Harman, Kay 1091, **1137–50**
Harnischfeger, A. 783, 791
Harre-Hindmarsh, J. 856, 866
Harris, D. 214
Harris, M. 366, 376
Harrison, P. 177–8, 188
Hart, A. 929, 1328
Harwood, J. 393
Hasan, Parween 804, 806
Hasegawa, T. 498, 506
Hastings, T. J. 111, 120
Hatano, G. 366, 372, 375, 376, 377
Hattie, J. 449, 453, 454, 455, 456, 503, 508, 991, 999
Hatton, E. 1069, 1075
Hatton, M. I. 333
Hau, K. T. 454, 497, 498, 500, 502, 506, 508, 991, 999
Havighurst, R. J. 309, 320
Haw, G. W. 653
Hawke, A. 728
Hawley, J. 329, 333
Hayamizu, T. 498, 506
Hayashi, T. 496, 506, 1071, 1075
Hayden, M. 1140, 1149
Hayes, D. 743, 753
Hayes, J. 512, 523
Hayhoe, R. 1217, 1220
Hayton, G. 718, 728
He, S. M. 190, 194, 198, 201
Hearn, W. E. 108, 120
Heater, D. B. 556, 567
Heath, S. B. 594
Heaton, C. 827, 837

Heck, Debbie **569–84**, 582, 583, 1001, 1002, 1011, 1013
Hedges, L. V. 447, 454, 742, 753
Hegarty, P. 790
Heider, F. 496, 506
Heinich, R. 525, 536, 1268
Heller, K. A. 201, 202
Heller, P. 221, 229
Hemara, W. 451, 454
Henderson, J. 1219
Heng, M. 791
Herman, S. 519, 523
Herr, E. 321–2, 333, 660, 661–2, 665, 671
Herr, K. 1085–6, 1093
Herriman, M. L. 486, 492, 493
Hersch, R. 604, 613
Hess, R. D. 355, 356, 357, 362, 498, 506, 988, 989, 992, 994, 999, 1120, 1121
Hextall, I. 542, 554
Hiebert, J. 356, 363, 518–19, 520, 524, 546, 554, 997, 1000, 1097
Higginson, F. 869, 880
Hil, P. W. 1240, 1242
Hill, Kathryn **629–40**, 633, 637, 638, 639, 640
Hill, S. 587, 596
Hine, P. 472, 473
Hines, G. 495, 506
Hinton, F. 866
Hipkins, Rosemary **615–27**, 620, 621, 626
Hirata, S. 464, 473
Hiratsuka, Mansumori 125, 1194
Hirayama, S. 366, 376
Hiroki, K. 1067, 1069, 1075
Hirono, T. 536
Hirumi, Atsusi 1261, 1268
Hite, S. 1086, 1094
Hladczuk, J. 596, 597
Ho, H. 499, 506, 508
Ho, H. Z. 515, 519, 523
Ho, I. T. 454, 498, 506
Ho, S. C. 1071, 1075
Ho Shin 316
Ho Wah Kam 7, 10, 11, 15, 201, **585–97**, 587, 592, 594, 596, **733–40**, 740, 768, 770, 779, 780, 784, 791, 887, 889, 891, 896, 911, 974, 975, 978, 985, 1002, 1003, 1012, 1291, 1293, 1299, 1324, 1328
Hobsbawm, E. J. 243, 244, 255
Hodgens, J. 941, 942
Hoffman, D. L. 423
Hofstede, G. H. 995, 999
Hogan, D. 675, 685
Hoi, P. 449, 454
Hoijtink, H. 410, 423
Holbrook, A. 134, 135, 140, 1142, 1144, 1147, 1149, 1199, 1206, 1288, 1299

Holdaway, D. 586, 587, 588, 596
Holloway, S. D. 990, 992, 1120, 1121
Holmes, B. 1126, 1135
Holsinger, D. 1096, 1104
Holton, D. 601, 603, 613
Homer-Dixon, T. 217, 218, 226, 229
Hong, E. 756, 758, 759, 760, 763, 766
Hong, H. J. 968, 969, 971
Hong, J. 514, 524
Hong, S. 515, 523
Hong, Y. Y. 498, 499, 500, 502, 506, 508
Hood, D. 725, 729
Hoosain, R. 507
Hoover, W. A. 486, 493
Hoover-Dempsey, K. V. 758, 766
Hope, J. 891, 896
Hopkins, D. 929
Hopkins, S. 729
Hopper, R. 834, 837, 845, 852
Hori, S. 384, 391, 392
Horio, T. 1100, 1105
Hossain, S. I. 325, 333
Hossein, S. 1051, 1061
Hou, L. 45, 57
Houang, R. T. 1106
Houcan Zhang 596
Hounsell, D. 443, 455
House, E. 778, 779
Houtz, L. E. 1261, 1268
Hoyle, E. 255, 256
Hruda, L. 508
Hsieh, H. S. 1218
Hsu, H. G. 333
Hu, R. P. 1020, 1028
Hu, W. 1016, 1028
Hua, S. 596
Huang, C. T. 1020, 1028
Huang, H. 70, 71
Huang, T.-C. I. 469, 470, 472
Huber, G. 1122
Huber, S. 1013
Huberman, A. M. 940, 943
Huda, H. 633, 640
Hufne, K. 685
Hughes, P. 451, 455, 1237
Hughes, Phillip W. 653, **1231–42**, 1242
Huguet, P. 220, 221, 229
Hui, C. H. 444, 455
Hui, H. 980, 985
Hui, P. 917, 926, 1028
Hui, Philip Kwok-Fai **1031–46**
Hui, X. 905, 911
Hummel, K. 729
Hun, C. 1264, 1268
Hung, Y. Y. 496, 506
Hunt, B. 6, 14
Hunt, M. 498, 507
Huntley, I. 605, 613
Husén, T. 105, 106, 188, 319, 334, 464, 468, 473, 952, 957,

1084, 1085, 1093, 1108, 1111, 1122, 1127, 1135, 1167–8, 1179, 1182, 1191, 1335, 1345
Husér, T. 1027
Hwa Kee, G. 1089, 1093
Hwang, Y. Y. 497, 506

Ibn Khaldun 1334
Ichikawa, F. V. 498, 506
Ichikawa, S. 766
Ichilov, O. 558, 567
Ichioka, F. 1122
Idol, L. 490, 493
Idris, N. 1299
Ikeda, M. 529, 536
Inagaki, K. 366, 376
Inayatullah **293–304**
Indrijathno, B. 1299
Indriyanto, B. 1062
Ingersoll, R. 1098, 1105
Ingram, D. 640
Ingulsrud, J. E. 587, 596
Inhelder, B. 308, 320
Innes-Brown, M. 325, 333, 556, 563, 567
Inoki, T. 324, 333
Ip, Kin Yuen 925, **1015–29**, 1016, 1028
Irvine, J. 157, 167, 169
Isaacs, I. 713
Isawa, Eiko **1063–77**
Ishida, H. 46, 56
Isidro, Grau 1261, 1268
Islam, M. 229
Islam, R. 704, 705, 706, 709, 713
Ismagilova, N. 249, 255
Ismail, M. 456, 499, 509
Istance, D. 874, 880
Ito, M. 956
Ivaiti, H. 687, 699
Iwashita, N. 639
Izawa, Eiko 919, **945–58**

Jackson, G. B. 1083, 1093
Jackson, P. W. 1198, 1206
Jackson, R. 204, 215
Jacobs, G. M. 55, 56, 591, 596
Jain, Sharada **279–90**
Jakwerth, P. 1106
Jamaluddin, W. 1061
James, – 1036
James, D. 713, 1219
James, W. 96, 105, 1039
Jamison, D. T. 328, 333
Jangira, N. K. 207–8, 214
Järvelä, S. 508
Jay, A. 98, 106
Jayaram, N. 1216, 1219
Jayaweera, S. 1215, 1216, 1219
Jehng, J. C. J. 515, 524
Jelas, Z. M. 210, 214
Jenkins, E. 620, 621, 625, 626, 627
Jensen, B. B. 580, 583
Jiang, M. 1051, 1061
Jiguang, B. 1149

Jilani, A. A. 336, 344, 347
Jimenez, E. 39, 41
Jin, K. 635, 640
Jin, L. 450, 454, 743, 745, 753, 990, 994, 996, 999
Jin, Y. S. 382, 392
Jitjang, A. 1299
Jiyono 101, 106, 118, 120
Jiyono, S. A. 1062
Johanson, R. K. 1051–2, 1061
Johnson, A. 551, 553
Johnson, A. W. 936, 937–8, 944
Johnson, M. B. 372, 376, 551
Johnson, R. 860, 866
Johnson, R. C. 386, 392
Johnson, T. 1149
Johnston, S. 1288, 1299
Johnstone, B. D. 1218, 1219
Jones, A. 626
Jones, A. M. E. 336, 338, 340, 341, 342, 347
Jones, B. F. 490, 493
Jones, D. P. 258, 267
Jones, G. 219, 220, 221, 222, 224, 229
Jones, K. 211, 215, 429, 439
Jones, R. 353, 362
Jöreskog, K. G. 939, 943
Jorgenson, D. W. 943, 944
Josephs, J. 1068, 1072, 1075
Joshi, M. M. 850, 852
Junger-Tas, J. 439
Juran, J. M. 945, 957
Juvonen, T. 425, 438

Kachru, B. B. 633, 640
Kaestle, C. F. 1085, 1093
Kaew Dang, Rung **1167–79**
Kai, Y. Y. 449, 454
Kaiser, G. 605, 613
Kallaghan, T. 120
Kamens, D. H. 120, 557, 558, 565, 567
Kamens, J. 1105
Kamil, M. L. 597
Kan, S. 500, 507
Kanaev, A. 254, 255, 563, 565, 567
Kane, T. 721, 728
Kanes, C. 493–4
Kang, S. J. 466, 471, 474
Kanjani, J. 101, 106
Kant, Immanuel 1332
Kantamara, P. 976, 977, 985, 1002, 1003, 1006, 1009, 1013
Kaplan, A. 500, 507
Kapperman, G. 211, 215
Karimov, Islam 248, 251
Karmel, P. 310, 320, 1173, 1179
Kasenda, S. 1212, 1219
Kashiwagi, K. 1120, 1121
Kawanaka, T. 1120, 1122
Kearins, J. 369, 371–2, 376
Kearney, G. E. 370, 376
Keeves, John P. xii–xxv, 55, 56, 97, 98, 106, **107–21**, 112, 120, **123–40**, **257–68**, 258, 264, 267, **305–20**, 353, 362, 363, 386, 392, 455, 468, 473, 517, 524, 758, 766, 839, 852, 1076, 1114, 1121, 1167, **1167–79**, 1178, 1179, **1193–1206**, 1262, 1267, **1331–45**
Keital, C. 554
Keith, M. L. 1251, 1256
Kellaghan, T. 805, 806
Keller, R. 211, 215
Kelley-Laine, K. 1063, 1075
Kelly, D. L. 590, 595, 605, 612, 613, 1121, 1122, 1255
Kelly, G. P. 557, 566
Kelly, M. 596
Kember, D. 444, 455, 991, 993, 999
Kemelfield, G. 595
Kemmis, S. 541, 554
Kemp, D. 833, 837
Kemp, M. 487, 492
Kenkyuujo, K. K. 949, 957
Kennedy, Kerry J. **217–30**, 225, 229, 362, 558, 567, 738–9, **867–81**, 880
Kenny, K. S. 1170, 1171, 1179
Kenny, M. 613
Kenway, J. 1071, 1075
Kenyon, R. 728
Kerr, D. 558, 567
Kerstin, N. 1122
Khan, A. R. 824, 825
Khan, G. R. 289, 290
Khan, Qamar Uddin 666, 671
Khander, S. R. 806
Khaniya, T. 159, 169
Khaparde, M. S. **1301–13**
Khine, M. S. 465, 468, 473, 474, 1290, 1299
Kholi, T. 203, 214
Khoo, H. S. 465, 467, 474
Kida, Hiroshi 126, 140
Kidd, J. R. 866
Kidston, P. 588, 596
Kiers, H. A. L. 411, 423
Kiesler, S. B. 1198, 1206
Kilpatrick, J. 554
Kilpatrick, S. 325, 331, 332
Kim, A. N. 964, 967, 969, 971
Kim, Anna **1063–77**
Kim, G. J. 962, 971
Kim, H. 113, 120, 465, 466, 470, 474, 770, 779
Kim, H. S. 960, 964, 967, 969, 971, 1070, 1076
Kim, I. 432, 434, 438
Kim, M. 640
Kim, T. 432, 434, 438
Kim, U. 497, 498, 507, 1065, 1071, 1076
Kim, V. 444, 455
Kim, Y. 432, 434, 438
Kim, Y. C. 963, 971

Index of Names 1355

Kim, Y. H. 7, 10, 15, 916, 923–4, **959–71**, 961, 968
Kim Young Sam 1040
Kimko, D. D. 1088, 1093, 1098, 1105
King, H. W. 207, 215
King, K. 1093, 1094
Kioh Jeong 326, 333, 668, 671
Kiper, J. 1261, 1268
Kirby, J. 486, 492
Kirsch, I. 320
Kirsner, K. 493
Kirst, M. W. 8, 13, 918, 929
Kish, L. 1197, 1206
Kitamura, K. 764, 766
Kitayama, S. 357, 362
Klauer, K. C. 424
Kleiner, A. 1329
Klicka, C. J. 1065, 1076
Knight, B. 713
Knipprath, Heidi 919, **945–58, 1063–77**
Knoll, S. 1120, 1122
Ko, C. T. 1099, 1105
Ko, K. W. 950, 957
Ko, P. 791
Ko Peng Sim 587, 596
Kobayashi, V. N. 762, 766
Kogan, M. 105, 124, 140, 1082–3, 1085, 1089, 1093, 1182, 1191
Koike, K. 324, 333
Komolkiti, S. 846, 851
Kong, C. K. 500, 506
Konstantopoulos, S. 742, 753
Koo, Ramsay Ding-Yee 333, 917, 925, **1015–29**, 1024, 1025, 1028, 1029
Koroteyeva, V. 247, 252, 255
Kosonen, K. 335, 347
Koteka, F. 687, 699
Kounin, J. S. 744, 753
Kouzou, Y. 955, 958
Kowalski, T. J. 861, 866
Kraemer, J. 613
Krans, J. 936, 943
Krathwohl, D. R. 111, 120
Kruiswijk, J. 438
Ku, B. 432, 434, 438
Ku-Yu, H. S. Y. 193, 201
Kubasek, N. K. 1263, 1268
Kuhn, D. 377
Kumano, Y. 623, 626
Kunnunkal, T. V. 644, 652
Kurganskaia, V. 250, 251, 255
Kuruppu, L. 55, 56
Kutnick, P. 752
Kwak, B. S. 960, 971
Kwak, K. 432, 435, 438
Kwan, T. 791
Kwan-Terry, A. 788, 791
Kwiek, M. 1209, 1219
Kwok, Y. 50, 56
Kwon, J. 432, 438
Kwong, J. 1017, 1018, 1028

Lai, K. C. 950, 957
Lai, S. 500, 508
Lakatos, I. 604, 613
Lake, J. 902, 911
Lakomski, G. 1139, 1149
Laksana, S. 648, 652
Lakshmi, T. K. S. 1139, 1150
Lam, A. G. 515, 523, 861, 862, 866
Lam, J. 1001, 1007–8, 1013
Lamb, S. 61, 71, 264, 267, 717, 729
lampel, J. 671
Landbeck, R. 444, 449, 455
Lang, Y. 627
Langeheine, R. 423, 424
Langer, J. A. 806
Langley, J. 965, 971
Lankshear, C. 895, 896
Lao, R. C. 496, 506, 1174
Lapointe, A. E. 1110, 1114, 1122
Lapp, D. 594
Larkin, A. 1259, 1262, 1267, 1268
Laskey, L. 941, 942
Laslett, R. 784, 791
Lasnik, H. 1267
Lau, K. L. 498, 507
Lau, P. 338, 347
Lau, S. P. 1025, 1027, 1028
Laughlin, J. E. 414, 419, 423
Lave, J. 603, 613
LaVine, R. A. 372, 377
Law, S. S. 330, 333
Lawson, M. J. 308, 320, 358–9, 386, 392, **511–24**, 517, 518, 524
Lawton, D. 1222, 1229
Lazimy, Y. 1265, 1268
Le Heron, J. 1266, 1268
Le Tendre, G. K. 47, 56
Le Thac Can 314, 319, 1061
Le Van Tac 212, 215
Leach, J. 626
Lean, G. 609, 613
Leask, M. 918, 929
Leavitt, H. B. 884, 896
Lebra, T. S. 770, 779
Ledbetter, C. 472, 473
Lee, A. 330, 333
Lee, C. 432, 435, 438, 509, 677, 685, 788, 791
Lee, C. J. 771, 779, 1040, 1041, 1045
Lee, C. K.-E. 745, 753
Lee, D. Y. 44, 55
Lee, F. M. F. 888, 896
Lee, H. 432, 438, 832, 837
Lee In-Hyo 919, **945–58**
Lee, J. C. K. 1099, 1105
Lee, J. W. 842, 843, 851
Lee, K. 756, 758, 759, 760, 763, 766
Lee, K. C. 544, 545, 551, 554
Lee, K. H. 1210, 1219
Lee, K. T. 1259, 1260, 1268
Lee, K.-W. L. 521, 522, 524
Lee, M. 1102, 1105
Lee, M. H. 968, 969, 971, 1318, 1328
Lee, M. N. N. 6, 7, 10, 15, 834, 837, 909, 911, **1207–20**
Lee, M. O. C. 518, 524
Lee, N. 482, 491
Lee, S. 46, 56, 760, 763, 766, 1218
Lee, S. S. U. 465, 470, 474
Lee S-Y. 588, 596, 991, 992, 993, 1000
Lee, W. 640
Lee, Wing On 144, 154, 260, 267, 333, 559, 567, 644, 652, 956, 958, 1028, 1105
Lee, Y.-H. 332
Lefrere, P. 1266, 1269
Leggett, E. L. 498, 506
Lehmann, R. 1119, 1122
Leibniz, G. W. 1332
Leicester, M. 439
Leithwood, K. 929, 985, 1328
Leitz, P. 1120, 1122
Lenahan, Robert 29, **29–42**
Lendon, R. J. 371, 377
Lene, Perive Tanuvasa 687, **687–99**, 699
Lenour, N. 407
Leong, L. T. 1061
Leong, Y. C. 761, 765
Lerner, R. M. 377
Lester, F. K. Jr. 481, 492
LeTendre, G. K. 209, 215, 1097, 1105
Leung, F. K. S. 554
Leung, J. Y. M. 905, 911
Leung, K. 497, 507
Levack, A. 289, 290
Levinson, D. 390, 392
Levy, A. 1323, 1328
Levy, J. 464, 471, 475
Lewin, K. M. 707, 713, 896, 1211, 1213, 1214, 1217, 1219
Lewis, C. C. 1247, 1256
Lewis, D. C. 454
Lewis, P. E. T. 325, 327, 333, 451, 1247
Leyser, Y. 211, 215
Li, A. K. F. 496, 507
Li, B. 46, 57, 1101, 1105
Li, C. 950, 957
Li, G. Q. 1017, 1028
Li, H. 428, 438
Li, K. D. 526, 536
Li, P. 428, 438
Li, W. C. 1002, 1013
Li, Yining 106
Liang, J. 488–9, 492
Liang, W. H. 496, 502, 509
Lieberman, A. 782, 791, 915, 929
Light, P. 753
Lijima, K. 682, 685
Likert, R. 352, 409, 412, 422, 423
Lillis, K. 675, 685

1356 Index of Names

Lim Cher Ping **899–911**
Lim, H. K. 1061
Lim, L. 211, 212, 215, 454
Lim, T. K. 190, 193, 201
Lim, T.-S. 393
Limoges, C. 1093
Lin, F. L. 1262, 1267
Lin, J. 980–2, 985, 1018, 1028
Lin, L. 1089, 1093
Lin, T. 333
Lin, W. Y. 446, 457
Lin, Y. 428, 438
Lindenberger, U. 381, 385, 391, 392
Lingens, H. G. 1179
Link, J. 943
Linkson, M. 622, 626
Linnenbrink, L. 508
Lipton, – 217, 229
Little, A. 1229
Little, J. W. 772, 779
Lituanas, P. 55, 56, 590–1, 596
Liu, C. 1212, 1219
Liu, D. 508
Liu, G. 243, 247, 255
Liu, Y. 429, 438
Liu, Z. P. 194, 201
Llewellyn, G. E. J. 1069, 1076
Lloyd, S. 10, 15, 594
Lo Bianco, J. 630, 640
Lo, M. 791
Lo, N. L. 769, 779
Lockheed, M. E. 39, 41, 174, 188, 1087, 1093
Loewenstein, M. 721, 729
Logan, L. 493, 1075
Long, Michael 54, 56, **715–30**, 717, 719, 720, 721, 729
Loo, S. 622, 626
Looi, C. K. 904, 911
Lopez, L. E. 401, 407
Loreman, T. J. 205, 215
Lou, Y. 745, 753
Louden, W. 594, 596, 627
Louis, K. S. 929
Lourdusamy, A. 897, 1264, 1268
Lovat, T. J. 889, 896
Lovitt, C. 897
Low, G. T. 1002, 1006–7, 1010, 1012, 1013
Low, L. 326, 332, 333
Low, S. H. 330, 333
Lowrie, T. 489, 492
Loxley, William A. 681, 686, 1091, **1151–64**, 1164
Lu, G. Q. 1016, 1017, 1018, 1028
Lubbers, – 322
Lucardie, D. 860, 866
Lucas, T. 1329
Luce-Kapler, R. 609, 613
Luke, A. 352, 585, 596
Lumelume, S. 595
Lumley, T. 633, 639
Lummis, J. M. 1071, 1076
Luna, E. 605, 613

Lundgren, U. P. 541, 554
Luo, Guanzhong 352, **409–24**, 414, 417, 418, 423
Luo, X. 1098, 1105
Luszcz, M. 386, 388, 392
Lynn, J. 98, 106
Lyon, P. E. 189, 201
Lyons, C. A. 592, 596
Lysaght, K. 438
Ma, Hing Tong 29, **29–42**, 324, 333, 429, 1029
Ma, K. H. 455
Ma Lang 425, **425–39**, 438
Ma Rhea, Z. 648, 652, 1226, 1230
McAdams, R. P. 992, 1000
MacBeath, John 733, 734, **767–80**, 768, 771, 777, 779, 780
MacCallum, J. 504, 507
McCary, M. 1001, 1010, 1013
McClelland, D. C. 495–6, 504, 507
McClure, J. 498, 507
McCombs, B. 478, 492
McCord, W. M. 505
McCormick, J. 503, 508
McDaniel, E. 517, 523
McDevitt, T. M. 498, 506
McDonald, M. 261, 268
McDonald, R. 728
McDonnell, L. 1136
McElwain, D. 370, 376
McGaw, B. 1140, 1146, 1149, 1182, 1191, 1198, 1203, 1204, 1206
McGillivary, K. 1261, 1268, 1269
McGinnes, E. 496, 507
McGregor, P. 1266, 1267
McGuckian, Peter **123–40**
Machida, S. 1262, 1268
McInerney, D. M. 500–1, 503, 505, 507, 509
McInerney, V. 501, 507
McIntyre, J. 35, 41, 728
McKague, M. 372, 376
McKay, P. 632, 640
McKenna, B. 745–6, 753
McKenzie, J. 1266, 1268
McKenzie, P. 1149
McKinley, E. 620, 622, 626
McKinnon, D. 454
McKinnon, G. E. 491
McKnight, C. C. 1106
McLaughlin, D. 1072, 1076
Maclean, Rupert 11, 13–14, **17–27**, **73–91**, 78, 91, **143–54**, **155–69**, 571, 583, 738, 739, 892, 895, 1144, 1145, 1146, 1149, **1181–91**, 1302, 1307, 1313, 1324, 1327
MacLeod, C. 493
McLoughlin, C. 1259, 1269
McMeniman, M. 1142, 1147, 1149

McMillan, J. 54, 56
McMullen, M. S. 1045, 1046
McMullen, P. 1241, 1242
McMurtrie, B. 70, 71
McMurtrie, J. 499, 506
McNamara, E. T. 1261, 1269
McNamara, Tim **629–40**, 640
McNaught, M. 595
McNaughton, S. 587, 596
McNay, M. 966, 971
McPartland, J. M. 959, 966, 971
Macpherson, R. J. S. 957
McPherson Waiti, P. 626
Macrae, S. 747, 752
McRobbie, C. 484–5, 493
Madaus, G. F. 111, 120
Madsen, D. 1288, 1299
Maehr, M. L. 500, 507, 508
Maercker, A. 392
Mager, R. F. 112, 120
Magindaan, C. 101, 106
Maglen, L. 729, 1051, 1061
Maher, J. 393
Maheshwari, A. N. 892, 896
Mahony, P. 542, 554
Majeed, A. 464, 474
Mak, G. C. L. 1210, 1212, 1219
Makarova, E. 247, 252, 255
Malen, B. 936, 943, 1106
Mallea, J. R. 1345
Malone, J. 627
Manasan, R. G. 1051, 1061
Mangubhai, F. 55, 56, 590, 595
Mani, R. 207, 215
Manset, G. 205, 206, 214
Mansfield, H. 493
Mansheng, Zhou **1193–1206**
Mao, C. J. 564, 567
Mao, L. R. 1019, 1029
Mao Ze-dong 563, 674
Mappa, S. 101, 106
Margianti, E. S. 465, 470, 474
Marginson, S. 1045 1041, 1043, 1211, 1219
Marimuthu, T. 1059, 1061
Marjoribanks, K. **43–57**, 49, 53, 54, 56, 120, 1071, 1076
Marks, G. N. 51, 54, 56
Markus, H. 357, 362, 372, 377
Marland, P. 887, 896
Maroske, M. 310, 320
Marsh, C. 1028
Marsh, H. W. 447, 455, 501, 507
Marshall, J. 1044, 1045
Martello, J. 487, 492
Martha, N. 535, 536
Martin, A. H. 1054, 1061
Martin, C. 743, 745, 748, 752, 753
Martin, M. O. 595, 833, 837, 1255
Martin, O. 605, 612, 613, 617, 626, 1115, 1121, 1122

Index of Names

Marton, F. 360, 361, 362, 442, 443, 455
Marx, Karl 1332
Marzano, R. 478, 492
Marzuki, S. 779
Masami, M. 961, 964, 971
Masia, B. B. 111, 120
Mason, J. 1266, 1269
Masters, Geoff N. 96, 106, 159, 169, 352, 353, 362, 594, 596, 736, **793–806**
Matane, P. 1072, 1076
Mathena, C. 1261, 1268
Matsuura, Koichiro 399
Maturana, H. 609, 613
Mau, R. 449, 454, 889, 896
Mauch, J. E. 1033, 1045, 1046
Maurer, H. 537
Maxwell, G. 437, 438
Maybery, M. 493
Mayer, V. 623, 626, 627
Mayor, F. 407
Mead, N. A. 1110, 1114, 1122
Meadows, S. 747, 753
Medin, D. L. 376
Medinnus, G. R. 386, 392
Meek, V. Lynn 737, **839–52**, 846, 852
Megarry, J. 255, 256, 258, 268
Mehan, H. 356, 363
Mehran, G. 1212–13, 1217, 1219
Meister, G. F. 597
Mel, Michael A. 919, **945–58, 1063–77**
Meng Hong Wei **107–21**, 119, 120, 121, 956, 1328
Menon, M. E. 836, 837
Menon, P. 862, 863, 866
Menon, R. 480, 494
Mercer, N. 479, 492
Merriam, S. B. 337, 338, 347
Meyer, J. W. 120, 557, 558, 565, 567, 1094, 1095, 1097, 1098, 1100, 1101, 1104, 1105, 1106, 1209, 1219
Miao, S. F. 1016, 1018, 1029
Michie, M. 622, 626
Middleton, J. 39, 41, 328, 332, 333, 659, 661, 662, 665, 667, 671, 682, 686, 1281, 1283
Milburn, G. 554
Miles, J. A. 353, 362
Miles, M. B. 940, 943
Milgram, R. M. 758, 766
Millar, R. 616, 618, 626, 627
Miller, J. L. 551, 554
Miller, P. 372, 377, 718, 729
Mills, M. 891, 896
Millwater, J. 472, 475, 897
Min, Wei-fang 683, 686, 1213, 1214, 1215, 1219
Ming, Weifang 106
Mingat, A. 36, 39, 41, 1211, 1219, 1280–1, 1283
Mintzberg, M. 657, 671
Mishra, G. 204, 214, 273

Mishra, R. C. 366, 376
Misson, S. 1149
Mitchell, D. **203–15**, 206, 209, 210, 215
Mitchell, I. 485, 490, 624, 627
Mitter, W. 254, 255
Mittler, P. 214
Miura, S. 315, 320
Mizoguchi, R. 529, 536
Moegiadi 101, 106, 1086, 1094, 1299
Moely, B. E. 455, 499, 508
Moffitt, J. E. 49, 55
Mogdil, C. 439
Mogdil, S. 439
Moghaddam, F. M. 63, 71
Mohamad, M. 337, 338, 347
Mohammed, Mahathir 6
Mohandas, Ramon **107–21**
Mok, A. 791
Mok, K. H. 831, 832, 837, 1012, 1102, 1105
Mok, Magdalena Mo Ching **915–29**, 916, 918, 919, 929, **945–58**, 1318, 1319, 1324, 1327, 1328
Molenda, M. 525, 536, 1268
Molnar, A. 746, 753
Monbusho 209, 215, 323, 333
Mong, H. W. 952, 957
Monkman, K. 1095, 1098, 1105, 1106
Monks, F. J. 201, 202
Montague, M. 478, 492
Montessori, M. 608
Moock, P. R. 328, 333
Moore, D. 437, 438, 590, 595, 596
Moore, M. 592, 597
Moore, P. J. 486, 492
Moos, R. H. 464, 474, 771, 780
Morgan, J. 1266, 1269
Moriarty, V. 748, 752, 753
Morita, Y. 425, 430, 431, 438, 439
Morris Matthews, K. 866
Morris, P. 566, 567, 770, 780, 787, 791, 883, 893, 896, 911, 1028, 1219, 1324, 1328
Morris, S. C. 372, 377, 1211–12
Morrison, K. 1024, 1029
Morrow, L. 613
Mortimore, P. 742, 743, 749, 752, 768, 779, 785, 791
Mosenthal, P. B. 597
Moskowitz, J. 890, 896
Mu, G. Z. 176, 188
Mu, X. 508
Mugler, F. 444, 449, 455
Mujanganja, Efison **701–14**
Mujue, Z. 1149
Mukherjee, H. 1061
Mukhopadhyay, M. 9, 15, 945, 958
Mulhauser, P. 595

Muljoatmodjo, S. 837
Muller, J. 899, 903, 911
Mullis, I. V. S. 595, 605, 612, 613, 626, 806, 1112, 1114, 1117, 1121, 1122, 1255
Mumford, L. 322, 333
Mummery, D. 671
Mundle, S. 681, 686
Munekata, T. 209, 215
Munroe, W. S. 111, 120
Murangi, K. 895
Murphy, J. 918, 929, 1001, 1013
Murray, H. A. 495, 507
Murray-Harvey, R. 455
Mussen, P. H. 490
Muta, H. 976, 979, 981, 985
Myers, C. A. 661, 671
Myers, K. 777, 780, 951, 957

Nabobo, Una 1225, 1229
Nabuka, J. 687, 699
Nagai, Y. 341, 347
Nagata, Yoshiyuki **641–53**
Nahaylo, B. 243, 255
Nair, V. K. K. 1263, 1269
Nakadome, T. 946, 958
Nakazawa, Y. 515, 523
Nam, S. S. 211, 212, 215
Nana, P. 1140, 1149
Nangia, P. 226, 229
Nannestad, C. 897
Nanzhao, Z. 1139, 1146, 1149
Narayan, D. 60, 71
Narayan, L. 341, 345, 347
Nash, R. 205, 214
Nation, I. S. P. 597
Nation, P. 591, 596
Naumann, J. 685
Neave, G. 109, 121
Nebres, B. F. 846, 852
Neemia, N. S. 687, 699
Neill, – 608
Nesdale, A. R. 486, 492, 493
Nesher, P. 608, 614
Neufeld, A. 215
Neugarten, B. 389, 390, 393
Newell, A. 513, 524
Newmann, F. 354, 363
Newson, J. 1045
Newton, Isaac 1332
Neyland, J. 604, 613
Ng, A. K. 761, 763, 766
Ng, Chi-Hung 355, 482–3, 492–3, **495–509**, 498, 500, 501, 503, 507
Ng, D. 498, 507
Ng, F. 791
Ng, H. M. 1017, 1029
Ng, K. H. 918, 929, 1318, 1319, 1322, 1323, 1328, 1329
Ng, M. 748, 751, 753
Ng, P. 615, 618, 626
Ng, S. F. 1210, 1219
Ng, S. H. 393
Ng, S. W. 1071, 1076

1358 Index of Names

Ng Seok Moi 55, 56, 587, 589, 596, 597
Ngok, L. 861, 862, 866
Ni, L. 496, 507
Nicholls, J. G. 497, 507
Nicholson, T. 588, 589, 591, 596, 597
Nicoll, W. 866
Nielsen, H. D. 1153, 1164, 1299, 1310, 1313
Nisbet, J. 1167, 1179
Nisbet, S. 255, 256
Niyozov, S. 248, 249, 253, 255
Njora, Hungi 1262, 1267, **1331–45**
Nkala, F. 454
Nkinyangi, J. 1190, 1191
Noah, H. 328, 333, 1345
Noble, A. 229
Noble, C. 728
Noesjirwan, J. 382, 393
Noh, T. H. 466, 471, 474
Nonglak, P. 101, 106
Noor Azmi, I. 892, 896
Norbeck, T. 505
Nordholm, L. A. 496, 507
Norris, D. M. 1266, 1269
North, B. 640
Northfield, J. 485, 490
Nothdurft, L. 482, 493
Nowotny, H. 1093
Nunnally, J. C. 445, 455
Nuthall, G. 485, 493
Nye, B. 742, 753
Nyerere, Julius 674

O' Donoghue, T. 1072, 1076
Oakes, J. 1136
Oanh Phan 332
O'Brien, A. M. 493
Ochiai, T. 209, 215
O'Connor, K. 626, 1122
O'Day, J. 1098, 1106
Ogawa, M. 617, 618–19, 620, 625–6, 627
Ogawa, N. 178, 188
Ogawa, R. T. 936, 943
Ogunmokun, G. O. 719, 729
Oh, L. W. 214
O'Higgins, N. 225, 229
Ohsako, T. 425, 438
Okamoto, Y. 515, 523
Okano, K. 52, 56
Olkin, I. 447, 454
Oller, J. 597
Olsen, N. J. 496, 507
Olssen, K. H. 897
Olssen, M. 866, 1044, 1045–6
Olweus, D. 425, 430, 431, 439
Oman, S. 1061
Omelich, C. L. 497, 505
Ordonez, Victor 1144, 1145, 1146, 1149, **1181–91**
O'Riordan, T. 583
Ornstein, A. C. 121
Orpen, C. 720, 729
Osborn, M. 791
Osborne, J. 627

Osborne, R. 603, 613, 616, 618–26, 627, 1035, 1046
Osherson, D. N. 1267
Osterman, P. 721, 729
Ota, H. 393
Outhred, L. 595
Owen, J. 1149
Owens, L. 427, 439

Packard, J. L. 595
Paige, R. M. 464, 474
Paik, S. J. 1049, 1059, 1061
Palakawongsa, Nai Nob 671
Palincsar, A. S. 479, 489, 490–1, 493, 514, 524
Palmer, A. 753
Palmer, Terry 919, **945–58**, **1063–77**
Pan, H. L. 770, 771, 780
Pandey, R. S. 207, 215
Pandey, S. 644, 645, 652
Pang, E. F. 1218
Pang, I Wah 917, 924, **1063–77**, 1067, 1071, 1075, 1076
Pang, N. S. K. 1003, 1013
Pang, S. K. 977, 985
Panizzolo, R. 719, 729
Papert, S. 535, 536
Parameter, L. 1098, 1105
Paris, S. G. 478, 487, 493, 597
Parish, W. L. 66, 67, 71
Park, D. K. 968, 971
Park, H. 432, 434, 438
Park, K. 432, 434, 439
Park, N. 1038, 1039, 1040, 1046
Park, Y. S. 497, 498, 507, 770, 779, 968–9, 970, 971, 1065, 1071, 1076
Parke, R. D. 392
Parker, J. G. 750, 753
Parmenter, T. 205, 214
Parnes, H. S. 657, 659, 661, 671
Parras, D. A. 343, 344, 348
Parry, O. 1288, 1299
Parry, S. 1140, 1149
Partridge, B. 250, 251, 255
Pascoe, S. 653
Passeron, J.-C. 59, 61, 71
Passow, A. H. 201, 202, 1335, 1345
Pate-Bain, H. 745–6, 753
Patel, S. J. 809, 825
Pateman, N. 493
Patrick, W. J. 945, 958
Patrinos, H. A. 333, 812, 825
Payutto, Prayudh 648
Pearson, M. 1288, 1299
Pearson, P. D. 597
Peddie, R. 855, 866
Pefianco, Erlinda **305–20**, 1262, 1269
Pell, A. 753
Pellegrino, J. W. 359, 363, 514, 520, 522, 524
Perkins, D. 768, 780

Perkins, P. G. 758, 766
Pernia, E. 334
Peters, M. 1044, 1045
Peterson, Candida C. 351, 372, 377, **379–93**, 390, 391, 393
Pfundt, H. 621, 627
Phaik-Choo Phuah 342, 343, 347
Pham, Q. S. 1055, 1061
Phelan, T. J. 132, 140, 1144, 1147, 1150, 1313
Philips, A. 1140, 1149
Phillips, G. 592, 596, 1110, 1114, 1122
Phillips, S. 372, 376
Phopruksawong, S. 1299
Phothisuk, U. 190, 192, 193, 201
Piaget, J. 308, 320, 358, 365, 366–7, 370, 371, 603
Pichert, J. W. 358, 362
Pickett, H. 373, 375, 376
Picot, B. 965, 971
Picus, L. 1136
Pierson, H. D. 393
Pillay, G. 326, 333
Pinar, W. F. 541, 551, 552, 554
Pinnell, G. S. 596
Pintor, R. L. 1336, 1345
Pintrich, P. 478, 493, 507, 508, 757, 766
Pischke, J. 721, 728
Pithers, B. 35, 41
Plewis, I. 792
Plomp, T. J. 1164
Pluck, M. L. 591, 593, 596
Poignant, R. 658, 660, 664, 671
Pok, T. 7, 15
Pol Pot 1213
Polestico, R. 713
Pollard, A. 785–6, 791
Pollitt, A. 632, 640
Polya, G. 603, 614
Pong, S.-L. 65, 66, 67, 71, 72
Poole, M. 1149
Poon-McBrayer, K. F. 205, 214
Poonwassie, A., 334, 671
Poonwassie, D. 334, 671
Pope, B. 324
Popper, K. R. 1194, 1206
Porras-Zuniga, J. 1125, 1136
Porter, P. 1043, 1046
Portes, A. 60, 71
Porteus, – 369–70
Post, D. 66, 72
Postiglione, G. 214, 845, 852, 956, 958, 1028, 1033, 1046, 1210, 1212, 1219
Postlethwaite, T. Neville 32, 41, **93–106**, 106, 188, 334, 353, 363, 788, 791, 1109, 1115, 1121, 1122, 1135, 1167
Poulsen, C. 745, 753

Powell, B. 938, 944
Power, Colin 351–63
Power, S. 941, 944
Pradhan, H. 345, 348
Prais, S. J. 742, 753
Prakash, S. 1032, 1046
Pratt, C. 367, 372, 376
Pravalpruk, K. 802, 806
Prazauskas, A. 246, 255
Pressick-Kilborn, K. 504, 507
Pressley, D. L. 491
Pressley, M. 478, 490
Preston, B. 902, 911
Price-Williams, D. 505
Print, M. 563, 567
Pritchard, A. 957
Pritchett, L. 1302, 1313
Prosser, M. 456
Provost, S. 455
Psacharopoulos, G. 663, 675–6, 681, 683, 686, 812, 825, 837, 1210, 1219
Pumwa, J. 833, 837
Punsalan, T. G. 647–8, 652–3
Purdie, N. 449, 453, 454, 455, 503, 508
Purves, A. C. 1119, 1121, 1122, 1178, 1179
Purwadi, A. 837, 1062
Putnam, R. D. 60, 68, 72
PuttI. 481, 490
Pye, W. 593, 596

Qi Dian Qiang 1252, 1256
Quah, M. L. 201, 211, 215, 788, 791
Quddus, M. 845, 852
Quek, C. L. 465, 474
Quine, W. V. 1206
Quisumbing, Lourdes R. 353, 395–407, 407, 647, 653

Ra, Y. S. 332
Radford, W. C. 134, 140, 1173, 1179
Rahim, T. 289, 290
Rahimah, H. A. 1001, 1013
Raina, V. K. 892, 896
Raizen, S. 1241, 1242
Rajput, J. S. 7, 15, 645, 653
Ralph, D. 874, 880
Ramanthan, R. 873, 880
Ramburuth, P. 503, 508
Ramirez, Francisco O. 7, 1088, 1091, 1094, 1095, 1095–1106, 1098, 1100, 1101, 1102, 1104, 1105, 1106
Ramsden, P. 442, 454, 455
Ramsey, P. D. K. 903, 911
Rana, P. B. 1053, 1061
Randall, E. V. 1086, 1094
Rao, I. 207, 215
Rao, N. 453, 455, 499, 502, 508
Rapley, P. 1299
Rasch, G. 412, 423
Rasher, S. P. 464, 475

Ratcliffe, M. 625, 627, 1253, 1256
Rattanavitch, S. 597
Rau, D. 329, 333
Raudenbush, S. W. 466, 473
Rauner, M. H. 560, 564, 567
Readings, B. 1209, 1219
Regmi, M. 445, 456, 509
Reid, J. 596
Reid, N. A. 594, 597
Reiko, Y. 1036, 1037, 1046
Rellinger, E. 478, 490
Renandya, W. A. 55, 56, 596
Rennie, L. 618, 619, 626, 627, 1243, 1255, 1287, 1299
Renshaw, Peter D. 351–63, 355, 363, 451, 479, 481, 492, 493, 495–509, 500, 501, 502–3, 504, 507, 508
Renzulli, J. S. 191, 201
Resnick, L. R. 491
Reyner, C. 338, 341, 344, 345, 348
Reynold, D. 733, 740
Reynolds, D. 786, 791, 993, 995, 996, 1000
Reynolds, W. M. 541, 554
Rhydwen, M. 594
Riah, H. 465, 468, 474
Rice, J. K. 747, 753
Richardson, J. T. E. 446, 455
Rickards, T. W. 468, 473
Ricketts, – 590
Ridoutt, L. 719, 729
Rigby, K. 425, 426, 427, 439
Riley, R. W. 215
Ritchie, J. 586, 597
Ritzen, J. M. 667–8, 671
Rivalland, J. 594, 596
Roberts, J. S. 414, 419, 423
Roberts, L. 1259, 1263, 1269
Roberts, P. 585, 597, 728
Robertson, S. 855, 866
Robinson, B. 335, 342, 343, 344, 348
Robinson, C. 724, 728, 729
Robinson, J. 65, 72
Robinson, P. 188
Robinson-Pant, A. 69, 72
Robitaille, D. F. 1112, 1122
Roche, L. A. 501, 507
Rodd, J. 1071, 1076
Roesgaard, M. 1100, 1105
Rogers, – 608
Rogers, G. 1258, 1269
Rogers, M. 719, 729
Rohl, M. 594
Rokicka, W. 1149
Rong, X. L. 338, 339, 343, 344, 348
Rorris, A. 1051, 1061
Rosch, E. 609, 614
Rosenblum, T. 44, 55
Rosenshine, B. 784, 785, 791
Rosier, M. J. 353, 363
Ross, K. N. 101, 1109, 1121
Rost, J. 423, 424

Rouse, B. 1268
Rowe, H. 511, 524
Rowe, K. J. 749, 753, 951, 958
Roy, O. 243, 244, 245, 246, 255
Roy-Singh, Raja 125
Rudduck, G. 787, 791
Rumberger, R. W. 45, 56
Rumble, G. 851, 1280, 1283
Rung, K. 7, 15
Russell, D. 447, 455
Russell, J. 1268
Russell, J. D. 525, 536
Russell, N. U. 1059, 1062
Russell, T. 624, 627
Ryan, D. 790, 1104
Ryan, E. B. 382, 392, 393
Ryan, R. 710, 720, 729
Rychen, D. S. 311, 320

Sachs, J. 455, 493, 499, 508, 902, 911, 1075
Sackney, L. E. 915, 929, 1323, 1329
Sacks, – 769
Sadak, J. 1149
Saga, Kabini 1226, 1229
Saha, Lawrence J. 55, 59–72, 71, 1081, 1085, 1091, 1092, 1093, 1123–36, 1182, 1191, 1207, 1220, 1288, 1299, 1334, 1345
Saihioo, P. 1299
Saini, A. 339, 348
Sainsbury, M. 595
Sakamoto, H. 955, 958
Sakamoto, T. 591, 597
Sako, M. 315, 320
Sako, T. 464, 473
Sakya, T. M. 184, 188, 339, 348
Salganik, L. H. 311, 320
Salili, F. 454, 497, 498, 500, 502, 506, 508, 515, 524, 990, 1000
Salisbury-Glennon, J. D. 513, 523
Säljö, R. 442, 455
Salleh, N. M. 1061
Salmi, J. 825
Samejima, F. 418, 423
Sammons, P. 791
San, G. 329, 333
Sandler, H. M. 758, 766
Santos, L. O. 895
Sanyal, B. 667, 833, 837
Sapianchai, P. 1295, 1299
Saragi, T. 591, 597
Sari, H 215
Sato, H. 956
Sato, M. 903, 911
Satter, M. A. 833, 837
Satterthwait, D. 891, 896
Saunders, L. 945, 958
Saunders, S. 669, 670, 671
Sawada, D. 520, 521, 524
Sawada, T. 762, 766
Saxby, – 588, 597

Scarino, A. 632, 640
Scarpetta, S. 1033, 1045
Scevak, J. J. 505
Schaie, K. W. 380, 392
Schallert, D. 790
Scharff, E. 1263, 1268
Schleicher, A. 119, 121, 1120, 1121
Schmeck, R. 446, 455
Schmidt, W. H. 617, 626, 1098, 1105
Schnack, K. 580, 583
Schneider, B. 60, 72
Schoenfeld, A. 478, 479, 480, 493
Schofer, E. 1081, 1092, 1094, 1095, 1098, 1100, 1105, 1106
Schofield, K. 724, 727, 729
Schön, D. 606, 614
Schoppa, L. 1100, 1106
Schroeder, W. L. 861, 866
Schultz, T. W. 809, 825
Schunk, D. H. 513, 524
Schwartz, S. 1149
Schwartzman, S. 1093
Schwille, J. 567
Scoll, B. W. 943
Scott, M. 866
Scott, P. 1093
Scott, R. 465, 470, 474
Scott, R. H. 1290, 1299
Se-Ho Shin 316, 320
Seagrim, G. N. 371, 377
Sedwal, M. 157, 169
Seetharam, K. 220, 221, 229
Segal, G. 895
Segerstrom, J. 681, 683, 684, 685
Segumpan, R. G. 1264, 1269
Selby Smith, C. 333, 669, 671, **715–30**, 719, 729, 730, 1146, 1150
Selvaratnam, V. 441, 453, 1055, 1062, 1218, 1219, 1220
Sen, A. 229, 651, 653, 1340, 1345
Seng, Q. K. 449, 454
Senge, P. 1329
Senturk, D. 515, 523
Seo, J. H. 967, 971
Sereyrath, S. 7, 15
Serpell, R. 1222, 1229
Serrano, A. 1120, 1122
Setijadi 1290, 1291, 1299
Sgro, P. 720, 728
Shaeffer, S. 1190, 1191
Shahid,Y. 702, 713
Shamsher, A. K. 851
Shan, Wen-Jing 7, 15, 919, **945–58**
Shao, J. R. 1016, 1029
Shapiro, B. 790, 1104
Shapson, S. M. 750, 753
Sharma, A. 207, 213, 759
Sharma, J. R. 1061

Sharma, U. 208, 215
Sharma, Y. 766
Sharp, S. 425, 439
Sharpe, I. 7, 15
Sharpe, L. 791, 908, 911
Sharpe, P. 790, 791
Shaughnessy, M. F. 515, 524
Shavelson, R. 100, 106, 1084, 1092, 1094, 1124, 1136, 1182, 1191
Shavit, Y. 1101, 1104
Shaw, M. E. 419, 423
Shaw, R. N. 729
Shayer, M. 309, 320
Shek, D. T. L. 201
Sheldon, S. 753
Shen, L. 429, 438
Shen, S. M. 1066, 1071, 1076
Shen, W. J. 976, 985
Shi, K. 500, 502, 508
Shi, T. 338, 339, 343, 344, 348
Shi Yuntal 643, 653
Shimada, S. 547, 554, 603, 612
Shimahara, N. 873, 880
Shimizu, H. 209, 210, 215
Shimizu, K. 956
Shimura, M. 529, 533, 536
Shinawatra, Thaksin 1246
Shiozawa, K. 1035, 1037, 1046
Shipman, N. 1001, 1013
Shkolnik, J. L. 746–7, 752
Shrestha, Mona **335–48**, 336, 348
Shu, – 591
Shuard, – 604
Shulman, L. S. 1253, 1256
Shute, R. 427, 439
Shweder, R. A. 372, 373, 377
Siddique, S. 1210, 1217, 1218
Siegal, M. 372, 377
Sieger, A. W. 596
Siegler, R. S. 368, 369, 377
Silva, P. A. 49, 55
Silvestri, P. 825
Sim, C. 1149
Sim, Hee-og 425, **425–39**, 439, 1248
Sim Wong-Kooi 136, 738, 739, 883, **883–97**, 885, 888, 889, 896, 1256, 1290, 1291, 1293, 1299
Simon, B. 781, 791
Simon, H. A. 358, 362, 513, 524
Simon, P. 750, 753
Sin Kuen-Fung 189, **189–202**, 201
Sinclair, B. J. 472, 473
Sinclair, K. E. 500, 501, 508
Singh, A. 207, 208, 214
Singh, G. 55, 56, 590, 595, 597
Singh, J. S. 1061, 1218
Singh, Madhu 333
Singh, R. 215, 464, 475
Singh, R. R. 172, 174, 188, 1178, 1237, 1242, 1302, 1313

Siniscalco, M. T. 270, 277
Sinnott, J. D. 386, 393
Sisavanh, K. 7, 15
Sison, R. 529, 533, 536
Siu Ping-kee 1028
Skeldon, R. 219, 221, 229
Skemp, R. 604, 614
Slade, Malcolm **257–68**, 264, 265, 266, 268
Slattery, P. 541, 554
Slavin, R. E. 447, 456
Slee, Phillip T. 352, 425, **425–39**, 426, 427, 439
Slengesol, I.-A. 708, 713
Sloper, D. 1055, 1061
Smaldino, S. 1268
Smart, D. 957
Smart, J. C. 1220
Smith, A. 728, 729
Smith, B. 860, 866, 1329
Smith, C. 784, 791
Smith, Ian David 456, 734, 735, 739, **755–66**
Smith, J. 310, 320, 384, 388, 391, 392, 393
Smith, J. W. A. 587, 593, 597
Smith, L. 500, 501, 508
Smith, M. L. 746, 753
Smith, M. S. 936, 943, 1098, 1106
Smith, P. 425, 439, 592, 596
Smith, R. M. 866
Smith, S. N. 451, 456
Smith, T. 605, 612, 613, 626, 1121, 1122, 1255
Smolicz, J. J. 248, 256
Smyth, J. 264, 268, 580, 583, 941, 943
Snyder, I. 895, 896
So, W. M. W. 1250, 1255
Soekamto, T. 1299
Soerjaningsih, W. 465, 470, 474
Soh, K. C. 887, 891, 896
Sohn, H. 432, 434, 439
Sokolovski, S. 246, 256
Somera, L. B. 393
Son, B. 521, 524
Son, S. N. 466, 474
Song, H. 432, 434, 439
Soo Hoo, S. 778, 780
Sörbom, D. 939, 943
Sorensen, C. W. 1071, 1076
Soydhurum, P. 1245, 1256
Spear, R. H. 1288, 1299
Spearritt, Donald 308, 320, 1091, **1107–22**, 1109, 1121
Spedding, S. F. 486, 493
Speelman, C. 493
Spence, J. C. 745, 753
Spinks, J. A. 201
Spinks, J. M. 918, 929, 932, 933, 937, 941, 942, 948, 956
Spletzer, J. 721, 729
Spreadbury, J. 1071, 1077
Spring, G. 944
Sriboonma, U. 976, 985

Index of Names

Srinivasan, A. 208, 214, **231–40**
Srivastava, Ashok K. **1301–13**
Stacey, K. 604, 613
Stalin, Josef 243, 244–5
Stanley, E. C. 945, 958
Stanley, G. 874, 880, 945
Stanton-Salazar, R. D. 50, 56
Staudinger, U. M. 379, 381, 384, 385, 386, 390, 391, 392
Staunton, M. 748, 753
Steelman, L. C. 938, 944
Steffe, L. 608, 614
Stein, B. S. 513, 523
Stein, R. 341, 348
Steiner, – 608
Stenhouse, L. 546, 554
Stephens, M. 890, 896
Sternberg, R. J. 50, 55, 56, 191, 195, 201, 363, 456, 768, 780
Stevenson, H. W. 63, 72, 355, 356, 363, 449, 456, 591–2, 596, 597, 758, 760, 763, 766, 786, 792, 988, 989, 990, 991, 992, 993, 995, 996, 998, 1000, 1065, 1071, 1077, 1098, 1106, 1120, 1122
Stevenson, J. 1149
Stigler, J. W. 63, 72, 355, 356, 363, 449, 456, 518–19, 520, 524, 546, 554, 591, 596, 597, 758, 760, 766, 786, 792, 988, 989, 990, 991, 993, 995, 996, 997, 998, 1000, 1065, 1071, 1077, 1097, 1098, 1106, 1120, 1122
Stiglitz, J. E. 702, 713
Stokes, S. 1066, 1069, 1075
Stoll, L. D. 791
Stott, K. 888, 896, 975, 978, 982, 984, 1002, 1006–7, 1010, 1012
Stow, H. 634, 640
Stromquist, N. 271, 273, 277, 1095, 1098, 1105, 1106
Stuart, J. S. 896
Sturman, A. 264, 268
Styles, I. M. 417, 423
Sucuoglu, B. 212, 214
Sugano, Y. 366, 377
Suk-Yong, W. 769, 772, 779
Sukarman, S. 1061
Suksmo, A. 1299
Sullivan, A. V. 9, 15
Sullivan, C. 589, 596
Sullivan, Keith 425, **425–39**, 436, 437, 439
Sully, – 1170
Sumara, D. 609, 611–12, 613
Sumida, M. 1067, 1071, 1077
Summers, A. A. 936–7, 944
Summers, L. H. 296, 304
Sun Tsu 657
Sun Yat-sen 563
Sung, I. 1262, 1269
Sung, J. 713, 1039, 1045, 1219

Suppes, P. C. 1201, 1206
Suryadi, Ace 101, 106
Sutaria, M. 1294, 1299
Sutherland, C. M. 437
Suzuki, H. 536
Suzuki, L. 357, 362
Suzuki, N. 1262, 1269
Suzuki, S. 7, 11, 15
Swaroop, S. 207, 208, 215
Sweet, R. 728, 1236, 1242
Sweeting, A. 770, 780
Sweller, J. 309, 320, 516, 524
Sykes, – 576, 582, 584

Tachiki, D. S. 682, 685
Taguchi, M. 366, 377
Takahashi, M. 380, 384, 385, 393
Takahashi, T. 530, 536
Takai, T. 215
Taki, Mitsura 425, **425–39**, 430, 431, 432, 439
Takuma, S. 209, 215
Tam Tim-kui, Peter 1028
Tam, W. M. 1071, 1077
Tan, A. L. 888, 896
Tan, E. 502, 505
Tan, J. 791, 909, 911
Tan, J. L. H. 707, 713, 740
Tan, K. S. 1259, 1269
Tan, L. L. 521, 524
Tanaka, N. 1262, 1269
Tang, C. 360, 362, 515, 524
Tang, F. H. 1024, 1029
Tang, K. C. 1024, 1029
Tang, M. S. 498, 506
Tang, X. 7, 8, 10, 15–16, 975, 979, 985
Tao, V. 500, 502, 508
Taplin, J. E. 372, 377
Tar, P. 204, 215
Taras, R. 255, 256
Tasker, R. 621, 627
Tate, G. 590, 597
Taubman, P. M. 541, 554
Taufe'ulungaki, Ana 1225, 1229–30
Tay-Koay, S. L. 734, 740, 773, 774, 776, 780
Taylor, H. 1261, 1269
Taylor, I. 626
Taylor, J. A. 454
Taylor, M. 321, 322, 334
Taylor, N. 1230
Taylor, P. 1299
Taylor, P. C. 469, 471, 473, 474
Taylor, W. 791
Taylor, William 136
Teasdale, G. R. 405, 407, **641–53**, 649, 652, 653, 893, 896–7, 1220, 1226, 1230
Teasdale, J. 405, 407, 649, 653, 1217, 1225, 1230
Teh, G. 51, 57, 465, 467, 474
Teicher, J. 720, 730
Teichler, U. 841, 852, 1149

Teo, C. H. 1249, 1256, 1294, 1299
Teo, C. T. 201, 877, 880
Teo, E. K. 763, 766
Teo, G. 500, 502, 505
Teruhisa, H. 1071, 1075, 1077
Teschner, W. 334
Thaman, Konai Helu **1221–30**, 1222, 1223, 1230
Thant, M. 825
Thapa, B. K. 1061
Tharp, R. 747, 753
Therborn, G. 1095, 1106
Thomas, Elwyn 911
Thomas, G. 484–5, 493, 1095, 1105
Thomas, R. M. 325, 332, 1051, 1061
Thomas, T. A. 456
Thompson, A. 518, 524
Thompson, E. 609, 614
Thompson, F. 61, 71
Thompson, G. B. 596, 597
Thong, L. K. 1061
Thongutai, U. 1299
Thorndike, E. L. 112, 121, 124
Thorndike, R. L. 589, 597, 1117, 1122
Thorp, H. 472, 474
Thurstone, L. L. 352, 409, 412, 419, 422, 423
Tienjun, Z. 1149
Tik, C. Y. 9, 16
Tilak, Jandhyala B. G. 172, 188, **673–86**, 682, 683, 686, 737, **809–26**, 812, 813, 820, 824, 825, 826, 832, 834, 837
Tilbury, D. 583, 1099
Tisher, R. P. 884, 890, 896, 897
Tizard, B. 785, 792
Tjeldvoll, A. 1167, 1168, 1179
Tobin, K. G. 53, 57, 470, 473, 474–5
Todeschini, M. 825
Toh, K. 621, 623, 624, 627
Toh, Kok-Aun **1243–56**
Toktomyshev, S. 252, 256
Tomlinson-Keasey, C. 392
Tomoda, Y. 567
Tong, A. 791
Torney-Purta, J. V. 558, 563, 567
Torres, N. 1095, 1104
Townsend, T. 3, 4, 5, 7, 10, 11, 14, 16, 779, 915, 929, 945, 953, 955, 957, 974, 984, 985, 1001, 1012, 1064, 1071, 1077, 1315, 1322–3, 1324, 1328, 1329
Toyokazu, U. 1071, 1075, 1077
Treiman, D. J. 46, 57
Triandis, H. C. 444, 455, 456
Trickett, E. J. 464, 474
Trigwell, K. 456
Trompenaars, L. 770, 779
Trow, M. 1093, 1167, 1179

Index of Names

Troy, D. 1268
Truran, J. 492
Truran, K. 492
Tsai, C. 621, 622, 623, 627
Tsang, C. L. J. 1250, 1255
Tsang, E. W. K. 502, 508
Tsang, M. C. 683, 686
Tse, Thomas Kwan-Choi **555–68**, 556, 557, 561, 563, 567, 946, 958
Tseng, A. S. 1020, 1029
Tsoi, Y. S. 1076
Tsuchida, M. 536, 1247, 1256
Tsui, K. 880, 895, 1327, 1328
Tuck, B. 499, 505, 596
Tuijnman, A. 124, 140, 307, 320, 952, 957, 1032, 1034, 1046, **1081–94**, 1082–3, 1084, 1089, 1091, 1093, **1123–36**, 1124, 1127, 1135, 1136, 1335, 1345
Tung, Y. W. 528, 536
Tunmer, W. E. 486, 492, 493, 589, 592, 595, 597
Tupuola, Anne-Marie 1225, 1230
Turay, A. 991, 1000
Turner, C. M. 746, 753
Turner, J. H. 1169–70, 1179
Turney, C. 738, 740, 886, 889, 897
Tuss, P. 498, 508
Tyler, R. W. 111–12, 121

Ullian, J. S. 1206
Unsworth, L. 597
Unterhalter, E. 338, 340, 341, 343, 348
Ushiogi, M. 766
Uzundemir, E. 212, 215

Van Adams, A. 39, 41, 333, 659, 661, 662, 665, 667, 671, 1283
van der Gaag, J. 328, 333
Van Etten, S. 503, 505, 507, 509
van Gramberg, B. 720, 730
van Kraayenoord, Christine **477–94**, 478, 487, 488, 493, 588, 594, 597
Van Schuur, W. H. 410, 411, 423, 424
Vandycke, N. 248, 256
VanSickle, R. L. 521, 524
Varela, F. 609, 613, 614
Varghese, N. V. 158, 169, 708, 714, 737, **827–38**, 832, 836, 837, 838
Varma, K. 229
Varma, V. 1288, 1299
Vedder, P. 1164
Veloo, P. 897
Venkataraman, M. 333
Venville, G. 624, 627
Verdisco, A. 1164
Verhelst, N. D. 413, 424

Verspoor, A. M. 174, 188, 823, 825, 826
Vestralen, H. H. F. M. 413, 424
Viboonlak, T. 101, 106
Vidovich, L. 1043, 1046
Vine, Ken **17–27**, **155–69**
Visaria, P. 225, 229
Visscher, A. J. 946, 958
Volet, S. 355, 363, 451, 500, 502–3, 504, 508
von Clausewitz, – 657
von Glasersfeld, E. 603, 614
Vulliamy, G. 745, 753
Vygotsky, L. 358, 367–8, 373, 377, 479, 493, 603, 757, 766

Wade, B. 592, 597, 790
Wagemaker, H. 589, 597
Wagner, – 248
Wagner, A. 917, 926, **1031–46**, 1034, 1046
Wagner, D. A. 320
Wai, F. L. 527, 536
Waiyawudh, S. 648, 652
Walberg, H. J. 48, 49, 57, 464, 473, 475, 991, 999
Walder, A. G. 46, 57, 1101, 1105
Walia, K. 645, 653
Walker, Allan 916, 922, 955, 957, **973–85**, 980, 981, 984, 985, 987, 988, 998, 999, 1001, 1003, 1009, 1012, 1013
Walker, D. A. 1120, 1122
Walker, I. 1064, 1071, 1077
Walker, R. 504, 507, 597
Walkey, F. 498, 507
Wall, D. 791
Wallace, J. 616, 627
Waller, T. G. 491
Wallerstein, I. 1095, 1106
Wang, B. H. 1069, 1077
Wang, B. L. C. 1215, 1220
Wang, C. P. 515, 523
Wang, D. 496, 508
Wang, G. W. 1207, 1216, 1220
Wang, H. 617, 626
Wang, H. H. 976, 977, 978, 983, 984–5, 1002, 1012
Wang, J. 428, 429, 438, 627
Wang, J. D. 190, 191, 201
Wang, M. 429, 439
Wang, M. C. 48, 49, 57, 752
Wang, P. 500, 507, 508
Wang, W. 508, 624, 627
Wang, X. 952, 957
Wang, Y. 9, 16, 429, 439, 918, 929
Wang, Z. M. 1016, 1029
Ward, C. 594, 596
Ward, C. D. 496, 507
Ward, D. 1266, 1269
Ward, J. 205, 214
Warren, E. 493–4
Warry, R. 1149
Wasser, J. D. 1261, 1269

Watanabe, Ryo xii–xxv, **123–40**
Watkins, C. 769, 777, 780
Watkins, D. 355, 359, 360, 362, 363, 989, 990, 995, 996, 1000
Watkins, David N. **441–62**, 444, 445, 446, 447, 448, 450, 452, 454, 456, 457, 497, 498, 499, 500, 508, 509, 514, 523, 524, 876, 881, 993
Watkins, K. 17, 27
Watson, J. 603, 614, 892, 897
Watson, K. 1213, 1215, 1220
Webster, D. 218, 221, 230
Webster, E. 728
Wee, J. 940, 944
Wei, S. 429, 438
Weick, K. 1106
Weidman, J. C. 1038, 1039, 1040, 1046
Weiner, B. 496, 497, 509, 515
Weiss, C. 99, 106, 1085, 1094, 1169, 1179
Welch, W. W. 991, 999
Wellman, H. M. 493
Wenger, E. 603, 613
Wenglinsky, H. 1261, 1269
Wenling Li 595
Wey, S.-C. 488, 493
Wheldhall, K. 592, 593, 595, 597
Whipple, G. M. 121
White, G. 624, 627
White, M. 756, 764, 766
White, R. 603, 614, 621, 622, 624, 625, 627, 1144, 1150
White, V. 1071, 1075
Whitton, D. 760, 766
Whitty, G. 941, 944, 1022, 1029
Whyte, W. F. 1085, 1094
Wi-vun Taiffalo Chiung 314, 320
Wideen, M. F. 884, 896, 897
Widman, K. 392
Wijemanne, E. L. 680, 686
Wildavsky, A. B. 1032, 1046
Wiley, D. 788, 791, 1115, 1122
Wiley, T. N. 363, 783
Wilkinson, I. 588, 597
Wilks, D. R. 465, 471, 475
Williams, A. 382, 384, 393
Williams, H. 613
Williamson, J. 883, 893, 896, 902, 911
Willis, R. J. 66, 67, 71
Willoughby, J. O. 1265, 1269
Wills, D. 204, 215
Wilson, David N. **321–34**, 322, 323, 325, 326, 327, 328, 331, 334, **657–71**, 658, 664, 665, 666, 671
Wilson, J. 480, 493–4, 1149
Wilson, J. D. 82, 91
Wilson, Steve **335–48**, 340, 342, 343, 346, 348

Wilson, W. H. 372, 376
Wilss, L. 451, 454
Winograd, P. 478, 493
Wirjomartono, S. A. 1062
Wiseman, A. 1105
Withers, G. 362, 592, 597
Witoelar, E. 226, 230
Witte, J. 943
Woessmann, L. 937–8, 944
Wolf, R. M. 1109, 1121
Wonacott, M. E. 323, 324, 334
Wong, A. F. L. 465, 466, 468, 473, 474, 475, **1285–99**
Wong, B. Y. L. 478, 494
Wong, F. L. A. 889, 895–6
Wong, H. W. 779
Wong, K. C. 955, 958, 981, 984, 993, 999, 1003, 1012
Wong, K. Y. 888, 897
Wong, M. 456
Wong, M. Y. 487, 494
Wong, N. 759, 766
Wong, N. C. M. 1022, 1029
Wong, N. Y. 446, 456, 457
Wong, R. 517, 524
Wong Ruth Y. L. 592, 596, 1291, 1293
Wong, S. K. 1264, 1268
Wong, Suk-Ying 108, 120, 558, 567, 568, 1101, 1104, 1105, **1207–20**
Wong, W. K. 500, 502, 505
Wongsthorn, T. 1102, 1106
Wood, D. 747, 753
Wood, F. 846, 852
Wood, H. 747, 753
Wooden, M. 718, 720, 728
Woodhall, M. 663, 826, 832, 838, 1210, 1219
Woodhead, M. 753
Wotipka, C. M. 1100, 1105, 1106
Wragg, T. 771, 777, 780
Wray, H. 1069, 1077
Wright, E. N. 753
Wright, J. L. 1262, 1269
Wright, J. M. 419, 423
Wright, R. 738, 740, 886, 897
Wu, K. L. 1029
Wu, W. T. 190, 194, 195, 197, 198, 201, 497, 509

Wu, X. 8, 10, 15–16
Wu, Z. 893, 897
Wubbels, Th. 464, 471, 475
Wyatt, T. 1124, 1136
Wylie, E. 640
Xiao, C. 429, 438
Xie, Y. 54, 56
Xu, G. Y. 1016, 1029
Xu, J. 428, 438
Xu, Z. 743, 751, 753
Yadav, M. S. 157, 169, 1139, 1150
Yadav, S. K. 207, 208, 214
Yam, S. C. 531, 537
Yamamoto, S. 677, 686
Yamauchi, K. 496, 498, 506, 509
Yang, C. L. 976, 979, 983, 985, 1002, 1013
Yang, J. 673, 686
Yang, K. S. 496, 498, 501, 502, 506, 509
Yang, N. 952, 957
Yang, S. S. 963, 967, 969, 971
Yaosaka, O. 949, 956, 958
Yarrow, A. 472, 475, 887, 897
Yates, L. 264, 268
Ye, C. H. 188
Yeap, B. 480, 482, 491, 494
Yee, A. H. 686, 826, 1210, 1220
Yencken, – 576, 582, 584
Yeo, H. 621, 624, 627
Yibing, W. 1102, 1106
Yip, J. S. K. 896
Yip, K. 500, 509
Yip, S. F. 1076
Yip, S. K. J. 125, 1248
Yiu, Y. B. 1017, 1029
Yoneyama, S. 53, 57
Yong, B. K. 531, 537
Yong, L. 1061
Yoon, H. K. 466, 475
Young, D. J. 51, 56, 464, 466, 473, 475
Young, E. 862, 866
Young, I. P. 959, 961, 970
Young, S. S. 537
Young, Y. 1019, 1029
Yu, A. B. 496, 501–2, 504, 509
Yu, C. 770, 771, 780
Yu, E. S. H. 496, 509

Yu, F. Z. 7, 16
Yu, Wai Sze 591, 597
Yuen, C. 207, 215
Yuen, M. T. 502, 508
Yuen-kwan, W. L. 892, 897
Yung, Andy Man-Sing 925, **1015–29**
Yung, K. K. 201, 1076
Yusuf, S. 230
Yuzawa, M. 488, 491
Zahorik, J. 753
Zajda, Joseph **241–56**
Zajda, Rea **241–56**
Zaslavsky, V. 243, 244, 256
Zeidner, M. 766
Zeng, K. 68, 72, 1059, 1062
Zha, Z. 194, 202
Zhang, G. 627
Zhang, J. 425, 429, 438
Zhang, L. F. 363, 456
Zhang, L. J. 487, 494
Zhang, M. 1052, 1062
Zhang, Tiedao **171–88**, 179, 188, 242, 246
Zhang, W. 429, 439
Zhang, Y. 255, 256
Zhang Yenming 919, **945–58**
Zheng Xin-rong 643, 653
Zhong, W. 1217, 1220
Zhou, M. 54, 57
Zhou Nanzhou 642, 643, 653
Zhou, W. 188
Zhou, X. 45, 57
Zhou, Y. 119, 120, 956, 1328
Zhu, J. H. 1252, 1256
Zhu Rongyi 734
Ziderman, A. 39, 41, 42, 333, 659, 661, 662, 665, 667, 671, 819, 826, 832, 838, 1281, 1282, 1283
Zimmer, J. 498, 508, 515, 519, 523
Zimmerman, B. J. 513, 524, 757, 766
Zou, Y. 429, 438
Zu-Guang Yu 273, 278
Zubrich, A. 1149
Zulkilfi, A. M. 779
Zuo, Y. 508

Index of Subjects

AAACE *see* Australian Association of Adult and Community Education
AAOU *see* Asian Association of Open Universities
AARE *see* Australian Association for Research in Education
ability grouping (streaming) 782, 783
　assignment 47
　criticism of 781
　family background 47–8
　gifted education 197
Aborigines 53, 369, 370–2
　learning approaches 451
　performance goals 500
　reading literacy 587
　socialisation 503
　traditional worldviews 622
　see also indigenous Australians
ABS *see* Australian Bureau of Statistics
absenteeism 286
absorptive capacity 660, 1058
academic freedom 1213
academic grades 446, 447, 448, 460–1
academic learning time (ALT) 735, 786
academic secondary education 665, 677
Academy of Sciences in China 1307
acceleration programs 193, 196, 197, 198
access
　Education for All 277
　elementary education 737
　equality of opportunity 143, 153
　and equity xix
　expansion of 1096
　females 90
　gender differences 279–90
　higher education 737
　remote areas 171–88
　secondary education 74, 78, 80, 84–5, 87, 90
　selection for higher education 839, 841, 846, 848–50
　South Asia 155
　universities 1213–14, 1215
　urban youth 222–3
accommodation 366, 367
accountability xix, 7, 107, 767, 1035, 1139
　decentralisation 1322
　definition 109–10
　educational changes 120
　educational management 915, 916, 918
　increasing demand for 8
　indicators 1125, 1126, 1135
　lack of 1312
　language education 636
　managerialism 542
　NGOs 340
　nonformal education 343
　private sector 1020
　public examinations 113–15
　quality assurance 946, 947, 948, 955
　reliable assessment 793
　research challenges 1316, 1321
　school effectiveness indicators 119
　school leadership 974, 976, 979
　self-managing schools 934, 939, 940
　teachers 768
　trends in educational reform 5
　Western influences 108
accreditation
　East Asia 711
　Pacific Islands TVET provision 694, 695, 699
　self-managing schools 921, 931, 942
　Singapore 909
ACCU *see* Asia-Pacific Cultural Centre for UNESCO
accumulated knowledge 385
ACEID *see* Asia-Pacific Centre of Educational Innovation for Development
ACER *see* Australian Council for Educational Research
achievement
　ability 497–8
　academic grades 446, 447, 448, 460–1
　attentiveness relationship 749
　attributional research 497–8
　case study of learning achievement in South Asia 155–69
　class size relationship 741–3, 749–50
　coaching 735, 739, 762
　comparative research 1107–22
　environmental factors 145–6
　gender differences 261–4, 265, 271, 1302
　homework relationship 735
　international studies 1088
　Malaysian schools 735–6
　monitoring 793, 794, 796, 797–9, 800, 802–3
　need for 495, 496
　quality assurance 955

1365

1366 Index of Subjects

socially-orientated/individual-orientated 501–2
socio-economic background relationship 145
survey studies 117–18
see also attainment; performance
achievement goal theory 499–501
achieving approach 443, 446, 448, 459–62
ACIRRT *see* Australian Centre for Industrial Relations Research and Training
ACSSO *see* Australian Council of State School Organisations
Action Aid 157
action competence 580
action research 550, 1183, 1197, 1286
  China 1139
  environmental education 582
  inclusive education 203
  metacognition 485, 490
  multiple intelligences 527
  nonformal education 341
  peace education 642, 646, 648–9, 650
  Project for Enhancing Effective Learning 485
  school-based 1145
  SERA objectives 137
  teachers 167
  user-oriented 1200
action research network 582
active citizens 226–7
active learning time 749
ACTS *see* Adult Cooperative Training Scheme
adaptive learning 502, 1262, 1264
ADB *see* Asian Development Bank
administration 1004, 1005, 1006, 1017
admission policies 839, 840, 848, 850–1
adolescents 1234
adopt-a-school program 1054
adult and community education (ACE) 335–6, 337, 338, 669
Adult Cooperative Training Scheme (ACTS) 330
adult education 301, 302, 304, 737–8
  China 1101, 1214
  environmental 571
  lifelong learning 305–20, 1274
  nonformal education 336, 338–9, 340
  universities 853–66
adult illiteracy 171, 1232, 1277
adult literacy 172, 293–304, 586, 1232
  Education for All 18, 24–5
  human development index 1340, 1342–3
  Lao PDR 1174
  Pakistan 164
  Vietnam 314
Adult Literacy and Lifeskills (ALL) survey 311
advances in the research field 1204
Advisory Committee on Education for Peace, Human Rights, Democracy, International Understanding and Tolerance 405
advisory services 87
AEC *see* Asian Environmental Council
AEPM *see* Pakistan Academy of Education Planning and Management
aesthetic education 1303
AFD *see* Agence Francaise de Development
affirmative actions 1215
Afghanistan
  female illiteracy 260
  higher education 843
  participation 305

Africa
  fees 1052
  irrelevance of schooling 177
  public expenditure 1049
  salaries 873
  war and violence 1233
age
  of beginning reading instruction 587
  beliefs about 383–4, 385
  lifespan human development 379–94
Agence Francaise de Development (AFD) 1158
Agenda on Education 879
aggressive behaviour 426, 428–9, 430, 750
Agha Khan University in Pakistan 1156
agriculture
  Barefoot College 239
  China literacy program 300
  nonformal education 337–8, 341
  Pacific Islands 1275, 1276
  social change 258
  subsistence farming 234
  women 285, 286, 344
AICTE *see* All India Council for Technical Education
aid *see* foreign aid
aid agencies 77, 298, 1091
AIDS 78, 226, 1233
AJP *see* Asian-Pacific Joint Production Program of Materials for Neo-literates in Rural Areas
alienation 153, 177
  bullying 427
  citizenship education 557
  girls 272
  social exclusion 227, 228
  young people 218
ALL *see* Adult Literacy and Lifeskills survey; Australian Language Levels project
All India Association for Educational Research xiii, 138
All India Council for Technical Education (AICTE) 849
Allama Iqbal Open University 906
Alliance Francais 1158
allocated time 735, 783
allocation theory 1208
ALT *see* academic learning time
alternative conceptions research 621, 624, 625
alternative school 232–40
American Educational Research Association 1286
American Samoa 114
American Society for Training and Development (ASTD) 661–2
analogy-mapping 374
animal husbandry 239
ANTA *see* Australian National Training Authority
anti-bullying interventions 428, 429, 436
anti-discrimination laws 204
ANTRIEP *see* Asian Network of Training and Research Institutions in Educational Planning
anxiety 499, 515–16, 765
APC *see* Australian Parents Council
APDMEN *see* Asia-Pacific Distance and Multimedia Education Network
APEC *see* Asia-Pacific Economic Cooperation
APEID *see* Asia and the Pacific Program of Educational Innovation for Development

Index of Subjects 1367

APERA *see* Asia-Pacific Educational Research Association
APJTED *see* Asia-Pacific Journal of Teacher Education and Development
APNEC *see* Asia-Pacific NGO Environmental Conference
APNIEVE *see* Asia-Pacific Network for International Education and Values Education
APPEAL *see* Asia-Pacific Programme of Education for All
APPEAL Training Materials for Literacy Personnel (ATLP) 182–4, 185
applied linguistics 630
applied research 99, 549, 1083, 1197–8, 1200
appraisal of teachers 964, 967
apprenticeships 711, 715, 1010
  Australia 723–4, 728
  New Zealand 726, 728
  training 669, 673
Approaches to Studying Inventory (ASI) 442, 443, 444, 446
Area Intensive Education Project 1306
articulation agreements 328, 346
articulation pathways 710
artificial intelligence 529, 533, 1264
ASAIHL *see* Association of Southeast Asia Institutions of Higher Learning
ASEAN *see* Association of South East Asian Nations
ASI *see* Approaches to Studying Inventory
Asia Foundation 1156
Asia Pacific Centre for Educational Leadership and School Quality 1310
Asia and the Pacific Program of Educational Innovation for Development (APEID) 125, 172, 174, 188, 571, 1237
  regional research cooperation 1304–5, 1307, 1308, 1313
  teacher education 883, 884, 895, 903, 904, 911
Asia-Pacific Bureau of Adult Education (ASPBAE) 571
Asia-Pacific Centre of Educational Innovation for Development (ACEID) 76, 80–2, 87, 138, 1304, 1305, 1313
Asia-Pacific Cultural Centre for UNESCO (ACCU) 181–2, 187
Asia-Pacific Distance and Multimedia Education Network (APDMEN) 533
Asia-Pacific Economic Cooperation (APEC) 571
  comparative statistics 1132, 1135
  HRDWG 1132, 1335, 1339, 1344
  school-based indicators of effectiveness 118
  teacher education 884, 888–9, 890, 895
Asia-Pacific Educational Research Association (APERA) xiii, xiv, xv, 139–40
Asia-Pacific Journal of Education 558, 567
Asia-Pacific Journal of Teacher Education and Development (APJTED) 5
Asia-Pacific Network for International Education and Values Education (APNIEVE) 353, 400, 402, 405, 647
Asia-Pacific NGO Environmental Conference (APNEC) 571
Asia-Pacific Programme of Education for All (APPEAL) 172, 182–4, 185, 571
Asia-Pacific Programme of Educational Innovation for Development *see* Asia and the Pacific Program of Educational Innovation for Development
Asian American students 54
Asian Association of Open Universities (AAOU) 847
Asian Centre of Educational Innovation for Development (ACEID) 1304, 1313
Asian Development Bank (ADB) 21, 80, 82, 87, 91, 226, 228, 323, 325
  Asia Key Indicators 702, 703, 704, 713
  donor aid 1055–7, 1154, 1156, 1159–60, 1163, 1164
  environmental education 570, 583
  financing 1051, 1060
  fugitive literature 666–7
  Industrial Manpower Survey 666
  national development 1208
  primary education 1033, 1045
  research 1087, 1139, 1145, 1149, 1181–2
  teaching profession 867
  vocational education and training 677, 685
  workforce education 327
Asian Development Bank Institute 1161
Asian economic miracle 1097
Asian Environmental Council (AEC) 571
Asian financial crisis 221, 1098
Asian Institute of Technology 864
Asian Model for Educational Development 172, 1303
Asian Network of Training and Research Institutions in Educational Planning (ANTRIEP) 1154
Asian Program of Educational Innovation for Development (APEID) 1303
  see also Asia and the Pacific Program of Educational Innovation for Development
Asian Tigers 293, 1211
Asian values 352, 356, 560, 566, 998, 1074
Asian-Pacific Joint Production Program of Materials for Neo-literates in Rural Areas (AJP) 181–2, 183
Asiaweek 761, 765
ASPBAE *see* Asia-Pacific Bureau of Adult Education
aspirations 49–50
assessment 610–11, 736, 1238
  China 450
  citizenship education 561–2
  cognitive 373
  constructivism 608
  curriculum 545–6
  definition 110
  as a diagnostic tool 24
  education for all 165–8
  enterprise education and training 725–6
  establishing a program 799–805
  formative 610
  high expectations 795–6
  Korean tertiary education 1041
  learning achievement
    India 157–9
    Nepal 159–61
    Pakistan 161–4
  learning technology 532
  managerialism 542
  methods 796–9
  new teachers 891

1368   Index of Subjects

oral language 796
psychometric 375
quality assurance 24
reading literacy 593-4
reform 951
reliable 793
research 101
resources 299
second language education 629-40
secondary education reform 86, 87, 88, 89
skills and competences 1035
student learning 450, 452, 453
student-based 532
teachers 963
Tyler Model 111-12
values education 404
see also formative assessment/evaluation; monitoring; Programme for International Student Assessment; summative assessment/evaluation
assessment research 1187
Assessment Research Centre, University of Melbourne 532, 536
Assessment Resource Banks 594
assimilation 366, 367, 623
Association of Commonwealth Universities 1208
Association of South East Asian Nations (ASEAN) 571, 1155
Association of Southeast Asia Institutions of Higher Learning (ASAIHL) 1208, 1210, 1218
Association of Tertiary Education Managers 1143
Association of Universities of Asia and the Pacific (AUAP) 533
associationism 607
ASTD see American Society for Training and Development
asynchronous feedback 1263
ATLP see APPEAL Training Materials for Literacy Personnel
attainment
  gender relationship 66-7
  social capital 61-2
  socio-economic status relationship 43, 45, 46, 48
  South Asia 157
  see also achievement
attention 365
attentiveness 749-50
attitudes 352, 770
  citizenship education 562
  Likert-style questionnaire 409-24
  nonformal education 307
  science 617
  vocational education and training 680
attributional influences 497-9, 515
AUAP see Association of Universities of Asia and the Pacific
AusAID see Australian Aid for International Development
Australia
  achievement goals 502
  adult and community education 335-6, 337, 338
  adult education participation 317, 318, 319
  alternative conceptions research 621
  Anglo-celtic culture 893
  anxiety research 499
  attitudes towards capital punishment 419, 421, 422

bullying 425-8, 431
Centre for Lifelong Learning and Development 312
citizenship education 563
classroom learning environments 464, 466
cognitive development research 365-6, 368, 369, 372, 373, 374-5
competencies 310-11
continuing education 854, 859-61, 863, 864
cultural contact 502-3
cultural values 504
curriculum 545
  integration 624
  reform 561
decentralisation 93
Department of Education 825, 1259, 1264, 1267
donor aid 1156, 1157, 1163
downsizing 1323
economic growth/development 828, 1088
educational research associations 134-5
effort attributions 499
enactivism 609
enrolment 32, 33
enterprise education and training 715-30
environmental education 573, 576, 578, 579
Europe/North America influence xv
family support 925
family/community participation 924
fees 1211
Fiji exports to 1275
gender differences 262, 263, 264-5
girls and science education 619
gross national income 31
higher education 811, 819, 841
  financing 827, 828, 829, 831, 832, 833, 844
  funding 836
  minority groups 845
  selection 842
Higher Education Contribution Scheme 1282
home-school communication 1065-6
homework policy 764
inclusive education for students with special needs 203-5
indigenous cultures 845, 1218
indigenous student learning 451
international comparative studies 1110-17
international students 70, 833, 844
IT strategy 11
language teaching 629-30, 631-2, 634, 636-8
large-scale testing programs 114-15
learning at home 1065
learning difficulties study 488
learning technology 531-2
lifespan studies 391
literacy 295, 486, 487
loans 1283
mathematics 481-2
national visions 7
nonformal education 337, 338, 339, 340
norms 390
Pacific Island students 691
paradigm shifts 12
parents
  involvement 1071, 1072, 1073, 1074
  parent education 1064
  volunteering 1066-7
participation 305

Index of Subjects

PISA 949
planning and policy 926
population 30, 31
primary to secondary school transition 472
private sector 949
problem solving 511
productive pedagogues 354
Project for Enhancing Effective Learning 485, 624–5
psychology 1198
public expenditure 36, 37, 40
public/private provision 34, 35–6
quality assurance 10, 946, 954, 955
reading literacy 586, 587, 588, 589, 591, 593–4
reforms 1172–4
research 147, 1086
  dissemination 1139, 1140, 1141, 1142, 1143–4, 1146–7
  institutions 127
  priorities 1204
  productivity 133
  training of researchers 1286, 1287, 1298
retention rates 264–5
school decision-making 1068–9
school leadership 1001
school-based management 948
science education 616, 619, 622, 1243
self-managing schools 10, 921, 931, 933–4, 939–40, 941, 942
Singapore comparison 468–9
Singapore students 451
situated cognition 623
social goals 501
staffing ratios 36, 38, 40
statistics 603
student learning 445, 448–9
Taiwan comparison 469
teachers 870
  monitoring 950
  preparation 738
  quality 11
  recruitment 901–3, 910
  teacher education 886–7, 889, 892, 900
teaching strategies 748
technical and vocational education 669, 670
technology research 604
tertiary education 737, 1041–4
transparency 952
universities 738
values in mathematics education 611
vocational education 35, 669, 670
workforce education 323, 324, 331
youth attitudes 265–6
see also Aborigines
Australian Aid for International Development (AusAID) 1156, 1158, 1308, 1309
Australian Association of Adult and Community Education (AAACE) 338, 347
Australian Association for Institutional Research 1143
Australian Association for Research in Education (AARE) xiii, 134–5, 136, 1143, 1286, 1290
Australian Bureau of Statistics (ABS) 717, 718–19, 724, 728
Australian Centre for Industrial Relations Research and Training (ACIRRT) 720, 728
Australian College of Educators 1143

Australian Council for Educational Research (ACER) 125, 127, 138, 169, 805, 1111, 1182, 1191
  dissemination of research 1141, 1142, 1149
  policy research 1167
  private sector 1156
  regional research cooperation 1305, 1306, 1310, 1313
Australian Council of State School Organizations Inc. (ACSSO) 1066, 1067, 1071, 1075
Australian Education Council 481, 490, 1179
Australian Human Rights and Equal Opportunity Commission 610, 612
Australian Language Levels (ALL) project 631
Australian National Centre for Vocational Education Research (NCVER) 331, 669, 724, 729, 1308, 1309
Australian National Training Authority (ANTA) 694, 722–3
Australian National University 132, 636, 865
Australian Parents Council Inc. (APC) 1066, 1071, 1075
Australian Research Council 1140
Australian Schools Commission 1172–4
Australian Science Education Project 466
Australian Vocational Education and Training Association 1143
authentic field experiences 1263
authentic pedagogy 354
authority, culture of 68–9
autocratic organisational structures 52–3
automaticity 359–60
automation 309
autonomous learning 611, 1261
autonomy
  Asian universities 1209–10
  local 1100
  private sector 1018, 1020, 1025, 1026
  public sector 1017, 1021, 1026
  subsidised schools 1021, 1022–3
average years of schooling, gender differences 280–1, 282

Bahrain, research 1141
Bali, environmental awareness 578, 579
Bangkok University 1156
Bangladesh
  basic skills 802
  boys' education 271
  colonial history 1153
  community financing 1052–3
  economic development 828
  enrolments 173, 175
  female illiteracy 260
  gender differences 279, 281–2
  higher education 819
    financing 828, 830
    private sector 834, 845
  Islamic Development Bank loans 1157
  Nonformal Primary Education Program 179–80
  participation 305
  population 293
  private sector 834, 1051
  private tutoring 1059
  repetition rate 174
  research environment 1312
  school retention 1160
  teacher-pupil ratio 872

1370 Index of Subjects

teachers 870, 906
universities 1155, 1213
vocational education and training 675, 677, 678, 679, 682
women 270, 285, 286
Bangladesh Institute of Development Studies (BIDS) 1155
Bangladesh Rural Advancement Committee (BRAC) 179
Barefoot College/barefoot teachers 233–40, 872
Bashkortostan 253
basic education 18, 19, 89
adult 338
COMPETE project 313
financing 1053
Indonesia/Malaysia 323, 331
nonformal 227
Thailand 1176, 1177
see also primary education
Basic Education for Skills Training (BEST) 330
basic equipment 94
basic learning needs 18
Basic Primary Education Project (BPEP), Nepal 159
basic research 99, 549, 604–5, 1083
basic skills 782, 802
basics for youth survival 227–8
Beginning Teacher Evaluation Study (BTES) 735, 786
behaviour of pupils 750
behaviourism 542, 546, 607, 608
Beijing Conference 269, 275
Beijing Normal University 526
beliefs 1195
culturally-shared 382–4, 385
student teachers 887
benchmarking 9–10, 802–3, 1126
Berlin Wisdom Paradigm 385, 390–1
BEST *see* Basic Education for Skills Training
best practice
language education 632
nonformal education 345, 346
Bhutan
community financing 1052
female illiteracy 260
gender differences 279, 281–2
school retention 1160
women 271, 285
bibliometric analysis 1144, 1147
BIDS *see* Bangladesh Institute of Development Studies
bilateral networks 1154, 1155–6
bilingual research 585
biliteracy 589
Bill Gates Foundation 1154, 1156
bioecological model of human development 44
biological decline 387–8
biology 372
birth rates
Australia 1174
East Asia 703
see also fertility
Board on Women Participation in Technical Education 849
BPEP *see* Basic Primary Education Project
BRAC *see* Bangladesh Rural Advancement Committee

brain activity 1265
brain drain 70, 697
Brain Korea 21 Project 1041
brain research 309
British Council 77, 81, 1158
Brunei Darussalam
classroom learning environments 464, 465, 468, 469, 470
colonial history 1153
donor support 1157
environmental awareness 576, 578, 579
QTI 471
reading literacy 55, 589
research training 1288–90, 1296
teacher education 889
teachers 870, 888
vocational education and training 678
BTES *see* Beginning Teacher Evaluation Study
Buddhism 384, 643, 648
budgets 934
bullying 52, 352–3, 425–39, 641
Bunkyo University of Tokyo 533
Burma (Myanmar)
ADB initiatives 1160
coaching 761, 764
higher education 811, 819, 1215
opposition to democracy 1336
research 1087
teachers 870
universities closed down 1213
vocational education and training 677, 678, 679
business studies 1101

CAGE (Chinese Association of Gifted Education) 192, 195, 200, 201, 202
calculators 600, 602, 604
Cambodia
ADB initiatives 1160
coaching 760, 761, 764
community-employed teachers 1053
compulsory education 7
culture of authority 68–9
enrolments 74
external aid 1058
female illiteracy 260
fertility 818
higher education 811, 813, 824
Khmer Rouge 1213
low incomes 323
national visions 7
private expenditure 1050–1
private tutoring 1059
public expenditure 1048
research 1087
teachers 869, 870, 879
violence 1235
vocational education and training 678
Cambridge Anthropological Expedition 369
Canada
influence on Asia-Pacific curriculum 606
parental involvement 9
Canadian International Development Agency (CIDA) 313, 1153, 1159
capital punishment 410, 412, 419–22
capitalism 1054, 1095
Marxist theory 244
taxation 1054
CARE Program 1289

Index of Subjects 1371

career ladders 966–7, 970
career long development 145, 154
career mobility 46
  see also occupational mobility; social mobility
caring environment 357
Carnegie Corporation of New York 125
Carnegie Foundation of New York 1141
case study approach 97
  gender sensitisation 276
  inclusive education for students with special needs 210
  literacy 299–303
  workforce education 328
caste system 232, 849
casual employment 1271, 1273
Catholic church 1052
cause and effect 97
CCE see Central Council on Education
CCEs see Centres for Continuing Education
CCP see Chinese Communist Party
CD-ROMS, language education 632, 635
CED see Continuing Education and Development Program
Center for Information Technology in School and Teacher Education, University of Hong Kong 527
Center for Scientific Documentation Information, Indonesian Institute of Sciences 534
Central Asia
  Asia-Pacific diversity 293
  education management reforms 296
  enrolments 1214
  higher education
    funding 829, 831
    private sector 834
  minorities 241–56
  post-communist transition 563
Central Council on Education (CCE), Japan 962, 970, 1069–70
Central Institute of Educational Research (CIER), China 128
centralisation 93–4
  planning 1032, 1054
  research/decision-making relationship 1188
Centre for Citizenship Education, Hong Kong Institute of Education 558
Centre for Educational Research and Innovation (CERI) 1084, 1090
  dissemination of research 1138, 1141, 1143, 1145, 1149
  INES project 1127
Centre for Gandhian Studies and Peace Research 645
Centre for Lifelong Learning and Development 312
Centre for Research and International Collaboration, Hong Kong 1305, 1307
Centre for Research in Pedagogy and Practice 1287, 1294
Centre for Research and Teaching in Civics, University of Sydney 558
Centres for Continuing Education (CCEs) 854, 855, 856, 860, 865
CERC see Comparative Education Research Centre
CERI see Centre for Educational Research and Innovation
certification 114, 308, 309

Indonesia 115
Japan 315
self-managing schools 921, 931, 942
teacher quality 950
teachers of language 632–3
certification examinations 114
Certified On-the-Job Training Centre (COJTC) 330
CES see Classroom Environment Scale
character development 546
child abuse 436
child rearing practices 149
child study movement 124, 1170
child-care centres 1021–2
child-centred approaches 561, 562
  pre-school 587
  reading 587, 588, 589
  Thailand 1246
child-rearing practices 372
Children's Fair 238
Children's Parliament 235–6, 239–40
children's rights 1157, 1162
Chile, salaries 873
China
  Academy of Sciences 1307
  ADB initiatives 1160
  adult education 1101, 1214
  ageing population 1214
  attributional research 498
  beliefs about old age 384
  bullying 425, 428–9
  Central Asia research 242
  civic curricula 563
  class size 742, 743, 751
  cognitive development 375
  community financing 1052, 1053
  Confucian culture/philosophy 642, 893
  cross-national problem solving studies 519–20
  curriculum reform 179
  decentralisation 10, 564, 982
  economic growth 1088
  educational research associations 135–6
  EFA goals 176
  effective schooling 920, 987, 988, 999
  effort 992–3
  enrolments 32, 33, 173, 707
  environmental education 573, 576, 578, 579, 1099
  ethnographic studies 453
  examinations 8, 114, 452, 992
  family background 45–6
  fees 1052
  gifted education 190, 194, 196–7, 198
  good educational outcomes 323
  graduate employment 1216
  gross national income 31
  higher education 819–20, 822–3, 1101, 1215
    financing 830, 831, 832, 833
    privatisation 844–5
  homework 734, 758, 991
  hours at school 988
  illiteracy 171
  inclusive education for students with special needs 205–6
  independent revenue-earning 1054
  influence on Macau education system 1024
  international comparative studies 1110–17

international students 70
Joint Innovative Project 1237-8
journals 1312
learning technology 526-7
literacy 294, 299-300
locus of control 496, 497
market economy 927, 1054, 1060
mathematics anxiety 516
mathematics software 528
memorisation 993
memory 360
metacognition 488-9
modernisation 1213
motivation 496
national visions 7
nonformal education 343
parent education 1064
parents 989-90, 991
participation 339
peace education 643-4
performance goals 500
performativity 769
political ideology 1212
population 29-31, 293, 1151, 1214
poverty 176-7
pressure to succeed 452
primary teachers 748
private sector 822-3, 1016, 1017-18, 1205, 1211
  higher education 1102
  private tutoring 1059
privatisation of tertiary education 8
problem solving 514
public expenditure 37, 1049
public/private provision 34, 35, 925, 1015-18, 1026, 1027
quality assurance 10
reading literacy 587-8, 589, 591
reform 1251-3
repetition rate 174
research
  dissemination 1137, 1139, 1141, 1142, 1143, 1146
  impact on practice 102
  institutions 128-9
  priorities 1204-5
  productivity 133
rural areas 343
school leadership 978-9, 980-1, 982, 1001-2
science education 616, 1251-3
SMILES 528
socialisation 990
socially-orientated achievement 502
staffing ratios 38
student activism 1213
student expectations 624
student learning 444, 449, 450-1
teacher education 893, 900, 901, 910
teachers 869, 870
  quality 11
  respect for 1255
  training 996
teaching practices 993-6, 997
technical assistance 1160
technical and vocational education 657
vocational education and training 325, 328, 329-30, 675, 676-7, 678, 679, 682
whole class teaching 745

women 344
World Bank loans 1161
World Education Indicators 1133
WTO entry 862
youth population 220
China National Institute for Educational Research (CNIER) 642, 1141, 1142, 1146, 1155
Chinese Communist Party (CCP) 1016, 1017
Chinese Educational Development and Research Center 905, 911
Chinese Society of Education (CSE) 135-6
Chinese State Commission 905, 910
Chinese University of Hong Kong 131
ch'onji 65-6
Christianity 647
Chulalongkorn University 1154
CIDA *see* Canadian International Development Agency
CIER *see* Central Institute of Educational Research
citizenship 231, 552, 1099, 1240, 1272
  Central Asia 241, 243, 251, 254
  democratic 1239
  environmental activism 577-80
citizenship education 352, 555-68, 641, 643, 1237
civic education 552, 555-68, 641, 1097, 1103, 1108
civic knowledge 643
civic responsibility 577
CIVITAS 564
class control, student teachers 889
class size 89, 90, 736, 741-54, 994
  achievement relationship 1119
  coaching 761-2
  Confucian heritage cultures 995
  lack of regulation 1059
  variation in 96
classification 367, 371
classroom
  achievement goals 502
  citizenship education 562
  contextual influences 744
  culture 481, 482
  gender differences in student perceptions 468
  learning 773-5
  management 733, 876, 1097
  processes 736, 743-4, 751
Classroom Environment Scale (CES) 464
classroom learning environment 51-2, 463-75
classroom practice 157, 355
  authentic pedagogy 354
  gifted education 196-7
  implemented curriculum 566
  Japan 997
  research 1146-7
  teachers as researchers 167
CLD *see* Comparative Lessons for Democracy
CLES *see* Constructivist Learning Environment Survey
climate 447
  achievement goals 502
  gender differences in student perceptions 468
cluster sample design 262
CMI *see* contextualised multiple intelligence; contextualised multiple intelligences
CNIER *see* China National Institute for Educational Research
Co-Construction theory 587
coaching 734, 735, 739, 755-66

Index of Subjects

Indian minority groups 849
 see also private tuition
Cockroft Report 602-3, 611, 613
cognition 562
 classroom learning 773
 definition 477
 knowledge of 488
 situated 603, 623-4
cognitive abilities 368
 wisdom 382, 385, 391
cognitive activity
 motivation 496
 problem solving 513
cognitive capabilities, gender differences 271
cognitive development 308-9, 352, 358-9, 365-77
cognitive disequilibrium 483
cognitive load theory 309, 516
cognitive processes 365, 374, 477, 615
cognitive psychology, Vygotskian 747
cognitive skills 757
cognitive strategies 358
COJTC *see* Certified On-the-Job Training Centre
COL *see* Commonwealth of Learning
collaboration xiv
 among educational researchers xvi, xix, xxii
 Asian teaching practices 994
 between teachers 1097
 community 1066-8
 cross-cultural 998
 curriculum aims 544
 gifted education research 196
 ICT research 1262
 Japanese teachers 1247
 NGOs 299
 PEEL initiative 625
 problem solving 514-15
 research 138, 1178
  APERA 140
  cognitive development 372-3, 375
  international platforms for 1084
  learning outcomes 361
  SERA objectives 137
  teacher education 894
  teacher 'scaffolding' 479, 481
collaborative decision-making 976, 980
collaborative group work 750
collaborative leadership 980
collaborative learning 450, 482
 Computer Supported Collaborative
  Learning 529
 virtual environments 530, 531
collaborative research, *see also* cooperation
collectivism 62-3, 357, 560, 1097
 Aboriginal students 451
 achievement motivation 496
 beliefs about old age 384
 Chinese culture 450
 civic curricula 563
 Confucian-heritage cultures 515
 extended families 65
 locus of control 497
 performance goals 500
 shift to individualism 556
 Taiwan 770
college graduates, East Asia 705
Colombo Plan aid 324
colonial history 1153

colonialism 557, 652
 vocational education and training 674
Columbia University 124
command economies 657, 665
commercial learning technology products 525-6, 534-5
commercialisation 737
Committee for the Review of Higher Education
 Financing and Policy 1043, 1045
common curriculum 108
Commonwealth of Learning (COL) 693-4, 695, 1156
 secondary education 77, 81
communication
 between Pacific Island nations 689, 696-7
 home-school 1065-6
 parental/community involvement 9
communication skills 876, 889, 907
 ICT benefits 1259
communications technology 1258-9
communicative competence 630, 635
communism 241, 253, 1054
 collapse of 242, 1273
Communist Party, China 1016, 1017
communitarian culture 62
community
 Barefoot College 237
 collectivist culture 62-3
 community-based materials 301
 context for learning 351
 effect on educational career 147-8
 empowerment 375
 financing 1052-3
 health education 224
 involvement 5, 8-9, 298, 915, 917, 919, 924-5, 975, 1320-1
  decline of 60
 gifted education 194, 197
 Thailand 1005
 learning within the 1177
 literacy projects 339, 340
 participation xx, 1063-77
 school relationship 150-1
 social capital 60
 as source of learning 1241
 volunteering 1066-8
 youth involvement 228
community colleges 668, 846, 862
 nonformal education 340
community development 186
 nonformal education 337, 340-2
community education 224
Community Learning Centres 24
community of practice 1265
community schools 151, 152
community service 225, 854
community-employed teachers 1053
comparability, assessment methods 797, 799
comparative education 1126
Comparative Education Research Centre
 (CERC) 324, 325
Comparative Lessons for Democracy (CLD) 564
comparative research studies 41, 353, 354
 achievement studies 1107-22
 educational indicators 1123, 1132, 1135
 effective schooling 998
 indigenous education 1226

mathematics curriculum 605
  regional cooperation 1312–13
  secondary education 82
  workforce education 324, 331
comparative schooling, effective schooling 921
compensatory education 147, 150–1, 152
COMPETE (Continuing Teacher Education Programme Utilizing Distance Education Technology and Materials) project 313–14
competence 309–12
  monitoring 794, 796
competences, new policy approaches 1035
competencies 309–12
  nonformal education 346
  South Asia 164
  teachers 313, 314
competency standards 722
competency testing 90
competency-based training 669, 723, 727, 728
competition 396
  amongst providers 1280, 1283
  class size 751
  global economic 1099, 1102
  international 1271
  Taiwan 748
competitive nature of learning 500
competitiveness
  Asian attitudes 770
  international 1139, 1271, 1318
completion of education 35
completion rates, gender differences 264, 265
Comprehensive Learning Hours 646
compulsory education 7
Compulsory Education Law, China 205
computational models 527
Computer Supported Collaborative Learning (CSCL) 529
computer technology
  China 1205
  Singapore 1249
computer-assisted learning/instruction 51, 307, 467, 522, 525, 535
computer-supported collaborative learning (CSCL) 1262
computers 932, 999
  compute-based farming 341
  evaluation studies 119
  lifelong learning 319
  mathematics 600, 602, 604
  reading literacy 594
  in schools 95
  see also information and communication technologies
conceptual change 483–5, 489
conceptual equivalence 444–5
conceptual understanding 484
conclusion-oriented research 98
concrete operational stage 367
confidence 940
  ICT benefits 1259
  poverty 177, 186
  see also self-esteem
conflict 1209
conflict perspective 1033, 1034
conflict resolution 336, 387, 641
Confucian culture 65
  teacher education 893

Confucian ethical values 925, 1015
Confucian heritage culture 354, 361
  coaching 761
  effective schooling 920
  international students 451
  Korea 1038
  learning 515
  moral education 563
  parental role 924–5
  repetition 359
  student learning 441
  value of schooling 452
  values 450
Confucian heritage cultures 987
  parental role 1065, 1073, 1074
  stereotypes 995
Confucian philosophy 642, 643
  filial piety 380, 384
Confucian tradition
  social evolution 1334
  values 1097
Confucianism, disabled students 205
Confucianist beliefs, collective good 770
consensus 1196
  research standards 1312
consent 1196
conservation 367, 370, 371
constructivism 51, 608
  curriculum 542, 545
  enactivism 609
  learning technology 526, 530, 531, 534, 536
  mathematics education 600, 603
  metacognition 624
  reading 590
  science education 621, 622
Constructivist Learning Environment Survey (CLES) 464, 467, 469, 470, 471
consultancy 550
consulting firms 1141
content management systems 1258
contextual classroom factors 744
contextualised multiple intelligence (CMI) 12
contextualised multiple intelligences (CMI) 1326, 1327
continuing education 306, 316, 737–8, 853–66
  teachers 313–14
  workforce education 321, 330
  see also adult education; lifelong learning
Continuing Education and Development Program (CED) 301
Continuing Education and Training (CET), Singapore 330
Continuing Teacher Education Programme Utilizing Distance Education Technology and Materials (COMPETE) project 313–14
contraception 226
controlled investigations 1197
Convention against Discrimination in Education 143
Convention on the Rights of the Child 143, 154
Cook Island
  information on 690
  technical and vocational education and training 687, 691
Cook Islands
  assessment 803
  continuing education 858

Index of Subjects 1375

cooperation
  Confucian-heritage cultures 515
  human resource development 668
  international 18, 1135, 1236–7
  regional
    research 1301–13
    values education 402
  research 1086–7, 1178, 1204, 1205
  values education 396, 398
Cooperation Programme for Educational Research in Asia 125
cooperative learning 207, 745, 750, 876
  ICT benefits 1259
  metacognitive knowledge 790
  technology and learning 525, 526, 536
Cooperative Research Centres (CRCs) 861
Cooperative Research Project 939, 940, 943
corporatisation 833, 834
corrections 94
corrective feedback 994
cost-effectiveness 742, 1126
cost-recovery 819, 820–1, 831, 836, 1047, 1052–4
cost-sharing 1047, 1052–4
costs
  educational provision xviii, 107
  efficiency 307
  higher education 819, 820–1
  Pacific Islands TVET provision 697–8, 699
  vocational education and training 682
Council of Australian Governments 639
Council of Europe 81, 631, 639
coursework in research methods 1287
craft knowledge 1004–5, 1009
craft training 340
CRCs see Cooperative Research Centres
creative work 549, 550
creativity 357, 386, 876, 932, 952
  curriculum reform 561–2
  gifted education 190, 191, 199
  Korea 546
  problem solving 511
  ROBOLAB 535
  Singapore 1099, 1250
Creativity-Action-Service Program 1239
crime 18, 1232
crisis of confidence in educational research 1085
critical issues and problems 1201–2
critical literacy skills 794–5
critical numeracy skills 794–5
critical theorists 1208–9, 1215
critical thinking 340, 770, 876
  curriculum reform 562
  Hong Kong 790
  Korea 546, 764
  Singapore 1099
  Thailand 1177
cross-cultural studies 358, 359, 371, 463
  effective schooling 998
  mathematics anxiety 515–16
  motivation 496–9
  parental expectations 990
  problem solving 519–20
  see also international studies
cross-national studies 1091, 1096–8
  children with reading difficulties 591–2
  citizenship education 565
  classroom learning environments 463, 468–9

  educational achievement 1107–22
  see also international studies
CSCL see Computer Supported Collaborative Learning; computer-supported collaborative learning
CSE see Chinese Society of Education
cultural capital xviii, 44, 45, 50, 59–72
cultural change 1325, 1326, 1334, 1338
cultural contact 502–3
cultural context
  class size 741, 751
  cognitive development 368, 372
  differences in student learning 441, 449–52
  effective schooling 987, 992–6
  learning 351–2, 355, 361
  problem solving 359, 514
  psychological development 379–80, 392
  school effectiveness 918, 920–1
  school leadership 980, 981, 984, 1003, 1006
  teacher education 893
  traditions xxiii
cultural crisis 124–5
cultural diversity 250, 398
cultural evolution 1332, 1334
cultural globalisation 1096, 1103, 1104
cultural heritage, Central Asia 254
cultural identity 629, 1303
cultural imperialism 557
cultural milieu 352
cultural orientations 149
cultural progress 18
cultural psychology 372, 373–4, 375
Cultural Revolution 45–6, 451, 904, 1016, 1213, 1251
cultural transmission 1208, 1216–17
cultural values 973, 979, 1216
  effective schooling 988, 998
  effort 498
  locus of control 497
  metacognition 483, 485
  motivation 495, 504
  Oceania 1221–2, 1226, 1227, 1228
  performance goals 500
  reading 587
  teaching practices 733
culturally inclusive education, Oceania 1221–30
culturally-shared beliefs 382–4, 385
culture
  China 1205
  ethnomathematics 600, 609–10
  gender bias 287, 288
  globalisation 309
  implemented curriculum 615
  influence on curriculum 563
  metacognition 482–3
  national 560
  traditional worldviews 622, 623
culture of authority 68–9
culture of peace 398–9, 405, 406
curriculum xv, xx, 541–54
  aims 543–4
  assessment methods 797
  Australia 1173
  Barefoot College approach 234, 235, 238–9
  changes in 600–1, 606, 619–20
  citizenship 555–6, 560–1, 563–4, 565–6
  common 108

1376 Index of Subjects

community schools   151
content   889
Cooperative Research Project   939
cross-national studies   1120–1
crowded   755
curriculum triangle   111–12
curriculum-evaluation diamond   113
development   111, 157, 547–9, 550
   case studies   178–84
   environmental education   581
   ICT   1325
   Korea   316
   mathematics   607, 611
   Oceania   1223, 1225, 1229
   school-based   876, 975
   state control   542
   textbooks   547
environmental education   575, 581, 582
evaluation   110, 111
framework documents   546–7
gender-sensitive   282
gifted education   190, 196, 197, 198
globalisation   1096–8
goals   630, 797
guidelines   570
higher education   1101–2
Hong Kong integrated curriculum initiative   1250–1, 1254
inclusive education   205, 209, 213
innovations   1103
integrated   1250–1, 1252, 1254
irrelevance   176
leadership   978, 1011
learning objectives   159
levels of   542–3
literacy   181, 182
Macau   1024
Malaysia   770
mathematics   599–614
needs-based   181, 186
nonformal education   340
objectives   111–13, 157, 159, 160–1
Oceania   1222, 1223, 1224, 1225, 1228, 1229
planning   783
reconceptualizing   611–12
reform   561–2, 625
   environmental education   581
   Korea   635
   metacognition   481
   secondary education   73, 78, 80, 86, 87, 89
   Singapore   764
   teacher education   903
relevance   176, 797–8, 1223
reorientation   186, 187
research   547, 549–50, 602–7, 1204, 1205
rural areas   178
science xxii, 615–27, 1243–56
second language education   630–8
sex stereotypes   272–3, 274, 277
Singapore   1099
skills and competences   1035
social studies   558–9
socially critical   428
Taiwan   528
Target Orientated Curriculum   787
teacher education   888–9
technology and science   1243–56

Thailand   1176, 1177
urban youth   223
values education   402, 403, 406–7
vocationalisation of   676–7
see also National Curriculum
Curriculum Corporation of Australia   631, 639
Curriculum Development Centres   86
Curriculum Development Council, Hong Kong   876, 880
Curtin University of Technology   1287, 1290, 1296–7, 1298
cycle of female disadvantage   288, 290
cycle of poverty   260
Cyprus, higher education   829, 836

Dakar Framework for Action   19, 805
   gender issues   269, 273
   teachers   1224
Dakar World Education Forum   73, 184
   Declaration   303
   gender stereotypes   275
   targets   304
Dakar Youth Empowerment Strategy   227, 228
data collection   1197
databases   298
   ISI   1144
   UNESCO Statistic Database on Education   339
De La Salle University, Manila   533
debt   18
decentralisation   5, 10, 93–4, 564, 975–6, 1100, 1157
   Australia   1043
   China   1017
   cross-national seminars   1178
   decision-making   87, 1184
   downsizing   1323
   educational administration   1017
   educational management   916, 918, 919
   governance structures   1103
   higher education   1215
   Hong Kong   1021, 1027
   Japan   1037
   Korea   1040
   Lao PDR   1175
   leadership   922
   management   1310
   new managerialism   926
   policy development and planning   1034–5, 1037, 1044
   principal's role   973, 979, 981, 982
   public sector   1026
   quality assurance   919–20, 947–9, 956
   reforms   1316, 1322
   secondary education   87, 88, 89
   self-managing schools   921–2, 931–44
   SWRC initiatives   233
   Taiwan   1019
   teacher education   888–9
   Thailand   1176
decision-making   374
   collaborative   976, 980
   family/community participation   1068–70
   new managerialism   926
   participatory   233
   principals   976–8
   research impact on   1181–91
decolonisation   557, 563
deep learning   355, 773, 993

Confucian-heritage cultures 515
cross-cultural perspective 442, 445, 446–7, 448, 449, 450, 459–62
mastery goals 500
deep understanding 354, 356, 357
Delors Report 77, 154, 259, 396, 402, 1196, 1333, 1338
  equity 1203
  learning entitlement 1241
  peace education 642, 643
  teachers 151, 1224
  values education 1240
demand
  Australia 1042–3
  Japan 1037–8
  policy development and planning 1034, 1044
democracy 145, 146, 641, 1169, 1176, 1240, 1344
  action competence 580
  APNIEVE 400
  Children's Parliament 236
  citizenship education 564, 566
  CIVITAS 564
  culture of peace 398, 399
  Dewey 1332
  erosion of 254
  globalisation 1332, 1336
  spread of 172
  values education 397, 402, 407
  workforce education 325
democratisation 265, 558, 559, 563
  literacy 294
  power relations 340
demographic changes
  East Asia 701, 703, 707–8
  see also population
Denmark, Danish Union of Teachers 771
Department of Education, New Zealand 1111
Department of Education, Science and Training (DEST), Australia 1264, 1267
Department of Education and Science and the Welsh Office (DESWO) 602–3, 611, 613
Department of Education, Training and Youth Affairs (DETYA), Australia 1259, 1267
Department for International Development (DFID), Great Britain 17, 27, 77, 81, 694, 1158
Department of Nonformal Education, Thailand 329
depression 427, 429, 435
deprofessionalisation 544
deregulation
  labour markets 1273
  Singapore 7
DeSeCo Steering Group 311
DEST *see* Department of Education, Science and Training
DESWO *see* Department of Education and Science and the Welsh Office
DETYA *see* Department of Education, Training and Youth Affairs
developing countries
  access to elementary education 737
  access to technology 738
  basic problems 313
  digital divide 851
  empowerment 187
  enrolments 172
  equality of opportunity 144, 145
  female illiteracy 270
  gender differences 281
  higher education 737, 809, 818, 819, 820–1, 824, 840–1
    open university 846–7
    private sector 835
    rates of return 1210
  HRD planning 664
  international comparative studies 1120
  lifelong education 319
  monitoring student learning 805–6
  nonformal education 335, 338, 339, 342, 345
  poverty 148, 177, 178
  primary education 1033
  public expenditure 173
  quality education 175–6
  research 146–7, 166–7
  self-managing schools 940–1
  structural adjustment 219
  UN World Programme of Action for Youth 1233
  urbanisation 178
  vocational education and training 674–5, 676, 682
  Western models 267
development 233
  Gender and Development 288
  indicators 702
development theory 1161
developmental change 387
developmental psychology 380, 381, 391
developmental tasks 309
devolution
  decision-making 1280
  management 1274, 1283
  Pacific Islands 1279, 1280
  of responsibilities 1034–5
DFID *see* Department for International Development
Dharma 644
diagnostic information 1265
dialogue 607
digital divide 851, 868, 892
direct instruction 784–5
Direct Subsidy Scheme (DSS) 1022–3, 1027
disabled students 153, 204–12, 1170
  access 90
  inclusiveness 1238
  Thailand 1176
disadvantaged students 149, 152, 153
  equity 1319
  inclusiveness 1238
  inequalities 1322
  new ideas 1201
  socio-economic environment 1019–20
discipline 750
  China 428
  student teachers 889
discrimination 143, 395, 1232–3
  Central Asia 251, 254, 255
  gender 269, 279, 282, 287–8, 344
  positive 146, 150
  state role 255
dissemination of research 1084, 1089, 1091, 1137–50, 1200, 1306
distal family contexts 44, 50, 53–4
distance education 76, 299, 319

Australia 860
COMPETE teacher education project 313-14
ICTs 851
information and communications
   technology 304, 307
Mongolia 342
primary teacher training 1160
research training 1296, 1298
rise of 839, 846-7
University of the South Pacific 864
urban youth programs 227
distance learning
  Asia-Pacific Distance and Multimedia Education
     Network 533
  EFA Assessment 21
  Korea 530
  Pacific Islands 688, 696-7, 699
  see also web-based learning
diversification 673-4, 676, 1315, 1319
division of labour, gender-based 276
domestic roles for women 272, 273
donor assistance/support xxi, 90, 298, 1151-64
  Lao PDR 1175
  NFPE 180
  Pacific Islands 688, 689, 692, 694, 695, 696,
     697-8
double hermeneutic process 1168, 1169, 1198, 1201
double-shift schooling 735-6, 787
downsizing 1323
drop-outs 89, 90, 153, 231-40, 1160
  boys 266
  East Asia 708-9
  female 85
  gender differences 266, 272, 276
  girls 266, 282
  illiteracy 296
  Macau 1025
  Murad Report 102
  Pacific Islands 553, 688, 691-2
  Pakistan 303
  primary education 20, 24
  research 101, 1186
  secondary education 76, 78, 85, 86
  socio-economic status 45
  see also school refusal
DSS *see* Direct Subsidy Scheme
dysfunctional families 388-9, 1236

e-knowledge 1266
e-learning 901, 1249, 1254, 1263
e-mail 696
EAI *see* East Asian Institute
early childhood education (ECE)
  Education for All 18, 22-3
  educational reform 8
  Hong Kong 1021-2
  nonformal 299
  Thailand 1176
early foundations of learning 351
Earth Summit 570, 571, 572
East Asia
  coaching 739
  economic crisis 296, 553, 836
  economic growth 87, 1211
  female illiteracy 270
  female workers 219
  financial crisis 701, 702, 706, 708
  higher education 811, 819, 820, 825, 830, 842-3

homework 735
illiteracy 260, 261, 295
leadership development 923
life expectancy 20
literacy 20
male/female illiteracy 260, 261
moral education 1344
participation rates and gender 259
private expenditure 1050
public expenditure 1049
reading literacy 592
school leadership 1003-4
teacher-pupil ratios 872
teachers 868, 869
tiger economies 293
transition from school to work 701-14
urban areas 218
vocational education and training 677-8, 682
youth population 220
East Asian Institute (EAI) 102
East Timor, teachers 870
Eastern Europe 1233
EC *see* European Commission
ECE *see* early childhood education
ecological psychology 744
economic analyses 1032
economic capital 59
  conversion to social capital 66
  family background 44, 45, 50
economic crisis 553, 570
economic development 7, 19, 146, 974, 1091
  China 1251
  differences in 20
  education relationship 158-9
  global 26
  higher education 810-16, 818, 824
  HRD planning 660-1, 665, 667
  investment in higher education 737
  learning outcomes 441
  Malaysia 6
  participation and expenditure 39, 41
  science education 619
  Singapore 1248
  unequal levels 810, 828
  university education 1207, 1210-12
  vocational education and training 681
  workforce education 321, 324-6
  youth contribution to 218
economic efficiency 716
economic globalisation 1095, 1096, 1100, 1101,
   1102, 1103, 1104
economic growth 18, 31, 293, 900, 1092, 1139,
   1222
  Central Asia 242
  curriculum aims 544, 547
  East Asia 87, 704, 707, 1211
  functionalism 1033
  globalisation 1274, 1332, 1337
  higher education 737, 810-16, 818
  human capital 553
  international studies 1088
  Korea 1038
  manpower requirements approach 659, 665
  mathematics/science relationship 1098
  Pacific Islands 687, 699
  science enrolments 1100
  secondary education 77

Singapore 1248
sustainable development 581
Taiwan 1212
teaching profession 868
university education 1207
vocational education and training 684
economic indicators, teaching profession 869
economic issues
  Central Asian collapse 249, 251
  education for all 296
  efficiency 164
  macro-economic policy 225
  macro-economics 660
  micro-economics 660
  national standards 551
  Pacific Islands education 1227, 1228
  regional economic downturns 217, 221
  stagnation of Pacific Island economies 293
  urbanisation 178
  women's contribution 283-7
  see also economic development; economic growth; poverty
economic miracle 1211
economic needs 1203
economic progress 18
Economic and Social Commission for Asia and the Pacific (ESCAP) 571
economic stagnation 18
economic well-being 1245, 1254, 1272
EDI *see* Educational Development Institute
EDICT Research Group 1262
EdNA 1258, 1268
educated unemployment 87
Education & Manpower Branch and Education Department, Hong Kong 977, 984
education of adolescents xxi
Education for All (EFA) xviii, 17-27, 175-6, 184-7, 304, 542
  access 277
  Conferences 1160
  economic crisis situations 296
  EFA 2000 Assessment 155, 157, 161, 165, 166-8, 223
  East Asia 709
  literacy 294
  Synthesis Report 298-9
  thematic studies 299
  evaluation and assessment 165-8
  gender-based discrimination 269
  gifted children 190
  Jomtien World Declaration 805
  monitoring student learning 793
  Pacific Islands 689
  Pakistan assessment 804
  Salamanca Statement (1994) 189
Education Commission, Hong Kong 206, 951, 957, 974, 984, 1023, 1028, 1075
  educational indicators 1133-4, 1135
  gifted education 191, 193, 200
  'learning to learn' 790, 791
  school-based management 935, 943
Education Department, Hong Kong 191, 193, 200, 206-7, 1023, 1028, 1066, 1075
Education Department, Singapore 952, 957
Education International, secondary education 77, 81

Education and Manpower Bureau, Hong Kong 11, 14, 950, 957, 1133, 1135
Education Ministers' Conferences of the Asia-Pacific region 1303, 1313
Education Queensland 362
Education Reserve Fund, China 1018
Education Sector Policy 323
Education Service Professional Development and Career Plan 910
Education to Fight Exclusion Project 226-7
educational administration 1004, 1005, 1006, 1017
educational aspirations 49-50
educational change xiv, xv, 3, 11
Educational Development Institute (EDI), Washington 1161-2
educational indicators *see* indicators
educational innovation 1303, 1305
educational inquiry 1196-7
Educational Planning and Research Division (EPRD) 105
educational priority areas (EPAs) 152
educational processes 1195
educational psychology 147, 189
educational reform *see* reform
Educational Reform Committee, Taiwan 1020
educational research *see* research
Educational Research Association, Singapore xiii, 1286, 1293
educational research associations 126, 134-8
Educational Research and Development Centre, Bahrain 1141
Educational Resources Information Center (ERIC) Clearinghouse 666
educational technologists 1261
EduCities 529
EET *see* enterprise education and training
EFA *see* Education for All
effective schooling 987-1000
  see also effectiveness
effectiveness
  classroom learning environments 463
  managerialism 542
  monitoring 805
  principal 1002-3
  school-based indicators 118-19
  teachers 167
  see also effective schooling; school effectiveness
efficiency 39, 41, 1103, 1151, 1181
  enterprise education and training 716
  external 87
  indicators 1128-9
  internal 85-6
  Pacific Islands 1279-80, 1283
effort 497-9, 992-3
egalitarianism 189, 190, 241, 789, 790
egocentricity 367
Eight Year Study 111
electronic measurement 535
elementary school
  investment 737
  mathematics 604
  see also primary education
elites/elitism 46, 189, 190, 845, 925, 1023
emancipation of women 1336
emergent literacy 586-7
emotional content 748-9
empirical research 95, 96

1380 *Index of Subjects*

employers 553, 660, 674, 877–8
  apprenticeships 723, 728
  enterprise education and training 715, 720, 725
  incentives 1283
  Singapore Skills Development Fund 682
employment
  Barefoot College 235
  East Asia 703–7
  formal education 345
  gender discrimination 279, 282
  gender-specific education 261
  globalisation 1337
  lifelong 315
  opportunities 657
  Pacific Islands 692, 698
  right to work 1336
  urban youth 219, 221, 222, 223, 224–6
  women 258, 272, 273, 274, 283–7, 288
  workforce education 321–34
  youth 701, 1234, 1235
  see also technical and vocational education; vocational education and training; work
empowerment 25
  community 375
  for development 184–7
  environmental education 580, 581
  internet 254
  learning opportunities 280
  nonformal education 328, 345
  parents 1068
  poverty reduction 177
  teachers 888, 1250
  values education 403
  women 288, 289, 302, 335, 340, 341, 344
enactivism 604, 609
Endowment Funds, Singapore 1055
energy consumption 1338
engaged time 735, 783
engineering 1100, 1101, 1103
England
  Qualifications and Curriculum Authority 558
  research 105
English as a Foreign Language 1108
English language
  Cook Islands 803
  teaching 733
English Proficiency Test for Indonesia (EPTI) 633–4
Enlightenment 241, 254, 1332, 1334, 1336
enlightenment effect 100, 105
enlightenment model 99, 100, 103
enrichment 193, 196, 197, 198, 199, 746, 1244
enrolments 173
  access to education 280
  Central Asia 248
  China 300
  early childhood education 23
  East Asia 707, 708
  expansion of 73, 74, 83–4, 172
  food supply program 175
  gender differences 259, 270, 276, 280, 281, 282
  girls in South Asia 284
  globalisation 1096
  growth in 1032–3, 1044
  higher education 809–10, 811, 813–18, 824, 1100–1, 1210–11, 1213–14
    China 905
  increasing 840, 851
  India 848, 850
  private institutions 822, 823, 834
  human capital measurement 1088
  human development index 1340, 1342–3
    India 158, 165
    Pakistan 164
  primary school 20, 22, 23
  private finance 1281
  private sector 1050, 1051–2
  sciences 1243–4
  social sciences 1103
  South Asia 155
  tertiary education 1031, 1032–3, 1044
    Australia 1041, 1042
    growth 1092
    Japan 1035–6, 1037
    Korea 1038, 1049
  TVET 328
  vocational education and training 328, 677–80, 681
  worldwide 1151, 1152
  see also gross enrolment ratio
enterprise education and training (EET) 553, 715–30
enterprise-based training 673, 682
enterprises 878, 1054
entitlement to educational services 267
entrepreneurship skills 225
environmental education 340, 552, 569–84, 1099, 1103, 1308
environmental issues 145–6, 147–8
  Darwin 1332
  degradation 18, 570, 668, 689, 1232
  donor aid 1159
  globalisation 1332, 1338
  harmony with nature 648
  Pacific Islands 689
  protection 232
environmental studies 616
EPAs *see* educational priority areas
EPRD *see* Educational Planning and Research Division
EPTI *see* English Proficiency Test for Indonesia
equal opportunity 97–8, 143–54, 1023
  Coleman study 100
  Delors report 1333
  gender issues 257
  inclusive education 204
  key-point schools 1017
  privatisation 1026
  women 868
  youth empowerment 227
  see also inequalities
equality 257, 651
  achievement outcomes 1173
  Central Asia 242, 249, 253
  culture of peace 398, 399
  gender 257, 261, 275, 277
  social 1208
Equality of Educational Opportunity (Coleman) 100
equilibration 366, 367
equity xix, 39, 41, 144, 641, 1103, 1272, 1274
  access to secondary education 74, 84–5, 87
  Central Asia 242, 249
  classroom environments 51
  disadvantaged students 1319

donor support for research 1157
enterprise education and training 716
financing of education 927, 1060, 1283
gender 78, 80, 87, 144, 153–4, 265, 267
   research 1147, 1157, 1160
   rural-urban migration 221
inclusiveness 1238
indicators 1128–9, 1133
New Zealand 856
Pacific islands 689
privatisation 1026
research 1181, 1203
rural education 336, 342–3
science curriculum 622–3
selection for higher education 839, 841, 846, 848–50, 851
social and racial justice 1203
student perceptions of 354
targets 298
technical and vocational education and training 688
values education 399
vocational education and training 675, 688
see also equality of opportunity; inequalities
equivalent usage 444
ER see extensive reading
Erebus Consulting Partners 637, 640
ERIC see Educational Resources Information Center
ESCAP see Economic and Social Commission for Asia and the Pacific
ethical issues 889, 1266
ethical values 402, 403
ethnic discrimination 1232–3
ethnic identity 559–60
ethnic minorities 22, 1214, 1215
ethnic nationalism 244
ethnicity
   Central Asia 241–56
   social capital 60
   Taiwan 564
   see also race
ethno-nationalism 241
ethnocentrism 252, 253, 254
ethnography
   ethnographic approach 69
   Soviet 244
   studies 453
ethnomathematics 600, 609–10, 1226
Euro-centrism 542
Europe
   fees 1052
   influence on Asia-Pacific education 108
   new mathematics 602
   pattern of formal schooling 172
   public expenditure 1049
   research 1083, 1086
   state provision of education 822
   vocational education and training 680
   workforce education 323, 324
European Commission (EC) 768, 1157, 1158, 1162, 1164
European Union (EU) 1162
   democracy 1336
   quality 1129, 1135
   statistical office 1128
evaluation xix, 107, 110–13

curriculum 110
definition 109
education for all 165–8, 186–7
educational changes 120
educational programs 466–7
evaluator training seminars 118
gifted education research 196
indicators 1123, 1124
language education 636–8
orientation 1238
research 1187
resources 299
school effectiveness indicators 119
secondary education 80
streamlined 298
teacher education 890, 891, 892
teachers 963, 964
values education 404
Western approaches/influences 108, 642
youth transition 713
see also formative assessment/evaluation; self-evaluation; summative assessment/evaluation
evaluatory research 550, 605
evaporated time 783
evolutionism 1169, 1170
examinations
   accountability 109, 113–15
   central 938
   coaching 734, 761, 762–3
   competitive 354
   cultural/social capital relationship 67–8
   family background 48
   India 848
   Indonesia 115–17
   Jesuit Order influence 108
   limitations of 155–6
   parental demand for good results 745
   primary schools in South Asia 155–7
   reforms 8, 920
   research priorities 1205
   secondary education reform 86, 87, 88
   Singapore 748
   student learning 452
   success 920, 988, 991–2, 1244
   university entrance 561
   see also assessment
excellence 354, 355, 356, 891
exclusion 397, 750
Exeter University 771
expansion of education 107, 109, 123, 125–6, 145
   higher education 1100–1, 1202, 1216, 1318
   planning and policy-making 1031, 1032–3
expectations 280
   assessment 795–6
   Australia 265
   motivation 498
   parental 990, 992
   of research 1186–7
   social 389
   stakeholders 1319–20, 1321
   student 624
   teachers 65–6, 487
expenditure xiv, xviii, 29–42, 1047–9, 1093, 1302
   accountability 107
   cutbacks 19
   decreasing 1102
   developing countries 173

Index of Subjects

human capital 722
Indonesia 325
Macau 1025
Pacific Islands 1277–8, 1282
per student 36
as percentage of GDP 36, 37
as percentage of GNP 173
private 1049–52
research 1141
rural areas 343
secondary education 85–6
Sri Lanka 907
tertiary education
  Japan 1037
  Korea 1039, 1040
see also finance
experiential learning 562
experimental psychology 124
experimentation 1197, 1199
expert behaviour 521–2
exploratory studies 550
extended families 65
extension activities 193, 196, 197, 199
extension tasks 756
extensive reading (ER) 590–1
external aid 1055–9, 1060
  see also foreign aid
external efficiency 87
external funding for higher education 835–6
external review 947, 948, 956
extra-curricular activities 562, 989
  gifted education 196, 197
  PTA 1067

failure 496, 498, 499, 515
fairness of assessment 797, 798
family 43–57, 989
  background 43, 44, 45–6
  cognitive development 366
  cultural capital 64–5
  dislocation 1234
  dysfunctional 1236
  early learning environments 54
  effect on educational career 147–8
  extended families 65
  gender issues 66–7, 290
  influence on bullying 433
  interaction patterns 45
  parent–child relationship 151
  participation 915, 917, 924–5, 1063–77
  school learning environments 51–2
  size 148, 258
  social capital 60, 61, 64–5
  values 402, 924–5
  see also parents
family capital 48–51
fatherhood 288
feedback 94
  assessment methods 797, 798
  corrective 994
  ICT 1263
  Japanese research lessons 1247
fees 84, 844, 845, 927, 1060
  Australia 1042–3, 1211
  China 1017, 1018
  cost-sharing 1052, 1053
  higher education 819, 820, 821–2, 831, 835
  Higher Education Contribution Scheme 1282

Korea 1039
public education 35, 40
FEL *see* Female Functional Literacy Program
FELP *see* Functional Education and Literacy Programme
female drop-out rates 85
Female Functional Literacy Program (FEL), Philippines 301
female retention rates 85
femininity 280, 288, 290
feminism 1100
fertility 159, 258, 260, 289, 296
  Australia 1173, 1174
  higher education 817–18
  see also birth rates
FfW *see* Kreditanstalt fur Wiederaufbau
field experiences 889, 1263
field supervisors 180
field trips 1068
Fiji
  continuing education 854, 858, 859
  economic/demographic indicators 1276
  educational provision 1277
  enrolments 1214
  environmental awareness 578, 579
  girls and science education 619
  manufacturing industry 1275, 1282
  mathematics 1226
  political stability 689
  private sector 1050
  public expenditure 1277, 1278, 1279
  reading literacy 55, 590
  student loans 833
  teachers 870
  technical and vocational education and training 687, 691, 694
filial piety 380, 384
finance 95, 1047–62, 1099–1100
  China 1017
  cost-effectiveness 1126
  donor support 1151–64
  educational services 919, 927
  higher education 819–22, 825, 827–38, 843–4, 1102
  international 1202
  Korea 1040–1
  Pacific Islands 1280–2, 1283
  private sector 1274, 1280–2, 1283
  research 101
  secondary education reform 76, 80, 84, 88, 90
  training 1271–2, 1274
  see also expenditure; funding
financial capacity 31
financial crisis 293, 701, 702, 706, 708, 710
Finn Committee 310, 311
First International Mathematics Study 258, 464
flexibility
  curriculum 551
  labour force 673
flexible delivery 307, 531
  apprenticeships 724
  competency-based training 723, 727
flexible learning environments, COMPETE project 313
Flinders University 1262, 1287, 1309
Ford Foundation 1086, 1153, 1154
foreign aid 830, 844, 927, 1055–9, 1060

foreign language education 629-40
foreign students
  Australia 833, 844
  UK 835
  see also international students
formal education 307, 308, 309
  enterprise education and training 715
  environmental protection 1338
  gender gap 269, 270
  globalisation 1332, 1335
  learning opportunities 312
  lifelong learning 336
  literacy rates 345
  Malaysia 337, 338
  research training 1285, 1286, 1297
  rural India 235
  social education 315
  Thailand 1176
  vocational programs 709
formal operational stage 367
formative assessment/evaluation 101, 111, 610, 1238
Framework for Action to Meet Basic Learning Needs (Dakar Framework for Action) 19
France
  donor aid 1158
  Enlightenment 1331-2
  French Revolution 1336
  influence on Asia-Pacific curriculum 606
  influence on Asia-Pacific education 108
  training 1281
free market economy 665, 667
free trade 1273
freedom 641, 651
French as a Foreign Language 1108
French Revolution 1336
fugitive literature 321, 326, 327, 666-7
full-cohort testing 800-1
Functional Education and Literacy Programme (FELP), Philippines 300-1
functional grammar approach 591
functional imaging techniques 1265
functional literacy 18, 24, 231
  Philippines 300-1
  Thailand 303
functional training 175
functionalism 1033, 1034, 1083, 1085, 1208, 1215
  educational reform 6
  structuration theory 1169, 1170
fundamental research 97, 549
funding
  higher education 737
  nonformal education 337, 340, 345-6
  private sector 737
  research 1188
  see also finance
further education
  Japan 314-15
  job skill equation 664

GAD see Gender and Development
Gadja Mada University 1154
GDP see Gross Domestic Product
Gekkan Seitosidou 430, 438
gender 269-90
  academic achievement 50
  access issues 90, 279-90
  achievement variation 66-7, 1302
  bias 287, 289
  bullying 427, 429, 430-1, 437
  Central Asia 249
  classroom learning environments 463, 467-8
  cognitive/metacognitive differences 1264-5
  cultural disadvantage 1302
  differences in outcomes 257-68
  discrimination 269, 279, 282, 287-8, 344
  disparities 20, 270
  donor aid 1157, 1159
  equality 232
  equity 78, 80, 87, 144, 153-4, 265, 267
    research 1147, 1157, 1160
    rural-urban migration 221
  family dynamics 66-7
  gap 269-70, 272, 277, 281, 282-3, 284
    literacy 296
  inclusiveness 1238
  inequalities 249, 1214, 1215, 1338
  literacy 296-8
  metacognition 487
  motivation 502
  out-of-school secondary-school age youth 74, 75
  perceptions of school life 51-2
  primary school enrolment 23
  research on differences 168
  retention rates 85
  science achievement 619
  sensitisation 270, 273-6, 277, 282
  Taiwan 564
  youth labour force participation in East Asia 705
  youth unemployment in East Asia 705
  see also women
Gender and Development (GAD) 288
gender development index 817
gender discrimination 1232-3
gender empowerment index 816-17
gender-sensitive education 270, 273-6, 277, 282
general education 673, 676, 683, 684
general human capital 553, 673
General Paper Constructivist Learning Environment Survey (GPCLES) 471
General Studies 1250-1, 1255
geography, Barefoot College 239
GER see gross enrolment ratio
German Technical Cooperation (GTZ) 1158
Germany
  donor aid 1158
  research 125
gifted education 189-202
gifted students 153, 189-202, 1176
giftedness 190-2, 497
global citizenship 557, 560, 566
global competition 857
global development 1331
global economy 707, 932, 1151, 1232, 1271, 1273, 1274, 1275
Global Plan for Education in the Twenty-first Century 22
global survival crisis 265
Global Technical Advisory Group (GTAG) 21
global village 12
globalisation xx, xxii-xxiii, 374, 770, 1091, 1095-1106, 1302, 1331-45
  Australian economy 265
  challenge of 790

1384 Index of Subjects

Chinese higher education reform   844
citizenship education   560
continuing education   864
cultural settings   309
economic growth   1274
educational management   915, 927
educational reforms   900, 1316, 1317, 1326
effective schooling   997
English language   629
ethnicity   254
higher education   733, 737, 809, 824
India   1172
influence on curriculum   544
Japan   857
language policy   638
market forces   26
need for tolerance   397
Pacific Islands   696
portability of qualifications   312
of production   1271
qualifications   755
quality assurance   86, 945, 949
school governance   1019
school leadership   980
secondary education reform   76, 77
South Asian women   287
staffing issues   924
teacher education   895
trends in educational reform   3, 7, 12
university education   1209, 1218
values   403
workforce education   322–3
globalised knowledge economy   1210
globalism   396
globalisation   217
GNI *see* gross national income
GNP *see* Gross National Product
goal theory   441
Goethe Institute   1158
governance   1099–1100, 1102
GPCLES *see* General Paper Constructivist Learning Environment Survey
grade repetition   94, 101, 174
graduate research training   1285–99
graduate unemployment   737, 1215–16
grammar   591
grants   927, 1058, 1060, 1283
  Direct Subsidy Scheme   1022
  Hong Kong   935
  nonformal education   340
  Thailand   1177
grassroots programs   300
Great Britain
  assessment   799
  Department for International Development (DFID)   1158
  donor aid   1158
  General Teaching Council   942
  influence on Asia-Pacific education   108
  Schools InterLink Project   532
  self-managing schools   941
  teacher training   752
Gross Domestic Product (GDP)
  allocation to secondary education   84
  East Asia   704
  external aid   1058
  higher education attainment ratio   814

human development index   1340, 1342–3
human resource development   1341
Lao PDR   1175
Pacific Islands   1275, 1276, 1277, 1278
taxation   1053
women's contribution   283
gross enrolment ratio (GER)
  expansion   73, 74, 83–4
  higher education   811, 813, 814, 815, 816, 817, 818, 824
  human development index   1340, 1342–3
gross national income (GNI)   31
Gross National Product (GNP)   1302
  Pacific Islands   1276
  public expenditure   1047–9
  public expenditure as percentage of   173
  taxation   1054
  vocational education and training   681
group placement   47
group work   996
GTAG *see* Global Technical Advisory Group
GTZ *see* German Technical Cooperation

hard technology   525
hard work *see* effort
Harvard Project Physics   464
Hawaii, reading literacy   590
HCM *see* hyperbolic cosine model
HEA *see* higher education attainment ratio
Headstart initiative   782
health education   222, 223–4, 239, 339
HECS *see* Higher Education Contribution Scheme
hegemony
  American   564
  state   1209
Hermannsburg project   371
hermeneutic processes   1169, 1198, 1201
hermeneutic research   1197
hidden curriculum   576
hierarchical model of intelligence   308
high culture   61
high-school leavers, East Asia   705
high-value-added manufacturing   325
higher degree programs   1285, 1286, 1287–98
higher education   xx, 736–8, 809–26, 1100–1
  curriculum   1101–2
  economic growth   810–16
  financing   819–22, 825, 827–38
  girls   282, 284
  increasing demand for   107
  investment   737
  privatisation   8
  rapid expansion   1318
  regional research   1309–10
  research priorities   1205
  selection   839–52
  student selection   737
  Thailand   1176
  vocational education and training link   685
  women   258
  see also continuing education; tertiary education; universities
higher education attainment ratio (HEA)   813, 814, 815, 816, 817, 818
Higher Education Contribution Scheme (HECS), Australia   1042, 1282
Higher Education Research and Development Society of Australasia   1143, 1308, 1309

higher-order thinking/skills 354, 511, 794–6
Hinduism 644
historical context 293–4
historical development of educational research xix
historical research 95, 1197
history 239, 1101
HIV/AIDS 78, 226, 1233
HKU *see* Hong Kong University
Hokkaido University of Education 529
home xviii
　background factors 1119
　collectivist culture 62
　learning at 1064–5
　school relationship 49, 64
home schooling 1065
home tutoring 48
home visit programs 150
home-school communication 1065–6
homelessness 1236
homework 94, 734, 735, 755–66, 920
　achievement relationship 1119, 1120
　Australia 1065
　effective schooling 988, 991, 992
　time spent on 788
Hong Kong
　academic curriculum 1212
　anxiety research 499
　attributional research 498
　child-centred approach 587
　civic education 557, 561
　cognitive orientation 615–16
　conflict perspective 1033
　continuing education 854, 861–2, 863–4
　Curriculum Development Council 876
　curriculum reform 561
　decentralisation 975–6
　economic growth 1088
　economy 1211
　education aims 790
　educational indicators 1133–4
　educational research associations 137–8
　effective schooling 920, 987, 999
　enrolments 32, 33, 707, 1214
　environmental education 576, 578, 579
　examination pressure 992
　examination reforms 950–1
　family/community participation 924
　fees 1052
　gender differences 66–7, 262, 263, 264
　General Studies 1250–1, 1255
　gifted education 190, 191, 193–4, 197, 199
　global civics 560
　gross national income 31
　high educational attainment 63, 769
　higher education 7, 811, 815, 819, 822, 824–5, 832, 1318
　home-school communication 1065, 1066
　homework 758, 759, 991
　IEA Civic Education Project 643
　inclusive education for students with special needs 206–7
　influence on Macau education system 1024
　Institute of Education 4, 131, 558, 1178, 1310
　integrated curriculum initiative 1250–1, 1254
　international studies 353, 1110–18
　IT strategy 11
　language 452
　leadership 922
　learning technology 527
　locus of control 497
　memorisation 360, 361, 993
　national visions 7
　paradigm shifts 12
　parents
　　involvement 1320
　　parent education 1064
　　role 925, 1065, 1071, 1072, 1073, 1074
　　volunteering 1067
　performance goals 500
　performance indicators 952
　performativity 769
　PISA 949
　policy emphasis 770
　population 30, 31
　post-colonial transition 563
　pressure to succeed 452, 992, 1244
　principals 977, 978, 981, 982, 983, 1003
　private sector 949, 1021–2, 1023
　private tuition 788, 1059
　public expenditure 36, 37, 40, 1049
　public/private education 925, 1020–3, 1027
　quality assurance 10, 946, 952–3, 954, 955, 974
　reading literacy 592
　repetition 360
　research 1143
　　institutions 128, 131
　　productivity 133
　school decision-making 1069
　school effectiveness research 768
　school leadership 1001, 1002, 1003, 1007–8
　school-based management 10, 948
　science education 617
　self-managing schools 921, 931, 934–5
　SMILES 528
　socially-orientated achievement 502
　staffing ratios 38
　student learning 441, 444, 446, 448–9, 450, 451
　student mobility 502
　Target Orientated Curriculum 787
　teacher education 892, 911
　teachers 870, 873, 876
　　evaluation 771
　　monitoring 950
　　quality 11
　　training 996
　teaching behaviour 734
　teaching practices 994, 997
　time allocation 736, 787, 788
　transparency 951
　values 451
　vocational education and training 678, 679, 681, 682
　workforce education 323, 330
Hong Kong Educational Research Association xiii, 137–8
Hong Kong University (HKU) 862, 863–4
hot-housing 734
household
　budget 1060
　cost 1050
　expenditure 164, 1050–1
HRD *see* human resource development
HRDWG *see* Human Resources Development Working Group

1386 Index of Subjects

human action 1201
human agency 217
human agents 1168, 1169
human capital 59, 553, 900, 1103
  Asian Tiger economies 1211
  East Asia 707
  economic growth 684
  enterprise education and training 716, 721
  expenditure on 722
  family background 45, 49
  formation 869
  general/specific distinction 673
  higher education 809, 841
  measuring 1087-8
  structural functionalist perspective 1207
  university education 1210
Human Cognitive Abilities (Carroll) 100
human computer interactions 1264, 1266
human development xix-xx, 309, 351-63, 1092, 1177
  bioecological model 44
  globalisation xxii, 1334, 1335, 1339-41, 1342-3
  higher education 816, 817
  indicators 1342-3
  lifespan 379-94
  motivation 495
  sustainable 20
  values education 395
  WCEFA 176
Human Development Index 817, 1339-41
Human Development Report Education Index 323
human intelligence *see* intelligence theories
human life cycle 382, 383
human needs 495
human resource development (HRD) 89, 325, 657, 658-68, 1159, 1161-2, 1210, 1228, 1341
human resource management 719
Human Resources Development Working Group (HRDWG) 1132, 1335, 1339, 1344
human rights 143, 145, 641, 1099, 1102, 1336
  APNIEVE 400
  citizenship education 557, 566
  education as a human right 1103
  values education 397, 399, 402, 407
Human Rights Charter 304
Humanistic Education Foundation 1019
Hungary, international studies 353
hyperbolic cosine model (HCM) 412-19
hypothesis testing 1197
hypothetico-deductive thinking 367, 1264

IAB *see Institute Ahminuddin Baki*
IAE *see* International Academy of Education
IALS *see* International Adult Literacy Study
IBE *see* International Bureau of Education
IBO *see* International Baccalaureate Organisation
ICE *see* International Conference of Ministers of Education
ICEQ *see* Individualised Classroom Environment Questionnaire
ICSED *see* International Standard Classification of Education
ICT *see* information and communications technology
IDB *see* Islamic Development Bank
IDEA *see* Institute for the Development of Educational Administrators
identity

  ethnic 247-8, 254
  transnational 255
identity politics 564
ideographic script 587-8
ideological education 1212
ideology 221
  inclusive education 213
  political 556, 557
IEA *see* International Association for the Evaluation of Educational Achievement
IEPs *see* individual education programs
IFA *see* Integrated Framework of Action for Peace, Human Rights and Democracy
IGES *see* Institute for Global Environmental Strategies
IGNOU *see* Indira Gandhi National Open University
IIEP *see* International Institute for Educational Planning
illiteracy 18, 73, 144, 295, 299, 395, 901, 1302
  adults 171, 1232, 1277
  APPEAL 571
  Asia 171, 174, 231
  ATLP initiative 182
  Education for All 19, 25
  gender differences 260-1, 270, 276
  India 905
  Indonesia 176
  Pacific Islands 1277
  Philippines 300-1
  rural poverty 177
  South Asia 296
  Thailand 303
  women in China 344
  see also literacy
ILO *see* International Labour Organisation
imagined community 559
IMF *see* International Monetary Fund
immigrants 1172-3
  Asian 54
  Hong Kong 1021
IMO *see* International Maritime Organisation
implementation
  of change xv
  policy 105
  reform 101
  of research findings xiv
implemented curriculum 566, 615, 617-18, 619, 624
import substitution industries 325
in-service teacher education 11, 167, 883-4, 885, 887-8, 890, 891-2
  Bangladesh 906
  Cambodia 869
  China 904, 905
  citizenship education 561
  COMPETE project 314
  educational administrators 901
  effective schooling 996
  environmental education 575, 582
  globalisation 895
  inclusive education for students with special needs 209
  Japan 903-4
  Korea 904
  lack of gender sensitisation 275
  Malaysia 908

Index of Subjects 1387

Pakistan 906
research impact on practice 102
Singapore 908, 909
Taiwan 950
workforce education 321, 328
INCA *see* International Review of Curriculum and Assessment Frameworks project
inclusion 1170
inclusive education 203–15, 242, 1238
income
  attainment relationship 48
  equity issues 144
  gender inequalities 285, 287
  Pacific Islands 1275
  per head 29, 36, 40
income contingent loans 832
independence 496
independent learning 876, 1099
India
  adult education 854
  classroom learning environments 464
  coaching 761
  colonial history 1153
  community service 225
  completion of schooling 1302
  continuing education 862–3
  curriculum 544
  economic growth 1088
  educational research associations 138
  Emperor Ashoka 651
  enrolments 173
  environmental education 573, 576, 578, 579, 582
  ethnographic studies 453
  examinations 114
  female illiteracy 260
  gender differences 279, 281–2
  Government of 851
  graduate unemployment 1215, 1216
  higher education 825, 839, 1211, 1215
    access and equity 847–50
    financing 830, 831, 832, 834
    participation 843
    private sector 834
  illiteracy 171
  inclusive education for students with special needs 207–9
  industrial training institutes 673
  international comparative studies 1110–17
  international students 70
  learning achievement assessment 157–9
  literacy 301–2
  manpower planning 666
  mathematics 609–10
  Minimum Learning Levels Program (MLLP) 178–9
  national visions 7
  nonformal education 341, 344, 346
  out-of-school children 231–40
  participation rates 339
  peace education 644–5, 649, 650, 651
  population 293, 1151
  primary education improvement 164–5
  private sector 834, 1051, 1102, 1211
  private tutoring 1059
  quality assurance 10
  reforms 1172
  religious bodies 1217
  repetition rate 174
  research 1138–9, 1143
    impact on practice 102
    institutions 129
    productivity 133
    research environment 1312
  science/engineering enrolments 1100
  sex stereotypes 273
  student distraction 786
  teacher education 893
  teachers 869, 870, 872, 878
    quality assurance 739
    recruitment 905–6
  Total Literacy Project 339
  UNICEF projects 1306
  universities 1155
  urban areas 218
  vocational education and training 673, 674, 675, 676, 677, 678, 679, 680–1, 682
  women 271, 285, 286
  workforce education 323
  World Bank loans 1161
  World Education Indicators 1133
  youth population 220
India University Grants Commission (UGC) 848–50
Indian Council of Social Science Research 1307
Indian Education Commission 1172
Indian Educational Abstracts 1306
Indian Educational Review 1306
indicators xix, 89, 90, 1091, 1123–36, 1322
  benchmarking 9–10
  comparative 1312–13
  Education for All 21
  enrolment rates 32, 33
  human development 1342–3
  internal efficiency 85
  monitoring change 1335
  outcomes 1123, 1128, 1129
  quality assurance 86, 920, 947, 949, 952, 955, 956
  school effectiveness 118–19
  school-based 118–19
  social status 65
  see also performance indicators
Indicators of Education Systems (INES) project 1123, 1126, 1127–8, 1134, 1136
indigenisation 884
Indigenous Australians 845
indigenous cultures 1216
  learning 352
  Oceania 1222
  Taiwan 564
indigenous knowledge 546, 1217–18
  Pacific Islands 1228, 1229
  school leadership development 1004–5, 1006, 1009
indigenous peoples
  Australian 365–6, 369–72, 375
  Central Asia 241, 246, 249, 252
  cognitive development 365–6, 369–72, 373, 375
  mathematics curriculum 609, 610
  nonformal education 341
  science education 619–20
  student learning 451
  values education 396
indigenous psychology 444

indigenous scholars 642
Indira Gandhi National Open University (IGNOU) 849–50
individual differences 189–90, 210
individual education programs (IEPs) 209
individual progress 793–4
individual work 745
individualisation xv, 5, 12, 562, 746, 748, 954, 1262, 1264, 1326
Individualised Classroom Environment Questionnaire (ICEQ) 464, 471
individualism 62–3, 187, 357, 451
  achievement motivation 496
  collectivism shift to 556
  locus of control 497
  Taiwan 770
individuality 315
Indonesia
  ageing population 707
  classroom learning environments 464, 465, 469, 470
  cognitive development research 375
  colonial history 1153
  completion of schooling 1302
  Composite Development Index 1120
  curriculum 545
  decentralisation 93
  decreased support for higher education 1102
  development indicators 702
  development plan targets 323
  economic growth 1088
  employment 703, 704
  English Proficiency Test 633–4
  enrolments 173, 1214
  environmental education 573, 578
  examinations 114, 115–17
  expenditure 37, 325
  external aid 1057
  good educational outcomes 323
  graduate unemployment 1215
  gross national income 31
  higher education 811, 824, 1211
    financing 833
    private sector 827, 837
  indigenous cultures 1216
  international comparative studies 1110–18
  international students 451
  Islam influence 563
  Islamic Development Bank loans 1157
  Islamic education 1217
  labour market signalling 665
  language education 630, 633–4
  National Assessment of Education Project 1171–2
  Office of Educational and Cultural Research and Development 118
  participation 339
  political ideology 1212
  population 30, 293, 703, 707
  private expenditure 1051
  private sector 711, 827, 837, 1051, 1102, 1211
  public/private provision 34, 36
  reading literacy 592
  religious bodies 1217
  repetition rate 174
  research 130, 1086, 1141
  research training 1290–1
  salaries 873
  science education 616
  self-managing schools 921, 931, 935
  staffing ratios 38
  street children 226
  student activism 1213
  teacher education 884, 885, 891
  teachers 738, 870
  technical assistance 1160
  technical and vocational education 710
  tracer studies 327
  TVET enrolment 328
  unemployment 704–6
  USAID 1159
  vocational education and training 677, 678, 679, 680, 683
  workforce education 331
  World Education Indicators 1133
  youth population 220
Indonesian Office of Educational and Cultural Research and Development 1141
induction training of teachers 950
industrial relations 719–20
industrialisation 1211, 1234
Industry Training Organisations (ITOs) 725–7
Industry-Based Training 330
inequalities
  Central Asia 241, 248–9, 254, 255
  China 1017, 1018
  class-based 45
  digital divide 851, 868, 892
  disadvantaged students 1322
  family background 43, 47
  gender 67, 85, 270, 276, 279, 285, 289, 1338
  higher education 1214–15
  learning divide 879
  private education 925, 1026
  private sector reliance 825
  private tutoring 1060
  regional 1053
  vocational education and training 680, 684
  see also equal opportunity; equity
INES see Indicators of Education Systems
infant mortality 572, 816, 817, 818
informal education 307, 308, 309, 782, 785
  East Asia 704, 706, 709
  environmental protection 1338
  globalisation 1332, 1335
  learning opportunities 312
  lifelong education/learning 154, 316, 336
  research training 1285, 1286–7, 1297
  Thailand 1176, 1177
informal training
  of educational research workers 1285, 1286–7, 1297
  enterprise education 715
Information Age 658, 664, 904, 910
information and communications technology (ICT) xxii, 266–7, 525, 536, 1257–69, 1344
  adult literacy 304
  applied research 1197–8
  Australia 265, 531–2
  China 526, 1205
  COMPETE project 314
  conceptual worlds 1194–5, 1200
  definitions 1258
  distance education 847, 851

Index of Subjects 1389

donor aid 1157
educational reforms 11–12
globalisation 1104, 1341
Indonesia 534
investment in 739
Japan 529
Korea 530
lifelong education 307–8, 314, 319
Macao 528
nonformal education 340, 346
Philippines 532–3
problem solving 522
quality assurance 949, 954
research 1147, 1202, 1324–5, 1327
secondary education 76, 80
Singapore 531, 909
Taiwan 528
teacher education 892, 901, 904, 909, 910–11
teachers 738, 867
Thailand 1177
see also computers; information technology
information function 418–19
information literacy 1257
information network management 904
Information Society 867, 876, 1336–7
see also knowledge society
information technology (IT) xv, 254, 975, 1244, 1254
  conceptual worlds 1196
  curriculum 545
  definitions 1258
  distance education 1296
  education for all goals 175
  Education For All 2000 Assessment Synthesis Report 298
  educational management 915, 916, 918
  educational reforms 3, 1316, 1317
  increased demand for 1102
  Pacific Islands 689, 696
  peri-urban areas 223
  research priorities 1205
  school leadership 1009, 1010
  Singapore 1249
  staffing issues 924
  training 1274
  uneven access 738, 739
  see also information and communications technology
innate ability 146, 992
  gender differences 257
  Japanese values 210
INNOTECH (Regional Centre for Educational Innovation and Technology) 1295
input-process-output model 919, 946–7
inquiry approach 1250
inspection 771, 947
Institute Ahminuddin Baki (IAB) 1004–5
Institute for the Development of Educational Administrators (IDEA), Thailand 1005
Institute for Global Environmental Strategies (IGES) 571
Institute for the Promotion of Science and Technology (IPST), Thailand 128, 1245
Institute for Scientific Information (ISI) 132, 1144
Institute of South East Asian Studies (ISEAS) 102, 1210
institutional self-evaluation 1037

institutional transfer 324
instructional methods, cross-national problem solving studies 518–21
instructional organisation 47–8
instructional technologies 1258, 1261
instructional time 783, 1119, 1120
instrumentalism 1092
integrated curriculum 1250–1, 1252, 1254
integrated education 206–7, 208, 211, 1170
Integrated Education of Disabled Children Scheme, India 208
Integrated Framework of Action for Peace, Human Rights and Democracy (IFA) 399, 400
integrated science 616
intellectual development 308–9
intellectual disabilities 478, 487
intelligence tests 782
intelligence theories 190, 191, 195, 199–200, 308
Intelligent Tutoring Systems (ITS) 529, 533, 1262
intended curriculum 566, 615, 617–18
inter-ethnic conflict, Central Asia 241, 248, 250, 251, 254, 255
Inter-governmental Conference on Environmental Education 570
interactive model 99
interactivity 1264
interest-free student loans 832
intergovernmental organisations 1032
internal efficiency 85–6
internalisation of values 400, 406
International Academy of Education (IAE) 97, 103, 106
International Adult Literacy Study (IALS) 310–11, 316–17, 717
international aid community 17
International Assessment of Educational Progress (IAEP) 1110, 1114
International Association for the Evaluation of Educational Achievement (IEA) 100, 111
  APEC report 1132
  Civic Education Project in Hong Kong 643
  cooperative research 1178
  cross-national studies 126, 449, 586, 757–8, 920, 949, 1107–9, 1110–19
  donor support 1154, 1156, 1163
  evaluator training seminars 118
  First International Mathematics Study 464
  gender differences 262–4
  homework 757–8
  indicators 1335
  lack of educational indicators 1135
  reading literacy 586
  reports 267
  sample design 262
  Second Science Study 258
International Association for the Evaluation of Educational Achievement in Mathematics 468
International Baccalaureate Organisation (IBO) 77, 81, 1239
international banks 1175
International Bureau of Education (IBE) 103, 1182, 1191
International Commission on the Development of Education 400–1
International Commission on Education for the Twenty-First Century 18, 77, 1233–4, 1333
  see also Delors report

international competitiveness 1139, 1271, 1318
International Conference of Ministers of Education (ICE) 401
International Conference on Population and Development 1236
International Consultative Forum on Education for All 21
international economic order 1103
International Institute for Child Study, Thailand 128
International Institute for Educational Planning (IIEP) 663, 666, 805, 1084, 1086, 1130, 1157, 1159, 1162
International Journal of Educational Research 558, 566, 567
International Journal of Social Education 558, 567
International Labour Organisation (ILO) 225, 229, 1159, 1224
  fugitive literature 666–7
  secondary education 77, 81
  teacher performance 739, 740
  teaching profession 867–8, 880
  VET study 327–8
  workforce education 323, 326
  workplace learning 877–8
International Maritime Organisation (IMO) 695
International Meeting on Educational Reform and Educational Research 1303
International Monetary Fund (IMF) 326
international organisations 1103
International Review of Curriculum and Assessment Frameworks (INCA) project 567
international schools 1023
International Schools Council 949
International Society for Technology in Education (ISTE) 1268
International Standard Classification of Education (ICSED) 1123, 1126, 1128, 1129–31
international students 451, 844
  see also overseas education
international studies 126–7, 353, 354, 1088, 1091
  see also comparative research studies; cross-cultural studies; cross-national studies
international understanding 400, 641, 645, 646, 652
internationalisation 315, 733, 1101
  business 1272
  citizenship education 560, 565
  higher education 1217
  influence on curriculum 544
  quality assurance 920, 947, 949
internationalism 396
internet 254, 525
  environmental education 582
  Pacific Islands 696
  teachers' networks 909
  see also web-based learning; World Wide Web
internships in research centres 1286
interpretative approach 1138, 1139
intolerance 395, 397, 398
investigator controlled applied research 1200
investigator-user linkages 1200
investment 164, 165, 1211
  elementary education 737
  formal education 345
  higher education 737, 809, 811, 824
  information and communication technologies 739

Pacific Islands 688
policy development and planning 1034
primary education 810, 811, 830
Singapore 1248
vocational education and training 682, 683, 684
invisible curriculum code 542
IOCADS 1264
IPST *see* Institute for the Promotion of Science and Technology
Iran, Islamic Republic of
  gender differences 263
  higher education 829
  Islamic education 1212, 1217
  research 1140
  universities 1212–13
  vocational education and training 678
irrelevance of education 176, 231–2
ISEAS *see* Institute of South East Asian Studies
ISI *see* Institute for Scientific Information
ISI database 1144
Islam 253, 560, 563, 622, 1053, 1334
Islamic Center for Technical and Vocational Training and Research, Bangladesh 1308
Islamic Development Bank (IDB) 1154, 1157, 1159, 1161, 1163
Islamic education 1212, 1217
Islamisation 1213
island nations *see* Pacific Islands
Israel, Perach Project 1241
ISTE *see* International Society for Technology in Education
IT *see* information technology
ITE *see* Singapore Institute of Technical Education
item bank 116
ITOs *see* Industry Training Organisations
ITS *see* Intelligent Tutoring Systems

Japan
  attitudes towards capital punishment 419, 421, 422
  beliefs about old age 384
  bullying 425, 429–32, 437
  capital investment conditions 703
  children with reading difficulties 591
  class size 741
  classroom learning environments 464
  coaching 734, 735, 756, 760–1, 764
  cognitive development research 366
  comparison with United States 64–5
  Confucian culture 893
  continuing education 854, 856–8, 863, 864
  cross-national problem solving studies 519
  curriculum 546
  decentralisation 93, 976
  donor aid 1156, 1157, 1163
  economic growth/development 828, 1088
  educational indicators 1131–2
  educational and instructional technology 1261
  educational reforms 12
  effective schooling 920, 987, 999
  effort 992–3
  enrolments 32, 33, 74, 1210
  environmental education 573–4, 576, 578, 579
  examinations 8, 114, 992
  family/community participation 924
  fertility 817
  gender differences 262, 263
  global civics 560

Index of Subjects 1391

gross national income 31
high educational attainment 63, 769, 1097
higher education 813, 822, 824, 841, 1210
  inequalities 1214–15
  private sector 822, 827, 834
home-school communication 1065, 1066
homework 991
hours at school 988, 989
human resource development 1210
inclusive education for students with special
  needs 209–10
international students 70
international studies 353, 1110–17
IT strategy 11
language education 638
learning technology 529–30
lesson planning 609
lifelong learning 314–15, 319
literacy 295
mathematics 519, 520, 547, 609
metacognition 1262
motivation 496
national heritage 560
national unity 1212
national visions 7
out of field teaching 1098
parents 989–90, 991
  involvement 1320
  parent education 1064–5
  role 925, 1065, 1071, 1072, 1073, 1074
  volunteering 1067
participation 305
peace education 645–6, 649, 650, 651
performance indicators 952
performativity 769
PISA 949
planning and policy 926
policy directions 102
population 30, 31
pressure to succeed 452, 1244
primary education 1281
principals 979, 981, 982, 983
private sector 822, 827, 834, 1036, 1038
  finance 1281
  higher education 1102
  private tuition 788–9, 1059
privatisation of tertiary education 8
public expenditure 37
public/private provision 34, 36, 40
quality assurance 946, 947–8, 953, 954, 955
questioning techniques 356
research 1137, 1139
  institutions 128
  productivity 133
salaries 873
school decision-making 1069–70
science education 616–17, 619, 620, 1246–7, 1254
science/engineering enrolments 1100
self-evaluation 948–9
shadow education 1100
social status 46
socialisation 990, 1120
Special Training Schools 323
staffing ratios 36, 38
student learning 441, 444, 449, 450
success attributions 770
teacher education 900, 901, 910
teachers 870, 923
  career ladder 966
  monitoring 950
  performance standards 964
  preparation 738
  recruitment 903–4, 962, 969–70
  salaries 756
  supply and demand 961
  training 996–7
teaching practices 993–6
technical and vocational education 668
tertiary education 737, 1035–8
time allocation 736, 788
TIMSS 758
transparency 952
universities 738
US comparison 519, 758, 763, 1120
vocational education and training 677, 678, 679, 682, 684
women 271
women's studies 1101
workers' roles 659
workforce education 323, 324
Japan Association for International Education 646
Japan International Cooperation Agency (JICA) 1156, 1158
Japan National Council of Parent-Teacher Associations 1069, 1075
Japanese Bank for International Cooperation (JBIC) 1158
Japanese Journal of Developmental Psychology 366
Japanese National Council on Educational Reforms 903
Japanese Peer Support program (JPSP) 432
JBIC *see* Japanese Bank for International Cooperation
Jesuit Order 108
JICA *see* Japan International Cooperation Agency
JIP *see* Joint Innovative Project
job analysis 634
job counselling 713
job opportunities 52
job satisfaction 888
job vacancy approach 658, 661, 664
job-referral system 52
Joint Innovative Project (JIP) 1237–8
Jomtien Conference (1990) 167, 175–6, 299, 1242
  aid flows 830
  goals 304
  right to education 1232
  universal primary education 337
  World Declaration on Education for All 19, 175, 805, 1232
journals 1142–4, 1148, 1306, 1310–12
  research training 1286, 1293
  science education research 1253
JPSP *see* Japanese Peer Support program
juku schools 756, 760–1, 762, 764, 788–9, 992, 1244
junior secondary schooling 34, 35
justice 20

Karachi Plan 172, 175, 1303
Kazakhstan 243, 244, 248, 250–1
  external aid 1057
  monitoring achievement 796
  private sector higher education 834

1392 *Index of Subjects*

KEDI *see* Korean Educational Development Institute
key competencies 310, 311
key-point schools 1017
Khmer Rouge 1213
KICE *see* Korean Institute of Curriculum and Evaluation
kindergartens 1021-2
Kiribati
  continuing education 858
  economic/demographic indicators 1276
  educational provision 1277
  information on 690
  maritime training 696, 698
  public expenditure 1277, 1279
  teachers 870
  technical and vocational education and training 687
KIYD *see* Korea Institute for Youth Development
knowledge 152, 351
  competence 310
  cultural capital 60-1
  curriculum 546
  domain-specific 522
  enactivism 609
  growth in 306
  indigenous 546, 1217-18
    Pacific Islands 1228, 1229
    school leadership development 1004-5, 1006, 1009
  knowledge-transforming strategies 517
  metacognition 477, 478, 480, 485
  nature of 551-2, 1194-8
  new subject knowledge 545
  organisation of 517-18
  pedagogical content knowledge 1253, 1254
  Piaget 366
  political 555, 556, 557
  prior 358-9
  professional 209
  research typology 549-50
  see also wisdom
knowledge economy 770, 851, 910, 1210
knowledge management 1085
knowledge society 841, 933, 942, 1002
  see also Information Society
knowledge workers 330, 658, 809, 876, 1041
knowledge-based economy 3-4, 7, 738, 915, 927, 1316, 1317
Korea
  ageing population 707, 1214
  beliefs about old age 384
  bullying 425, 432-5
  classroom learning environments 465, 466, 469, 470, 471
  coaching 734, 761, 764
  curriculum 546
  development indicators 702
  economic growth/development 828, 1088, 1211
  educational indicators 1132
  educational and instructional technology 1261
  employment 703, 704
  enrolments 32, 33, 74, 707, 708, 1210, 1214
  environmental education 574, 578, 579
  examinations 8, 114
  family background 46
  family/community participation 924

fertility 817
gender differences 262, 263
gifted education 192, 199
girls in business 273
gross national income 31
high educational attainment 63, 769, 1097
higher education 7, 811, 813, 824, 1210, 1214-15, 1318
  financing 820, 822, 823, 828
  participation 842, 843
  private sector 822, 827, 834, 837, 1102, 1211
home-school communication 1065, 1066
homework 758
HRD planning 667
international students 70
international studies 353, 1110-17
journals 1312
language education 630, 634-6
learning entitlement 1241
learning technology 530
lifelong learning 315-16, 319
locus of control 497
Mastery Learning Project 113
metacognition 1262
national heritage 560
national visions 7
paradigm shifts 12
parents
  involvement 1320
  parent education 1065
  parent volunteering 1068
  role 925, 1065, 1071-2, 1073, 1074
participation 305, 339
peace education 649, 650, 651
PISA 949
planning and policy 926
political ideology 1212
population 30, 703, 707, 1214
pressure to succeed 452
primary education 1281
private sector 1038-40, 1051
  finance 1281
  higher education 822, 827, 834, 837, 1102, 1211
  private expenditure 1049-50
  private tuition 788, 1059
privatisation of tertiary education 8
public expenditure 37, 1049, 1102
public/private provision 34, 36, 40
quality assurance 946, 947, 953, 954
relative wealth 323
research 131, 1141
rote learning reduction 764
rote memorisation 546
salaries 873
school decision-making 1070
science education 616, 617, 620, 1244
science/engineering enrolments 1100
shadow education 1100
social harmony 770
staffing ratios 38
structural adjustment 326
success attributions 770
teacher education 900, 901
teachers 870, 923
  beliefs 65
  career ladder 966, 967

monitoring 950
performance standards 962-4
placement 967-8
quality 11
recruitment 904, 910, 961-2, 969-70
research 968-9
supply and demand 959-60
technical and vocational education 670, 710
tertiary education policy and planning 1038-41
time allocation 736
TIMSS 758
TVET enrolment 328
unemployment 704-6
vocational education and training 676, 677-80, 681, 682, 683, 684, 1212
voucher programs 711
workforce education 323, 326-7, 331
Korea Institute for Youth Development (KIYD) 1068, 1076
Korean Educational Development Institute (KEDI) 131, 192, 315, 434, 1070, 1141
parent education 1065, 1075
quality assurance 947, 953, 954
regional research cooperation 1307, 1308, 1309
Korean Institute of Curriculum and Evaluation (KICE) 131
Korean Journal of Thinking and Problem Solving 511, 515
Korean Research Institute for Vocational Education and Training (KRIVET) 131, 331, 668
Kreditanstalt fur Wiederaufbau (FfW) 1158
KRIVET *see* Korean Research Institute for Vocational Education and Training
Kuala Lumpar Declaration of the Ministries of Education and Development of the Asia-Pacific Region (MINEDAP VI) 404
Kyrgyz Republic
external aid 1057
public expenditure 1048
Kyrgyzstan 243, 244, 247, 248, 250, 252

Labor Force Survey 325
laboratory skills 796-7
labour force
productivity 321, 326
quality 1087-8, 1098
women's participation 306
labour market xxii, 87, 553
demand 219, 325, 658, 664, 665
East Asia 701, 710
'old school tie' 62
Pacific Islands 1271-83
signalling 658, 659, 661, 665
women's participation 283-7, 288
see also unemployment
language
Barefoot College 238-9
Central Asia 241, 243, 245-6, 250-2
English language teaching 733
for learning 777-8
learning technology 526, 527
Pacific Islands 1228, 1229
Pakistan 804-5
patterns of 149
research 101
second language education 552, 629-40
student learning 452
testing 630, 632-4, 637-8

see also reading
language experience approach 588, 589
Lao PDR
ADB initiatives 1160
beliefs about old age 384
compulsory education 7
curriculum 545
economic development 828
enrolments 1214
female illiteracy 260
higher education 819, 824
HRD planning 667
low incomes 323
market economy 927, 1060
nonformal literacy program 227
participation 339
peace education 649, 650
public expenditure 1048-9
reforms 1174-5
repetition rate 174
research 1087
science education 616
taxation 1054
teachers 870
vocational education and training 678, 679
large-scale assessment 114-15, 797-8, 799
latent trait theory 352, 410
Latin America
fees 1052
salaries 873
LATIS *see* Learning and Technology in Schools project
law of comparative judgment (LCJ) 410, 411, 412
LCJ *see* law of comparative judgment
LD *see* learning disabilities
leadership 919, 922, 973-85, 1001-13
development 916, 918, 919, 922-3
research challenges 1322, 1324
research priorities 1204
learned helplessness 489
learning 768, 779
3P model 443, 453
achievement relationship 1119
adaptive 502, 1262, 1264
alternative conceptions research 621
Asian-Pacific Joint Production Program of Materials for Neo-literates in Rural Areas 181-2
at home 1064-5
autonomous 611
brain activity 1265
class size relationship 747, 748, 749, 751, 752
cognitive development 308-9, 365, 368, 369
cognitive-situative framework 503
competence 310
cross-cultural perspective 441-62
cultural contact 502-3
cultural influences 993
cultural values 498
curriculum objectives 542
education for all 186, 187
effective schooling 998-9
entitlement 1241
evaluation 112, 113
formal/nonformal/informal distinction 307
goals 500-1
homework/coaching 735, 756-7

human development   xix–xx, 351–63
ICT   1262, 1264, 1265, 1266
internal world of   734, 777
metacognition   484–5, 489, 490
minimum levels of   102
monitoring   736, 793–806
motivation   495–509
networks   875
opportunities for   280, 306–7, 312
out-of-school contexts   772
outcomes   351, 354–6, 361, 442
  3P model   443
  citizenship education   562
  classroom environment relationship   463, 465
  improving   453
  self-managing schools   921–2, 933, 936–41, 942
passive   751
performance comparison   769–70
problem solving   513, 514
problem-based learning   1009
quality of   1182
research priorities   1204
rural children   171
school leadership   1009, 1010
skills   953
socio-cultural factors   481, 483
styles   876
teacher evaluation   772, 773–8
technology   525–37
theories on   607–9
time   735, 782, 783–4
to learn   790
values education   396, 401
Vygotsky   368
workforce education   322
see also collaborative learning; lifelong learning; mastery learning
learning achievement   18, 24, 155–69
learning community   1240–1
learning difficulties   211, 478, 486, 487, 488, 490, 1173
see also reading difficulties
learning disabilities (LD)   488
learning environment   354–6, 463–75
  adaptive   1262
  student learning   446–7, 448–9, 453
  traditional/new   1260
  values education   406
Learning Environment Inventory (LEI)   464
Learning Federation, Australia   1264
learning for mastery   112, 113, 483, 590, 782, 784
learning materials
  COMPETE project   313–14
  sex stereotypes   272–3, 274, 275, 276–7
learning objects   1264
learning organisations   1002, 1010
Learning Process Questionnaire (LPQ)   442, 443, 444, 445–6
learning profession   877–9
Learning in Regular Classrooms movement   206
Learning School Project   775–7
Learning in Science Projects (LISP)   620
learning society   856, 863, 1241
learning space   1264
learning technologies   1258
Learning and Technology in Schools (LATIS) project   531

Learning and Working Programme   1239–40
least developed countries   19, 271
lecturing   736
legislation
  Central Asian republics   251
  early childhood education   23
  inclusive education   204, 205, 207, 210, 211, 212
  Korea   316
  lifelong education   316, 319
  Thailand   303
legitimatory research   97, 98
LEGO   535
LEI *see* Learning Environment Inventory
leisure time   316
length of the school day   101
levels of education   1131
Li Po Chun World College   1239
liberal education   338
liberalisation   265, 559, 563
  Chinese higher education reform   844
  Singapore   7
  trade   25, 26
liberation, nonformal education   328
libraries   532–3
life expectancy   20, 816, 817, 818, 1202, 1231
  human development index   1340, 1342–3
  human resource development   1341
  Lao PDR   1174
  Pacific Islands   1276
life sciences   1249
life skills
  Education for All   21, 25
  gender differences   271
  nonformal education   340
lifelong education   8, 77
  educational opportunity   145
  learning skills   899
  research priorities   1205
  rethinking   396
  structuration theory   1169
  teacher education   887
  teachers   950
  Thailand   1176
  urban youth   222
lifelong learning   12, 154, 305–20, 738, 769, 932, 954, 1034, 1274
  adult literacy   25
  continuing education   856, 864, 865
  culture of   877, 878
  curriculum aims   544
  and development   xv
  East Asia   711
  educational aims   953
  educational opportunity   145
  enterprise education and training   716
  entitlement   1043–4
  Hong Kong   790
  Japan   856–7, 858
  leadership   923
  new ideas   1201
  nonformal education   335–6
  peace education   648
  public/private education   1027
  school leadership   1007, 1009, 1010
  Singapore   1250
  teachers   867, 877, 878

Index of Subjects 1395

technical and vocational education and training 688
tertiary education 842, 1043–4
Thailand 1177
universal tertiary education 842
virtual learning communities 529
workforce education 321, 330
youth transition 712
lifelong learning centres 315
lifelong professional development 5, 10–11, 916, 1316, 1323–4
lifespan human development 379–94
Likert scales 409, 411–12, 413, 422
Likert-style questionnaire 409–24
linguistic analysis, Hindu texts 644
LISP *see* Learning in Science Projects
literacy 293–304, 552, 570, 585–97
  access to education 280
  ACCU learning materials 181
  assessment 799
  ATLP 182–4
  Barefoot College 234, 235, 236, 237
  curriculum 181, 182, 544
  definitions 294
  disparities 20
  Education for All 21, 22
  female 296–8
  gender differences 260–1, 270, 271, 276, 280, 281, 282–3, 284, 296
  higher-order skills 794, 795
  human development index 1340
  IEA studies 1108, 1117–18
  increase in 172
  India 158, 159, 231, 848
  Indonesia 175–6
  Kazakhstan 251
  metacognition 486–9, 490
  nonformal education 227, 338–9, 340, 344–5
  Pakistan 164
  parent education 1064
  PISA 1310
  poverty reduction 17
  projects 55
  rates 295, 297
  research 101, 1147
  sex stereotypes 274
  Singapore 1248
  Soviet education 245
  Sri Lanka 905
  UNESCO Learning and Training Programme 1240
  universal 146, 154
  Vietnam 314
  women 69–70, 341, 848
  workforce education 321
  see also illiteracy; reading; scientific literacy
literature, IEA studies 1108
loans 737, 927, 1058, 1060, 1282, 1283
local culture 544, 545
local management of schools 931, 934
  see also self-managing schools
localisation 12, 581
locus of control 446, 447, 448, 453, 462, 496–7
LOGO programming 518, 535
London Class Size Study 751
long-term memory 309
longitudinal studies

gifted education 192, 195
student progress 1306
LOTS 1264
low value-added manufacturing 325
LPQ *see* Learning Process Questionnaire
m-learning 1263
MacArthur Foundation 1156
Macau
  civic education 557, 561, 563
  learning technology 527–8
  post-colonial transition 563
  public/private education 925, 1023–5, 1027
  research 128–9
  teachers 870
macro-economics 225, 660
macro-level 5, 6, 13
  educational management 915, 917, 918, 919, 925–7, 928
  quality assurance 955
  research challenges 1315–16, 1317–21
macro-studies 1011
Magna Carta for Disabled Persons, Philippines 211
Mahub ul Haq Development Centre 282, 285, 286, 290
mainstreaming
  China 206
  Malaysia 210
  Philippines 211
Malaysia
  ageing population 707
  anxiety research 499
  attainment 67
  civic curricula 563
  coaching 761
  cognitive development research 375
  colonial history 1153
  curriculum 545, 546, 770
  decreased support for higher education 1102
  development indicators 702
  development plan targets 323
  donor support 1157
  economic growth 1088
  employment 704
  English-medium schools 735–6
  enrolments 32, 33, 707, 708, 850
  environmental education 574
  examinations 8
  formal education 337, 338
  higher education 7, 811, 824–5, 836, 1210, 1215
    enrolments 850
    financing 832–3, 834
    private sector 834
  inclusive education for students with special needs 210
  indigenous cultures 1216
  international comparative studies 1110–17
  Islamic education 622, 1217
  leadership 922
  learning technology 534
  Ministry of Education 118, 129
  monitoring achievement 794, 803
  moral education 560
  national vision 6
  nonformal education 337, 338
  parental involvement 1320
  peace education 649, 650

political ideology   1212
population   30, 703, 707
pressure for success   1244
private sector   834
  higher education   1102
  private tutoring   1059
public expenditure   36, 37, 40
public/private provision   34, 36
relative wealth   323
research
  impact on practice   102
  institutions   129
  productivity   133
  training of researchers   1291–2
salaries   873, 874
school effectiveness research   768
school leadership   922, 1001, 1002, 1003, 1004–5
school-based management   10
science education   617
science/engineering enrolments   1100
secondary education   1096
single-mother families   65
staffing ratios   36, 38
student activism   1213
student learning   450, 451
teacher education   884, 885, 892, 900
teachers   870, 876
  quality   11
  recruitment   907–10
teaching time   787
technical and vocational education   324, 328, 710
training   1281
unemployment   704–6
vocational education and training   324, 328, 676, 677, 678, 679
workforce education   323, 324, 331
World Education Indicators   1133
Malaysia-Toray Science Foundation   1292
Malaysian Educational Research Association (MERA)   138, 1292
Maldives
  teachers   870, 872
  unqualified teachers   739
malnutrition   375
management   xx, 734, 915–29
  Central Asia   296
  principals   1003
  school-based   6, 10, 931–44, 948, 955, 975
    Hong Kong   1021
    organisation of education   916, 918, 921–2
    research challenges   1316, 1322–3
    school leadership   973, 974, 978, 979, 982, 983
    school-to-home communication   1066
    Thailand   1005
  technologies   11–12
  training   87, 89
  see also self-managing schools
managerialism   542, 551, 926
  higher education   832
  time efficiency   789
manpower analyses   663, 681, 684
manpower demands   101
manpower planning   657–8, 662, 663, 666, 667, 684
manpower requirements   659, 660, 663, 665
manpower surveys   325
manufacturing
  Fiji   1275, 1282

women   285, 286
workforce education   325, 327
many-to-one interactions   1264
Maori   451, 453
  assessment   803
  enterprise education and training   718, 727
  science education   619
  traditional worldviews   622
  Treaty of Waitangi   856
marginalisation   1234–4
marginalised groups
  nonformal education   25–6
  urban youth   226–7
maritime training   695–6, 698
market economy   8, 927, 1054, 1060
  China   905, 910, 1054
  workforce education   325, 328
market forces   1320
market-based approaches   764, 926, 1043
marketisation   1102, 1319, 1320
  ethnicity   254
  higher education   819, 832
  Hong Kong   1023
  students with special needs   212
Marshall Islands
  continuing education   858
  economic/demographic indicators   1276
  educational provision   1277
  public expenditure   1277, 1279
Marxism   244
masculinity   280, 287–8, 290, 435
massification of higher education   1104
mastery
  goals   500, 501, 502
  learning   112, 113, 483, 590, 782, 784
  training   496
Matane Report   1072
maternity and childcare benefits   286
mathematical modelling   601
mathematical processes   600, 601, 603
mathematics   552, 599–614
  anxiety   515–16
  Asian teaching approaches   518–19
  Barefoot College   239
  class size   741, 747
  coaching   762
  Cook Islands   803
  economic growth relationship   1098
  Fiji   1226
  gender differences   262, 263, 467
  homework   759–60
  IEA studies   262, 263
  international studies   353, 1088, 1097, 1111–14, 1120
  Japan   547
  literacy   1099, 1111, 1120
  metacognition   479–83, 489, 490
  software   528
  South Asia learning achievement   156, 157–8, 159–64
  US/Japan comparison   758
mathematics for all   599
Mayer Committee   310, 311, 320
MCATS   1264
MCI see My Class Inventory
measurement   1197
measurement of attitude   409–24

Index of Subjects 1397

mechanisation 306
mechatronic environment 322
MECS *see* Ministry of Education, Culture and Sports
media, TIMSS reporting 101
mega cities 218, 226
mega-universities 847
Melanesia
  agricultural management programs 344
  nonformal education 337, 345
memorisation 444–5, 450, 608, 993
  Confucian-heritage cultures 515
  Korea 546
  see also rote learning
memory 309, 351, 358, 360–1
  cognitive load 516
  lifespan development 387
  optimisation research 389
  survival skills 371–2
men's issues 288–9
mental health 366
mental models 372
mental tests 124
MERA *see* Malaysian Educational Research Association
meritocracy 44–5, 48, 52, 53
meso-level 5, 6, 13
  educational management 915, 917, 918, 919, 924–5, 928
  quality assurance 955
  research challenges 1315–16, 1317–21
MESSC *see* Ministry of Education, Science, Sports and Culture
meta-analysis
  research 1312
  student learning 446–9, 452–3
metacognition 351, 477–94
  classroom learning 773
  conceptual worlds 1196
  curriculum decision-making 624–5
  ICT 1262, 1264
  language of 777
  metacognitive knowledge 790
  self-regulation 757
metacognitive awareness 477–9, 484, 485, 489
metacognitive development 480
metadata-associated learning object 1264
metalinguistics 486
micro-economics 660
micro-studies 1011
micro-teaching lessons 1247
Micronesia
  economic/demographic indicators 1276
  educational provision 1277
  higher education 835
  public expenditure 1277, 1279
  teachers 870
microteaching 891
Middle East
  colonial history 1153
  fees 1052
migration 293, 397
  East Asia 706
  Pacific Island student 691, 692
  rates of 218, 219, 220
mind, theory of 374
mindfulness 359–60

MINEDAP *see* Ministers of Education and Those Responsible for Economic Planning in Asia and the Pacific
miniaturisation of technology 1265
Minimum Learning Levels Program (MLLP) 178–9, 1306
Minimum Levels of Learning (MLL) 178–9, 1306
Ministers of Education and Those Responsible for Economic Planning in Asia and the Pacific (MINEDAP) 172
Ministry of Culture and Tourism, Korea 1068, 1076
Ministry of Education, China 179, 188, 911, 978–9, 1002, 1013
Ministry of Education, Culture and Sports (MECS), Philippines 1294–5
Ministry of Education and Human Resource Development (MOEHRD), Korea 960, 962, 963, 967, 968, 971
Ministry of Education, India 847, 848, 852, 863, 866, 906, 911, 1172, 1179
Ministry of Education, Indonesia 130, 880
Ministry of Education, Japan 209, 431, 760, 766, 903, 964, 971
  budget 1156
  family/community involvement 1064–5, 1067, 1070
Ministry of Education, Korea 1039, 1070, 1076
Ministry of Education, Lao PDR 1174–5, 1179
Ministry of Education, Malaysia 118, 129, 907, 909
Ministry of Education, New Zealand 438, 609, 613, 965
  information and communications technology 1258–9, 1264, 1269
  research 1085, 1090, 1094, 1140
Ministry of Education, Science, Sports and Culture (MESSC), Japan 766, 1036, 1037, 1038, 1045, 1132, 1135
Ministry of Education, Singapore 481, 492, 764, 1007, 1264, 1269
  quality assurance 947, 948, 952, 957
  research training 1294
  teacher training 907–8, 909–10
Ministry of Education, Taiwan 877, 878, 949, 1018, 1019, 1029
Ministry of Education, Thailand 329, 1005, 1013, 1295
Ministry of Education, Vietnam 880
Ministry of Human Resource Development, India 347
minorities 90, 153
  Central Asia 241–56
  China 300
  higher education 845, 849, 851
  India 849, 850
  lack of educational opportunities 144
  women in China 344
'mis-oriented perceptions' 177
mixed ability groups, whole class teaching 745
MLLP *see* Minimum Learning Levels Program
Model of School Learning (Carroll) 100
models
  research utilisation 99–100
  Tyler Model 111–12
Modern Educational Technology Research Center, Beijing Normal University 526

modernisation 1205, 1302
  China 1213
  coaching 761
  higher education 809
  Iran 1213
  Japan 903
Modular Skills Training (MOST) 330
MOEHRD *see* Ministry of Education and Human Resource Development
Monash University 1243
Mongolia
  citizenship education 556
  distance education 342
  external aid 1058
  gender issues 271
  higher education 831, 832, 834
  independent revenue-earning 1054
  participation 339
  post-communist transition 563
  private expenditure 1050
  taxation 1054
  teachers 870
  urban youth program 227
  vocational education and training 678, 679
monitoring 89–90, 1035
  achievement 117
  curricula 1120
  educational changes xxiii, 120, 1339
  EFA 2000 Assessment 168
  globalisation 1334–5
  information and communications technology 954
  language education 636
  lifelong education 316–17, 319
  problem solving 518
  research challenges 1322
  resources 299
  school effectiveness 118, 119
  school performance 767
  schools 918, 919–20, 945–58
  secondary education reform 88
  skills 518
  streamlined 298
  student learning 736, 793–806
  teachers 950
  tertiary education 1037, 1043
  youth transition 713
  see also assessment
moral curriculum code 541
moral development 352–3, 1222
moral education 340, 402, 560, 561, 563, 641, 1341–4
  Confucian tradition 1097
  Hong Kong 1134
  regional research 1303, 1308
  research priorities 1205
  Singapore 1099
  vocational schools 677
moral values xv, 1172, 1195
morality 770
mortgage loans 832
MOST *see* Modular Skills Training
mother-child relationships 366
mothers
  educational attainment 66–7
  values 67
motivation 495–509, 990–1

achievement relationship 1119
  coaching 757
  comparative studies 1109
  homework 757, 759, 760
  ICT 1259
  metacognition 478, 479, 483, 488, 490
  motive/strategy model of learning 443, 446
  problem solving 513
  socio-cultural environment 483
  student learning 445, 446
  teachers 887–8
  to learn 952
  whole class teaching 745
motoric intelligence 367
MTDFS 1264
multi-level curriculum 205
Multi-Media University, Kuala Lumpur 1156
multi-method approach 747
multiculturalism
  Central Asia 247–8, 252, 253
  citizenship education 557, 559, 560, 566
  culture of peace 399
  migrant students 483
multidirectional lifespan approach 387, 390–1
multidisciplinarity 1082, 1083, 1198–9
multilateral networks 1154, 1156–7
multilevel nature of educational research 1199
multimedia 530, 536, 1259, 1282
  Asia-Pacific Distance and Multimedia Education Network 533
  China 526
  lifelong learning 315–16
  Malaysia 909
multiple intelligences 12, 1242
  contextualised 1326, 1327
  gifted students 191, 194, 195–6, 199
  learning technology 527–8, 536
multiple talents 191, 194, 195–6, 199
multivariate nature of educational research 1199
My Class Inventory (MCI) 464
Myanmar (Burma)
  ADB initiatives 1160
  coaching 761, 764
  higher education 811, 819, 1215
  opposition to democracy 1336
  research 1087
  teachers 870
  universities closed down 1213
  vocational education and training 677, 678, 679

Nanyang Technological University 1007, 1248, 1262, 1287, 1293
nation-building 7, 1209, 1248
  Central Asia 241, 242, 248, 252–3, 254
  youth role 221
national achievement 100–1
National Adult Education Program, India 862–3
National Assessment of Education Progress, United States 795, 800
National Assessment of Education Project, Indonesia 1171–2
National Center of Education Statistics, United States 1127
National Center for the Gifted and Talented, Thailand 193
National Central University of Taiwan 529
National Centre for Vocational Education Research

Index of Subjects 1399

(NCVER), Australia 331, 669, 724, 729, 1308, 1309
National Council of Educational Research and Training (NCERT), India 102, 129, 157–8, 188, 645, 1143
 regional research cooperation 1305, 1306–7, 1308, 1309, 1313
 teacher training reforms 906
National Council for Teacher Education (NCTE), India 878
National Council of Teachers of Mathematics (NCTM) 601, 613
national culture 560
National Curriculum 543, 544, 615, 994
 Korea 968, 969
 science education 622
 Singapore 748
 United Kingdom 783, 786
national development xx–xxi, 7–8, 186, 187, 217, 1317
 adult literacy programs 299
 Pacific Islands 688, 689, 690
 research relationship 1081, 1092
 Singapore 1099
 teachers' roles 874, 876
 university education 1207–20
National Education Act, Thailand 935–6
National Education Commission, Thailand 5, 118, 128, 304, 1175, 1179, 1295
National Educational Monitoring Project (NEMP), New Zealand 594, 596
national examinations xix
 accountability 108–9, 113–15
 Indonesia 115–17
National Federation of UNESCO Associations in Japan (NFUAJ) 646
national identity 544
 Central Asia 243, 252–3, 254
 citizenship education 558
 curriculum aims 543
 university education 1208, 1209
National Institute of Education, Colombo 1155
National Institute of Education, Hong Kong 1154
National Institute of Education, Singapore 130, 531, 1007, 1154
 research training 1286, 1287, 1289, 1292–4
 teacher training/recruitment 908–9
National Institute of Educational Planning and Administration, India 1143
National Institute for Educational Research (NIER), Japan xxii, 91, 1155, 1182, 1191
 bullying 431
 curriculum 543, 544, 545, 554
 dissemination of research 1140–1, 1149
 donor aid 1158
 environmental education 582, 583
 evaluator training seminars 118
 family/community involvement 1063, 1066, 1076
 higher education financing 831, 832, 833, 837
 international seminar xiii–xiv, 4, 1178
 peace education 646, 649
 regional research cooperation 1303, 1305, 1306, 1307, 1308, 1309, 1313
 research programs 125, 126
 values education 401–2, 403, 404, 405, 407
National Institute for Educational Research and Training, Korea 904

National Institute for Learning Reform 1177
National Institute of Special Education, Japan 128, 1306, 1308, 1309
National Institution for Academic Degrees, Japan 1037
national investment in primary education 164, 165
National Schools Network (NSN) 902
National Society for the Scientific Study of Education (NSSE) 124
national standards 551
 New Zealand 725
 Pacific Islands 694
 see also standards
National Taiwan Normal University 329
national testing programs 156, 157
National Union of Teachers, United Kingdom 771
national unity 1208, 1212
National University of Singapore 531
national visions 6–7
nationalism 254, 1218
 Central Asia 243, 244, 248, 251
 citizenship education 557, 559–60, 566
nationality, Central Asia 244
natural variation 96
Nauru
 continuing education 858
 information on 690
 technical and vocational education and training 687
NCERT see National Council of Educational Research and Training
NCTE see National Council for Teacher Education
NCTM see National Council of Teachers of Mathematics
NCVER see National Centre for Vocational Education Research
NDF see Nordic Development Fund
needs assessment 182, 329, 658
needs-based empowerment curriculum 181, 186
NEMP see National Educational Monitoring Project
neo-liberalism 855, 926, 1044, 1100
neo-technic revolution 322
Nepal
 completion of schooling 1302
 economic development 828
 external aid 1057–9
 female illiteracy 260
 fertility 817–18
 gender differences 279, 281–2
 higher education 813, 828, 829
 independent revenue-earning 1054
 Industrial Manpower Survey 666
 learning achievement assessment 159–61
 nonformal education 336
 participation 305
 school retention 1160
 science/engineering enrolments 1100
 student learning 444, 445
 teachers 872
 textbooks 872
 unqualified teachers 739
 vocational education and training 677, 682
 women 270, 285, 286, 287
net enrolment ratio 32, 33
 gender differences 259, 270, 281
 India 158

1400 Index of Subjects

Pakistan 164
Netherlands
  bullying 431
  influence on Asia-Pacific education 108, 606
  research 1086
NETTLAP *see* Network for Environmental Training at Tertiary Level in Asia
Network for Environmental Training at Tertiary Level in Asia (NETTLAP) 571
networks
  learning 875
  Pacific Island 696
  social capital 50–1, 60, 62
neural nets 374
neuroscience 768, 1202
new ideas 1201, 1202–3
new managerialism 926
new mathematics 600, 601, 602, 608
New Right 855
new subject knowledge 545
New Zealand
  adult education participation 317, 318, 319
  alternative conceptions research 621
  Anglo-celtic culture 893
  anxiety research 499
  attributional research 497–8
  beliefs about age boundaries 383–4
  bullying 425, 435–7
  class size 736
  continuing education 854–6, 863, 864
  contribution to higher education funding 836
  curriculum 545, 546, 561
  donor aid 1156, 1157
  economic growth 1088
  educational research associations 136
  enactivism 609
  enterprise education and training 715–30
  environmental education 574, 576, 578, 579
  Europe/North America influence xv
  gender differences 262, 263, 264
  girls and science education 619
  global civics 560
  higher education 811, 813, 819, 841
    alternatives 846
    financing 827, 828, 829, 831, 832, 833
  inclusive education for students with special needs 203
  indigenous cultures 1218
  indigenous student learning 451
  international comparative studies 1110–18, 1120
  large-scale testing programs 114
  learning technology 532
  literacy 295
  locus of control 496
  mathematics curriculum for indigenous people 609
  national visions 7
  Pacific Island students 691
  PISA 949
  practice-orientated research 1085
  private sector 949
  quality assurance 946, 953
  reading literacy 586–7, 588–9, 590, 591, 592, 593–4
  research 147, 1139, 1140, 1141, 1144
    institutions 127–8
    productivity 133
    training of researchers 1298
  school-based management 948
  science education 616, 619–20, 622
  self-governing schools 10
  self-managing schools 921, 931, 941, 942
  statistics 603
  strategic research initiative 1090
  teacher education 891, 900
  teachers 870, 923
    performance standards 964–6
    preparation 738
    recruitment 901–3, 910
  tertiary education 737
  universities 737–8
New Zealand Association for Research in Education (NZARE) xiii, 136
New Zealand Council for Educational Research (NZCER) 127–8, 594, 1140, 1141, 1149, 1307
New Zealand Education Act 948
New Zealand Qualifications Authority (NZQA) 310, 311, 320, 549, 554, 694, 725, 726
NFE *see* nonformal education
NFPE *see* Nonformal Primary Education Program
NFUAJ *see* National Federation of UNESCO Associations in Japan
NGOs *see* non-government organisations; non-governmental organisations
NIER *see* National Institute for Educational Research
Niue
  continuing education 858
  information on 690
  reading literacy 55, 590
  technical and vocational education and training 687, 691
noise levels 750
non-governmental organisations (NGOs)
  adult education 301, 302
  adult literacy funding 25
  collaboration 299
  community participation 1067, 1069
  continuing education 859
  disabled students 208
  donor support 1156
  environmental education 571, 574, 575, 583
  informal sector training 712
  nonformal education 337, 339–40, 342
  Pacific Islands 688, 692, 698
  parent education 1064
  peace education 646, 650
  UNICEF collaboration 1162
  urban youth 226
nonformal education (NFE) 25–6, 231, 298, 307, 308, 309, 335–48, 1033, 1034, 1239
  Bangladesh 906
  Barefoot College 238
  basic education 227
  community participation 1072
  definitions 335–6
  East Asia 709, 711–12
  environmental protection 1338
  gender gap 269, 270
  globalisation 1335
  ICT 307–8
  Korea 316, 319
  learning centres 232
  learning opportunities 312

lifelong education/learning 154, 316
literacy 227, 299–300, 301
  Pakistan 179
  peace education 646
  research 101, 1306
  secondary education 76, 87, 89
  social education 315
  technical and vocation education and training 88
  Thailand 329, 1176
  tolerance 397
  training 673
  urban youth 223, 224
  WCEFA 175
Nonformal Primary Education Program (NFPE) 179–80
Nordic Development Fund (NDF) 1158
norms
  citizenship education 556, 557
  'social clock' 389–90
North America, public expenditure 1049
North Korea
  political ideology 1212
  teachers 870
Norway, bullying 431
novice teachers 890, 908
NSN see National Schools Network
NSSE see National Society for the Scientific Study of Education
numeracy
  assessment 799
  Barefoot College 234, 235, 237
  curriculum aims 544
  gender differences 261, 271
  higher-order skills 794, 795
  India 158
  Pakistan 164
  parent education 1064
  poverty reduction 17
  rural areas 179
  Singapore 1248
  UNESCO Learning and Training Programme 1240
NZARE see New Zealand Association for Research in Education
NZCER see New Zealand Council for Educational Research
NZQA see New Zealand Qualifications Authority

objectives, curriculum 111–13
observation 1197
observational data 166
occupational aspirations 49–50
occupational classifications 659
occupational education 338
occupational mobility 716, 1101
  see also career mobility
occupational training see on-the-job training; workforce education
Oceania
  culturally inclusive education 1221–30
  female illiteracy 270
  labour market xxii
  participation rates and gender 259
  public expenditure 1049
  teacher-pupil ratios 872
  teachers 868, 869
  see also Pacific Islands; South Pacific

ODA see official development assistance; Overseas Development Administration
ODE see Open Distance Education
OECD see Organisation for Economic Cooperation and Development
Office of Educational and Cultural Research and Development, Indonesia 118, 1155, 1290–1
Office of the National Education Commission (ONEC), Thailand 128, 935–6, 943, 1155
Office of Training and Further Education (OTFE) 729
official development assistance (ODA) 1055, 1056
OFTE see Office of Training and Further Education
OJT see on-the-job training
on-line questionnaires 471
on-the-job training (OJT) 321, 324, 325, 327, 715, 820
  apprenticeships 726
  Asian teachers 1098
  Certified On-the-Job Training Centre 330
  planning technical and vocational education 661, 673, 674
  Project InSPIRE 1292
ONEC see Office of National Education Commission
online learning systems 1262
Open Distance Education (ODE), Mongolia 342
open university 839, 846–7, 850, 851
openness 920, 947, 951–2
operational level 6, 916, 918, 928, 1316, 1324–7
opportunity costs 155
optimisation research 381, 389
ORACLE Research 785, 786
oral communication skills 796, 797
Organisation for Economic Cooperation and Development (OECD)
  Adult Literacy and Lifeskills survey 311
  democracy 1336
  devolved decision-making 1280
  education for all 17, 27
  Education at a Glance 1127–8, 1136
  employment 1272, 1273, 1283
  enterprise education and training 717–18, 720, 721, 729
  family/community involvement 1063, 1065, 1066, 1067, 1072, 1076
  foreign aid 1156, 1157
  Frascati Manual 1082, 1094
  higher education 841–2, 852
  HRD planning 657, 660–1
  IALS 311, 316–17, 320
  indicators 29, 41, 119, 949
    comparative 1123, 1126–8, 1131–4, 1136
    enrolments 32, 33
    expenditure 36, 37
    globalisation 1335, 1345
  Indicators of Education Systems project 1123, 1126, 1127–8, 1134, 1136
  lifelong learning 312, 320, 1034
  literacy/numeracy skills 17
  part-time employment 1236, 1242, 1273
  PISA 126, 311, 618, 949, 1110–11, 1120, 1310
  policy-makers 768
  public expenditure 1277–8
  regional research cooperation 1310

research   1084, 1085, 1090, 1094, 1138, 1141, 1144–5, 1182, 1191
salaries   873
Schooling for Tomorrow   874
secondary education   77, 81
self-managing schools   936, 943
sustainable consumption   577, 583
teaching profession   867, 880
tertiary education   1033, 1045
unemployment   1272
vocational education and training   680, 682, 686
young workers   707
youth population   225, 229
youth transition   702, 703, 709, 712, 713
organisation of education   xx
Osakafu Kyouiku Iinkai   1066, 1076
out-of-school children   1232, 1234
   gender differences   281
   nonformal education   301
   Pakistan   302–3
outcomes   94, 96
   equality of achievement   1173
   evaluation   111, 112–13
   gender differences   153, 257–68
   inclusive education   213
   indicators   1123, 1128, 1129
   learning   351, 354–6, 361, 442
      3P model   443
      citizenship education   562
      classroom environment relationship   463, 465
      improving   453
      self-managing schools   921–2, 933, 936–41, 942
   measuring   877
   Pacific Islands   1275
   quality assurance   947, 956
   school effectiveness indicators   119
   school-based management   1323
   standardised tests   111
   teacher education   891
over-crowded classrooms   208
over-qualification   841
over-supply of teachers   903, 960
Overseas Development Administration (ODA)   1305, 1306
overseas education   32, 70, 1296, 1297
   see also international students
Oxfam   17

Pacific Association of Teacher Educators (PATE)   1224–5
Pacific Island Maritime Institutions and Maritime Authorities Association (PIMIMAA)   695
Pacific Islands   xxi, 293, 1221–30
   cultural traditions   1222
   cultural transmission   1216
   enterprise education and training   718
   foreign aid   827, 835–6, 1156
   girls and science education   619
   higher education financing   827, 830, 835–6
   labour market and educational reform   1271–83
   moral education   1344
   national unity   1212
   reading literacy   589–90, 592
   student learning   444
   teachers   769
   technical and vocational education and training   687–99
   values   352
   vocational education and training   553, 687–99
   youth   296
   see also Oceania; South Pacific
Pacific Regional Association of TVET Providers   693–4
Pacific TVET Council   693–4, 695
pairwork   745
Pakistan
   assessment   803–5
   colonial history   1153
   completion of schooling   1302
   enrolments   173
   female illiteracy   260
   gender differences   279, 281–2
   graduate unemployment   1215
   higher education, financing   830
   illiteracy   260, 296
   inclusive education for students with special needs   210–11
   Islamic Development Bank loans   1157
   learning achievement assessment   161–4
   literacy   302–3
   nonformal education   179
   opposition to democracy   1336
   participation   305
   population   293, 296
   school retention   1160
   science/engineering enrolments   1100
   teachers   871, 906
   vocational education and training   676, 677, 678, 679, 682
   women in labour force   285, 286
   youth population   220
Pakistan Academy of Education Planning and Management (AEPM)   161
Palau
   economic/demographic indicators   1276
   educational provision   1277
   public expenditure   1277, 1279
Papua New Guinea (PNG)
   Board of Management/Board of Governors   1070
   economic/demographic indicators   1276
   educational provision   1277
   examination reforms   950–1
   family/community participation   924, 1063, 1072, 1073, 1074
   girls and science education   619
   higher education   842, 846
   international comparative studies   1110–17
   nonformal education   341
   parent education   1064
   parent volunteering   1068
   population   1275
   public expenditure   1277, 1279
   quality assurance   947, 954
   research   1142–3
   teachers   871, 950
   universities   833
   vocational education and training   678, 679
   women   271
PAR see Participatory Action Research
para schools   316
paradigm controversy   1084–5
paradigm shifts   12
parent-teacher associations (PTA)   1067, 1069, 1071

parenting 1064–5
parents 43, 1241
  assessment results 801
  attitudes 100, 148–9, 150
  child relationship 151
  choice 1320
  ch'onji 65–6
  declining influence 402
  dedication 763
  demands for good exam results 745
  effective schooling 987, 988–91
  expectations 498
  family size 148
  human capital 45
  interest in education 148–9
  involvement 5, 8–9, 48, 55, 149, 758–9, 975, 1320–1
    gifted education 194
    organisation and management of education 915, 917, 924–5
    Taiwan 977
  parenting 1064–5
  pause, prompt and praise method 592
  proximal family capital 48–51
  social capital 62
  strong belief in education 1244–5
  student perceptions of school life 51
  student performance 938
  support from 588
  values education 403
Parents and Citizens Associations 1066–7
part-time employment 1273
partial credit 159
participation xviii, xx, 29, 34, 35, 39–40, 305–6
  adult education 312, 317, 318
  barriers to 312
  East Asia 707–9
  Education For All 2000 Assessment Synthesis Report 298
  enterprise education and training 718
  family/community 1063–77
  gender issues 258, 259–60
  higher education 840, 842–3
  human resource development 1341
  increase in 542
  lifelong learning 312
  nonformal education 345
  regional cooperative research 1305
  rural areas 343
  school leadership 1011
  South Asia 155
  tertiary education 1031
    Japan 1035, 1036
    Korea 1038, 1039
    Thailand 1176, 1177
  UNESCO statistics 339
  variation in 84
  willingness to participate 952
  women 258, 335, 344
  workforce 1273
  youth 227
Participatory Action Research (PAR) 648–9
participatory approaches 1239
participatory decision-making 233
participatory learning 562
PATE *see* Pacific Association of Teacher Educators
patriarchy 66, 279, 282, 287, 289, 290

Index of Subjects 1403

patriotism 544, 545, 559
patron-client relationships 68
patronage politics 68
pause, prompt and praise method 592–3
payment by results 108
PBL *see* problem-based learning
PDA *see* portable digital assistants
peace 353, 362, 552
  APNIEVE 400
  culture of 398–9, 405, 406
  values education 395, 396, 398–9, 402
peace education 641–53
PEC *see* Principals' Executive Centre
PECR (Primary Education Curriculum Renewal) project 102
pedagogical content knowledge 1253, 1254
pedagogical practice 1198
PEEL *see* Project for Enhancing Effective Learning
peer assessment, teacher language proficiency 635, 636
peer critique 1247
Peer Relations Questionnaire (PRQ) 426
peer relationships 53
  bullying 432
  class size relationship 750–1
peer tutoring 207, 592, 1239, 1241
Perach Project 1241
perception 365, 367, 1197
performance
  boys 264–5, 271
  Confucian heritage countries 441
  girls 261–2, 264–5, 271
  goals 500, 501, 502
  international 768–9
  research 132–4
  school-based management 936–7
  South Asian learning achievement studies 158, 160–1, 162–3, 164
  teachers 923, 962–6, 970
  TIMSS 937–8
  variations in mean levels 158, 164
  see also achievement
performance indicators 310, 952, 1139
performance management system (PMS) 965–6
peri-urbanisation 219, 221
persistence 496
personal capital 49
personal development 1272
personality 444, 453
Personalized System of Instruction 525
Persons with Disabilities Act, India 207
phenomenography 442
Philippines
  ageing population 707
  coastal communities 343
  colonial history 1153
  Commission on Educational Reform 846
  COMPETE teacher education program 313–14, 319
  Composite Development Index 1120
  development indicators 702
  economic growth 1088
  employment 704
  enrolments 32, 33, 1214
  environmental education 574
  gender differences 263
  good educational outcomes 323

graduate unemployment 1215, 1216
gross national income 31
higher education 813, 815, 824, 834, 1211, 1215
  enrolments 850
  participation 842
  private sector 846
inclusive education for students with special needs 211
informal sector 712
international comparative studies 1110–18
international students 451
learning technology 532–3
lifelong learning 313–14, 319
literacy 300–1
Muslim minorities 1217
national visions 7
participation in secondary education 35, 40
peace education 647–8, 649, 650, 651
population 30, 31, 703, 707
private expenditure 1050
private sector 711, 846, 1051–2, 1211
  higher education 1102
  universities 1155
privatisation of tertiary education 8
public expenditure 37
public/private provision 34, 36
reading literacy 55, 592
religious bodies 1217
research 1087, 1294–5
salaries 739, 873
science education 616, 617
science/engineering enrolments 1100
staffing ratios 38
teacher education 884, 885
teachers 871
teaching time 787
technical and vocational education 668
unemployment 704–6
urban youth program 227
values education 403–4
vocational education and training 668, 676, 677, 680, 683
workforce education 323
World Education Indicators 1133
youth population 220
phonemic awareness 486, 588
phonics 587, 588
phonological re-coding 486
physical punishment 428, 436
physical sciences 1243
Piagetian theories 308, 358, 365, 366–7, 370–1, 483
Piagetian-Kohlbergian theory 561
PIED see Project Integrated Education of the Disabled
PIMIMAA see Pacific Island Maritime Institutions and Maritime Authorities Association
PISA (Programme for International Student Assessment) 126, 311, 618, 949, 1110–11, 1120, 1310
placement 47, 967–8
placement counselling 47
plagiarism 1266
planning 86–7, 95, 166, 926
  Hong Kong universities 861–2
  human resource development 657–70
  national contexts 175
  research 103

tertiary education 1031–46
plasticity 381, 388–9
Plowden Report 100, 782
pluralistic society 1023
PMS see performance management system
policy 102, 217, 926
  adoption 980
  coaching 764
  continuing education 863
  East Asian labour market 709, 710, 711
  effect on student learning 453
  enterprise education and training 716–17, 721–7
  formulation 980, 1327
  gender issues 287–9
  gifted education 190, 193, 194, 195, 199
  growth 1032–4
  higher education 818–23, 823–4
  homework 763–4
  implementation 105, 980, 1001
  investment in higher education 737
  language education 629, 630, 638
  monitoring 793
  peace education 649–50
  research 1083–4, 1085, 1146, 1148, 1157, 1181–2, 1187, 1189
  sex stereotypes 273
  staffing 924, 970
  students with special needs 204, 205
  teacher recruitment 961
  teacher self-evaluation 767–9
  tertiary education 1031, 1033, 1034–44
  urban youth 218, 227, 228
policy analysis 1167
policy-makers xiv, xvi, xxiii, 96
  clarification of roles 88
  dilemmas faced by 1320
  EFA goals 187
  HRD planning 664
  ICT 1325
  management technologies 12
  national visions 1318
  New Zealand 1090
  problem-solving model 99
  R&D influence 669
  research 97–100, 103–5, 166, 1139, 1145, 1148, 1182, 1183–4, 1189, 1190
  science curricula 1247–53, 1254
  secondary education reform 90
  self-learning 1327
  structural change 1319
  teaching practices 733, 734
  trends in educational reform 3, 8, 12–13
  university education 1207
  urban youth 221
policy-making xv, xviii
  achievement monitoring 793
  indicators 1125, 1134, 1135
  research 96–105, 1167, 1168, 1181–2, 1186, 1190
  priorities 1205
  trends in educational reform 4, 13
policy-oriented research 924, 1167, 1168, 1186, 1188
political development, university education 1207, 1212–13
political elites 1212
political globalisation 1096, 1103, 1104
political ideology 1185, 1188, 1212

Index of Subjects 1405

political issues
  Central Asia 243–4
  Children's Parliament 235–6, 239–40
  Chinese Cultural Revolution 1016
  citizenship education 555–6, 566
  control of curriculum 551, 552
  decision-making 1185, 1187–8, 1189
  external aid 1055, 1058–9, 1060
  finance 927
  globalisation 1332, 1336
  India 645
  neo-liberalism 855
  Pacific Islands 689–90
  parental/community involvement 1321
  policy priorities 97
  research 166, 167–8, 1144
  social indicators 1125
  stability 900
political knowledge 555, 556, 557
political mobilisation 60
political model 99
political socialisation 555, 1212, 1213
politicisation of education, Australia 1174
pollution 668
polytechnics
  New Zealand 725
  vocational education and training 673, 677
Popper, Karl 778
population 20, 29–31
  ageing 707, 1214, 1274
  change 29–31
  mobility 690–1
  Pacific Islands 687, 688, 690–1, 1275, 1276, 1278
  school-aged 107
  urban youth 217, 218, 219, 220
population growth 18, 172, 260, 296, 305, 570
  East Asia 702, 703, 707
  female literacy relationship 296–8
  illiteracy 299
  Lao PDR 1174
  Pacific Islands 553, 687, 688
  South Asia 304
  TVET planning 668
  world 1231, 1236
portability of qualifications 310, 312
portable digital assistants (PDA) 1263, 1265
Portugal
  influence on Asia-Pacific education 108
  influence on Macau education system 1024
positive discrimination 146, 1215
positivism 1138–9
post-communist countries 563, 564
post-compulsory education and training 324
post-literacy programs 296, 300, 304
postgraduate education 1147, 1285–99
poverty 17, 19, 176–8, 184, 395, 570, 1233, 1235
  Barefoot College 235
  Central Asia 241, 249
  cognitive development relationship 375
  cycle of 260
  East Asia 702, 706
  effect on educational career 148
  empowerment 186
  eradication 20
  gender issues 260, 282, 344
  higher education relationship 816, 818
  lack of educational opportunities 144

Lao PDR 1175
  least developed countries 271
  plasticity of development 389
  reduction 1157, 1159, 1160, 1161
  social capital investment 228
  social exclusion 227
  TVET planning 668
  urban 217, 221
poverty line 20
power, culture of authority 68
power distance 978, 980, 981
PPP see purchasing power-parity
practical communicative skills 630
practice exercises 756
practice teaching 884
practice-oriented research 1085
practicum 889, 891
pragmatism 541–2
pre-employment training 673
pre-school education
  compensatory education 147, 150
  research 102
pre-service teacher education 883–4, 885, 886–7, 888–9, 890–1, 892–3
  Bangladesh 906
  China 904, 905
  citizenship education 561
  environmental education 575, 582
  globalisation 895
  inclusive education 212
  Korea 961
  lack of gender sensitisation 275
  Malaysia 908
  mathematics teachers 611
  research impact on practice 102
  research training 1286
  Singapore 908
pre-service workforce education 321, 323
preoperational stage 367
preparatory assignments 756
presage-process-product paradigm 891
President's Commission on Education Reform, Korea 1040, 1041
primary education 83, 305, 1281, 1302
  adult literacy link 304
  community financing 1052–3
  developing countries 1033
  drop-outs 20
  East Asia 708
  Education for All 18, 19, 22, 23–4
  enrolments 708
  expansion of 145
  gender disparity 270
  girls 282, 284
  gross enrolment ratios 32, 33
  increasing demand for 107
  India 158, 164–5
  Malaysia 794, 803
  Nepal 159–61
  Nonformal Primary Education Program 179–80
  Oceania 1228
  Pacific Islands 1275–7
  Pakistan 161–4, 302–3
  participation rates and gender 259
  Primary Education Curriculum Renewal project 102
  private expenditure 1051

rates of return 810, 811, 830
sex stereotypes 272–3
South Asia 155–6, 164
teacher recruitment 906, 907
teacher supply in Korea 960–1
Thailand 303
transition to secondary schooling 471
universal 172–5, 1092, 1275
  developing countries 338, 339
  East Asia 708
  India 850
  Jomtien Conference 337
universalisation 146, 172–5, 187
see also basic education; elementary school
Prime Project 604, 614
principals 966–7, 1001–13
  effectiveness 1002–3
  inclusive education for students with special needs 208
  leadership style 980–1
  role 922, 973, 975, 976, 979–80, 982, 983, 1001
  school leadership 973–85
  self-managing schools 939–40, 942
Principals' Executive Centre (PEC), Singapore 1007
principle of right to information 951
principle of unwarranted harm 951
priorities of educational research 1194, 1203–5
priorities for research xxi
private provision of education 29, 34, 35–6, 39, 40, 41
private rates of return
  higher education 1210–11
  private tutoring 1060
private schools 96, 1100
  costs 86
  high-income families 48
  social capital 62
private sector xx, 319, 925–6, 1015–29
  China 1205
  donor support 1156
  East Asia 709, 711
  enrolments 1050, 1051–2
  enterprise education and training 718
  expenditure 1049–52
  finance 76, 84, 90, 1274, 1280–2, 1283
  higher education 737, 820–3, 827–8, 834–5, 836–7, 844–6, 1102–3, 1104, 1211
  increased role 1273
  inequalities 825
  Korean para schools 316
  Pacific Islands 687, 688
  productivity growth 1272
  quality assurance 949
  secondary education 76, 84, 87, 90
  tertiary education
    Japan 1036, 1038
    Korea 1038–40
  urban youth 226
  vocational education and training 681–2, 685
private tuition 39, 98, 339, 734, 788–9, 1047, 1059–60, 1065, 1244
see also coaching
private universities 737, 822–3, 844–6, 1102, 1155
  donor support 1156
  financing of higher education 827, 834–5, 836–7
  Japan 1036, 1038

privatisation 87, 88, 975, 1100
  educational management 915, 917
  efficiency 39
  globalisation 1102
  higher education 828, 830–4, 839, 842–6
  Hong Kong 1022, 1023, 1027
  reforms 1315, 1319, 1320
  Singapore 7
  Taiwan 1018–19, 1020, 1026
  trends in educational reform 5, 8
problem creation 1098
problem representation 516
problem situation 512–13, 519, 522
problem solving computer-assisted tutorial (PSCAT) system 522
problem students 427
problem translation 522
problem-based learning (PBL) 521, 525, 526, 536, 1009
problem-centred teaching 547, 603
problem-solving 351, 511–24, 575, 738, 932
  Asian teaching practices 994
  curricular reforms 1100
  direct instruction 784
  educational aims 953
  gifted education 197, 199
  information literacy 1257
  Japanese curriculum 1098
  mathematical 479–83
  mathematics 156, 601, 603, 1120
  metacognition 479–83
  model 99
  nonformal education 340
  numeracy 795
  private tuition 789
  psychological development 388
  reforms 974
  ROBOLAB 535
  simulations 1264
  situated learning 359
  skills 858, 1249–50
process monitoring 919
processing loads 374
productive pedagogues 354
productivist model 872, 877
productivity
  East Asia 702, 710
  educational researchers 132–3
  enterprise education and training 720, 721
  growth 1272
  HRD planning 660, 662, 663, 664
  indicators 1128–9
  labour force 321, 326
professional associations 1142, 1143
professional development 611, 771
  career-long 80
  China 893
  class sizes 752
  continuing education 854, 892, 908
  continuous 916, 918, 923
  effective schooling 920, 988, 997
  Hong Kong 734
  ICT 1261–4
  inadequate provision 979
  Japan 904, 997
  knowledge creation 779
  LATIS project 531

Index of Subjects 1407

lifelong 5, 10–11, 916, 918, 1316, 1323–4
principals 981–2
reform 975
research priorities 1203
research training 1286
school leadership 1007, 1010
self-managing schools 939, 940, 941, 942
strengthening 78
teacher research 606
Tokyo Declaration xiv
professional doctorates 1286, 1287, 1297–8
professional practice 550
professional standards 1176
professionalism 604, 736, 867, 884, 902, 949, 1224
profit-making 1016, 1018
program activities, UNESCO secondary education activities 78–80, 81
Programme for International Student Assessment (PISA) 126, 311, 618, 949, 1110–11, 1120
progressive education movement 111
Project for Enhancing Effective Learning (PEEL) 485, 624–5
Project InSPIRE 1292
Project Integrated Education of the Disabled (PIED), India 207
Project Radio Education in Adult Literacy 1306
promotion system 962–3, 964, 966–7
prospective accountability study 1171
prospective evaluation 1171
proximal family capital 48–51
proximal settings 44, 45, 53, 54, 55
PRQ *see* Peer Relations Questionnaire
PSCAT *see* problem solving computer-assisted tutorial system
psychological development 379–94
 see also human development
psychological structures 367
psychology 95, 147, 1198
 cultural 372, 373–4, 375
 developmental 380, 381, 391
 ecological 744
 experimental 124
 gifted children 189
 group size and participation 749
 indigenous 444
 learning 525, 772
 research institutes 132
psychometric approaches 782
psychosocial development 309
PTA *see* parent-teacher associations
public education 338, 1015–29
public examinations
 accountability 109, 113–15
 Indonesia 115–17
 reforms 920, 947, 950–1
public expenditure 36, 37, 40, 1047–9, 1093, 1302
 accountability 107
 decreasing 1102
 developing countries 173
 Korea 1102
 Macau 1025
 Pacific Islands 1277–8, 1282
 as percentage of GNP 173
 secondary education 85
 Singapore 1102
 social services 1032
 Sri Lanka 907

Taiwan 1102
tertiary education
 Japan 1037
 Korea 1039, 1040
 vocational education and training 682
public funding of higher education 822, 825, 827, 828–30
public post-secondary education 35, 36
public sector 925–6
 accountability 1139
 enterprise education and training 718
 higher education 822, 823
 management 1273–4
 productivity growth 1272
 universities 1153–4, 1155
 vocational education and training 681–2
public-private partnerships 710
publication of research 98, 132–3
publicly provided education 29, 34, 35–6, 39, 41
punishment, physical 428, 436
purchasing power-parity (PPP) 31

QERC *see* Quality of Education Review Committee
QTI *see* Questionnaire of Teacher Interaction
qualifications 11, 755
 East Asia 711
 elite professions 46
 Japan 315
 New Zealand 725
 Pacific Islands TVET provision 694, 695, 697, 699
 portability 310, 312
 teachers 869–72, 901, 909, 950, 1059
qualitative research 166, 470–1, 651
quality 280, 974
 achievement levels 1096
 developing countries 175–6
 disadvantaged students 1319
 East Asia 708–9
 educational management 916, 918
 equality of opportunity 143
 gender gap 272, 277
 higher education 1318
 indicators 1128, 1133
 learning 156, 164, 165, 1182
 Pacific Islands TVET provision 697
 private tutoring 1060
 quantity relationship 171, 174
 research 1089, 1322
 school-based indicators 119
 self-managing schools 932
 teacher recruitment 900, 901, 904, 908, 910
 teachers 151, 736, 739, 889, 891, 923, 1316, 1323–4
 teaching workforce 867, 869–72, 877
 UN World Programme of Action for Youth 1233
 upgrading 1181
quality assurance 24, 916, 918, 919–20, 945–58, 974, 1035
 cross-national seminars 1178
 educational reform 9, 10
 indicators 1126
 nonformal education 343
 paradigm shifts 1326
 planning and policy 926
 research challenges 1322
 secondary education 76, 78, 80, 86–7

teachers   739
tertiary education   1037, 1043, 1044
Thailand   1176, 1177
quality education for all   199
Quality Education Fund   1064
Quality of Education Review Committee (QERC), Australia   310, 311
quality of teaching, self-evaluation   767
quantification   1197
quantitative research   166
   learning environments research   470–1
   peace education   651
   Western approaches   642
quaternary phase   306, 308, 312
question difficulty gradient   159–60, 162
questioning   356–7
Questionnaire of Teacher Interaction (QTI)   464, 467, 468–9, 470, 471
questionnaires
   attitudes   409–24
   classroom learning environments   463, 464, 465–6, 467, 469–70, 471
   environmental awareness   576
   peace education   649
   self-esteem   447
   student learning   442, 443, 444–6, 449, 458, 459–62

R and D model   99
race
   Aboriginal studies   372
   inclusiveness   1238
   see also ethnicity
racial discrimination   1232–3
racial justice, research priorities   1203
racism   254
   Aboriginal students   53
   bullying   437
radical constructivism   603
Rainbow Reading Program   593
Rajasthan State Institute of Education Research and Training   157, 158
Rasch model   159–60, 162, 412, 414
rates of return   662, 665, 683, 684
   enterprise education and training   720–1
   higher education   810–11, 812, 1210–11
   investment in higher education   737
   primary education   810, 811, 830
   private tutoring   1060
   studies   325, 328
rational curriculum code   541–2
rational paradigm   1032
RDD model *see* research-development-dissemination model
re-training   321, 322, 661
reactivity   1264
reading   552, 795
   Asian children   989
   assessment   799–800
   comprehension   1108, 1117
   difficulties   372, 591–3
   gender differences   262, 263, 264
   how children learn to read   586–91
   IEA studies   262, 263, 264, 1108, 1117–18, 1120
   literacy   1108, 1111, 1117–18, 1120
   metacognition   486–7, 488–9
   to learn   590

Reading and English Acquisition Program (REAP)   589
reading literacy   585–97
Reading Literacy Study   949
Reading Recovery program   588, 592
real world problem solving   601
realistic curriculum code   541
REAP *see* Reading and English Acquisition Program
reasoning   351, 367
   curriculum aims   544
   metacognition   477
reciprocal teaching   489
recognition of prior learning (RPL)   864
recruitment of teachers   78, 80, 738, 884, 899–911, 904–5, 907–10, 961–2, 969–70
RECSAM *see* Regional Education Centre for Science and Mathematics
recurrent education   306
   see also lifelong learning
redundancy of information   309
reflection   606
reflective practice   1138
reform   xviii, xxi–xxii, 1098–9
   China   1251–3
   educational management   915, 916–17
   globalisation   1100
   implementation   101
   India   906
   Japan   315
   labour market   1271–83
   opposition to   954–5
   Pacific Islands   1227, 1271–83
   parent/community involvement   1072
   principal role   922
   public examinations   920, 947, 950–1
   research   95–6, 98, 1168, 1170, 1171–9, 1205, 1315–29
   rural education   179
   school leadership   973, 974–5, 979, 980, 983, 984, 1001
   science and technology curricula   1243–56
   secondary education   73–91, 1231–42
   self-managing schools   933, 941, 942
   social/economic   152
   teacher education   947
   teachers   900
   tertiary education   1043
   Thailand   1005–6
   trends   3–16
   UK/US   781
   workplace education   329–30
refugees   342
regional aggregate expenditures   1058
regional collaboration   xiv, xvi, xix, xxii, 175, 1301–13
regional database on comparative studies   1313
regional development   1092
regional differences   144, 149–50, 167–8
Regional Education Centre for Science and Mathematics (RECSAM)   1291, 1292
regional identity   1212
Regional Institute of Higher Education (RIHED)   102
Regional Language Centre (RELC), Singapore   591
Regional Seminar on Educational Research in

Relation to Educational Reform in Asia and Oceania 126
Regional Technical Advisory Groups (RTAGs) 21
regulation
  coaching 765
  teacher education 910
reinforcement learning 533
Reinforcement Theory 525
relational complexity theory 372, 374, 375
RELC *see* Regional Language Centre; SEAMEO-Regional Language Centre
relevance of curriculum 1223
reliability 445, 793, 797–8, 799
reliability index 421
religion 68, 293, 1217
  Catholic Church 1052
  decline in authority of religious institutions 1236
  India 644
  Islam 1053
  value systems 642
religious education 561, 563
remedial reading programs 592–3
repetition 24, 76, 89, 174, 359–60, 361
  Aboriginal students 451
  Macau 1025
  see also grade repetition
replication studies 166
Report Card on Inclusive Education in Australia 204–5
reproduction theory 1208–9
research 93–106, 123–40, 1167–79, 1193–1206
  Asian classrooms 354
  bullying 429, 432, 435, 437
  Central Asia 241–3, 244–5, 246–9
  citizenship education 558, 565–6
  class size 744, 745–8
  classroom learning environments 463, 465, 470–2
  coaching 760–3, 764
  cognitive development 309, 365–6, 368–9, 372–3, 374–5
  continuing education 854, 863–5
  Cooperative Research Centres 861
  cross-cultural studies 358, 359, 371, 444, 446–9, 452–3
    effective schooling 998
    mathematics anxiety 515–16
    motivation 496–9
    parental expectations 990
    problem solving 519–20
  cross-national studies 1091, 1096–8
    children with reading difficulties 591–2
    citizenship education 565
    classroom learning environments 463, 468–9
    educational achievement 1107–22
  curriculum 547, 549–50, 602–4
  definition 1081–3
  developing countries 146–7, 166–8
  dissemination 1084, 1089, 1091, 1137–50, 1200, 1306
  donor support 1151–64
  effective schooling 920–1, 997–8
  family/community involvement 925, 1063, 1070–2, 1073–5
  fugitive literature 321
  gaps 1204
  gifted education 191, 192, 195–6, 199, 200

homework 757–60, 763
HRD planning 665–70
ICT 308, 1262, 1265–6
  impact of 324, 1181–91, 1199–1201
inclusive education 203, 204–5, 208, 212, 213
language education 629–40
learning 351, 355, 361
lifespan human development 380, 381–2, 390–1
mathematics 602–7
metacognition 479–89, 490
motivation 495, 503–4
new strategies 1238
nonformal education 337, 340–1, 345, 346
paucity of 166
peace education 641–2, 643–51
policy-making 96–101
policy-oriented 924
prior knowledge 359
problem solving 511, 513–14, 518–22, 523
public/private education 925–6
reform 1315–29
regional cooperation 1301–13
regional and national development 1081–94
school effectiveness 768
school leadership 1010–11
science education 620–5, 1253
self-managing schools 936–40
Soviet 244–5
staffing issues 923–4, 968–9
syntheses 96, 102, 605
teacher education 738, 883–97
teacher-based 1253
technology 602
time allocation 785–6
training research workers 1285–99
types of 604–6
utilisation 1137, 1144–8, 1169
workforce education 323–9, 331–2
see also comparative research studies
'research lessons' 1246–7
Research School of Social Sciences, Australian National University 132
research-development-dissemination (RDD) model 547–8, 607
research-oriented model 99–100
research-teaching-study nexus 823
resource management skills 757
resources 299, 1121
  access to 1337
  achievement relationship 1119
  allocation 939, 940, 947, 1133
  community involvement 9
  economic 59, 1151
  Education for All 27
  gifted children 189–90
  human capital 59
  indicators 1133
  internal efficiency 85
  language education 632–6
  material 1338
  Pacific Islands 1279, 1280
  policy development and planning 1034
  poverty 177
  primary school enrolment 23–4
  research 1090
  social/cultural capital 60–1
retention rates 83–4, 1160

1410 Index of Subjects

Australia 1173
BRAC students 180
China 300
examination results 114
female 85
gender issues 260, 261, 264, 265
retirement and attrition 909, 960
retraining 715, 716
returns
  enterprise education and training 716, 720–1
  higher education 810–11, 812, 1210–11
  investment in higher education 737
  workforce education 321
reversibility in thought 367
revision 736
right to education 17–18, 27, 143, 144–5, 171, 304, 1232
right to information 951
right to work 1336
RIHED *see* Regional Institute of Higher Education
ROBOLAB 535
Rockefeller Foundations 1153, 1154, 1156
romanised script 314
rote learning 450, 452, 587, 608, 782
  civics education 565
  effective schooling 993
  Korea 546, 764
  see also memorisation
Royal Melbourne Institute of Technology 531
RPL *see* recognition of prior learning
RTAGs *see* Regional Technical Advisory Groups
Runaway World 1331, 1332, 1341, 1344
rural areas 94, 150, 171–88
  China 300
  class sizes 748
  coaching 760
  community participation 1068
  curriculum 178
  disadvantaged groups 153
  equity 335, 342–3
  gender-based wage disparities 286–7
  Indonesia 534
  knowledge of institutions 239
  nonformal education 336, 337–8, 339, 343, 345
  primary school enrolment 23
  private tutoring 1059
  Rajasthan case study 232, 234, 235
  research priorities 1205
  students with special needs 206, 207
  Vietnam 1055
  vocational education and training 674, 675, 680
rural poverty 176–7
rural-urban migration 220–1
Russia 241–2, 246
  decentralisation 564
  economic growth 1088
  influence on Asia-Pacific curriculum 606
  influence on Asia-Pacific education 108
  post-communist transition 563
  research institutions 129–30
Russian Academy of Education 130
Russian Academy of Sciences 241
Russian Federation
  gender differences 262, 263
  international comparative studies 1110–17
  research productivity 133

SACMEQ *see* Southern Africa Consortium for Monitoring Educational Quality
safety nets for young people at risk 712
SAGE *see* Wisconsin Student Achievement Guarantee in Education
SAL *see* Student Approaches to Learning position
Salamanca Statement (1994) 189, 201
Salamanca Statement and Framework for Action on Special Needs Education 203, 210, 215
salaries 85, 738–9, 755, 756, 765, 869, 873–4, 1151
  educational expenditure 36, 39, 40, 41
  Japan 964, 997
  Korea 962–3
  low level 1049
  private institutions 835
  raising 910
  see also wages
Samoa
  continuing education 858
  economic/demographic indicators 1276
  educational provision 1277
  higher education 835
  information on 690
  maritime training 696
  public expenditure 1277, 1279
  reading literacy 590
  salaries 697
  teachers 871
  technical and vocational education and training 687, 691, 694
  transport 689
Samoan Government Statement of Economic Strategies 690
sample surveys 800–1
SASEANEE *see* South and South-east Asia Network for Environmental Education
satellite access 859
SATs *see* Scholastic Achievement Tests
SBM *see* school-based management
scaffolding 757
schemes/schemas 367
scholarship 549, 550, 606
  citizenship conflict 561
  cultural respect for 624
Scholastic Achievement Tests (SATs), Singapore 1250
School Based Management Scheme, Hong Kong 1021
school buildings 94
school capital 51–3
school charter 934, 948
school climate 100
school effectiveness xix, 733, 918, 920–1, 955
  principal role 1002, 1003
  research 768
School Excellence Model (SEM) 947, 948, 952
school governance 1020, 1021
school leadership 1001–13
  see also leadership
School of Professional and Continuing Education (SPACE) 862, 863–4, 866
school refusal 52, 53, 209
school sizes 85–6, 89
school violence 641
school-based action research 1145
school-based curriculum development 876, 975

school-based management (SBM) 6, 10, 931–44, 948, 955, 975
  Hong Kong 1021
  organisation of education 916, 918, 921–2
  research challenges 1316, 1322–3
  school leadership 973, 974, 978, 979, 982, 983
  school-to-home communication 1066
  Thailand 1005
  see also self-managing schools
school-to-work transition 327, 329, 701–14
schools
  Asian/American comparison 64
  audits 947
  bullying 425–39
  community relationship 150–1
  culture 1002
  distance 282
  double-session 735
  drop-outs 231–40
  effective schooling 987–1000
  external evaluation 1322
  indicators of effectiveness 118–19
  individualist culture 62, 63
  instructional organisation 47–8
  as learning communities 1240–1
  learning environments 51–2
  monitoring 918, 919–20, 945–58
  networked 875
  organisational structure 52–3
  progressive 789
  retention 1160
  reviews 948, 956
  self-evaluation 1322
  self-management 919
  self-review 948
  social capital 62
  student achievement relationship 1119
  subsidised 1021, 1022–3, 1027
Schools of the Future (SOF) 939–40
Schools InterLink Project 532
science 552, 615–27, 1096, 1098
  Barefoot College 239
  class size 741, 747
  cross-national studies 468–9
  curricular reform 1243–56
  economic globalisation 1100
  economic growth relationship 1098
  gender differences 262–4
  globalisation 1100, 1332, 1334, 1336–7
  human capital 1103
  IEA studies 258, 262, 263, 264, 1108, 1114–17
  Indonesian Center for Scientific Documentation Information 534
  international studies 353, 1088
  laboratory skills 758, 796–7
  literacy 1099, 1111, 1120
  metacognition 483–5, 489, 490
  Newton 1332
  technology 526, 527, 528, 534, 535
science of education 96
science education community 1253–4
science education research 1253
Science Laboratory Environment Inventory (SLEI) 464, 466, 467, 470, 471
Science, Technology and Society (STS) model 621, 1252–3
scientific abstract thinking 367

scientific epistemology 124
scientific literacy 530, 615, 618, 619, 1243, 1254
scientific and technological literacy 18
scoring 156
Scotland 773
Scottish Consultative Council on the Curriculum 773, 780
SEABAS see Southeast Asian Bibliographic and Abstracting Service
SEAMEO see South-East Asian Ministers of Education Organisation
SEAMEO-Regional Language Centre (RELC) 102
SEARRAG see South-East Asia Research Review and Advisory Group
SEASAME see South-East Asian Science and Mathematics Experiment
Second IEA Science Study 949
Second Indochina War 314
Second International Conference on Technical and Vocational Education 329
Second International Mathematics Study 258, 949, 1111, 1112
Second International Science Study 353, 1111, 1115
second language education 552, 629–40
second-chance education 1241
secondary education xix, xxi, 305, 1281
  advanced countries 1033
  completion 35
  East Asia 708
  expansion 7, 145, 1096
  girls 282, 284
  gross enrolment ratios 32, 33
  increasing demand for 107
  Pacific Islands 691–2
  participation 40, 259–60
  poor quality 851
  primary education transition to 471
  rates of return 810
  reform 73–91, 1231–42
  teacher supply in Korea 960
  technical schools 325
  universalisation 841
  vocational 329
Sedc see State Education Commission
segregation 1170
  gifted children 196, 198, 199
  students with special needs 206, 211
selection
  bias 262, 264
  examinations 108, 114, 115, 117
  higher education 737, 839–52
  lower secondary schooling 156
  principals 982–3
  teacher education 884, 887, 908
  universities 108, 115
self 62–3
self-assessment
  metacognition 478
  teacher language proficiency 635, 636
self-concept 406, 446
self-directed learning 1202, 1259, 1261, 1263
self-discipline 789
self-efficacy 478, 488, 499, 759
self-esteem 351, 354, 406, 1235
  bullying effect on 427
  classroom learning environments 466

effort attribution   498, 499
  ICT benefits   1259
  motivation   497
  student learning   446, 447, 448, 453, 459
  see also confidence
self-evaluation   1322
  Japanese tertiary education   1037
  teachers   767-80
  teaching practices   734
self-explanation training   517
self-government   236
self-learning   1327
self-management   734
self-managing schools   10, 916, 918, 919, 921-2, 931-44, 1323
self-questioning   484
self-regulation
  learning   441, 757, 760, 903, 1261
  metacognition   477-9, 482, 483, 489
  problem solving   513, 518
self-reliance   177, 225-6
self-taught ICT users   1261
SEM *see* School Excellence Model
Seminar on Learning and the Educational Process (SOLEP)   126
Senate Standing Committee on Adult and Community Education   348
senior secondary education   34, 35
sensory-motor stage   367
separation index   421
SERA *see* Singapore Educational Research Association
service sector, women   285, 286
sex differences   258, 269
sex education   224
sex stereotypes   272-3, 274, 275, 276, 287-8, 290, 619
sexism   269, 275
sexual abuse   226
sexual harassment   271
sexual health education   21
sexual violence   435
Shanghai Education Commission   742
SHBIE *see* Sultan Hassanal Bolkiah Institute of Education
Shiksa Karmi Project   872
SIDA *see* Swedish International Development Agency
simulated experience   1198
simulation software   527
simulations   1264
Singapore
  academic curriculum   1212
  ageing population   1214
  attitudes towards capital punishment   419, 421, 422
  Australia comparison   468-9
  character development   546
  class size   741, 742
  classroom learning environments   464, 465-6, 467, 471
  coaching   735, 761, 762-3, 765
  collegiality   978
  continuing education   864
  cooperative learning   745
  curriculum   543-4, 545, 546, 551, 764, 1212
  decentralisation   975

economic growth/development   974, 1088, 1211
education aims   790
educational and instructional technology   1261
educational research associations   136-7
effective schooling   988
Endowment Funds   1055
enrolments   33, 707, 1210-11, 1214
environmental education   574, 576, 578, 579
examinations   8
fees   1052
gender differences   263, 264, 468
gifted education   193, 199
global civics   560
gross national income   31
high educational attainment   63, 739, 769, 1097
higher education   811, 815, 822, 823, 824-5, 829, 1210-11
human resource development   1210
inclusive education for students with special needs   211-12
independent revenue-earning   1054, 1055
international studies   353, 1110-18
IT strategy   11
leadership   922
learning technology   530-1
literacy   487
Masterplan for IT   909
mastery learning   784
mathematical problem solving   480, 481, 482
metacognition   1262
Muslim minorities   1217
national heritage   560
national vision   7
open classrooms   750
paradigm shifts   12
passive learning   751
performance goals   500
performance indicators   952
performativity   769
PISA   949
political ideology   1212
population   30, 31, 1214
pre-reading skills   587
pressure to succeed   452, 1244
primary education   1281
principals   981, 982
private sector   823
private tuition   789, 1059
problem solving   521, 522
public expenditure   36, 37, 40, 1102
public/private provision   34, 36
quality assurance   10, 946, 954
reading literacy   587, 589, 591, 592
reforms   1099
research
  impact on practice   102
  institutions   130
  productivity   133
  training of researchers   1292-4, 1298
School Excellence Model   947, 948, 952
school leadership   922, 1002, 1003, 1006-7, 1010
school-based management   10
science education   617, 619, 620, 1244, 1247-50
situated cognition   623
staffing ratios   38
students
  activism   1213

activity 773–4, 776
  expectations 624
  learning 449, 450
  mobility 502
  perceptions 354
teacher education 884, 885, 887, 889, 892, 900, 901, 905, 911
teachers 871, 876, 923
  career ladder 967
  job satisfaction 888
  quality 11
  recruitment 907–10
  salaries 739, 756
Teachers' Network 894, 908
teaching behaviour 734
technical and vocational education 668, 670
time allocation 787, 788
TIMSS 758
tracer studies 327
transparency 952
TVET 324
values 451
vocational education and training 7, 677, 678, 682
whole class teaching 748
workforce education 323, 324, 325–6
Singapore Educational Research Association (SERA) 136–7
Singapore Institute of Technical Education (ITE) 330
single-mother families 65
site-level 5–6
  educational management 916, 918, 919–24, 928
  quality assurance 955
  research challenges 1316, 1321–4
situated activity 514
situated cognition 603, 623–4
situated learning 359, 526, 530, 536, 623
size of classes *see* class size
Skill New Zealand 718, 725, 726, 727, 730
skilling 711
skills 357–8
  Barefoot College 238
  basic 782, 802
  cognitive 370, 757
  demand for skilled labour 325
  East Asia 707
  enterprise education and training 715, 716, 719
  entrepreneurship 225
  essential 310, 311
  gifted education 193
  higher-order 794–6
  ICT 308, 1259
  monitoring 518
  new policy approaches 1035
  numerical 69
  psychological development 388
  research 532
  rural poverty 177–8
  second language education 630
  Singapore Skills Development Fund 682
  social 794
  survival 371–2
  teachers 889
  technological change 322
  thinking 1249–50
  upgrading 321, 332

vocational education and training 673, 674, 675, 681, 684
  workforce education 321, 326, 332
  youth transition 712
  see also social skills
Skills Training 25–6, 330
SLEI *see* Science Laboratory Environment Inventory
small enterprises 718–19, 723
Smart School Project 909
SMILES (School-based Multiple Intelligences Learning Evaluation System) 527–8
social action 1196, 1197, 1200
social background 39
social capital xviii, 59–72, 100
  family background 45, 49, 50–1
  immigrant groups 54
  nonformal education 335
  urban youth 221, 227, 228
social change 1151, 1198, 1218
  developing countries 219
  globalisation 1334, 1336, 1338
  India 1172
  women's roles 258
social class
  cultural capital 61
  home-school relations 1071
  inequalities 45
  private education 1020
  reproduction 46, 1208–9
  reproduction of 1020, 1033
  social capital 60
social cohesion 1209, 1272
social constructivism 603, 608
  reading 590
social context
  bullying 433
  homework 757
  psychological development 379, 389–90
social contexts 361
  cognitive development 368, 374
  cultural psychology 373, 374
social control, social capital 60
social development 375, 816–18
  China 1251
  nonformal education 342
social disharmony 1190
social education 315, 319
social education centres 315, 319
social engineering 245
social equality 1208
social equity 1272
social evolution 1332, 1334
social exclusion 226–7, 228, 750
social goals 500, 501
social growth 687
social harmony 770, 1212
  curriculum aims 544
  India 645
social indicators 1125
social interaction 481
  ICT 307, 308
  problem solving 514
social justice
  Australia 264
  higher education 841
  research priorities 1203

women 341, 344
youth policy 267
Social Learning Theory 428
social mobilisation 60
social mobility 60, 187, 235, 356
  see also career mobility
social needs 1203
social policy 1234
social progress 18
social psychology 749
social rates of return 325
social relations 751
social responsibility 1177, 1222
social science research 1083, 1201
social scripts 359
social security 1053, 1060
social selection 187
social services 1032
social skills 794
  ICT benefits 1259
  Japanese schools 432
social status 267
social studies 558–9
social values 1172, 1195
social well-being 1245, 1254
Social Work and Research Centre (SWRC), Rajasthan 232-3, 240
social-cognitive theory 513, 756
socialisation 94, 149, 353, 361, 495, 504, 629, 809
  Aboriginal Australians 503
  Asian collectivist model 357
  attributional research 498
  citizenship education 555
  comparative studies 1120, 1121
  effective schooling 987, 990
  political 555, 1212, 1213
  sexist 275
  structural functionalist perspective 1208
  values 921
socialising 750
socialism 556, 1016–17, 1058
socio-cultural development
  psychological 379, 389–90
  university education 1207, 1213–18
socio-cultural environment
  motivation 503, 504
  motivation and learning strategies 483
socio-cultural theory of cognition 358
socio-economic status 147, 231
  attainment relationship 43, 45, 46, 48, 67, 145, 1214
  EFA objectives 175
  equity issues 144
  higher education 845–6
  nonformal education 340
  private schooling 39
  privatisation in Taiwan 1019
  research favouring higher status groups 1187
  teacher beliefs 65
  United States 1026
sociology of education 147
SOF *see* Schools of the Future
soft technology 525
software 527, 528, 530, 532
  home-made 1325
  reading literacy 594
solar power 240

SOLEP *see* Seminar on Learning and the Educational Process
solidarity 54, 396, 398
  Asian students in Australia 483
  culture of peace 398, 399
  social goals 501
  youth 228
Solo Taxonomy 100
Solomon Islands
  continuing education 858, 859
  economic/demographic indicators 1276
  educational provision 1277
  girls and science education 619
  information on 690
  maritime training 696
  political stability 689
  public expenditure 1277, 1279
  reading literacy 55, 590
  teachers 871
  technical and vocational education and training 687, 694
Soros Foundation 251, 256, 1156
South Asia
  access to education 153
  adult literacy 25
  case study of learning achievement 155–69
  drop-out rates 24
  female illiteracy 270
  gender differences 154, 259, 279, 280–8
  higher education 824, 827, 843
  illiteracy 260, 261, 270, 295
  learning achievement 24
  life expectancy 20
  literacy 20
  out-of-school children 231
  participation 259, 305
  population control 304
  poverty 176
  problems with educational services provision 1339
  public expenditure 1049
  teacher preparation 738
  teacher-pupil ratios 872
  teachers 868, 869
  vocational education and training 678, 681, 682
South Asian Association for Regional Co-operation (SAARC) 1154, 1155
South Central Asia, youth population 220
South Korea *see* Korea
South Pacific
  continuing education 858–9
  reading literacy 589–90, 592
  universities 738
  see also Oceania; Pacific Islands
South Pacific Association for Teacher Education 883
South Pacific Regional Environment Programme (SPREP) 571, 583
South and South-east Asia Network for Environmental Education (SASEANEE) 571
South-East Asia
  economic crisis 296
  higher education 811, 824, 827
  leadership development 923
  life expectancy 20
  literacy 20
  youth population 220

South-East Asia Research in Education Group
    (SEAREG) 126
South-East Asia Research Review and Advisory
    Group (SEARRAG) 883, 1292, 1305, 1306,
    1307
South-East Asian Bibliographic and Abstracting
    Service (SEABAS) 1292
South-East Asian Ministers of Education
    Organisation (SEAMEO) 313, 669-70, 833,
    837, 1154, 1155, 1210, 1220, 1304, 1305-6, 1313
  INNOTECH 1262, 1295
  RECSAM 1291, 1292
  Regional Centre for Educational Innovations and
    Technology 1304-5, 1306, 1309
  teacher education 894
South-East Asian Science and Mathematics
    Experiment (SEASAME) 1291
Southern Africa Consortium for Monitoring
    Educational Quality (SACMEQ) 98, 103, 805
Soviet ethnography 244
Soviet Language Policy 245-6
Soviet Union, former 241-56, 293, 294
  external aid 1057, 1058
  technical and vocational education 657
SPACE *see* School of Professional and Continuing
    Education
special education 204, 206, 207, 211
  gifted children 189
  teachers 208, 210, 211
  Thailand 1176
special needs 203-15, 1065
specialisation 1254-5
specific human capital 553, 673
spiritual poverty 177
spirituality 402, 642
split attention 309
SPQ *see* Student Process Questionnaire
SPREP *see* South Pacific Regional Environment
    Programme
Sri Lanka
  coaching 760, 761
  conflict resolution 336
  environmental education 574-5
  graduate underemployment 1216
  higher education 811-12, 820, 1215
  population ageing 1214
  private tutoring 1059
  reading literacy 55
  repetition rate 174
  science education 616
  science/engineering enrolments 1100
  teacher recruitment 905, 906-7
  teachers 871, 872
  technical colleges 673
  universities 1155, 1213
  unqualified teachers 739
  vocational education and training 673, 676, 677,
    680
  World Education Indicators 1133
Srinakarinwirot University 128
staffing 919, 923-4, 959-71
  ratios 36-8, 40
  turnover 697
stakeholders 919, 1321-2
  accountability 109-10
  educational reform 9
  effective schooling 987

expectations 1319-20, 1321
indicators 1124
quality assurance 953
school effectiveness 119
standardisation 954
standardised tests 111, 801
  Cook Islands 803
  language education 637
  New Zealand 114
  secondary education reform 86, 89, 90
standards 767, 990, 1316
  cross-national seminars 1178
  curriculum 551
  evaluation 112, 113
  international 1217
  language education 631, 637
  maintenance of 156
  monitoring 799
  Pacific Islands 694
  policy approaches 926
  reporting against 802-3
  skills and competences 1035
  teacher education 878, 879
  teacher responsibility 768
  teachers 923, 962-6, 970
  Thailand 1176
standards of living 18
Stanford University 126
STAR project 741-2, 743, 744
State Education Commission (Sedc), China 330,
    334
state finance 927
state provision of higher education 822, 825,
    836-7
state-trait debate 443-4
statistical analysis 1199
statistics 599, 600, 601, 603
Statistics Canada 311, 316, 320
stereotypes
  age 384
  Asian teachers 449
  Confucian heritage cultures 995
  cultural 355, 484
  sex 272-3, 274, 275, 276, 287-8, 290, 619
sticky probing 356-7
strategic research 549, 1083, 1090
strategies, problem solving 516, 517
streaming *see* ability grouping
street children 226
stress
  bullying 431-2, 437
  teachers 888, 889
stressful lifestyles 388
structural adjustment 326, 824, 830
structural functionalist perspective 1208
structural unemployment 224-5
structuration theory 1168, 1169-70, 1171
structure of school systems 94
STS *see* Science, Technology and Society model
student age population 31
Student Approaches to Learning (SAL)
    position 441-2, 444
student assistance for living costs 40
student fees 819, 820, 821-2, 831, 835, 844, 845,
    927, 1060
  Australia 1042-3
  China 1017, 1018

1416 Index of Subjects

cost-sharing 1052
Higher Education Contribution Scheme 1282
Korea 1039
student loan schemes 832-3, 1282
Student Process Questionnaire (SPQ) 442, 443, 444, 445-6, 450
student teachers
  anxiety 889
  assessment 891
  attitudes 892
  beliefs 887, 892
student-centred learning 995, 1005, 1009
student-teacher interactions 743
student-teacher ratio 36-8, 40, 85, 90, 742, 743, 872, 1277, 1302
students
  activism 1213
  assessment of performance 110, 111-12
  at education risk 1147
  classroom activity 773-4
  Fielding taxonomy 778
  growth in numbers 1231
  learning 441-62
  Learning School Project 775-7
  perceptions of
    Australia-Singapore comparison 468-9
    classroom learning environments 466, 467, 468, 469
    gender differences 467-8
  selection for higher education 737
  subjective experience sampling 774
students with special needs (SWSN) 203-15
studying 757, 758
subcultures 62
subjective experience sampling 774
subordination of women 279, 287-8
subsidies
  enterprise education and training 716, 723, 725, 727-8
  higher education 827, 830
  Macau 1025
  private education 35, 40
subsidised schools 1021, 1022-3, 1027
success 496, 497-8, 515
successful intelligence 191, 195
suicidal ideation 427, 429
Sultan Hassanal Bolkiah Institute of Education (SHBIE) 1288-9
summative assessment/evaluation 101, 111, 500-1, 610, 625, 1238
supervision
  higher degrees by research 1287-8
  teachers 884, 891
supply of teachers 738, 899, 900-1, 906, 909, 923, 959-61, 968, 969
Suranaree University of Technology, Thailand 533
surface approach 442, 444-5, 446, 448, 449, 459-62
surface learning 500, 773
surveys 96, 1197
  attitudes towards inclusive education 203, 205, 208, 211, 212
  educational achievement 117-18
  enterprise education and training 717, 718-19
  human resource development 658, 662, 666
  International Adult Literacy Survey 717
survival skills 371-2

sustainable development
  environmental education 552, 569, 571, 572, 575-6, 580-1, 582, 583
  values education 400, 402
Swedish International Development Agency (SIDA) 17, 27, 1305, 1306
SWRC *see* Social Work and Research Centre
SWSN *see* students with special needs
symbolic modelling 1264
synchronous feedback 1263
System of National Accounts 283-5
system science 623
systemic grammar 591
systems analysis 1032

tactical model 99
TAFE *see* technical and further education; Technical and Further Education institutes
TAI *see* technology achievement index
Taiwan
  Australia comparison 469
  children with reading difficulties 591-2
  Chinese cultural identity 559
  civic curriculum 563-4
  class size 741, 742
  classroom learning environments 465, 469
  coaching 734
  collectivism/individualism tension 770
  competition 748
  cross-national problem solving studies 519
  curriculum reform 561
  decentralisation 975-6
  decision-making 976-7
  economic growth 1088, 1211
  educational and instructional technology 1261
  effective schooling 920, 987, 988, 999
  enrolments 1210
  examination pressure 992
  examination reforms 950-1
  family background 47-8
  female illiteracy 260
  gender 67
  gifted education 190, 191, 195, 197, 199, 200
  girls and science education 619
  high student achievement 63, 1097
  higher education 7, 822, 1210-11, 1318
    participation 842
    private sector 822, 834
  homework 991
  hours at school 988, 989
  human resource development 1210
  influence on Macau education system 1024
  international students 70
  international studies 353, 1110-17
  learning technology 528-9
  locus of control 496, 497
  mathematics anxiety 516
  metacognition 1262
  national visions 7
  paradigm shifts 12
  parental involvement 1320
  performance goals 500
  political ideology 1212
  pressure to succeed 452, 992
  primary education 1281
  principals 978, 979, 981-3
  private finance 1281

Index of Subjects   1417

private sector   822, 834, 949, 1018, 1019–20, 1026, 1211
private tutoring   1059
privatisation of tertiary education   8
problem solving computer-assisted tutorial system   522
public expenditure   1102
public/private education   925, 1018–20, 1026, 1027
research productivity   133
science education   616, 619
self-efficacy study   488
situated cognition   623
SMILES   528
socialisation   990
socially-orientated achievement   501–2
student expectations   624
student learning   449
teacher education   911
teachers   870, 877, 878
  evaluation   771
  monitoring   950
  quality   11
  respect for   1255
teaching practices   993–5
technical and vocational education   668, 670
time allocation   736, 788
traditional worldviews   622
training   329
US comparison   763
values in mathematics education   611
vocational education and training   7, 676, 680, 681, 682, 683, 1212
whole class teaching   745
workforce education   323
Tajikistan   243, 244, 249, 250, 253, 819
talented children *see* gifted children
talented learners   153
talents
  definition   190–2
  multiple   191, 194, 195–6
Tamagawa University, Tokyo   1156
Taoism   643
taped stories   593
Target Orientated Curriculum (TOC), Hong Kong   787
targets
  Dakar World Forum   304
  Education For All 2000 Assessment Synthesis Report   299
  indicators   1126, 1128
Task Force on Higher Education and Society (TFHES)   825, 1046
Tata Institute of Social Sciences in Bombay   1156
tax rebates   1177
taxation   1047, 1053–4, 1060
  high levels of   1273
  loans   1283
Taxonomy of Educational Objectives (Bloom)   100, 111
TEAC *see* Tertiary Education Committee
teacher education   xx, 11, 738–9
  community   1072
  COMPETE project   313–14
  environmental education   569, 575, 580–2
  India   878
  Korea   961

language proficiency   635–6
NGO programs   342
Oceania   1224–6, 1228
peace education   648
Philippines   313–14
recruitment of teachers   899–911
reform   947, 1170
research   883–97, 1324
secondary education reform   88
Thailand   879
  see also teacher training
Teacher Education for Peace Project   642, 648–9
teacher educators   738, 884, 886, 887
  collaborative research   894
  environmental education   581–2, 583
  Oceania   1224–5
  Singapore   905
teacher evaluation   771–3
teacher induction   884, 890, 908, 950
Teacher Proficiency Tests   633–4, 635
Teacher Registration Board (TRB), New Zealand   965, 971
teacher research
  informal   550
  mathematics curriculum   606
teacher support   354
teacher training   94, 157, 1098–9
  anti-bullying   428
  Barefoot College   234–5, 237
  citizenship education   561
  class size   751, 752
  effective schooling   996–7
  gifted education   194, 195
  ICT   1261
  inclusive education for students with special needs   208–9, 212
  India   302
  Korea   959–60
  secondary education   76, 86, 88, 89
  values education   403, 404, 405
  see also teacher education
teacher training college   101
teacher unions   938, 955, 964, 1174
teacher-student interaction   52
teacher-student ratio   36–8, 40, 85, 90, 742, 743, 872, 1277, 1302
teachers   734–6
  attitudes towards homework   759
  Barefoot College   233–5, 236–7
  BRAC selection system   180
  ch'onji   65–6
  class size   743, 744, 745–9, 751–2
  coaching   755
  collaboration between   1097
  collegiality   978
  community-employed   1053
  continuing education program in the Philippines   313–14
  curriculum effect on   544
  demand for   738
  dialogue   607
  direct instruction   784–5
  education for all   186
  effective schooling   994
  effectiveness   167
  expectations   65–6, 487, 498
  female   282

General Studies 1251
gifted education 197, 198, 199
ICT skills 1261, 1264, 1265
implemented curriculum 624
inclusive education for students with special needs 205, 207, 208, 210, 211, 212
Japan 1246-7
language proficiency 632, 633, 634, 635-6, 638
learning environment assessments 471
monitoring 950
Oceania 1222, 1223-6
Pacific Islands 697, 1279
paradigm shifts 1326
peace education 647, 649
performance standards 962-6, 970
preparation 736, 738, 752
professional standards 1176
professionalism 604
qualification examination 962, 969
qualifications 869-72, 901, 909, 950, 1059
quality 151, 923, 947, 949-50, 1316, 1323-4
questioning techniques 356-7
Questionnaire of Teacher Interaction 464, 468-9, 471
Rahman Arshad Report 102
reconceptualization of curriculum 552
recruitment 78, 80, 738, 884, 899-911, 904-5, 907-10, 961-2, 969-70
research 1145, 1146-7, 1204, 1205
 as researchers 167, 1183, 1298
respect for 1255, 1320
'scaffolding' 479, 481, 489, 747, 757
science education 1254-5
self-evaluation 767-80
self-management 921
shortage 967-8
shortage of 900, 906
Singapore 1250
social constructivism 608
specialisation 1254-5
student achievement relationship 1119
supply of 738, 899, 900-1, 906, 909, 923, 959-61, 968, 969
surplus 960, 961
teaching profession 867-81
technology 534-5
tertiary education 548-9
Thailand 1246
time issues 783-4
workload 743
see also professional development; salaries
Teachers College, Columbia University 124
Teachers Council of Thailand 879
teachers' guides 547, 548
Teachers' Network 894, 908
teaching behaviours 966, 970
teaching hours 968
teaching practices 733, 734
 Asian schools 1097
 class size 745-9
 student achievement relationship 1119
teaching profession 867-81
teaching time 735, 736, 739, 746, 747
Teaching-Learning Cycle 406
team teaching 1255
teamwork 329, 544
technical assistance 21, 90, 168, 1160

technical colleges
 increase in number of 305, 306
 Japan 315
 Sri Lanka 673
technical education xx
 curriculum influenced by industry 548
 foreign aid 1057
 increasing demand for 107
 sex stereotypes 273
 Singapore 1248
technical and further education (TAFE) 669
 Australian State Government Institutes 338, 722, 723
 institutions 338
technical schools 667
 Indonesia 325, 665
 Japan 677
Technical and Vocational Education Research Centre 329
technical and vocational education and training (TVET) 88, 89, 321, 324, 325, 327
 expenditure 86
 Indonesia/Malaysia 331
 meta-research 328
 Pacific Islands 687-99
 program activities 80
 see also workforce education
technical and vocational education (TVE) 35, 657-71, 701, 709-10, 711-12
technological change 322-3, 1271
 cultural change 1325
 enterprise education and training 716
 globalisation 1336-7
 school-based management 1323
technological developments 899
technology xx, 525-37, 1231
 curriculum 1101
 economic globalisation 1100
 enterprise education and training 719
 global changes 857, 864
 globalisation 1332, 1334, 1336-7
 HRD planning 664
 impact of 1202
 literacy 294
 mathematics curriculum 600, 601-2, 604
 Newton 1332
 nonformal education 346
 Pacific Islands 1280
 reading literacy 593
 science curriculum 616, 1243-56
 technical and vocational education and training 688, 692, 699
 uneven access 738
 vocational education and training 674, 688, 692, 699
 women's labour force participation 306
 see also computers; information and communications technology
technology achievement index (TAI) 815, 816
telecommunications 859, 932, 1258-9, 1280
television 307, 315-16, 319
 reading literacy 593
 Thailand 1177
temporary employment 1273
tertiary education 39, 305, 1031-46
 curriculum 542, 547, 548
 East Asia 708, 711

Index of Subjects 1419

enrolments 32, 33, 1092
expansion of 145
Pacific Islands 688, 691–2, 694, 697
participation rates and gender 259
planning and policy-making 926
private provision 40, 41
rewarding careers 737
see also higher education; universities
Tertiary Education Committee (TEAC), New Zealand 726, 730
test development for cross-national studies 1108–9
testing
   gender differences 262
   see also examinations; mental tests; standardised tests
textbooks 547, 548
   citizenship education 556
   Macau 1024
   mathematics curriculum 600
   Nepal 872
   problem solving 520
TFHES *see* Task Force on Higher Education and Society
Thailand
   ADB initiatives 1160
   ageing population 707, 1214
   children per family 703
   class size 743
   coaching 761
   cognitive development research 375
   Composite Development Index 1120
   curriculum 544–5
   decentralisation 976
   decreased support for higher education 1102
   development indicators 702
   economic growth 1088
   employment 703, 704
   enrolments 32, 33, 1214
   environmental education 575, 576, 578, 579
   gender differences 263, 264
   gifted education 192–3, 199
   gross national income 31
   higher education 811, 815, 824, 1214–15
     alternatives 846
     enrolments 850
     private sector 827, 834, 837
   human resource development 666
   international comparative studies 1110–19
   leadership 922
   learning technology 533
   literacy 303
   Muslim minorities 1217
   national assessment 802
   National Education Commission 5, 118, 128, 1175, 1179
   national heritage 560
   national visions 7
   nonformal education 341, 342, 709
   parents, involvement 1320
   peace education 648, 649, 650, 651
   political ideology 1212
   population 30, 703, 707, 1214
   principals 978, 981
   private sector 827, 834, 837, 1051
     higher education 1102
     universities 1155
   public expenditure 36, 37, 40
   public/private provision 34, 36
   quality assurance 10
   reading literacy 589, 592
   reforms 1175–7
   relative wealth 323
   repetition rate 174
   research institutions 128
   research training 1295–6, 1297
   school leadership 922, 1002, 1003, 1005–6
   school-to-work transition 329
   science education 616, 1245–6
   science/engineering enrolments 1100
   secondary education 1096
   self-managing schools 921, 931, 935–6
   social relations 977
   staffing ratios 36, 38
   student revolution 1213
   teacher education 879, 884, 885, 892
   teachers 11, 739, 873–4
   technical and vocational education 668, 710
   unemployment 704–6
   vocational education and training 668, 677, 678, 679, 680, 683, 710
   workforce education 323, 324
   World Education Indicators 1133
   youth population 220
theory-practice relationship 1089–90, 1296
thinking skills 1249–50
Third International Mathematics and Science Study (TIMSS) 101, 353, 354, 605, 949, 1108, 1112–14, 1115–17, 1244, 1310
   age levels 1109
   APEC report 1132
   Asian schools 1097
   homework 758
   Pakistan 804
   policy-makers 768
   science content 617
   self-managing school 921, 931, 937–8
Thurstone scales 410, 412, 422
time 735, 736, 739, 781–92
   allocation of 785–6, 787, 788–9, 790
   class size 746, 747
   instructional 1119, 1120
   spent in school 988–9
   on task 592, 749, 781, 782, 783, 785, 1259
time-series data 1132
TIME *see* Training Initiative for Mature Employees
TIMSS *see* Third International Mathematics and Science Study
TIMSS-R, time allocation 787
Tokelau
   continuing education 858
   information on 690
   technical and vocational education and training 687, 691
   transport 689
Tokyo Declaration xiii–xiv
tolerance 18, 353, 362, 562, 651
   Central Asia 253–4
   culture of peace 398, 399
   values education 397–8, 406, 407
   wisdom 385
Tonga
   continuing education 858, 859
   economic/demographic indicators 1276
   educational provision 1277

1420 *Index of Subjects*

information on 690
maritime training 696
outcomes 1275
private sector 1050
public expenditure 1277, 1278, 1279
technical and vocational education and training 687, 691
Torres Strait Islanders 369, 451
Total Literacy Campaigns 1306
Total Literacy Project, India 339
total quality management 9
tourism 1271, 1275, 1282
tracer studies 327
traineeships 724
training 322, 332, 1274
  Certificate Course in Information Technology 533
  competency-based 669
  East Asia 711
  educational research workers xiv, xxii, 126, 134, 168, 1285–99
  enterprise education and training 715–30
  essential skills 25–6
  evaluators 118
  finance 1271–2
  HRD planning 658, 661
  IALS 317, 318
  in-service 11
  indicators 669, 670
  Japan 315
  Korea 316
  materials 181, 182
  needs assessment 329
  NFPE 180
  nonformal literacy programs 301
  Pacific Islands 1275, 1278–9
  regional research cooperation 1312–13
  school leadership 1004–8, 1011
  UNESCO Learning and Training Programme 1239–40
  VET meta-research 327
  workplace 1281
  youth unemployment 225
  see also on-the-job training; technical and vocational education and training; vocational education and training; workshops
Training Initiative for Mature Employees (TIME) 330
transfer of knowledge 359
transition from school to work 327, 329
transition pathways 709, 710–12
transitive inference 374
transnational organisations 1095
transparency 920, 947, 948, 951–2, 953
TRB *see* Teacher Registration Board
Treaty of Waitangi 855–6
Tree of Opportunity 1227
Trends in Mathematics and Science Study, *see also* Third International Mathematics and Science Study
Trends in Mathematics and Science Study (TIMSS) 1310
tuition centres 756, 764
tuition fees *see* fees
Turkey 212, 242
Turkmenistan 243, 244, 247, 250
Turtle Geometry 535

tutoring, *see also* private tuition
Tuvalu
  continuing education 858
  economic/demographic indicators 1276
  educational provision 1277
  information on 690
  maritime training 696, 698
  public expenditure 1277, 1279
  technical and vocational education and training 687, 691
TVE *see* technical and vocational education
TVET *see* Technical-Vocational Education and Training
Tyler Model of evaluation 111–12

UGC *see* India University Grants Commission; University Grants Committee
UN *see* United Nations
underemployment 704, 706, 1216, 1272
understanding 356–7, 360, 450
  conceptual 484
  knowledge organisation 517–18
UNDP *see* United Nations Development Programme
unemployment 1215–16, 1271, 1282
  crisis 701
  East Asia 701, 702–3, 704–6, 710, 712, 713
  educated 87
  enterprise education and training 719
  family background relationship 49
  graduate 737
  OECD countries 1272
  urban youth 221, 224–5
  vocational education and training 674, 675, 681
  youth 553, 1233, 1235–6, 1272
    Australia 723
    East Asia 702–3, 704–6, 710, 712, 713
    family background relationship 49
UNEP *see* United Nations Environment Programme
UNEVOC 696
unfolding models 410
UNFPA 288
  Global Technical Advisory Group 21
UNICEF *see* United Nations Children's Emergency Fund
United Kingdom
  bullying 431
  class size 742, 743
  cognitive developmentalists 375
  contribution to higher education funding 836
  curriculum research 625
  foreign students 835
  influence on Asia-Pacific curriculum 606
  international students 70
  National Curriculum 783, 786
  National Union of Teachers 771
  new mathematics 602
  Plowden Report 782
  poor performance 768
  primary teachers 748
  reforms 781
  research 124, 125, 147, 1086
  research productivity 133
  simulation software 527
  teaching styles 782, 785
  technology research 604
  time allocation 785–6, 787, 788

Index of Subjects 1421

universal suffrage 1336
within-class groups 745
youth unemployment 710
United Nations (UN) 154, 188, 1154, 1157, 1159, 1162-3, 1232
  Convention on the Rights of the Child 143, 154
  democracy 1336
  Economic and Social Commission for Asia and the Pacific (ESCAP) 571
  General Assembly 1233, 1242
  poverty 176
  rural areas 178
  Universal Declaration of Human Rights 171, 188
United Nations Children's Emergency Fund (UNICEF) 105, 229, 571, 1305, 1306
  decentralisation in Indonesia 935, 944
  donor support 1157, 1159, 1162
  EFA indicators 21
  fatherhood 288
  Kazakhstan Monitoring Learning Achievement project 796
  secondary education 77, 81
  self-managing schools 941, 944
  studies 157
  World Declaration on Education for All 1232
United Nations Development Programme (UNDP) 570, 583, 1057, 1086
  donor support 1157, 1159, 1163
  fugitive literature 666-7
  Global Technical Advisory Group 21
  human development index 1339-41, 1342-3, 1345
  Human Development Report 826
  human rights 1336
  indicators 1335, 1337, 1338, 1345
  men's issues 289
  Oceania curriculum 1223
  secondary education 77, 81
  technology 1337
  technology achievement index 815
United Nations Educational, Scientific and Cultural Organisation (UNESCO) xiii, xiv, 29, 42, 154, 188
  ACEID 138
  Asia-Pacific Cultural Centre 181-2, 187
  Asia-Pacific Program of Education for All 172, 182-4, 185
  Australian National Advisory Committee 1173
  Bangkok Centre xxii
  citizenship education 564
  community participation 1063, 1072
  Constitution 1303-4
  Convention against Discrimination in Education 143, 154
  cross-national seminars 1178
  Dakar Framework for Action, gender-based discrimination 269
  decentralisation in Indonesia 935, 944
  Declaration on the Principles of Tolerance 397, 407
  Delors Report 1224, 1333
  donor support 1157, 1159, 1162, 1164
  Education For All 20, 22, 27, 172, 182-4, 185, 304
    EFA 2000 Assessment 169, 229
      literacy 294

  Synthesis Report 298-9
    thematic studies 299
  Education to Fight Exclusion Project 226-7
  environmental education 570, 581, 583
  fugitive literature 666-7
  functional curriculum package 183
  funding for Certificate Course in Information Technology 533
  gender issues 275-6, 277, 278
  Global Technical Advisory Group 21
  gross enrolment ratios 32
  higher education 813, 824, 826, 836, 837, 1102, 1106
  indicators 1126, 1128, 1130, 1132, 1133, 1136, 1277
  Institute for Statistics 41, 805, 1130
  International Commission on Education for the Twenty-First Century 1233-4
  international conferences 76, 82
  international cooperation 1237
  International Institute for Educational Planning 663, 666
  international seminar xiii, 4
  Kazakhstan Monitoring Learning Achievement project 796
  Learning and Working Programme 1239-40
  literacy 295, 296, 297, 303, 304
  mathematics for all 599
  Oceania curriculum 1223
  Oceania teacher education 1224, 1225
  Pacific Islands 693-4
  participation rates 259
  peace 398-9, 642, 646, 647, 648-9
  primary education 1033, 1233
  Principle Regional Office for Asia and the Pacific 125, 126, 1086-7, 1184, 1237, 1238, 1242
    regional research cooperation 1304, 1305, 1307, 1309, 1312, 1313
    school-to-work transition 707, 709, 713
  private expenditure 1050
  public expenditure 36, 37, 1048, 1062
  reform 1178, 1179
  regional research cooperation 1303, 1304-5, 1308-10
  research 1084, 1086-7, 1145, 1186, 1190
  Salamanca Statement 189, 201, 203, 210, 215
  Second International Conference on Technical and Vocational Education 329
  secondary education 77, 78-80, 81, 82, 91
  self-managing schools 941, 944
  sex stereotypes 272-3
  Statistic Database on Education 339, 348
  Statistical Reports 169
  studies 157
  teacher education 883, 900, 901, 902, 903, 904, 911
  teacher performance 739, 740
  teaching profession 867-8, 869, 872, 873-4, 877, 880
  technical and vocational education 668, 669-70
  tertiary education 1039, 1046
  Universal Declaration of Human Rights 1232
  universal primary education 172
  values education 398-9, 400-1, 402
  vocational education and training 668, 669-70, 676, 679, 683, 686

1422 Index of Subjects

Workshop on Technical and Vocational
  Education for Girls 273
World Education Report 144–5, 171, 174, 188,
  1232, 1242, 1260, 1269
  see also Asia and the Pacific Program of
  Educational Innovation for Development
United Nations Environment Programme
  (UNEP) 570, 571, 583
United States
  children with reading difficulties 591–2
  citizenship education 564
  civil war 1336
  class size 736, 741–3, 746
  comparative studies 1120
  comparison with Asian schools 64
  cross-national problem solving studies 519–20
  decline of community involvement 60
  Department of Education 102–3, 106
  educational research 124
  foreign aid 1058
  higher education 813
  homework 758
  influence on Asia-Pacific education 108, 606
  influence on Australasia 559
  innate ability 992
  Japan comparison 519, 758, 763, 1037, 1120
  mathematics anxiety 516
  nation at risk proposals 1099
  National Assessment of Education Progress 795, 800
  new mathematics 602
  norms 390
  out of field teaching 1098
  parental expectations 990
  parental involvement 9
  poor performance of students 449, 768
  primary teachers 748
  private higher education institutions 820
  questioning techniques 356
  Reading Recovery program 592
  reading resources 1120
  reforms 781
  research 102–3, 133, 147, 1083, 1086
  salaries 873
  school leadership 1001
  school-to-home communication 1066
  science 1243
  social studies 558
  socio-economic advantage 1026
  student distraction 786
  teaching styles 782
  time allocation 783, 786, 788
  workforce education 323, 324
  workplace learning 878
  youth unemployment 710
United States Aid for International Development
  (USAID) 77, 81, 1159
unity of educational research xvi
unity of inquiry 1193
Universal Declaration of Human Rights 17, 143, 145, 154, 171, 188, 1232
universal literacy 146, 154
universal primary education (UPE) 172–5, 184, 1092, 1275
  developing countries 338, 339
  East Asia 708
  India 850

Jomtien Conference 337
universal secondary education 708
universal suffrage 1336
universalisation 73, 178
  primary education 146, 164, 172–5, 187
  secondary education 841
Universiti Brunei Darussalam 1286, 1291, 1296
Universiti Malaysia, Sarawak 534
Universiti Sains Malaysia 1292
Universiti Technologi Malaysia 1262
universities xxi
  adult education 737–8
  Asia-Pacific Distance and Multimedia Education
    Network 533
  Australia 1041–2, 1043
  China literacy program 300
  coaching 756, 761, 764
  continuing education 853–66
  corporatization 737
  donor support 1163
  elite 46, 47
  entrance examinations 561
    India 848
    preparation for 756, 764
  family background 46, 53–4
  gifted education 196
  income generating activities 833–4, 836
  increase in number of 305, 306
  India 847–50
  Japan 315, 1037
  national development 1207–20
  overseas study 70
  Pacific Islands 688
  private 36, 737, 822–3, 844–6, 1102, 1155
    donor support 1156
    financing of higher education 827, 834–5, 836–7
    Japan 1036, 1038
  public sector 1153–4, 1155
  selection 86, 108, 115
  Singapore 1055
  widespread availability 380
  see also higher degree programs; higher
    education; tertiary education
University of Adelaide 860
University of Auckland 855
University of Chicago 124
University of Delhi 645
University of Goroka 609, 1142–3
University Grants Commission, India 862, 863
University Grants Committee, Hong Kong 1021, 1029
University Grants Committee, New Zealand 831
University of Hong Kong 131, 324, 527, 831
University of Macao 527
University of Malaya 1004, 1286, 1291–2
University of Melbourne 532, 536
University of New England, Australia 860
University of Newcastle, Australia 860
University of Papua New Guinea 846
University of the Philippines 1154
University of Queensland 860
university reform movement 858
University of San Carlos, Philippines 533
University of the South Pacific 444, 449, 590, 1223
  continuing education 846, 854, 858–9, 863, 864, 866

Pacific Islands education symposium 1226–7
  teacher education 1224–6
University of Southern Queensland 860
University of Sydney 558, 860, 866
university-based research 1140, 1147
unwarranted harm 951
upward mobility 1216
urban areas 153
  nonformal education 338
  private tutoring 1059
urban conglomerates 218–19
urban youth 217–30
urbanisation 178, 217, 218–21, 222, 397
  entrepreneurship development 225
  reduction of agriculture 258
  TVET planning 668
U.S. Embassy, Beijing 1252, 1256
USAID see United States Aid for International Development
user-oriented action research 1200
utilisation of research 1137, 1144–8, 1169
utility of social science research 100
Uzbekistan 243, 244, 247, 249, 250, 251–2, 1057

value judgements 105, 156–7
value orientations 149, 355
values 145, 920, 921, 973, 979, 1121, 1341–4
  Asian 352, 356, 560, 566, 991, 998, 1074
  child rearing practices 149
  China 643, 644
  citizenship education 556, 557, 560, 562
  clarification 1097
  Confucian 450–1, 925, 1015, 1097
  curriculum aims 543
  Delors report 1333
  diversity of 928
  effective schooling 988, 995
  gender bias 287
  inculcation 1097
  India 644, 1172
  internalisation 400, 406
  Japanese cultural 210
  learning outcomes 351, 352
  mathematics education 611
  nonformal education 307
  Oceania 1221–2, 1223, 1226, 1227, 1228
  outcome measures 355
  religion 642, 1217
  school leadership 981
  shared 362
  socio-cultural approach 998
  Western 327
  see also cultural values; moral values
values education 352, 395–407, 558, 1237, 1240
  Central Asia 253–4
  peace 641, 647
  Philippines 647–8
  Singapore 546
values-orientation 76
Van Leer Foundation 1154, 1156
Vanuatu
  continuing education 858, 859
  economic/demographic indicators 1276
  educational provision 1277
  information on 690
  maritime training 696
  political stability 689
  public expenditure 1277, 1278, 1279

reading literacy 55, 590
technical and vocational education and training 687, 694
VET see Vocational Education and Training; vocational education and training
victimisation 427, 435
video materials
  reading literacy 593
  teacher language proficiency 635, 636
videotaping 353, 519, 1247
Vietnam xix
  ADB initiatives 1160
  adult literacy program 314
  colonial history 1153
  compulsory education 7
  curriculum 546
  decentralisation 93
  enrolment 32, 33
  environmental education 575, 582
  fees 40
  good educational outcomes 323
  gross national income 31
  higher education 811, 824, 1215
  inclusive education for students with special needs 212
  independent revenue-earning 1055
  lifelong learning 314, 319
  market economy 927, 1060
  peace education 649, 650
  population 30, 31
  private finance 1050–1, 1281–2
  private sector 1102, 1211
  private tutoring 1059
  public expenditure 37, 1048
  public/private provision 34, 35, 36
  rate-of-return study 328
  research 103, 104, 1087
  science education 616
  staffing ratios 38
  student learning 450
  taxation 1054
  teachers 11, 869, 879
  violence 1235
  vocational education and training 678
  women 271
violence 395, 397, 641, 1232, 1233, 1235
  Australian schools 425–6
  Japanese schools 430
  Korean schools 434
  New Zealand schools 436
violent crime 18
virtual chemistry laboratory 531
virtual environments 1264
virtual facilitator 1264
virtual learning communities 529, 530
virtual reality 528–9, 530, 531, 534
virtual university 847
virtue 1177
visual-spatial memory skills 371–2
VITB see Vocational and Industrial Training Board
vocabulary acquisition 590, 591
vocational education 657–71, 1212, 1281
  Australia 35
  costs 87
  Education for All 25
  educational reforms 7, 8
  entrepreneurship development 225

Indonesia 325
Japanese employers 315
key competencies 310
Korea 1038, 1068
nonformal education 340
privatisation 1018, 1019–20, 1026
secondary level 39, 40, 41
sex stereotypes 273
Taiwan 1018, 1019–20, 1026
teacher training 905
Thailand 1176
see also technical and vocational education and training
Vocational Education and Training (VET) 321, 327–8, 553, 673–86,
 Australia 722, 723, 724, 727
 New Zealand 725, 727
 research 331
 see also workforce education
Vocational and Industrial Training Board (VITB), Singapore 330
vocational schools 673–4, 677, 1019–20
Vocational Secondary Schools 325
volunteering 225, 1066–8
vouchers 711, 926, 1027, 1043, 1100

wages 720, 721
 East Asia 706, 707
 gender-based disparities 286–7
 see also salaries
war 1231, 1232, 1233
wastage 165, 174
wearable ICT 1265
WEAs *see* Workers' Educational Associations
web-based learning 528, 530, 531–2, 1249, 1254
 see also internet
welfare of humankind 17
Western culture 998, 1334
Western influences 108
Western research methods 642
What is Happening in this Class (WIHIC) questionnaire 464, 465–6, 467, 469, 470
WHO *see* World Health Organisation
whole class teaching 450, 745, 748, 994, 995
whole-school approaches 570
WID *see* Women in Development
WIHIC *see* What is Happening in this Class questionnaire
willingness to participate 952
Wireless Application Protocol 1263
wireless slates 1263, 1265
Wisconsin Student Achievement Guarantee in Education (SAGE) 746
wisdom 382, 384–6, 391, 1222
WISE *see* Worker Improvement through Secondary Education
within-construct validity 445–6
women 340, 932, 1201
 Central Asia 249
 changing roles 258, 265, 283
 employment 283–7
 empowerment 288, 289, 302, 335, 340, 341, 344
 equal opportunity 868
 Female Functional Literacy Program 301
 folk sayings 270–1
 greater inclusion of 1103
 higher education 809–10, 845, 848–9, 1100–1
 illiteracy 144, 270

 labour force participation 283–7, 306
 literacy 69–70
 participation 335, 344
 regional research 1310
 rights 1101
 status of 1100
 stereotypes 272–3
 teaching profession 868, 869
 universal suffrage 1336
 see also gender
Women in Development (WID) 288
women's studies 1101, 1103
word identification 486
word problems 163–4
work 553
 competition for high paid jobs 761
 school transition to 327, 329, 701–14
 see also employment; vocational education and training
work experience programs 225, 713, 715–16, 1176
Worker Improvement through Secondary Education (WISE) 330
worker productivity 324, 326
Workers' Educational Associations (WEAs) 338
workforce education 321–34
working memory 309, 516
workplace 154
 knowledge 701
 learning 877–8
 problem solving in China 514
Workplace New Zealand 719–20
workshops 1286, 1295, 1306, 1307–8
World Bank 27, 172, 804, 899, 1103
 achievement studies 1302
 classification of nations 323
 Development Indicators 29
 Development in Practice 158, 164, 169
 donor aid 1154, 1156, 1159, 1161–2, 1163, 1164
 East Asian educational investment 1211, 1220
 Education Sector Review 1223
 environmental education 570, 583, 584
 female education and fertility 296
 financing 1051, 1052, 1053, 1057, 1062
 fugitive literature 666–7
 funding for Malaysia 1004
 gender gap 269, 278
 Global Technical Advisory Group 21
 health education 224, 230
 higher education 737, 813, 826, 830, 831, 832, 838, 840, 852
 investment 165
 labour market signalling 659
 Lao PDR 1175
 malnutrition 375
 Pacific Islands 1275–7, 1282, 1283
 Pakistan assessment 804
 primary education 1033, 1281
 research 1087
 secondary education 77, 81
 self-managing schools 940–1
 teacher recruitment 899, 900, 906, 907, 911
 teaching profession 867, 881
 time allocation 786, 792
 training outcomes 332
 transition countries 328
 vocational education and training 327–8, 334, 676, 683–4, 686

World Education Indicators 1128, 1133
World Commission on Environment and
   Development 581, 584
World Conference on Education for All
   (WCEFA) 19, 175–6, 184
World Declaration on Education for All 19, 175,
   805, 1232
World Development Report 1162
world economy *see* global economy
World Education Forum 1224
   Education for All 19, 22, 298
   secondary education 73
World Education Indicators 32, 37, 1128, 1133
World Health Organisation (WHO) 226, 230
World Links for Development Program 1162
World Programme of Action for Youth to the Year
   2000 1233
World Resources Institute 570, 584
world system of nation-states 1095
World Trade Organisation (WTO) 1026
World Watch Institute 570, 584
World Wide Fund for Nature 570, 571, 584
World Wide Web
   Schools InterLink Project 532
   see also internet
worldwide cultural rationalisation 1095
writing
   assessment 799–800
   IEA studies 1108, 1118–19
   metacognition 487
   US national assessments 795
written composition, IEA studies 1108, 1118–19
youth
   changing attitudes 265–6
   employment 701, 1234, 1235
   Pacific Islands 296
   policy 267
   population 217, 218, 219, 220
   in transition 701, 702–3
   unemployment 553, 1233, 1235–6, 1272
      Australia 723
      East Asia 702–3, 704–6, 710, 712, 713
      family background relationship 49
   values education 398
zest for living 952
zone of proximal development (ZPD) 368, 479,
   481, 504, 747
ZPD *see* zone of proximal development

Kluwer International Handbooks of Education

Volume 1

International Handbook of Educational Leadership and Administration
Edited by Kenneth Leithwood, Judith Chapman, David Corson,
Philip Hallinger, and Ann Hart
ISBN 0-7923-3530-9

Volume 2

International Handbook of Science Education
Edited by Barry J. Fraser and Kenneth G. Tobin
ISBN 0-7923-3531-7

Volume 3

International Handbook of Teachers and Teaching
Edited by Bruce J. Biddle, Thomas L. Good, and Ivor L. Goodson
ISBN 0-7923-3532-5

Volume 4

International Handbook of Mathematics Education
Edited by Alan J. Bishop, Ken Clements, Christine Keitel, Jeremy Kilpatrick,
and Collette Laborde
ISBN 0-7923-3533-3

Volume 5

International Handbook of Educational Change
Edited by Andy Hargreaves, Ann Leiberman, Micheal Fullan,
and David Hopkins
ISBN 0-7923-3534-1

Volume 6

International Handbook of Lifelong Learning
Edited by David Aspin, Judith Chapman, Micheal Hatton,
and Yukiko Sawano
ISBN 0-7923-6815-0

Volume 7

International Handbook of Research in Medical Education
Edited by Geoff R. Norman, Cees P.M. van der Vleuten, and David I. Newble
ISBN 1-4020-0466-4

Volume 8

Second International Handbook of Educational Leadership and Administration
Edited by Kenneth Leithwood and Philip Hallinger
ISBN 1-4020-0690-X

Volume 9

International Handbook of Educational Evaluation
Edited by Thomas Kellaghan and Daniel L. Stufflebeam
ISBN 1-4020-0849-X

Volume 10

Second International Handbook of Mathematics Education
Edited by Alan J. Bishop, M.A., (Ken) Clements, Christine Keitel,
Jeremy Kilpatrick, and Frederick K.S. Leung
ISBN 1-4020-1008-7

Volume 11

International Handbook of Educational Research in the Asia-Pacific Region
Edited by John P. Keeves and Ryo Watanabe
ISBN 1-4020-1007-9

Printed by Publishers' Graphics LLC